MILADY

Joel Gerson

CONTRIBUTING AUTHORS:
Janet D'Angelo
Sallie Deitz
Shelley Lotz

SERIES EDITOR:
Jean Harrity

FUNDAMENTALS
ESTHETICS

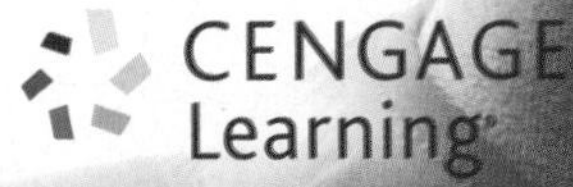

Australia Brazil Japan Korea Mexico Singapore Spain United Kingdom United States

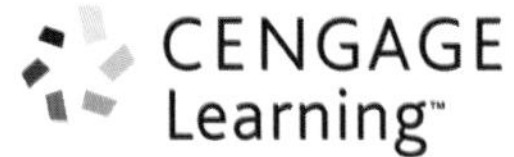

Milady Standard Esthetics: Fundamentals, Eleventh Edition

Joel Gerson, Janet D'Angelo, Sallie Deitz, and Shelley Lotz

President, Milady: Dawn Gerrain

Director of Content and Business Development: Sandra Bruce

Acquisitions Editor: Martine Edwards

Associate Acquisitions Editor: Philip Mandl

Senior Product Manager: Jessica Mahoney

Editorial Assistant: Elizabeth A. Edwards

Director of Marketing and Training: Gerard McAvey

Senior Production Director: Wendy A. Troeger

Production Manager: Sherondra Thedford

Senior Content Project Manager: Nina Tucciarelli

Senior Art Director: Benjamin Gleeksman

Cover and Title page photo: Bruce Talbot/Getty Images

For product information and technology assistance, contact us at
Cengage Learning Customer & Sales Support, 1-800-354-9706

For permission to use material from this text or product, submit all requests online at **www.cengage.com/permissions**
Further permissions questions can be emailed to
permissionrequest@cengage.com

Library of Congress Control Number: 2011943910

ISBN-13: 978-1-111-30689-2

ISBN-10: 1-111-30689-3

Milady
Executive Woods
5 Maxwell Drive
Clifton Park, NY 12065
USA

Cengage Learning is a leading provider of customized learning solutions with office locations around the globe, including Singapore, the United Kingdom, Australia, Mexico, Brazil, and Japan. Locate your local office at **www.cengage.com/global**

Cengage Learning products are represented in Canada by Nelson Education, Ltd.

To learn more about Milady, visit **milady.cengage.com**

Purchase any of our products at your local college store or at our preferred online store **www.cengagebrain.com**

Printed in the United States of America
2 3 4 5 6 7 16 15 14 13 12

Contents in Brief

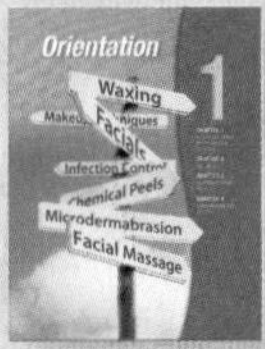

ORIENTATION / 1

GENERAL SCIENCES / 71

SKIN SCIENCES / 225

ESTHETICS / 353

BUSINESS SKILLS / 621

Table of Contents

15 Facial Treatments / 381

16 Facial Massage / 427

17 Facial Machines / 447

18 Hair Removal / 471

19 Advanced Topics and Treatments / 527

20 The World of Makeup / 557

PART 5 BUSINESS SKILLS / 621

Procedures at a Glance

MINI PROCEDURES

Preface

Milady Standard Esthetics: Fundamentals

You are about to begin a journey into a career ripe with opportunity for success and personal satisfaction. The need for professional estheticians continues to grow in new and exciting ways, providing ample room for personal success in a variety of career paths.

As your school experience begins, consider how you will approach your course of study through attitude, study skills and habits, and perseverance—even when the going gets tough. Stay focused on your goal—to become a licensed esthetician and begin your career—and talk to your instructor should any problems arise that might prevent you from succeeding in attaining it.

Foreward

You have one decision to make today: Are you going to be your very best self or just get by? That's it. After all, 90 percent of success is showing up, mentally—*and* physically. Are you committed to putting a laser focus on learning?

Education makes your life better, happier, richer. Specialized learning builds confidence, leads to a specific career, and opens dozens of unexpected doors. And if you listen to those who have already traversed the path before you, esthetics training will provide you with the foundation for an exciting, artistic, limitless career.

The Benchmark for Esthetics Education

Milady's Standard Textbook for Professional Estheticians was first published in 1978, the creation of Joel Gerson. It soon became the textbook choice of esthetics educators and has seen 11 revisions. Throughout this period, it has consistently been the most widely used esthetics textbook in the world. As the science and business of skin care evolve, new editions of the text are needed periodically, and Milady is committed to publishing the best in esthetics education. We have thoroughly updated the content and design of this textbook to bring you the most valuable, effective educational resource available. To get the most out of the time you will spend studying, take a few minutes now to learn about the text and how to use it before you begin.

© Bachrach.

Joel Gerson

This 11th Edition of *Milady Standard Esthetics: Fundamentals* provides you with the basic information you need in an esthetics training course up to 600 hours. Before beginning this revision, Milady conducted extensive research to learn what needed to be changed, added, or deleted. We went to some of the top experts in the field to learn how the changing esthetics field should be reflected in this new edition of the textbook. We involved top educators in the revision process, providing firsthand knowledge of current esthetics classes. Finally, we sent the finished manuscript out for yet more reviews. What you hold in your hands is the finished result.

Milady Standard Esthetics: Fundamentals, 11th Edition, contains comprehensive information on many subjects including infection control, spa body treatments, choosing a product line, and more. In addition, a new chapter entitled "Life Skills" has been added to align with other Milady textbooks placing a greater emphasis on goal setting, time management, study skills, and ethics. As a part of your esthetics education, this book provides you with a valuable guide for learning the techniques you will be performing, as well as detailed information for gaining insight into how to interact with clients and even to run a business. No matter which career path you choose in the esthetics field, you will refer to this text again and again as the foundation upon which to build your success.

Features of this Edition

In response to the suggestions of the esthetics educators and professionals who reviewed the *Milady Standard Esthetics: Fundamentals* and to those submitted by students who use this text, this edition includes many new features and learning tools.

Alignment

Milady has carefully aligned all of its core textbooks. This means that information appearing in more than one text—whether it is esthetics, nail technology, or cosmetology—now matches from one book to another.

Design

Milady has also dramatically changed the design of the textbook—it now has an exciting magazine feel—to reflect the innovative and unique energy and artistry found in the skin care business.

Photography and Art

Over 100 new, four-color photographs and illustrations have been added throughout the text, appearing in both chapter content and step-by-step procedures.

Pre- and Post-Service Procedures

To drive home the point that pre-service cleaning, disinfecting, and preparing for the client are important, you will find that a unique *Pre-Service Procedure* has been created in Chapter 14, *The Treatment Room*, to specifically address setting up your facial room and for meeting, greeting, and escorting your client to your service area. Additionally, a *Post-Service Procedure* has been created to address cleaning, disinfecting, and organizing after servicing a client.

Pre-Service and *Post-Service* Procedure icons with page numbers appear in every chapter with procedures, so you can quickly and easily refer to them when needed.

Why Study This?

Milady knows, understands, and appreciates how excited students are to delve into the newest and most exciting products and equipment, and we recognize that students can sometimes feel restless spending time learning the basics of the profession. To help you understand why you are learning each chapter's material and to help you see the role it will play in your future career as an esthetician, Milady has added this new section to each chapter. The section includes three or four bullet points that tell you why the material is important and how you will use the material in your professional career.

New Organization of Chapters

By learning and using the tools in this text together with your teachers' instruction, you will develop the abilities needed to build a loyal and satisfied clientele. To help you locate information more easily, the chapters are now grouped into five main parts:

Part 1: Orientation

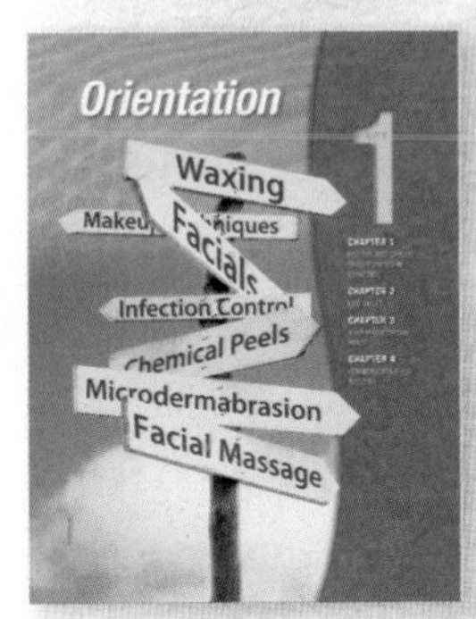

Orientation includes four chapters that cover the past, present, and future of the field of esthetics. Chapter 1, "History and Career Opportunities in Esthetics," outlines the origin of esthetics, tracing its evolution through the twenty-first century and speculating on where it will go in the future. Chapter 2, "Life Skills," is a new addition to this edition that stresses the importance of setting goals, time management, and establishing a solid foundation for a successful career. Chapter 3, "Your Professional Image," stresses the importance of personal hygiene and deportment and discusses interacting with managers, coworkers, and clients. Chapter 4, "Communicating for Success," is a blueprint for using your special skills and personality to build a successful career in esthetics and outlines how to service and retain a loyal client base.

Part 2: General Sciences

General Sciences includes important information that you need to know to keep you and your clients safe and healthy. Chapter 5, "Infection Control: Principles and Practices," offers the most current, vital facts about cleaning and disinfection procedures, hepatitis, HIV, and other infectious viruses and bacteria and tells how to prevent them from being transmitted. Chapters 6 through 8—"General Anatomy and Physiology," "Basics of Chemistry," and "Basics of Electricity"—provide essential information that will help guide your work with clients and enable you to make decisions about treatments. Chapter 9, "Basics of Nutrition," is the final chapter in Part 2. This chapter is vital for estheticians who seek to understand the effects of nutrition on the

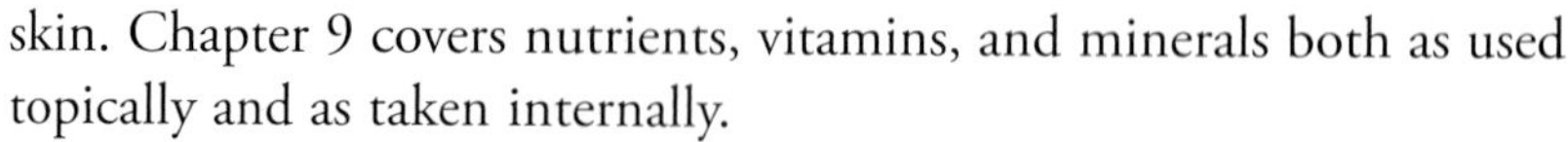

skin. Chapter 9 covers nutrients, vitamins, and minerals both as used topically and as taken internally.

Part 3: Skin Sciences

Skin Sciences offers clear, up-to-date content on every aspect of the skin. Chapter 10, "Physiology and Histology of the Skin," includes skin anatomy and skin function; Chapter 11, "Disorders and Diseases of the Skin," explores the many maladies of the skin including acne, sensitive skin, and the danger of sun exposure. Chapter 12, "Skin Analysis," addresses skin types and conditions, stressing the necessity of a thorough client consultation. The foundation on which almost every retail sale is built is covered in Chapter 13, "Skin Care Products: Chemistry, Ingredients, and Selection."

Part 4: Esthetics

Esthetics focuses on actual practices performed by the esthetician. Setting up the treatment room and creating the correct atmosphere for both the client and for the esthetician are covered in Chapter 14, "The Treatment Room." Chapter 15, "Facial Treatments," instructs in the methods used during several types of facials and their benefits and contraindications, as well as the unique considerations and techniques of the men's facial. Chapter 16, "Facial Massage," covers the benefits of massage along with contraindications and basic massage movements. Chapter 17, "Facial Machines," is devoted to machines used in esthetic treatments and provides instruction on the use of the steamer, galvanic machine, Wood's Lamp, and more. Chapter 18, "Hair Removal," covers the critical information you'll need for these increasingly requested services. Chapter 19, "Advanced Topics and Treatments," provides an overview of the body and clinical procedures used with cosmetic surgery and also covers the increasingly popular spa body treatments. Color theory, face shapes, and advice about selecting a product line are some of the topics addressed in Chapter 20, "The World of Makeup," which will provide a reference in the future, with appearance-enhancement services growing in demand.

Part 5: Business Skills

Business Skills contains a wealth of new information on creating financial and operational success as an esthetician. Chapter 21, "Career Planning," provides practical instruction on setting goals, preparing a resume, and preparing for an interview. Information on the skills of money management and communication is also included.

"The Skin Care Business," Chapter 22, includes valuable information on establishing your own business, as well as tips to help you recognize a successful business to join as an employee. Lastly, Chapter 23, "Selling Products and Services," stresses market-related topics including product knowledge, understanding your clients' needs, and tracking your success.

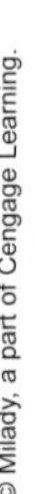

Additional Features of this Edition

As part of this edition, many features are available to help you master key concepts and techniques.

Throughout the text, short paragraphs in the outer column draw attention to various skills and concepts that will help you reach your goal. The **Focus On** pieces target sharpening technical skills, sharpening personal skills, ticket upgrading, client consultation, and building your client base. These topics are key to your success as a student and as a professional.

Did You Know?

These features provide interesting information that will enhance your understanding of the material in the text and call attention to a special point.

The Activity boxes describe hands-on classroom exercises that will help you understand the concepts explained in the text.

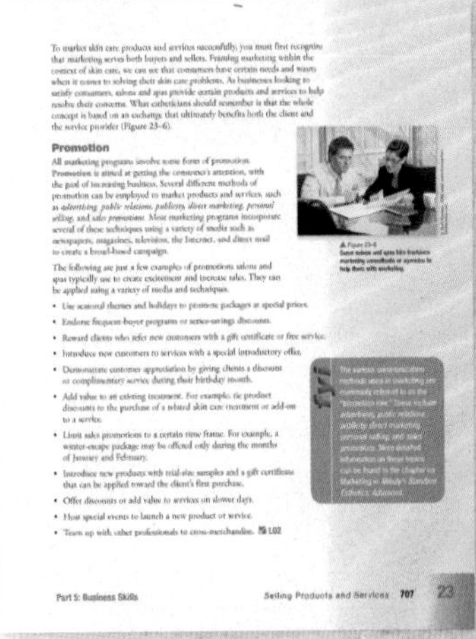

FYI's offer important, interesting information related to the content. Often **FYI** boxes direct you to a Web site or other resource for further information.

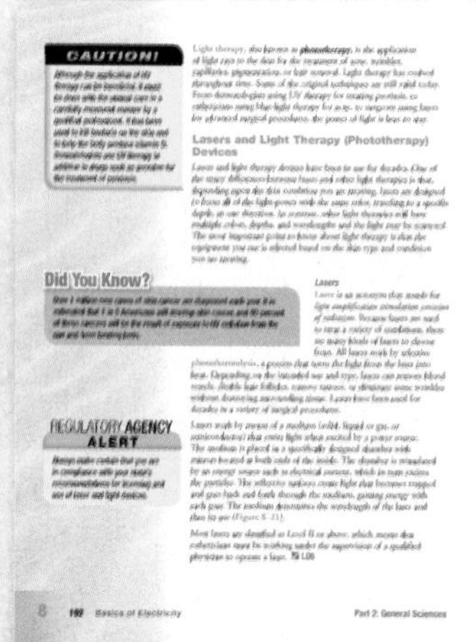

CAUTION!

Some information is so critical for your safety and the safety of your clients that it deserves special attention. The text directs you to this information in the **CAUTION** boxes found in the margins.

REGULATORY **AGENCY** **ALERT**

This feature alerts you to check the laws in your region for procedures and practices that are regulated differently from state to state. It is important, while you are studying, to contact state boards and provincial regulatory agencies to learn what is allowed and not allowed. Your instructor will provide you with contact information.

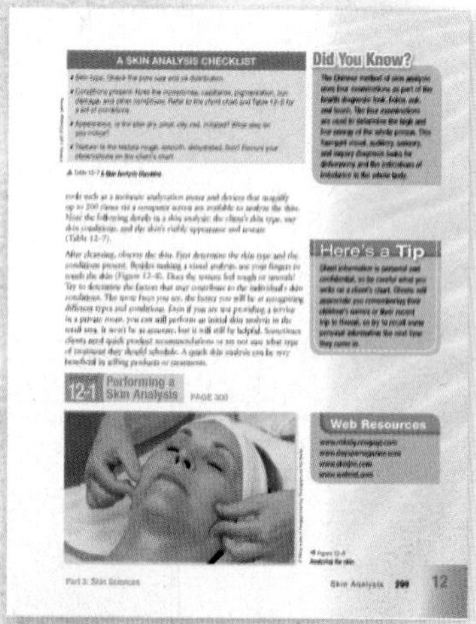

Here's a **Tip**

These helpful tips draw attention to situations that might arise and provide quick ways of doing things. Look for these tips throughout the text.

Web Resources

The **Web Resources** provide you with Web addresses where you can find more information on a topic and references to additional sites for more information.

Educational Chapter Formatting

Each chapter of *Milady Standard Esthetics: Fundamentals* includes specialized formatting and strategies for the presentation of material to enhance your experience while working with the chapter and to facilitate the learning process.

Learning Objectives

At the beginning of each chapter is a list of learning objectives that tell you what important information you will be expected to know after studying the chapter. Throughout the chapter you will see a special icon that indicates you have finished reading the material that corresponds to one of these Learning Objectives. **LO1**

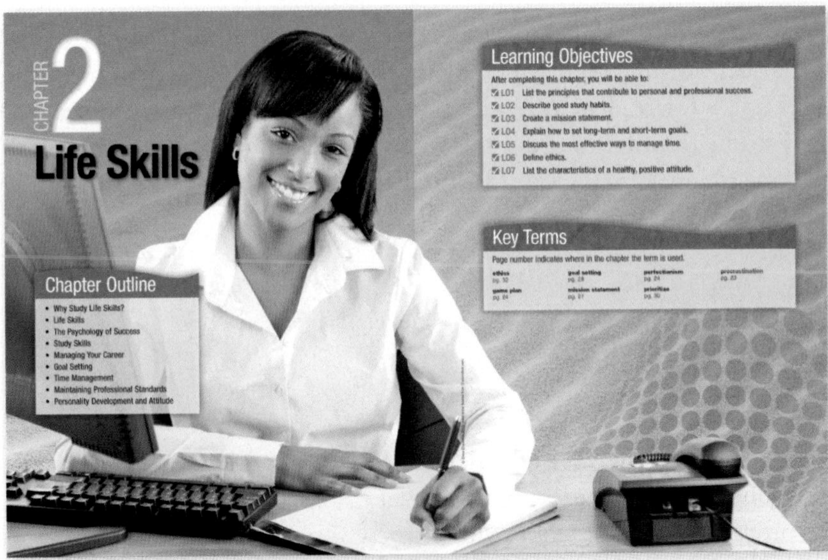

Key Terms

The words you will need to know in a chapter are given at the beginning, in a list of **Key Terms.** When the word is discussed for the first time within the chapter, it appears in boldface type. If the word is difficult to pronounce, a phonetic pronunciation appears after it in parentheses.

Procedures

All step-by-step procedures offer clear, easy-to-understand directions and multiple photographs for learning the techniques. At the beginning of each procedure, you will find a list of the needed implements and materials, along with any preparation that must be completed before the procedure begins.

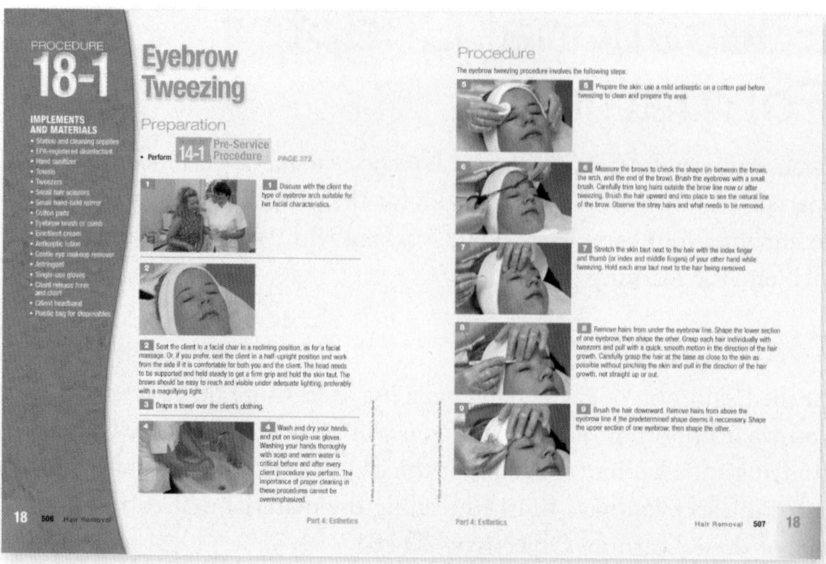

In previous editions, the procedures (which are detailed, illustrated, and in-depth) interrupted the flow of the main content, often making it necessary for readers to flip through many pages before continuing their study. In order to avoid this interruption, all of the procedures have been moved to a special **PROCEDURES** section at the end of each chapter.

PAGE 506

Some students may want to review a procedure at the time it is mentioned in the main content. To make it easy for you to find the procedure you are looking for at these times, Milady has added Procedural Icons. These icons appear where each procedure is mentioned within the main content of the chapter, and they direct you to the page number where the entire procedure appears.

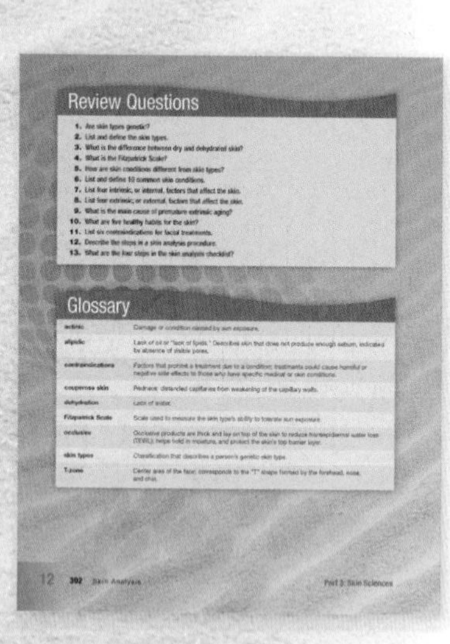

Review Questions

Each chapter ends with questions designed to test your understanding of the chapter's information. Your instructor may ask you to write the answers to these questions as an assignment or to answer them orally in class. If you have trouble answering a chapter review question, go back to the chapter to review the material and then try again. The answers to the **Review Questions** are in your instructor's *Course Management Guide*.

Chapter Glossary

All key terms and their definitions are included in the **Chapter Glossary** at the end of each chapter, as well as in the **Glossary/Index** at the end of the text.

Extensive Learning and Teaching Package

While *Milady Standard Esthetics: Fundamentals* is the center of the curriculum, students and educators have a wide range of supplements from which to choose. All supplements have been revised and updated to complement the new edition of the textbook, except for the DVD series.

STUDENT SUPPLEMENTS	
SUPPLEMENT TITLE	**DELIVERY FORMAT**
Milady Standard Esthetics: Fundamentals Student Workbook	• Designed to reinforce classroom and textbook learning. • Helps students recognize, understand, and retain the key concepts as covered in the textbook. • Provides fill-in-the-blank, multiple-choice, matching, crossword puzzles, and labeling exercises that reinforce practical applications.
Milady Standard Esthetics: Fundamentals Exam Review	• Contains chapter-by-chapter questions in multiple-choice format to help prepare for the written portion of licensure exams. • Aids in overall classroom preparation. • Revised to meet the most stringent test-development guidelines. • Questions are for study purposes only and are not the exact questions that will be seen on licensure exams.

Milady Standard Esthetics: Fundamentals Student CD-Rom	• Interactive resource designed to reinforce classroom learning, stimulate the imagination, and aid in preparation for board exams.
	• Featuring:
	  • Video clips to demonstrate procedures and theoretical concepts
	  • Chapter quizzes that provide 20 questions at a time but draw from a quiz bank of 1,000 multiple-choice questions
	  • An 'arcade' with 4 different types of games
	  • An audio glossary that pronounces each term and provides the definition
	• Content follows and enhances Milady Standard Esthetics: Fundamentals.

STUDENT SUPPLEMENTS	
SUPPLEMENT TITLE	DELIVERY FORMAT

 **Milady U Online Licensing Preparation: Fundamental Esthetics**	• Provides an alternative way to study for licensure exams, whether taken on a computer or on paper.
	• Offers familiarity with a computerized test environment during licensure exam preparation.
	• Features include:
	  • 24x7 availability and students have the flexibility to study from any computer
	  • Chapter tests, quizzes, and comprehensive exams that draw from 1,000 multiple-choice questions
	  • All questions are available in both English and Spanish
	  • Immediate results with rationales to assist with knowledge acquisition
	  • Robust reports that help students determine areas of study they need to focus on
	www.miladyonline.cengage.com

 **Milady Standard Esthetics: Fundamentals Step-by-Step Procedures**	• Full-color, spiral-bound guide. • Used in conjunction with the textbook, or on its own to brush up on key procedures. • Each step is clearly explained and is accompanied throughout by full-color photos. • List of rubrics appear at the end of each chapter; the rubric is a clearly-developed scoring document used to differentiate between levels of development in a specific skill performance or behavior. • Notes section inserted to comment on your performance of each of the key tasks.
 **Milady Standard Esthetics: Fundamentals E-Book**	• Electronic version of Milady Standard Esthetics: Fundamentals for instant online access. • Requires an Internet connection. • Enables highlighting, note-taking, and bookmarking. • Has search capabilities. • Contains an audio glossary. • Ability to print pages one at a time while connected to the Internet.
 **Milady Standard Esthetics: Fundamentals Coursemate**	• Content-rich, online learning environment that presents information in a new and different way to accommodate the ever-changing learning styles. • Simple, user-friendly interface. • Provides an Engagement Tracker, a Web-based reporting and tracking tool, allowing instructors to monitor students' use of course material and assess their engagement and preparation. • Contains an Enhanced eBook providing students with an interactive, online-version of the printed textbook. • Consists of a Student Learning Pathway, featuring a variety of integrated resources including: Learning Objectives, FAQs, PowerPoint, Study Notes, Crosswords, Chapter Overviews, Flashcards, Discussion Topics, Web Links, Glossary, and Interactive Quizzing.

Educator Supplements

Milady proudly offers a full range of innovative products created especially for esthetics educators to make classroom preparation and presentation easy, effective, and enjoyable.

SUPPLEMENT TITLE
Milady Standard Esthetics: Fundamentals Course Management Guide Print Binder
Milady Standard Esthetics: Fundamentals Course Management Guide CD
Milady Standard Esthetics: Fundamentals DVD Series
Milady Standard Esthetics: Fundamentals Instructor Support Slides CD
Milady Standard Esthetics: Fundamentals Student CD School / Network Version
Milady Standard Esthetics: Fundamentals Interactive Games CD

Thank you for choosing Milady as your Total Learning Solutions Provider. For additional information on the above resources or to place an order please contact your Milady Sales Representative or visit us online at www.milady.cengage.com

About the Authors

Joel Gerson

© Bachrach.

Joel Gerson, Ph.D., set the standards for esthetic skin care schools in the United States when he authored *Standard Textbook for Professional Estheticians* as the result of many years of research and experience. Before the book was published, no state offered a separate license in esthetic skin care. Since the publication of the first edition, 48 states now offer separate licenses for the practice of facial treatments and skin care.

Joel Gerson has been called the "master of skin care education" by *American Salon Magazine* because he is a firm believer in education and enjoys sharing his knowledge with others. He has presented his dynamic and comprehensive lectures and seminars throughout the United States, Canada, Europe, and the Far East.

Joel's professional credentials include resident makeup artist for the House of Revlon; spokesman for Lever Brothers; vice president of Education for Christine Valmy, Inc.; national training director for Pivot Point International; and director of skin care training for Redken Laboratories. Joel is currently serving as a technical consultant to several major manufacturers and has appeared on radio and television talk shows. His articles on facial treatments and skin care have appeared in many publications, including *Les Nouvelles Esthétiques, Dermascope, Modern Salon,* and *American Salon.* He has hosted for the last ten years the International Congress of Esthetics, sponsored by the American edition of *Les Nouvelles Esthétiques* and the *Dermascope Magazine.* Joel Gerson has a doctorate in Allied Health Science and holds a teaching license for Scientific Facial Treatments from the University of the State of New York. He has served as an esthetic examiner with the New York Department of State.

Janet M. D'Angelo

Courtesy of Janet D'Angelo. Photography by Gretje Ferguson.

Janet M. D'Angelo, M.Ed., is founder and president of J.Angel Communications, LLC, a Marketing & Public Relations firm specializing in the health, beauty, and wellness industry. With more than 25 years of experience developing marketing and management strategies and a strong background in education, Janet is a featured speaker at trade shows and conferences in the U.S. and abroad, where she educates on a wide range of business topics. She is also an adjunct professor in the College of Management at the University of Massachusetts Boston.

Janet began her career in the skin care industry in 1979 as one of the first separately licensed estheticians in Massachusetts. Since then she has worked tirelessly to raise industry awareness and promote professional standards, serving on trade association advisory boards and research committees, addressing legislative boards, conducting business seminars, and writing articles for consumer and trade publications.

In addition to her work on this text, Janet D'Angelo is the author of *Spa Business Strategies: A Plan for Success,* (Cengage Learning, 2006; 2010), a contributing editor and author of the "Business Communication Skills" of *Milady's Standard Comprehensive Training for Estheticians* (Milady, 2003) and *Milady's Standard Esthetics: Advanced* (Cengage Learning, 2010; 2013). D'Angelo is a member of several professional organizations including the American Marketing Association (AMA), Associated Skin Care Professionals (ASCP), and the International Spa Association (ISPA). She can be reached at janet@jangelcommunications.com.

Sallie Deitz

Photo courtesy of Sallie Deitz.

Sallie Deitz serves in education and product development with Bio Therapeutic, Inc., and the Bio Therapeutic Institute of Technology, in Seattle, Washington. Deitz has been a licensed esthetician for 26 years, and has 12 years of clinical experience. She is the author of *The Clinical Esthetician: An Insider's Guide to Succeeding in a Medical Office* (Milady, 2004) and *Amazing Skin: A Girl's Guide to Naturally Beautiful Skin* (Drummond Publishing Group, 2005). Sallie Deitz is a contributing author to *Milady's Standard Comprehensive Training for Estheticians* (Milady, 2004); *Milady('s) Standard Esthetics: Fundamentals*, 10th and 11th eds. (Milady, 2009; 2012); and *Milady('s) Standard Esthetics: Advanced* (Milady, 2010; 2012). Deitz is also the author of *Skin Care Practices and Clinical Protocols* (2013) published by Milady, a part of Cengage Learning.

Sallie has a Bachelor's Degree from The Evergreen State College in Olympia, WA., in liberal arts with a concentration in education. She has completed numerous graduate courses in adult education, learning styles, and the multiple intelligences.

Sallie speaks at various esthetic tradeshows, hosts webinars, and presents at select seminars. She is an advisory board member with the Northwest Aestheticians' Guild, Seattle, WA; an advisory board member for The Salon Professional Academy (Tacoma, WA); and has served as a committee member in test development for NIC (National Interstate Council of State Board of Cosmetology Esthetics Division).

Shelley Lotz

Photo courtesy of Shelley Lotz. Photography by Judith Pavlik.

Shelley Lotz started her career in esthetics over 25 years ago and has been involved in many aspects of the industry including business management, training, marketing, retailing, and teaching. She is a contributing author of *Milady's Standard Esthetics: Fundamentals* (9th and 10th eds.). Shelley is the former owner and an instructor at the Oregon Institute of Aesthetics, an undergraduate and advanced graduate-level esthetician school. She co-developed the school's esthetic procedures and curriculum.

Before starting the school, she owned her own esthetics business and worked at salons and spas. Shelley is now a consultant and educator. She has taught workshops and worked as a makeup artist for photographers and film/video. Shelley has been a member of the Oregon Department of Education curriculum committee and the Board of Cosmetology's item-writing committee.

Shelley Lotz has a Bachelor of Science degree in Biology, Geography, and Communications from Southern Oregon University. For her, the most rewarding part of teaching is making a difference in the lives of students. She is passionate about this exciting industry and loves sharing information through writing and education. Shelley currently works at a spa and as a green business consultant.

Her other career interest is teaching Sustainable Living Programs, including the Certified Sustainable Building Advisor Program. A life-long passion for sustainability and the spa industry has led her to combine both fields into a complementary blend of green business and holistic beauty. Shelley is writing a new book on Green Salons and Spas.

Editorial Contributors

Courtesy of Jean Harrity.

Jean Harrity

Jean Harrity has been working in the beauty industry since 1991. Throughout her career, she has worn many hats that include Nail Technician, Esthetician, Medical Aesthetician, Esthetic and Nail Teacher, Salon Manager, Makeup Artist, and Permanent Makeup Artist. She has worked with many different types of skin, their many imperfections and disorders, and has a strong knowledge and understanding of a wide variety of skin care, nail care, and makeup products.

As a freelance makeup artist, Jean has been performing makeup services since 1996. Working with organizations such as *Spri, Maybelline, Teen People, Nexxus* and *DiamondJack's Casino,* she has been published in various media formats including magazines, books, and on-line. Jean continues to pursue the creativity that makeup artistry brings by continuing to work with models and photographers.

Jean currently serves on the Board of Barber, Cosmetology, Esthetics, Hair Braiding, and Nail Technology for the state of Illinois. As a board member she is able to help create, change, and enforce the rules for this profession to protect the public.

Contributing Authors for Previous Editions of Milady Standard Esthetics: Fundamentals

Catherine M. Frangie

John Halal

Acknowledgments

Milady recognizes, with gratitude and respect, the many professionals who have offered their time to contribute to this edition of *Milady Standard Esthetics: Fundamentals* and wishes to extend enormous thanks to the following people who have played a part in this edition:

- The staff members at Bio-Therapeutic, Inc., for all of their support and patience while working on the various chapters and clinical trials.
- Dino Petrocelli, Rob Werfel, and Alison Pazourek, professional photographers, whose photographic expertise helped bring many of these pages to life.
- Allison Provenzano, professional makeup artist, licensed cosmetologist, New York State Examiner, and instructor at Orlo School of Hair Design, for her artfully inspired makeup applications.
- Vanessa Crewe, Owner of Elegant Esthetics and Licensed Esthetician, for generously performing all of the chemical exfoliation services at the photo shoot.
- Michelle D'Allaird, Owner of Aesthetic Science Institute, Latham, NY, who, along with her instructors and students, welcomed the Milady team to their school in order to conduct this edition's photoshoot, and who were whole-heartedly kind and hospitable to our entire team.
- Barbara Acello, M.S., R.N., Denton, TX, for her important contribution on the Standard and Universal Precautions content appearing in Chapter 5, Infection Control: Principles and Practices.
- Randy Brenner, Dimensions in Aesthetic Advancement, Latham, NY, for all of his help in acquiring products for the photoshoot and providing instruction on proper home care.
- Helen Bickmore, for graciously sharing her time and waxing expertise at the photoshoot.
- David Suzuki, owner of Bio-Therapeutic, Inc., for providing photos showcased throughout this edition.
- Many thanks to the following for their assistance with Parts 3 and 4 of the text: Gretchen Facey, Crystal Koebrick, Janet Bocast, Renee Norman-Martin, Marcella Arana, Danika Blood, Kathy Lystra, Suzanne Mathis McQueen, Feather Gilmore, Serena Beach, Panos Photinos, and the students at the Oregon Institute of Aesthetics for their support and editing.

Reviewers of Milady Standard Esthetics: Fundamentals, 11th Edition

Lurana S. Bain, LMT, Elgin Community College, Elgin, IL

Yota G. Batsaras, QueenB Cosmetics, Cypress, CA

Christen Brummett, Clary Sage College, Tulsa, OK

Linda Burmeister, International Dermal Institute, Carson, CA

Toni Campbell, Sullivan South High School, Kingsport, TN

Christi Cano, Innovative Spa Productions, Henderson, NV

Suzanne Casabella, NYS Licensed Esthetician

Kimberly Coleman, Ofallon, MO

Linda Cowin, Tukwila, WA

Lisa W. Crawford, Bellefonte Academy, Maysville, KY

Vanessa Crewe Ntabona, owner of Elegant Esthetics in Albany, NY

Jessica Cummings, Face Forward Inc., Peabody, MA

Rhonda Cummings, Face Forward Inc., State Approved Advanced Training Institute, Peabody, MA

Denise DeFilippo Podbielski, Making Faces, Glenville, NY

Debbie Eckstine-Weidner, DeRielle Cosmetology Academy and Revelations Day Spa, Mechanicsburg, PA

Jennifer A. Errigo, LE, LMP, Esthetic Sciences, Clover Park Technical College, Lakewood, WA

Bianca Felice, High Brow Studio & Skin, Miami Beach, FL

Amy Fields Rumley, Merle Norman Cosmetics & Skin Care Center, Greensboro, NC

Nichole Fox, L.E., Office of Dr Robert Sarro, Dermatology Associates, PA of the Palm Beaches

Denise Fuller, Editor of Les Nouvelles Esthétiques & Spa Magazine - American Edition, Founder of the National Aesthetic Spa Network, Miami, FL

Sheilah D. Fulton, Atlanta, GA

Cindy German-Day, Nuance Skin Boutique, Athens, GA

Laureen Gillis, Kent Career Technical Center, Grand Rapids, MI

Shari Golightly, Entanglements Training Center, Greeley, CO

Valerie Gora, LMT, Excellent Bodywork, Inc., North Palm Beach, FL

Mona Green, Clary Sage College, Tulsa, OK

Jeanne Valek Healy, Carolina Skin Care Academy, Inc., Columbia, SC

Larissa Harbert, San Diego, CA

Celia G. Hines, American Spirit Institute, Williamsburg, VA

Ruth Ann Holloway, Dermal Dimensions Skin Care, Providence, UT

Kim Jarrett, B Street Design, Overland Park, KS

Donna L. Joy, Spa Consultant, Dundee, NY

Dr. Carolyn R. Kraskey, 2933 Pentagon Dr., Minneapolis, MN

Becky Larsen-Kunc, College of Hair Design, East Campus, Lincoln, NE

Austine Mah, Consultant, Educator, and Esthetician, Plano, TX

Yolanda Matthews, The Cosmetology Connection, Houston, TX

Debbie Messinger, Roebuck, SC

Sandra Peoples, Pickens Technical College, Aurora, CO

Beth Phillips, Heritage College, Kansas City, MO

Patricia Powers Stander, Independent Skin Care Consultant, Licensed Esthetician & Esthetics Instructor, Florence, MA

Darlene Ray, LMT, NMT, MNT, Miller-Motte Technical College, Chattanooga, TN

Lisa Reinhardt, Arcadia, CA

Robin Roberts Cochran, Gadsden State Community College-Ayers Campus, Anniston, AL

Denise Sauls, Lurleen B. Wallace Community College, Opp, AL

Mona Shattell, Greensboro, NC

Melissa Siedlicki, Clover Park Technical College and Brassfields Salon & Spa, Tacoma, WA

Donna Simmons, Tulsa Tech, Collinsville, OK

Karlee Sorensen, Northwest Skin Center, Lakewood, WA

Lisa Sparhawk, Self-employed Private Educator, Albany, NY

Karen Sutera, Karen Sutera Salon, New Hartford, NY

Bonnie J. Swiatkkowski, Vogue Beauty College, Mishawaka, IN

Maureen C. Thacker, Academy of Career Training, Kissimmee, FL

Nancy Tomaselli, Instructor, Cerritos Community College, Norwalk, CA

Nadine Toriello, All About You Day Spa/Keys To Esthetics Education Center, Key West, FL

Madeline Udod, Eastern Suffolk BOCES, Long Island, NY

Daria V. Wright, Skin & Beauty Expert, Chicago, IL

Tamara A. Yusupoff, Bellus Academy: The Academy of Beauty and Spa, San Diego, CA

Tina Marie Zillmann, V.P./Owner, Advanced Rejuvenating Concepts, San Antonio, TX

Special thanks to Milady's Infection Control Advisory Panel

- Barbara Acello, M.S., R.N., Denton, TX
- Ronald S. Hampton Sr., President of Hampton Manufacturing, Inc., Fayetteville, GA
- Mike Kennamer, Ed.D., Director of Workforce Development & Skills Training, Northeast Alabama Community College, AL
- Janet McCormick, MS, Cidesco, FL
- Leslie Roste, R.N., National Director of Education & Market Development, King Research/Barbicide, WI
- Robert T. Spalding Jr., DPM, TN
- David Vidra, CLPN, WCC, MA, President Health Educators, Inc., OH

Orientation

PART 1

CHAPTER 1

History and Career Opportunities in Esthetics

Chapter Outline

- Why Study History and Career Opportunities in Esthetics?
- Brief History of Skin Care
- Style, Skin Care, and Grooming Throughout the Ages
- Career Paths for an Esthetician
- A Bright Future

Learning Objectives

After completing this chapter, you will be able to:

- ✓ **LO1** Describe the cosmetics and skin care practices of earlier cultures.
- ✓ **LO2** Discuss the changes in skin care and grooming in the twentieth and twenty-first centuries.
- ✓ **LO3** Name and describe the career options available to licensed estheticians.
- ✓ **LO4** Explain the development of esthetics as a distinct, specialized profession.

Key Terms

Page number indicates where in the chapter the term is used.

esthetician (aesthetician)
pg. 9

esthetics (aesthetics)
pg. 9

henna
pg. 5

medical aesthetics (esthetics)
pg. 10

nanotechnology
pg. 8

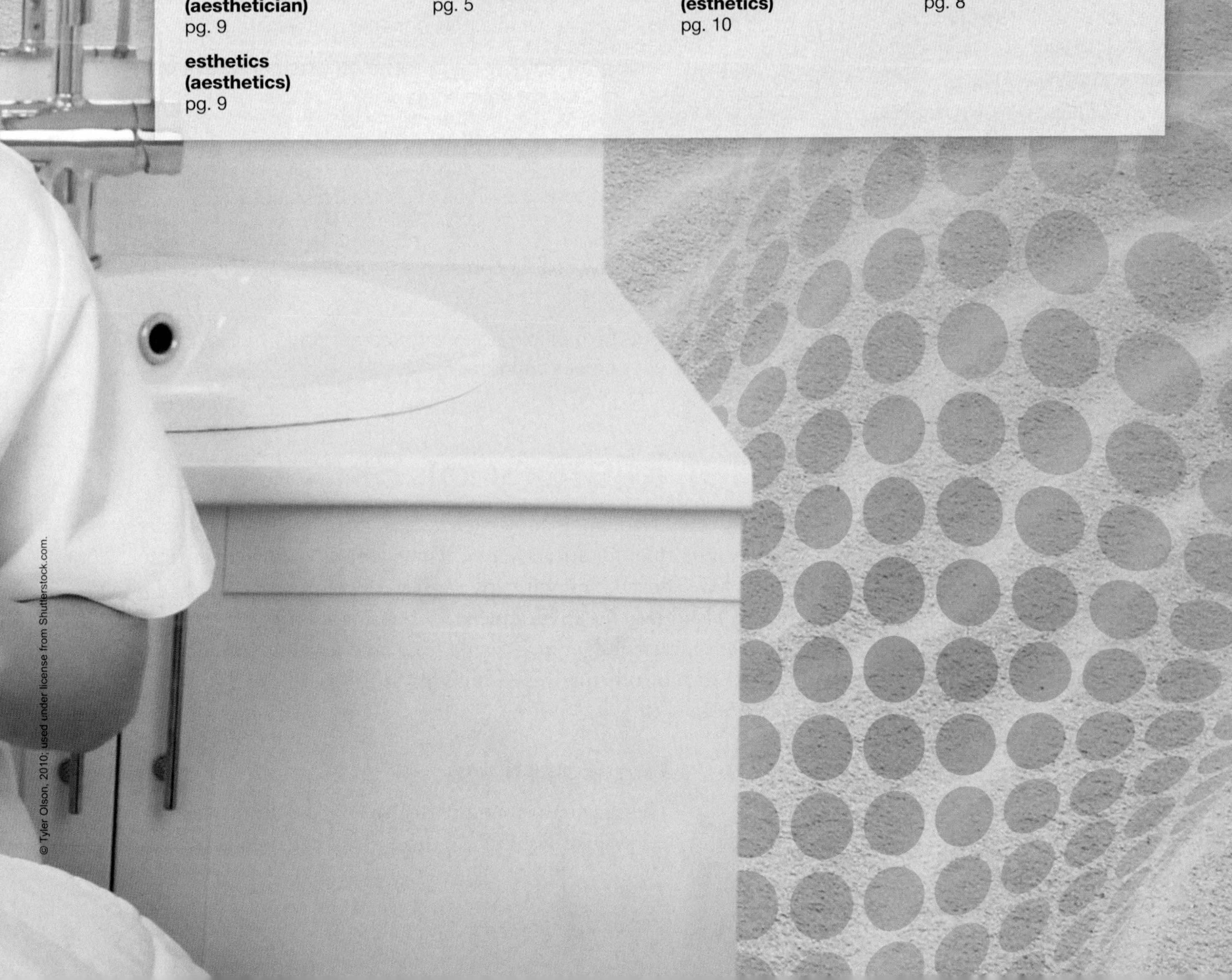

Much of today's skin and body care therapies are rooted in the practices and attempts of earlier civilizations to ward off disease in order to live healthier, longer lives. The brief history outlined in this chapter will acquaint you with some of the ways men and women have tried to improve upon skin health and nature by changing and enhancing their appearance.

Why Study History and Career Opportunities in Esthetics?

Esthetics (es-THET-iks) is a career in which you can grow, thrive, and make a difference in the lives of others every day. Whether you are coming to esthetics as your first, second, or third career choice, it holds the promise of independence, pride, and community. Being a professional esthetician opens many doors that are not available in other industries. Once you become proficient and master the basics, the only limits that you will experience are those that you allow to define you. While you are studying History and Career Opportunities in Esthetics, here are some good reasons for learning as much as possible on these topics.

- It is good to have a historical perspective on where we have been in order to know how far we have come.
- It is helpful to understand what materials used in early beauty preparations may have been instrumental in determining how materials are used today, such as in color formulations and cosmetics.
- To understand how culture can shape fashion and how it can bring about the necessity for change.
- To learn about the multiple options for career opportunities, and then to expand your career upon them.

The simple but effective implements used at the dawn of history were shaped from sharpened flints, oyster shells, or bone. Animal sinew or strips of hide were used to tie the hair back or as adornment. Ancient people around the world used coloring matter on their hair, skin, and nails, and they practiced tattooing. Pigments were made from kohl, berries, tree bark, minerals, insects, nuts, herbs, leaves, and other materials. Many of these colorants are still used today.

Brief History of Skin Care

In early times, grooming and skin care were practiced more for self-preservation than for attractiveness. For example, an ancient African might have adorned himself with a variety of colors that would allow him to blend into his environment for hunting. During the reign of Elizabeth I, men and women would have used lead and arsenic face powder to adorn themselves because it was the social trend in the mid-1500s.

The Egyptians

The Egyptians were the first to cultivate beauty in an extravagant fashion (**Figure 1–1**). They used cosmetics as

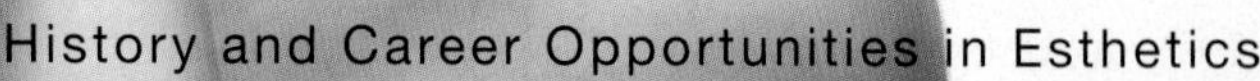

part of their personal beautification habits, for religious ceremonies, and in preparing the deceased for burial. One of the earliest uses of **henna**, a dye obtained from the powdered leaves and shoots of the mignonette tree used as a reddish hair dye and in tattooing, was as an adornment in ancient Egypt for body art and on fingernails. The Egyptians also placed great importance on the animals that surrounded them. Each animal of prominence had a corresponding god or goddess that was artfully mimicked from the animal's physical characteristics. The Egyptians incorporated these traits into their grooming and beautification habits, as well as their mummification rites. To the early Egyptians, cleanliness was also very important—it was a means of protection from evil as well as from disease.

▲ Figure 1–1
The Egyptians were the first to cultivate beauty in an extravagant fashion.

The Hebrews

The early Hebrews had a wealth of grooming and skin care techniques. Due to their nomadic history, they adopted many techniques from other cultures. Hebrew grooming rituals were based on the principle that their bodies were gifts to be cared for. Cosmetics were primarily used for cleansing and maintenance of the skin, hair, teeth, and overall bodily health.

The Hebrews used olive and grapeseed oils to moisten and protect the skin. They prepared ointment from hyssop (an aromatic plant originally found near the Black Sea and in central Asia) for cleansing, and they used cinnamon balms to keep in body heat. Myrrh and pomegranate were the Hebrews' most useful grooming and health aids. Myrrh in powder form was used to repel fleas, and in tincture form it was used for oral hygiene. Pomegranate was used as an antiseptic and was helpful in expelling intestinal worms.

The Greeks

The words *cosmetics* and *cosmetology* come from the Greek word *kosmetikos* (kos-MET-i-kos), meaning "skilled in the use of cosmetics." In ancient Greece, beauty was determined by how one looked when naked. It was the naked Grecian athlete who defined the balance between mind and body. The Greeks viewed the body as a temple. They frequently bathed in olive oil and then dusted their bodies in fine sand to regulate their body temperature and to protect themselves from the sun. They were very aware of the effects of the natural elements on the body and the aging process. They used both honey and olive oil for elemental protection and were always in search of ways to improve their health and appearance. It was this drive for perfection that made the Greeks so prominent in advancing grooming and skin care (**Figure 1–2**).

▲ Figure 1–2
The Greeks were prominent in advancing grooming and skin care.

The Romans

The ancient Romans are famous for their baths, which were magnificent public buildings with separate sections for men and women. Ruins of these baths survive to this day. Steam therapy, body scrubs, massage, and

▲ Figure 1–3
The Romans applied various preparations to the skin to maintain attractiveness.

other physical therapies were all available at bathhouses. After bathing, Romans applied rich oils and other preparations to their skin to keep it healthy and attractive (Figure 1–3). Fragrances made from flowers, saffron, almonds, and other ingredients were also part of bathing and grooming rituals.

The Asians

The Asians, like the Egyptians, blended nature, animal, and self into a sophisticated and elaborate culture that adhered to a high standard of grooming and appearance. Both the Chinese and Japanese cultures blended the edges of their natural scenery into their looks.

History also shows that during the Shang dynasty (1600 BC), Chinese aristocrats rubbed a tinted mixture of gum arabic, gelatin, beeswax, and egg whites onto their nails to turn them crimson or ebony.

▲ Figure 1–4
The geisha personifies the Japanese ideal of beauty.

The ancient Japanese geisha not only exemplified the ideal of beauty, she was also able to incorporate it into intricate rituals (Figure 1–4). Geishas removed their body hair by a technique similar to what we call *threading* today—they wrapped a thread around each hair and pulled it out. From the tenth to the nineteenth centuries, blackened teeth were considered beautiful and appealing. It was common for both the married woman and the courtesan to black out their teeth with a paste made from sake, tea, and iron scraps.

The Africans

Traditional African medicine features diverse healing systems estimated to be about 4,000 years old. Since ancient times, Africans have created remedies and grooming aids from the materials found in their natural environment (Figure 1–5). Even today in parts of North Africa, people use twigs from the mignonette tree as toothpicks. The twigs have an antiseptic quality and help prevent oral and tooth disease. ☑ **L01**

▲ Figure 1–5
Africans created remedies and grooming aids from materials found in their natural environment.

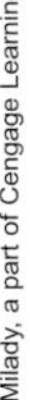

Style, Skin Care, and Grooming Throughout the Ages

Style and personal grooming took many turns throughout history and reflected the social mores of specific time periods. Beautification and adornment slowly moved away from the spiritual and the medicinal and began to reflect the popular culture of the day.

The Middle Ages

The Middle Ages is the period in European history between classical antiquity and the Renaissance. It began with the downfall of Rome in AD 476 and lasted until about 1450. During that time, religion played a prominent role in people's lives. Healing, particularly with herbs, was largely in the hands of the church. Beauty culture was also practiced.

Tapestries, sculptures, and other artifacts from this period show towering headdresses, intricate hairstyles, and the use of cosmetics on skin and hair (Figure 1–6). Women wore colored makeup on their cheeks and lips, but not on their eyes. Bathing was not a daily ritual, but those who could afford them used fragrant oils.

▲ Figure 1–6
Tapestries, sculptures, and other artifacts from the Middle Ages show towering headdresses, intricate hairstyles, and the use of makeup on skin and hair.

The Renaissance

During the Renaissance period, Western civilization made the transition from medieval to modern history. One of the most unusual practices was the shaving or tweezing of the eyebrows and the hairline to show a greater expanse of forehead—a bare brow was thought to give women a look of greater intelligence (Figure 1–7). Fragrances and cosmetics were used, although highly colored preparations for lips, cheeks, and eyes were discouraged. The hair was carefully dressed and adorned with ornaments or headdresses. Many women used bleach to make their hair blond, which was a sign of beauty.

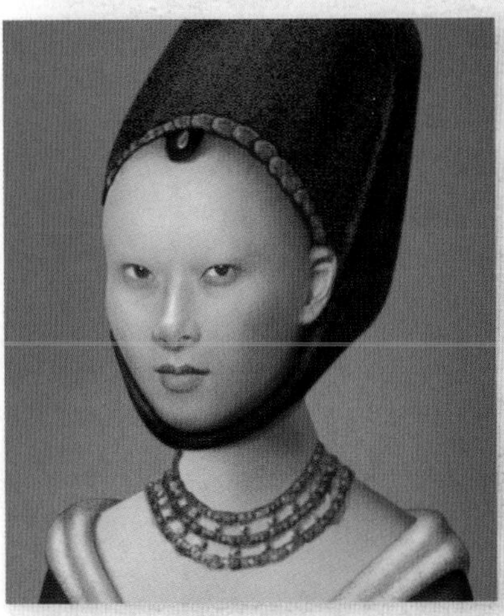

▲ Figure 1–7
Shaving or tweezing the eyebrows and hairline to show a greater expanse of forehead was thought to make women appear more intelligent.

The Age of Extravagance

Marie Antoinette was queen of France from 1755 to 1793. This era was called the Age of Extravagance. Women of status bathed in strawberries and milk and used various extravagant cosmetic preparations, such as scented face powder made from pulverized starch (Figure 1–8). Lips and cheeks were often brightly colored in pink and orange shades. Small silk patches were used to decorate the face and conceal blemishes. Some hairstyles extended high into the air, using elaborate wire cages with springs to adjust the height. The hairstyles might have even contained gardens and menageries with live animals, which could attract lice and other parasites.

The Victorian Age

The Victorian Age spans the reign of Queen Victoria of England (1837–1901). Modesty was greatly valued, and makeup and showy clothing were discouraged except in the theater (Figure 1–9). Hairstyles were sleek and demure, often knotted in the back with hairpins. Men kept their hair short and grew sideburns, a mustache, and/or a beard. To preserve skin health and beauty, women used beauty masks and packs made from honey, eggs, milk, oatmeal, fruits, vegetables, and other natural ingredients. Victorian women are said to have pinched their cheeks and bitten their lips to induce natural color rather than use cosmetics such as lipstick and rouge.

▲ Figure 1–8
Women of status used various extravagant cosmetic preparations, such as scented face powder made from pulverized starch.

▲ Figure 1–9
During the Victorian period, makeup and showy clothing were discouraged, except in the theater.

▼ Figure 1–10
Beauty and fashion images through the decades.

The Twentieth Century

The twentieth century brought about many changes in style, skin care, and innovation of the beauty culture. Each decade seemed to have an inherently different look, whereas in earlier history it may have taken a century to bring about a change (**Figure 1–10**). These changes were primarily due to greater exposure to other cultures (because more people were traveling) and to the industrialization of civilizations. Newspapers, magazines, radio, and motion pictures were important sources of information on fashions in the United States as well as in other countries. The twentieth century brought about Tretinoin (Retin-A®), Botox®, alpha hydroxy acid, and a myriad of sought-after cosmetic surgery procedures.

The Twenty-First Century

The beginning of the twenty-first century brought about a more relaxed approach to clothing, hair, and makeup. Styles became less elaborate, with a focus on a great-looking pair of jeans with simple tops, and skin care continued to top the list of purchases for the average consumer.

With information on facial services, treatments, and product ingredients readily available, consumers would go armed to their favorite shopping venue, including the Internet, to make informed, discerning decisions about cosmetics in general. Never before did the esthetician have so much competition—from the 11 to 18 percent increase in skin care centers popping up all the way to the growth of the skin care knowledge base of their clients.

Advancements spiked dramatically in the field of esthetics with the use and layering of technologies. Lasers, light therapies, microcurrent, ultrasonic, and chemical compounds have been modified and recalibrated to incorporate a busy client with no time to spend recovering from a procedure. Technology continues to become smaller, smarter, and more mobile.

The use of **nanotechnology**, the art of manipulating materials on an atomic or molecular scale, becomes more prevalent in use by product manufacturers. By changing the chemistry of product ingredients and breaking them into smaller units, nanotechnology rejuvenated the older tried-and-true ingredients and created new ones. The future of skin health appears promising as researchers continually develop new products that decrease adverse reactions in the skin. ✔ **LO2**

Today and Beyond

The birth of the medical spa has created growth in a segment of the skin care industry. Cosmetic surgery continues to be popular and is a multibillion-dollar industry. According to the American Society for Aesthetic Plastic Surgery, cosmetic procedures in 2010 increased by 147 percent over those performed since 1997. Nonsurgical procedures, however, such as injectibles (Botox®, Juvederm®), laser hair reduction, chemical peels, and microdermabrasion, still lead all cosmetic surgical procedures in every category.

Private Labeling and Branding

Private-label product lines have become important to many spas and medical spas (medi-spas). An esthetician can create a line as simple or as complex as desired, depending on the type of branding he or she chooses to promote sales.

Compounding Pharmacies

For estheticians working with and for physicians, skin care has a pharmaceutical component. Many compounding pharmacies have taken a market share of the cosmetic industry by offering more advanced preparations. Compounding pharmacies build preparations according to the requests of the physician for a given patient or client. It is possible to make special compounds which may include exfoliants, lighteners, antioxidants, and prescriptions such as retinoic acid for cell renewal. These products must be recommended, prescribed, and administered by a physician.

New ingredients and therapies for wrinkles, skin cancer, and general skin health will continue to be developed. As the technology improves, these methods will be less invasive and allow the client to spend less time away from her regular daily activities. Baby boomers will continue to retire and younger clients will take a lead in driving the market. The esthetician is well positioned to benefit from all of the future endeavors related to skin care development, technology, health, and fashion.

Career Paths for an Esthetician

Esthetics, also known as **aesthetics**, from the Greek word *aesthetikos* (meaning "perceptible to the senses"), is a branch of anatomical science that deals with the overall health and well-being of the skin, the largest organ of the human body. An **esthetician**, also known as **aesthetician**, is a specialist in the cleansing, beautification, and preservation of the health of skin on the entire body, including the face and neck.

Estheticians provide preventive care for the skin and offer treatments to keep the skin healthy and attractive. They may also manufacture, sell, or apply cosmetics. They are trained to detect skin problems that may require medical attention. However, unless an esthetician is also a licensed dermatologist, physician, or physician's assistant, he or she cannot prescribe medication, make a diagnosis, or give medical treatments.

Did You Know?

You will see the spelling of *esthetician* vary slightly depending on where you are working. In the medical realm, you will more often see the word spelled as *aesthetician* in reference to the original Greek word *aesthetikos*. Many cosmetic surgeons, nurses, and clinical estheticians prefer the original spelling. In recent history the initial letter *a* has been dropped in Western Europe and in the United States because the word *esthetician* relates more to the newer spa culture and has become a more modern term.

Esthetics is an exciting, ever-expanding field. Over the past few decades, it has evolved from a minor part of the beauty industry into an array of specialized services offered in elegant, full-service salons, day spas, and wellness centers. As a licensed esthetician, you can choose from a wide range of career options.

Salon or Day Spa Esthetician

Estheticians in a salon or day spa are skin care specialists and consultants. They perform facials and facial massage, waxing, and body treatments, applied both manually and with the aid of machines. They may also offer makeup. To be successful and build their clientele, estheticians must keep records of the services they provide and the products they use. They must always behave pleasantly toward clients, and they must become skillful at selling products.

Estheticians are employed in full-service salons, skin care salons, or day spas. These may be independent businesses or national chains, and they may operate within hotels or department stores.

As an esthetician, you can work your way up to management and supervisory positions. With the experience you gain in these positions, you may decide to open your own salon or buy an established business or franchise. Most private salon or franchise owners have multiple responsibilities. Besides running the business, you may perform any or all of the services your business offers; or, you may choose to limit your services to the areas of skin care and makeup.

Medical Aesthetician

Medical aesthetics, also known as medical **esthetics**, involves the integration of surgical procedures and esthetic treatments. In this setting, the physician concentrates on surgical work while the esthetician assists in esthetic treatments. Career opportunities are available in many different medical settings, where estheticians perform services ranging from working with pre- and postoperative patients to managing a skin care department in a medical spa. These tasks may involve patient education, marketing, buying and selling products, camouflage makeup, and—with a physician's supervision—performing advanced treatments including laser and light therapies (depending on state licensing rules). In addition, an experienced esthetician may manage the cosmetic surgery office or act as a patient care coordinator (**Figures 1–11, 1–12, and 1–13**). Some estheticians are also licensed practical nurses (LPNs) and registered nurses (RNs) or medical assistants. The settings for such work may include outpatient clinics, dermatology clinics, medical spas, laser clinics, or research and teaching hospitals.

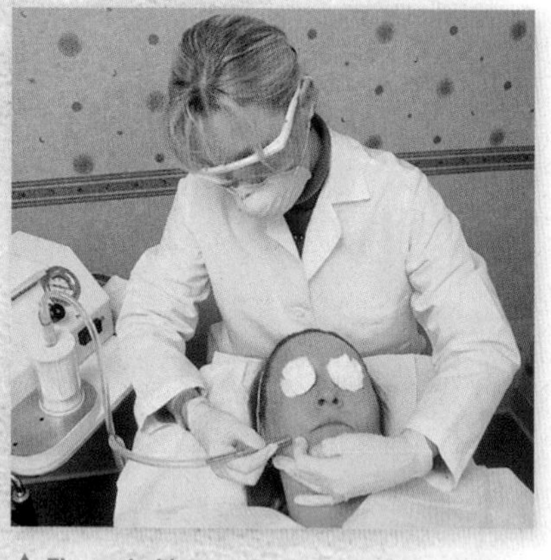
Courtesy Scherrer Photography.

▲ Figure 1–11
Microdermabrasion is a common treatment offered in most skin care centers.

If you are interested in pursuing a career in medical aesthetics, you will want to learn not only basic skin care skills but also cosmetic chemistry, makeup and camouflage techniques, and business skills. A thorough understanding of skin anatomy, medical terminology, and skin disorders is also a must, as is the ability to communicate effectively and compassionately with clients. This type of work is very demanding, and it is important to be adaptable. Many rules and regulations must be observed and followed in a medical setting, and there is much at stake. You must be a good leader, but also be able to follow instructions explicitly. Teamwork is the number one priority in a medical organization. Contact your state board for rules and regulations for estheticians working in a medical setting.

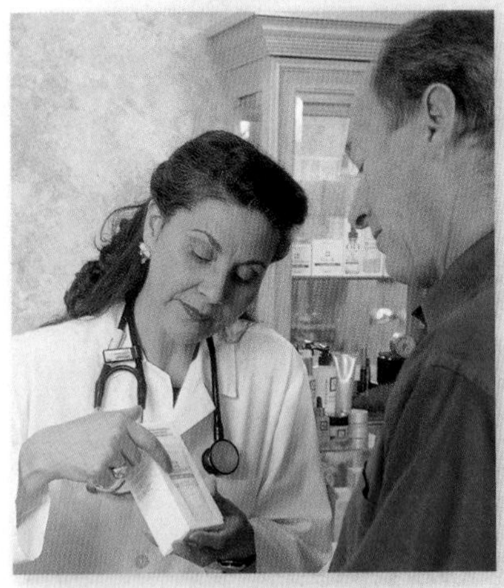
Courtesy Scherrer Photography.

▲ Figure 1–12
Physicians instruct patients on proper home-care protocols.

Makeup Artistry and Camouflage Therapy

As a makeup artist, you must develop a keen eye for color and color coordination in order to select the most flattering cosmetics for each client. You may offer facials and facial massage as part of your services, or concentrate only on applying makeup.

Makeup artists in salons, spas, and department stores work for an hourly wage, commission, salary, or various combinations of all three.

- Commercial photographers often employ full- or part-time makeup artists. In fashion photography, a makeup artist works with models (**Figure 1–14**). Magazine and advertising layouts often require ultrafashionable hairstyles and makeup to call attention to products or clothing. The makeup artist may also be a photographer's assistant, helping with set designs or assisting with bridal photographs.
- Another exciting avenue for makeup artistry can be found in television, theater, movies, and fashion shows. In this highly competitive field, you may need a lengthy apprenticeship and acceptance into a union. Most major television and motion picture productions are shot on the East or West Coast, which may limit the number of jobs available. The same holds true for theatrical productions and large fashion shows. However, many cities and towns support Community Theater, and most large department stores produce fashion shows. In many cases, when full-time work as a makeup artist is not available, the position may be combined with other duties.
- A particularly rewarding field related to makeup artistry is camouflage therapy. Clients require this service for varying reasons: as a temporary measure while recovering from surgery, such as a face lift; to disguise a congenital defect; or to hide scars and other effects of an accident. The principles of standard makeup application also apply to camouflage makeup, particularly in terms of shading and blending. But working with clients desiring camouflage makeup also requires patience, compassion, a reassuring manner, and the ability to teach new techniques to an often traumatized individual.
- Another option for makeup artists is a career in mortuary science. Many people believe that viewing the deceased has a comforting psychological effect on the bereaved family and friends, and the

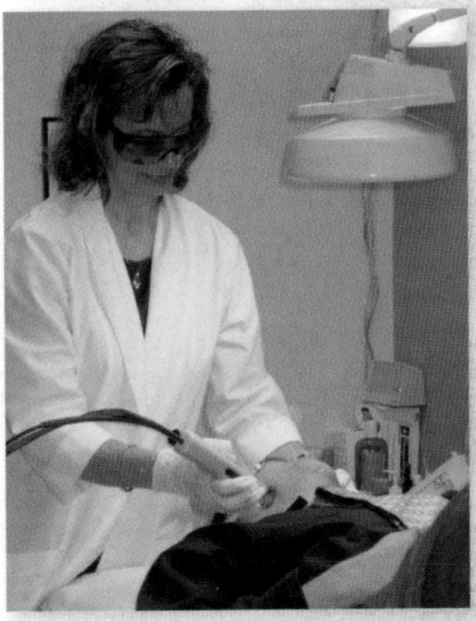
© Caddell's Laser Clinic.

▲ Figure 1–13
Depending upon state licensing regulations, estheticians work as laser technicians.

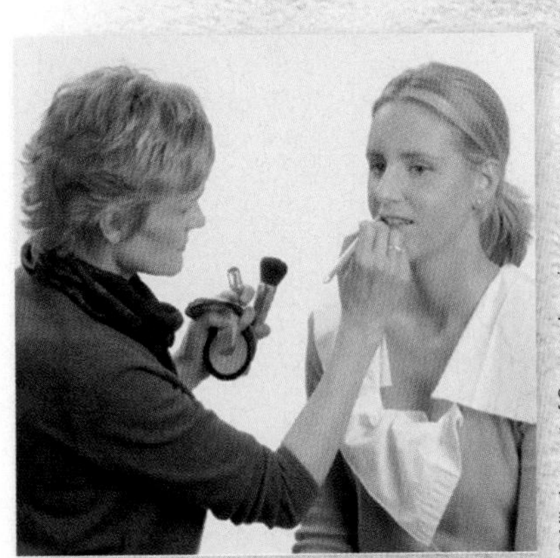
© Milady, a part of Cengage Learning. Photography by Larry Hamill.

▲ Figure 1–14
Makeup artists often work with models.

fyi

It is advisable to have some professional experience working in a spa, salon, or clinic as an esthetician since today's students are savvy and many going through initial training have come to esthetics as a second or third career. In order to be an effective educator, experience in the field is necessary.

custom is widely practiced. Training includes the study of restorative art, which is the preparation of the deceased. Restoration work requires a high degree of skill and must be performed under the direction of a mortician. In this career, the esthetician or cosmetologist works only on preparing and applying cosmetics.

Manufacturer's Representative

Manufacturer's representatives are responsible for training estheticians and other staff members on product knowledge, the proper use of products and where they fit into treatments sequences, and how to retail and merchandise. Representatives call on spas, salons, drugstores, department stores, and specialty businesses to help build clientele and increase product sales. For this position, you must have a professional appearance, an outgoing personality, and sales ability. You can expect to travel a great deal, and you will often exhibit products at trade shows and conventions.

▲ Figure 1–15
An esthetician can pursue a successful career in sales.

Salesperson or Sales Manager

Salons, spas, department stores, boutiques, and specialty businesses employ estheticians as salespersons and sales managers. Estheticians who fill these slots often work their way up to top management positions and ownership. As a salesperson, your duties would include keeping records of sales and stock on hand, demonstrating products, selling to clients, and cashiering (Figure 1–15). You must thoroughly know the products you sell and be able to help clients select cosmetics that suit their particular skin type and color. Salespeople do not have to be licensed estheticians, but smart companies hire licensed estheticians because they are well trained to present cosmetics to the public, are polished in appearance, and are specialists in the art and science of skin care and can cross-sell services and treatments.

Cosmetics Buyer

A cosmetics buyer in department stores, salons, or specialty businesses must keep up with the latest products and be able to recognize and anticipate trends in skin care. Buyers travel frequently visiting markets, trade shows, and manufacturers' showrooms. As a buyer, you must estimate the amount of stock your operation will need over a particular period, and you must keep records of purchases and sales.

▲ Figure 1–16
A writer with a background in esthetics can write for magazines, newspapers, television, or book publishers.

Esthetics Writer or Beauty Editor

If you have talent and training in journalism, you may wish to pursue a career as an esthetics writer or editor for a magazine or newspaper (Figure 1–16). Journalists in this field write feature articles, daily or weekly columns, and "question and answer" columns. Some also review new products, medical breakthroughs, and salon techniques. Writers produce educational books and brochures for the esthetics and cosmetology market, do fashion coordination and commentary, and make media appearances.

Cosmetics and skin care products are heavily advertised on television and radio and in magazines and newspapers. Copywriters design ads and commercials and write the information enclosed in packages and printed on labels. They often work with photographers and television producers to create commercial messages. Some are involved in producing the multimedia programs used in classrooms to educate the consumer.

Travel Industry

Many cruise ships, airlines, and airport organizations are employing estheticians to work and manage esthetic departments. Airports today have licensed massage therapists as well as estheticians and manicurists to serve the traveling public. In addition, some private airline companies may employ estheticians to travel along to meet the needs of special clients with esthetics services. Cruise ship companies have mirrored the practices of land-based spa owners to keep up with demand for esthetic services onboard.

ACTIVITY

Begin a journal dedicated to creating the ideal esthetics position for you. Make a wish list detailing the perfect job description. Ask yourself what tasks you might be performing, and consider the types of settings you think would be exciting and interesting. Then describe the type of people you would enjoy working with and the clients you would like to serve. Add to your journal whenever you can, and you will begin to develop an idea of your ideal esthetics position. THINK BIG.

Educator

If you want to teach esthetics in a public, vocational, industrial, or technical high school, you must meet the same requirements as other teachers of career preparation courses. You must be trained in curriculum and lesson planning, classroom management, and presentation techniques. If you are interested in heading a department of esthetics or cosmetology in a public or private school, you will need supervisory skills as well as the necessary certification. Contact your local state board for the requirements of becoming a licensed esthetics instructor.

Many private cosmetology or esthetics schools have teacher-training programs for promising graduates (Figure 1–17). Some states require a teacher to train in teaching all subjects. Others require teachers to specialize in one area such as skin care, makeup styling, theatrical makeup, or hair removal. Some basic teacher-training courses are also generally required. As an instructor, you must keep up with developments in the education field as well as in beauty products and skin care techniques. Many teachers attend workshops and conferences to stay abreast of industry changes and trends.

▲ Figure 1–17
Estheticians become educators.

Many school owners and directors begin their careers as general practitioners. The director of a school or a department within a school has many duties, including preparing the curriculum and ensuring that the school's physical layout and equipment meet state standards. The director works closely with teachers, counsels students about licensing and placement, and maintains relationships with trade organizations and industry experts.

To be a successful teacher, supervisor, director, or school owner requires a good sense of commercial operations, a thorough knowledge of the business, and the ability to direct people and get along with them. Professionals in education dedicate themselves to improving the beauty industry by working together in associations at the national, state, and local level. They help establish, amend, and repeal state laws and regulations, improve and standardize curriculums, and ensure the professionalism of the entire industry.

Manufacturers of cosmetics and other products frequently employ licensed cosmetologists and estheticians as education directors. These professionals educate the public about the manufacturer's products and conduct seminars for teachers of consumer education. As part of the manufacturer's consumer-education program, education directors appear at conventions to display products, talk with teachers about the merits of the products, and distribute educational materials for classroom use. Education directors may also be workshop or seminar leaders, lecturers, and/or writers.

▼ Fgure 1–18
Estheticians own and manage skin care corporations.

Skin Care Company Owner

For the ambitious entrepreneurial esthetician or skin specialist, the possibilities are endless for building a skin care business. Being the owner of a company will involve a strong business acumen which may involve developing skin care products and technologies, teaching and training, research and development, sales and marketing, human resources and team-building, accounting and processing, and traveling the world while building your business (**Figure 1–18**). Often these individuals become leaders in the skin care industry and set the standards for years to come.

Product Development

For estheticians interested in cosmetic chemistry and ingredients, working in product development for a skin care company is another career choice. Creating new products and developing new technologies is very exciting for the individual desiring to be on the cutting-edge of the industry (**Figure 1–19**). Seeing a product or skin care device go from being a concept to the marketplace is a rewarding experience. There are classes in cosmetic chemistry to help interested estheticians offered as extension programs through universities such as the University of California of Los Angeles (UCLA) and other select community and vocational colleges.

▲ Figure 1–19
Estheticians work in product development.

Mobile Esthetician

An emerging concept for estheticians and skin therapists is to serve as a mobile esthetician—willing to make house and office calls. With more individuals working from home today, and office workers putting in longer hours, this makes a nice option as a business venture for enterprising estheticians. Some estheticians have invested in multi education and licensure in the areas of esthetics, cosmetology/hair, and manicuring and massage to provide a greater range of options for a demanding public interested and fascinated by personal services. A mobile esthetician may purchase a special vehicle, a light-weight mobile chair, and use specific devices and products for on-the-go treatments to serve busy clients (Figure 1–20). With a good business plan in place and diligence on your part, this career path can be lucrative and provide an untapped opportunity with rich rewards. Some states will have restrictions for this career opportunity. Be sure to check with your state regulatory agency first if you are interested in pursuing a career as a mobile esthetician.

Courtesy of Bio-Therapeutic, Inc.

▲ Figure 1–20
Mobile estheticians make office and house calls.

State Licensing Inspector or Examiner

Most states have laws governing cosmetology and other personal services and give examinations for cosmetology and related licenses. As a licensed, experienced cosmetologist and/or esthetician, you may become a state inspector or examiner. Inspectors conduct regular salon and spa inspections to ensure that managers and employees are following state rules and regulations and meeting ethical standards. State examiners prepare and conduct examinations, enforce rules and regulations, investigate complaints, and conduct hearings.

State Board Member

Members of state licensing organizations must be highly qualified and experienced in their professions. They conduct examinations, grant licenses, and inspect schools to see that certain physical standards, such as those for space and equipment, are maintained. In addition, they make sure that educational materials meet certain specifications. The chairperson of the state board is usually a full-time employee, but other members may be school owners or people in related professions. ☑ L03

Did You Know?

Look Good . . . Feel Better (LGFB) is a free public service program that teaches beauty techniques to women with cancer, helping them boost their self-image and camouflage their hair loss. The program is open to all women cancer patients actively undergoing treatment for cancer.

Look Good . . . Feel Better

800-395-LOOK (800-395-5665)

www.lookgoodfeelbetter.org

A Bright Future

The future for esthetics is promising; experts predict that the biotechnology industry will continue to create compounds, ingredients, and products that promote dramatically younger-looking skin. Device manufacturers will continue to innovate and improve on existing technologies and create new ones. The demand is being driven by a working consumer who will remain in the workforce longer than previous generations. Healthy-looking and healthy-acting skin, along with lifestyle commitments, will keep them vital well into their later years.

Did You Know?

The baby boomers—Americans born between 1946 and 1964—constitute the largest generation in U.S. history. They are also the largest single market for skin care products and services. This trend continues with baby boomers' younger siblings, and both generations' children coming up behind them, enjoying the benefits of the skin care market.

Skin care products will be more effective and will contain both chemical and natural ingredients. Product ingredient-delivery systems and device-treatment applications are continually evolving and will mimic the body's own natural health requirements. The interest in less invasive technology is here to stay. Prevention will serve as a number one priority. Cell and tissue protectants will be sought by the consumer—studies over the last 25 years have demonstrated that in the nature vs. nurture concept, nurture takes the lead role when defining antiaging methodologies.

These trends bode well for the esthetician. The average life span of people in the United States has doubled since 1900. Life has become more fast-paced and stressful for most Americans, and environmental assaults on the skin have increased. These factors enhance the value of an esthetician's services, particularly to consumers who are more knowledgeable and more affluent than in previous generations. Skin care options today are more science-based and the results are more dramatic. Consumers view these personal services and products as necessary to their health and sense of well-being and consider them more as a routine rather than a luxury.

Web Resources

For more information about the esthetics profession, visit these Web sites:

www.lookgoodfeelbetter.org
www.ncea.tv
www.dol.gov
www.cosmeticplasticsurgerystatistics.com
www.themakeupgallery.info
www.beauty.about.com

Opportunity for Estheticians

The U.S. Department of Labor predicts the rapid growth of full-service day spas and a growing demand for practitioners licensed to provide a broad range of services. There will be plenty of opportunities for estheticians in newer settings, such as lifestyle and retirement centers. Whole communities are being designed for the baby boomers, who have grown accustomed to having these esthetic services. We are seeing a multidisciplinary approach to medicine and a further blending of them with subspecialties such as esthetics, massage, wellness, and women's fitness centers that may be partnered with an Obstetrician-Gynecologist (OB-GYN) facility, for example. Cosmetic dentists are partnering with cosmetic surgeons. Teaching hospitals that run clinical studies in human potential will also have medical spas and fitness centers to enhance the benefits of these studies. We will see more estheticians as independent practitioners who make home, office, and hotel visits. ☑ L04

This is a time of revolutionary changes in what we know about the skin and the ways we care for it. Keeping the skin healthy and youthful looking for decades is no longer just a fantasy. As an esthetician, you are part of an exciting, rewarding, and well-respected profession that will only grow in importance and earning power in the years ahead. If you can dream of your ideal career, it is there waiting for you.

Review Questions

1. Name some of the materials that ancient people used as color pigments in cosmetics.
2. What did the ancient Hebrews use to keep their skin healthy and moist?
3. The word *cosmetics* comes from what Greek word? What does it mean?
4. In ancient Rome, what body therapies were provided by bathhouses for patrons?
5. Describe the facial masks women used during the Victorian Age.
6. Which important cosmetic products and procedures were introduced in the late twentieth century?
7. What career options are available to estheticians in salons and day spas?
8. What is medical aesthetics? In what ways can estheticians practice their skills in a medical setting?
9. Describe the different environments in which makeup artists can be employed.
10. What are the duties of a manufacturer's representative? Of a cosmetics buyer?
11. Discuss the employment options open to an esthetics educator.
12. Describe additional opportunities for estheticians and the subspecialties that they may pursue.

Glossary

esthetician	Also known as *aesthetician*; a specialist in the cleansing, beautification, and preservation of the health of skin on the entire body, including the face and neck.
esthetics	Also known as *aesthetics*; from the Greek word *aesthetikos* (meaning "perceptible to the senses"); a branch of anatomical science that deals with the overall health and well-being of the skin, the largest organ of the human body.
henna	A dye obtained from the powdered leaves and shoots of the mignonette tree; used as a reddish hair dye and in tattooing.
medical aesthetics	Also known as medical *esthetics*; the integration of surgical procedures and esthetic treatments.
nanotechnology	The art of manipulating materials on an atomic or molecular scale.

CHAPTER 2

Life Skills

Chapter Outline

- Why Study Life Skills?
- Life Skills
- The Psychology of Success
- Study Skills
- Managing Your Career
- Goal Setting
- Time Management
- Maintaining Professional Standards
- Personality Development and Attitude

Learning Objectives

After completing this chapter, you will be able to:

- ✓ **LO1** List the principles that contribute to personal and professional success.
- ✓ **LO2** Describe good study habits.
- ✓ **LO3** Create a mission statement.
- ✓ **LO4** Explain how to set long-term and short-term goals.
- ✓ **LO5** Discuss the most effective ways to manage time.
- ✓ **LO6** Define ethics.
- ✓ **LO7** List the characteristics of a healthy, positive attitude.

Key Terms

Page number indicates where in the chapter the term is used.

ethics
pg. 32

game plan
pg. 24

goal setting
pg. 28

mission statement
pg. 27

perfectionism
pg. 24

prioritize
pg. 30

procrastination
pg. 23

Why Study Life Skills?

As an esthetician your primary job responsibility is promoting skin health and beauty. To be successful in this people-oriented business you will need excellent life skills.

- Practicing good life skills will lead to a more rewarding and productive career in the beauty and wellness industry.
- Estheticians work with many different types of people. Developing good life skills will help you to keep those interactions positive in all situations.
- Well-developed life skills will help you to manage your personal and professional life in a meaningful and productive manner.
- Good life skills promote healthy self-esteem, which in turn helps you achieve your personal best.

Life Skills

All of the technical skills you are now acquiring in school are vastly important. But the way you handle yourself and behave toward others will ultimately determine whether you can attain—and sustain—success. Even the best technical skills must rest on a solid foundation of life skills, which are tools and guidelines that prepare you for living as a mature adult in a complicated world. Acquiring life skills empowers you to move beyond the personal and professional challenges that all of us face in our daily lives. Keeping an open mind and learning as much as you can about who you are is the first step in reaching your personal best and developing a rewarding career. Becoming a lifelong learner will help you to stay fresh, motivated, and engaged in your life and in the lives of those around you.

Many life skills will lead to a satisfying and productive existence. Some of the most important are:

- Demonstrating that you care about others.
- Adapting to situations around you.
- Staying the course with your goals.
- Seeing projects to completion.
- Developing meaningful relationships.
- Building a professional network.
- Learning how to take care of your finances.
- Using common sense and reasoning things out.
- Staying calm in stressful situations.
- Taking responsibility seriously.

- Mastering techniques that will help you to be more organized.
- Maintaining a sense of humor.
- Acquiring patience.
- Always striving to do your best.
- Remaining honest and true to yourself in all your endeavors.

As you practice these skills, be prepared to reinvent yourself from time to time. A wise mentor can be an invaluable resource, steering you to books, tapes, and free classes on personal development. Use every social and business opportunity to apply the knowledge you acquire to hone your interpersonal and communication skills. Seek out new friends who are on a path of personal growth and meet regularly to share new and exciting information about what you are learning. When you let people see you in new and different ways, you expand your consciousness and create space for the unlimited possibilities that are available to you.

The Psychology of Success

Well-developed life skills are the cornerstone of a successful career. The real test lays in endurance. Are you passionate about learning and committed to reaching your highest potential? Do you see yourself sustaining this passion 1 year, 5 years, or even 10 years from now? While esthetics school is challenging, it becomes much easier when you put that extra amount of effort, enthusiasm, and excitement into your studies. If your talent is not fueled by the passion necessary to sustain you over the course of your career, you can have all the talent in the world and still not be successful (**Figure 2–1**).

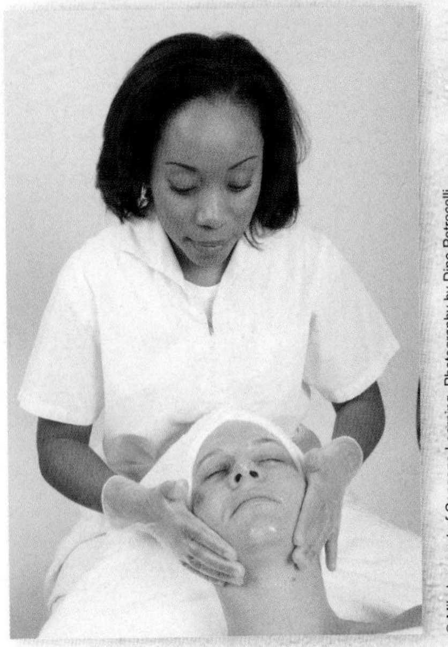

▲ Figure 2–1
Loving your work is critical to your success.

Guidelines for Success

Defining *success* is a very personal matter. Some basic principles, however, form the foundation of personal and professional success. You can begin your journey to success right now by examining and putting the following principles into practice.

- **Build self-esteem.** Self-esteem is based on inner strength and begins with trusting your ability to reach your goals.
- **Visualize your success.** Imagine yourself working in a successful skin care salon where clients perceive you as a person of confidence, competence, and maturity. See yourself as a polished professional with many requests for your services and a full appointment book. The more you visualize yourself as a successful esthetician, the more easily you can turn the possibilities in your life into realities.
- **Build on your strengths.** Practice doing whatever helps you to maintain a positive self-image—playing the piano, cooking, or

▲ Figure 2–2
Spend time on the things you do well.

teaching yoga, for example (Figure 2–2). How do you feel when you have mastered something difficult? If you can apply the same discipline and commitment to esthetics, you are bound to achieve similar success at work. There are many work-related skills, such as eyebrow shaping and makeup artistry, that you can strive to perfect. The things you are good at do not have to be things you can see, touch, or feel. Perhaps you are a good listener, or a caring friend, or a conscientious parent or considerate coworker; such attributes are equally important to the esthetician's success.

- **Learn from your mistakes.** There is very little room for error in esthetic procedures, especially when working with chemicals and sophisticated equipment that have the potential to cause injury or harm to a client, so it is important to practice until you are confident. If you do make a mistake, rather than wasting precious energy on self-critical and negative thoughts, think about how you could have avoided it and what you will do to prevent the same mistake from happening a second time. When you see the opportunity for growth in everyday challenges, you are a problem solver, not a victim. This level of maturity benefits everyone involved: you, your clients and your employer, and it ultimately gives people the confidence they need to have faith in your skills and abilities.
- **Define success for yourself.** While there may be many people you look up to and admire, do not depend on other people's definition of success. What is right for your father, your sister, or your best friend may not be right for you.
- **Practice your presentation skills.** Develop good communication skills, such as speaking with confidence, standing tall, and using good grammar when you speak. An awareness of how you come across to others will not only help you to earn the respect and trust of your clients, it is critical to networking with colleagues and other business associates who have the potential to influence key decision makers.
- **Develop good networking skills.** There are many ways to connect with colleagues and business associates to further your career. The list in Chapter 21, Career Planning, will help you to get started. If time and finances are an issue, investigate on-line social networks in which you can participate. Do not overlook local business and higher-education opportunities within your community. Participating in networking groups and seminars outside of the industry will help you to broaden your perspective and build business.
- **Keep your personal life separate from your work.** People who talk about themselves or others at work lower morale and cause the whole team to suffer. It may be tempting to share day-to-day happenings, but too much information can lead to a host of problems at work. Putting the focus on your personal life rather than the task at hand can leave you vulnerable to the judgment of others. It also

undermines efficiency and is something most bosses frown upon. We will talk more about this topic and the best way to manage relationships with coworkers in Chapter 4, Communicating for Success, and Chapter 21, Career Planning.

- **Keep your energy up.** A healthy lifestyle is a tremendous asset in reaching your goals. Be sure to get enough rest and pace yourself. Success means having a clear head, a fit body, and the ability to refuel and recharge throughout the day. (Take the Self-Care Test in **Figure 2–3** to determine how well you take care of yourself.)
- **Respect others.** Use good manners. Avoid interrupting. Do not discuss your personal life with a neighboring coworker, even if you think clients cannot hear you. (They can and do.) As your awareness grows, this kind of respect will become a way of life. When you treat people kindly, they will respect you, and their respect helps build your self-esteem.
- **Stay productive.** Work on eliminating any bad habits that can keep you from maintaining peak performance. Three key bad habits that can keep you from maintaining peak performance are: (1) procrastination, (2) perfectionism, and (3) the lack of a game plan.

Procrastination is putting off until tomorrow what you can do today. This destructive yet common habit can lead to a host of unwanted problems. For example, a well-intentioned, "I'll study tomorrow," may

The Self-Care Test

Some people know intuitively when they need to stop, take a break, or even take a day off. Other people forget when to eat. You can judge how well you take care of yourself by noting how you feel physically, emotionally, and mentally. Here are some questions to ask yourself to see how you rate on the self-care scale.

1. Do you wait until you are exhausted before you stop working?
2. Do you forget to eat nutritious food and substitute junk food on the fly?
3. Do you say you will exercise and then put off starting a program?
4. Do you have poor sleep habits?
5. Are you constantly nagging yourself about not being good enough?
6. Are your relationships with people filled with conflict?
7. When you think about the future are you unclear about the direction you will take?
8. Do you spend most of your spare time watching TV?
9. Have you been told you are too stressed and yet you ignore these concerns?
10. Do you waste time and then get angry with yourself?

Score 5 points for each yes. A score of 0-15 says that you take pretty good care of yourself, but you would be wise to examine those questions you answered yes to. A score of 15-30 indicates that you need to rethink your priorities. A score of 30-50 is a strong statement that you are neglecting yourself and may be headed for high stress and burnout. Reviewing the suggestions in these chapters will help you get back on track.

◀ Figure 2–3
Self-Care Test.

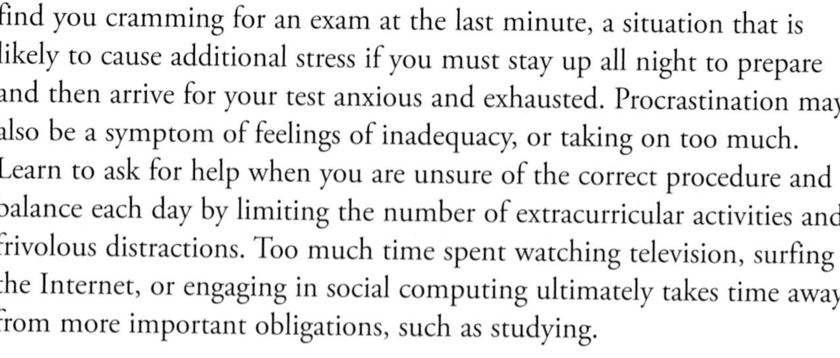

find you cramming for an exam at the last minute, a situation that is likely to cause additional stress if you must stay up all night to prepare and then arrive for your test anxious and exhausted. Procrastination may also be a symptom of feelings of inadequacy, or taking on too much. Learn to ask for help when you are unsure of the correct procedure and balance each day by limiting the number of extracurricular activities and frivolous distractions. Too much time spent watching television, surfing the Internet, or engaging in social computing ultimately takes time away from more important obligations, such as studying.

ACTIVITY

Develop your definition of success. What does it look like to you? You may draw it, paint it, create a vision board from images or words cut from a magazine, or write it out in outline form. Whichever method you use be sure to post it somewhere so that you can see it every day, and your definition of success will become more real to you.

Perfectionism is an unhealthy compulsion to do things perfectly. There are times when estheticians must adhere to strict protocol performing tasks exactly as specified. For example, when practicing cleaning and disinfection procedures, applying chemicals, or using equipment that has the potential to cause injury or harm. In this case striving for perfection is a worthy goal. In other situations, exceptionally high standards can interfere with your ability to get the job done in an efficient manner. Here is where self-imposed, irrational, or unattainable goals—such as a need to shine counter tops and equipment until you can see your image—may be unnecessary and counterproductive. A more practical and less frustrating approach to work is one that focuses on achieving the best results in the most efficient way possible.

Lacking a game plan. Having a **game plan** is the conscious act of planning your life, instead of just letting things happen. While an overall game plan is usually organized into large blocks of time (5 or 10 years ahead), it is just as important to set daily, monthly, and yearly goals. Where do you want to be in your career 5 years from now? What do you have to do this week, this month, and this year to get closer to your goal?

Rules for Success

If you were to ask several successful estheticians what the key to their success is, you will likely find one single trait in common—a lifelong commitment to learning. Education is a powerful tool that can open many new doors, but to be successful you must take ownership of your education. During this beginning stage of your esthetic training, your instructors will be there to support and guide you in the learning process, but the ultimate responsibility for learning is *yours*. To derive the greatest benefit from your education, you must commit yourself to the following rules:

- Attend all classes.
- Arrive for class early.
- Have all necessary materials ready.
- Listen attentively to your instructor.
- Highlight important points.

- Take notes for later review.
- Pay close attention during summary and review sessions.
- When something is not clear, ask questions to gain a better understanding.

Following these simple rules will help you to gain the most from your current program, but it is important to remember that your learning will not stop here. Education is the foundation of your career and the basis from which you will continue to grow as a professional. Finishing school is not the end of learning. The esthetic industry is constantly changing. There are always new trends, techniques, products, and information. Read industry magazines and trade journals, develop a library of reference books, attend trade shows, and continue your education with advanced educational classes throughout your career. Developing good habits at the onset will take you a long way on the road to success. ☑ L01

Motivation and Self-Management

Motivation propels you to do something; self-management is a well-thought-out process to achieve what you want in the long term. When you are hungry, for example, you are motivated to eat. But it is self-management that helps you to decide how you will nourish your body, where you will get food, and how much of it you will actually ingest. A motivated student finds it much easier to learn. The best motivation for you to learn comes from an inner desire to grow your skills as a professional—a lifelong pursuit that is motivated by the ever-changing world of professional beauty and a strong desire to be the best esthetician you can be.

If you are personally drawn to skin care, then you are likely to be interested in the material you will be studying in school. If your motivation comes from some external source—for instance, your parents, teachers, friends, or a vocational counselor—you will need to determine if their well-intentioned encouragement fits with your career goals and desires. To achieve success, you need more than a passing interest or an external push; you must feel a sense of personal excitement and a good reason for staying the course. Remember—you are the one in charge of managing your own life and learning. To do this successfully, you need good self-management skills.

Tapping into the Creative Mind

Self-management requires a strong commitment to owning one's personal power. There are many inner resources that can be called upon to accomplish this goal. One important self-management skill we can draw on is the creative mind. Creativity is often equated with artistic talents such as painting, acting, and writing. In the beauty business, creativity is generally associated with applying makeup, hairstyling, or doing artificial nails. The creative mind is also an unlimited inner resource for solving problems and generating new ideas. To enhance your creativity, keep these guidelines in mind:

▲ Figure 2–4
Build strong relationships for support.

- **Do not be self-critical.** Criticism blocks the creative mind from exploring ideas and discovering solutions to challenges.
- **Do not depend on others for motivation.** Inspiration may come from many sources, but tapping into your own creativity is the best way to manage your success.
- **Change your vocabulary.** Build a positive vocabulary by using active problem-solving words like *explore*, *analyze*, *solve*, *create*, and so on.
- **Do not try to go it alone.** In today's high-pressured world, many talented people find that they are more creative in an environment where people work together and share ideas. This is where the value of a strong salon and spa team comes into play (**Figure 2–4**).

Study Skills

Developing good study habits is an important part of the learning process and the initial yardstick from which you can begin to measure your success. If you find studying overwhelming, break it down into more manageable tasks. For example, instead of trying to study for 3 hours at a stretch and suffering a personal defeat when you fold after 40 minutes, set the bar lower by studying in smaller chunks of time. If your mind tends to wander in class, try writing down key words or phrases as your instructor discusses them. Any time you lose your focus, request additional help, but be prepared with questions based on your notes.

▲ Figure 2–5
Studying with friends can be effective and fun.

Another way to get a better handle on studying is to find other students who are open to being helpful and supportive. The more you discuss new material with others, the more comfortable you will become with it, and the more successful you will be. If possible, study together (**Figure 2–5**).

Establishing Good Study Habits

Part of developing consistently good study habits is knowing where, when, and how to study.

Where

- Establish a comfortable, quiet spot where you can study uninterrupted.
- Have everything you need—books, pens, paper, proper lighting, and so on—before you begin studying.

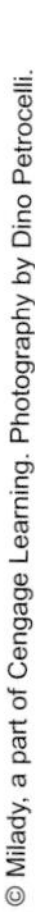

- Remain as alert as possible by sitting upright. Reclining will make you sleepy!

When

- Start out by estimating how much study time you need.
- Study when you feel most energetic and motivated.
- Make good use of your time by planning study periods at peak attention times.
- Be creative and take advantage of any down time that is available—for example, while waiting for a doctor's appointment, haircut, oil change, and so on; during work breaks; or while commuting to work or school if you take the bus or train.

How

- Study a section of a chapter at a time, instead of the entire chapter at once.
- Make a note of key words and phrases as you go along and use these as a quick study guide to prepare for vocabulary tests, etc.
- Test yourself on each section to ensure that you understand and remember the key points of each chapter.
- If you are time challenged, consider using audio recordings of your lessons and review these while running, walking, or driving, instead of listening to the radio or music.

Remember that every effort you make to follow through on your education is an investment in your future. The progress you make with your learning will increase your confidence and self-esteem across the board. In fact, when you have mastered a range of information and techniques, your self-esteem will soar right along with your grades. ☑ **LO2**

Managing Your Career

No matter how hard you study, or how creative, talented, and motivated you are, you are bound to face a few challenges along the way. Knowing how to manage your career will make all the difference in overcoming those challenges and staying focused on your goals.

Design a Mission Statement

Every successful business has a business plan. An essential part of this plan is the **mission statement**, which establishes the values that an individual or institution lives and works by, as well as future goals (Figure 2–6). If you are going to succeed in life, you too will need a well thought-out sense of purpose and a reason for being.

▼ Figure 2–6
A vision board with a personal mission statement.

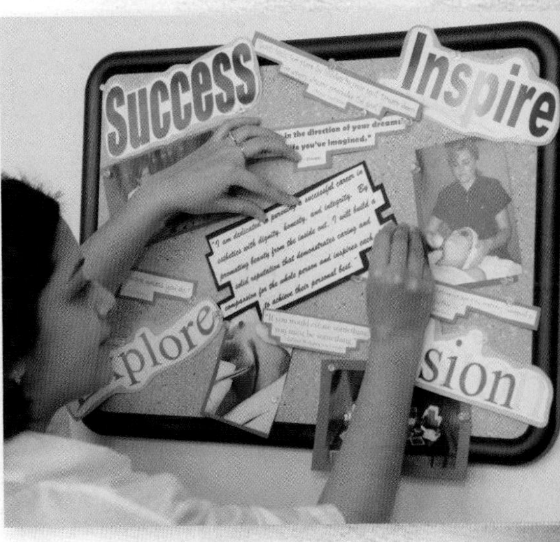

FOCUS ON

Your Plan for Success

Invest in yourself by coming up with a game plan. You may think it is easier to just coast along from day to day, but the road to success is best reached with a clear vision that will lead you to exactly where you want to go. By consciously planning your life instead of just letting things happen, you become an active participant in the manifestation of your goals. Begin by asking yourself where you want to be in 10 days, 10 months, or 10 years. What kind of resources and training will you need to get there? It may seem harder at first to approach life in this way, but you will find it brings greater rewards. Winners are people who decide what they want to do, set a goal, and stick to it. *Remember you are a winner.*

FOCUS ON

The Goal

Make this commitment to yourself: I have taken the first steps on my journey to success. I have given myself the courage to enroll in school. By taking this step, I have made the conscious decision that I want more from my life for myself and for those for whom I am responsible. This decision will help me to accomplish my dreams.

Your personal mission statement does not have to be elaborate. Start with one or two sentences that communicate who you are and what you want for your life. One example of a simple yet thoughtful mission statement is: "I am dedicated to pursuing a successful career in esthetics with dignity, honesty, and integrity. By promoting beauty from the inside out, I will build a solid reputation that demonstrates caring and compassion for the whole person and inspires each client to achieve their personal best." Whatever you want for your future will be based on the mission statement you make now. It will point you in a solid direction and help you feel secure when things are temporarily not working out as planned. For reinforcement, keep a copy of your mission statement where you can see it and read it every day. ✓ **L03**

Goal Setting

Some people never have a fixed goal in mind. They go through life one day at a time without really deciding what they want, where they can find it, or how they are going to live their lives once they get it. They drift from one activity to the next with no direction. Does this describe you? Or do you have drive, desire, and a dream? If so, do you have a reasonable idea of how to go about meeting your goal?

Goal setting is the identification of long-term and short-term goals that helps you decide what you want out of your life. When you know what you want, you can draw a circle around your destination and chart the best course to get you there. By mapping out your goals, you will see where you need to focus your attention and what you need to learn in order to fulfill your dreams.

How Goal Setting Works

What are you working toward at this time in your life? Can you picture your goal in your mind? Is it working with patients in a dermatology clinic or a skin care salon? Perhaps you have a vision of owning your own profitable day spa.

There are two types of goals: short-term goals and long-term goals. Examples of short-term goals are to get through a midterm exam successfully or to finish your esthetics course. Short-term goals are usually those you wish to accomplish within a year at the most. Long-term goals are measured in larger sections of time such as 2 years, 5 years, 10 years, or even longer. Examples of long-term goals are owning your own salon or writing a book on skin care.

The important thing is to have a plan and re-examine it often to make sure you are staying on track (**Figures 2–7 and 2–8**). The most successful professionals continue to set goals for themselves even after they have accumulated fame, fortune, and respect. They adjust their goals and action plans as they go along, but never forget that their goals are what keep them going. ✓ **L04**

HERE'S A SAMPLE OF HOW TO SET AND TRACK SHORT-TERM GOALS.			
NUMBER	GOAL SETTING CHECKLIST	COMPLETION DATE	DONE
1.	Read Chapter 2. Action Steps: Read first part at lunch; finish it after dinner.	6/09/2013	❑
2.	Practice speaking to clients in a pleasing voice. Action Steps: Do with family tonight.	6/10/2013	❑
3.	Create my own mission statement. Action Steps: Review sample in Chapter 2; write my own.	6/15/2013	❑
4.	Start researching trends. Action Steps: Search on-line, read trade and beauty magazines. Make a 5-word "trend list."	6/20/2013	❑
5.	Prepare to pass the Chapter 2 exam. Action Steps: Review what I read, ask instructor any questions, have study session with 2 friends.	7/10/2013	❑
6.	Practice being on time! Action Steps: Set alarm for 15 minutes earlier. Give self $1 every time get to class 10 minutes early.	Start 6/20 5 days in a row by 7/20	❑
7.	Build my vocabulary. Action Steps: Buy book or find Web site. Learn 1 new word a day.	Daily	❑

▲ Figure 2–7
Here's a sample of how to set and track short-term goals.

MY GOALS			
NUMBER	GOAL SETTING CHECKLIST	COMPLETION DATE	DONE
1.			
2.			
3.			
4.			
5.			
6.			
7.			

▲ Figure 2–8
Use this as a template and fill in your own goals!

Time Management

Time management is essential to goal setting. It is also an integral component in living a healthy life. We need time for rest, time to exercise, time to eat, time to play, time to work, and time to spend with friends and family. If we are able to manage our time carefully, we can live more fulfilling lives and actually contribute more to the lives of others. Some ideas for managing your time as efficiently as you can are as follows:

- Learn to **prioritize**. Make a list of tasks that need to be done in the order of most-to-least important. To-do lists for the day or week are very helpful (**Figure 2–9**).
- Never take on more than you can handle. Learn to say no firmly but kindly, and mean it. You will find it easier to complete your tasks if you limit your activities and do not spread yourself too thin.
- Learn problem-solving techniques, and use them.
- Give yourself a time-out whenever you are frustrated, overwhelmed, irritated, worried, or feeling guilty about something. Brooding only reinforces frustration and will cost you valuable time and energy.
- Plan to make dates with friends and family members; doing so helps us to be well-rounded and provides a solid support structure.
- Reward yourself with a special treat for work well done and time managed efficiently.
- Exercise to stimulate clear thinking and planning.
- Develop your own personal mission statement. This can help you stay on track, and it is useful to determine whether a project or job is good for you.
- Commit to making effective time management a habit.

▲ Figure 2–9
Write out a plan to help you reach your goals.

Time Management in Esthetics

When it comes to esthetics, being on time is a large part of being professional. We would not stay in practice very long if we were unable to be on time, and balance that time with each client wisely. On the job, punctuality is a professional responsibility. Time means money, as

Real-Life Goal Setting

Many salon managers will assist you in setting goals, based on the salon's criteria. One common goal you may be asked to reach is to retail a certain dollar amount or percentage of gross sales, for instance, "Must retail a minimum of $2,000 per month or 30 percent of gross service income."

Goals may also be tied to your performance and income level. For example, you may be required to maintain a certain client retention rate or increase the number of services sold to repeat clients to receive a bonus or increase your sales commission. In turn, estheticians are generally encouraged to set goals that will support higher earnings for the salon, like increasing retail or service sales. Salon managers will help you break down financial goals into attainable, daily goals. For instance, if you are looking to increase your gross income by $10,000 more a year, you will need to bring in an additional $27.39 a day. Of course, you don't work 7 days a week. A more realistic number is based on working 5 days a week, 52 weeks a year, or 260 days. That's $38.46 per day more you need to gross. There may be several different ways to increase your income depending on how you are paid. For example, you may try to sell more retail products to half your clients, or increase the number of add-on services and back-bar treatments if your salary also includes a commission on services.

the saying goes. If you cannot perform a certain number of services or allow enough time to maximize the results of treatments clients will become dissatisfied, and you will quickly fall behind in monetary goals. To achieve long-term financial success and client satisfaction, you must carefully plan each day (**Figure 2–10**).

You must have a solid understanding of how long each treatment will take as well as a method for maintaining an organized approach. If you are just starting out, this means practicing each treatment until timing becomes second nature. Most facials require at least 1 hour to perform. When combined with additional consultation and retail responsibilities, the average treatment time generally totals about 1 hour and 15 minutes.

Getting used to working within these parameters requires training and discipline. Probably the most helpful advice you will receive as an esthetician is "Be prepared." The following guidelines will help you do just that.

- At the end of the day, begin organizing for the next day. Clean and organize your treatment room, and replenish supplies as needed.
- Pull each scheduled client's record and review the last treatment. Decide on *possible* treatment procedures based on previous notations. Make sure all necessary equipment is sanitized and ready for use.
- Note any special considerations. Depending upon your employer's policy, ask a new client to arrive 10 minutes early to fill out a client intake form. While the client is changing, review the history.
- For clients with special needs, know that you may need to spend more time with them, and plan your schedule accordingly.
- Look at the retail products the client is using, and have them available. Leave enough time to review progress on home-care or to recommend a program if the client is new.
- Build time into your schedule for making important follow-up or sales calls.
- Make time for lunch and a few minutes to visit with a friend or coworker to enjoy your day. ☑ **LO5**

We live in a hurried world. An important part of your work that should not be overlooked is the added benefit of relaxation that most clients expect. If you are rushed, your clients will not be able to relax and fully enjoy the treatment. By taking time to prepare in advance, you can give your clients your undivided attention. A few minutes of deep breathing or silent meditation can also help to relax and refresh your mind in-between clients. This is probably the best way to demonstrate your professionalism.

ACTIVITY

It's estimated that as much as 4 hours a day are spent checking e-mail, texting, looking at Web sites, and watching videos. To find out if you are managing your time well, try this:

- **Write down the time in the morning when you first go on-line, check e-mail, or send a text message.**
- **Do what you normally do, then note the end time for these activities.**
- **Throughout the day, try to estimate and add to your list how much time you spend on these activities.**
- **Add up the total time at the end of your day.**

Are you surprised? Time-management experts recommend that you work for the first 45 minutes or hour of the day and avoid e-mailing, Web browsing, and texting. Instead, plan your day, review reading materials for school, or do other work. This can be the best time to accomplish something concrete, because it is quiet and often interruption-free. Starting your day being productive helps you develop good time-management skills for life.

© Photodisc.

▲ Figure 2–10
Organize your to-do list for the day, week, and month.

fyi

Real-Life Time Management

There are two critical areas of time management in the salon. Showing up for work on time each day is the first step in managing your day successfully. The second, and perhaps the most important aspect of time management, is to stay on time with your treatments, so you can give each client the undivided quality time they deserve and avoid keeping the next client waiting for her scheduled appointment. This means mastering the service during the time allotted. Salons vary in how they book facials, which may range anywhere from 30 minutes for a mini-facial to 90 minutes for an advanced or signature treatment. Scheduling an additional 10 to15 minutes in-between treatments gives the service provider time to review home-care treatment protocols and recommend additional service and retail products. In most cases you will also need to allow time to clean up and prepare for the next client.

Many salons today use computerized systems to help practitioners stay on schedule. Some employ personal digital assistants (PDAs) or pagers to alert service providers when the next client has arrived. A simple digital text sent to the front desk can be a tremendous help if you would like to know if there is time to add on a service immediately. With experience, you'll learn to accommodate late clients and add-on services like a pro.

Maintaining Professional Standards

An important part of professional development is a commitment to upholding ethical standards. **Ethics** are the moral principles by which we live and work. Good character, proper conduct, and moral judgment expressed through personality and human relations skills are ethics in action. Ethics are sometimes referred to more simply as a code of conduct. In different professions, codes of ethics are classified by boards or commissions. In esthetics this is most often generated by the Board of Cosmetology; for example, each state board of cosmetology sets the ethical standards that must be followed by all estheticians who work in that state. These guidelines are essential to maintaining the credibility and integrity of our profession, protecting consumers, and earning the public's trust. Ethical dilemmas tend to arise when we are confused about our boundaries or inexperienced in how to handle situations.

To be clear, estheticians are expected to be knowledgeable about skin care. They are trained to perform specialized skin care services and to advise and educate clients on products and techniques. To do this well, they must maintain competency, act responsibly, protect client confidentiality, avoid exploitation, and demonstrate exemplary conduct.

Obtaining the appropriate state license or certificate to practice esthetics is the first step in establishing credibility (**Figure 2–11**). Estheticians should always adhere to the regulations and guidelines of their state licensing board and should be aware that each state may vary in what an esthetician may or may not do in that particular state. Estheticians should also be conscious of regulations set forth by the Food and Drug Administration (FDA) and other government agencies, such as the Federal Trade Commission (FTC) and the Consumer Product Safety Commission (CPSC), whose function is to protect the consumer and prevent the public from being duped by false claims and advertising. ☑ **LO6**

As skin care professionals, we can all appreciate the consumer who is wary of purchasing the ever-present "miracle in a jar." So how do we gain the public's trust? Here are some general guidelines that will help you maintain credibility and build confidence.

- Obtain the necessary credentials to practice in your state.
- Join and participate in professional organizations that take an unbiased approach to esthetics.
- Make sure your behavior and actions match your values. For example, if you believe it is unethical to sell products just to turn a profit, then do not do so. However, if you believe a client

needs products and additional services for healthy skin maintenance, it would be unethical not to give the client that information.

- Show respect for your colleagues and supervisors. Do not make derogatory comments about other practitioners or undermine your employer's policies and price structure.
- Know your boundaries. Do only what you are trained to do. Do not offer advice or make recommendations outside of your area of expertise. This means understanding when to decline a service or opinion and refer the client to the appropriate professional.
- Keep client relationships professionally friendly. Clients often confide very personal information. Practice respectful listening, maintain professional boundaries, and do not gossip. Do not give advice or share personal information.
- Be honest and truthful. Do not make false claims about products and techniques. When you do not have the answer, simply say, "I don't know, but I'll find out for you."
- Do not rely on promotional literature by manufacturers to ensure a product's efficacy. Conduct your own research, particularly on controversial methods or ingredients, by having the staff try the products before you make claims about them (Figure 2–12). Also, it is fine to tell a client that a product is new in the office, and that you are trying it out. Make sure you can stand behind the products you use or recommend.
- Be open to seeking consultation from more experienced colleagues or other professionals.
- Stay informed. Attend as many continuing-education seminars as you can (but recognize that one workshop does not make you an expert). Subscribe to professional trade publications and read as much as possible.

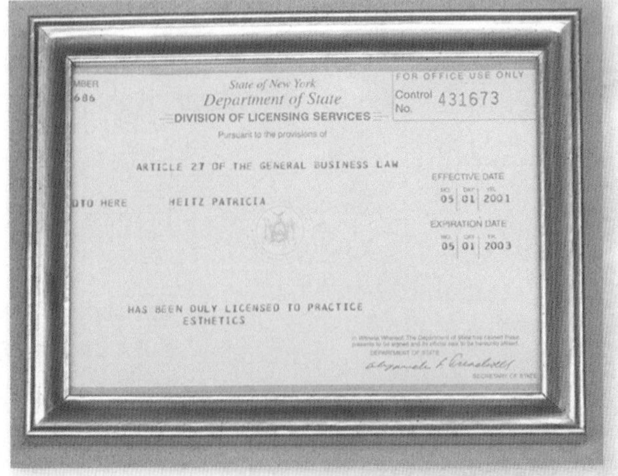

▲ Figure 2–11
A license establishes that an esthetician is a qualified practitioner.

FOCUS ON
Stress Management

Deep breathing is a simple but very effective practice. Breathe deeply into the lungs through the nose. Your abdomen should extend outward as you inhale. When you fully exhale, the abdomen will contract inward. Try to integrate deep breathing into your day as often as possible. Deep breathing calms and energizes simultaneously. It can also lower blood pressure and is a true stress-buster!

Personality Development and Attitude

Professional standards set the tone for the esthetician's personal endorsement of proper business protocol. Some occupations require minimal human interaction. For example, a bookkeeper may have limited opportunity to interact with clients and colleagues. As an esthetician, though, you will be dealing face-to-face with people from all walks of life throughout your day. While a good deal of the services you provide will be performed working one-on-one with clients, you

▲ Figure 2–12
Always try products yourself before recommending them to others.

Did You Know?

The National Coalition of Estheticians, Manufacturers/Distributors & Associations (NCEA) is an organization that was developed to support estheticians and the public in which they serve. The following is their mission statement:

The mission of the NCEA is to represent the esthetic profession by defining and conveying standards of practice, while educating the industry and the public.

The code of ethics as printed by the NCEA is as follows:
NCEA Code of Ethics

Client Relationships

- Estheticians* will serve the best interests of their clients at all times and will provide the highest quality service possible.
- Estheticians will maintain client confidentiality, keep treatment and documentation records, and provide clear, honest communication.
- Estheticians will provide clients with clear and realistic goals and outcomes and will not make false claims regarding the potential benefits of the techniques rendered or products recommended.
- Estheticians will adhere to the scope of practice of their profession and refer clients to the appropriate qualified health practitioner when indicated.

Scope of Practice

- Estheticians will offer services only within the scope of practice as defined by the state within which they operate, if required, and in adherence with appropriate federal laws and regulations.
- Estheticians will not utilize any technique/procedure for which they have not had adequate training and shall represent their education, training, qualifications and abilities honestly.
- Estheticians will strictly adhere to all usage instructions and guidelines provided by product and equipment manufacturers, provided those guidelines and instructions are within the scope of practice as defined by the state, if required.
- Estheticians will follow, at minimum, infection control practices as defined by their state regulatory agency, Centers for Disease Control & Prevention (CDC) and Occupational Safety & Health Administration (OSHA).

Professionalism

- Estheticians will commit themselves to ongoing education and to provide clients and the public with the most accurate information possible.
- Estheticians will dress in attire consistent with professional practice and adhere to the Code of Conduct of their governing board.

*For the purpose of the NCEA Code of Ethics, the use of the term Esthetician applies to all licensed skin care professionals as defined by their state law.

All information printed with permission of NCEA.

will also be expected to work as part of a team. A good understanding of your own personality will help you to blend more easily with the many different personalities you will encounter in clients, coworkers, and your employer. Some of the most important elements of a healthy, positive lifestyle are attitude, work ethic, and teamwork. Making sure these characteristics are personal assets will help you to make the most of your day.

Attitude

Attitude can be defined as your outlook, and it underlies the way you live your life. Attitude stems from what you believe and can be influenced by your parents, teachers, friends, and even books and movies. You may not be able to change a characteristic that you were born with, but you can change your attitude.

In business and in your personal life, a pleasing attitude will gain you more associates, clients, and friends. Here are some ingredients of a healthy, well-developed attitude.

- **Diplomacy.** Be tactful in your dealings with others. This means being straightforward, but not critical.
- **Emotional stability.** It is essential to have feelings and express them appropriately. Self-control—learning how to handle a confrontation as well as letting people know how you feel without going overboard—is an important indicator of maturity.
- **Receptivity.** To be receptive means being interested in other people and being responsive to their opinions, feelings, and ideas. Receptivity involves taking the time to really listen instead of pretending to do so.
- **Sensitivity.** Your personality shines when you show genuine concern for the feelings of others. Sensitivity is a combination of understanding, empathy, and acceptance. A sensitive person is aware of how damaging criticism can be and always offers criticisms constructively. Being sensitive does not mean you have to let people take advantage of you; it means being compassionate and responsive. It is strength, not weakness.
- **Values and goals.** Neither values nor goals are inborn characteristics. You acquire these beliefs about what constitutes appropriate behavior and how you will focus your energy as you move through life. A strong value system is bolstered by two very important skills: good manners and good judgment. These are the basis for all good business practices.
- **Communication skills.** Communication is your way of ensuring that you understand the needs and desires of the people around you. And because communication is a two-way street, it ensures that your

Did You Know?

In a medical setting, including skin care clinics and medical spas, federal privacy standards to protect clients' and patients' medical records and health information has been enacted in the United States. The Department of Health and Human Services (HHS) developed the Health Insurance Portability Accountability Act (HIPAA) to protect individuals with regard to obtaining information about their health in a medical setting. But the act also states that all communication that takes place in a medical setting must be kept confidential. This means that clients or patients visiting a medical spa or clinical skin care setting can file formal complaints about practitioners engaging in a breach of confidentiality. Estheticians can be held liable for sharing information with others about clients or patients. The bottom line is, information shared about a client in the office is on a need-to-know basis as it pertains to properly treating a client. Do not gossip about clients with other estheticians or with other clients. For more information, visit www.hhs.gov/ocr/hipaa.

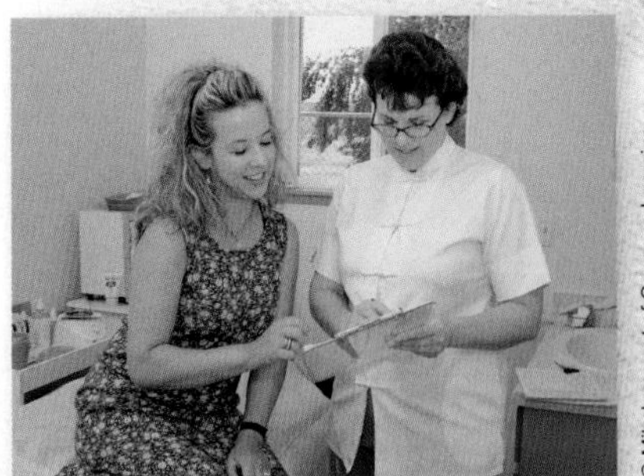

▲ Figure 2–13
Communicating during a client consultation should be a two-way street.

Did You Know?

When you smile, a number of physiological changes take place. Laughter can rev up your immune system, lower your blood pressure, and help you sleep better. Laughing is good for the soul, whether at work or at play.

FOCUS ON

The Positive

Some say that attitude is everything and that, with a winning attitude, you cannot miss being a success. So ask yourself: "Am I a winner?"; "Do I have faith in my success?"; "Do I get along with others?" If you can answer yes, then you may be able to create the life you want. If the answer is no, then you have more work to do on the attitude front. This is a process that continues throughout your life.

clients will understand your ideas and suggestions as well. Clients can go virtually anywhere to receive skilled treatments, but they stay with estheticians who create the best atmosphere, treat them with respect, and have good interpersonal skills (Figure 2–13, page 35).

- **Discretion and confidentiality.** Do not share your personal problems with your clients or tell other people the concerns they may have shared with you. This is not simply a matter of courtesy, in esthetics it is a professional responsibility.
- **Maintain boundaries.** Have a one-minute rule on sharing information about yourself and respect the limits of your esthetics license. Remember the appointment is about the client and her skin, and you are an esthetician, not a counselor. ☑ L07

Work Ethic

As employees we all want to be valued for the contributions we make. Employers are equally concerned about the contribution you will make and are looking for people who are loyal and committed to doing a good job. But it takes more than getting up in the morning and showing up at work to earn that respect. Establishing a good work ethic requires you to be mindful about how you approach each day, how you treat others, and how you support your employer's needs. A willingness to give the best of yourself, accept constructive criticism, grow and learn from your mistakes, and adapt to changes in the workplace demonstrates a positive attitude that will get you off to a good start. A good work ethic includes being trustworthy, reliable, hardworking, respectful, and supportive of others.

Teamwork

Today's salon and spa environment can be hectic and fast-paced. To maintain a stress-free and productive environment, every staff member must be focused on working cooperatively. Teamwork is essential to developing a positive work ethic in a salon environment. Staff members need to know they can rely on each other for help and support. When each person pulls their own weight and is dedicated to sharing responsibility, stress is alleviated and common goals are achieved.

Team members who are equally invested in providing quality service in a relaxing, supportive, and nurturing environment are also better able to encourage one another to do the best job possible. The result is a caring and respectful work environment where everyone can be successful.

Review Questions

1. List several principles that you can put into practice to create personal and professional success.
2. How do you describe good study habits?
3. How do you create a mission statement? (Give an example.)
4. How do you go about setting long-term and short-term goals?
5. What are some of the most effective ways to manage time?
6. What is the definition of ethics?
7. What are the characteristics of a healthy, positive attitude?

Glossary

ethics	The moral principles by which we live and work.
game plan	The conscious act of planning your life, instead of just letting things happen.
goal setting	The identification of long-term and short-term goals that helps you decide what you want out of your life.
mission statement	A statement that establishes the values that an individual or institution lives and works by, as well as future goals.
perfectionism	An unhealthy compulsion to do things perfectly.
prioritize	To make a list of tasks that need to be done in the order of most-to-least important.
procrastination	Putting off until tomorrow what you can do today.

CHAPTER 3

Your Professional Image

Chapter Outline

- Why Study the Importance of Your Professional Image?
- Beauty and Wellness
- Appearances Count
- Your Physical Presentation
- Professional Conduct

Learning Objectives

After completing this chapter, you will be able to:

- ☑ **LO1** Explain the characteristics of a professional image.
- ☑ **LO2** Understand the importance of professional hygiene.
- ☑ **LO3** Demonstrate proper standing and sitting posture.
- ☑ **LO4** Understand how your personal conduct affects your professional image.

Key Terms

Page number indicates where in the chapter the term is used.

ergonomically correct posture
pg. 43

ergonomics
pg. 43

personal hygiene
pg. 41

physical presentation
pg. 43

professional image
pg. 40

Judging others by their appearance might seem rather shallow, yet research shows that first impressions are tied closely to our physical appearance. Because you are in the image business, how you look and present yourself will have an even greater impact on how others perceive you. If you are recommending skin care services, it is critical that your own skin be well-cared for. If you are advising clients on the perfect eyebrow shape for their face, then your eyebrows must be in harmony with your facial features. If you are advising your clients about makeup, then your makeup must be current and beautifully applied. When your appearance and the way that you conduct yourself are in harmony with the beauty business, your chances of being successful in the field of esthetics increases by as much as 100 percent! After all, when you look great, your clients will assume that you can make them look great, too.

Why Study the Importance of Your Professional Image?

The way you look, act, and speak is critical to presenting a polished professional image in the skin care business.

- Clients expect skin care professionals to have skin that is well-cared for and makeup that is current and skillfully applied.
- When you follow your own advice and practice good skin care, clients will develop confidence in your ability to do the same for them.
- The esthetician's work is physically demanding. Maintaining an ergonomically correct posture while working is an important part of staying healthfully and gainfully employed for years to come.
- Your professional image extends to how well you interact with managers, coworkers, and clients. Understanding what behaviors are appropriate in the workplace is vital to flourishing in your career.

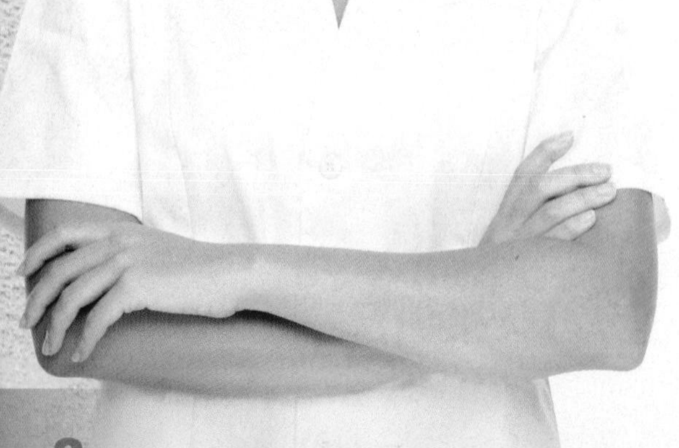

Beauty and Wellness

Your **professional image** is the impression projected by a person engaged in the profession of esthetics, consisting of outward appearance and conduct exhibited in the workplace (**Figure 3–1**). Your appearance, attitude, and abilities create a mental picture in the minds of your clients and associates. You want that image to earn their respect, trust, and eagerness for your knowledge.

Your professional image is also tied to your role as a model for your clients. You not only help your clients look their best but also alert them to lifestyle decisions that can affect their beauty and health. That means you will need to look your best and make lifestyle choices that express your commitment to your own well-being. Adequate sun protection, exercise, and avoidance of harmful stimuli, such as alcohol and tobacco, are just a few examples of healthy lifestyle choices. Remember: If you do not make every effort to look good, your clients may assume that you cannot make *them* look good. ✓ **L01**

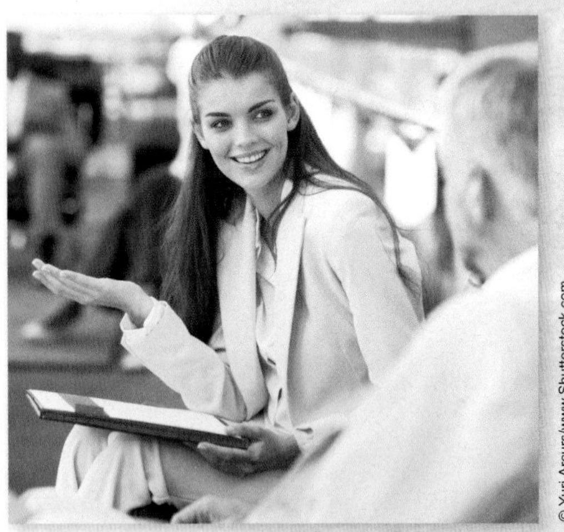

▲ Figure 3–1
Project a professional image at all times.

Personal Hygiene

Personal hygiene (HY-jeen) is the daily maintenance of cleanliness and healthfulness through certain sanitary practices. The basics of personal hygiene include:

- Daily bathing or showering, shaving for men, and freshening up throughout the day as necessary.
- Shampooing, conditioning, and styling your hair as required to keep it fresh, clean, and contemporary.
- Following a regular skin care regimen.
- Brushing and flossing your teeth, as well as using a mouthwash or breath mints throughout the day as needed.
- Paying attention to what you eat and drink during work hours. The smell of certain foods and beverages, like coffee and onions, can linger long after ingestion.
- Using underarm deodorant or antiperspirant.
- Washing your hands throughout the day as required, such as when beginning and ending a service or after visiting the bathroom.
- Avoiding the use of heavy perfumes. To prevent allergic reactions some salons may ask you to avoid using perfume altogether.

CAUTION!

Fragrances

Many salons have a no-fragrance policy for staff members during work hours because a significant number of people are sensitive or allergic to a variety of chemicals, including perfume oils. For some individuals this sensitivity may also apply to the use of essential oils. Whether or not your salon has a no-fragrance policy, the use of perfume and heavily scented lotions should be saved for after work and always used in moderation.

Nail care is particularly important for estheticians. Keep both fingernails and toenails clean, trimmed, and filed (**Figure 3–2**). Nails that are too long or pointed can scratch your client's skin or interfere with your work. Be meticulous about your manicure and pedicure. Take care of hangnails immediately. Keep your hands and feet well moisturized. ✓ **L02**

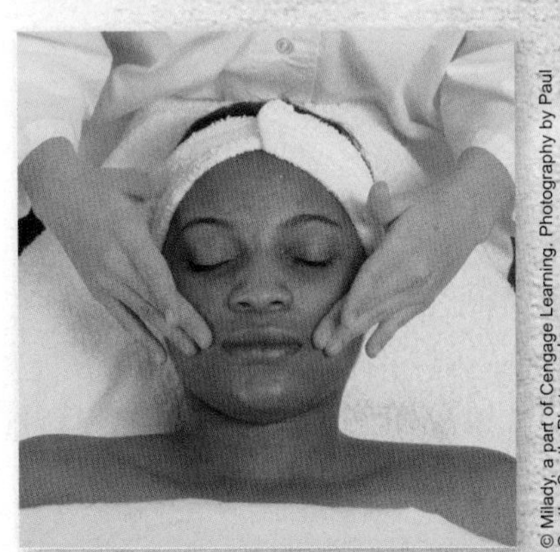

▲ Figure 3–2
An esthetician's nails must be trimmed and filed smooth.

Appearances Count

As a skin care specialist, your poised and attractive appearance will ensure that your clients think of you as a professional. Many salon and spa managers consider appearance and poise to be just as important for success as technical knowledge and skills. So it is a good idea to establish habits of good health and grooming from the start.

Creating Balance

Real beauty begins with health and stays grounded in health. Good health greatly affects your energy level, your attitude, and, ultimately, your appearance. One of the most important factors in promoting and maintaining health is balance.

Balance can be hard to achieve in the frantic pace of modern life. For many of us, it can be a challenge to manage stress. Being in balance enables us to make the right choices for ourselves. If you consistently undermine your well-being with poor choices, you may be putting yourself at risk for disease. Achieving balance is crucial to leading a healthy, productive life (**Figure 3–3**). You can help create balance by eating a nutritious diet, exercising regularly, getting adequate rest and recreation, and avoiding such habits as smoking, drinking excessively, and taking drugs.

▲ Figure 3–3
Learn to balance your professional life with personal time.

Dress for Success

At the salon, strive to have your hair, makeup, and clothing express a professional image that is consistent with the image of the salon. You should always comply with the dress code, but the following guidelines are generally appropriate:

- Clothing should be clean and fresh. Uniforms should be comfortable and provide good mobility, especially in the shoulder and elbow areas, but should not be too loose fitting (**Figure 3–4**).
- Wear clean undergarments every day, and keep them out of view. Underwear elastic peeking out of your pants or exposed bra straps, as well as cleavage exposure and a bare midriff, are inconsistent with a professional image.
- Hair should be neatly coiffed and swept up and off the shoulders if it is long.
- Socks or hosiery should be free of runs and harmonize with your attire.
- Keep shoes clean and comfortable, with good support.
- A clean, natural approach is generally best when applying makeup.
- Dangling jewelry is inappropriate, and it is hazardous to your clients.

▲ Figure 3–4
Clothing should be clean, functional, and comfortable.

Wearing Makeup in the Salon

Makeup is an exciting category for beauty professionals and may include a wide range of menu options in the skin care salon, such as natural or mineral cosmetics, camouflage, and permanent makeup. Worn tastefully to accentuate your best features, makeup can help promote your professional image and represents profitable sales for salons. That said, it is important to be conscious of the focus of the esthetician's work—

beautiful, healthy skin. When working, take a lighter approach to your makeup regime and reserve trendier looks such as heavily made-up eyes and black nail polish for after hours.

Your Physical Presentation

Another important aspect of your professional image is physical presentation. To a large degree, **physical presentation** is made up of a person's physical posture, walk, and movements. It can enhance or detract from your attractiveness and is an important part of your well-being. Unhealthy or defective body postures can cause a number of physical problems, particularly when these postures become a habit.

Ergonomics is the science of designing the workplace, its equipment, and tools to make specific body movements more comfortable, efficient, and safe. We will talk more about ergonomics in Chapter 14, The Treatment Room. Learning how to control your own body in the workplace will give you a head-start.

Posture

Good posture conveys an image of confidence. When you stand tall with your back straight, stomach in and shoulders back, you appear competent and poised. How you carry yourself can also prevent fatigue and other physical problems. As an esthetician, you will spend a lot of time in one of two positions: standing on your feet or sitting behind the treatment bed or table on a stool. Under these conditions it is essential to maintain an **ergonomically correct posture**, or one that is healthy for the human spine. Hydraulic chairs, stools, and treatment tables that can be raised and lowered to accommodate the individual practitioner's needs are ideal for maintaining healthy work conditions. You will learn more about how to set up an ergonomically viable treatment room in Chapter 14, The Treatment Room. When you are conscious of how you move your body and practice good posture, you not only look more confident, you will feel better throughout the day.

Standing Posture

Here are some guidelines for achieving and maintaining good standing posture (follow **Figure 3–5**):

- Keep the neck elongated and balanced directly above the shoulders.
- Lift your upper body so that your chest is out and up (do not slouch).
- Hold your shoulders level and relaxed, not scrunched up.
- Keep your back straight.
- Pull your abdomen in so that it is flat.
- Flex your knees slightly and position them over your feet.

CAUTION!

Not only can wearing inappropriate shoes at work be uncomfortable, it could be dangerous. Flip-flops and open-toed shoes are just two examples of footwear that are not safe to wear around chemicals, electricity, or sharp implements. Estheticians must adhere to state board regulations and health code requirements for appropriate footwear in the salon.

Did You Know?

Physical exercise is a great way to relieve stress. Going for a vigorous walk or run, biking, swimming, yoga, or aerobic dancing can make productive use of valuable personal time, allowing you to put aside the demands of your work. This kind of exercise is relaxing and has beneficial physiological effects. One exercise session can generate up to 2 hours of the relaxation response.

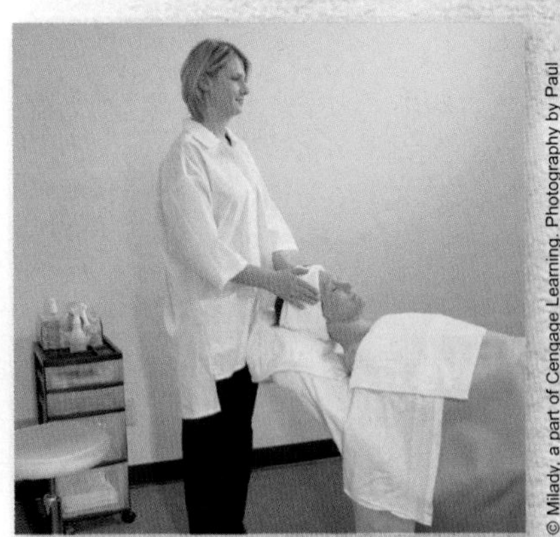

▲ **Figure 3–5**
Good standing posture can help prevent back strain and other problems.

ACTIVITY

Practice these quick exercises, which will help you relieve stress from repetitive movements or from standing or sitting in one position for too long:

For Wrists

1. Stand up straight.
2. Raise both of your arms straight out.
3. Bend your wrists so your fingers point upward and hold for 5 seconds.
4. Hold your wrists steady and turn your hands, so your fingers face the floor.
5. Hold for 5 seconds.
6. Repeat the cycle five times.

For Fingers

1. Get a ball the size of a tennis ball or a tension ball.
2. Grip it tightly for a count of five, then release.
3. Repeat five times.

For Shoulders

1. Stand up straight and shrug your shoulders upward.
2. Now, roll your shoulders back and hold for a count of five.
3. Reverse direction and roll your shoulders forward for a count of five.
4. Repeat five times.

Sitting Posture

Guidelines for a proper sitting position (follow Figure 3–6) include:

- Keep your back straight.
- Keep the soles of your feet entirely on the floor.
- Do not cross your legs or your feet at the ankles.
- Do not bend forward from the waist or stoop forward from the shoulders. Bend from the hips, or sit on a chair or wedge-shaped cushion that tilts forward. ✓ LO3

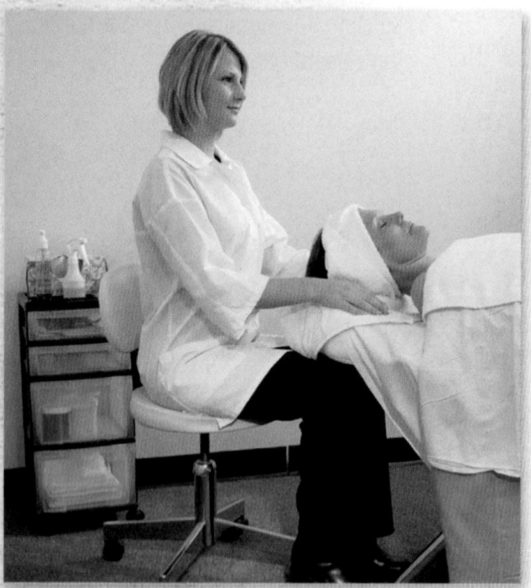

▲ Figure 3–6
Proper body alignment while sitting is important for an esthetician.

Professional Conduct

In addition to your appearance, your professional image consists of your conduct in the workplace—or how you behave and get along with your clients, coworkers, and your employer.

Good manners are the hallmark of all professional interactions. In business, no matter what the day brings you must be prepared to deal with it in a positive and professional manner. Ask yourself: "Am I warm, pleasant, and friendly to each person that I come in contact with?"; "Do I maintain appropriate boundaries and treat even the most benign client information as privileged?"; "Do I keep my ego in check and compromise as needed to maintain professional relationships?" Before you cross a line that you might later regret, think about how you would feel if salon guests overheard you and your client discussing the details of your's and your client's personal life, or if a colleague you trusted was overheard judging your ability to maintain a clientele in the lunchroom with several other coworkers.

Beyond the very serious legal ramifications associated with breaking HIPPA rules and regulations or the unsavory repercussions of workplace politics, how you look, listen, and engage with clients, coworkers, and supervisors are all factors in your professional presentation. When you steer clear of the gossip mill, practice confidentiality, and treat everyone with the respect and kindness that you would want for yourself throughout the course of your day, your professional image is greatly enhanced.

Mastering Self-Control

Practicing proper etiquette in the workplace is a must; however, as long as we are working for and with people, there will always be some who are more difficult than others.

While they do present a challenge, you need to remember that you are in a professional setting, and your standards for dealing with others must be high. Difficult clients are still a source of income, and difficult coworkers may not go away. We will discuss best practices for communicating with clients and coworkers further in Chapter 4, Communicating for Success. For now, the important thing to remember is that you always have the power to make positive choices.

When conflicts arise consider the following coping mechanisms:

- Count to 10 and think before you speak.
- Distance yourself from a situation to regain your composure.
- Avoid engaging in a no-win situation or argument.
- Get another opinion before making a judgment.
- Stand your ground when necessary. You can be assertive without being overbearing when you use proper business etiquette.
- Direct a situation to a higher authority if necessary.
- Take the high road and refrain from criticizing.
- Help others meet their goals by assuming more responsibility (**Figure 3–7**).

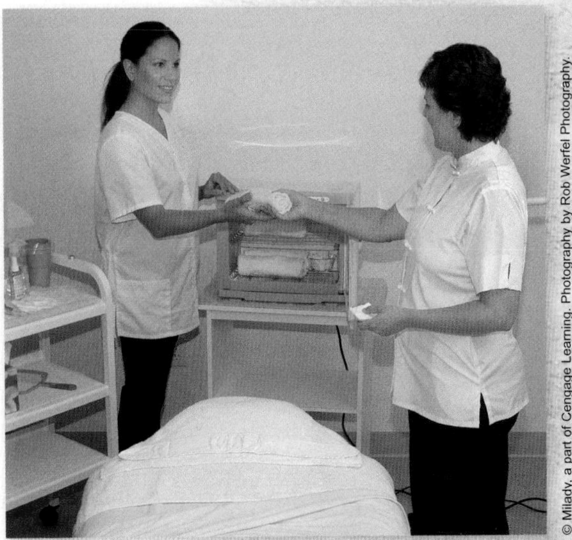

▲ **Figure 3–7**
Pitching in wherever help is needed is part of being a team player.

Ultimately, if you are invested in working cooperatively with others, have a strong work ethic, use proper etiquette, and practice good communication techniques the potential for conflict is greatly decreased. ☑ **LO4**

Review Questions

1. Define the term professional image.
2. What practices can you incorporate into your everyday routine to create balance and promote health?
3. List the basic habits of personal hygiene.
4. What is the best way to ensure you are dressed for success?
5. What is the role of good posture in professional presentation and health?
6. How can you avoid ergonomically related injuries?
7. What is the most important factor in professional conduct?
8. List five ways you can master self-control in the workplace.

Glossary

ergonomically correct posture	One that is healthy for the human spine.
ergonomics	The science of designing the workplace, its equipment, and tools to make specific body movements more comfortable, efficient, and safe.
personal hygiene	Daily maintenance of cleanliness and healthfulness through certain sanitary practices.
physical presentation	A person's physical posture, walk, and movements.
professional image	The impression projected by a person engaged in any profession, consisting of outward appearance and conduct exhibited in the workplace.

CHAPTER

4 Communicating for Success

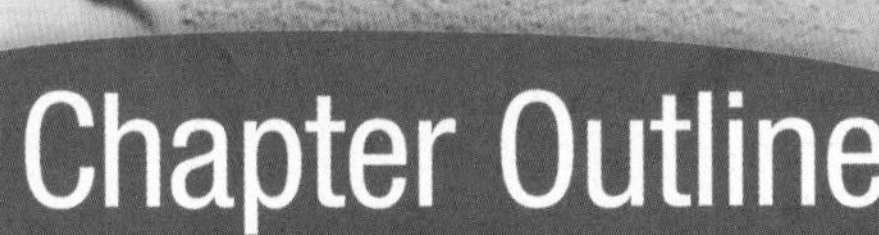

Chapter Outline

- Why Study Communicating for Success?
- Human Relations
- Communication Basics
- The Client Consultation
- Special Issues in Communication
- In-Salon Communication

Learning Objectives

After completing this chapter, you will be able to:

- ☑ LO1 List the golden rules of human relations.
- ☑ LO2 Explain the importance of effective communication.
- ☑ LO3 Conduct a successful client consultation.
- ☑ LO4 Handle delicate communications with your clients.
- ☑ LO5 Build open lines of communication with coworkers and salon managers.

Key Terms

Page number indicates where in the chapter the term is used.

client consultation (needs assessment) pg. 54

communication pg. 52

consent form pg. 54

reflective listening pg. 58

Do you have outstanding technical skills? Gifted hands? A flair for makeup artistry? If you do, you are definitely on your way to becoming successful in your chosen career path within the field of esthetics. It is important to realize, though, that technical and artistic skills can only take you so far. To thrive in the field of esthetics, you must also master the art of communication. Effective human relations and communication skills build lasting client relationships, aid in your growth as a practitioner, and help prevent misunderstandings and unnecessary tension in the workplace (**Figure 4–1**).

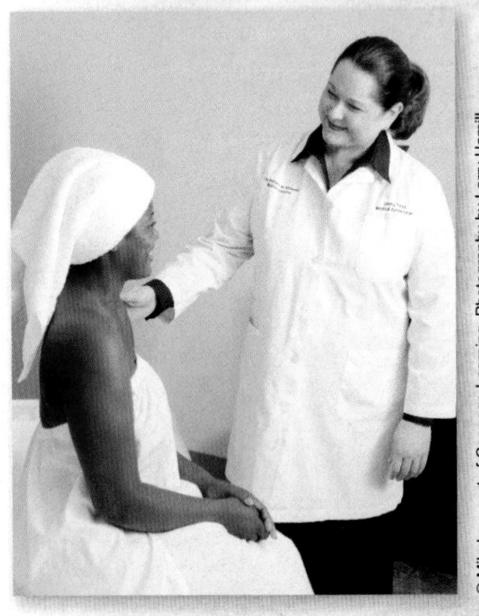

▲ Figure 4–1
Good communication is essential to building positive client relations.

Why Study Communicating for Success?

Estheticians work face-to-face with clients—a distinct advantage in determining their needs, wants, likes, and dislikes. To make the most of this prime time together, estheticians must have excellent communication skills.

- Communicating effectively is the basis of all long-lasting relationships with clients and coworkers.
- Strong professional relationships are based on trust. To be successful in building trust, you must be able to verbalize your thoughts and ideas with clients, colleagues, and supervisors in a positive and purposeful way.
- The close-knit salon and spa environment will present complex and sometimes difficult interpersonal dynamics. In order to navigate them successfully, you will need effective ways to communicate.
- Practicing and perfecting professional communication ensures that clients will enjoy their experience with you, and will encourage their continued patronage.
- The ability to control communication and express your ideas in a professional manner is a primary ingredient for success in any career. This is particularly true in one as personal as skin care.

Human Relations

No matter where you work, you will not always get along with everyone. It is not possible to always understand what people need, even when you know them well. Even if you do think you understand what people want, you cannot always be sure that you will satisfy them. This can lead to tension and misunderstanding.

The ability to understand people is the key to operating effectively in many professions. It is especially important in esthetics, where customer service is central to success. Most of your interactions will depend on your ability to communicate successfully with a wide range of people:

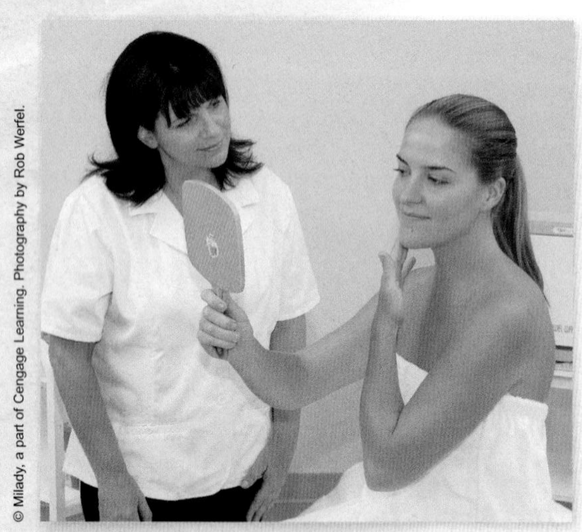
© Milady, a part of Cengage Learning. Photography by Rob Werfel.

▲ Figure 4–2
Be attentive to your client's needs.

your boss, coworkers, clients, and the different vendors who come into the skin care salon or spa to sell and educate you about their products. When you clearly understand the motives and needs of others, you are in a better position to do your job professionally and easily (**Figure 4–2**).

The best way to understand others is to begin with a firm understanding of yourself. When you are conscious of your own needs and desires, it is easier to appreciate others and to help them get what they need. Basically, we all have similar needs. When we are treated with respect and people listen to us, we feel good about them and ourselves. When we create an atmosphere where customers and staff have confidence in us, we will get the respect we deserve. Good relationships are built on mutual respect and understanding. Here is a brief look at the basics of human relations, along with some practical tips for dealing with situations that you are likely to encounter.

- A fundamental factor in human relations has to do with how secure we are feeling. When we feel secure, we are happy, calm, and confident, and we act in a cooperative and trusting manner. When we feel insecure, we become worried, anxious, overwhelmed, perhaps angry and suspicious, and usually we do not behave very well. We might be uncooperative, hostile, or withdrawn.
- Human beings are social animals. When we feel secure, we like to interact with other people. We enjoy giving our opinions, we take pleasure from having people help us, and we take pride in our ability to help others. When people feel secure with us, they react positively and are a joy to be with. You can help people feel secure around you by being respectful, trustworthy, and honest.
- No matter how secure you are, there will be times when you will be faced with people and situations that are difficult to handle. You may already have had such experiences. There are always some people who create conflict wherever they go. They can be rude, insensitive, or so self-centered that being considerate just does not enter their minds. Even though you may wonder how anyone could be so insensitive, just try to remember that this person at that particular time feels insecure, or he or she would not be acting this way.

To become skilled in human relations, learn to make the best of situations that could otherwise drain both your time and your energy. Here are some good ways to handle the ups and downs of human relations.

- **Respond calmly instead of overreacting.** A fellow was asked why he did not get angry when a driver cut him off. "Why should I let someone else dictate my emotions?" he replied. A wise fellow, don't you think? The ability to think thoughtfully rather than react impulsively will help you to maintain control of your emotions. In situations like this, not reacting with "an eye for an eye" mentality might even have saved a life.
- **Believe in yourself.** When you do, you trust your judgment, uphold your own values, and stick to what you believe is right. It is easy to believe in

yourself when you have a strong sense of self-worth. It comes with the knowledge that you are a good person and deserve to be successful. Believing in yourself makes you feel strong enough to handle almost any situation in a calm, helpful manner.

- **Talk less, listen more.** There is an old saying that we were given two ears and one mouth for a reason. You get a gold star in human relations when you listen more than you talk. When you are a good listener, you are fully attentive to what the other person is saying. If there is something you do not understand, ask a question to gain understanding.
- **Be attentive.** Each client is different. Some are clear about what they want; others are aggressively demanding, while others may be hesitant. If you have an aggressive client who is not responding to your best efforts to communicate effectively, instead of trying to handle it by yourself, ask your manager for advice. You will likely be told that what usually calms difficult clients down is listening without interruption, agreeing with them, and then asking what you can do to make the service more to their liking. This approach works nine out of ten times.
- **Take your own temperature.** If you are tired or upset about a personal problem, or have had an argument with a fellow student, you may be feeling down about yourself and wish you were anywhere but in school. If this feeling lasts a short time, you will be able to get back on track easily enough and there is no cause for alarm. If, however, you begin to notice certain chronic behaviors about yourself once you are in a job, pay careful attention to what is happening. An important part of being in a service profession is taking care of yourself first and resolving whatever conflicts are going on so that you can take care of your clients. Trust can be lost in a second without even knowing it—and, once lost, trust is almost impossible to regain.

The Golden Rules of Human Relations

Keep the following guidelines in mind for a crash course in human relations that will always keep you in line and where you should be:

- Communicate from your heart; solve problems from your head.
- A smile goes a long way in establishing rapport and making people feel comfortable.
- Be kind to others. Treat people in a way that allows them to maintain their dignity.
- Every action brings about a reaction. Think twice before impulsively reacting to a situation.
- Learn to ask for help when you are overwhelmed.
- Show people you care by listening to them and trying to understand their point of view.

- Give compliments freely. An encouraging word at the right moment brings out the best in people.
- Being right is different from acting righteous. Avoid being a know-it-all and offering your unsolicited opinion on every topic.
- Balance your service to others with personal time to renew your own mind, body, and spirit.
- Develop a sense of humor. The ability to laugh makes coping with the demands of life a lot easier.
- Show patience with other people's flaws.
- Take time to evaluate your own attitude and actions.
- Make amends when you are wrong.
- Learn to forgive yourself and others.
- Be compassionate toward others, demonstrating your support in difficult times.
- Build shared goals; be a team player and a partner to your clients.
- A simple thank-you goes a long way in showing your appreciation to clients and colleagues.
- Remember that listening is the best relationship builder. ✓ LO1

Communication Basics

Communication is the act of successfully sharing information between two people, or groups of people, so that it is effectively understood. There are many facets to communication. You can communicate through words, voice inflections, facial expressions, body language, and visual tools (e.g., before and after photos).

▼ Figure 4–3
First impressions are often lasting impressions. When meeting a client for the first time, maintain good eye contact, smile, and extend a warm handshake.

As you develop effective communication skills, consider that many times it is not *what* we say, but rather *how* we say it. Paying attention to the nonverbal cues we use can help us to improve the quality of our relations with both clients and colleagues. The list of positive and negative nonverbal cues in Table 4-1 will help you to become more aware of how you are coming across to others (**Table 4–1**).

When you and your client are both communicating clearly about an upcoming service, your chances of pleasing that person soar.

Meeting and Greeting New Clients

One of the most important communications you will have with a client is the first time you meet that person. Be polite, genuinely friendly, and inviting—and remember that your clients are coming to you for services they are paying for. This means it is your job to provide them with excellent customer service every time they come to see you; otherwise, if you don't, you may lose them to another esthetician or salon (**Figure 4–3**).

POSITIVE AND NEGATIVE NONVERBAL CUES	
POSITIVE NONVERBAL CUES	**NEGATIVE NONVERBAL CUES**
• A pleasant tone of voice	• A loud and overpowering voice
• An even rate of speech	• Rapid and jumbled speech
• A moderate tone of voice	• A soft and unassertive voice
• Good eye contact	• Looking away from a person
• A simple nod to demonstrate you are listening	• Yawning, fidgeting with pens, paperclips, etc., or other distracting gestures
• Warm and enthusiastic facial gestures	• Pursing the lips or folding arms in an off-putting manner
• A smile	• A frown
• Appropriate body distance	• Standing uncomfortably close to a person
• The gentle touch of a hand	• Using hand gestures to scold or embarrass

▲ Table 4–1 **Positive and Negative Nonverbal Cues.**

To earn clients' trust and loyalty, you need to:

- Always approach a new client with a smile on your face. If you are having a difficult day or have a problem of some sort, keep it to yourself. The time you spend with your client is for her needs, not yours.
- Always introduce yourself. Names are powerful, and they are meant to be used. Many clients have had the experience of being greeted by the receptionist, ushered back to the service area, and when the service has been performed and the appointment is over, they have not learned the name of a single person.
- Set aside a few minutes to take new clients on a quick tour of the salon.
- Introduce clients to the people they may have interactions with while in the salon, including potential service providers for other services such as nail care or makeup.
- Be yourself. Do not try to trick your clients into thinking you are someone or something that you are not. Just be who you are. You will be surprised at how well this will work for you. ☑ L02

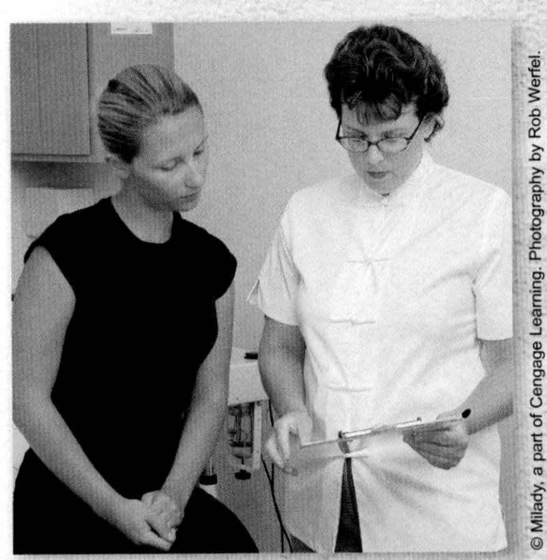

▲ Figure 4–4
The initial intake form is a critical consultation and communication tool.

Intake Form

An intake form—also called a *client questionnaire* or *consultation card*—should be filled out by every new client before receiving services. Whether in the salon or in school, this form can prove to be extremely useful (Figure 4–4).

Some salon intake forms ask for a lot of detailed information, and some do not. In esthetics school, the intake form may be accompanied by a release statement in which the client acknowledges that the service is being provided by a student who is still learning. This helps protect the school and the student from any legal action by a client who may be unhappy with the service. The salon you work in is likely to be equally cautious when it comes to accepting risk, asking clients to sign and date the intake form at each visit, especially when more advanced higher-risk procedures are involved. In the event a client does not disclose a previous treatment that has an adverse affect, the signed intake form may serve as tangible evidence that the information was not disclosed.

How to Use the Client Intake Form

The client intake form should be mentioned the moment a new client calls the skin care salon or spa to make an appointment. When scheduling the appointment, let the client know that you and the salon will require some information before you can begin the service. Some salons ask clients to arrive 15 minutes before their appointment time for this purpose. You will also have to allow time in your schedule to conduct a 5- to 15-minute **client consultation**, also known as **needs assessment**, the verbal communication with a client to determine desired results, depending on the type of service you will be performing and the client's needs (Figure 4–5).

Consent Form

Having a client sign a consent form is standard practice for more aggressive treatments. A **consent form** is a customary written agreement between the client and esthetician (spa/salon) for applying a particular treatment, whether routine or preoperative. It is a legal document that is kept in the client's chart. Typically it states that the client agrees to the treatment, application, or procedure, as well as understands and accepts all risks involved. It is important not to create an atmosphere of apprehension when introducing this form to clients. What you do want to accomplish is a thorough understanding of the benefits and features of the service or product in question. You also want the client to have a complete understanding of any contraindications to its use. Making these things clear at the outset can help reduce any fears or anxiety the client may have and allow the client to feel more comfortable with the treatment process.

How to Use the Consent Form

When introducing the consent form to clients, take time to review all the steps involved in the treatment process. Be sure to carefully explain any home-care directions that may be necessary. Provide the client with a copy of the consent form, and keep the original for your files. It is also wise to maintain a treatment log and have the client initial and date all subsequent treatment procedures. These extra precautionary measures go a long way in safeguarding both you and the client.

The Client Consultation

The client consultation is the verbal communication that determines the desired results. It is the single most important part of

CONFIDENTIAL SKIN HEALTH INTAKE FORM

PLEASE PRINT CLEARLY

Today's Date: ______________________

First Name: ______________ Last Name: ______________ Date of Birth: __/__/______

Street ______________ Apt # _____ City ______________ State _____

Phone: Home (____) _____-______ Work: (____) _____-______ Mobile: (____) _____-______

Primary Care Physician: ______________________

Dermatologist: ______________________

Emergency Contact: ______________________

Your Occupation: ______________________

Referred by: ______________________

☐ Friend ☐ Mailer ☐ Walk/Drive-by ☐ Yellow Pages ☐ Gift Certificate ☐ Other

Esthetician Name: ______________________

1. Is this your first visit to the salon/spa? ☐ Yes ☐ No
2. What is the primary reason for your visit today? ______________________
3. What special areas of concern do you have? Please check all that apply.

   ☐ Acne Management
   ☐ Acne Scarring
   ☐ Age Management
   ☐ Age Spots
   ☐ Broken Capillaries
   ☐ Enlarged Pores
   ☐ Fine Lines and Wrinkles
   ☐ Hair Removal
   ☐ Pigmentation
   ☐ Rejuvenation
   ☐ Scarring
   ☐ Stretch Marks
   ☐ Sun Damage
   ☐ Other

Please explain your concerns in detail here: ______________________

____

____

4. Have you ever had a facial treatment before? ☐ Yes ☐ No
   If yes, when was your last treatment? ______________________
5. How would you describe your experience? ☐ Positive ☐ Negative
   Additional Comments: ______________________

   ____
6. Have you ever had any of the following? If yes, please state the date of last treatment next to all that apply.

☐ Microdermabrasion
If yes, date of last treatment. ______________

☐ Hair Removal
  ☐ Electrolysis ☐ Laser ☐ IPL
  ☐ Waxing ☐ Other
If yes, date of last treatment.
____

☐ Botox® Injections
If yes, date of last treatment. ______________

☐ Collagen Injections
If yes, date of last treatment. ______________

☐ Restylane® Injections
If yes, date of last treatment. ______________

☐ Cosmetic Fillers
Please list all here: ______________
____
If yes, please state date of last treatment.
____

☐ Facial or Cosmetic Surgery
If yes, please describe and state date of last procedure. ______________
____

☐ Chemical Peels
If yes, date of last treatment. ______________

☐ Natural Peels
If yes, date of last treatment. ______________

☐ Laser Skin Resurfacing
If yes, date of last treatment. ______________

☐ Massage
If yes, date of last treatment. ______________

☐ Body Treatments
If yes, date of last treatment. ______________

☐ Permanent Makeup/Tattooing
If yes, date of last treatment. ______________

☐ Other
Please list any other cosmetic procedures or injections you have had here:
____
____
Please state date of last treatment. ______________
____

Please continue to next page

▲ Figure 4–5
The client intake form gives you an opportunity to build an excellent relationship with your client.

Did You Know?

Confidentiality

Estheticians can be held liable for a breach of confidentiality. This can result in lawsuits for both the salon and individuals. As a reminder, always adhere to HIPAA rules and regulations when handling client information and remember that the intake information supplied by clients is strictly confidential and should be handled with the utmost discretion at all times and in all situations. Never conduct a client consultation in an area where other guests or service providers might overhear, or discuss client information in public places or open salon areas.

Estheticians working in upscale salons must be particularly cautious when it comes to dealing with celebrity and high-profile clients. Asking for a client's autograph, taking photos of the client in the spa, or disclosing information about the client to the media without consent is a violation of privacy that can have significant legal repercussions. If you work in such a setting, you must be able to balance the celebrity factor with excellent service and the utmost discretion.

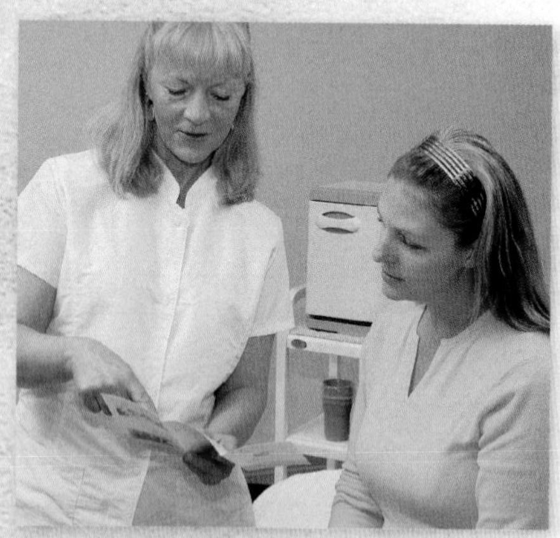

▲ Figure 4–6
Before and after photos are an excellent way to demonstrate the results of a product or treatment.

any service and should always be done *before* beginning any part of the service. Some professionals skip the client consultation altogether, or they make time for it only on a client's first visit to the salon. These professionals are making a serious mistake. A consultation should be performed, to some degree as part of every single service and salon visit. It keeps good communication going, and it allows you to keep your clients feeling satisfied with your services. Most importantly, it helps to reduce the risk of doing harm to a client.

Once you are clear about what a client is looking for, and whether or not there are any contraindications to the desired treatments, you can work together to develop a strategy for meeting these needs.

Preparing for the Client Consultation

So that your time is well spent during the client consultation, it is important to be prepared. To facilitate the consultation process, you should have certain important items on hand. A pen and intake form along with vendor-supplied or salon-manufactured pamphlets, photos, articles, or clinical research papers will help you to present the services or explain the benefits of certain ingredients that will be used to perform a treatment.

As skin care treatments become more sophisticated, many clients will have very specific questions about the outcome. Before and after photos are often a good way to demonstrate the results of a product or treatment. Step-by-step photos of the actual treatment process can also be helpful in letting clients know what to expect. Photos of satisfied customers are ideal for demonstrating the efficacy of a product or service, but they are not always suitable. Although many skin care clinics and medical spas will use before and after photos to document a client's progress, it is important to remember that such client information is confidential. If you have a client whose progress is significant, it is extremely important to gain her permission to use such photos for promotional purposes.

Vendor pamphlets that contain before and after photos are often a better resource for demonstrating the details of more aggressive treatments (**Figure 4–6**). When presenting such photos, be sure to explain how the procedure is conducted in your salon and to point out any differences. A discussion about whom the best candidates are for specific treatments can help clients to decide if the treatment is suitable for them. Even if a client appears to be a good candidate, it is wise to let clients know that you will be conducting a thorough analysis of their skin before making a final determination as to whether or not you can administer a treatment. Helping new clients understand why certain things can or cannot be achieved will also reassure them that you are knowledgeable and serious about their needs.

On occasion, you will find yourself consulting with a client who insists on a specific treatment or service that is not appropriate for them. In some cases a client may even misrepresent the truth about a situation to get you to perform a treatment that could have serious consequences. If you decide to perform a treatment that goes against your best judgment and causes harm to a client, guess who will catch the blame? In this situation, it is important to consult with a qualified superior. Refusing to perform a treatment can be difficult, but it is always better to be safe than sorry.

Letting clients know up front that every treatment is subject to further skin analysis sets the tone for professional conduct and lets clients know that all treatments are subject to specific guidelines. If there is any doubt as to whether or not you should proceed, never be afraid to get a second opinion from your supervisor or a more experienced colleague. As a final measure, always have the client sign the intake form to be sure they understand what the service involves and have fully disclosed any contraindications to treatment. For example, if the client is having a microdermabrasion treatment, you will want to be assured they have not recently undergone a chemical peel, waxing, or laser hair removal. When you frame more aggressive treatments in terms of proper skin analysis and the right skin condition, you let the client know that you are a professional that truly has their best interest at heart.

The Consultation Area

Presentation counts for a lot in a business that is concerned wtih appearances. Once you have brought a client to the consultation or treatment room to begin the consultation process, make sure she is comfortable. You and she are about to begin an important conversation that will clue you in to her needs and preferences. Your work area needs to be freshly cleaned and uncluttered. Have any pamphlets, photos, and literature that you will use to describe the benefits, features, or any contraindications to a service available. All other appropriate tools to perform the desired service should be ready for use. Review the intake form carefully with the client, and refer to it often during the consultation process. Throughout the consultation and especially once a course of action is decided on, make notes on the intake form. Record any formulations or products that you use, and include any specific techniques you follow, or goals you are working toward, so that you can remember them for future visits.

The 10-Step Consultation Method

Every complete consultation needs to be structured in such a way that you cover all the key points that consistently lead to a successful conclusion. While this may seem like a lot of information to memorize, it will become second nature as you become more experienced and conduct many consultations. Depending on the service requested, the consultation will vary to some degree. For example, a chemical peel will require a more detailed consultation than a makeup application. To ensure that you are always thorough, keep a list of the following

FOCUS ON

Understanding the Client's Goals

The initial consultation is the most important interaction you will have with a client. Information gathered at this point will help you to define the client's goals and objectives and create a positive working relationship. Remember that each client is an individual with a personal agenda. Some clients may be interested in age management, while others will be looking to remedy or control a certain skin condition. Many clients will simply want to experience the relaxation benefit associated with skin care services. When you reinforce how these goals will be met, through treatment and at-home treatment products, the client feels heard, and your chances of increasing their satisfaction is high.

To determine the best outcome, you will want to gather as much information as possible without invading the client's privacy or making them feel uncomfortable. This generally includes information about any health problems, allergies, and medications, as well as the use of any prescription skin care products, cosmeceuticals, or other skin care treatments the client has recently received that could adversely affect treatment. When conducting a consultation, remember that the information a client provides is considered privileged and should be held strictly confidential.

10 key points at your station for referral, and modify it as needed for the actual service.

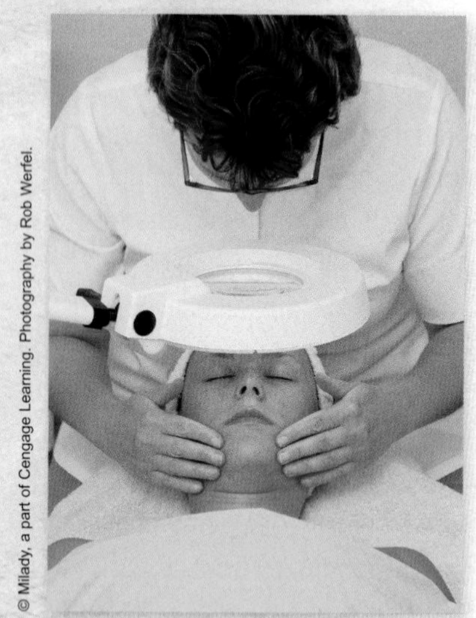

▲ Figure 4–7
Analyze your client's skin for type, texture, and skin conditions.

1. **Review** the intake form that your client has filled out and take a few minutes to develop rapport with the client and get the consultation going.
2. **Assess** your client's current goals and objectives. Is she looking to remedy a skin condition? Rejuvenate her appearance? Relax and unwind?
3. **Preference.** Ask your client what skin care products she is currently using. Does she love the fact that she only has to spend 10 minutes a day taking care of her skin? What professional treatments has she had in the past? Was she happy with the results? What is the reason for today's visit?
4. **Analyze.** Use a magnifying loupe and/or Wood's lamp to assess the client's skin. Note the skin type, texture, and any skin conditions on the consultation analysis form. Determine the client's Fitzpatrick type (more detailed information on the Fitzpatrick scale will be discussed in Chapter 12, Skin Analysis). Are there any contraindications, allergies, or sensitivities that will affect treatment (**Figure 4–7**)?
5. **Lifestyle.** Ask your client about her career and personal lifestyle.
   - Does she spend a great deal of time outdoors? Does she swim every day?
   - Is she a businesswoman? An artist? A stay-at-home mom?
   - Does she have a strong personal style that she wishes to project?
   - What are her skin care habits? How often does she have facials? How much time does she want to spend taking care of her skin each day?
   - Note all of the intrinsic and extrinsic factors.
6. **Show and tell.** Review the various treatment options. This is a good time to get a real grasp on whether the client's goals are realistic. What does the client hope to achieve? If she says she wants to look like a certain celebrity, does this mean she likes the shape of the celebrity's eyebrows or is interested in having dermatological or plastic surgery? Reinforcing your words with literature and before and after photos is critical to having a clear understanding of what both of you are really saying.

   Listening to the client and then repeating, in your own words, what you think the client is telling you is known as **reflective listening**. Mastering this listening skill will help you to always be on target with your services and to build a deep trust with your clients.
7. **Suggest.** Once you have enough information to make valid suggestions, narrow the treatment options based on the following factors:
   - ***Lifestyle.*** The products and services you recommend must fit the client's needs in terms of time and effort, stress level, medical conditions, and other intrinsic and extrinsic factors such as hormonal issues, poor nutrition, smoking or alcohol habits, and personal appearance goals.
   - ***Skin type.*** You must base your recommendations on whether your client has dry, normal, oily, combination, or sensitive skin.

- ***Skin conditions.*** Point out any contraindications to treatment or special considerations related to conditions, such as acne and hyper- or hypopigmentation.
- ***Fitzpatrick typing.*** Determine the client's Fitzpatrick type, and explain how this will affect any of the treatments or services you recommend. Advise the client on the appropriate sun protection products.

  When making suggestions qualify them by referencing the preceding factors. For example: "This treatment will help to improve the overall tone and texture of your skin." Tactfully discuss any unreasonable expectations the client may have shared with you by pointing out any contraindications or limitations to the product or service that are unrealistic based on her personal goals. If the client's skin is damaged, you may need to address the need for a series of treatments, better home-care products, or lifestyle changes, or refer the client to a medical professional who is better able to meet her needs.

  Never hesitate to suggest additional services that will provide added value to the treatment or enhance the service. For example, adding an enzyme to a basic facial will help to improve skin tone and texture, while an eyebrow wax and new makeup palette can give the client a completely new look that will better suit her lifestyle, fulfill her desire to improve her appearance, and so on.

8. **Sun exposure.** Instructions regarding proper sun protection should be part of every consultation service. Use the Fitzpatrick scale to recommend the appropriate level of sun-protection products and caution all clients against the harmful effects of overexposure to the sun. Estheticians should stress to clients that overexposure to the sun may not only lead to skin cancer but can also contribute to aging, hyperpigmentation, capillary damage, free-radical damage, and collagen and elastin deterioration (these will be discussed in detail in upcoming chapters). It is especially important to advise clients who have exfoliating treatments to keep out of the sun to avoid serious side effects.
9. **Maintenance.** Counsel every client on proper skin care, a regular schedule of salon treatments, the benefit of a series of treatments, lifestyle limitations, and home maintenance that she will need to commit to in order to look her best.
10. **Repeat.** Reiterate everything that you have agreed upon. Make sure to speak in measured, precise terms and use visual tools to demonstrate the end result. This is the most critical step of the consultation process because it ultimately determines the service(s) you will perform. Take your time, and be thorough. ☑ LO3

Concluding the Service

Once the service is finished and the client has let you know whether she is satisfied, take a few more minutes to enter the results on the consultation form. Ask for her reactions, and record them. Note anything you did that you might want to do again, as well as anything that does not bear repeating. Also make note of the final results and any retail products that you have recommended. This is the perfect time to review the client's goals and objectives. Always supply the client with a written recommendation of the products and treatments you have suggested, with specific directions for product use and recommended time frames for in-salon treatments. This is an excellent tool that the client can use for future reference if they are not ready to purchase at the time of service. Be sure to review your recommendations with the client verbally as well, otherwise the client may ignore them or view them as an impersonal sales pitch. When you take time to make a personal connection with the client, you will be seen as a caring professional who is invested in helping clients stay on track. You also have a better chance of increasing the benefit of salon services. Before moving on to the next client be sure to date your notes and file them in the proper place (Figure 4–8).

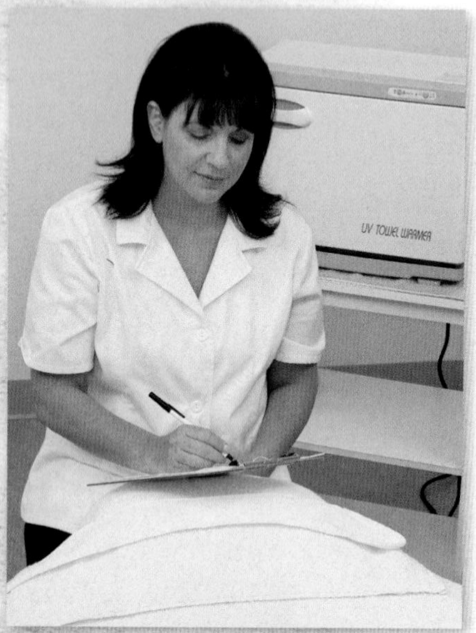

▲ Figure 4–8
Take time to record your results on the client consultation form after each and every service.

Special Issues in Communication

Although you may do everything in your power to communicate effectively, you will sometimes encounter situations that are beyond your control. The solution is not to try to control the circumstances, but to communicate past the issue. Your reactions to situations, and your ability to communicate in the face of problems, are critical to being successful in a "people" profession such as the esthetics industry.

Handling Tardy Clients

Tardy clients are a fact of life in every service industry. Because skin care professionals are so dependent on appointments and scheduling to maximize working hours, a client who is very late for an appointment, or one who is habitually late, can cause problems. One tardy client can make you late for every other client you service that day, and the pressure involved in making up for lost time can take its toll. You also risk inconveniencing the rest of your clients who are prompt for their appointments.

Here are a few guidelines for handling late clients.

- Know and abide by the salon's tardy or late policy. Many salons set a limited amount of time they allow a client to be late before they require them to reschedule. Generally, if clients are more than 15 minutes late, they should be asked to reschedule. Most will accept responsibility and be understanding about the rule, but you may come across a few clients who insist on being seen immediately. In many skin care salons, the front desk manager or receptionist handles this type of problem, but sometimes a client will insist on speaking to the service provider. If you are called upon, explain that you have other appointments and are responsible to those clients as well. Also explain that rushing through the service is unacceptable to both of you. If there is enough time to go ahead with the treatment be sure the client understands that you may not be able to conduct the full treatment given the shortened time period; for example, there may be less time for a relaxing massage. In certain instances you may consider offering an alternative treatment, such as a 60-minute facial instead of the 90-minute signature service that was scheduled. Most salons also have policies in place when it comes to fees for late arrivals and missed appointments. The client should be made aware of these policies prior to scheduling or it will be hard to enforce them.

- If your tardy client arrives and you have the time to take her without jeopardizing other clients' appointments, let your client know why you are taking her even though she is late. You can deliver this information and still remain pleasant and upbeat. Say, "Oh, Ms. Lee, we're in luck! Even though you're a bit late, I can still take you because my next appointment isn't scheduled for another hour. Isn't it great that it worked out?" This lets her know that being late is not acceptable under normal circumstances, but that if you can accommodate her, you will.
- As you get to know your clients, you will learn who is habitually late. You may want to schedule such clients for the last appointment of the day or ask them to arrive earlier than their actual appointment time.
- Imagine this scenario: Despite your best efforts, you are running late. You realize that no matter what has happened in the salon that day, your clients want and deserve your promptness. If extenuating circumstances beyond your control have placed you in a position where the next client will be kept waiting for longer than 15 minutes, have the receptionist look up your client's records and call them to advise them of the situation. Give them the opportunity to reschedule, or to come a little later than their scheduled appointments. If you cannot reach them beforehand, be sure to approach them when they come into the salon and let them know that you are delayed. Tell them how long you think the wait will be, and give them the option of changing their appointment. Apologize for the inconvenience and show a little extra attention by personally offering them a beverage. Even if these clients are not happy about the delay, or they need to change their appointment, at least they will feel informed and respected.

CAUTION!

A client who continually disrupts your schedule or a unique mishap is one thing, but continually asking clients to check in because you are always running late is another and is not recommended as a routine fix. Estheticians must learn to perform treatments within the allotted time frame for services. Salons have equal responsibility when it comes to abiding by their policies for tardy clients. When you are on time for clients and abide by salon and spa policies, you show clients that you are a professional and your time is valuable.

Handling Scheduling Mix-Ups

We are all human, and we all make mistakes. Chances are you have gone to an appointment on a certain day, at a certain time, only to discover that you are in the wrong place, at the wrong time. The way you are treated at that moment will determine if you ever patronize that business again. The number one thing to remember when you, as a professional, get involved with a scheduling mix-up is to be polite and never argue about who is correct. Being right may sound good, but this kind of situation is not about being right; it is about preserving your relationship with your client. If you handle the matter poorly, you run the risk of never seeing that client again.

Even if you know for sure that she is mistaken, tell yourself that the client is always right. Assume the blame if it helps keep her happy. *Do not, under any circumstances, argue the point with the client.*

Once you have the chance to consult your appointment book, you can say, "Oh, Mrs. Montez, I have you in my appointment book for 10 a.m. tomorrow, and unfortunately I already have a fully scheduled day today. I'm so sorry about the mix-up. Is it possible for you to come in at 10 a.m. tomorrow? Or shall I reschedule you for another time?" Even though the client may be fuming, you need to stay disengaged. Your focus is to move the conversation away from who is at fault, and squarely in the direction of resolving the confusion. Make another appointment for the client and be sure to get her telephone number so that you can call and confirm the details of the appointment in advance. When the client does return, be sure to add something of value to her service to make amends for the inconvenience, such as a complimentary hand and foot massage.

▲ Figure 4–9
Accommodate an unhappy client promptly and calmly.

Handling Unhappy Clients

No matter how hard you try to provide excellent service to your clients, once in a while you will encounter a client who is dissatisfied with the service. The way you and the salon handle this difficult situation will have lasting effects on you, the client, and the salon, so you need to know how best to proceed (**Figure 4–9**).

Once again, it is important to remember the ultimate goal: make the client happy enough to pay for the service and return for more of the same.

Many salons and spas will have set guidelines for handling difficult situations. When in doubt, here are some guidelines to follow.

- The first thing you should do is express your most sincere apology for the client's displeasure. Let the client know that your goal is to have every client walk out of the salon or spa completely satisfied. While you may not be able to remedy the situation immediately—for instance if the client just had a chemical peel, it would not be appropriate to repeat the service—it is important to let the client know you are interested in fixing the problem.

- Give the client an opportunity to vent. In many cases the client simply wants to be heard. Listen attentively without interrupting, paying close attention as to why the client is dissatisfied. Most clients will be able to identify the cause of their displeasure in a few minutes, although some clients may be vague. If the client has a difficult time expressing herself, look for clues by asking several open-ended questions but do not get caught up in a detailed interrogation, as this may only serve to fuel the client's dissatisfaction. If it is possible to change what she dislikes, do so immediately. If that is not possible, ask the client what would satisfy her and work toward achieving that goal as quickly as possible. You may need to enlist the help of the receptionist or front desk manager in rescheduling your other appointments or arranging for another practitioner to step in. If the client seems open to the suggestion of rescheduling, ask her to return to the salon at a time when you are free. If this is not possible, and you will be relying on help from another practitioner, explain who will be working with her and what the other practitioner will be doing. The bottom line is: Do whatever you have to do to make her happy.
- If you cannot change what the client is unhappy with, or it is simply impossible to change, you must honestly and tactfully explain the reason why you cannot make any changes. The client will not be happy, but you can offer any options that may be available to remedy the situation. A follow-up note with a gift certificate or special offer, such as a complimentary makeup session or eye treatment that can be redeemed at her next facial appointment, is generally a nice way to make amends.
- When engaging with clients under difficult circumstances it is extremely important to keep your emotions in check at all times. Never argue with the client, resort to disparaging remarks, or try to force your opinion. Unless you can change what has caused the dissatisfaction, arguing will just fuel the fire.
- Do not hesitate to call on the spa director, front desk manager, or a senior staff member for help. They have encountered a similar situation at some point in their careers and have insights that can help you.
- If, after you have tried everything, you are unable to satisfy the client, defer to your manager's advice on how to proceed. The client may be too upset to handle the situation maturely, and it may be easier for her to deal with someone else. This does not mean that you have failed; it simply means that another approach is needed. In some cases a disgruntled client will only be satisfied by taking their complaint to a higher authority. Listen to how the message is being conveyed to you. Can you pinpoint the client's emotions? Does she feel that her concerns are being ignored or feel that she is being taken advantage of? Does she want to be sure the manager is informed? This is valuable information for the next customer service agent.

FOCUS ON

Communication

At some point in your career, you will no doubt have a disgruntled client who is unhappy about something that was done either during the service or in scheduling. No matter how well you communicate, handling a situation like this can be difficult. The best way to prepare is to practice. Role-play with a classmate, taking turns being the client and the practitioner. Role-playing both sides of the issue will give you a better understanding of the entire situation.

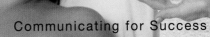

- Some clients may express their unhappiness in a disrespectful tone. Do not let this throw you into a tailspin. Another person's rudeness is not necessarily a reflection on you if you have handled the situation appropriately. Most clients do not resort to irrational behavior or disrespectful language; however, if someone behaves so badly that you feel abused or threatened, never hesitate to call for additional support.
- Confer with your salon manager or spa director after the experience. A good manager will not hold the event against you, but view it instead as an inevitable fact of life that you can learn from. Follow your manager's advice and move on to your next client. Use whatever you may have learned from the experience to perform future client consultations and services better.

FOCUS ON Professionalism

A long-time client reveals to you one day that she and her husband are going through a messy divorce. You care for her and try to be understanding as she reveals increasingly personal details. You want to be helpful and supportive, but realize you need to establish boundaries. What can you do?

Try this: Tell her you understand the situation is very difficult, but while she is in the salon or spa, you want to do everything in your power to give her a break from it. Let her know that while she is in your care, you should both concentrate on her enjoyment of the services and not on the things that are stressing her. She will appreciate the suggestion, and you will have put her back on the track of her real reason for coming to see you.

Handling Difficult People

The first thing you must realize when dealing with difficult clients, coworkers, and bosses is that the issues involved are not always about you. Do not take offensive words or actions personally. You must be prepared to deal with all kinds of personality types; not everyone who comes into your salon will be easygoing and trust your judgment. In fact, you may have clients who will take advantage of the fact that you are a novice.

The following guidelines or coping strategies will help you to maintain control.

- **Respect professional boundaries.** Remember you are an esthetician, not a life coach or counselor.
- **Keep conversation on a professional level.** Steer inappropriate commentary back to the task at hand.
- **Do not give personal or health advice.**
- **Post rules in a visible place.** Make sure clients are aware of the salon's policies.
- **Be assertive but respectful.**
- **Learn to censor your dialogue, and think before you speak.** Avoid engaging in gossip.
- **Practice positive communication skills such as active listening.**
- **Use positive body language.** Maintain good eye contact and nod to let the client know you are listening. Avoid crossing your arms, frowning, or looking sternly at the person.
- **Give the client the opportunity to vent without interrupting.**
- **Use language that evokes a positive response.** Whenever possible, find a middle ground.
- **Be clear.** State the facts simply, courteously, and succinctly, in a manner that does not provoke controversy or argument.

- **Acknowledge concerns, and state how you can address them.** Assure clients as necessary.
- **Compliment coworkers, managers, or bosses for a job that is well done.** Everyone benefits from a well-deserved and genuine compliment. ✓ L04

Getting Too Personal

Sometimes when a client forms a bond of trust with her esthetician, she may have a hard time differentiating between a professional and a personal relationship. That will be *her* problem, but you must not make it *your* problem. Your job is to handle your client relationships tactfully and sensitively. You cannot become your client's counselor, career guide, parental sounding board, or motivational coach. Your job and your relationship with your clients are very specific: The goal is to advise and service clients with their skin care needs, and nothing more.

In-Salon Communication

Behaving in a professional manner is the first step in making meaningful in-salon communication possible. Unfortunately, some skin care professionals act immaturely and get overly involved in the salon rumor mill.

The salon community is usually a close-knit one in which people spend long hours working together. For this reason, it is important to maintain boundaries around what you will and will not do or say at the salon. Remember, the salon is your place of business and, as such, must be treated respectfully and carefully.

Communicating with Coworkers

As with all communication, there are basic principles that must guide your interactions. In a work environment, you will not have the opportunity to handpick your colleagues. There will always be people you like or relate to better than others, and there will always be people whose behaviors or opinions you find yourself in conflict with. These people can try your patience and your nerves, but they are your colleagues and are deserving of your respect.

Here are some guidelines to keep in mind as you interact and communicate with fellow staffers.

- **Treat everyone with respect.** Regardless of whether you like someone, your colleagues are professionals who, just like you, provide services to clients who bring revenue into the salon. And, as practicing professionals, they have information they can offer you. Look at these people as having something to teach you, and hone in on their talents and their techniques.
- **Remain objective.** Different types of personalities working in the same treatment rooms over long and intense hours are likely to breed

some degree of dissension and disagreement. To learn and grow, you must make every effort to remain objective and resist being pulled into spats and cliques. Under no circumstances should you resort to shouting, name-calling, racist remarks, or other inappropriate language when engaging with coworkers. If at any point you feel you are about to lose self-control, give yourself permission to take a "time-out" and remove yourself from the situation immediately. When one or two people in the salon behave disrespectfully toward one another, the entire team suffers because the atmosphere changes. Not only will this be unpleasant for you, but it will also be felt by the clients—who may decide to take their business elsewhere if they find the atmosphere in your salon too tense. In some cases inappropriate behavior could even result in a law suit. This can have long-term damaging repercussions that could not only cost you your job, but prevent you from future employment.

- **Be honest and be sensitive.** Many people use the excuse of being honest as a license to say anything to anyone. While honesty is always the best policy, using unkind words or actions with regard to your colleagues is never a good idea. Be sensitive. Put yourself in the other person's place, and think through what you want to say before you say it. That way, any negative or hurtful words can be suppressed.
- **Remain neutral.** Undoubtedly, there will come a time when you are called on to make a statement or to "pick a side." Do whatever you can to avoid getting drawn into the conflict. If you have a problem with a colleague, the best way to resolve it is to speak with her or him directly and privately.

  Speaking to, or gossiping with, others about someone never resolves a problem. It only makes it worse and is often as damaging to you as it is to the object of your gossip.
- **Seek help from someone you respect.** If you find yourself in a position where you are at odds with a coworker, you may want to seek out a third party—someone who is not involved and who can remain objective—such as the manager or a more experienced practitioner. Ask for advice about how to proceed, and really listen to what this mentor has to say. Since this person is not involved, he or she is more likely to see the situation as it truly is and can offer you valuable insights.
- **Do not take things personally.** This is often easier said than done. How many times have you had a bad day, or been thinking about something totally unrelated, when a person asks you what is wrong, or wonders if you are mad at them? Just because someone is behaving in a certain manner and you happen to be there, do not interpret the words

or behaviors as being meant for you. If you are confused or concerned by someone's actions, find a quiet and private place to ask the person about it. The person may not even realize he or she was giving off any signals.

- **Keep your private life private.** There is a time and a place for everything, but the salon is never the place to discuss your personal life and relationships. It may be tempting to engage in that kind of conversation, especially if others in the salon are doing so, and to solicit advice and opinions, but that is why you have friends. Coworkers can become friends, but those whom you selectively turn into friends are different from the ones whose facial or massage room happens to be next to yours (**Figure 4–10**).

▲ Figure 4–10
Getting along with coworkers is in everyone's best interest.

Communicating with Managers

Another important relationship for you within the salon is the one you will build with your manager. The salon manager is generally the person who has the most responsibility on how the salon is run in terms of daily maintenance, operations, and client service. The manager's job is a demanding one. In some cases, in addition to running a busy salon, the manager may also be a service provider. This person deserves your utmost respect and cooperation.

Your manager is likely to be the one who hired you and is responsible for your training and how well you move into the salon culture; therefore, your manager has a vested interest in your success. As a salon employee, you will see the manager as a powerful and influential person, but it is also important to remember that she is a human being. She is not perfect, and she will not be able to do everything you think should be done in every instance. Whether she personally likes you or not, her job is to look beyond her personal feelings and make decisions that are best for the salon as a whole. The best thing you can do is to try to understand the decisions and rules that she makes whether you agree with them or not.

Many salon professionals utilize their salon managers in inappropriate ways by asking them to solve personal issues between staff members.

Inexperienced managers, hoping to keep everything flowing smoothly, sometimes make the mistake of getting involved in petty issues. You and your manager must both understand that her job is to make sure the business is running smoothly, not to babysit temperamental practitioners.

CAUTION!

In this age of technology there may be a number of communication tools that you rely on to keep you informed throughout the day, such as a cell phone, iPhone, or iPad device. Some salons may specify how, where, and when you can use these items during work hours. It is important to respect these rules. But even if you are not given specific guidelines, it is imperative for estheticians to exercise caution when revealing private information in public areas. A personal conversation or private photos overheard or seen by guests, coworkers, or your supervisor can quickly become the target of unwanted gossip and innuendo. Save the sharing of very personal information for a time when you can be assured of your privacy.

Here are some guidelines for interacting and communicating with your salon manager.

- **Be a problem solver.** When you need to speak with your manager about some issue or problem, think of some possible solutions beforehand. This will indicate that you are working in the salon's best interest and are trying to help, not make things worse.
- **Get your facts straight.** Make sure that all your facts and information are accurate before you speak to your salon manager. This way you will avoid wasting time solving a "problem" that really does not exist.
- **Be open and honest.** When you find yourself in a situation you do not understand or do not have the experience to deal with, tell your salon manager immediately and be willing to learn.
- **Do not gossip or complain about colleagues.** Going to your manager with gossip or to "tattle" on a coworker tells your manager that you are a troublemaker. If you are having a legitimate problem with someone and have tried everything in your power to handle the problem yourself, then it is appropriate to go to your manager. But you must approach her with a true desire to solve the problem, not just to vent.
- **Check your attitude.** The salon environment, although fun and friendly, can also be stressful, so it is important to take a moment between clients to "take your temperature." Ask yourself how you are feeling. Do you need an attitude adjustment? Be honest with yourself. Perhaps you are being overly sensitive or feeling insecure. Lots of times our unhappiness does not stem from the situation directly at hand, instead it may be a reflection of our own insecurities, or something else that is going on in our lives at the time.
- **Be open to constructive criticism.** It is never easy to hear that you need improvement in any area, but keep in mind that part of your manager's job is to help you achieve your professional goals. She is supposed to evaluate your skills and offer suggestions on how to increase them. Keep an open mind, and do not take her criticism personally.
- **Do not challenge a manager's authority unless there is a legitimate reason to do so.** Some employees challenge everything a manager says. This is counterproductive to team building and undermines the manager's authority. On the other hand, there are times when unethical or inappropriate behaviors, such as sexual harassment, verbal abuse, or misappropriating funds and clients, are legitimate cause for concern. If you find yourself in a difficult situation in which you must go over the head of your immediate supervisor, be prepared with detailed documentation to state your case and take the time to think it through with a trusted confidant beforehand. If a number of coworkers are experiencing the same

FOCUS ON

The Goal

Too much time spent on your personal life means time away from the task of perfecting your skills and building up the business for yourself and the salon.

situation, there may be strength in numbers. Still, the road to arbitration can be difficult, so it is critical to distinguish between a personality problem, a petty annoyance, and a legitimate concern. In some cases the best solution may be to seek employment elsewhere.

Communicating During an Employee Evaluation

Salons that are well run will make it a priority to conduct frequent and thorough employee evaluations. Sometime in the course of your first few days of work, your salon manager will tell you when you can expect your first evaluation. If she does not mention it, you might ask her about it and request a copy of the form she will use or the criteria on which you will be evaluated.

Take some time to look over this document. Be mindful that the behaviors and/or activities you will be evaluated on are most likely to be the ones listed on your job description. This is useful information. You can begin to watch and rate yourself in the weeks and months ahead so you can assess how you are doing. Remember, everything you are being evaluated on is there for the purpose of helping you improve. Make the decision to approach these communications positively. As the time draws near for the evaluation, try filling out the form yourself. In other words, give yourself an evaluation, even if the salon has not asked you to do so. Be objective, and carefully think about your comments. Then, when you meet with the manager, show her your evaluation and tell her you are serious about your improvement and growth. She will appreciate your input and your desire. And, if you are being honest with yourself, there should be no surprises (**Figure 4–11**).

Many salons have performance standards that clearly identify their human resource policies on wage increases and the protocol for advancement. If the salon you work at does not, be prepared to raise these important issues yourself. Before your evaluation meeting, write down any thoughts or questions you may have so you can share them with your manager. Do not be shy. If you want to know when you can take on more services, when your pay scale will be increased, or when you might be considered for promotion, this meeting is the appropriate time and place to ask. Many beauty professionals never take advantage of this crucial communication opportunity to discuss their future because they are too nervous, intimidated, or unprepared. Do not let that happen to you. Participate proactively in your career and in your success by communicating your desires and interests.

While it is important to be prepared for your evaluation, it is also important to remember who is in charge of the meeting. Be respectful toward your supervisor and demonstrate the appropriate professional courtesies at all times. At the end of the meeting, thank your manager for taking the time to do an evaluation and for the feedback and guidance she has given you. ☑ **LO5**

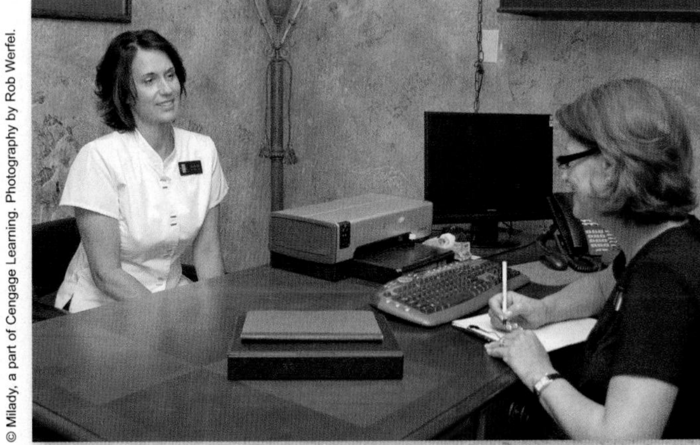

▲ **Figure 4–11**
The employee evaluation provides an excellent opportunity to solicit your manager's advice on the best way to improve your skills.

Review Questions

1. List the golden rules of human relations.
2. Define communication.
3. How should you prepare for a client consultation?
4. List and describe the 10 elements of a successful client consultation.
5. Name some types of information that should go on a client consultation card.
6. How should you handle tardy clients?
7. How should you handle a scheduling mix-up?
8. How should you handle an unhappy client?
9. List at least five things to remember when communicating with your coworkers.
10. List at least four guidelines for communicating with salon managers.

Glossary

client consultation	Also known as the needs assessment; the verbal communication with a client that determines what the client's needs are and how to achieve the desired results.
communication	The act of successfully sharing information between two people, or groups of people, so that it is effectively understood.
consent form	A customary written agreement between the client and esthetician (salon/spa) for applying a particular treatment, whether routine or preoperative.
reflective listening	Listening to the client and then repeating, in your own words, what you think the client is telling you.

General Sciences

PART 2

CHAPTER 5

Infection Control: Principles and Practices

Chapter Outline

- Why Study Infection Control?
- Regulation
- Principles of Infection
- Principles of Prevention
- Universal and Standard Precautions
- The Professional Salon Image
- Procedures

Learning Objectives

After completing this chapter, you will be able to:

- ☑ LO1 Understand state laws and rules and the differences between them.
- ☑ LO2 List the types and classifications of bacteria.
- ☑ LO3 Define hepatitis and Human Immunodeficiency Virus (HIV) and explain how they are transmitted.
- ☑ LO4 Explain the differences between cleaning, disinfecting, and sterilizing.
- ☑ LO5 List the types of disinfectants and how they are used.
- ☑ LO6 Discuss Universal and Standard Precautions.
- ☑ LO7 List your responsibilities as a salon professional.
- ☑ LO8 Describe how to safely clean and disinfect salon and spa tools and implements.

Key Terms

Page number indicates where in the chapter the term is used.

acquired immune deficiency syndrome (AIDS) pg. 84

acquired immunity pg. 86

allergy pg. 88

antiseptics pg. 96

aseptic procedures pg. 95

asymptomatic pg. 99

autoclave pg. 87

bacilli pg. 80

bacteria pg. 79

bactericidal pg. 79

binary fission pg. 81

bioburden pg. 90

bloodborne pathogens pg. 83

body substance isolation (BSI) pg. 97

chelating soaps (chelating detergents) pg. 95

clean (cleaning) pg. 78

cocci pg. 80

contagious disease (communicable disease) pg. 82

contamination pg. 83

cross-contamination pg. 94

decontamination pg. 86

dermatophytes pg. 85

diagnosis pg. 83

diplococcic pg. 80

direct transmission pg. 80

disease pg. 76

disinfectants pg. 76

disinfection pg. 78

efficacy pg. 89

exposure incident pg. 100

flagella (cilia) pg. 80

folliculitis (barber's itch)pg. 85

fungi pg. 85

fungicidal pg. 79

hepatitis pg. 84

hospital disinfectants pg. 76

human immunodeficiency virus (HIV) pg. 84

human papillomavirus (HPV, plantar warts) pg. 84

immunity pg. 86

indirect transmission pg. 80

infection pg. 78

infection control pg. 78

infectious pg. 77

infectious disease pg. 78

Key Terms

Page number indicates where in the chapter the term is used.

inflammation
pg. 81

local infection
pg. 81

Material Safety Data Sheet (MSDS)
pg. 76

methicillin-resistant staphylococcus aureus (MRSA)
pg. 82

microorganism
pg. 79

mildew
pg. 85

motility
pg. 80

multiuse (reusable)
pg. 93

mycobacterium fortuitum
pg. 77

natural immunity
pg. 86

nonpathogenic
pg. 79

nonporous
pg. 76

occupational disease
pg. 83

parasites
pg. 86

parasitic disease
pg. 83

pathogenic
pg. 79

pathogenic disease
pg. 83

personal protective equipment (PPE)
pg. 97

phenolic disinfectants
pg. 91

porous
pg. 93

pus
pg. 81

quaternary ammonium compounds (quats)
pg. 91

sanitizing
pg. 74

scabies
pg. 86

single-use (disposable)
pg. 93

sodium hypochlorite
pg. 92

spirilla
pg. 80

Standard Precautions
pg. 97

staphylococci
pg. 80

sterilization
pg. 88

streptococci
pg. 80

systemic disease
pg. 83

tinea pedis
pg. 85

tinea versicolor (sun spots)
pg. 85

toxins
pg. 80

tuberculocidal disinfectants
pg. 76

tuberculosis
pg. 76

Universal Precautions
pg. 99

virucidal
pg. 79

virus
pg. 81

Publisher's Note: In previous editions of this chapter the term **sanitizing** was used interchangeably to mean ***clean*** or ***cleaning***. You will also find that many commercially-available products used in the cleaning and disinfecting process continue to use the words sanitize and sanitizing. However, the publisher's goal is to clearly define these terms below and within the glossary because:

- There is much confusion about and misuse of the terms cleaning, sanitizing, disinfecting, and sterilizing within the beauty industry. In an effort to do what we can to clarify these critical terms, Milady opted to consistently use cleaning, instead of using cleaning in one sentence and sanitizing in another sentence.
- Professionals in the health care and scientific communities (of disease prevention and epidemiology) and associations, such as The Association for Professionals in Infection Control and Epidemiology, generally do not use the terms interchangeably either. Instead, it is more common for infection control professionals to use the term cleaning. Infection control professionals consider sanitation a layperson's term or a product marketing term (as in hand sanitizers).

The term clean is defined: A mechanical process (scrubbing) using soap and water or detergent and water to remove all visible dirt, debris, and many disease-causing germs. Cleaning also removes invisible debris that interferes with disinfection. Cleaning is what cosmetologists and estheticians are required to do before disinfecting.

The term sanitize is defined: A chemical process for reducing the number of disease-causing germs on cleaned surfaces to a safe level.

The term disinfection is defined: A chemical process that uses specific products to destroy harmful organisms (except bacterial spores) on environmental surfaces.

Why Study Infection Control: Principles and Practices?

Estheticians should study and have a thorough understanding of infection control principles and practices because this is a foundational element that ensures the safety of both clients and technicians and is required by law.

- To be a knowledgeable, successful, and responsible professional in the field of esthetics, you are required to understand the types of infections you may encounter in the salon, spa, or medical facility.
- Understanding the basics of cleaning and disinfecting and following federal and state rules will ensure that you have a long and successful career as an esthetician.
- Understanding the chemistry of the cleaning and disinfecting products that you use and how to use these products is essential to keep yourself, your clients, and your environment safe.

Regulation

Many different federal and state agencies regulate the practice of esthetics. Federal agencies set guidelines for the manufacturing, sale, and use of equipment and chemical ingredients along with safety in the workplace. State agencies regulate licensing, enforcement, and conduct when working in a salon, spa, or medical facility.

Web Resources

You can find an EPA-approved list of hospital and tuberculocidal disinfectants by going to the EPA's Web site at www.epa.gov and entering a search on the homepage for "EPA-registered disinfectants."

Federal Agencies

Occupational Safety and Health Administration (OSHA)

The Occupational Safety and Health Administration (OSHA) was created as part of the U.S. Department of Labor to regulate and enforce safety and health standards to protect employees in the workplace. Regulating employee exposure to potentially toxic substances and informing employees about the possible hazards of materials used in the workplace are key points of the Occupational Safety and Health Act of 1970. This regulation created the Hazard Communication Standard (HCS), which requires that chemical manufacturers and importers assess and communicate the potential hazards associated with their products. The Material Safety Data Sheet (MSDS) is a result of the HCS.

The standards set by OSHA are important to the esthetics industry because of the products used in salons, spas, and medical offices. OSHA standards address issues relating to the handling, mixing, storing, and disposing of products; general safety in the workplace; and your right to know about any potentially hazardous ingredients contained in the products you use and how to avoid these hazards.

Material Safety Data Sheet (MSDS)

Federal and state laws require that manufacturers supply a **Material Safety Data Sheet (MSDS)** for all products sold. The MSDS contains information compiled by the manufacturer about product safety including the names of hazardous ingredients, safe handling and use procedures, precautions to reduce the risk of accidental harm or overexposure, and flammability warnings. The MSDS also provides useful disposal guidelines and medical and first aid information. When necessary, the MSDS can be sent to a medical facility so that a doctor can better assess and treat the patient. OSHA and state regulatory agencies require that MSDSs be kept available in the salon, spa, or medical office for all products. OSHA and state board inspectors can issue fines for salons, spas, medical offices, or medi-spas for not having MSDS documents available during regular business hours.

Did You Know?

The term Hospital Grade is not a term used by the EPA. The EPA does not grade disinfectants; a product is either approved by the EPA as a hospital disinfectant or it is not.

Federal and state laws require salons, spas, and medical offices to obtain Material Safety Data Sheets from the product manufacturers and/or distributors for each professional product that is used. MSDSs often can be downloaded from the product manufacturer's or the distributor's Web site. Not having MSDSs available poses a health risk to anyone exposed to hazardous materials and violates federal and state regulations. All employees must read the information included on each MSDS and verify that they have read it by adding their signatures to a sign-off sheet for the product. These sign-off sheets must be available to state and federal inspectors upon request.

Environmental Protection Agency (EPA)

The Environmental Protection Agency (EPA) registers all types of disinfectants sold and used in the United States. **Disinfectants** (dis-in-FEK-tents) are chemical products that destroy all bacteria, fungi, and viruses (but not spores) on surfaces. The two types that are used in salons, spas, medical offices, and medi-spas are hospital disinfectants and tuberculocidal disinfectants.

- **Hospital disinfectants** (HOS-pih-tal dis-in-FEK-tents) are effective for cleaning blood and body fluids. They can be used on any nonporous surface in the salon. **Nonporous** (nahn-POHW-rus) means that an item is made or constructed of a material that has no pores or openings and cannot absorb liquids. Hospital disinfectants control the spread of **disease** (dih-ZEEZ), an abnormal condition of all or part of the body, or its systems or organs, that makes the body incapable of carrying on normal function.
- **Tuberculocidal disinfectants** (tuh-bur-kyoo-LOH-sy-dahl dis-in-FEK-tents) are proven to kill the bacteria that cause **tuberculosis** (tuh-bur-kyoo-LOH-sus), a disease caused by bacteria that are transmitted through coughing or sneezing. These bacteria are capable of forming spores, so they are difficult to kill. Tuberculocidal disinfectants are one kind of hospital disinfectant. The fact that

Did You Know?

Estheticians, nail techs, and cosmetologists can put themselves and their clients at risk unless stringent infection control guidelines are performed every day. A case in point was the spread of a bacterium called **Mycrobacterium fortuitum** (MY-koh-bak-TIR-ee-um for-TOO-i-tum), a microscopic germ that normally exists in tap water in small numbers. Until an incident occurred, health officials considered the germ to be completely harmless and not **infectious** (in-FEK-shus), caused by or capable of being transmitted by infection.

In the year 2000, over 100 clients from one California salon developed serious skin infections on their legs after getting pedicures. The infection caused ugly sores that lingered for months, required the use of strong antibiotics, and permanently scarred some of the clients' legs. The source of the infection was traced to the salon's whirlpool foot spas. Salon staff did not clean and disinfect the foot spas properly, resulting in a build-up of hair and debris in the foot spas that created the perfect breeding ground for bacteria. As a result, the state of California issued specific requirements for pedicure equipment in the hope of preventing future outbreaks.

The outbreak was a catalyst for change in the esthetics industry because, due to the media and advertising, the public views all salon or spa professionals similarly regardless of their chosen discipline, as we often work in the same facilities and have the same risk potentials for infection transmission (Figure 5–1).

Incidents such as this demonstrate how important it is for estheticians to use the proper disinfectants on all tools such as comedone extractors, microdermabrasion hand pieces, and other esthetic devices and accessories. When in doubt about the disinfectant you should use, consult federal and state regulations.

tuberculocidal disinfectants are more powerful does not mean that you should automatically reach for them. Some of these products can be harmful to salon, spa, and esthetic tools and equipment, and these products require special methods of disposal. Check the rules in your state to be sure that the product you choose complies with state requirements.

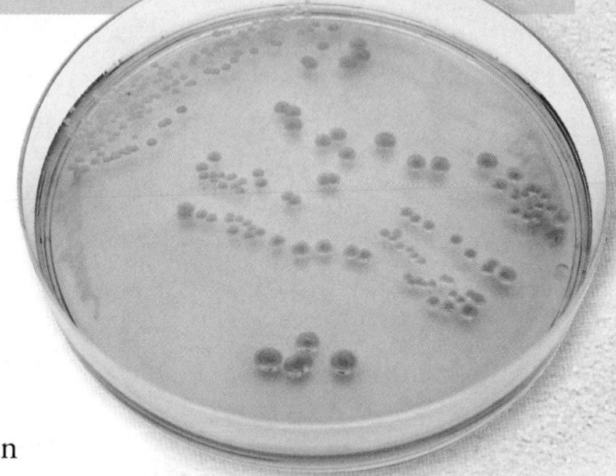

▲ Figure 5–1
Bacteria growing in a petri dish.

It is against federal law to use any disinfecting product contrary to its labeling. Before a manufacturer can sell a product for disinfecting surfaces, tools, implements, or equipment, it must obtain an EPA-registration number that certifies that the disinfectant may be used in the manner prescribed by the manufacturer's label. Misusing a product for disinfecting may cancel its efficacy for disinfecting. This also means that if you do not follow the label instructions for mixing, contact time, and the type of surface the disinfecting product can be used on, you are not complying with federal law. If there is a lawsuit, you can be held responsible.

State Regulatory Agencies

State regulatory agencies exist to protect salon and spa professionals and to protect consumers' health, safety, and welfare while they receive salon and spa services. State regulatory agencies include licensing agencies, state boards of cosmetology, commissions, and health departments. Regulatory agencies require that everyone working in a salon or spa follow specific procedures. Enforcement of the rules through inspections and investigations of consumer complaints is also part of an agency's responsibility. An agency can issue penalties against both the salon owner and the esthetician's license.

Penalties vary and include warnings, fines, probation, and suspension or revocation of licenses. It is vital that you understand and follow the laws and rules of your state at all times. Your salon, spa, or medical facility's reputation, your license, and everyone's safety depend on it.

Laws and Rules—What is the Difference?

Laws are written by both federal and state legislatures that determine the scope of practice (what each license allows the holder to do) and that establish guidelines for regulatory agencies to make rules. Laws are also called statutes.

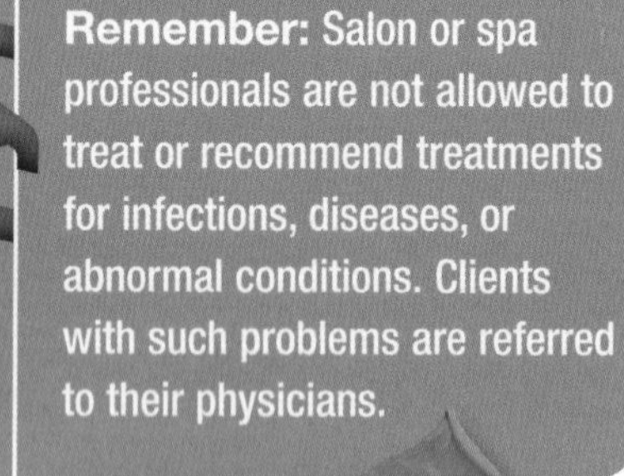

fyi

Remember: Salon or spa professionals are not allowed to treat or recommend treatments for infections, diseases, or abnormal conditions. Clients with such problems are referred to their physicians.

Rules and regulations are more specific than laws. Rules are written by the regulatory agency or the state board, and they determine how the law must be applied. Rules establish specific standards of conduct and can be changed or updated frequently. Esthetician's must be aware of any changes or updates to the rules and regulations, and they must comply with them. ✓ L01

Principles of Infection

Being an esthetician is fun and rewarding, but it is also a great responsibility. One careless action could cause injury or **infection** (in-FEK-shun), the invasion of body tissues by disease-causing pathogens. If your actions result in an injury or infection, you could lose your license and ruin the salon's or spa's reputation. Fortunately, preventing the spread of infections is easy when you know proper procedures and follow them at all times. Prevention begins and ends with you (Figure 5–2).

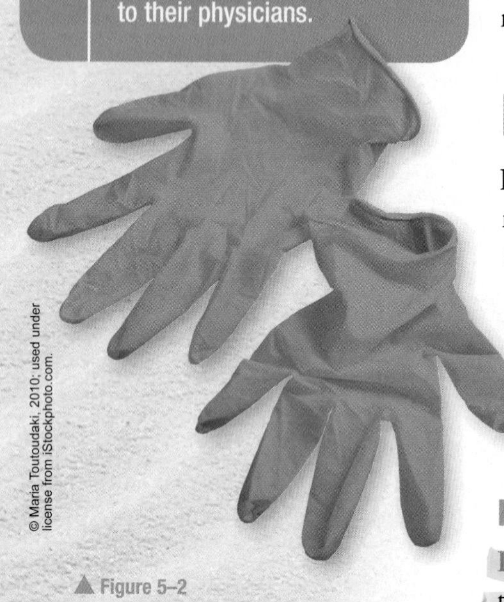

▲ Figure 5–2
Gloves are worn during treatments and services in the salon and spa.

Infection Control

Infection control are the methods used to eliminate or reduce the transmission of infectious organisms. Estheticians must understand and remember the following four types of potentially harmful organisms:

- Bacteria
- Viruses
- Fungi
- Parasites

Under certain conditions, many of these organisms can cause infectious disease. An **infectious disease** (in-FEK-shus dih-ZEEZ) is caused by pathogenic (harmful) organisms that enter the body. An infectious disease may or may not be spread from one person to another person.

In this chapter, you will learn how to properly clean and disinfect the tools and equipment you use in the salon, spa, or medical facility so they are safe for you and your clients (Figure 5–3). To **clean** (cleaning) is a mechanical process (scrubbing) using soap and water or detergent and water to remove all visible dirt, debris, and many disease-causing germs from tools, implements, and equipment. The process of **disinfection** (dis-in-FEK-shun) destroys most, but not necessarily all, harmful organisms on environmental surfaces. Disinfection is not effective against bacterial spores.

▲ Figure 5–3
Gloves are worn for cleaning and disinfecting all surfaces.

Cleaning and disinfecting procedures are designed to prevent the spread of infection and disease. Disinfectants used in salons, spas, and medical facilites must be **bactericidal** (back-teer-uh-SYD-ul), capable of destroying bacteria; **virucidal** (vy-ru-SYD-ul), capable of destroying viruses; and **fungicidal** (fun-jih-SYD-ul), capable of destroying fungi. Be sure to mix and use these disinfectants according to the instructions on the labels so they are safe and effective.

Contaminated salon or spa tools and equipment can spread infections from client to client if the proper disinfection steps are not taken after every service. You have a professional and legal obligation to protect clients from harm by using proper infection control procedures. If clients are infected or harmed because you perform infection control procedures incorrectly, you may be found legally responsible for their injuries or infections.

Bacteria

Bacteria (bak-TEER-ee-ah) (singular: bacterium, back-TEER-ee-um) are one-celled microorganisms that have both plant and animal characteristics. A **microorganism** (my-kroh-OR-gah-niz-um) is any organism of microscopic or submicroscopic size. Some bacteria are harmful and some are harmless. Bacteria can exist almost anywhere: on skin, in water, in the air, in decayed matter, on environmental surfaces, in body secretions, on clothing, or under the free edge of nails. Bacteria are so small they can only be seen with a microscope.

Types of Bacteria

There are thousands of different kinds of bacteria that fall into two primary types: pathogenic and nonpathogenic. Most bacteria are **nonpathogenic** (non-path-uh-JEN-ik); in other words, they are harmless organisms that may perform useful functions. They are safe to come in contact with since they do not cause disease or harm. For example, nonpathogenic bacteria are used to make yogurt, cheese, and some medicines. In the human body, nonpathogenic bacteria help the body break down food and protect against infection. They also stimulate the immune system.

Pathogenic (path-uh-JEN-ik) bacteria are harmful microorganisms that can cause disease or infection in humans when they invade the body. Salons, spas, medical facilities, and schools must maintain strict standards for cleaning and disinfecting at all times to prevent the spread of pathogenic microorganisms. It is crucial that estheticians learn proper infection control practices while in school to ensure that you understand the importance of following them throughout your career. Table 5-1, Causes of Disease (pg. 80), presents terms and definitions related to pathogens.

Classifications of Pathogenic Bacteria

Bacteria have three distinct shapes that help to identify them. Pathogenic bacteria are classified as described below.

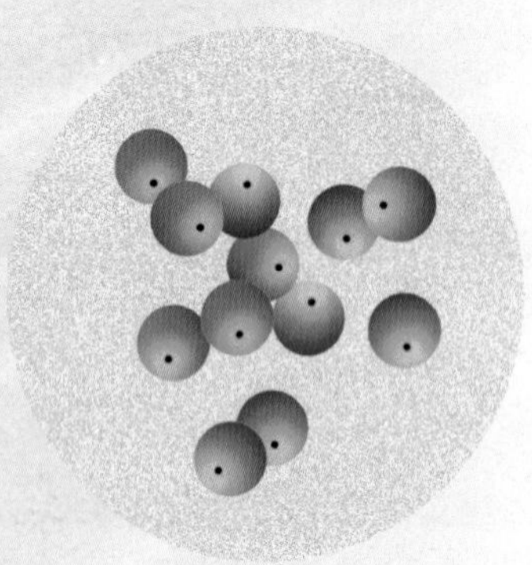

▲ Figure 5–4
Cocci.

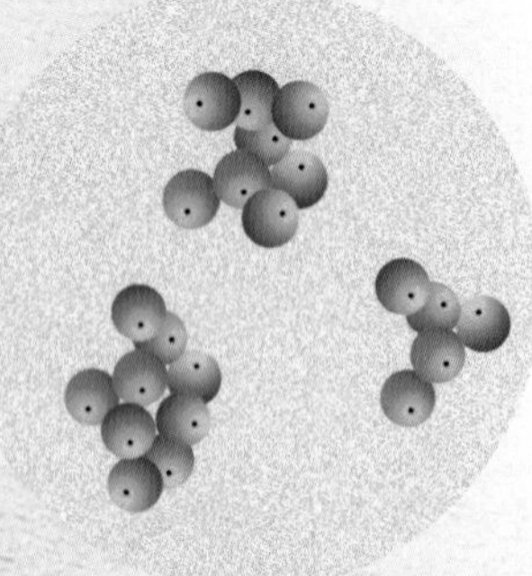

▲ Figure 5–5
Staphylococci.

- Cocci (KOK-sy) are round-shaped bacteria that appear singly (alone) or in groups (Figure 5–4).
    - Staphylococci (staf-uh-loh-KOK-sy) are pus-forming bacteria that grow in clusters like bunches of grapes. They cause abscesses, pustules, and boils (Figure 5–5). Some types of staphylococci (or staph as many call it) may not cause infections in healthy humans.
    - Streptococci (strep-toh-KOK-sy) are pus-forming bacteria arranged in curved lines resembling a string of beads. They cause infections such as strep throat and blood poisoning (Figure 5–6).
    - Diplococci (dip-lo-KOK-sy) are spherical bacteria that grow in pairs and cause diseases such as pneumonia (Figure 5–7).
- Bacilli (bah-SIL-ee) are short rod-shaped bacteria. They are the most common bacteria and produce diseases such as tetanus (lockjaw), typhoid fever, tuberculosis, and diphtheria (Figure 5–8).
- Spirilla (spy-RIL-ah) are spiral or corkscrew-shaped bacteria. They are subdivided into subgroups, such as treponema pallidum, which causes syphilis, a sexually transmitted disease (STD), and borrelia burgdorferi, which causes Lyme disease (Figure 5–9).

Movement of Bacteria

Different bacteria move in different ways. Cocci rarely show active motility (MOH-til-eh-tee), which means self-movement. Cocci are transmitted in the air, in dust, or within the substance in which they settle. Bacilli and spirilla are both capable of movement and use slender, hair-like extensions called flagella (fluh-JEL-uh) for locomotion (moving about). You may also hear people refer

CAUSES OF DISEASE	
TERM	**DEFINITION**
Bacteria	One-celled microorganisms having both plant and animal characteristics. Some are harmful and some are harmless.
Direct Transmission	Transmission of blood or body fluids through touching (including shaking hands), kissing, coughing, sneezing, and talking.
Indirect Transmission	Transmission of blood or body fluids through contact with an intermediate contaminated object such as a razor, extractor, nipper, or an environmental surface.
Infection	Invasion of body tissues by disease-causing pathogens.
Germs	Nonscientific synonym for disease-producing organisms.
Microorganism	Any organism of microscopic to submicroscopic size.
Parasites	Organisms that grow, feed, and shelter on or in another organism (referred to as the host), while contributing nothing to the survival of that organism. Parasites must have a host to survive.
Toxins	Various poisonous substances produced by some microorganisms (bacteria and viruses).
Virus	A parasitic submicroscopic particle that infects and resides in cells of biological organisms. A virus is capable of replication only through taking over the host cell's reproductive function.

▲ Table 5–1 **Causes of Disease.**

to **cilia** (SIL-ee-uh) as the hair-like extensions on cells. Cilia are shorter than flagella. Both flagella and cilia move cells, but they have a different motion. Flagella move in a snake-like motion while cilia move in a rowing-like motion.

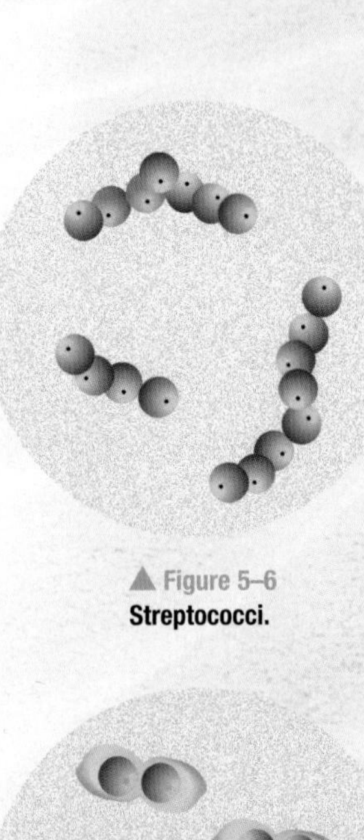

▲ Figure 5–6
Streptococci.

Bacterial Growth and Reproduction

When seen under a microscope, bacteria look like tiny bags. They generally consist of an outer cell wall that contains liquid called protoplasm. Bacterial cells manufacture their own food through what they absorb from the surrounding environment. They give off waste products, grow, and reproduce. The life cycle of bacteria consists of two distinct phases: the active stage and the inactive or spore-forming stage.

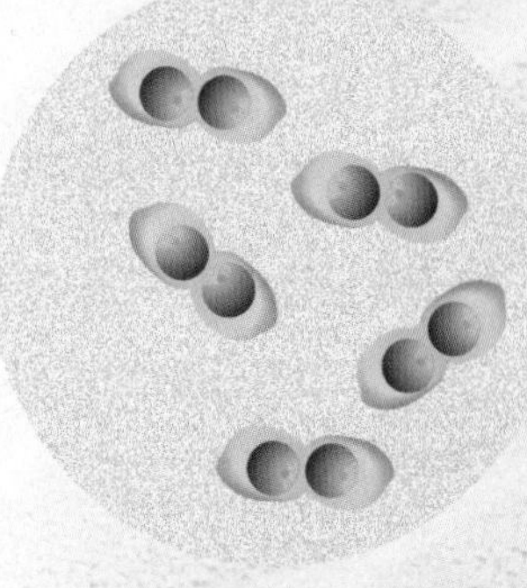

▲ Figure 5–7
Diplococci.

Active stage. During the active stage, bacteria grow and reproduce. Bacteria multiply best in warm, dark, damp, or dirty places. When conditions are favorable, bacteria grow and reproduce. When they reach their largest size, they divide into two new cells. This division is called **binary fission** (BY-nayr-ee FISH-un). The cells that are formed are called daughter cells and are produced every 20 to 60 minutes, depending on the bacteria. The infectious pathogen staphylococcus aureus undergoes cell division every 27 to 30 minutes. When conditions become unfavorable and difficult for them to thrive, bacteria either die or become inactive.

Inactive or spore-forming stage. Certain bacteria, such as the anthrax and tetanus bacilli, coat themselves with wax-like outer shells. These bacteria are able to withstand long periods of famine, dryness, and unsuitable temperatures. In this stage, spores can be blown about and are not harmed by disinfectants, heat, or cold. When favorable conditions are restored, the spores change into the active form and begin to grow and reproduce.

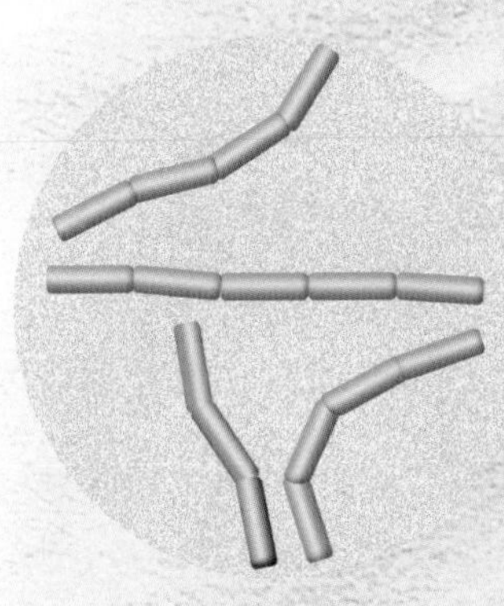

▲ Figure 5–8
Bacilli.

Bacterial Infections

There can be no bacterial infection without the presence of pathogenic bacteria. Therefore, if pathogenic bacteria are eliminated, clients cannot become infected. You may have a client who has tissue **inflammation** (in-fluh-MAY-shun), a condition in which the body reacts to injury, irritation, or infection. An inflammation is characterized by redness, heat, pain, and swelling. **Pus** is a fluid created by infection. It contains white blood cells, bacteria, and dead cells. The presence of pus is a sign of a bacterial infection. A **local infection**, such as a pimple or abscess, is confined to a particular part of the body and appears as a lesion containing pus. Staphylococci are among the most common bacteria that affect humans and are normally carried by about a third of the population. Staph bacteria can be picked up on doorknobs, countertops, and other surfaces but in salons, spas, medical facilities, and medi-spas they are more frequently spread through skin-to-skin contact (such as shaking hands) or through the use of unclean tools or implements. If these bacteria get into the wrong place, they can be very dangerous. Although lawsuits are rare considering the number of services performed in a salon or spa or medi-spa, every year many facilities are sued for allegedly causing staph infections.

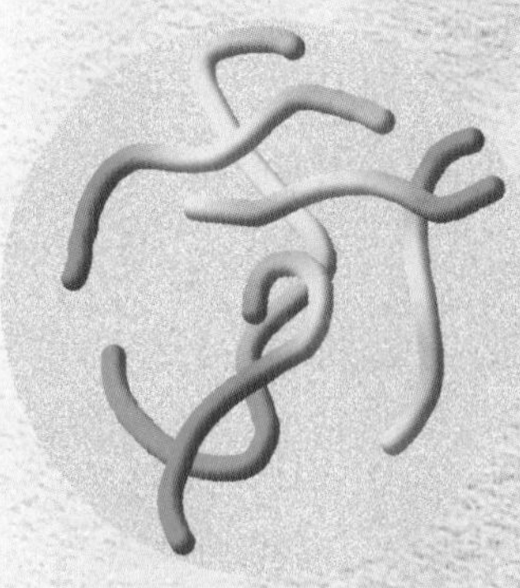

▲ Figure 5–9
Spirilla.

Staph is responsible for food poisoning and a wide range of diseases, including toxic shock syndrome. Some types of infectious staph bacteria are highly resistant to conventional treatments such as antibiotics. An example is the staph infection called **methicillin-resistant staphylococcus aureus (MRSA)** (METH-eh-sill-en-ree-ZIST-ent staf-uh-loh-KOK-us OR-ee-us). Historically, MRSA occurred most frequently among persons with weakened immune systems or among people who had undergone medical procedures. Today, it has become more common in otherwise healthy people. Clients who appear completely healthy may bring this organism into the salon where it can infect others. Some people carry the bacteria and are not even aware of their infection, but the people they infect may show more obvious symptoms. MRSA initially appears as a skin infection such as pustules, rashes, and boils that can be difficult to cure. Without proper treatment, the infection becomes systemic and can have devastating consequences that can result in death. Because of these highly resistant bacterial strains, it is important to clean and disinfect all tools and implements used in the salon or spa. You owe it to yourself and your clients! Also, do not perform services if the client's skin, scalp, neck, hands, or feet show visible signs of abrasion or infection. ☑ L02

When a disease spreads from one person to another person, it is said to be a **contagious disease** (kon-TAY-jus dih-ZEEZ), also known as **communicable disease** (kuh-MYOO-nih-kuh-bul dih-ZEEZ). Some of the more common contagious diseases that prevent a salon or spa professional from servicing a client are the common cold, ringworm, conjunctivitis (pinkeye), viral infections and natural nail, toe, or foot infections. The most common way these infections spread is through dirty hands, especially under the fingernails and in the webs between the fingers. Be sure to always wash your hands after using the restroom and before eating. Contagious diseases can also be spread by contaminated implements, cuts, infected nails, open sores, pus, mouth and nose discharges, shared drinking cups, telephone receivers, and towels. Uncovered coughing or sneezing and spitting in public also spread germs.

Table 5–2, Terms Related to Disease, lists terms and definitions that are important for a general understanding of disease.

Viruses

A **virus** (VY-rus) (plural: viruses) is a parasitic submicroscopic particle that infects and resides in the cells of a biological organism. A virus is capable of replication only through taking over the host cell's reproductive function. Viruses are so small that they can only be seen under the most sophisticated and powerful microscopes. They cause common colds and other respiratory and gastrointestinal (digestive tract) infections. Other viruses that plague humans are measles, mumps, chicken pox, smallpox, rabies, yellow fever, hepatitis, polio, influenza, and HIV, which causes AIDS.

TERMS RELATED TO DISEASE	
TERM	**DEFINITION**
Allergy	Reaction due to extreme sensitivity to certain foods, chemicals, or other normally harmless substances.
Contagious Disease	A disease that is spread from one person to another person. Some of the more contagious diseases are the common cold, ringworm, conjunctivitis (pinkeye), viral infections, and natural nail or toe and foot infections.
Contamination	The presence, or the reasonably anticipated presence, of blood or other potentially infectious materials on an item's surface or visible debris or residues such as dust, hair, and skin.
Decontamination	The removal of blood or other potentially infectious materials on an item's surface and the removal of visible debris or residue such as dust, hair, and skin.
Diagnosis	Determination of the nature of a disease from its symptoms and/or diagnostic tests. Federal regulations prohibit salon or spa professionals from performing a diagnosis.
Disease	An abnormal condition of all or part of the body, or its systems or organs, that makes the body incapable of carrying on normal function.
Exposure Incident	Contact with nonintact (broken) skin, blood, body fluid, or other potentially infectious materials that is the result of the performance of an employee's duties.
Infectious Disease	Disease caused by pathogenic (harmful) microorganisms that enter the body. An infectious disease may or may not be spread from one person to another person.
Inflammation	Condition in which the body reacts to injury, irritation, or infection. An inflammation is characterized by redness, heat, pain, and swelling.
Occupational Disease	Illnesses resulting from conditions associated with employment, such as prolonged and repeated overexposure to certain products or ingredients.
Parasitic Disease	Disease caused by parasites, such as lice and mites.
Pathogenic Disease	Disease produced by organisms including bacteria, viruses, fungi, and parasites.
Systemic Disease	Disease that affects the body as a whole, often due to under-functioning or over-functioning internal glands or organs. This disease is carried through the blood stream or the lymphatic system.

▲ Table 5–2 **Terms Related to Disease.**

One difference between viruses and bacteria is that a virus can live and reproduce only by taking over other cells and becoming part of them, while bacteria can live and reproduce on their own. Also, bacterial infections can usually be treated with specific antibiotics, but viruses are not affected by antibiotics. In fact, viruses are hard to kill without harming the body's own cells in the process. Vaccinations prevent viruses from growing in the body. There are many vaccines available for viruses, but not all viruses have vaccines. There is a vaccine available for hepatitis B, and all salon, spa, and medical facility practitioners should receive this vaccine. Health authorities recommend that service providers in industries with direct contact to the public—including estheticians, cosmetologists, teachers, florists, and bank tellers—ask their doctor about getting vaccinated for hepatitis B.

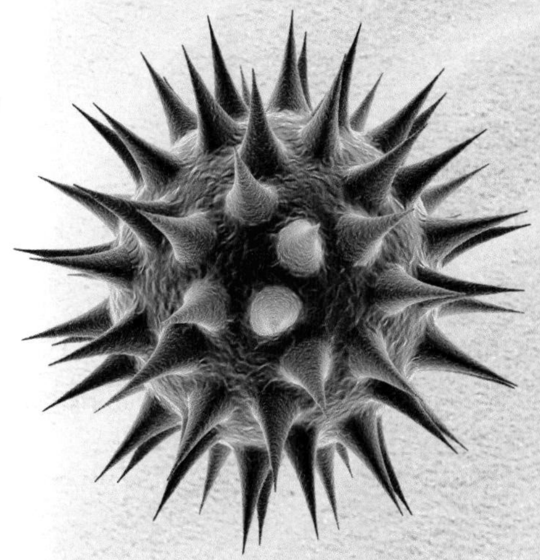

Bloodborne Pathogens

Disease-causing microorganisms that are carried in the body by blood or body fluids, such as hepatitis and HIV, are called **bloodborne pathogens**.

Did You Know?

An example of a common viral infection often seen in salons, spas, and medical facilities is the **human papillomavirus (HPV)**, also known as **plantar warts**. This virus can infect the bottom of the foot and resembles small black dots, usually in clustered groups. HPV is highly contagious, difficult to kill, and can be passed from client to client by the use of contaminated devices, implements, and tools. Even though the esthetician does not perform pedicures, unless they are licensed to do so, it is important to refer the client to a physician if you see signs of HPV.

In salons, spas, and medi-spas the spread of bloodborne pathogens is possible through performing facial treatments such as during facials and performing extractions, using microdermabrasion equipment, performing peels or working with postoperative patients in a medical offices or spas, while waxing, tweezing, or whenever the skin is broken. Use great care to avoid cutting or damaging clients' skin during any type of service.

Cutting living skin is considered outside the scope of the estheticians licensed and approved practices. Federal law allows only qualified medical professionals to cut living skin, since this is considered a medical procedure. This means that estheticians are not allowed to cut or remove live tissue.

Hepatitis

Hepatitis (hep-uh-TY-tus), is a bloodborne virus that causes disease and can damage the liver. In general, it is difficult to contract hepatitis; however, hepatitis is easier to contract than HIV because hepatitis can be present in all body fluids of those who are infected. In addition, unlike HIV, hepatitis can live on a surface outside the body for long periods of time. For this reason, it is vital that all surfaces that come in contact with a client are thoroughly cleaned and disinfected.

There are three types of hepatitis that are of concern in the salon, spa, or medical facility: hepatitis A, hepatitis B, and hepatitis C. Hepatitis B is the most difficult to kill on a surface, so check the label of the disinfectant you use to be sure that the product is effective against hepatitis B. Hepatitis B and C are spread from person to person through blood and, less often, through other body fluids, such as semen and vaginal secretions.

HIV/AIDS

Human immunodeficiency virus (HIV) (HYOO-mun ih-MYOO-noh-di-FISH-en-see VY-rus), abbreviated HIV, is the virus that causes **acquired immune deficiency syndrome (AIDS)** (uh-KWY-erd ih-MYOON di-FISH-en-see sin-drohm), abbreviated AIDS. AIDS is a disease that breaks down the body's immune system. HIV is spread from person to person through blood and, less often, through other body fluids such as semen and vaginal secretions. A person can be infected with HIV for many years without having symptoms, but testing can determine whether a person is infected within six months after exposure to the virus. Sometimes, people who are HIV-positive have never been tested and do not know they have the potential to infect other people.

The HIV virus is spread mainly through the sharing of needles by intravenous (IV) drug users and by unprotected sexual contact. Less commonly, HIV is spread through accidents with needles in healthcare settings. The virus is less likely to enter the bloodstream through cuts and sores. It is not spread by holding hands, hugging, kissing, sharing food, or using household items such as the telephone or toilet seats. There are no documented cases that indicate the virus can be spread by food handlers, insects, or casual contact during hair, skin, nail, and pedicure salon services.

If you accidentally cut a client who is HIV-positive, the tool will be contaminated. You cannot continue to use the implement without cleaning and disinfecting it. Continuing to use a contaminated implement without cleaning and disinfecting it puts you and others in the salon, spa, or medical facility at risk of infection. ✓ L03

Fungi

Fungi (FUN-jI) (singular: fungus, FUN-gus) are microscopic plant parasites that include molds, mildews, and yeasts. They can produce contagious diseases, such as ringworm. Mildew (MIL-doo), another fungus, affects plants or grows on inanimate objects but does not cause human infections in the salon. Depending upon the type, they grow in single cells or in colonies. Fungi, also called vegetable parasites, obtain nourishment from dead organic matter or from living organisms. Most fungi are nonpathogenic and make up many of the body's normal flora. Fungal infections usually affect the skin as they live off of keratin, a protein that makes up the skin. The most basic cause of fungal infections are dermatophytes (DUR-mah-toh-fytes), the fungi that cause skin, nail, and hair infections.

Common types of fungal infections are tinea pedis, a ringworm fungus of the foot or athlete's foot; tinea corporis, or ringworm; and onychomycosis, a nail infection (Figure 5–10). Folliculitis, also known as **folliculitis barbae, sycosis barbae**, or **barber's itch**, is an inflammation of the hair follicles caused by a bacterial infection from ingrown hairs due to shaving or other epilation methods. It is primarily limited to the bearded areas of the face and neck or around the scalp. This infection occurs almost exclusively in older adolescent and adult males. A person with folliculitis may have deep, inflamed or noninflamed patches of skin on the face or the nape of the neck.

Other types of fungal infections are those brought about by yeast—such as tinea versicolor, also known as **sun spots**—which are characterized by white or varicolored patches on the skin and are often found on arms and legs. Intertrigo is another type of fungal infection found in the body folds of the skin in areas such as the underarms and in the groin, while thrush is found in the mouth and vaginal areas; both are caused by candida albicans, a yeast that thrives in dark, moisture-rich environments.

Both bacterial and fungal infections will spread to others unless all implements, surfaces, towels, and everything that touches the client is properly cleaned and disinfected before reuse or is thrown away after use. It is always important to assume that all clients may have infections and to use proper infection control measures at all times.

fyi

Pathogenic bacteria, viruses, or fungi can enter the body through:

- Broken or inflamed skin, such as a cut or a scratch. They also can enter through a bruise or a rash. Intact skin is an effective barrier to infection.
- The mouth (contaminated water, food, or fingers).
- The nose (inhaling different types of dust or droplets from a cough or sneeze).
- The eyes or ears (less likely, but possible).
- Unprotected sex.

The body prevents and controls infections with:

- Healthy, unbroken skin—the body's first line of defense.
- Body secretions, such as perspiration and digestive juices.
- White blood cells that destroy bacteria.
- Antitoxins that counteract the toxins.

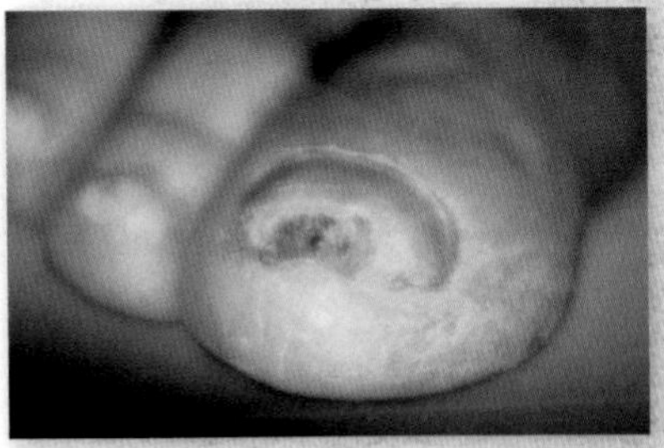

▲ Figure 5–10
Nail Fungus.

▲ Figure 5–11
Head Lice.

Parasites

Parasites are organisms that grow, feed, and shelter on or in another organism (referred to as a host), while contributing nothing to the survival of that organism. They must have a host to survive. Parasites can live on or inside of humans and animals. They also can be found in food, on plants and trees, and in water. Humans can acquire internal parasites by eating fish or meat that has not been properly cooked. External parasites that affect humans on or in the skin include ticks, fleas, and mites.

Head lice are a type of parasite responsible for contagious diseases and conditions (Figure 5–11). One condition caused by an infestation of head lice is called pediculosis capitis (puh-dik-yuh-LOH-sis KAP-ih-tus). Scabies (SKAY-beez) is also a contagious skin disease and is caused by the itch mite, which burrows under the skin. Contagious diseases and conditions caused by parasites should only be treated by a doctor. Contaminated countertops, tools, and equipment should be thoroughly cleaned and then disinfected with an EPA-registered disinfectant for the time recommended by the manufacturer or with a bleach solution for 10 minutes.

Did You Know?

In most states estheticians are not allowed to use needles, lancets, and probes that penetrate the skin nor are they allowed to offer any invasive services. You should check your state's regulations about using any implement that may penetrate the skin. If you are allowed to use these implements in your state, be sure to receive the proper training before using them in the salon, spa, or medical facility.

Immunity

Immunity is the ability of the body to destroy and resist infection. Immunity against disease can be either natural or acquired and is a sign of good health. Natural immunity is partly inherited and partly developed through healthy living. Acquired immunity is immunity that the body develops after overcoming a disease, through inoculation (such as flu vaccinations), or through exposure to natural allergens such as pollen, cat dander, and ragweed.

Principles of Prevention

Proper decontamination can prevent the spread of disease caused by exposure to potentially infectious materials on an item's surface. Decontamination also will prevent exposure to blood and visible debris or residue such as dust, hair, and skin.

Decontamination (dee-kuhn-tam-ih-NAY-shun) is the removal of blood or other potentially infectious materials on an item's surface and the removal of visible debris or residue such as dust, hair, and skin. There are two methods of decontamination.

▲ Figure 5–12
A variety of disinfectants are available for salon and spa use.

- **Decontamination Method 1:** Cleaning and then disinfecting with an appropriate EPA-registered disinfectant (Figure 5–12).
- **Decontamination Method 2:** Cleaning and then sterilizing.

Many state regulatory agencies believe there is a lower risk of infection in salons than in medical facilities, where sterilizing is a major concern. Therefore, most salons and spas are concerned with Decontamination Method 1: cleaning and disinfecting. Estheticians working in medical facilities will use a combination of both Decontamination Method 1 and Decontamination Method 2. Some states have upgraded their infection control standards in salons and spas that perform nail services to Decontamination Method 2: cleaning and sterilizing. When done properly, Decontamination Method 2 results in the destruction of all microbes through heat and pressure in an autoclave (Figure 5–13).

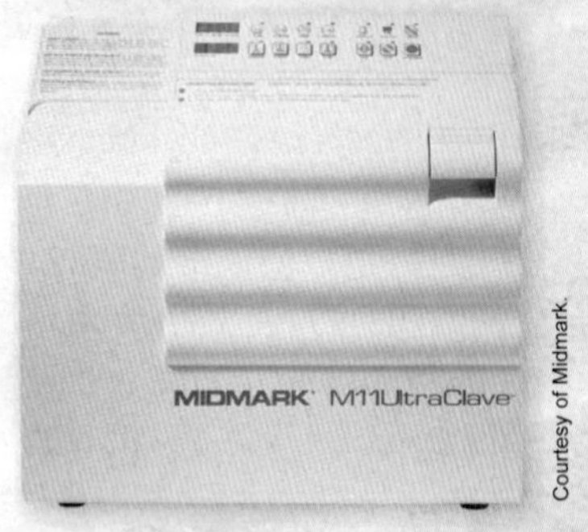

▲ Figure 5–13
An autoclave is for use in sterilization, which is the highest level of decontamination.

Decontamination Method 1

Decontamination Method 1 has two steps: cleaning and disinfecting. Remember that when you clean, you must remove all visible dirt and debris from tools, implements, and equipment by washing with liquid soap and warm water and by using a clean and disinfected nail brush to scrub any grooved or hinged portions of the item.

A surface is properly cleaned when the number of contaminants on the surface is greatly reduced. In turn, this reduces the risk of infection. The vast majority of contaminants and pathogens can be removed from the surfaces of tools and implements through proper cleaning. This is why cleaning is an important part of disinfecting tools and equipment. A surface must be properly cleaned before it can be properly disinfected. Using a disinfectant without cleaning first is like using mouthwash without brushing your teeth—it just does not work properly!

Benefits of Sterilizing

Not every tool or implement can be sterilized. Therefore, most state regulatory agencies do not require salons or spas to sterilize tools and implements. Check with your state regulatory agency to determine whether sterilization of tools and implements is required in your state.

The benefits of sterilization are:

- Sterilization is the most reliable means of infection control.
- Sterilized tools and implements in sealed bags assure clients that you are using fresh instruments during the service. The bag should be opened just before the service to show clients that the tools and implements have been sterilized, and that the salon or spa owners and staff care about the safety of their clients.

Cleaned surfaces can still harbor small amounts of pathogens, but the presence of fewer pathogens means infections are less likely to be spread. Putting antiseptics on your skin or washing your hands with soap and water will drastically lower the number of pathogens on your hands. However, it does not clean them properly. The proper cleaning of the hands requires rubbing hands together and using liquid soap, warm running water, a nail brush, and a clean towel. (See Procedure 5–3, Proper Hand Washing, later in this chapter.) Do not underestimate the importance of proper cleaning and hand washing. They are the most powerful and important ways to prevent the spread of infection.

There are three ways to clean your tools or implements:

- Washing with soap and warm water, then scrubbing them with a clean and properly disinfected nail brush.
- Using an ultrasonic unit.
- Using a cleaning solvent (e.g., on comedone extractors).

The second step of Decontamination Method 1 is disinfection. Remember that disinfection is the process that eliminates most, but not necessarily all, microorganisms on nonliving surfaces. This process is not effective against bacterial spores. In the salon or spa setting, disinfection is extremely effective in controlling microorganisms on surfaces such as comdeone extractors, microdermabrasion tips, and other tools and

CAUTION!

Read labels carefully! Manufacturers take great care to develop safe and highly effective products, however, when used improperly, many otherwise safe products can be dangerous. If you do not follow proper guidelines and instructions, any professional salon or spa product can be dangerous. As with all products, disinfectants must be used exactly as the label instructs (Figure 5–14).

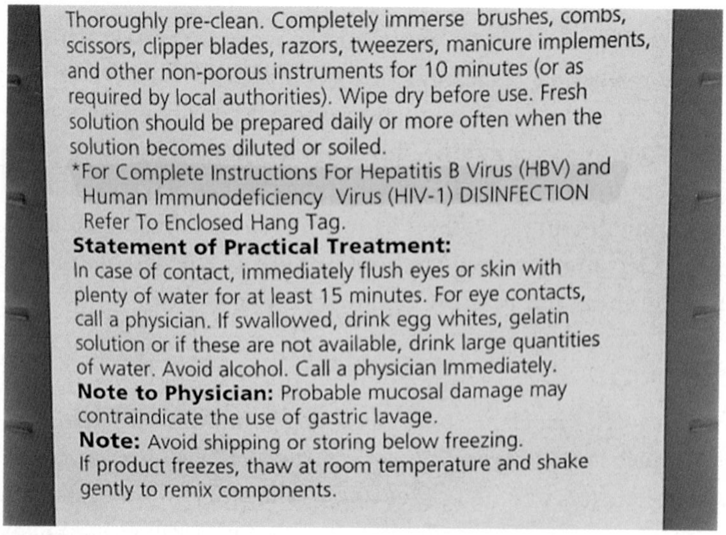

Thoroughly pre-clean. Completely immerse brushes, combs, scissors, clipper blades, razors, tweezers, manicure implements, and other non-porous instruments for 10 minutes (or as required by local authorities). Wipe dry before use. Fresh solution should be prepared daily or more often when the solution becomes diluted or soiled.
*For Complete Instructions For Hepatitis B Virus (HBV) and Human Immunodeficiency Virus (HIV-1) DISINFECTION Refer To Enclosed Hang Tag.
Statement of Practical Treatment:
In case of contact, immediately flush eyes or skin with plenty of water for at least 15 minutes. For eye contacts, call a physician. If swallowed, drink egg whites, gelatin solution or if these are not available, drink large quantities of water. Avoid alcohol. Call a physician Immediately.
Note to Physician: Probable mucosal damage may contraindicate the use of gastric lavage.
Note: Avoid shipping or storing below freezing.
If product freezes, thaw at room temperature and shake gently to remix components.

▲ Figure 5–14
A product label.

equipment (multiuse and single-use tools are discussed later in this chapter). Any disinfectant used in the salon or spa should carry an EPA-registration number and the label should clearly state the specific organisms the solution is effective in killing when used according to the label instructions.

CAUTION!

Improper mixing of disinfectants—to be weaker or more concentrated than the manufacturer's instructions—can dramatically reduce their effectiveness. Always add the disinfectant concentrate to the water when mixing and always follow the manufacturer's instructions for proper dilution.

Safety glasses and gloves should be worn to avoid accidental contact with eyes and skin (Figure 5–15).

Remember that disinfectants are products that destroy all bacteria, fungi, and viruses (but not spores) on surfaces. Disinfectants are not for use on human skin, hair, or nails. Never use disinfectants as hand cleaners since this can cause skin irritation and **allergy** (AL-ur-jee), a reaction due to extreme sensitivity to certain foods, chemicals, or other normally harmless substances. All disinfectants clearly state on the label that you should avoid skin contact. This means avoid contact with your skin as well as the client's. Do not put your fingers directly into any disinfecting solution. Disinfectants are pesticides and can be harmful if absorbed through the skin. If you mix a disinfectant in a container that is not labeled by the manufacturer, the container must be properly labeled with the contents and the date it was mixed. All concentrated disinfectants must be diluted exactly as instructed by the manufacturer on the container's label.

Decontamination Method 2

Decontamination Method 2 also has two steps: cleaning and *sterilizing*. The word sterilize is often used incorrectly. **Sterilization** is the process that completely destroys all microbial life, including spores.

The most effective methods of sterilization use high-pressure steam equipment called autoclaves. Simply exposing instruments to steam is not enough. To be effective against disease-causing

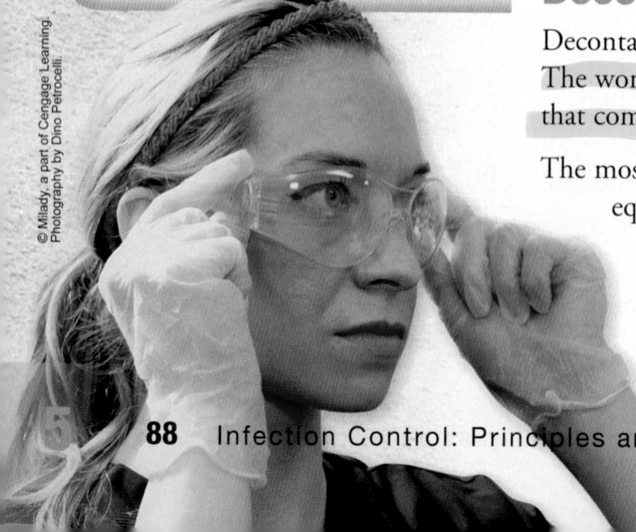

◀ Figure 5–15
Wear safety goggles and gloves while handling disinfectants.

pathogens, the steam must be pressurized in an autoclave so that the steam penetrates the spore coats of the spore-forming bacteria. Dry-heat forms of sterilization are less efficient and require longer times at higher temperatures. Dry-heat sterilization is not recommended for use in salons or spas.

It is important to understand how to use an autoclave correctly. For example, dirty implements cannot be properly sterilized without first being properly cleaned. Autoclaves need regular maintenance and testing to ensure they are in good working order. The color indicator strips that are used on autoclave bags can provide false readings, so they should never be used solely to determine whether instruments have been sterilized. These strips are only an indication, not verification that the autoclave is working. The Centers for Disease Control and Prevention (CDC) requires that autoclaves be tested weekly to ensure they are properly sterilizing implements. The accepted method is called a spore test. Sealed packages containing test organisms are subjected to a typical sterilization cycle and then sent to a contract laboratory that specializes in autoclave performance testing. You can find laboratories to perform this type of test by simply doing an Internet search for autoclave spore testing. Other regular maintenance is also required to ensure the autoclave reaches the correct temperature and pressure. Keep in mind that an autoclave that does not reach the intended temperature for killing microorganisms may create a warm, moist place where pathogenic organisms can grow and thrive.

Salons should always follow the autoclave manufacturer's recommended schedule for cleaning, changing the water, service visits, replacement parts, and any required maintenance. Be sure to keep a logbook of all usage, testing, and maintenance for the state board to inspect. Showing your logbook to clients can provide them with peace of mind and confidence in your ability to protect them from infection. ✔ L04

Choosing a Disinfectant

You must read and follow the manufacturer's instructions whenever you are using a disinfectant. Mixing ratios (dilution) and contact time are very important. Not all disinfectants have the same concentration, so be sure to mix the correct proportions according to the instructions on the label. If the label does not have the word *concentrate* on it, the product is already mixed. It must be used directly from the container and must not be diluted. All EPA-registered disinfectants, even those sprayed on large surfaces, will specify a contact time in their directions for use. Contact time is the amount of time the surface must stay moist with disinfectant in order for the disinfectant to be effective.

Disinfectants must have efficacy claims on the label. **Efficacy** (ef-ih-KUH-see) is the ability to produce an effect. As applied to disinfectant claims, efficacy means the effectiveness with which a disinfecting solution kills organisms when used according to the label instructions.

CAUTION!

Disinfectants must be registered with the EPA. Look for an EPA-registration number on the label.

Did You Know?

The EPA has recently approved a new disinfectant that can be used in the salon, spa, and medical facility which is available in a spray and an immersion form, as well as wipes.

- Accelerated hydrogen peroxide (AHP). This disinfectant is based on stabilized hydrogen peroxide. AHP disinfectant needs to be changed only every 14 days and is nontoxic to the skin and the environment. There is an AHP formula that is available for disinfecting pedicure tubs.

Read the labels of all types of disinfectants closely. Choose the one that is most appropriate for its intended use and is the safest for you and your clients.

Professionals have many disinfectants available to them and should choose the one best suited for their specialty. The ideal disinfectant would:

- Maintain efficacy in the presence of **bioburden**, the number of viable organisms in or on an object or surface or the organic material on the surface of an object before decontamination or sterilization.
- Require that it be changed after a longer length of time (at least a week or more, not daily).
- Be inexpensive.
- Be nontoxic and nonirritating.
- Include strips for checking effectiveness.
- Be readily available from multiple manufacturers.
- Be EPA-approved.
- Be environmentally friendly (can be disposed down the salon drain).
- Have no odor.
- Be noncorrosive.

CAUTION!

For salon and spa use, bleach is not a magic potion! All disinfectants, including bleach, are inactivated (made less effective) in the presence of many substances, including oils, lotions, creams, hair, skin, nail dust, and nail filings. If bleach is used to disinfect equipment, it is critical to use a detergent first to thoroughly clean the equipment and remove all debris. Never mix detergents with the bleach.

Did You Know?

Not all household bleaches are effective as disinfectants. To be effective, the bleach must have an EPA-registration number and contain at least 5 percent sodium hypochlorite and be diluted properly to a 10 percent solution—9 parts water to 1 part bleach.

Estheticians working in salons, spas, and medical facilities must be aware of the types of disinfectants that are on the market. Additionally, it is important to learn about new disinfectants that become available, as there are constant upgrades and improvements being made in these products. Salons and spas pose a lower infection risk when compared to hospitals. For this reason, hospitals must meet much stricter infection control standards. They often use disinfectants that are too dangerous for the salon environment. Even though salons pose a lower risk of spreading certain types of infections, it is still very important to clean and then disinfect all tools, implements, surfaces, and equipment correctly. When salon and spa implements accidentally contact blood, body fluids, or unhealthy conditions, they should be properly cleaned and then completely immersed in an EPA-registered hospital disinfectant solution that shows effectiveness against HIV, hepatitis, and tuberculosis. They also can be immersed in a 10 percent bleach solution. Always wear gloves and follow the proper Universal Precautions protocol for cleaning up after an exposure incident (described later in this chapter).

Proper Use of Disinfectants

Implements must be thoroughly cleaned of all visible matter or residue before being placed in disinfectant solution. This is because residue will interfere with the disinfectant and prevent proper disinfection. Properly cleaned implements and tools, free from all visible debris, must be completely immersed in disinfectant solution. Complete immersion means there is enough liquid in the container to cover all surfaces of the item being disinfected, including the handles, for 10 minutes or for the time recommended by the manufacturer.

Disinfectant Tips

- Use only on precleaned, hard, nonporous surfaces.
- Always wear gloves and safety glasses when handling disinfectant solutions.
- Always dilute products according to the instructions on the product label.
- An item must remain submerged in the disinfectant for 10 minutes unless the product label specifies differently.
- To disinfect large surfaces such as tabletops, carefully apply the disinfectant onto the precleaned surface and allow it to remain wet for 10 minutes, unless the product label specifies differently.
- If the product label states, "Complete Immersion," the entire implement must be completely immersed in the solution.
- Change the disinfectant according to the instructions on the label. If the liquid is not changed as instructed, it will no longer be effective and may begin to promote the growth of microbes.
- For spas, proper disinfection of a whirlpool pedicure spa requires that the disinfecting solution circulate for 10 minutes, unless the product label specifies otherwise.

Types of Disinfectants

Disinfectants are not all the same. Some are appropriate for use in the salon or spa and some are not. Some disinfectants should be used on tools and implements that are immersed and some should be used on nonporous surfaces. You should be aware of the different types of disinfectants and the ones that are recommended for salon use.

Disinfectants Appropriate for Salon Use

Quaternary ammonium compounds (KWAT-ur-nayr-ree uh-MOH-neeum KAHM-powndz), also known as **quats** (KWATZ), are disinfectants that are very effective when used properly in the salon or spa. The most advanced type of these formulations is called *multiple quats*. Multiple quats contain sophisticated blends of quats that work together to dramatically increase the effectiveness of these disinfectants. Quat solutions usually disinfect implements in 10 minutes. These formulas may contain antirust ingredients, so leaving tools in the solution for prolonged periods can cause dulling or damage. They should be removed from the solution after the specified period, rinsed (if required), dried, and stored in a clean, covered container.

Phenolic disinfectants (fi-NOH-lik dis-in-FEK-tents) are powerful tuberculocidal disinfectants. They are a form of formaldehyde, have a very high pH, and can damage the skin and eyes. Phenolic disinfectants can be harmful to the environment if put down the drain. They have been used reliably over the years to disinfect salon tools; however, they do have drawbacks. Phenol

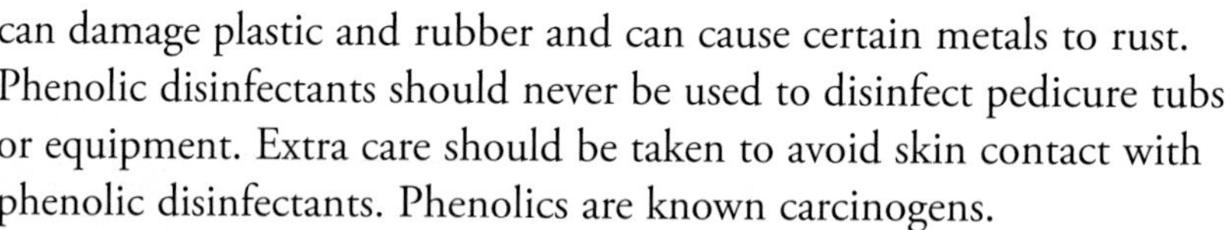

can damage plastic and rubber and can cause certain metals to rust. Phenolic disinfectants should never be used to disinfect pedicure tubs or equipment. Extra care should be taken to avoid skin contact with phenolic disinfectants. Phenolics are known carcinogens.

fyi Another word that is used (most often in marketing and sales copy) to describe multiuse items is *disinfectable*, which means these items can be disinfected and used again.

Bleach

Household bleach, 5.25 percent **sodium hypochlorite** (SOH-dee-um hy-puh-KLOR-ite), is an effective disinfectant and has been used extensively as a disinfectant in the salon. Using too much bleach can damage some metals and plastics, so be sure to read the label for safe use. Bleach can be corrosive to metals and plastics and can cause skin irritation and eye damage.

To mix a bleach solution, always follow the manufacturer's directions. Store the bleach solution away from heat and light. A fresh bleach solution should be mixed every 24 hours or when the solution has been contaminated. After mixing the bleach solution, date the container to ensure that the solution is not saved from one day to the next. Bleach can be irritating to the lungs, so be careful about inhaling the fumes.

Disinfectant Safety

Disinfectants are pesticides (a type of poison) and can cause serious skin and eye damage. Some disinfectants appear clear while others are cloudy. Always use caution when handling disinfectants, and follow the safety tips below.

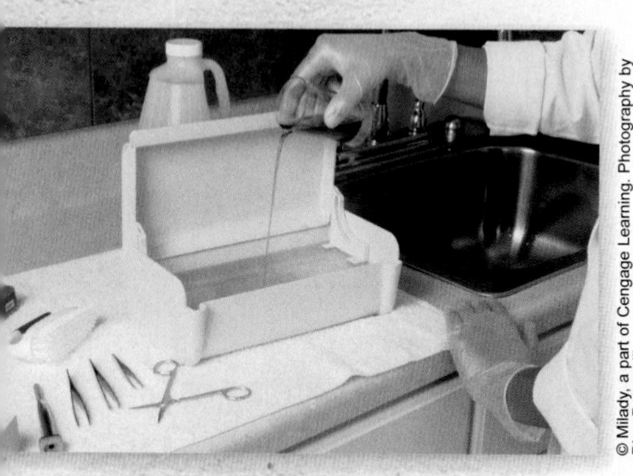

▲ Figure 5–16
Wear gloves while mixing disinfectants.

Safety Tips for Disinfectants

Always

- Keep an MSDS on hand for the disinfectant(s) you use.
- Wear gloves and safety glasses when mixing disinfectants (**Figure 5–16**).
- Avoid skin and eye contact.
- Add disinfectant to water when diluting (rather than adding water to a disinfectant) to prevent foaming, which can result in an incorrect mixing ratio.
- Use tongs, gloves, or a draining basket to remove implements from disinfectants.
- Keep disinfectants out of reach of children.
- Carefully measure and use disinfectant products according to label instructions.
- Follow the manufacturer's instructions for mixing, using, and disposing of disinfectants.

- Carefully follow the manufacturer's directions for when to replace the disinfectant solution in order to ensure the healthiest conditions for you and your client. Replace the disinfectant solution every day—more often if the solution becomes soiled or contaminated.

Never

- Let quats, phenols, bleach, or any other disinfectant come in contact with your skin. If you do get disinfectants on your skin, immediately wash the area with liquid soap and warm water. Then rinse the area and dry the area thoroughly.
- Place any disinfectant or other product in an unmarked container. All containers should be labeled (Figure 5–17).

Jars or containers used to disinfect implements are often incorrectly called wet sanitizers. The purpose of disinfectant containers is to disinfect, not to clean. Disinfectant containers must be covered, but not airtight. Remember to clean the container every day and to wear gloves when you do. Always follow the manufacturer's label instructions for disinfecting products. ☑ L05

CAUTION!

Porous or absorbent items must be disposed of properly if the skin is broken during the service or if they come into contact with unhealthy skin or nails.

Remember: When in doubt, throw it out!

Disinfect or Dispose?

How can you tell which items in the salon can be disinfected and reused? There are two types of items used in salons: multiuse (reusable) items and single-use (disposable) items.

▲ Figure 5–17
All containers must be labeled.

Multiuse, also known as **reusable**, items can be cleaned, disinfected, and used on more than one person even if the item is accidentally exposed to blood or body fluid. These items must have a hard, nonporous surface. Examples of multiuse items are comedone extractors, metal diamond tips on microdermabrasion devices, and tweezers.

Single-use, also known as **disposable**, items cannot be used more than once. These items cannot be properly cleaned so that all visible residue is removed—such as cotton tips, balls and rounds, sponges, gauze, tissues, and paper towels. Single-use items must be thrown out after each use.

Porous means that an item is made or constructed of a material that has pores or openings. These items are absorbent. Some porous items can be safely cleaned, disinfected, and used again. Examples of porous items are towels, chamois, and linens.

If a porous item contacts broken skin, blood, body fluid, or any unhealthy skin or nails, it must be discarded immediately. Do not try to disinfect the item. If you are not sure whether an item can be safely cleaned, disinfected, and used again, throw it out.

CAUTION!

Ultraviolet (UV) sanitizers are useful storage containers, but they do not disinfect or sterilize.

Keep a Logbook

Salons and spas should always follow manufacturers' recommended schedules for cleaning and disinfecting tools and implements, and sinks and basins. It is necessary to schedule regular service visits for

CAUTION!

Electric sterilizers, bead sterilizers, and baby sterilizers cannot be used to disinfect or sterilize implements. These devices can spread potentially infectious diseases and should never be used in salons or spas. Also, UV light units will not disinfect or sterilize implements. State rules require that you use liquid disinfecting solutions! Autoclaves are effective sterilizers. If you decide to use an autoclave, be sure that you know how to operate it properly.

equipment, and replace parts when needed. Although your state may not require you to keep a logbook of all equipment usage, cleaning, disinfecting, testing, and maintenance, it is advisable to keep one. Showing your logbook to clients provides them with peace of mind and confidence in your ability to protect them from infection and disease.

Disinfecting Nonelectrical Tools and Implements

State rules require that all multiuse tools and implements must be cleaned and disinfected before and after every service—even when they are used on the same person. Mix all disinfectants according to the manufacturer's directions, always adding the disinfectant to the water, not the water to the disinfectant (Figure 5–18).

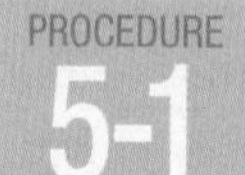
PROCEDURE 5-1 Disinfecting Nonelectrical Tools and Implements PAGE 104

▲ Figure 5–18
Carefully pour disinfectant into the water when preparing disinfectant solution.

Disinfecting Electrical Tools and Equipment

Electrotherapy tools such as microcurrent devices and galvanic accessories, microdermabrasion hand pieces, and other types of electrical equipment may have contact points that cannot be immersed in liquid. These items should be cleaned and disinfected using an EPA-registered disinfectant designed for use on these devices (Figure 5–19). Follow the procedures recommended by the disinfectant manufacturer for preparing the solution and follow the item's manufacturer directions for cleaning and disinfecting the device.

Disinfecting Work Surfaces

Before beginning every client service, all work surfaces must be cleaned and disinfected. Be certain to clean treatment beds, counters, trays, tables, sinks, stainless bowls, back-bar product bottles, and any other points of contact that you may have touched after having exposure to a client's skin. Clean doorknobs and handles daily to reduce transferring germs to your hands. Continue to wash your hands routinely after every service and task.

PROCEDURE 5-2 Aseptic Procedure PAGE 106

▲ Figure 5–19
Clean and disinfect implements.

Cross-Contamination

Any disinfected item that has been touched or exposed to air is contaminated. **Cross-contamination** occurs when you, the esthetician, touch an object such as the skin without cleaning your hands, and then touch an object or product with the same hand or utensil. You must use properly disinfected tools, and you must never touch clean items with hands that have been exposed to the client's skin. **Aseptic procedures**, the process of properly handling sterilized and disinfected equipment and supplies to reduce contamination, are an important part of client and practitioner safety guidelines.

Cleaning Towels and Linens

All linens should be used once and then cleaned by laundering with detergent and bleach. Soiled laundry should be folded into itself, handled with gloves and placed in a closed, lined receptacle until it is washed.

Laundry hampers or bins are to be cleaned daily with disinfectant. Laundry should be done regularly rather than left for the next day. Be sure that towels and linens are thoroughly dried. Items that are not dry may grow mildew and bacteria. Keep clean towels in a closed closet or cabinet until needed. Store soiled linens and towels in covered or closed containers, away from clean linens and towels, even if your state regulatory agency does not require that you do so. Whenever possible, use disposable towels, especially in restrooms.

Soaps and Detergents

Chelating soaps (CHE-layt-ing SOHPS), also known as **chelating detergents**, work to break down stubborn films and remove the residue of products such as scrubs, salts, and masks. The chelating agents in these soaps work in all types of water, are low-sudsing, and are specially formulated to work in areas with hard tap water. Hard tap water reduces the effectiveness of cleaners and disinfectants. If your area has hard water, ask your local distributor for soaps that are effective in hard water. This information will be stated on the product's label.

Additives, Powders, and Tablets

There is no additive, powder, or tablet that eliminates the need for you to clean and disinfect. Products of this type cannot be used instead of EPA-registered liquid disinfectant solutions. You cannot replace proper cleaning and disinfection with a shortcut. Water sanitizers do not properly clean or disinfect equipment. They are designed for Jacuzzis and hydrotherapy tubs where no oils, lotions, or other enhancements are used. Therefore, water sanitizers do not work well in a salon or spa environment. Never rely solely on water sanitizers to protect your clients from infection. Products that contain Chloramine T, for example, are not effective disinfectants for equipment. These products only treat the water and have limited value in the salon or spa. They do not replace proper cleaning and disinfection. Remember: There are no shortcuts!

Dispensary

The dispensary must be kept clean and orderly, with the contents of all containers clearly marked. Always store products according to the

CAUTION!

Products and equipment that have the word *sanitizer* on the label are merely cleaners. They do not disinfect. Items must be properly cleaned and disinfected after every use before using them on another client.

CAUTION!

Some states require that all procedures for cleaning and disinfecting tools, implements, and equipment must be recorded in a salon, spa, or medical facility logbook. Check with your state's regulatory agency to determine whether you are required to do so. It is a good practice to complete a logbook, even if not required, as it shows clients you are serious about protecting their health.

CAUTION!

Follow this rule for all tools and supplies: If you cannot disinfect your tools or supplies, you must discard them.

CAUTION!

When washing hands, use liquid soaps in pump containers. Bar soaps can grow bacteria.

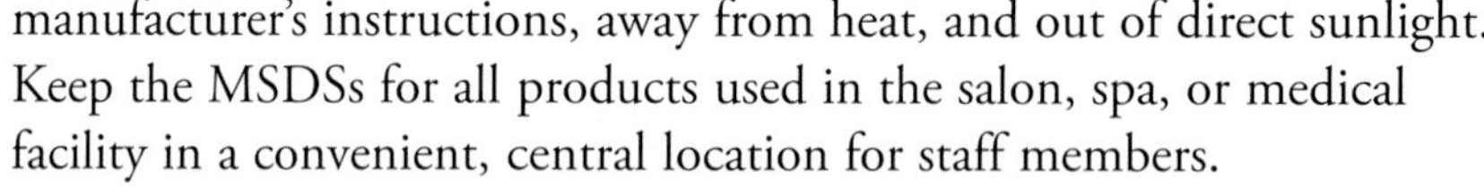

manufacturer's instructions, away from heat, and out of direct sunlight. Keep the MSDSs for all products used in the salon, spa, or medical facility in a convenient, central location for staff members.

Handling Single-Use Supplies

All single-use supplies, such as mascara wands, makeup applicators, cotton, gauze, wipes, and paper towels, should be thrown away after one use. Anything exposed to blood, including skin care treatment debris, must be double-bagged and marked with a biohazard sticker, separated from other waste, and disposed of according to OSHA standards.

CAUTION!

Taking the time to conduct a thorough facial skin analysis will enable you to determine whether a client has any open wounds or abrasions. If the client does have an open wound or abrasion, do not perform services of any kind for the client.

Hand Washing

Properly washing your hands is one of the most important actions you can take to prevent spreading germs from one person to another. Proper hand washing removes germs from the folds and grooves of the skin and from under the free edge of the nail plate by lifting and rinsing germs and contaminants from the surface.

You should wash your hands thoroughly before and after each service. Follow the hand washing procedure in this chapter. Antimicrobial and antibacterial soaps can dry the skin, and medical studies suggest that they are no more effective than regular soaps or detergents. Therefore, it is recommended that you minimize the use of antimicrobial and antibacterial soaps. Repeated hand washing can also dry the skin, so using a moisturizing hand lotion after washing is a good practice. Be sure the hand lotion is in a pump container, not a jar.

PROCEDURE 5-3 Proper Hand Washing PAGE 108

Avoid using very hot water to wash your hands because this is another practice that can damage the skin. Remember: You must wash your hands thoroughly before and after each service, so do all you can to reduce any irritation that may occur.

Waterless Hand Sanitizers

Antiseptics (ant-ih-SEP-tiks) are germicides formulated for use on skin and are registered and regulated by the Food and Drug Administration (FDA). Antiseptics can contain either alcohol or benzalkonium chloride (ben-ZAHL-khon-ee-um KLOHR-yd), which is less drying to the skin than alcohol. Alcohol solutions containing 60 percent to 95 percent alcohol are most effective. Lower and higher concentrations are less potent. Most alcohol-based products contain skin-conditioning agents to reduce the risk of irritation. Antiseptics cannot clean the hands of dirt and debris; this can only be accomplished with liquid soap, a soft-bristle brush, and water. If the hands are soiled, use hand sanitizers only after properly cleaning your hands. Never use an antiseptic to disinfect instruments or other surfaces. They are ineffective for that purpose.

Universal and Standard Precautions

The Centers of Disease Control and Prevention (CDC) studies diseases and provides guidance to prevent their spread. AIDS was a major public health crisis in the 1980s. In 1985, the CDC responded by introducing Universal Precautions (UP). Using this system, workers evaluated each client care situation and applied gloves if there was a risk of contact with visible blood. Sometimes blood is present but not visible. If blood was not visible, gloves were not needed. In 1987, a hospital developed a new system called **body substance isolation (BSI)**. The guidelines were published and widely adopted. When using BSI, **personal protective equipment (PPE)** is to be worn for contact with all body fluids, even if blood is not visible.

Standard Precautions (SP) were introduced by the CDC in 1996 to replace Universal Precautions. Workers must assume that all blood and body fluids are potential sources of infection, regardless of the perceived risk. The precautions are used for all clients whenever exposure to bloodborne pathogens is likely. Standard Precautions took information from both Universal Precautions and BSI. The importance of all body fluids, secretions, and excretions was recognized as a factor in the spread of disease. PPE is worn any time contact with blood, body fluid, secretions, excretions, mucous membranes, or nonintact skin is likely. The name *Standard Precautions* was selected to prevent confusion with other types of precautions. One goal was to be as simple anduser-friendly as possible.

The most common method for spreading infection is through the hands. In 2002, the CDC published the "Guidelines for Hand Hygiene." Investigators studied different methods of cleansing hands. They found that products containing alcohol were more effective in removing germs than using soap and water, unless the hands were visibly soiled. Most health care facilities and many other businesses began using alcohol-based products for routinely cleansing the hands. This includes the operating room, which is the most sterile area in a hospital. Standard Precautions were updated in 2007 by the CDC. The 2002 handwashing guidelines were included, as were precautions to prevent the spread of respiratory infections.

When the CDC publishes a change, it takes several years for the new information to get to everyone who needs it. From 1970 to 1996, infection control changes were frequent. Some workers had a hard time keeping up with all the changes and became confused. Many continue to use a combination of both Universal Precautions and BSI to this day. Many experienced workers consider Standard Precautions the equivalent of

BRIEF COMPARISON OF UNIVERSAL AND STANDARD PRECAUTIONS

UNIVERSAL PRECAUTIONS (UP)	STANDARD PRECAUTIONS (SP)
Overview	**Overview**
Everyone is considered a potential threat for transmission of bloodborne pathogens. Workers are expected to evaluate the risk and use universal precautions to protect themselves and others.	Workers must assume that all blood and body fluids are potential sources of infection, regardless of the perceived risk. Workers are expected to use standard precautions to protect themselves and others.
Universal Precautions apply to: • Blood • Other body fluids containing visible blood, semen, vaginal secretions • Body tissues • Fluids: cerebrospinal, synovial (knee), pleural (lung), peritoneal (abdomen), pericardial (heart), and amniotic fluid (bag of water that protects the fetus during pregnancy) **Universal Precautions do not apply to:** • Feces • Sputum • Tears • Vomitus • Breast milk • Nasal secretions • Sweat • Urine • Saliva ***Unless these substances contain visible blood.*** Wear gloves when contact with body fluids containing *visible blood* is likely.	**Standard Precautions apply to:** • Blood • All body fluids • All secretions (except sweat) • Excretions • Mucous membranes • Nonintact (broken) skin • Breast milk Wear gloves when contact with *any* blood or body fluid is likely. Wear gloves for all contact with body substances and tissues, even if you cannot see blood. Gloves are not required for contact with perspiration (sweat).
Gloves	**Gloves**
Changing gloves during care not required. Change gloves after each contact.	Apply gloves when contact with the substances listed above is likely. Change gloves *immediately prior to* contact with mucous membranes and nonintact skin.
Items and Surfaces in Room	**Items and Surfaces in Room**
Apply UP to items and surfaces that may have contacted substances to which UP apply.	Apply SP to items and surfaces that may have contacted substances to which SP apply.
Environmental contamination not an issue.	Avoid environmental contamination with used gloves. (This means counters, faucets, door knobs, etc.)

▲ Table 5–3 **Brief Comparison of Universal and Standard Precautions.**

Universal Precautions. This is incorrect. They are very different systems. Refer to Table 5–3 for a brief comparison of Universal and Standard precautions.

As you can see, infection control procedures change frequently as new information becomes available. Keep up with changes by reading professional journals, looking on-line, and going to continuing education classes. As an esthetician, you must understand the differences between UP and SP. By using Standard Precautions, you can be sure that you are

BRIEF COMPARISON OF UNIVERSAL AND STANDARD PRECAUTIONS	
UNIVERSAL PRECAUTIONS (UP)	**STANDARD PRECAUTIONS (SP)**
Needles and Sharps	**Needles and Sharps**
Avoid recapping needles. Place used sharps in a puncture-resistant container near the area of use.	Avoid recapping needles. Handle needles and sharps carefully to prevent injury to the user and others who may contact the soiled device. Place used sharps in a puncture-resistant container near the area of use.
Splashing of Blood and Body Fluids	**Splashing of Blood and Body Fluids**
No guidelines; splashing of blood or body fluids not addressed.	Apply a mask, eyewear, or gown if splashing is likely.
Additional Information	
For additional information, refer to: Hand Hygiene in Healthcare Settings go to: www.cdc.gov/handhygiene/ 2007 Guideline for Isolation Precautions: Preventing Transmission of Infectious Agents in Healthcare Settings go to: www. inyurl.com/4zxfunz	

▲ Table 5–3 **(continued)**

meeting the highest standards of practice. To protect yourself and your clients, learn all you can and be very diligent with infection control!

OSHA and Universal Precautions

OSHA publishes a set of standards for **Universal Precautions (UP)** that require the employer and employee to assume that there are pathogens present in human blood that can spread disease in humans. (These standards can be found in the OSHA publication, *Standard 1910.1030, Bloodborne Pathogens*.) Because it may not be possible to identify clients with infectious diseases, strict infection-control practices should be used with all clients. In most instances, clients who are infected with the hepatitis B virus or other bloodborne pathogens are **asymptomatic**, which means that they show no symptoms or signs of infection. Bloodborne pathogens are more difficult to kill than germs that live outside the body.

CAUTION!

Since estheticians work with an array of sharp implements and tools, cutting yourself is a very real possibility. If you do suffer a cut and blood is present, you must follow the steps for an exposure incident outlined in this chapter for your safety and the safety of your client.

OSHA sets safety standards and precautions that protect employees in situations where they could be exposed to bloodborne pathogens. Precautions include proper hand washing, wearing gloves, and properly handling and disposing of sharp instruments and any other items that may have been contaminated by blood or other body fluids. It is important that specific procedures are followed if visible blood is present.

An Exposure Incident: Contact with Blood or Body Fluid

You should never perform a service on any client who comes into the salon or spa with an open wound or an abrasion. Sometimes accidents happen while a service is being performed, and it is important to know what to do if this happens.

An **exposure incident** is contact with nonintact (broken) skin, blood, body fluid, or other potentially infectious materials that is the result of the performance of an employee's duties. Should the client suffer a cut or abrasion that bleeds during a service, follow these steps for the client's safety, as well as your own:

1. Stop the service.
2. Put on gloves to protect yourself from contact with the client's blood.
3. Stop the bleeding by applying pressure to the area with a clean cotton ball or piece of gauze.
4. When bleeding has stopped, clean the injured area with an antiseptic wipe. Every salon, spa, and medical facility must have a first aid kit.
5. Bandage the cut with an adhesive bandage.
6. Clean and disinfect your workstation or styling station, using an EPA-registered disinfectant designed for cleaning blood and body fluids.
7. Discard all single-use contaminated objects such as wipes or cotton balls by double-bagging (place the waste in a plastic bag and then in a trash bag). Place a biohazard sticker (red or orange) on the bag, and deposit the bag into a container for contaminated waste. Deposit sharp disposables in a sharps box (Figure 5–20).
8. Before removing your gloves, make sure that all multiuse tools and implements that have come into contact with blood or other body fluids are thoroughly cleaned and completely immersed in an EPA-registered disinfectant solution designed for cleaning blood and body fluids or 10 percent bleach solution for at least 10 minutes or for the time recommended by the manufacturer of the product. Be sure that you do not touch other work surfaces in the workplace, such as faucets and counters. If you do, these areas must also be properly cleaned and disinfected. Remember: Blood may carry pathogens, so you should never touch an open sore or a wound.
9. Remove your gloves and seal them in the double bag along with the other contaminated items for disposal. Thoroughly wash your hands and clean under the free edge of your nails with soap and warm water before returning to the service.
10. Recommend that the client see a physician if any signs of redness, swelling, pain, or irritation develop. ✓ LO6

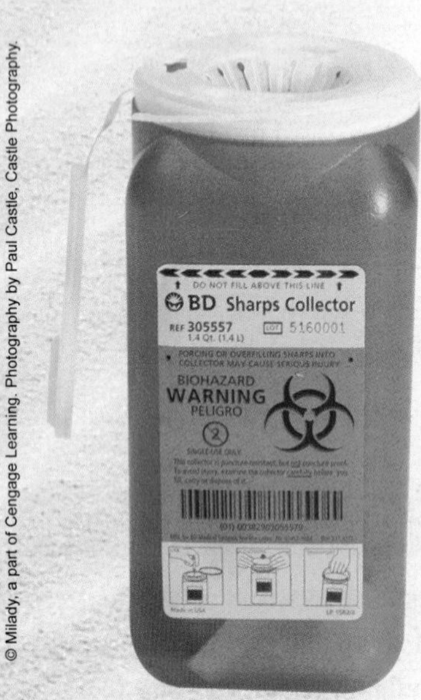

▲ Figure 5–20
Always use a sharps box to dispose of sharp, disposable implements.

First Aid

Because emergencies arise in every line of business, knowledge of basic first aid is invaluable. Every esthetician should know CPR (cardiopulmonary resuscitation) and should have some first aid training. You can obtain this training through your local trade or technical college. Emergency medical technicians (EMTs) or an ambulance should be called as soon as possible after any accident has occurred. Do *not* recommend treatment for specific emergencies—always call a medical professional or 911.

In Case of Emergency

Every salon, spa, and medical facility should have current emergency contact information posted clearly by each telephone and in a central and known location. The emergency contact list should include the following information: fire department, police (local and state), ambulance, nearest hospital emergency room, poison control center.

Each employee should know where exits are located and how to evacuate the building efficiently in case of fire or other emergency. Yearly fire drills or evacuation procedures should be performed just to keep everyone informed on how to clear safely out of a building. Fire extinguishers should be placed where they can be reached easily, and employees should know how to use them. Employees should have regular training on how to operate these devices, and they should know exactly where they are located. A well-stocked first aid kit should be kept within easy reach (Figure 5–21).

Did You Know?

You should never attempt to clean or disinfect any used tool or implement at your workstation. Proper cleaning and disinfecting should only be accomplished in a specified area of the salon and requires the use of clean, warm running water, a scrub brush, and liquid soap for cleaning and disinfectant solution for disinfecting. Tools and implements must also be completely rinsed after being disinfected and then dried and kept in a dry, covered container until use.

Basic First Aid Knowledge

Estheticians are not medical personnel, but anyone who works with the public should have a working knowledge of first aid as it pertains to the work environment. People who can administer first aid are also good citizens in their community. It makes good sense to know how to apply pressure to a bleeding wound, or how to dress a burn, or what to do if someone chokes, and it will certainly come in handy should you come across a situation that requires such knowledge.

Did You Know?

A first aid kit at a minimum should include these items: small bandages, gauze, antiseptic, and a blood-spill kit that contains disposable bags, gloves, and hazardous waste stickers.

Burns

There are four levels of burns (Figure 5–22 on pg. 102). They are identified as follows:

1. ***First degree***. A minor burn affecting the upper layers of the skin, primarily the epidermis, with some redness and irritation, but no blisters or open skin.
2. ***Second degree***. This level of burn affects the top two layers of the skin, the epidermis, and the dermis. It is more painful than the first-degree burn and will show redness and blisters.
3. ***Third degree***. This burn affects all layers of the skin and will blister, swell, and scar. The pain associated with a third-degree burn depends on the amount of nerve damage that has taken place.
4. ***Fourth degree***. These are burns that have injured the muscle, ligaments, tendons, nerves, blood vessels, and bones. These burns always require medical attention.

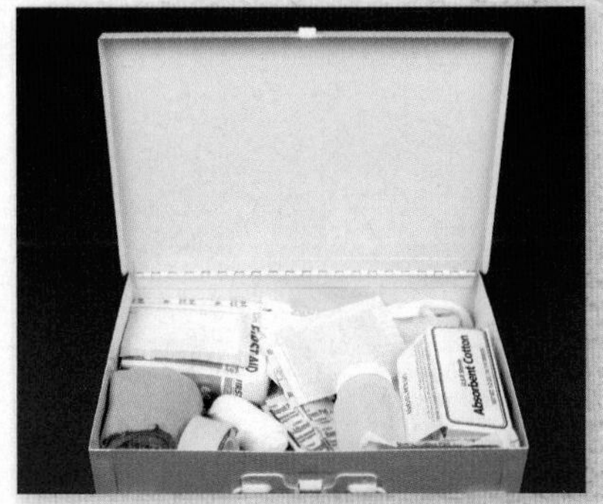

▲ Figure 5–21
Having a well-stocked first aid kit is necessary.

Eye Flush

Eye-flushing stations are important to an esthetician working in any type of setting and are a requirement for every business using chemicals to maintain, according to OSHA Standards. As always, prevention is

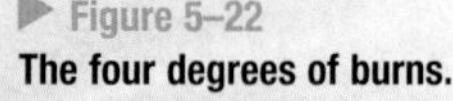
Figure 5–22
The four degrees of burns.

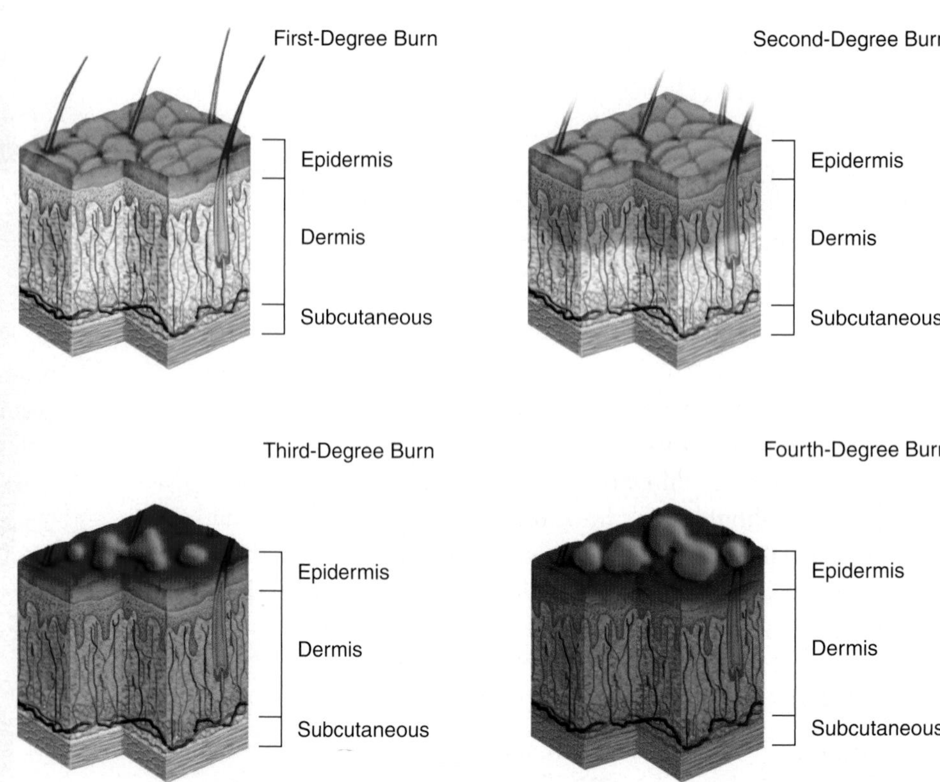

the best answer to warding off problems of product getting into a client's eye. Place eye protection on clients during all appropriate treatments; however, accidents do happen, and when they do, you must be proactive. Take the client to the nearest available sink or eye-flushing station. Gently flush the eye with water for 15 minutes and have the client seek medical attention immediately.

The Professional Salon Image

Infection control practices should be a part of the normal routine for you and your coworkers so that the salon or spa and staff project a steadfast professional image. The following are some simple guidelines that will keep the workplace healthy and looking its best.

- Keep floors and workstations dust-free. Sweep hair off the floor after every client. Mop floors and vacuum carpets every day.
- Control dust, hair, and other debris.
- Keep trash in a covered waste receptacle to reduce chemical odors and fires.
- Clean fans, ventilation systems, and humidifiers at least once each week.
- Keep all work areas well-lit.
- Clean and disinfect restroom surfaces, including door handles.

- Provide toilet tissue, paper towels, liquid soap, properly disinfected soft-bristle nail brushes, and a container for used brushes in the restroom.
- Do not allow the salon or spa to be used for cooking or living purposes.
- Never place food in the same refrigerator used to store salon or spa products.
- Prohibit eating, drinking, and smoking in areas where services are performed or where product mixing occurs (e.g., back-bar area). Consider having a smoke-free salon. Even when you do not smoke in the service areas, the odor can flow into those areas.
- Empty waste receptacles regularly throughout the day. A metal waste receptacle with a self-closing lid works best.
- Make sure all containers are properly marked and properly stored.
- Never place any tools or implements in your mouth or pockets.
- Properly clean and disinfect all multiuse tools before reusing them.
- Store clean and disinfected tools in a clean, covered container. Clean drawers may be used for storage if only clean items are stored in the drawers. Always isolate used implements away from disinfected implements.
- Avoid touching your face, mouth, or eye areas during services.
- Clean and disinfect all work surfaces after every client.
- Have clean, disposable paper towels for each client.
- Always properly wash your hands before and after each service.
- Use clean linens and disposable towels on clients. Keep soiled linens separate from clean linens. Use effective exhaust systems in the salon spa or medical facility. This will help ensure proper air quality in the workplace.

Your Professional Responsibility

You have many responsibilities as a salon professional, but none is more important than protecting your clients' health and safety. Never take shortcuts for cleaning and disinfecting. You cannot afford to skip steps or save money when it comes to safety.

- It is your professional and legal responsibility to follow state and federal laws and rules.
- Keep your license current and notify the licensing agency if you move or change your name.
- Check your state's Web site weekly for any changes or updates to rules and regulations. ☑ LO7

PROCEDURE 5-1

Disinfecting Nonelectrical Tools and Implements

Nonelectrical tools and implements include items such as comedone extractors, microdermabrasion hand pieces, galvanic accessories, makeup brushes, and tweezers.

1 It is important to wear safety glasses and gloves while disinfecting nonelectrical tools and implements to protect your eyes from unintentional splashes of disinfectant and to prevent possible contamination of the implements by your hands and to protect your hands from the powerful chemicals in the disinfectant solution.

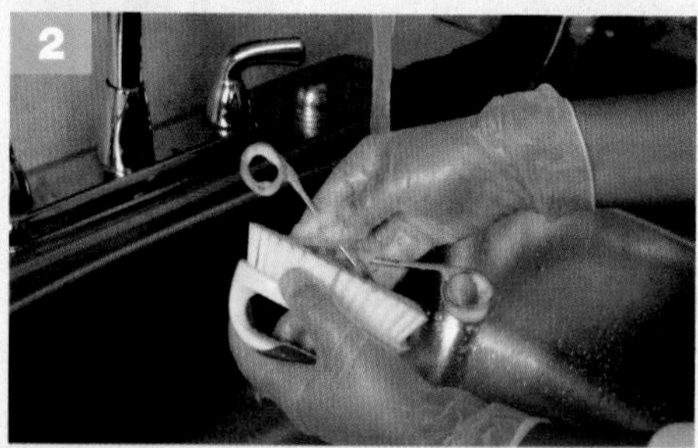

2 Rinse all implements with warm running water, and then thoroughly clean them with soap, a nail brush, and warm water. Brush grooved items, if necessary, and open hinged implements to scrub the revealed area.

3 Rinse away all traces of soap with warm running water. The presence of soap in most disinfectants will cause them to become inactive. Soap is most easily rinsed off in warm, not hot, water. Hotter water is not more effective. Dry implements thoroughly with a clean or disposable towel, or allow them to air dry on a clean towel. Your implements are now properly cleaned and ready to be disinfected.

4 It is extremely important that your implements be completely clean before you place them in the disinfectant solution. If implements are not clean, your disinfectant may become contaminated and ineffective. Immerse cleaned implements in an appropriate disinfection container holding an EPA-registered disinfectant for the required time (at least 10 minutes or according to the manufacturer's instructions). Remember to open hinged implements before immersing them in the disinfectant. If the disinfection solution is visibly dirty, or if the solution has been contaminated, it must be replaced.

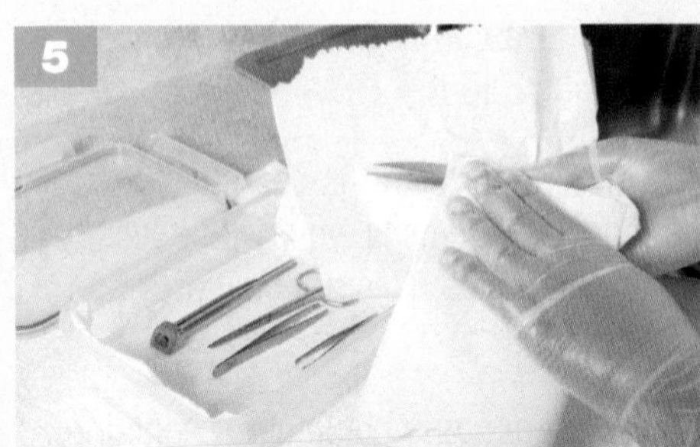

5 After the required disinfection time has passed, remove tools and implements from the disinfection solution with tongs or gloved hands, rinse the tools and implements well in warm running water, and pat them dry.

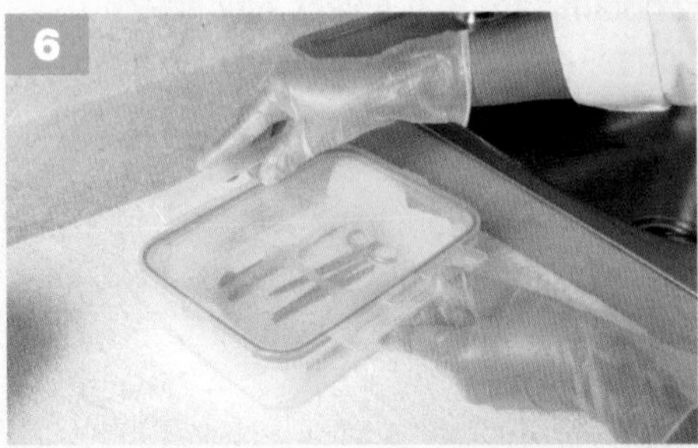

6 Store disinfected tools and implements in a clean, covered container until needed.

7 Remove gloves and thoroughly wash your hands with warm running water and liquid soap. Rinse and dry hands with a clean fabric or disposable towel. ✓ LO8

PROCEDURE 5-2

Aseptic Procedure

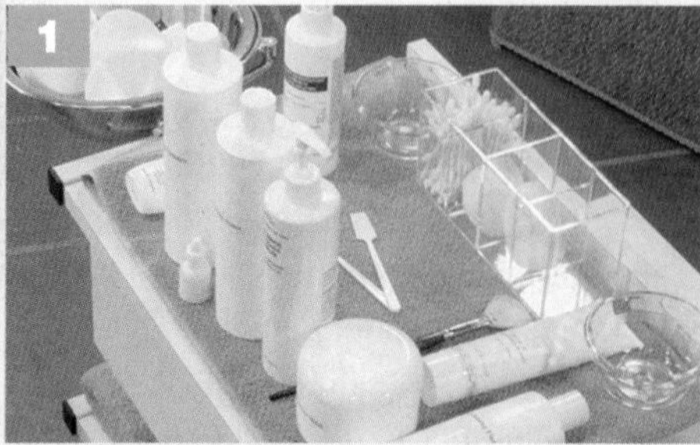
© Milady, a part of Cengage Learning. Photography by Larry Hamill.

1 Before beginning any treatment, wash your hands using proper decontamination methods.

2 Lay out on a clean towel all implements that you will use during the treatment, such as cotton, swabs, sponges, and so forth.

3 To prevent airborne contact, cover with another clean towel until you are ready to start the treatment. By prearranging these utensils, you will be less likely to need to open a container to get more supplies. This not only prevents cross-contamination but is also more efficient.

4 Once you have begun a treatment, never open any package or container or touch a product without a spatula or tongs. Touching any object with gloved hands that have touched the client will contaminate that object. Any object touched during treatment must be discarded, disinfected, or autoclaved.

© Milady, a part of Cengage Learning. Photography by Rob Werfel.

5 Use clean towels, sheets, headband or plastic cap, and gown for each client.

© Milady, a part of Cengage Learning. Photography by Rob Werfel.

6 Wash your hands after touching a client's hair.

7 Put on gloves at the beginning of every treatment and wear them throughout the treatment. This is especially important during and after extraction, waxing, and the performance of microdermabrasion, skin peels, or electrolysis.

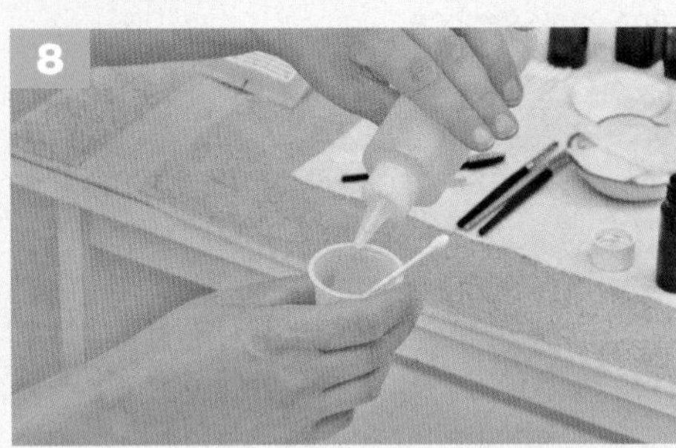

8 Remove creams and products from containers using pumps, squeeze bottles with dispenser caps, or disinfected spatulas. It is best to remove products before the treatment and place them in small disposable cups. This way, you will not have to touch bottles or jars with soiled gloved hands. Spatulas should be disinfected or discarded after each use.

9 After completing the treatment, fold linens in toward their center, then place them in a covered laundry receptacle. Throw away disposable items in a closed trash container. Place sharps in a sharps box. Disinfect or sterilize all items to be reused. Discard any unused product that has been removed from its container.

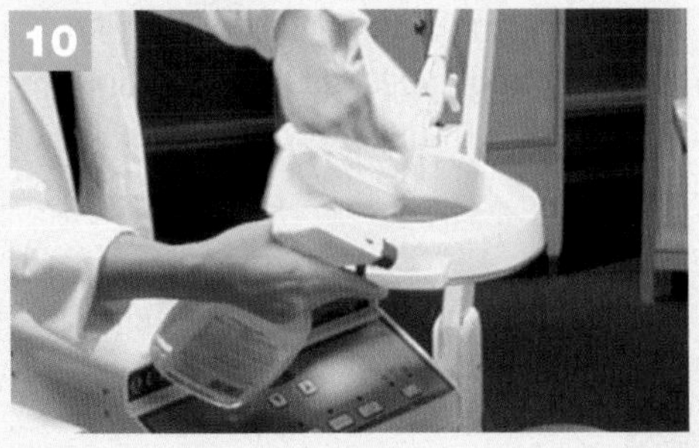

10 Wipe down all surfaces touched during treatment with a disinfectant before the next client is seated.

PROCEDURE 5-3

Proper Hand Washing

Hand washing is one of the most important procedures in your infection control efforts and is required in every state before any service.

1 Turn on the warm water, wet your hands, and then pump soap from a pump container onto the palm of your hand. Rub your hands together, all over and vigorously, until a lather forms. Continue for a minimum of 20 seconds.

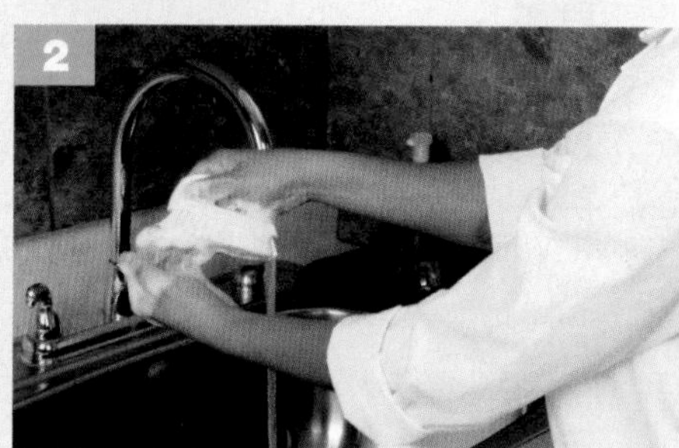

2 Choose a clean, disinfected nail brush. Wet the nail brush, pump soap on it, and brush your nails horizontally back and forth under the free edges. Change the direction of the brush to vertical and move the brush up and down along the nail folds of the fingernails. The process for brushing both hands should take about 60 seconds to finish. Rinse hands in running warm water.

fyi

Dirty nail brushes should be stored together in a closed container until you are ready to clean and disinfect them. Then nail brushes should be properly cleaned, rinsed, dried, and immersed for the required disinfection time in a disinfectant that does not harm plastics. After they have been disinfected, rinse the brushes in clean, warm water, dry them, and place them in a clean storage location.

3 Use a clean cloth or paper towel, according to the salon policies, for drying your hands.

4 After drying your hands, turn off the water with the towel and dispose of the towel.

Review Questions

1. What is the primary purpose of regulatory agencies?
2. What is an MSDS? Where can you get it?
3. List the four types of organisms that estheticians must know about and remember.
4. What are bacteria?
5. Name and describe the two main classifications of bacteria.
6. What are some of the beneficial functions performed by nonpathogenic bacteria?
7. Name and describe the three forms of pathogenic bacteria.
8. What is a contagious disease?
9. Is HIV a risk in the salon or spa? Why or why not?
10. What is the difference between cleaning, disinfecting, and sterilizing?
11. What is complete immersion?
12. List at least six precautions to follow when using disinfectants.
13. How do you know if an item can be disinfected?
14. Can porous items be disinfected?
15. How often should disinfectant solutions be changed? How often should an AHP disinfectant be changed?
16. What are Universal Precautions?
17. What are Standard Precautions?
18. What is an exposure incident?
19. Describe the procedure for handling an exposure incident in the salon or spa.
20. Explain how to clean and disinfect nonelectrical tools and implements.
21. Explain how to clean and disinfect electrical tools and equipment.

Glossary

acquired immune deficiency syndrome	Abbreviated AIDS; a disease that breaks down the body's immune system. AIDS is caused by the human immunodeficiency virus (HIV).
acquired immunity	Immunity that the body develops after overcoming a disease, through inoculation (such as flu vaccinations), or through exposure to natural allergens such as pollen, cat dander, and ragweed.
allergy	Reaction due to extreme sensitivity to certain foods, chemicals, or other normally harmless substances.
antiseptics	Chemical germicides formulated for use on skin; registered and regulated by the Food and Drug Administration (FDA).
aseptic procedures	A process of properly handling sterilized and disinfected equipment and supplies to reduce contamination.
asymptomatic	Showing no symptoms or signs of infection.
autoclave	A device for sterilization by steam under pressure.

Glossary

bacilli	Short rod-shaped bacteria. They are the most common bacteria and produce diseases such as tetanus (lockjaw), typhoid fever, tuberculosis, and diphtheria.
bacteria (singular: bacterium)	One-celled microorganisms that have both plant and animal characteristics. Some are harmful; some are harmless.
bactericidal	Capable of destroying bacteria.
binary fission	The division of bacteria cells into two new cells called daughter cells.
bioburden	The number of viable organisms in or on an object or surface or the organic material on a surface or object before decontamination or sterilization.
bloodborne pathogens	Disease-causing microorganisms carried in the body by blood or body fluids, such as hepatitis and HIV.
body substance isolation	Abbreviated BSI; a system of precautions developed by a Seattle hospital in 1987 to prevent contact with bodily substances and fluids by using protective apparel to prevent the spread of communicable disease.
chelating soaps	Also known as *chelating detergents*; detergents that break down stubborn films and remove the residue of products such as scrubs, salts, and masks.
clean	Also known as *cleaning*; a mechanical process (scrubbing) using soap and water or detergent and water to remove all visible dirt, debris, and many disease-causing germs. Cleaning also removes invisible debris that interferes with disinfection.
cocci	Round-shaped bacteria that appear singly (alone) or in groups. The three types of cocci are staphylococci, streptococci, and diplococci.
contagious disease	Also known as *communicable disease*; a disease that is spread from one person to another person. Some of the more contagious diseases are the common cold, ringworm, conjunctivitis (pinkeye), viral infections, and natural nail or toe and foot infections.
contamination	The presence, or the reasonably anticipated presence, of blood or other potentially infectious materials on an item's surface or visible debris or residues such as dust, hair, and skin.
cross-contamination	Contamination that occurs when you touch one object and then transfer the contents of that object to another, such as touching skin, then touching a product without washing your hands.
decontamination	The removal of blood or other potentially infectious materials on an item's surface and the removal of visible debris or residue such as dust, hair, and skin.
dermatophytes	A type of fungi that causes skin, hair, and nail infections.
diagnosis	Determination of the nature of a disease from its symptoms and/or diagnostic tests. Federal regulations prohibit salon professionals from performing a diagnosis.
diplococci	Spherical bacteria that grow in pairs and cause diseases such as pneumonia.
direct transmission	Transmission of blood or body fluids through touching (including shaking hands), kissing, coughing, sneezing, and talking.
disease	An abnormal condition of all or part of the body, or its systems or organs, that makes the body incapable of carrying on normal function.

Glossary

disinfectants	Chemical products that destroy all bacteria, fungi, and viruses (but not spores) on surfaces.
disinfection	Also known as *disinfecting*; the process that eliminates most, but not necessarily all, microorganisms on nonporous surfaces. This process is not effective against bacterial spores.
efficacy	The ability to produce an effect.
exposure incident	Contact with nonintact (broken) skin, blood, body fluid, or other potentially infectious materials that is the result of the performance of an employee's duties.
flagella	Also known as *cilia*; slender, hair-like extensions used by bacilli and spirilla for locomotion (moving about).
folliculitis	Also know as folliculitis barbae, sycosis barbae, or barber's itch. Inflammation of the hair follicles caused by a baterial infection from ingrown hairs. The cause is typically from ingrown hairs due to shaving or other epilation methods.
fungi (singular: fungus)	Microscopic plant parasites, which include molds, mildews, and yeasts; can produce contagious diseases such as ringworm.
fungicidal	Capable of destroying fungi.
hepatitis	A bloodborne virus that causes disease and can damage the liver.
hospital disinfectants	Disinfectants that are effective for cleaning blood and body fluids.
human immunodeficiency virus	Abbreviated HIV; a pathogen that is most often the precursor to acquired immune deficiency syndrome (AIDS). By impairing or killing the immune system affected with it, HIV progressively destroys the body's ability to fight infections or certain cancers.
human papillomavirus	Abbreviated HPV and also known as *plantar warts*; a virus that can infect the bottom of the foot and resembles small black dots, usually in clustered groups.
immunity	The ability of the body to destroy and resist infection. Immunity against disease can be either natural or acquired and is a sign of good health.
indirect transmission	Transmission of blood or body fluids through contact with an intermediate contaminated object such as a razor, extractor, nipper, or an environmental surface.
infection	The invasion of body tissues by disease-causing pathogens.
infection control	The methods used to eliminate or reduce the transmission of infectious organisms.
infectious	Caused by or capable of being transmitted by infection.
infectious disease	Disease caused by pathogenic (harmful) microorganisms that enter the body. An infectious disease may or may not be spread from one person to another person.
inflammation	Condition in which the body reacts to injury, irritation, or infection; characterized by redness, heat, pain, and swelling.
local infection	An infection, such as a pimple or abscess, that is confined to a particular part of the body and appears as a lesion containing pus.
Material Safety Data Sheet	Abbreviated MSDS; information compiled by the manufacturer about product safety, including the names of hazardous ingredients, safe handling and use procedures, precautions to reduce the risk of accidental harm or overexposure, and flammability warnings.

Glossary

methicillin-resistant staphylococcus aureus	Abbreviated MRSA; a type of infectious bacteria that is highly resistant to conventional treatments such as antibiotics.
microorganism	Any organism of microscopic or submicroscopic size.
mildew	A type of fungus that affects plants or grows on inanimate objects, but does not cause human infections in the salon.
motility	Self-movement.
multiuse	Also known as *reusable*; items that can be cleaned, disinfected, and used on more than one person, even if the item is accidentally exposed to blood or body fluid.
mycobacterium fortuitum	A microscopic germ that normally exists in tap water in small numbers.
natural immunity	Immunity that is partly inherited and partly developed through healthy living.
nonpathogenic	Harmless microorganisms that may perform useful functions and are safe to come in contact with since they do not cause disease or harm.
nonporous	An item that is made or constructed of a material that has no pores or openings and cannot absorb liquids.
occupational disease	Illness resulting from conditions associated with employment, such as prolonged and repeated overexposure to certain products or ingredients.
parasites	Organisms that grow, feed, and shelter on or in another organism (referred to as the host), while contributing nothing to the survival of that organism. Parasites must have a host to survive.
parasitic disease	Disease caused by parasites, such as lice and mites.
pathogenic	Harmful microorganisms that can cause disease or infection in humans when they invade the body.
pathogenic disease	Disease produced by organisms, including bacteria, viruses, fungi, and parasites.
personal protective equipment	Abbreviated PPE; protective clothing and devices designed to protect an individual from contact with bloodborne pathogens; examples include gloves, fluid-resistant lab coat, apron, or gown, goggles or eye shield, and face masks that cover the nose and mouth.
phenolic disinfectants	Powerful tuberculocidal disinfectants. They are a form of formaldehyde, have a very high pH, and can damage the skin and eyes.
porous	Made or constructed of a material that has pores or openings. Porous items are absorbent.
pus	A fluid created by infection.
quaternary ammonium compounds	Also known as *quats*; disinfectants that are very effective when used properly in the salon.

Glossary

sanitizing	A chemical process for reducing the number of disease-causing germs on cleaned surfaces to a safe level.
scabies	A contagious skin disease that is caused by the itch mite, which burrows under the skin.
single-use	Also known as *disposable*; items that cannot be used more than once. These items cannot be properly cleaned so that all visible residue is removed, or they are damaged or contaminated by cleaning and disinfecting in exposure incident.
sodium hypochlorite	Common household bleach; an effective disinfectant for the salon.
spirilla	Spiral or corkscrew-shaped bacteria that cause diseases such as syphilis and Lyme disease.
Standard Precautions	Abbreviated SP; precautions such as wearing personal protective equipment to prevent skin and mucous membrane where contact with a client's blood, body fluids, secretions (except sweat), excretions, nonintact skin, and mucous membranes is likely. Workers must assume that all blood and body fluids are potential sources of infection, regardless of the perceived risk.
staphylococci	Pus-forming bacteria that grow in clusters like a bunch of grapes. They cause abscesses, pustules, and boils.
sterilization	The process that completely destroys all microbial life, including spores.
streptococci	Pus-forming bacteria arranged in curved lines resembling a string of beads. They cause infections such as strep throat and blood poisoning.
systemic disease	Disease that affects the body as a whole, often due to under-functioning or over-functioning of internal glands or organs. This disease is carried through the blood stream or the lymphatic system.
tinea pedis	A ringworm fungus of the foot or athlete's foot.
tinea versicolor	Also known as *sun spots*; a noncontagious fungal infection which is characterized by white or varicolored patches on the skin and is often found on arms and legs.
toxins	Various poisonous substances produced by some microorganisms (bacteria and viruses).
tuberculocidal disinfectants	Disinfectants that kill the bacteria that causes tuberculosis.
tuberculosis	A disease caused by bacteria that are transmitted through coughing or sneezing.
Universal Precautions	Abbreviated UP; a set of guidelines published by OSHA that require the employer and the employee to assume that all human blood and body fluids are infectious for bloodborne pathogens.
virucidal	Capable of destroying viruses.
virus (plural: viruses)	A parasitic submicroscopic particle that infects and resides in the cells of biological organisms. A virus is capable of replication only through taking over the host cell's reproductive function.

CHAPTER 6

General Anatomy and Physiology

Chapter Outline

- Why Study Anatomy and Physiology?
- Cells
- Tissues
- Organs and Body Systems
- The Skeletal System
- The Muscular System
- The Nervous System
- The Circulatory System
- The Lymphatic/Immune System
- The Endocrine System
- The Digestive System
- The Excretory System
- The Respiratory System
- The Integumentary System
- The Reproductive System

Learning Objectives

After completing this chapter, you will be able to:

- ☑ LO1 Define and explain why the study of anatomy, physiology, and histology is important to the esthetician.
- ☑ LO2 Describe cells, their structure, and their reproduction.
- ☑ LO3 Define tissue and identify the types of tissues found in the body.
- ☑ LO4 Name the 9 major body organs and the 11 main body systems and explain their basic functions.

Key Terms

Page number indicates where in the chapter the term is used.

abductors pg. 131

absorption pg. 146

adductors pg. 131

adipose tissue pg. 120

adrenal glands pg. 145

anabolism pg. 120

anatomy pg. 118

angular artery pg. 141

anterior auricular artery pg. 142

aorta pg. 140

arteries pg. 140

arterioles pg. 140

atrioventricular valves (ATV) pg. 140

atrium pg. 138

auricularis anterior pg. 128

auricularis posterior pg. 128

auricularis superior pg. 128

auriculotemporal nerve pg. 136

autonomic nervous system (ANS) pg. 132

axon pg. 134

belly pg. 127

biceps pg. 130

blood pg. 140

blood vessels pg. 140

body systems (systems) pg. 121

brachial artery pg. 143

brain pg. 133

brain stem pg. 134

buccal nerve pg. 137

buccinator pg. 129

capillaries pg. 140

cardiac muscle pg. 126

carpus (wrist) pg. 126

catabolism pg. 120

cell membrane pg. 119

cells pg. 118

central nervous system (CNS) pg. 132

cerebellum pg. 133

cerebrum pg. 133

cervical cutaneous nerve pg. 137

cervical nerves pg. 137

cervical vertebrae pg. 124

circulatory system (cardiovascular system, vascular system) pg. 138

clavicle (collarbone) pg. 125

common carotid arteries pg. 141

connective tissue pg. 120

corrugator muscle pg. 128

cranium pg. 123

cytoplasm pg. 119

defecation pg. 146

deltoid pg. 130

dendrites pg. 134

deoxyribonucleic acid (DNA) pg. 119

depressor anguli oris (triangularis muscle) pg. 129

depressor labii inferioris (quadratus labii inferioris muscle) pg. 129

diaphragm pg. 146

diencephalon pg. 133

Key Terms

Page number indicates where in the chapter the term is used.

digestion
pg. 145

digestive enzymes
pg. 145

digestive system (gastrointestinal system)
pg. 145

digital nerve
pg. 137

eleventh cranial nerve (accessory nerve)
pg. 137

endocrine glands (ductless glands)
pg. 144

endocrine system
pg. 145

epicranial aponeurosis
pg. 128

epicranius (occipitofrontalis)
pg. 127

epithelial tissue
pg.120

ethmoid bone
pg. 124

excretory system
pg. 146

exhalation
pg. 146

exocrine glands (duct glands)
pg. 144

extensors
pg. 131

external carotid artery
pg. 141

external jugular vein
pg. 142

facial artery (external maxillary artery)
pg. 141

fifth cranial nerve (trifacial, trigeminal nerve)
pg. 136

flexors
pg. 131

frontal artery
pg. 142

frontal bone
pg. 124

frontalis
pg. 128

glands
pg. 144

greater auricular nerve
pg. 137

greater occipital nerve
pg. 137

heart
pg. 138

hemoglobin
pg. 141

histology (microscopic anatomy)
pg. 118

hormones
pg. 146

humerus
pg. 125

hyoid bone
pg. 124

inferior labial artery
pg. 141

infraorbital artery
pg. 142

infraorbital nerve
pg. 136

infratrochlear nerve
pg. 136

ingestion
pg. 145

inhalation
pg. 146

insertion
pg. 127

integumentary system
pg.146

internal carotid artery
pg. 141

internal jugular vein
pg. 142

interstitial fluid
pg. 143

joint
pg. 123

kidneys
pg. 128

lacrimal bones
pg. 124

lateral pterygoid
pg. 128

latissimus dorsi
pg. 130

levator anguli oris (caninus)
pg. 129

levator labii superioris (quadratus labii superioris)
pg. 129

liver
pg. 121

lungs
pg. 146

lymph
pg. 143

lymph capillaries
pg. 144

lymph nodes
pg. 143

lymphatic/immune system
pg. 143

mandible
pg. 124

mandibular nerve
pg. 136

masseter
pg. 128

maxillary bones
pg. 124

maxillary nerve
pg. 136

medial pterygoid
pg. 128

median nerve
pg. 138

melasma
pg. 147

mental nerve
pg. 136

mentalis
pg. 130

metabolism
pg. 120

metacarpus (palm)
pg. 126

middle temporal artery
pg. 142

mitosis
pg. 119

mitral valve (bicuspid valve)
pg. 139

motor nerves (efferent nerves)
pg. 134

muscular system
pg. 126

muscle tissue
pg. 120

myology
pg. 126

nasal bones
pg. 124

nasal nerve
pg. 136

nasalis muscle
pg. 129

nerve tissue
pg. 120

nerves
pg. 134

nervous system
pg. 132

neurology
pg. 132

neuron or nerve cell
pg. 134

nonstriated muscles (involuntary, visceral, smooth)
pg. 126

nucleoplasm
pg. 119

nucleus
pg. 119

occipital artery
pg. 142

occipital bone
pg. 124

occipitalis
pg. 128

Key Terms

Page number indicates where in the chapter the term is used.

ophthalmic nerve
pg. 136

orbicularis oculi
pg. 129

orbicularis oris
pg. 130

organelle
pg. 119

organs
pg. 120

origin
pg. 127

os
pg. 122

osteology
pg. 122

ovaries
pg. 145

palatine bones
pg. 124

pancreas
pg. 144

parasympathetic division
pg. 132

parathyroid glands
pg. 144

parietal artery
pg. 142

parietal bones
pg. 124

pectoralis major and minor
pg. 130

pericardium
pg. 138

peripheral nervous system (PNS)
pg. 132

peristalsis
pg. 145

phalanges (digits)
pg. 126

physiology
pg. 118

pineal gland
pg. 144

pituitary gland
pg. 144

plasma
pg. 141

platelets (thrombocytes)
pg. 141

platysma
pg. 128

posterior auricular artery
pg. 142

posterior auricular nerve
pg. 137

procerus
pg. 129

pronators
pg. 131

protoplasm
pg. 119

pulmonary circulation
pg. 138

radial artery
pg. 143

radial nerve
pg. 138

radius
pg. 125

red blood cells (red blood corpuscles, erythrocytes)
pg. 141

reflex
pg. 134

reproductive system
pg. 147

respiration
pg. 121

respiratory system
pg. 146

ribs
pg. 125

risorius
pg. 130

scapula (shoulder blade)
pg. 125

sensory nerves (afferent nerves)
pg. 134

serratus anterior
pg. 130

seventh cranial nerve (facial nerve)
pg. 137

skeletal system
pg. 122

skin
pg. 121

smaller occipital nerve (lesser occipital nerve)
pg. 137

sphenoid bone
pg. 124

spinal cord
pg. 134

sternocleidomastoid (SCM)
pg. 128

sternum (breastbone)
pg. 125

striated muscles (skeletal, voluntary)
pg. 126

submental artery
pg. 141

superficial temporal artery
pg. 141

superior labial artery
pg. 141

supinator
pg. 131

supraorbital artery
pg. 142

supraorbital nerve
pg. 136

supratrochlear nerve
pg. 136

sympathetic division
pg. 132

systemic or general circulation
pg. 138

temporal bones
pg. 124

temporal nerve
pg. 137

temporalis muscle
pg. 128

testes
pg. 145

thorax
pg. 125

thyroid gland
pg. 144

tissue
pg. 120

transverse facial artery
pg. 142

trapezius
pg. 130

triceps
pg. 130

tricuspid valve
pg. 139

turbinal bones
pg. 139

ulna
pg. 125

ulnar artery
pg. 143

ulnar nerve
pg. 138

valves
pg. 138

vascular system
pg. 138

veins
pg. 140

ventricle
pg. 138

venules
pg. 140

vomer bone
pg. 139

white blood cells (white corpuscles, leukocytes)
pg. 141

zygomatic bones (malar bones, cheekbones)
pg. 139

zygomatic nerve
pg. 137

zygomaticus major and minor
pg. 130

Whether applying product, giving a treatment, or doing a skin care analysis, as licensed estheticians, we are permitted to touch people as part of our profession. This is true of very few other occupations, and it is an honor to be able to aid others in a greater sense of well-being.

Anatomy (ah-NAT-ah-mee) is the study of the structures of the human body that can be seen with the naked eye, and of what substances they are made. It is the science of the structure of organisms, or of their parts.

Physiology (fiz-ih-OL-oh-jee) is the study of the functions and activities performed by the body structures.

Histology (his-TAHL-uh-jee), also known as **microscopic anatomy**, is the study of the tiny structures found in living tissue.

Estheticians focus primarily on the muscles, bones, nerves, and circulation of the head, face, neck, arms, and hands. Understanding this anatomy and physiology will help you develop your skills and perform your work safely.

Why Study Anatomy and Physiology?

As an esthetic professional, an overview of human anatomy and physiology will enable you to perform your services knowledgeably and effectively on a consistent basis.

- Estheticians need to understand how the human body functions as an integrated whole.
- As a service provider, you must be able to recognize changes from the norm.
- A scientific basis is needed for the proper application of services and products such as facials and hand and arm massages.
- Estheticians must understand the effect that services will have on tissues, organs, and body systems.
- Decisions on which treatment plans and protocols to provide for a client are based on the foundation and structures within the body. ☑ LO1

Cells

Cells are the basic unit of all living things, from bacteria to plants to animals to human beings. Without cells, life does not exist. As a basic functional unit, the cell is responsible for carrying on all life processes. There are trillions of cells in the human body, and they vary widely in size, shape, and purpose.

Basic Structure of the Cell

The cells of all living things are composed of a substance called **protoplasm** (PROH-toh-plaz-um), a colorless, jellylike substance in which food elements such as proteins, fats, carbohydrates, mineral salts, and water are present. You can visualize the protoplasm of a cell as being similar to the clear gel of a raw egg.

In addition to protoplasm, most cells also include a nucleus, an **organelle** (small organ), cytoplasm, and the cell membrane (Figure 6–1).

- The **nucleus** (NOO-klee-us) is the dense, active protoplasm found in the center of the cell. It plays an important part in cell reproduction and metabolism. You can visualize the nucleus as the yolk of a raw egg. Within the nucleus of the cell is the **nucleoplasm**, which is a fluid that contains proteins, and a very important acid known as **deoxyribonucleic acid (DNA)** (DEE-ok-see-RYE-boh-noo-KLEE-ik ASS-id). DNA is what determines our genetic makeup, including the color of our eyes, skin, and hair.
- The **cytoplasm** (sy-toh-PLAZ-um) is all the protoplasm of a cell except that found in the nucleus. This watery fluid contains the food material necessary for cell growth, reproduction, and self-repair.
- The **cell membrane** is the part of the cell that encloses the protoplasm and permits soluble substances to enter and leave.

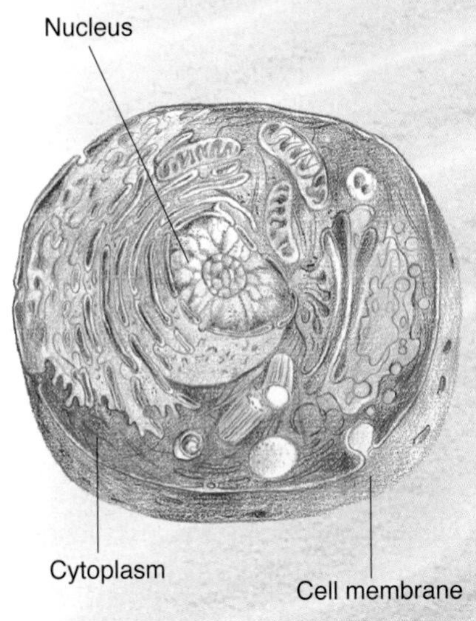

▲ Figure 6–1
Anatomy of the cell.

Cell Reproduction and Division

Cells have the ability to reproduce, thus providing new cells for the growth and replacement of worn or injured ones. **Mitosis** (my-TOH-sis) is the usual process of cell reproduction in human tissues that occurs when the cell divides into two identical cells called daughter cells. Two small structures near the nucleus called centrioles (SEN-tree-olz) move to each side during mitosis to help divide the cell. As long as conditions are favorable, the cell will grow and reproduce. Favorable conditions include an adequate supply of food, oxygen, and water; suitable temperatures; and the ability to eliminate waste products. If conditions become unfavorable, the cell will become impaired or may be destroyed. Unfavorable conditions include toxins (poisons), disease, and injury (Figure 6–2). ☑ **LO2**

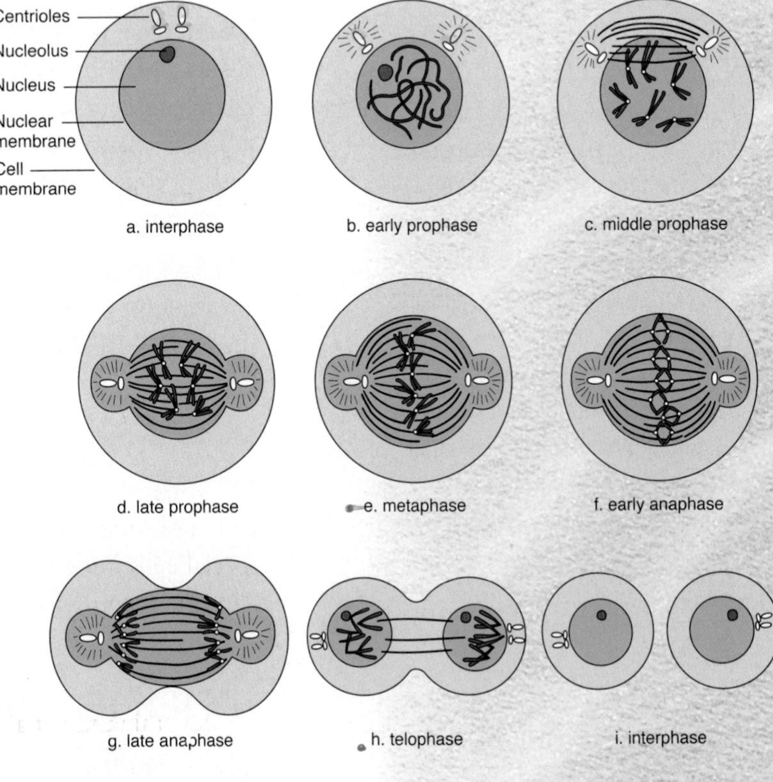

▲ Figure 6–2
Phases of mitosis.

Cell Metabolism

Metabolism (muh-TAB-uh-liz-um) is a chemical process that takes place in living organisms. Through metabolism, cells are nourished and carry out their activities. Metabolism has two phases, anabolism and catabolism, that are carried out simultaneously and continually within the cells.

- **Anabolism** (uh-NAB-uh-liz-um) is constructive metabolism, the process of *building up* larger molecules from smaller ones. During this process, the body stores water, food, and oxygen for the time when these substances will be needed for cell growth and repair.
- **Catabolism** (kuh-TAB-uh-liz-um) is the phase of metabolism in which complex compounds within the cells are broken down into smaller ones. This process releases energy that is stored by special molecules to be used in muscle contractions, body secretions, or heat production.

Did You Know?

According to Jeffrey Utz, M.D., from the department of Neuroscience at Allegheny University, an average adult body is 50 to 65 percent water—which equals roughly 45 qt (42.5 l). Men's bodies contain more water than women's bodies do. A man's body is 60 to 65 percent water, compared to 50 to 60 percent for a woman. In infants, the figure is amazingly more at 70 percent. Water content differs throughout various tissues in the body; for instance, blood is made up of 83 percent water, and muscle is 75 percent water.

Tissues

Tissue (TISH-oo) is a collection of similar cells that perform a particular function. Each tissue has a specific function and can be recognized by its characteristic appearance. Body tissues are composed of large amounts of water, along with various other substances. There are four types of tissue in the body.

- **Connective tissue** supports, protects, and binds together other tissues of the body. Examples of connective tissue are bone, cartilage, ligaments, tendons, fascia (which separates muscles), and fat or **adipose tissue** (ADD-ih-pohz TISH-oo), which gives smoothness and contour to the body. Collagen and elastin are protein fibers also located in the connective tissue.
- **Epithelial tissue** (ep-ih-THEE-lee-ul TISH-oo) is a protective covering on body surfaces. Examples are skin, mucous membranes, the lining of the heart, digestive and respiratory organs, and the glands.
- **Muscle tissue** contracts and moves the various parts of the body.
- **Nerve tissue** carries messages to and from the brain and controls and coordinates all bodily functions. Nerve tissue is composed of special cells known as neurons, which make up the nerves, brain, and spinal cord. ☑ LO3

Did You Know?

Have you ever wondered why someone has green eyes instead of brown, or red hair instead of blond? It is because of the genetic information enclosed within the DNA located in the nucleus of the cell. The DNA determines all of the cell's functions and characteristics, and the information is transferred at conception. As an esthetician working with all sorts of people, you will become aware of how a person's genetic code will largely determine his or her appearance.

Organs and Body Systems

Organs are structures composed of specialized tissues designed to perform a specific functions in plants and animals. Table 6–1 lists some of the most important organs of the body.

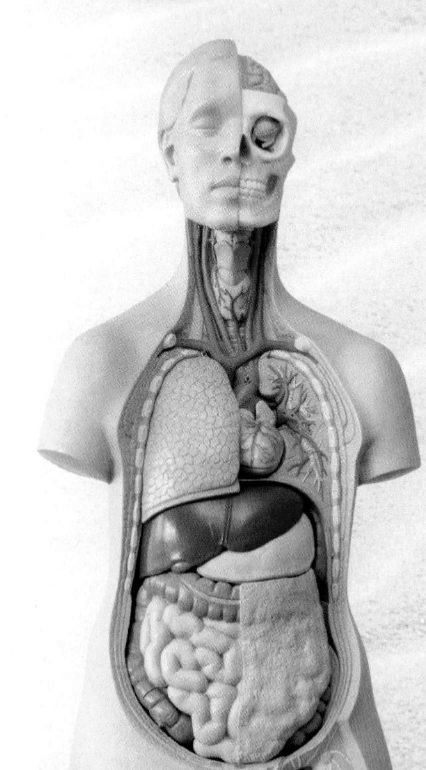

NINE MAJOR BODY ORGANS AND THEIR FUNCTIONS	
ORGAN	**FUNCTION**
Brain	Controls the body.
Eyes	Control the body's vision.
Heart	Circulates the blood.
Kidneys	Excrete water and waste products.
Lungs	Supply oxygen to the blood.
Liver	Removes waste created by digestion.
Skin	External protective coating that covers the body.
Stomach	Digests food, along with the intestines.
Intestines	Digests food, along with the stomach.

▲ Table 6–1 **Nine Major Body Organs and Their Functions.**

ELEVEN MAIN BODY SYSTEMS AND THEIR FUNCTIONS	
SYSTEM	**FUNCTION**
Skeletal	Physical foundation of the body; consists of the bones and movable and immovable joints.
Muscular	Covers, shapes, and supports the skeleton tissue; also contracts and moves various parts of the body; consists of muscles.
Nervous	Carries messages to and from the brain and controls and coordinates all bodily functions; consists of the brain, spinal cord, and nerves.
Circulatory	Controls the steady circulation of the blood through the body by means of the heart and blood vessels.
Lymphatic/Immune	Protects the body from disease by developing immunities and destroying disease-causing toxins and bacteria.
Endocrine	Affects growth, development, sexual activities, and health of the body; consists of specialized glands.
Digestive	Changes food into nutrients and wastes; consists of mouth, stomach, intestines, salivary and gastric glands.
Excretory	Purifies the body by elimination of waste matter; consists of kidneys, liver, skin, intestines, and lungs.
Respiratory	Enables breathing, supplies the body with oxygen, and eliminates carbon dioxide as a waste product; consists of lungs and air passages.
Integumentary	Serves as a protective covering for the body and helps in temperature regulation; consists of skin, accessory organs such as oil and sweat glands, sensory receptors, hair, and nails.
Reproductive	The reproductive system performs the function of reproducing and perpetuating the human race.

▲ Table 6–2 **Eleven Main Body Systems and Their Functions.**

Body systems, also known as **systems**, are groups of bodily organs acting together to perform one or more functions. The human body is composed of 11 major systems (Table 6–2). ✔ **LO4**

Figure 6–3
The skeletal system.

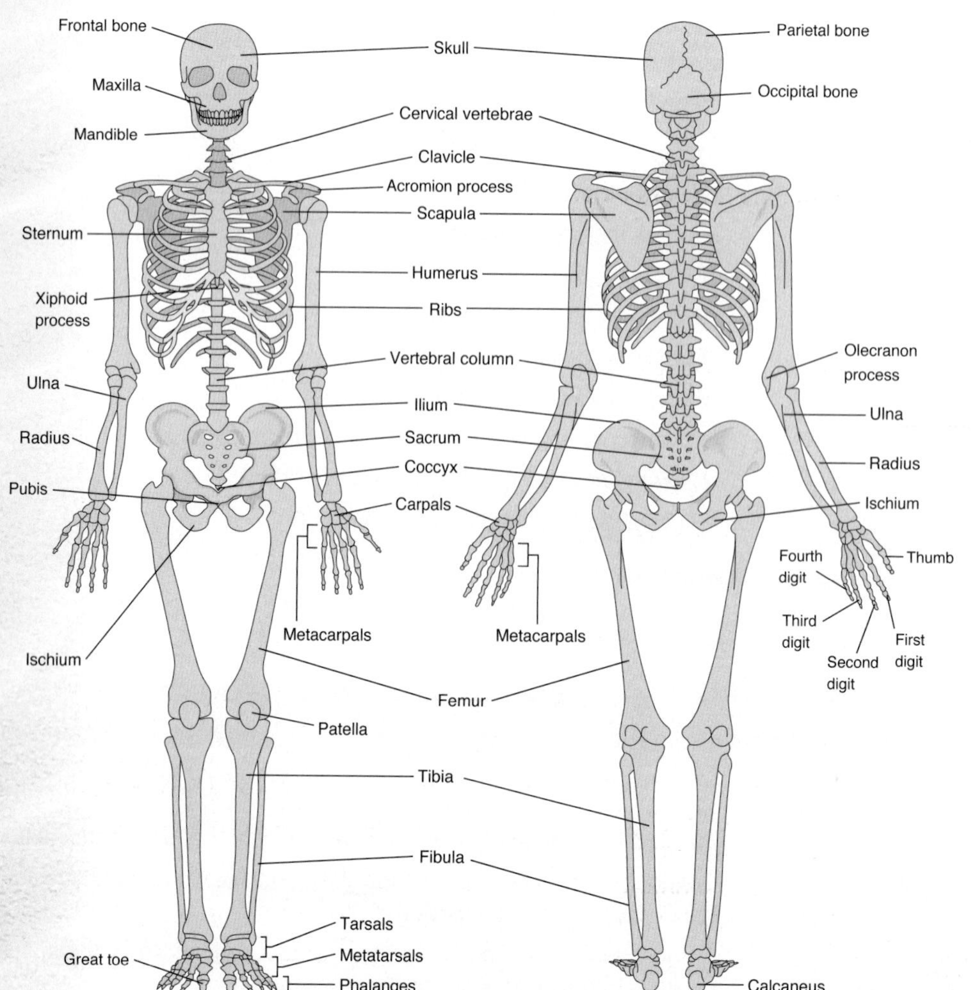

The Skeletal System

The **skeletal system** forms the physical foundation of the body (**Figure 6–3**). The skeletal system serves many important functions; it provides the shape and form for our bodies in addition to supporting, protecting, allowing bodily movement, producing blood for the body, and storing minerals such as calcium carbonate and calcium phosphate.

Osteology (ahs-tee-AHL-oh-jee) is the study of the anatomy, structure, and function of the bones. **Os** (AHS) means *bone* and is used as a prefix in many medical terms, such as osteoarthritis, a joint disease.

The skeleton has 206 bones that form a rigid framework to which the softer tissues and organs of the body are attached. Muscles are connected to bones by tendons. Bones are connected to each other by ligaments. The place where bones meet one another is typically called a joint. Joint is where 2 or more bones where connected

The bone tissue is composed of several types of bone cells embedded in a web of inorganic salts (mostly calcium and phosphorus) and collagenous and ground fibers. The web gives the bone strength, and the fibers give the bone flexibility.

Did You Know?

People often complain of joint pain; however, the pain is usually caused by inflammation of the tissue surrounding the joint and not by the joint itself.

You have over 230 moveable and semi-moveable joints in your body.

The primary functions of the skeletal system are to:

- Give shape and support to the body.
- Protect various internal structures and organs.
- Serve as attachments for muscles and act as levers to produce body movement.
- Help produce both white and red blood cells (one of the functions of bone marrow).
- Store most of the body's calcium supply as well as phosphorus, magnesium, and sodium.

A **joint** is the connection between two or more bones of the skeleton. There are two types of joints: movable, such as elbows, knees, and hips; and immovable, such as the pelvis or skull, which allow little or no movement.

Bones of the Skull

The human head contains 22 bones divided into two groups: the cranium and the facial bones. The **cranium** (KRAY-nee-um) is an oval, bony case that protects the brain, formed by 8 bones; and the face consists of 14 bones including the maxilla (upper jaw) and mandible (lower jaw). The skull has many small openings in its base that allow the cranial nerves to travel to their destinations (**Figure 6–4**).

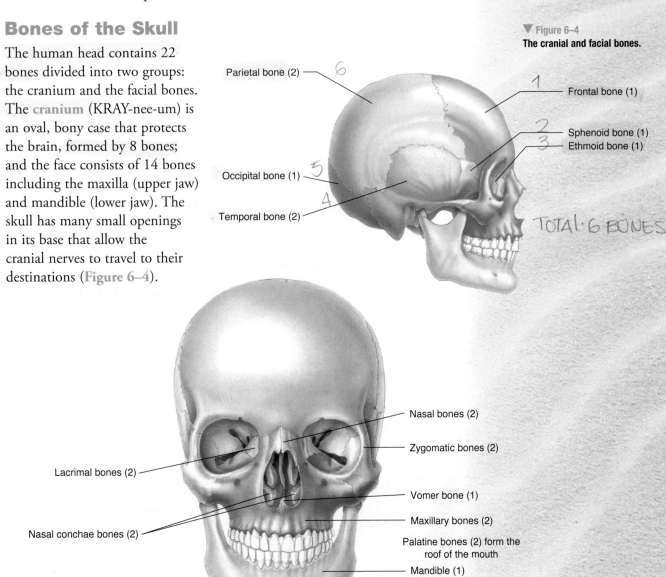

▼ Figure 6–4
The cranial and facial bones.

Bones of the Cranium

The cranium is made up of eight bones:

- The **occipital** (ahk-SIP-ih-tul) **bone** is the hindmost bone of the skull; it forms the back of the skull above the nape.
- The two **parietal** (puh-RY-uh-tul) **bones** form the sides and crown (top) of the cranium.
- The **frontal** (FRUNT-ul) **bone** forms the forehead.
- The two **temporal** (TEM-puh-rul) **bones** form the sides of the head in the ear region.
- The **ethmoid** (ETH-moyd) **bone** is the light, spongy bone between the eye sockets that forms part of the nasal cavities.
- The **sphenoid** (SFEEN-oyd) **bone** joins all the bones of the cranium together.

Did You Know?

Painful inflammation involving the carpus area can be caused by repetitive motions, such as flexing your wrist excessively or locking it in a bent position. Keeping the wrist straight can help prevent these injuries.

Bones of the Face

The 14 bones of the face include:

1–2. Two **nasal** (NAY-zul) **bones** form the bridge of the nose.

3–4. Two **lacrimal** (LAK-ruh-mul) **bones**, the smallest and most fragile bones of the face, are situated at the front inside part of the eye socket.

5–6. Two **zygomatic** (zy-goh-MAT-ik) **bones**, also known as **malar bones** or **cheekbones**, form the prominence of the cheeks, or cheekbones.

7–8. Two **maxillary** (mak-SIL-AIR-EE) **bones** form the upper jaw.

9. The **mandible** (MAN-duh-bul) forms the lower jawbone, the largest and strongest bone of the face.

10–11. Two **turbinal** (TUR-bih-nahl) **bones** (also referred to as turbinate bones); these are thin layers of spongy bone on either of the outer walls of the nasal depression.

12. The **vomer** (VOH-mer) **bone** is a flat, thin bone that forms part of the nasal septum.

13–14. Two **palatine bones** form the hard palate of the mouth.

Bones of the Neck

The main bones of the neck are the **hyoid** (HY-oyd) **bone**, a U-shaped bone at the base of the tongue that supports the tongue and its muscles, and the **cervical vertebrae** (SUR-vih-kul VURT-uh-bray), the seven bones of the top part of the vertebral column located in the neck region (Figure 6–5).

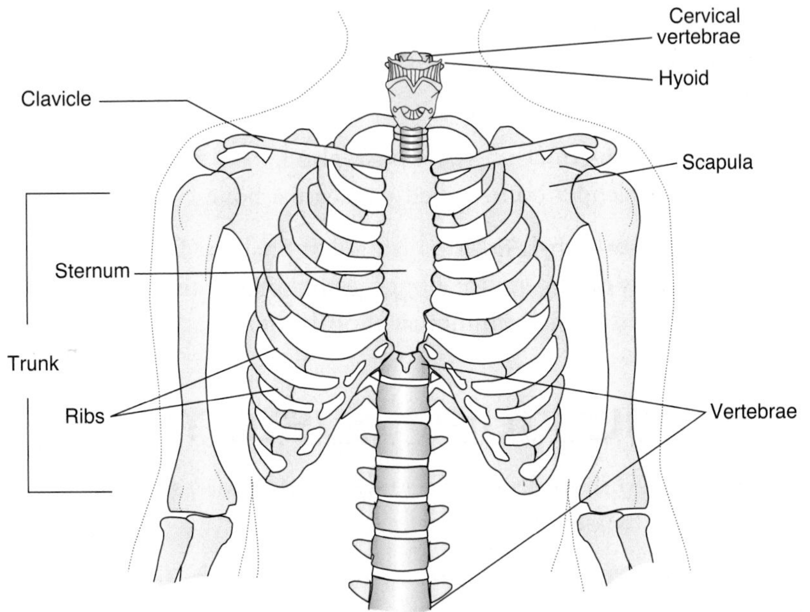

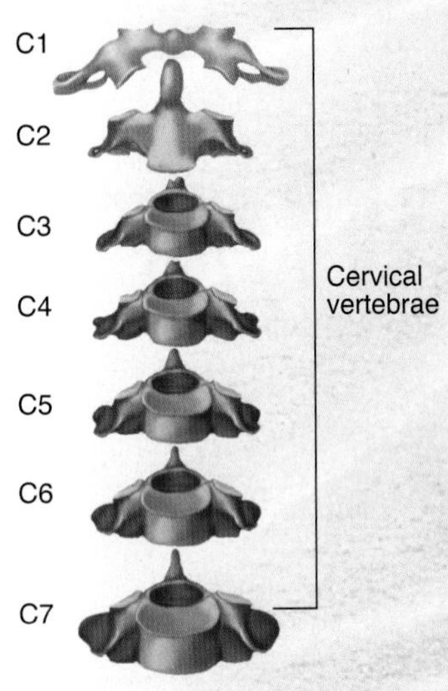

▲ Figure 6–5
Bones of the neck, shoulder, and back.

Bones of the Chest

The bones of the trunk or torso are comprised of:

- Thorax (THOR-aks). The chest or pulmonary trunk consisting of the sternum, ribs, and thoracic vertebrae. It is an elastic, bony cage that serves as a protective framework for the heart, lungs, and other internal organs.
- Ribs. Twelve pairs of bones forming the wall of the thorax.
- Scapula (SKAP-yuh-luh) also known as **shoulder blade**. The large, flat, triangular bone of the shoulder. There are two scapulas.
- Sternum (STUR-num), also known as **breastbone**. The flat bone that forms the ventral (front) support of the ribs.
- Clavicle (KLAV-ih-kul), also known as **collarbone**. The bone that joins the sternum and scapula.

Bones of the Arms and Hands

The important bones of the arms and hands are as follows (Figures 6–6 and 6–7):

- The humerus (HYOO-muh-rus) is the uppermost and largest bone of the arm, extending from the elbow to the shoulder.
- The ulna (UL-nuh) is the inner and larger bone of the forearm (lower arm), attached to the wrist and located on the side of the little finger.
- The radius (RAY-dee-us) is the smaller bone in the forearm on the same side as the thumb.

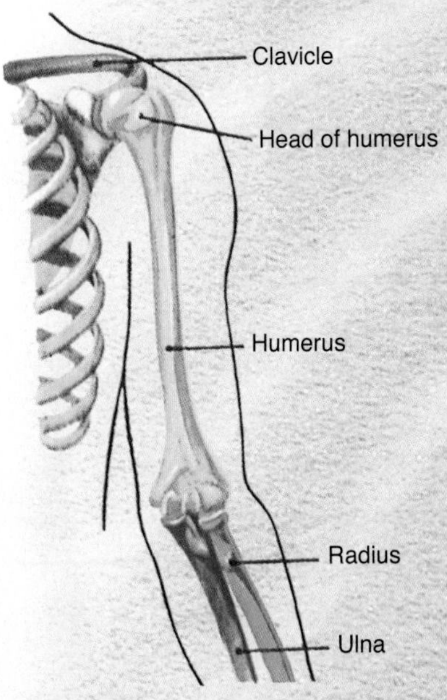

▲ Figure 6–6
Bones of the arm.

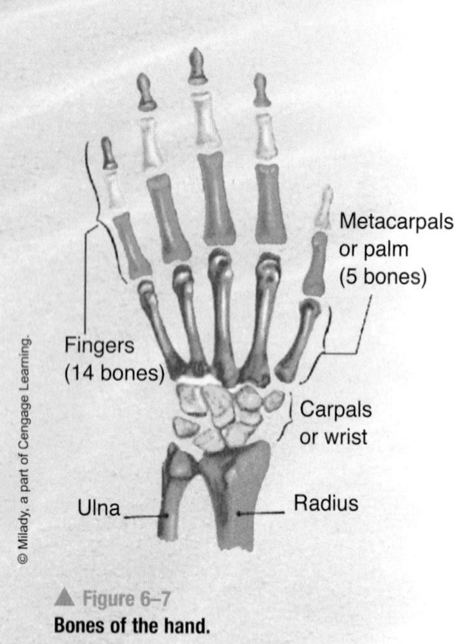

▲ Figure 6–7
Bones of the hand.

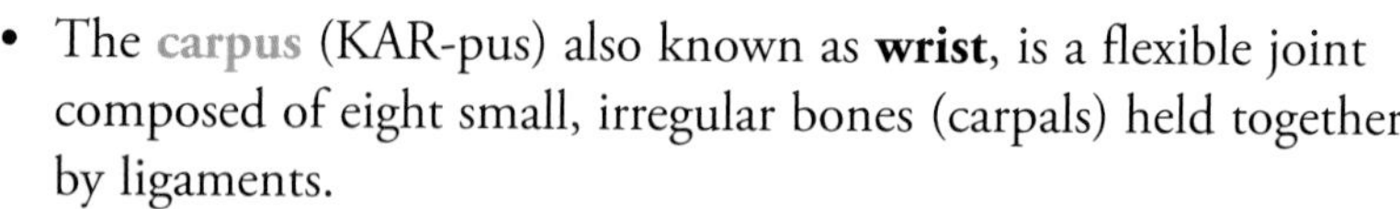

- The carpus (KAR-pus) also known as **wrist**, is a flexible joint composed of eight small, irregular bones (carpals) held together by ligaments.
- The metacarpus (met-uh-KAR-pus), also known as **palm**, consists of five long, slender bones called metacarpal bones.
- The phalanges (fuh-LAN-jeez) (singular: phalanx, FAY-langks), also known as **digits**, are the bones in the fingers, three in each finger and two in each thumb, totaling 14 bones.

The Muscular System

Myology (my-AHL-uh-jee) is the study of the nature, structure, function, and diseases of the muscles.

The muscular system covers, shapes, and supports the skeletal tissue. It contracts and moves various parts of the body. The human body has over 630 muscles, which are responsible for approximately 40 percent of the body's weight. Out of the over 630 muscles, 30 of them are facial muscles. Muscles are fibrous tissues with the ability to stretch and contract according to the demands of the body's movements.

Did You Know?

About 40 to 50 percent of body weight is in muscles. And there are over 630 muscles that make your body move.

There are three types of muscular tissue.

- Striated (STRY-ayt-ed) muscles, also known as **skeletal** or **voluntary**, are attached to the bones and make up a large percentage of body mass and are controlled by the will (Figure 6–8). Nerve impulses trigger a reaction from the muscle which contracts, moving its associated bone or joint.
- Nonstriated muscles, also known as **involuntary**, **visceral**, or **smooth**, function automatically, without conscious will (Figure 6–9). These muscles are found in the digestive and circulatory systems as well as some internal organs of the body.
- Cardiac muscle is the involuntary muscle that makes up the heart (Figure 6–10). This type of muscle is unique and not found in any other part of the body. It is striated and has a crossing, banding

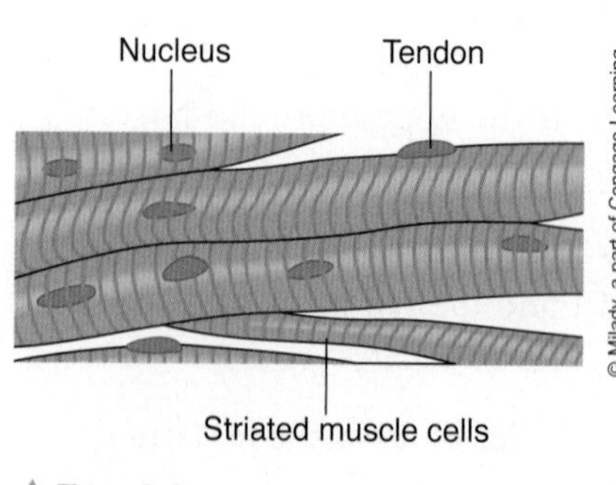

▲ Figure 6–8
Striated muscle cells.

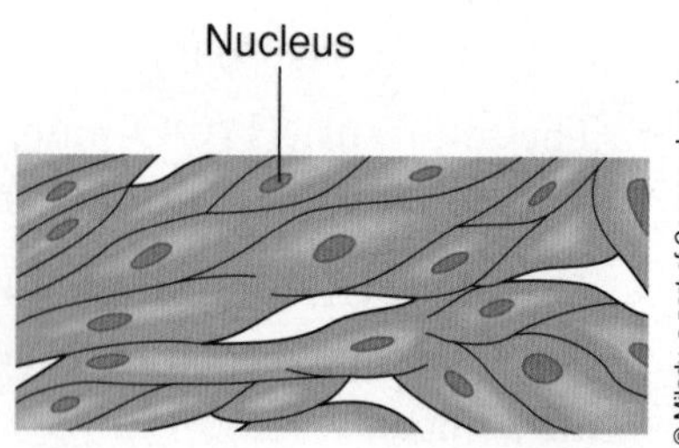

▲ Figure 6–9
Nonstriated muscle cells.

pattern that allows contraction and thus the beating of the heart. It is under the control of the autonomic nervous system.

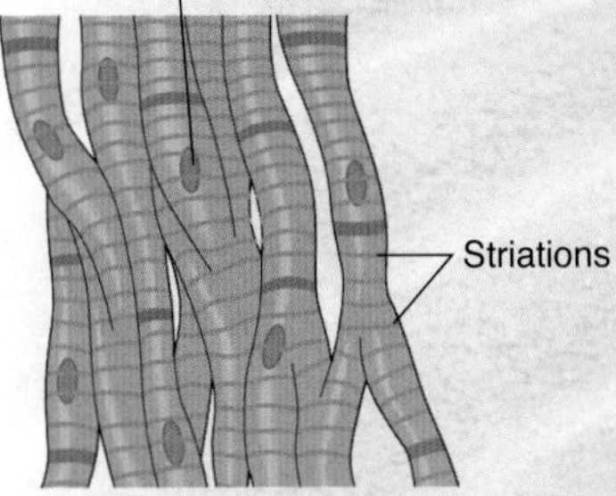

▲ Figure 6–10
Cardiac muscle cells.

A muscle has three parts:

- The **origin** is the more fixed part of the muscle closest to the skeleton, which flexes, but remains stationary.
- The **belly** is the middle part of the muscle.
- The **insertion** is the part of the muscle which is the movable attachment and farthest from the skeleton. Pressure in massage is usually directed from the insertion to the origin.

Muscular tissue can be stimulated by:

- Massage (hand or electric vibrator)
- Electrical therapy current (See Chapter 8, Basics of Electricity, for additional information on high-frequency, galvanic, or microcurrent.)
- Light rays (infrared light, light-emitting diode [LED] or ultraviolet radiation)
- Heat rays (heating lamps or heating caps)
- Moist heat (steamers or moderately warm steam towels)
- Nerve impulses (through the nervous system)
- Chemicals (certain acids and salts)

Muscles of the Scalp

There are four muscles of the scalp:

- The **epicranius** (ep-ih-KRAY-nee-us), also known as **occipitofrontalis** (ahk-SIP-ihtoh-frun-TAY-lus), is a broad muscle that covers the top of the skull. It consists of two parts, occipitalis and frontalis (Figure 6–11).

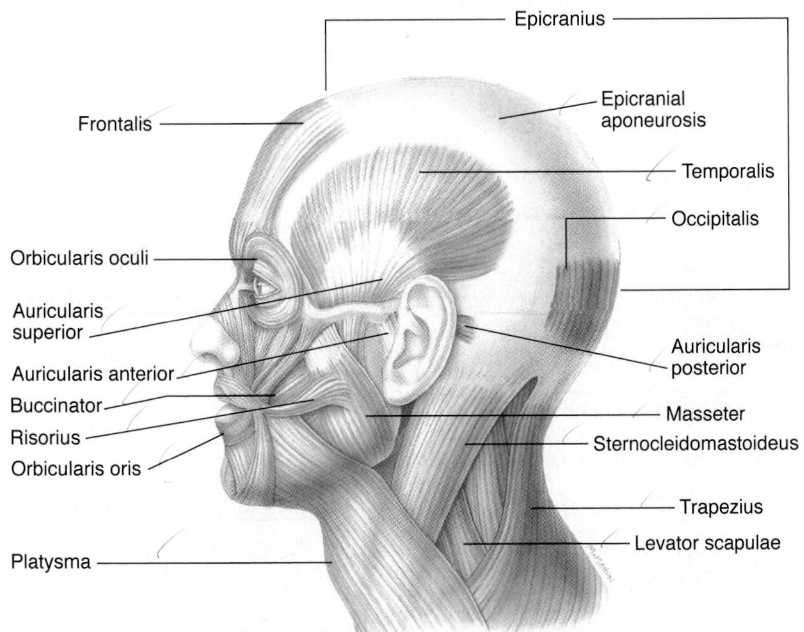

◀ Figure 6–11
Muscles of the head, face, and neck.

- The **occipitalis** (ahk-SIP-i-tahl-is), the back of the epicranius, is the muscle that draws the scalp backward.
- The **frontalis** (frun-TAY-lus) is the anterior (front) portion of the epicranius. It is the scalp muscle that raises the eyebrows, draws the scalp forward, and causes wrinkles across the forehead.
- The **epicranial aponeurosis** (ep-ih-KRAY-nee-al ap-uh-noo-ROH-sus) is a tendon connecting the occipitalis and the frontalis.

Muscles of the Ear

These muscles are attached to the ear.

- The **auricularis** (aw-rik-yuh-LAIR-is) **superior** is the muscle above the ear that draws the ear upward.
- The **auricularis anterior** is the muscle in front of the ear that draws the ear forward.
- The **auricularis posterior** is the muscle behind the ear that draws the ear backward.

Muscles of Mastication (Chewing)

The main muscles of mastication coordinate to open and close the mouth and bring the jaw forward or backward. These muscles, listed below, are sometimes referred to as the *chewing muscles.*

- **Masseter** (muh-SEE-tur)
- **Temporalis** (tem-poh-RAY-lis)
- **Medial pterygoid** (MEE-dee-ul TEHR-ih-goyd)
- **Lateral pterygoid** (LAT-ur-ul TEHR-ih-goyd)

Muscles of the Neck

Muscles of the neck include the following.

- The **platysma** (plah-TIZ-muh) is a broad muscle extending from the chest and shoulder muscles to the side of the chin. It is responsible for lowering the lower jaw and lip.
- The **sternocleidomastoid (SCM)** (STUR-noh-KLEE-ih-doh-mas-TOY-d) is the muscle extending along side of the neck from the ear to the collarbone. It acts to rotate the head from side to side and up and down.

Muscles of the Eyebrow

Muscles of the eyebrow include the following.

- The **corrugator** (KOR-oo-gay-tohr) is the muscle located beneath the frontalis and orbicularis oculi. It draws the eyebrow down and wrinkles the forehead vertically (Figure 6–12).

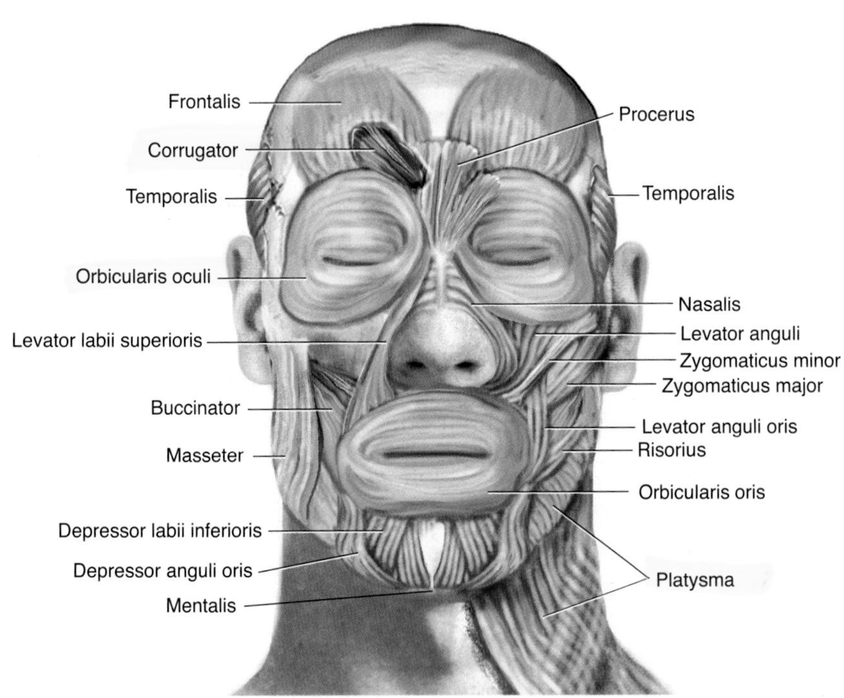

Figure 6–12
Muscles of the face.

- The orbicularis oculi (or-bik-yuh-LAIR-is AHK-yuh-lye) is the ring muscle of the eye socket; it closes the eyes.

Muscles of the Nose

The two primary muscles of the nose are:

- The procerus (prah-sir-us or pro-SAARH-us) lowers the eyebrows and causes wrinkles across the bridge of the nose.
- The nasalis is a two part muscle which covers the nose that includes the *transverse part* and the *alar part*, which flair the nostrils.

Did You Know?

You have over 30 muscles in your face that control your expressions.

Muscles of the Mouth

The following are important muscles of the mouth (see Figure 6–12).

- The buccinator (BUK-sih-nay-tur) is the thin, flat muscle of the cheek between the upper and lower jaw that compresses the cheeks and expels air between the lips, as in when blowing a whistle.
- The depressor anguli oris, also known as **triangularis** (try-ang-gyuh-LAY-rus) **muscle**, is the muscle extending alongside the chin that pulls down the corners of the mouth.
- The depressor labii inferioris (dee-PRES-ur LAY-bee-eye in-FEER-eeor-us), also known as **quadratus labii inferioris**, is a muscle surrounding the lower lip that depresses the it and draws the lower lip to one side.
- The levator anguli oris (lih-VAYT-ur ANG-yoo-ly OH-ris), also known as **caninus** (kay-NY-nus), is a muscle that raises the angle of the mouth and draws it inward.
- The levator labii superioris (lih-VAYT-ur LAY-bee-eye soo-peer-ee-OR-is), also known as **quadratus** (kwah-DRA-tus) **labii superioris**,

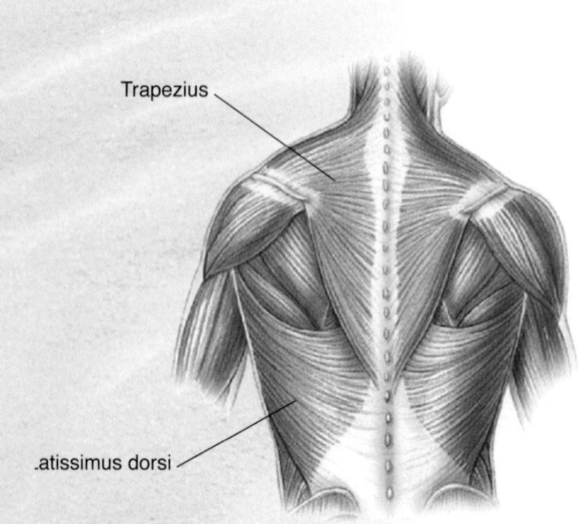

▲ Figure 6–13
Muscles of the back and neck that attach the arms to the body.

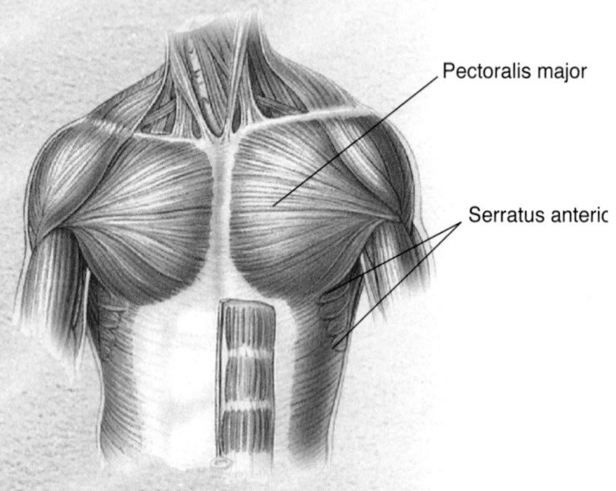

▲ Figure 6–14
Muscles of the chest that attach the arms to the body.

is a muscle that elevates the lip and dilates the nostrils, as in expressing distaste.

- The **mentalis** (men-TAY-lis) is the muscle that elevates the lower lip and raises and wrinkles the skin of the chin.
- The **orbicularis oris** (or-bik-yuh-LAIR-is OH-ris) is the flat band around the upper and lower lips that compresses, contracts, puckers, and wrinkles the lips.
- The **risorius** (rih-ZOR-ee-us) is the muscle that draws the corner of the mouth out and back, as in grinning.
- The **zygomaticus** (zy-goh-MAT-ih-kus) **major** and **zygomaticus minor** are muscles extending from the zygomatic bone to the angle of the mouth that elevate the lip, as in laughing.

Muscles that Attach the Arms to the Body

Muscles attaching the arms to the body include the following.

- The **latissimus dorsi** (lah-TIS-ih-mus DOR-see) is a large, flat, triangular muscle that covers the lower back. It comes up from the lower half of the vertebral column and iliac crest (hip bone) and narrows to a rounded tendon attached to the front of the upper part of the humerus (Figure 6–13).
- The **pectoralis major** (pek-tor-AL-is) and **pectoralis minor** are muscles of the chest that assist the swinging movements of the arm.
- The **serratus anterior** (ser-RAT-us an-TEER-ee-or) is a muscle of the chest that assists in breathing and in raising the arm (Figure 6–14).

Muscles of the Shoulder and Arm

Here are the principal muscles of the shoulders and upper arms (Figure 6–15).

- The **trapezius** (trah-PEE-zee-us) muscle covers the back of the neck, shoulders, and upper and middle region of the back; shrugs shoulders and stabilizes the scapula.
- The **biceps** (BY-seps) muscles produce the contour of the front and inner side of the upper arm; they lift the forearm, flex the elbow, and turn the palms outward.
- The **deltoid** (DEL-toyd) is a large, triangular muscle covering the shoulder joint that allows the arm to extend outward and to the side of the body.

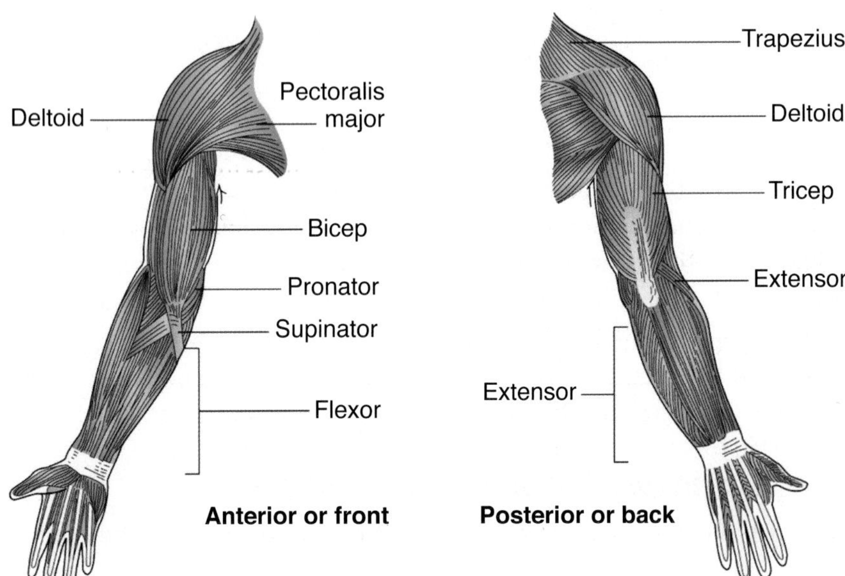

◀ Figure 6–15
Muscles of the anterior and posterior shoulder and arm.

- The **triceps** (TRY-seps) is a large muscle that covers the entire back of the upper arm and extends the forearm.

The forearm is made up of a series of muscles and strong tendons. As an esthetician, you will be concerned with the following muscles.

- The **extensors** (ik-STEN-surs) are muscles that straighten the wrist, hand, and fingers to form a straight line.
- The **flexors** (FLEK-surs), extensor muscles of the wrist, are involved in flexing the wrist.
- The **pronators** (proh-NAY-tohrs) are muscles that turn the hand inward so that the palm faces downward.
- The **supinator** (SOO-puh-nayt-ur) muscle rotates the radius outward and the palm upward.

Muscles of the Hand

The hand is one of the most complex parts of the body, with many small muscles that overlap from joint to joint, providing flexibility and strength to open and close the hand and fingers. During the aging process, these muscles lose mobility, causing stiffness in the joints. Massage can help relax and maintain the pliability of these muscles.

Important muscles to know include the:

- **Abductors** (ab-DUK-turz). Muscles that draw a body part, such as a finger, arm, or toe, away from the midline of the body or of an extremity. In the hand, abductors separate the fingers.
- **Adductors** (ah-DUK-turz). Muscles that draw a body part, such as a finger, arm, or toe, inward toward the median axis of the body or of an extremity. In the hand, adductors draw the fingers together (**Figure 6–16**).

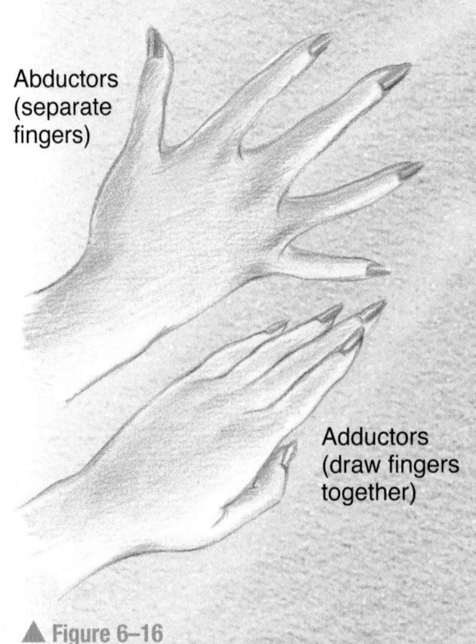

▲ Figure 6–16
Muscles of the hand.

Did You Know?

If you did not have a central nervous system, you could not taste, smell, see, hear, think, breathe, move, run, sleep, remember, sing, laugh, or write, to name just a few things.

The Nervous System

The **nervous system** is an exceptionally well-organized system that is responsible for coordinating all the many activities that are performed by the body. Every square inch (2.5 square centimeters) of the human body is supplied with fine fibers known as *nerves*; there are over 100 billion nerve cells, known as *neurons*, in the body. The scientific study of the structure, function, and pathology of the nervous system is known as **neurology** (nuh-RAHL-uh-jee). An understanding of how nerves work will help you perform massage more proficiently and understand the effects of these treatments on the body as a whole.

Divisions of the Nervous System

The nervous system, as a whole, is divided into three main subdivisions.

- The **central nervous system (CNS)** consists of the brain, spinal cord, spinal nerves, and cranial nerves. It controls consciousness and many mental activities, voluntary functions of the five senses (seeing, hearing, feeling, smelling, and tasting), and voluntary muscle actions including all body movements and facial expressions.
- The **peripheral nervous system (PNS)** (puh-RIF-uh-rul NURV-vus SIS-tum) is a system of nerves that connects the peripheral (outer) parts of the body to the central nervous system; it has both sensory and motor nerves. Its function is to carry impulses, or messages, to and from the central nervous system.
- The **autonomic nervous system (ANS)** (aw-toh-NAHM-ik NURV-us SIS-tum) is the part of the nervous system that controls the involuntary muscles; it regulates the action of the smooth muscles, glands, blood vessels, heart, and breathing (Figure 6–17).

The peripheral nervous system (PNS) is further divided into two sections, the afferent peripheral system and the efferent peripheral system. From the efferent peripheral system, there are two subcategories, the somatic nervous system, which causes us to react to our external environment; and the autonomic nervous system (ANS), which is responsible for the internal regulation of impulses from the central nervous system to smooth muscles, such as the heart, and blood vessels and glands. The autonomic nervous system is considered involuntary.

The organs affected by the autonomic system receive nerve cells or fibers from its two divisions, the sympathetic and the parasympathetic. The **sympathetic division** stimulates or speeds up activity and prepares the body for stressful situations, whereas the **parasympathetic division** operates under normal, nonstressful conditions and helps restore and slow down activity, thus keeping the body in balance.

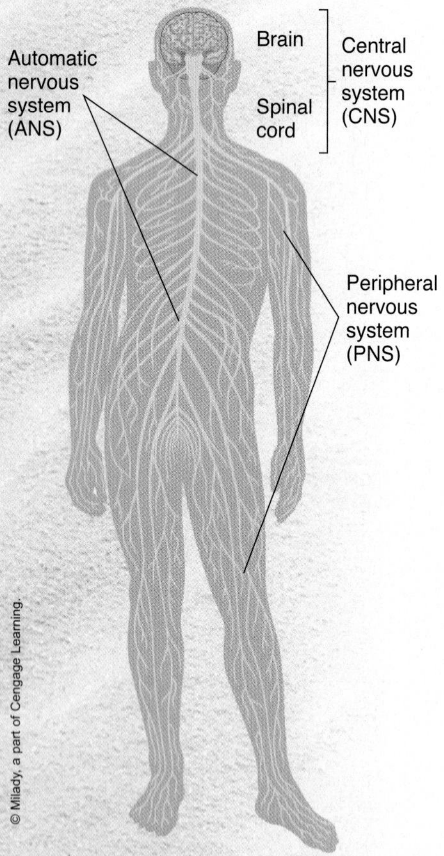

▲ Figure 6–17
Principal parts of the nervous system.

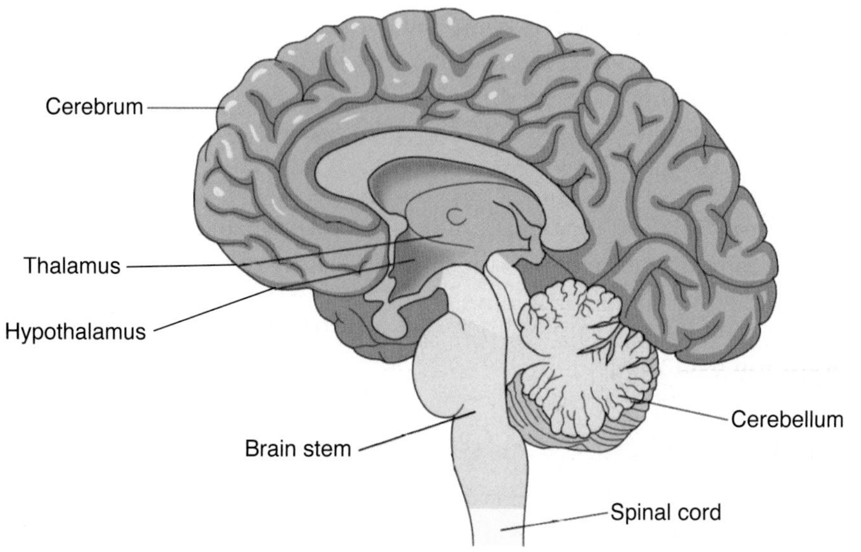

◀ Figure 6–18
Principal parts of the brain.

The Brain and Spinal Cord

The **brain** is the largest and most complex mass of nerve tissue in the body. The brain is contained in the cranium, weighs an average of 44 to 48 ounces (1.25 to 1.35 kilograms), and has four main parts. They are the cerebrum, the cerebellum, the diencephalon, and the brain stem. The brain controls sensation, muscles, glandular activity, and the power to think and feel. It sends and receives telegraphic messages through 12 pairs of cranial nerves that originate in the brain and reach various parts of the head, face, and neck (Figure 6–18).

The brain is divided into four parts.

- The **cerebrum** makes up the bulk of the brain. It is located in the front, upper part of the cranium. It has an inner core of white matter, composed of bundles of axons each coated with a sheath of myelin, and an outer core of gray matter, composed of masses of cell bodies and dendrites. Within the cerebrum is the *cerebral cortex*, located in the part of the cerebrum from which most messages from the brain are sent—such as those conveying thought, hearing, and sight.
- The term **cerebellum** is Latin for *little brain*. It lies at the base of the cerebrum and is attached to the brain stem. It acts to control movement, coordinate voluntary muscular activity, and maintain balance and equilibrium.
- The **diencephalon** (Dy-en-sef-ah-lon) is located in the uppermost part of the midbrain and has two main parts, called the *thalamus* and the *hypothalamus*. The thalamus, located in the upper part of the diencephalon, acts as a relay station for sensory impulses and plays a role in the recognition of pain and temperature in the body. The hypothalamus, located in the lower part of the diencephalon, controls many bodily functions such as body temperature. The hypothalamus also controls the pituitary gland.

- The **brain stem** connects the spinal cord to the brain. It consists of three parts—the *midbrain, pons*, and *medulla oblongata*—all of which connect sections of the brain with the spinal cord. The brain stem is involved in regulating such vital functions as breathing, heartbeat, and blood pressure.

The **spinal cord** is a continuation of the brain stem and originates in the brain, extends down to the lower extremity of the trunk, and is protected by the spinal column. Thirty-one pairs of spinal nerves extending from the spinal cord are distributed to the muscles and skin of the trunk and limbs.

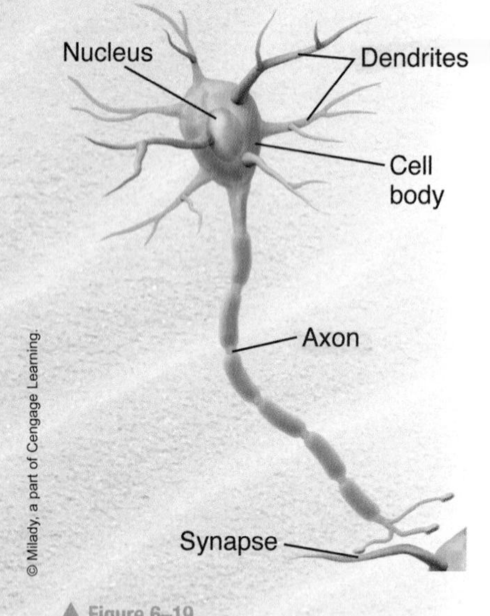

▲ Figure 6–19
A neuron or nerve cell.

Nerve Cell Structure and Function

A **neuron** (NOO-rahn) or **nerve cell** is the primary structural unit of the nervous system (Figure 6–19). It is composed of a cell body and nucleus; **dendrites** (DEN-dryts), nerve fibers extending from the nerve cell that receive impulses from other neurons; and an **axon** (AK-sahn), which sends impulses away from the cell body to other neurons, glands, or muscles.

Nerves are whitish cords, made up of bundles of nerve fibers held together by connective tissue, through which impulses are transmitted. Nerves have their origin in the brain and spinal cord and send their branches to all parts of the body.

Types of Nerves

There are two types of nerves:

- **Sensory nerves**, also known as **afferent nerves** (AAF-eer-ent NURVS), carry impulses or messages from the sense organs to the brain, where sensations such as touch, cold, heat, sight, hearing, taste, smell, pain, and pressure are experienced. Sensory nerve endings called receptors are located close to the surface of the skin. As impulses pass from the sensory nerves to the brain and back through the motor nerves to the muscles, a complete circuit is established, resulting in movement of the muscles.

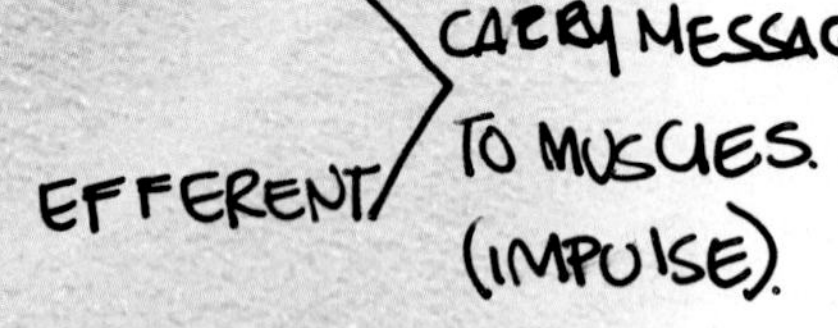

- **Motor nerves**, also known as **efferent nerves** (EF-uh-rent NURVS), carry impulses from the brain to the muscles or glands. These transmitted impulses produce movement.

A **reflex** (REE-fleks) is an automatic nerve reaction to a stimulus that involves the movement of an impulse from a sensory receptor along the afferent nerve to the spinal cord and a responsive impulse back along an efferent neuron to a muscle, causing a reaction (for example, the quick removal of the hand from a hot object). Reflexes do not have to be learned, they are automatic.

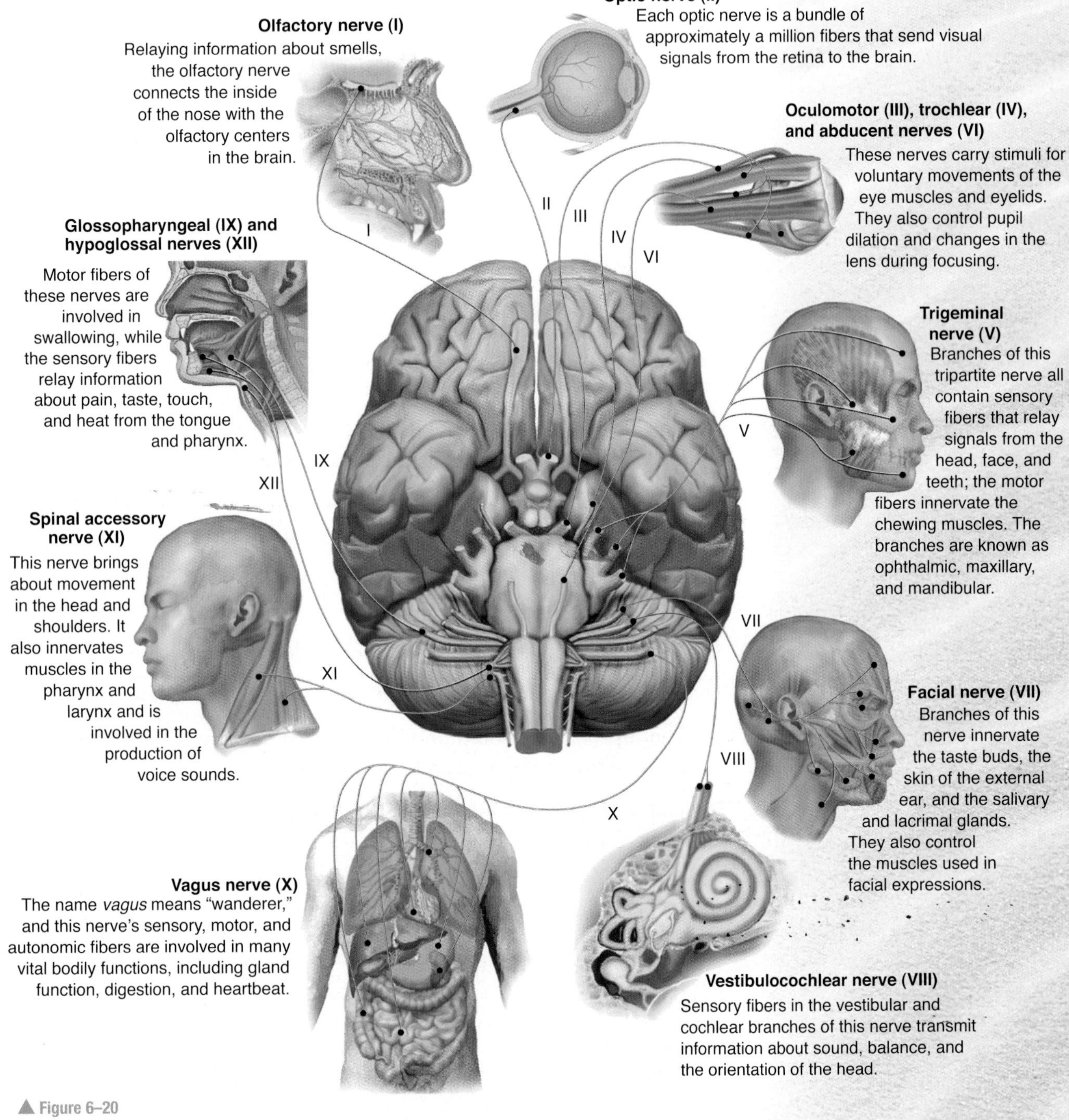

Olfactory nerve (I)
Relaying information about smells, the olfactory nerve connects the inside of the nose with the olfactory centers in the brain.
Optic nerve (II)
Each optic nerve is a bundle of approximately a million fibers that send visual signals from the retina to the brain.
Oculomotor (III), trochlear (IV), and abducent nerves (VI)
These nerves carry stimuli for voluntary movements of the eye muscles and eyelids. They also control pupil dilation and changes in the lens during focusing.
Glossopharyngeal (IX) and hypoglossal nerves (XII)
Motor fibers of these nerves are involved in swallowing, while the sensory fibers relay information about pain, taste, touch, and heat from the tongue and pharynx.
Trigeminal nerve (V)
Branches of this tripartite nerve all contain sensory fibers that relay signals from the head, face, and teeth; the motor fibers innervate the chewing muscles. The branches are known as ophthalmic, maxillary, and mandibular.
Spinal accessory nerve (XI)
This nerve brings about movement in the head and shoulders. It also innervates muscles in the pharynx and larynx and is involved in the production of voice sounds.
Facial nerve (VII)
Branches of this nerve innervate the taste buds, the skin of the external ear, and the salivary and lacrimal glands. They also control the muscles used in facial expressions.
Vagus nerve (X)
The name vagus means "wanderer," and this nerve's sensory, motor, and autonomic fibers are involved in many vital bodily functions, including gland function, digestion, and heartbeat.
Vestibulocochlear nerve (VIII)
Sensory fibers in the vestibular and cochlear branches of this nerve transmit information about sound, balance, and the orientation of the head.
I
II
III
IV
VI
V
IX
XII
VII
XI
VIII
X

▲ Figure 6–20
The cranial nerves and their functions.

Nerves of the Head, Face, and Neck

There are 12 pairs of cranial nerves arising at the base of the brain and the brain stem. The cranial nerves activate the muscles and sensory structure of the head and neck including skin, membranes, eyes, and ears (Figure 6–20).

Estheticians are primarily concerned with nerves V, VII, and XI, and each one has several branches.

The largest of the cranial nerves is the **fifth cranial nerve**, also known as **trifacial** (try-FAY-shul) or **trigeminal** (try-JEM-un-ul) nerve. It is the chief sensory nerve of the face, and it serves as the motor nerve of the muscles that control chewing. It consists of three branches:

- **Ophthalmic nerve** (ahf-THAL-mik). Affects the skin of the forehead, upper eyelids, and interior portion of the scalp, orbit, eyeball, and nasal passage.
- **Mandibular nerve** (man-DIB-yuh-lur). Affects the muscles of the chin and lower lip.
- **Maxillary nerve** (MAK-suh-lair-ee). Affects the upper part of the face.

The following branches of the fifth cranial nerve are affected by facial or lymphatic massage (**Figure 6–21**).

- The **auriculotemporal** (aw-RIK-yuh-loh-TEM-puh-rul) **nerve** affects the external ear and skin above the temple, up to the top of the skull.
- The **infraorbital** (in-fruh-OR-bih-tul) **nerve** affects the skin of the lower eyelid, side of the nose, upper lip, and mouth.
- The **infratrochlear** (in-frah-TRAHK-lee-ur) **nerve** affects the membrane and skin of the nose.
- The **mental nerve** affects the skin of the lower lip and chin.
- The **nasal nerve** affects the point and lower side of the nose.
- The **supraorbital** (soo-pruh-OR-bih-tul) **nerve** affects the skin of the forehead, scalp, eyebrow, and upper eyelid.
- The **supratrochlear** (soo-pruh-TRAHK-lee-ur) **nerve** affects the skin between the eyes and upper side of the nose.

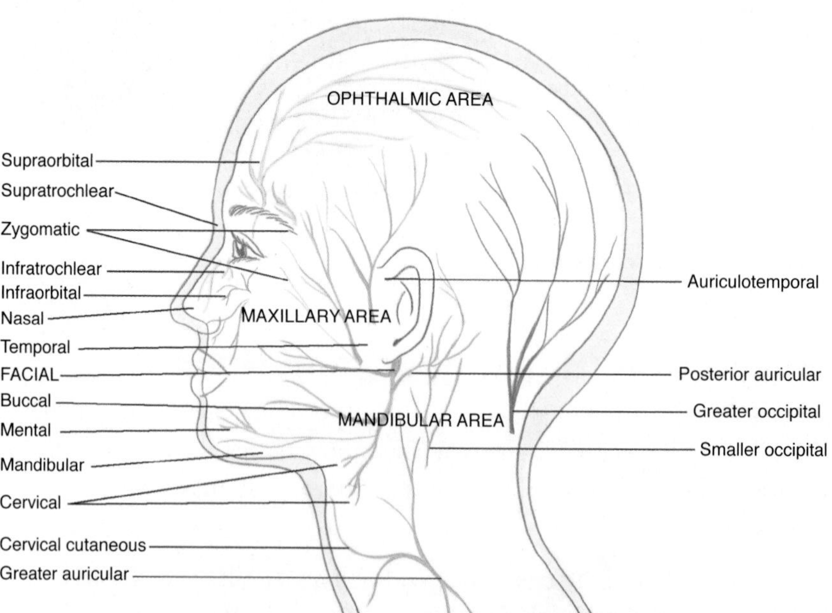

Figure 6–21
Nerve and nerve branches of the head, face, and neck.

- The zygomatic (zy-goh-MAT-ik) nerve affects the muscles of the upper part of the cheek.

The seventh cranial nerve, also known as **facial nerve**, is the chief motor nerve of the face. It emerges near the lower part of the ear and extends to the muscles of the neck. Its divisions and their branches supply and control all the muscles of facial expression and the secretions of saliva. The following are the most important branches of the facial nerve.

- The buccal (BUK-ul) nerve affects the muscles of the mouth.
- The cervical (SUR-vih-kul) nerves (branches of the facial nerve) affect the side of the neck and the platysma muscle.
- The mandibular nerve affects the muscles of the chin and lower lip.
- The posterior auricular nerve affects the muscles behind the ear at the base of the skull.
- The temporal nerve affects the muscles of the temple, side of the forehead, eyebrow, eyelid, and upper part of the cheek.
- The zygomatic nerve (upper and lower) affects the muscles of the upper part of the cheek.

The eleventh cranial nerve, also known as **accessory nerve**, is a type of motor nerve that controls the motion of the neck and shoulder muscles. This nerve is important to estheticians because it is affected during facials, primarily with massage.

Cervical nerves originate at the spinal cord, and their branches supply the muscles and scalp at the back of the head and neck as follows.

The cervical cutaneous (kyoo-TAY-nee-us) nerve, located at the side of the neck, affects the front and sides of the neck as far down as the breastbone.

- The greater auricular nerve, located at the side of the neck, affects the face, ears, neck, and parotid gland.
- The greater occipital nerve, located in the back of the head, affects the scalp as far up as the top of the head.
- The smaller occipital nerve, also known as **lesser occipital nerve**, located at the base of the skull, affects the scalp and muscles behind the ear.

Nerves of the Arm and Hand

The principal nerves supplying the superficial parts of the arm and hand are as follows (Figure 6–22).

- The digital nerve (DIJ-ut-tul) is a sensory-motor nerve that, with its branches, supplies the fingers.

Did You Know?

The ulnar nerve runs along the bottom of the elbow. This explains why leaning on the elbows for long periods can cause the little fingers to go numb. This is due to localized inflammation (irritation and swelling) around the nerve.

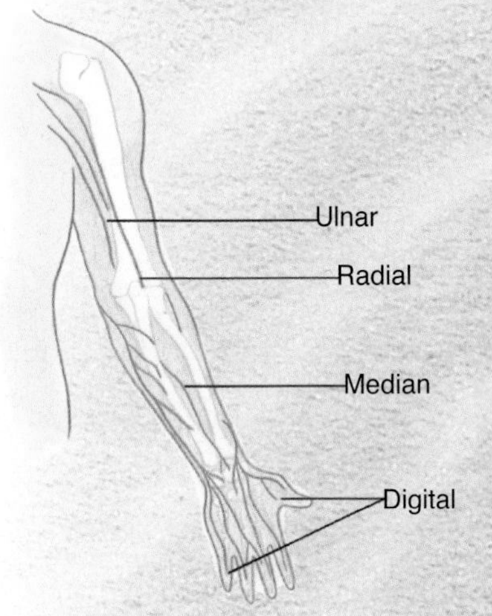

▲ Figure 6–22
Nerves of the arm and hand.

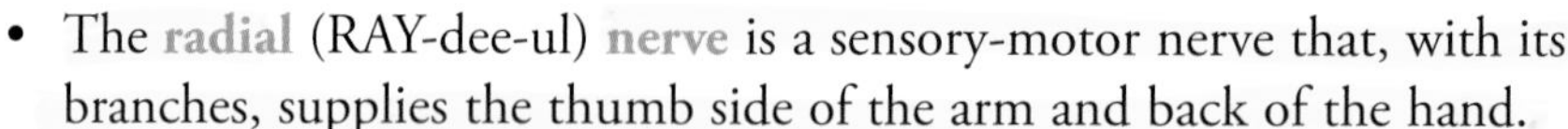

- The **radial** (RAY-dee-ul) **nerve** is a sensory-motor nerve that, with its branches, supplies the thumb side of the arm and back of the hand.
- The **median** (MEE-dee-un) **nerve** is a smaller sensory-motor nerve than the ulnar and radial nerves; with its branches, it supplies the arm and hand.
- The **ulnar** (UL-nur) **nerve** is a sensory-motor nerve that, with its branches, affects the little-finger side of the arm and palm of the hand.

The Circulatory System

The **circulatory system**, also known as **cardiovascular system** or **vascular system**, controls the steady circulation of the blood through the body by means of the heart and blood vessels (veins and arteries). The **vascular system** consists of the heart, arteries, veins, and capillaries for the distribution of blood throughout the body.

The Heart

The **heart** is often referred to as the body's pump (Figure 6–23 on page 30); it is a muscular, cone-shaped organ that keeps the blood moving within the circulatory system. It is enclosed by a membrane known as the **pericardium** (payr-ih-KAR-dee-um). The heart is about the size of a closed fist, weighs approximately 9 ounces (255 grams), and is located in the chest cavity. The heartbeat is regulated by the vagus (tenth cranial) nerve and other nerves in the autonomic nervous system. In a normal resting state, the heart beats 72 to 80 times per minute.

The interior of the heart contains four chambers and four valves. The upper, thin-walled chambers are the right **atrium** (AY-tree-um) and left atrium. The lower, thick-walled chambers are the right **ventricle** (VEN-truh- kul) and left ventricle. **Valves** between the chambers allow the blood to flow in only one direction. With each contraction and relaxation of the heart, the blood flows in, travels from the atria (plural of *atrium*) to the ventricles, and is then driven out, to be distributed throughout the body.

The blood is in constant and continuous circulation from the time it leaves the heart until it returns to the heart. Two systems attend to this circulation:

- **Pulmonary circulation** sends the blood from the heart to the lungs to be oxygenated.
- **Systemic or general circulation** carries the oxygenated blood from the heart throughout the body and back to the heart again.

The following is a brief explanation of how the pulmonary circulation system and the systemic circulation system work.

1. Deoxygenated (oxygen-poor) blood flows from the body into the right atrium.

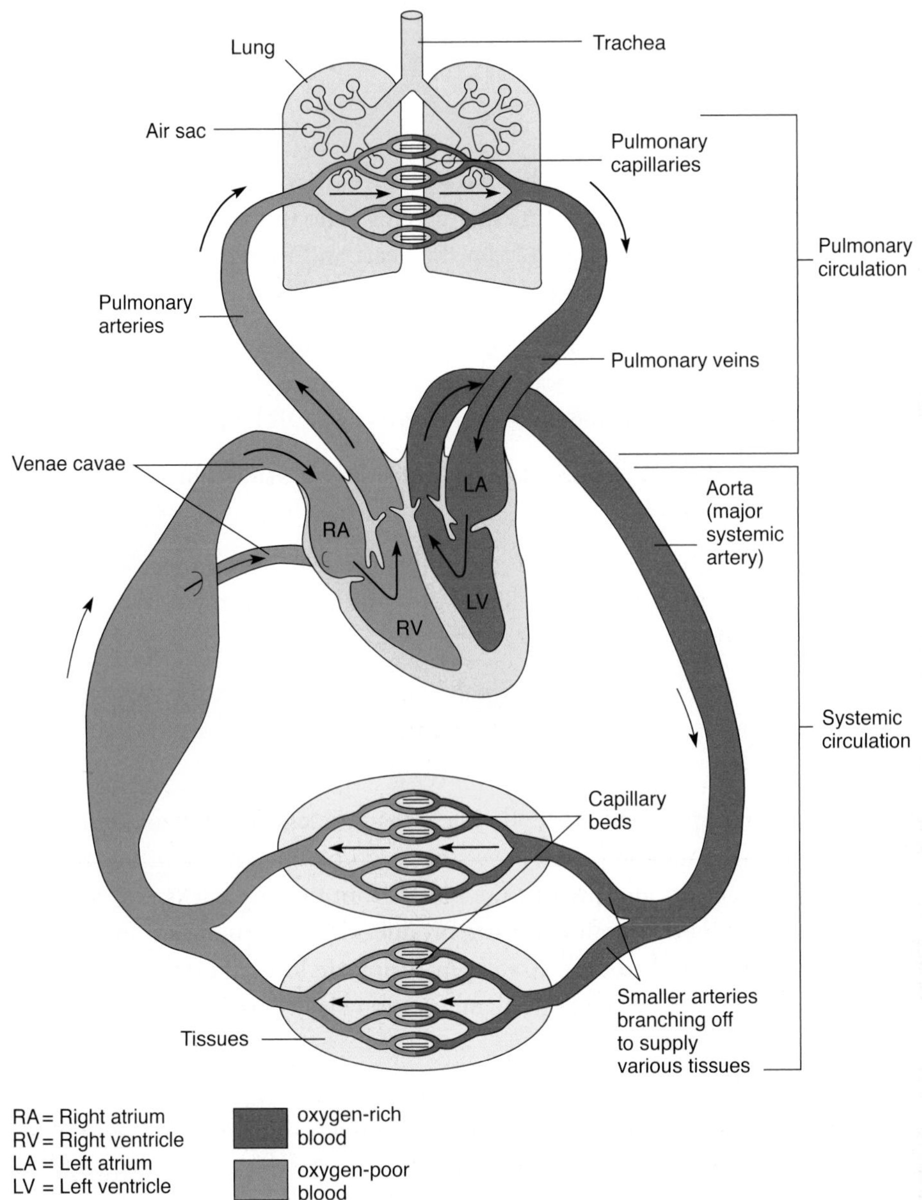

◀ Figure 6–23
Drawing of blood flow through the heart.

2. From the right atrium, it flows through the **tricuspid valve** (try-KUS-pid VALV) into the right ventricle.
3. The right ventricle pumps the blood to the pulmonary arteries, which move the deoxygenated blood to the lungs. When the blood reaches the lungs, it releases waste gases (carbon dioxide) and receives oxygen. The blood is then considered to be oxygen-rich.
4. The oxygen-rich blood returns to the heart through the pulmonary veins and enters the left atrium.
5. From the left atrium, the blood flows through the **mitral valve**, also known as **bicuspid valve** (by-KUS-pid VALV), into the left ventricle.
6. The blood then leaves the left ventricle and travels to all parts of the body.

The tricuspid and bicuspid (mitral) valves are anatomically known as the **atrioventricular valves (AV)**.

Blood Vessels

The **blood vessels** are tube-like structures that include the arteries, arterioles, capillaries, venules, and veins. The function of these vessels is to transport blood to and from the heart and then on to various tissues of the body. The types of blood vessels found in the body are:

- **Arteries** (AR-tuh-rees). Thick-walled, muscular, flexible tubes that carry oxygenated blood away from the heart to the arterioles. The largest artery in the body is the **aorta** (ay-ORT-uh).
- **Arterioles** (ar-TEER-ee-ohls). Small arteries that deliver blood to capillaries.
- **Capillaries.** Tiny, thin-walled blood vessels that connect the smaller arteries to venules. Capillaries bring nutrients to the cells and carry away waste materials.
- **Venules** (VEEN-yools). Small vessels that connect the capillaries to the veins. They collect blood from the capillaries and drain it into the veins.
- **Veins.** Thin-walled blood vessels that are less elastic than arteries. They contain cup-like valves that keep blood flowing in one direction to the heart and prevent the blood from flowing backward. Veins carry blood containing waste products back to the heart and lungs for cleaning and to pick up oxygen. Veins are located closer to the outer skin surface of the body than arteries (**Figure 6–24**).

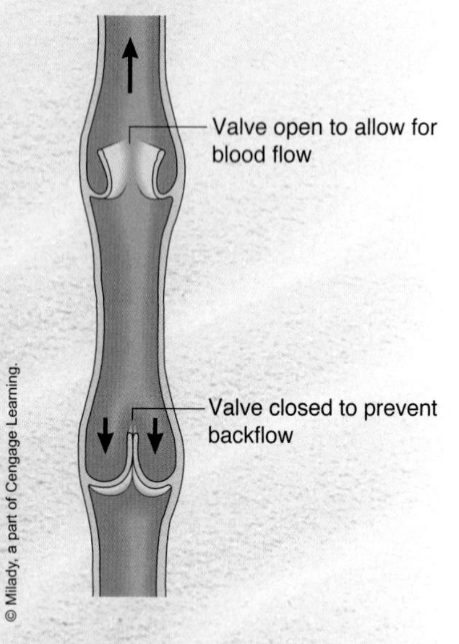

▲ Figure 6–24
Valves in the veins.

The Blood

Blood is a nutritive fluid circulating through the circulatory system and is considered connective tissue. There are 8 to 10 pints (3.8 to 4.7 liters) of blood in the human body, accounting for about one-twentieth of the body's weight. Blood is approximately 83 percent water. It is sticky and salty, with a normal temperature of 98.6 degrees Fahrenheit (36 degrees Celsius). It is bright red in the arteries—except for the pulmonary artery—and dark red in the veins. The color change occurs during the exchange of carbon dioxide for oxygen as the blood passes through the lungs, and the exchange of oxygen for carbon dioxide as the blood circulates throughout the body.

Blood performs the following critical functions.

- It carries water, oxygen, food, and secretions to all cells of the body.
- It carries away carbon dioxide and waste products to be eliminated through the lungs, skin, kidneys, and large intestines.
- It helps to equalize the body's temperature, thus protecting the body from extreme heat and cold.

- It aids in protecting the body from harmful bacteria and infections through the action of the white blood cells.
- It closes injured minute blood vessels by forming clots, thus preventing blood loss.

Did You Know?

An adult heart beats about 30 million times a year and pumps nearly 4,000 gal (15,142 l) of blood every day.

Composition of the Blood

Blood is composed of red blood cells, white blood cells, plasma, and platelets.

Red blood cells, also known as **red corpuscles** (KOR-pus-uls) or **erythrocytes** (ih-RITH-ruh-syts), are produced in the red bone marrow. They contain **hemoglobin** (HEE-muh-gloh-bun), a complex iron protein that gives the blood its bright red color. The function of red blood cells is to carry oxygen to the body cells. **White blood cells**, also known as **white corpuscles** or **leukocytes** (LOO-koh-syts), perform the function of destroying disease causing germs. **Platelets**, also known as **thrombocytes** (THRAHM-buh-syts), are much smaller than red blood cells. They contribute to the blood-clotting process, which stops bleeding.

Plasma (PLAZ-muh) is the fluid part of the blood in which the red and white blood cells and platelets flow. It is about 90 percent water and contains proteins, sugars, and oxygen. The main function of plasma is to carry food and secretions to the cells and to take carbon dioxide away from the cells.

Arteries of the Head, Face, and Neck

The **common carotid** (kuh-RAHT-ud) **arteries** are the main source of blood supply to the head, face, and neck. They are located on either side of the neck, and each one is divided into an internal and external branch.

Did You Know?

An adult has over 60,000 miles (96,561 km) of blood vessels in their body. If you tied all of your blood vessels together, they would go around the Earth about two and one-half times!

The **internal carotid artery** supplies blood to the brain, eyes, eyelids, forehead, nose, and internal ear. The **external carotid artery** supplies blood to the anterior (front) parts of the scalp, ear, face, neck, and side of the head (Figure 6–25). The external carotid artery subdivides into several branches. Of particular interest to the esthetician are the following arteries:

The **facial artery**, also known as **external maxillary artery**, supplies blood to the lower region of the face, mouth, and nose. Here are some of its branches.

- The **submental** (sub-MEN-tul) **artery** supplies blood to the chin and lower lip.
- The **inferior labial** (LAY-bee-ul) **artery** supplies blood to the lower lip.
- The **angular artery** supplies blood to the side of the nose.
- The **superior labial artery** supplies blood to the upper lip and region of the nose.

The **superficial temporal artery** is a continuation of the external carotid artery and supplies blood to the muscles of the front, side, and top of the head. Some of its important branches are as follows.

▶ Figure 6–25
Arteries of the head, face, and neck.

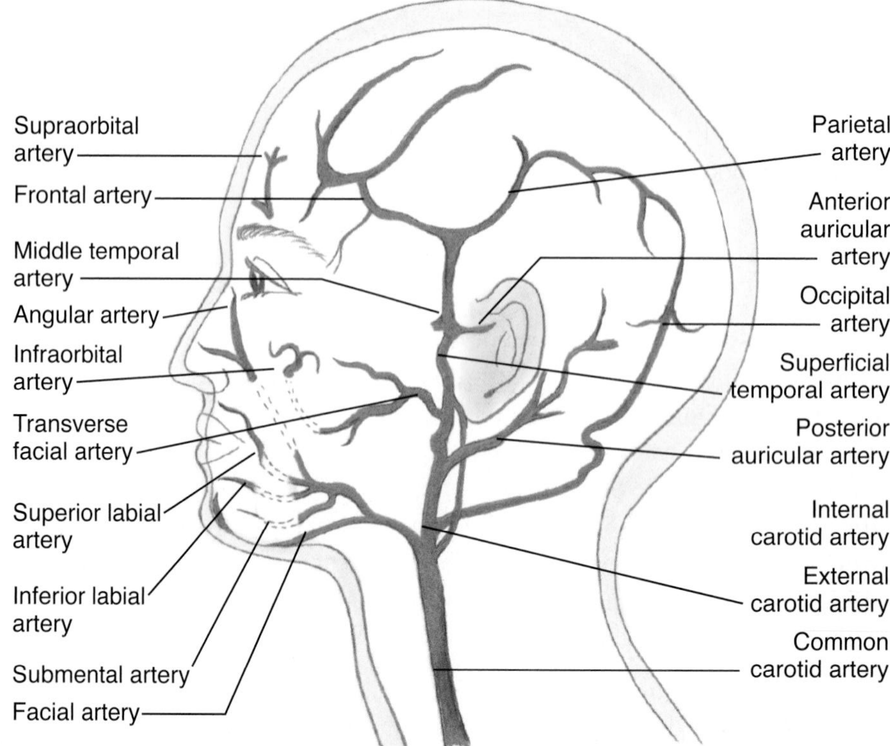

- The **frontal artery** supplies blood to the forehead and upper eyelids.
- The **parietal artery** supplies blood to the side and crown of the head.
- The **transverse facial** (tranz-VURS) **artery** supplies blood to the skin and masseter.
- The **middle temporal artery** supplies blood to the temples.
- The **anterior auricular artery** supplies blood to the front part of the ear.

Two other arteries that branch from the external carotid artery are as follows.

- The **occipital artery** supplies blood to the skin and muscles of the scalp and back of the head up to the crown.
- The **posterior auricular artery** supplies the scalp, the area behind and above the ear, and the skin behind the ear.

Here are two branches of the internal carotid artery that are important to know.

- The **supraorbital** (soo-pruh-OR-bih-tul) **artery** supplies blood to the upper eyelids and forehead.
- The **infraorbital** (in-frah-OR-bih-tul) **artery** supplies blood to the muscles of the eye.

Veins of the Head, Face, and Neck

The blood returning to the heart from the head, face, and neck flows on each side of the neck in two principal veins: the **internal jugular** (JUG-yuh-lur) **vein** and **external jugular vein**. The most important veins of the face and neck are parallel to the arteries and take the same names as the arteries, however, there are no jugular arteries; rather, they are known as the carotid arteries.

Blood Supply to the Arm and Hand

The ulnar and radial arteries are the main blood supply of the arms and hands and are branches of the **brachial artery** (Figure 6–26). The **ulnar artery** and its numerous branches supply the little-finger side of the arm and palm of the hand. The **radial artery** and its branches supplies blood to the thumb side of the arm and the back of the hand, as well as the muscles of the skin, hands, fingers, wrist, elbow, and forearm.

The important veins are located almost parallel with the arteries and take the same names as the arteries. While the arteries are found deep in the tissues, the veins lie nearer to the surface of the arms and hands.

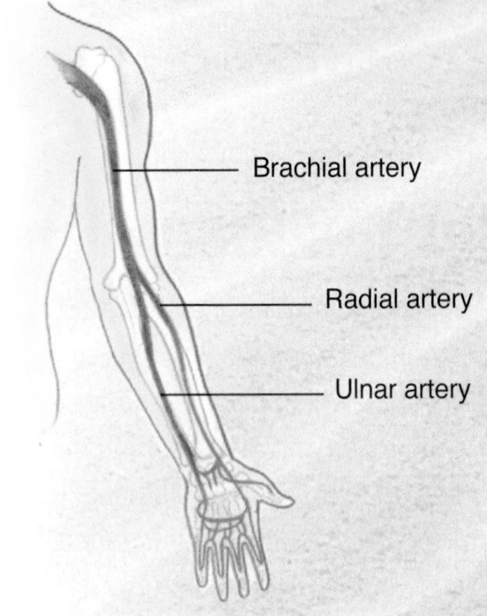

▲ Figure 6–26
Arteries of the arm and hand.

The Lymphatic/Immune System

The **lymphatic/immune system** is a vital factor to the circulatory and immune systems and is made up of lymph, lymph nodes, the thymus gland, the spleen, and lymph vessels that act as an aid to the blood system; the lymphatic and immune systems are closely connected in that they protect the body from disease by developing immunities and destroying disease-causing microorganisms. **Lymph** is a colorless, watery fluid derived from blood plasma as a result of filtration through the capillary walls into the tissue spaces. The function of the lymphatic system is to protect the body from disease by developing immunities, to destroy disease-causing microorganisms, and to drain tissue spaces of excess **interstitial fluid** (blood plasma found in the spaces between tissue cells) in the blood. It then carries waste and impurities away from the cells.

The lymphatic system is closely connected to the blood and the cardiovascular system for the transportation of fluids. The difference is that the lymphatic system transports lymph fluid.

The lymphatic vessels start as tubes that are closed at one end (Figure 6–27). They can occur individually or in clusters that are called **lymph capillaries**. The lymph capillaries are distributed throughout most of the body, except the nervous system.

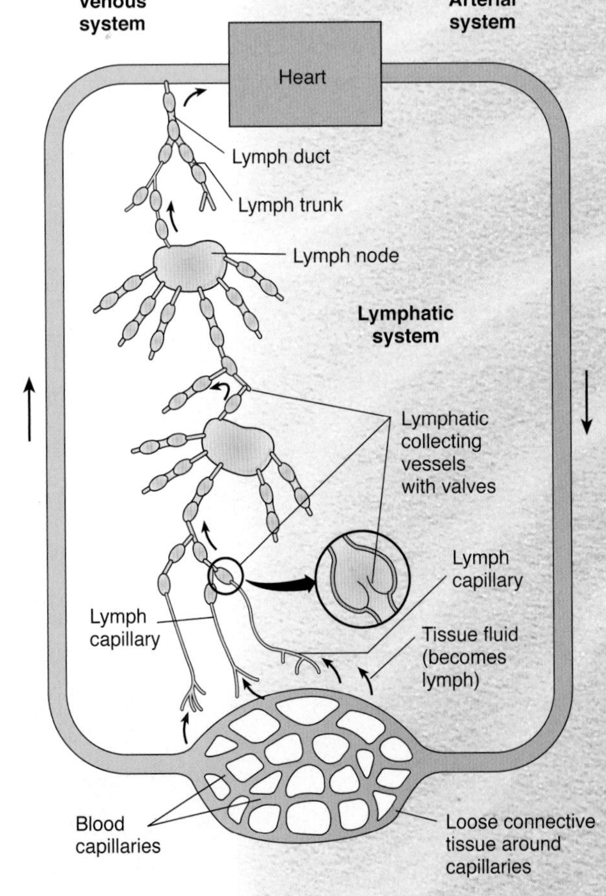

▲ Figure 6–27
The lymphatic system.

The lymphatic vessels are filtered by the **lymph nodes**, which are gland-like structures found inside the vessels. This filtering process helps to detoxify and fight infection before the lymph is reintroduced into the bloodstream.

Did You Know?

As estheticians we may learn techniques such as lymphatic drainage, which has been found to improve lymphatic flow and to stimulate circulation. Additionally, lymphatic drainage may create a sense of well-being and provide relaxation for the client.

The primary functions of the lymphatic system are:

- To act as a defense against invading bacteria and toxins.
- To remove waste material from the body cells to the blood.
- To aid in reducing swelling, inflammation, and accumulations in the blood vessels.

The Endocrine System

The **endocrine** (EN-duh-krin) **system** is a group of specialized glands that affect the growth, development, sexual activities, and health of the entire body. **Glands** are specialized organs that remove certain elements from the blood to convert them into new compounds. There are two main types of glands.

- **Exocrine** (EK-suh-krin) **glands**, also known as **duct glands**, produce a substance that travels through small, tube-like ducts. Sweat and oil glands of the skin belong to this group.
- **Endocrine glands**, also known as **ductless glands**, release secretions called *hormones* directly into the bloodstream, which in turn influence the welfare of the entire body (Figure 6–28).

Hormones, such as insulin, adrenaline, and estrogen, stimulate functional activity or secretion in other parts of the body.

Did You Know?

Hormones are actually chemicals. There are over 30 hormones telling your body what it should do every day.

Here is a list of the endocrine glands and their functions.

- The **pineal gland** plays a major role in sexual development, sleep, and metabolism.
- The **pituitary gland** is the most complex organ of the endocrine system. It affects almost every physiologic process of the body: growth, blood pressure, contractions during childbirth, breast-milk production, sexual organ functions in both women and men, thyroid gland function, the conversion of food into energy (metabolism).
- The **thyroid gland** controls how quickly the body burns energy (metabolism), makes proteins, and how sensitive the body should be to other hormones.
- The **parathyroid glands** regulate blood calcium and phosphorus levels so that the nervous and muscular systems can function properly.
- The **pancreas** secretes enzyme-producing cells that are responsible for digesting carbohydrates, proteins, and fats. The islet of Langerhans cells within the pancreas control insulin and glucagon production.

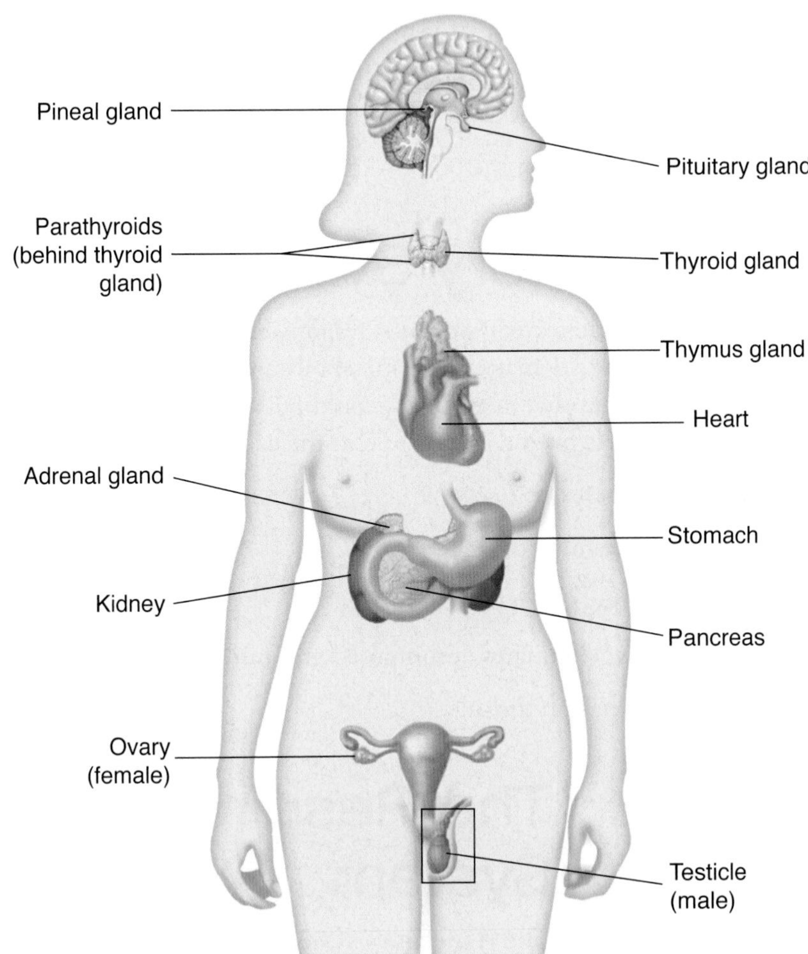

◀ Figure 6–28
The endocrine glands and other body organs.

- The adrenal glands secrete about 30 steroid hormones and control metabolic processes of the body, including the fight-or-flight response.
- The ovaries and testes function in sexual reproduction as well as determining male and female sexual characteristics.

Did You Know?

The average adult has about 25 ft (7.6 m) of intestines. In your lifetime, your digestive system handles about 50 tons (45 metric tons) of food.

The Digestive System

The digestive system, also called the **gastrointestinal** (gas-troh-in-TES-tun-ul) **system**, is responsible for changing food into nutrients and waste. Digestive enzymes (EN-zymz) are chemicals that change certain kinds of food into a form that can be used by the body. The food, now in soluble form, is transported by the bloodstream and used by the body's cells and tissues.

The digestive system prepares food for use by the cells through five basic activities.

- Eating or ingestion—taking food into the body
- Moving food along the digestive tract—known as peristalsis
- Breakdown of food by mechanical and chemical means—known as digestion

Web Resources

www.innerbody.com

www.getbodysmart.com

- **Absorption** of the digested food into the circulatory systems for transportation to the tissues and cells
- Elimination of waste from the body—known as **defecation**

The Excretory System

The **excretory** (EK-skre-tor-ee) **system** is responsible for purifying the body by eliminating waste matter. The metabolism of body cells forms various toxic substances that, if retained, could poison the body. Each of the following organs plays a crucial role in the excretory system.

- The kidneys excrete urine.
- The liver discharges bile.
- The skin eliminates perspiration.
- The large intestine eliminates decomposed and undigested food.
- The lungs exhale carbon dioxide.

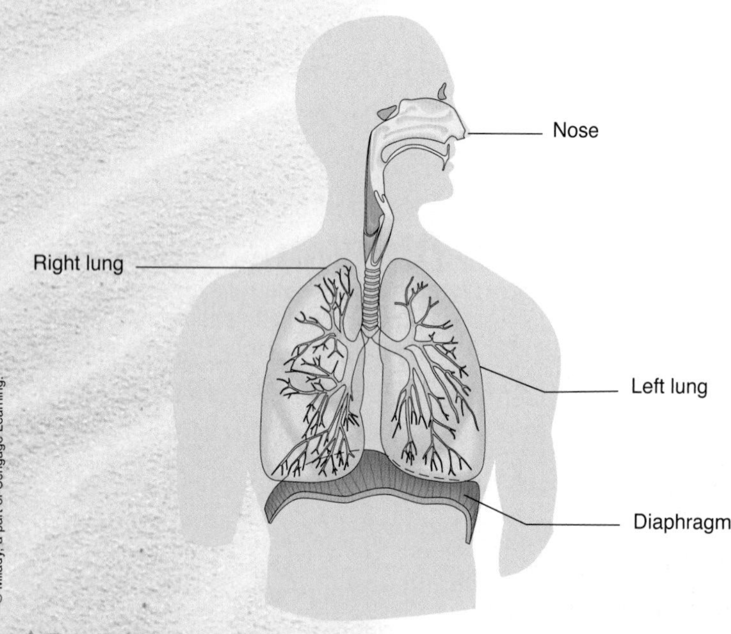

▲ Figure 6–29
The respiratory system.

The Respiratory System

The **respiratory system** (RES-puh-ra-tor-ee SIS-tum) enables breathing (**respiration**) and consists of the lungs and air passages. The **lungs** are spongy tissues composed of microscopic cells in which inhaled air is exchanged for carbon dioxide during one breathing cycle. The respiratory system is located within the chest cavity and is protected on both sides by the ribs. The **diaphragm** is a muscular wall that separates the thorax from the abdominal region and helps control breathing (Figure 6–29).

With each breathing cycle, an exchange of gases takes place. During **inhalation** (in-huh-LAY-shun), or breathing in, oxygen is absorbed into the blood. During **exhalation** (eks-huh-LAY-shun), or breathing outward, carbon dioxide is expelled from the lungs.

The Integumentary System

The **integumentary system** is made up of the skin and its various accessory organs, such as the oil and sweat glands, sensory receptors, hair, and nails (Figure 6–30). (Skin anatomy and physiology are discussed in detail in Chapter 10, Physiology and Histology of the Skin.)

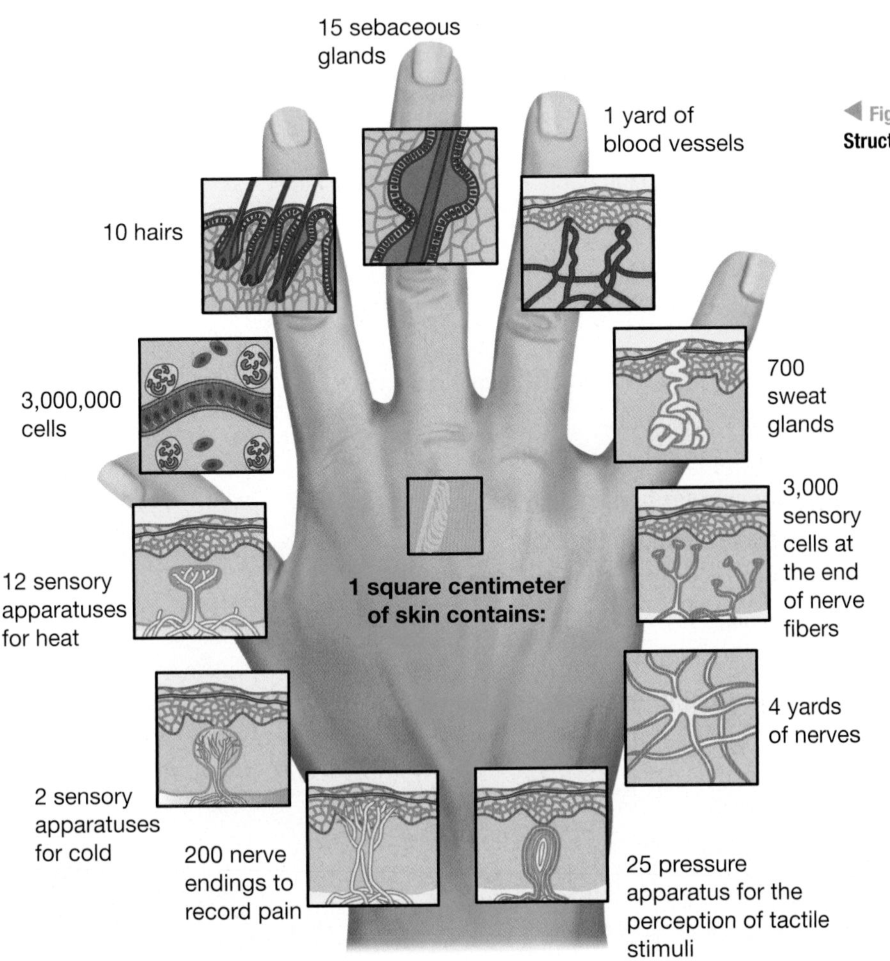

◀ Figure 6–30
Structures of the skin.

The word integument means a natural covering. So, you can think of the skin as a protective overcoat for your body against the outside elements that you encounter every day such as germs, chemicals, and sun exposure.

The Reproductive System

The **reproductive system** (ree-proh-DUK-tiv SIS-tum) includes the ovaries, uterine tubes, uterus, and vagina in the female and the testes, prostate gland, penis, and the urethra in the male. It performs the function of producing children and passing on our genetics from one generation to another.

The reproductive system produces hormones—estrogen in females and testosterone in males. These hormones, or lack thereof, affect and change the skin in several ways as we age. Acne, loss of collagen and elastin, loss of scalp hair, facial hair growth and color, and changes in skin pigmentation such as **melasma** (pregnancy mask) are some of the results of changing or fluctuating hormones. Estheticians today have many resources—including products, treatments, and lifestyle modification recommendations—for helping clients.

Did You Know?

Your lungs contain almost 1,500 miles (2,414 km) of airways so you can breathe. Every minute you breathe in about 13 pt (6 l) of air.

Did You Know?

Every minute you shed about 30,000 to 40,000 dead skin cells from your body. That can total up to about 40 lb (18 kg) of skin in your lifetime.

Review Questions

1. Define anatomy, physiology, and histology.
2. Why is the study of anatomy, physiology, and histology important to the esthetician?
3. Name and describe the basic structures of a cell.
4. Explain cell metabolism and its purpose.
5. List and describe the functions of the four types of tissue found in the human body.
6. What are organs?
7. List and describe the functions of the most important organs found in the body.
8. Name the 11 body systems and their main functions.
9. List the primary functions of the skeletal system.
10. Name and describe the three types of muscular tissue found in the body.
11. Name and describe the two types of nerves found in the body.
12. Name and briefly describe the five types of blood vessels found in the body
13. List and describe the components of blood
14. What are the primary functions of the lymphatic system?
15. What two types of glands make up the endocrine system?
16. List the organs of the excretory system and their function.

Glossary

abductors	Muscles that draw a body part, such as a finger, arm, or toe, away from the midline of the body or of an extremity. In the hand, abductors separate the fingers.
absorption	The transport of fully digested food into the circulatory system to feed the tissues and cells.
adductors	Muscles that draw a body part, such as a finger, arm, or toe, inward toward the median axis of the body or of an extremity. In the hand, adductors draw the fingers together
adipose tissue	A specialized connective tissue considered fat, which gives smoothness and contour to the body and cushions and insulates the body.
adrenal glands	Glands that secrete about 30 steroid hormones and control metabolic processes of the body, including the fight-or-flight response.
anabolism	Constructive metabolism; the process of building up larger molecules from smaller ones.
anatomy	The study of human body structure that can be seen with the naked eye and how the body parts are organized and the science of the structure of organisms or of their parts.
angular artery	Artery that supplies blood to the side of the nose.
anterior auricular artery	Artery that supplies blood to the front part of the ear.
aorta	The body's largest artery. The arterial trunk that carries blood from the heart to be distributed by branch arteries through the body.
arteries	Thick-walled muscular and flexible tubes that carry oxygenated blood from the heart to the capillaries throughout the body.

Glossary

arterioles	Small arteries that deliver blood to capillaries.
atrioventricular valves	Abbreviated ATV; valves which are designed to prevent the blood from flowing back into the pumping chamber.
atrium	Thin-walled, upper chamber of the heart through which blood is pumped to the ventricles. There is a right atrium and a left atrium.
auricularis anterior	Muscle in front of the ear that draws the ear forward.
auricularis posterior	Muscle behind the ear that draws the ear backward.
auricularis superior	Muscle above the ear that draws the ear upward.
auriculotemporal nerve	Nerve that affects the external ear and skin above the temple, up to the top of the skull.
autonomic nervous system	Abbreviated ANS; the part of the nervous system that controls the involuntary muscles; regulates the action of the smooth muscles, glands, blood vessels, and heart.
axon	The extension of a neuron through which impulses are sent away from the cell body to other neurons, glands, or muscles.
belly	Middle part of a muscle.
biceps	Muscle producing the contour of the front and inner side of the upper arm.
blood	Nutritive fluid circulating through the circulatory system (heart, veins, arteries, and capillaries) to supply oxygen and nutrients to cells and tissues and to remove carbon dioxide and waste from them.
blood vessels	Tube-like structures that transport blood to and from the heart, and to various tissues of the body; include arteries, arterioles, capillaries, venules, and veins.
body systems	Also known as *systems*; groups of bodily organs acting together to perform one or more functions. The human body is composed of 11 major systems.
brachial artery	Located in the upper arm, the brachial artery is a major blood vessel which runs down the arm and ends by dividing into the radial and ulnar arteries, which run down through the forearm.
brain	Part of the central nervous system contained in the cranium; largest and most complex nerve tissue; controls sensation, muscles, glandular activity, and the power to think and feel.
brain stem	Structure that connects the spinal cord to the brain.
buccal nerve	Nerve that affects the muscles of the mouth.
buccinator	Thin, flat muscle of the cheek between the upper and lower jaw that compresses the cheeks and expels air between the lips.
capillaries	Tiny, thin-walled blood vessels that connect the smaller arteries to the veins. Capillaries bring nutrients to the cells and carry away waste materials.
cardiac muscle	The involuntary muscle that is the heart. This type of muscle is not found in any other part of the body.
carpus	Also known as *wrist*; a flexible joint composed of eight small, irregular bones (carpals) held together by ligaments.

Glossary

catabolism	The phase of metabolism that involves the breaking down of complex compounds within the cells into smaller ones, often resulting in the release of energy to perform functions such as muscular efforts, secretions, or digestion.
cell membrane	Part of the cell that encloses the protoplasm and permits soluble substances to enter and leave the cell.
cells	Basic unit of all living things; minute mass of protoplasm capable of performing all the fundamental functions of life.
central nervous system	Abbreviated CNS; cerebrospinal nervous system; consists of the brain, spinal cord, spinal nerves, and cranial nerves.
cerebellum	Lies at the base of the cerebrum and is attached to the brain stem; this term is Latin for "little brain."
cerebrum	Makes up the bulk of the brain and is located in the front, upper part of the cranium.
cervical cutaneous nerve	Nerve located at the side of the neck that affects the front and sides of the neck as far down as the breastbone.
cervical nerves	Nerves that originate at the spinal cord, whose branches supply the muscles and scalp at the back of the head and neck; affect the side of the neck and the platysma muscle.
cervical vertebrae	The seven bones of the top part of the vertebral column, located in the neck region.
circulatory system	Also known as *cardiovascular system* or *vascular system*; system that controls the steady circulation of the blood through the body by means of the heart and blood vessels.
clavicle	Also known as *collarbone*; bone joining the sternum and scapula.
common carotid arteries	Arteries that supply blood to the face, head, and neck.
connective tissue	Fibrous tissue that binds together, protects, and supports the various parts of the body such as bone, cartilage, and tendons.Examples of connective tissue are bone, cartilage, ligaments, tendons, blood, lymph, and fat.
corrugator muscle	Facial muscle that draws eyebrows down and wrinkles the forehead vertically.
cranium	Oval, bony case that protects the brain.
cytoplasm	All the protoplasm of a cell except that which is in the nucleus; the watery fluid containing food material necessary for cell growth, reproduction, and self-repair.
defecation	Elimination of feces from the body.
deltoid	Large, triangular muscle covering the shoulder joint that allows the arm to extend outward and to the side of the body.
dendrites	Tree-like branching of nerve fibers extending from a nerve cell; short nerve fibers that carry impulses toward the cell and receive impulses from other neurons.
deoxyribonucleic acid	Abbreviated DNA; the blueprint material of genetic information; contains all the information that controls the function of every living cell.
depressor anguli oris	Also known as *triangularis muscle*; muscle extending alongside the chin that pulls down the corner of the mouth.

Glossary

depressor labii inferioris	Also known as *quadratus labii inferioris*; muscle surrounding the lower lip that depresses the lower lip and draws it to one side.
diaphragm	Muscular wall that separates the thorax from the abdominal region and helps control breathing.
diencephalon	Located in the uppermost part of the midbrain; consists of two main parts the thalamus and the hypothalamus.
digestion	Breakdown of food by mechanical and chemical means.
digestive enzymes	Chemicals that change certain kinds of food into a form that can be used by the body.
digestive system	Also called the *gastrointestinal system*; responsible for changing food into nutrients and wastes; consists of the mouth, stomach, intestines, salivary and gastric glands and other organs.
digital nerve	Sensory-motor nerve that, with its branches, supplies impulses to the fingers.
eleventh cranial nerve	Also known as *accessory nerve*; a motor nerve that controls the motion of the neck and shoulder muscles.
endocrine glands	Also known as *ductless glands*; release secretions called hormones directly into the bloodstream which in turn influence the welfare of the entire body.
endocrine system	Group of specialized glands that affect the growth development, sexual activities, and health of the entire body.
epicranial aponeurosis	Tendon connecting the occipitalis and the frontalis.
epicranius	Also known as *occipitofrontalis*; the broad muscle that covers the top of the skull and consists of the occipitalis and frontalis.
epithelial tissue	Protective covering on body surfaces, such as the skin, mucous membranes, and lining of the heart; digestive and respiratory organs; and glands.
ethmoid bone	Light, spongy bone between the eye sockets that forms part of the nasal cavities.
excretory system	Group of organs—including the kidneys, liver, skin, large intestine, and lungs—that purify the body by elimination of waste matter.
exhalation	Breathing outward; expelling carbon dioxide from the lungs.
exocrine glands	Also known as *duct glands*; produce a substance that travels through small, tube-like ducts. Sweat and oil glands of the skin belong to this group.
extensors	Muscles that straighten the wrist, hand, and fingers to form a straight line.
external carotid artery	Artery that supplies blood to the anterior parts of the scalp, ear, face, neck, and side of the head.
external jugular vein	Vein located on the side of the neck that carries blood returning to the heart from the head, face, and neck.
facial artery	Also known as *external maxillary artery*; supplies blood to the lower region of the face, mouth, and nose.
fifth cranial nerve	Also known as *trifacial* or *trigeminal nerve*; it is the chief sensory nerve of the face, and it serves as the motor nerve of the muscles that control chewing. It consists of three branches.

Glossary

flexors	Extensor muscles of the wrist, involved in flexing the wrist.
frontal artery	Artery that supplies blood to the forehead and upper eyelids.
frontal bone	Bone forming the forehead.
frontalis	Front (anterior) portion of the epicranius; muscle of the scalp that raises the eyebrows, draws the scalp forward, and causes wrinkles across the forehead.
glands	Specialized organs that remove certain elements from the blood to convert them into new compounds.
greater auricular nerve	Nerve at the sides of the neck affecting the face, ears, neck, and parotid gland.
greater occipital nerve	Nerve located in the back of the head, affects the scalp as far up as the top of the head.
heart	Muscular cone-shaped organ that keeps the blood moving within the circulatory system.
hemoglobin	Iron-containing protein in red blood cells that binds to oxygen.
histology	Also known as *microscopic anatomy*; the study of the structure and composition of tissue.
hormones	Secretions produced by one of the endocrine glands and carried by the bloodstream or body fluid to another part of the body, or a body organ, to stimulate functional activity or secretion, such as insulin, adrenaline, and estrogen.
humerus	Uppermost and largest bone in the arm, extending from the elbow to the shoulder.
hyoid bone	U-shaped bone at the base of the tongue that supports the tongue and its muscle.
inferior labial artery	Supplies blood to the lower lip.
infraorbital artery	Artery that originates from the internal maxillary artery and supplies blood to the eye muscles.
infraorbital nerve	Nerve that affects the skin of the lower eyelid, side of the nose, upper lip, and mouth.
infratrochlear nerve	Nerve that affects the membrane and skin of the nose.
ingestion	Eating or taking food into the body.
inhalation	Breathing in through the nose or mouth, and thus oxygen is absorbed by the blood.
insertion	Point where the skeletal muscle is attached to a bone or other more movable body part.
integumentary system	The skin and its accessory organs, such as the oil and sweat glands, sensory receptors, hair, and nails.
internal carotid artery	Artery that supplies blood to the brain, eyes, eyelids, forehead, nose, and internal ear.
internal jugular vein	Vein located at the side of the neck to collect blood from the brain and parts of the face and neck.
interstitial fluid	Blood plasma found in the spaces between tissues.
joint	Connection between two or more bones of the skeleton.
kidneys	One of the organs which supports the excretory system by eliminating water and waste products.
lacrimal bones	Small, thin bones located in the anterior medial wall of the orbits (eye sockets).
lateral pterygoid	Muscles that coordinate with the masseter, temporalis, and medial pterygoid muscles to open and close the mouth and bring the jaw forward; sometimes referred to as chewing muscles.

Glossary

latissimus dorsi	Large, flat, triangular muscle covering the lower back.
levator anguli oris	Also known as *caninus*; is a muscle that raises the angle of the mouth and draws it inward.
levator labii superioris	Also known as *quadratu labii superioris*; muscle surrounding the upper lip that elevates the upper lip and dilates the nostrils, as in expressing distaste.
liver	One of the organs which supports the excretory system by removing toxic waste products of digestion.
lungs	Spongy tissues composed of microscopic cells in which inhaled air is exchanged for carbon dioxide during one respiratory cycle.
lymph	Clear, yellowish fluid that circulates in the lymph spaces (lymphatic) of the body; carries waste and impurities away from the cells.
lymph capillaries	Lymphatic vessels that occur in clusters and are distributed throughout most of the body.
lymph nodes	Gland-like structures found inside lymphatic vessels; filter the lymphatic vessels and help fight infection.
lymphatic/immune system	Vital to the circulatory and to the immune system made up of lymph, lymph nodes, the thymus gland, the spleen, and lymph vessels that act as an aid to the blood system; the lymphatic and immune system are closely connected in that they protect the body from disease by developing immunities and destroying disease-causing microorganisms.
mandible	Lower jawbone; largest and strongest bone of the face.
mandibular nerve	Branch of the fifth cranial nerve that supplies the muscles and skin of the lower part of the face; also, nerve that affects the muscles of the chin and lower lip.
masseter	One of the muscles that coordinate with the temporalis, medial pterygoid, and lateral pterygoid muscles to open and close the mouth and bring the jaw forward; sometimes referred to as chewing muscles.
maxillary bones	Form the upper jaw.
maxillary nerve	Branch of the fifth cranial nerve that supplies the upper part of the face.
medial pterygoid	One of the muscles that coordinate with the masseter, temporalis, and lateral pterygoid muscles to open and close the mouth and bring the jaw forward; sometimes referred to as chewing muscles.
median nerve	Nerve, smaller than the ulnar and radial nerves, that supplies the arm and hand.
melasma	Also referred to as *pregnancy mask*; skin condition that is triggered by hormones that causes darker pigmentation in areas such as on the upper lip and around the eyes and cheeks.
mental nerve	Nerve that affects the skin of the lower lip and chin.
mentalis	Muscle that elevates the lower lip and raises and wrinkles the skin of the chin.
metabolism	(1) Chemical process taking place in living organisms whereby the cells are nourished and carry out their activities. (2) The process of changing food into forms the body can use as energy. Metabolism consists of two parts: anabolism and catabolism.
metacarpus	Also known as *palm*; consists of five long, slender bones called metacarpal bones.
middle temporal artery	Artery that supplies blood to the temples.

Glossary

mitosis	Cells dividing into two new cells (daughter cells); the usual process of cell reproduction of human tissues.
mitral valve	Also known as *bicuspid valve*; a valve in which, from the left atrium, the blood flows through into the left ventricle.
motor nerves	Also known as *efferent nerves*; carry impulses from the brain to the muscles or glands. These transmitted impulses produce movement.
muscle tissue	Tissue that contracts and moves various parts of the body.
muscular system	Body system that covers, shapes, and supports the skeleton tissue; contracts and moves various parts of the body.
myology	Study of the nature, structure, function, and diseases of the muscles.
nasal bones	Bones that form the bridge of the nose.
nasal nerve	Nerve that affects the point and lower sides of the nose.
nasalis muscle	Two-part muscle which covers the nose.
nerve tissue	Tissue that controls and coordinates all body functions.
nerves	Whitish cords made up of bundles of nerve fibers held together by connective tissue, through which impulses are transmitted.
nervous system	Body system composed of the brain, spinal cord, and nerves; controls and coordinates all other systems and makes them work harmoniously and efficiently.
neurology	The scientific study of the structure, function, and pathology of the nervous system.
neuron or nerve cell	The basic unit of the nervous system, consisting of a cell body, nucleus, dendrites, and axon.
nonstriated muscles	Also known as *involuntary, visceral*, or *smooth* muscles; function automatically, without conscious will.
nucleoplasm	Fluid within the nucleus of the cell that contains proteins and DNA; determines our genetic makeup.
nucleus	The central part, core. 1) In histology the dense, active protoplasm found in the center of a eukaryotic cell that acts as the genetic control center; it plays an important role in cell reproduction and metabolism. 2) In chemistry, the center of the atom, where protons and neutrons are located.
occipital artery	Artery that supplies blood to the skin and muscles of the scalp and back of the head up to the crown.
occipital bone	Hindmost bone of the skull, below the parietal bones; forms the back of the skull above the nape.
occipitalis	Back of the epicranius; muscle that draws the scalp backward.
ophthalmic nerve	Branch of the fifth cranial nerve that supplies the skin of the forehead, upper eyelids, and interior portion of the scalp, orbit, eyeball, and nasal passage.
orbicularis oculi	Ring muscle of the eye socket; closes the eyelid.
orbicularis oris	Flat band around the upper and lower lips that compresses, contracts, puckers, and wrinkles the lips.

Glossary

organelle	Small structures or miniature organs within a cell that have their own function.
organs	Structures composed of specialized tissues and performing specific functions in plants and animals.
origin	Part of the muscle that does not move; it is attached to the skeleton and is usually part of a skeletal muscle.
os	Means *bone* and is used as a prefix in many medical terms, such as *osteoarthritis*, a joint disease
osteology	Study of anatomy, structure, and function of the bones.
ovaries	Function in sexual reproduction as well as determining male and female sexual characteristics.
palatine bones	Two bones that form the hard palate of the mouth.
pancreas	Secretes enzyme-producing cells that are responsible for digesting carbohydrates, proteins, and fats. The islet of Langerhans cells within the pancreas control insulin and glucagon production.
parasympathetic division	Part of the autonomic nervous system, it operates under normal nonstressful situations, such as resting. It also helps to restore calm and balance to the body after a stressful event.
parathyroid glands	Regulate blood calcium and phosphorus levels so that the nervous and muscular systems can function properly.
parietal artery	Artery that supplies blood to the side and crown of the head.
parietal bones	Bones that form the sides and top of the cranium.
pectoralis major and minor	Muscles of the chest that assist the swinging movements of the arm.
pericardium	Double-layered membranous sac enclosing the heart; made of epithelial tissue.
peripheral nervous system	Abbreviated PNS; system of nerves and ganglia that connects the peripheral parts of the body to the central nervous system; has both sensory and motor nerves.
peristalsis	Moving food along the digestive tract.
phalanges (singular: phalanx)	Also known as *digits*; are the bones in the fingers, three in each finger and two in each thumb, totaling 14 bones.
physiology	Study of the functions or activities performed by the body's structures.
pineal gland	A gland located in the brain. Plays a major role in sexual development, sleep, and metabolism.
pituitary gland	A gland found in the center of the head. The most complex organ of the endocrine system. It affects almost every physiologic process of the body: growth, blood pressure, contractions during childbirth, breast-milk production, sexual organ functions in both women and men, thyroid gland function, and the conversion of food into energy (metabolism).
plasma	Fluid part of the blood and lymph that carries food and secretions to the cells and carbon dioxide from the cells.
platelets	Also known as *thrombocytes*; much smaller than red blood cells; contribute to the blood-clotting process, which stops bleeding.

Glossary

platysma	Broad muscle extending from the chest and shoulder muscles to the side of the chin; responsible for depressing the lower jaw and lip.
posterior auricular artery	Artery that supplies blood to the scalp, behind and above the ear.
posterior auricular nerve	Nerve that affects the muscles behind the ear at the base of the skull.
procerus	Muscle that covers the bridge of the nose, depresses the eyebrows, and causes wrinkles across the bridge of the nose.
pronators	Muscles that turn the hand inward so that the palm faces downward.
protoplasm	Colorless, jellylike substance in cells; contains food elements such as protein, fats, carbohydrates, mineral salts, and water.
pulmonary circulation	Sends the blood from the heart to the lungs to be purified, then back to the heart again.
radial artery	Artery, along with numerous branches, that supplies blood to the thumb side of the arm and the back of the hand; supplies the muscles of the skin, hands, fingers, wrist, elbow, and forearm.
radial nerve	Nerve that, with its branches, supplies the thumb side of the arm and back of the hand.
radius	Smaller bone in the forearm on the same side as the thumb.
red blood cells	Also known as *red corpuscles* or *erythrocytes*; produced in the red bone marrow; blood cells that carry oxygen from the lungs to the body cells and transport carbon dioxide from the cells back to the lungs.
reflex	Automatic reaction to a stimulus that involves the movement of an impulse from a sensory receptor along the sensory nerve to the spinal cord. A responsive impulse is sent along a motor neuron to a muscle, causing a reaction (for example, the quick removal of the hand from a hot object). Reflexes do not have to be learned; they are automatic.
reproductive system	Body system that includes the ovaries, uterine tubes, uterus and vagina in the female and the testes, prostate gland, penis and urethra in the male. This system performs the function of producing offspring and passing on the genetic code from one generation to another.
respiration	Process of inhaling and exhaling; the act of breathing; the exchange of carbon dioxide and oxygen in the lungs and within each cell.
respiratory system	Body system consisting of the lungs and air passages; enables breathing, which supplies the body with oxygen and eliminates carbon dioxide as a waste product.
ribs	Twelve pairs of bones forming the wall of the thorax.
risorius	Muscle of the mouth that draws the corner of the mouth out and back, as in grinning.
scapula	Also known as *shoulder blade*; one of a pair of large, flat triangular bone of the shoulder.
sensory nerves	Also known as *afferent nerves*; carry impulses or messages from the sense organs to the brain, where sensations such as touch, cold, heat, sight, hearing, taste, smell, pain, and pressure are experienced. Sensory nerve endings called receptors are located close to the surface of the skin.

Glossary

serratus anterior	Muscle of the chest that assists in breathing and in raising the arm.
seventh cranial nerve	Also known as *facial nerve*; it is the chief motor nerve of the face. It emerges near the lower part of the ear and extends to the muscles of the neck.
skeletal system	Physical foundation of the body, composed of the bones and movable and immovable joints.
skin	External protective coating that covers the body. The body's largest organ; acts as a barrier to protect body systems from the outside elements.
smaller occipital nerve	Also known as *lesser occipital nerve*; located at the base of the skull, affects the scalp and muscles behind the ear.
sphenoid bone	Bone that joins all the bones of the cranium together.
spinal cord	Portion of the central nervous system that originates in the brain, extends down to the lower extremity of the trunk, and is protected by the spinal column.
sternocleidomastoid	Abbreviated SCM; muscle of the neck that depresses and rotates the head.
sternum	Also known as *breastbone*; the flat bone that forms the ventral support of the ribs.
striated muscles	Also known as *skeletal* or *voluntary* muscles; attached to the bones and make up a large percentage of body mass; controlled by the will.
submental artery	Artery that supplies blood to the chin and lower lip.
superficial temporal artery	A continuation of the external carotid nerve artery; artery that supplies blood to the muscles of the front, side, and top of the head.
superior labial artery	Artery that supplies blood to the upper lip and region of the nose.
supinator	Muscle of the forearm that rotates the radius outward and the palm upward.
supraorbital artery	Artery that supplies blood to the upper eyelid and forehead.
supraorbital nerve	Nerve that affects the skin of the forehead, scalp, eyebrow, and upper eyelid.
supratrochlear nerve	Nerve that affects the skin between the eyes and upper side of the nose.
sympathetic division	Part of the autonomic nervous system that stimulates or speeds up activity and prepares the body for stressful situations, such as in running from a dangerous situation, or competing in a sports event.
systemic or general circulation	Circulation of blood from the heart throughout the body and back again to the heart.
temporal bones	Bones forming the sides of the head in the ear region.
temporal nerve	Nerve affecting the muscles of the temple, side of the forehead, eyebrow, eyelid, and upper part of the cheek.
temporalis muscle	Temporal muscle; one of the muscles involved in mastication (chewing).
testes	Male organs which produce the male hormone testosterone.
thorax	Also known as *chest* or *pulmonary trunk*; consists of the sternum, ribs, and thoracic vertebrae; elastic, bony cage that serves as a protective framework for the heart, lungs, and other internal organs.

Glossary

thyroid gland	A gland located in the neck; controls how quickly the body burns energy (metabolism), makes proteins, and how sensitive the body should be to other hormones.
tibial nerve	Division of the sciatic nerve, passes behind the knee; subdivides and supplies impulses to the knee, the muscles of the calf, the skin of the leg, and the sole, heel, and underside of the toes.
tissue	Collection of similar cells that perform a particular function.
transverse facial artery	Artery that supplies blood to the skin and the masseter.
trapezius	Muscle that covers the back of the neck and upper and middle region of the back; stabilizes the scapula and shrugs the shoulders.
triceps	Large muscle that covers the entire back of the upper arm and extends the forearm.
tricuspid valve	The heart valve that prevents backflow between the right atrium and the right ventricle.
turbinal bones	Thin layers of spongy bone on either of the outer walls of the nasal depression.
ulna	Inner and larger bone of the forearm, attached to the wrist on the side of the little finger.
ulnar artery	Artery that supplies blood to the muscle of the little-finger side of the arm and palm of the hand.
ulnar nerve	Sensory-motor nerve that, with its branches, affects the little-finger side of the arm and palm of the hand.
valves	Structures that temporarily close a passage or permit flow in one direction only.
vascular system	Body system consisting of the heart, arteries, veins, and capillaries for the distribution of blood throughout the body.
veins	Thin-walled blood vessels that are less elastic than arteries; they contain cuplike valves to prevent backflow and carry impure blood from the various capillaries back to the heart and lungs.
ventricle	A thick-walled, lower chamber of the heart that receives blood pumped from the atrium. There is a right ventricle and a left ventricle.
venules	Small vessels that connect the capillaries to the veins. They collect blood from the capillaries and drain it into veins.
vomer bone	Flat, thin bone that forms part of the nasal septum.
white blood cells	Also known as *white corpuscles* or *leukocytes*; perform the function of destroying disease causing germs.
zygomatic bones	Also known as *malar bones* or *cheekbones*; bones that form the prominence of the cheeks; the cheekbones.
zygomatic nerve	Nerve that affects the skin of the temple, side of the forehead, and upper part of the cheek.
zygomaticus major and minor	Muscles on both sides of the face that extend from the zygomatic bone to the angle of the mouth. These muscles elevate the lip, pull the mouth upward and backward, as when you are laughing or smiling.

CHAPTER 7

Basics of Chemistry

Chapter Outline

- Why Study Chemistry?
- Chemistry
- Matter
- Potential Hydrogen (pH)
- Chemical Reactions
- Chemistry as Applied to Cosmetics

Learning Objectives

After completing this chapter, you will be able to:

- ☑ LO1 Define chemistry and its branches: organic and inorganic chemistry.
- ☑ LO2 Explain matter and its structure.
- ☑ LO3 Discuss the properties of matter and how matter changes.
- ☑ LO4 Understand how acid, alkaline, and pH affect the skin.
- ☑ LO5 Explain pH and the pH scale.
- ☑ LO6 Explain the difference among solutions, suspensions, and emulsions.

Key Terms

Page number indicates where in the chapter the term is used.

acid mantle
pg. 168

acid-alkali neutralization reactions
pg. 170

acids
pg. 167

air
pg. 166

alkalis (bases)
pg. 167

anion
pg. 167

antioxidants
pg. 170

atoms
pg. 163

cation
pg. 167

chemical change
pg. 165

chemical compounds
pg. 165

chemical properties
pg. 165

chemistry
pg. 161

combustion
pg. 170

compound molecules (compounds)
pg. 163

element
pg. 162

elemental molecules
pg. 163

emulsions
pg. 172

free radicals
pg. 170

gases
pg. 164

hydrogen
pg. 165

hydrogen peroxide
pg. 166

hydrophilic
pg. 172

hydroxide
pg. 167

immiscible
pg. 171

inorganic chemistry
pg. 162

ion
pg. 167

ionization
pg. 167

lipophilic
pg. 173

liquids
pg. 164

logarithmic scale
pg. 168

matter
pg. 162

miscible
pg. 171

molecule
pg. 163

nitrogen
pg. 166

oil-in-water (O/W) emulsion
pg. 173

organic chemistry
pg. 161

oxidation
pg. 165

oxidation-reduction (redox)
pg. 170

oxidize
pg. 171

oxygen
pg. 165

pH
pg. 166

pH scale
pg. 166

physical change
pg. 165

physical mixtures
pg. 165

physical properties
pg. 165

redox reaction
pg. 170

reduction
pg. 170

solids
pg. 164

solute
pg. 171

solutions
pg. 171

solvent
pg. 171

states of matter
pg. 164

surfactants
pg. 172

suspensions
pg. 172

water
pg. 166

water-in-oil (W/O) emulsion
pg. 174

As an esthetician, you will be working with chemistry every day. As you will see, chemistry (one of the physical sciences), along with chemicals and chemical changes, makes life on earth possible. The daily functioning of our bodies is based on chemical reactions. The skin is made of chemicals. Creams, lotions, masks, and makeup—whether they come from natural sources such as plant extracts or from ingredients manufactured in a laboratory—are made from chemicals (Figure 7–1).

The effects of cosmetics and skin care products are based on how the skin reacts to chemicals. To understand how different chemicals affect the skin, and to choose the correct products and cosmetics for each client's skin type, estheticians must have a basic knowledge of chemistry.

▲ Figure 7–1
All skin care products are made of chemicals.

Why Study Chemistry?

Estheticians need to understand basic chemistry as it is crucial in performing services safely, effectively, and with the best results for clients.

- Without an understanding of basic chemistry, you would not be able to use professional products effectively and safely.
- Every product used in the salon and spa and in skin care services contains some type of chemical.
- With an understanding of chemistry, you will learn how to layer products in services and know how the skin may react with products and services.
- With an understanding of chemistry, you will be able to troubleshoot and solve common problems you may encounter with esthetic services.

Chemistry

Chemistry is the science that deals with the composition, structure, and properties of matter and how matter changes under different conditions. There are two branches of chemistry—organic and inorganic.

Organic chemistry is the study of substances that contain the element carbon. All living things, whether they are plants or animals, contain carbon. Although the term *organic* is often used to mean safe or *natural* because of its association with living things, the term also applies to anything that has ever been alive. Gasoline, plastics, synthetic fabrics, pesticides, and fertilizers are all organic substances. These products are manufactured from natural gas and oil, which are the remains of plants and animals that died millions of years ago. Organic compounds are flammable and will burn.

Inorganic chemistry is the branch of chemistry dealing with compounds that do not contain the element carbon, but may contain the element hydrogen. Inorganic substances are not flammable and will not burn because they do not contain carbon. Inorganic substances are not, and never were, alive. Metals, minerals, glass, pure water, and air are examples of inorganic substances. ☑ L01

Matter

Matter is any substance that occupies space and has mass (weight). All matter has physical and chemical properties and exists in the form of a solid, liquid, or gas. Since matter is made from chemicals, everything made out of matter is a chemical.

Although matter has physical properties that we can touch, taste, smell, or see, not everything that we can see is matter. For instance, we can see visible light and electric sparks, but these are forms of energy, and energy is not matter. Everything known to exist in the universe is either made of matter or energy. There are no exceptions to this rule.

Energy does not occupy space or have physical properties, such as mass (weight). Energy is discussed in Chapter 8, Basics of Electricity.

Elements

An element is the simplest form of chemical matter. It cannot be broken down into a simpler substance without a loss of identity. There are about 90 naturally occurring elements, each with its own distinctive physical and chemical properties. All matter in the universe is made up of one or more of these 90 different elements.

Each element is identified by a letter symbol, such as O for oxygen, C for carbon, H for hydrogen, N for nitrogen, and S for sulfur (Figure 7–2).

▶ Figure 7–2
The periodic table of elements.

1 H Hydrogen 1.0079																	2 He Helium 4.0026
3 Li Lithium 6.941	4 Be Beryllium 9.0122											5 B Boron 10.881	6 C Carbon 12.0107	7 N Nitrogen 14.0067	8 O Oxygen 15.9994	9 F Fluorine 18.9984	10 Ne Neon 20.1797
11 Na Sodium 22.9897	12 Mg Magnesium 24.305											13 Al Aluminum 26.9815	14 Si Silicon 28.0855	15 P Phosphorus 30.9738	16 S Sulfur 32.065	17 Cl Chlorine 35.453	18 Ar Argon 39.948
19 K Potassium 39.098	20 Ca Calcium 40.078	21 Sc Scandium 44.9559	22 Ti Titanium 47.867	23 V Vanadium 50.9415	24 Cr Chromium 51.9961	25 Mn Manganese 54.938	26 Fe Iron 55.845	27 Co Cobalt 58.9332	28 Ni Nickel 58.6934	29 Cu Copper 63.546	30 Zn Zinc 65.409	31 Ga Gallium 69.723	32 Ge Germanium 72.64	33 As Arsenic 74.9216	34 Se Selenium 78.96	35 Br Bromine 79.904	36 Kr Krypton 83.798
37 Rb Rubidium 85.4678	38 Sr Strontium 87.62	39 Y Yttrium 88.9059	40 Zr Zirconium 91.224	41 Nb Niobium 92.9064	42 Mo Molybdenum 95.94	43 Tc Technetium (98)	44 Ru Ruthenium 101.07	45 Rh Rhodium 102.9055	46 Pd Palladium 106.42	47 Ag Silver 107.8682	48 Cd Cadmium 112.411	49 In Indium 114.818	50 Sn Tin 118.71	51 Sb Antimony 121.76	52 Te Tellurium 127.6	53 I Iodine 126.9045	54 Xe Xenon 131.293
55 Cs Cesium 132.9055	56 Ba Barium 137.327		72 Hf Hafnium 178.49	73 Ta Tantalum 180.9479	74 W Tungsten 183.84	75 Re Rhenium 186.207	76 Os Osmium 190.23	77 Ir Iridium 192.217	78 Pt Platinum 195.078	79 Au Gold 196.9665	80 Hg Mercury 200.59	81 Tl Thallium 204.3833	82 Pb Lead 207.2	83 Bi Bismuth 208.9804	84 Po Polonium (209)	85 At Astatine (210)	86 Rn Radon (222)
87 Fr Francium (223)	88 Ra Radium (226)		104 Rf Rutherfordium (261)	105 Db Dubnium (262)	106 Sg Seaborgium (266)	107 Bh Bohrium (264)	108 Hs Hassium (277)	109 Mt Meitnerium (268)	110 Ds Darmstadtium (271)	111 Rg Roentgenium (272)	112 Uub Ununbium (277)						
			57 La Lanthanum 138.9055	58 Ce Cenium 140.116	59 Pr Praseodymium 140.9077	60 Nd Neodymium 144.24	61 Pm Promethium (145)	62 Sm Samarium 150.36	63 Eu Europium 151.964	64 Gd Gadolinium 157.25	65 Tb Terbium 158.9253	66 Dy Dysprosium 162.5	67 Ho Holmium 164.9303	68 Er Erbium 167.259	69 Tm Thulium 168.9342	70 Yb Ytterbium 173.04	71 Lu Lutetium 174.967
			89 Ac Actinium 227.03	90 Th Thorium 232.0381	91 Pa Protactinium 231.0359	92 U Uranium 238.0289	93 Np Neptunium (237)	94 Pu Plutonium (244)	95 Am Americium (243)	96 Cm Curium (247)	97 Bk Berkelium (247)	98 Cf Californium (251)	99 Es Einsteinium (252)	100 Fm Fermium (257)	101 Md Mendelevium (258)	102 No Nobelium (259)	103 Lr Lawrencium (262)

Atoms

Atoms are the particles from which all matter is composed. An atom is the smallest particle of an element that still retains the properties of that element.

The atoms of each element are different in structure from the atoms of all other elements. The structural differences of the 90 different atoms account for the 90 different elements and their distinct properties. All the atoms of the same element are identical. Atoms cannot be divided into simpler substances by ordinary chemical means. Atoms consist of smaller particles; protons, which have a positive electrical charge; neutrons, with a neutral charge; and electrons, with a negative charge (Figure 7–3). The number of protons in an atom equals the number of electrons.

Carbon Atom

Proton

Neutron

Electron

▲ Figure 7–3
An atom consists of negatively charged electrons, positively charged protons, neutral neutrons, and electrons orbiting the unit.

Molecules

A **molecule** (MAHL-uh-kyool) is formed by joining two or more atoms chemically. For example, water is made from hydrogen atoms and oxygen atoms. Carbon dioxide is made from carbon atoms and oxygen atoms. There are two types of molecules.

- **Elemental molecules** (el-uh-MEN-tuhl MAHL-uuh-kyools) contain two or more atoms of the same element that are united chemically (Figure 7–4). When all the atoms that form a molecule are the same, the molecule is made of the same element, and the molecule is called an elemental molecule. Atmospheric oxygen, in the air we breathe, is the elemental molecule O_2. In the atmosphere, the ozone that protects us from ultraviolet radiation is the elemental molecule O_3.
- **Compound molecules** ((KAHM-pownd MAHL-uh-kyools), also known as **compounds**, are chemical combinations of two or more atoms of different elements that are united chemically. An example would be sodium chloride (NaCl) which is common table salt. It is a chemical compound that contains one atom of the element sodium (Na) and one atom of the element chlorine (Cl) (Figure 7–5). **L02**

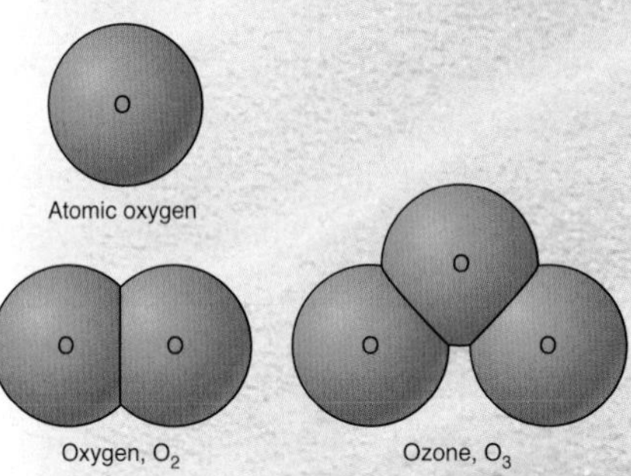

▲ Figure 7–4
Elemental molecules contain two or more atoms of the same element in definite (fixed) proportions.

States of Matter

All matter exists in one of three different physical forms:

- Solid
- Liquid
- Gas

The difference in these physical forms depends on temperature. These

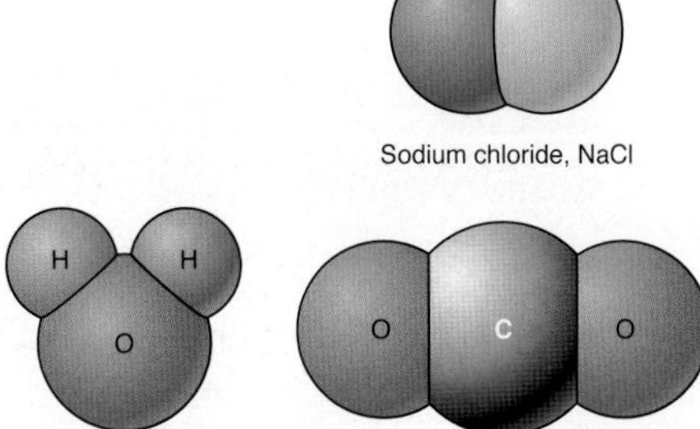

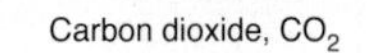

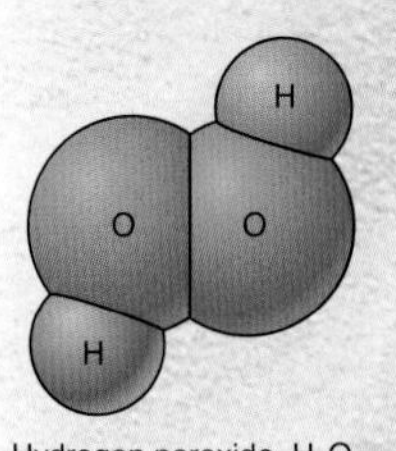

◀ Figure 7–5
Compound molecules contain two or more atoms of different elements in definite (fixed) proportions.

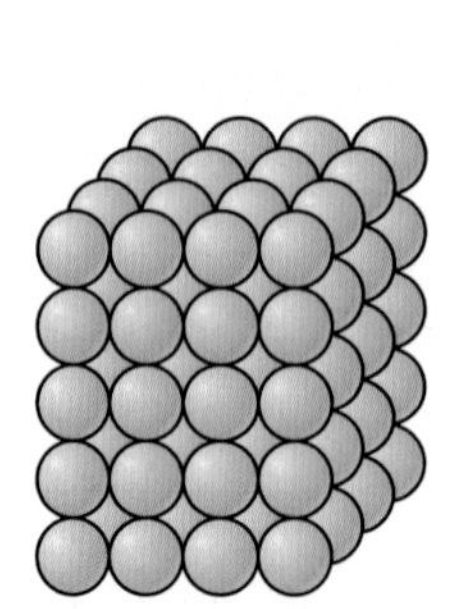

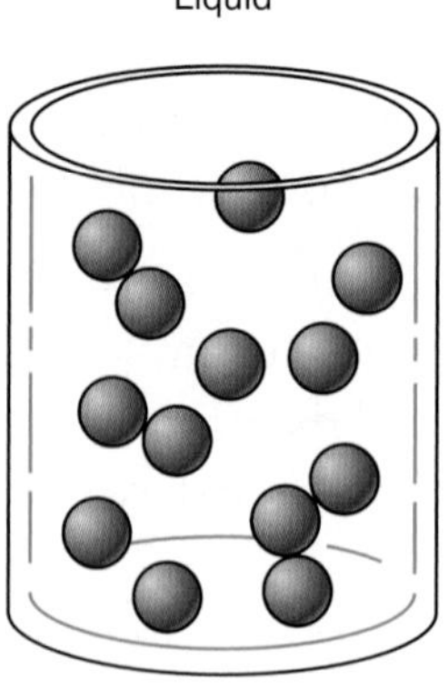

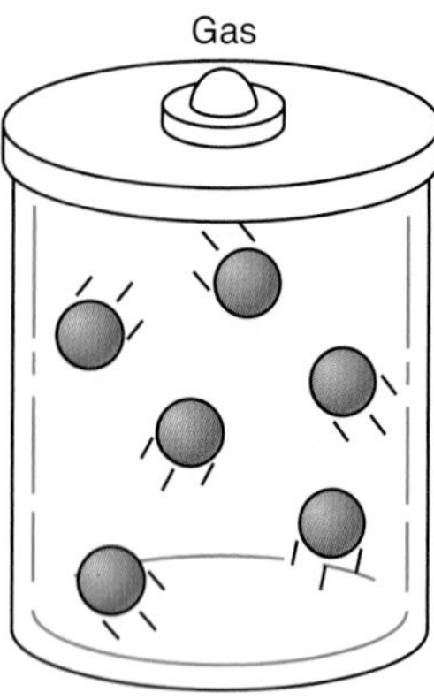

▶ Figure 7–6
The states of matter: solid, liquid, and gas.

Did You Know?

Everything except light and electricity is a chemical. Water is a *chemical.* Using the word chemical to describe something does not mean it is dangerous or harmful. The vast and overwhelming majority of chemicals you come in contact with every day are safe and harmless. Manufacturers are required to list potentially harmful ingredients on their labels.

There is no such thing as a chemical-free product, these types of claims are misleading. Even your body is completely composed of chemicals.

three different physical forms of matter—solid, liquid, gas—are called **states of matter** (Figure 7–6).

Like most other substances, water (H_2O) can exist in all three states of matter, depending on its temperature. Ice turns to water as it melts, and water turns to steam as it boils. The form of water is different due to a change of state, but it is still water (H_2O). It is not a different chemical. It is the same chemical in a different physical form. This is called a physical change.

The three different states of matter have the following distinct characteristics (Table 7–1):

- **Solids** have a definite size (volume) and a definite shape. Ice is an example of a solid. Ice has a definite size and shape. Ice is solid water (H_2O) at a temperature of less than 32 degrees Fahrenheit (0 degrees Celsius).
- **Liquids** have a definite size (volume) but not a definite shape. Liquids take on the shape of the container they are in. Water is an example of a liquid. Water has a definite size, but it does not have a definite shape. Water is a liquid (H_2O) at a temperature between 32 degrees Fahrenheit (0 degrees Celsius) and 211 degrees Fahrenheit (100 degrees Celsius).
- **Gases** do not have a definite size (volume) or a definite shape. Steam is an example of a gas. Steam does not have a definite size or a definite shape. Steam is gaseous water (H_2O) at a temperature above 212 Fahrenheit (100 degrees Celsius).

STATES OF MATTER		
STATE	**DESCRIPTION**	**EXAMPLES**
Solid	Rigid fixed shape and volume	Ice, brushes, chair
Liquid	Definite volume but takes shape of container	Water, cleansers, serums
Gas	No fixed volume or shape; takes shape and volume of container	Steams/vapor, propane, ozone

▲ Table 7–1 **States of Matter.**

Physical and Chemical Properties of Matter

Every substance has unique physical and chemical properties that allow us to identify it.

Physical properties are characteristics that can be determined without a chemical reaction and that do not cause a chemical change in the identity of the substance. Physical properties include color, odor, weight, density, specific gravity, melting point, boiling point, and hardness.

Chemical properties are characteristics that can be determined only with a chemical reaction and that cause a chemical change in the identity of the substance. Rusting iron and burning wood are examples of a change in chemical properties. In both of these examples, the chemical reaction known as **oxidation**, the addition of oxygen or the loss of hydrogen, creates a chemical change in the identity of the substance. The iron is chemically changed to rust, and the wood is chemically changed to ash.

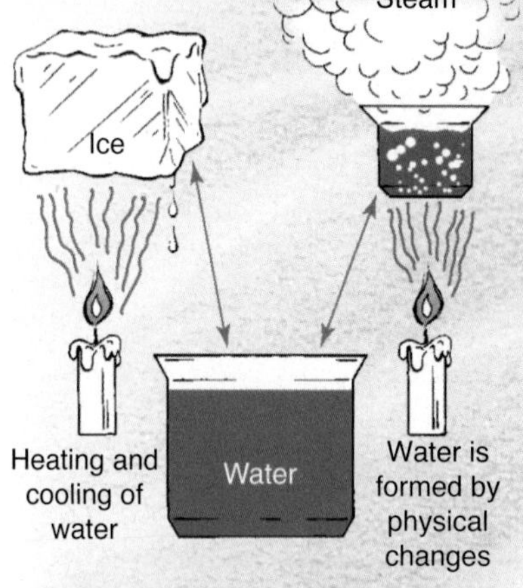

▲ Figure 7–7
Physical changes.

Physical and Chemical Changes

Matter can be changed in two different ways: physically and chemically.

- A **physical change** is a change in the form or physical properties of a substance without the formation of a new substance. There is no chemical reaction involved, and no new chemicals are formed. A change in the state of matter is an example of a physical change. Solid ice undergoes a physical change when it melts into liquid water (Figure 7–7).
- A **chemical change** is a change in the chemical composition of a substance, in which a new substance or substances are formed having properties different from the original. It is the result of a chemical reaction (Figure 7–8). As previously described (iron into rust, wood into ash), oxidation is an example of a chemical reaction that causes a chemical change. ☑ L03

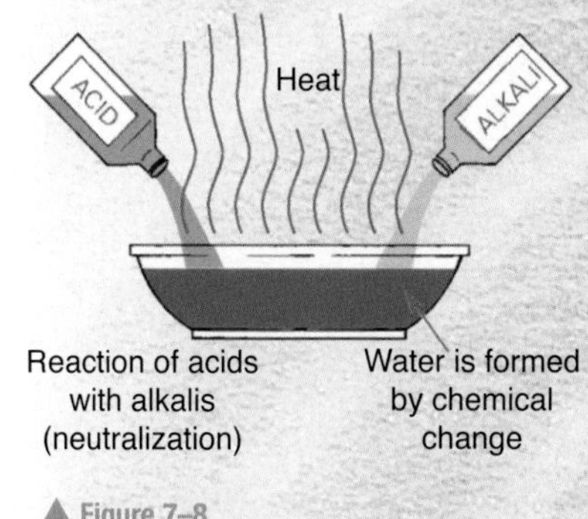

▲ Figure 7–8
Chemical changes.

Properties of Common Elements, Chemical Compounds, and Physical Mixtures

A familiarity with the properties of some of the most common elements, chemical compounds, and physical mixtures can help you understand why certain cosmetic products act the way they do. **Chemical compounds** are a combination of two or more atoms of different elements united chemically with a fixed chemical composition, definite proportions, and distinct properties. **Physical mixtures** are a combination of two or more substances that are united physically, in any proportions with combined properties.

Hydrogen (H) is a colorless, odorless, tasteless gas and is the lightest element known. It is found in chemical combination with oxygen in water and with other elements in most organic substances. Elemental hydrogen is flammable and explosive when mixed with air.

Oxygen (O), the most abundant element found on earth, is a colorless, odorless, tasteless gas. It comprises about half of the Earth's crust, half of the

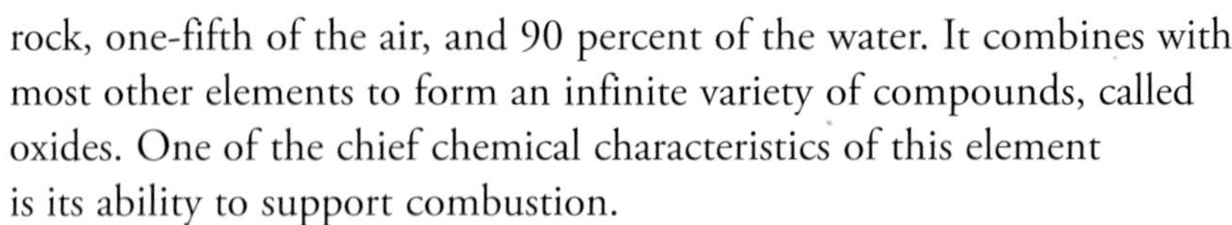

rock, one-fifth of the air, and 90 percent of the water. It combines with most other elements to form an infinite variety of compounds, called oxides. One of the chief chemical characteristics of this element is its ability to support combustion.

Nitrogen (N) is a colorless, gaseous element. It makes up about four-fifths of the air in our atmosphere and is found chiefly in the form of ammonia and nitrates.

Air is the gaseous mixture that makes up the Earth's atmosphere. It is odorless, colorless, and generally consists of about 1 part oxygen and 4 parts nitrogen by volume. It also contains a small amount of carbon dioxide, ammonia, and organic matter, which are all essential to plant and animal life.

Water (H_2O) is the most abundant of all substances, comprising about 75 percent of the Earth's surface and about 65 percent of the human body. Water is seldom pure. Natural spring water contains dissolved minerals, bacteria, and other substances.

Water makes up a large part of the skin. All cells require water to live, and even dying cells in the upper layer of the skin contain water. Water is also the most commonly used cosmetic ingredient. It replenishes moisture on the surface of the skin, helps keep other ingredients in solution, and helps spread products across the skin.

Hydrogen peroxide (H_2O_2), a chemical compound of hydrogen and oxygen, is a colorless liquid with a characteristic odor and a slightly acid taste. There are many uses for hydrogen peroxide in spas, salons, and skin care clinics. In haircoloring developers, for example, the solution known as a 20-volume peroxide is a solution of 6 percent hydrogen peroxide; and 10-volume peroxide is a solution of 3 percent hydrogen peroxide and can be used as an antiseptic.

Potential Hydrogen (pH)

Danish biochemist Soren Sorensen invented the pH scale for measuring the acidity of a substance in 1909. The **pH scale** is a measure of the acidity and alkalinity of a substance; the pH scale has a range of 0 to 14, with 7 being neutral. A pH below 7 is an acidic solution; a pH above 7 is an alkaline solution.

The **pH** (potential hydrogen) of a substance is its relative degree of acidity or alkalinity and is measured on a scale of 0 to 14. Notice that the term pH is written with a small p (which represents a quantity) and a capital H (which represents the hydrogen ion). The symbol pH represents the quantity of hydrogen ions. Understanding pH and how it affects the hair, skin, and nails is essential to understanding all salon and spa services.

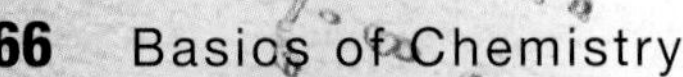

Water and pH

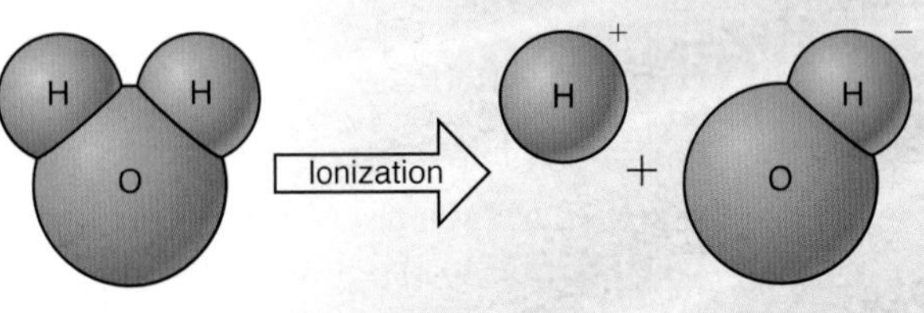

▲ Figure 7–9
Ionization.

Understanding pH requires that we learn the term *ion*. An **ion** (EYE-on) is an atom or molecule that carries an electrical charge. **Ionization** (eye-on-ih-ZAY-shun) causes an atom or molecule to split in two, creating a pair of ions with opposite electrical charges. An ion with a negative electrical charge is an **anion** (AN-eye-on). An ion with a positive electrical charge is a **cation** (KAT-eye-on).

In water, some of the water (H_20) molecules naturally ionize into hydrogen ions and **hydroxide** ions, which is an anion with one oxygen and one hydrogen atom. The pH scale measures ions (Figure 7–9). The hydrogen ion (H^+) is acidic. The more hydrogen ions there are in a substance, the more acidic it will be. The hydroxide ion (OH^-) is alkaline. The more hydroxide ions there are in a substance, the more alkaline it will be. pH is only possible because of this ionization of water. Only products that contain water can have a pH.

In pure (distilled) water, each water molecule that ionizes produces one hydrogen ion and one hydroxide ion. Pure water has a neutral pH because it contains the same number of hydrogen ions as hydroxide ions. It is an equal balance of 50 percent acid and 50 percent alkaline. The pH of any substance is always a balance of both acidity and alkalinity. As acidity increases, alkalinity decreases. The opposite is also true; as alkalinity increases, acidity decreases (Figure 7–10). Even the strongest acid also contains some alkalinity.

CAUTION!

As estheticians, we must safeguard our hands while using various chemicals, peels, and products with varying pH levels. Make certain to wear gloves and follow manufacturer's recommendations for using products both for treatments and services, and for disinfecting.

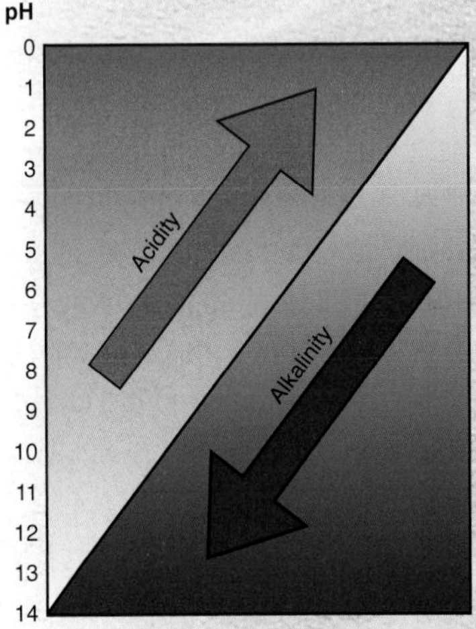

▲ Figure 7–10
Each step in the pH scale represents a tenfold change in pH.

Acids and Alkalis

Acids are substances that have a pH below 7.0, taste sour, and turn litmus paper from blue to red. The lower the pH number, the greater the degree of acidity. **Alkalis**, also known as **bases**, have a pH above 7.0, taste bitter, and turn litmus paper from red to blue. The higher the pH number, the greater the degree of alkalinity (Figure 7–11). A pH of 7 is a neutral solution.

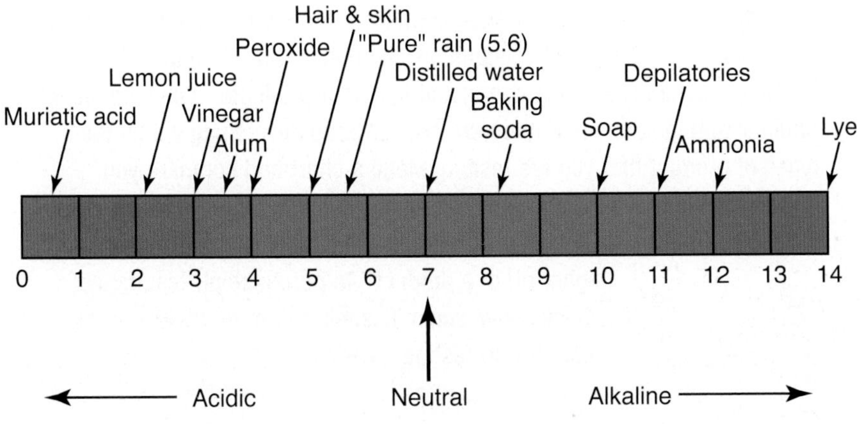

◀ Figure 7–11
The pH scale.

Did You Know?

It is important to have products contain the proper pH for a given skin type. For example, if a client has dry dehydrated skin, giving that client a product that is too acidic could further dry and irritate their skin. Conversely, if a client has an oily skin type, a product that is slightly alkaline may contribute to oil and sebum buildup and possibly create acne. This client may need a more acidic pH to their product.

The natural pH of the skin is slightly acidic at 5.5. The skin produces both sebum and sweat to create a barrier on the skin's surface known as the acid mantle. The **acid mantle** is a protective barrier against certain forms of bacteria and other microorganisms. We can influence our clients by selecting and using products that are developed for their skin type and condition.

pH and Skin Care Products

When the skin is exposed to extremes in pH levels, dryness, dehydration, inflammation, and even bacteria can grow if the product is incorrect for a given skin type. It is important to give a client with an oily skin type a product that will help reduce oil and bacteria, rather than have them use the same product as their friend who may have very dry skin, for instance. The pH will be slightly different in these two products. It is important to note that while many estheticians cross over in product lines, using a cleanser from one line and a serum from another, it may not be beneficial to the skin as pH values can differ from line to line and might have different delivery systems within the ingredients. Additionally, it is important to layer products from the lowest viscosity to the highest. For example, the following products would be applied in this order: a light serum or ampoule, a lotion, then a cream. Products that are heavier, such as creams, may have larger molecules, varying pH values, and could potentially block a product from penetrating into the skin and therefore should be applied last. ✓ L04

Even at levels that are not nearly as severe, extreme variations in pH can damage the skin's barrier function and cause irritation. Buffering agents are frequently added to skin care products to maintain the pH at the correct level to produce the desired effect while keeping the product safe and nonirritating to the skin. This is why it is important for estheticians to understand the chemistry of products and to make selections based on the skin type and condition being treated.

Did You Know?

The pH scale is a **logarithmic scale**. This means that in a pH scale, a change of one whole number represents a tenfold change in pH. A pH of 8 is 10 times more alkaline than a pH of 7. A change of two whole numbers indicates a change of 10 times 10, or a hundredfold change. A pH of 9 is 100 times more alkaline than a pH of 7.

ACTIVITY

For a product to have a pH, it must contain water. Cleaners, toners, serums, and moisturizers have a pH. Search on-line under "pH test papers", purchase some pH testing papers, and test your products. Document your findings and look to see if there are any patterns developing within the types of product that you are testing. Make a chart and compare your findings with what your classmates found. How will the pH of these various products affect the skin? What skin types will require lower pH versus a higher pH in a product? To purchase pH test papers check www. scientificsonline.com or www.enasco. com for pH testing papers.

pH WORKSHEET FORM				
NORMAL	DRY	OILY	COMBINATION	SENSITIVE
Product name & pH level	Product name & pH level	Product name & pH level	Product name & pH level	Product name & pH level
NORMAL	DRY	OILY	COMBINATION	SENSITIVE
Product name & pH level	Product name & pH level	Product name & pH level	Product name & pH level	Product name & pH level

Table 7–2 **pH Worksheet Form.**

Testing pH in Products

As an esthetician, it is helpful to learn to test the pH in products regularly when you are considering what to buy for your salon, spa, clinic, or for research. This is a great habit to begin as a student. Refer to Table 7–2 as a sample worksheet to chart your findings. Look for patterns in the pH of products for various skin types, and then test how they perform. Begin testing products with your classmates, and then continue that practice once you have clients of your own. Ask yourself: Is the product well tolerated by my client? Is the product made for oily skin more acidic? Is the product made for dry skin more alkaline? Document your findings. ☑ **LO5**

Chemical Reactions

Two types of chemical reactions are of importance to estheticians because they explain how skin care products work. They are acid-alkali neutralization reactions and oxidation-reduction reactions.

Acid-alkali neutralization reactions occur when an acid is mixed with an alkali, also called a base, in equal proportions to neutralize each other

Did You Know?

When you see a rusty nail, tarnish on a silver spoon, or corrosion on metal, you are observing oxidation.

and form water (H_2O) and a salt. For example, hydrochloric acid (HCl) reacts with sodium hydroxide (NaOH) to form sodium chloride (NaCl) which is common table salt, and water (H_2O). These are examples of acid-alkali neutralization reactions.

Oxidation-reduction, also known as **redox**, is a chemical reaction in which the oxidizing agent is reduced and the reducing agent is oxidized. An *oxidizing agent* is a substance that releases oxygen. Hydrogen peroxide (H_2O_2) is an example of an oxidizing agent. Hydrogen peroxide can be thought of as water with an extra atom of oxygen. When hydrogen peroxide is mixed with haircolor, facial bleaching cream, or brow tint, oxygen is added to the preparation and thus it becomes oxidized. At the same time, oxygen is subtracted from the hydrogen peroxide and the hydrogen peroxide is reduced. In this example, the haircolor, the facial bleach, or the brow tint is a reducing agent. Redox reactions are always an exchange. When a substance is oxidized, the oxidizer is always reduced. A **reduction** is the subtraction of oxygen or the addition of hydrogen. The chemical reaction is called a **redox reaction**.

Web Resources

For some fun with chemistry, check out these Web sites:

www.chem4kids.com (This is not just for kids!)

www.ehow.com

www.scienceclarified.com

www.answers.com

www.wisegeek.com

www.kangenwaterreport.com

Oxidation reactions can take place without oxygen. Oxidation also can occur when hydrogen is subtracted from a substance. Thus, oxidation is the result of either the addition of oxygen, or the subtraction of hydrogen. Reduction can also occur when hydrogen is added to a substance. Consequently, reduction is the result of either the loss of oxygen or the addition of hydrogen. The desired chemical changes created by processing of haircolors, facial bleaching creams, or brow tinting products would not be possible without oxidation–reduction (redox) reactions.

Combustion is the rapid oxidation of a substance, accompanied by the production of heat and light. Lighting a match is an example of rapid oxidation. You cannot have a fire without oxygen.

Did You Know?

The sugar in grapes is chemically converted into ethyl alcohol by certain types of yeast when wine is fermented in a wooden vat. This is an example of a chemical reaction.

As estheticians, we learn about the process of oxidation by using antioxidants in skin care products. **Antioxidants** are used to stabilize skin care products by preventing oxidation that would otherwise cause a product to turn rancid and decompose. They are vitamins such as A, C, and E, which can be applied topically in products or taken internally to increase healthy body functions.

Antioxidants prevent oxidation by neutralizing **free radicals**. Free radicals are *super* oxidizers that cause an oxidation reaction and produce a new free radical in the process. Because they are created by highly reactive atoms or molecules (often oxygen), free radicals are unstable. If left alone they will create inflammation, damage DNA, and eventually cause disease and death. One free radical can **oxidize** (combine or cause a substance to combine with oxygen) millions of other substances. Antioxidants are free radical scavengers that stop the oxidation reaction from continuing.

SOLUTIONS, SUSPENSIONS, AND EMULSIONS		
SOLUTIONS	**SUSPENSIONS**	**EMULSIONS**
Miscible	Slightly miscible	Immiscible
No surfactant	No surfactant	Surfactant
Small particles	Larger particles	Largest particles
Usually clear	Usually cloudy	Usually a solid color
Stable mixture	Unstable mixture	Limited stability through an emulsifier
Example: solution of hydrogen peroxide	Example: calamine lotion	Example: shampoos and conditioners

Table 7–3 **Solutions, Suspensions, and Emulsions.**

Chemistry as Applied to Cosmetics

To better serve their clients, estheticians should have an understanding of the chemical composition, preparation, and uses of cosmetics that are intended to cleanse and beautify the skin. Most of the products an esthetician uses are solutions, suspensions, and emulsions.

Solutions, Suspensions, and Emulsions

Solutions, suspensions, and emulsions are all physical mixtures of two or more different substances (Table 7–3). The distinction between solutions, suspensions, and emulsions depends on the size of the particles and the solubility of the components.

Solutions

Solutions (soh-LOO-shuns) are stable physical mixtures of two or more substances. A **solute** (SOL-yoot) is any substance that is dissolved by a solvent to form a solution. A **solvent** (SOL-vent) is any substance that dissolves the solute to form a solution.

Miscible (MIS-eh-bel) liquids are mutually soluble. Water and alcohol are examples of miscible (mixable) liquids. **Immiscible** liquids are not mutually soluble (Figure 7–12). Water and oil are examples of immiscible (nonmixable) liquids. You have probably heard the saying, "oil and water don't mix."

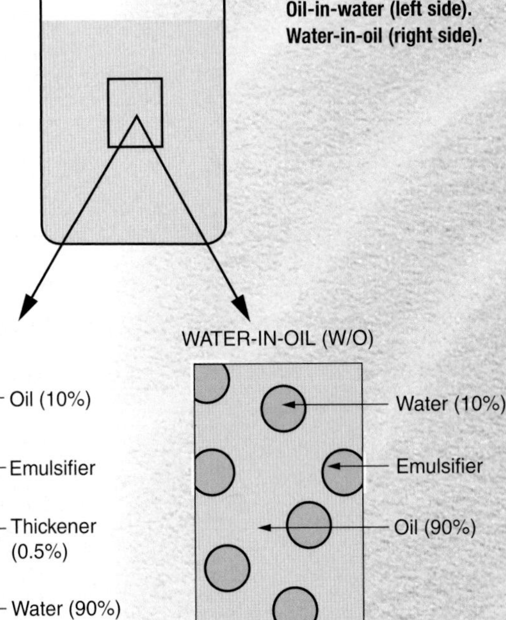

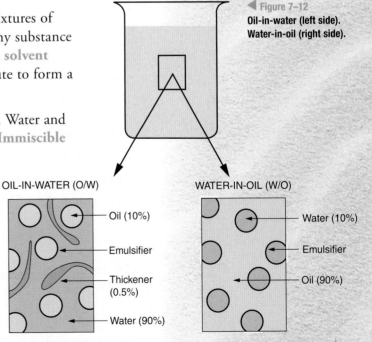

Figure 7–12 **Oil-in-water (left side). Water-in-oil (right side).**

Solutions contain particles the size of a small molecule that are invisible to the naked eye. Solutions are usually transparent, although they may be colored. Solutions do not separate on standing. Salt water is a solution of a solid dissolved in a liquid. Water is the solvent that dissolves the salt and holds it in solution. Air, salt water, and hydrogen peroxide are examples of solutions.

Suspensions

Suspensions are uniform mixtures of two or more substances. Suspensions differ from solutions due to the size of the particles. Suspensions contain larger particles than solutions do. The particles in a suspension are large enough to be visible to the naked eye. Suspensions are not usually transparent and may be colored. Suspensions have a tendency to separate over time.

Oil and vinegar salad dressing is an example of a suspension with oil suspended in vinegar. Salad dressing will separate on standing and should be shaken well before use. Salad dressing, paint, and aerosol hair spray are examples of suspensions.

Emulsions

Emulsions (ee-MUL-shuns) are mixtures of two or more immiscible substances united with the aid of an emulsifier. The term *emulsify* means "to form an emulsion," with one liquid dispersed in another. Although emulsions tend to separate over time, a properly formulated emulsion, when stored correctly, should be stable for at least 3 years. Without adequate dispersion, emulsions can become unstable over time and break (separate) into two insoluble layers. Once this occurs, the emulsion should usually be discarded. ✔ L06

Surfactants

Surfactants (sur-FAK-tants) are used to emulsify oil and water to create an emulsion. The word *surfactant* is an acronym for surface active agent. Surfactants are able to wet the skin and emulsify oil and water. A surfactant molecule has two distinct parts that make the emulsification of oil and water possible (Figure 7–13). One end of the surfactant molecule is **hydrophilic** (water loving), and the other end is **lipophilic** (oil loving). Since "like dissolves like," the hydrophilic end dissolves in water and the lipophilic end dissolves in oil, so, a surfactant molecule dissolves in both oil and water and joins them together to form an emulsion.

Most skin care products are emulsions of oil and water. Two types of emulsions are used in cosmetic preparations: oil-in-water (O/W) and

▲ Figure 7–13
A surfactant molecule.

water-in-oil (W/O). As a skin moisturizer, the purpose of an emulsion is to apply a uniform layer of the emulsion's oil phase evenly on the skin. Once contact is made with the skin, the oil phase is deposited on the surface. The oil phase acts as an external lubricant to smooth and protect the surface of the epidermis. The water phase restores the natural moisture content of the epidermis, making the skin soft and smooth. Thus, the water in the emulsion acts as an internal lubricant. One advantage of O/W emulsions is that they are easily rinsed away with water. An O/W cleansing lotion, for example, can be removed easily with wet cotton pads or sponges.

O/W emulsions are often milky, free-flowing liquids, although thickeners may be added to form gels or thick creams. O/W emulsions include moisturizing and cleansing lotions.

Oil-in-Water (O/W) Emulsions

In an **oil-in-water (O/W) emulsion**, droplets of oil are dispersed in water. The droplets of oil (micelles) are surrounded by surfactants with their "tails" (lipophilic ends) pointing in and their "heads" (hydrophilic ends) pointing out, which keeps the oil dispersed in water. In O/W emulsions, the water is the continuous or external phase and the oil is the discontinuous or internal phase (**Figure 7–14**). O/W emulsions usually contain a small amount of oil and a greater amount of water. Salons and spas primarily use O/W emulsions.

Did You Know?

Soaps were the first synthetic surfactants. Soaps were made more than 5,000 years ago by boiling oil or animal fat with wood ashes. Modern soaps are made from animal, vegetable, or synthetic fats or oils by a process called *saponification.* Traditional bar soaps are highly alkaline and combine with the minerals in hard water to form an insoluble film that coats skin and can cause hands to feel dry, itchy, and irritated. Modern synthetic surfactants have overcome these disadvantages and are superior to soaps; many are milder on the skin than soaps used in the past.

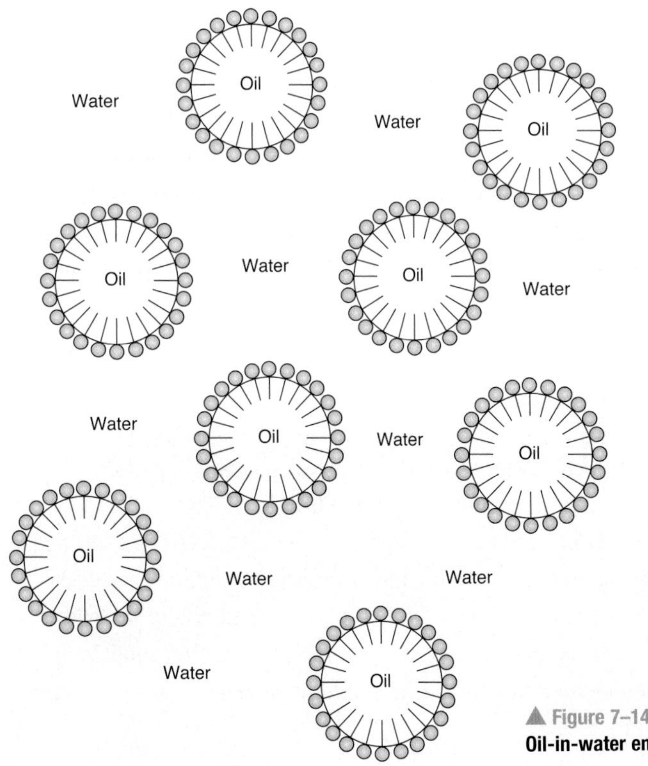

▲ **Figure 7–14**
Oil-in-water emulsion.

▶ Figure 7–15
Water-in-oil emulsion.

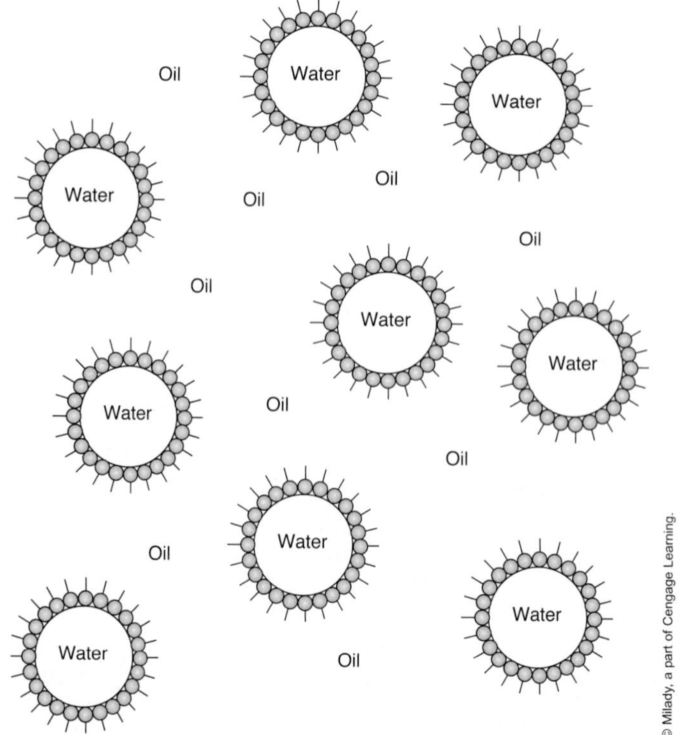

ACTIVITY

Experiment: Water-in-oil emulsion, Oil-in-water emulsion

Pour water into one glass, and olive oil into another glass. Put two drops olive oil into the water glass, and mix. Then add two drops of water to the glass of olive oil, and mix. Which mixture is a W/O emulsion, and which one is an O/W emulsion?

Water-in-Oil (W/O) Emulsions

In a **water-in-oil (W/O) emulsion**, droplets of water are dispersed in oil. The droplets of water (inverse micelles) are surrounded by surfactants with their "heads" (hydrophilic ends) pointing in and their "tails" (lipophilic ends) pointing out. In W/O emulsions, the oil is the continuous or external phase and the water is the discontinuous, or internal phase (Figure 7–15).

Water-in-oil emulsions usually contain a smaller amount of water and a greater amount of oil. W/O emulsions are heavier, greasier, and more water resistant than O/W emulsions because the oil is in the external phase. These emulsions remove grime and help prevent moisture loss from the skin. Examples include cleansing creams, cold creams, night creams, massage creams, baby creams, suntan lotions, and hair-grooming creams.

Did You Know?

Mayonnaise is an oil-in-water emulsion of two immiscible liquids. Although oil and water are immiscible, the egg yolk in mayonnaise emulsifies the oil and disperses it uniformly in the water. Without the egg yolk as an emulsifying agent, the oil and water would separate into two insoluble layers. Mayonnaise should not separate on standing. Many of the lotions and creams used by estheticians are oil-in-water emulsions. Mayonnaise, skin cleansers, moisturizers, and body washes are examples of oil-in-water emulsions.

Review Questions

1. Define chemistry.
2. What is the difference between organic and inorganic chemistry?
3. Define matter.
4. What are the differences between solids, liquids, and gases?
5. Define element.
6. What are atoms?
7. Define molecule.
8. What is the difference between a chemical compound and a physical mixture?
9. What are physical properties? How are they different from chemical properties?
10. How can matter be changed? Give an example of each kind of change.
11. Describe hydrogen, oxygen, and nitrogen.
12. How is water important in skin care?
13. Define pH. Why do you need to know the pH of products you work with?
14. Define oxidation and reduction.
15. Explain the differences between solutions, suspensions, and emulsions.
16. Explain the structure of the two types of emulsion products used in skin care.
17. What types of products are made with oil-in-water (O/W) emulsions? With water-in-oil (W/O) emulsions?

Glossary

acid mantle	Protective barrier of lipids and secretions on the surface of the skin.
acid-alkali neutralization reactions	When an acid is mixed with an alkali in equal proportions to neutralize each other and form water (H_2O) and a salt.
acids	Substances that have a pH below 7.0, taste sour, and turn litmus paper from blue to red.
air	The gaseous mixture that makes up the Earth's atmosphere. It is odorless, colorless, and generally consists of about 1 part oxygen and 4 parts nitrogen by volume.
alkalis	Also known as *bases*; compounds that react with acids to form salts; have a pH above 7.0 (neutral), taste bitter, and turn litmus paper from red to blue.
anion	An ion with a negative electrical charge.
antioxidants	Used to stabilize skin care products by preventing oxidation that would otherwise cause a product to turn rancid and decompose. They are vitamins such as A, C, and E, which can be applied topically in products or taken internally to increase healthy body functions.
atoms	The smallest chemical components (often called particles) of an element that still retains the properties of that element.
cation	Ion with a positive electrical charge.
chemical change	Change in the chemical properties of a substance that is the result of a chemical reaction in which a new substance or substances are formed that have properties different from the original.

Glossary

chemical compounds	Combinations of two or more atoms of different elements united chemically with a fixed chemical composition, definite proportions, and distinct properties.
chemical properties	Those characteristics that can only be determined by a chemical reaction and a chemical change in the identity of the substance.
chemistry	Science that deals with the composition, structures, and properties of matter and how matter changes under different conditions.
combustion	Rapid oxidation of any substance, accompanied by the production of heat and light.
compound molecules	Also known as *compounds*; a chemical combination of two or more atoms of different elements in definite (fixed) proportions.
element	The simplest form of matter; cannot be broken down into a simpler substance without loss of identity.
elemental molecules	Molecule containing two or more atoms of the same element in definite (fixed) proportions.
emulsions	An unstable physical mixture of two or more immiscible substances (substances that normally will not stay blended) plus a special ingredient called an emulsifier.
free radicals	Unstable molecules that cause inflammation, disease, and biochemical aging in the body, especially wrinkling and sagging of the skin. Free radicals are super oxidizers that cause an oxidation reaction and produce a new free radical in the process that are created by highly reactive atoms or molecules (often oxygen).
gases	Matter without a definite shape or size. No fixed volume or shape; takes the shape of its container.
hydrogen	Colorless, odorless, tasteless gas; the lightest element known.
hydrogen peroxide	Chemical compound of hydrogen and oxygen; a colorless liquid with a characteristic odor and a slightly acid taste.
hydrophilic	Easily absorbs moisture; in chemistry terms, capable of combining with or attracting water (water-loving).
hydroxide	An anion (an ion with a negative electrical charge) with one oxygen and one hydrogen atom.
immiscible	Liquids that are not capable of being mixed together to form stable solutions.
inorganic chemistry	The study of substances that do not contain the element carbon, but may contain the element hydrogen.
ion	An atom or molecule that carries an electrical charge.
ionization	The separation of an atom or molecule into positive or negative ions.
lipophilic	Having an affinity for or an attraction to fat and oils (oil-loving).
liquids	Matter that has volume, no definite shape and will take shape of its container, such as water.
logarithmic scale	A method of displaying data in multiples of 10.
matter	Any substance that occupies space and has mass (weight).
miscible	Capable of being mixed; liquids that are mutually soluble, meaning that they can be mixed together to form stable solutions.

Glossary

molecule	A chemical combination of two or more atoms.
nitrogen	A colorless gaseous element that makes up about four-fifths of the air in our atmosphere and is found chiefly in ammonia and nitrates.
oil-in-water (O/W) emulsion	Oil droplets dispersed in a water with the aid of an emulsifying agent.
organic chemistry	Study of substances that contain carbon.
oxidation	Either the addition of oxygen or the loss of hydrogen; a chemical reaction that combines a substance with oxygen to produce an oxide.
oxidation-reduction	Also known as *redox*; chemical reaction in which the oxidizing agent is reduced and the reducing agent is oxidized.
oxidize	To combine or cause a substance to combine with oxygen.
oxygen	The most abundant element on Earth.
pH	The abbreviation used for potential hydrogen; relative degree of acidity and alkalinity of a substance. pH represents the quantity of hydrogen ions.
pH scale	A measure of the acidity and alkalinity of a substance; the pH scale has a range of 0 to 14, with 7 being a neutral. A pH below 7 is an acidic solution; a pH above 7 is an alkaline solution.
physical change	Change in the form or physical properties of a substance without a chemical reaction or the formation of a new substance.
physical mixtures	Combination of two or more substances united physically, not chemically, without a fixed composition and in any proportions.
physical properties	Characteristics that can be determined without a chemical reaction and that do not cause a chemical change in the identity of the substance.
redox reactions	Chemical reaction in which the oxidizing agent is reduced and the reducing agent is oxidized.
reduction	The process through which oxygen is subtracted from or hydrogen is added to a substance through a chemical reaction.
solids	A state of matter that is rigid with a definite size and shape, such as ice.
solute	A substance that dissolves the solute to form a solution.
solutions	A uniform mixture of two or more mutually miscible substances.
solvent	A substance that dissolves another substance to form a solution.
states of matter	The three different physical forms of matter: solid, liquid, and gas.
surfactants	Acronym for *surface active agent*; reduce surface tension between the skin and the product to increase product spreadability; allow oil and water to mix, or emulsify.
suspensions	Unstable mixtures of two or more immiscible substances.
water	Most abundant of all substances, comprising about 75 percent of the Earth's surface and about 65 percent of the human body.
water-in-oil (W/O) emulsion	Droplets of water dispersed in an oil.

CHAPTER 8

Basics of Electricity

Chapter Outline

- Why Study Basics of Electricity?
- Electricity
- Electrical Equipment Safety
- Electrotherapy
- Light Energy, Lasers, and LED (Light-Emitting Diode)

Learning Objectives

After completing this chapter, you will be able to:

- ☑ LO1 Define the nature of electricity and the two types of electric current.
- ☑ LO2 Define electrical measurements.
- ☑ LO3 Understand the principles of electrical equipment safety.
- ☑ LO4 Describe the types of electrotherapy and their uses.
- ☑ LO5 Explain electromagnetic radiation and the visible spectrum of light.
- ☑ LO6 Describe what the acronym *laser* stands for.
- ☑ LO7 Describe the colors of light in LED therapy and their benefits for the skin.

Key Terms

Page number indicates where in the chapter the term is used.

active electrode
pg. 186

alternating current (AC)
pg. 182

ampere (A, amp)
pg. 182

anaphoresis
pg. 186

anode
pg. 186

blue light
pg. 193

cataphoresis
pg. 186

cathode
pg. 186

chromophore
pg. 193

circuit breaker
pg. 184

complete electric circuit
pg. 181

conductor
pg. 180

converter
pg. 182

desincrustation
pg. 186

direct current (DC)
pg. 182

electric current
pg. 180

electricity
pg. 180

electrode (probe)
pg. 185

electromagnetic spectrum
pg. 189

electrotherapy
pg. 185

fuse
pg. 183

galvanic current
pg. 186

green light
pg. 193

grounding
pg. 184

inactive electrode
pg. 186

infrared light
pg. 190

insulator (nonconductor)
pg. 181

intense pulse light
pg. 194

invisible light
pg. 190

iontophoresis (ionization)
pg. 186

kilowatt (K)
pg. 183

laser (light amplification stimulation emission of radiation)
pg. 192

LED (light-emitting diode)
pg. 193

light therapy (phototherapy)
pg. 192

microcurrent
pg. 186

milliampere (mA)
pg. 183

modalities
pg. 185

ohm (O)
pg. 183

photothermolysis
pg. 192

plug
pg. 182

polarity
pg. 186

rectifier
pg. 182

red light
pg. 193

Tesla high-frequency current (violet ray)
pg. 188

ultraviolet (UV) radiation
pg. 190

visible light
pg. 190

volt (V, voltage)
pg. 182

watt (W)
pg. 183

wavelength
pg. 190

white light
pg. 191

yellow light
pg. 193

▲ Figure 8–1
Electricity.

Electricity or electrical current powers all of the devices that we use as estheticians. To use equipment and tools effectively and safely, all esthetic professionals need to have a basic working knowledge of electricity. The more we know and understand about electricity and its functions in skin care, the better we can ensure positive outcomes in our services and treatments. Additionally, we can prevent potential electrical problems in the salon, spa, or medical facility (Figure 8–1).

Why Study Basics of Electricity?

Estheticians should study and have a thorough understanding of the basics of electricity as it is a component of many service devices and so that technicians practice proper safety precautions and procedures and do not endanger either themselves or their clients.

- Most facial devices operate with electricity.
- It is important to understand how electricity functions so that you can use your devices safely and appropriately.
- It is important to have a good basic education in electricity as esthetics devices routinely undergo upgrades and improvements, and you will be able to transfer that knowledge to newer versions more easily.

Did You Know?

Electricity travels very fast: 186,000 miles (299,338 km) per second. If you traveled that fast, you could go around the world eight times in the few seconds that it takes you to turn on a light switch.

Did You Know?

One lightning bolt has enough electricity to service 200,000 homes.

Electricity

Lightning on a stormy night is an effect of electricity. If you plug a poorly wired appliance into a socket and sparks fly out, you are also seeing the effects of electricity. You are not really "seeing" electricity, but its visual effects on the surrounding air. Electricity does not occupy space or have physical or chemical properties; therefore, electricity is not matter. If it is not matter, then what is it? **Electricity** (ee-lek-TRIS-ih-tee) is the movement of particles around an atom that creates pure energy. Electricity is a form of energy that, when in motion, exhibits magnetic, chemical, or thermal effects.

An **electric current** (ee-LEK-trik KUR-unt) is the flow of electricity along a conductor in a complete circuit. All materials can be classified as conductors or nonconductors (insulators), depending on how easily an electric current can be transmitted through them.

A **conductor** (kahn-DUK-tur) is any material that easily conducts electricity. This means that electricity will pass through the material easily. Metals are good conductors, and copper is a particularly good conductor used in electric wiring and electric motors. Water makes a good conductor. This explains why one should not swim in a lake during an electrical storm, since the electrical current can pass though the water and electrocute the swimmer.

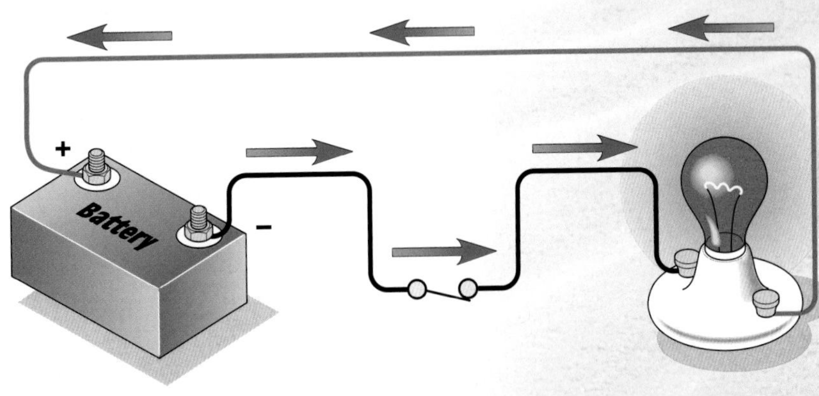

▲ Figure 8–2
A complete direct current (DC) electric circuit.

An **insulator**, also known as **nonconductor** (nahn-kun-DUK-tur), is a substance that does not conduct electricity. Rubber, silk, wood, glass, and cement are good insulators. Electric wires are composed of twisted metal threads (conductor) covered with rubber (insulator). A **complete electric circuit** (SUR-kit) is the path of negative and positive electric currents moving from the generating source through the conductors and back to the generating original source or to the ground (Figure 8–2).

Did You Know?

Hydropower (water-powered) plants today make up our country's largest renewable energy source. Hydropower plants rely on a dam that holds back water and creates a large lake known as a reservoir. The water comes from melting snow from the mountains, traveling via groundwater, creeks, streams and rivers, and of course, rain.

When large doors on the dam open, water flows from the reservoir into a pipe. As the water flows into the pipe it builds up pressure, which turns a turbine (a big disc with blades) attached to a generator. As the turbine blades turn, so do a series of magnets inside the generator. Giant magnets rotate past copper coils, producing alternating current by moving electrons. The alternating current (AC) is converted to a higher-voltage current by a transformer. Going out of the power plant are large wires that become power lines, and the electrical current that is passing through the lines supplies the community with electricity (Figure 8–3).

▼ Figure 8–3
Electricity flow chart.

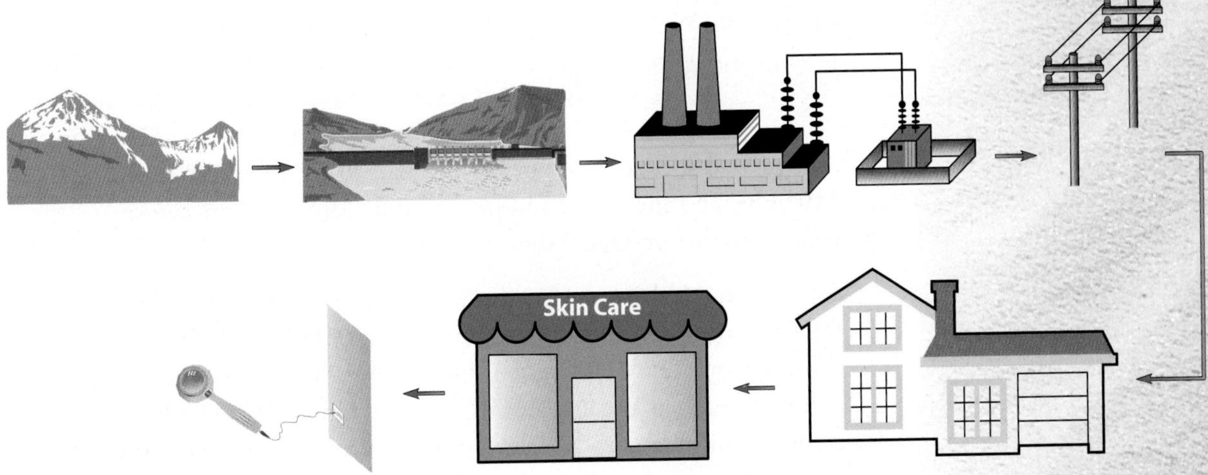

Types of Electric Current

There are two kinds of electric current.

Direct current (DC) is a constant, even-flowing current that travels in one direction only. Flashlights, cellular telephones, and cordless hand-held devices use the direct current produced by batteries. The battery in your car stores direct current electrical energy. Without it, your car would not start in the morning. A **converter** is an apparatus that changes direct current to alternating current. Today, some cars, appliances, and even skin care devices contain converters which allow us to use them without the use of an electrical wall outlet.

Alternating current (AC) is a rapid and interrupted current, flowing first in one direction and then in the opposite direction. This change in direction happens 60 times per second. All devices that use a **plug**, a two- or three-prong connector at the end of an electrical cord, to connect an apparatus into a wall outlet such as corded hair dryers, flat irons, magnifying lamps, and microdermabrasion devices are using alternating current. Alternating current is produced by mechanical generators.

A **rectifier** (REK-ti-fy-ur) is an apparatus that changes alternating current to direct current. Cordless electric clippers and mobile phone chargers use a rectifier to convert the AC current from an electrical wall outlet in a building to the DC current needed to recharge their batteries. ☑ L01

Electrical Measurements

The flow of an electric current can be compared to water flowing through a garden hose. Individual electrons flow through a wire in the same way that individual water molecules flow through a hose.

Did You Know?

THE DIFFERENCE BETWEEN ALTERNATING AND DIRECT CURRENT

Direct Current (DC)	Alternating Current (AC)
• Constant, even flow	• Rapid and interrupted flow
• Travels in one direction	• Travels in two directions

A **volt (V)**, also known as **voltage**, is the unit that measures the pressure or force that pushes the flow of electrons forward through a conductor, much like the water pressure that pushes the water molecules through the hose (Figure 8–4). Without pressure, neither water nor electrons would flow. Car batteries are 12 volts, normal wall sockets that power your hair dryer and curling iron are 110 volts, and most air conditioners and clothes' dryers run on 220 volts. A higher voltage indicates more pressure or force.

An **ampere** (AM-peer) **(A)**, also known as **amp**, is the unit that measures the amount of an electric current (the number of electrons flowing through a conductor). Like a water hose, which must be able to expand as the amount of water flowing through it increases, a conductor must also be large enough to transmit the amount of electrons (amps) that flow through it. A hair dryer rated at 12 amps must have a cord that is twice as thick as one rated at 5 amps to handle the extra amperage, otherwise, the cord might overheat and potentially could start a fire. A higher amp rating indicates a greater number of electrons and a stronger current (Figure 8–5).

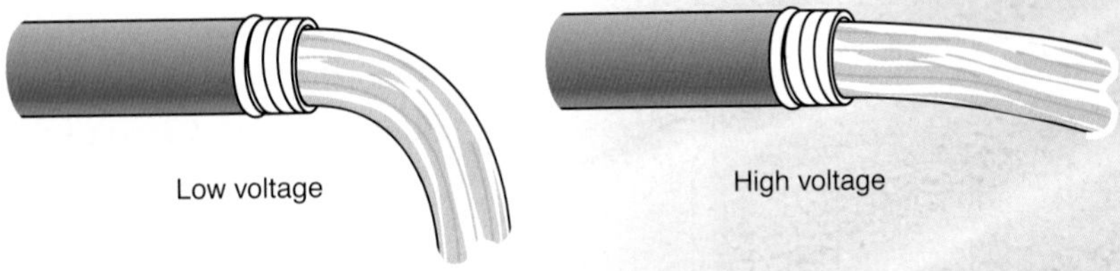

Low voltage

High voltage

▲ Figure 8–4
Volts measure the pressure or force that pushes electrons forward.

A **milliampere (mA)** (mill-ee-AM-peer) is one-thousandth (1/1000) of an ampere. The current for facial and scalp treatments is measured in milliamperes; as reference, an ampere current would be too strong and would damage the skin or body.

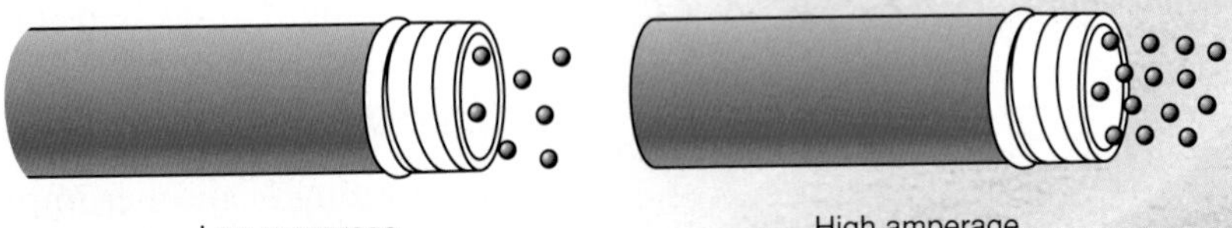

Low amperage

High amperage

▲ Figure 8–5
Amps measure the number of electrons flowing through the wire.

An **ohm (O)** is a unit that measures the resistance of an electric current. Current will not flow through a conductor unless the force (volts) is stronger than the resistance (ohms).

A **watt (W)** is a measurement of how much electric energy is being used in 1 second. A 40-watt light bulb uses 40 watts of energy per second.

A **kilowatt (K)** is 1,000 watts. The electricity in your house is measured in kilowatts per hour (kwh). A 1,000-watt (1-kilowatt) hair dryer uses 1,000 watts of energy per second. ☑ **L02**

Did You Know?

Wattage does not define the brightness of a light bulb; it refers to the amount of electricity consumed while the bulb is being used. Newer bulbs that are more efficient can produce more light using less electricity.

Electrical Equipment Safety

When working with electricity, you must always be concerned with your own safety as well as that of your clients. All electrical equipment should be inspected regularly to determine whether it is in safe working order. Poor electrical connections and overloaded circuits can result in an electrical shock, a burn, or even a serious fire.

Safety Devices

A wire that is not large enough to carry the electrical current passing through it will overheat and possibly cause a fire. There are two electrical safety devices that you may encounter when working in a salon, spa, or medical facility. They are called a fuse and a circuit breaker.

- A **fuse** (FYOOZ) prevents excessive current from passing through a circuit. It is designed to blowout or melt when the wire becomes too hot from overloading the circuit with too much current. This occurs when too many appliances or faulty equipment are connected to an electricity source. This mechanism will automatically shut off your device or appliance. To re-establish the circuit, disconnect the appliance, check all connections and insulation, insert a new fuse, then reconnect the appliance (Figure 8–6).

▲ Figure 8–6
Fuse box.

▲ Figure 8–7
Circuit breaker.

- A **circuit breaker** (SUR-kit BRAYK-ar) is a switch that automatically interrupts or shuts off an electric circuit at the first indication of an overload. Circuit breakers have replaced fuses in modern electric circuits. They have all the safety features of fuses but do not require replacement and can simply be reset. For example, your hair dryer has a circuit breaker located in the electric plug that is designed to protect you and your client in case of an overload or short circuit. When a circuit breaker shuts off, you should disconnect the appliance and check all connections and insulation before resetting it (Figure 8–7).

Grounding

Grounding is another important way of promoting electrical safety. All electrical appliances must have at least two electrical connections. The *live* connection supplies current to the circuit. The *ground* connection completes the circuit and carries the current safely away to the ground. If you look closely at electrical plugs with two rectangular prongs, you will often see that one is slightly larger than the other. This guarantees that the plug can be inserted only one way, and it protects you and your client from electrical shock in the event of a short circuit.

For added protection, some appliances have a third, circular, electrical connection that provides an additional ground. This extra ground is designed to guarantee a safe path for electricity if the first ground fails or is improperly connected. Appliances with a third circular ground offer the most protection for you and your client (Figure 8–8).

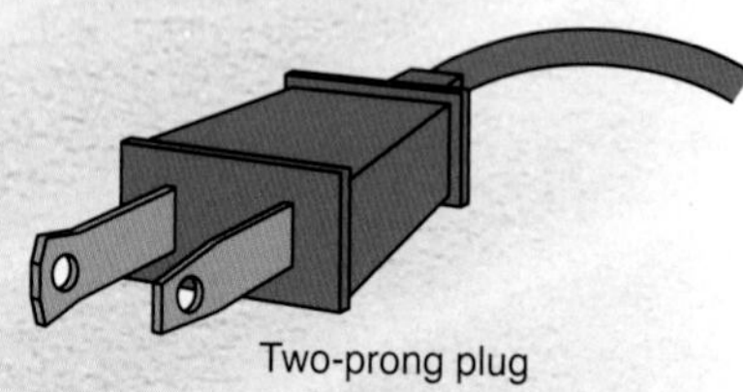

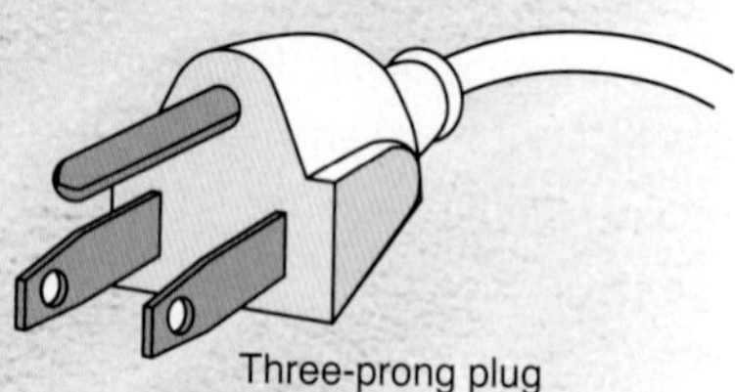

▲ Figure 8–8
Two-prong and three-prong plugs.

Guidelines for Safe Use of Electrical Equipment

Careful attention to electrical safety helps to eliminate accidents and to ensure greater client satisfaction. The following reminders will help ensure the safe use of electricity.

- All the electrical appliances you use should be UL certified (**Figure 8–9**).
- Read all instructions carefully before using any piece of electrical equipment.
- Disconnect all appliances when not in use.
- Inspect all electrical equipment regularly.
- Keep all wires, plugs, and electrical equipment in good repair.
- Use only one plug to each outlet; overloading may cause the circuit breaker to pop. If more than one plug is needed in an area, use a power strip with a surge protector (Figure 8–10).
- Unplug electrical devices or connections that get hot.

Underwriter's Laboratory

▲ Figure 8–9
UL symbol as it appears on electrical devices. Always check for the UL symbol.

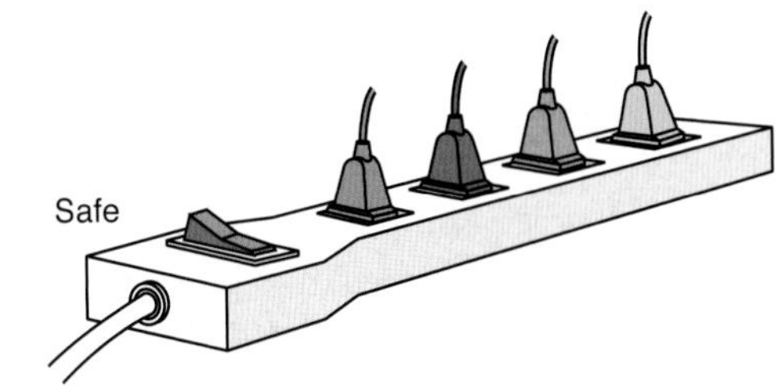

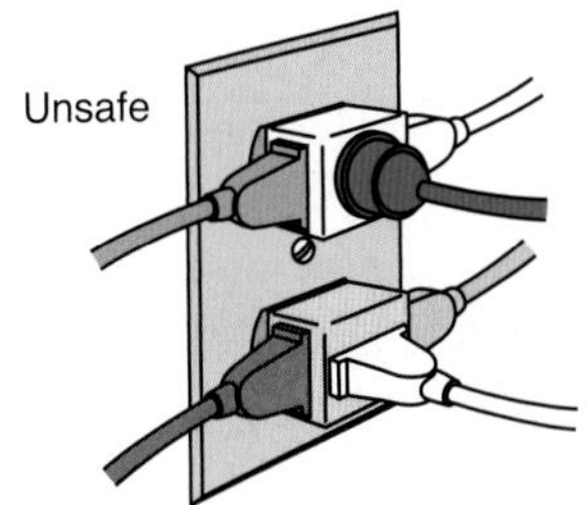

▲ Figure 8–10
Safe and unsafe use of outlets.

CAUTION!

Underwriter's Laboratory (UL®) certifies the safety of electrical appliances. Electric mitts, facial masks, and other tools that are UL approved are certified to be safe when used according to the manufacturer's directions. Always look for the UL symbol on electrical appliances, and take the time to read and follow the manufacturer's directions.

- You and your client should avoid contact with water and metal surfaces when using electricity; do not handle electrical equipment with wet hands.
- Do not leave your client unattended while he or she is connected to an electrical device.
- Keep electrical cords off the floor and away from people's feet; getting tangled in a cord could cause you or your client to trip.
- Do not attempt to clean around electric outlets while equipment is plugged in.
- Do not touch two metal objects at the same time if either is connected to an electric current.
- Do not step on or place objects on electrical cords.
- Do not allow an electrical cord to become twisted; this can cause a short circuit.
- Disconnect appliances by pulling on the plug, not the cord.
- Do not attempt to repair electrical appliances unless you are qualified.
- If you have a problem with electrical wiring or an electrical device or appliance tell your supervisor immediately, take the device in for repair, or call a qualified electrician or repair representative to resolve the issue. ☑ LO3

CAUTION!

Never tamper with wiring or electrical plugs to get them to fit into a receptacle for purposes that they were not designed.

Electrotherapy

Electrical facial treatments are commonly referred to as **electrotherapy**. These treatments are often called **modalities**. Each modality produces a different effect on the skin.

An **electrode**, or **probe**, is an applicator for directing the electric current from the device to the client's skin. It is usually made of carbon, glass, or metal. Each modality (except for Tesla high frequency) requires two electrodes—one negative and one positive—to conduct the flow of electricity through the body (Figure 8–11).

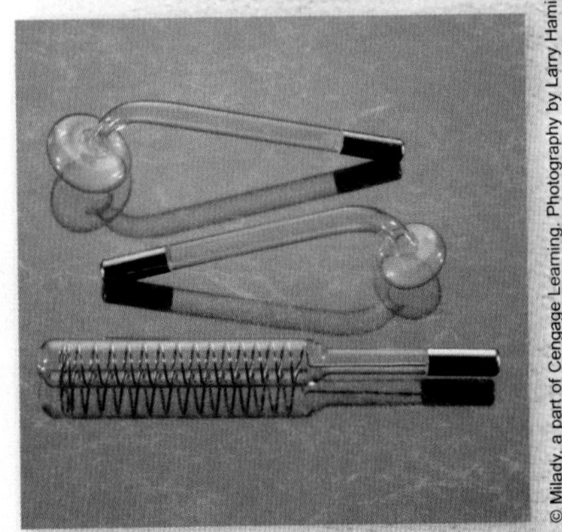

▲ Figure 8–11
Electrodes come in a variety of shapes.

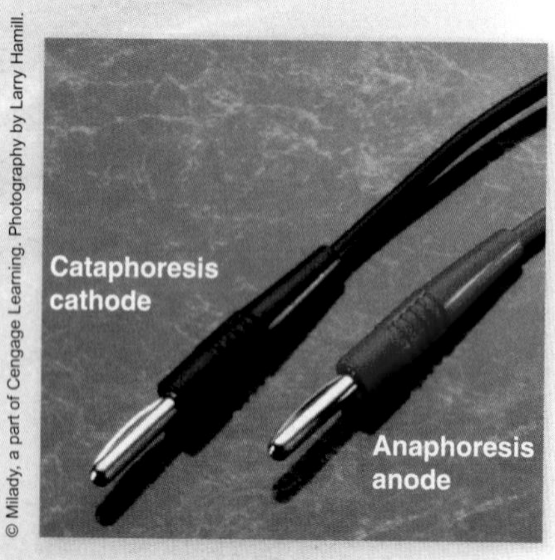

▲ Figure 8–12
Cathode and anode.

Polarity

Polarity (poh-LAYR-ut-tee) indicates the negative or positive pole of an electric current. Electrotherapy devices always have one negatively charged pole and one positively charged pole. The positive electrode is called an anode (AN-ohd). The anode is usually red and is marked with a "P" or a plus (+) sign. The negative electrode is called a cathode (KATH-ohd). It is usually black and is marked with an "N" or a minus (-) sign (Figure 8–12). If the electrodes are not marked, ask your instructor, salon manager, or supervisor to help you determine the positive and negative poles.

Modalities

The primary modalities used in esthetics today are galvanic current, microcurrent, and Telsa high-frequency current.

Did You Know?

Galvanic current is named after a doctor named Luigi Galvani who was born in Italy and lived there until his death in 1798.

Galvanic Current

Galvanic current (gal-VAN-ik KUR-unt) is a constant and direct current (DC). It has a positive and negative pole and produces chemical changes when it passes through the tissues and fluids of the body.

Two different chemical reactions are possible, depending on the polarity (negative or positive) that is used (see Table 8–1). The active electrode (AK-tiv ih-LEK-trohd) is the electrode used on the area to be treated. The inactive electrode (in-AK-tiv- ee-LEK-trohd) is the opposite pole from the active electrode. Note that the effects produced by the positive pole are the exact opposite of those produced by the negative pole.

Iontophoresis (eye-ahn-toh-foh-REE-sus), also known as **ionization,** is the process of introducing water-soluble products into the skin with the use of electric current.

Cataphoresis (kat-uh-fuh-REE-sus) refers to infusing a positive (acid) product into the skin with the use of electric current, and anaphoresis (an-uh-for-EES-sus) is the process of infusing a negative (alkaline) product into the skin. Desincrustation (des-inkrus-TAY-shun) is a form of anaphoresis and is a process used to soften and emulsify grease deposits (oil) and blackheads in the hair follicles. This process is frequently used to treat acne, milia (small, white, bead-like mass), and comedones (blackheads and whiteheads).

CAUTION!

Do not use negative galvanic current on skin with broken capillaries or pustular acne conditions, or on a client with high blood pressure or metal implants.

Microcurrent

Microcurrent is an extremely low level of electricity that mirrors the body's own natural electrical impulses. Microcurrent can be used for iontophoresis, firming, toning, and soothing skin. Additionally, it can aid in the healing of tissue, such as in the case of acne, as it is technology that works with the body's own natural processes.

Newer microcurrent devices use polarity within one set of probes, which are applied by the esthetician, that allows the client to relax rather than actively participate in the service or treatment (Figure 8–13).

EFFECTS OF GALVANIC CURRENT

POSITIVE POLE (ANODE)	NEGATIVE POLE (CATHODE)
Cataphoresis	**Anaphoresis**
• Produces acidic reactions	• Produces alkaline reactions
• Closes the pores	• Opens the pores
• Soothes the nerves	• Stimulates and irritates the nerves
• Decreases blood supply	• Increases blood supply
• Contracts blood vessels	• Expands blood vessels
• Hardens and firms tissues	• Softens tissues

▲ Table 8–1 **Effects of Galvanic Current.**

CAUTION!

As with all electrical current devices, microcurrent should not be used on clients with the following health conditions: pacemakers, epilepsy, cancer, pregnancy, phlebitis, or thrombosis. Microcurrent should also not be used on anyone currently under a doctor's care for a condition that may be contraindicated. If you are unsure about treating a client, refer them back to their physician to obtain consent.

Additionally, microcurrent does not travel throughout the entire body, but rather serves the specific area being treated.

Microcurrent can be effective in the following ways:

- Improves blood and lymph circulation
- Produces acidic and alkaline reactions opens and closes hair follicles/pores
- Increases muscle tone
- Restores elasticity
- Reduces redness and inflammation
- Minimizes healing time in acne lesions
- Improves barrier functions of the skin
- Increases metabolism

When used in treatments for aging-skin, the results may be a softer, firmer, more hydrated appearance of the skin (Figures 8–14 and 8–15). As with all electrical equipment, microcurrent should not be used

Did You Know?

In the past, Faradic- and sinusoidal-current devices, which used alternating and interrupted current to produce a mechanical reaction without a chemical effect, were used in both scalp and facial treatments. These devices caused a visible muscular contraction and have been replaced with newer technology. Devices which visibly contract muscles may be considered a Class 2 or above and out of the scope of practice for the esthetician.

Courtesy of David Suzuki, BioTherapeutic.

▲ Figure 8–13
Microcurrent probes.

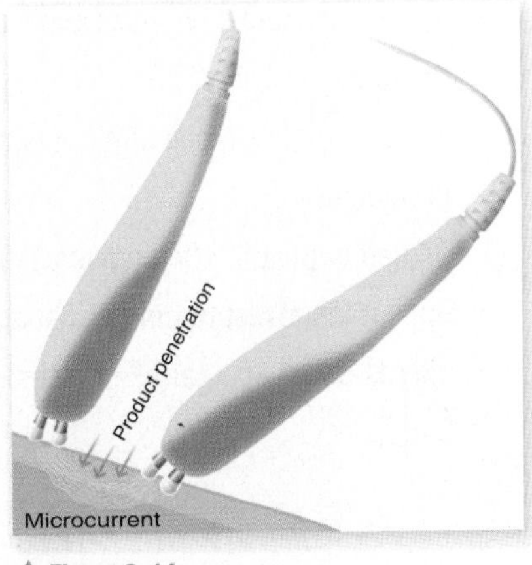

Courtesy of David Suzuki, BioTherapeutic.

▲ Figure 8–14
Iontophoresis with microcurrent.

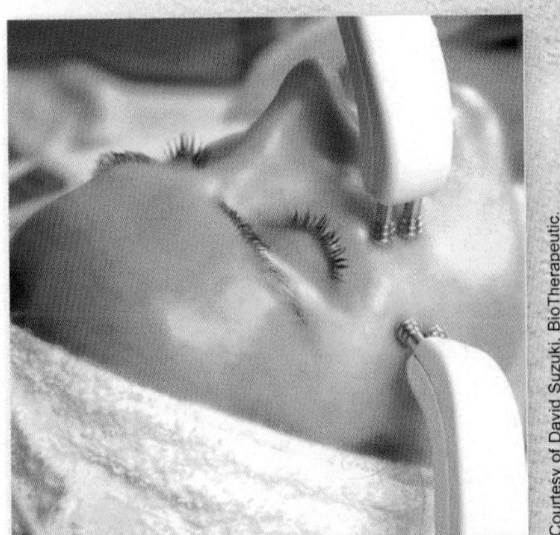

Courtesy of David Suzuki, BioTherapeutic.

▲ Figure 8–15
Ionizing with microcurrent.

on people with pacemakers, epilepsy, cancer, pregnancy, phlebitis, thrombosis, or on anyone currently under a doctor's care.

CAUTION!

Tesla high-frequency current should not be used on clients who are pregnant; suffer from epilepsy (seizures) or asthma; or have high blood pressure, a sinus blockage, a pacemaker, metal implants, or body piercings from the waist up. The client should avoid any contact with metal—such as chair arms, jewelry, and metal bobby pins—during the treatment. A burn may occur if such contact is made.

Tesla High-Frequency Current

Tesla high-frequency current, also known as **violet ray**, is a thermal or heat-producing current with a high rate of oscillation or vibration. It is commonly used for both scalp and facial treatments. Tesla current does not produce muscle contractions, and its effects can be either stimulating or soothing depending on the method of application. The electrodes are made from either glass or metal, and only one electrode is used to perform a service. Here are some benefits of using Tesla high-frequency current:

- Stimulates blood circulation
- Increases elimination and absorption
- Increases metabolism
- Improves germicidal action
- Relieves congestion

CAUTION!

As with all facial services and treatments, it is important to take a full history before performing electrotherapy. If you are unsure about whether you should perform a service on a client, ask them to check with their physician to obtain a signed written consent form from their physician and put it in the client file for documentation. If your client has any of the following conditions, it is not advisable to treat them with electrotherapy:

- Pacemaker/heart conditions/high blood pressure
- Taking multiple medications
- Mental health disorders
- Epilepsy
- Bleeding disorders
- Open cuts, sores, pustular acne, or abrasions
- Diabetes
- Metal dental or facial implants including braces, pins, or plates
- Pregnancy
- Dilated capillaries (telangiectasias, or spider veins)
- Recent laser resurfacing or chemical peel (check with physician)
- Clients using Accutane® or retinoids (check with physician)
- Cancer

REGULATORY AGENCY ALERT

Always make certain that you are in compliance with your state's recommendations for licensing and use of electrical current devices.

There are two methods for applying high-frequency current.

- ***Direct surface application.*** The esthetician holds the handpiece, where the glass electrode is inserted, and applies it directly to the client's skin, moving it slowly over the entire face for stimulation (Figure 8–16). When applying and removing the electrode from the skin, you must hold your finger on the glass electrode to prevent sparking. Remove your finger once the electrode has been placed on the skin. Apply the electrode to areas for healing acne and disinfecting.
- ***Indirect application.*** The client holds the tube electrode (with the metal coil inside) while the esthetician massages the face with her hands (Figure 8–17). At no time should the esthetician hold the electrode. To prevent shock, turn on the current only after the client has firmly grasped the electrode. Turn the current off before removing the electrode from the client's hand. The indirect application stimulates all cell functions without the irritation that could occur with direct application. This treatment is beneficial for sensitive, dehydrated skin. ☑ L04

CAUTION!

As you learn more about facials and treatments, you will become familiar with the term *contraindication.* A contraindication is a predetermined condition that exists in your client that excludes them from using certain ingredients or products and/or from having treatments.

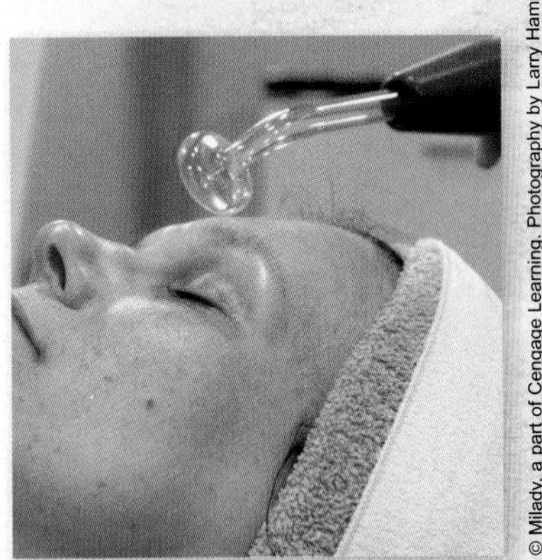

▲ Figure 8–16
Direct high-frequency application.

Light Energy, Lasers, and LED (Light-Emitting Diode)

There are three types of electromagnetic energy: visible light, invisible infrared light, and invisible ultraviolet radiation. The **electromagnetic spectrum** (Figure 8–18) is a form of energy that travels through space in waves and has both electric and magnetic properties.

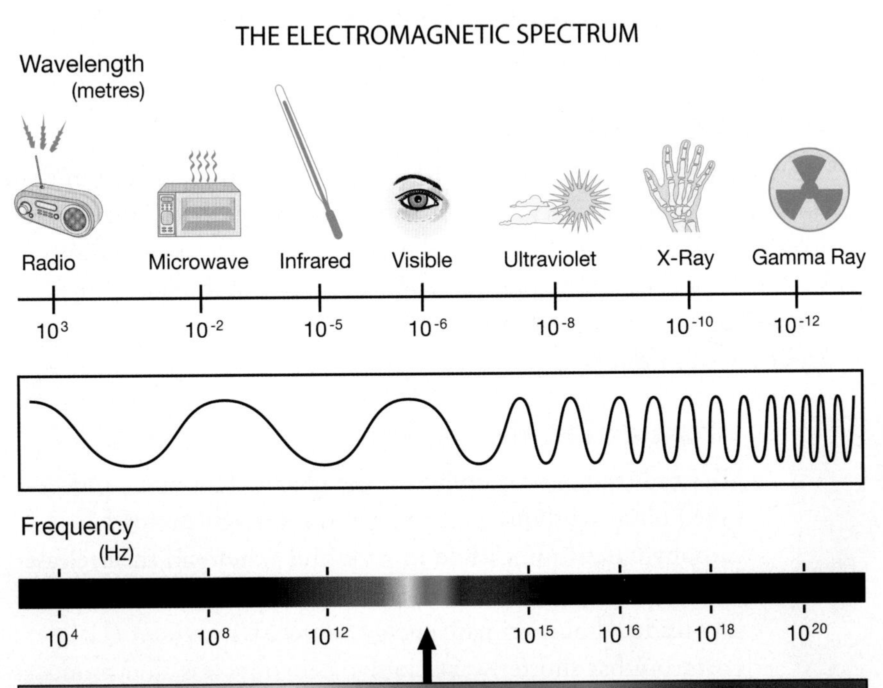

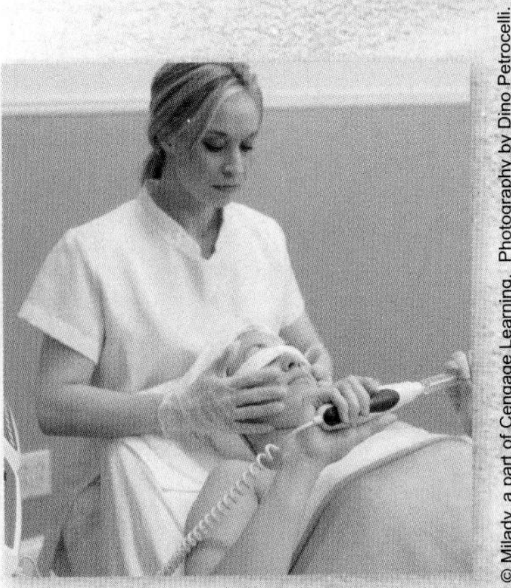

▲ Figure 8–17
Indirect high-frequency application.

◀ Figure 8–18
The electromagnetic spectrum.

LONG WAVELENGTHS AND SHORT WAVELENGTHS

LONG WAVELENGTHS	SHORT WAVELENGTHS
Low Frequency	High Frequency
Penetrate Deeper	Penetrate Less
Have Less Energy	Have More Energy

Did You Know?

If light from the sun is passed through a glass prism, it will appear in seven different colors, known as the rainbow, arrayed in the following manner: violet (the shortest wavelength), indigo, blue, green, yellow, orange, and red (the longest wavelength). These colors, which are visible to the eye, constitute visible light.

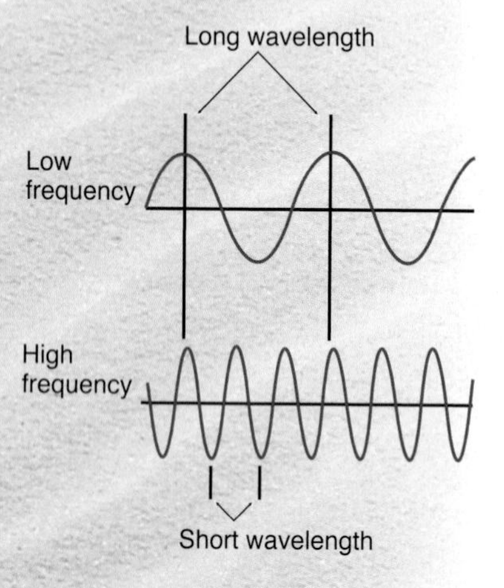

▲ Figure 8–19
Long and short wavelengths.

Visible Light

Visible light is electromagnetic radiation that we can see. Electromagnetic radiation is also called *radiant energy* because it carries, or radiates, energy through space on waves. These waves are similar to the waves caused when a stone is dropped on the surface of the water. The distance between two successive peaks is called the **wavelength**.

Long wavelengths have low frequency, meaning the number of waves is less frequent (fewer waves) within a given length. Short wavelengths have higher frequency because the number of waves is more frequent (more waves) within a given length (Figure 8–19).

Invisible Light

Scientists have discovered that at either end of the visible spectrum there is **invisible light** that the naked eye cannot perceive. Before the visible violet light is ultraviolet light; it is the shortest and least penetrating light of the spectrum. Beyond the visible red light of the spectrum is **infrared light**, which produces heat (Figure 8–20). ☑ L05

Natural sunlight is made up of three types of electromagnetic radiation:

- Visible Light = 35 percent
- Invisible Infrared Light = 60 percent
- Invisible Ultraviolet Light = 5 percent

Ultraviolet Radiation

We need sunlight to survive on the planet. Through a process called photosynthesis, green plants use sunlight to form carbohydrates from carbon dioxide and water and then release oxygen as a by-product. Sunlight also controls our weather and is considered our ultimate energy source. **Ultraviolet (UV) radiation** has shorter wavelengths, penetrate less, and produces

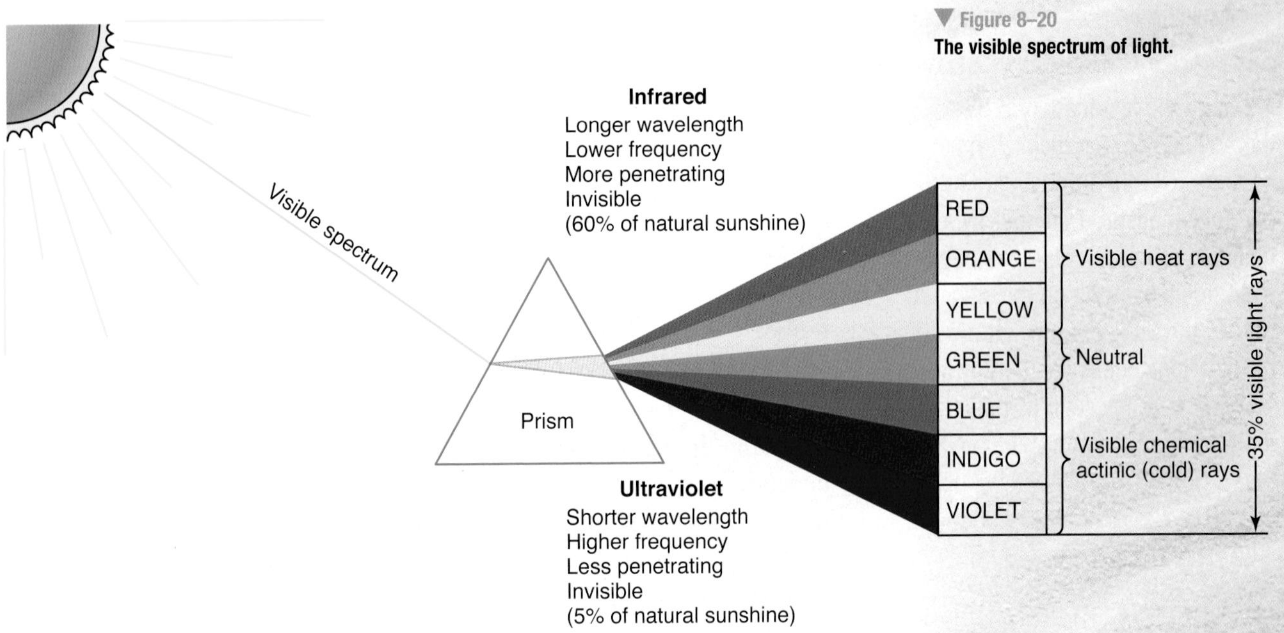

▼ Figure 8–20
The visible spectrum of light.

less heat than visible light does. UV also produces chemical effects and kills germs.

Small amounts of exposure to the sun can be beneficial in the production of vitamin D; however, recent studies have shown that overexposure to the sun causes skin damage, premature aging, and skin cancer. There are three types of UV radiation:

- ***Ultraviolet A (UVA).*** Ultraviolet A has the longest wavelength of the UV light spectrum and penetrates directly into the dermis of the skin, damaging the collagen and elastin. Ultraviolet A is often called the aging ray. UVA light is the light that is often used in tanning beds.
- ***Ultraviolet B (UVB).*** Ultraviolet B is often called the burning ray, because it is most associated with sunburns. Both UVA and UVB light cause skin cancers.
- ***Ultraviolet C (UVC).*** Ultraviolet C is blocked by the ozone layer. If the Earth loses the protective layer of the ozone, life will no longer exists as we know it. UVC radiation will virtually *cook* the Earth. We do not want to deplete the ozone layer, because it protects us from UVC radiation.

fyi

We all need to strike a delicate balance with sunlight exposure. Keep in mind that tanned skin is damaged skin. Tanning will eventually cause photoaging (premature aging due to sun exposure) and irreversibly damage the skin's collagen-building properties.

Did You Know?

Some animals can see parts of the electromagnetic spectrum that humans cannot. For example, many insects can see ultraviolet (UV) radiation.

Did You Know?

When we hear the term white light it is actually referring to combination light because it is a combination of all the visible rays of the spectrum.

Did You Know?

We often hear the term "rays" used in association with sun light, such as UV rays, UVA and UVB rays, or light rays. The word ray in these cases represents the term *radiation.*

CAUTION!

Although the application of UV therapy can be beneficial, it must be done with the utmost care in a carefully measured manner by a qualified professional. It has been used to kill bacteria on the skin and to help the body produce vitamin D. Dermatologists use UV therapy in addition to drugs such as psoralen for the treatment of psoriasis.

Light therapy, also known as **phototherapy,** is the application of light rays to the skin for the treatment of acne, wrinkles, capillaries, pigmentation, or hair removal. Light therapy has evolved throughout time. Some of the original techniques are still valid today. From dermatologists using UV therapy for treating psoriasis, to estheticians using blue-light therapy for acne, to surgeons using lasers for advanced surgical procedures, the power of light is here to stay.

Lasers and Light Therapy (Phototherapy) Devices

Lasers and light therapy devices have been in use for decades. One of the many differences between lasers and other light therapies is that, depending upon the skin condition you are treating, lasers are designed to focus all of the light-power with the same color, traveling to a specific depth, in one direction. In contrast, other light therapies will have multiple colors, depths, and wavelengths and the light may be scattered. The most important point to know about light therapy is that the equipment you use is selected based on the skin type and condition you are treating.

Did You Know?

Over 1 million new cases of skin cancer are diagnosed each year. It is estimated that 1 in 5 Americans will develop skin cancer, and 90 percent of those cancers will be the result of exposure to UV radiation from the sun and from tanning beds.

Lasers

Laser is an acronym that stands for *light amplification stimulation emission of radiation.* Because lasers are used to treat a variety of conditions, there are many kinds of lasers to choose from. All lasers work by selective **photothermolysis**, a process that turns the light from the laser into heat. Depending on the intended use and type, lasers can remove blood vessels, disable hair follicles, remove tattoos, or eliminate some wrinkles without destroying surrounding tissue. Lasers have been used for decades in a variety of surgical procedures.

REGULATORY AGENCY ALERT

Always make certain that you are in compliance with your state's recommendations for licensing and use of laser and light devices.

Lasers work by means of a medium (solid, liquid or gas, or semiconductor) that emits light when excited by a power source. The medium is placed in a specifically designed chamber with mirrors located at both ends of the inside. The chamber is stimulated by an energy source such as electrical current, which in turn excites the particles. The reflective surfaces create light that becomes trapped and goes back and forth through the medium, gaining energy with each pass. The medium determines the wavelength of the laser and thus its use (Figure 8–21).

Most lasers are classified as Level II or above, which means that estheticians must be working under the supervision of a qualified physician to operate a laser. ✓ **LO6**

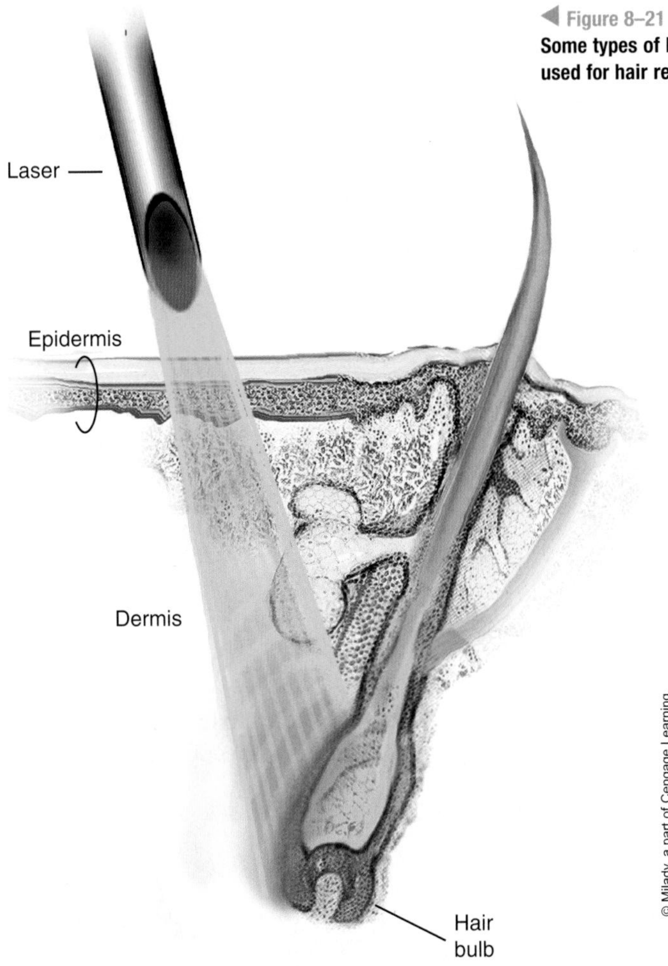

◀ Figure 8–21
Some types of lasers are used for hair removal.

Did You Know?

Some 40 years ago, NASA in space studies found LED (light-emitting diode) to improve human tissue in the areas of healing and tissue growth. These original studies have laid the foundation for LED use in skin rejuvenation using light energy with specific colors to obtain responses in the skin such as increasing collagen reproduction and killing certain types of bacteria that create acne.

LED or Light-Emitting Diode

LED is the acronym for *light-emitting diode*, a device used to reduce acne, increase skin circulation, and improve the collagen content in the skin. The LED works by releasing light onto the skin to stimulate specific responses, at precise depths of the skin. Each color of light corresponds to a different depth (nanometer) in the skin. The LED color of light is also seeking color in the skin known as a chromophore. The term chromophore is derived from the Greek term *chroma* meaning color. A **chromophore** is a color component within the skin such as blood or melanin. When the colored light reaches a specific depth in the skin, it triggers a reaction such as the stimulation of circulation or reducing the amount of bacteria.

Depending on the type of equipment, the LED can be blue, red, yellow, or green (Table 8–2 on page 194). LED in **blue light** has been shown to reduce acne, and **red light** increases circulation and improves the collagen and elastin production in the skin. **Yellow light** has been shown to reduce swelling and inflammation, and **green light** reduces hyperpigmentation. (Figure 8–22).

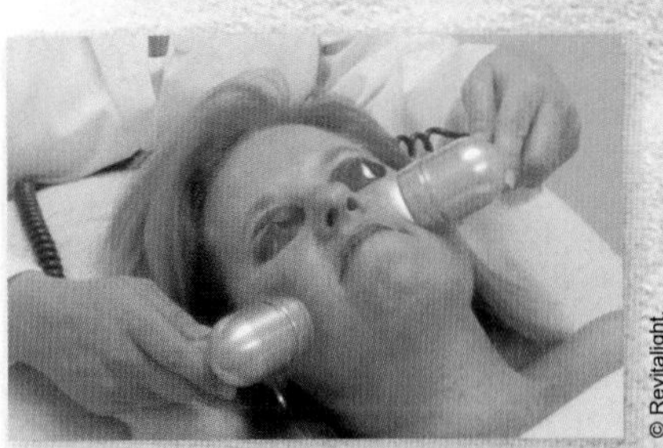

▲ Figure 8–22
LED treatment reduces redness and improves collagen content in the skin.

EFFECTS OF LED (LIGHT-EMITTING DIODE) THERAPY	
COLOR NM (NANOMETERS)	BENEFICIAL EFFECTS
Red light 640 nm	Increases cellular processes Boosts collagen and elastin production Stimulates wound healing
Yellow light 590 nm	Reduces inflammation Improves lymphatic flow Detoxifies and increases circulation
Green light 525 nm	Lessens hyperpigmentation Reduces redness Calms and soothes
Blue light 570 nm	Improves acne Reduces bacteria *Used with medications for precancerous lesions (medical procedure only)

▲ Table 8–2 **Effects of LED (Light-Emitting Diode) Therapy.**

As with all light therapies, it is important to make certain that you have viewed the client consultation form for any contraindications. Light therapy should not be performed on anyone who has light sensitivities (photosensitivities), phototoxic reactions, is taking antibiotics, has cancer or epilepsy, is pregnant, or is under a physician's care. If you are unsure whether you should apply a treatment, always refer the client to their physician. ☑ **LO7**

Web Resources

Several Web sites can provide additional information about electricity. Try these:
www.ezistim.com
www.eia.doe.gov
www.howto.altenergystore.com
www.loc.gov
www.bio-therapeutic.com

Infrared Light

Infrared lamps have been used in salons for heating conditioners and chemicals in hair treatments. They are also used in spas and saunas for relaxation and warming up muscles. There are uses of near infrared light for signs of aging (such as for wrinkles), wound healing, and increasing circulation as it has the longest wavelength of all of the light therapy's and thus can penetrate the deepest into the skin.

Intense Pulse Light

Intense pulse light is a medical device that uses multiple colors and wavelengths (broad spectrum) of focused light to treat spider veins, hyperpigmentation, rosacea/redness, wrinkles, enlarged hair follicles/pores, and excessive hair. As with most devices, multiple treatments are required. A thorough medical history is taken, and these treatments are provided under the supervision of a qualified physician.

Review Questions

1. Why is it important for estheticians to have a basic understanding of electricity?
2. What is the difference between conductors and insulators?
3. Describe the two types of electric current, and give examples of each.
4. Define volt, amp, ohm, and watt.
5. Why should you look for the UL symbol on electrical devices?
6. What are the modalities used in electrotherapy? What kind of current is each one?
7. List the effects of the positive pole and the negative pole of a galvanic current.
8. What is iontophoresis? What is desincrustation?
9. What is microcurrent and what are its benefits?
10. Name the benefits of Tesla high-frequency current.
11. What is the electromagnetic spectrum? What is visible light?
12. List and describe the five main types of light therapy.
13. Why must exposure to ultraviolet rays be carefully monitored?
14. What does the acronym *laser* stand for?

Glossary

active electrode	Electrode of an electrotherapy device that is used on the area to be treated.
alternating current	Abbreviated AC; rapid and interrupted current, flowing first in one direction and then in the opposite direction; produced by mechanical means and changes directions 60 times per second.
ampere	Abbreviated A and also known as *amp*; unit that measures the amount of an electric current (quantity of electrons flowing through a conductor).
anaphoresis	Process of infusing an alkaline (negative) product into the tissues from the negative pole toward the positive pole.
anode	Positive electrode; the anode is usually red and is marked with a P or a plus (+) sign.
blue light	A light-emitting diode for use on clients with acne.
cataphoresis	Process of forcing an acidic (positive) product into deeper tissues using galvanic current from the positive pole toward the negative pole; tightens and calms the skin.
cathode	Negative electrode; the cathode is usually black and is marked with a N or a minus (-) sign.
chromophore	The colored cells or target in the epidermis or dermis that absorbs the laser beam's thermal energy, causing the desired injury or destruction of the material.
circuit breaker	Switch that automatically interrupts or shuts off an electric circuit at the first indication of overload.
complete electric circuit	The path of an electric current from the generating source through conductors and back to its original source.

Glossary

conductor	Any substance, material, or medium that easily transmits electricity.
converter	Apparatus that changes direct current to alternating current.
desincrustation	Process used to soften and emulsify sebum and blackheads in the follicles.
direct current	Abbreviated DC; constant, even-flowing current that travels in one direction only and is produced by chemical means.
electric current	The flow of electricity along a conductor.
electricity	The movement of particles around an atom that creates pure energy; form of energy that, when in mothion, exhibits magnetic, chemical, or thermal effects; a flow of electrons.
electrode	Also known as *probe*; applicator for directing the electric current from an electrotherapy device to the client's skin.
electromagnetic spectrum	Also known as *electromagnetic spectrum of radiation*; made up of all forms of energy whose spectrum ranges from the longest waves to the shortest.
electrotherapy	The use of electrical devices to treat the skin and for therapeutic benefits.
fuse	A special device that prevents excessive current from passing through a circuit.
galvanic current	A constant and direct current (DC); uses a positive and negative pole to produce the chemical reactions (desincrustation) and ionic reactions (iontophoresis).
green light	A light-emitting diode for use on clients with hyperpigmentation or for detoxifying the skin.
grounding	The *ground* connection completes the circuit and carries the current safely away to the ground.
inactive electrode	Opposite pole from the active electrode.
infrared light	Infrared light has longer wavelengths, penetrates more deeply, has less energy, and produces more heat than visible light; makes up 60 percent of natural sunlight.
insulator	Also known as *nonconductor*; substance that does not easily transmit electricity.
intense pulse light	Abbreviated IPL; a medical device that uses multiple colors and wavelengths (broad spectrum) of focused light to treat spider veins, hyperpigmentation, rosacea and redness, wrinkles, enlarged hair follicles and pores, and excessive hair.
invisible light	Light at either end of the visible spectrum of light that is invisible to the naked eye.
iontophoresis	Also know as *ionization*; process of infusing water-soluble products into the skin with the use of electric current, such as the use of positive and negative poles of a galvanic machine or a microcurrent device.
kilowatt	Abbreviated K; 1,000 watts.
laser	Acronym for *light amplification stimulation emission of radiation*; a medical device that uses electromagnetic radiation for hair removal and skin treatments.
LED	Acronym for *light-emitting diode*; a device used to reduce acne, increase skin circulation, and improve the collagen content in the skin.

Glossary

light therapy	Also known as *phototherapy*; the application of light rays to the skin for the treatment of acne, wrinkles, capillaries, pigmentation, or hair removal.
microcurrent	An extremely low level of electricity that mirrors the body's natural electrical impulses.
milliampere	Abbreviated mA; one-thousandth of an ampere.
modalities	Currents used in electrical facial and scalp treatments.
ohm	Abbreviated O; unit that measures the resistance of an electric current.
photothermolysis	Process by which light from a laser is turned into heat.
plug	Two- or three-prong connector at the end of an electrical cord that connects an apparatus to an electrical outlet.
polarity	Negative or positive pole of an electric current.
rectifier	Apparatus that changes alternating current to direct current.
red light	A light-emitting diode for use on clients in the stimulation of circulation and collagen and elastin production.
Tesla high-frequency current	Also known as *violet ray*; thermal or heat-producing current with a high rate of oscillation or vibration that is commonly used for scalp and facial treatments.
ultraviolet (UV) radiation	Invisible rays that have short wavelengths, are the least penetrating rays, produce chemical effects, and kill germs.
visible light	The primary source of light used in facial and scalp treatments.
volt	Abbreviated V and also known as *voltage*; unit that measures the pressure or force that pushes the flow of electrons forward through a conductor.
watt	Abbreviated W; measurement of how much electric energy is being used in one second.
wavelength	Distance between two successive peaks of electromagnetic waves.
white light	Referred to as *combination light* because it is a combination of all the visible rays of the spectrum.
yellow light	A light-emitting diode which aids in reducing inflammation and swelling

CHAPTER 9

Basics of Nutrition

Chapter Outline

- Why Study Nutrition?
- Nutrition Recommendations
- Nutrition for the Skin
- Macronutrients
- Micronutrients: Vitamins and Minerals
- Nutrition and Esthetics
- Water and the Skin
- Self-Care and the Esthetician

Learning Objectives

After completing this chapter, you will be able to:

- ✓ **LO1** Describe the dietary guidelines for foods.
- ✓ **LO2** Identify macro- and micronutrients.
- ✓ **LO3** Understand vitamins and minerals and their benefits.
- ✓ **LO4** Explain how nutrition relates to healthy skin.
- ✓ **LO5** Discuss the benefits of proper nutrition.
- ✓ **LO6** Explain the importance of water intake.
- ✓ **LO7** Describe why it is important for the esthetician to have good self-care habits.

Key Terms

Page number indicates where in the chapter the term is used.

adenosine triphosphate (ATP)
pg. 203

amino acid
pg. 202

arteriosclerosis
pg. 206

B vitamins
pg. 214

bioflavonoids
pg. 217

calories
pg. 207

carbohydrates
pg. 203

cholesterol
pg. 206

complementary foods
pg. 203

disaccharides
pg. 204

enzymes
pg. 207

fats (lipids)
pg. 205

fortified
pg. 213

glycosaminoglycans
pg. 203

hypoglycemia
pg. 205

linoleic acid
pg. 206

macronutrients
pg. 202

micronutrients
pg. 208

minerals
pg. 217

monosaccharides
pg. 204

mucopolysaccharides
pg. 203

nonessential amino acids
pg. 202

omega-3 fatty acids
pg. 206

osteoporosis
pg. 213

polysaccharides
pg. 204

proteins
pg. 202

retinoic acid (Retin-A®)
pg. 211

tretinoin
pg. 211

vitamin A (retinol)
pg. 211

vitamin C (ascorbic acid)
pg. 216

vitamin D
pg. 213

vitamin E (tocopherol)
pg. 213

vitamin K
pg. 214

All bodily functions, including the building of tissues, are directly related to nutrition. The foods we eat and the water we drink are the basic building blocks of life. Foods are broken down into basic molecules that are then delivered to every cell in the human body. These molecules are used by the cells to repair damage, form new cells, and conduct all biochemical reactions that run the body's systems. They provide energy that enables our bodies to perform numerous functions. The skin is nourished by the blood through the arteries and capillaries in the circulatory system. Think of the body or the cell as a factory. All the necessary systems, departments, units, and components for the factory to function optimally are contained within the foods we consume (Figure 9–1).

As we know, estheticians are not licensed dietitians, nor are we adequately trained in nutrition to legally recommend dietary changes to our clients. Clients may be taking medications for health conditions such as diabetes or high blood pressure which can be negatively affected by misleading advice, including supplement recommendations; however, it is beneficial for anyone practicing personal-care services, such as esthetics, to have a good working knowledge of nutrition and how the body is affected by the foods we consume. Good nutrition is necessary for healthy skin.

Why Study Nutrition?

Here are some very good reasons for studying and learning about nutrition that will benefit both you and your clients.

- As estheticians we need to have a strong, healthy body as it is vitally important to the health of your practice, and your practice is related to nutrition and wellness in many ways.
- Understanding proper nutrients for the body in order to maintain optimum energy levels throughout the day is beneficial for all practitioners and their clients.
- Clients will directly benefit from the information and referrals that we can make based on having a basic understanding of nutrition.

Nutrition Recommendations

Nutritional needs depend on various factors such as age, sex, weight, physical activity, and body type. The United States Department of Agriculture (USDA) is the governmental agency that regulates nutrition-related affairs. The USDA issues recommended dietary allowances (RDAs) for certain nutrients, including vitamins and minerals.

The USDA's *MyPlate* is a recommended guideline for food groups that individuals should consume daily and can be personalized based upon an individual's needs. *MyPlate* was issued by the USDA in 2011 to replace

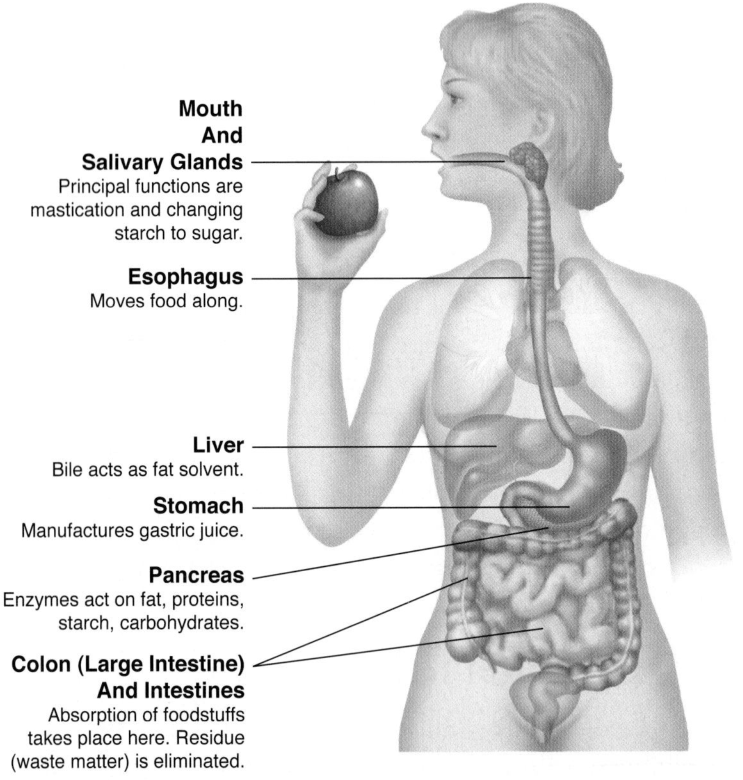
Mouth
And
Salivary Glands
Principal functions are mastication and changing starch to sugar.
Esophagus
Moves food along.
Liver
Bile acts as fat solvent.
Stomach
Manufactures gastric juice.
Pancreas
Enzymes act on fat, proteins, starch, carbohydrates.
Colon (Large Intestine)
And Intestines
Absorption of foodstuffs takes place here. Residue (waste matter) is eliminated.
© Milady, a part of Cengage Learning.

Figure 9–1
The digestive system and food consumption.

the food pyramid. The nutritional tool now emphasizes healthy food choices using a visual representation of a plate setting by breaking out the food groups by recommended proportions. Grains, vegetables, dairy, fruits, and protein are the five basic food categories in the *MyPlate* icon (Figure 9–2). Nutritional tips, recipes, and other tools for building healthy diets according to individual needs can be found at www.ChooseMyPlate.gov. Three examples of food guidelines are the USDA Food Guide; the Dietary Approaches to Stop Hypertension (DASH) Eating Plan; and the Institute of Medicine's nutrient intake recommendations.

Interestingly, as consumers we have never had more detailed information about the foods we are purchasing and consuming, yet as a nation we have never been more overweight. Many nutritional reports say that much of the population consumes more calories than needed. To safeguard against this, choose foods that are high in nutrients but lower in calories. People of all ages are encouraged to eat foods with more calcium, potassium, fiber, magnesium and vitamins A, C, and E. Other recommended dietary changes are to avoid oversized meal portions and reduce calories, saturated and trans fats, cholesterol, sugars, and salt.

Individual needs such as pregnancy and lactation can affect women's nutritional needs. Diseases or medications that affect the ability to digest food

Figure 9–2
The USDA MyPlate illustrates the five food groups to help build healthier diets.

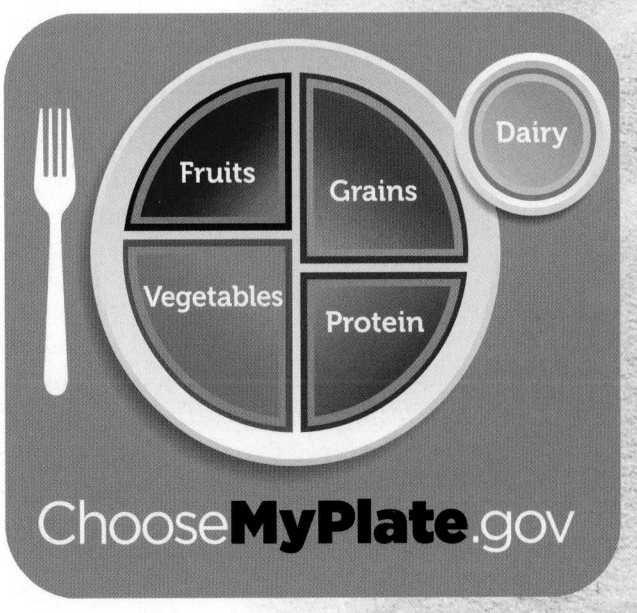
Fruits
Grains
Dairy
Vegetables
Protein
ChooseMyPlate.gov
US Department of Agriculture.

Did You Know?

The USDA updated the food pyramid to the easy-to-use *MyPlate* in 2011. Did you know there are other food guidelines you may find interesting? Some of these alternatives reflect healthful eating habits from cultures around the world (Asian, Mediterranean, or Latin American for example). Some guidelines emphasize seafood; others are based on a vegetarian diet, while still others address specific health problems. Whichever guidelines you choose to follow depends largely on your nutritional goals, your lifestyle, and your taste buds.

▲ Figure 9–3
Find beneficial nutrients from an abundance of food sources.

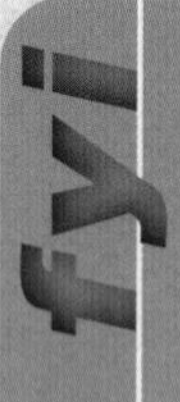

It is not a function of the esthetician to make vitamin and mineral supplement recommendations, and it is necessary to refer clients to qualified, licensed practitioners.

interrupt the normal process of nutrients reaching the bloodstream and, consequently, the cells. See a dietitian or doctor for nutritional advice. ☑ **L01**

Nutrition for the Skin

Understanding how to maintain skin and body health is beneficial to the esthetician personally, as well as to the client. Healthy skin begins with diet and water intake. The adage, "You are what you eat," still holds true. Proper dietary choices help regulate hydration (maintaining a healthy level of water in the body), oil production, and overall cell function. Skin disorders, fatigue, stress, depression, and some diseases are often the result of a poorly balanced diet. Vitamins and minerals are a necessary part of a balanced diet. The benefits and effects of nutrients and their food sources are discussed in this chapter (**Figure 9–3**).

Macronutrients

Macronutrients are the basic building blocks necessary for bodily functions, including the functioning of the skin. The **macronutrients** are the three basic food groups: proteins, carbohydrates, and fats. They make up the largest part of the nutrition we eat. Eating foods found in all three of these basic food groups is necessary to support the health of the body. The recommended intake is protein: 20 percent (105 grams); carbohydrates: 54 percent (281 grams); and fat: 26 percent (60 grams). This is based on an intake of 2,000 calories per day according to the USDA's DASH Eating Plan.

Proteins

Proteins are chains of **amino acid** molecules that are used by every cell of the body to make other usable proteins. These building blocks carry out various functions required by the cells and the body. Proteins are used in the duplication of DNA, the blueprint material containing all the information that controls the function of every living cell. Proteins are needed to make muscle tissue, blood, and enzymes as well as the keratin that is present in skin, nails, and hair. Proteins are used by the immune system in making antibodies. Collagen and elastin are also made from protein.

Proteins contain essential amino acids. Although there are more than 100 naturally occurring amino acids, the proteins of all plants and animals are made from just 20 "common amino acids." Eleven of the twenty common amino acids are called the **nonessential amino acids** because they can be synthesized by the body and do not have to be in our diet. The remaining nine are the essential amino acids that must be in our daily diet because they cannot be synthesized by the human body.

Dietary Sources of Proteins

Although meat, fish, poultry, eggs, and dairy products are complete proteins that provide essential amino acids, they should be limited in the diet for various reasons. One example would be with eggs: if you eat too many eggs, you may raise your cholesterol count. Many plant sources are low in fat and also a good source of fiber, but they are not complete proteins because they all lack at least one of the essential amino acids. **Complementary foods** are combinations of two incomplete proteins that, together, provide all the essential amino acids and make a complete protein. Some complementary proteins are peanut butter and bread, rice and beans, beans and corn, and blackeyed peas and cornbread.

Vegetarians must be careful to obtain their daily protein requirements. Those who consume dairy products have an easier time obtaining a sufficient amount of protein. Vegans, people who eat strictly plant products with no dairy products, must be especially careful to consume enough protein in their diets through nuts, grains, legumes, and vegetables. Soy products are particularly beneficial in the vegetarian diet.

Dietary sources of protein come from animal meats as well as fish, eggs, dairy products, nuts, grains, and beans. Although most vegetables also contain protein, it is in smaller proportions. Protein deficiencies can cause anemia, low resistance to infection, and organ impairment.

Did You Know?

According to the newest information from the United States Department of Agriculture (USDA), the 2010 *Dietary Guidelines for Americans* recommendations focuses on nutrients from food, rather than supplements.

Carbohydrates

Carbohydrates break down the basic chemical sugars that supply energy for the body. They are frequently called *carbs*. The most important carbohydrate is glucose, because it provides the majority of the body's energy. Glucose is stored in the muscles and liver as glycogen, or animal starch. When muscles are used, glycogen is broken down to provide the energy needed for muscular work. Nutrients are broken down into **adenosine triphosphate (ATP)** (uh-DEE-nuh-zeen tri-FOS-fate), the substance that provides energy to cells. ATP also converts oxygen to carbon dioxide, a waste product we breathe out (Figure 9–4).

Carbohydrates can be combined with proteins to produce many important body chemicals. For example, **mucopolysaccharides** (mew-ko-poly-SACK-uh-rides) are carbohydrate–lipid complexes that are good water binders. These are important to the skin and are present in the dermis as **glycosaminoglycans** (gly-kose-ah-mee-no-GLY-cans), a water-binding substance between the fibers of the dermis.

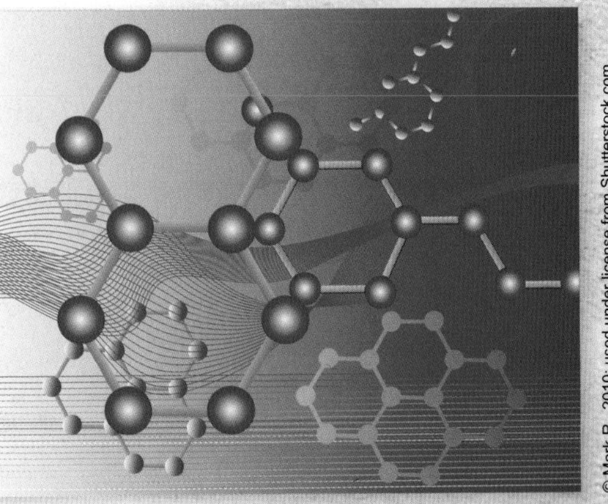

▲ Figure 9–4
Adenosine Triphosphate (ATP) provides energy to the cells.

Monosaccharides, Disaccharides, and Polysaccharides

There are three basic structural carbohydrate divisions: monosaccharides, disaccharides, and polysaccharides.

Monosaccharides. The most basic unit of a carbohydrate is glucose, the simplest of all carbohydrates. The glucose molecule is known as a monosaccharide (mah-no-SACK-uh-ride; *mono* means *one*, and *saccharide* means *sugar*), a one-unit sugar molecule that all cells use for energy. Fruit sugar (fructose) is a naturally occurring monosaccharide.

Disaccharides (dye-SACK-uh-rides). These are made up of two molecular sugar units (*di* means *two*). Lactose (milk sugar) and sucrose (sugar) are both disaccharides.

Polysaccharides (poly-SACK-uh-rides). These complex compounds consist of a chain of sugar unit molecules (*poly* is from the Greek *polu*, meaning *many*). A digestible polysaccharide starch can be broken down by the digestive system into simpler, usable glucose molecules. Starch is the storage form of glucose for plants. Fiber is also a polysaccharide but is not digestible.

The Three Basic Types of Carbohydrates

The three basic types of carbohydrates are simple sugars, starches, and fiber.

Simple sugars. These are present in table sugar (also known as sucrose), fruit sugars (fructose), and milk sugars (lactose).

Starches. These are also called complex carbohydrates and are present in many vegetables and grains. Starch is a white, odorless, complex carbohydrate that is an important food. In plants, carbohydrates are stored chiefly as starch.

Fiber. Fiber, another type of carbohydrate, is commonly called roughage. It is divided into two categories: soluble and insoluble. These carbohydrates help to move food particles from the digestive tract and on into the colon, where they are ultimately expressed as waste or stool. A lack of fiber is associated with constipation and, in the long term, with colon cancer.

Dietary Sources of Carbohydrates

The dietary sources of carbohydrates include:

- Simple carbohydrates such as sweets, syrups, honey, fruits, and many vegetables.
- Starches, including grains, cereals, breads, and other flour products; potatoes; rice; legumes (beans); and pasta.
- High-fiber foods, including grain, brans (such as oat bran or wheat bran), whole-grain breads, beans, apples, and vegetables such as carrots and corn.

Some foods are listed in two different categories because there is more than one type of saccharide group in many foods. For example, potatoes are a starch source and also contain fiber. Fruits and vegetables have both simple sugars and fiber (Figure 9–5).

Glucose

Blood glucose or blood sugar can drop too low without adequate carbohydrates. This condition is known as **hypoglycemia** (high-poh-gly-SEE-me-ah). Low blood sugar causes symptoms such as fatigue, anxiety, and food cravings. Fluctuating blood sugar levels and food cravings are triggered if the brain is energy starved. Simple carbs, such as table sugar, have no fiber and are quickly absorbed into the bloodstream. Refined carbohydrates such as white bread have their natural fiber and bran milled away, so they enter the bloodstream more quickly but do not provide long-term energy. Eating *good* or complex carbohydrates such as whole grains will help to slow absorption of glucose into the bloodstream and balance glucose levels.

▲ Figure 9–5
Dietary sources of simple carbohydrates.

The hormone insulin, produced in the pancreas, brings nutrients and glucose into cells and stores fat. Without insulin, the body cannot utilize glucose. Consequently, there is a high level of glucose in the blood and a low level of glucose absorption by the tissues. Diabetes results from this imbalance. Regulating hormone and glucose levels through proper nutrition is important to maintain good health.

Fats

Fats, also known as **lipids**, are the third group of macronutrients. Fats are used as energy, but not as readily as carbohydrates. Although many people associate fats with obesity, some fat is required in the diet, and it is an essential component of good health. The layer of fat in the body also helps retain heat. Fats are used to produce the materials in the sebaceous glands that lubricate the skin. Lipids are fats or fatlike substances used by the body to make hormones, create cell membranes, and assist in absorption of the fat-soluble vitamins A, D, E, and K.

Fatty Acids

Fats are organic compounds made up of a glycerol molecule and fatty acids. The chemical composition of the carbon and hydrogen molecules that combine with glycerol determine the type of fatty acid. Fatty acids make up triglycerides, the main fat in foods. Triglycerides are fats and oils representing 95 percent of fat intake. Phospholipids (the main lipids in cell membranes) and sterols are the remaining 5 percent.

The three types of fatty acids are saturated, monounsaturated, and polyunsaturated.

- ***Saturated fats*** such as processed foods have more rigid molecules, and this can cause hardening of the arteries.
- ***Monounsaturated fats*** from olive oil and canola oil are more fluid molecules and are important for cell integrity and membrane phospholipids.

- ***Polyunsaturated fats*** are liquid at room temperature and are more easily oxidized. Polyunsaturated fats are found in fish, corn, safflower, and nut oils.

The body has the capacity to manufacture fats for use as needed. These fats can be made from carbohydrates and proteins. Essential fatty acids are acids that the body cannot manufacture on its own, and therefore they need to be extracted internally by the body from ingested food. Fatty acids from food protect against disease and help produce hormones.

Did You Know?

Body fats can store unabsorbed drugs you may have taken years ago.

Disease-preventing omega-3 and omega-6 fatty acids are polyunsaturated fatty acids necessary for brain and body development, metabolism, and hair and skin growth; however, too much omega-6 in the diet can lead to health problems. The typical American diet has an excess of omega-6, while the healthy Mediterranean diet has more omega-3. The dietary amount for omega-3 is recommended to be three times more than omega-6.

Linoleic acid (lyn-uh-LAY-ick AH-sid) is omega-6, an essential fatty acid used to make important hormones and maintain the lipid barrier of the skin. Linoleic acid is found in oils made from safflower, sunflower, corn, soybean, borage, and flaxseed.

Omega-3 fatty acids (Alpha-linolenic) are a type of *good* polyunsaturated fat that may decrease the likelihood of cardiovascular diseases by reducing **arteriosclerosis** (are-TEER-ee-oh-sklur-OH-sis), clogging and hardening of the arteries. Omega-3 fatty acids are largely present in cold-water fish. Salmon is highest in omega-3 acids, but mackerel, tuna, herring, trout, and cod are also high in omega-3. Nutritionists suggest that these fish should be a regular part of the diet and consumed two to three times a week. Alpha-linoleic acid, an omega-3, is a popular nutrient for healthy skin and reducing inflammation. Sources of omega-3 include fish oil, walnuts, flax, pumpkin seeds, and algae (Figure 9–6).

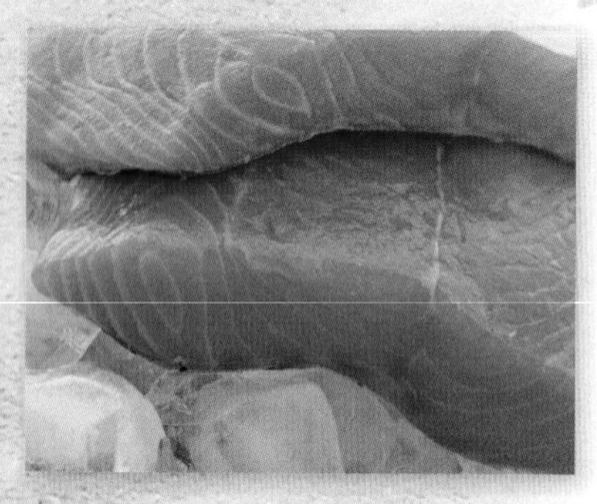

Figure 9–6
Salmon rich in omega-3 fatty acids.

Trans Fatty Acids

Trans fatty acids can increase the *bad* type of cholesterol in the blood, known as low-density lipoprotein (lie-po-PRO-teen) (LDL). LDLs are composed largely of cholesterol. Conversely, high-density lipoproteins (HDLs) are *good* lipoproteins with high protein content. Lipoproteins contain protein and lipids that transport water-insoluble lipids through the blood.

The body makes cholesterol, so we do not need to consume large amounts of it in the diet. **Cholesterol** is a waxy substance found in your body that is needed to produce hormones, vitamin D, and bile. Cholesterol protects nerves, the structure of cells, and is vitally important in the body—until we begin to show signs that we have too much in the body.

Cholesterol and phospholipids, along with some triglycerides, are absorbed into the lymph system because they are insoluble in water (blood).

Saturated fats are unhealthy, highly processed fats that raise serum cholesterol. Hydrogenated fats are also detrimental to health because they elevate blood lipids and cholesterol. Saturated fats are found mostly in animal sources and coconut and palm oils.

Too much cholesterol or fat in the diet can result in clogged blood vessels, slowing and blocking blood flow. High levels of blood cholesterol can lead to high blood pressure, heart disease, and stroke. High cholesterol is also genetically determined.

Calories

Fats are very high in **calories**, the measure of heat units. Calories fuel the body by making energy available for work. A gram of fat has 9 calories, while a gram of carbohydrate or a gram of protein has 4 calories. When people take in too many calories, and do not use them in body functions, the body stores the excess calories as body fat. It takes about 3,500 extra calories for the body to store 1 pound (453 grams) of fat. These extra calories can come from the intake of fat, carbohydrates, or even protein.

The number of calories required to run the body varies with individual lifestyles. Obesity in the United States has doubled in the past 2 decades. Nearly one-third of adults are obese; that is, they have a body mass index (BMI) of 30 or greater. Changing our diets and lifestyle is necessary to slow down this prevalent trend. Conversely, some individuals are underweight and malnourished, which is not healthy either. An average weight and balanced diet are the optimum goals for good health.

Dietitians generally believe that 55 to 60 percent of all calories should be obtained from carbohydrates—mainly grains, breads, pasta, vegetables, and fruit. Candy is also a carbohydrate, but sweets should be limited to no more than 240 calories per day for women and 310 calories per day for men.

Most nutritional authorities generally recommend limiting fats to no more than 30 percent of the diet. No more than 10 percent of this amount should come from saturated fats. Saturated fats come primarily from meats and dairy products. Polyunsaturated and monounsaturated fats come primarily from vegetable oils. Foods such as pastries, fast foods, fried foods, snack foods (junk foods), and products containing cream are high in fat and should be avoided or eaten in moderation.

Protein requirements make up the balance of the diet, around 15 to 20 percent. Remember that protein sources, such as meat, also contain fats and carbohydrates.

Enzymes

Enzymes are biological catalysts made of protein and vitamins. Enzymes break down complex food molecules into smaller molecules to utilize

USDA Guidelines are recommended daily allowances (RDAs) for a balanced nutritional consumption. Recommended intake for calories is 2,300 to 3,000 for men and 1,900 to 2,200 for women. As a general range for food categories, 45 to 65 percent of the diet should be complex carbohydrates; 15 to 35 percent proteins; and 30 percent unsaturated fats. It is necessary, however, to consult your physician regarding dietary advice and refer clients to a qualified professional for specific health recommendations.

Web Resources

To calculate your BMI, check out www.healthatoz.com.

CAUTION!

Food allergies are common and can be severe. In other cases a food allergy may go undetected. For example, allergies to shellfish, seaweed, and peanuts can mean adverse reactions to body treatments at spas if product ingredients contain seaweed or peanut oil. Be sure the spa intake form includes questions about allergies and discuss them with your client. Learn as much as you can about ingredients and the potential for allergic reactions clients may have with certain ingredients. Know the ingredients that are contained within the products you are using on the skin. If you have allergies, remember to tell other service providers so that they can best serve you.

the energy extracted from food. Enzymes are also necessary to bring about reactions or speed up reactions in the body. Materials in the body are reduced by enzymes into carbon dioxide, water, and unnecessary end-products that are excreted. Vitamins also assist in breaking down molecules.

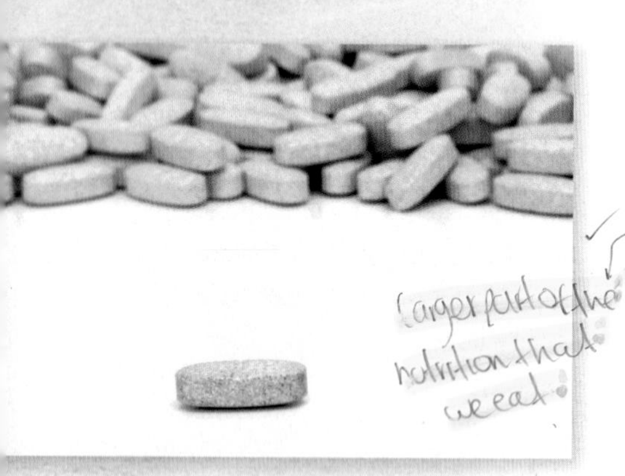

▲ Figure 9–7
Micronutrients: vitamins and minerals.

Micronutrients: Vitamins and Minerals

Micronutrients are essential trace vitamins and minerals that we need for proper body functions including copper, iodine, zinc, and selenium. They are used in processes carried out by the cells for the production of many biochemicals necessary for life. Vitamins and minerals must be part of the diet because the body cannot synthesize all vitamins on its own. Vitamins are required for many chemical reactions that break down and reconstruct proteins, convert amino acids, and synthesize fatty acids. Many vitamins are also involved in energy release from carbohydrates (Figure 9–7).

Vitamins play an important role in the skin's health by aiding in healing, softening, and fighting diseases of the skin. Antioxidants such as A, C, and E have all been shown to have positive effects on skin health. Experts agree that eating foods rich in nutrients and loaded with vitamins and minerals is the most important way to achieve health in general; however, taking vitamin and mineral supplements may provide additional skin-health support.

Beyond general health, external applications of vitamins and minerals have shown great benefit to achieve skin health as well. As mentioned, ideally, the nutrients the body needs for proper functioning and survival should come primarily from the foods we eat, however, if a person's daily food consumption is lacking in nutrients, vitamin and mineral supplements can help provide some additional nutrients (making sure not to exceed the RDA) (Table 9–1). Medications can interfere with the body's ability to absorb vitamins and minerals. As with all supplements, herbal preparations, and medications, it is necessary to consult with a qualified professional for the proper dosage and implementation of products into one's diet. ☑ L02

Did You Know?

Did you know that 1 pound (453 grams) of fat is equal to 3,500 calories?

Vitamins

Vitamins fall into two categories: fat-soluble (vitamins A, D, E, and K), and water-soluble (vitamins B and C).

Fat-soluble vitamins A, D, E, and K are generally present in fats within foods. The body stores them in the liver and in adipose (fat) tissue. Because they can be stored in the body, it is possible to get too much of certain vitamins, namely vitamins A and D. Fat-soluble vitamins protect the outside membrane of cells.

A NUTRITION CHART: VITAMINS, MINERALS, AND FOOD SOURCES			
VITAMIN RDA	**NATURAL SOURCES**	**FUNCTIONS**	**DEFICIENCY SYMPTOMS**
A 5,000 IU	Yellow and green fruits and vegetables, carrots, dairy products, fish liver oil, yellow fruits	Growth and repair of body tissues, bone formation, vision	Night blindness, dry scaly skin, loss of smell and appetite, fatigue, bone deterioration
B-1 (Thiamine) 1.5 mg	Grains, nuts, wheat germ, fish, poultry, legumes, meat	Metabolism, appetite maintenance, nerve function, healthy mental state, muscle tone	Nerve disorders, cramps, fatigue, loss of appetite, loss of memory, heart irregularity
B-2 (Riboflavin) 1.7 mg	Whole grains, green leafy vegetables, liver, fish, eggs	Metabolism, health in hair, skin, nails; cell respiration; formation of antibodies and red blood cells	Cracks and lesions in corners of mouth, digestive disturbances
B-6 (Pyridoxine) 2 mg	Whole grains, leafy green vegetables, yeast, bananas, organ meats	Metabolism, formation of antibodies, sodium/potassium balance	Dermatitis, blood disorders, nervousness, weakness, skin cracks, loss of memory
B-7 (Biotin) 300 mcg	Legumes, eggs, grains, yeast	Metabolism, formation of fatty acids	Dry, dull skin; depression, muscle pain, fatigue; loss of appetite
B-12 (Cobalamine) 6 mcg	Eggs, milk/milk products, fish, organ meats	Metabolism, healthy nervous system, blood cell formation	Nervousness, neuritis, fatigue
Choline (no RDA)	Lecithin, fish, wheat germ, egg yolk, soybeans	Nerve metabolism and transmission; regulates liver, kidneys, and gallbladder	Hypertension, stomach ulcers, liver and kidney conditions
Folic acid (Folacin) 400 mcg	Green leafy vegetables, organ meats, yeast, milk products	Red blood cell formation, growth and cell division (RNA and DNA)	Gastrointestinal disorders, poor growth, loss of memory, anemia
Inositol (no RDA)	Whole grains, citrus fruits, yeast, molasses, milk	Hair growth, metabolism, lecithin formation	Elevated cholesterol, hair loss, skin disorders, constipation, eye abnormalities
B complex (Niacin) 20 mg	Meat, poultry, fish, milk products, peanuts	Metabolism, healthy skin, tongue and digestive system, blood circulation, essential for synthesis of sex hormones	Fatigue, indigestion, irritability, loss of appetite, skin conditions
B complex (PABA) (no RDA)	Yeast, wheat germ, molasses	Metabolism, red blood cell formation, intestines, hair coloring, sunscreen	Digestive disorders, fatigue, depression, constipation
B-15 (Pantothenic acid) 10 mg	Whole grains, pumpkin and sesame seeds	Metabolism, stimulates nerve and glandular systems, cell respiration	Heart disease, glandular and nerve disorders, poor circulation
C Ascorbic acid 60 mg	Citrus fruits, vegetables, tomatoes, potatoes	Aids in healing, collagen maintenance, resistance to disease	Gum bleeding, bruising, slow healing of wounds, nosebleeds, poor digestion

▲ Table 9–1 **A Nutrition Chart: Vitamins, Minerals, and Food Sources.**

(continued)

A NUTRITION CHART: VITAMINS, MINERALS, AND FOOD SOURCES			
VITAMIN RDA	**NATURAL SOURCES**	**FUNCTIONS**	**DEFICIENCY SYMPTOMS**
D 400 IU	Egg yolks, organ meats, fish, fortified milk	Healthy bone formation, healthy circulatory functions, nervous system	Rickets, osteoporosis, poor bone growth, nervous system irritability
E 30 IU	Green vegetables, wheat germ, organ meats, eggs, vegetable oils	Red blood cells, inhibits coagulation of blood, cellular respiration	Muscular atrophy, abnormal fat deposits in muscles, gastrointestinal conditions, heart disease, impotency
F (no RDA)	Wheat germ, seeds, vegetable oils	Respiration of body organs, lubrication of cells, blood coagulation, glandular activity	Brittle nails and hair, dandruff, diarrhea, varicose veins, underweight, acne, gallstones
K (no RDA)	Green leafy vegetables, milk, kelp, safflower oil	Blood clotting agent, important to proper liver function and longevity	Hemorrhage
P (Bioflavonoids) (no RDA)	Fruits	For healthy connective tissue, aids in utilization of vitamin C	Tendency to bleed easily, gum bleeding, bruising, similar to vitamin C's symptoms
Calcium 1000–1400 mg	Dairy products, bone meal	Resilient bones, teeth, muscle tissue, regulating heartbeat, blood clotting	Soft, brittle bones; osteoporosis, heart palpitations
Chromium (no RDA)	Corn oil, yeast, clams, whole grains	Body's use of glucose, energy, effective use of insulin	Atherosclerosis, diabetic sugar intolerance
Copper 2 mg	Whole grains, leafy green vegetables, seafood, almonds	Healthy red blood cells, bone growth and formation, joins with vitamin C to form elastin	Skin lesions, general weakness, labored respiration
Iodine .15 mg	Iodized table salt, shellfish	Part of the hormone thyroxine which controls metabolism	Dry skin and hair, obesity, nervousness, goiters
Iron 18 mg	Meats, fish, leafy green vegetables	Hemoglobin formation, blood quality, resistance to stress and disease	Anemia, constipation, breathing difficulties
Magnesium 400 mg	Nuts, green vegetables, whole grains	Metabolism	Nervousness, agitation, disorientation, blood clots
Manganese 2 mg	Egg yolks, legumes, whole grains	Carbohydrate and fat production, sex hormone production, bone development	Dizziness, lacking muscle coordination
Phosphorus 800 mg	Proteins, grains	Bone development, important in protein, fat, and carbohydrate utilization	Soft bones, rickets, loss of appetite, irregular breathing
Potassium 2000 mg	Grains, vegetables, bananas, fruits, legumes	Fluid balance; controls activity of heart muscle, nervous system, and kidneys	Irregular heartbeat, muscle cramps (legs), dry skin, general weakness

▲ Table 9–1 *(continued)*

A NUTRITION CHART: VITAMINS, MINERALS, AND FOOD SOURCES			
VITAMIN RDA	NATURAL SOURCES	FUNCTIONS	DEFICIENCY SYMPTOMS
Sodium 500 mg	Table salt, shellfish, meat and poultry	Maintains muscular, blood, lymph, and nervous systems; regulates body fluid	Muscle weakness and atrophy, nausea, dehydration
Sulphur (no RDA)	Fish, eggs, nuts, cabbage, meat	Collagen and body tissue formation, gives strength to keratin	N/A
Zinc 15 mg	Whole grains, wheat bran	Healthy digestion and metabolism, reproductive system, aids in healing	Stunted growth, delayed sexual maturity, prolonged wound healing
Selenium 055 mcg	Whole grains, liver, meat, fish	Part of important antioxidant: glutathione peroxidase	Heart damage, reduces body's resistance to chronic illnesses
Fluoride (no RDA)	Fluoridated water and toothpaste	Bone and tooth formation	Increased tooth decay

▲ Table 9–1 *(continued)*

Vitamin A

Vitamin A, also known as **retinol**, is an ingredient used in skin care products designed for aging skin. It is has been found to stimulate collagen production and is used in acne treatments. Vitamin A is also a group of compounds called retinoids. Retinol and retinoic acid (re-tuh-NO-ik AH-cid), also known as **Retin-A®**, are examples of retinoids.

Vitamin A is necessary for proper eyesight, especially at night. A deficiency in vitamin A can result in a condition known as night blindness, or the impaired ability of the eyes to adapt to the dark. Vitamin A is also important for the proper maintenance of epithelial tissue, which makes up the surface of the lungs, intestines, mucous membranes, the bladder, and the skin. These surfaces produce mucus, which is important for protection and flexibility.

Fat-Soluble Vitamins

Vitamin A supports the overall health of the skin. This vitamin aids in the functioning and repair of skin cells. Vitamin A is an antioxidant that can help prevent certain types of cancers, including skin cancer, and it has been shown to improve the skin's elasticity and thickness.

Topically, vitamin A can be used to treat many different types of acne and other skin conditions, primarily wrinkles. It is found in many over-the-counter (OTC) creams and lotions. Derivatives of vitamin A are used in many skin prescription creams called retinoic acid or Retin-A®, known as *retinoids*. Tretinoin, better known as Retin-A® or Renova™,

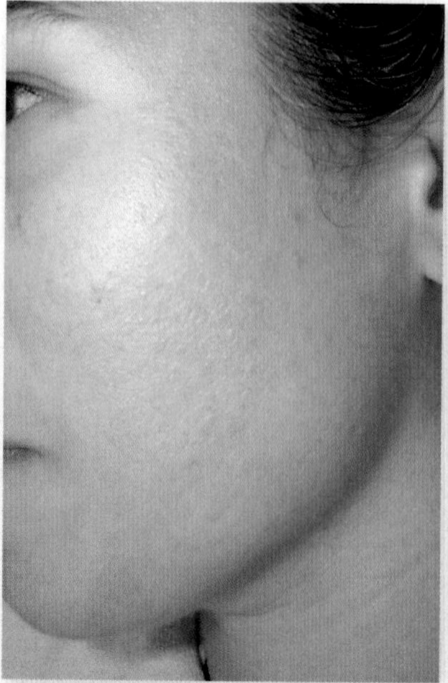

▲ Figure 9–8
Before Retin-A® use for mild acne.

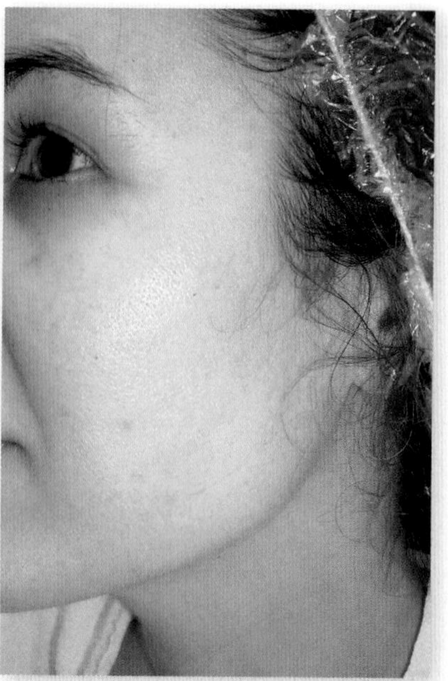

▲ Figure 9–9
After Retin-A® use for mild acne.

Courtesy of Mark Lees Skin Care.

is used to treat both acne and sun-damaged skin (Figure 9–8 and Figure 9–9). Retinoids are also used in skin care formulations. Retinol helps improve the appearance of sun-damaged skin, and it may help other esthetic disorders. Retinyl palmitate polypeptide and beta-carotene are also used in skin care, primarily for their antioxidant properties.

Without vitamin A, a hard keratin protein forms in the body, impairing cellular function of epithelial tissues, replacing mucus, and sometimes resulting in bacterial infection. These surfaces are also a frequent site for cancer development. Research is ongoing to determine the role of vitamin A in preventing cancer.

Since the body stores vitamin A, consuming too much of it can result in vitamin A toxicity. This condition can be serious, resulting in hair loss, very dry lips, and damage to the liver, spleen, and other organs. People should avoid taking more than about 15,000 retinol equivalents (RE) per day. This condition is generally a problem only when people take too many vitamin A supplements.

FOCUS ON
Your Skin

Although a healthy diet does not always guarantee healthy skin, you are what you eat. Your body cannot produce healthy skin without the proper nutrients. Antioxidants are your skin's best friend.

Beta-carotene is a provitamin A. Provitamins, also called *precursors*, are vitamin-containing substances that are converted to the actual vitamin once they are in the body. Beta-carotene is responsible for the bright color of many fruits and vegetables. The carotenes consumed in the diet are important in controlling the free radicals formed during biochemical reactions in the body. Research also points to the possibility that carotenes may play an important role in the formation and function of immune system cells.

Beta-carotene is found in colorful vegetables such as carrots, dark green vegetables such as spinach, and in fruits that are orange in color.

Most people get about half their vitamin A from retinol and half from beta-carotene. Milk that has been fortified contains vitamin A. **Fortified** means that a vitamin has been added to a food product. Carrots, pumpkin, yams, fish, and eggs all contain vitamin A.

Vitamin D

Vitamin D is sometimes called the *sunshine vitamin* because the skin synthesizes vitamin D from cholesterol when exposed to sunlight. This is not a recommendation for tanning, because the skin is also severely damaged by sun exposure. Minimal amounts of sunshine are all that is necessary for vitamin D synthesis.

The main function of vitamin D is to enable the body to properly absorb and use calcium, the element needed for proper bone development and maintenance. Vitamin D also promotes healthy, rapid healing of the skin. Because vitamin D helps to support the bone structure of the body, it is found in many fortified foods and dietary supplements. Dietary sources include fortified milk, fish oils, egg yolks, and butter. Foods from plants are not a good source of vitamin D. Some skin care companies are including Vitamin D in their topical formulas for skin health improvements and as an antioxidant as well.

Deficiencies of vitamin D result in a condition called rickets, which is seen in children. Children with rickets do not develop bones normally. In adults, vitamin D deficiency results in a condition called osteomalacia, or adult rickets, which is the gradual softening and bending of the bones. This disease is more common in women than men, and it often first develops during pregnancy.

Osteoporosis (ahs-tee-oh-puh-ROH-sis) is a reduction in the quality of bone or atrophy of the skeletal tissue. It is an age-related disorder affecting 20 million Americans, 80 percent of them women age 45 and older. Lack of vitamin D is a contributory cause of the disorder. Psoriasis also appears to be linked to deficiency of vitamin D.

Vitamin D is stored in the body, so it is possible—though rare—to have toxic symptoms from too much vitamin D. Most vitamin D toxicity is the result of taking too many vitamin D supplements.

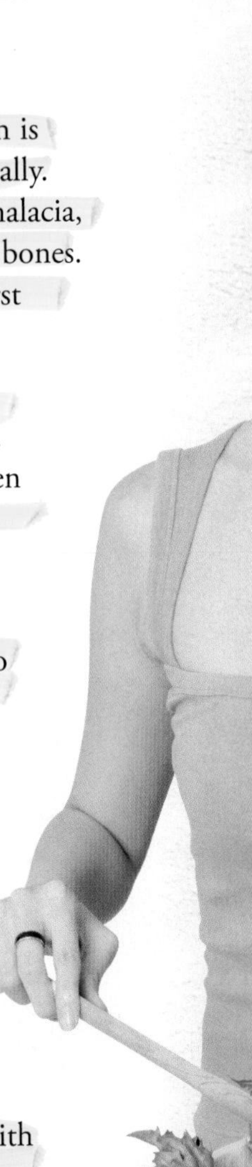

Vitamin E

Vitamin E, also known as **tocopherol** (toe-KAH-fah-roll), is primarily an antioxidant. Antioxidants are important in protecting the body from damage caused by free radicals (the wild molecules that steal electrons from other molecules).

Tocopherol helps to stop free radicals so that cell membranes are not damaged. Continual damage from free radicals is associated with many diseases, tumor formation, and the aging process of the body as well as the skin. Vitamin E generally works to protect many tissues of the body from damage so that they can function normally (**Figure 9–10**).

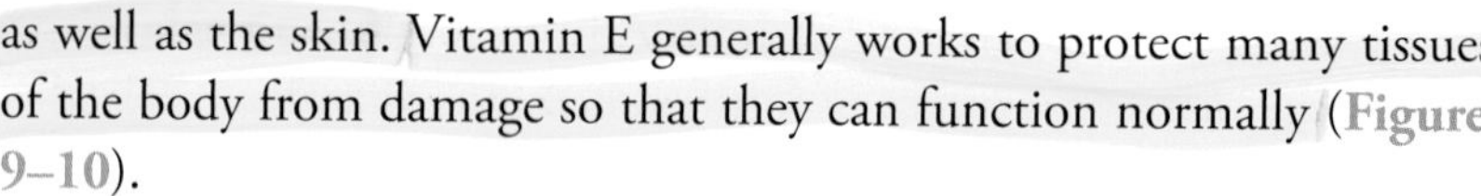

▲ Figure 9–10
Fat-soluble vitamins.

Used in conjunction with vitamin A, vitamin E helps protect the skin from the harmful effects of the sun's rays. Vitamin E also helps heal damage to tissues when used both internally and externally. When used externally in topical lotions or creams, vitamin E may help heal structural damage to the skin, including burns and stretch marks. Vitamin E is excellent as an antioxidant and as a preservative in skin care products.

Good sources of vitamin E include vegetable oils and seed oils (safflower oil is very high in vitamin E); green, leafy vegetables; and avocados, wheat germ, egg yolks, and butter.

Vitamin K

Vitamin K is essential for the synthesis of proteins necessary for blood coagulation. Coagulation is the clotting factor that allows bleeding to stop. Vitamin K applied topically in skin care products has been shown to improve the appearance and the presence of abnormal capillaries, or spider veins, by strengthening capillary walls.

Vitamin K is found in beans; dark, leafy vegetables such as spinach and broccoli; and egg yolks. Deficiencies of vitamin K, although rare, result in hard-to-control bleeding and can be related to certain disorders that prevent proper absorption of fats by the intestines.

Water-Soluble Vitamins

Water-soluble vitamins, B and C, benefit the inside of cells. Water-soluble vitamins do not stay in the body very long. The body must have regular supplies of the water-soluble vitamins because they are used in almost every metabolic reaction and are then excreted—not retained—by the body. Most of these are easily obtained through many foods.

B Vitamins

There are eight **B vitamins:** *B complex (niacin), B_1 (thiamine), B_2 (riboflavin), B_6 (pyridoxine), B_7 (biotin), B_{12} (cobalamine), folic acid (folacin),* and *B_{15} (pantothenic acid)*. These interact with other water-soluble vitamins and act as coenzymes (catalysts) to facilitate enzymatic reactions.

- ***Niacin*** (ny-ah-sin) is a necessary part of many metabolic reactions. Most of these complex reactions are important in the release of energy from carbohydrates. Niacin is required by the body for manufacturing steroids as well as red blood cells. Proteins are the best source of niacin: peanuts, beans, milk, eggs, and meats. Some niacin is found in whole-grain products and in enriched foods.

Pellagra is a disease associated with niacin deficiency. Pellagra can affect the skin, mental functions, the intestinal tract, and can cause death.

- ***Riboflavin*** (ry-bo-flaa-vin) (vitamin B_2) is a water-soluble vitamin that works with enzymes to produce energy in cells. Cells use vitamin B_2 to manufacture various amino acids and fatty acids. Vitamin B_2 is found in milk; meats; liver; dark green leafy vegetables; broccoli; eggs; and salmon and tuna. Grains and bread are often fortified with riboflavin. Deficiencies can result in retarded growth, nerve tissue damage, dryness of the skin, and cracks at the corners of the mouth, known as cheilosis (chay-low-sis)
- ***Thiamine*** (thy-ah-meen) (vitamin B_1) removes carbon dioxide from cells and converts carbohydrates stored as fat. Vitamin B1 is found in pork, beef, fortified cereals, whole wheat products, and nuts. Beriberi is the disease caused by B_1 deficiency. Beriberi affects the nervous system, and it can slow the heart rate as well as cause mental dysfunction. In children it can stunt growth. Vitamin B_1 deficiency can also be caused by alcohol abuse.

- ***Pyridoxine*** (py-ride-ox-ene) (vitamin B_6) is important in the metabolism of proteins, both for breaking down and reconstructing amino acids as needed by the body. Several important chemicals, including histamine, are produced in conjunction with vitamin B_6. Research has shown vitamin B_6 can help improve the effects of premenstrual syndrome (PMS) and irritability. Vitamin B_6 is present in meats, soybeans, fish, and walnuts as well as in vegetables and fruits such as bananas, potatoes, prunes, and avocados. Vitamin B_6 deficiency results in many symptoms, including poor coordination and mental acuity problems, and it can affect the level of white blood cells. Vitamin B_6 is strongly connected to protein synthesis. Many problems are associated with a deficiency and create a domino effect on many other reactions.

- ***Folacin*** (foll-ah-sin), also known as *folic acid*, is an important B vitamin. It is involved in processing amino acids and in transporting certain molecules. This is important for cells that make chemicals conducive to mental health. Vitamin B_{12} and vitamin C must be present for folacin to work properly. Like many other important vitamins, folacin is found in dark green leafy vegetables. Asparagus, cantaloupe, sweet potatoes, and green peas are all good sources of folacin. Deficiencies can cause various mental problems, including moodiness, hostility, and loss of memory. There is a connection between low intakes of folacin and birth defects, as well as colorectal cancer.
- ***Biotin*** (bio-tin) (vitamin B_7) is involved in energy formation by cells, as well as in the synthesis of both proteins and fatty acids. It is produced in the intestinal tract by microbes (good bacteria) and is present in milk, liver, and other organ meats. Deficiencies are primarily

caused by intestinal disorders or by poor absorption. Antibiotics can kill off good bacteria along with the bad, causing lower levels of biotin.

- ***Cobalamine*** (co-bol-a-meen) (vitamin B_{12}) is important in the activation of folacin, fatty acid synthesis, and DNA synthesis in conjunction with proper red blood vessel formation by the bone marrow. Liver, salmon, clams, oysters, and egg yolks are some good food sources of vitamin B_{12}. A disorder known as pernicious anemia is caused by a lack of vitamin B_{12}, or from poor absorption of the vitamin caused by other diseases. Absorption of this vitamin decreases with age, making deficiency symptoms more likely to occur in older persons.
- ***Pantothenic acid*** (pant-o-then-ik ah-sid) (vitamin B_{15}) is important in various processes involved in synthesizing fatty acids and in metabolizing proteins and carbohydrates. Its role in fatty acid synthesis includes the synthesis of hormones, cholesterol, and phospholipids. The latter two are important in the barrier function of skin (the lipid matrix that protects the skin's surface). This vitamin also aids in the functioning of the adrenal glands. Pantothenic acid deficiency is practically nonexistent. Pantothenic acid is present in many foods, but not in fruits.

Vitamin C

Vitamin C, also known as **ascorbic acid** (uh-SKOR-bick AH-cid), is an antioxidant that helps protect the body from many forms of oxidation and from problems involving free radicals. Research indicates that an adequate intake of vitamin C may help prevent cancer because of its ability to scavenge free radicals that attack DNA. DNA damage can lead to the formation of cancerous cells. Vitamin C performs numerous functions in the body.

Vitamin C is an important vitamin needed for proper repair of the skin and tissues. Vitamin C is important in fighting the aging process and promotes collagen production in the dermal tissues, keeping the skin healthy and firm. It is required for collagen formation in skin as well as in cartilage and spinal discs. Vitamin C also renews vitamin E by allowing it to neutralize more free radicals. When applied topically in serums, lotions, and creams, vitamin C has been found to increase collagen and to lighten skin.

Vitamin C also helps prevent damage to capillary walls and can help prevent easy bruising, bleeding gums, and capillary distension.

Vitamin C acts to prevent cardiovascular disease by helping to maintain blood vessel walls and by preventing oxidation of bad cholesterol, which can lead to clogging in the blood vessels. Vitamin C assists the body in dealing with stress, and it is easily depleted during times of great stress. This vitamin supports the healing process of the body. Studies also show that vitamin C helps reduce the time and severity of colds.

Vitamin C is found in citrus fruits; dark green leafy vegetables; tomatoes; and other fruits and vegetables. Vitamin C is easily depleted in smokers, which is important because smokers have more free radicals forming in their bodies. Researchers suggest that smokers need twice as much vitamin C as nonsmokers do. Symptoms of scurvy from vitamin C deficiency include easy bruising, bleeding gums, poor wound healing, and anemia. Scurvy is rare, but it can occur in people with very poor diets and is occasionally seen in senior citizens.

Bioflavonoids (by-oh-FLAH-vuh-noids), which are referred to as vitamin P, enhance absorption of vitamin C. Bioflavonoids relieve pain and bruises. They also protect capillary blood vessels. Bioflavonoids promote circulation, have an antibacterial effect, and can reduce the symptoms of oral herpes. Bioflavonoids are antioxidants found in citrus peel, peppers, grapes, garlic, berries, and green tea.

Minerals

The body requires many **minerals**, inorganic materials essential in many cell reactions and bodily functions. Most are required in relatively small quantities, but they are, nevertheless, necessary for life.

Some of the important minerals and their functions are as follows:

- ***Calcium*** is important in forming and maintaining teeth and bones. It helps prevent osteoporosis, a degenerative disease that results in brittle bones.
- ***Magnesium*** is required for energy release and protein synthesis, preventing tooth decay, and maintaining nerve and muscle movement.
- ***Phosphorus*** is present in DNA and is involved in energy release. It is needed for bone formation and cell growth, and it assists vitamin and food energy processes.
- ***Potassium*** is required for energy use, water balance, and muscular movement. It aids in maintaining blood pressure and regulates cell nutrient transfers and reactions. It is also important in heart and nervous system functions.

Did You Know?

Vegetarians need more protein, iron, and vitamin B_{12} as well as calcium and vitamin D. One egg, ½ ounce (14 g) of nuts, or ¼ cup (57 g) of legumes is equivalent to 1 ounce (28 g) of meat.

fyi

The term *moderately* active means an activity level equal to walking 1.5 to 3 miles (2.4 to 4.8 km) at a pace of 3 to 4 mph (3.8 to 6.4 km/h) and daily light physical activity. The term *active* includes activity equal to walking more than 3 miles (4.8 km) per day.

Walking burns 280 calories per hour. Running burns 590 calories per hour.

- ***Sodium*** moves carbon dioxide, regulates water levels, and transports materials through cell membranes. It also regulates blood pH and helps in stomach, nerve, and muscle function. To limit sodium intake, people should consume less than 2,300 mg (approximately 1 teaspoon [5 milliliters] of salt) of sodium per day. Choose and prepare foods with little salt. Sodium and potassium need to be balanced, so consume potassium-rich foods such as fruits and vegetables. On average, the higher an individual's salt (sodium chloride) intake is, the higher his or her blood pressure will be. Nearly all Americans consume substantially more salt than they need. Decreasing salt intake is advisable to reduce the risk of elevated blood pressure.

Trace Minerals

Other minerals needed in the body are trace minerals. These are required in very small quantities. All of these minerals are necessary for correct body functions, and many are present in cells and tissues. The following are brief descriptions of trace mineral functions, but they are by no means complete.

- ***Iron*** is used in the production of hemoglobin and oxygenation of red blood cells. It is also essential for enzymes and for the immune system.
- ***Iodine*** helps metabolize excess fat and is important in development and thyroid health.
- ***Zinc*** is important for protein synthesis and collagen formation. It also promotes wound healing and helps the immune system.
- ***Copper*** aids in formation of bone, hemoglobin, cells, and elastin. It is involved in healing, energy production, and is essential for collagen formation.
- ***Chromium*** (chro-me-um) helps with energy and the metabolism of glucose and aids in synthesizing fats and proteins. Chromium also stabilizes blood sugar levels.
- ***Fluoride*** is needed for healthy teeth and bone formation.
- ***Selenium*** (sil-en-e-um) is a vital antioxidant protecting the immune system. It works with vitamin E to produce antibodies and to maintain a healthy heart; it is also needed for tissue elasticity.
- ***Manganese*** (man-gun-eze) assists protein and fat metabolism, promotes healthy nerves, and supports immune system function. Manganese also aids in energy production and bone growth. **L03**

ACTIVITY

Keep a log of your day's food intake by reading labels and recording calories and nutritional values. Compare these values to the RDAs. How close did you come to eating the recommended portions? A daily food log can help you be more aware of what you are eating and inspire healthy habits.

Nutrition and Esthetics

Proper nutrition is a primary factor in maintaining the skin's health. Some foods directly affect certain conditions of the skin, but there are also many myths about food and the skin. An example is the widely held belief that chocolate can cause or worsen acne. The truth is that junk foods and sweets are unhealthy and should not be consumed in large quantities, but they may not directly affect acne; however, excess iodine in one's diet may trigger acne in some cases. It is best to refer a client to a qualified physician for further evaluation (Figure 9–11).

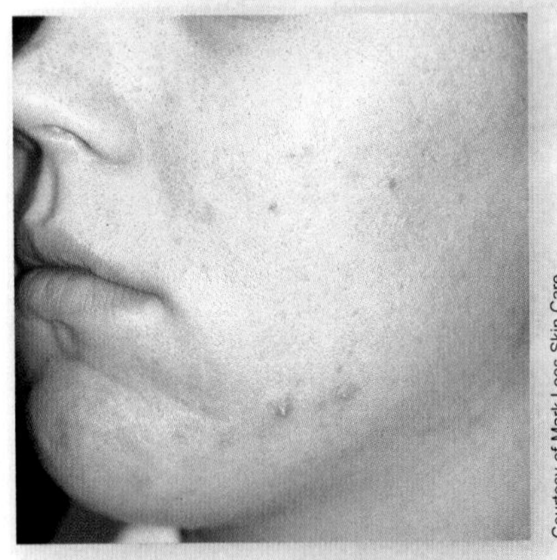

▲ Figure 9–11
Excess iodine can trigger acne in some cases.

As scientific studies continue, the correlation between foods and acne will become clearer. It is well known that spicy foods and alcohol consumption can induce rosacea flare-ups. Diet will affect the skin, and skin is an indicator of the body's overall health. Some women have such low-fat diets that their body fat drops too low, resulting in hormonal imbalances that can cause skin problems, including hyperpigmentation and forms of acne. Chapter 13, Skin Care Products: Chemistry, Ingredients, and Selection, discusses the effects of topical vitamins and antioxidants on the skin. ☑ LO4

Client Health Concerns

Obesity and weight loss are concerns for many clients. Although clients may talk to you about their health-related issues, it is important to remember that unless you are formally educated in nutrition, you are not a source of counsel for persons with nutritional concerns. To do so might endanger your client's health and have legal consequences. All clients who have serious questions about nutritional issues should be referred to a registered dietitian. Fad diets are rampant. Every week there is some new, magical weight-loss gimmick or plan.

Here is the truth about weight loss:

- The only way to lose weight is to burn more calories than you consume.
- Certain diets can cause chemical imbalances that may damage the body.
- Vitamins and supplements are not substitutes for proper nutrition. You can get most of the vitamins and minerals you need from a balanced diet.
- Vitamin and mineral supplements have little nutritional value because they do not provide the basics—the carbohydrates, proteins, and fats necessary for life processes.
- You must eat a balanced diet for the vitamins and minerals to have any effect. If you look at nutrition as building and maintaining a house, the nails (vitamins and minerals) are no good without the wood and the bricks (macronutrients).
- No magical ingredient can cause weight loss without having other, sometimes harmful, effects on the body.
- The best way to lose weight, and to maintain proper weight, is to adopt a healthy diet along with proper exercise.

fyi

Some skin care product companies manufacture vitamin and mineral supplements that are designed for healthy skin.

Food Choices

Healthier food choices are more readily available in today's health-conscious world. The abundance of choices makes it easier to eat nutritious, high-quality foods.

Education and scientific advances have increased our knowledge of nutrition and how foods affect our health. Organic foods are grown without pesticides or added chemicals and are becoming more popular as awareness increases. Farmer's markets and health-food sections of grocery stores have become common. Fast-food restaurants are offering healthier alternatives. Selecting what we put in our bodies is a choice, and eating fresh foods without preservatives is one of them. Nutritional and herbal supplements are another topic altogether. A wealth of information is available on nutrition and health. As with anything else, doing research and checking facts for accuracy is recommended. As scientific research improves, what may be true today could change tomorrow.

Web Resources

www.choosemyplate.gov

www.health.gov

www.ams.usda.gov

www.fda.gov

www.quickstudycharts.com

Fad Diets

Fad diets are those which promise quick weight loss. They may vary from eating one type of food exclusively to eating multiple foods in a systematic format. As we know, there are no limits to what you might find in the way of a fad diet today. Most fad diets should be looked at from a discerning perspective, as they can be unhealthy for the body. One of the major problems with eating in an imbalanced manner is that it likely will create just that in the body. Eating balanced nutritional foods is vital for our health on many levels: from the energy that we acquire to supporting proper blood sugar level needs to making certain that we have the required essential vitamins and minerals in the body in order to ward off illnesses, health problems, and weight gains.

Here are some situations to be aware of when looking at a potential fad diet:

- Exaggerated claims or promises that sound too good to be true
- The purchase of a product is necessary to obtain weight loss
- The elimination of various food groups (all meat or all carbohydrate)
- Studies that cannot be supported
- Selling the product becomes part of the weight-loss program

Always follow the nutritional advice of your healthcare provider, and refer clients to qualified practitioners for this advice as well. This is a wonderful referral service that we can provide for our clients, and it can work as a tremendous networking benefit to you and your clients. ☑ L05

▲ Figure 9–12
Water is an essential nutrient.

Water and the Skin

There is one essential nutrient no person can live without, and that is water (Figure 9–12). To function properly, the body and skin both rely heavily on water. Water composes 50 to 70 percent of the body's weight. Drinking pure water is essential to keeping the skin and body healthy; it sustains cell health, aids in elimination of toxins and waste, helps regulate body temperature, and aids in proper digestion. When all of these functions perform properly, they help the skin stay healthy, vital, and attractive. Drinking 9 to 12 cups (2 to 3 liters) of water a day is an average recommendation.

Here's a Tip

Keep a large bottle of water on hand daily to keep the body hydrated. Offer clients water during their services (Figure 9–13).

▲ Figure 9–13
Encourage clients to drink water to maintain healthy skin.

Water Facts

- An estimated 75 percent of Americans are chronically dehydrated. Research suggests that the benefits of water on human health and functioning are many.
- Even mild dehydration will slow metabolism by as much as 3 percent.
- Drinking lots of water can help stop hunger pangs for many dieters.
- Lack of water is the number one cause of daytime fatigue.
- A 2 percent drop in body water can trigger fuzzy short-term memory, trouble with basic math, and difficulty in focusing on a computer screen or printed page.

Water Intake Requirements

The amount of water needed by an individual varies, depending on body weight and level of daily physical activity. Here is an easy formula to help you determine how much water is needed every day for maximum physical health: Take your body weight and divide by 2. Divide this number by 8. The resulting number approximates how many 8-ounce glasses of water you should drink every day. For instance, if you weigh 160 pounds, you should drink 10 glasses of water a day. If you engage in intense physical activity each day, add two extra glasses of water to the final number. This will help replace extra fluids lost while exercising. Drinking excessive amounts of water is not recommended, so increase the amount only if you are thirsty or dehydrated. As with all healthy habits, moderation is usually the best choice for nutritional balance. ✔ LO6

Self-Care and the Esthetician

As estheticians it is vital that we develop and use good health habits to set an example for our clients and to increase our own age prevention while enjoying excellent health. Here are 14 essential tools for practicing wellness inside and out:

- Exercise: Move your body (walking, running, hiking) for ½ hour at least three times a week

▲ Figure 9–14
Make sure you are drinking enough water.

- Hydrate: Make certain that you are getting enough water (Figure 9-14)
- Eat: Fresh fruits and vegetables of all colors everyday for antioxidant benefits
- Balance the fats: Eat no more that 30 percent of overall caloric intake in fats, and 10 percent or less in *bad* saturated fats
- Reduce inflammation: Minimize sugar and processed food intake
- Manage your protein: Keep protein at 20 percent of total caloric daily intake
- Cook lightly: Steam, poach, or stir-fry foods instead of grilling, broiling, or baking
- Frequent the fiber: Add more whole grains, nuts and seeds, or cereals to your diet
- Drink green tea: Sipping on green tea helps to lower cholesterol, reduces blood sugar levels, and provides additional antioxidant benefits
- Have regular massages: Trade services with other practitioners
- DO NOT SMOKE: By now, we all know that smoking is detrimental to our health, both inside and outside; start a smoking cessation program as soon as possible if you are still smoking; visit: www.smokefree.gov
- Make healthy friends: Maintain good healthy relationships; the esthetics' profession demands your best
- Schedule routine health checks: Make certain to have your regular dental cleanings, physicals, and other health screenings (Figure 9–15)
- Have fun: Remember your passion for esthetics and make time for you! ☑ LO7

ACTIVITY

We have presented a basic overview of nutrition in this chapter. If you are interested in learning more about this subject, check out nutrition courses or textbooks to give yourself a better knowledge base for both nutrition and health issues.

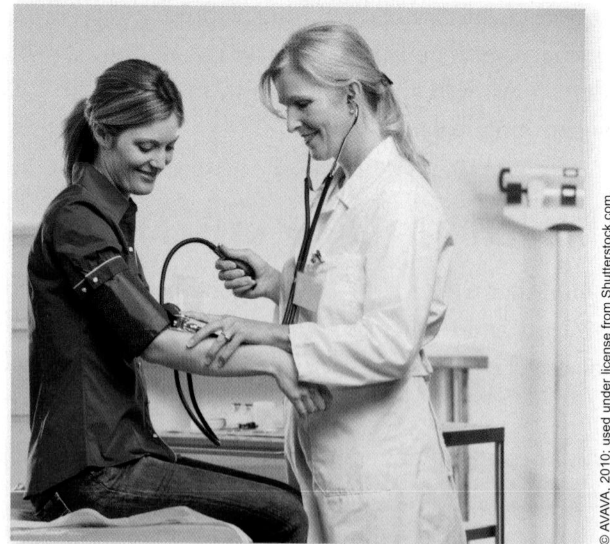

▶ Figure 9–15
Schedule your routine health screenings.

Review Questions

1. What is MyPlate?
2. What are calories?
3. What are the three macronutrients?
4. What are proteins?
5. What are carbohydrates?
6. Why is fat necessary in the diet?
7. What are the micronutrients?
8. What are the fat-soluble vitamins?
9. What are the water-soluble vitamins?
10. Which vitamins are antioxidants?
11. How is vitamin A beneficial for the skin?
12. Name the eight B vitamins.
13. List the minerals and trace minerals.
14. Why is water essential for the body?
15. How does vitamin C affect the skin?
16. What is a "fad" diet and why should we avoid them?
17. Why is it important for the esthetician to have good health and nutritional habits?

Glossary

adenosine triphosphate	Abbreviated ATP; the substance that provides energy to cells and converts oxygen to carbon dioxide, a waste product we breathe out.
amino acid	Organic acids that form the building blocks of protein.
arteriosclerosis	Clogging and hardening of the arteries.
B vitamins	These water-soluble vitamins interact with other water-soluble vitamins and act as coenzymes (catalysts) by facilitating enzymatic reactions. B vitamins include niacin, riboflavin, thiamine, pyridoxine, folacin, biotin, cobalamine, and pantothenic acid.
bioflavonoids	Biologically active flavonoids; also called vitamin P; considered an aid to healthy skin and found most abundantly in citrus fruits.
calories	A measure of heat units; measures food energy for the body.
carbohydrates	Compounds that break down the basic chemical sugars and supply energy for the body.
cholesterol	A waxy substance found in your body that is needed to produce hormones, vitamin D, and bile; also important for protecting nerves and for the structure of cells.
complementary foods	Combinations of two incomplete foods; complementary proteins eaten together provide all the essential amino acids and make a complete protein.
disaccharides	Sugars made up of two simple sugars such as lactose and sucrose.
enzymes	Catalysts that break down complex food molecules to utilize extracted energy.

Glossary

fats	Also known as *lipids*; macronutrients used to produce energy in the body; the materials in the sebaceous glands that lubricate the skin.
fortified	A vitamin has been added to a food product.
glycosaminoglycans	A water-binding substance between the fibers of the dermis.
hypoglycemia	A condition in which blood glucose or blood sugar drops too low; caused by either too much insulin or low food intake.
linoleic acid	Omega-6, an essential fatty acid used to make important hormones; also part of the skin's lipid barrier.
macronutrients	Nutrients that make up the largest part of the nutrition we take in; the three basic food groups: protein, carbohydrates, and fats.
micronutrients	Vitamins and substances that have no calories or nutritional value, yet are essential for body functions.
minerals	Inorganic materials required for many reactions of the cells and body.
monosaccharides	Carbohydrates made up of one basic sugar unit.
mucopolysaccharides	Carbohydrate–lipid complexes that are also good water-binders.
nonessential amino acids	Amino acids that can be synthesized by the body and do not have to be obtained from the diet.
omega-3 fatty acids	Alpha-linoleic acid; a type of "good" polyunsaturated fat that may decrease cardiovascular diseases. It is also an anti-inflammatory and beneficial for skin.
osteoporosis	A thinning of bones, leaving them fragile and prone to fractures; caused by the reabsorption of calcium into the blood.
polysaccharides	Carbohydrates that contain three or more simple carbohydrate molecules.
proteins	Chains of amino acid molecules used in all cell functions and body growth.
retinoic acid	Also known as *Retin-A®*; vitamin A derivative that has demonstrated an ability to alter collagen synthesis and is used to treat acne and visible signs of aging; side effects are irritation, photosensitivity, skin dryness, redness, and peeling.
tretinoin	Transretinoic acid, a derivative of Vitamin A used for collagen synthesis, hyperpigmentation, and for acne.
vitamin A	Also known as *retinol*; an antioxidant that aids in the functioning and repair of skin cells.
vitamin C	Also known as *ascorbic acid;* an antioxidant vitamin needed for proper repair of the skin and tissues; promotes the production of collagen in the skin's dermal tissues; aids in and promotes the skin's healing process.
vitamin D	Fat-soluble vitamin sometimes called the *sunshine vitamin* because the skin synthesizes vitamin D from cholesterol when exposed to sunlight. Essential for growth and development.
vitamin E	Also known as *tocopherol*; primarily an antioxidant; helps protect the skin from the harmful effects of the sun's rays.
vitamin K	Vitamin responsible for the synthesis of factors necessary for blood coagulation.

Skin Sciences

PART 3

CHAPTER 10

Physiology & Histology of the Skin

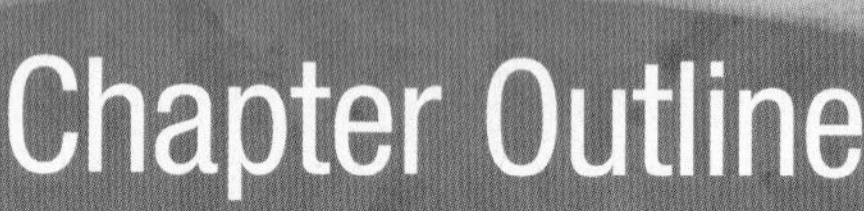

- Why Study Physiology and Histology of the Skin?
- Skin Facts
- Skin Functions
- Layers of the Skin
- Hair Anatomy
- Nail Anatomy
- Nerves
- Glands
- Skin Health

Learning Objectives

After completing this chapter, you will be able to:

- LO1 Explain the functions of the skin.
- LO2 Describe the layers of the skin.
- LO3 Describe how skin gets its color.
- LO4 Define collagen and elasticity.
- LO5 Name the glands of the skin.
- LO6 Discuss how sun damage affects skin.
- LO7 Understand free radical damage.
- LO8 Understand the effects of hormones on the skin.
- LO9 Explain how the skin ages.

Key Terms

Page number indicates where in the chapter the term is used.

apocrine glands pg. 243
arrector pili muscle pg. 232
barrier function pg. 230
ceramides pg. 244
collagen pg. 238
corneocytes pg. 234
dermal papillae pg. 239
dermis pg. 237
desmosomes pg. 235
eccrine glands pg. 243
elastin pg. 238
epidermal growth factor (EGF) pg. 230
epidermis pg. 233
eumelanin pg. 237
fibroblasts pg. 230
follicles pg. 232
glycation pg. 248
hair papillae pg. 239
hyaluronic acid pg. 239
hydrolipidic pg. 230
intercellular matrix pg. 230
keratin pg. 234
keratinocytes pg. 234
Langerhans immune cells pg. 235
leukocytes pg. 244
lymph vessels pg. 238
melanin pg. 236
melanocytes pg. 236
melanosomes pg. 236
papillary layer pg. 239
pheomelanin pg. 237
pores pg. 232
reticular layer pg. 239
rosacea pg. 250
sebaceous glands (oil glands) pg. 232
sebum pg. 232
stratum corneum (horny layer) pg. 234
stratum germinativum (basal cell layer) pg. 235
stratum granulosum (granular layer) pg. 235
stratum lucidum pg. 235
stratum spinosum (spiny layer) pg. 235
subcutaneous layer (hypodermis) pg. 239
subcutis tissue (adipose tissue) pg. 239
sudoriferous glands (sweat glands) pg. 232
T-cells pg. 244
telangiectasia pg. 250
transepidermal water loss (TEWL) pg. 230
tyrosinase pg. 237
UVA radiation (aging rays) pg. 245
UVB radiation (burning rays) pg. 245

Estheticians have an opportunity to study a most fascinating science. The science of skin *histology* and *physiology* includes the functions, layers, and anatomy of the skin. Skin histology is the study of the structure and composition of the skin tissue. Physiology is the study of the functions of living organisms. These are the foundational sciences estheticians need to learn before caring for the skin.

Estheticians who specialize in the health and beauty of skin are sometimes referred to as *technicians, skin therapists,* or *specialists.* There is much more to being an esthetician than simply performing facials and selling products. As scientific research in the industry changes constantly, estheticians must continue their education at all times. Clients value an esthetician's understanding of their skin and personalized treatment suggestions (**Figure 10–1**). By educating clients, estheticians are sharing their knowledge and expertise. An esthetician's primary focus is on preserving, protecting, and nourishing the skin.

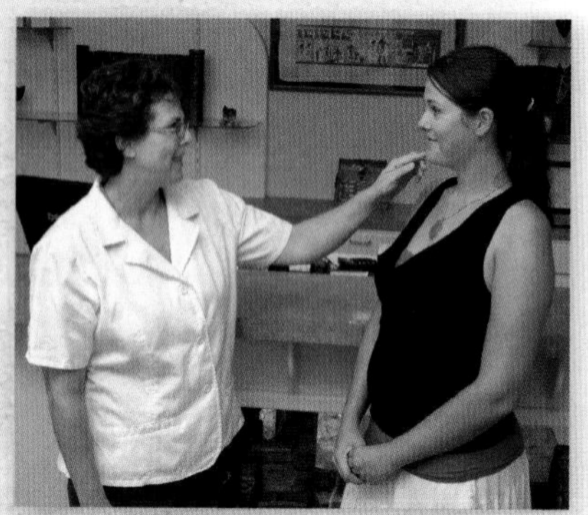

▲ Figure 10–1
Consulting with a client.

The complexity of the skin is amazing. The layers, components, and functions all work to protect and regulate the skin and the body. There is much to study about the body's largest organ and how to best maintain its optimum health. The aging process, sun exposure, hormones, and nutrition affect the skin's health and appearance. By understanding skin physiology, estheticians can be confident in treating this intricate system.

Why Study Physiology and Histology of the Skin?

Estheticians should study and have a thorough understanding of the physiology and histology of the skin because they must understand the skin and how it functions in order to effectively treat their clients.

- The functions, layers, and anatomy of the skin are the foundations estheticians need to learn before caring for the skin.
- By understanding skin physiology, estheticians can be confident in treating the skin and sharing their knowledge with clients.
- Understanding how the skin cell layers function is important in choosing ingredients and treatments for clients.
- Part of providing skin care services is understanding how the aging process, sun exposure, hormones, and other influencing factors affect the skin's health and appearance.

Skin Facts

Skin, or the *integumentary system*, is the largest organ in the body. It is a strong barrier designed to protect us from the outside elements. The body systems that make up our outermost layer are incredibly complex. Skin layers, nerves, cellular functions, hair follicles, and glands all work together harmoniously to regulate and protect the body.

Hormones, growth factors, and other biochemicals control the skin's intricate functions.

The basic material and building blocks for our body's tissues are proteins. Proteins are made up of amino acids. Amino acids form peptides (part of a protein) and proteins. Peptide bonds are what hold these amino acids together. Chains of amino acids then become polypeptides. Proteins are the foundation of our cells and skin.

Our skin is a cell-making factory with miles (kilometers) of blood vessels, millions of sweat glands, and an array of nerves within a network of fibers (**Figure 10–2**). Appendages of the skin include hair, nails, sweat glands, and oil glands. Healthy skin is slightly moist, soft, smooth, and somewhat acidic. Skin is thickest (4 millimeters or 1⁄5 inch) on the palms of the hands and soles of the feet. It is thinnest on the eyelids (1.5 millimeters or 1⁄16 inch). The skin of an average adult weighs 7 pounds (3 kilograms) and averages an area of about 22 square feet (6.5 square meters) in size. It contains one-half to two-thirds of the blood in the body and one-half of the primary immune cells.

fyi

Each square inch (2.5 square cm) of skin contains:

- Millions of cells.
- 8 feet (2.5 m) of blood vessels.
- 32 (10 m) feet of nerves.
- 650 sweat glands.
- 100 oil glands.
- 65 hairs.
- 1,300 nerve endings.
- 155 pressure receptors.
- 12 cold and heat receptors.

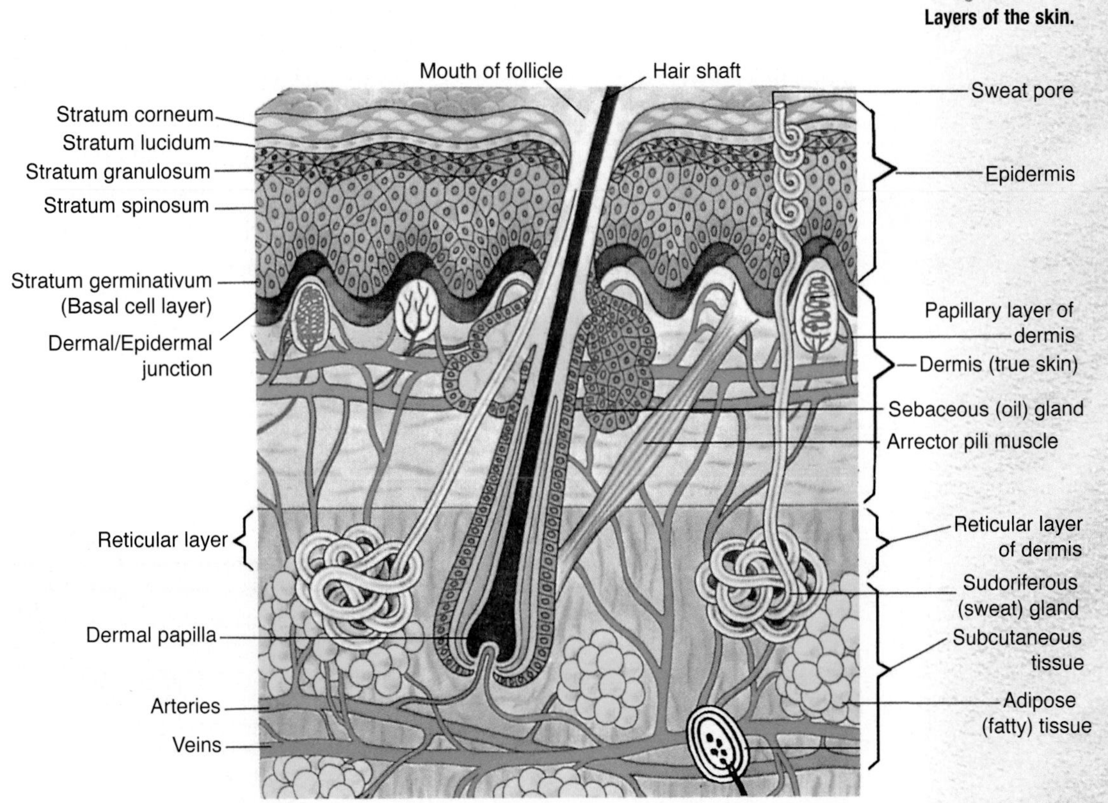

▼ **Figure 10–2**
Layers of the skin.

Did You Know?

Touch is one of the first senses to develop. Nerve fibers in the skin sense when we are touched. Depending on the type of stimulation, sensations felt on our skin cause us to feel, react, or move. Massage sends messages to the brain through nerve stimulation and lowers stress in the body. Studies have shown stress reduction in babies and older adults when they experience more touch and interaction with others.

Skin Functions

The six primary functions of the skin are protection, sensation, heat regulation, excretion, secretion, and absorption.

Protection

The skin is a thin, yet strong, protective barrier to outside elements and microorganisms. It has many defense mechanisms to protect the body from injury and invasion. Sebum (oil) on the epidermis gives protection from external factors such as invasion by certain bacteria. The acid mantle is the protective barrier made up of sebum, lipids, sweat, and water. These components form a **hydrolipidic** film to protect the skin from drying out and from exposure to external factors. The acid mantle has an average pH of 5.5. The balanced pH of the skin is important for maintaining the proper acidic level of 5.5 to protect from pathogens and for regulating enzymatic functions.

The acid mantle is part of the skin's natural barrier function. The **barrier function** is the skin's mechanism that protects us from irritation and intercellular **transepidermal water loss (TEWL)**, the water loss caused by evaporation on the skin's surface. Lipids are substances that contribute to the barrier function of the epidermis. Lipids are protective oils and are part of the **intercellular matrix** (fluid) between epidermal cells. Damage to our barrier layer is the cause of many skin problems including sensitivities, aging, and dehydration (**Figure 10–3**).

fyi The microscopic view of the structure of the epidermis resembles a brick wall—the cells are the bricks, and the intercellular matrix is the cement mortar between the bricks that holds everything together.

The skin's most amazing feature is the ability to heal itself. Skin can repair itself when injured, thus protecting the body from infection and damage from injury. Through a hyperproduction of cells and blood clotting, injured skin can restore itself to its normal thickness. Hormones such as **epidermal growth factor (EGF)** stimulate skin cells to reproduce and heal. Proteins and peptides trigger **fibroblasts** (cell stimulators) and cells to rejuvenate. Skin cells are activated to quickly repair the skin. Other protective components of the skin include cells and the immune system. These processes are discussed later in this chapter.

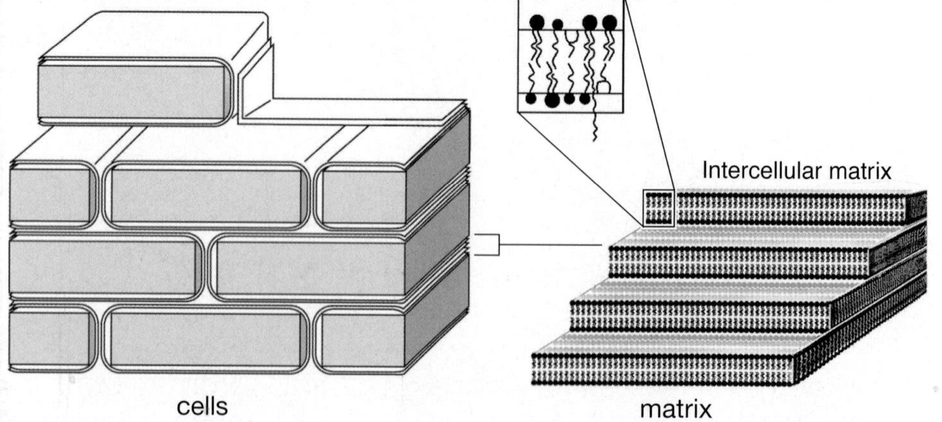

▶ Figure 10–3
Barrier layer function: the brick-and-mortar concept.

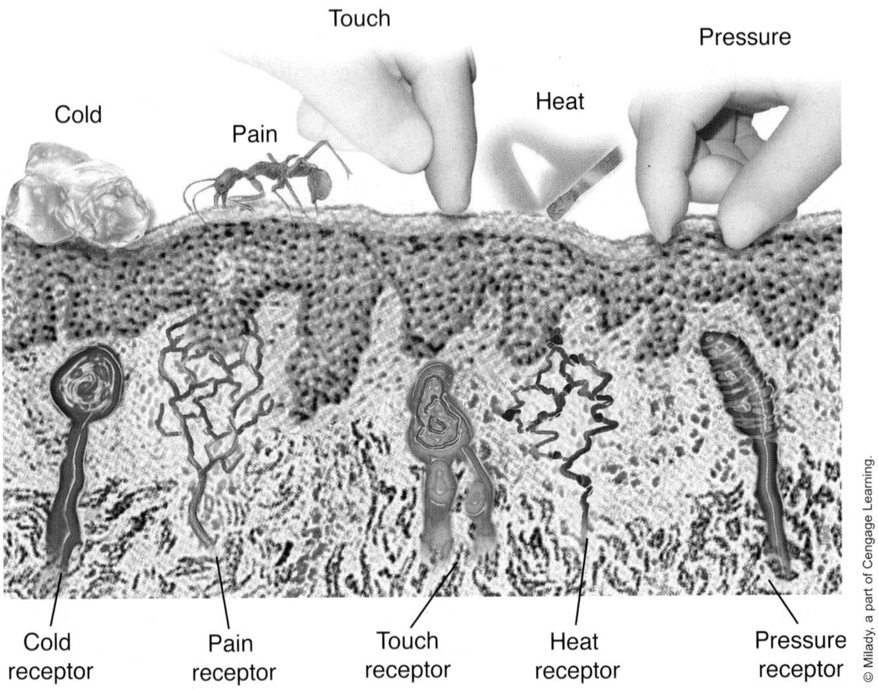

▲ Figure 10–4
Sensory nerve endings in the skin.

Another form of protection in the skin is melanin, the pigment that protects us from the sun. Melanin is the pigment in the eyes, hair, and skin that gives us some protection from the UV rays emitted by the sun.

Sensation

Sensory nerve endings in the dermis respond to touch, pain, cold, heat, and pressure (**Figure 10–4**). When the body senses touch, it affects our body's functions. Massage and product application produce physiological benefits to the body such as increased circulation. Millions of nerve-end fibers on the surface of the skin detect stimuli. These sensations send messages to the brain as a protective defense mechanism or as a positive message that something is stimulating the surface. These signals also cause other nerves or muscles to react. Sensory nerve fibers are most abundant in the fingertips and thus are designed to be one of the most sensitive parts of the body.

fyi

Hydro means *water. Lipidic* means *oil.* A *hydrolipidic film* is an oil–water balance on the skin's surface.

Heat Regulation

The body's average internal thermostat is set at 98.6 degrees Fahrenheit (37 degrees Celsius). When the outside temperature changes, the skin automatically adjusts to warm or cool the body.

The body maintains thermoregulation through evaporation, perspiration, radiation, and insulation. Millions of sweat glands release heat from the body through perspiration to keep us from overheating. We then cool ourselves through evaporation on the skin's surface. Blood flow and blood vessel dilation also assists in cooling the body.

fyi

Sometimes the terms *pore* and *follicle* are used interchangeably. Pores are actually sweat gland openings, not follicles. Pore is a common term that clients usually use when describing their skin. These are technically follicles they are referring to, not pores.

Follicles are tube-like depressions with oil glands attached to them. Some follicles have hair and others are hairless.

We protect ourselves from the cold by constriction of the blood vessels and decreasing blood flow. Additionally, the body's fat layers help to insulate and warm the body.

Hair follicles also help regulate body temperature and protect from heat loss. When we are cold, the **arrector pili muscles** attached to the hair follicles contract and cause "goose bumps." This reaction is thought to warm the skin by the air pocket that is created under the hairs that stand up when the muscle contracts. Shivering is also an automatic response to cold and a way to warm up the body.

Excretion

The **sudoriferous glands** (soo-duh-RIF-uh-rus), also known as **sweat glands**, excrete perspiration and detoxify the body by excreting excess water, salt, and unwanted chemicals through the pores. Sweat, just like sebum, is also part of the acid mantle. **Pores** are the openings for sweat glands, however, the word pore is used as a lay term for *follicle*, because both are openings on the top of the epidermis. These gland functions are discussed later in the chapter.

Secretion

Sebum is an oily substance that protects the surface of the skin and lubricates both the skin and hair. **Sebaceous glands**, (sih-BAY-shus GLANZ), also known as **oil glands**, are appendages attached to follicles that produce sebum. These oils help keep the skin soft and protected from outside elements. The skin is approximately 50 to 70 percent water. Sebum coating the surface of the skin slows down the evaporation of water, also known as transepidermal water loss (TEWL), and helps maintain water levels in the cells. Emotional stress and hormone imbalances can stimulate oil glands to increase the flow of sebum, which can lead to skin problems.

Absorption

Absorption of ingredients, water, and oxygen is necessary for our skin's health. Vitamin D is also synthesized and produced in the skin upon exposure to the sun. The skin selectively absorbs topical products and creams through the cells, hair follicles, and sebaceous glands. While absorption is limited, some ingredients with a smaller molecular size can penetrate into the skin. The penetration ability of the ingredient is determined by the size of the molecule and other characteristics of the product. Lipid-soluble products penetrate better. The routes of penetration into the skin are through the follicle walls, sebaceous glands, intercellular, or transcellular (**Figure 10–5**).

Absorption of select topical products helps keep skin moisturized, nourished, and protected. Scientific advances continually result in the creation of new products that are more readily absorbed by the skin, thus making them more effective. Many chemicals and prescription

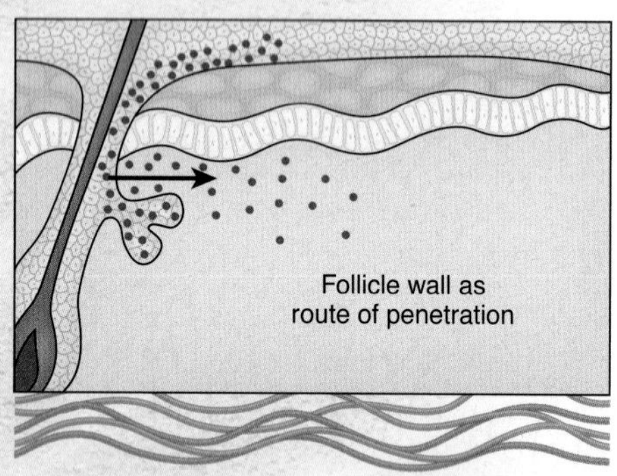

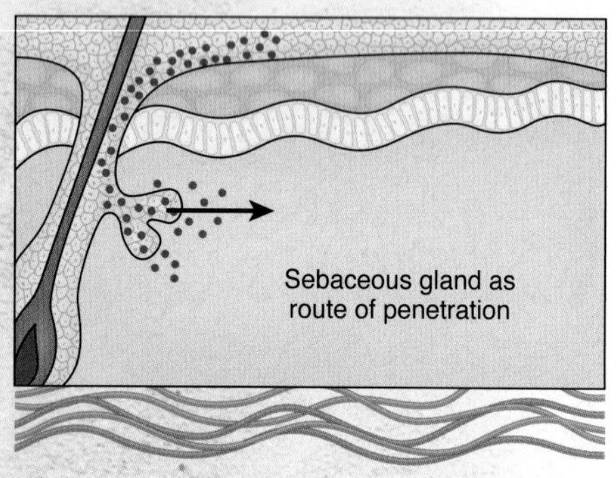

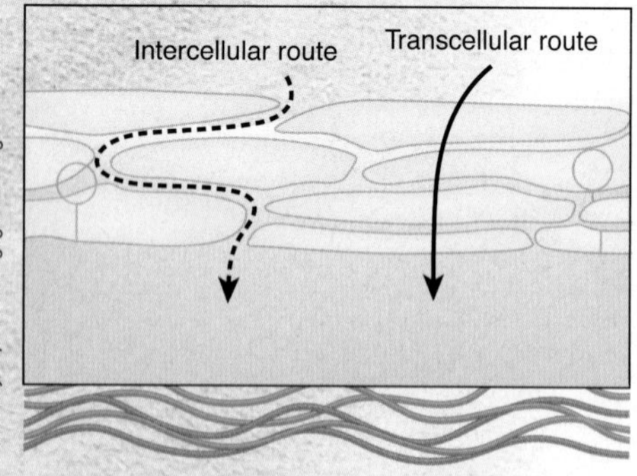

▲ Figure 10–5
Primary routes of penetration.

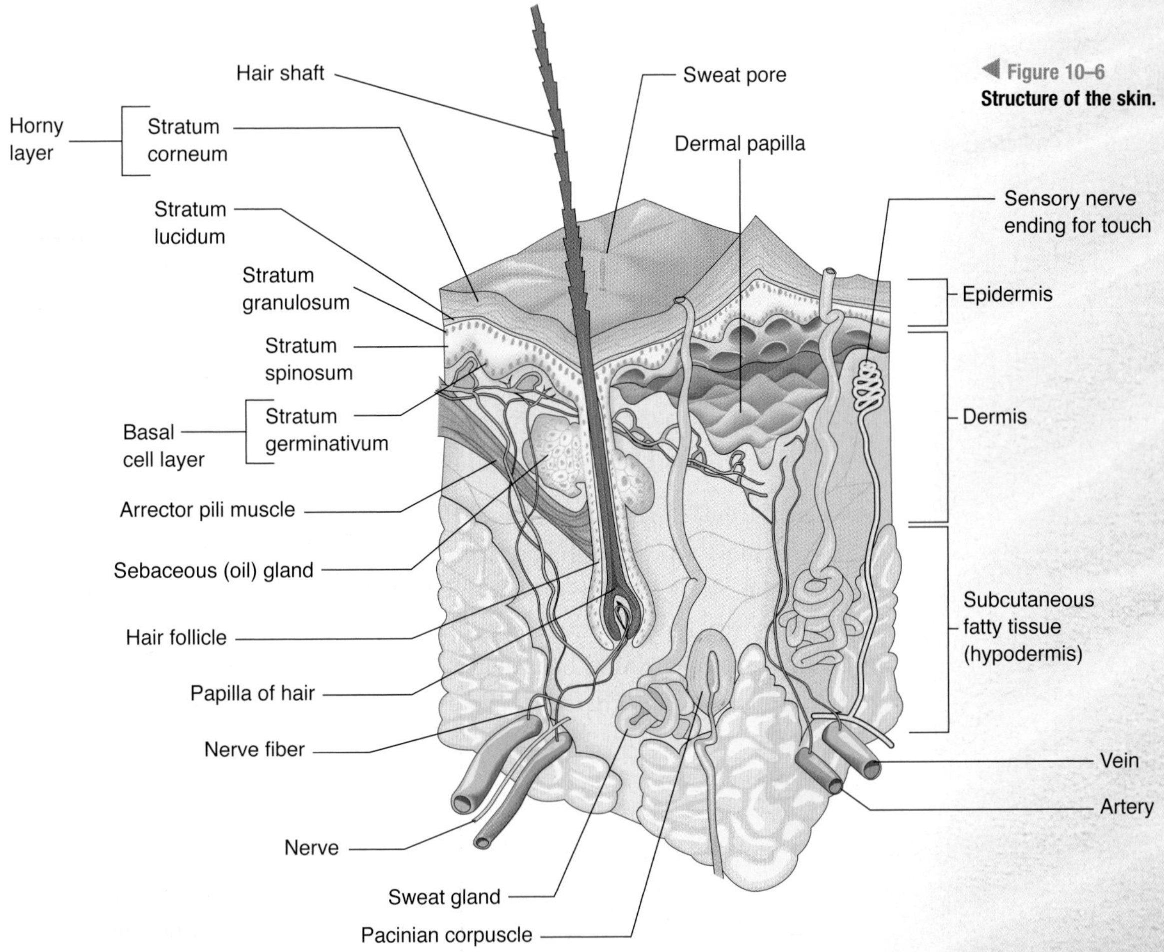

◀ Figure 10–6
Structure of the skin.

creams can penetrate the skin. This effect can be either harmful or beneficial, depending on the chemicals. ✔ LO1

fyi Intercellular means "between" the cells and transcellular is "across" or through the cells.

Layers of the Skin

The skin is comprised of two main layers, the epidermis and the dermis (Figure 10–6).

The Epidermis

The **epidermis** is the outermost layer of the skin. This is the epithelial tissue that covers our body. It is a thin, protective covering with many nerve endings. The epidermis is composed of five layers called strata (singular: stratum). The uppermost surface layer is the stratum corneum, followed by the stratum lucidum, stratum granulosum, and stratum spinosum; the bottom layer is the stratum germinativum (the basal layer) (Figure 10–7). Understanding how the skin cell layers function is important in choosing ingredients and treatments. Estheticians are licensed

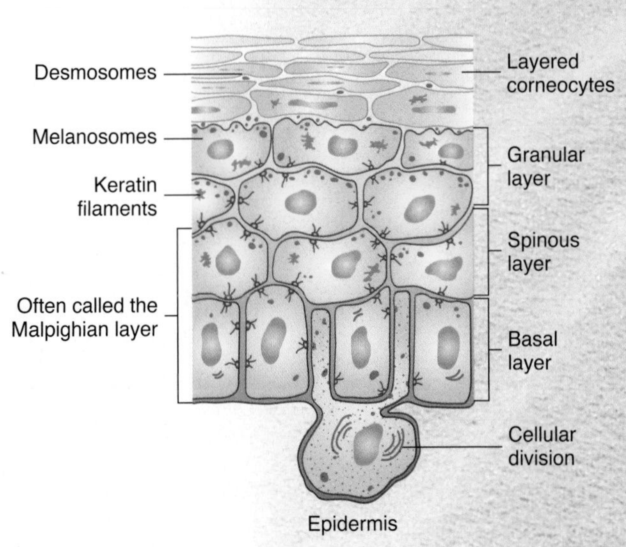

▲ Figure 10–7
Individual layers of the skin.

Did You Know?

The epidermis and dermis combined is 1.5 to 4 mm (1⁄16 to 1⁄5 in) thick. The epidermis is only .04 mm to 1.5 mm (1⁄1,000 to 1⁄16 in) thick. The dermis is much thicker than the epidermis.

fyi

The epidermis is composed of the following layers (strata):

- Stratum corneum—"the horny cells"
- Stratum lucidum—"the clear cells"
- Stratum granulosum—"the grainy cells"
- Stratum spinosum—"the spiny cells"
- Stratum germinativum—"the germination or growth layer"

to work only on the epidermis, not the dermis, unless they are working with a physician or another licensed medical practitioner.

Keratinocytes

Keratinocytes (kair-uh-TIN-oh-sytes), composed of keratin, comprise 95 percent of the epidermis. These cells contain both proteins and lipids. Surrounding the cells in the epidermis are lipids, which protect the cells from water loss and dehydration.

Keratin (KAIR-uh-tin) is a fiberous protein that provides resiliency and protection to the skin. Keratin is found in all layers of the epidermis. Hard keratin is the protein found in hair and nails.

Keratinocytes have many different functions and go through changes as they move up through the layers to the top layer of the stratum corneum. Stem cells are the mother cells that divide in the basal layer forming new daughter cells. These daughter cells move up through the layers before becoming hardened corneocytes of the stratum corneum. Keratinocytes and other cells protect the epidermis. Other cells in the epidermis include melanocytes, immune cells, and Merkel cells (nerve receptors).

The Stratum Corneum

The **stratum corneum** (STRAT-um KOR-nee-um), also known as **horny layer**, is the top, outermost layer of the epidermis. The esthetician is primarily concerned with this layer. The stratum corneum is very thin, yet it is waterproof, permeable, regenerates itself, detoxifies the body, and responds to stimuli. Keratinocytes on the surface have hardened into **corneocytes** (KOR-nee-oh-sytes), the waterproof, protective cells. These "dead" protein cells have dried out and lack nuclei. This layer is referred to as the *horny layer* because of these scale-like cells.

Keratinocytes are continually shed from the skin in a process called *desquamation* (DES-kwuh-may-shun). These cells are replaced by new cells coming to the surface from the lower stratums. This process of desquamation and replacement is known as *cell turnover*. The average adult cell turnover rate is every 28 days depending on a person's age, lifestyle, and health. The cell turnover rate slows down with age.

Cells and oil combine to form a protective barrier layer on the stratum corneum. This is the acid mantle. Stratum corneum cells are surrounded by bilayers of oil and water. Lipids of the cell membranes, such as phospholipids and essential fatty acids, determine the health of this protective barrier.

In general, the stratum corneum has 15 to 20 layers of cells. The stratum corneum has a thickness between 0.01 to 0.04 mm. The keratinocytes on the surface of the skin are also called *squamous* (flat, scaly) keratinized cells. There are different terms used to describe the same cells, so it is helpful to remember these surface cells are both flat and hardened (squamous and cornified).

The Stratum Lucidum

The **stratum lucidum** (STRAT-um LOO-sih-dum) is a thin, clear layer of dead skin cells under the stratum corneum. It is a translucent layer made of small cells that let light pass through. This layer is thickest on the palms of the hands and soles of the feet. The keratinocytes in this layer contain clear keratin. The cells here release lipids forming bilayers of oil and water. The thicker skin on the palms and soles is composed of epidermal ridges that provide a better grip while walking and using our hands. This layer also forms our unique fingerprints and footprints.

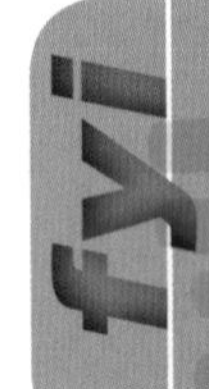

Contrary to popular belief, the stratum lucidum is found all over the body, not just on the palms and soles, where it is most apparent.

The Stratum Granulosum

The **stratum granulosum** (STRAT-um gran-yoo-LOH-sum), also known as **granular layer**, is composed of cells that resemble granules and are filled with keratin. The production of keratin and intercellular lipids also takes place here. In this layer, enzymes dissolve the structures (desmosomes) that hold cells together. As these cells become keratinized, they move to the surface and replace the cells shed from the stratum corneum.

Natural moisturizing substances such as triglycerides, ceramides, waxes, fatty acids, and other intercellular lipids are made here and are excreted from cells to form components of the skin's waterproofing barrier function of the top layer. These water-soluble compounds are referred to as natural moisturizing factors (NMFs) and hydrate the lipid layer surrounding cells, absorb water, and prevent water loss.

The Stratum Spinosum

The **stratum spinosum** (STRAT-um spy-NOH-sum), also known as **spiny layer**, is above the stratum germinativum. Cells continue to divide and change shape here, and enzymes are creating lipids and proteins. Cell appendages, which resemble prickly spines, become desmosomes, the intercellular structures that assist in strengthening and holding cells together. **Desmosomes** (DEZ-moh-somes) are keratin filaments—the protein bonds that create the junctions between the cells. These strengthen the epidermis and assist in intercellular communication.

Also found here are the **Langerhans** (läng-ER-häns) **immune cells**, which protect the body from infections by identifying foreign material (antigens). The immune cells help destroy these foreign invaders. Keratinocytes and melanocytes work in synergy here forming the even placement of pigment granules. The spinosum is the largest layer of the epidermis.

Stratum Germinativum (the basal cell layer) is where everything starts or germinates. Basal means the fundamental, or basic, layer.

The Stratum Germinativum

The **stratum germinativum** (STRAT-um jur-min-ah-TI-vum), also known as **basal cell layer**, is located above the dermis, composed of a single layer of basal cells laying on a "basement membrane." In this active layer, stem cells undergo continuous cell division (mitosis) to replenish the regular loss of skin cells shed from the surface. Stem cells are basically mother cells that divide to produce daughter cells.

Mother cells divide to form two daughter cells. Some stem cells and daughter cells always remain undifferentiated and keep dividing for constant self-renewal over a lifetime. These either remain stem cells or are programmed to become something else, such as a keratinocyte. In the body, some daughter cells go on to become skin cells. Other cells become glands, follicles, tissues, or organs. Daughter cells that are not able to divide anymore are now programmed to end up as one specific type of cell. This is known as *terminal differentiation*. Cells such as these keratinocytes begin their journey of terminal differentiation as they migrate to the surface and eventually become strong and protective.

Cells in the basal layer produce the necessary lipids that form cell membranes and hold the cells together. Merkel cells (sensory cells) are touch receptors also located in the basal layer. The stratum germinativum also contains **melanocytes** (muh-LAN-uh-sytes), which are cells that produce pigment granules in the basal layer (**Figure 10–8**). About 5 to 10 percent of the basal cells are melanocytes. The pigment carrying granules, called **melanosomes** (MEL-uh-noh-sohms), then produce a complex protein, **melanin** (MEL-uh-nin), which determines skin, eye, and hair color. LO2

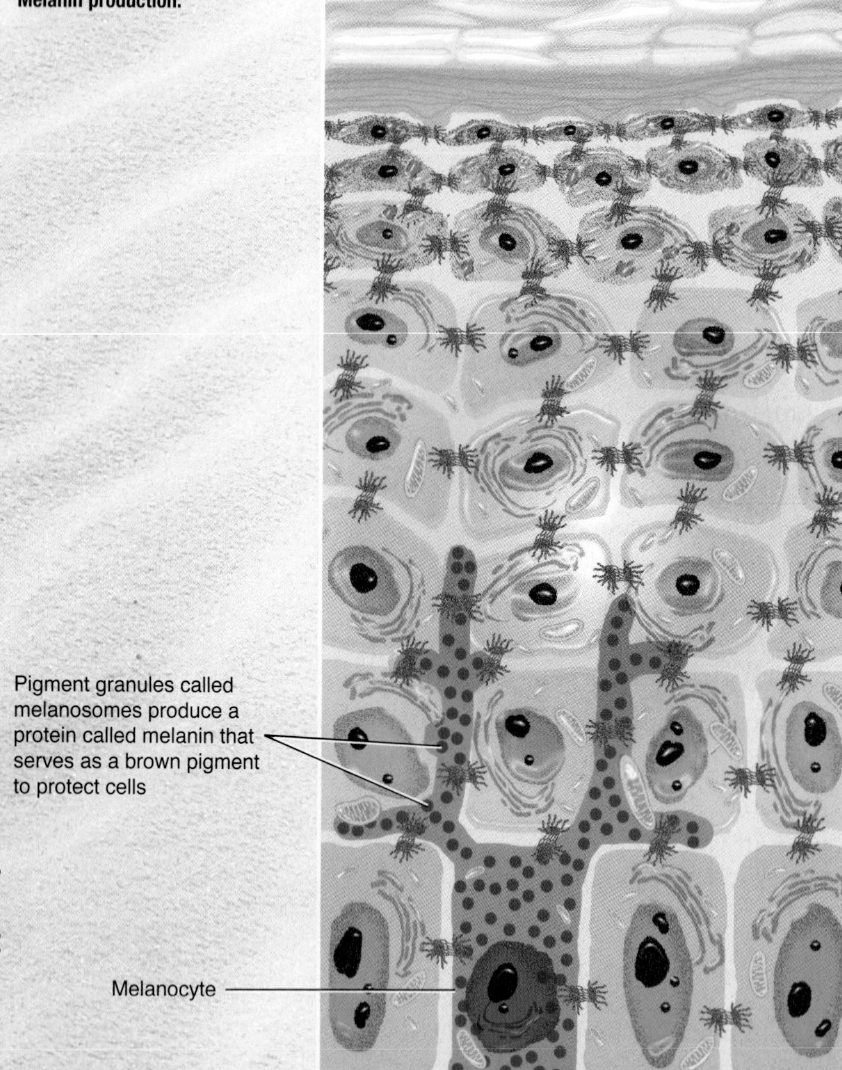
Pigment granules called melanosomes produce a protein called melanin that serves as a brown pigment to protect cells
Melanocyte
Basement membrane
© Milady, a part of Cengage Learning.

Figure 10–8
Melanin production.

Skin Color: Melanin, Melanocytes, and Melanosomes

Melanin is the pigment that protects us from the sun. Damage to DNA triggers melanocyte stimulating hormones to produce melanin. Melanocyte cells make melanosome spheres which are transferred to keratinocytes (**Figure 10–9**). Melanosomes carry the pigment granules that provide skin's color. One melanocyte will deposit pigment-carrying melanosomes into about 30 keratinocytes through its dendrites. Dendrites are the arms, or cellular projections, that branch out to interact with other cells in the extracellular matrix between cells. This process is how pigment darkening occurs.

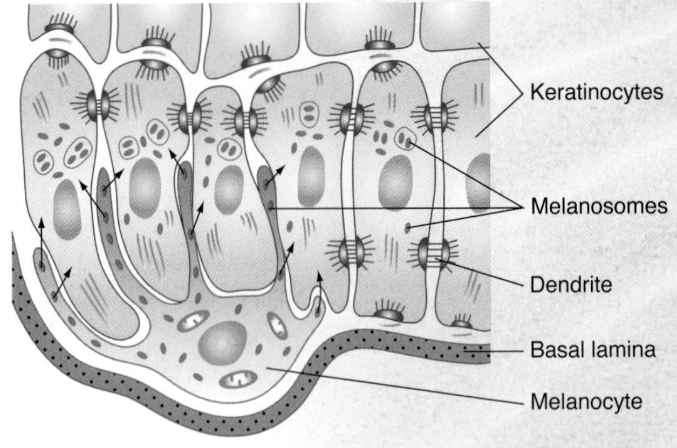

▲ Figure 10–9
Melanin protects the skin.

Melanin is transferred into the cells through dendrites (branches) that move up to the skin's surface. Melanin production is stimulated by exposure to sunlight and protects the cells below by absorbing and blocking UV radiation. **Tyrosinase** (TY-ruh-sin-ays) is the enzyme that stimulates melanocytes and thus produces melanin. It is estimated that there are over 1,000 melanocytes per square mm (⅛ square inch) of skin.

Every person has approximately the same number of melanocytes. Differences in genetic skin color are due to the amount of melanin activated in the skin and the way it is distributed. Individuals with darker skin and melanin have more activity in their melanocytes. Both internal and external factors affect melanin activation and production.

The body produces two types of melanin: **pheomelanin** (fee-oh-MEL-uh-nin), which is red to yellow in color, and **eumelanin** (yoo-MEL-uh-nin), which is dark brown to black. People with light-colored skin mostly produce pheomelanin, while those with dark-colored skin mostly produce eumelanin. Fair skin individuals have approximately 20 melanosomes per keratinocyte and dark skin contains about 200 melanosomes per keratinocyte.

Products that suppress melanin production by interrupting biochemical processes are referred to as *brightening agents*. Some are called *tyrosinase inhibitors*. These products are designed to reduce hyperpigmentation. Pigmentation disorders are discussed in Chapter 11, Disorders and Diseases of the Skin. Products and treatments for hyperpigmentation are discussed in other chapters. ☑ L03

FOCUS ON

Melanin

Melanocytes **are cells that produce pigment granules, called** ***melanosomes.***

↓

Melanosomes **carry and produce the protein, called** ***melanin.***

↓

Melanin **is transferred to cells from melanosomes through dendrite branches.**

The Dermis

The **dermis** (DUR-mis), also called the derma, corium (KOH-ree-um), cutis (KYOO-tis), or true skin, is the support layer of connective tissues below the epidermis. The dermal/epidermal junction connects the dermis to the epidermis. This junction consists of layers of a connective collagen tissue with many small pockets and holes. Collagen fibrils from the dermis are embedded into these layers to provide strength and adhesion. Keratin filaments on the epidermis side also ensure strength and adhesion to the junction.

The dermis, which is about 25 times thicker than the epidermis, consists of two layers: the papillary layer (PAP-uh-lair-ee LAY-ur) above and the reticular layer below. The dermis is primarily comprised of connective tissues made of collagen protein and elastin fibers. The dermis also supplies the skin with oxygen and nutrients.

Did You Know?

Melanoma is a cancer that begins in melanocytes. It is the most serious type of skin cancer because it can spread rapidly throughout the body. This metastasis (spreading of cells within the body) is why melanoma is so dangerous.

Did You Know?

Collagen is the most abundant protein in the body and is derived from the Greek words *kolla* for "glue" and *gennan* for "to produce."

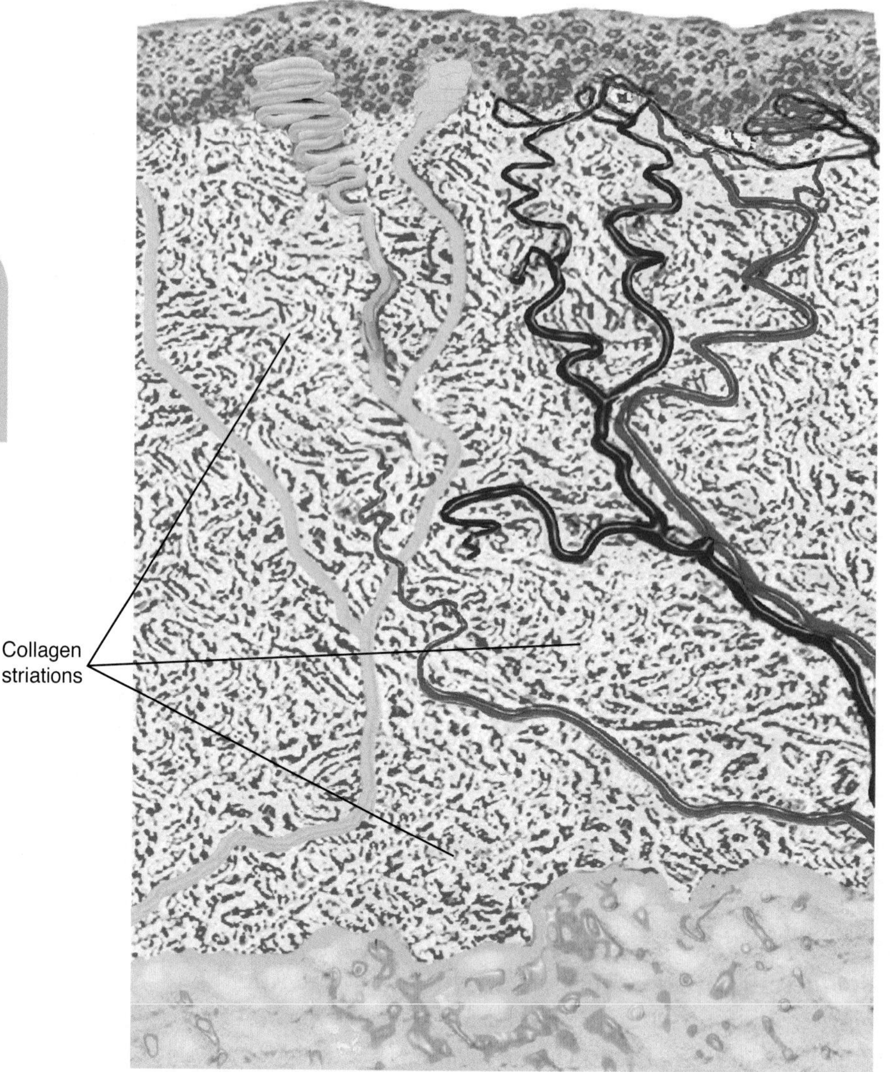

▲ Figure 10–10
Collagen in the dermis.

Collagen (KAHL-uh-jen) is a protein substance of complex fibers that gives skin its strength and is necessary for wound healing. Produced by fibroblasts, collagen makes up 70 percent of the dermis (**Figure10–10**). Fibroblast cells produce proteins and aid in the production of collagen and elastin.

In contrast, the quantity of elastin is a small percentage of the dermis. Elastin is only about one-fifteenth compared to the amount of collagen. **Elastin** is the fibrous protein that forms elastic tissue and gives skin its elasticity.

Blood and lymph vessels, capillaries, follicles, sebaceous glands, sweat glands, sensory nerves, additional receptors, and the arrector pili muscles are all located in the dermis. **Lymph vessels** remove waste products, bacteria, and excess water. ✓ L04

Fibroblasts (cell stimulators), lymphocytes (fight infections), Langerhans cells (guard cells), mast cells (involved in allergic reactions), and leukocytes (white blood cells to fight infections) are all found in the dermis.

Collagen and extracellular matrix proteins give support and function to the skin. Other components give tautness or firmness to the skin by interacting with elastin and hyaluronic acid. Hormones such as epidermal growth factor (EGF) and fibroblast growth factor (FGF) stimulate fibroblasts, cells, proteins, and DNA synthesis.

In the dermis is a fluid matrix called *ground substance*. It is also referred to as the *extracellular matrix* (ECM) composed of collagen, other proteins, and GAGs (Glycosaminoglycans). These intercellular substances are comprised of water and other components to maintain water balance, provide dermal support and assist cell metabolism, growth, and migration.

Glycosaminoglycans are large protein molecules and water-binding substances found between the fibers of the dermis. GAGs are polysaccharides–protein and sugar complexes. Beneficial hydrating fluids such as **hyaluronic acid** (HY-uh-luhr-ahn-ik A-sid) are part of this dermal substance. Hyaluronic acid is a GAG. Ingredients that duplicate these natural intercellular fluids are important in esthetics and skin care products and are discussed in other chapters.

Did You Know?

Collagenase and elastase are enzymes that help protect collagen and elastin; however, when excessive levels are produced from UV radiation or other damage, it causes dermal breakdown and premature aging.

The Papillary Layer

The **papillary layer** connects the dermis to the epidermis, forming the epidermal/dermal junction. The **dermal papillae** are membranes of ridges and grooves that attach to the epidermis. Attached to the dermal papillae are either looped capillaries that nourish the epidermis or tactile corpuscles, the nerve endings sensitive to touch and pressure. Note that papillae in the hair follicle are called **hair papillae** (puh-PILL-ay)—the small, cone-shaped structures at the bottom of hair follicles. The blood supplies nourishment within the skin through capillaries. The papillary layer comprises 10 to 20 percent of the dermis. Collagen and elastin is more widely spaced here than in the reticular layer.

The Reticular Layer

The **reticular layer**, the denser and deeper layer of the dermis, is comprised mainly of collagen and elastin. Damage to these elastin fibers as they break down are the primary cause of sagging, wrinkles, and aging—loss of elasticity in the skin. Stretch marks are caused by damaged elastin fibers. Collagen and elastin are broken down by ultraviolet (UV) damage and other factors.

Growth factors such as epidermal growth factor (EFG) are chemicals that induce cells to divide and grow.

Subcutaneous Tissue

Below the reticular layer is a **subcutaneous layer**, also known as **hypodermis**, composed of loose connective tissue or **subcutis** (sub-KYOO-tis) **tissue**, also known as **adipose tissue**. This layer is 80 percent fat. This tissue creates a protective cushion that gives contour and smoothness to the body, as well as providing a source of energy for the body. Fat storage in the body is also influenced by hormones.

Vessels, nerves, fibers, adipose cells, fibroblasts, and other cells are just some of the components of the hypodermis. This layer decreases and thins with age.

A summary of the main components and functions in the skin's layers is included for the following terms.

Epidermis: Layers of the epidermis include keratinocytes, immune cells, and intercellular fluids.

Stratum Corneum: Hardened corneocytes (also referred to as flattened squamous cells), melanin, barrier layer, acid mantle, desquamation.

Stratum Lucidum: Clear cells; thickest on the palms and soles.

Stratum Granulosum: Production of keratin granules in cells; additional lipid production and excretion; desmosomes dissolved by enzymes.

Stratum Spinosum: Large layer, cell activity, desmosomes created, Langerhans immune cells, melanosome pigment distribution.

Stratum Germinativum: Single layer of cells, cell mitosis, stem cells, merkel cells. Keratinocytes, melanocytes, and lipids are all produced here.

Dermis: Collagen, elastin, and intercellular fluids are the main components of the dermis. Fibroblasts and immune cells are found here.

Papillary Layer: Touch receptors, blood vessels, capillaries, dermal papilla.

Reticular Layer: Collagen and elastin, glands, blood and lymph vessels, nerve endings, intercellular fluids.

ACTIVITY

To become more familiar with the layers of the skin, use an unlabeled, blank skin chart to draw in and label all of the parts and layers. Use a different color to represent each layer and each component. What could you do to show the difference between each layer? Have fun with this and compare each other's diagrams in the classroom.

Hair Anatomy

Hair is an appendage of the skin—it is a slender, threadlike outgrowth of the skin and scalp. **Figure 10–11** shows the structure of the hair follicle. There is no sense of feeling in the hair, due to the absence of nerves.

Much of the hair on the body is invisible to the naked eye. The heavier concentration of hair is on the head, under the arms, around the genitals, and on the arms and legs. Due to hormonal influence, there are different male and female hair growth patterns. Genetics influence the distribution of each person's hair, its thickness, quality, color, rate of growth, and whether the hair is curly or straight. Hair on the scalp grows an average of .35 millimeters (1⁄60 inch) per day.

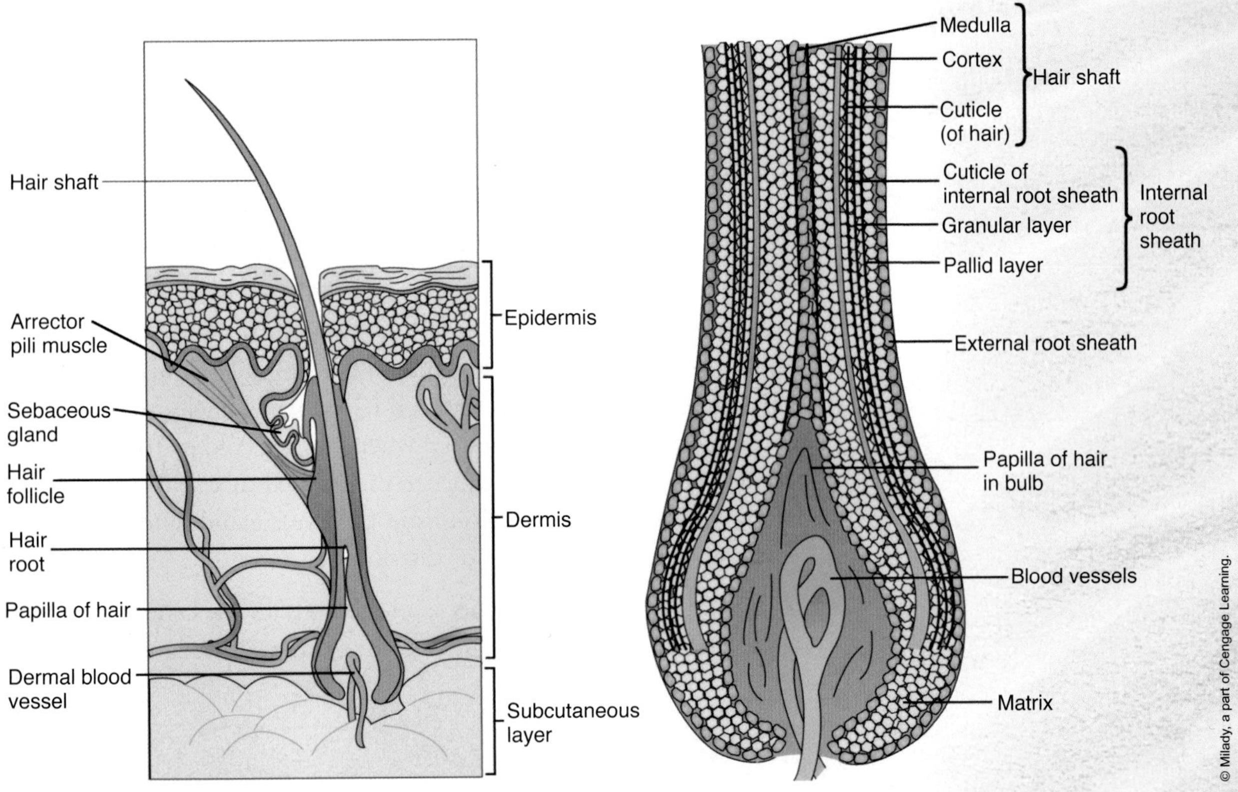

Figure 10–11
Hair follicle structure.

The hair contains 90 percent hard keratin. It has a lower moisture and fat content than soft keratin, and is a particularly tough, elastic material. Keratin forms continuous sheets (fingernails) or long, endless fibers (hair). Hard keratin does not normally break off or flake away. It remains a continuous structure. Hair also contains melanin, which determines hair color.

The hair follicle structure is partially the cause of some skin disorders such as ingrown hairs or folliculitis (a bacterial infection). Hair growth is discussed extensively in Chapter 18, Hair Removal.

Nail Anatomy

The nail, an appendage of the skin, is a hard translucent plate that protects fingers and toes. The nail is composed of hard keratin. Figure 10–12 shows the nail structure. *Onyx* (AH-niks) is the technical term for the nail. The hard, or horny, nail plate contains no nerves or blood vessels. Nails grow approximately 1⁄10 of an inch (3.7millimeters) per month.

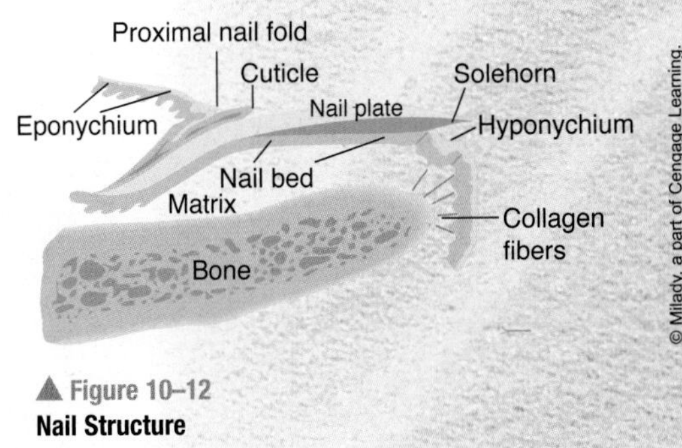

Figure 10–12
Nail Structure

Secretory nerves are motor nerves, so there are two main categories of nerves, not three categories, as stated in the past.

Nerves

Nerves are cordlike bundles of fibers made up of neurons through which sensory stimuli and motor impulses pass between the brain or other parts of the central nervous system and the eyes, glands, muscles, and other parts of the body. Nerves form a network of pathways for conducting information throughout the body. There are two types of nerves: motor and sensory.

- *Motor*, or *efferent*, nerve fibers convey impulses from the brain or spinal cord to the muscles or glands. These stimulate muscles, such as the arrector pili muscles, attached to the hair follicles. Arrector pili muscles cause "goose bumps" when you are cold or frightened. *Secretory* nerve fibers are motor nerves attached to sweat and oil glands. They regulate excretion from the sweat glands and control sebum output to the surface of the skin.
- *Sensory*, or *afferent*, nerve fibers send messages to the central nervous system and brain to react to heat, cold, pain, pressure, and touch.

Glands

The dermis of the skin contains two types of duct glands, each producing different substances. The sebaceous glands secrete oil, while the sudoriferous glands excrete sweat (**Figure 10–13**).

The Sebaceous (Oil) Glands

Sebaceous glands are connected to the hair follicles and produce oil, which protects the surface of the skin. Glandular sacs open into

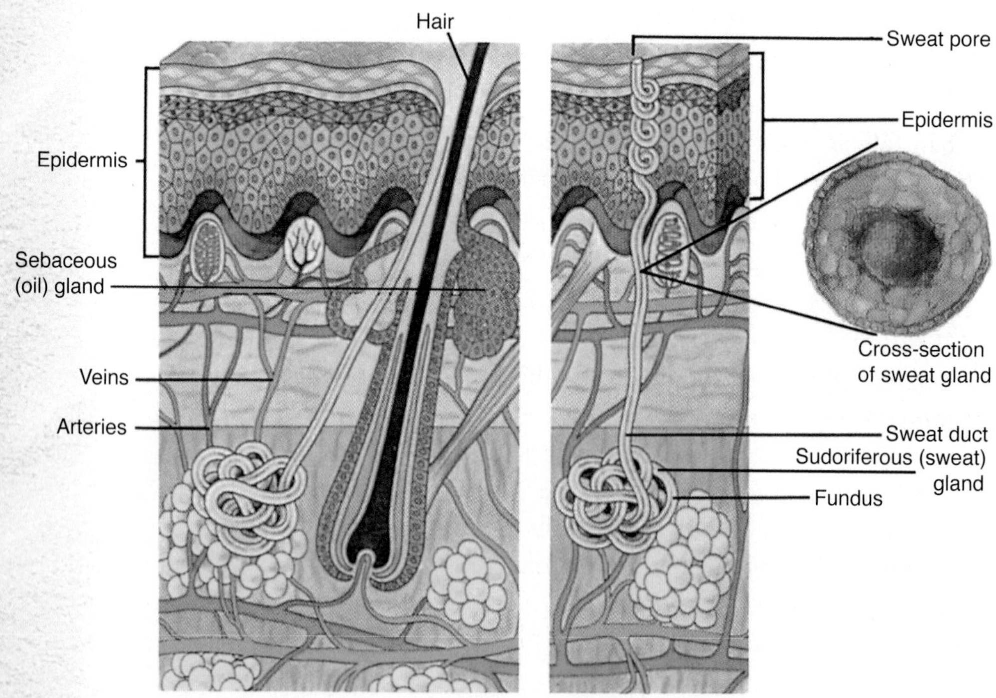

▶ Figure 10–13
Oil and sweat glands.

the follicles through ducts. If the ducts become clogged, comedones (blackheads) are formed. The oily secretions lubricate both the skin and hair. Sebaceous glands are larger on the face and scalp than on the rest of the body. Other chapters include further discussion on sebaceous glands and acne.

The Sudoriferous (Sweat) Glands

Sudoriferous glands help to regulate body temperature and eliminate waste products by excreting sweat. They have a coiled base and duct openings at the surface, known as pores. Liquids and salts are eliminated daily through these pores. The excretion of sweat is controlled by the nervous system. Normally, 1 to 2 pints (.5 to 1 liter) of liquids containing salts are eliminated daily through sweat pores in the skin. There are two kinds of sweat glands—the apocrine and the eccrine.

Did You Know?

Apocrine glands produce chemicals known as *pheromones*. Pheromones are hormones that trigger biological reactions or communicate signals to others. This reaction is thought to attract others through scent production and is sometimes referred to as body chemistry.

The **apocrine glands** (AP-uh-krin GLANZ) are coiled structures attached to the hair follicles found under the arms and in the genital area. Their secretions are released through the oil glands. These are more active during emotional changes. Odors associated with these glands are due to the interaction of the secretions and bacteria on the surface of the skin. According to some authorities, apocrine glands are not true sweat glands because their openings connect to oil glands instead of pore openings directly on the skin's surface.

The **eccrine glands** (EK-run GLANZ) are found all over the body, primarily on the forehead, palms, and soles. They have a duct and pore through which secretions are released on the skin's surface. These glands are not connected to hair follicles. Eccrine glands are more active when the body is subjected to physical activity and high temperatures. Eccrine sweat does not typically produce an offensive odor. ✓ L05

Skin Health

In order to survive, cells need these important elements: nourishment, protection, the ability to function properly, and continual replacement or proliferation.

Skin health and aging of the skin are both influenced by many different factors including heredity, sun exposure, the environment, health habits, and general lifestyle. This topic is discussed thoroughly in Chapter 12, Skin Analysis.

The Immune System and the Skin

Our immune system is a complex defense mechanism that protects the body from foreign substances. The immune system is activated when antigens (foreign invaders) are identified. Antibodies are molecules

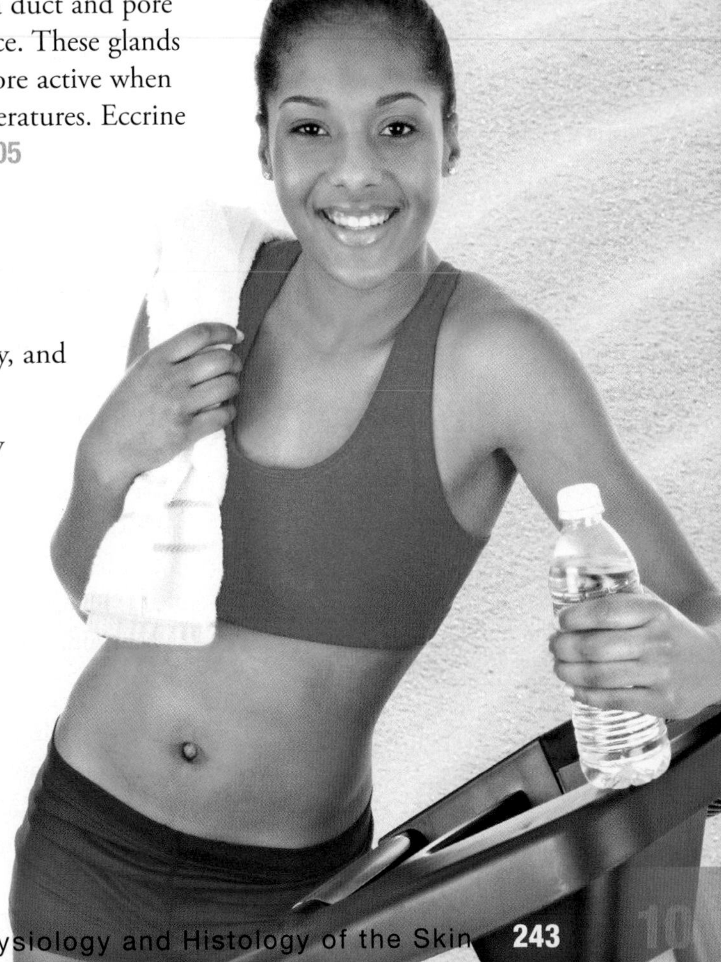

formed to fight and neutralize bacteria, viruses, and antigens. Langerhans cells, T-cells, and leukocyte cells are part of the immune system.

A primary part of the system are the Langerhans cells (guard cells) that sense unrecognized foreign invaders such as bacteria and then process these antigens for removal through the lymph system.

The immune system also produces **T-cells**, which identify molecules that have foreign peptides and also help regulate immune response. Another part of the immune system is **leukocytes**, the white blood cells that have enzymes to digest and kill bacteria and parasites. These white blood cells also respond to allergies.

Other components of the immune system are enzymes and other cells that protect the body from foreign substances, bacteria, and infections. Infections and allergic reactions speed up cell growth and migration rates for faster healing. The skin's capacity to heal, fight infection, and protect itself is truly extraordinary.

Skin Nourishment

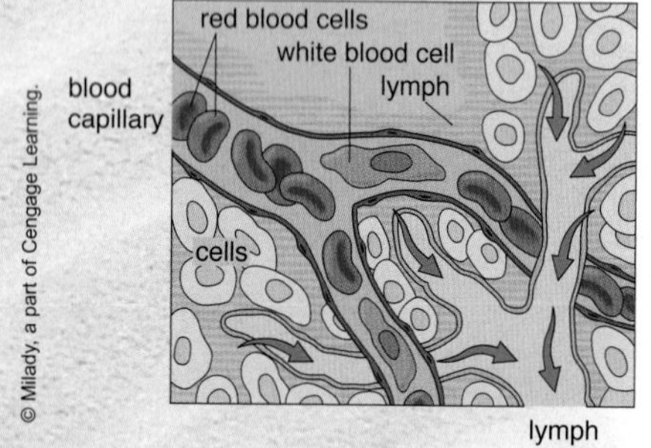

▲ Figure 10–14
Nourishment through the blood and lymph systems.

Blood and lymph are the fluids that nourish the skin (**Figure 10–14**). Networks of arteries and lymphatics send essential materials for growth and repair throughout the body. Water, vitamins, and nutrients are all important for skin health. Blood supplies nutrients and oxygen to the skin. Nutrients are molecules from food such as protein, carbohydrates, and fats. Topical products also nourish the epidermis.

Lymph, the clear fluids of the body that resemble blood plasma but contain only colorless corpuscles, bathe the skin cells, remove toxins and cellular waste, and have immune functions that help protect the skin and body against disease. Networks of arteries and lymph vessels in the subcutaneous tissue send their smaller branches up to dermal papillae, follicles, and skin glands.

Cell Protection

The health of skin cells depend on the cellular membrane and the water-holding capacity of the stratum corneum. Phospholipids, glycolipids, cholesterol, triglycerides, squalene, and waxes are all different types of lipids found in the stratum corneum and cell membranes. Intercellular lipids and proteins surround cells and provide protection, hydration, and nourishment to the cells. **Ceramides** are a group of waxy lipid molecules important to barrier function and water-holding capacity such as glycolipids. Fifty percent of the lipids in the stratum corneum are ceramides. Fatty acids are also components of the intercellular substances.

Lipids are reduced if the skin is dry, damaged, or mature. Topical products containing ceramides and other lipids benefit wrinkled skin and expedite healing. Exfoliation removes and depletes lipids, so topical product reapplication is necessary to balance what was lost in exfoliation.

Cell recovery depends on water to function properly, so drinking water and keeping skin hydrated is essential to keep cells healthy.

Did You Know?

Proteins, enzymes, vitamins, and metabolites are natural antioxidants in the body.

Cell Replacement

The body replaces billions of cells daily. Organs such as the skin, heart, liver, and kidneys have their cells replaced every 6 to 9 months. Cells of the bones are replaced every 7 years. Unfortunately, elastin and collagen are not easily replaced by the body, and the skin does not regain its once pliable shape after being stretched or damaged by UV radiation; however, research shows that certain procedures and ingredients, such as vitamin A and alpha hydroxy acids (AHAs), stimulate skin cell turnover and reduce visible signs of aging. Regular cell turnover is necessary to keep skin healthy.

Sun Damage

The sun and its ultraviolet (UV) electromagnetic radiation have the greatest impact on how our skin ages. According to the U.S. Department of Health and Human Services, ultraviolet radiation (UVR) is a proven carcinogen. UV exposure alters DNA and can cause skin cancer. Approximately 80 to 85 percent of our aging is caused by sun exposure. As we age, the collagen and elastin fibers of the skin naturally weaken. This weakening happens at a much faster rate when the skin is frequently exposed to ultraviolet radiation.

UV reaches the skin in two different forms, as UVA and UVB radiation. Each of the UV forms affects the skin at different levels (Figure 10–15). Cell damage is cumulative, and photodamage (from the sun) causes photoaging. Pigment dysfunction, wrinkles, sagging, collagen and elastin breakdown, and skin cancer are the results of exposure to UV radiation.

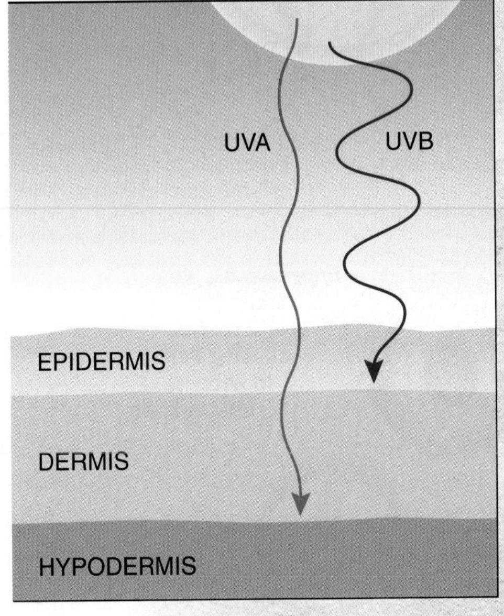

▲ Figure 10–15
UV rays penetrate into the skin at different levels.

UVA radiation, also known as **aging rays**, contributes up to 95 percent of the sun's ultraviolet radiation reaching the Earth's surface. The longer wavelengths of UVA (320 to 400 nanometers) penetrate deeper into the skin and cause genetic damage and cell death. UVA weakens the skin's collagen and elastin fibers causing wrinkling and sagging in the tissues. UVA can also penetrate glass and clouds. UVA is present all year and more prevalent than UVB.

UVB radiation, also known as **burning rays**, causes burning of the skin as well as tanning, aging, and cancer. UVB wavelengths range between 290 to 320 nanometers. Although UVB penetration is shorter than and not as deep as UVA, these wavelengths are stronger and more damaging to the skin and can damage the eyes as well. On a positive note, UVB radiation contributes to the body's synthesis of vitamin D and other important minerals.

Melanin is designed to help protect the skin from the sun's UV radiation, but melanin can be altered or destroyed when large, frequent doses of UV are allowed to penetrate the skin. It is important that you advise your clients about the necessary precautions to take when they are exposed to the sun. Sun protection does more than protect the skin; it defends cells from radiation, cell death, tissue breakdown, and aging.

In addition to taking sun protection precautions, clients should be advised to see a physician specializing in dermatology for regular skin checkups, especially if they detect any changes in the coloration, size, or shape of a mole.

Home self-examinations can also be an effective way to check for signs of potential skin cancer between scheduled doctor visits. When performing a self-care exam, clients should be advised to check for any changes in existing moles and to pay attention to any new visible growths on the skin. Sun damage, skin cancer, and sunscreens are discussed further in Chapter 12, Skin Analysis, and in other chapters. ✓ L06

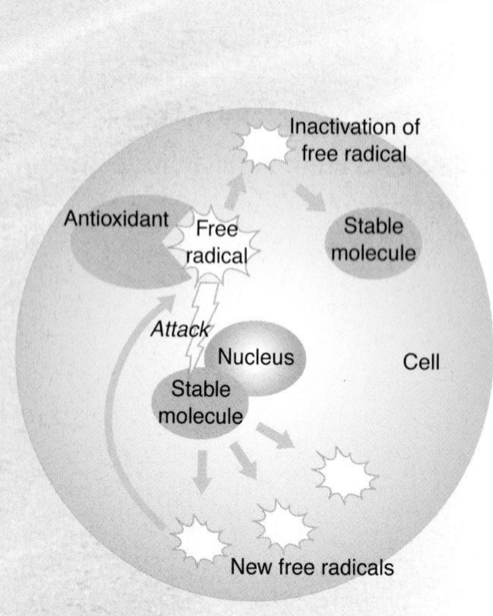

▲ Figure 10–16
Free radicals.

Free Radical Damage

Free radicals are chemically active atoms or molecules with unpaired electrons. They have an unequal number of electrons and an unbalanced electrical charge. Consequently, these are unstable and steal electrons from other molecules, which then damages the other molecules (**Figure 10–16**).

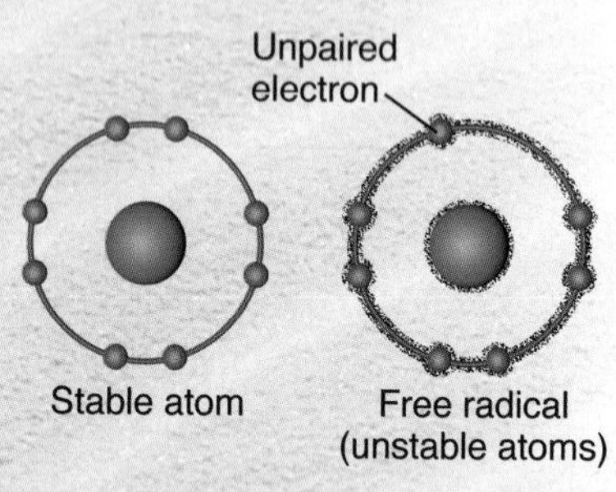

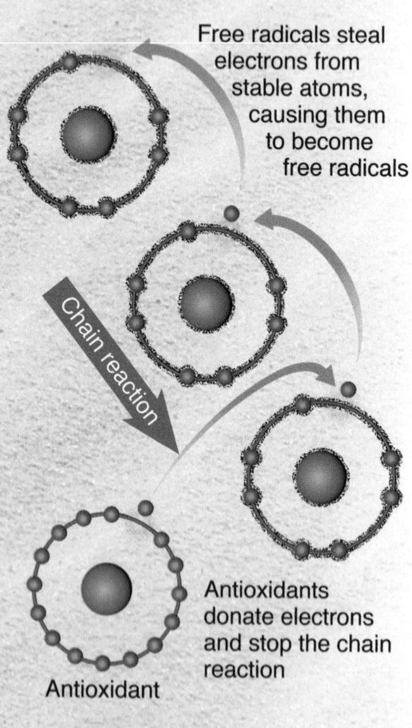

▲ Figure 10–17
Free radicals and antioxidants.

Free radicals are reactive oxidants (derived from reactions with oxygen molecules) that search the body for other electrons that will allow them to become stable, neutral molecules again. Free radicals take electrons from compounds in the body such as proteins, lipids, or DNA; this process destabilizes and oxidizes the once healthy molecules and creates more free radicals, starting a chain reaction of cellular destruction (**Figure 10–17**). Free radicals are super-oxidizers that not only cause an oxidation reaction but also produce new free radicals in the process.

Normal oxidation deactivates the oxidizer and stops the oxidation from continuing, but the oxidation caused by free radicals continues in a chain reaction that can oxidize millions of other compounds. The donating molecules are now missing an electron and become an unstable new free radical. This process is then repeated in other cells. This is an oxidation process that continues and expands, damaging more cells.

The prevention of free radical formation is a critical process and complex task that is necessary for cells to survive. Antioxidants are vital to neutralize this chain reaction by donating their electrons to stabilize the free radical's electrons. Proteins, enzymes, vitamins, and metabolites are all antioxidants.

Free radicals are generated by many factors including exposure to UV, unhealthy foods, chemicals, smoke, and trauma from medical treatments. The free radicals generated when the skin is exposed to sunlight will damage skin cells. When sunlight contacts the skin, it reacts with oxygen to create free radicals. These free radicals attack cell membranes. UV light can also kill cells by damaging their DNA.

The melanin pigment produced by tanning darkens the skin and absorbs UV radiation to help keep cells from being damaged. Skin cells have built-in antioxidants to protect against sun damage, but their ability to protect cells deteriorates with sun exposure. Inflammation also causes free radical damage and leads to aging, skin pigmentation, and disease. Red and inflamed skin is another indication of free radical damage. ☑ L07

Many free radicals are related to the oxygen molecule and are by-products of our use of oxygen in the energy cycle. In our bodies, free radicals cause the same type of oxidative damage that is observed as fruit decays and turns brown, or when a car rusts as the metal is exposed to oxygen. Our organs also experience damage over time from free radicals.

Skin Health and the Environment

While the sun may play the predominant role in how the skin ages, changes in our environment also greatly influence this aging process. Pollutants in the air from factories, automobile exhaust, and even secondhand smoke can all influence the appearance and overall health of our skin. While these pollutants affect the surface appearance of the skin, they can also change the health of the underlying cells and tissues, thereby speeding up the aging process.

Climate, humidity levels, and other factors also affect the skin. Routine cleansing at night helps to remove the buildup of pollutants that have settled on the skin's surface throughout the day. Applying daily moisturizers, protective lotions, sunscreen, and even foundation products all help to protect the skin from airborne pollutants and the environment.

Did You Know?

By inhaling just one puff of one cigarette, we create three trillion free radicals in the lungs. Free radicals attack our cells and produce a tremendous inflammatory response.

Skin Health and Lifestyle Choices

What we choose to put into our bodies significantly affects our overall health. The impact of poor choices can be seen most visibly on the skin. Smoking, drinking, drugs, and poor dietary choices all greatly influence the aging process. It is the esthetician's responsibility to be aware of how these habits affect the skin and to tactfully point out these effects to clients without stepping outside the scope of practice into the medical arena.

Smoking and tobacco use may not only cause cancer but are linked to the premature aging and wrinkling of the skin. Nicotine in tobacco causes contraction and weakening of the blood vessels and small capillaries that supply blood to the tissues, causing decreased circulation. Eventually, the tissues are deprived of essential oxygen, and the skin's surface may appear yellowish or gray in color and can look dull (Figure 10–18). Lack of oxygen and nutrients accelerates skin aging.

▼ Figure 10–18
Smoking ages the skin.

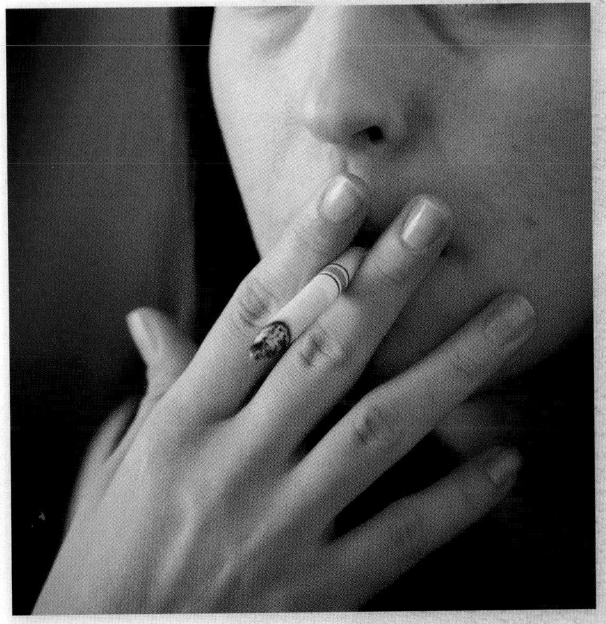

Using prescription or illegal drugs also affects the skin. Certain drugs have been shown to interfere with the body's intake of oxygen, thus affecting healthy cell growth. Some drugs can even aggravate serious skin conditions, such as acne. Others can cause dryness and allergic reactions on the skin's surface.

Similarly, consuming alcohol has a damaging effect on the skin. Heavy or excessive intake of alcohol dilates the blood vessels and capillaries. Over time, this constant over-dilation and weakening of the fragile capillary walls can cause them to expand and burst. This causes a constant flushed appearance of the skin and red splotches in the whites of the eyes. Alcohol can also dehydrate the skin by drawing essential water out of the tissues, making the skin appear dull and dry. When dehydrated, skin is in an inflammatory state that also accelerates the aging process. Alcohol in excess results in a rapid and sustained increase in blood sugar, which causes inflammation and a glycation reaction. In addition, alcohol is metabolized by the liver into chemicals which are toxic to cells.

Both smoking and drinking contribute to the aging process on their own, but the combination of the two can be even more damaging to the tissues. The constant dilation and contraction of the tiny capillaries and blood vessels, as well as the constant deprivation of oxygen and water to the tissues, quickly makes the skin appear lifeless and dull. It is very difficult for the skin to adjust and repair itself. Usually, the damage done by these lifestyle habits is hard to reverse or even diminish.

Glycation

Recent research indicates that an intrinsic part of the aging process involves damaged structures and tissues that gradually accumulate in the body through a destructive process called *glycation*, which is caused by an elevation in blood sugar. **Glycation** is the binding of a protein molecule to a glucose molecule resulting in the formation of damaged, nonfunctioning structures known as *advanced glycation end products.* Glycation alters protein structures and decreases biological activity. For example, glycation contributes to the aging of skin, contributing to wrinkles and age spots. Many age-related diseases such as arterial stiffening, cataracts, and neurological impairment are partially attributed to glycation.

Scientists have established that anything that causes a rise in our blood sugar results in inflammation on a cellular level. When blood sugar goes up rapidly and continually, the sugar can actually attach to the collagen in the skin, making it stiff and inflexible. This is glycation. When collagen is cross-linked by sugar, it leads to stiff and sagging skin.

When blood sugar is elevated we are in an inflammatory state. For example, lack of sleep elevates the hormone cortisol. On the days we do not get enough sleep, we tend to crave carbohydrates because cortisol raises blood sugar and insulin levels, setting up this craving. Even though it is an essential hormone in the body, cortisol has many negative side effects in excess quantities. For example, it can break down muscle tissue, thin skin, decalcify bones, and elevate blood sugar. In summary, glycation is an unhealthy biological process for many reasons. A healthy lifestyle and a diet with low sugar intake can help keep sugar levels balanced in the body.

Aging Skin and Hormones

As we age, our skin changes significantly. This is partially because of shifts in the hormone balance. Hormones are the internal messengers for most of the body's systems and are significant internal factors in the skin's appearance, strength, and health. Estrogen (present in both men and women, but predominantly in women) is a crucial hormone for good health and the appearance of skin. Estrogen is anti-inflammatory, an antioxidant, and a key factor in tissue repair. The hormone is also responsible for maintaining health in several body functions such as coordination, balance, skin moisture, vision, bones, and the nervous system. Estrogen has even been linked to memory and emotions.

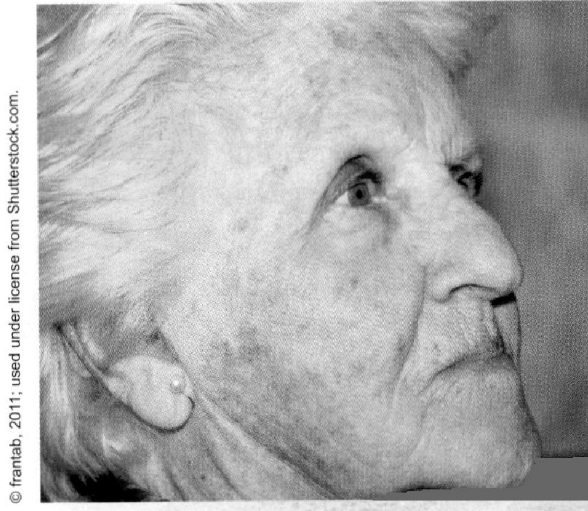

▲ Figure 10–19
Aging of the skin.

Changes to the skin begin as women enter perimenopause in their forties, and these changes continue into menopause (fifties) and beyond, because of the decrease in estrogen. All tissues begin to thin and change. This affects the skin's protective barrier, epithelial (external covering) tissue, and dermis. As skin ages, vascular and capillary walls begin to weaken, lipids are reduced, the lymphatic system is less efficient, glands slow down, and there are fewer fibroblasts, thus affecting cells, collagen, and elastin (**Figure 10–19**, page 249). Collagen loses its ability to respond to physical changes from aging and sun damage (**Figure 10–20**, page 249).

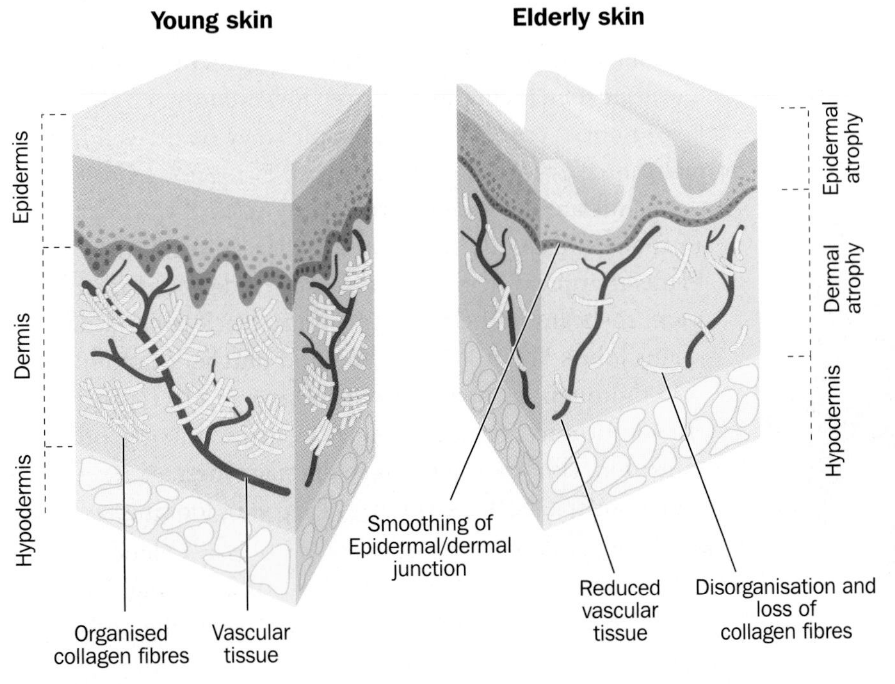

◀ Figure 10–20
The physiology of aging skin.

As estrogen is depleted, skin begins to lose its tone. Reduced glycosaminoglycans mean less moisture in the tissues; keratinocytes are reduced (slower cell mitosis); melanocytes are reduced (less protective pigment); and cellular exchanges are reduced. Testosterone levels become dominant as estrogen decreases, which can increase sebum production, pore size, and hair growth on the face. This partially explains the unwanted hair growth and unexpected adult acne. ✓ LO8

Web Resources

www.skincancer.org
www.ncbi.nlm.nih.gov (National Library of Medicine, National Institute of Health)
www.medicinenet.com

Microcirculation

Microcirculation is the circulation of blood from the heart to arterioles (small arteries), to capillaries, to venules (small veins), and then back to the heart. Hormonal changes are one cause of the microcirculation problems common in mature skin. One such problem is couperose (KOO-per-ohs) skin, or **telangiectasia** (tell-ann-jee-ek-TA-zhuh), the dilation of the capillary walls. As the endothelium (wall of the capillary) atrophies and loses its elasticity, the walls dilate and fill with blood, sometimes bursting.

Other causes of couperose skin or spider veins are heredity, alimentary (digestive) problems, alcohol, smoking, sun damage, harsh cosmetics, trauma, pregnancy, excess localized heat, topical corticosteroids, inflammation, and heat/cold fluctuations. These all lead to permanent dilation of the capillaries.

Rosacea (roh-ZAY-see-uh) is a chronic vascular disorder characterized by couperose veins and congestion of the skin. Acne rosacea includes papules and pustules. In some cases, rosacea may be caused by parasitic microorganisms (mites). Skin disorders are discussed in Chapter 11, Disorders and Diseases of the Skin.

Hormone Replacement Therapy

Hormone replacement therapy (HRT) is often suggested to balance estrogen for women experiencing menopause, however, some HRT may be linked to breast cancer. These therapies may be derived from animal-source estrogens or plant-source estrogens. Estrogens from plants are called *phytoestrogens* (fy-toh-ES-tro-jins); they are about 200 to 400 times weaker than animal estrogens. Plants that provide phytoestrogens include Mexican wild yam, soybeans, red clover, sage, hops, black cohash, flax, Saint John's Wort, licorice root, and butcher's broom. Do thorough research before choosing an HRT program. In addition to hormone balancing, maintaining good nutrition, skin care, lymphatic drainage massage, exercise, and a positive outlook will help keep skin looking radiant at any age. ✓ LO9

Review Questions

1. What are the six main functions of the skin?
2. What does barrier function mean?
3. How does sebum protect the skin?
4. What is the acid mantle?
5. Name the five layers of the epidermis.
6. What glands help regulate the body's temperature?
7. What are keratinocytes?
8. What are melanocytes?
9. Name the two layers of the dermis.
10. What is collagen?
11. Why is skin elasticity important?
12. Name the two main types of nerves and describe what they do.
13. What are the two main glands associated with the skin?
14. What are the two types of sweat glands?
15. How does skin get its nourishment?
16. Describe the difference between UVA wavelengths and UVB wavelengths.
17. How does UVA and UVB radiation affect the skin?
18. What are free radicals?

Glossary

apocrine glands	Coiled structures attached to hair follicles found in the underarm and genital areas that secrete sweat.
arrector pili muscle	Small, involuntary muscles in the base of the hair follicle that cause goose flesh when the appendage contracts, sometimes called goose bumps and papillae.
barrier function	Protective barrier of the epidermis; the corneum and intercellular matrix protect the surface from irritation and dehydration.
ceramides	Glycolipid materials that are a natural part of skin's intercellular matrix and barrier function.
collagen	Fibrous, connective tissue made from protein; found in the reticular layer of the dermis; gives skin its firmness. Topically, a large, long-chain molecular protein that lies on the top of the skin and binds water; derived from the placentas of cows or other sources.
corneocytes	Another name for a stratum corneum cell. Hardened, waterproof, protective keratinocytes; these "dead" protein cells are dried out and lack nuclei.
dermal papillae	Membranes of ridges and grooves that attach to the epidermis; contains nerve endings and supplies nourishment through capillaries to skin and follicles.
dermis	Also known as the *derma*, *corium*, *cutis*, or *true skin*; support layer of connective tissue, collagen, and elastin below the epidermis.
desmosomes	The structures that assist in holding cells together; intercellular connections made of proteins.

Glossary

eccrine glands	Sweat glands found all over the body with openings on the skin's surface through pores; not attached to hair follicles, secretions do not produce an offensive odor.
elastin	Protein fiber found in the dermis; gives skin its elasticity and firmness.
epidermal growth factor	Abbreviated EGF; stimulates cells to reproduce and heal.
epidermis	Outermost layer of skin; a thin, protective layer with many cells, mechanisms, and nerve endings. It is made up of five layers: stratum corneum, stratum lucidum, stratum granulosum, stratum spinosum, and stratum germinativum.
eumelanin	A type of melanin that is dark brown to black in color. People with dark-colored skin mostly produce eumelanin. There are two types of melanin; the other type is pheomelanin.
fibroblasts	Cells that stimulate cells, collagen, and amino acids that form proteins.
follicles	Hair follicles and sebaceous follicles are tube-like openings in the epidermis.
glycation	Caused by an elevation in blood sugar, glycation is the binding of a protein molecule to a glucose molecule resulting in the formation of damaged, nonfunctioning structures, known as Advanced Glycation End products(a.k.a. AGES). Glycation alters protein structures and decreases biological activity.
hair papillae	Cone-shaped elevations at the base of the follicle that fit into the hair bulb. The papillae are filled with tissue that contains the blood vessels and cells necessary for hair growth and follicle nourishment.
hyaluronic acid	Hydrating fluids found in the skin; hydrophilic agent with water-binding properties.
hydrolipidic	Hydrolipidic film is an oil–water balance that protects the skin's surface.
intercellular matrix	Lipid substances between corneum cells that protect the cells from water loss and irritation.
keratin	Fiberous protein of cells that is also the principal component of skin, hair, and nails; provides resiliency and protection.
keratinocytes	Epidermal cells composed of keratin, lipids, and other proteins.
Langerhans immune cells	Guard cells of the immune system that sense unrecognized foreign invaders, such as bacteria, and then process these antigens for removal through the lymph system.
leukocytes	White blood cells that have enzymes to digest and kill bacteria and parasites. These white blood cells also respond to allergies.
lymph vessels	Located in the dermis, these supply nourishment within the skin and remove waste.
melanin	Tiny grains of pigment (coloring matter) that are produced by melanocytes and deposited into cells in the stratum germinativum layer of the epidermis and in the papillary layers of the dermis.It is a protein that determines hair, eye, and skin color; a defense mechanism to protect skin from the sun.
melanocytes	Cells that produce skin pigment granules in the basal layer.
melanosomes	Pigment carrying granules that produce melanin, a complex protein.
papillary layer	Top layer of the dermis next to the epidermis.
pheomelanin	A type of melanin that is red and yellow in color. People with light-colored skin mostly produce pheomelanin. There are two types of melanin; the other is eumelanin.

Glossary

pores	Tube-like opening for sweat glands on the epidermis.
reticular layer	Deeper layer of the dermis that supplies the skin with oxygen and nutrients; contains fat cells, blood vessels, sudoriferous (sweat) glands, hair follicles, lymph vessels, arrector pili muscles, sebaceous (oil) glands, and nerve endings.
rosacea	Chronic condition that appears primarily on the cheeks and nose and is characterized by flushing (redness), telangiectasis (distended or dilated surface blood vessels), and, in some cases, the formation of papules and pustules.
sebaceous glands	Also known as *oil glands*; protect the surface of the skin. Sebaceous glands are appendages connected to follicles.
sebum	Oil that provides protection for the epidermis from external factors and lubricates both the skin and hair.
stratum corneum	Also known as *horny layer*; outermost layer of the epidermis, composed of corneocytes.
stratum germinativum	Also known as *basal cell layer*; active layer of the epidermis above the papillary layer of the dermis; cell mitosis takes place here that produces new epidermal skin cells and is responsible for growth.
stratum granulosum	Also known as *granular layer*; layer of the epidermis composed of cells filled with keratin that resemble granules; replaces cells shed from the stratum corneum.
stratum lucidum	Clear, transparent layer of the epidermis under the stratum corneum; thickest on the palms of hands and soles of feet.
stratum spinosum	Also known as *spiny layer*; layer of the epidermis above the stratum germinativum (basal) layer containing desmosomes, the intercellular connections made of proteins.
subcutaneous layer	Also known as *hypodermis*; subcutaneous adipose (fat) tissue located beneath the dermis; a protective cushion and energy storage for the body.
subcutis tissue	Also known as *adipose tissue*; fatty tissue found below the dermis that gives smoothness and contour to the body, contains fat for use as energy, and also acts as a protective cushion for the outer skin.
sudoriferous glands	Also known as *sweat glands*; excrete perspiration, regulate body temperature, and detoxify the body by excreting excess salt and unwanted chemicals.
t-cells	Identify molecules that have foreign peptides and also help regulate immune response.
telangiectasia	Capillaries that have been damaged and are now larger, or distended, blood vessels; commonly called *couperose skin*.
transepidermal water loss	Abbreviated TEWL; water loss caused by evaporation on the skin's surface.
tyrosinase	The enzyme that stimulates melanocytes and thus produces melanin.
UVA radiation	Also known as *aging rays*; longer wavelengths ranging between 320 to 400 nanometers that penetrate deeper into the skin than UVB; cause genetic damage and cell death. UVA contributes up to 95 percent of the sun's ultraviolet radiation.
UVB radiation	Also known as *burning rays*; UVB wavelengths range between 290 to 320 nanometers. UVB rays have shorter, burning wavelengths that are stronger and more damaging than UVA rays. UVB causes burning of the skin as well as tanning, skin aging, and cancer.

CHAPTER 11

Disorders and Diseases of the Skin

Chapter Outline

- Why Study Disorders and Diseases of the Skin?
- Dermatology and Esthetics
- Lesions of the Skin
- Disorders of the Sebaceous (Oil) Glands
- Disorders of the Sudoriferous (Sweat) Glands
- Inflammations of the Skin
- Pigmentation Disorders
- Hypertrophies of the Skin
- Contagious Diseases
- Skin Cancer
- Acne

Learning Objectives

After completing this chapter, you will be able to:

- LO1 Understand the different types of skin lesions.
- LO2 Understand gland disorders.
- LO3 Understand skin inflammations.
- LO4 Recognize pigmentation disorders.
- LO5 Identify which disorders are contagious.
- LO6 Recognize potential skin cancer growths.
- LO7 Understand acne and the causes of the disorder.
- LO8 Recognize the different grades of acne.
- LO9 Identify common skin conditions and disorders.
- LO10 Know which disorders to refer to a physician.

Key Terms

Page number indicates where in the chapter the term is used.

acne
pg. 261

acne excoriee
pg. 260

actinic keratoses
pg. 267

albinism
pg. 266

anhidrosis
pg. 262

asteatosis
pg. 261

atopic dermatitis
pg. 263

basal cell carcinoma
pg. 270

bromhidrosis
pg. 262

bulla
pg. 258

carbuncle
pg. 261

chloasma (liver spots)
pg. 266

comedo
pg. 261

comedogenic
pg. 274

conjunctivitis (pinkeye)
pg. 268

contact dermatitis
pg. 263

crust
pg. 260

cyst
pg. 258

dermatitis
pg. 263

dermatologist
pg. 258

dermatology
pg. 258

eczema
pg. 263

edema
pg. 264

erythema
pg. 264

excoriation
pg. 260

fissure
pg. 260

folliculitis
pg. 264

furuncle (boil)
pg. 261

herpes simplex virus 1
pg. 268

herpes simplex virus 2
pg. 268

herpes zoster (shingles)
pg. 268

hyperhidrosis
pg. 262

hyperkeratosis
pg. 267

hyperpigmentation
pg. 265

hypertrophy
pg. 267

hypopigmentation
pg. 265

impetigo
pg. 268

keloid
pg. 260

keratoma
pg. 267

keratosis
pg. 267

keratosis pilaris
pg. 267

lentigo
pg. 266

lesions
pg. 258

leukoderma
pg. 266

macule
pg. 259

malignant melanoma
pg. 271

Key Terms

Page number indicates where in the chapter the term is used.

milia
pg. 261

miliaria rubra (prickly heat)
pg. 263

mole
pg. 267

nevus (birthmark)
pg. 266

nodules
pg. 259

papule
pg. 259

perioral dermatitis
pg. 263

primary lesions
pg. 258

pruitis
pg. 264

pseudofolliculitis (razor bumps)
pg. 264

psoriasis
pg. 264

pustule
pg. 259

retention hyperkeratosis
pg. 272

rosacea
pg. 264

scale
pg. 261

scar
pg. 261

sebaceous filaments
pg. 273

sebaceous hyperplasia
pg. 262

seborrhea
pg. 262

seborrheic dermatitis
pg. 262

secondary lesions
pg. 260

skin tag
pg. 267

squamous cell carcinoma
pg. 270

stain
pg. 266

steatoma
pg. 262

tan
pg. 266

tinea
pg. 268

tinea corporis (ringworm)
pg. 268

tubercle
pg. 260

tumor
pg. 260

ulcer
pg. 261

urticaria (hives)
pg. 264

varicose veins
pg. 264

vasodilation
pg. 264

verruca (wart)
pg. 268

vesicle
pg. 260

vitiligo
pg. 267

wheal
pg. 260

Skin disorders and diseases are interesting and complex subjects. Estheticians must be knowledgeable about skin disorders and diseases. Recognizing these conditions can help the esthetician work with clients effectively and safely. The medical field is progressing and the treatment of skin disorders and diseases is becoming easier with advances in technology, ingredients, and medicine. Although there are hundreds of disorders and diseases, only the most common are discussed in this chapter. Knowledge of skin problems takes years of experience and study, but reference books are helpful in identifying these disorders and diseases.

Estheticians can provide client education and help clients with many of their skin concerns. Individuals that have skin problems can be affected emotionally by dealing with such a visible problem. Be sensitive to people's modesty and to how their experiences may have a lifetime effect on their self-esteem and health. Even in the classroom, baring our skin to close examination by others can be uncomfortable. Use positive words of encouragement and be mindful of how you discuss skin problems tactfully.

Never work on any skin condition you do not recognize. When in doubt, stop the service. Let clients know if you do not recognize a condition or lesion, and they will appreciate your honesty and caution. Trying to extract a sebaceous hyperplasia mistaken for a comedone can lead to scarring and a potentially worse problem. Advanced classes and experience are necessary to learn more about disorders. Treatments and products formulated for some of the common disorders are addressed in subsequent chapters.

Why Study Disorders and Diseases of the Skin?

Estheticians should study and have a thorough understanding of disorders and diseases of the skin in order to effectively and safely treat clients.

- Recognizing skin disorders and diseases is necessary to work with clients effectively and safely, especially for those conditions that are contagious or that need to be referred to a physician.
- Estheticians can help clients with many common disorders and conditions such as rosacea and minor acne.
- By understanding acne and the causes of the disorder, estheticians have a rewarding opportunity to help people with acne and make a difference in their lives.
- As an esthetician, it is important to keep current on the treatments of skin disorders and diseases along with the advances in technology, ingredients, and medicine used to treat the skin.

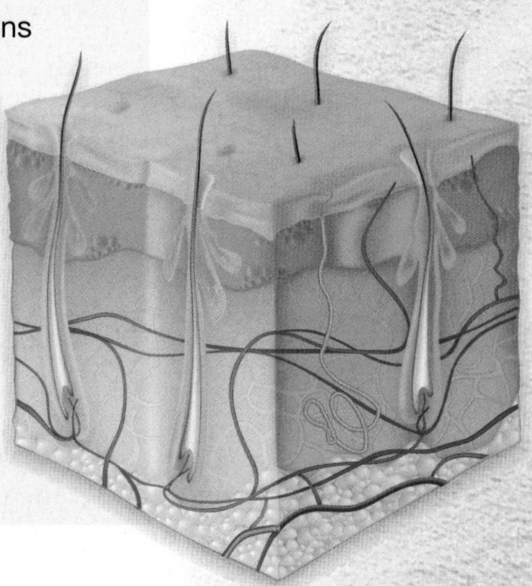

Dermatology and Esthetics

Dermatology is the branch of medical science that studies and treats the skin and its disorders and diseases. A **dermatologist** is a physician who treats these disorders and diseases. Recognizing skin disorders and diseases is important for the protection of both the technician and the client. Estheticians may not perform services on clients who have contagious or infectious diseases. Any skin abnormality you do not positively recognize must be referred to a physician.

Dermatologists and physicians are qualified to treat skin problems, but estheticians may not diagnose or treat disorders and diseases of the skin beyond their scope of practice; however, estheticians can help clients with many common disorders and conditions such as rosacea, minor acne, and sensitive skin. Caution and strict infection control practices are imperative when working with skin disorders. Knowledge of skin conditions that *contraindicate* (prohibit) a treatment is also necessary.

CAUTION!

Do not attempt to diagnose or treat medical conditions. Estheticians are not licensed to diagnose skin disorders or diseases. Refer clients to a physician if you think they have a disorder or disease that needs medical attention.

Causes and treatments for all of the disorders and diseases are not addressed here due to the limited scope of practice and vast amount of advanced medical information that it would require. Some lesions fit into more than one category and have more than one name or definition. Skin disorders are not easy to categorize as they can be as diverse as the individuals dealing with the ailments.

Lesions of the Skin

Lesions (LEE-zhuns) are structural changes in the tissues caused by damage or injury. Any mark, wound, or abnormality is described as a lesion. The three types of lesions are primary, secondary, and tertiary. Some books refer to the tertiary, or third, type of lesions as *vascular lesions*. Vascular lesions involve the blood or circulatory system.

Primary Lesions

Primary lesions are lesions in the early stages of development or change. Primary lesions are characterized by flat, nonpalpable changes in skin color or by elevations formed by fluid in a cavity, such as vesicles or pustules. Primary lesions of the skin include the following (**Figure 11–1**):

- **Bulla** (BULL-uh) (plural: bullae, BULL-ay). A large blister containing watery fluid. It is similar to a vesicle, but larger.
- **Cyst** (SIST). A closed, abnormally developed sac containing fluid, infection, or other matter above or below the skin. An acne cyst is one type of cyst.

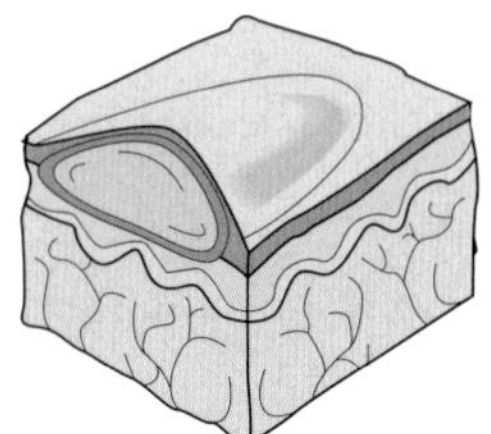

Bulla:
Same as a vesicle only greater than 0.5 cm
Example:
Contact dermatitis, large second-degree burns, bulbous impetigo, pemphigus

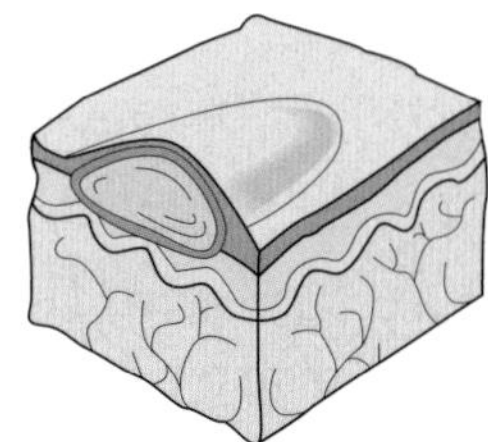

Vesicle:
Accumulation of fluid between the upper layers of the skin; elevated mass containing serous fluid; less than 0.5 cm
Example:
Herpes simplex, herpes zoster, chickenpox

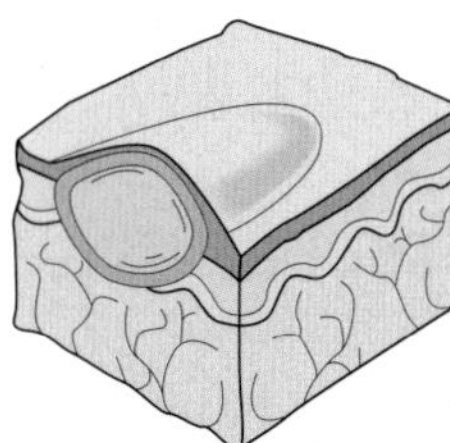

Tubercle:
Solid and elevated; however, it extends deeper than papules into the dermis or subcutaneous tissues, 0.5-2 cm
Example:
Lipoma, erythema, nodosum, cyst

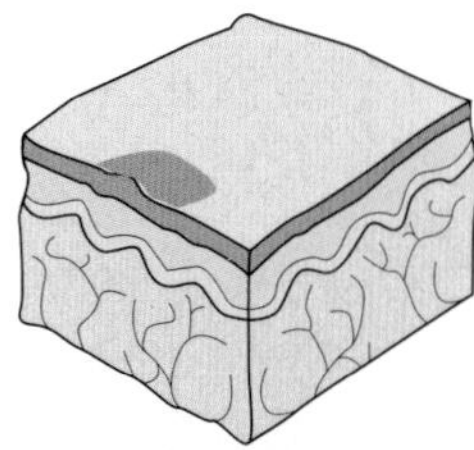

Macule:
Localized changes in skin color of less than 1 cm in diameter
Example:
Freckle

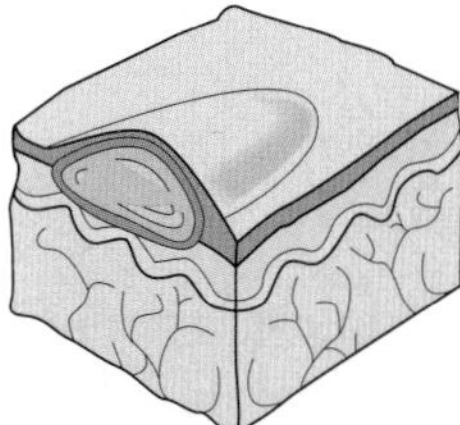

Pustule:
Vesicles or bullae that become filled with pus, usually described as less than 0.5 cm in diameter
Example:
Acne, impetigo, furuncles, carbuncles, folliculitis

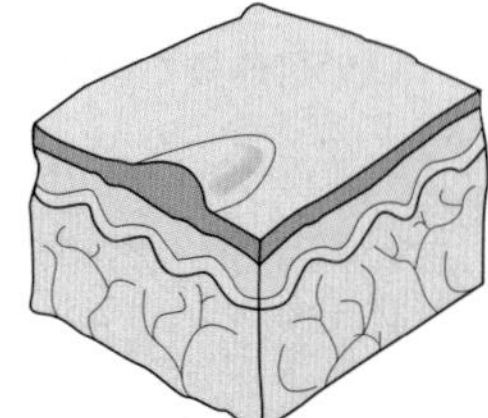

Papule:
Solid, elevated lesion less than 0.5 cm in diameter
Example:
Warts, elevated nevi

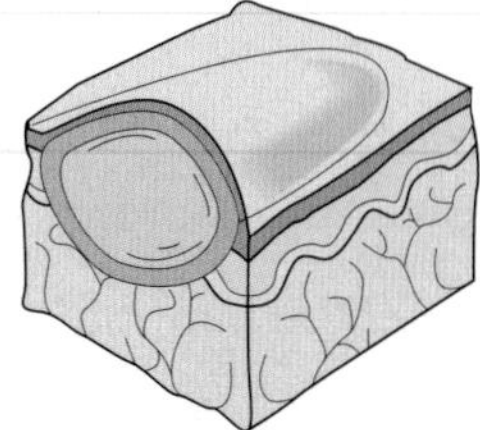

Nodule/Tumor:
The same as a nodule only greater than 2 cm
Example:
Carcinoma (such as advanced breast carcinoma); **not** basal cell or squamous cell of the skin

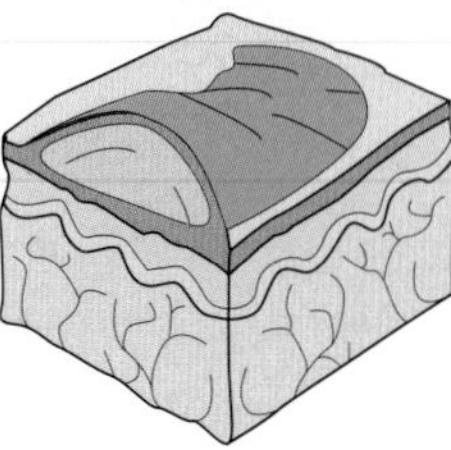

Wheal:
Localized edema in the epidermis causing irregular elevation that may be red or pale
Example:
Insect bite or a hive

▲ Figure 11–1
Primary lesions of the skin. These illustrations show the size, elevation or depression, and layers of the skin that are affected in each type of lesion.

- **Macule** (MAK-yool), (plural: maculae, MAK-yuh-ly). A flat spot or discoloration on the skin, such as a freckle or a red spot, left after a pimple has healed. Macules are neither raised nor sunken.
- **Nodules** (NOD-yool). These are often referred to as tumors, but they are smaller bumps caused by conditions such as scar tissue, fatty deposits, or infections.
- **Papule** (PAP-yool). A small elevation on the skin that contains no fluid, but may develop into a pustule (**Figure 11–2**). Papules are less than half an inch (1.25 centimeters) in diameter and may have a varied appearance in color and are either rounded, smooth, or rough.
- **Pustule** (PUS-chool). An inflamed papule with a white or yellow center containing pus, a fluid consisting of white blood cells, bacteria, and other debris; a small pus-containing blister that may or may

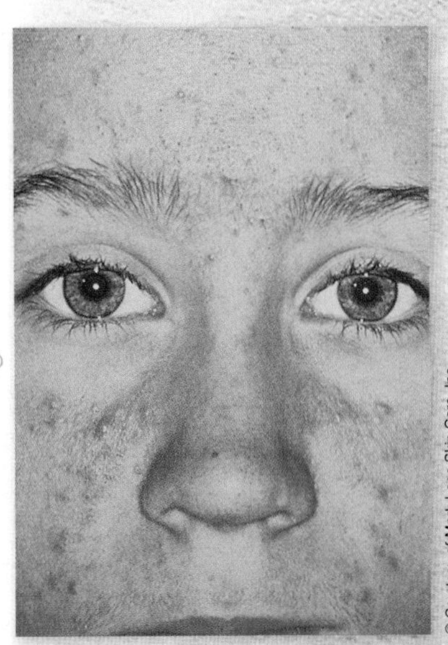

▲ Figure 11–2
Papules.

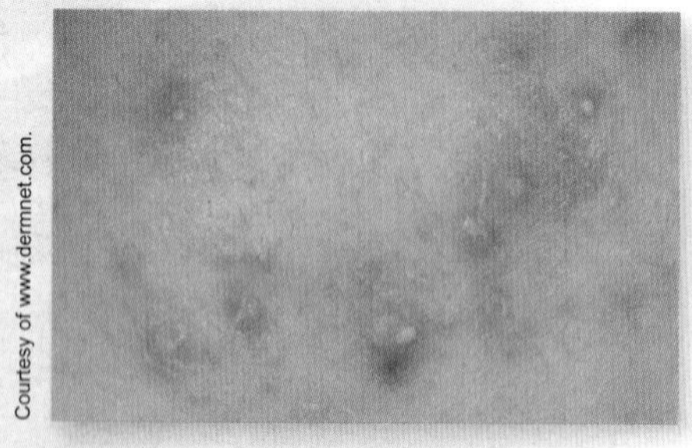

▲ Figure 11–3
Pustules.

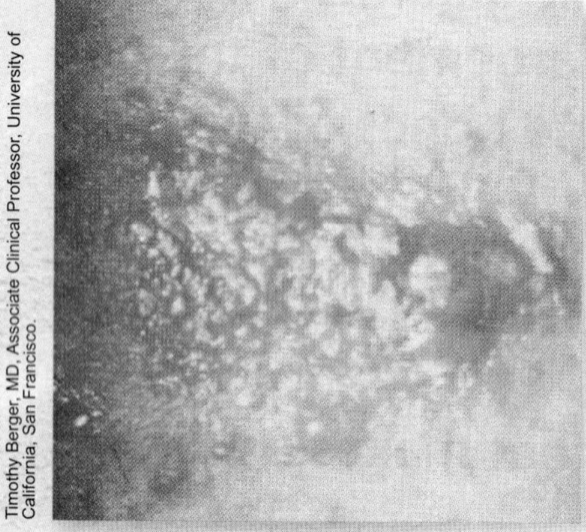

▲ Figure 11–4
Vesicles.

not be caused by an infection. Acne pustules in hair follicles are not infectious (Figure 11–3).

- **Tubercle** (TOO-bur-kul). An abnormal rounded, solid lump; larger than a papule.
- **Tumor** (TOO-mur). A large nodule; an abnormal cell mass resulting from excessive cell multiplication, varying in size, shape, and color.
- **Vesicle** (VES-ih-kel). A small blister or sac containing clear fluid. Poison ivy and poison oak produce vesicles (Figure 11–4).
- **Wheal** (WHEEL). An itchy, swollen lesion caused by a blow, insect bite, skin allergy reaction, or stings. Hives and mosquito bites are wheals. Hives are called urticaria (ur-tuh-KAYR-ee-ah) and can also be caused by exposure to allergens used in products.

Secondary Lesions

- **Secondary lesions** of the skin develop in the later stages of disease and change the structure of tissues and organs (Figure 11–5).
- **Crust**. Dead cells formed over a wound or blemish while it is healing, resulting in an accumulation of sebum and pus, sometimes mixed with epidermal material. An example is the scab on a sore.
- **Excoriation** (ek-skor-ee-AY-shun). A skin sore or abrasion produced by scratching or scraping.
- **Acne excoriee** (ak-nee ek-SKOR-ee). A disorder where clients purposely scrape off acne lesions, causing scarring and discoloration.
- **Fissure** (FISH-ur). A crack in the skin that may penetrate into the dermis. Chapped lips or hands are fissures.
- **Keloid** (KEE-loyd). A thick scar resulting from excessive growth of fibrous tissue (collagen). Keloids are usually found in those that are

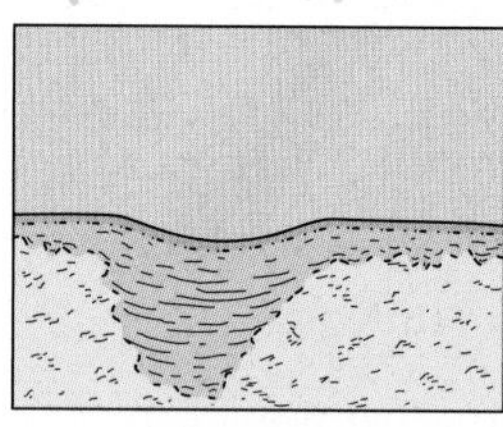

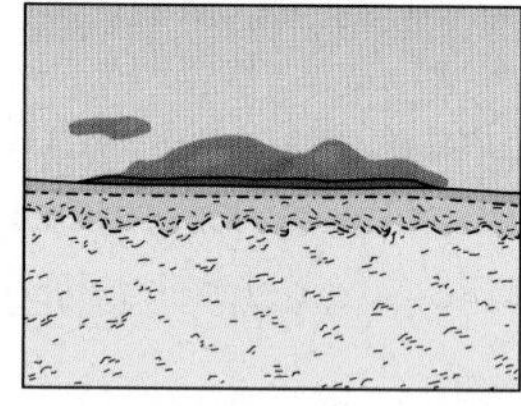

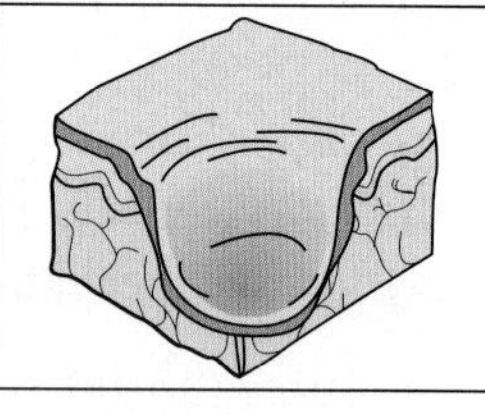

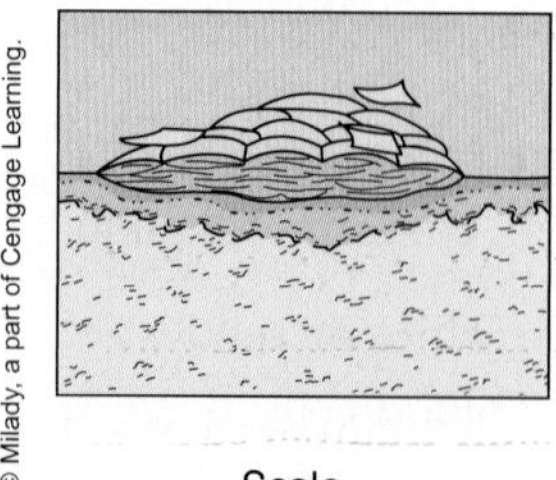

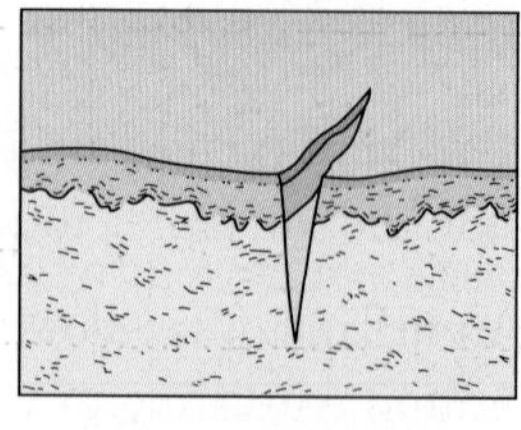

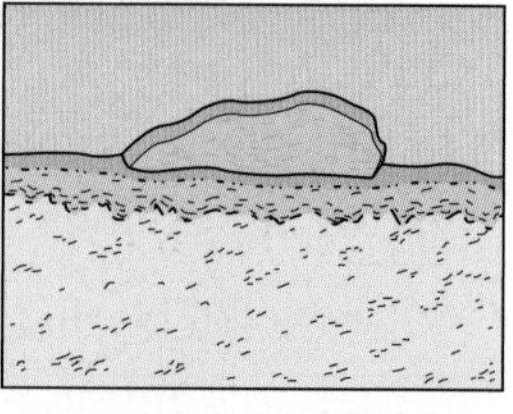

▶ Figure 11–5
Secondary skin lesions.

genetically predisposed to them and may occur following an injury or surgery (**Figure 11–6**).

- **Scale**. Excessive shedding of dead skin cells; flaky skin cells; any thin plate of epidermal flakes, dry or oily. An example is abnormal or excessive dandruff or psoriasis.
- **Scar**. Discolored, slightly raised mark on the skin formed after an injury or lesion of the skin has healed. The tissue hardens to heal the injury. Thick, elevated scars are *hypertrophic*.
- **Ulcer**. An open lesion on the skin or mucous membrane of the body, accompanied by pus and loss of skin depth; a deep erosion or depression in the skin, normally due to infection or cancer. Requires medical referral. ✓ LO1

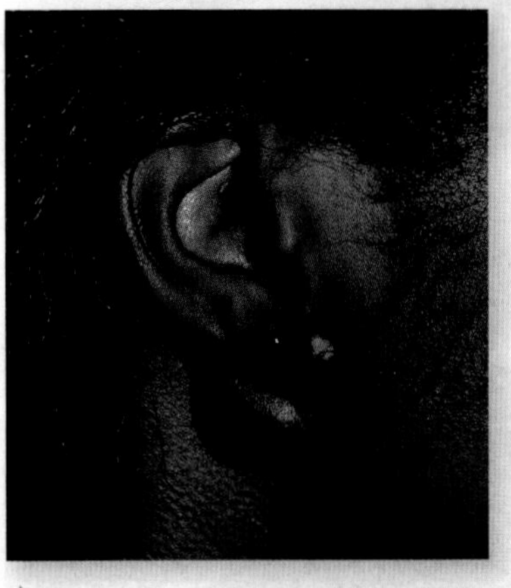

▲ Figure 11–6
Keloids.

Disorders of the Sebaceous (Oil) Glands

Notable sebaceous gland disorders include the following:

- **Acne**. A chronic inflammatory skin disorder of the sebaceous glands characterized by comedones and blemishes. There are many types of acne. Common acne is known as *acne simplex* or *acne vulgaris*. Inflammation of the sebaceous glands results from retained oil secretions, cells, and excessive *Propionibacterium acne* (*P. acne*) bacteria.
- **Asteatosis** (as-tee-ah-TOH-sis). Dry, scaly skin from sebum deficiency; can be due to aging, internal disorders, alkalies of harsh soaps, or cold exposure.
- **Comedo** (KAHM-uh-doe) (plural: comedones; KAHM-uh-dohnz). A noninflamed buildup of cells, sebum, and other debris inside follicles. An *open comedo* is a blackhead open at the surface and exposed to air. When the follicle is filled with an excess of oil a blackhead forms. It is dark because it is exposed to oxygen and oxidation occurs (**Figure 11–7**). A *closed comedo* forms when the openings of the follicles are blocked with debris and white cells. Also referred to as a *whitehead*, but should not be confused with the more hardened white type of papules called milia.
- **Furuncle** (FYOO-rung-kul), also known as **boil**. A subcutaneous abscess filled with pus. Furuncles are caused by bacteria in glands or hair follicles.
- **Carbuncles**. (KAHR-bung-kuls) Groups of boils.
- **Milia** (MIL-ee-uh). These epidermal cysts are small, firm white papules. Milia are whitish, pearl-like masses of sebum and dead cells under the skin with no visible opening often mistakenly called whiteheads (whiteheads look similar but are soft). Hardened and closed over, milia are more common in dry skin types and may form after skin trauma, such as a laser resurfacing or chronic exposure to UV radiation (**Figure 11–8**).

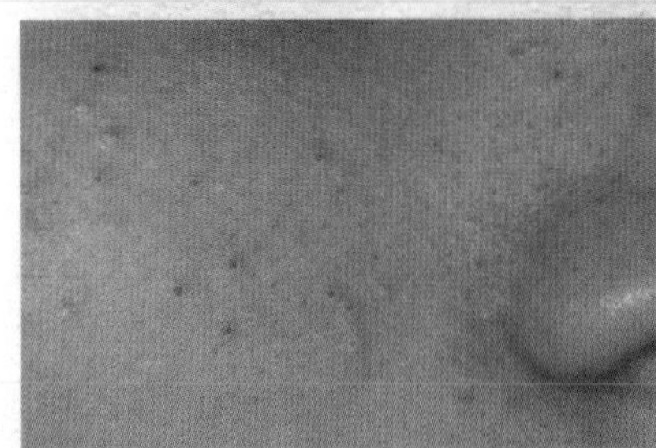
▲ Figure 11–7
Comedones.

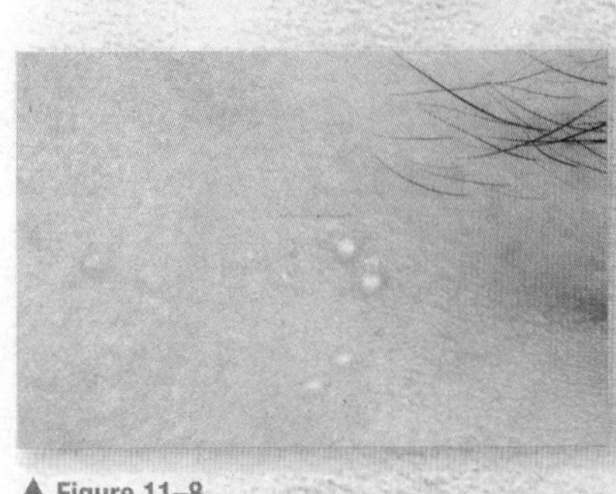
▲ Figure 11–8
Milia.

They resemble small sesame seeds and are almost always perfectly round. They are usually found around the eyes, cheeks, and forehead; also caused by blocked follicular openings from thick moisturizers. Depending on the state, milia can be treated in the salon or spa. Milia must be lanced, or opened, to be extracted.

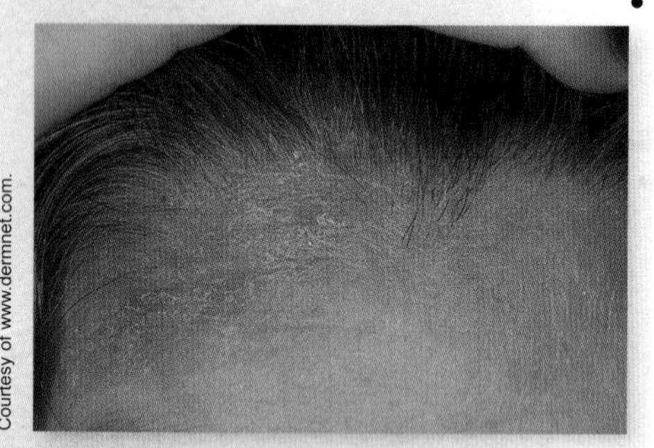

Courtesy of www.dermnet.com.

▲ Figure 11–9
Sebaceous hyperplasia.

- **Sebaceous hyperplasia** (sih-BAY-shus hy-pur-PLAY-zhuh). Benign lesions frequently seen in oilier areas of the face. They are often white, yellow, or flesh colored. Sebaceous hyperplasia is described as doughnut-shaped with an indentation in the center. Sebaceous material may be found in the center. As cell turnover rate slows with age and decreased androgen levels, this causes abnormal cell buildup with very little oil that crowds and enlarges sebaceous glands. Do not mistake these overgrowths of the sebaceous gland for comedones or milia, which may look similar at first. These harmless lesions cannot be removed by extraction, only surgically (**Figure 11–9**).
- **Seborrhea** (seb-oh-REE-ah). Severe oiliness of the skin; an abnormal secretion from the sebaceous glands.
- **Seborrheic dermatitis** (seb-oh-REE-ick derm-ah-TIE-tus). A skin condition characterized by inflammation, dry or oily scaling or crusting, and/or itchiness. The red, flaky skin often appears in the eyebrows, in the scalp and hairline, the middle of the forehead, and along the sides of the nose. One cause is an inflammation of the sebaceous glands. This condition is sometimes treated with cortisone creams. Severe cases should be referred to the dermatologist. Seborrheic dermatitis is also a common form of eczema.
- **Steatoma** (stee-ah-TOH-muh). A sebaceous cyst or subcutaneous tumor filled with sebum and ranging in size from a pea to an orange. It usually appears on the scalp, neck, and back; also called a *wen*.

Disorders of the Sudoriferous (Sweat) Glands

Disorders of the sudoriferous glands include the following:

- **Anhidrosis** (an-hy-DROH-sis). A deficiency in perspiration due to failure of the sweat glands; often results from a fever or skin disease. Anhidrosis requires medical treatment.
- **Bromhidrosis** (broh-mih-DROH-sis). Foul-smelling perspiration, usually in the armpits or on the feet. Bromhidrosis is caused by bacteria and yeast that break down the sweat on the surface of the skin.
- **Hyperhidrosis** (hy-pur-hy-DROH-sis). Excessive perspiration caused by heat, genetics, medications, or medical conditions. Also called *diaphoresis*.

- **Miliaria rubra** (mil-ee-AIR-ee-ah ROOB-rah), also known as **prickly heat**. Acute inflammatory disorder of the sweat glands; results in the eruption of red vesicles and burning, itching skin from excessive heat exposure. LO2

Inflammations of the Skin

Inflammations of the skin include the following:

- **Dermatitis**. An inflammatory condition of the skin; various forms include lesions such as eczema, vesicles, or papules. The three main categories of dermatitis are atopic, contact, and seborrheic.
- **Atopic dermatitis**. Atopic dermatitis is a chronic, relapsing form of dermatitis (*atopic* is "excess inflammation from allergies"). Irritants and allergens trigger reactions that include dry, cracking skin. The redness, itching, and dehydration of the dermatitis make the condition worse. Use of humidifiers and lotion can help keep the skin more hydrated. Topical corticosteroids can relieve the symptoms.
- **Contact dermatitis**. An inflammatory skin condition caused by an allergic reaction from contact with a substance or chemical. Contact dermatitis can be caused by either an allergic reaction or contact with an irritant. Makeup, skin care products, detergents, dyes, fabrics, jewelry, and plants can all cause red, itchy skin. Allergies to red dyes in products and nickel in jewelry are common. *Allergic contact dermatitis* is caused by exposure to allergens (Figure 11–10). Poison ivy is an example. A rash occurs when the immune system responds to allergens such as fragrances and preservatives. *Irritant contact dermatitis* is a localized inflammatory reaction caused by exposure to caustic irritants. Occupational disorders from ingredients in cosmetics and chemical solutions can cause contact dermatitis, or *dermatitis venenata*. Contact with allergens and caustic chemicals can also cause skin sensitivity or disorders. Allergies and skin eruptions are common. Wearing gloves or protective skin creams while working with chemicals or irritating substances can help prevent contact dermatitis. Irritant contact dermatitis can become worse and lead to allergic contact dermatitis.

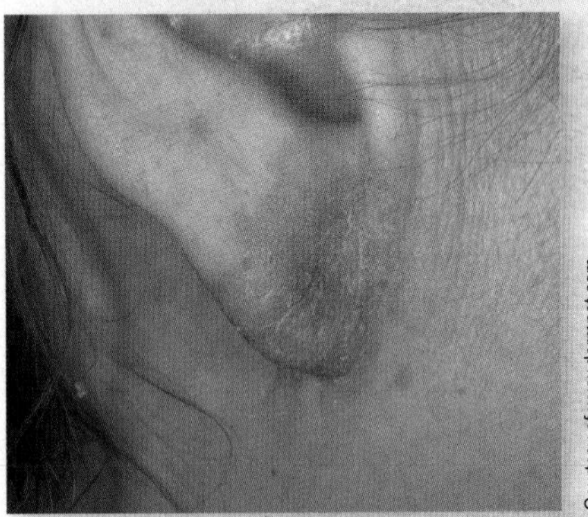

Courtesy of www.dermnet.com.

▲ Figure 11–10
Contact dermatitis.

- **Perioral dermatitis** (pair-ee-OR-ul derm-a-TIE-tuss). An acne-like condition around the mouth; consists mainly of small clusters of papules. It may be caused by toothpaste or products used on the face. It is not contagious. Antibiotics can help treat the condition.
- **Eczema** (EG-zuh-muh). An inflammatory, painful, itching disease of the skin; acute or chronic in nature, with dry or moist lesions. This should be referred to a physician (Figure 11–11). Avoid contact and skin care treatments if a client has eczema. *Seborrheic dermatitis* is a common form of eczema as well as a sebaceous gland disorder; characterized by scaling around the nose, ears, scalp, eyebrows, and mid-chest areas. This flaking mainly affects oilier areas.

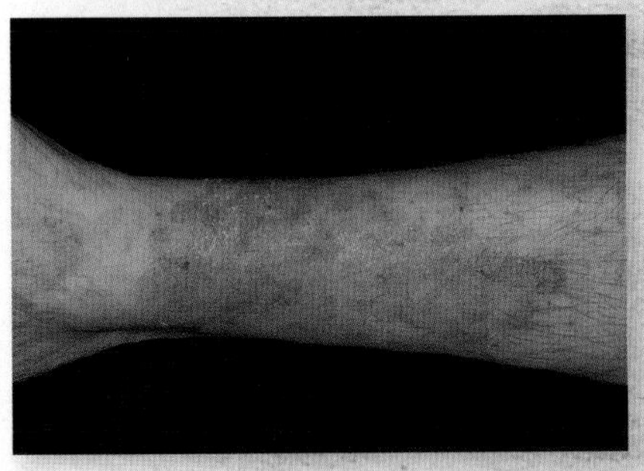

Courtesy of www.dermnet.com.

▲ Figure 11–11
Eczema.

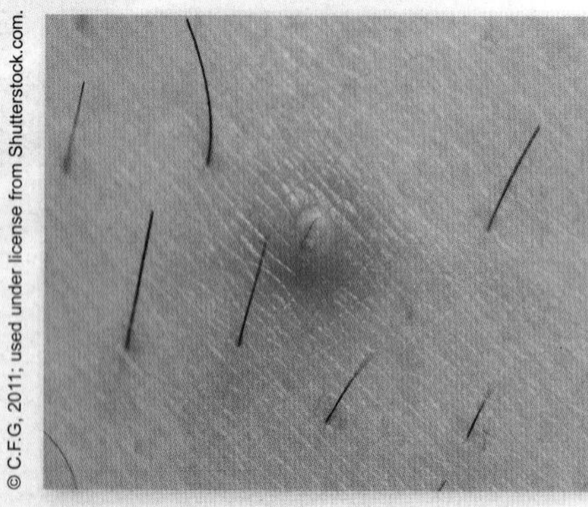

© C.F.G, 2011; used under license from Shutterstock.com.

▲ Figure 11–12
Folliculitis.

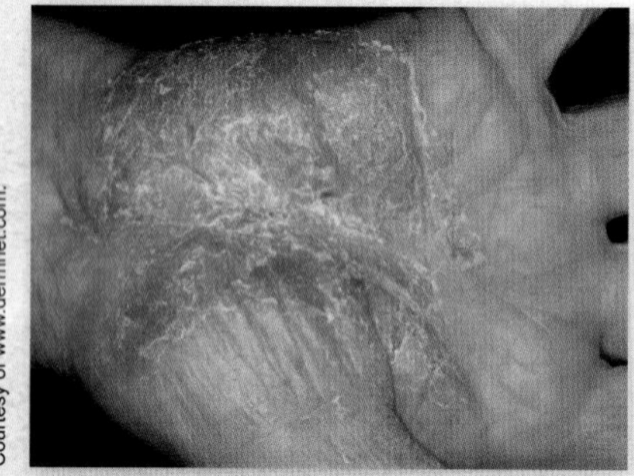

Courtesy of www.dermnet.com.

▲ Figure 11–13
Psoriasis.

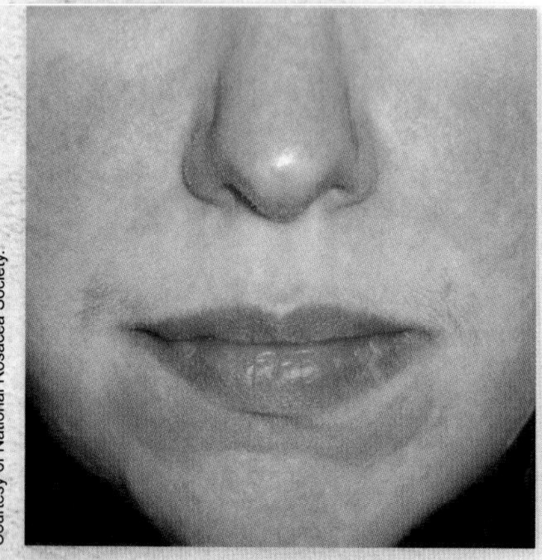

Courtesy of National Rosacea Society.

▲ Figure 11–14
Rosacea.

- **Edema** (ih-DEE-muh). Swelling from a fluid imbalance in the cells or from a response to injury, infection, or medication.
- **Erythema** (er-uh-THEE-muh). Redness caused by inflammation.
- **Folliculitis** (fah-lik-yuh-LY-tis). Hair grows under the surface instead of growing up and out of the follicle, causing a bacterial infection. These ingrown hairs are common in men, usually from shaving (referred to as *barbae folliculitis, folliculitis barbae, sycosis barbae, or barber's itch*) (Figure 11–12). **Pseudofolliculitis** (SOO-doe-fah-lik-yuh-LY-tis), also known as **razor bumps**, resembles folliculitus without the pus or infection.
- **Pruitis** (proo-RYT-us). The medical term for itching; persistant itching.
- **Psoriasis** (suh-RY-uh-sis). An itchy skin disease characterized by red patches covered with white-silver scales; caused by an over-proliferation of skin cells that replicate too fast (Figure 11–13). Psoriasis is usually found in patches on the scalp, elbows, knees, chest, and lower back. If patches are irritated, bleeding can occur. Psoriasis is not contagious but can be spread by irritating the affected area.
- **Urticaria** (ur-tuh-KAYR-ee-ah), also known as **hives**. An allergic reaction by the body's histamine production.

Vascular Lesions

- **Rosacea** (roh-ZAY-see-uh). An inflammation of the skin characterized by extreme redness, dilation of blood vessels, and in severe cases the formation of papules and pustules (Figure 11–14). It is chronic congestion primarily on the cheeks and nose. The cause and treatment of rosacea is a primary skin care concern. The cause is unknown, but may be due to heredity, bacteria, mites, or fungus. Certain factors are known to aggravate the condition. **Vasodilation** (vascular dilation) of the blood vessels makes rosacea worse. Spicy foods, alcohol, caffeine, temperature extremes, heat, sun, and stress aggravate rosacea. Soothing and calming ingredients and treatments will help calm the skin and decrease the inflammation. Rosacea and couperose conditions are discussed further in other chapters.
- **Telangiectasia** (tel-an-jee-ek-TAY-zhuh). A vascular lesion; describes capillaries that have been damaged and are now larger, or distended blood vessels. Commonly called *couperose skin* and characterized by redness.
- **Varicose veins**. Vascular lesions that are abnormally dilated and twisted veins which can occur anywhere in the body. Sometimes treated with *sclerotherapy*, a nonsurgical injection into the vein. Surgery is a treatment option for serious vein problems.

Allergic Contact Dermatitis

Allergic contact dermatitis is caused by exposure and direct skin contact to an allergen. Normally the immune system protects us from pathogens and disease, but in an allergic reaction the immune system actually causes the problem by trying to do its job too well. An allergic reaction occurs when our immune system mistakes a substance for a toxic one and initiates a major defense against it.

Initial exposure to an allergen does not always cause an allergic reaction. The development of hypersensitivity is the result of repeated exposure to an allergen over time. This process is called *sensitization* (SEN-sih-tiz-A-shun), and it may take months or years depending on the allergen and the intensity of exposure. Also remember that different people develop allergies to different allergens. Individual predisposition to allergies may be inherited because sensitivity seems to run in families.

Poison ivy is a common allergen. Although approximately 75 percent of the population is allergic to poison ivy, the remaining 25 percent will never have a reaction no matter how many times they are exposed. Individuals who are not predisposed never become sensitized and will not develop allergies.

Irritant Contact Dermatitis

Irritant reactions affect everyone who comes in contact with an irritant, although the degree of irritation will vary depending on the individual. In acute cases, symptoms are noticed immediately or within just a few hours. Chronic cases may be delayed reactions that take weeks, months, or years to develop. Symptoms range from redness, swelling, scaling, and itching to serious, painful chemical burns. Irritating substances will temporarily damage the epidermis. Caustic substances are examples of irritants. When the skin is damaged by irritating substances, the immune system springs into action. It floods the tissue with water, trying to dilute the irritant. This is why swelling occurs.

The immune system also releases histamines, which enlarge the vessels around the injury. Blood can then rush to the area more quickly and help remove the irritating substance. The extra blood under the skin is easily visible. The entire area becomes red, warm, and may throb. Histamines cause the itchy feeling that often accompanies contact dermatitis. After everything calms down, the swelling will go away. The surrounding skin is often left damaged, scaly, cracked, and dry. Fortunately, irritations are not permanent. If you avoid repeated and/or prolonged contact with the irritating substance, the skin will usually quickly repair itself; however, continued or repeated exposure may lead to permanent allergic reactions and skin damage. ✓ LO3

CAUTION!

Reactions from chemicals are commonly seen in the salon:

- On the practitioner's fingers, palms, or on the back of the hand.
- On the practitioner's face, especially the cheeks.
- On the client's scalp, hairline, forehead, or neckline

If you examine the area where the problem occurs, you can usually determine the cause.

For example, technicians may react to chemicals from using disinfectants or strong skin care products. This is both prolonged and repeated contact! Sensitization is an increased or exaggerated sensitivity to products. Wear gloves to avoid potential reactions. Eyes and lungs can also be affected by exposure to strong chemicals or ingredients.

Pigmentation Disorders*

The genetic background of a person influences pigmentation disorders. Abnormal pigmentation, referred to as *dyschromia* (diz-KRO-me-ah), can be caused by various internal or external factors. Sun exposure is the biggest external cause of pigmentation disorders and can make existing pigmentation disorders worse. Drugs may also cause skin pigmentation abnormalities. **Hyperpigmentation**, overproduction of pigment, and **hypopigmentation**, lack of pigment, are the two types of pigmentation disorders. Hyperpigmentation is a frequent concern for clients and is discussed in subsequent chapters.

Did You Know?

Severe allergic reactions can result in high fever and anaphylactic (an-ah-fah-LAK-tik) shock, which can be life threatening.

© Milady, a part of Cengage Learning. Photography by Visual Recollection.

▲ Figure 11–15
Hyperpigmentation.

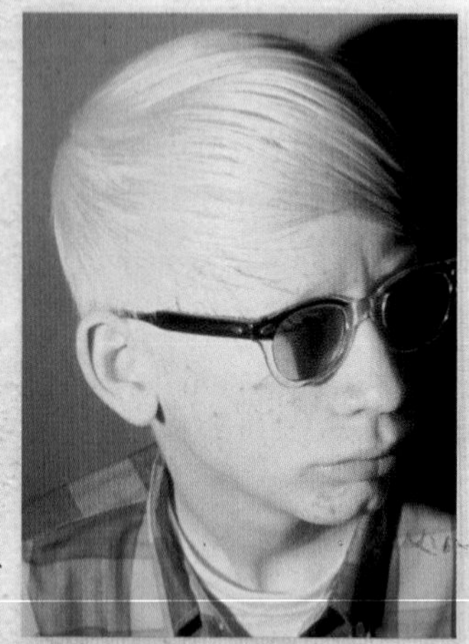

Courtesy of www.dermnet.com.

▲ Figure 11–16
Albinism.

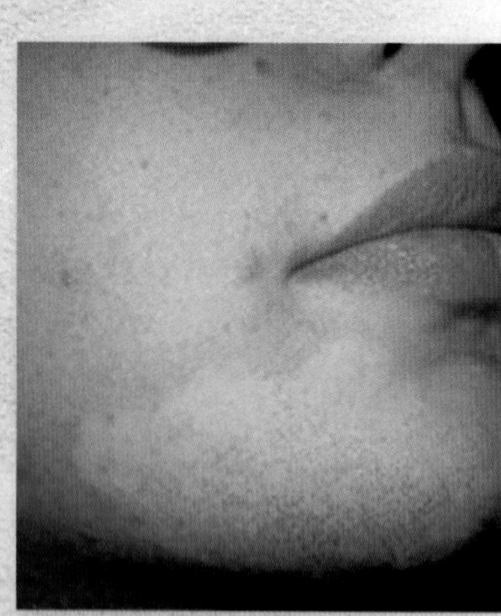

Courtesy of www.dermnet.com.

▲ Figure 11–17
Vitiligo.

Hyperpigmentation

Hyperpigmentation appears in the following forms:

- **Chloasma** (klo-AZ-ma), also known as **liver spots**. Increased pigmentation; from sun exposure or pigmentation from other causes. Melasma is a type of chloasma, which appears during pregnancy. They can be helped by exfoliation treatments or can be treated by a dermatologist.
- **Hyperpigmentation**. An overproduction of pigment (**Figure 11–15**). Increased melanin causes excess pigment. Sun exposure, acne, medications, and post-inflammatory hyperpigmentation from skin damage can cause darkened pigmentation.
- **Lentigo** (len-TY-goh). A flat, pigmented area similar to a freckle; small, yellow-brown spots. Lentigenes (len-tih-JEE-neez) are multiple freckles. Lentigenes that result from sunlight exposure are liver spots called *actinic*, or solar, lentigenes. Freckles are tiny round or oval pigmented skin on areas exposed to the sun, referred to as *macules*, the small flat colored spots on the skin.
- **Melasma** (muh-LAZ-muh). A term for hyperpigmentation triggered by hormonal changes, often during pregnancy or with birth control use. *Pregnancy mask* is a condition where brown pigmentation appears on the face during pregnancy. It usually fades with time, but is worsened by sun exposure.
- **Nevus** (NEE-vus), also known as **birthmark**. A malformation of the skin from abnormal pigmentation or dilated capillaries.
- **Stain**. Abnormal brown or wine-colored skin discoloration with a circular or irregular shape. A *port wine stain* is a birthmark, which is a vascular type of nevus. Stains may also occur after certain diseases.
- **Tan**. Exposure to the sun causes tanning, a change in pigmentation due to melanin production as a defense against UV radiation that damages the skin. A tan is basically visible skin and cell damage.

Hypopigmentation

Hypopigmentation occurs in various forms.

- **Albinism** (AL-bi-niz-em). A rare genetic condition characterized by the lack of melanin pigment in the body including the skin, hair, and eyes (**Figure 11–16**). The person is at risk for skin cancer, is sensitive to light, and ages early without normal melanin protection. The technical term for albinism is *congenital leukoderma* or *congenital hypopigmentation*.
- **Leukoderma** (loo-koh-DUR-ma). Loss of pigmentation; light, abnormal patches of depigmented skin; congenital, acquired due to immunological and post-inflammatory causes. Vitiligo and albinism are leukodermas.
- **Vitiligo** (vih-til-EYE-goh). A pigmentation disease characterized by white irregular patches of skin that are totally lacking pigment (**Figure 11–17**).

The condition can worsen with time and sunlight. The disease can occur at any age and is believed to be an autoimmune disorder causing an absence of melanocytes. ✓ LO4

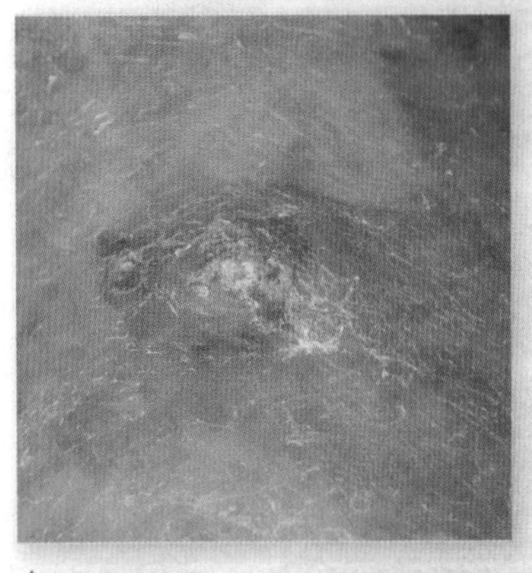

▲ Figure 11–18
Actinic keratosis.

Courtesy of www.dermnet.com.

Hypertrophies of the Skin

Hyphertrophies are defined as abnormal growths and include the following forms:

- **Hypertrophy** (hy-PUR-truh-fee). An abnormal growth; many are *benign*, or harmless, however, some growths are premalignant or malignant and can be dangerous or cancerous. *Hypertrophic* is used to describe thickening of a tissue. The opposite of hypertrophy is *atrophy*, which means "wasting away or thinning." Keloids are an example of hypertrophies.
- **Actinic keratoses.** Pink or flesh-colored precancerous lesions that feel sharp or rough that are a result of sun damage and should be checked by a dermatologist (**Figure 11–18**).
- **Hyperkeratosis.** Thickening of the skin caused by a mass of keratinocytes.
- **Keratoma** (kair-uh-TOH-muh). An acquired, thickened patch of epidermis. A callus caused by pressure or friction is a keratoma. If the thickening also grows inward, it becomes a corn.
- **Keratosis** (kair-uh-TOH-sis) (plural: keratoses, kair-uh-TOH-seez). An abnormally thick buildup of skin cells.
- **Keratosis pilaris** (kair-uh-TOH-sis py-LAIR-us). Redness and bumpiness in the cheeks or upper arms; caused by blocked follicles. Exfoliation can help unblock follicles and alleviate the rough feeling (**Figure 11–19**).

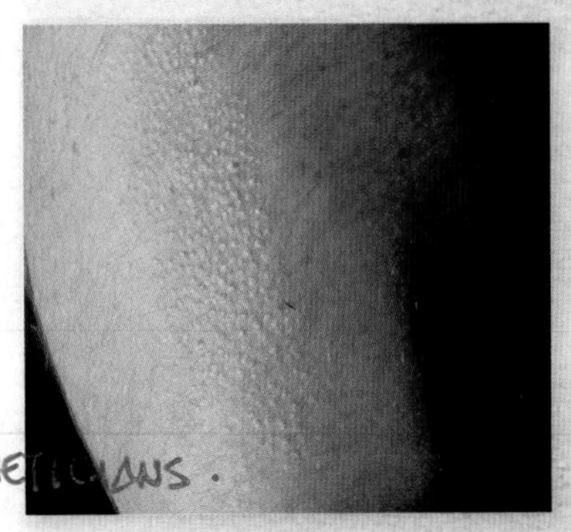

▲ Figure 11–19
Keratosis pilaris.

Courtesy of www.dermnet.com.

- **Mole.** A pigmented nevus; a brownish spot ranging in color from tan to bluish black. Some are flat, resembling freckles; others are raised and darker. Most are benign, but changes in mole color or shape should be checked by a physician. Hairs in moles are common and should not be removed unless by a physician because it may irritate or cause structural changes to the mole.
- **Skin tag.** Small outgrowths or extensions of the skin that look like flaps; they are benign and are common under the arms or on the neck from friction or where skin is rubbed together (**Figure 11–20**).
- **Verruca** (vuh-ROO-kuh), also known as **wart**. A hypertrophy of the papillae and epidermis caused by a virus. Infectious and contagious, verrucas can spread (**Figure 11–21**).

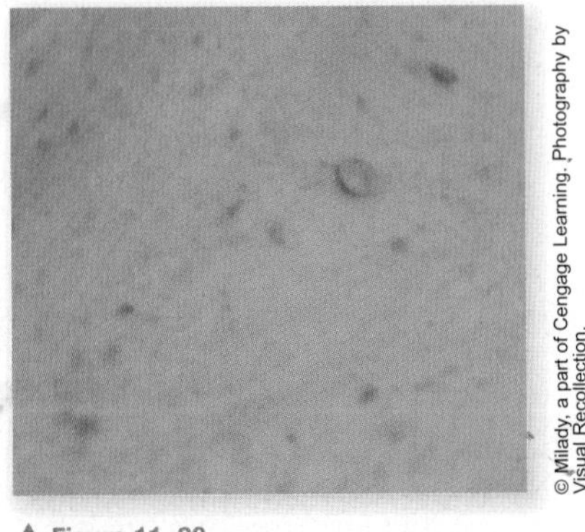

▲ Figure 11–20
A skin tag.

© Milady, a part of Cengage Learning. Photography by Visual Recollection.

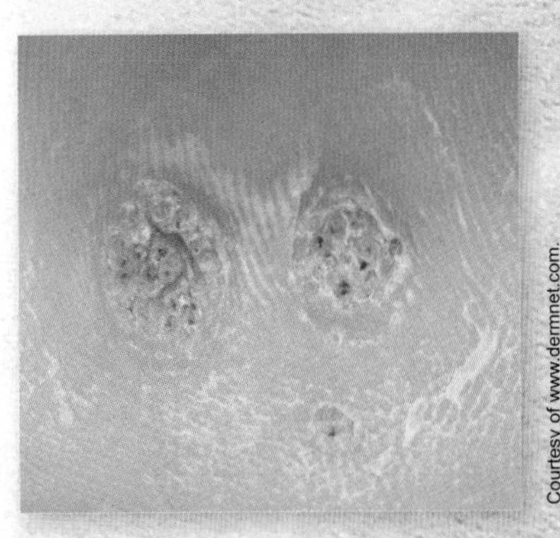

▲ Figure 11–21
Verruca.

Courtesy of www.dermnet.com.

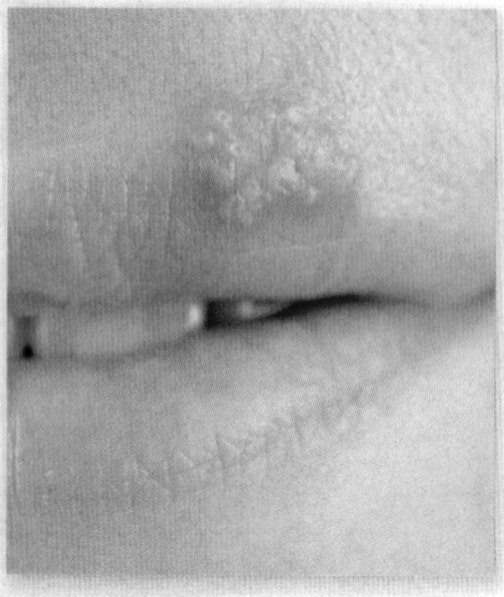

▲ Figure 11–22
Herpes type 1.

Contagious Diseases

The term *contagious disease* is used interchangeably with the terms *infectious* or *communicable* disease. Do not perform services on anyone with a contagious disease because it can spread and infect others. Refer them to a physician.

The following are contagious diseases.

- **Conjunctivitis** (kun-junk-tuh-VY-tus) also known as **pinkeye**. Inflammation of the mucous membrane (conjunctiva) around the eye due to chemical, bacterial, or viral causes; very contagious; treated with antibiotics.
- **Herpes simplex virus 1** (HER-peez SIM-pleks VY-rus). Fever blisters or cold sores; recurring viral infection. A vesicle or group of vesicles on a red, swollen base. The blisters usually appear on the lips or nostrils. Herpes simplex virus 1 causes cold sores and lesions around the mouth; it is a contagious disease (Figure 11–22).
- **Herpes simplex virus 2**. Genital herpes; never work on clients with a current herpes lesion. Peels, waxing, or other stimuli may cause a breakout, even if the condition is not currently active. The virus can be spread to other areas on the person that is infected or to other people. Understanding a client's health history from her intake form may prevent potential problems.

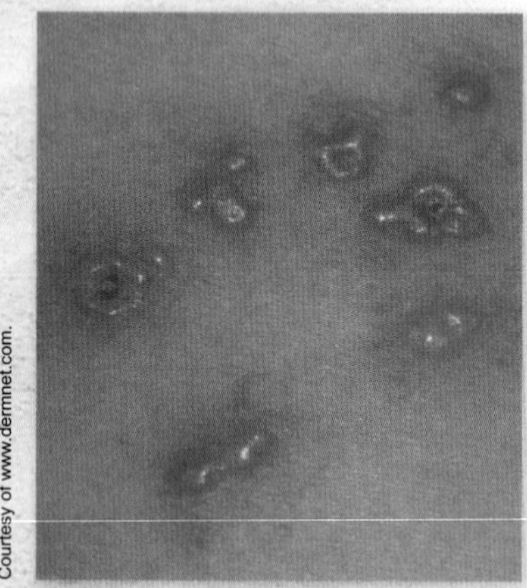

▲ Figure 11–23
Shingles.

- **Herpes zoster** (HER-peez ZOHS-tur), also known as **shingles**. A painful skin condition from the reactivation of the chickenpox virus; also known as the varicella-zoster virus (VZV). Shingles is a viral infection of the sensory nerves characterized by groups of red blisters that form a rash that occurs in a ring or line (Figure 11–23). The rash is typically confined to one side of the body. VZV can cause nerve and organ damage and severe pain that can last for months or years. Treated with antiviral drugs.
- **Impetigo** (im-puh-TEE-go). A bacterial infection of the skin that often occurs in children; characterized by clusters of small blisters or crusty lesions filled with bacteria. It is extremely contagious.
- **Tinea** (TIN-ee-uh). Fungal infections. Fungi feed on proteins, carbohydrates, and lipids in the skin. Tinea pedis, athlete's foot, is a fungal infection.
- **Tinea corporis** (TIN-ee-uh KOR-pur-is), also known as **ringworm**. Highly contagious; it forms a ringed red pattern with elevated edges (Figure 11–24).
- **Wart**. Verruca; a hypertrophy of the papillae and epidermis caused by a virus. Infectious and contagious, verrucas can spread. Wear gloves and avoid contact with warts. ☑ LO5

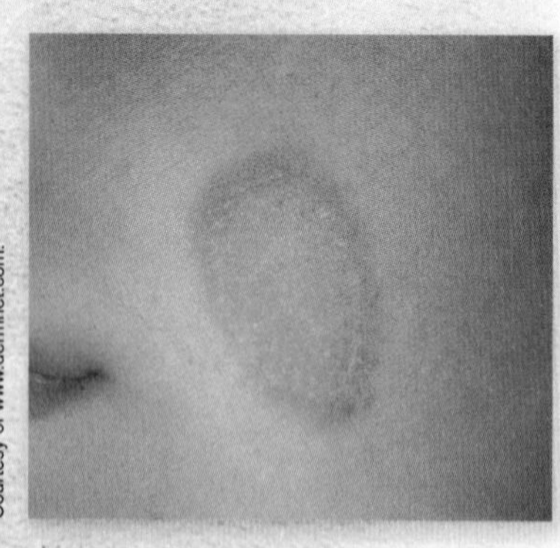

▲ Figure 11–24
Tinea corporis (ringworm).

ACTIVITY

To help learn the lesions, make an outline of the lesions using the categories and the names of each lesion. Continue listing the categories in columns and the conditions below each category.
For example:

Primary Lesions	Secondary Lesions	Contagious	Inflammations	Hypertrophies	Glands	Pigment
bulla	crust	herpes	dermatitis	keloid	milia	hyper

A Noncontagious Fungal Infection

Tinea versicolor (TIN-ee-uh VUR-see-kuh-lur), also called *pityriasis versicolor*, is a fungal condition that inhibits melanin production (**Figure 11–25**). It is not contagious because it is caused by yeast, a normal part of the human skin. It is characterized by white, brown, or salmon-colored flaky patches from the yeast on the skin. This sun fungus can be treated with antifungal cream or medication. Selenium sulfide shampoos can also treat the condition. High humidity and summer heat stimulate the condition. It usually fades in the cold winter season and recurs in the warm season.

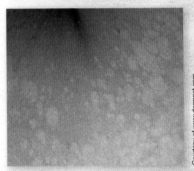

Courtesy of www.dermnet.com.

▲ Figure 11–25
Tinea versicolor.

Skin Cancer

Skin cancer risk increases with cumulative ultraviolet (UV) sun exposure and is found in three distinct forms that vary in severity. Each form is named for the type of cells that are affected. Skin cancer is caused by damage to DNA. Skin cancer tumors form when cells begin to divide rapidly and unevenly. See **Table 11–1**, on page 270, for some facts on skin cancer.

If detected early, these abnormal growths can be removed. If not taken care of, they can be deadly. It is important for estheticians to recognize serious skin disorders so they can refer clients to physicians. Tactfully suggest that the client seek medical advice without diagnosing or speculating about the disorder. Annual exams are recommended to check for cancerous lesions. Sun damage and sunscreens are discussed in other chapters.

CAUTION!

Do not work on clients if you have a verruca or any other contagious conditions on any area that would touch or infect the client! Do not touch clients' warts or plantar warts on the feet, because these are also contagious.

fyi

Benign means "not harmful"; *malignant* means "cancerous."

Carcinoma is a cancerous tumor.

FACTS ABOUT SKIN CANCER AND SUN EXPOSURE

- Melanoma is rising faster than any other cancer, and it causes 8,000 deaths every year.
- Death from skin cancer occurs at the rate of one death per hour in the United States.
- More than 1.3 million skin cancers are diagnosed annually in the United States.
- One in five Americans will get skin cancer.
- More than 90% of all skin cancers are caused by sun exposure.
- Only 33% of the population uses sunscreen.
- The risk of skin cancer doubles if a person has had five or more sunburns in their lifetime, or even one severe sunburn as a child.
- Most parents do not correctly use sunscreen on their children or protect them with hats or clothing.
- Most of the people diagnosed with melanoma are white men over age 50.
- Skin cancer is the number one cancer in men over age 50.
- Men over age 40 spend the most time outdoors and have the most exposure to UV radiation.
- Skin cancer has tripled in women under age 40 in the past 30 years.
- Skin cancer kills more women in their late 20s and early 30s than breast cancer does.
- The effects of photoaging from sun exposure or indoor tanning can be seen as early as age 20 or before.
- There is a 75% increase of melanoma risk among those who use tanning beds in their teens and twenties.
- UVA wavelengths pass through clouds and window glass.
- There is no safe way to tan.

▲ Table 11–1 **Facts About Skin Cancer and Sun Exposure.**

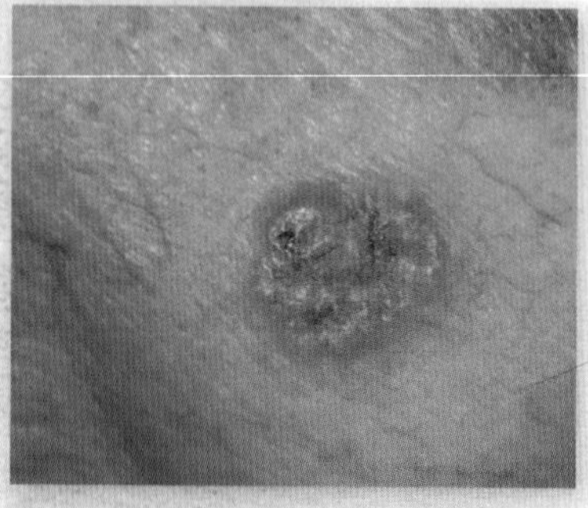

▲ Figure 11–26
Basal cell carcinoma.

Basal Cell Carcinoma

Basal cell carcinoma (BAY-zul CEL kar-si-NOH-mah) is the most common and the least severe type of carcinoma (Figure 11–26). Typical characteristics include open sores, reddish patches, or a smooth growth with an elevated border. It often appears as shiny bumps that are either colored or as light, pearly nodules. Sometimes blood vessels run through the nodules.

Basal cells do not spread as easily as squamous or melanoma cells. It is caused primarily by overexposure to UV radiation. They can be removed by surgery or other medical procedures.

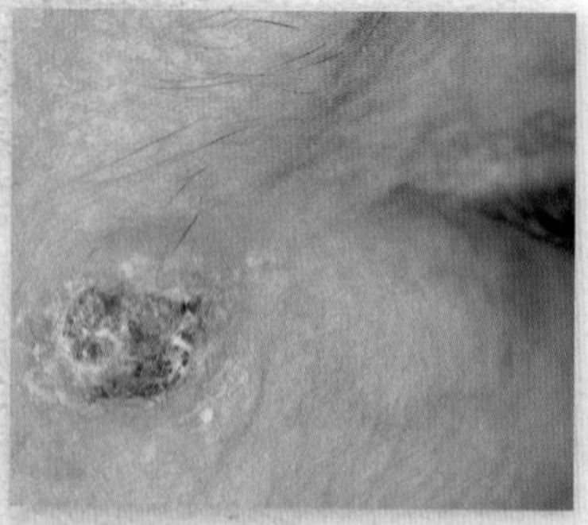

▲ Figure 11–27
Squamous cell carcinoma.

Squamous Cell Carcinoma

Squamous cell carcinoma (SKWAY-mus CEL kar-si-NOH-mah) is a more serious condition than basal cell carcinoma (Figure 11–27). It is characterized by red or pink scaly papules or nodules. Sometimes they are characterized by open sores or crusty areas that do not heal and may bleed easily. Squamous cell carcinoma can grow and spread to other areas of the body.

Malignant Melanoma

Malignant melanoma (muh-LIG-nent mel-ah-NOH-muh) is the most serious form of skin cancer. Black or dark patches on the skin are usually uneven in texture, jagged, or raised (Figure 11–28). It can be tan and even white. Melanomas may have surface crust or bleed. Many appear in preexisting moles. It is not always found on areas exposed to sunlight and is often found on feet, toes, backs, and legs.

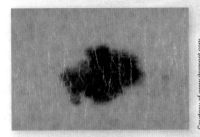

Courtesy of www.dermnet.com.

▲ Figure 11–28
Malignant melanoma.

Malignant melanoma is more deadly because it can spread (metastasize) throughout the body and to internal organs via the lymphatics and blood stream. Early detection of melanomas and regular checkups are vital. Many young people can die from this dangerous cancer. Infrequent, intense UV exposure may cause a higher risk for melanoma than chronic continuous exposure does. Caucasians who have a tendency to burn are more susceptible to skin cancer.

fyi

ABCDE's of Melanoma Detection

The American Cancer Society recommends using the ABCDE Cancer Checklist to help make potential skin cancer easier to recognize. When checking existing moles, look for changes in any of the following:

- A—Asymmetry: the two sides of the lesion are not identical.
- B—Border: the border is irregular on these lesions.
- C—Color: melanomas are usually dark and have more than once color or colors that fade into one another.
- D—Diameter: the lesion in a melanoma is usually at least the size of pencil eraser.
- E—Evolving: melanoma as a lesion often changes appearance.

Changes to any of these characteristics should be examined by a physician (Figure 11–29). For more information, contact the American Cancer Society at www.cancer.org or (800) ACS-2345.

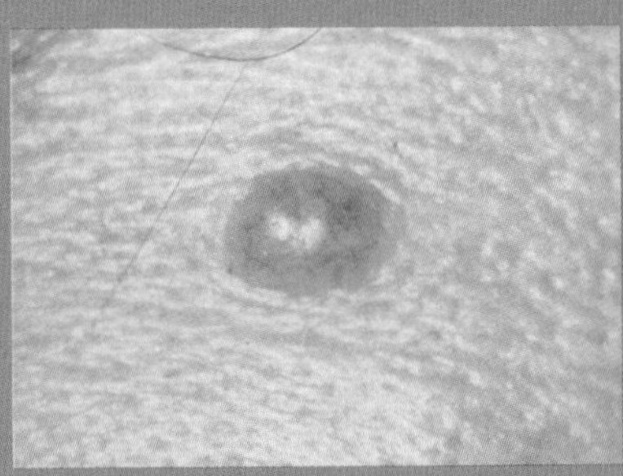

Benign mole—symmetrical

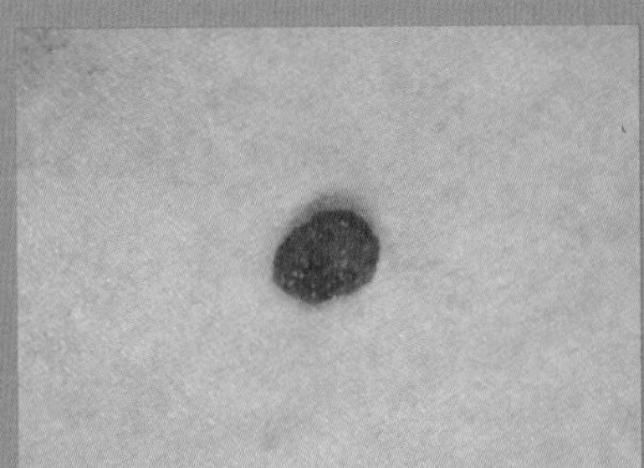

Benign mole—one shade

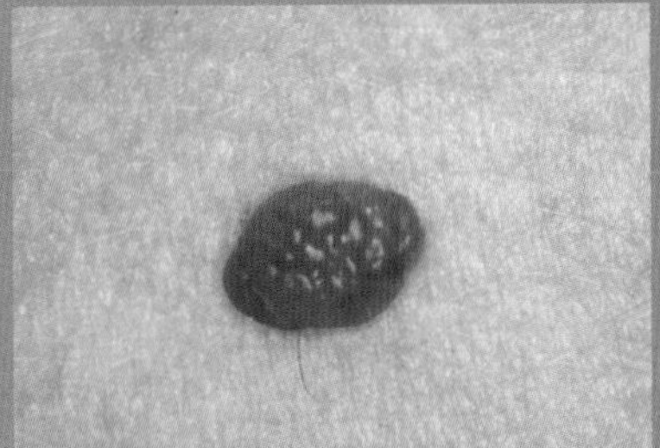

Benign mole—even edges

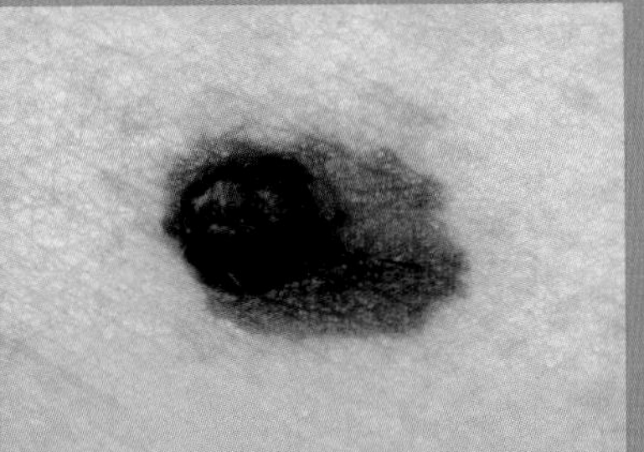

Melanoma—asymmetrical

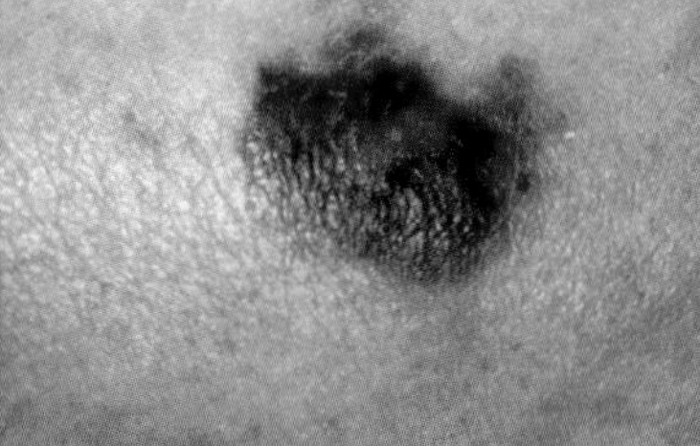

Melanoma—two or more shades

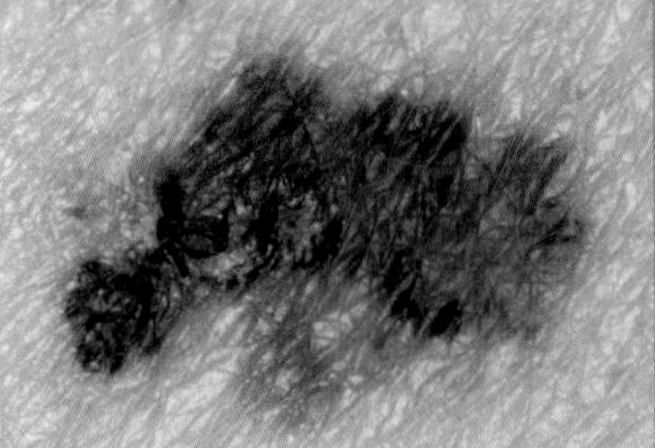

Melanoma—uneven edges

Courtesy of the Skin Cancer Foundation, http://www.skincancer.org.

▲ Figure 11–29 **ABCDE checklist.**

ACTIVITY

Do your own mole and lesion check. Record where they are located and write down the description of the lesions now that you are familiar with wording used to describe various skin conditions.

You can use a blank chart of the body to track moles. Take photos of suspicious lesions. Get a partner to assist in checking the back area and back of the legs. How many lesions look suspicious?

You can also use this type of information to record in client charts.

Example of tracking moles:

Date: *May 5, 2010*

Location: *Chest area: right side by collar bone.*

Description (A,B,C,D, E's): *Small, light brown freckle, 1 cm (3/8 in) in diameter, flat, evenly shaped border.*

Changes/Evolution: *Darker than last year.*

Follow up: *Doctor checked for moles in April, 2009.*

Get check-ups once a year.

The ABCDE Cancer Checklist is a method of evaluating possible skin cancer lesions; each letter corresponds to specific melanoma characteristics (Refer to Figure 11–29). Melanoma mole-like lesions are *asymmetrical*, have uneven *borders*, uneven *color*, are larger in *diameter* than a pencil eraser, and they change or *evolve*. ✓ L06

Acne

Acne is a primary concern for many clients seeking skin care help from an esthetician. This severe skin problem can greatly affect a person's self-esteem. Acne, a skin disorder of the sebaceous glands, is characterized by comedones and blemishes and is hereditary. It is usually triggered by hormonal changes. It begins to flare up when a person reaches puberty, but adult acne is also prevalent.

Acne ranges from mild breakouts to disfiguring cysts and scarring (**Figure 11–30**). Acne can be controlled with proper medications, but medications have side effects and treatment may sometimes be a lifelong battle. Estheticians have a great opportunity to help people with less severe acne and make a difference in their lives. Acne can be a challenge to work with, but seeing visible improvement in a client's skin is very rewarding.

ACTIVITY

Go to the skin cancer foundation at skincancer.org or another Web site to get more information on skin cancer facts. What is the most interesting or significant thing you learned from the Web site research?

Causes of Acne

Causes of acne include the following:

- Genetics/heredity
- Clogged follicles
- Bacteria
- Triggers include hormones, stress, cosmetics, skin care products, and foods

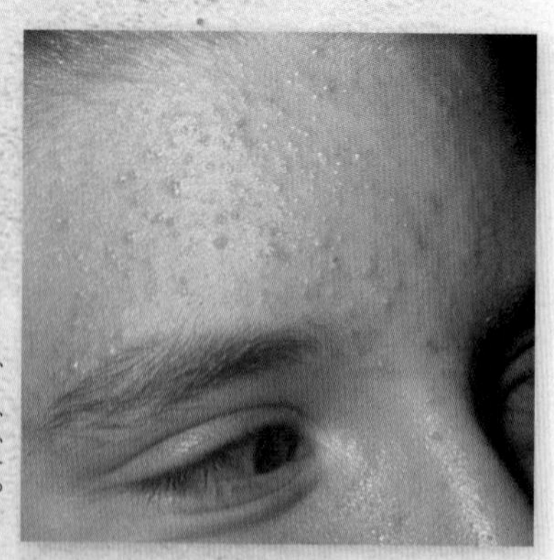

▲ Figure 11–30
Acne.

Genetics and Clogged Follicles

Clogged follicles are caused by a number of factors, including excess oil, retention hyperkeratosis, and sebaceous filaments.

The *pilosebaceous unit* (py-loh-see-BAY-shus unit) is the term for the entire follicle that includes the hair shaft, sebaceous gland, and the sebaceous duct or canal to the surface. The hairless follicle (with attached sebaceous glands) is the main follicle involved in acne (**Figure 11–31**).

Retention hyperkeratosis (ree-TEN-shun hy-pur-kair-uh-TOH-sis) is a hereditary factor in which dead skin cells build up because they do not shed from the follicles as they do on normal skin. Additionally, excessive sebum production can overtax the sebaceous follicles and cause further cell buildup. Sebum mixed with cells in the follicle become comedos (plugs in the follicles). Consequently, open and closed comedones are formed. While not inflamed, these comedones are the beginning of acne problems if they are not treated with proper skin care to alleviate the impaction. Another reason follicles get clogged is that the opening, or ostium (AHS-tee-um), of the follicle may be too small to let impactions out.

Sebaceous filaments, similar to open comedones, are mainly small, solidified impactions of oil without the cell matter. These filaments also block the follicle and can cause an acne breakout. They are often found on the nose.

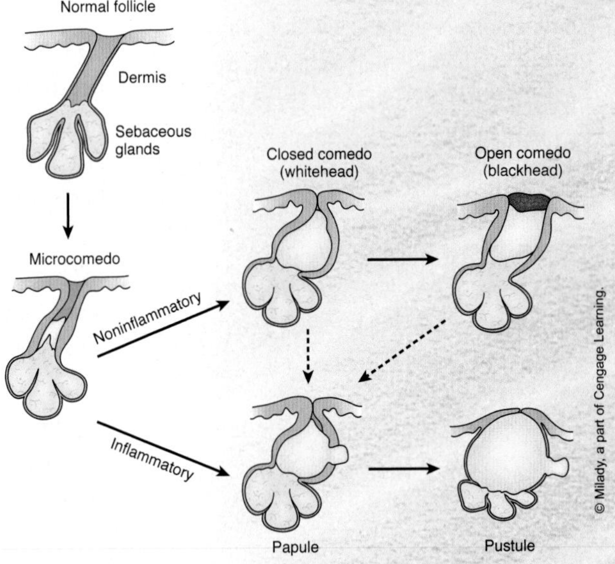

▲ Figure 11–31
Acne and sebaceous follicles.

Bacteria

Bacteria in the follicles are anaerobic. This means bacteria cannot live in the presence of oxygen. When follicles are blocked with sebum and dead skin buildup, oxygen cannot reach the bottom of the follicle. This results in excessive P. bacteria (propionibacterium) proliferation.

Sebum can irritate follicles and cause inflammation. As bacteria and inflammation grow, pressure is exerted on the follicle wall. If the wall ruptures, it becomes infected and debris spills out into the dermis. Redness and inflammation occur when a foreign object is detected in the skin, and white blood cells move in to fight the infection. Papules are red, inflamed lesions caused by this process. Papules may become more infected and pus develops. These infected papules become pustules and are filled with fluid from the dead white blood cells that fought the infection.

Cysts are nodules made up of deep pockets of infection. Skin forms hardened tissue around the infection to stop the spread of bacteria, which can lead to both depressed and raised scars from damage to the dermal tissue. Because it is in the dermis, this variety of acne—called *cystic acne*—can be treated only by a physician.

Acne Triggers

Hormonal changes, stress, products, and certain foods may aggravate acne. Climate, sun, friction, and medications also trigger skin flare-ups.

Hormones

Male hormones, known as *androgens* (AN-droh-jins), stimulate sebaceous glands. High levels of the male hormone testosterone (tes-TOSS-tur-own) cause an increase in oil production, which leads to oily skin and possible acne. These hormones increase during puberty, when teen acne is first evident. In females, acne is not as severe because there is less testosterone production.

FOCUS ON
Scientific Research

When researching topics, keep an open mind and determine the reliability of the source providing the information. What is found to be true one year may change with new evidence and discoveries. This is true of many topics, including the skin and health sciences. There is an overwhelming amount of information being shared out there especially with today's Internet access. It's important to dig deeper to verify and analyze what we are reading—just because it's in print or on the Internet does not make it true or factual.

Web Resources

www.dermatologyabout.com
www.dermnet.com
www.phil.cdc.gov
www.medicinenet.com
www.medicineplus.gov
www.rosacea.org
www.skincancer.org

Adult acne is more common in females for various reasons. Adrenal glands responding to stress produce extra hormones. Hormonal fluctuations from birth control pills, premenstrual changes, pregnancy, and menopause can all lead to acne inflammations in women. Hormonal acne is often seen on the chin.

Hormones during premenstrual cycles cause water retention, consequently swelling the epidermis and blocking pilosebaceous ducts (oil gland ducts). In the first trimester of pregnancy, women have more progesterone that converts to testosterone, making breakouts common. Estrogenic hormones (estrogen, progesterone, etc.) are produced from androgens. Changes are noticeable as the pregnancy progresses. Hormones also change with the seasons, and skin is also affected by the climate in other ways. Hormonal problems are becoming more evident in the effects they have on the skin.

Stress

Stress causes hormonal fluctuations and increased sebum production. The adrenal gland responds to stress and secretes adrenalin, which helps us cope with stressful events. Male hormones are also produced by the adrenal gland and stimulate the sebaceous gland. Unfortunately, when we have a big event and want to look our best, blemishes may appear because of the increased stress level and sebum production.

Cosmetics and Products

Certain ingredients in products can aggravate acne. Fatty ingredients such as waxes and some oils can clog or irritate follicles. These **comedogenic** ingredients can block follicles, which causes cell buildup, resulting in comedones. *Acnegenic* products also cause acne inflammation. Products rich in emollients and occlusive products are too heavy for problem skin types. Moisturizers and sunscreens should be lighter formulas such as oil-in-water (O/W) emulsions, not water-in-oil (W/O) emulsions. Many makeup products are comedogenic, especially foundations and powders that are made with solids and fatty ingredients. Other products for hair and skin can also trigger or irritate acne. Products are discussed thoroughly in Chapter 13, Skin Care Products: Chemistry, Ingredients, and Selection.

Foods

Foods blamed for triggering acne may not affect it directly, although our eating habits do affect our body's functions. Excessive iodides in salt, MSG, kelp, cheese, processed and packaged foods (especially fast foods), and minerals obtained from an ocean source found in vitamins can all irritate acne. The excess iodides are excreted through pores and are thought to irritate them. Eating fresh vegetables and fruits and increasing water intake seems to help those with acne experience fewer breakouts. Different scientific opinions exist about how our diet affects acne. Ongoing research is progressing regarding this subject.

Other Irritations

Pressure or friction from rubbing or touching the face, phone use, or wearing hats can contribute to *acne mechanica* breakouts. Pillows or makeup brushes can also transfer bacteria to the face, so it's important to wash them often. Keeping hands and items that touch the face clean can help reduce breakouts.

Prolonged pressure or heat will likely cause skin problems. Swelling caused by heat, sweating or a moist, humid climate will clog and irritate follicles. Various drugs will also affect the body and are known to irritate skin. LO7

Grades of Acne

Acne is broken down into four grades (Table 11–2). The number of lesions, comedones, papules, pustules, or cysts present determines the severity of the acne. LO8

Treating Acne

There are many ways to help clients control acne. Good skin care treatments, products, and proper nutrition will help with skin problems. Estheticians can educate clients in caring for their skin and what causes acne flare-ups. Ingredients that can cause acne, acne treatments, and extractions are covered in Chapter 15, Facial Treatments.

Physicians may prescribe medications to treat Grade III and IV acne. A few of the acne medications are listed here in Table 11–3, page 275. Ask a physician for more information on acne medications and the potential side effects of the drugs.

GRADES OF ACNE	
GRADE I	Minor breakouts, mostly open comedones, some closed comedones, and a few papules (Figure 11–32).
GRADE II	Many closed comedones, more open comedones, and occasional papules and pustules (Figure 11–33).
GRADE III	Red and inflamed, many comedones, papules, and pustules (Figure 11–34).
GRADE IV	Cystic acne. Cysts with comedones, papules, pustules, and inflammation are present (Figure 11–35). Scar formation from tissue damage is common.

▲ Table 11–2 **Grades of Acne.**

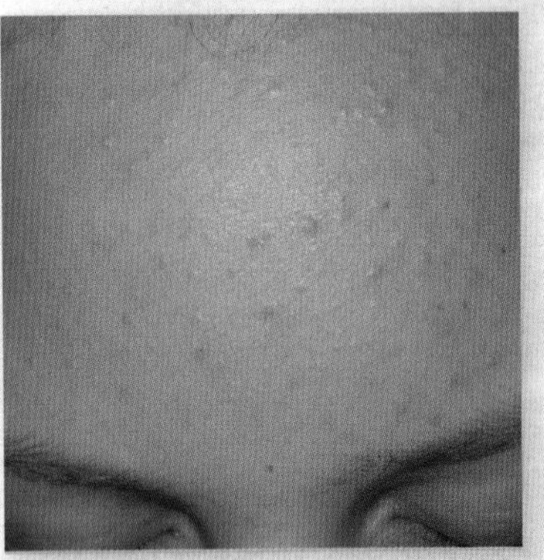

▲ Figure 11–32
Grade I acne.

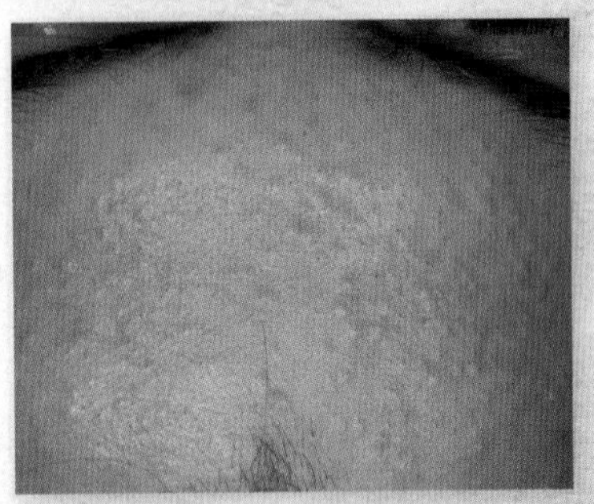

▲ Figure 11–33
Grade II acne is characterized by many closed comedones and is difficult to treat.

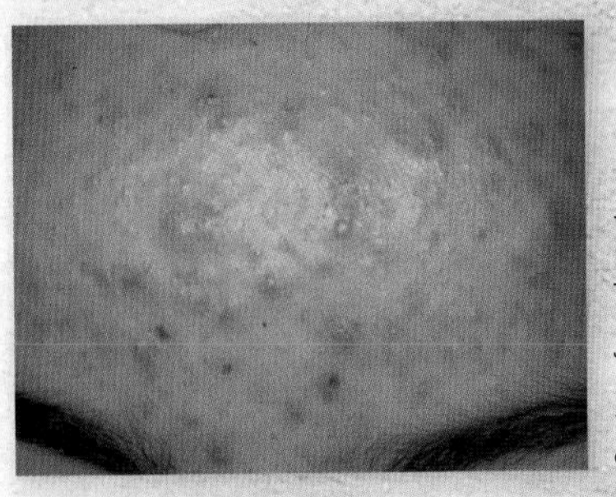

▲ Figure 11–34
Grade III acne.

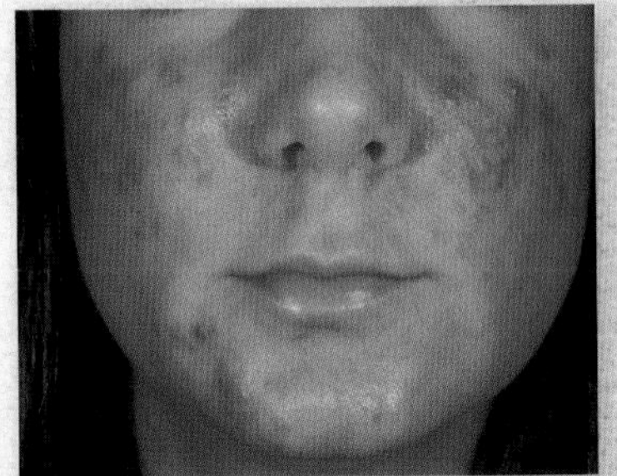

▲ Figure 11–35
Grade IV acne.

COMMON MEDICATIONS USED IN THE TREATMENT OF ACNE

DRUG	ACTIONS	POTENTIAL SIDE EFFECTS
Adapalene (Differin®)	A topical peeling agent similar to retinoic acid. May be less irritating than tretinoin.	Drying, redness, and irritation; photosensitivity.
Azelaic acid (Azelex®)	A topical acidic agent that flushes out follicles.	Drying, redness, and irritation; photosensitivity.
Clindamycin	Topical antibiotic; kills bacteria.	Very drying.
Isotretinoin (Accutane®)	An oral medication similar to retinoic acid; used for severe acne. Pulled from the U.S. market in 2009 for extreme side effects, but is still prescribed. Similar products may be harmful.	Severe dryness, birth defects, other health problems; possible depression.
Tazarotene (Tazorac®)	Another retinoid; a topical peeling agent that may be less irritating than tretinoin.	Drying, redness, and irritation; photosensitivity.
Tretinoin (Retin-A®)	A topical vitamin A acid. A strong peeling agent that is drying and also flushes out follicles.	Very drying, causes redness and irritation; photosensitivity.

▲ Table 11–3 **Common Medications Used in the Treatment of Acne.**

ACTIVITY

With a partner, examine each other's face for skin conditions and disorders. See if you can properly identify them. Don't be shy: everyone has skin issues and it's important to know what they are. It is your job now to care for the skin. Ask your instructor to guide you on this as it can be tricky. Once you learn skin analysis and use a magnifying lamp further into your studies, it will be easier to identify these. Never guess on identifying a client's skin conditions. It's okay to say you are not sure what it is you are looking at. ☑ LO9 ☑ LO10

Review Questions

1. Name and define the primary lesions.
2. Name and define the secondary lesions.
3. What is a comedone?
4. Name and define the sebaceous gland disorders.
5. List the inflammations of the skin.
6. What is contact dermatitis?
7. What is rosacea?
8. List three disorders characterized by hyperpigmentation.
9. What are four types of hypertrophies?
10. Name and define six of the contagious diseases.
11. Do contagious diseases contraindicate working on a client?
12. Describe the differences between the three types of skin cancer.
13. Explain the checklist system used to identify skin cancers.
14. What are the main causes of acne?
15. What may trigger an acne flare-up?
16. Describe the four grades of acne.
17. List three potential side effects of acne drugs.

Glossary

acne	Chronic inflammatory skin disorder of the sebaceous glands that is characterized by comedones and blemishes; commonly known as *acne simplex* or *acne vulgaris*.
acne excoriee	Disorder where clients purposely scrape off acne lesions, causing scarring and discoloration.
actinic keratoses	Pink or flesh-colored precancerous lesions that feel sharp or rough; resulting from sun damage.
albinism	Absence of melanin pigment in the body, including skin, hair, and eyes; the technical term for albinism is *congenital leukoderma* or *congenital hypopigmentation.*
anhidrosis	Deficiency in perspiration, often a result of a fever or skin disease, that requires medical treatment.
asteatosis	Dry, scaly skin from sebum deficiency, which can be due to aging, body disorders, alkalies of harsh soaps, or cold exposure.
atopic dermatitis	Excess inflammation; dry skin, redness, and itching from allergies and irritants.
basal cell carcinoma	Most common and the least severe type of skin cancer, which often appears as light, pearly nodules; characteristics include sores, reddish patches, or a smooth growth with an elevated border.
bromhidrosis	Foul-smelling perspiration, usually in the armpits or on the feet.

Glossary

bulla (plural: bullae)	Large blister containing watery fluid; similar to a vesicle, but larger.
carbuncle	Cluster of boils; large inflammation of the subcutaneous tissue caused by staphylococci bacterium; similar to a furuncle (boil) but larger.
chloasma	Also known as *liver spots*; condition characterized by hyperpigmentation on the skin in spots that are not elevated.
comedo (plural: comedones)	Mass of hardened sebum and skin cells in a hair follicle; an open comedo or blackhead when open and exposed to oxygen. Closed comedones are whiteheads that are blocked and do not have a follicular opening.
comedogenic	Tendency for an ingredient to clog follicles and cause a buildup of dead skin cells, resulting in comedones.
conjunctivitis	Also known as *pinkeye*; very contagious infection of the mucous membranes around the eye; chemical, bacterial, or viral causes.
contact dermatitis	Inflammatory skin condition caused by contact with a substance or chemical. Occupational disorders from ingredients in cosmetics and chemical solutions can cause contact dermatitis (a.k.a. dermatitis venenata). Allergic contact dermatitis is from exposure to allergens; irritant contact dermatitis is from exposure to irritants.
crust	Dead cells form over a wound or blemish while it is healing, resulting in an accumulation of sebum and pus, sometimes mixed with epidermal material. An example is the scab on a sore.
cyst	Closed, abnormally developed sac containing fluid, infection, or other matter above or below the skin.
dermatitis	Any inflammatory condition of the skin; various forms of lesions such as eczema, vesicles, or papules; the three main categories are atopic, contact, and seborrheic dermatitis.
dermatologist	Physician who specializes in diseases and disorders of the skin, hair, and nails.
dermatology	Medical branch of science that deals with the study of skin and its nature, structure, functions, diseases, and treatment.
eczema	Inflammatory, painful itching disease of the skin, acute or chronic in nature, with dry or moist lesions. This condition should be referred to a physician. *Seborrheic dermatitis*, mainly affecting oily areas, is a common form of eczema.
edema	Swelling caused by a fluid imbalance in cells or a response to injury or infection.
erythema	Redness caused by inflammation; a red lesion is erythemic.
excoriation	Skin sore or abrasion produced by scratching or scraping.
fissure	Crack in the skin that penetrates the dermis. Chapped lips or hands are fissures.
folliculitis	Also known as *folliculitis barbae, sycosis barbae,* or *barber's itch*. Inflammation of the hair follicles caused by a bacterial infection from ingrown hairs. The cause is typically from ingrown hairs due to shaving or other epilation methods.
furuncle	Also known as *boil;* a subcutaneous abscess filled with pus; furuncles are caused by bacteria in the glands or hair follicles.

Glossary

herpes simplex virus 1	Strain of the herpes virus that causes fever blisters or cold sores; it is a recurring, contagious viral infection consisting of a vesicle or group of vesicles on a red, swollen base. The blisters usually appear on the lips or nostrils.
herpes simplex virus 2	Strain of the herpes virus that infects the genitals.
herpes zoster	Also known as *shingles*; a painful viral infection skin condition from the chickenpox virus; characterized by groups of blisters that form a rash in a ring or line.
hyperhidrosis	Excessive perspiration caused by heat, genetics, medications, or medical conditions; also called *diaphoresis*.
hyperkeratosis	Thickening of the skin caused by a mass of keratinized cells (keratinocytes).
hyperpigmentation	Over-production of pigment.
hypertrophy	Abnormal growth of the skin; many are benign, or harmless.
hypopigmentation	Absence of pigment, resulting in light or white splotches.
impetigo	A contagious skin infection caused by staphylococcal or streptococcal bacteria, characterized by clusters of small blisters or crusty lesions and often occurring in children.
keloid	Thick scar resulting from excessive growth of fibrous tissue (collagen).
keratoma	Acquired, superficial, thickened patch of epidermis. A callus is a keratoma caused by continued, repeated pressure or friction on any part of the skin, especially the hands and feet.
keratosis (plural: keratoses)	Abnormally thick buildup of cells.
keratosis pilaris	Redness and bumpiness common on the cheeks or upper arms; it is caused by blocked hair follicles. The patches of irritation are accompanied by a rough texture and small pinpoint white milia.
lentigo	Freckles; small yellow-brown colored spots. Lentigenes that result from sunlight exposure are actinic, or solar, lentigenes. Patches are referred to as *large macules*.
lesions	Mark, wound, or abnormality; structural changes in tissues caused by damage or injury.
leukoderma	Skin disorder characterized by light, abnormal patches; congenital, acquired, post-inflammatory, or other causes that destroy pigment-producing cells. Vitiligo and albinism are leukodermas.
macule (plural: maculae)	Flat spot or discoloration on the skin, such as a freckle. Macules are neither raised nor sunken.
malignant melanoma	Most serious form of skin cancer as it can spread quickly (metastasize). Black or dark patches on the skin are usually uneven in texture, jagged, or raised. Melanomas may have surface crust or bleed.
milia	Epidermal cysts; small, firm papules with no visible opening; whitish, pearl-like masses of sebum and dead cells under the skin. Milia are more common in dry skin types and may form after skin trauma, such as a laser resurfacing.

Glossary

miliaria rubra	Also known as *prickly heat*; acute inflammatory disorder of the sweat glands resulting in the eruption of red vesicles and burning, itching skin from excessive heat exposure.
mole	Pigmented nevus; a brownish spot ranging in color from tan to bluish black. Some are flat, resembling freckles; others are raised and darker.
nevus	Also known as *birthmark*; malformation of the skin due to abnormal pigmentation or dilated capillaries.
nodules	These are often referred to as tumors, but these are smaller bumps caused by conditions such as scar tissue, fatty deposits, or infections.
papule	Pimple; small elevation on the skin that contains no fluid but may develop pus.
perioral dermatitis	Acne-like condition around the mouth. These are mainly small clusters of papules that could be caused by toothpaste or products used on the face.
primary lesions	Primary lesions are characterized by flat, nonpalpable changes in skin color such as macules or patches, or an elevation formed by fluid in a cavity, such as vesicles, bullae, or pustules.
pruitis	Persistent itching.
pseudofolliculitis	Also known as *razor bumps*; resembles folliculitis without the pus or infection.
psoriasis	Skin disease characterized by red patches covered with white-silver scales. It is caused by an overproliferation of skin cells that replicate too fast. Immune dysfunction could be the cause. Psoriasis is usually found in patches on the scalp, elbows, knees, chest, and lower back.
pustule	Raised, inflamed papule with a white or yellow center containing pus in the top of the lesion referred to as the head of the pimple.
retention hyperkeratosis	Hereditary factor in which dead skin cells build up and do not shed from the follicles as they do on normal skin.
scale	Flaky skin cells; any thin plate of epidermal flakes, dry or oily. An example is abnormal or excessive dandruff.
scar	Light-colored, slightly raised mark on the skin formed after an injury or lesion of the skin has healed up. The tissue hardens to heal the injury. Elevated scars are hypertrophic; a keloid is a hypertrophic (abnormal) scar.
sebaceous filaments	Similar to open comedones, these are mainly solidified impactions of oil without the cell matter.
sebaceous hyperplasia	Benign lesions frequently seen in oilier areas of the face. An overgrowth of the sebaceous gland, they appear similar to open comedones; often doughnut-shaped, with sebaceous material in the center.
seborrhea	Severe oiliness of the skin; an abnormal secretion from the sebaceous glands.
seborrheic dermatitis	Common form of eczema; mainly affects oily areas; characterized by inflammation, scaling, and/or itching.
secondary lesions	Skin damage, developed in the later stages of disease, that changes the structure of tissues or organs.

Glossary

skin tag	Small, benign outgrowths or extensions of the skin that look like flaps; common under the arms or on the neck.
squamous cell carcinoma	Type of skin cancer more serious than basal cell carcinoma; characterized by scaly, red or pink papules or nodules; also appear as open sores or crusty areas; can grow and spread in the body.
stain	Brown or wine-colored discoloration with a circular and/or irregular shape. Stains occur after certain diseases, or after moles, freckles, or liver spots disappear. A port wine stain is a birthmark, which is a vascular type of nevus.
steatoma	Sebaceous cyst or subcutaneous tumor filled with sebum; ranges in size from a pea to an orange. It usually appears on the scalp, neck, and back; also called a *wen*.
tan	Increase in pigmentation due to the melanin production that results from exposure to UV radiation; visible skin damage. Melanin is designed to help protect the skin from the sun's UV radiation.
tinea	A contagious condition caused by fungal infection and not a parasite; characterized by itching, scales, and, sometimes, painful lesions.
tinea corporis	Also known as *ringworm*; a contagious infection that forms a ringed, red pattern with elevated edges.
tubercle	Abnormal rounded, solid lump; larger than a papule.
tumor	Large nodule; an abnormal cell mass resulting from excessive cell multiplication and varying in size, shape, and color.
ulcer	Open lesion on the skin or mucous membrane of the body, accompanied by pus and loss of skin depth. A deep erosion; a depression in the skin, normally due to infection or cancer.
urticaria	Also known as *hives*; caused by an allergic reaction from the body's histamine production.
varicose veins	Vascular lesions; dilated and twisted veins, most commonly in the legs.
vasodilation	Vascular dilation of the blood vessels.
verruca	Also known as *wart*; hypertrophy of the papillae and epidermis caused by a virus. It is infectious and contagious.
vesicle	Small blister or sac containing clear fluid. Poison ivy and poison oak produce vesicles.
vitiligo	Pigmentation disease characterized by white patches on the skin from lack of pigment cells; sunlight makes it worse.
wheal	Itchy, swollen lesion caused by a blow, insect bite, skin allergy reaction, or stings. Hives and mosquito bites are wheals. Hives (urticaria) can be caused by exposure to allergens used in products.

CHAPTER 12

Skin Analysis

Chapter Outline

- Why Study Skin Analysis?
- Skin Types are Genetically Determined
- Sensitive Skin
- The Fitzpatrick Scale
- Diverse Skin Pigmentation
- Skin Types versus Skin Conditions
- Factors That Affect the Skin
- Healthy Habits for the Skin
- Contraindications
- Client Consultations
- Performing a Skin Analysis
- Procedures

Learning Objectives

After completing this chapter, you will be able to:

- ✓ LO1 Identify skin types.
- ✓ LO2 Identify skin conditions.
- ✓ LO3 Explain the causes of skin conditions.
- ✓ LO4 Understand how UV radiation affects the skin.
- ✓ LO5 Explain healthy habits for the skin.
- ✓ LO6 Determine treatment contraindications.
- ✓ LO7 Conduct client consultations.
- ✓ LO8 Fill out skin analysis charts.
- ✓ LO9 Perform a skin analysis.

Key Terms

Page number indicates where in the chapter the term is used.

actinic
pg. 291

alipidic
pg. 285

contraindications
pg. 284

couperose skin
pg. 287

dehydration
pg. 286

Fitzpatrick Scale
pg. 288

occlusive
pg. 286

skin types
pg. 284

T-zone
pg. 285

Learning about individual skin types and conditions is one of the most interesting aspects of skin care. It is never boring because every face is unique. Client skin analysis is a vital part of an esthetician's skills, since recommending the appropriate skin care products and regime must be individualized to suit each person. Before performing services or selecting products, an individual's skin type and conditions must be analyzed correctly.

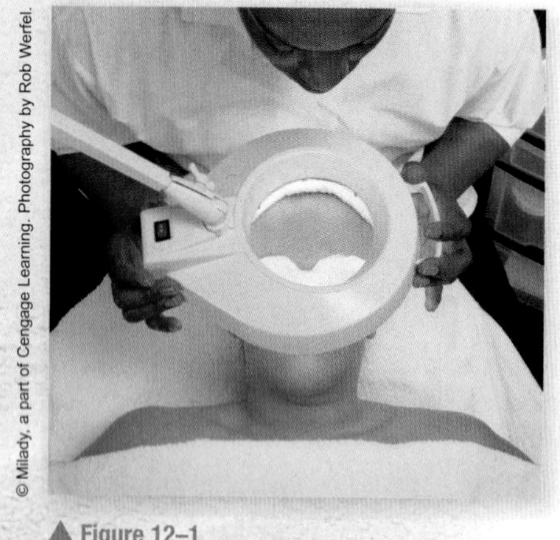

▲ **Figure 12–1**
Conducting a skin analysis with a magnifying light.

People want to know what their skin conditions are and what they can do to improve their skin's appearance. They rely on estheticians for information and education. Clients need to be educated about the benefits of professional skin care treatments. Skin analysis and consultations are also good marketing tools to introduce services and products to prospective clients. The first-time facial client may have specific skin concerns, or may just want to experience a relaxing spa service. Be sure to let the client know what services are offered. This is an opportunity to promote all services in the spa.

The consultation and skin analysis will help determine which products to use and recommend. It is also a guide to determine the type of service to perform (**Figure 12–1**). A client chart is used to record the analysis and consultation notes, an important part of record keeping. Additionally, estheticians need to know which services and products are contraindicated (prohibited). These **contraindications** are factors that prohibit a treatment due to a condition. Certain treatments could cause harmful or negative side effects to those who have specific medical or skin conditions.

Skin conditions may be caused by both internal and external factors and are unique to each individual. Ethnic skin also has unique conditions and challenges. Products are formulated for different **skin types** (the classification that describes a person's genetic skin type) and conditions, and the number of new product lines grows annually. Skin care products and treatments are discussed in other chapters. The consultation, health screening questions, and client chart are all used as part of an in-depth skin analysis.

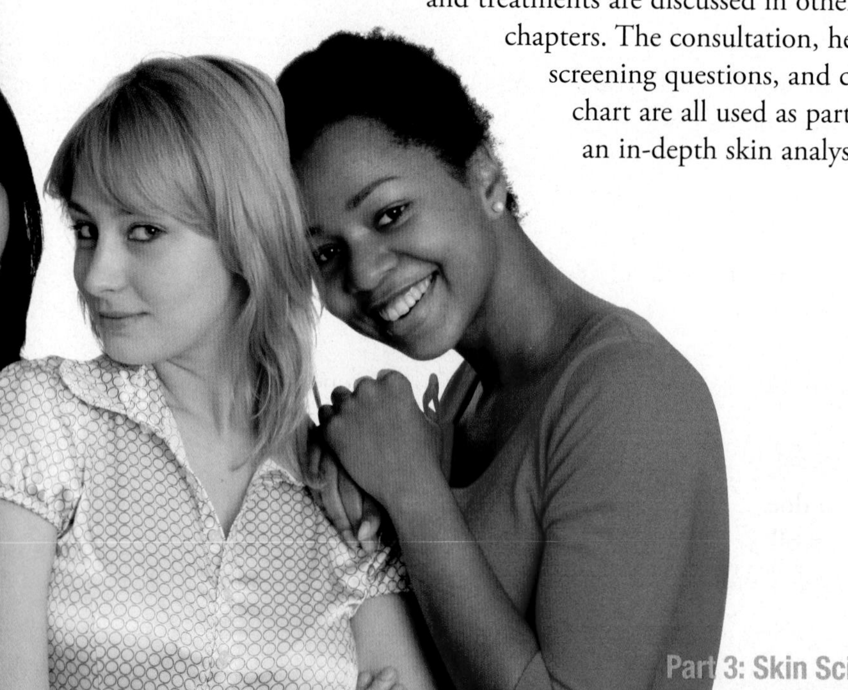

Why Study Skin Analysis?

Estheticians should study and have a thorough understanding of skin analysis in order to understand each client's skin type and provide the best treatment regimen possible for each individual's skin type and condition.

- Before performing services or selecting products, an individual's skin type and conditions must be analyzed correctly to determine the appropriate treatment and products.
- A thorough skin analysis and client consultation is especially important to determine the causes of skin conditions and any contraindications that the client may have.
- Knowledge of healthy habits and "enemies" of the skin will give you a better understanding of how to help clients, as clients rely on estheticians for information about their skin conditions and how to improve their skin's appearance.

Skin Types are Genetically Determined

People are born with their skin type, which is determined by their genetics and ethnicity. Like everything else, skin can change over time. An individual's skin type is based primarily on how much oil is produced in the follicles from the sebaceous glands and on the amount of lipids found between the cells. The **T-zone** is the center area of the face, corresponding to the "T" shape formed by the forehead, nose, and chin (Figure 12–2). How large the pores are in the T-zone and throughout the face can help determine the skin type. Generally, an individual's skin becomes drier over time. Our cellular metabolism and oil/lipid production slow down as we age.

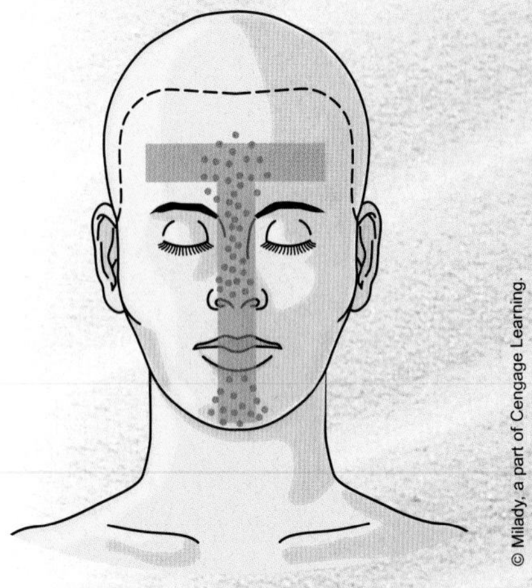

▲ Figure 12–2
The T-zone area of the face.

Skin types include dry, normal, combination, and oily. Sensitive skin is sometimes discussed as a skin type; but it is primarily a condition. Acne is considered a disorder, as explained in Chapter 11, Disorders and Diseases of the Skin. All skin types need proper cleansing, exfoliating, and hydrating. Finding the right care for each individual can be challenging, and this makes the esthetician's job even more interesting. The focus of this chapter is to identify skin types and conditions. Mastering this skill is necessary before learning about which products and treatments to choose for each person.

Skin types are categorized as follows:

- Dry
- Normal
- Combination
- Oily

Dry Skin

Dry skin does not produce enough oil. **Alipidic** (al-lah-PID-ik) skin lacks oil (lipids). The follicles are usually small and the sebum is minimal. If you can barely see the follicles or they are small, this

indicates a dry skin type. The natural oil secretions in our follicles help protect us from environmental damage and aging. Dry skin needs extra care because it lacks this normal protection.

Dry skin is more sensitive because the acid mantle and barrier function are not as healthy due to the lack of lipids. Skin texture can be slightly rough and feel tight. Stimulating oil production and protecting the surface is imperative to taking care of dry skin. **Occlusive** (uh-KLOO-sive) products are thick and lay on top of the skin to reduce transepidermal water loss, also known as TEWL. These products help hold in moisture and protect the skin's top barrier layer, which combats dryness.

Dry versus Dehydrated Skin

While common for someone with dry skin, **dehydration,** or lack of water, is a condition that can be seen with all skin types. Dehydrated skin lacks water. This is different from dry skin that lacks oil. It is important to remember the difference, because even oily skin can be dehydrated and need to be hydrated.

Dehydrated skin can look thin or flaky and can feel tight and dry. It is sometimes described as *crepey* or *papery*, like crepe paper. Skin that needs moisture tends to absorb products quickly. Dehydrated skin can be caused by internal and external factors such as medications, coffee, alcohol, sun, over-exfoliation, and harsh products. Drinking plenty of water and hydrating the skin with moisturizers and humectants can help minimize the negative effects of dryness and dehydration. Hydrating products such as gel masks are discussed in Chapter 13, Skin Care Products: Chemistry, Ingredients, and Selection.

Normal Skin

Normal skin has a good oil–water balance. It can fluctuate and sometimes will be a little drier or a little oilier. The follicles are a normal size, and the skin is usually free of blemishes. If the follicle size is smaller to medium just on the edge of the T-zone by the nose, measuring outward from the center of the face, this is typical of a normal skin type. Follicles are not usually that visible towards the cheeks or the outside of the face. Maintenance and preventative care are the goals for this type of skin.

Combination Skin

Combination skin can be both oily and dry, or both oily and normal at the same time. The T-zone through the middle of the face on the forehead, nose, and chin is oilier. This area has more sebaceous glands and larger pores. The outer areas of the face can be either normal or dry and can even appear flaky from either dehydration or buildup of dead skin cells. If you can see the follicle size is more obvious and looks medium to larger outside the T-zone on the cheeks, this is an indication of a combination skin type.

Combination skin needs to be balanced and requires more care than normal skin does. To care for combination skin, the oil–water balance can be achieved by treating both the oily and dryer areas of the face. Proper maintenance including cleansing and regular exfoliation help to keep skin clear and blemishes minimal. Water-based products work best for combination skin. Avoid harsh products, excessive cleansing, and rough exfoliating on all skin types.

Oily Skin

Oily skin, also known as *lipidic skin*, is characterized by excess sebum (oil) production. The follicle size is larger and contains more oil. If the follicle size is visible or larger over most of the face, this indicates an oily skin type. Oily skin requires more cleansing and exfoliating than other skin types do. It is prone to blemishes because the pores get clogged with oil and a buildup of dead skin cells. This excess oil and buildup on the surface can make the skin appear thicker and sallow. Blemishes and comedones are common.

Balancing the skin's oil production through treatments and products is important. Over-cleansing can make matters worse by stripping the skin's acid mantle and irritating it. If skin is stripped of oil, it is unbalanced. This causes the body's protection mechanism to produce additional oil to compensate for the dryness on the surface. Remember that no matter what the skin type, the goal is to balance the barrier function.

Educating clients (especially teenagers with hormonal flare-ups) on how to care for their skin will help them tremendously. Proper treatment, exfoliation, and a water-based hydrator will help keep oily skin clean and balanced. The positive side to having oily skin is that it ages more slowly because of the protection provided by oil secretions. Oily skin is more prone to acne, so people with this skin type need professional treatments more often than those with normal skin. After a deep-cleansing facial and good home-care, visible improvements are noticeable (**Figure 12–3**).

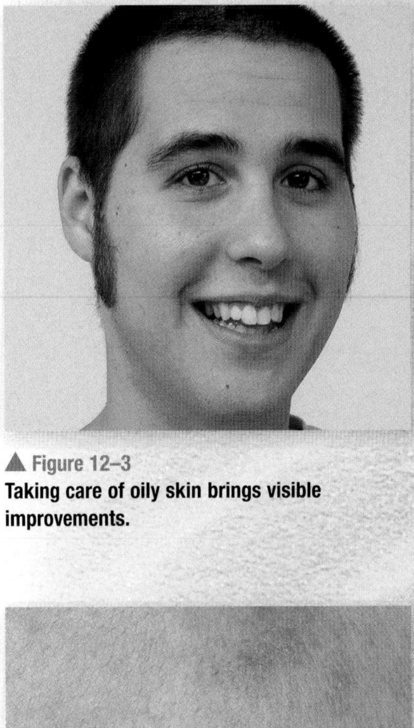

▲ Figure 12–3
Taking care of oily skin brings visible improvements.

Sensitive Skin

Sensitive skin is increasingly common. We are constantly bombarded by environmental stimuli, stress, sun exposure, and other unhealthy elements. Sensitive skin is a condition, but it is also genetically predisposed. Sensitive skin is characterized by fragile, thin skin and redness. Northern European descendants tend to have fair, light-colored skin that is thinner and more sensitive. It flushes easily and may appear red due to the blood flow being closer to the surface. Individuals with darker skin can also have naturally sensitive skin, but it is not as visible.

Sensitive skin is easily irritated by products and by exposure to heat or sun (**Figure 12–4**). Telangiectasia, or **couperose skin** conditions, which appear as red, distended capillaries, are noticeable on sensitive skin.

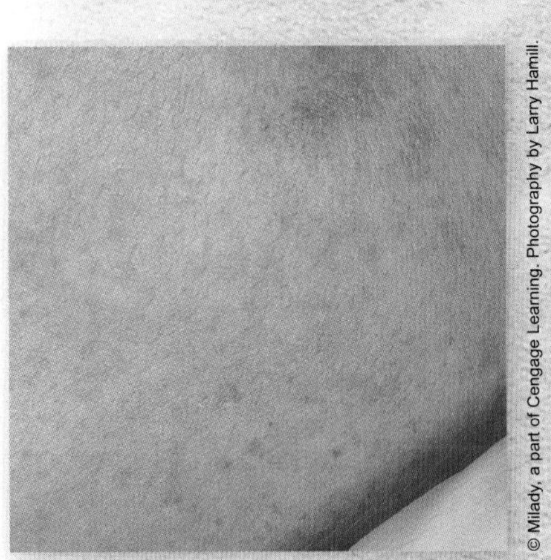

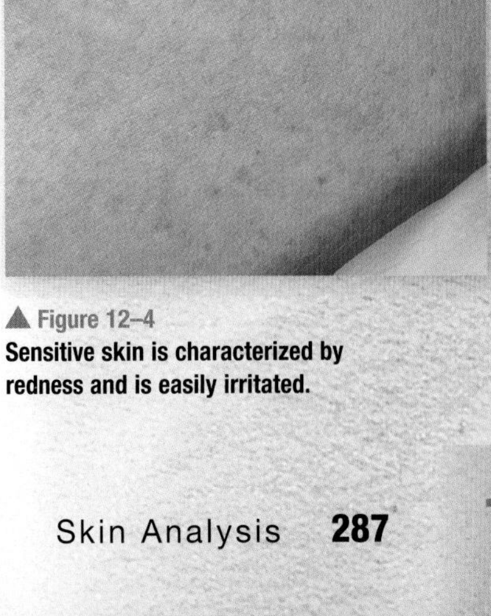

▲ Figure 12–4
Sensitive skin is characterized by redness and is easily irritated.

Rosacea and vascular conditions are more common with this type of skin. Sometimes these conditions may be a protective visible reaction to let us know something is irritating our skin.

Fragile or thin skin can also be the result of age or medications. Anyone's skin can become reactive and sensitized from exposure to things such as chemicals, harsh products, heat, or even chapping from cold weather.

Rosacea is thought to be more prevalent now due to an aging population as well as the increased use of medications, strong exfoliating products, and treatments in today's society.

Sensitive or sensitized skin can be difficult to treat because of its low tolerance to products and stimulation. Avoid irritating products and procedures. For example, excessive rubbing, heat, exfoliation, or extractions can cause damage and increase redness. Sensitive skin needs to be treated very gently with nonirritating, calming products. Many companies have product lines designed specifically for sensitive skin. It is important to find out what is causing sensitive conditions by completing a thorough skin analysis. Is it a natural part of their skin condition or is it something the client is exposed to? Primary treatment goals for sensitive skin are to soothe, calm, and protect. ✓ L01

The Fitzpatrick Scale

Developed by Dr. Thomas Fitzpatrick, the **Fitzpatrick Scale** is used to measure the skin type's ability to tolerate sun exposure (**Table 12–1**). It is important to be familiar with this method when determining treatments and products for your clients. Everyone's tolerance level is different for peels and treatments. Lighter skin types are generally more sensitive and reactive. Individuals with darker skin have more melanin, which gives more protection from the sun, but they have other sensitivities and concerns. There is not one true phototype classification due to mixed genetic characteristics; therefore the scale is just a guideline.

Other Skin Classification Systems

Glogau Scale

The ***Glogau scale*** evaluates photodamage (sun) based on wrinkling categorized by age.

- Type I is minimal to no wrinkles; age 20 to 30 or younger.
- Type II shows wrinkles only visible while in motion when making facial expressions. Early to moderate photoaging, light keratosis; age 30 to 40s.
- Type III shows wrinkles at rest, advanced photoaging, hyperpigmentation, telangiectasia, keratosis, age 40 to 50s.
- Type IV shows predominate wrinkles, severe photoaging, severe scarring may be noticable. Ages are not specified.

THE FITZPATRICK SCALE		
FITZPATRICK SKIN TYPE	APPEARANCE/GENERAL CHARACTERISTICS	REACTION TO UV SUN EXPOSURE AND LASER TREATMENT DAMAGE RISKS
Type I	Very fair; blond or red hair; light-colored eyes; freckles common.	Always burns, never tans. High risk for skin cancer, vascular damage.
Type II	Fair-skinned; light eyes; light hair.	Burns easily, tans with difficulty. High risk for skin cancer, vascular damage.
Type III	Very common skin type; fair; eye and hair color vary.	Sometimes burns, gradually tans. Risk of hyper/hypopigmentation. Moderate risk of skin cancer and vascular damage.
Type IV	Mediterranean Caucasian skin; dark brown hair; medium to heavy pigmentation.	Rarely burns, tans easily. High risk of hyper/hypopigmentation. High risk for scarring. Moderate risk for vascular damage.
Type V	Middle Eastern skin; dark and black hair; brown eyes; rarely sun sensitive.	Skin darkens; may never burn. High risk of hyper/hypopigmentation. High risk for scarring from treatments and trauma. Moderate risk for vascular damage. Lower risk for solar-pigmented conditions and actinic aging (from sun exposure).
Type VI	Black skin, brown eyes; rarely sun sensitive.	Tans easily; may never burn. Very high risk of hyper/hypopigmentation. Very high risk for scarring from treatments and trauma. Moderate risk for vascular damage. Lower risk for solar-pigmented conditions and actinic aging.

▲ Table 12–1 **The Fitzpatrick Scale.**

Rubin's Classification

Rubin's Classifications of Photodamage uses levels to classify photodamage by the depth of skin changes or damage. This indicates what kind of treatment is appropriate for the skin's conditions.

- Level 1 includes superficial pigment and changes in the epidermis. Superficial chemical exfoliation and antioxidants will be beneficial for skin at this level.
- Level 2 includes changes in the epidermis and papillary dermis, actinic keratosis, pigmentation, and increased wrinkles. This client will benefit from medium-depth peels and stronger products such as retinoids.
- Level 3 shows deeper changes down to the reticular dermis. Skin looks leathery and shows severe sun damage. Laser resurfacing and other cosmetic procedures are suggested for this level of damage.

Diverse Skin Pigmentation

▲ Figure 12–5
Ethnic skin is more fragile than it looks.

Darker skin types contain more melanin than lighter Caucasian skin types do. We all have different heritages with unique combinations of ethnic backgrounds, so skin categories and descriptions are only general guidelines. Black, Hispanic, Asian, and Native American skin types all have different amounts of melanin. The number of melanocytes is the same, but the melanin transferred to keratinocytes by the melanosome (MEL-uh-noh-sohm) is greater in dark skin. Melanosomes are pigment granules from melanocyte cells that produce melanin in the basal layer. While darker skin types are considered oilier and thicker, they can also be fragile. Reactions are hard to see on darker skin, but they may be just as intense as those on lighter skin (**Figure 12–5**).

Hyperpigmentation is a greater problem for darker skin types. Other pigmentation disorders also include hypopigmentation such as vitiligo.

Post-inflammatory hyperpigmentation can result from hormones, trauma, extractions, sun damage, or exfoliation. Hyperpigmentation can also be caused by peels, lightening agents, and laser treatments so use caution with these products and treatments.

Black skin is prone to hyperkeratosis (excessive cell turnover and dead skin-cell buildup), so it needs more exfoliation and deep pore cleansing. Abnormal hypertrophic scarring (keloids) is also problematic for black skin. Black skin does not age as quickly, because it is thicker and has more melanin for additional sun protection; however, dark skin still needs protection from sun damage.

Asian skin is considered to be one of the most sensitive skin types. It has great elasticity and firmness, and it does not show signs of aging as quickly as Caucasian skin does. Nevertheless, Asian skin can become hyperpigmented from treatments or exfoliating agents such as alpha hydroxy acids (AHAs). Gentler exfoliating products such as enzymes are recommended. Sun protection is necessary to slow down hyperpigmentation.

Caution clients that receiving lightening treatments for their age spots (dark areas) can actually make things worse. If exfoliated areas produce melanin in an uneven pattern, lightening treatments can lead to splotchiness. Avoiding sun exposure and using sun protection daily is a must for anyone prone to hyperpigmentation. A personalized skin care routine will keep your client's skin looking beautiful for years to come.

Care and precautions for other skin types including Native American, Indian, and Hispanic skin are the same as for other ethnic skin types. These groups typically have thicker skin that is usually characterized by more oil production and needs more deep-cleansing treatments. Additionally, individuals that have thicker hair and thicker roots in the follicle can make waxing more difficult. If you want to specialize in ethnic skin care, explore the educational resources and advanced classes for this area of study. No matter what the skin type or ethnic background, everyone needs an individualized skin care consultation and program to maintain healthy skin.

Skin Types versus Skin Conditions

Many internal and external factors affect the condition of a person's skin. Skin conditions are not just a result of our genetic makeup. These conditions are what the esthetician is most concerned about, and they are the focus of skin treatments. Some of the most common skin conditions estheticians see today are adult acne, **actinic** (ak-TIN-ik) aging (from sun damage), and problems from hormonal fluctuations.

Dehydration, pigmentation disorders, and rosacea are also significant concerns to clients. Other skin conditions include comedones, hyperkeratinization, redness, sensitivities, and of course, aging. We can improve some of these conditions through routine facials, by using specialized products, and by avoiding the factors that affect the conditions. On the client's chart, you will want to note other conditions that you learn about here and in Chapter 11, Disorders and Diseases of the Skin, which may not be listed in **Table 12–2**, page 292.

☑ L02

SKIN CONDITIONS AND DESCRIPTIONS	
SKIN CONDITION	**DESCRIPTION**
Actinic keratosis	A rough area resulting from sun exposure, sometimes with a layered scale or scab that sometimes falls off. Can be precancerous.
Adult acne	Acne breakouts from hormonal changes or other factors.
Asphyxiated	Smokers have asphyxiated skin from lack of oxygen. Characterized by clogged pores and wrinkles; dull and lifeless-looking. Can be yellowish or gray in color.
Comedones	*Open comedones* are blackheads and clogged pores caused by a buildup of debris, oil, and dead skin cells in the follicles. *Closed comedones* are not open to the air or oxygen; they are trapped by dead skin cells and need to be exfoliated and extracted.
Couperose skin; Telangiectasia	Redness; distended capillaries from weakening of the capillary walls; internal or external causes.
Cysts	Fluid, infection, or other matter under the skin.
Dehydration	Lack of water (also caused by the environment, medications, topical agents, aging, or dehydrating drinks such as caffeine and alcohol).
Enlarged pores	Larger pores due to excess oil and debris trapped in the follicles or expansion due to elasticity loss or trauma.
Erythema	Redness caused by inflammation.
Hyperkeratinization	An excessive buildup of dead skin cells/keratinized cells.
Hyperpigmentation	Brown or dark pigmentation; discoloration from melanin production due to sun or other factors.
Hypopigmentation	White, colorless areas from lack of melanin production.
Irritation	Usually redness or inflammation; from a variety of causes.
Keratosis (plural: Keratoses)	A buildup of cells; a rough texture.
Milia	Hardened, pearl-like masses of oil and dead skin cells trapped beneath the surface of the skin. Milia are not exposed to oxygen and have to be lanced to open and remove them.
Papules	Raised lesions; also called *blemishes*.
Poor elasticity	Sagging; loose skin from damage, sun, and aging.
Pustules	An infected papule with fluid inside.
Rosacea	A vascular disorder; chronic redness. Papules and pustules may be present.
Sebaceous hyperplasia	Benign lesions seen in oilier areas of the face. Described as looking like doughnut holes. Cannot be extracted.
Seborrhea	Oiliness of the skin.
Sensitivities	Reactions from internal or external causes.
Solar comedones	Large blackheads, usually around the eyes, due to sun exposure.
Sun damage	UV damage to the epidermis and dermis; primary effects are wrinkles, collagen and elastin breakdown, pigmentation, and cancer.
Wrinkles/Aging	Lines and damage from internal or external causes.

▲ Table 12–2 **Skin Conditions and Descriptions.**

Factors That Affect the Skin

Habits, diet, and stress all play a part in our health, which in turn is reflected in our skin's appearance. Skin conditions can be caused by allergies/reactions, genetics/ethnicity, medications, medical conditions, and many other internal or external factors. Being aware of what can affect the skin will help the esthetician determine why the client may be experiencing problems. Knowledge of healthy habits and "enemies" of the skin will give you a better understanding of how to help clients with their concerns.

Internal Factors

Our body's internal (*intrinsic*) health affects how we feel as well as how our body and skin looks. Stress, our lifestyle, and even our attitude can contribute to our skin's health. Free radicals in the body, dehydration (lack of water), vitamin deficiency, improper nutrition, alcohol, caffeine, hormones, and menopause all affect our skin's well-being. Unfortunately, cumulative sun damage shows up at the same time as menopause—an unfair double attack on a woman's body. Hormonal imbalances can lead to sensitivity, dehydration, hyperpigmentation, and microcirculation problems that affect capillaries. Additionally, lack of exercise, lack of sleep, smoking, medications, and drugs will have negative effects both inside and out (Table 12–3).

ACTIVITY

What are some examples of contraindications you may see as a skin care specialist? Write down any medications, contagious diseases, skin disorders, medical conditions, and skin irritations you can think of that would contraindicate a facial service.

External Factors

Sun damage is the main external (*extrinsic*) cause of aging (Figure 12–6). Environmental exposure, pollutants, air quality, and humidity also affect the skin's health (Table 12–4, on page 294). Poor maintenance and home-care can also contribute to skin problems. Misuse of products or poor facial treatments can be detrimental to maintaining a healthy and attractive complexion. This is another reason why correct skin analysis and product recommendations are so important. ✓ LO3

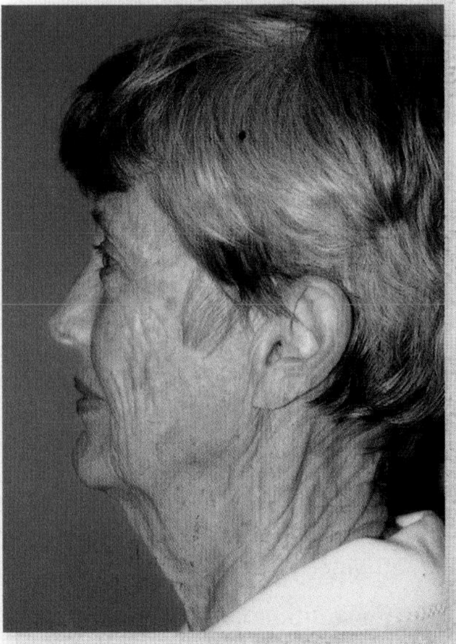

▲ Figure 12–6
Sun damage causes photoaging.

INTERNAL EFFECTS ON THE SKIN	
• Genetics and ethnicity-influenced conditions	• Lack of exercise
• Stress, lifestyle, negative attitude	• Lack of sleep
• Free radicals	• Smoking
• Dehydration	• Medications, drugs
• Vitamin deficiency	• Medical conditions
• Improper nutrition, alcohol, caffeine	• Aging
• Hormones and menopause	• Glycation

▲ Table 12–3 **Internal Effects on the Skin.**

Did You Know?

Approximately 80 percent of premature extrinsic aging is caused by the sun.

EXTERNAL EFFECTS ON THE SKIN
• UV exposure and sun damage
• Sunlamps and tanning booths
• Environmental exposure, pollutants, and air quality
• Environment, climate, and humidity
• Poor maintenance and skin care
• Misuse of products or treatments, over-exfoliation, or harsh products
• Allergies and reactions to environmental factors or products
• Photosensitivity to the sun from medications or products

▲ Table 12–4 **External Effects on the Skin.**

Sunlight and Interaction with the Skin—UV Radiation

Sunlight is energy. Both UVA and UVB wavelengths are absorbed, scattered, and reflected by the skin. UVC wavelengths are even shorter and more energetic but are mainly absorbed by the ozone layer. See **Table 12–5** for a comparison on UVA and UVB radiation. UV is a proven carcinogen, suppresses the immune system, and causes eye damage.

The amount of energy organisms get from sunlight depends on how much exposure and how strong or intense the exposure is. This is referred to as the dosage. *Minimal erythemal dose* (MED) is the term used to describe how

ULTRAVIOLET LIGHT COMPARISONS	
UVA RADIATION (320–380 NM)	**UVB RADIATION (280–320 NM)**
UVA has longer wavelengths that penetrate deeper into the dermis than UVB.	UVB has shorter wavelengths and are stronger than UVA because they deliver more energy.
UVA wavelengths are less energetic because of the lower frequency.	UVB have more energy because the wavelengths have a higher frequency.
UVA radiation is absorbed by the epidermis and dermis. Wavelengths above 320 nm penetrate more readily into the dermis.	UVB penetrates less because the shorter wavelengths are scattered or reflected more by the epidermis.
Long wavelengths have low energy, or frequency, so are less intense; but 95% of solar radiation is UVA, so it is up to 50 times more prevalent than UVB.	Short wavelengths have higher energy. The higher energy from UVB causes more interaction and has a greater effect directly on DNA, molecules, and cells in the epidermis.
UVA affect the dermis, collagen, and elastin. It also causes DNA damage from free radicals, leading to skin cancer.	UVB are the main cause of sunburns, tanning, skin aging, and skin cancers.
UVA is the dominant cause of tanning, wrinkling, and premature aging.	UVB is stronger in the U.S. during summer months. UVB exposure is doubled when reflected by snow or ice and is greater at higher altitudes.
Tanning beds use UVA light and have 12 times the dosage of the sun, which is equal to 12 times the amount of damage and aging.	

▲ Table 12–5 **Ultraviolet Light Comparisons.**

Here are some helpful tips for using physical sunscreen:

- Wear a moisturizer or protective lotion with a sunscreen of *sun protection factor* (SPF) 30 on all areas of potential exposure. Apply 20 minutes before sun exposure.
- Avoid exposure during peak hours, when UV exposure is highest. In the U.S. this is usually between 10 a.m. and 4 p.m.
- Apply sunscreen liberally after swimming or any activities that result in heavy perspiration. Better yet, sunscreen should be reapplied every hour or immediately after swimming.
- All sunscreen used for protection should be full- or broad-spectrum to filter out both UVA and UVB radiation. Check the expiration date printed on the bottle to make sure that the sunscreen has not expired.

Protection from damaging effects of UV exposure:

- Avoid exposing children younger than 6 months of age to the sun.
- Wear a hat and protective clothing when participating in outdoor activities. Redheads are particularly susceptible to sun damage. Wear swim shirts while swimming.
- Remember that UVA comes through clouds and windows; UVA is even stronger through glass.
- Wear sunglasses to protect the eyes and the eye area.
- Avoid tanning beds. Research is showing more evidence on how damaging tanning beds are to the skin.
- UV damage and aging is accelerated with the intense, strong bulbs in tanning beds. Cancer is linked to use of tanning beds.

long it takes to become red (erythema) from sun exposure. The dosage is the intensity of the sun multiplied by the time exposed: Dosage = Intensity × Time. Erythema is redness and the result of cell damage and blood vessel dilation in the dermis. It can appear hours after exposure and last for several days. ✓ LO4

Healthy Habits for the Skin

Preventative measures for skin care include avoiding the sun and wearing protective clothing, hats, and sunscreen. This is the best protection for our skin. Proper home-care, skin treatments, and ingredients such as antioxidants, peptides, lipids, and alpha hydroxy acids (AHAs) are all beneficial (See Chapter 13, Skin Care Products: Chemistry, Ingredients, and Selection, for more information). A good diet, vitamins, water intake, regular exercise, and other healthy practices all have a positive effect on our health and our complexion. Some authorities even believe positive thinking can decrease premature aging. ✓ LO5

CAUTION!

Many medications and topical products are *photosensitizers* that make people more sensitive to sun exposure and can cause severe reactions such as burning, hyperpigmentation, and allergic reactions.

Contraindications

Contagious diseases, skin disorders, medical conditions, medications, and skin irritation can all contraindicate, or prohibit, a service (**Table 12–6**, on page 296). Legally, you may not ask clients about contagious diseases, but they may list them on the client questionnaire. Recognizing diseases is vital to avoid causing harm to clients or to you. Also, medications or topical peeling agents can make the skin too sensitive for facials or waxing.

Here's a Tip

Top ten healthy habits for the skin:

1. Avoid sun exposure.
2. Eat healthy nutritious food.
3. Do not smoke.
4. Avoid excessive alcohol.
5. Drink plenty of water.
6. Get plenty of rest.
7. Stay active and exercise regularly.
8. Use beneficial products and home-care.
9. Get regular facials for good skin maintenance.
10. Avoid stress and maintain a calm, positive attitude.

Certain medical conditions and illnesses may contraindicate any stimulation to the face or body. Additionally, allergies and sensitivities to products and ingredients are common. Contraindications are also discussed in other chapters. Clients who have obvious skin conditions such as open sores, fever blisters (herpes simplex), or other abnormal-looking conditions should be referred to a physician for treatment. ✓ LO6

Client Consultations

A thorough client consultation is important for many reasons. The most important is to find out about any contraindications that the client may have. A consultation will help you to determine why a client may be experiencing skin problems. Their health, lifestyle, occupation, and product use will all affect their skin. Sometimes estheticians are like detectives, trying to determine why the client is having a certain skin problem. The more you know about your client, the more you discover what they need for their skin.

ACTIVITY

What do you think your skin type is? What skin conditions do you have? After doing your skin analysis in class with other students, see how closely the analysis matches your original answers to these questions. Did you learn anything new about your skin after an analysis?

CONTRAINDICATIONS FOR SKIN TREATMENTS
• Certain skin diseases, disorders, or irritations.
• Use of Accutane® or any skin-thinning or exfoliating drug, including Retin-A®, Renova™, Tazorac®, Differin®, and so on. Avoid waxing, exfoliation, peeling treatments, or stimulating treatments if a client uses these.
• Pregnancy—The client should not have any electrical treatments, or any questionable treatment, without her physician's written permission. Some pregnant clients also experience sensitivities from waxing.
• Metal bone pins or plates in the body—Avoid all electrical treatments.
• Pacemakers or heart irregularities—Avoid all electrical treatments.
• Allergies—Any allergic substances listed should be strictly avoided. Clients with multiple allergies should use fragrance-free products designed for sensitive skin.
• Seizures or epilepsy—Avoid all electrical and light treatments.
• Use of oral steroids (cortisones) like prednisone—Avoid any stimulating, exfoliating treatments or waxing, as skin may be more fragile and bruise easier.
• Autoimmune diseases such as lupus—Avoid any harsh or stimulating treatments.
• Diabetes—Be aware that due to their poor blood circulation, many diabetics heal very slowly and may not readily feel pain, especially in the feet. If you are in doubt, get approval from the client's physician before treatment.
• Blood thinners—No extraction or waxing.

▲ Table 12–6 **Contraindications for Skin Treatments.**

Ask questions relating to skin conditions and the client's personal health. You may have three forms for a client: a questionnaire, a release form, and a client chart that includes their skin analysis. Have clients fill out a confidential questionnaire. A *client release form* is also highly recommended. A client release form is a document that a client reads and signs, releasing you from liability before you perform services. A *client chart* is a record all of your notes from the skin analysis, what you used in the treatment, and your home-care recommendations (**Figure 12–7**, on page 298).

Once you learn about ingredients and start giving facials, you will be recommending products. Think about how you can help the client through treatments, home-care suggestions, and preventative measures. Conduct the consultation, discuss what you see with the client, and give advice during the analysis or after the treatment. Use a client chart to record the analysis, the type of treatment performed, products used, and other consultation notes. It is beneficial to practice skin analysis before diving into products and treatments. Each subject you study gives you a foundation to build upon for the next step. ✓ L07 ✓ L08

ACTIVITY

Analyze the faces of your friends and family to determine their skin type and conditions. Ask questions, note the contraindications, and fill out the client charts. Consult with them about healthy habits and taking care of their skin. They might be your best clients!

Questions to ask during the consultation include the following:

- **Do you have allergies to products or scents?**
- **Why are you here? (What brought the client in? Is it for deep cleansing or just relaxation?)**
- **What are your skin concerns? (What does he or she care about?)**
- **What products do you use? (What is the client's home-care routine? What are the ingredients, and how often are they used?)**
- **Have you had treatments before? (Is this the client's first facial?)**
- **Is this a normal state for your skin? (Is it normally more clear? Is it usually less irritated?)**
- **How does your skin feel during different times of the day? (What is the degree of oiliness or dryness?)**

Performing a Skin Analysis

Knowing how to analyze skin is the first step in providing skin care. Identifying conditions and contraindications, as well as providing thorough consultations and charting client notes, are all elements of good facial treatments.

Educating clients on healthy habits and the causes of skin conditions is part of the service. Products, ingredients, different types of facials, and a home-care regime for preventative maintenance are all beneficial in caring for the skin. A series of treatments may be necessary to effectively help the client's conditions. Twenty years of sun damage cannot be helped overnight. Realistically, it could take weeks or months to see a visible difference in the skin for some other conditions as well, such as acne.

Beneath the surface, however, treatments have positive benefits and do make a difference, even if the effects are not instantly visible. Information on choosing products for treatments and home-care is presented in Chapter 13, Skin Care Products: Chemistry, Ingredients, and Selection. While at first skin analysis seems difficult, practice and experience will build confidence in using this important skill. Soon you will automatically notice skin conditions.

CAUTION!

Contraindications such as medications, contagious diseases, skin disorders, medical conditions, and skin irritation can all make a service inappropriate.

Knowing skin types, conditions, and the factors affecting the skin's health enables you to give an accurate skin analysis. The best tool for analyzing the skin is a magnifying lamp/light. A Wood's lamp can also be useful to see the deeper levels of pigmentation and condition of the skin (discussed in Chapter 17, Facial Machines). Other hand-held

CLIENT CONSULTATION FORM: SKIN TREATMENTS

Date:
Name:
Address:
City: State: Zip:
Phone: Cell:
E-mail:
Referred by:
Main reason for visit:

Have you had facials before? Yes No
Do you have any skin concerns?
Circle those that apply below:
Aging Dryness Redness Wrinkles Sun Damage
Acne Blemishes Oiliness Peeling Rough Texture
Pigmentation (dark or light discolored areas)

Do you have any allergies? Yes No
Please list:
Are you allergic to any ingredients? Yes No
Please list:
Have you recently seen a dermatologist? Y N
Have you had any recent surgeries, laser procedures, or strong exfoliation treatments? Y N
Type of Treatment: When?
Please list any medications you take:
Do you have any health issues or skin conditions? Y N
Please list:
What facial care products do you use?
Circle those that apply below:
Soap Cleanser Toner Moisturizer Sunscreen Mask
Night cream Exfoliant, Scrub, or Peeling product
Favorite product line:

SKIN ANALYSIS CHART

Skin Type: Dry (Normal) Combination Oily Acne

Conditions:		**Facial Area:**
Dehydrated		
Aging	*X*	*all*
Wrinkles	*X*	
Sun damage	*X*	
Redness		
Couperose	*X*	*T-zone*
Pigmentation:		
Hyper or hypo	*X*	*cheeks*
Comedones (open or closed)		
Milia		
Hyperkeratinization (rough, cell build up)	*X*	
Psoriasis		
Other:		

Esthetician: *SL* **Date:** *10/15/2012*

Conditions:		**Facial Area:**
Poor Elasticity	*X*	
Rosacea		
Sensitive		
Oiliness		
Acne - Grade: 1 2 3 4		
Cysts		
Papules		
Pustules		
Asphixiated		
Sunburn		
Moles		
Scarring		

Contraindications:

SKIN CARE TREATMENT RECORD

Date	**Type of Treatment**	**Esthetician**
10/15/ 2012	*One-hour Facial*	*SL*

Notes/Comments:
Skin sensitive, wants series of exfoliation treatments, advised no waxing with chemical treatments

	Products Used:	**Products recommended**	**Products purchased**
Cleanser:	*Normal*	*X*	*X*
Exfoliant:	*Exfoliating enzyme mask*		
Mask	*Antiaging Clay*	*Hydrating*	*X*
Massage	*Rose-based lotion*	*n/a*	
Toner	*Calming*		
Serum	*Antioxidant*	*X*	*X*
Eyes/lips	*Eye gel, lip treatment*	*X*	
Moisturizer, Sunscreen	*Cream w/SPF 30*	*X*	*X*
Other:	*5% Glycolic cream: prep for exfoliation treatments*	*X*	*X*

Date	**Type of Treatment**	**Products recommended**	**Products purchased**	**Esthetician**
10/30/2012	*Chemical Exfoliation - #1 in series: AHA 30%, 5 minutes*	*Continue same*	*no*	*SL*

Notes/Comments:_
Good results with home-care, smoother texture, no reaction to treatment #1. Likes the products

▲ **Figure 12–7**
A client intake form and client chart.

A SKIN ANALYSIS CHECKLIST

- Skin type: Check the pore size and oil distribution.
- Conditions present: Note the comedones, capillaries, pigmentation, sun damage, and other conditions. Refer to the client chart and Table 12–2 for a list of conditions.
- Appearance: Is the skin dry, clear, oily, red, irritated? What else do you notice?
- Texture: Is the texture rough, smooth, dehydrated, firm? Record your observations on the client's chart.

▲ Table 12–7 **A Skin Analysis Checklist.**

Did You Know?

The Chinese method of skin analysis uses four examinations as part of the health diagnosis: look, listen, ask, and touch. The four examinations are used to determine the high and low energy of the whole person. This four-part visual, auditory, sensory, and inquiry diagnosis looks for disharmony and the indications of imbalance in the whole body.

tools such as a moisture analyzation meter and devices that magnify up to 200 times via a computer screen are available to analyze the skin. Note the following details in a skin analysis: the client's skin type, any skin conditions, and the skin's visible appearance and texture (Table 12–7).

After cleansing, observe the skin. First determine the skin type and the conditions present. Besides making a visual analysis, use your fingers to touch the skin (Figure 12–8). Does the texture feel rough or smooth? Try to determine the factors that may contribute to the individual's skin conditions. The more faces you see, the better you will be at recognizing different types and conditions. Even if you are not providing a service in a private room, you can still perform an initial skin analysis in the retail area. It won't be as accurate, but it will still be helpful. Sometimes clients need quick product recommendations or are not sure what type of treatment they should schedule. A quick skin analysis can be very beneficial in selling products or treatments.

Here's a Tip

Client information is personal and confidential, so be careful what you write on a client's chart. Clients will appreciate you remembering their children's names or their recent trip to Hawaii, so try to recall some personal information the next time they come in.

PROCEDURE 12-1 **Performing a Skin Analysis** PAGE 300

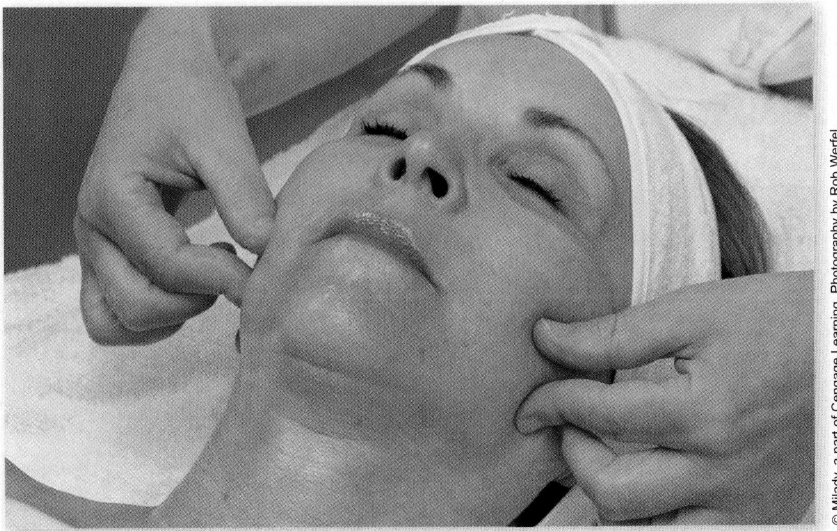

◀ Figure 12–8 **Analyzing the skin.**

Web Resources

www.milady.cengage.com
www.dayspamagazine.com
www.skininc.com
www.webmd.com

PROCEDURE

12-1

Performing a Skin Analysis: Step by Step

Supplies

- EPA-registered disinfectant
- Hand sanitizer
- Antibacterial soap
- Covered trash container
- Bowl
- Spatula
- Hand towels
- Headband
- Clean linens
- Bolster

Single-use Items

- Gloves
- Cotton pads (4" x 4" for cleansing)
- Cotton rounds
- Cotton swabs
- Plastic bag
- Paper towels
- Tissues

Products

- Eye makeup remover or cleanser
- Facial cleanser
- Toner
- Moisturizer

Preparation

- Perform 

PAGE 372

Procedure

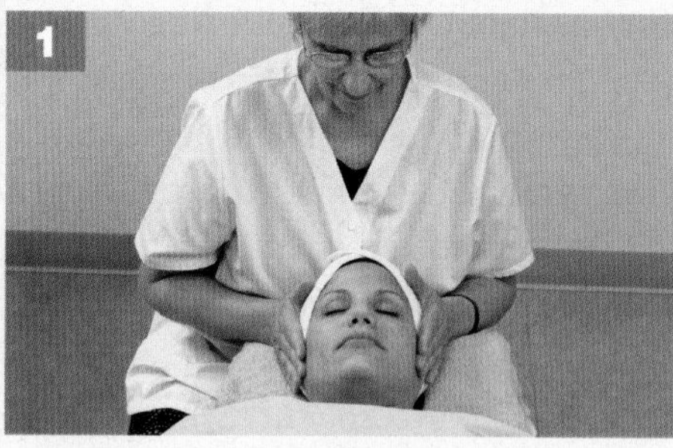

1 Look briefly at your client's skin with your naked eye or a magnifying light. You cannot do an accurate analysis if your client is wearing makeup.

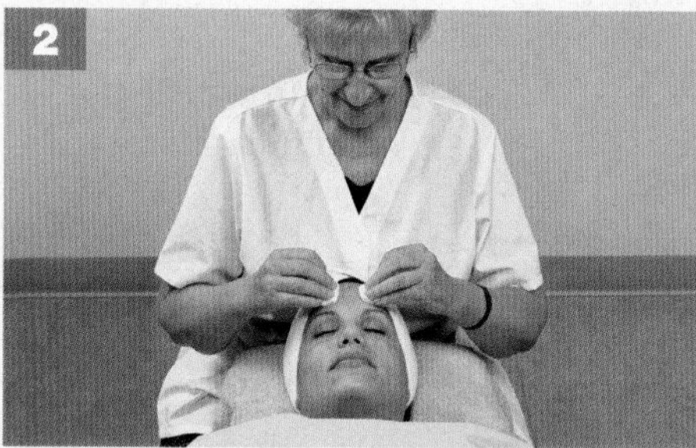

2 Cleanse the skin (a client's normal state of dryness or oiliness may not be as visible immediately after cleansing).

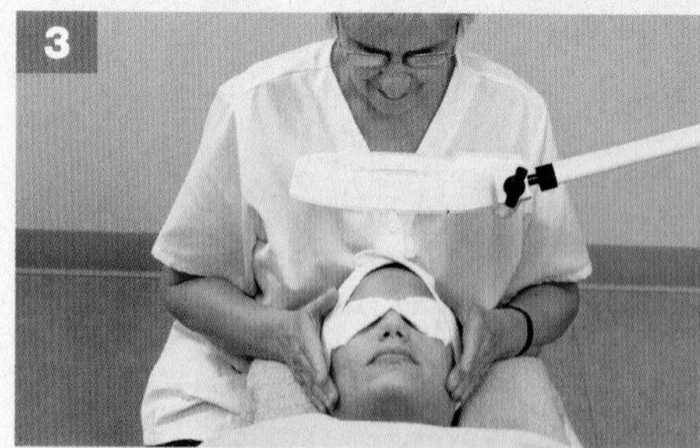

3 Use a magnifying light to examine the skin more thoroughly. Cover the eyes with eye pads. (In addition to the magnifying light, a Wood's lamp can be used here.)

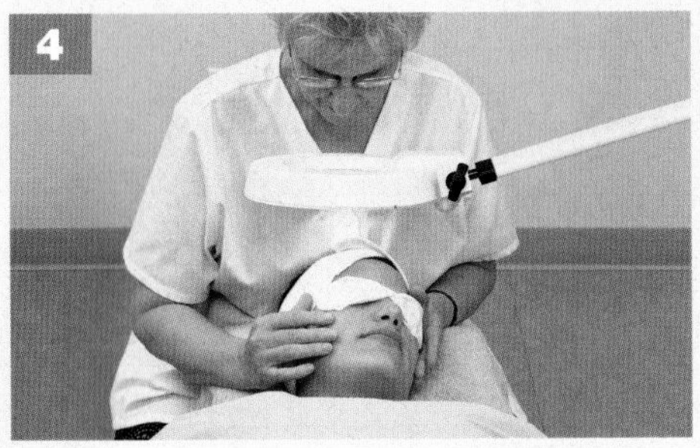

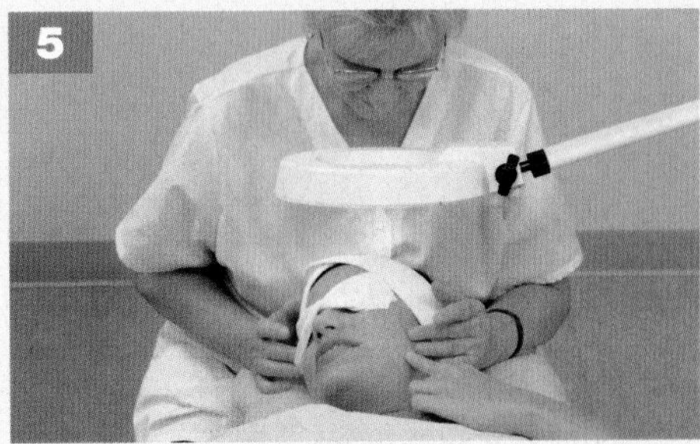

The four components of skin analysis are *look*, *feel*, *ask*, and *listen*.

4 Look closely at the client's skin type, the conditions present, and the appearance; also *touch* the skin with the fingertips to feel its texture.

5 Listen: Conduct a brief *consultation* while continuing to analyze with the magnifying lamp.

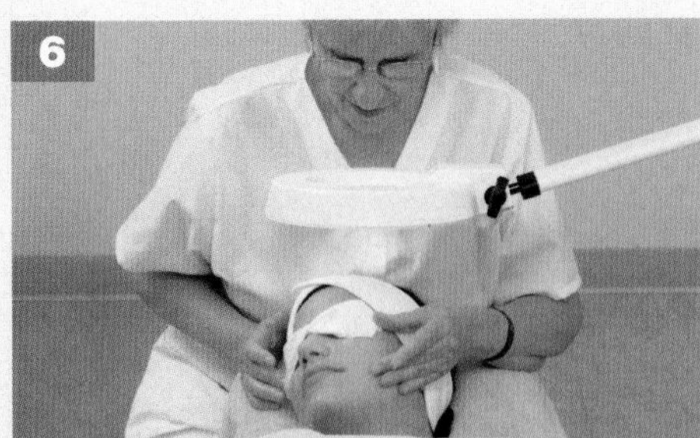

6 Ask questions relating to the skin's appearance and the client's personal health or lifestyle. Discuss what you see with the client; also recommend products and a home-care routine.

7 Reapply a toner and moisturizer or sunscreen to balance and protect the skin.

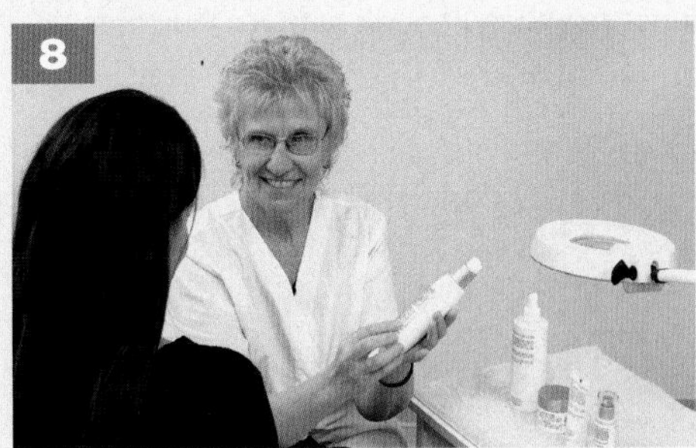

8 Choose products for treatment and home-care. (Refer to Chapter 13, Skin Care products: Chemistry, Ingredients, and Selection.)

9 Record the information on the client chart at the appropriate time—usually after the treatment is completed. ☑ LO9

Post-Service

- **Complete**

PAGE 375

Review Questions

1. Are skin types genetic?
2. List and define the skin types.
3. What is the difference between dry and dehydrated skin?
4. What is the Fitzpatrick Scale?
5. How are skin conditions different from skin types?
6. List and define 10 common skin conditions.
7. List four intrinsic, or internal, factors that affect the skin.
8. List four extrinsic, or external, factors that affect the skin.
9. What is the main cause of premature extrinsic aging?
10. What are five healthy habits for the skin?
11. List six contraindications for facial treatments.
12. Describe the steps in a skin analysis procedure.
13. What are the four steps in the skin analysis checklist?

Glossary

actinic	Damage or condition caused by sun exposure.
alipidic	Lack of oil or "lack of lipids." Describes skin that does not produce enough sebum, indicated by absence of visible pores.
contraindications	Factors that prohibit a treatment due to a condition; treatments could cause harmful or negative side effects to those who have specific medical or skin conditions.
couperose skin	Redness; distended capillaries from weakening of the capillary walls.
dehydration	Lack of water.
Fitzpatrick Scale	Scale used to measure the skin type's ability to tolerate sun exposure.
occlusive	Occlusive products are thick and lay on top of the skin to reduce transepidermal water loss (TEWL); helps hold in moisture, and protect the skin's top barrier layer.
skin types	Classification that describes a person's genetic skin type.
T-zone	Center area of the face; corresponds to the "T" shape formed by the forehead, nose, and chin.

CHAPTER 13

Skin Care Products: Chemistry, Ingredients, and Selection

Chapter Outline

Learning Objectives

After completing this chapter, you will be able to:

- ✓ LO1 Understand product components used in formulating products.
- ✓ LO2 Understand FDA regulations regarding cosmetic claims and product safety.
- ✓ LO3 Recognize the most common cosmetic ingredients and their benefits.
- ✓ LO4 List and describe the main categories of professional skin care products.
- ✓ LO5 Explain the basic products used in facials.
- ✓ LO6 Understand product formulations for different skin types.
- ✓ LO7 Explain the benefits of numerous skin care products.
- ✓ LO8 Safely use a variety of salon products while providing client services.
- ✓ LO9 Recommend home-care for different skin types and conditions.

Key Terms

Page number indicates where in the chapter the term is used.

alpha hydroxy acids (AHAs)
pg. 315

alcohol (ethanol)
pg. 324

algae
pg. 326

allantoin
pg. 326

aloe vera
pg. 326

alpha lipoic acid
pg. 319

alum
pg. 324

ampoules
pg. 340

anhydrous
pg. 308

aromatherapy
pg. 330

astringents
pg. 334

azulene
pg. 326

benzyl peroxide
pg. 324

beta hydroxy acids (BHAs)
pg. 315

beta-glucans
pg. 317

binders
pg. 320

botanicals
pg. 314

calendula
pg. 326

carbomers
pg. 313

carrot
pg. 326

certified colors
pg. 314

chamomile
pg. 326

chelating agent
pg. 313

chemical exfoliation
pg. 330

clay masks
pg. 338

cleansers
pg. 312

coenzyme Q10
pg. 319

colorants
pg. 314

comedogenicity
pg. 311

cosmeceuticals
pg. 308

cosmetics
pg. 307

delivery systems
pg. 316

detergents
pg. 311

DMAE (dimethylaminoethanol)
pg. 319

echinacea
pg. 326

emollients
pg. 308

emulsifiers
pg. 312

enzyme peels
pg. 326

essential oils
pg. 313

exfoliants
pg. 315

exfoliation
pg. 315

fatty acids
pg. 310

fatty alcohols
pg. 310

Key Terms

Page number indicates where in the chapter the term is used.

fatty esters
pg. 310

fragrances
pg. 313

fresheners
pg. 334

functional ingredients
pg. 307

glycerin
pg. 324

glycoproteins
pg. 317

gommage (roll-off masks)
pg. 337

grapeseed extract
pg. 326

green tea
pg. 326

healing agents
pg. 314

herbs
pg. 324

horsechestnut
pg. 326

humectants
pg. 314

hydrators
pg. 314

hydrophilic agents
pg. 314

jojoba
pg. 326

keratolytic
pg. 318

kojic acid
pg. 326

lakes
pg. 314

lanolin
pg. 324

lavender
pg. 326

licorice
pg. 327

lipids
pg. 315

liposomes
pg. 316

lubricants
pg. 310

mask (pack, masque)
pg. 337

mechanical exfoliation
pg. 335

methylparaben
pg. 324

mineral oil
pg. 309

modelage masks (thermal masks)
pg. 339

moisturizers
pg. 341

noncertified colors
pg. 314

oil soluble
pg. 312

olfactory system
pg. 331

papaya
pg. 327

parabens
pg. 324

paraffin wax masks
pg. 339

peptides
pg. 317

performance ingredients
pg. 306

petroleum jelly
pg. 324

pH adjusters
pg. 314

phytotherapy
pg. 330

polyglucans
pg. 317

polymers
pg. 316

potassium hydroxide
pg. 324

preservatives
pg. 313

propylene glycol
pg. 325

quaternium 15
pg. 325

retinol
pg. 317

rose
pg. 327

salicylic acid
pg. 325

seaweed
pg. 327

serums
pg. 340

silicones
pg. 310

sodium bicarbonate
pg. 325

sorbitol
pg. 325

sphingolipids
pg. 325

squalane
pg. 325

squalene
pg. 325

stem cells
pg. 317

sulfur
pg. 325

sun protection factor (SPF)
pg. 319

tea tree
pg. 327

tissue respiratory factor (TRF)
pg. 317

titanium dioxide
pg. 325

toners
pg. 334

urea
pg. 325

vehicles
pg. 316

water soluble
pg. 312

witch hazel
pg. 327

zinc oxide
pg. 325

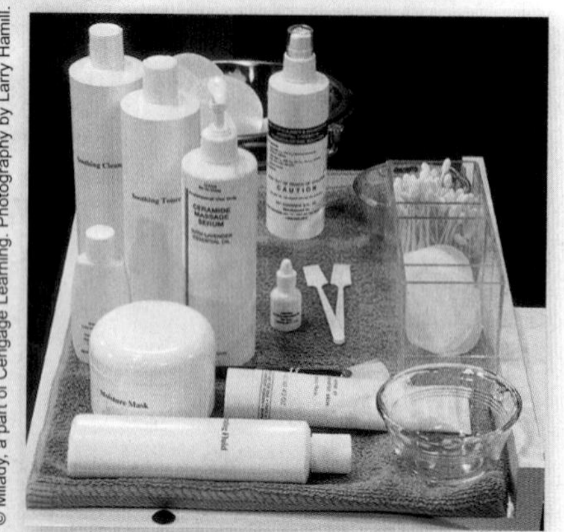

▲ Figure 13–1
Treatment products are the esthetician's most important tools.

The products an esthetician uses are the lifeblood of the facial treatment (**Figure 13–1**). The **performance ingredients** in products do the actual work of cleansing, normalizing, moisturizing, or otherwise treating the skin. Products come in many forms and types: solids, liquids, gases, or combinations of these. They may be formulated as cleansers, moisturizers, exfoliants, or other types of products. Within each category they are further differentiated by skin type.

In addition to understanding basic chemistry and cosmetic ingredients, estheticians need to know about new advanced ingredients and treatments, particularly those to which "antiaging" benefits are ascribed. While estheticians may not be allowed to claim the actual benefits of these products, you should understand them.

The cosmetics industry is continually developing new products to improve the appearance of the skin. Products used in treatments and for home-care can make a significant difference in the skin's health and appearance. The effectiveness of skin care formulations has increased as our knowledge of skin biology expands. From phytotherapy (therapeutic benefits from plants) to clinical formulations, product ingredients are one of the most exciting subjects in skin care. The chemistry of ingredients can be studied at the molecular level, but product chemistry and biochemistry are complex subjects. This can be explored further when researching ingredients and the effects on the skin.

As an esthetician, you will need to know what a wide spectrum of skin care products do, how they work, and how they are used. You will need to make decisions about products that will best suit your client's skin type and current condition. A person's skin care needs can change depending upon the season or life's activities. Be sure to check with clients to see if changes in their products are necessary. Educate them about the product or ingredient that is being used, what it does for them, and why it is effective.

Product ingredients are derived from a variety of sources including herbs, essential oils, plants, and synthetic performance ingredients. It's important to be familiar with each ingredient in the product and know its potential side effects. Read the manufacturer's literature and follow their instructions. This extensive chapter covers three main topics: chemistry, ingredients, and product selection.

Why Study Skin Care Products: Chemistry, Ingredients, and Selection?

Estheticians should study and have a thorough understanding of skin care products in order to provide clients with the appropriate treatment and products for maintaining healthy, beautiful skin.

- As an esthetician, you will need to know what skin care ingredients and products do, how they work, and how they are used.
- The most important step in selecting products is determining which ingredients are best for an individual's needs and understanding product formulations for different skin types.
- In addition to understanding basic chemistry and cosmetic ingredients, you will need to stay current with new developments in cosmetic chemistry and advanced ingredients.
- Products used in treatments and for home-care have many benefits and can make a significant difference in the skin's health and appearance.
- Being aware of a client's allergies and the ingredients being used in products is very important to avoid problems or reactions to products.

Cosmetic Chemistry

The FDA views cosmetics according to the Cosmetic Act of 1938, which distinguishes between drugs and cosmetics. **Cosmetics** are defined by the FDA as: articles that are intended to be rubbed, poured, sprinkled or otherwise applied to the human body or any part thereof for cleansing, beautifying, promoting attractiveness, or altering the appearance. In contrast, *drugs* are products (other than food) intended to affect the structures and/or functions of the body of humans or other animals. These definitions are important because they state that estheticians cannot make claims that a product or treatment can affect the structure or function of the skin. Estheticians focus on improving the skin's cosmetic appearance.

Every ingredient used in cosmetic chemistry has a function in the finished product. These ingredients are divided into two basic types: functional ingredients and performance ingredients. See **Table 13–1** and **Table 13–2** on pages 320 and 321, for a summary of some common functional and performance ingredients.

Functional ingredients make up the majority of a product; they allow products to spread, give them body and texture, and give them a specific form such as a lotion, cream, or gel. These ingredients do not affect the appearance of the skin but are necessary to the product formulation. A preservative is an example of an inactive functional ingredient.

Performance ingredients cause the actual changes in the appearance of the skin. Examples include glycerin, which hydrates the skin's surface; alpha hydroxy acids (AHAs), which exfoliate the corneum; and lipids, which help patch the skin's barrier. Performance ingredients are sometimes referred to as active agents—or erroneously called *active ingredients*, which is an official term for use in the drug industry to indicate ingredients that chemically cause physiological changes.

fyi

Some products and drugs are absorbed into the skin and the blood stream through the routes of penetration: skin cells, follicles, and glands.

A third category, **cosmeceuticals**, are products intended to improve the skin's health and appearance. Cosmeceuticals are stronger performance ingredients that may cause biochemical reactions and physiological effects to the skin. This category is not yet recognized by the FDA.

Product Components

Ingredients can be derived from plants, vitamins, or animals. They are also synthesized from chemicals in a lab. The terms *natural* and *organic* are often used in referring to skin product ingredients, but these terms have no specific regulated definition. The FDA regulates USA food labels and certifications, but skin care product labels are not yet regulated for these terms. *Hypoallergenic* describes ingredients that may be less likely to cause allergic reactions. *Noncomedogenic* describes ingredients that will not clog pores or cause comedones.

Many of the terms used in relation to products used by estheticians are descriptive and are for consumer marketing purposes. Research or testing of products varies, and product chemistry is complicated, so it may be difficult to predict how a certain product will work for an individual. Some ingredients perform multiple roles in products and function as both a functional and performance ingredient.

Water

Water makes up a large part of the skin. It is also the most frequently used cosmetic ingredient—it is both a vehicle and a performance ingredient. As a vehicle, it helps keep other cosmetic ingredients in solution and helps spread products across the skin. As a performance ingredient, water replenishes moisture in the surface of the skin. Almost all skin care products are a mixture of oil and water, or emulsions.

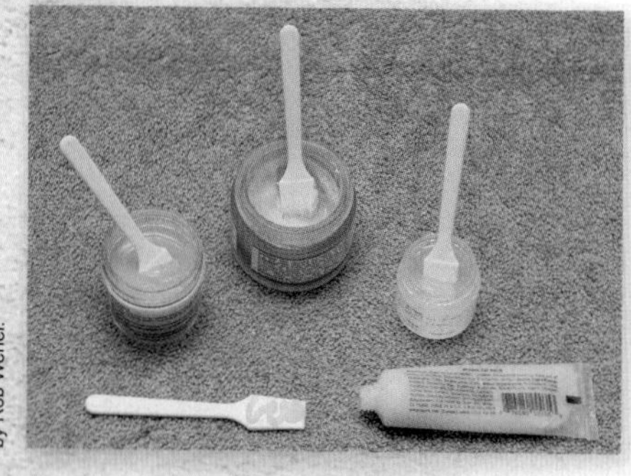

▲ Figure 13–2
Anhydrous products do not contain water.

Products that do not contain any water are called **anhydrous** (an-HY-drus). These include oil-based serums, petrolatum-based products such as lip balm, and silicone serums (Figure 13–2). Anhydrous products are designed for dry skin.

Emollients

Emollients are "fatty" materials (derived from oils or fats) used to lubricate and moisturize the skin. They can act as either vehicles or

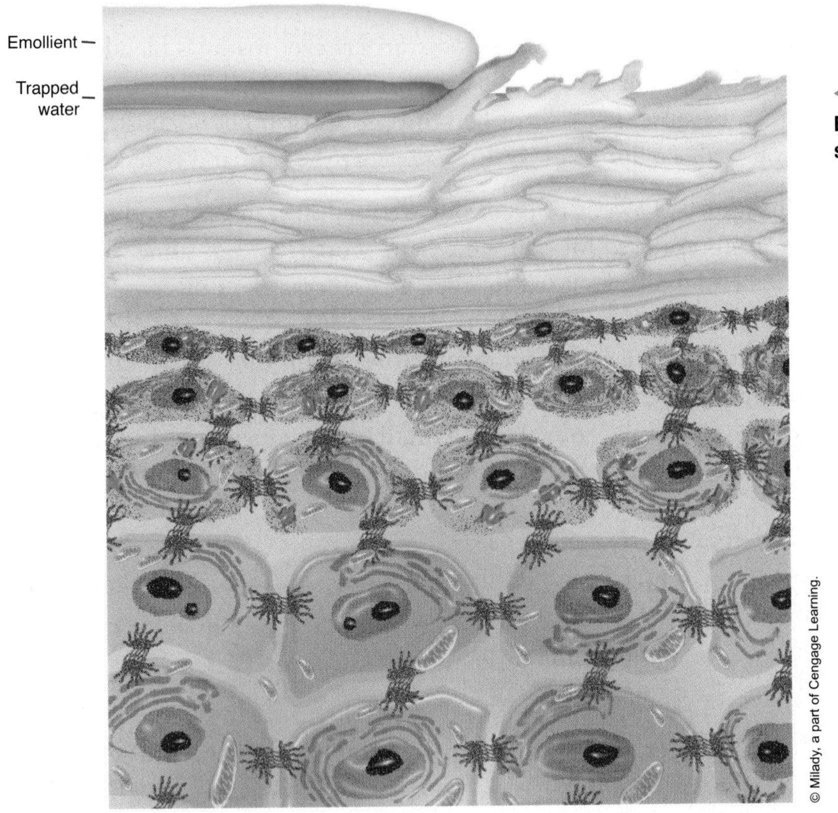

Emollient
Trapped water

© Milady, a part of Cengage Learning.

◀ Figure 13–3
Emollients trap moisture in the skin by the process of occlusion.

performance ingredients. As vehicles, emollients help place, spread, and keep other substances on the skin. For instance, emollients in sunscreen help spread the sunscreen agents across the skin and hold them in place. Emollients in loose powder help the powder slip evenly across and adhere to the skin.

As performance ingredients, emollients lubricate the skin's surface and guard the barrier function. Emollients lie on top of the skin and prevent dehydration by trapping water and decreasing transepidermal water loss (TEWL). This moisturizing technique is called *occlusion* (Figure 13–3). Silicones and oils are both emollients.

Oils

Many oils are used in skin care. They vary in density, fat content, and heaviness. They also vary in their tendency to cause comedones in oily or acne-prone skin. Different oils are appropriate for different degrees of dryness in the skin. Oils come from many sources.

Oils from the Earth. Mineral oil and petrolatum come from the earth, specifically from petroleum sources. Both emollients are time-tested, offer excellent protection against dehydration, and help prevent irritant skin contact. They are completely nonreactive and biologically inert, which means that they do not react with other chemicals involved in the skin's function. They can be combined with water and blended with an emulsifier into a cream, lotion, or fluid, which makes them much less oily.

ACTIVITY

Did you know that you can easily and safely test the pH of a solution? pH test papers (litmus papers and pH papers) can be used to indicate the pH of any aqueous solution. You can test any skin care product. You will need pH test papers, several small open containers, bottled drinking water, stirring sticks, and some white towels. Place the product you want to test in a small open cup or bowl. If the product is a powder or is extremely thick, add a small amount of bottled water and stir thoroughly. Dip the test paper into the product. Immediately place the paper on a white towel, and compare the color obtained to the color chart on the package to determine the pH level. Test anything you can think of. Be creative! What you discover may surprise you.

Classic cold cream, one of the first moisturizers ever made, is blended with mineral oil. Mineral oil and petrolatum can be used with no added preservatives because they do not harbor bacteria or other organisms. Mineral oil is also a lubricant. **Lubricants** coat the skin and reduce friction.

Oils from Plants. Dozens of plant oils are used in skin care products. Most plant oils are used for their emollient properties, but some, such as aromatic essential oils, are used for their fragrances. Plant oils contain fatty acids, which are beneficial for skin that does not produce enough sebum. The oils help keep the skin from dehydrating. Plant oils vary in fatty acid content and heaviness. Coconut oil and palm oil are two of the fattiest and heaviest oils. Some lighter and less comedogenic natural oils are safflower, sunflower, canola, and jojoba (huh-HOH-buh) oil.

Other Emollients

Literally hundreds of emollients exist. Some come from natural sources, and others are synthesized in a laboratory or derived from other oils or fatty materials.

Fatty acids are lubricant ingredients derived from plant oils or animal fats. Although these ingredients are acids, they are not irritating. Fatty acids are actually more like oils. Common fatty acids that you will see are oleic acid, stearic acid, and caprylic acid.

Fatty alcohols are fatty acids that have been exposed to hydrogen. They are not drying; they have a wax-like consistency and are used as emollients or spreading agents. Examples of fatty alcohols are cetyl alcohol, lauryl alcohol, and stearyl alcohol.

Fatty esters are produced from combining fatty acids and fatty alcohols. Esters are easily recognized on labels because they almost always end in *–ate,* such as octyl palmitate. They often feel better than natural oils and lubricate more evenly. Frequently used fatty esters are isopropyl myristate, isopropyl palmitate, and glyceryl stearate.

Silicones are a group of oils that are chemically combined with silicon and oxygen and leave a noncomedogenic protective film on the surface of the skin. They also act as vehicles (for spreading) in some products, including makeup foundations. They are excellent protectants, helping to keep moisture trapped in the skin yet allowing oxygen in and out of the follicles. Silicones also add an elegant, non-greasy feel to products. Examples of silicones are dimethicone, cyclomethicone, and phenyl trimethicone. These ingredients are frequently used in sunscreens, foundations, and moisturizers.

Emollients and Comedogenicity

Many emollient ingredients such as oils and fatty acids can cause or worsen the development of comedones in the skin. These emollients are said to be comedogenic, which means they block pores.

Comedogenicity (kahm-uh-do-jen-IS-suh-tee) is the tendency of any topical substance to cause or to worsen a buildup of dead cells in the follicle, leading to the development of a comedo (blackhead).

Emollients that are comedogenic are not intended for clog-prone or acne-prone skin. Oilier skin produces enough of its own emollient, as sebum, and thus does not need more. Dry skin that does not produce enough sebum may need heavier emollient ingredients to protect the skin from dehydration. This type of skin does not clog easily and is not acne prone. Not all emollients and oils are comedogenic. Common comedogenic ingredients are shown in Table 13–7 on page 329.

Surfactants

One of the biggest categories of cosmetic ingredients is ***surfactants***. Surfactants reduce the surface tension between the skin and the product, and increase the spreadability of cosmetic products. Detergents and emulsifiers are surfactants.

Detergents

The main types of surfactants used in skin-cleansing products are **detergents**. They reduce the surface tension of the dirt and oil on the skin's surface and form an emulsion to lift them from the skin (Figure 13–4). These are not the type of detergents you associate with washing clothes, but they are from the same chemical family. Detergents are used primarily in cleansing products.

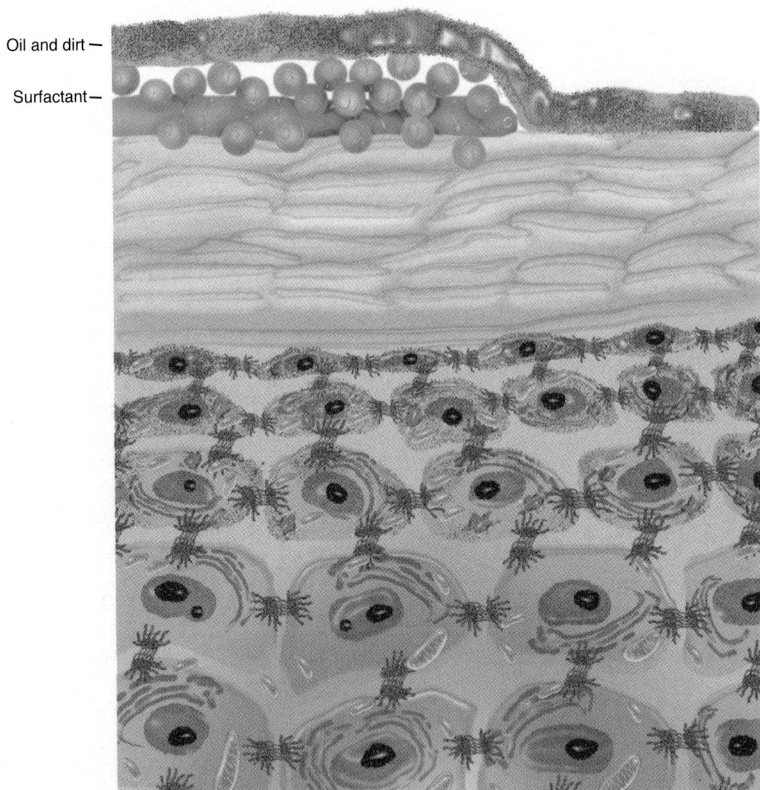

Figure 13–4
Detergents reduce the surface tension of dirt and oils and lift them from the skin.

They are also the agents that cause cleansers to foam. Detergents that are too strong can remove too much sebum and actually damage the lipid barrier function of the skin.

Some common detergent examples are sodium lauryl sulfate, sodium laureth sulfate (derived from coconut oil), and ammonium lauryl sulfate. There is scientific debate on the health concerns regarding sodium lauryl sulfate, but it can be a skin irritant. Do not confuse lauryl and laureth, as they are two very different things.

Cleansers are soaps and/or detergents that clean the skin. Soaps may be combined with detergents to make cleansers.

Emulsifiers

Emulsifiers are another category of surfactants. In fact, some detergents can also act as emulsifiers. **Emulsifiers** are surfactants that cause oil and water to mix to form an emulsion. Without emulsifiers, oil and water would separate into layers. Emulsifiers surround oil particles, allowing them to remain evenly distributed throughout the water (**Figure 13–5**).

When skin care products are mixed, materials that are compatible with oil are mixed in with the oil. These substances are called **oil soluble**, and they are mixed into the oil phase of the product during manufacturing. Substances that are mixable with water are known as **water soluble** and are mixed in the water phase. Examples of emulsifiers are polysorbate and potassium cetyl sulfate.

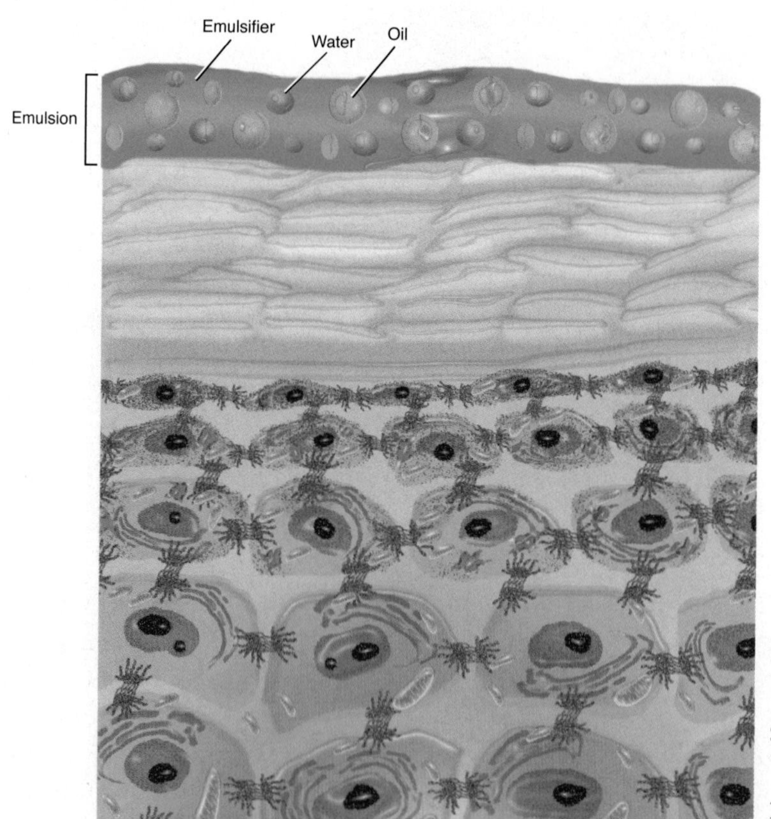

▶ Figure 13–5
In an emulsion, an emulsifier is added to the oil and water process.

Gellants and Thickeners

Gellants are agents that are used to give a product a gel-like consistency. Certain vehicle ingredients are added to thicken products or to help suspend ingredients that are hard to mix into a product. One example is **carbomers** (KAHR-boh-murz), which are used to thicken creams and are frequently used in gel products.

Fragrances

People love wonderful scents, especially in products they associate with relaxation, such as bath oils and bath salts. **Fragrances** can come from plant, animal, or synthetic sources, but plant oils are especially popular. These perfumes give products their scent. Essential oils are often used for their natural fragrance.

Aromatherapy is the therapeutic use of plant aromas and essential oils for beauty and health treatment purposes. **Essential oils** are highly concentrated plant oils with properties that can have various effects on the skin. Essential oils are also used to relax, stimulate, or balance the psyche (Figure 13–6). Aromatherapy has been used medically for thousands of years, and it is still used today in treatments and products.

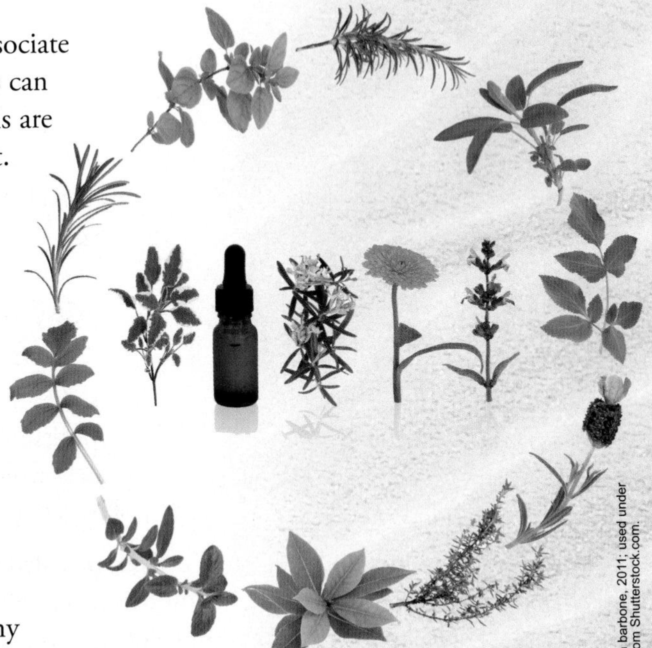

▲ Figure 13–6
Essential oils are frequently used in skin care products.

Preservatives

Preservatives are an important functional ingredient in many skin care and cosmetic products. **Preservatives** prevent bacteria and other microorganisms from living in a product. Without preservatives, products could easily be contaminated with bacteria, fungi, molds, or other microorganisms that could cause disease in the person using the product. Examples of preservatives used in skin care products are chelating agents.

A **chelating agent** (CHE-layt-ing A-junt) is a chemical that is added to cosmetics to improve the efficiency of the preservative. Chelating agents work by breaking down the cell walls of bacteria and other microorganisms. Common chelating ingredients are disodium EDTA, trisodium EDTA, and tetrasodium EDTA. EDTA is an acronym for the chemical name *ethylene-diamine-tetra-acetic acid.* These ingredients are usually on the bottom of the ingredient list because they are used in small quantities. Parabens, quaternium (kwah-TAYR-nee-um) 15, and urea are all preservatives and some of these remain controversial due to their irritancy or other health concerns. There are debates on whether parabens accumulate in the body and disrupt hormones.

FOCUS ON
Aromatherapy
Essential oils are the fragrant soul of the plant.

Besides fighting bacteria, preservatives help protect products from chemical changes that can adversely affect the product. *Antioxidants* are substances that inhibit oxidation reactions. They are used to help the condition of the skin by combating free radicals as well as stopping the oxidation that causes products to turn rancid and spoil. Common antioxidants used as preservatives are ascorbic acid, BHA, BHT and tocopherol.

Color Agents

Color agents serve several purposes. In skin care products, they add color, which mainly enhances a product's visual appeal. In color cosmetics, of course, the color agents are responsible for most of the product's cosmetic effects. They give color to products such as eye shadows, lipsticks, and foundations. **Colorants** are vegetable, pigment, or mineral dyes that give products color.

The FDA closely regulates color agent ingredients. There are two types of color ingredients: certified colors and noncertified colors.

Certified colors are synthetic, inorganic, and are known as metal salts. These are colorants that have been batch certified and approved by the FDA.

Noncertified colors are organic (carbon-based) compounds from animal or plants extracts and can also be natural mineral pigments. Noncertified colors are less irritating than certified colors, making them more useful for cosmetics applied to the eye area, for example. They are listed on ingredient labels as "D&C," which stands for *drug & cosmetic* or "FD&C," which stands for *food, drug, & cosmetic.*

Lakes are insoluble pigments made by combining a dye with an inorganic material and are commonly used in colorful cosmetics. These colorants can be blended to produce many different colors for skin care products and makeup.

Exempt colors, those that do not require certification, include zinc oxide, iron oxides, carmine, mica, and the ultramarine colors. They are less intense in color than certified colors. Nonetheless, zinc oxide and iron oxide help with opacity, meaning that they provide a solid color that is not transparent. They are used extensively in coverage makeup products such as foundations.

Other Product Components

pH adjustors—Substances called pH adjusters are acids or alkalis (bases) used to adjust the pH of products. Buffering ingredients stabilize products and prevent changes in pH. Sodium hydroxide and citric acid are often used as pH adjusters. These are functional ingredients.

Solvents—These are substances, such as water or alcohol, that dissolve other ingredients. These are functional ingredients.

Botanicals—Ingredients derived from plants. Performance ingredients used in phytotherapy are derived from plants and have many functions.

Healing agents—These are substances such as chamomile, licorice, azulene, and aloe that heal the skin. These are performance ingredients.

Hydrators and Moisturizers

Hydrators, **humectants** (hyoo-MEK-tents), and **hydrophilic agents** are ingredients that attract water to the skin's surface. They can lock water on the skin, reducing dehydration. Many humectants are available including glycerin, sodium PCA, sorbitol, seaweed extracts, algae (AL-jee) extract, hyaluronic acid (HY-uh-lur-AHN-ik A-sid), and propylene glycol.

Most moisturizing products are combinations of emollients and humectants. Thousands of possible combinations exist. These combinations determine the differences between moisturizers, creams, lotions, and fluids. Thicker creams have more emollients than lotions or fluids.

Lipids

Lipids are used to improve hydration, plumpness, and smoothness of the skin. They can also reduce sensitivity by making the skin more resistant to irritants and dehydration. Common lipid ingredients are sphingolipids, phospholipids, and glycosphingolipids. These ceramides (a family of lipid molecules), also found naturally in the intercellular matrix, are all known to improve the barrier function of the skin.

Exfoliating Ingredients

Exfoliation (eks-foh-lee-AY-shun), or the removal of dead corneum cells on the epidermis, improves the skin's appearance. **Exfoliants** are mechanical and chemical ingredients that exfoliate the skin. Mechanical exfoliating ingredients are added to products to physically scrape dead cells from the skin's surface. The ingredients include polyethylene and jojoba beads, ground nuts such as almonds, and various seeds.

Exfoliation can also be achieved through chemical action (**Figure 13–7**). **Alpha hydroxy acids (AHAs)** and **beta hydroxy acids (BHAs)** are naturally occurring mild acids used as chemical exfoliants. Glycolic, lactic, malic, citric, and tartaric are AHA's. Salicylic (sal-uh-SIL-ik) acid is a BHA, which is not as strong as an AHA. Citric acid was originally cited as a BHA, but is now considered a mild AHA. This has to do with the chemical composition of the acids.

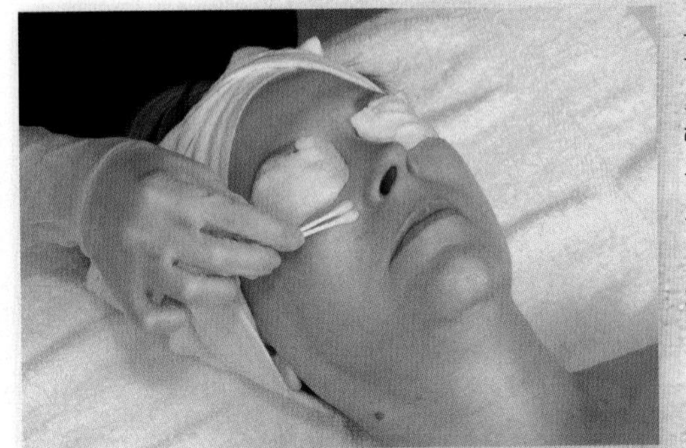

▲ Figure 13–7
Applying an AHA product.

These exfoliants work by loosening the bond between cells in the epidermis. They can also help to lighten pigmented areas, soften rough skin, and heal areas that are prone to breakouts. Any of these exfoliants can be added to other products. Acids come in a variety of concentrations and pH levels that affect the potency and irritancy of a given product. A product with the same concentration of hydroxy acid is more irritating at a lower pH. A concentration of 10 percent or less and a pH of 3.5 or greater is recommended for over-the-counter products and home use. Sun protection is necessary when using chemical exfoliants.

Enzymes

Enzymes such as papain, bromelain, and pancreatin (pan-cre-a-tin) are also used in exfoliating products. These ingredients are designed to dissolve keratin proteins on the surface of the skin to make it softer, smoother, and help maintain the hydration level of the epidermis. Once the dead skin cells are gently removed, the skin is clearer and can absorb products more easily. This is true for all types of exfoliants.

Lighteners and Brighteners

Lighteners and brighteners are ingredients that are used in the bleaching or lightening of the skin, actually "lifting" a darker pigmented area to a lighter color. Commonly used ingredients are hydroquinone, kojic acid, arbutin, vitamin C, licorice root, bearberry, green tea extract, and alpha hydroxy and beta hydroxy acids. These ingredients work either by bleaching the upper layers of the epidermis or by slowing down the pigment factories in the skin, known as melanocytes, thus blocking the production of melanin. These ingredients are also known as tyrosinase inhibitors. *Tyrosinase* (TY-ruh-sin-ays) is the enzyme that converts tyrosine, an amino acid, into melanin. When using these products, it is important for clients to wear sunscreen to protect the skin and to prevent the pigmented areas from returning. Hydroquinone is another controversial ingredient due to health concerns.

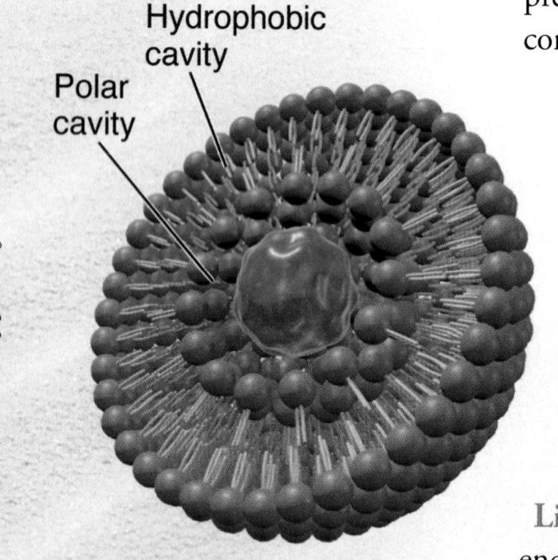

▲ Figure 13–8
Liposomes can encapsulate and transport water-soluble ingredients in their polar cavity and oil-soluble ingredients in their hydrophobic cavity.

Delivery Systems

Delivery systems are chemical systems that deliver ingredients to specific areas of the epidermis. Vehicles, liposomes, and polymers are three types of delivery systems.

Vehicles are spreading agents and carrying bases necessary to the formulation of a cosmetic. Water and emollients are both vehicles. Vehicles carry or deliver other ingredients into the skin and make them more effective.

Liposomes (LY-puh-zohms) are closed lipid bilayer spheres that encapsulate ingredients, target their delivery to specific areas of the skin, and control their release (Figure 13–8). The bilayer structure of liposomes mimics cell membranes and is therefore compatible with cells—in contrast to standard *micelle* emulsions, which disrupt and damage cell membranes in the delivery process.

Polymers (PAHL-uh-murs) are chemical compounds formed by a number of small molecules. One use of polymers is in delivery systems. They are used as advanced vehicles that release substances onto the skin's surface at a microscopically controlled rate. They are also referred to as microsponges.

Performance Ingredients That Improve Cell Metabolism

A major goal of advanced skin care treatments is to help the skin function at its maximum capacity at any age. Improvements in cell turnover that emulates younger skin together with nutrients to facilitate this process can slow the appearance of aging. While it is impossible to reverse major damage, a well-planned skin care program can reduce the signs of aging. A number of high-tech ingredients serve as antioxidants and actually stimulate metabolic processes. Many of these ingredients are found naturally in the body and are designed to be compatible with natural cellular functions. Other high-tech ingredients are also briefly discussed here.

Polyglucans (PAHL-ee-glue-kans) and **beta-glucans** (BAY-tuh GLUE-kans) are used to enhance the skin's defense mechanism and stimulate cell metabolism. They are normally derived from yeast cells and have a natural affinity for the skin. A polyglucan is hydrophilic, absorbing more than 10 times its weight in water. Polyglucans also help preserve hydration, collagen, and elastin by forming a protective film on the skin. Beta-glucans help reduce the appearance of fine lines and wrinkles by stimulating the formation of collagen.

Tissue respiratory factor (TRF) is also derived from yeast cells. TRF functions as an anti-inflammatory and moisturizing ingredient.

Stem cells are being derived from plants to protect or stimulate our own skin stem cells. This is for health and antiaging benefits. Stem cell ingredients derived from grapes and apples may help protect the stem cells in the skin. There will be many developments in this research science in the years to come.

Epidermal Growth Factor (EGF) stimulates cell division and is used for healing wounds or burns. Skin contains its own natural EGF. The research on these and other ingredients continues to advance rapidly.

Peptides

Peptides are chains of amino acids used in skin care products to produce changes in the skin's appearance. Peptides have been shown to help aging skin by improving tissue repair and skin functions such as cell and fibroblast activity. Collagen, elasticity, and skin firmness are all considered to be enhanced by peptides. Two of the more common peptide ingredients are palmitoyl pentapeptide-3 and palmitoyl oligopeptide. Copper peptides are another effective formulation. Peptides are less irritating than some of the other ingredients for aging skin, and they are often used along with other ingredients such as hydrators and antioxidants.

Glycoproteins (gly-koh-PRO-teens), also called glycopolypeptides, another yeast cell derivative, have been found to enhance immune response and cellular metabolism, which boosts oxygen uptake in the cell. This revitalizing capacity strengthens the skin's natural ability to protect itself against damaging environmental influences. Glycoproteins are skin conditioning agents derived from carbohydrates and proteins. These are especially beneficial to skin that appears unhealthy, is dull from smoking, has diffused redness, or has environmental damage.

Retinol and Retinoic Acid (Retin-A®)

A natural form of vitamin A, **retinol** (RET-in-all) stimulates cell repair and helps to normalize skin cells by generating new cells. It has been used in serums, creams, and lotions and varies in concentration when used either as a cosmetic or a drug. As with many cosmetic ingredients, more than a trace amount is necessary

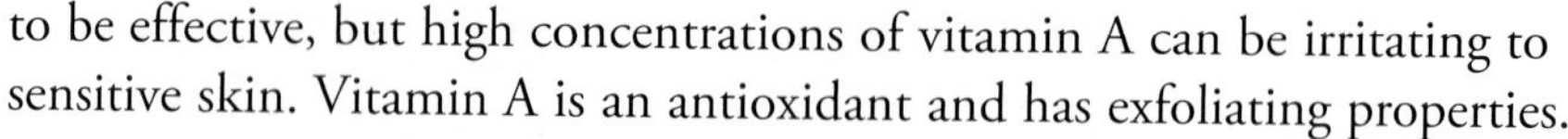

to be effective, but high concentrations of vitamin A can be irritating to sensitive skin. Vitamin A is an antioxidant and has exfoliating properties.

Retinoic acid (Retin-A®, Renova®, Tazorac®) is also a form of vitamin A approved as an active drug ingredient. It is of the **keratolytic** (kair-uh-tuh-LIT-ik) group, meaning that it causes sloughing, or exfoliating, of skin cells. It is used for skin problems such as acne, sun-damaged skin, and wrinkles. Because many people have moderate to severe reactions to retinoic acid, a physician must be treating anyone using retinoids.

Vitamins and Other Antioxidants

Antiaging products and treatments are a main focus of the skin care industry. Antioxidants are one of the most effective treatments for the skin. *Antioxidants* are vitamins, amino acids, and other natural substances that neutralize the damaging effects of free radicals and help skin cope with the damaging effects of environmental influences. Aging or sun-damaged skin needs antioxidants both topically and orally.

Antioxidants, applied topically, neutralize free radicals before they can attach themselves to cell membranes and destroy the cells. These are also added to cosmetic formulations to prevent the oxidation that causes a product to turn rancid and spoil.

Antioxidants play a vital role in maintaining the quality, integrity, and safety of cosmetic products. Typical cosmetic antioxidants include reducing agents and free radical scavengers.

Vitamins A, C, and E have been used in skin care products as antioxidants for many years. It is believed that they work by interfering with inflammation, thus reducing the production of enzymes that injure and destroy skin cells. Other antioxidants include alphalipoic acid, idebenone, stearyl glycyrrhizinate, green tea, and grapeseed. When used in combinations, these formulas are called broad-spectrum antioxidants that give a greater range of protection.

Antioxidants can help prevent wrinkles, promote skin healing, and reduce the formation of scar tissue (presurgical and postsurgical). Vitamins A and E (fat soluble) protect the phospholipid structure of the cell membrane. Vitamin C (water soluble) guards the inside of cells and DNA.

Free Radicals

Antioxidants are included in many skin care formulas designed to combat free radicals. *Free radicals* are aggressive, unstable, oxygen-containing molecules. They have lost an electron and need to steal other electrons from other molecules, thereby damaging the cells they steal from.

Free radicals are *super* oxidizers that not only cause an oxidation reaction but also produce a new free radical in the process. Normal oxidation deactivates the oxidizer and stops the reaction from continuing, but the oxidation reaction caused by free radicals continues in a chain reaction that can go on forever. One free radical can oxidize millions of other compounds.

Free radicals damage cell membranes and normal cellular metabolism systems. They can also damage DNA and RNA, and they contribute to the hardening of collagen and elastin cells. This all leads to premature aging and increases skin sensitivity, irritation, age spots, and dryness.

Antioxidant Ingredients

Here are some of the most widely used antioxidants:

- **Vitamin C** (L-ascorbic acid) is a water-soluble antioxidant. It strengthens the white blood cells and immune system and is essential for producing collagen.
- **Ester Vitamin C**, also called *Ester C*, is joined by a chemical ester bond with a fatty acid derived from palm oil (palmitic acid). It is oil-soluble and is absorbed into the skin much more easily than water-soluble ingredients are. It is highly stable and maintains its effectiveness when mixed with other ingredients. Vitamin C ester stimulates fibroblasts and cell metabolism.
- **Alpha lipoic acid** is a natural molecule found in every cell in the body. It is a powerful antioxidant and is soluble in water and oil. This antioxidant increases cellular metabolism and the effects of other antioxidants. Alpha lipoic acid is also anti-inflammatory and reduces redness.
- **DMAE (dimethylaminoethanol)** (dy-meth-il-uh-MEEN-noh-eth-uh-nol) is an antioxidant that stabilizes cell membranes. It also boosts the effects of other antioxidants. DMAE increases chemicals that control muscle tone, thus improving the appearance of sagging skin.
- **Coenzyme Q10** is considered a powerful antioxidant that protects and revitalizes skin cells. It is often formulated with other natural protective ingredients to strengthen the capillary network and increase energy to epidermal cells. It seems to fortify the skin's immune function and activate metabolic functions. Use of CoQ10 often results in visible reduction of wrinkles and fine lines.

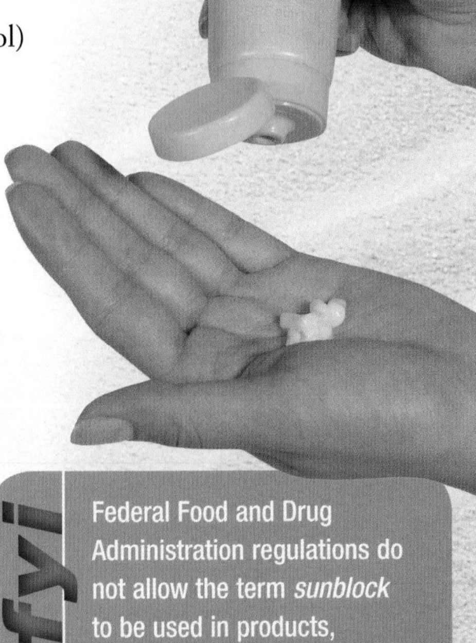

Sunscreen Ingredients

There are two types of active sunscreen ingredients. Chemical sunscreens are organic (carbon based) compounds that chemically absorb ultraviolet radiation. Physical sunscreens are inorganic (without carbon) compounds that physically reflect or scatter ultraviolet radiation. The **sun protection factor (SPF)** of ingredients is the ability of a product to delay sun-induced erythema, the visible sign of sun damage. SPF is based on the UVB protection, not the UVA protection. This is why the UVA exposure can be greater when using sunscreens. The estimated SPF is not just based on the exposure time, but also on the sun's intensity, skin type, product application, and other factors.

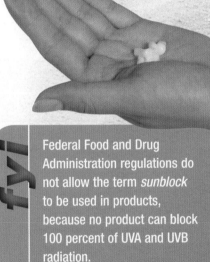

fyi
Federal Food and Drug Administration regulations do not allow the term *sunblock* to be used in products, because no product can block 100 percent of UVA and UVB radiation.

The reactions of chemicals and additives in sunscreen formulas are complex. The photostability of products exposed to UV radiation and the potential photoallergic reactions from using sunscreen in susceptible individuals are considerations in product choices. Fragrances and preservatives in sunscreens can also cause skin allergies and irritation.

FOCUS ON

Chemistry

PEG is the acronym for *polyethylene glycol.* PEGs are blended into many formulations as solvents, binders (substances such as glycerin that bind, or hold, products together), vehicles, humectants, and bases for enhanced results. The number listed with the name (PEG-4, PEG-75) is the weight of the molecular chain as measured in moles.

Examples of *organic* chemical sunscreens are:

- Octinoxate (octyl methoxycinnimate)
- Octisalate (octyl salicylate)
- Oxybenzone (benzophenone)

Examples of *inorganic* physical sunscreens are:

- Titanium dioxide
- Zinc oxide

Natural versus Synthetic Ingredients

A combination of both natural and synthetic ingredients is one of the best chemical formulations. Natural products directly from nature can have powerful skin benefits; however, some of the most effective cosmetic ingredients are not derived from plants. Synthetically produced ingredients can be just as effective and may have certain advantages over ingredients derived naturally from plants.

Natural and synthetic ingredients can both have drawbacks. Natural ingredients may cause allergies in people who are sensitive, while synthetic versions of the same ingredients may not. Certain synthetic ingredients are effective cell renewal stimulants. It should be remembered, though, that synthetic ingredients may have unhealthy chemicals and do not harness the real essence or purity of plants or oils.

Many manufacturers are combining natural ingredients and synthetic ingredients to obtain the best of both worlds. Clients will prefer one

▼ Table 13–1
Functional Ingredients.

FUNCTIONAL INGREDIENTS		
COMPONENTS	**CATEGORIES OF INGREDIENTS**	**EXAMPLES OF INGREDIENTS**
Water	liquid	water
Emollients	oils, fatty acids, fatty alcohols, fatty esters, silicones	jojoba oil, olive oil, sesame, mineral oil
Surfactants	detergents, emulsifiers	laurel PCA, decyl polyglucose, polysorbate, sodium cocoate, sodium lauryl sulfate, TEA (triethanolamine)
Gellants/Thickeners	carbomers (polymers)	carbomer 934, carboxymethyl cellulose (cellulose gum), xanthan gum (cornstarch gum)
pH Adjusters	buffers	citric acid, sodium bicarbonate
Color Agents	certified, noncertified, exempt, lakes	D&C organic, zinc oxide, mica, mineral dyes, metal salts, inorganic (iron oxide)
Preservatives	antioxidants, antimicrobial, chelating agents	ascorbyl palmitate, imidazolidinyl urea, BHT, BHA EDTA, parabens, urea
Fragrances	natural, synthetic	lavender, essential oils
Solvents	alcohol, water	isopropyl alcohol, butylene glycol
Delivery Systems	vehicles, liposomes, polymers	cyclomethicone (silicone)

PERFORMANCE INGREDIENTS	
COMPONENTS	EXAMPLES OF INGREDIENTS
Antioxidants	vitamins A, C, and E, green tea (polyphenols), idebenone, coenzyme Q10 (ubiquinone)
Botanicals	plants, herbs
Brighteners	licorice root, kojic acid, vitamin C, mulberry extract
Chemical Exfoliants	AHA's, BHA's
Enzymes	papain (papaya), bromelain (pineapple), pumpkin
Healing Agents	licorice, aloe, chamomile
Hydrators	humectants (glycerin), hyaluronic acid, polyglucans, sodium PCA, sorbitol
Lipids	phospholipids, ceramides, sterols
Peptides	palmitoyl pentapeptide 4, palmitoyl oligopeptide

◀ Table 13–2
Performance Ingredients.

philosophy over the other and will be attracted to either natural or more clinical products. Knowing the benefits of both is important for estheticians and for those selling products.

Sometimes it can be difficult to know when to choose natural ingredients or synthetic ones—both make tremendous contributions to skin care formulations.

Manufacturers do extensive research and development to bring the latest technologies into cosmetic formulations. For example, hyaluronic acid, an ingredient used to bind moisture, was initially derived from roosters' combs. Synthetic production of this ingredient was developed, and today it is derived from synthetic sources for use in cosmetics. The synthetic version is more stable and has more effective water-binding properties.

To make informed choices, estheticians must stay current with developments in cosmetic chemistry. Combining both natural and synthetic ingredients is effective in product formulations. The quality and the sources of ingredients are both important factors to consider when choosing products.

Organic Ingredients

Organic ingredients are intended to be natural products that are grown without the use of pesticides or chemicals. Ideally, they are harvested and manufactured in a more natural way. Unfortunately there is no organic labeling standard for cosmetics in the United States at this time.

The USDA may certify organic products that meet the standards through the National Organic Program as applied to agricultural products. The content of organically produced ingredients must be

CAUTION!

If a client has an allergic reaction to a product that requires medical treatment, the manufacturer of the product is responsible—unless the product was purchased in bulk, repackaged by the salon in smaller containers, and resold, in which case the salon is at fault. If the product is made in the salon, the salon is also responsible. Malpractice insurance does not generally cover products formulated or repackaged in the salon.

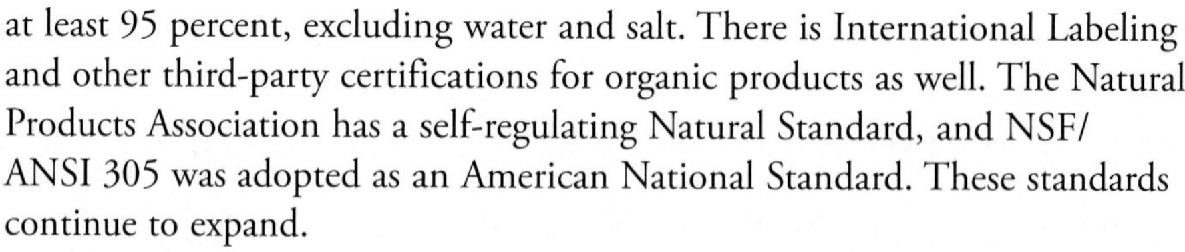

at least 95 percent, excluding water and salt. There is International Labeling and other third-party certifications for organic products as well. The Natural Products Association has a self-regulating Natural Standard, and NSF/ANSI 305 was adopted as an American National Standard. These standards continue to expand.

It is difficult to formulate products without preservatives and other functional ingredients to stabilize the product. Additionally, most products are 60 to 90 percent water, so the product may be labeled organic by the water alone. Marketing statements do not always tell the whole story. False claims are common in the billion-dollar skin care industry.

On a positive note, green chemistry is becoming more common with manufacturers that are improving their processing to reduce their effects on the environment. Many ingredients such as herbs, fruits, and oils are grown organically. Society is more aware of environmental effects on the planet and the health benefits of using more "organic" products.

Products that are considered "green" are more sustainable, which generally means they are not as harmful to the environment due to practices such as the ingredients used, the manufacturing processes, or the resources that are conserved.

Scientific research is expanding the knowledge of how chemicals and ingredients affect our health. Organic ingredients are becoming more popular as consumer demand increases. New organic product lines are flourishing. Technological advances have also made it easier to blend effective skin care products from organic and natural sources. ✓ L01

Product Safety

The FDA does not require approval of cosmetics before their manufacture and sale. The FDA does require that all drugs be proven safe and effective before their manufacture and sale. The FDA regulates cosmetics only in the areas of safety, labeling, and the claims made for a product. If a cosmetic product makes a drug claim, is not properly labeled, or has been reported as unsafe, the FDA can take legal action against the manufacturer. Drugs may claim to change a function of the body. Cosmetics may claim only to change the appearance of the body.

FDA regulations for cosmetic labeling state that cosmetic companies must list the company's name, location, or distribution point as well as all the ingredients in the product. This allows consumers to check for ingredients they may be allergic to. Ingredients must be listed in descending order of predominance, starting with the ingredient having the highest concentration and ending with the ingredient having the lowest concentration. Ingredients with a concentration of less than 1 percent may be listed in any order. A fragrance must be listed as "fragrance," but the ingredients need not be listed.

Allergic Reactions

Many ingredients used in skin care products—including fragrances, essential oils, and preservatives—may cause adverse skin reactions. Being aware of a client's allergies and the ingredients being used in treatments is very important to avoid problems or reactions. Sometimes a product or treatment will cause a reaction. If the skin becomes excessively red or the client complains of burning, immediately remove the product and rinse the skin with cold water. Having a cortisone cream available and products to calm skin reactions is a recommended precaution.

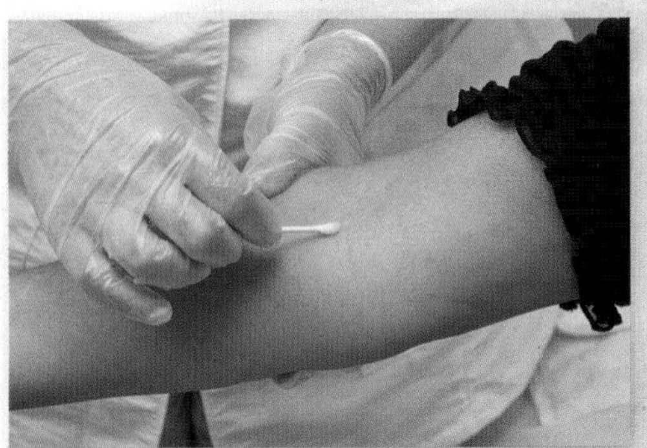

▲ Figure 13–9
A patch test is the best way to determine if a client is allergic to a product.

Fragrances and some preservatives are among the most common allergens. Allergic reactions may not be detected until several days later. Symptoms may include inflammation of the skin, burning or itching, blisters, blotches, or rashes. The eyes may swell, puff, or produce tears.

The best way to guard against allergic reactions is to pretest a small quantity of the product with a test patch (Figure 13–9). Before the treatment, conduct a patch test on clients with reactive skin. Try the product on the inside of the arm, near the elbow, or on a small area of the face.

If there is any reaction within 24 hours, the product should not be used. If the reaction is serious, the product should be taken to a physician who can determine what has caused the problem and then treat the condition appropriately. The manufacturer of the product should be notified immediately.

Always follow strict cleaning procedures in treatment areas and elsewhere in the salon. Products must be kept clean and stored properly. Close containers when not in use. Do not share cosmetics with anyone else. Never use saliva to moisten eye makeup or other cosmetics; use only fresh, clean water. Discard outdated, rancid, or stale products. Products stored in dark containers and in cooler temperatures will last longer. ✓ LO2

Ingredients

Choosing products that are effective for a person's individual needs is the most important part of any treatment and home-care regime. Results are more noticeable when products are used correctly. The next section in this chapter includes a partial list of ingredients used in skin care and beauty products. Their definitions and properties are included in Tables 13–3 through 13–7 on the following pages.

Many products are made synthetically rather than from plants or animal products. It is important to know the source of the ingredient, particularly if clients have a preference for one type over another. The source of the ingredient and the manufacturing process determine the quality and effectiveness of the product.

FOCUS ON

Controversial Ingredients

Controversial ingredients used in products include sodium lauryl sulfate; parabens and other preservatives; color agents; nanoparticles; and phthalates (plasticizers). Accutane and hydroquinone are also controversial. Scientific research and testing continues to determine potential side effects from using certain chemicals. Some concerns are valid, while others are not yet proven. There are many rumors and incorrect information is prevalent on the Internet. Estheticians and consumers need to research and verify facts from reliable sources to determine what the real concerns are.

COMMON PRODUCT COMPONENTS AND INGREDIENTS (Natural and Synthetic)	
INGREDIENT	**DESCRIPTION**
AHAs/BHAs	Chemical exfoliators. Glycolic, lactic, malic, citric, and tartaric are AHA's. Salicylic, a BHA, is not as strong. These exfoliants work by loosening the bond between cells in the epidermis.
Alcohol	Used as an antiseptic and solvent in perfumes, lotions, and astringents. There are many types of alcohols; not all are drying.
Alum	A compound made of aluminum, potassium, or ammonium sulfate. An astringent, antiseptic, and stimulating. Good for oily skin; also stops bleeding.
Benzyl Peroxide	A drying ingredient with antibacterial properties commonly used for blemishes and acne. It can be a skin allergen and irritant.
Ceramides	A family of lipid materials found in skin's intercellular matrix; a natural moisturizing factor; products help lipid replacement and combat dryness, aging, and dehydration.
Collagen	Protein derived from animals or synthetically manufactured. Plumps the surface of the skin and prevents water loss.
Essential Oils	Oils derived from plants and herbs; they have many different properties and effects on the skin and psyche.
Glycerin	Formed by a decomposition of oils or fats, glycerin is an excellent skin softener and humectant as well as a very strong water binder.
Herbs	These, along with plant extracts, contain phytohormones. Hundreds of different herbs are used in skin care products and cosmetics to help heal, stimulate, soothe, and moisturize. Herbs are also used as astringents.
Hyaluronic Acid	A hydrophilic agent with excellent water-binding properties.
Lanolin	An emollient with moisturizing properties, lanolin is a sheep's wool derivative formed by a secretion of the sheep's sebaceous glands.
Lipids	Fat or fat-like substances; improves hydration and the barrier function of the skin.
Liposomes	Closed-lipid bilayer spheres that encapsulate ingredients, targeting their delivery to specific tissues of the skin, and controlling their release.
Methylparaben	One of the most frequently used preservatives because of its very low sensitizing potential; one of the oldest preservatives in use to combat bacteria and molds. It is noncomedogenic. May be an irritant. See parabens.
Mineral Oil	An emollient and lubricant; mineral oil is a clear, odorless substance derived from petroleum.
Mucopolysaccharides	Made of carbohydrate–lipid complexes; good water binders.
Parabens	One of the most commonly used groups of preservatives in the cosmetic, pharmaceutical, and food industries, parabens provide antibacterial and antifungal activity against a diverse number of organisms. There are health debates on parabens as to whether they accumulate in the body and disrupt hormones.
Peptides	Chains of amino acids that stimulate fibroblasts, cell metabolism, and improve skin's firmness. Larger chains are called polypeptides.
Petroleum Jelly	An occlusive agent that protects the barrier layer by holding in water. It is used after laser surgery to protect the skin as it heals.
Potassium Hydroxide	A strong alkali used in soaps and creams.

▲ Table 13–3
Common Product Components and Ingredients.

continued

COMMON PRODUCT COMPONENTS AND INGREDIENTS (Natural and Synthetic)

INGREDIENT	DESCRIPTION
Propylene Glycol	A humectant often used in dry or sensitive skin moisturizers.
Quaternium 15	An all-purpose preservative active against bacteria, mold, and yeast, this ingredient is probably the greatest formaldehyde-releaser among cosmetic preservatives; may cause dermatitis and allergies.
Retinoic Acid	A vitamin A derivative, retinoic acid has demonstrated an ability to alter collagen synthesis. It is used to treat acne and visible signs of aging. Side effects are irritation, photosensitivity, skin dryness, redness, and peeling.
Salicylic Acid	A beta hydroxy acid with exfoliating and antiseptic properties, its natural sources include sweet birch, willow bark, and wintergreen. Check for client allergies to this acid and to aspirin.
Silicone	Oil that is chemically combined with silicon and oxygen and leaves a noncomedogenic, protective film on the surface of the skin.
Sodium bicarbonate	Baking soda; an inorganic salt used as a buffering agent, neutralizer, and a pH adjuster.
Sorbitol	A humectant that absorbs moisture from the air to prevent skin dryness. In dry climates, if the skin's moisture content is greater than the atmosphere, humectants such as sorbitol will draw moisture out of the skin. It is obtained from the leaves and berries of mountain ash. It also occurs in other berries, cherries, plums, pears, apples, seaweed, and algae.
Sphingolipids	A ceramide; lipid materials that are a natural part of the intercellular matrix. Glycosphingolipids and phospholipids are also natural lipids found in the barrier layer.
Squalane	Derived from olives, squalane is an emollient, desensitizing agent, and nourishing.
Squalene	Originally from shark-liver oil, squalene occurs in small amounts in olive oil, wheat germ oil, and rice bran oil. It is also found in human sebum. Insoluble in water, it is a lubricant and perfume fixative.
Sulfur	Sulfur reduces oil-gland activity and dissolves the skin's surface layer of dry, dead cells. This ingredient is commonly used in acne products. It can cause allergic skin reactions in some sensitive people and those allergic to sulfur or sulfates.
Titanium Dioxide	An inorganic sunscreen that reflects UVA and UVB. When applied, it remains on the skin surface, basically scattering the UV radiation. Used in sunscreen, makeup bases, and daytime moisturizers; also used to give cosmetics a white color.
Urea	Properties of urea include enhancing the penetration abilities of other substances. It is anti-inflammatory and an antiseptic; its deodorizing action protects the skin's surface and helps maintain healthy skin.
Vitamins	Vitamins are organic compounds and essential nutrients. Vitamins A, C, E, and K are beneficial to the skin for many reasons.
Zinc Oxide	An inorganic sunscreen that reflects UVB and UVA. Also used to protect, soothe, and heal the skin. Zinc oxide is somewhat astringent, antiseptic, and antibacterial. It is obtained from zinc ore and is nonallergenic.

▲ Table 13–3 **(continued)**

INGREDIENTS FROM NATURE

Some of the following natural ingredients are derived from plants (phytotherapy), and some are also produced synthetically.

INGREDIENT	DESCRIPTION	PRIMARY BENEFITS
Algae	Derived from seaweed; contains minerals	Moisturizing, nourishing
Allantoin	Derived from the comfrey plant or uric acid; used in soothing products	Healing, promotes healthy tissue growth
Almond meal	Ground almonds; commonly used in scrubs	Soothing and exfoliating
Aloe vera	A versatile plant used in many products	Healing, soothing, hydrating, anti-inflammatory
Arnica	Healing; great for sore muscles, bruising	Anti-inflammatory
Avocado	An emollient; contains vitamins A and C	Moisturizing, soothing
Azulene	Derived from the chamomile plant; used for sensitive skin and calming	Anti-inflammatory, soothing
Bayberry	Root bark; good for oily skin	Antiseptic, astringent
Birch leaf	Good for oily skin	Antiseptic, stimulating
Calendula	From the marigold plant; good for itching, swelling, and acne	Healing, soothing, anti-inflammatory
Carrot	Used in creams and masks; rich in vitamin A	Antioxidant, moisturizing, soothing
Chamomile	Plant extract; used for sensitive skin	Calming, anti-inflammatory
Cocoa butter	Softens and lubricates; from the cocoa tree	Moisturizing
Coconut	Commonly used for oils, soaps, and creams	Lathers, cleanses, lubricates
Comfrey	Has many beneficial and soothing qualities; contains allantoin	Healing, moisturizing, emollient
Coneflower	Echinacea (ek-uh-NAY-shah) is from the coneflower; used internally to support the immune system	Healing, preventing infection
Cucumber	Commonly used for masks and the eye area to reduce puffiness	Antiseptic, soothing
Eucalyptus	From the gum tree; used for acne and oily skin	Antiseptic, antimicrobial, astringent, stimulating
Evening primrose	Soothing; known to help women's menstrual pain	Treats dry skin, flakiness; healing
Geranium	Calm irritation, an anti-irritant	Astringent, anti-inflammatory
Grapeseed extract	A soothing antioxidant derived from grapes	Healing, moisturizing, antiaging
Green tea	Many health benefits include lipid protection; antibacterial, stimulating	A strong antioxidant and anti-inflammatory
Horsechestnut	A plant extract with bioflavonoids (vitamin P); strengthens capillary walls	Good for couperose skin and redness
Jojoba	A widely used noncomedogenic oil derived from a desert shrub; healing	A soothing emollient, moisturizer, and lubricant
Kojic acid	A tyrosinase inhibitor; usually derived from mushrooms	A skin-lightening agent for hyperpigmentation
Lavender	A popular herb and oil used for aromatherapy and calming	Soothing, anti-inflammatory, antiseptic properties

▲ Table 13–4
Ingredients from Nature.

continued

INGREDIENTS FROM NATURE Some of the following natural ingredients are derived from plants (phytotherapy), and some are also produced synthetically.		
Licorice	An anti-irritant good for sensitive skin; also inhibits melanin production	Soothing, used to lighten surface hyper-pigmentation
Mint	An herb good for circulation	Stimulating, also an antiseptic
Oatmeal	Good for skin irritation, rashes, and sunburns; used in masks and scrubs	Soothing, anti-inflammatory, healing
Olive	Olive tree extracts are used for many beauty products	Moisturizing and calming
Orange	Soothing with an aromatic, uplifting scent	Anti-inflammatory, antibacterial, and an astringent
Papaya	Contains papain, an enzyme used in enzyme peels	Exfoliating, softening, moisturizing
Peppermint	Cools skin and constricts capillaries; has refreshing properties; contains menthol	Reduces irritation and itching
Pineapple	Contains bromelain, an enzyme with stimulating and antiseptic properties	Good for exfoliation and treating blemishes
Pomegranate	A powerful antioxidant; treats sun damage	Healing, fights free radicals
Rose	One of the most common ingredients in skin care products; used for dry, aging skin	Soothing and moisturizing
Sandalwood	An exotic scent used for aromatherapy; good for skin irritations	Soothing and antiseptic properties
Seaweed	Derivatives such as algae have many nourishing minerals and properties; detoxifies, stimulates metabolism; *may be a serious allergen if allergic to seaweed, shellfish, or iodine!*	Humectant and moisturizing properties, firming
Sesame	Used in massage and moisturizing products	Moisturizing
Shea butter	A natural fat used as heavier occlusive moisturizer.	Moisturizing and healing
Soy	A protein and a source of vitamins; an isoflavonoid (phytoestrogen) with antioxidant and anti-inflammatory properties	Anti-inflammatory, moisturizing
Tea tree	Good for oily skin and scalp treatments	Germicidal, healing antifungal, antiseptic
Witch hazel	From the hamanelis shrub; good for toning the skin	An astringent and antiseptic

▲ Table 13–4 **(continued)**

FOCUS ON

Nanotechnology

Nanoparticles are submicroscopic particles of matter that range from 1 to 100 nanometers in size. The width of one hair is about 70,000 nanometers. Substances in nanoparticle form can penetrate deeper into the skin and have a higher reactivity. Because of their unique properties, the use of nanoparticles in skin care products has exciting potential applications, but also may raise health concerns. Normally inert chemicals can trigger chemical reactions and disrupt cell activity when combined in nanoparticles. Additionally, these particles do not dissolve as readily so they may stay in the body longer. Research continues on this fascinating technology.

▶ Table 13–5
Essential Oils and Herbs.

ACTIVITY

Why are some products better than others? Take this opportunity to do some research. Go to a drugstore and compare its product prices and ingredients to those of a professional line. Comparing ingredients often reveals the answer to this question. Use a cosmetic ingredients dictionary to look up ingredients and learn more about the benefits or potential side effects.

ESSENTIAL OILS AND HERBS

Here are some common essential oils or herbs used for their aromatherapeutic properties as well as skin benefits.

INGREDIENT	PRIMARY PROPERTIES	SKIN BENEFITS
Benzoin	astringent	oily skin; acne
Bergamot	soothing	oily skin; acne
Birch leaf	stimulating	moisturizing
Eucalyptus	stimulating	increases circulation
Evening primrose	soothing	moisturizing
Frankincense	soothing	healing; rejuvenating
Geranium	stimulating	antiseptic; healing
Jasmine	soothing	moisturizing
Lavender	soothing	healing
Lemon	stimulating	antiseptic for acne; oily skin
Lemongrass	stimulating	antiseptic for acne; oily skin
Melissa (lemon balm)	soothing	soothes irritation
Myrrh	healing	soothes irritation; acne
Neroli	soothing	antiseptic for acne; oily skin
Orange	stimulating, uplifting	astringent
Patchouli	soothing	moisturizing
Peppermint	cooling	decreases circulation
Rose	soothing	moisturizing
Rosemary	stimulating	increases circulation
Rosewood	stimulating	healing; dry skin
Sandalwood	soothing	anti-inflammatory
Tea tree	stimulating	antiseptic; acne
Ylang-ylang	soothing	antiseptic; enhances circulation

▶ Table 13–6
Natural Food Ingredients and Their Benefits.

NATURAL FOOD INGREDIENTS AND THEIR BENEFITS

- Avocado—rich in vitamins and oil; beneficial for dry and sensitive skin.
- Cucumber—soothing and healing; commonly used as a mask or for eye pads.
- Eggs—egg white masks tone and tighten the skin.
- Herbs—many herbs and teas such as chamomile are used for masks and compresses.
- Honey—hydrating, toning, and tightening effects; used in masks and scrubs.
- Lemon— brightening, astringent.
- Oatmeal—soothing, healing; used in face and body masks.
- Papaya—exfoliating with enzymatic properties; papaya enzyme peels are popular.
- Potatoes—used for oily skin or to reduce puffiness in the eye area.
- Tea—reduces puffiness; great for the eyes.
- Yogurt—cleansing and mildly astringent; used in masks.

COMMON COMEDOGENIC INGREDIENTS		
HIGHLY COMEDOGENIC	**MODERATELY COMEDOGENIC**	**MILDLY COMEDOGENIC**
Linseed Oil	Decyl Oleate	Corn Oil
Olive Oil	Sorbitan Oleate	Safflower Oil
Cocoa Butter	Myristyl Lactate	Laury Alcohol
Oleic Acid	Coconut Oil	Lanolin Alcohol
Coal Tar	Grapeseed Oil	Glyceryl Stearate
Isopropyl Isostearate	Sesame Oil	Lanolin
Squalene	Hexylene Glycol	Sunflower Oil
Isopropyl Myristate	Tocopherol	Avocado Oil
Myristyl Myristate	Isostearyl Neopentanoate	Mineral Oil
Acetylated Lanolin	Most D & C Red Pigments	
Oleyl Alcohol	Octyldodecanol	
Octyl Palmitate	Peanut Oil	
Isostearic Acid	Lauric Acid	
Myreth 3 Myristate	Mink Oil	
Butyl Stearate		
Lanolic Acid		
*Note: Mildly comedogenic ingredients are generally not a problem when used in diluted concentrations. Check to see their ranking of concentration on the ingredient label.		
NONCOMEDOGENIC		
Glycerin	Water	Sodium Hyaluronate
Squalane	Iron Oxides	Octylmethoxycinnimate
Sorbitol	Dimethicone	Oxybenzone
Sodium PCA	Cyclomethicone	Petrolatum
Zinc Stearate	Polysorbates	Butylene Glycol
Octyldodecyl Stearate	Cetyl Palmitate	Tridecyl Stearate
SD Alcohol	Propylene Glycol Dicaprate	Tridecyl Trimellitate
Propylene Glycol	Propylene Glycol Dicaprylate	Octyldodecyl Stearoyl Stearate
Allantoin	Jojoba Oil	Phenyl Trimethicone
Panthenol	Isopropyl Alcohol	

▲ Table 13–7
Common Comedogenic Ingredients.

Herbs and Plant Properties

Another classification system is to list ingredients by the category or properties. The following is a partial list of plant and herbal properties that have astringent, stimulating, calming and/or soothing, healing, and hydrating properties. Many of the plants or herbs listed have more than one property or effect on the skin or senses. Check out aromatherapy and herb books for more information on this intriguing subject.

CAUTION!

Many people are allergic to seaweed and other ingredients such as salicylic acid and sulfur. A thorough consultation is imperative to avoid serious allergic reactions.

Herb and Plant properties:

- **Aromatic:** lavender, mint, rose, orange, eucalyptus
- **Antiseptic:** peppermint, tea tree, clove
- **Astringent:** comfrey root, witch hazel, alum root, lemon
- **Stimulating:** eucalyptus, wintergreen, spearmint
- **Calming:** comfrey root (allantoin), chamomile (azulene), almond
- **Cleansing:** lemongrass, aloe
- **Healing:** chamomile, comfrey, aloe
- **Moisturizing:** rose, chamomile

fyi

A necessary book for estheticians to have on hand is an ingredients dictionary, which lists the properties of hundreds of natural and synthetic ingredients. One example is *Milady's Skin Care and Cosmetic Ingredients Dictionary*, 2nd ed., published by Milady, a part of Cengage Learning.

Aromatherapy

Aromatherapy is an ancient healing practice using essential oils and aromas from plants to treat the body, mind, and spirit (**Figure 13–10a and b**). These plant components have medicinal and healing properties. The practice is used therapeutically for physical ailments and for mental balancing. Essential oils can affect the brain and emotions. The psychological benefits from essential oils depend on the oil chosen. Aromatherapy incorporated in esthetic services can make a treatment even more relaxing and effective.

To retain the plant's natural living properties, it must be extracted properly. Synthetically produced oils do not have the therapeutic value that natural oils retain. **Phytotherapy** is the use of plant extracts for therapeutic benefits. The different parts of the plants used for making products from oils and essences are the roots, bark, stem, seeds, and flowers. The extraction process can be expensive, and the way that essences are extracted determines their strength and quality.

Aromatherapy, a form of phytotherapy, must be used with caution. The pure oils are powerful and can irritate the skin or the senses if overused.

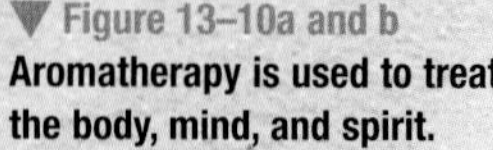

▼ Figure 13–10a and b
Aromatherapy is used to treat the body, mind, and spirit.

One or two drops of pure oil are usually enough. Some people are allergic to certain fragrances, and a wonderful facial could turn into an unpleasant experience if that oil is used. Study aromatherapy and the contraindications before using oils on clients.

There are many benefits of using aromatherapy oils for the skin. Oils can moisturize, stimulate, cleanse, soothe, and nourish. Plant extracts, teas, flowers, and fruits have therapeutic value when applied as compresses, masks, sprays, oils, or lotions.

The Olfactory System

The body's **olfactory system** gives us our sense of smell, which is the strongest of the five senses. Scents have a strong effect on our reactions to places, products, and other people. Memories are also brought on by familiar scents. Aromatherapy scents affect us because of the sensitive olfactory system. Fragrances are a large part of our everyday life, from food scents to our perfume. Notice how fragrance influences our moods and how much more relaxed we are when the scent of a favorite candle diffuses across the room. Different blends of scents have different effects, both physically and mentally.

Ingredients for Mature Skin

When working with mature skin, estheticians are expected to inform clients about the causes of their skin changes. Knowledge of hormone replacement, diet, and lifestyle influences is useful. Consider clients' needs, and use care when selecting treatments and suggesting home-care products.

Many ingredients are available to support the needs of mature skin. Topical ingredients need to have high-tech delivery systems, such as liposomes, to carry or deliver the ingredients effectively into the skin. One example of an effective formula to combat premature aging is a combination of alpha lipoic acid, vitamin C ester, DMAE, and glycolic acid. In addition to peptides and other antioxidants, the following ingredients are proven to have a positive effect on mature skin and rosacea:

- Green tea
- Dipotassium glycyrrhizate (licorice root)
- Squalane oil (vegetable oil from green olives)—rich in vitamins A, D, and E
- Seaweed
- Chamomile
- Micronized vitamin E
- Panthenol—vitamin B_5

Here's a Tip

Essential oils can be used in a variety of ways. Lighting a cinnamon candle in the winter can give the salon a cozy feeling, cheering up both clients and the staff. You can use a spray bottle to diffuse well-diluted essential oils in the treatment room, or spray it on the sheets and towels. You can create your own aromatherapy massage oil by adding a few drops of essential oil to a massage oil, cream, or lotion. Remember people are sensitive to scents, so do not overuse it. A little bit goes a long way in aromatherapy.

CAUTION!

Essential oils are powerful. To prevent allergic reactions, they should be used with caution and only after proper training.

- Allantoin
- Guarana (an anti-inflammatory and decongestant)
- Rose essential oil

Green tea (from China and Japan) is an excellent everyday source of help for microcirculation problems. It contains polyphenols (strong antioxidants); essential oils; salts; calcium; potassium; manganese; copper; zinc; fluoride; vitamins A, B, and C; and caffeine. It is one of the best antioxidants available and provides effective lipid protection. Green tea is antibacterial, an anti-irritant, and provides UV protection.

Licorice root is 50 to 100 times sweeter than sugar and contains sugar, flavonoids (found in plants with yellow pigment), estrogens, amino acids, and polysaccharides. It is anti-inflammatory and a natural replacement for hydrocortisone (used to reduce rashes and redness). Licorice root also inhibits histamine release in allergic reactions. An antioxidant, licorice root lightens skin because it inhibits tyrosinaze activity (melanin production).

Vitamin K has been used in products for blood coagulation. It is helpful for clients with telangiectasias and spider veins. ✓ LO3

© Katusha/www.Shutterstock.com.

▲ Figure 13–11
There is a limitless selection of facial products to choose from.

Product Selection

All products are formulated for different skin types and conditions. The most important step in recommending products is determining which ingredients are best for an individual's needs. Learning about ingredients is necessary, and it takes time. Before applying a product, be sure to do a consultation and ask the client discreetly about any allergies she may have. No matter what the skin type, using the correct ingredients and following the proper steps in a home-care routine is essential for healthy skin.

Most skin care products (Figure 13–11) can be grouped into the following main categories:

- Cleansers
- Exfoliants
- Hydrators and moisturizers
- Sunscreens
- Toners
- Masks
- Serums and ampoules

Cleansers

Cleansers come in many forms and should be used twice a day as the first step in a skin care routine. Cleansers that rinse clean with water and do not strip the skin's natural acid mantle are the best choices. Different skin types require different ingredients to achieve this balance. All cleansers should leave the skin pH-balanced. Soap is not usually recommended; it can leave a film on the skin and can be quite alkaline, causing dryness and other problems.

Cleanser Benefits

Skin cleansers have the following benefits:

- Cleansers dissolve makeup and dirt to keep pores clean and prepare the skin for other products.
- Cleansers may have emollients that soften dry skin.
- Cleansers may contain ingredients to counteract various skin problems.
- Additional ingredients can help certain skin conditions such as sensitivity, dehydration, or capillary problems.

Types of Cleansers

Cleansers for all skin types and conditions come in three basic forms: gels, lotions, and creams. All products are unique and depend on the ingredients in that particular product. Keep this in mind when reading about each product category. These are general categories, not absolutes.

A ***cleansing gel*** is a detergent-type "foaming" cleanser with a neutral or slightly acidic pH. Foaming cleansers are designed to dissolve more oil. Many people are accustomed to the foaming type of bar soap and want that "squeaky clean" feeling. Gels leave the skin feeling clean, but often a little tight or dry. Clients with oily or combination skin prefer foamy cleansers.

For acne-prone skin, an antimicrobial agent may be added to kill bacteria. Recommend gel cleansers with caution because they can dry out the skin. This often leads to irritation, stimulates an overproduction of oil in the skin, and can exacerbate acne.

A ***cleansing lotion*** is a water-based emulsion for normal and combination skin. For dry skin, "milky" lotion cleansers containing more oils or emollients that soften the skin are recommended. These cleansers do not strip the skin's natural oil or pH balance. Additional ingredients can be added to cleansers to suit certain skin conditions such as sensitivity, dehydration, or capillary problems.

A ***cleansing cream*** is a water-in-oil emulsion used primarily to dissolve makeup and dirt. It is suitable for very dry and mature skin. Cleansing creams are heavier than cleansing lotions. Actors and other performers use these products to remove heavy stage makeup. Remember that like dissolves like, so oil dissolves oil. Cleansing cream should be removed with a sponge or a soft cloth; otherwise, a residue may be left on the skin. Cleansing creams may be followed by a toner or another cleanser to remove any residue.

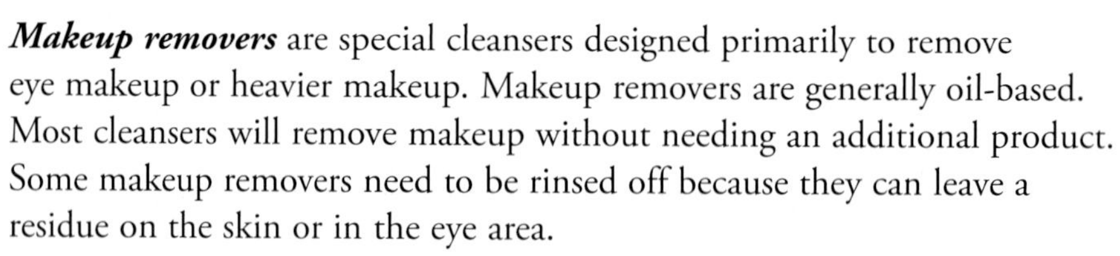

Makeup removers are special cleansers designed primarily to remove eye makeup or heavier makeup. Makeup removers are generally oil-based. Most cleansers will remove makeup without needing an additional product. Some makeup removers need to be rinsed off because they can leave a residue on the skin or in the eye area.

Toners

Toners, fresheners, tonics, and astringents are all essentially the same type of product; these terms are sometimes used interchangeably.

Toner Benefits

Here are some benefits of using toners:

- Toners and similar products remove residue left behind by cleansers or other products.
- Fresheners restore the skin's natural pH after cleansing and hydrate the skin.
- Astringents have a temporary tightening effect on both the skin and follicle openings.
- Some products can help certain skin conditions, depending on the ingredients.

Types of Toners

Toners, fresheners, and astringents have different properties and vary in alcohol content. These are watery liquids, used after cleansing in the skin care routine and generally before a moisturizer is applied. Toners can be applied to the face with a cotton pad or can be sprayed directly onto the skin (avoid the eyes).

- **Fresheners,** or skin freshening lotions, have the lowest alcohol content and are beneficial for dry and mature skin as well as for sensitive skin.
- **Toners** have a higher alcohol content and are designed for use on normal and combination skin. They tone, or tighten, the skin.
- **Astringents** have the highest alcohol content and are used for oily and acne-prone skin. They help oily and acneic conditions and remove excess oil on the skin, but some are too drying and should be used carefully.

Exfoliants

Exfoliation Benefits (Mechanical or Chemical)

Removing dead epidermal cells benefits the skin in many ways:

- Skin texture is smoother and softer.

- Follicle openings are cleaner.
- Deep pore cleansing and extraction are easier.
- The cell turnover rate is increased, bringing new cells to the surface more rapidly.
- The skin's ability to retain moisture and lipids is improved.
- Product penetration is improved, and delivery of ingredients into the epidermis is more effective.
- Blood flow and circulation are stimulated.
- Makeup application is smoother and more even.

Exfoliation is especially beneficial for the following conditions:

- Oily, clogged skin with blackheads, whiteheads, and minor acne breakouts
- Dry or dehydrated skin with cell buildup, flaking, and a tight, dry surface
- Dull, lifeless-looking skin (this skin condition actually has a tremendous buildup of dead cells that produces a slight gray color on the surface)

The term *exfoliation* refers to the peeling or sloughing of the horny (outer) layer of the skin, also known as the *corneum*. Many different types of peeling and exfoliation treatments are available, ranging from brushing treatments and light enzyme peels to strong surgical peels that can be administered only by dermatologists and plastic surgeons.

Alpha hydroxy acids (AHAs), gentle scrubs, and peeling creams all exfoliate dead skin cells that clog pores. Exfoliating the skin can treat a variety of skin problems and is necessary for healthy skin.

Use caution when exfoliating the skin. It is important to note that the esthetician's domain is the superficial epidermis, not treatments that involve the live layers of the skin below the epidermis. There are two basic types of exfoliation treatments: mechanical and chemical.

CAUTION!

As a student, you should always receive hands-on training from your instructor before attempting exfoliation procedures. Exfoliation can cause irritation and damage to the skin and capillaries if overused, or used incorrectly.

Mechanical Exfoliants

Mechanical exfoliation is a method of physically rubbing dead cells off of the skin. Examples of mechanical peeling treatments include granular scrubs, such as those made with almond meal or jojoba beads, or treatments that use a brushing machine. The movement of the brushes or scrubs removes cells from the surface of the corneum.

Granular scrubs are usually used after cleansing from one to two times per week and are rinsed with water. Frequency of use depends on the skin conditions. Exfoliation should be avoided if someone has sensitive or irritated skin. Microdermabrasion, a strong type of mechanical exfoliation, is covered in Chapter 19, Advanced Topics and Treatments.

Chemical Exfoliants

In **chemical exfoliation**, dead skin cells and the intercellular matrix, or "glue" that holds them together (desmosomes), are dissolved by chemical agents such as AHAs (**Figure 13–12**). Chemical exfoliation products and procedures are discussed in Chapter 19, Advanced Topics and Treatments.

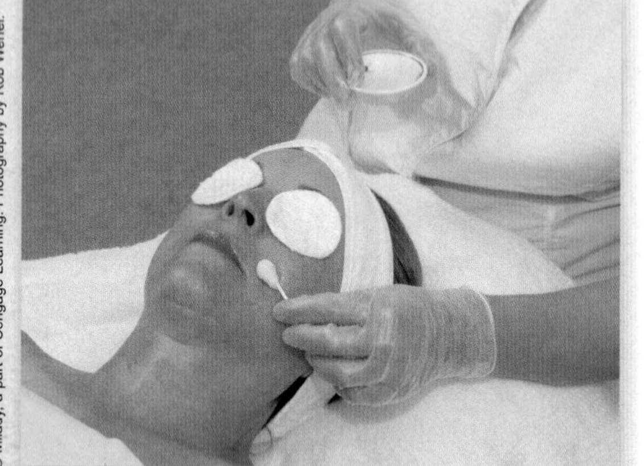

▲ Figure 13–12
Chemical exfoliation with AHAs.

Enzyme Peels

Unlike AHAs, enzymes digest only the dead cells on the surface. Superficial enzyme peels are mild. AHAs are much stronger than enzymes.

Enzyme peels involve the use of keratolytic enzymes, which help speed up the breakdown of keratin, the protein in skin. One enzyme often used is papain, which is derived from the papaya. Another frequently used enzyme is pancreatin (derived from beef by-products). Pumpkin and pineapple (bromelain) are other popular enzymes.

The enzyme peel is an exfoliating treatment for clients who are Retin-A® users and for ultrasensitive clients who have skin that is too sensitive for glycolic acid peels. Many acne clients (when first starting treatments) fall into this category. These peels digest keratinized epidermal cells, dislodge "sebaceous filaments" (sebum and other cellular wastes accumulated in the follicles), prepare the skin for extraction, and help fade and even out superficial irregular skin tone.

There are two basic types of enzyme treatments: masks and gommage. The most popular type of enzyme peel uses a powdered form of enzyme that is either mixed by the esthetician with warm water or can be purchased premixed in a base similar to a treatment mask. Other ingredients are combined in the peel formula to address different skin types and conditions. This type of enzyme treatment generally produces

CAUTION!

To avoid damaging skin, do not use brushing machines, scrubs, or any harsh mechanical exfoliation techniques on these skin conditions:

- **Sensitive skin**
- **Skin with many visible capillaries**
- **Thin skin that reddens easily**
- **Older skin that is thin and bruises easily**
- **Acne-prone skin with inflamed papules and pustules**
- **Skin medically treated with tretinoin (retinoic acid or Retin-A®), Accutane®, adapalene (Differin®), other acne drugs, azelaic acid, alpha hydroxy acids (AHAs), or salicylic acid (found in many common skin products)**

a more even exfoliation of the cell buildup and helps to dilate the follicle openings slightly.

A second type of enzyme peel is a **gommage** (go-MAHJ), also known as **roll-off mask**, in a cream form that is applied and then massaged or "rolled" off the skin. This cream may contain paraffin or oatmeal. This treatment is actually a combination of an enzyme and a mechanical exfoliation (Figure 13–13).

Masks

Mask Benefits

Masks provide many benefits for the skin. Depending on their ingredients, they can do the following:

- Tighten and tone the skin
- Draw impurities out of the pores
- Clear up blemishes
- Hydrate
- Nourish
- Calm and soothe
- Rejuvenate the skin
- Brighten the complexion

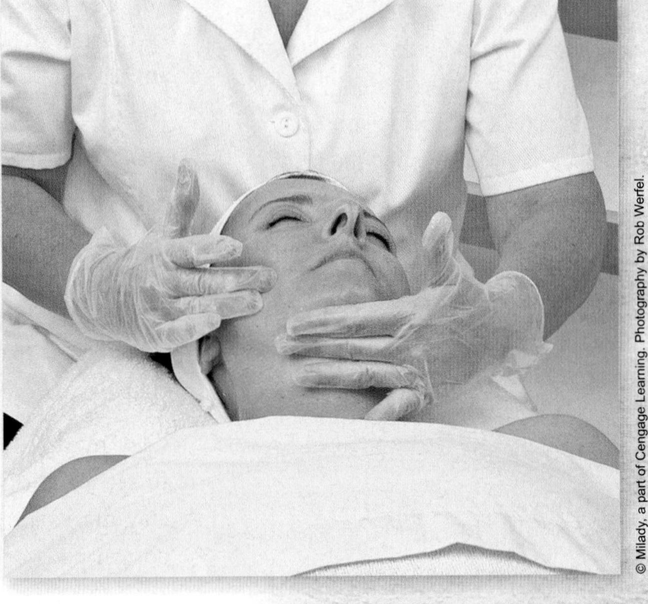

▲ Figure 13–13
Gommage is used for exfoliation.

Types of Masks

A good **mask**, also known as **pack** or **masque**, can do wonders for the skin and, like most beauty treatments, the benefits of masks have been known for hundreds of years. Mask ingredients include herbs and vitamins, which can be combined in clay, seaweed, or hydrating bases. Masks come in powder form or premixed. Masks allow an esthetician to treat a variety of skin conditions at the same time.

There are two types of mask categories: *nonsetting* and *setting*. Nonsetting masks do not dry or "set up." Setting masks harden or dry.

Nonsetting Masks. Nonsetting masks, such as cucumber or aloe, are designed to stay moist and are more hydrating. For home-care, masks are usually applied once a week, after exfoliation for best results and penetration. Also referred to as cream masks or gel masks, nonsetting masks are not formulated to dry. These nourish or treat the skin rather than give it a deep cleaning. They are highly beneficial for sensitive, couperose, aging, or dry skin because ingredients such as collagen, aloe, and seaweed have excellent hydrating properties.

Cream masks, which do not dry on the skin like clay masks do, are often used for dry skin. They often contain oils and emollients as well as humectants, and they have a strong moisturizing effect.

Did You Know?

The Inflammation Cascade

Inflammation can be caused by too much irritation from exfoliation or other factors and lead to premature aging. Stimulating the body's histamine activity that reacts to irritants and allergens causes the enzyme *collagenase* to break down collagen and the enzyme *elastase* to break down elastin. Natural hydrators in the skin, such as hyaluronic acid, are also lost when the skin is excessively irritated. Over-exfoliating can break down our natural protection and impede normal cellular functions. This is an example of "too much of a good thing."

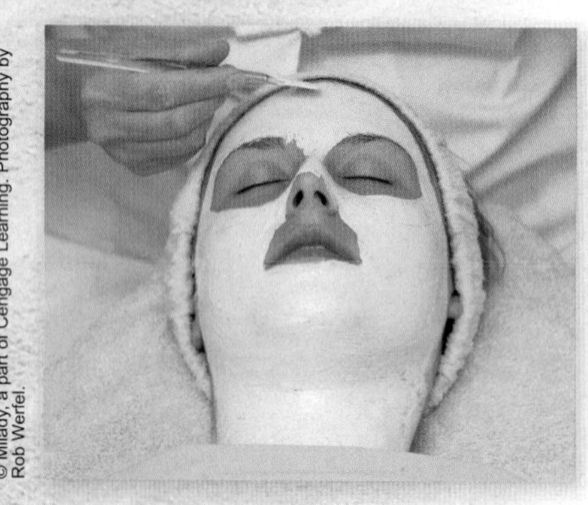

▲ Figure 13–14
Applying a clay mask.

CAUTION!

Remember that many people are allergic to seaweed and even shellfish, which is usually a contraindication for seaweed products. Serious reactions to marine-based products do occur, so use caution when using these ingredients.

Gel masks can be used for sensitive or dehydrated skin. They often contain hydrators and soothing ingredients and thus help plump surface cells with moisture, making the skin look more supple and hydrated.

Collagen masks are another great mask choice with many benefits such as plumping, calming, and diminishing wrinkles. Freeze-dried collagen sheets infused with ingredients are applied wet on the skin.

Setting Masks. Setting masks harden and contain setting ingredients, which dry and provide a complete barrier on top of the skin. Ingredients such as clay, alginate, paraffin wax, and gypsum (a kind of plaster) account for this effect. Keep in mind that some of these ingredients do not always set up, depending on the formulation and the purpose of the product.

Clay Masks. Clay masks draw impurities to the surface of the skin as the mask dries and tightens. Clay also stimulates circulation and temporarily contracts the pores of the skin. These masks contain clay, kaolin, bentonite, or silica for their tightening and sebum-absorbing effects. Stronger clay masks are used on oily and combination skin. Clay-based masks with sulfur have healing and antiseptic properties that have a beneficial effect on acne.

Clay masks are applied with a mask brush or the fingers and are allowed to set for about 10 minutes (**Figure 13–14**). After they are fully dried, clay masks are softened with towels or steam and then removed with cotton pads or towels.

Algae and Seaweed Masks. Alginate masks (AL-jun-ate) are often seaweed based. They come in powder form and are mixed with water or sometimes serums. After mixing, they are quickly applied to the face and then dry to form a rubberized texture. A treatment cream or serum is generally applied under them. The alginate mask forms a seal that encourages the skin's absorption of the serum or cream underneath. These professional masks are generally used only in the salon and are not retailed for home use.

Algae (derived from seaweed) is also used in other types of masks and products for its moisturizing properties, ability to smooth wrinkles, and detoxification. Seaweed is high in mineral content and therapeutic ingredients.

Modelage Masks (MA-dell-ahj), also known as **thermal masks**, contain special crystals of gypsum, a plaster-like ingredient. Modelage masks are used with nourishing products underneath. Mixed with water immediately before application and applied about ¼-inch (.6 centimeters) thick, the modelage mask sets up and hardens (**Figure 13–15**). The chemical reaction that occurs when the plaster and the crystals mix with water produces a gradually increasing temperature that reaches approximately 105 degrees Fahrenheit

(40.5 degrees Celsius). Left on the skin, the mask gradually cools. The setting time for modelage masks is approximately 20 minutes.

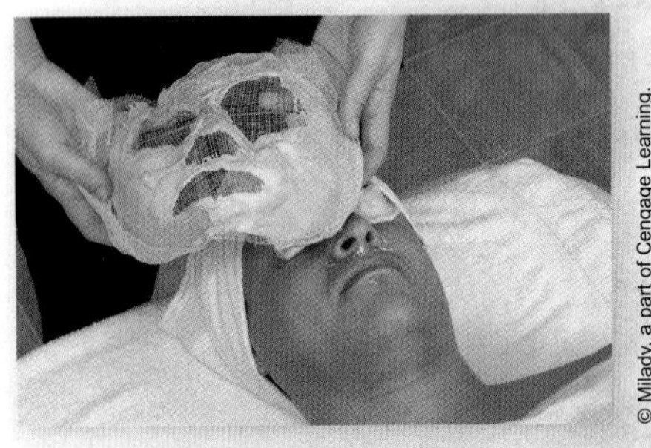

▲ Figure 13–15
The modelage mask.

Like other heat-creating treatments that increase circulation, modelage masks are very beneficial for dry, mature skin or dull-looking skin. This type of mask is not typically recommended for use on sensitive skin, skin with capillary problems, oily skin, or skin with blemishes. Massage is not recommended either before or after a modelage mask application, because blood circulation will already be increased from the mask. These masks can become heavy on the face and should not be applied to the lower neck or to clients who suffer from claustrophobia. These masks are used in the salon and are not retailed.

Paraffin Wax Masks. Paraffin masks are used to warm the skin and promote penetration of ingredients deeper into the skin through the heat trapped under the paraffin. The heat increases blood circulation and is beneficial for dry, mature skin or skin that is dull and lifeless. It has a plumping and softening effect on the skin.

Paraffin masks are specially prepared facial masks containing paraffin and other beneficial ingredients. They are melted at a little more than body temperature (98.6 degrees Fahrenheit or 37 degress Celsius) before application. When applied, the paraffin quickly cools to a lukewarm temperature and hardens to a candle-like consistency (**Figure 13–16**). Paraffin masks are applied on top of a treatment cream as the paraffin, which has no treatment properties of its own, allows for deeper penetration of the cream's ingredients into the skin. The paraffin mask procedure is presented in Chapter 15, Facial Treatments.

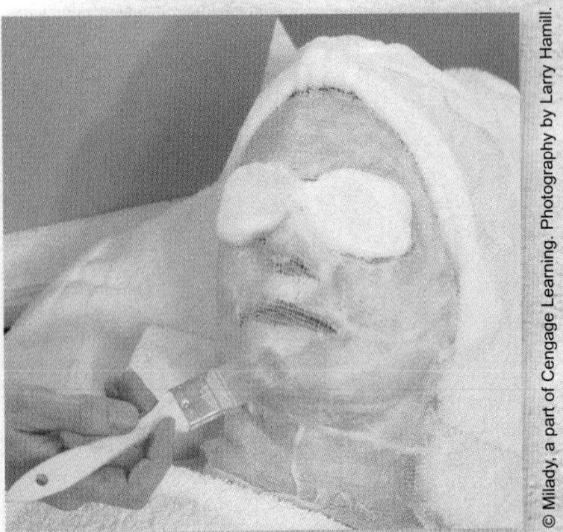

▲ Figure 13–16
The paraffin wax mask.

Custom-designed Masks. Homemade masks derived from fresh fruits, vegetables, milk, yogurt, or eggs have been used traditionally for many years. Ingredients such as honey and almond meal or oatmeal can be mixed with milk into a paste for use as a mask. These masks are beneficial unless the person is allergic to a particular substance. Custom-designed masks can be fun to experiment with, but they are usually done at home rather than in a professional setting. Sanitation, regulations, and convenience preclude the use of homemade masks in the salon. Additionally, products not packaged by a manufacturer may not be covered under your employer's insurance. While problems are unlikely, there are insurance liability issues about any skin reactions to homemade products.

Paraffin and thermal masks are not recommended for use on sensitive skin, skin with capillary problems, oily skin, or skin with blemishes. These masks are designed for dry and mature skin; the heat is too stimulating for other skin conditions and may cause redness or irritation.

A client may ask about homemade products. It is important for estheticians to be familiar with these ingredients and to know why the quality of prepackaged professional products give more predictable results. Additionally, some product lines are designed to custom-blend products and estheticians can add ingredients to various products. This is a good way to customize treatments.

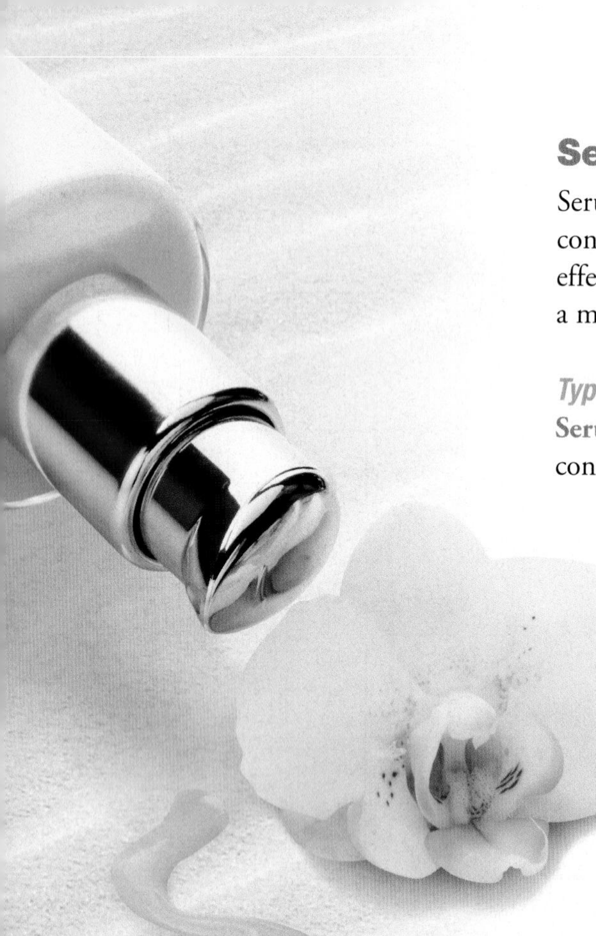

Serums and Ampoules

Serums and ampoules are essentially the same type of product containing concentrated and specialized ingredients designed for effective penetration into the skin. These products are applied under a moisturizer, mask, or massage cream.

Types of Serums and Ampoules

Serums (SIR-ums) are concentrated ingredients that target specific skin conditions. Serums are chemically formulated with smaller molecules that are able to penetrate further into the skin and thus are more effective. Serums are thin liquids made with performance ingredients such as vitamins, lipids, and antioxidants.

Ampoules (AM-pyools) are small, sealed vials containing a single application of highly concentrated extracts in a water or oil base. They are designed for a wide variety of skin types and problems. The advantage of ampoules is that they deliver highly concentrated performance ingredients in a premeasured amount. The extract is applied to the client's face with light massage movements until it has been completely absorbed.

Eye Creams

Benefits

Eye creams have several benefits, including the following:

- Protecting thin, delicate tissue
- Firming
- Reducing lines
- Decreasing puffiness

Types of Eye Creams

Eye creams are usually thicker to protect thin, delicate tissue. Products made for the eye area include ingredients for firming and reducing lines. Eye masks, tea bags, or compresses are beneficial for the eye area and can be used in facial treatments. Products formulated for the eye area are similar to concentrated specialty creams and gels.

Lip Treatments

Lip treatments include moisturizing balms and products. Some contain collagen derivatives or other ingredients to plump-up the lips. Exfoliating and healing ingredients are also used in lip conditioners.

Moisturizers and Hydrators

Benefits

The following are some benefits of using moisturizers and hydrators:

- Protecting skin from the elements
- Nourishing skin through ingredients
- Balancing the oil–water content of skin
- Treating various skin conditions such as redness, aging, or dryness

Types of Moisturizers

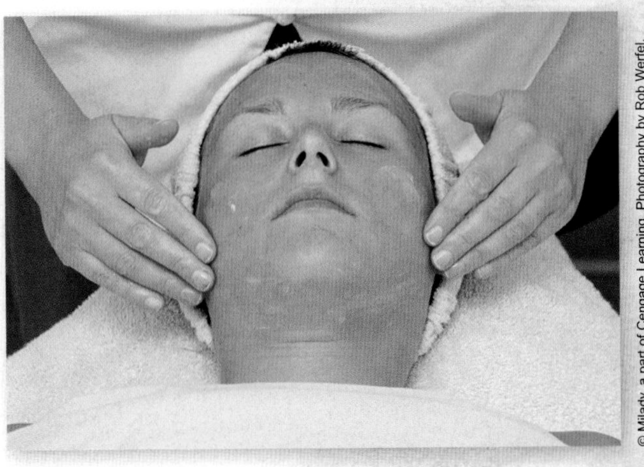

▲ Figure 13–17
Applying a moisturizer.

Moisturizers are products formulated to add moisture to the skin. Lotions, hydrators, and creams are all referred to as *moisturizers*. These products are used twice a day after cleansing to protect and nourish the skin. They are applied at the end of the facial and are intended for daily use as a day cream or makeup base (**Figure 13–17**). Moisturizer is a good general term to use with clients, even though technically there are differences in the products. Moisturizers are available for various skin types and conditions, from acne-prone skin to dry and mature skin.

Treatment creams and massage lotions are different forms of moisturizers. Moisturizers contain an ingredient that helps retain water within the surface layers of the skin. Hydrators are formulated with humectants that attract water to the skin.

Oil-based moisturizers contain emollients and are heavier and occlusive, designed to protect the surface and trap water under the cream. It is important to use a moisturizer to hydrate and balance the oil–water moisture content of the skin. Water-based moisturizers are lighter emulsions for combination to oily skin and are absorbed quickly and leave no residue on the skin's surface. Even oily skin needs the hydration and protection found in a hydrator. This skin type will try to overcompensate for dryness and produce more oil, or it will become dehydrated if it is not balanced.

A valuable ingredient included in some day creams is sunscreen. These creams are good only for incidental sun exposure. For direct sun exposure, stronger sunscreens must be used and reapplied often.

Treatment Creams. Treatment creams, also referred to as *nourishing creams*, are designed to moisturize and condition the skin—especially during sleep, when normal tissue repair is taking place. Treatment creams are often heavier in consistency and texture than moisturizers are and they contain more emollient and active ingredients. Specialty treatment products for oily skin usually have very little or no emollient.

Massage Creams. Massage creams, lotions, or oils have a variety of bases and ingredients. These are designed to provide slip (gliding ability) for massage while also nourishing and treating skin conditions. Massage lotions are also blended with aromatherapy oils to use during

Here's a Tip

With all product usage, choose the right formulas for your client's skin. Be sure to apply the appropriate amount of product; using too much can have adverse affects on the skin and wastes money on products.

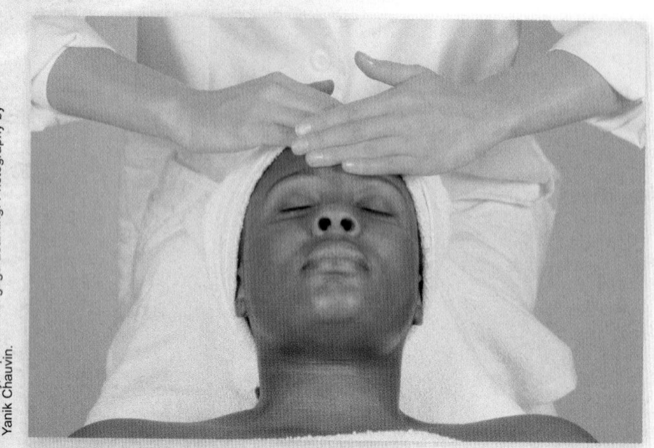

▲ Figure 13–18
Applying massage cream.

treatments (Figure 13–18). Choose the appropriate massage blend for the skin type.

Sunscreens

Daily sunscreen is helpful to protect skin from UV radiation. An important part of an esthetician's job is to recommend sunscreen. Estheticians should stress to clients that sun exposure leads to skin cancer as well as to aging, hyperpigmentation, capillary damage, free radical damage, and collagen and elastin deterioration. Daily sunscreen can be in moisturizer form and comes in all weights and formulas.

Oil-free, light lotions that will not clog pores are available for oily skin. The amount of SPF labeled on products does not always match the protection level. The amount of face powders and lotions may need to be much thicker than the amount typically applied on the skin in order to match the SPF rating. Remind clients that these products are only for incidental sun exposure.

Sunscreen Ingredients

Full-spectrum sunscreens protect the skin from both UVA and UVB exposure. Sunscreens absorb or reflect ultraviolet radiation. Categories of compounds that absorb UVB are salicylates and cinnamates. UVA-absorbing compounds are benzophenones. Most sunscreens now combine ingredients to target both UVB and UVA radiation.

Sunscreens that protect the skin from UVB include: octyl salicylate, octyl methoxycinnamate, oxybenzone, octylhomosalate, octocrylene, zinc oxide, and titanium dioxide.

Some of the sunscreens that protect the skin from UVA are: oxybenzone, avobenzone (Parsol 1789), benzophenone-3, butyl methoxydibenzoylmethane, mexoryl®, titanium dioxide, and zinc oxide.

Physical (nonchemical) sunscreens are broad spectrum sunscreens: zinc oxide and titanium dioxide.

SPF refers to the sun protection factor in sunscreens that delays sun-induced *erythema.* An SPF 2 sunscreen blocks 50 percent of UVB, allowing you to stay in the sun twice as long as you could with no sun protection. Increasing the SPF increases the protection. An SPF 15 sunscreen blocks 93.3 percent of UVB; and an SPF 30 sunscreen blocks 96.9 percent of UVB. But notice that doubling the SPF from 15 to 30 does not double the protection. In this case it increases UVB protection by only 3.6 percent, and at higher SPFs the increase is even less. Although doubling the SPF does not double the protection, the higher SPF increases the potential for sensitivity to the product due to the increase in the concentration of active ingredients. The SPF can be misleading and is based on many factors, not just the exposure time.

ACTIVITY

Choose products and ingredients for different skin types and conditions according to your product line. Write-in ingredients and product types you think you would use. Use the ingredient tables in this chapter or a cosmetic ingredients dictionary to research your products.

PRODUCT TYPE AND INGREDIENTS FOR DIFFERENT SKIN TYPES AND CONDITIONS	Mature	Sensitive	Dry	Normal	Combo	Oily	Acne
cleansers	Example: *cleansing cream with antioxidants*						
exfoliants		*enzyme peel*					
masks	*collagen*						
massage lotions							
additives and oils		*calming—chamomile*					
toners							
serums							
moisturizers and sunscreen	*ceramides*						
eye and lip care products							

Self-Tanners

Self-tanning lotions are formulated with dihydroxyacetone (DHA), an ingredient that reacts with the proteins (keratin) on the surface cells of the skin and turns them darker. Most self-tanners have no sunscreen protection; sunscreen should still be applied. Looking tan does not mean the skin has protection from sunburns or photoaging. Keep in mind that the "tan" look from self-tanners can disguise redness or sunburn. ☑ LO4 ☑ LO5 ☑ LO6 ☑ LO7 ☑ LO8

Home-Care Products

Products the client can use at home are as important as those you use during the facial. The same principles that you use in determining products for treatments apply here. Give clients simple, precise instructions as to how and when to use the product. It is a good idea to give a home-care sheet to clients who may not remember what you told them. Your product line and specific treatments will determine what to

CLIENT HOME-CARE INSTRUCTION SHEET Write-in recommendations for clients from the product line you carry. Most product companies provide home-care sheets to give out to clients.			
DAY	NIGHT	WEEKLY	PRODUCT RECOMMENDATIONS
1. Cleanser	1. Cleanser	1. Cleanser	
2. Toner	2. Toner	2. Exfoliation: 1-2 times/week	
3. Serums/eye cream	3. Serums/eye cream	3. Masks: 1-2 times/week	
4. Moisturizer	4. Moisturizer	4. Toner	
5. Sunscreen		5. Serums/eye cream	
		6. Moisturizer	

▲ Table 13–8
Client Home-Care Instruction Sheet.

▲ Figure 13–19
The home-care consultation.

recommend. Explaining instructions, precautions, and realistic expectations will be beneficial to both you and your clients.

Use Table 13–8 as a general home-care guideline for clients. Giving out product samples saves money for you and your clients: they help you determine what works best, and your clients will appreciate being able to try a product without investing a lot of money. A product guarantee and refund policy will depend on the place where you work. Satisfied clients are good for business and will be loyal if you take care of them.

Retailing products is not just about making sales. You are helping your clients take care of their skin. As you begin to work with clients, you become familiar with the needs of their skin and are more knowledgeable in recommending personalized products. Professional products sold only by licensed professionals (estheticians) are generally better formulated for individual needs. While professional products may cost more initially, they are usually more effective due to a higher concentration of performance ingredients—and this means less product is needed. With proper products chosen just for them, clients will see better results in their home-care (Figure 13–19). This saves your clients money in the long run because they will avoid wasting money in trying different products that might not be suited to their individual needs.

ACTIVITY

Using the client home-care instruction sheet, practice recommending products to someone you know. Pull out the retail products, explain each one, the benefits, a few of the main ingredients, and how to use them.

Choosing a Product Line

Deciding what product lines to use and retail can be one of the biggest business decisions an esthetician can make. Whether a technician is self-employed or involved in choosing product lines for a salon owner, the product line and retail sales affect the success of the business. If the staff likes the product and use it at home, it will be easy to use in treatments.

It will also be easier to promote and sell.

When choosing a product line, take into consideration the following points:

- Are the ingredients high quality and beneficial?
- Are the products versatile—that is, effective for all skin types?
- Are the wholesale cost and the retail pricing affordable?
- Is the product name recognizable and reputable? Many clients choose a product based on its name and how it is marketed.
- How are the products packaged?
- What fragrances are used?
- What can clients in your area afford?
- What support can you anticipate from the company or supplier? The costs of samples and brochures, return policies, and marketing promotions affect your business.
- What educational opportunities and training are provided by the supplier? These can help you become more knowledgeable and successful.

There are countless skin care ingredients and hundreds of product lines for the esthetician to choose from. Researching the different product options will help estheticians become familiar with these choices. Knowing the daily skin care steps for maintaining healthy skin is necessary in making product recommendations. Choosing the correct product formulas for clients is important to effectively and safely treat the skin.

Understanding what ingredients do for the skin will make it easier to recommend and choose products. Ingredient and product technology is an exciting part of esthetics. It is an area demanding continuous attention and review, but it is also one of the most interesting aspects of the industry.

Product Prices and Costs

Pricing and costs of products are a consideration for both you and your client. Product costs can be expensive if you do not choose wisely. Generally, the markup for retail products is 100 percent, or doubled from the wholesaler cost. Let your client know why professional products available only from licensed estheticians cost more than those they can purchase over the counter. Consider the quality of the ingredients and the concentration of performance ingredients in the products when comparing prices. When comparing skin care product lines, determine what you and your clientele like. Use Table 13–9 on page 346 to compare and rate product lines. ✓ LO9

Here's a Tip

To save time and be ready for the post-consultation, pull out recommended home-care products while the client is getting dressed after a facial. Show them what you recommend before they check out at the front desk.

Here's a Tip

A good way to determine product cost is to break down the costs into daily or weekly amounts. This gives clients a better idea of how affordable the product is and how much they are spending on the recommended products, which is usually not more than a cup of coffee per day.

For example, if you have a product that costs $50 for 2 ounces (56 g) and is estimated to last 6 months, then the cost is $8.33/per month (the cost of $50 divided by 6 months).

The cost per week is $2.08 ($8.33 for 1 month divided by 4 weeks in a month).

This is only .30 cents/per day ($2.08 per week divided by 7 days/week).

A very good price for maintaining beautiful skin. How much would it cost for your product line? Use three products and figure out the total cost per day for all three.

CHART FOR COMPARING AND RATING PRODUCT LINES Use your own rating system—for example, rate products from 1 to 5 or from excellent to fair.						
PRODUCT LINE	CLEANSER	TONER	MOISTURIZER	EXFOLIANT	MASK	OTHER
Skin types						
Main ingredients						
Cost						
Quality						
Texture						
Scent						
Color						
Packaging						
Overall rating						

▲ Table 13–9 **Chart for Comparing and Rating Product Lines.**

ACTIVITY

Use Table 13–9 to compare and rate product lines. Make a copy of the chart, or create your own and fill in the blanks while sampling and testing different products.

Web Resources

www.ams.usda.gov
www.cir-safety.org
www.cosmeticscop.com
www.cosmeticsdatabase.org
www.cosmeticsdesign.com
www.fda.gov
www.medscape.com
www.nsf.org

Review Questions

1. What is the FDA definition of cosmetics?
2. What is the main difference between functional and performance ingredients?
3. What functions does water serve in cosmetic formulations?
4. What are emollients?
5. Name three emollients other than oil that are used in skin care products.
6. Define comedogenicity.
7. What are essential oils?
8. Why are preservatives necessary in cosmetic products?
9. What is the function of humectants in skin care products?
10. What are the two basic types of sunscreen products?
11. What is the difference between a physical sunscreen and a chemical sunscreen?
12. Describe the symptoms of an allergic reaction to cosmetic products.
13. What two main product components are the most common allergens?
14. List five antioxidant ingredients.
15. What are the primary functions and benefits of antioxidants?
16. List four ingredients beneficial for mature or aging skin.
17. List two ingredients beneficial for acne.
18. List two ingredients beneficial for sensitive skin.
19. What are the main categories of professional skin care products?
20. What are the benefits of toners?
21. Describe the two basic types of exfoliation treatments.
22. What are five benefits of exfoliation?
23. List the benefits of a mask.
24. What is the difference between a nonsetting and a setting mask?
25. Why are moisturizers necessary?
26. What does SPF refer to?
27. Why is using sunscreen important?
28. List the steps in a good daily skin care routine.
29. What considerations are important in choosing product lines?

Glossary

alpha hydroxy acids	Abbreviated AHAs; acids derived from plants (mostly fruit) that are often used to exfoliate the skin; mild acids: glycolic, lactic, malic, and tartaric acid. AHAs exfoliate by loosening the bonds between dead corneum cells and dissolve the intercellular matrix. Acids also stimulate cell renewal.
alcohol	Antiseptic and solvent used in perfumes, lotions, and astringents. SD alcohol is a special denatured ethyl alcohol.
algae	Derived from minerals and phytohormones; remineralizes and revitalizes the skin.

Glossary

allantoin	An anti-inflammatory compound isolated from the herb comfrey; it is used in creams, hand lotion, hair lotion, aftershave, and other skin-soothing cosmetics for its ability to heal wounds and skin ulcers and to stimulate the growth of healthy tissue.
aloe vera	Most popular botanical used in cosmetic formulations; emollient and film-forming gum resin with hydrating, softening, healing, antimicrobial, and anti-inflammatory properties.
alpha lipoic acid	A natural molecule found in every cell in the body; it is a powerful antioxidant and is soluble in water and oil.
alum	Compound made of aluminum, potassium, or ammonium sulfate with strong astringent action.
ampoules	Small, sealed vials containing a single application of highly concentrated extracts in a water or oil base.
anhydrous	Describes products that do not contain any water.
aromatherapy	Therapeutic use of plant aromas and essential oils for beauty and health treatment purposes; involves the use of highly concentrated, nonoily, and volatile essential oils to induce such reactions as relaxation and invigoration, or to simply create a pleasant fragrance during a service.
astringents	Liquids that help remove excess oil on the skin.
azulene	Derived from the chamomile plant and characterized by its deep blue color; has anti-inflammatory and soothing properties.
benzyl peroxide	Drying ingredient with antibacterial properties commonly used for blemishes and acne.
beta-glucans	Ingredients used in antiaging cosmetics to help reduce the appearance of fine lines and wrinkles by stimulating the formation of collagen.
beta hydroxy acids	Abbreviated BHAs; exfoliating organic acid; salicylic acid; milder than alpha hydroxy acids (AHAs). BHAs dissolve oil and are beneficial for oily skin.
binders	Substances such as glycerin that bind, or hold, products together.
botanicals	Ingredients derived from plants.
calendula	Anti-inflammatory plant extract.
carbomers	Ingredients used to thicken creams; frequently used in gel products.
carrot	Rich in vitamin A, commonly derived from seeds and as an oil; also used as product colorant.
certified colors	Inorganic color agents also known as metal salts; listed on ingredient labels as D&C (drug and cosmetic).
chamomile	Plant extract with calming and soothing properties.
chelating agent	A chemical added to cosmetics to improve the efficiency of the preservative.
chemical exfoliation	Chemical agent that dissolves dead skin cells and the intercellular matrix, or "glue," that holds them together (desmosomes).
clay masks	Oil-absorbing cleansing masks that draw impurities to the surface of the skin as they dry and tighten.
cleansers	Soaps and detergents that clean the skin.

Glossary

coenzyme Q10	Powerful antioxidant that protects and revitalizes skin cells.
colorants	Substances such as vegetable, pigment, or mineral dyes that give products color.
comedogenicity	Tendency of any topical substance to cause or to worsen a buildup in the follicle, leading to the development of a comedo (blackhead).
cosmeceuticals	Products intended to improve the skin's health and appearance.
cosmetics	As defined by the FDA: articles that are intended to be rubbed, poured, sprinkled or otherwise applied to the human body or any part thereof for cleansing, beautifying, promoting attractiveness, or altering the appearance.
delivery systems	Systems that deliver ingredients to specific tissues of the epidermis.
detergents	Type of surfactant used as cleansers in skin-cleansing products.
DMAE	Dimethylaminoethanol; antioxidant that stabilizes cell membranes and boosts the effect of other antioxidants.
echinacea	Derivative of the purple coneflower; prevents infection and has healing properties; used internally to support the immune system.
emollients	Oil or fatty Ingredients that lubricate, moisturize, and prevent water loss.
emulsifiers	Surfactants that cause oil and water to mix and form an emulsion; an ingredient that brings two normally incompatible materials together and binds them into a uniform and fairly stable blend.
enzyme peels	Enzyme products that dissolve keratin proteins (dead skin cells) and exfoliate the skin.
essential oils	Oils derived from herbs; have many different properties and effects on the skin and psyche.
exfoliants	Mechanical and chemical products or processes used to exfoliate the skin.
exfoliation	Peeling or sloughing of the outer layer of skin.
fatty acids	Emollients; lubricant ingredients derived from plant oils or animal fats.
fatty alcohols	Emollients; fatty acids that have been exposed to hydrogen.
fatty esters	Emollients produced from fatty acids and alcohols.
fragrances	Give products their scent.
fresheners	Skin-freshening lotions with a low alcohol content.
functional ingredients	Ingredients in cosmetic products that allow the products to spread, give them body and texture, and give them a specific form such as a lotion, cream, or gel. Preservatives are also functional ingredients.
glycerin	Formed by a decomposition of oils or fats; excellent skin softener and humectant; very strong water binder; sweet, colorless, oily substance used as a solvent and as a moisturizer in skin and body creams.
glycoproteins	Skin-conditioning agents derived from carbohydrates and proteins that enhance cellular metabolism and wound healing.
gommage	Also known as *roll-off mask*; exfoliating creams that are rubbed off the skin.

Glossary

grapeseed extract	Powerful antioxidant with soothing properties.
green tea	Powerful antioxidant and soothing agent; antibacterial, anti-inflammatory, and a stimulant.
healing agents	Substances such as chamomile or aloe that help to heal the skin.
herbs	Hundreds of different herbs that contain phytohormones are used in skin care products and cosmetics; they heal, stimulate, soothe, and moisturize.
horsechestnut	Extract containing bioflavonoids; also known as vitamin P. Helps strengthen capillary walls; used for couperose areas or telangiectasia.
humectants	Ingredients that attract water. Humectants draw moisture to the skin and soften its surface, diminishing lines caused by dryness.
hydrators	Ingredients that attract water to the skin's surface.
hydrophilic agents	Ingredients that attract water to the skin's surface.
jojoba	Oil widely used in cosmetics; extracted from the bean-like seeds of the desert shrub. Used as a lubricant and noncomedogenic emollient and moisturizer.
keratolytic	Agent that causes exfoliation, or sloughing, of skin cells.
kojic acid	Skin-brightening agent.
lakes	Insoluble pigments made by combining a dye with an inorganic material.
lanolin	Emollient with moisturizing properties; also an emulsifier with high water-absorption capabilities.
lavender	Antiallergenic, anti-inflammatory, antiseptic, antibacterial, balancing, energizing, soothing, and healing.
licorice	Anti-irritant used for sensitive skin; helps lighten pigmentation.
lipids	Fats or fat-like substances; lipids help repair and protect the barrier function of the skin.
liposomes	Closed-lipid bilayer spheres that encapsulate ingredients, target their delivery to specific tissues of the skin, and control their release.
lubricants	Coat the skin and reduce friction; mineral oil is a lubricant.
mask	Also known as *pack* or *masques*; concentrated treatment products often composed of herbs, vitamins, mineral clays, moisturizing agents, skin softeners, aromatherapy oils, beneficial extracts, and other beneficial ingredients to cleanse, exfoliate, tighten, tone, hydrate, and nourish and treat the skin.
mechanical exfoliation	Physical method of rubbing dead cells off of the skin.
methylparaben	One of the most frequently used preservatives because of its very low sensitizing potential; combats bacteria and molds; noncomedogenic.
mineral oil	Lubricant derived from petroleum.
modelage masks	Also known as *thermal masks*; thermal heat masks; facial masks containing special crystals of gypsum, a plaster-like ingredient.

Glossary

moisturizers	Products formulated to add moisture to the skin.
noncertified colors	Colors that are organic, meaning they come from animal or plant extracts; they can also be natural mineral pigments.
oil soluble	Compatible with oil.
olfactory system	Gives us our sense of smell, which is the strongest of the five senses.
papaya	Natural enzyme used for exfoliation and in enzyme peels.
parabens	One of the most commonly used groups of preservatives in the cosmetic, pharmaceutical, and food industries; provide bacteriostatic and fungistatic activity against a diverse number of organisms.
paraffin wax masks	Mask used to warm the skin and promote penetration of ingredients through the heat trapped under the surface of the paraffin.
peptides	Chains of amino acids that stimulate fibroblasts, cell metabolism, collagen, and improve skin's firmness. Larger chains are called polypeptides.
performance ingredients	Ingredients in cosmetic products that cause the actual changes in the appearance of the skin.
petroleum jelly	Occlusive agent that restores the barrier layer by holding in water; used after laser surgery to protect the skin while healing.
pH adjusters	Acids or alkalis (bases) used to adjust the pH of products.
phytotherapy	Use of plant extracts for therapeutic benefits.
polyglucans	Ingredients derived from yeast cells that help strengthen the immune system and stimulate the metabolism; also hydrophilic and help preserve and protect collagen and elastin.
polymers	Chemical compounds formed by combining a number of small molecules (monomers) into long chain-like structures; advanced vehicles that release substances onto the skin's surface at a microscopically controlled rate.
potassium hydroxide	Strong alkali used in soaps and creams.
preservatives	Chemical agents that inhibit the growth of microorganisms in cosmetic formulations. These kill bacteria and prevent products from spoiling.
propylene glycol	Humectant often used in dry- or sensitive-skin moisturizers.
quaternium 15	All-purpose preservative active against bacteria, mold, and yeast. It is probably the greatest formaldehyde-releaser among cosmetic preservatives; may cause dermatitis and allergies.
retinol	Natural form of vitamin A; stimulates cell repair and helps to normalize skin cells by generating new cells.
rose	Credited with moisturizing, astringent, tonic, and deodorant properties; found in the forms of rose extracts, oil, or water.
salicylic acid	Beta hydroxy acid with exfoliating and antiseptic properties; natural sources include sweet birch, willow bark, and wintergreen.

Glossary

seaweed	Seaweed derivatives such as algae have many nourishing properties; known for its humectant and moisturizing properties, vitamin content, metabolism stimulation and detoxification, and aiding skin firmness.
serums	Concentrated liquid ingredients for the skin designed to penetrate and treat various skin conditions.
silicones	Oil that is chemically combined with silicon and oxygen and leaves a noncomedogenic, protective film on the surface of the skin.
sodium bicarbonate	Baking soda; an alkaline inorganic salt used as a buffering agent, neutralizer, and a pH adjuster.
sorbitol	Humectant that absorbs moisture from the air to prevent skin dryness.
sphingolipids	Ceramides, or lipid material, that are a natural part of the intercellular matrix. Glycosphingolipids and phospholipids are also natural lipids found in the barrier layer.
squalane	Derived from olives; desensitizes and nourishes; an emollient.
squalene	Originally from shark liver oil; also occurs in small amounts in olive oil, wheat germ oil, and rice bran oil; also found in human sebum. A lubricant and perfume fixative.
stem cells	Derived from plants to protect or stimulate our own skin stem cells; for health and antiaging benefits.
sulfur	Sulfur reduces oil-gland activity and dissolves the skin's surface layer of dry, dead cells. This ingredient is commonly used in acne products.
sun protection factor	Abbreviated SPF; ability of a product to delay sun-induced erythema, the visible sign of sun damage. The SPF rating is based only on UVB protection, not UVA exposure.
tea tree	Soothing and antiseptic; antifungal properties.
tissue respiratory factor	Abbreviated TRF; ingredient derived from yeast cells that functions as an anti-inflammatory and moisturizing ingredient.
titanium dioxide	Inorganic physical sunscreen that reflects UV radiation.
toners	Also known as *fresheners* or *astringents*; liquids designed to tone and tighten the skin's surface.
urea	Properties include enhancing the penetration abilities of other substances; anti-inflammatory, antiseptic, and deodorizing action that protects the skin's surface and helps maintain healthy skin.
vehicles	Spreading agents and ingredients that carry or deliver other ingredients into the skin and make them more effective.
water soluble	Mixable with water.
witch hazel	Extracted from the bark of the hamanelis shrub; can be a soothing agent or, in higher concentrations, an astringent.
zinc oxide	Inorganic physical sunscreen that reflects UVA radiation. Also used to protect, soothe, and heal the skin; is somewhat astringent, antiseptic, and antibacterial.

Esthetics

4

©EvaStory, 2011; used under license from Shutterstock.com

CHAPTER 14

The Treatment Room

Chapter Outline

- Why Study The Treatment Room?
- The Esthetician's Presentation
- Creating a Professional Atmosphere
- Furniture, Equipment, and Room Setup
- Treatment Room Supplies, Disposables, and Products
- Three-Part Procedure
- Room Preparation
- After the Facial: Decontamination Procedures
- Saving Resources and Money with Green Practices
- Procedures

Learning Objectives

After completing this chapter, you will be able to:

- ✓ LO1 Understand the components of creating a professional atmosphere.
- ✓ LO2 Describe what equipment and supplies are needed for facials.
- ✓ LO3 Prepare and set up the treatment room for services.
- ✓ LO4 Explain why the room setup should be comfortable for the esthetician.
- ✓ LO5 Properly clean and disinfect the treatment room.

Key Terms

Page number indicates where in the chapter the term is used.

dispensary
pg. 360

implements
pg. 365

LOHAS (Lifestyle of Health and Sustainability)
pg. 371

sharps container
pg. 359

sustainability
pg. 370

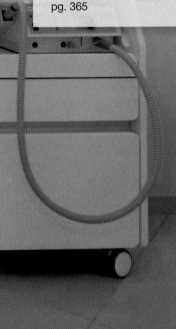

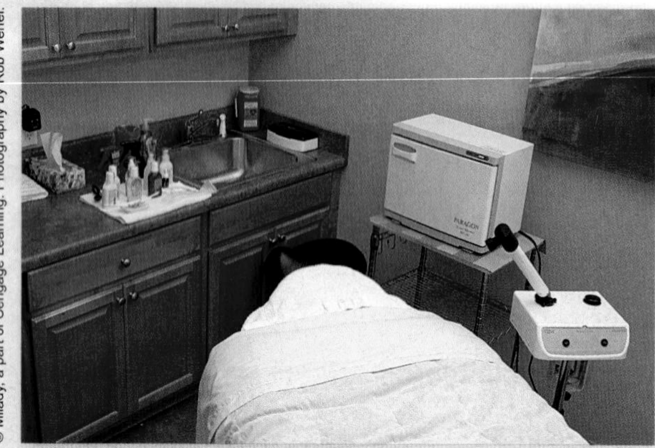

▲ Figure 14–1
A prepared treatment room.

This chapter is designed to help estheticians learn to prepare the treatment room for services. Included are easy-to-use checklists and advice for setting up, cleaning, and keeping the room well stocked. Just about everything needed for basic room preparation is listed in this chapter. Treatment room setup and preparation are integral parts of giving treatments (Figure 14–1). Creating a professional atmosphere involves many details. After the facial service, proper decontamination measures are needed to prepare the room for the next client. Treatment room setup includes choosing furniture, equipment, supplies, and products.

Why Study The Treatment Room?

Estheticians should study and have a thorough understanding of the treatment room topics in order to provide a comfortable and clean environment for both the client and technician so that the client's experience is enjoyable and relaxing.

- Planning and preparing a well-stocked and organized room is necessary to function efficiently and provide good service.
- Creating a clean, comfortable, and relaxing atmosphere is part of your service that clients expect.
- Estheticians/students are responsible for the cleanliness of the treatment rooms, and a clean environment is necessary for client safety and to comply with the laws of your state board regulations.
- Your success depends on many factors, including your appearance and professionalism, and you will feel confident if you are organized and prepared.

▲ Figure 14–2
The technician's presentation.

The Esthetician's Presentation

Making a good first impression is important in any business setting. Your success depends on many factors, including your image and attitude. An esthetician's appearance and professionalism reflect on the business. Practicing good hygiene, dressing professionally, and having a neat appearance all convey a polished image (Figure 14–2). Additionally, employers, coworkers, and clients appreciate working with someone who has a positive attitude. This positive attribute will contribute favorably to the team.

Being dependable and providing excellent customer service is imperative. Professionalism includes being a self-starter and taking the initiative to prepare the treatment room. Plan enough time to set up the room before the day begins. You will project a calm, confident image if you are prepared. Refer to Chapter 3, Your Professional Image, for more information on professionalism.

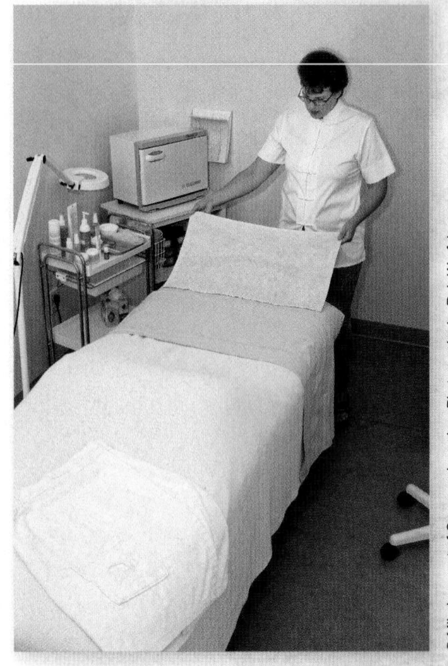

▲ Figure 14–3
Preparing the facial room.

Creating a Professional Atmosphere

Planning and preparing the treatment room for clients is the first step in performing services (Figure 14–3). The setup and supplies will vary, depending on the workplace and treatments offered. Whether you are an employee or self-employed, a well-stocked and organized room is necessary to function efficiently. You can provide services with minimal equipment, if necessary. Creating a clean, comfortable, and relaxing atmosphere is part of your service. A pleasant ambiance also improves the work environment for the staff.

A facility needs to be professional looking and clutter-free. Stations and supplies must be spotless. Consider the clients' comfort and yours when choosing equipment. The goal is to give quality service in a nice, quiet atmosphere. In this service-oriented business, the primary focus is the client and their entire experience while they are in your care.

Furniture, Equipment, and Room Setup

Treatment room furnishings can range from the basics to high-end designer equipment. A spa environment is usually more relaxing than a clinical one. Relaxing colors, music, and décor are preferable in a spa (Figure 14–4). Room esthetics is vital to create a relaxing, professional

CAUTION!

A workstation that is uncomfortable for the body and posture could cause neck, back, and hand problems over time.

◀ Figure 14–4
A beautifully appointed treatment room.

Did You Know?

Clients form their opinion of you and your business during the first few minutes of their visit. No matter how good the service is, they might not return if they are not greeted politely, if the treatment room is in disarray, or if they are treated poorly after the service. Customer service and teamwork affect everyone in the salon.

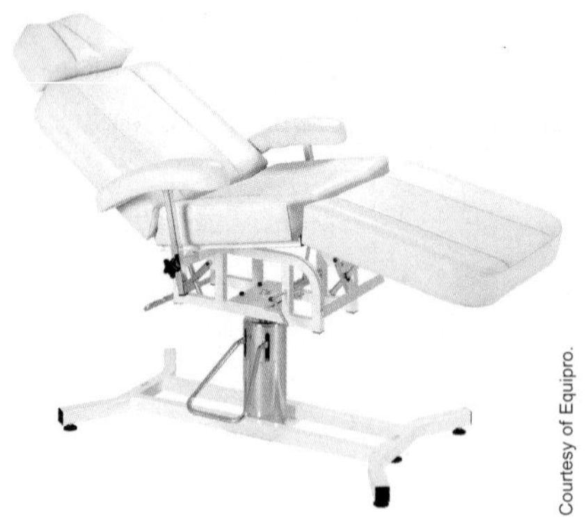
Courtesy of Equipro.

▲ Figure 14–5
An adjustable facial bed.

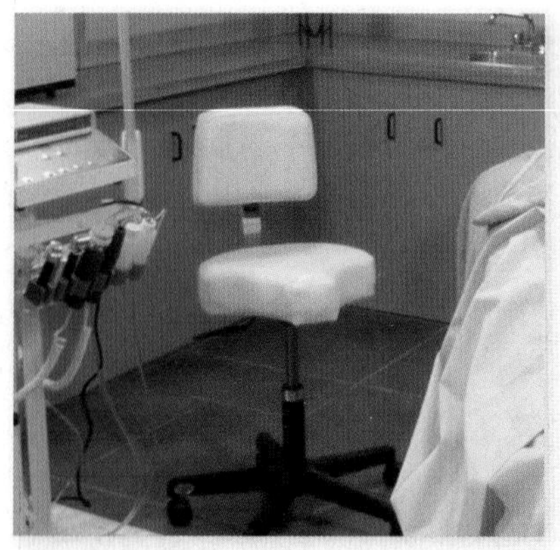
© Milady, a part of Cengage Learning. Photography by Larry Hamill.

▲ Figure 14–6
The esthetician's stool.

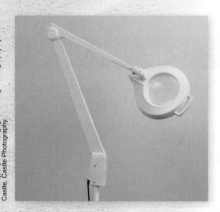

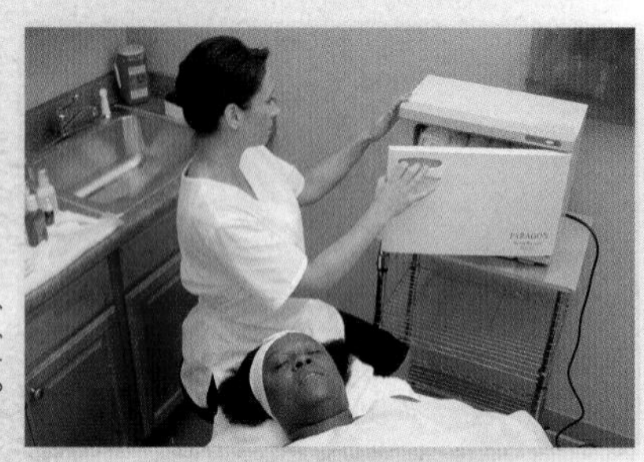
© Milady, a part of Cengage Learning. Photography by Rob Werfel.

▲ Figure 14–7
The towel warmer.

© Milady, a part of Cengage Learning. Photography by Paul Castle, Castle Photography.

▲ Figure 14–8
The magnifying lamp.

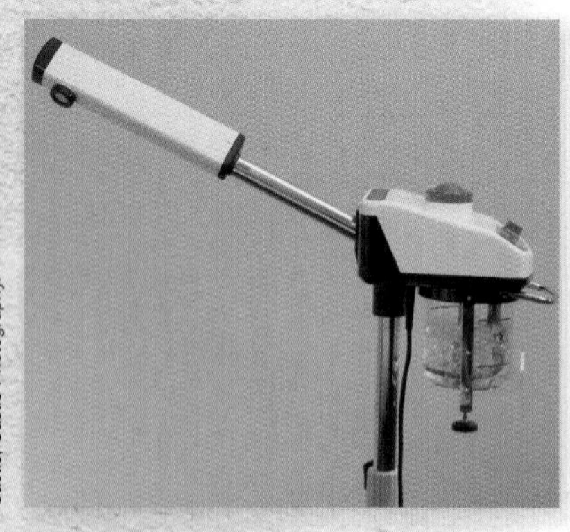
© Milady, a part of Cengage Learning. Photography by Paul Castle, Castle Photography.

▲ Figure 14–9
The steam machine.

atmosphere which includes scents, music, and both visual and thermal comfort. When setting up a room for treatments, think about the services you will perform and how you will work at the station. Another consideration is how comfortable the client will be on the treatment table (be sure to consider the needs of the male client). Client safety and following health regulations are the two most important considerations before, during, and after treatments. Facial equipment and machines are reviewed in Chapter 17, Facial Machines. ☑ L01

A Checklist of Furniture and Equipment

Equipment for the facial treatment consists of the following items:

- ***Treatment Table*** (also called a facial chair or bed). The treatment table can be a massage table or an esthetician's table. Make sure it is large enough to accommodate clients comfortably and is suitable for body waxing (Figure 14–5).
- ***Esthetician's chair***, or operator's stool (Figure 14–6). The technician's stool needs to be *ergonomically correct*: healthy for the body and spine. Make sure it is comfortable for you while you perform services and that it can roll around easily. Back support and adjustable height is preferable.
- ***Towel warmer***, or "hot cabbie." A towel warmer keeps towels warm and can also be used to warm products and cotton pads (Figure 14–7). Plastics will melt in a towel warmer, so use glass or ceramic dishes for warming products. Professional product warmers are also available.
- ***Magnifying lamp*** or ***light***. Also referred to as a "mag" lamp; used to analyze the skin and to perform detail work such as tweezing (Figure 14–8).
- ***Steamer*** (Figure 14–9). Steamers are great tools for warming and softening the skin. Steam is part of a standard facial procedure.

- ***Stepstool.*** A stepstool helps clients get on and off the bed safely. Make sure the stool is stable. Assist clients if they need help.
- ***Utility cart.*** A cart holds tools, supplies, and products. This can be a stationary table or roll cart.
- ***Galvanic, high-frequency, brush, vacuum*** and ***spray machines*** (Figure 14–10). These can either be individual machines or multifunctional machines all on one stand. See Chapter 17, Facial Machines, for information about machines.
- ***EPA-registered Disinfectant.*** A wet disinfectant should be located in each treatment room for disinfecting tools and equipment (Figures 14–11). Implements must be thoroughly cleaned of all visible matter before being placed in disinfectant solution.

  Note: An ultraviolet (UV) sanitizer unit does not disinfect tools and is only used for storage.
- Optional: An ***autoclave*** is a sterilizer for implements (Figure 14–12). This is necessary for a medical facility.
- ***Wax heater.*** The wax heater is an electric warming device used for soft-wax, paraffin, or hard-wax application (Figure 14–13). They are usually kept activated during the day for walk-ins or unexpected requests. Waxing is discussed in Chapter 18, Hair Removal.
- Closed, covered ***waste container.*** A metal receptacle with a self-closing lid and foot pedal is required for preventing contamination.
- Closed, covered ***laundry hamper.***
- ***Sharps container.*** A sharps container is a biohazard container for disposal of lancets. It is red, labeled, and puncture-proof (Figure 14–14). Follow OSHA and state regulations for proper disposal. Not all facilities perform services that require a sharps container.

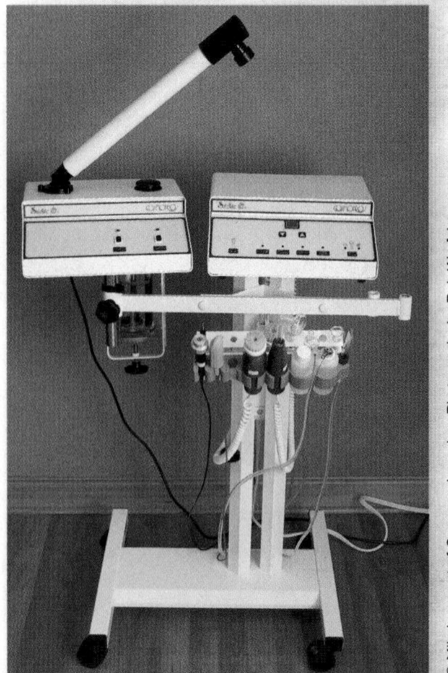

▲ Figure 14–10
Multifunctional machines.

▲ Figure 14–11
Wet sanitizer.

MIDMARK M11UltraClave

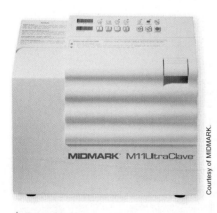

▲ Figure 14–12
Autoclave.

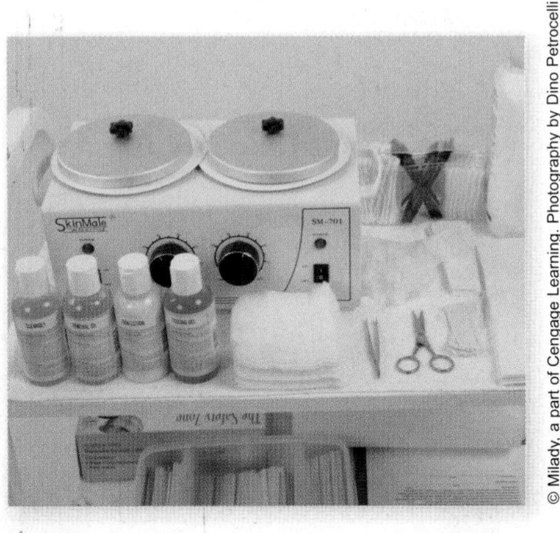

▲ Figure 14–13
Wax heaters.

▲ Figure 14–14
A sharps container.

▲ Figure 14–15
A neat dispensary helps maintain and control inventory.

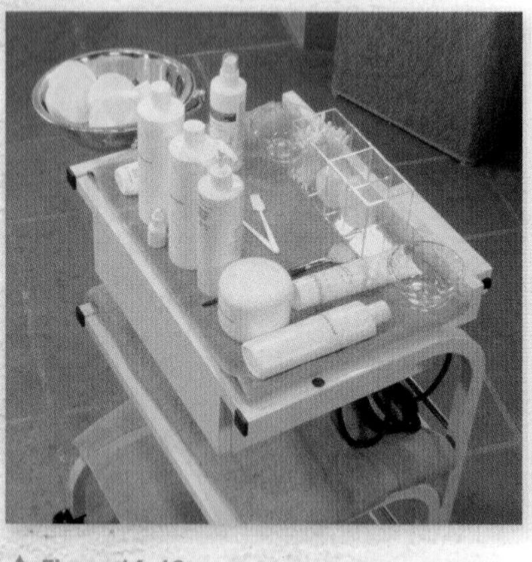

Treatment Room Supplies, Disposables, and Products

The Dispensary

If supplies and products are not kept in the treatment room or at the workstations, then they are kept in a **dispensary**, which is a separate room for mixing products and storing supplies (Figure 14–15). Supplies are kept in clean, covered, labeled containers. Proper storage is necessary to keep items from being contaminated. The amount of supply usage depends on the facility. Different setups require different numbers of towels or cotton supplies. Each instructor or manager will have a special setup procedure to follow (Figure 14–16). The following section presents an example of what is needed for a basic facial. Refer to the waxing and makeup chapters to set up for those services.

▲ Figure 14–16
Proper setup of supplies helps the treatment go smoothly.

Facial Supplies

Facial supplies include the following (Figure 14–17):

- Hand cleanser or antibacterial soap for hand washing
- Face and hand towels
- Disinfectant to decontaminate implements, equipment, and surfaces
- Bowls to warm or mix product in; also used to hold cotton pads or other supplies
- Spatulas to disperse products from jars
- Fan and mask brushes to apply masks or massage lotions
- Client headband to protect the hair and hold it out of the way
- Client gown/wrap for the client to change into
- Clean sheets/linens/bath towels (depending on the setup, use either sheets or towels)
- Blankets to cover the client
- Finger cots to use during extractions

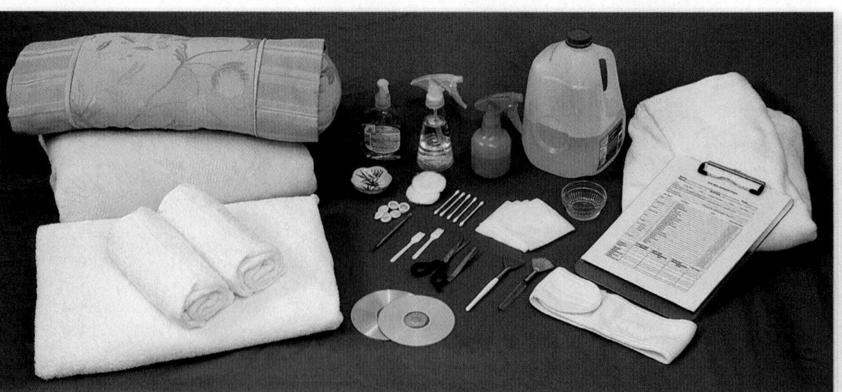

▶ Figure 14–17
Facial supplies.

- A bed warmer
- A bolster for back support, placed under the knees
- A pillow or rolled hand towel for neck support
- Implements: tweezers; an extraction tool
- Tongs to handle hot towels and retrieve clean items
- Distilled water for the steamer
- Client chart and home-care prescription card/pad
- Relaxing music
- Product retail brochures

Single-Use Items

Single-use items are disposable and can only be used once. This supply usage depends on your facility and may include the following:

- Paper towels
- Cotton 4" × 4" (10 cm × 10 cm) pads or single-use sponges to remove product from the skin (sponges are porous and cannot be disinfected or reused)
- Gauze squares for use with certain facial treatments
- Cotton or cotton pads, or 2" × 2" (5 cm × 5 cm) pads, for toner application and to make eye pads and cleansing pads
- Tissues for blotting the face
- Cotton swabs for product application, removing eye makeup, or performing extractions
- One pair of vinyl or nitrile gloves (latex is not recommended, as many people are allergic to latex and oil can break down the latex, compromising the protection of the gloves)
- A sealable plastic bag for proper disposal of single-use items
- Extraction supplies: cotton, swabs, lancets/needles, or extraction tool (see state regulations for extraction rules)
- Wax supplies (see Chapter 18, Hair Removal)

CAUTION!

Do not put an electric blanket beneath the bed linens. This is a fire hazard and can scorch the treatment table. Use only specified bed warmers made for this purpose. Electric blankets must go on top of the blankets. Bed warmers are a nice addition for client comfort.

Products

Products are the main ingredients in performing services. Chapter 13, Skin Care Products: Chemistry, Ingredients, and Selection, addresses the guidelines for choosing products. Have the correct products for all client services on hand. Basic products used in facials include the following (Figure 14–18):

- Cleanser
- Mask
- Exfoliant
- Face massage cream or lotion

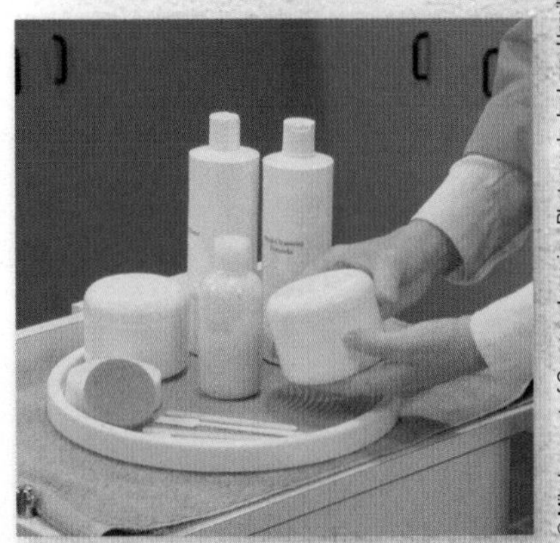

▲ Figure 14–18
Gather all products to be used before beginning the service.

- Toner or astringent
- Moisturizer
- Sunscreens
- Serums, eye cream, lip balm ☑ LO2

Three-Part Procedure

It is easier to keep track of what you are doing, to remain organized, and to give consistent service if you break your skin care procedures into three individual parts. The Three-Part Procedure consists of: 1) pre-service, 2) actual service, and 3) post-service.

Part One: Pre-Service Procedure

The pre-service procedure is an organized step-by-step plan for making sure your tools, implements, and materials are clean and disinfected; for setting up your facial room; and for meeting, greeting, and escorting your client to your service area.

PAGE 372

Part Two: Service Procedure

The service procedure is an organized, step-by-step plan for accomplishing the actual service the client has requested such as a basic facial, hair removal, or makeup application.

Part Three: Post-Service Procedure

The post-service procedure is an organized step-by-step plan for caring for your client after the procedure has been completed. It details helping your client through the scheduling and payment process and provides information for you on how to prepare for the next client.

PAGE 375

Here's a Tip

When setting up for a facial, preheat your towel warmer, towels, and steamer first. They take the longest to heat up (approximately 15 minutes).

Room Preparation

Before setting up the room, refer to the setup checklist that the facility uses. Look at your schedule to see what supplies are needed. If specified, put the clean laundry away. Have the client's chart notes ready, and review the product retail consultation forms if applicable. After practicing for a while, you will find that setting up becomes easier. The following guidelines are for a standard facial setup. It takes approximately 10 to 15 minutes to set up for a service and 10 to15 minutes to clean up after a service. A checklist of equipment, supplies, and single-use items is summarized in Chapter 15, Facial Treatments. Once you have gathered all that you need for treatments, you can start setting up.

Equipment Preparation

To prepare equipment, use the following guidelines:

1. Turn on the wax heater as needed. Check and adjust the temperature.
2. Preheat the towel warmer and put in wet towels, product dishes/bowls, and cotton cleansing pads to warm.
3. Preheat the steamer. First check the steamer water level (it should be just slightly below the fill line). If necessary, refill the steamer—using only distilled water. Follow the manufacturer's directions for care. Refer to Chapter 17, Facial Machines, for steamer information.
4. Preheat any other equipment needed.

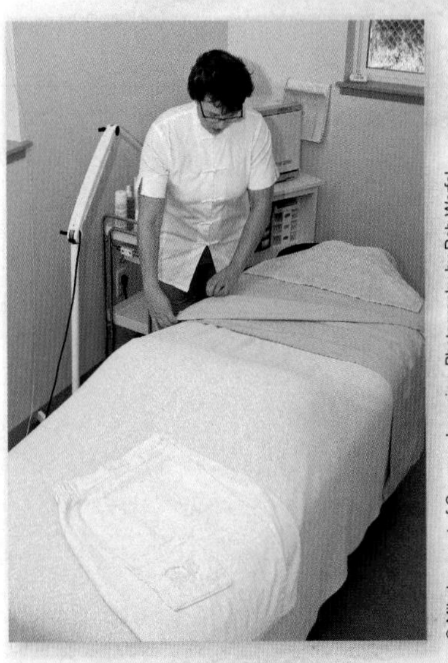

▲ Figure 14–19
Prepare the facial bed properly.

Prepare the Treatment Table

Procedures for preparing the treatment table are as follows (Figure 14–19):

1. Place clean linens neatly on the treatment table.
2. Place a blanket on top of the linens to keep the client warm and comfortable.
3. Lay out one hand towel to place under the head and one for placement over the décolleté (day-call-TAY) on the upper chest area if applicable.
4. Have a clean headband and gown or wrap ready for the client.
5. Have a bolster and pillow available.

Setting Up Supplies

Follow these procedures for setting up supplies:

1. Wash your hands with soap and warm water before setting up and touching clean items.
2. Check to make sure the disinfectant is ready. Wet disinfectants are filled and changed according to manufacturer's instructions (check to see that the strength is maintained by regular refilling).
3. Place supplies on a clean towel (paper or cloth) on the clean and disinfected workstation. (Put out supplies in the order used, lined up neatly, and cover with another towel until you are ready to use them.)

ACTIVITY

Time yourself to see how fast you can set up the workstation for a facial. See if you can set up from memory after practicing for a while.

Setting Out Single-Use Items

Single-use items are kept in clean, covered containers or closed cupboards to prevent contamination. After washing your hands, dispense only the amount needed for the service. Use clean forceps or tongs to retrieve additional supplies during a service.

Set out single-use supplies on a clean towel in the order they will be used. Do not put clean or soiled supplies on bare counter surfaces. Contaminated, single-use items must be disposed of properly in a covered waste receptacle.

Here's a Tip

Use a checklist to set up and clean up the treatment room—put an outline of the steps on 3" × 5" (7.5 cm × 12.5 cm) index cards for easy reference.

fyi A bolster can be a rolled-up towel or blanket in a pillowcase. Comfortable pillows are also important to a client's neck comfort and make a difference in how relaxing the facial is for the client. Check-in with clients to avoid causing neck or back pain from uncomfortable positions.

Arranging the Products

Set out the treatment products in order of the procedure application: cleanser, massage cream or lotion, masks, toner, moisturizer, and other products as determined by the client's skin analysis.

Setting Up the Dressing Area

Set up the dressing area for the client, if appropriate. Arrange a place for the client to sit while changing. Get water or tea ready for the client, and have a client chart and release form prepared.

Remember to explain to the client where to put their personal belongings and how to put on the spa wrap. Explain how to get into the bed and where to position their head (if you leave the room for them to change). Some clients have not had a facial or wax service and do not know exactly what they are expected to do. ☑ L03

Here's a Tip

Keep a clean nail brush in your room to scrub your nails and hands before performing services. Be sure to clean and disinfect the nail brush after every use.

Ergonomics

Ergonomics is the study of adapting work conditions to suit the worker. The equipment and the positions we use should be healthy for the spine and body. Adjust the facial table height, if possible. When setting up, remember to align the stool with the facial table for the correct height and position for performing services. The technician's feet should be flat on the floor, and hands should be below chest level (Figure 14–20). A good stool with back support is essential for esthetic work. It is worth paying a little more for a well-padded and quality stool. The room setup should be comfortable for the technician to avoid strain on the hands, body, and back.

Arrange the supply cart or counter as close to the facial table as possible. When reaching for a product or implement, or to adjust equipment, get up out of the chair. Do not overstretch your back to reach for something. Be aware of the position of your back, and remind yourself to sit up straight. Pay attention to your posture. Stretching and loosening up the hands before and after working is helpful in maintaining the health and flexibility of the wrists and hands. ☑ L04

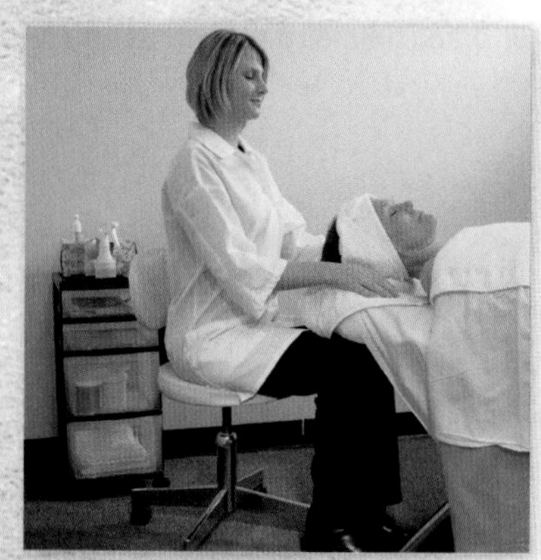

▲ Figure 14–20
Correct sitting posture for an esthetician.

After the Facial: Decontamination Procedures

Now that the facial setup has been reviewed, this is a good time to discuss the clean-up procedures, even though the facial procedure has not been performed yet. It is helpful to learn and practice each phase of a service before moving on to the next step. This way you can focus on the procedure since you will already be familiar with the pre- and post-service steps.

After completing the post-consultation with the client, be sure to record the client chart notes and write up retail sales. Then prepare the room for the

FOCUS ON

Exercises for Strengthening the Hands and Wrists

1. Hold the hands at chest level with fists clenched. Make a fist, squeezing as hard as you can, while holding for a count of five. Release the hands, spreading the fingers wide for a count of five. Repeat 10 to 20 times. This exercise is excellent for strengthening the hands and wrists (Figure 14–21).
2. Place both hands, palms down, on a flat surface. Tap each finger, beginning with the thumbs, and count each finger from thumb to little finger, as it is tapped in rhythm. Count 1, 2, 3, 4, 5. Then, starting with the little finger, tap each finger to the count of 5, 4, 3, 2, 1. This exercise is similar to playing the piano and is especially good for building coordination and hand control (Figure 14–22).
3. Place the palms together at chest level. Keep them together as you bend the left wrist as far back as it will go, and then do the same with the right wrist. Keep bending the wrists in rhythm for 20 counts. This exercise strengthens the hands and wrists and makes them more flexible (Figure 14–23).

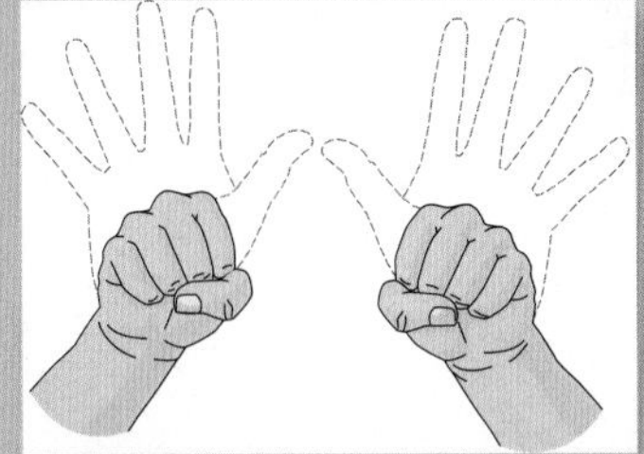

▲ Figure 14–21
Strengthening hands and wrists.

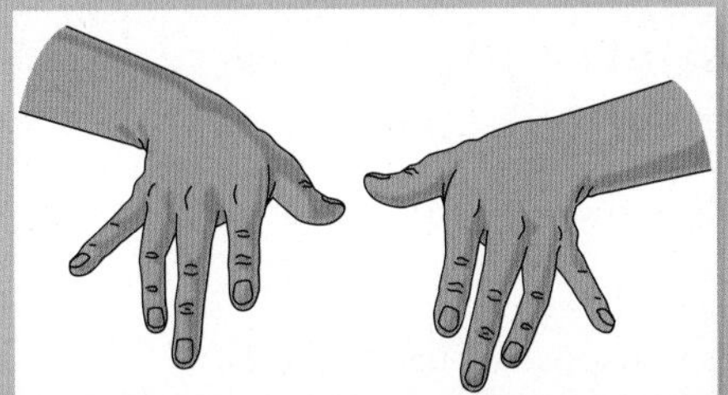

▲ Figure 14–22
Building coordination and hand control.

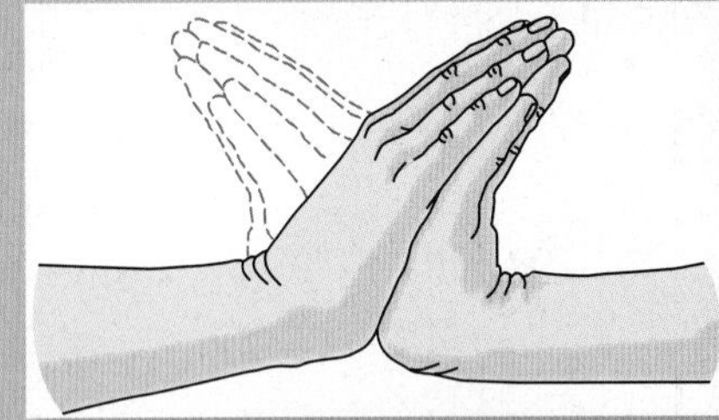

▲ Figure 14–23
Increasing flexibility of the hands and wrists.

next client, or clean the room in preparation for the end of the day. Remember that the order of the clean up varies with each facility's guidelines and that decontamination procedures improve as laws and technology evolve.

As discussed in Chapter 5, Infection Control: Principles and Practices, there are two methods of decontamination:

- Decontamination Method 1: Cleaning and then disinfecting with an appropriate EPA-registered disinfectant.
- Decontamination Method 2: Cleaning and then sterilizing.

Cleaning and Disinfecting Implements

Appropriate cleaning and disinfecting involves the following:

- Wear gloves for all decontamination procedures to prevent contamination and protect hands from the strong chemicals. Wash hands after completing decontamination procedures.
- Wash and disinfect all brushes, tweezers, and other nondisposables. **Implements** are multiuse items and tools such as brushes, tweezers, and comedone extractors.
- Wash implements thoroughly with antibacterial soap and dry them off first before placing in the disinfectant. This process is important to maintain the wet disinfectant strength and keep it from becoming dirty or diluted.

Here's a Tip

To avoid cross-contamination, roll the used side of linens and sheets inward so the dirty side is inside the laundry bundle. This also keeps product or hair off the floor and saves cleaning time. For additional cleanliness, do not let the linens or other items touch your clothing before or after use.

- Be sure all implements remain in the disinfectant for the appropriate amount of time according to the manufacturer's instructions. Do not leave implements in longer than the recommended time—doing so will ruin certain items that will break down and have to be replaced more often.
- Remove, rinse, dry, and put them away.
- Store clean items in a covered container in a drawer or cupboard when not in use.
- Clean and disinfect bowls and other multiuse items. Dry and store properly.

- Change the disinfectant to comply with manufacturer's directions and infection control regulations. If required, record on a dated log when the disinfectant is changed (Table 14–1).

Disinfecting Equipment and the Treatment Room

Disinfecting the equipment and facial room involves the following procedures:

- Properly dispose of used supplies.
- Turn off the table warmer if used.
- Clean the wax machine (and turn it off at the end of the day).
- Disinfect the steamer and mag lamp.
- Disinfect the bottom tray and the inside of the towel warmer after removing all used items.
- Disinfect any other equipment used, and turn it off.
- Clean all containers, and wipe off dirty product containers with a disinfectant.
- Clean all counters, sinks, surfaces, and floor mats with disinfectant.

DISINFECTANT LOG

Change the high-level disinfectant solution in the container according manufacturer's directions or if it is cloudy and seems to require changing. Record when it is changed.

DATE CHANGED	YOUR INITIALS
3/5/13	*S.L.*

▲ Table 14–1 **Disinfectant Log.**

Laundry and Linens

Clean-up procedures for laundry and linens:

- Remove dirty linens, and remake the treatment table for the next client or leave it unmade.
- Place the used linens, towels, and sheets in the appropriate covered container or laundry hamper.
- Fasten the Velcro® on the headbands and client wraps before putting them in the laundry to keep lint from sticking to the Velcro®.

Single-Use Items

Appropriate handling of single-use items involves the following:

- Soiled items such as gloves and extraction supplies must be placed in a sealable plastic bag and then in a covered waste container or biohazard container.
- While in use, single-use items must be placed on surfaces that can be disinfected or disposed of, such as a paper towel.
- Keep the clean supplies separate from the used ones. Take out only what is needed for each service.
- Disposable extraction lancets and needles go in a biohazard/sharps container. (Check OSHA and state rules for proper handling.)

REGULATORY AGENCY ALERT

Check with the regulatory agencies on extraction laws and the disposal of extraction supplies.

End-of-the-Day Clean-Up

In most facilities, estheticians/students are responsible for the cleanliness of the treatment rooms. Technicians must be prepared to clean up areas they use. Be sure to alert the manager about areas of the facility that may need repair or deep cleaning. Clean-up procedures are regulated by regional laws, so be aware of these regulations.

End-of-the-Day Checklist

At the end of the day, be sure to follow these procedures:

- Prepare the room, and check the schedule for the next shift or workday.
- Use a clean-up checklist to make sure you did not forget anything.
- Turn off all equipment.
- Leave the towel-warmer door open to dry, and empty the tray underneath before cleaning and disinfecting it.
- Clean anything that has not been cleaned after the last service including the bed, sink, counters, and doorknobs.
- Refill all containers, supplies, and the steamer.
- Check floors; sweep or mop as required. Check for wax spills.
- Empty waste containers. Replace with clean trash liners.
- Remove personal items from the area.

Here's a Tip

Do not put wet brushes in a closed drawer or container because they will mildew and not dry. Lay brushes out to dry, covered with a clean towel, before storing them in a closed container.

ACTIVITY

It is interesting to find out what setting up a treatment room might cost. On your own, make a list of suppliers that carry the tools and supplies you need. Check out beauty supply houses, Internet sites, trade journals, and trade shows to get an idea of what is available. Research the supplies and equipment costs to determine what you would need to spend to set up your own room (Table 14–2).

DETERMINING THE COSTS OF SETTING UP A TREATMENT ROOM	
ITEMS	ESTIMATED COSTS
Sink/water supply	
Treatment table/chair	
Esthetician stool	
Hot cabinet/towel warmer	
Utility cart	
Magnifying lamp	
Steamer	
Stepstool	
Waxers	
Optional electrical equipment	
Furniture	
Linens	
Products	
Supplies	
Single-use items	
CD player/music	
Total Cost: $	

▲ Table 14–2 **Determining the Costs of Setting Up a Treatment Room.**

FOCUS ON Professionalism

Being a team player means going out of your way to help others with cleaning, setting up, and assisting clients. Taking the initiative to build your own clientele is how you become successful. Never gossip or discuss pay or tips in the workplace. The primary focus is on taking care of clients; personal gain is a secondary goal and benefit. When you are happy and truly enjoy your job, it is easy to share positive enthusiasm and energy with everyone else.

You now have a good idea about how much work goes into preparing for services. Once you have a good setup and all of the tools needed, it is easy to stay organized and work efficiently. A clean environment is necessary for client safety and to comply with the laws of your local regulatory agencies. Clients will be confident in your ability and feel safe in your hands when they know your facility is clean. Keeping the room organized is necessary for a smooth, efficient operation. Now you are ready to welcome clients. The chapters following this one will cover facial, waxing, and makeup procedures. ☑ LO5

Saving Resources and Money with Green Practices

It is practical to think about saving resources and costs when planning the facility, treatment room, amenities, and what services to offer. Businesses that strive to be sustainable are more balanced, healthy, and successful. Green practices such as reducing energy and water use lead to many positive results. The conscious movement to improve the way we live and lessen the impact on the world is at the forefront of today's culture. Customers expect businesses to use green practices and be socially responsible (Figure 14–24).

Sustainability and green business models are becoming mainstream. It is an opportunity to make a difference in the way the beauty industry does business. While the industry is known for the focus on caring for others, it is often wasteful in the excessive use of packaging, water, supplies, and other resources. It's a natural extension for the holistic nature of the beauty and spa industry to take better care of the planet and people, and not to exist just for profit. Sustainability balances these three aspects: people, planet, and profit. Greening the business strengthens relationships between employees and customers that share these same values.

Green Facility Operations

Beauty services, products, supplies, operations, utilities, green building, and responsible facility management are all components of a green facility. Many salons are implementing energy and water conservation practices that save both money and natural resources. Buying organic and healthier products and fewer disposable supplies are ways to green up the facial room. Consider what could save natural resources when purchasing items for the facility.

Treatment Rooms

Choosing equipment, supplies, and other needs for the treatment rooms makes an impact on the business. Purchasing equipment that lasts will save money and time in the long run. Having dependable equipment also makes the services more reliable. A good magnifying light or steamer may last 10 years, whereas an inexpensive one may only last 2 years. Quality linens improve the client experience and quality of the service. Water conservation is another important practice that can be implemented in the facility by using low-flow fixtures and instant hot-water taps.

◀ **Figure 14–24 Greening the facility is good for business.**

The Treatment Menu

When designing a treatment menu consider the equipment, products, and supplies that will be needed. These all contribute to the overhead and cost of providing services. As a case in point, a complicated treatment such as a body mask that takes excessive water for rinsing could be altered to use less water by changing to a product that is easier to rinse off. Using locally-sourced natural products such as local clay or herbs are also popular treatment choices.

Did You Know?

What is Sustainability? Sustainability is meeting the needs of the present without compromising the ability of future generations to meet their needs. The three facets of sustainability are the three E's: the *Environment*, the *Economy*, and social *Equity*.

Choosing Green Products

Research the ingredients and packaging when choosing retail and back bar products. Many clients want organic, healthy products in recycled packaging. Plastic bottles replaced with recycled content packaging is a positive step in the packaging industry. Some buyers now want to know how responsibly products are manufactured and how toxic the chemicals are in producing our goods.

Using Fewer Supplies

With strict client safety and cleanliness standards, it is challenging to get away from using single-use, disposable supplies. It is essential to adhere to laws and regulations. Check local regulations for rules on using single-use items, such as using glass drinking cups for clients in the facility. Using washable drinking glasses is not legal in some areas that require single-use, throw-away cups. There are compostable alternatives to plastic cups. Of course only disinfected or clean items are used for clients, but changes can be made to save on throw-away supplies.

Choosing washable alternatives for single-use items, such as 4″ × 4″ (10 cm × 10 cm) esthetic wipes saves throwing away thousands of cotton pads and other items. This also saves money and time spent on purchasing in the long run. Microfiber esthetic wipes are great choices to replace the cotton wipes or sponges. Another way to save resources and money is to use towels instead of single-use, throw-away paper items. Using smaller towels and fewer towels and linens leads to saving water and time used in doing laundry.

Other ways to save money and time are to be conscious of the products and supplies used. Try and use less without sacrificing the quality of the service. Does the client need to put on a gown or can she just slip under the sheet? Give them the option. Spatulas and other nonporous items can be disinfected instead of thrown away. It's good for business to work more efficiently and keep costs down.

Conscious Purchasing

When purchasing other supplies, paper, packaging, front-desk items and office supplies, try to minimize packaging. Look for recycled paper, products, and containers. Print minimal marketing materials on recycled paper. Do more Internet marketing and save on printing expensive brochures.

Waste Reduction

The Three *R's* of waste reduction are: *Reduce, Reuse*, and *Recycle*. Precycling by buying less is the first step in reducing waste. This helps save money and storage space. Be creative with displays and use what you have on hand or can reuse later when buying things. Reducing plastic material and switching to glass is another easy way to help green up the facility. Glass can be recycled much easier than plastic.

The Green Facility

Energy conservation is the primary focus to save money and resources. Heating and cooling a building is expensive. Reducing energy use by monitoring the temperature, using energy efficient light fixtures, and turning off power strips that are not in use can save thousands of dollars per year in a typical facility. Water conservation is an important and scarce resource. Using conservation methods both indoors and outdoors in landscaping can also save hundreds of dollars per year for a facility. Letting water run full blast at the sink wastes thousands of gallons of water and dollars.

Another component of a green building is healthy indoor environmental quality. Using green materials such as nontoxic paint has many healthy benefits. The green choices for furniture and interiors are definitely expanding. Healthy indoor air quality is important for the staff and clients. Good ventilation and use of nontoxic products without chemicals are essential to the occupants' health. Indoor environmental quality includes comfortable room temperatures, acoustics, visual aesthetics, and scents. It is interesting to note that these healthy practices are all aspects that spas offer as part of the client's relaxing experience.

When greening the facility, consider the stations, client lounge, changing rooms, front desk, reception area, office, retail area, staff break room, and bathrooms. Start with small steps and goals to make your facility more sustainable. Share your progress with coworkers and clients. It is also a great team builder and marketing promotion.

Did You Know?

The LOHAS, acronym for **Lifestyle of Health and Sustainability**, consumers are forward-thinking individuals who consider the impact on the environment and society when making purchasing decisions. In 2010 the LOHAS market comprised 20% of the adult population and was a $200 billion market that is expected to double by 2012.

Web Resources

www.americansalon.com

www.dayspamagazine.com

www.greenspanetwork.com

www.milady.cengage.com

www.modernsalon.com

www.skininc.com

www.estheticians.com

PROCEDURE 14-1

Pre-Service Procedure

Service Tip

Before servicing a client, take a moment to sit on your facial chair and take a good look around. Based on what you see, hear, and feel, ask yourself this question: What kind of an experience will my client have while she is here?

Answering the following questions will enable you to provide your client with a positive experience:

- Is my room clean and organized or cluttered and messy?
- Will the music and the temperature be comfortable for the client?
- Am I wearing too much perfume/cologne? Am I carrying an unpleasant food or tobacco odor? Is my breath pleasant-smelling?
- When I look at myself in the mirror, do I see the professional I want to be? Does my personal grooming—my hair, makeup, and clothing—look professional?
- Do I look as if I am happy and enjoying my work?
- Is there some problem bothering me today that is affecting my ability to concentrate on the needs of my client?

Remember the old adage: You only get one chance to make a good first impression. Stack the odds in your favor!

A. Preparing the Facial Room

Check your room supply of linens (towels and sheets) and replenish as needed. For the first appointment of the day, preheat your towel warmer, towels, wax heater, steamer, and any other equipment as needed.

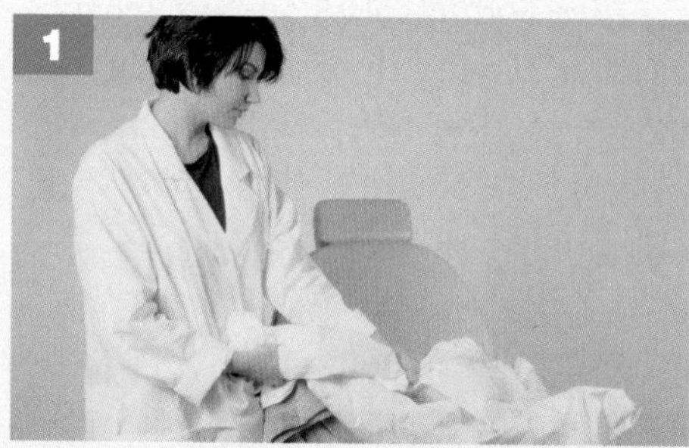

1 Change the bed or treatment chair linens.

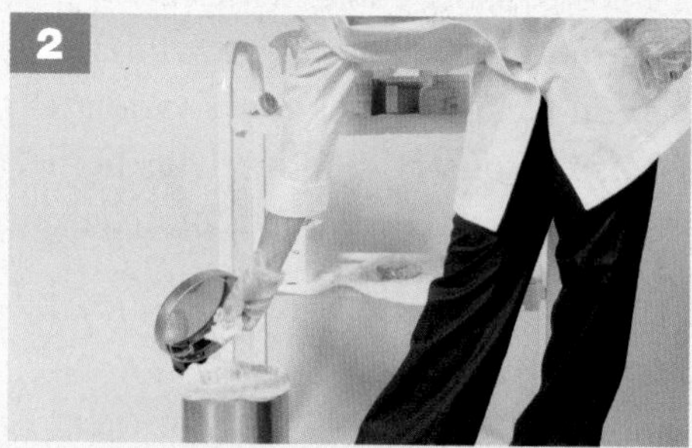

2 Throw away any disposables used during the previous service.

3 Clean and disinfect any used brushes or implements such as mask brushes, comedo extractors, tweezers, machine attachments, and electrodes. See Procedure 5–1, Disinfecting Nonelectrical Tools and Implements on page 104, to clean and disinfect implements properly.

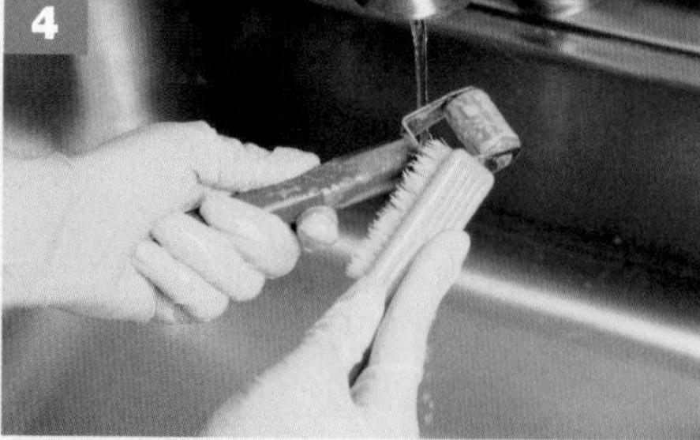

4 Clean and disinfect any machine parts used during the previous service.

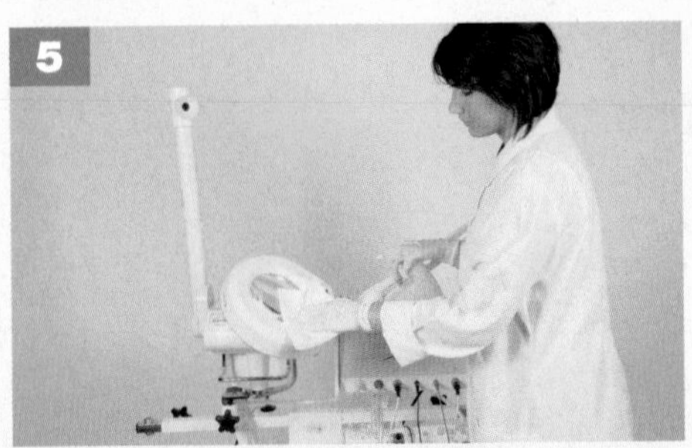

5

5 Clean and disinfect counters and magnifying lamp or lens.

6 Check the water level on the steamer/vaporizer as needed.

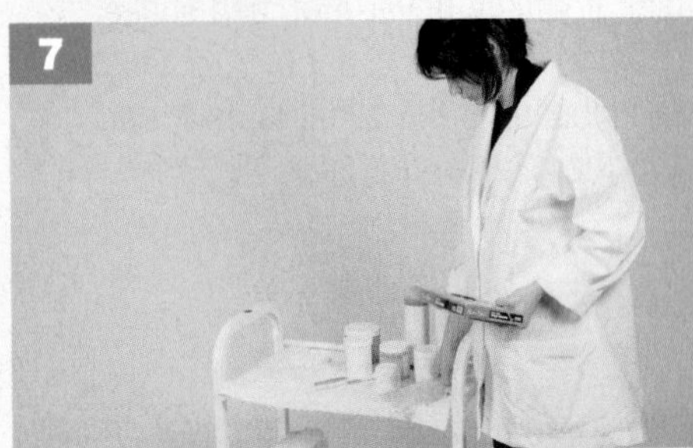

7

7 Replace any disposable implements you may need such as gloves, sheet cotton, gauze squares, sponges for cleansing and makeup, disposable makeup applicators (mascara wands, lip brushes, other brushes), spatulas and tongue-depressor wax applicators, cotton swabs, facial tissue, and wax strips.

8 Prepare to greet your next client.

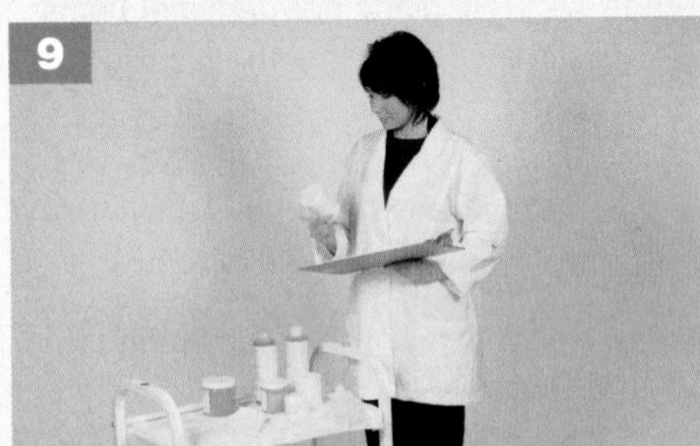

9

9 Review your client schedule for the day and decide which products you are likely to need for each service. Make sure you have enough of all the products you will be using that day. You may have to retrieve additional product from the dispensary. This is also a good time to refresh your mind about each repeat client you will be seeing that day and his or her individual concerns.

10 Place supplies on a clean towel or cloth in the order to be used, lined up neatly, and cover with another towel until you are ready to use them.

11 Your room should be ready to go from the previous night's thorough cleaning. (See "At the End of the Day" in Procedure 14–2, Post-Service Procedure.)

B. Preparing for the Client

12 Retrieve the client's intake form or service record card and review it. If the appointment is for a new client, let the receptionist know that the client will need an intake form.

13 Organize yourself by taking care of your personal needs before the client arrives—use the restroom, get a drink of water, return a personal call—so that when your client arrives, you can place your full attention on her needs.

14 Turn off cell phone, pager, or PDA. Be sure that you eliminate anything that can distract you from your client while she is in the salon.

15 Take a moment to clear your head of all your personal concerns and issues. Take a couple of deep breaths and remind yourself that you are committed to providing your clients with fantastic service and your full attention.

16 Wash your hands using Procedure 5–3, Proper Hand Washing on page 108, before going to greet your client.

C. Greet Client

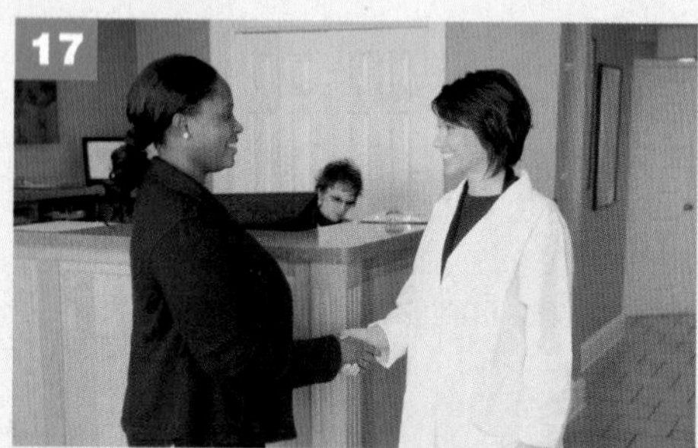
17

17 Greet your client in the reception area with a warm smile and in a professional manner. Introduce yourself if you've never met, and shake hands. The handshake is the first acceptance by the client of your touch, so be sure your handshake is firm and sincere. If the client is new, ask her for the intake form she filled out in the reception area.

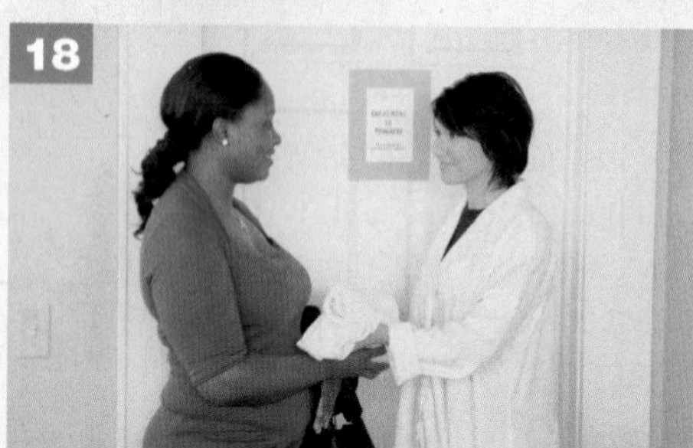
18

18 Escort the client to the changing area for her to change into a smock or robe. Make sure you tell her where to securely place her personal items. If you do not have a changing room or lockers, she will need to change in the treatment room.

19 Ask the client to remove all jewelry and put in a safe place because you do not want to stop the service for her to remove the jewelry later.

20 Invite her to take a seat in the treatment chair or to lie down on the treatment table.

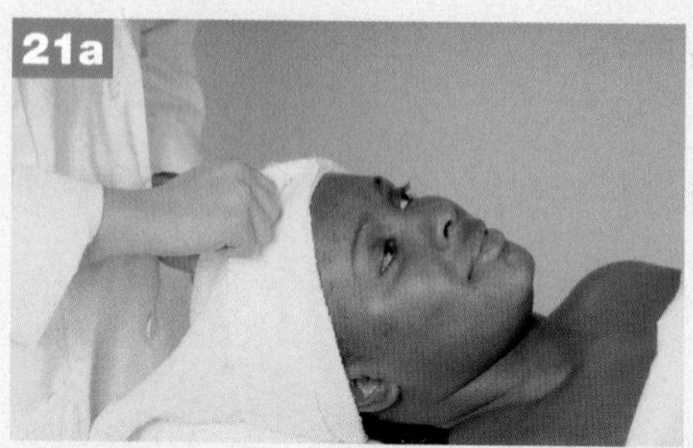
21a

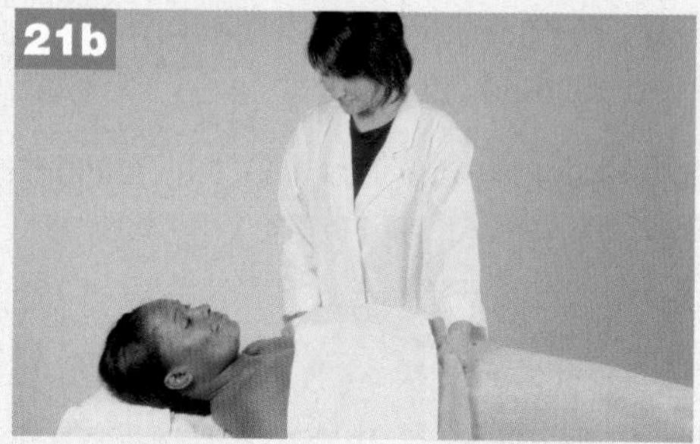
21b

21 Drape the client properly and either place her hair in a protective cap or use a headband and towels to drape her hair properly. Give her a blanket and make sure she is comfortable before beginning the service. Remember, the client is not just a facial or another service, but a person you want to build a relationship with. By first showing clients respect, you will begin to gain their trust in you as a professional. Openness, honesty, and sincerity are always the most successful approach in winning clients' trust, respect, and, ultimately, their loyalty.

22 Perform a consultation before beginning the service. If you are servicing a returning client, ask how her skin has been since her last treatment. If the client is new, discuss the information on the intake form, and ask any questions you have regarding her skin or any conditions listed on the form. Determine a course of action for the treatment, and briefly explain your plan to the client.

PROCEDURE
14-2 Post-Service Procedure

A. Advise Clients and Promote Products

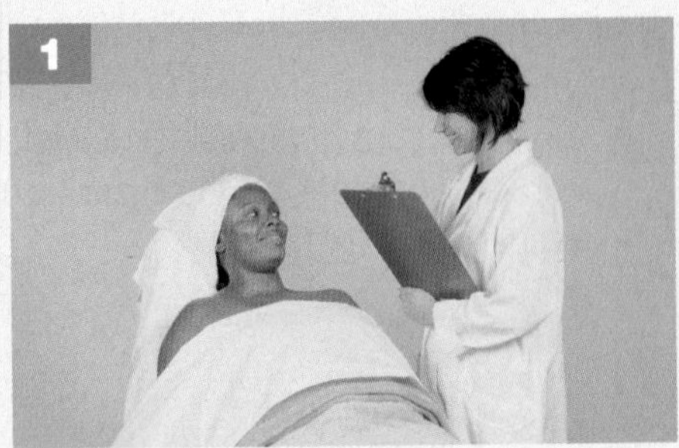

1

2

1 Before the client leaves your treatment area, ask her how she feels and if she enjoyed the service. Explain the conditions of her skin and your ideas about how to improve them. Be sure to ask if she has any questions or anything else she wishes to discuss. Be receptive and listen. Never be defensive. Determine a plan for future visits. Give the client ideas to think over for the next visit.

2 Advise client about proper home-care and explain how the recommended professional products will help to improve any skin conditions that are present. This is the time to discuss your retail product recommendations. Explain that these products are important and how to use them.

B. Schedule Next Appointment and Thank Client

3

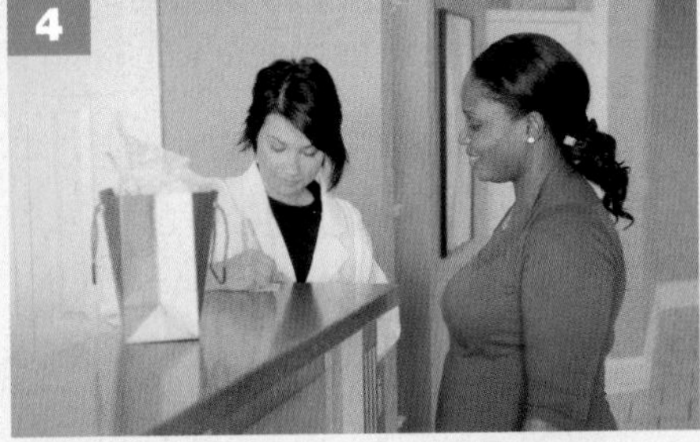

4

3 Escort the client to the reception desk and write up a service ticket for the client that includes the service provided, recommend home-care, and the next visit/service that needs to be scheduled. Place all recommended professional retail home-care products on counter for the client. Review the service ticket and the product recommendations with your client.

4 After the client has paid for her service and take-home products, ask if you can schedule her next appointment. Set up the date, time, and type of service for this next appointment, write the information on your business card, and give the card to the client.

PROCEDURE

14-2 Post-Service Procedure (continued)

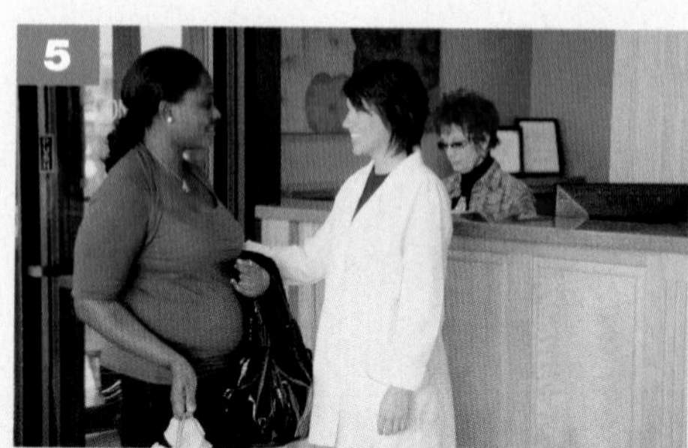

5 Thank the client for the opportunity to work with her. Express an interest in working with her in the future. Invite her to contact you should she have any questions or concerns about the service provided. If the client seems apprehensive, offer to call her in a day or two in order to check-in with her about any issues she may have. Genuinely wish her well, shake her hand, and wish her a great day.

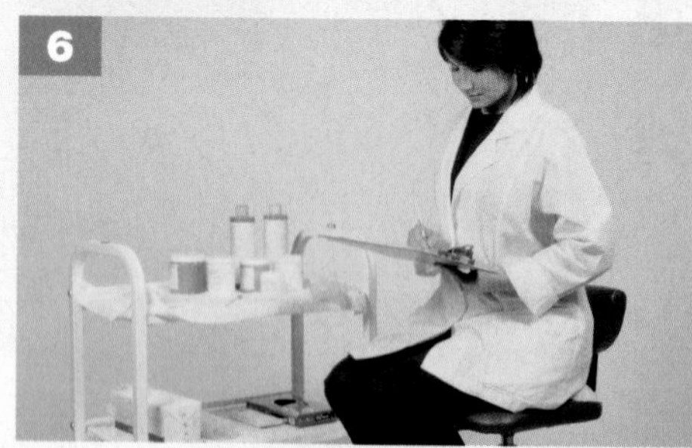

6 Be sure to record service information, observations, and product recommendations on the client record, and be sure you return it to the proper place for filing.

At the End of the Day

1 Put on a fresh pair of gloves to protect yourself from contact with soiled linens and implements.

2 Turn off all equipment.

3 Remove all dirty laundry from the hamper. Spray the hamper with a disinfectant aerosol spray or wipe it down with disinfectant. Mildew grows easily in hampers.

4 Remove all dirty spatulas, used brushes, and other utensils. Most of these should have been removed between clients during the day.

5 Thoroughly clean and disinfect all multiuse tools and implements.

6 Wipe down all counters, the facial chair, machines, and other furniture with an approved disinfectant. The magnifying lamp should be cleaned on both sides in the same manner.

7 Replenish the room with fresh linens, spatulas, utensils, and other supplies so it is ready for the next day.

8 Change disinfection solution.

9 Maintain vaporizer as necessary.

10 Check the room for dirt, smudges, or dust on the walls, on the baseboards, in corners, or on air vents. Vacuum and mop the room with a disinfectant.

11 Replenish any empty jars. If you are reusing jars for dispensing creams from a bulk container, always use up the entire content of the small jar and thoroughly cleanse the jar before replenishing. Never add cream to a partially used jar. Rinse the empty jar well with hot water and then disinfect, rinsing thoroughly. Allow the jar to dry before refilling.

12 Empty waste containers. Replace with clean trash liners.

PROCEDURE

14-3 & 14-4

IMPLEMENTS AND MATERIALS

- Roll of cotton
- Bowl
- Water
- Disinfectant
- Covered container or sealable plastic bag for storage

Preparation: Making Cleansing Pads and Butterfly Eye Pads

Preparation of Cotton Pads and Compresses

If prepackaged 4" × 4" (10 cm × 10 cm) esthetic wipes or sponges are not available, cotton pads can be made from a roll of cotton. You can prepare all cotton cleansing pads, eye pads, and the cotton compress pads that are used in a facial before the treatment begins. In a busy salon, the esthetician should check the appointment book at the beginning of each work day to see how many appointments are booked for that day. To save time, enough pads and compresses can then be made for the entire day if they are kept clean. Store pads and compresses in a covered container.

Remove enough pads from the container before each treatment and place them in a bowl that is kept within easy reach during the facial treatment. For each client, you may need a minimum of one pair of eye pads, one cotton compress mask, and four to six cleansing pads. The pads and compresses that are not used on the day they are made can be stored safely in an airtight, covered container or placed in a plastic bag and refrigerated for use the next day.

PROCEDURE

14-3 Making Cleansing Pads

IMPLEMENTS AND MATERIALS

- Roll of cotton
- Bowl
- Water
- Disinfectant
- Covered container or sealable plastic bag for storage

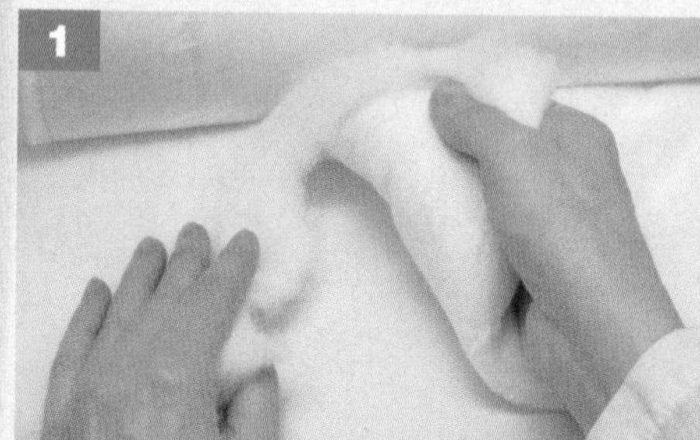

1 Divide a roll of cotton into strips approximately 4-inches (10 centimeters) wide. This is about the width of the average hand. Tear the cotton (do not cut) so that the edges are frayed and the cleansing pads are less lumpy when the edges are folded under.

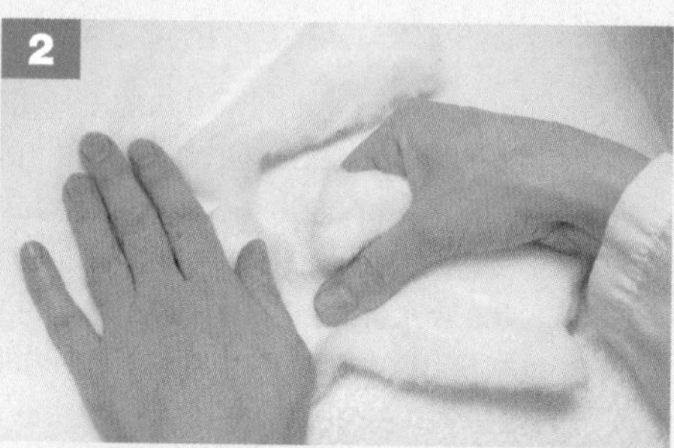

2 To make cleansing pads, hold one of the cotton strips in one hand and pull downward with the other hand until the cotton tears, making a cotton square approximately 4-inches (10 centimeters) wide by 5-inches (12.5 centimeters) long. Four to six of these pieces will be needed for each facial treatment.

3 Submerge the cotton in water while supporting the pad with your fingers.

4 Tuck the edges of the cotton under while turning it in your hands. Place the round pad in the palm of your hand, placing the other palm over the pad. Squeeze out excess water from the pad.

PROCEDURE

14-4 Making Butterfly Eye Pads

IMPLEMENTS AND MATERIALS

- Roll of cotton
- Bowl
- Water
- Disinfectant
- Covered container or sealable plastic bag for storage

Eye pads can be made from either 4" × 4" (10 cm × 10 cm) cotton squares, prepackaged round cotton pads, or pieces of cotton. There are two types of eye pads: round and butterfly. Both styles of eye pads are correct, and the choice of which to use is up to the esthetician. The pads should be large enough to cover the entire eye area, but not so large that they interfere with product application or treatment. The advantage of the butterfly pad over the round pad is that it will not fall off of the eyes as easily. Round eye pads are made following the same procedure as for round cleansing pads, but the cotton piece should measure about 2½" × 2½" (6.25 cm × 6.25 cm).

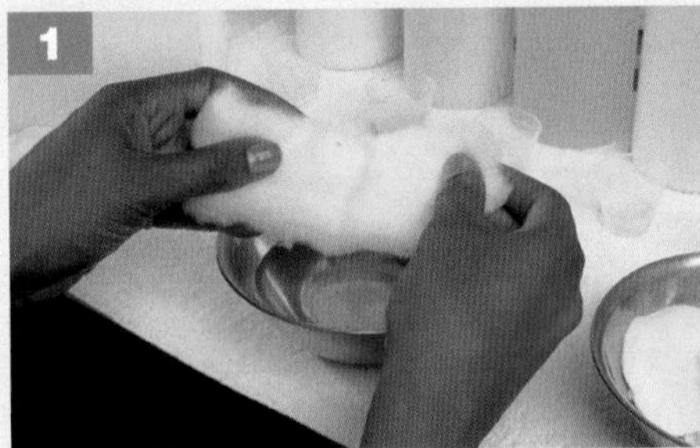

1 Dip a piece of cotton measuring approximately 2" × 6" (5 cm × 15 cm) into the water.

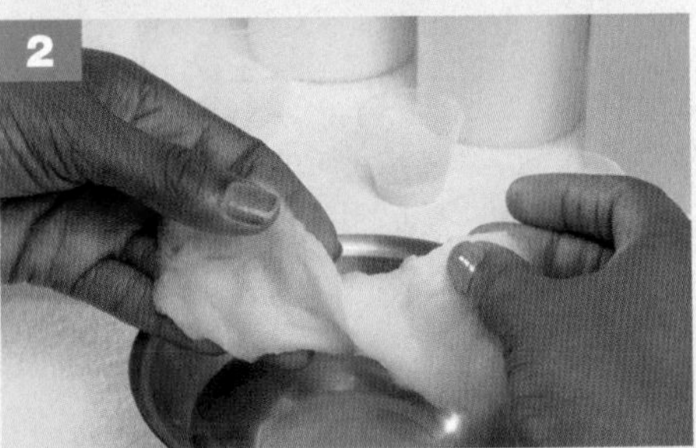

2 Twist the cotton in the center with a one-half turn.

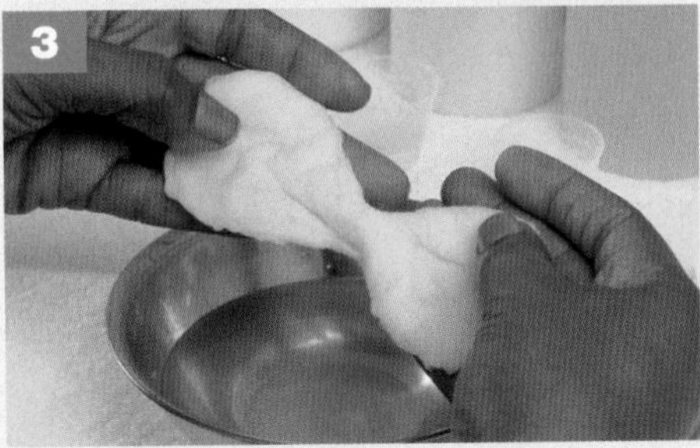

3 Fold the pad in half and squeeze out the excess water.

Optional: Take a prepackaged esthetics square 4" × 4" (10 cm × 10 cm) pad, unfold lengthwise, and twist it in the middle.

Clean-Up

- **Perform** PROCEDURE 5-2 Aseptic Procedure PAGE 106
- **Complete** PROCEDURE 14-2 Post-Service Procedure PAGE 375

Review Questions

1. What type of salon atmosphere is it important to create?
2. What are the two most important considerations in preparing and cleaning the room?
3. What essential equipment do you need for facials?
4. What does ergonomically correct mean?
5. How long does it take to set up for a facial?
6. How do you disinfect implements?
7. Where do you put soiled single-use items when you have completed the service?
8. What steps are involved in cleaning the room or workstation at the end of the day?

Glossary

dispensary	Room or area used for mixing products and storing supplies.
implements	Multiuse items and tools such as brushes, tweezers, and comedone extractors.
LOHAS	Acronym for *Lifestyle of Health and Sustainability;* forward-thinking consumers who consider the impact on the environment and society when making purchasing decisions.
sharps container	Plastic biohazard containers for disposable needles and anything sharp. The container is red and puncture-proof and must be disposed of as medical waste.
sustainability	Meeting the needs of the present without compromising the ability of future generations to meet their needs. The three facets of sustainability are the three E's: the *Environment*, the *Economy*, and social *Equity*.

CHAPTER 15

Facial Treatments

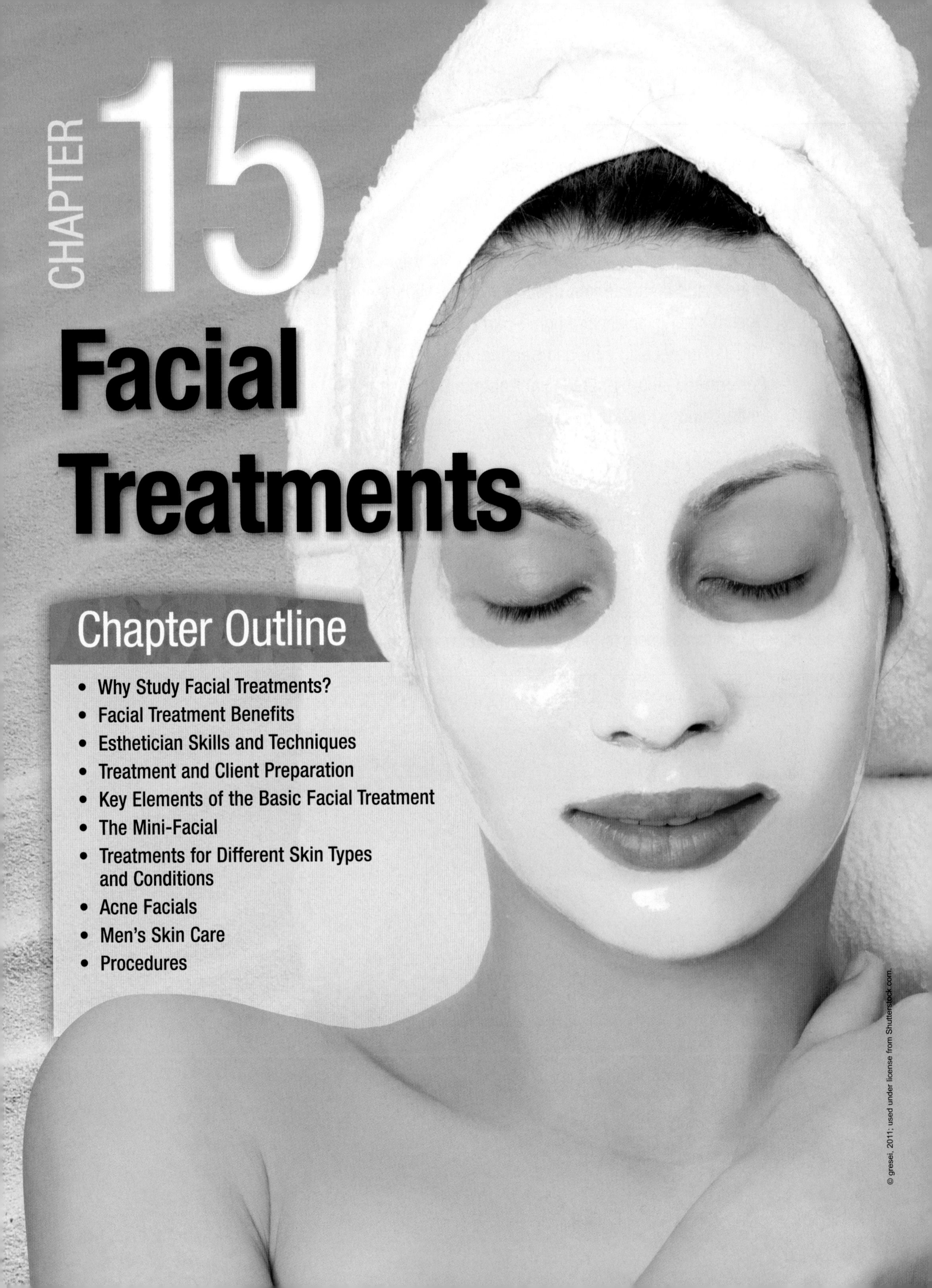

Chapter Outline

- Why Study Facial Treatments?
- Facial Treatment Benefits
- Esthetician Skills and Techniques
- Treatment and Client Preparation
- Key Elements of the Basic Facial Treatment
- The Mini-Facial
- Treatments for Different Skin Types and Conditions
- Acne Facials
- Men's Skin Care
- Procedures

Learning Objectives

After completing this chapter, you will be able to:

- ☑ LO1 Describe the benefits of a facial treatment.
- ☑ LO2 Perform the facial set up procedures.
- ☑ LO3 Explain the key elements of the basic facial treatment.
- ☑ LO4 Understand the treatment needs for dry, dehydrated, mature, sensitive, and oily skin.
- ☑ LO5 Describe acne facials and home-care.
- ☑ LO6 Discuss men's skin care and treatments.
- ☑ LO7 Perform the step-by-step facial treatment.
- ☑ LO8 Understand extraction methods.

Key Terms

Page number indicates where in the chapter the term is used.

extraction
pg. 391

facial
pg. 384

vasoconstricting
pg. 400

The skin care field has advanced rapidly in recent years due to the growing interest in health and beauty. This increase in the popularity of skin care has brought the field of esthetics to the forefront of the beauty and spa industry. Once considered luxuries, regular facials and skin care maintenance are now regarded as necessities by many. Facial treatments are also welcome breaks from the stresses of life in today's fast-paced society.

Stress reduction and caring for our health go hand in hand. Facials offer both benefits at the same time: they improve the skin's health while offering a relaxing service (**Figure 15–1**). Regular treatments result in noticeable improvements in the skin's texture and appearance. Clinical esthetics and technological advances, such as light therapy and lasers, are constantly expanding the skin care industry. (See Chapter 19, Advanced Topics and Treatments.)

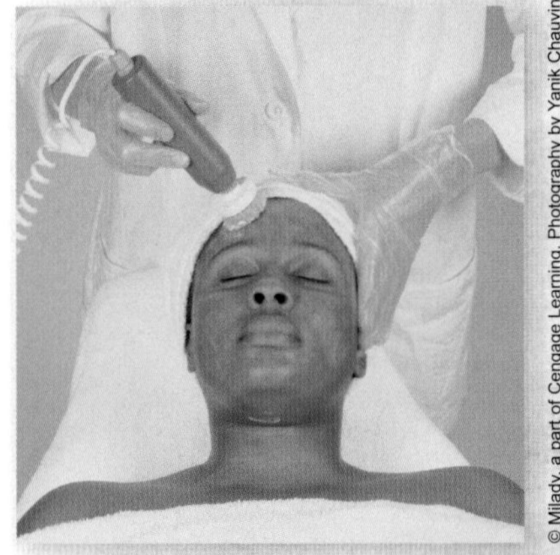

▲ Figure 15–1
Facials improve and rejuvenate the skin.

Facial treatments are the core treatments that estheticians perform. Giving a facial is both interesting and enjoyable. You were probably attracted to esthetics because you wanted a rewarding career that allows you to give to others. This is the perfect job to help others feel good and make a positive impact on their self-image. After a treatment, clients are rejuvenated and feel good when they walk out the door to face the world again.

The basic facial treatment procedure is covered here; however, there are many different types of facials and methods. It is best to get a basic routine memorized before implementing new steps or changing the routine. For example, the steps, products, focus of corrective treatments, and massage methods can all be varied. Once you are comfortable with routine procedures, your creativity will begin to flow naturally as you incorporate new ideas into your treatments.

Why Study Facial Treatments?

Estheticians should study and have a thorough understanding of facial treatments because this is a foundational skill for all skin care services, and you must be able to provide services that are safe, healthy, and beneficial for your clients.

- Facial treatments are the core treatments that estheticians perform; educated, well-trained estheticians that understand various treatment protocols will be the most successful.
- Facials help maintain the health of the skin and correct certain skin conditions through deep cleansing, massage, the use of masks and other products, and various treatment methods.
- Understanding the key elements and benefits of facials gives you confidence that you are making a difference in treating the client's skin, and this also helps you communicate those benefits to your clients.

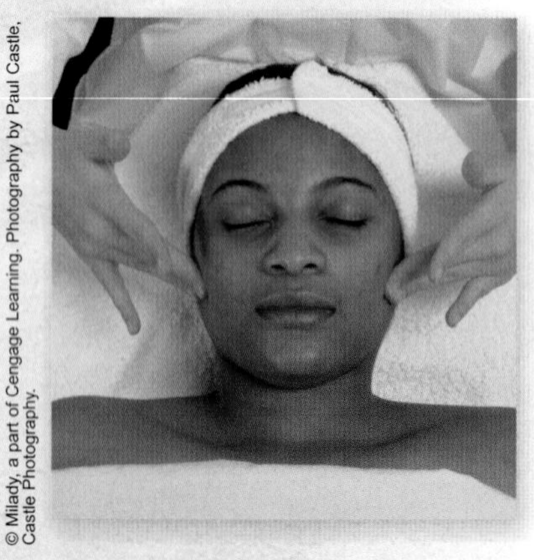

© Milady, a part of Cengage Learning. Photography by Paul Castle, Castle Photography.

▲ Figure 15–2
A facial treatment is one of the most relaxing services in a salon.

Facial Treatment Benefits

What is a facial treatment? A **facial** is a professional service designed to improve and rejuvenate the skin. What can a facial/skin treatment do for your client? A skin treatment has many benefits (Figure 15–2). Facials help maintain the health of the skin and correct certain skin conditions through deep cleansing, massage, the use of masks and other products, and various treatment methods. Clinical services in a medical office usually focus more on corrective skin treatments, whereas spa treatments may focus more on the relaxation experience. Blending a results-oriented treatment with a relaxing experience leads to the best overall service.

Providing education and consultations are also part of a facial. The benefits of the facial procedure are outlined below. Understanding what the benefits of treatments are gives you confidence that you are making a difference in the client's skin. This knowledge also helps you communicate those benefits to your clients.

Facial treatments include the following benefits:

- Deep cleanses
- Exfoliates
- Increases circulation and detoxifies
- Relaxes the senses, nerves, and muscles
- Stimulates the skin functions and metabolism
- Slows down premature aging
- Treats conditions such as dryness, oiliness, or redness
- Softens wrinkles and aging lines
- Helps clear up blemishes and minor acne ☑ L01

FOCUS ON

Your Success

The following skills are valuable in creating and maintaining success (Figure 15–3).

- **Technical skills**
- **Customer service**
- **Retail sales**
- **Knowledge**
- **Education**
- **Communication**

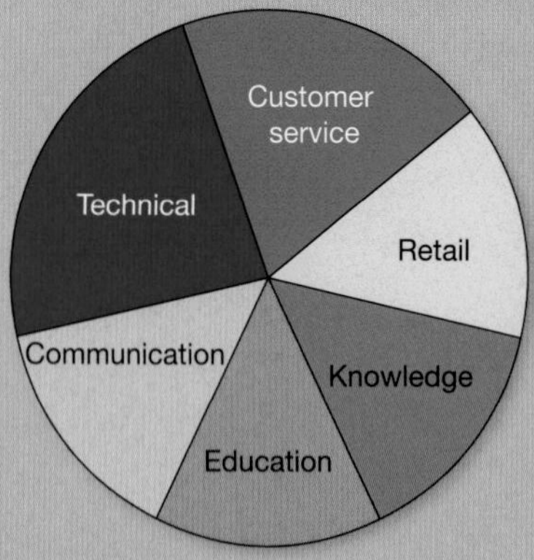

© Milady, a part of Cengage Learning.

▲ Figure 15–3
Esthetician skills.

Esthetician Skills and Techniques

What skills are needed to be successful at giving facials? Knowledge of skin histology, skin analysis, and skin care products is essential for an esthetician to make informed decisions for the client. Additionally, knowledge of contraindications, technological advances, and facial equipment is important. Client-relation skills are another facet and important element of being an esthetician. Connecting with the client and knowing how to communicate with him or her will partially determine your success. Massage techniques and your touch, pressure, and flow in the facial are valuable parts of your skills. Retailing and client consultations are another part of the job.

Some of these skills may seem to come more naturally to you, but as you get more experience, you will improve in all of these areas. Pay attention to little details that make the client comfortable. Knowing how to communicate well will also help build client loyalty. Educated, well-trained technicians are the best promotion for the esthetics industry. Facials are a valuable service with wonderful benefits. The market will continue to expand as more people discover these benefits.

Continuing your education with advanced classes and attendance at conferences and trade shows will keep you informed, excited, and motivated. It is essential to continue your education annually. A true professional will not miss these opportunities for growth. Make a commitment to yourself to attend at least one esthetics class or conference every year—this will make a difference in your potential career success.

Facial Treatment Protocol

To be successful and to maintain client loyalty, follow these treatment guidelines:

- Help the client to relax by speaking in a quiet and professional manner.
- Explain the benefits of the products and service you offer, and answer any questions the client may have.
- Provide a skin analysis and educational consultation.
- Provide a quiet atmosphere and work quietly and efficiently.
- Make sure clients are warm and comfortable.
- Maintain neat and clean conditions in the facial work area. Arrange supplies in an orderly fashion.
- If your hands are cold, warm them before touching the client's face.
- Keep your nails smooth and short to avoid scratching the client's skin.
- Remove rings, bracelets, and other jewelry that may injure the client, get in the way, or cause a distraction during the treatment.
- Follow systematic procedures.
- Be moderate in all treatment and product applications. Too much of a good thing can counteract the benefits.
- Be aware of your touch and the amount of pressure you apply to the face.
- Massage and apply or remove products in a smooth, consistent pattern. What you do for the right side, do for the left using the same order for the same number of times.
- Apply and remove products neatly: avoiding getting it in the eyes, mouth, and nostrils.
- Do not let water or products drip down the client's neck or in the eyes or ears.
- Be genuine in your concern for your client and focus on her or his needs.
- Give the client your full attention at all times.

FOCUS ON

Building Your Business

Share the benefits of your facial services with others as you meet new contacts or clients. Many people are not aware of these benefits!

THE FACIAL SUPPLY CHECKLIST			
SUPPLIES		SINGLE-USE ITEMS	PRODUCTS
Disinfectant	Implements	Paper towels	Cleanser
Hand sanitizer/antibacterial soap	Implement Tray	Gloves/finger cots	Exfoliant
Covered waste container	Hand towels	Cotton pads	Mask
Bowls	Client wrap	Cotton rounds	Toner
Spatulas	Clean linens	Sealable plastic bags	Moisturizer
Fan and mask brushes	Blanket	Tissues	Sunscreen
Tongs	Headband	Extraction supplies	Optional: serums, eye cream, lip balm
Mirror	Sharps container		
Distilled water	Bolster		
Equipment: Choose as needed: steamer, towel warmer, mag lamp, etc.	Client chart		

▲ Table 15–1
The Facial Supply Checklist.

▲ Figure 15–4
Professionally greeting the client.

Treatment and Client Preparation

Use the following resources to prepare for client treatments:

- Refer to the treatment room setup checklist in Table 15–1 and the room setup information in Chapter 14, The Treatment Room.
- Review the contraindication information in Chapter 12, Skin Analysis.
- Use the client charts and consultation information in Chapter 12, Skin Analysis.

Meeting and Greeting Clients

One of the most important communications you will have with a client occurs the first time you meet (Figure 15–4). Be polite, friendly, and inviting. You need to give great service every time clients come to see you; otherwise, you may lose them to another esthetician. The following are good customer service practices:

- Always approach a client with a smile.
- Even if you are having a difficult day or have a problem of some sort, keep it to yourself. The time you are with your client is for your client and her needs, not yours.
- Always introduce yourself to new clients and greet returning clients by name. A brief yet warm handshake will make the client feel welcome.

FOCUS ON

Customer Service

Think of a time when you were treated well as a client and how it made you feel. Share an example with the class.

- Set aside a few minutes to take new clients on a quick tour of the facility. Introduce them to the receptionist and other coworkers. This helps clients to feel comfortable and at home.
- Be yourself. Your clients can sense when you are being genuine and open, and they will have more confidence in you and in your expertise.

> **FOCUS ON**
>
> **Client Services**
>
> Facial clients are typically asked to come in 15 minutes prior to their appointments so they can fill out their consultation form, get into a robe, and prepare for their treatment. Clients are called the day before to confirm their appointments. The receptionist will check-in the client and have them prepare for the service. Have a consultation form ready to use. This practice keeps technicians on schedule and is an everyday practice in the industry.

Setup, Products, and Supplies Checklist

It is important to assemble supplies in an organized, efficient manner (Figure 15–5).

Refer to the checklist in Table 15–1 to set up for a facial. ✓ L02

Preparing the Client for the Facial Treatment

After warmly greeting the client, assist her in preparing for the facial (Figure 15–6). The receptionist or technician will show the client where to change and store any belongings. Clients can change into their wrap and remove their shoes in a changing room or the treatment room. Explain what clothing can be removed: shoes, restrictive pants, and bras. Let the client know the neck and shoulders are usually bare for facials. Dark fabric will collect lint from sheets, so it is best to remove clothing that will be under the sheets. Let clients decide what clothing they are comfortable removing.

Instruct the client how to prepare for the treatment and how to put on the facial wrap. There are many styles of wraps or gowns. For example, men wear a kimono-type robe or a wrap around the waist.

Show the client how to get on the facial bed safely and where to position the head. Assist the client in getting comfortable.

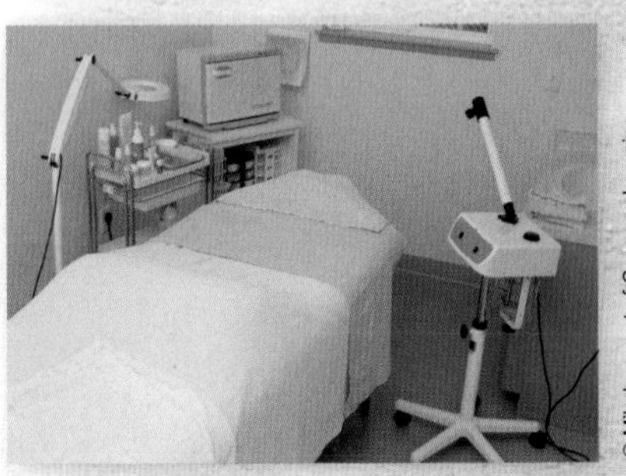

▲ Figure 15–5
An efficient workstation is organized.

Adjust the head drape, pillow, and linens following your instructor's method. Place a towel across the client's chest and a cover over the body as directed. Drape the hair with a towel or headband as necessary. Check to make sure the headband is not too tight and that all of the hair is covered. Consider efficiency and laundry costs when determining what to use for draping. A bolster placed under the knees (supports the back) and a neck pillow are also used for the client's comfort.

Draping the Hair

To drape the client's head: fasten a clean headband, towel, or other head covering around the client's head to protect the hair.

To drape the head with a towel, follow these steps:

1. Place the towel on the headrest. Fold the towel lengthwise from one of the top corners to the opposite lower corner, and place it over the headrest with the fold facing down.

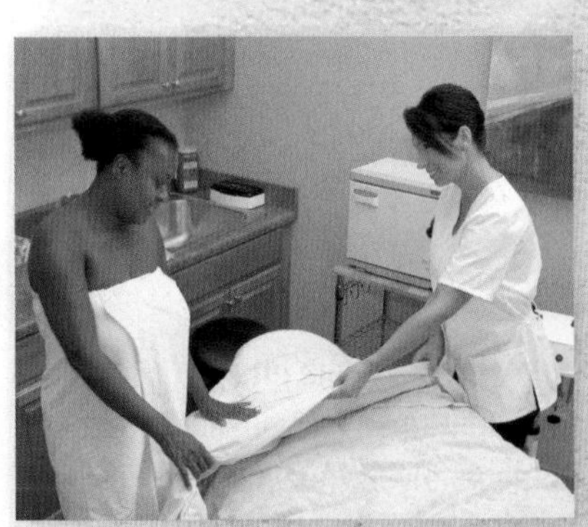

▲ Figure 15–6
Help the client prepare for the facial.

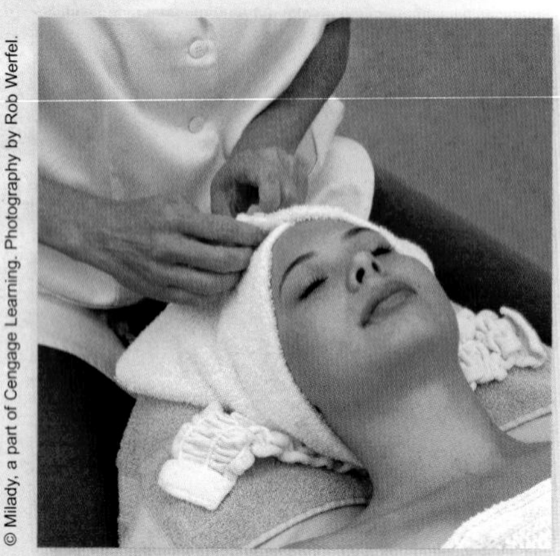

▲ Figure 15–7
Draping the hair with a towel.

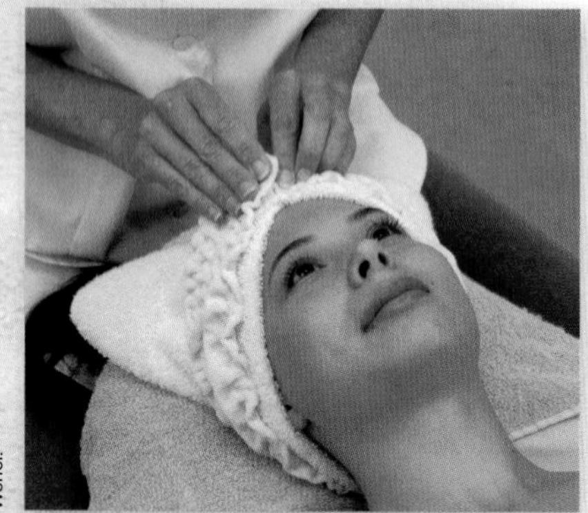

▲ Figure 15–8
Make sure the headband is comfortable.

2. When the client is in a reclined position, the back of the head should rest on the towel, so that the sides of the towel can be brought up to the center of the forehead to cover the hairline (Figure 15–7).
3. Use a headband with a Velcro® closure or a fastener to hold the towel in place (Figure 15–8). Make sure that all strands of hair are tucked under the towel, that the earlobes are not bent, and that the towel is not wrapped too tightly.

Key Elements of the Basic Facial Treatment

Each step in the facial process is described below. A more thorough explanation of the steps is given before the actual steps of the procedure are listed. This way you can become familiar with the steps before having to perform the procedure. As you practice facials, follow the chart (Table 15–2) to memorize the steps. Adapt this basic procedure to fit your local facility and regulations. Most basic facials take approximately 1 hour.

Refer to Table 15–5 on page 393 for timing suggestions.

The Initial Consultation and Analysis

The initial consultation and skin analysis determine the products and procedures to be used and give you time to discuss the client's home-care needs. Many estheticians schedule at least 15 minutes extra for a client's first visit. Before cleansing, inspect the skin type and conditions: is it dry, normal, or oily? Is the skin texture smooth or rough? Are there fine lines or creases? Are there blackheads or acne conditions? Are dilated capillaries visible? Is the skin color even?

You want to see the skin's natural state before cleansing and then again after cleansing, especially if the client is wearing makeup. Complete a thorough analysis with a magnifying lamp after cleansing (Table 15–3). Check for any other conditions or contraindications prohibiting a facial (Table 15–4).

CAUTION!

If any product gets into the eyes, have the client rinse and flush the eyes immediately at the sink. Then resume the procedure. If they wear contacts, they may need to remove them before receiving a treatment. Avoid the eye area if appropriate.

Cleansing and Analysis

After the initial dry skin analysis, apply warm towels for a few minutes. Warm towels are used before cleansing to prepare the client for your touch, to warm and moisten the skin, and to make cleansing more effective and enjoyable.

Cleanse to remove impurities and makeup before the in-depth skin analysis and facial treatment (Figure 15–9). Use a milky or creamy cleanser that rinses easily. During a facial, it is hard to remove foam or gel cleansers. Avoid overrubbing or stimulating the skin and thoroughly, but efficiently, complete the cleansing. If there is makeup residue, do a

THE FACIAL PROCEDURE CHECKLIST The basic facial procedure is divided into the following steps:
1. Client consultation, including review of contraindications and initial skin analysis
2. Client draping
3. Warm towels and cleansing
4. In-depth skin analysis (refer to Table 15–3)
5. Exfoliation product or mask
6. Softening with steam or warm towels (aromatherapy optional)
7. Extractions (and/or brow waxing, if applicable)
8. Massage (massage and mask steps can be reversed)
9. Mask (clay or hydrating)
10. Toner
11. Moisturizer and/or sunscreen (serums, eye creams optional)

▲ Table 15–2
The Facial Procedure Checklist.

SKIN ANALYSIS CHECKLIST: LOOK, TOUCH, ASK, LISTEN Analyze the skin using a magnifying lamp. Place eye pads on the eyes. Try not to cover what you need to look at around the eyes. Perform the following checklist:
1. Look for any obvious skin conditions and note the skin type.
2. Touch the skin, noting its elasticity, softness, texture, skin condition, and so on.
3. Continue the consultation, asking questions while analyzing.
4. Choose the products.
5. Note the information on the client chart (this can be done before, during, or after the facial).

▲ Table 15–3
Skin Analysis Checklist: Look, Touch, Ask, Listen.

FACIAL CONTRAINDICATIONS (refer to Chapter 12, Skin Analysis)
• Contagious diseases such as HIV, herpes or hepatitis, pinkeye, or ringworm
• Skin disorders or diseases
• Medical conditions, including pregnancy
• Certain medications
• Use of acne drugs or other topical peeling agents
• Skin irritation
• Allergies to products and ingredients
• Severe, uncontrolled hypertension
• Electrical contraindications as listed in Chapter 17, Facial Machines

▲ Table 15–4 **Facial Contraindications.**

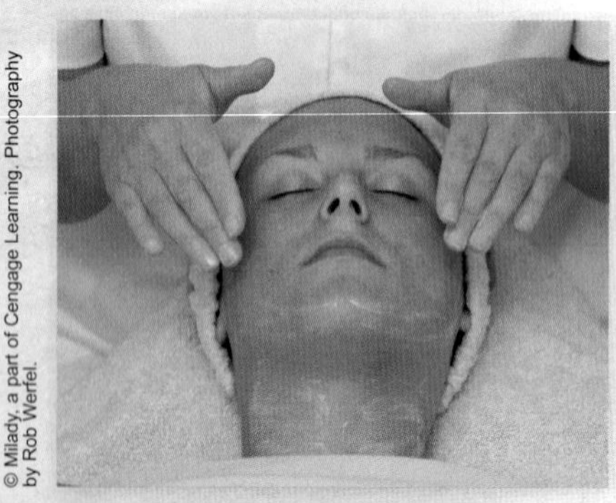

▲ Figure 15–9
Cleansing the skin is the first step in the facial process.

double cleansing—once before using the towels and once after. Some estheticians use a toner between facial steps to remove any makeup or product residue. Most facial products can be applied with fingertips and removed with cotton pads or sponges.

Make sure the client is not wearing contacts. Before starting the cleansing procedure, the client's eye and lip color can be removed. Do not use too much cleanser because it can run into the eye. Some clients prefer to leave their eye makeup on, and it is appropriate to work around it. Analyze the skin after cleansing.

PAGE 409

PROCEDURE 15-2 **Applying Cleansing Product** PAGE 411

PROCEDURE 15-3 **Removing Product** PAGE 413

Here's a Tip

To remove makeup from under the eye, try to use light, inward strokes around the eye area towards the nose under the lower lashes to avoid tugging outward on the delicate skin. Use this technique when applying or removing products.

Exfoliation

Exfoliation can be achieved by using products such as peels, or you can use the brush machine to remove dead skin cells that make the skin feel rough and clog the follicles. Exfoliation makes the skin smoother, helps product penetration by unblocking the surface, and promotes stimulation, which increases the cell turnover rate (**Figure 15–10**). A clay-lifting mask or enzyme mask can also help exfoliate the skin. This step can be performed before steam, extractions, or a mask. It is most effective in the beginning of the treatment after cleansing. Exfoliation is discussed in Chapter 13, Skin Care Products: Chemistry, Ingredients, and Selection.

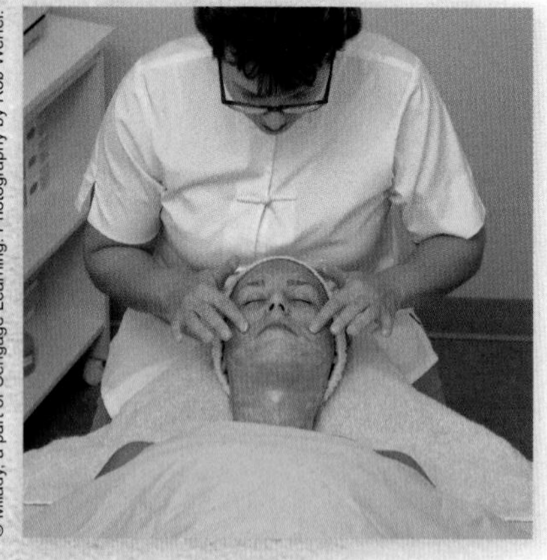

▲ Figure 15–10
Exfoliating the skin can be achieved by a number of methods.

Steam or Warm Towels

Warmth softens the follicles, promotes more effective cleansing, prepares the skin for extractions or product penetration, softens superficial lines, and increases circulation (**Figure 15–11**). Towels or steam should never be too warm or used too long because they can damage capillaries and cause overstimulation, redness, and irritation.

Always check the towel temperature on the inside of your wrist before applying. Keep towels away from the nostrils. Warm towels can be used in place of steam or for product removal during treatments.

Steam is typically used before deep cleansing. The steamer nozzle is placed approximately 18 inches (45 centimeters) away from the client. Check to make sure the client is comfortable and does not feel claustrophobic. The nozzle can be positioned above or below the client's face.

There are many different variations of a facial procedure. The order of steps can be changed. This will depend on what you are trying to achieve in the facial, the client's needs, the product line, the facility where you work, or your school's individual training program. Be flexible and enjoy the variety.

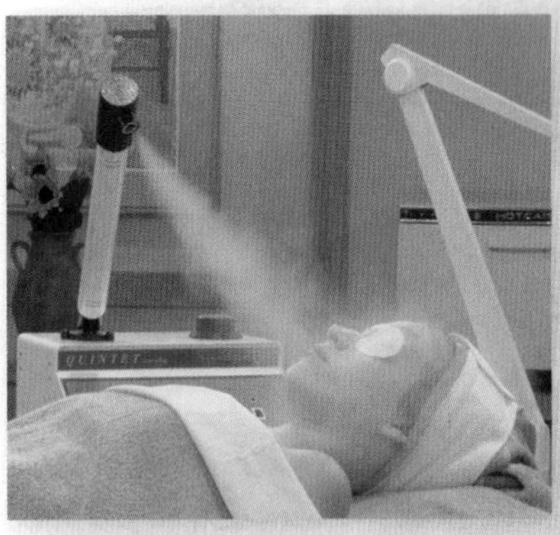

▲ Figure 15–11
Steam softens the follicles.

Extractions and/or Deep Pore Cleansing

The technique of manually removing impurities and comedones from follicles is called **extraction** (Figure 15–12). Cleaning out the debris that expands them allows the follicles to contract back to their natural size. Manual extraction is often the only way to expel impurities and clean out the follicles. It is also necessary to extract papules and pustules in order to release bacteria and fluids so they can heal more rapidly.

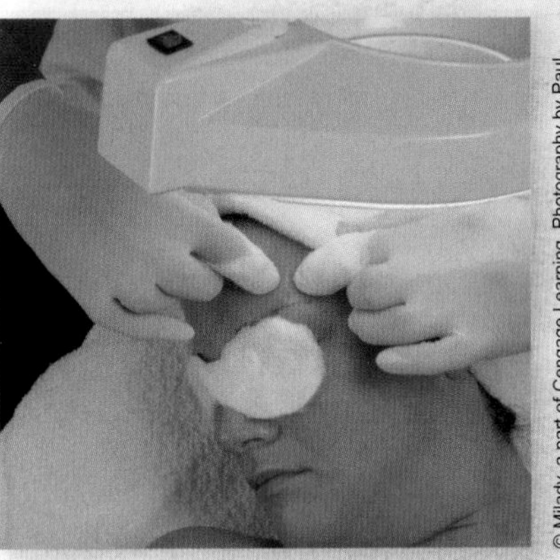

▲ Figure 15–12
Extractions remove impurities.

Massage

Massage promotes physiological relaxation, increases circulation and metabolism, and increases product penetration (Figure 15–13). Additionally, the products used for massage have many benefits. Refer to Chapter 16, Facial Massage, for facial massage steps and protocol. Memorize all steps of the massage or procedure before doing a complete facial. This way you will not have to memorize everything at the same time. The massage can be performed at different times during treatments, depending on the order of your procedures. Massage products are applied warm, with fingertips or a fan brush.

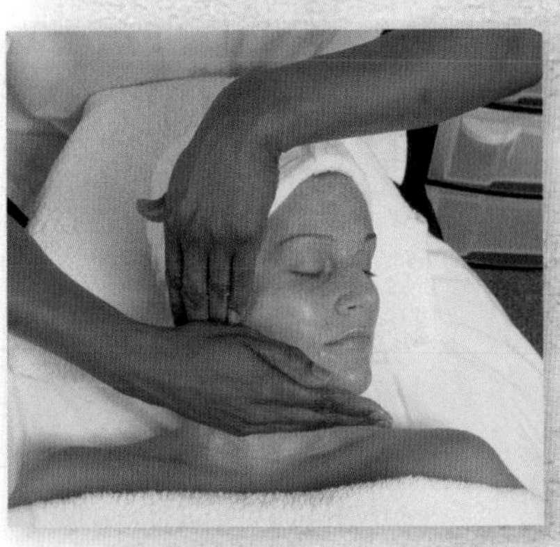

▲ Figure 15–13
The most soothing and relaxing part of the facial is the massage.

Treatment Masks

As discussed previously, masks can draw out impurities, clear up blemishes, tighten and tone skin and also hydrate, calm, or rejuvenate the skin.

Depending on their function, masks are applied at different times during a treatment (Figure 15–14). If you are drawing impurities out of the skin, it may be beneficial to apply the mask before using steam and doing extractions. If it is a calming, hydrating mask, then it is applied at the end of a facial to calm the skin and leave it hydrated.

Towels, sponges, or cotton 4″ × 4″ (10 cm × 10 cm) pads are used to remove products. Cotton compresses are also used for removing the mask.

PROCEDURE 15-5 Applying the Cotton Compress PAGE 420

PROCEDURE 15-6 Removing the Cotton Compress PAGE 421

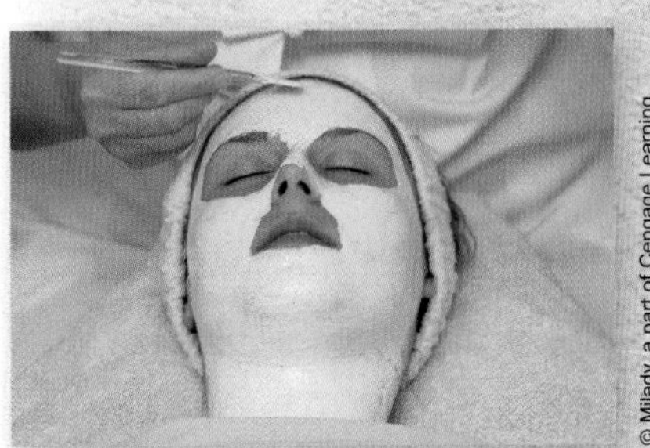

▲ Figure 15–14
The mask is applied with a brush or the fingers.

Paraffin Masks

Paraffin masks are used to warm the skin and promote penetration of ingredients deeper into the skin through the heat trapped under the paraffin. The heat increases blood circulation and is beneficial for dry, mature skin or skin that is dull and lifeless. It has a plumping and softening effect on the skin.

Paraffin masks are melted at a little more than body temperature (98.6 degrees Fahrenheit or 37 degrees Celsius) before application. When applied, the paraffin quickly cools to a lukewarm temperature and hardens to a candle-like consistency. Paraffin masks are applied on top of a treatment cream as the paraffin, which has no treatment properties of its own, allows for deeper penetration of the cream's ingredients into the skin.

Paraffin masks are not recommended for use on sensitive skin, skin with capillary problems, oily skin, or skin with blemishes. These masks are designed for dry and mature skin; the heat is too stimulating for other skin conditions and may cause redness or irritation.

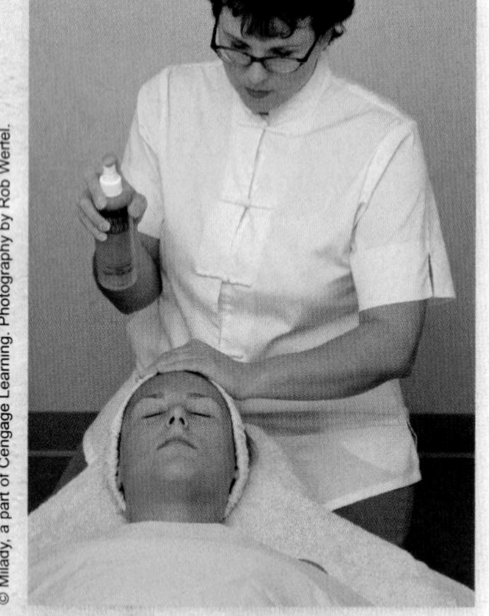

▲ Figure 15–15
Toners can be applied with a cotton pad or sprayed on.

PAGE 424

Toners

Toners finish the cleansing process by removing any products left on the skin and help balance the skin's pH (Figure 15–15). Different formulas can also help skin problems such as dehydration or acne. Toners, fresheners, and astringents are all referred to as toners for simplicity in the textbook. Toners can be misted onto the face or applied with a saturated cotton pad.

Serums, Eye, and Lip Treatments

Serums are concentrated ingredients used for specific corrective treatments. Serums or ampoules are applied with fingertips under a mask or moisturizer. These are also used with facial machines in a variety of treatments. Eye and lip creams are usually thicker and are applied with fingertips or cotton swabs.

Moisturizers

Depending on the formula, moisturizers seal in moisture and protect the barrier layer of the skin. They can also hydrate and balance the oil–water moisture content of the skin. Products with performance ingredients will be even more effective when left on the skin and are applied at the end of a treatment.

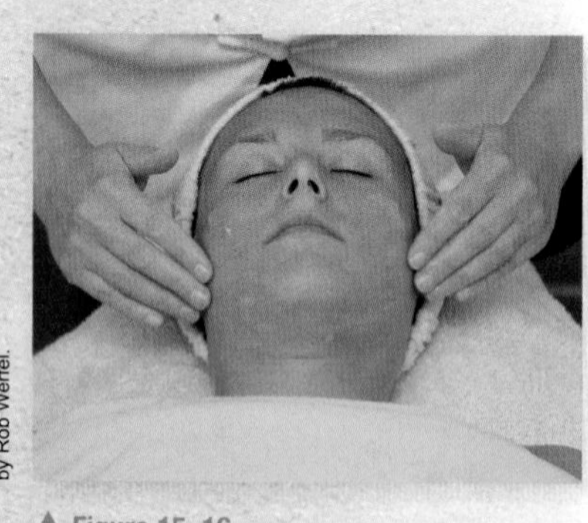

▲ Figure 15–16
Apply sunscreen after the facial.

Sunscreens

Daily application of sunscreen is essential to help protect the skin (Figure 15–16). After finishing a stimulating, nourishing facial, do not send your client out with a newly exfoliated face without sun protection. Sunscreens are often formulated in a moisturizing base.

Completing the Service

After completing the facial service, quietly and slowly let the client know you are finished. Tell her to take her time sitting up, offer to assist her in getting off the table, and then leave the room so she can change.

- Explain to the client what to do next—for example, meet you outside in the reception area or other appropriate instructions. Offer her some water to rehydrate after the service.
- The client consultation after the service includes recommending products and rebooking their next appointment. Show the client which products you recommend, and write them down on a home-care instruction sheet for her to keep (Figure 15–17).
- Explain that you will also record the products you recommend in her file. Recommend that she reschedule once a month for a facial and any other services you believe would benefit her, such as a brow wax.
- Ask her what products she would like to take home with her, and recommend a time for scheduling the next appointment.
- Thank her for coming, and let her know you enjoyed meeting her.
- Make your chart notes and file them away. Clean up the room and prepare for the next client (Table 15–5).

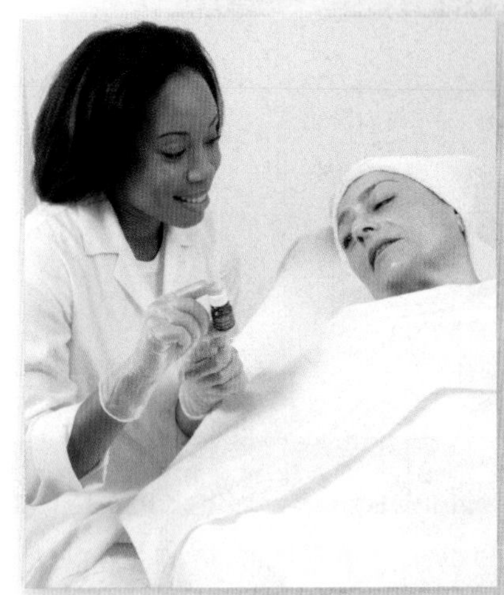

▲ Figure 15–17
After the facial, discuss home-care products with your client.

▼ Table 15–5
Timing the Facial Procedure.

TIMING THE FACIAL PROCEDURE				
	SUGGESTED TIME: (IN MINUTES)	ACNE FACIAL	MINI-FACIAL	WRITE IN YOUR PROTOCOL HERE
Setup time	10-15			
• Consultation	3		Brief	
• Draping	2			
• Towels	2			
• Cleansing	3			
• Skin analysis	3		Brief	
• Exfoliation or mask	8-10			
• Steam or towels	8			
• Extractions	8		Skip	
• Massage	10	Skip or brief	Skip or brief	
• Mask	8-10		Brief	
• Toner	1			
• Moisturizer	2			
• Cleanup time and post consultation	10-15			
Total time:	**60**	**45**	**30**	
Note: There are many variations to these basic guidelines.	minutes plus ½-hour cleanup/setup time			

Consultation and Home-Care

Home-care is probably the most important factor in a successful skin care program. The key word here is program. Clients' participation is essential to achieve results. A program consists of a long-range plan involving home-care, salon treatments, and client education.

Every new client should be thoroughly consulted about home-care for her skin conditions. After the first treatment, block out about 15 minutes to explain proper home-care for the client.

CAUTION!

To avoid overstimulation and damage to capillaries, do not use excessive steam or hot towels on couperose skin. Towels do not have to be steaming to feel good. Inform clients why excessive heat or steam is not good for the skin.

After the treatment is finished, have the client sit in the facial chair, or invite her to move to a well-lit consultation area. A mirror should be provided, so that she can see the conditions you will be discussing.

Explain, in simple terms, the client's skin conditions, informing her of how you propose to treat the conditions. Inform her about how often treatments should be administered in the salon, and very specifically explain what she should be doing at home.

Set out the products you want the client to purchase and use. Explain each one, and tell her in which order to use them. Make sure to have written instructions for the client to take home.

It is important to have products available for the client that you believe in and that produce results. Retailing products for clients to use at home is important to the success of your treatments and to your business.

Post-Treatment Checklist

After the facial, complete the post-service procedures (Table 15–6). These were thoroughly discussed in Chapter 14, The Treatment Room, Procedure 14–2, Post-Service Procedure. LO3

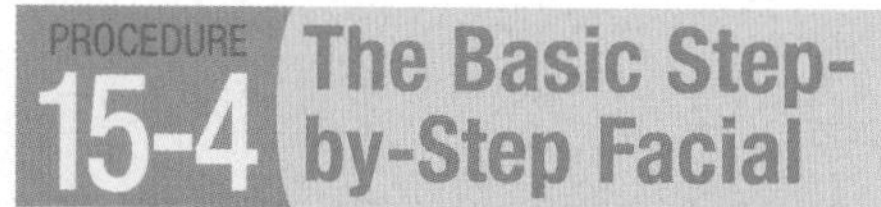

PROCEDURE
15-4
The Basic Step-by-Step Facial

PAGE 415

Variations of the Basic Facial

Remember that the steps of the facial procedure will vary depending on the focus of the facial. Sometimes the massage is the last step after the mask, and sometimes two masks are used. Sometimes steam or massage is omitted. The procedure used depends on what you are trying to achieve. Are you trying to hydrate and calm the skin, or deep-cleanse and stimulate it? For example, if the client needs hydrating, you may choose to omit the cleansing mask and the extractions. Do not be too concerned about utilizing different methods or procedures right now. As you continue your practice, you can vary the treatments you offer.

Different Facial Philosophies and Methods

There are many different types of facials. Some incorporate different massage philosophies, and others focus on specific results from

THE POST-TREATMENT CHECKLIST

POST-FACIAL	EQUIPMENT/ROOM	SUPPLIES	SINGLE-USE ITEMS
Wash your hands.	Clean the wax machine and turn it off at the end of the day.	Wash and disinfect brushes, spatulas, tweezers, and other nondisposable implements used during the process.	Soiled items such as gloves and extraction supplies must be placed in a sealable plastic bag and then in a covered waste container.
Say good-bye to the client after the post-consultation.	Clean and disinfect the steamer. Refill with distilled water.	Clean and disinfect bowls and other multiuse items. Dry and store properly.	Disposable extraction lancets go in a biohazard sharps container.
Make the client chart notes.	Wipe and disinfect the equipment used.	Remove the dirty linens and remake the bed.	
Write up retail sales.	Clean all containers and wipe off dirty product containers with a disinfectant.	Turn off the bed warmer if used.	
Prepare the room for the next client or carry out end-of-the-day cleanup tasks.	Clean and disinfect all counters, sinks, surfaces, and floor mats.	Put the linens, towels, and sheets in the appropriate covered laundry hamper.	
Wear gloves during cleaning procedures.		Change the disinfectant solution to comply with state agency regulations.	
		Remove or change the towels on the workstation tables.	
		Put away the supplies.	

▲ Table 15–6
The Post-Treatment Checklist.

a product manufacturer. Some facials have specific goals, such as stimulating or calming the skin, body, and mind. Philosophies range from holistic Ayurvedic Treatments (**Figure 15–18**) to Chinese Face Mapping (**Figure 15–19**). Using different facial zones (as related to different parts the face) to target treatments has also become more popular. Machines such as microdermabrasion and light therapy are another type of treatment focus.

Different nations also practice different methods. It is interesting to learn about European techniques, such as those practiced by the French and Germans, who have been instrumental in developing skin care for hundreds of years. Eastern Europe is well known for an abundance of Natural Mineral Springs and European massage techniques.

European-trained beauty therapists learn many aspects of skin and beauty care beyond basic esthetics. They perform esthetics,

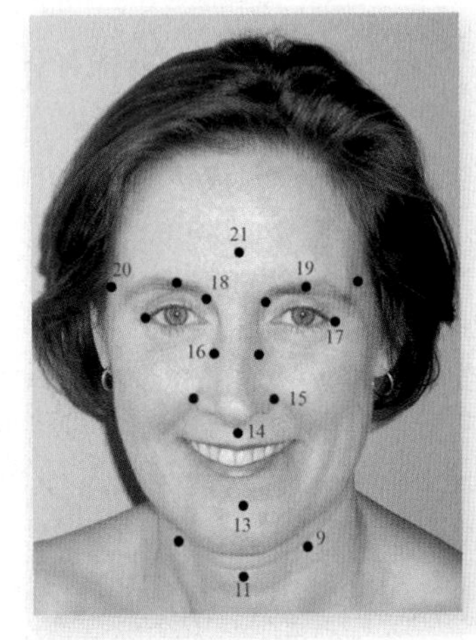

▲ Figure 15–18
Ayurvedic Treatments.

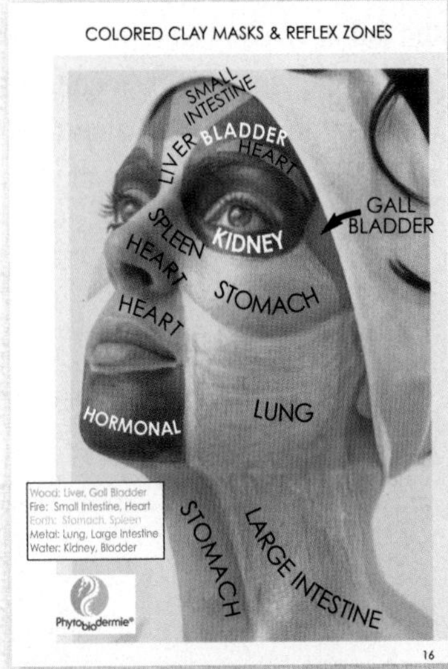

▲ Figure 15–19
Chinese Face Mapping.

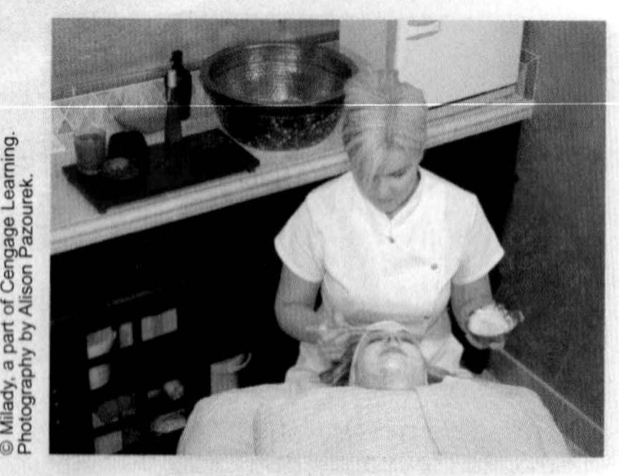

▲ Figure 15–20
An exotic facial treatment.

massage, and cosmetology services. The American industry tends to be oriented toward the newest technology available, with a focus on advanced performance ingredients. Regions such as India and Asia have their own fascinating methods and products, bringing their native philosophies and ingredients to the skin care world. For example, Asian treatments for lightening skin pigmentation are popular. These different philosophies and methods offer many choices to incorporate into the treatment menu (**Figure 15–20**).

The Mini-Facial

The main differences between a mini-facial and a basic facial are the time and the number of steps. Mini-facials may take only 30 minutes and do not include all the steps of a full, 60-minute facial. Omitted steps may include the comprehensive skin analysis, steaming, massage, or extractions. Deep cleansing and masking are the most important elements of the mini-facial because they produce the most visible results.

The mini-facial gives clients a treatment that can be completed quickly if they are pressed for time. It will introduce them to a light, refreshing facial that may lead to rebooking for a more in-depth, relaxing facial to address specific skin concerns and conditions.

ACTIVITY

Explore other interesting cultures and their beauty secrets. Do some research on different facial techniques and procedures. Check out books, the Internet, and professional trade journals to learn more about a variety of services offered in the industry. What treatments are interesting to you? Which cultures do you want to learn more about? Share an article with your fellow students.

Mini Procedure

THE MINI-FACIAL

1. Perform a quick cleansing to remove makeup. Rinse well.
2. Analyze with a magnifying lamp.
3. Perform a second quick cleansing with an exfoliant or a cleanser. Rinse thoroughly. A brush machine can be used as a quick exfoliating method.
4. Apply a mask for approximately 10 minutes.
5. Remove the mask. (Steam is optional before or after mask.)
6. Apply a toner appropriate to the client's skin type.
7. Apply a moisturizer (and sunscreen for daytime).
8. Recommend a treatment for the client's next visit.
9. Recommend initial home-care products and complete the home-care chart.

Treatments for Different Skin Types and Conditions

Skin conditions and products have been covered in previous chapters, so review ingredients and the factors that affect the skin's health to choose treatments for the individual client. The following treatments incorporate the same procedures as the basic facial, but certain steps and products are added or omitted, based on the condition and skin type being treated. Too many product choices can be overwhelming, so it is appropriate to offer a basic facial with ingredients designed for a normal skin type. This service can be effective for almost any client.

Dry Skin

Skin is often dry due to inactivity of the sebaceous glands, which produce the sebum (oil) that lubricates the skin. Dry skin may appear to be thin, and in some cases small capillaries can be seen near the surface of the skin. Dry skin can appear to be fine in texture but coarse to the touch. Facial treatments and home-maintenance can help minimize dryness and stimulate the production of sebum.

The skin may have dry and oily areas that can be treated separately. Serums and creams for dry skin are important. Occlusive products are necessary to protect and balance dry skin. Conversely, there is a theory that using a heavy cream or oil on dry skin may inhibit its production of natural oils, so moderation is the key. When discussing the client's dry skin condition, the esthetician can explain that the excessive application of heavy creams may in some cases interfere with the production of sebum and that stimulating the natural oil of the skin is far more beneficial than just applying heavy oils or creams. Balance and protect skin with the appropriate products and in the proper amounts.

FOCUS ON

Your Health

Remember to take a break during the day and drink water to stay hydrated. Make sure you eat regularly to avoid low blood sugar. Maintain your health so you can focus on your client.

Treatments for Dry Skin

For dry or mature skin, the treatment goals are similar: to hydrate and nourish the skin. The purpose of the treatment is to stimulate the cell metabolism by using performance ingredients. Massage and exfoliation are beneficial to dry skin. Protecting the barrier function and keeping dry skin well lubricated is important.

Follow the facial steps using products designed for dry skin. Complete procedures and facial steps are not included here—only the additions to the facial.

- Use a gentle enzyme peel, or a gentle alpha hydroxy acid peel, to exfoliate the skin.
- For a mask a collagen, hydrating, paraffin wax, or thermal mask can be used.
- The galvanic machine or the massage can be used to assist in the penetration of a hydrating serum or other nourishing product.
- A moisturizing cream with an oil base, antioxidants, and a sunscreen finish the treatment.

Dehydrated Skin That Lacks Water

A client's skin may have enough oil, but still feel dry and flaky due to lack of water in the skin. The skin may become dehydrated from drying

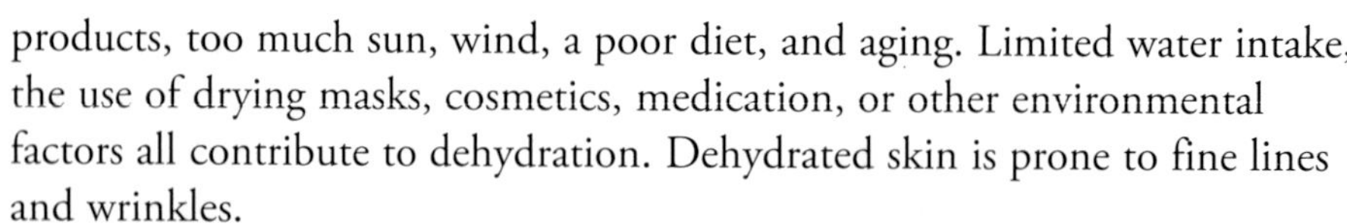

products, too much sun, wind, a poor diet, and aging. Limited water intake, the use of drying masks, cosmetics, medication, or other environmental factors all contribute to dehydration. Dehydrated skin is prone to fine lines and wrinkles.

If the client's skin seems to be dehydrated from factors that require medical attention (such as diet, lack of fluids, or medication), the esthetician should recommend that the client seek the advice of his or her physician or dermatologist. In the meantime, facial treatments to improve the general health of the skin and to help it to retain moisture are beneficial.

Dehydration of the skin may be a temporary condition, varying from season to season and due to various factors in the environment. Use a treatment similar to the one for dry, mature, or sensitive skin. The goal is to hydrate and nourish the skin. Adapt the products for the individual's needs.

Treatments for Mature or Aging Skin

Dry skin is often due to the natural aging process of the body. As a person advances in years, the body's processes slow down, and cells and lipids are not replaced as rapidly as they were when the person was younger. It is not difficult to diagnose aging skin, but skin ages at different rates due to the following factors:

- The skin ages due to neglect and the external treatment it has received.
- Exposure to extreme climates; too much sun, wind, or polluted air will hasten the aging process.
- Physiological disease, poor health, and psychological (emotional) problems can cause the skin to appear older.
- Extreme weight loss can result in loss of muscle tone and lined and sagging skin, which in turn gives the skin an "aged" appearance.
- Medications, a poor diet, smoking, and the misuse of alcoholic beverages affect the skin's appearance.

The mature client's skin can be improved; but the natural aging process cannot be reversed, nor will the skin be restored to the same vital condition of youth. The client should be advised that treatments can make the skin look and feel better, but there are no miracle treatments that restore aging skin. Prevention and healthy habits are the key to beautiful skin at any age.

Elasticity of the Skin

Aging skin often lacks elasticity. One way to test the skin for elasticity is by taking a small section of the facial skin or neck between the thumb and forefinger and giving the skin a slight outward pull. When the skin is released, and if the elasticity is good, the skin will immediately return to its normal shape. If the skin is slow to resume its normal shape, it is lacking elasticity. Firming ingredients and treatments are beneficial for skin's elasticity.

Ingredients for Mature Skin

Aging or sun-damaged skin needs antioxidants topically and orally. Antioxidants such as vitamins A, C, and E, minerals, green tea, and grapeseed extract all help protect the body from free radicals. Other beneficial care for aging skin includes protecting the barrier function of the skin and wearing sunscreen. Additionally, alpha hydroxy acids can help combat the signs of aging and sun damage. Hydrating ingredients such as hyaluronic acid, sodium hyaluronate, sodium PCA, and glycerin all bind water to the skin and retain the moisture that is essential to maturing skin. Peptides, lipids, polyglucans, coenzyme Q10, and liposomes are all beneficial performance ingredients.

Treatment goals for mature skin are to hydrate and revitalize the skin. Stimulating the metabolism and firming the skin are also part of an antiaging facial. Facial treatments are wonderful rejuvenators for clients with mature, aging, or sun-damaged skin. Remember all of the benefits derived from each of the facial steps.

Mature Skin Treatments

Here are some suggestions for treating mature skin:

- Use procedures similar to those designed for dry skin, adapting the ingredients.
- Massage with a deep-penetrating serum and cream.
- Collagen or hydrating masks are both beneficial in a facial treatment for mature skin.
- A thermal or paraffin mask will also plump and force-feed nutrients into the skin.
- Firming products can be effective in visibly tightening the skin.
- AHA treatments and products have many benefits.
- Advanced treatments such as light therapy and microcurrent are effective tools for mature skin. (See Chapter 17, Facial Machines.)

Treatments for Sensitive Skin or Rosacea

For sensitive skin, the primary goal is to calm and cool the skin. Increasing the skin's barrier function is another important part of treating sensitive skin. Rosacea is treated much the same because it is also characterized by red, couperose, and sensitive conditions. Calming ingredients such as aloe vera, chamomile, allantoin, azulene, and licorice extracts are all effective on sensitive or irritated skin.

Individuals with sensitive (or sensitized) skin should avoid stimulating, drying products and heat. Advise these clients to avoid vasodilators that dilate capillaries: heat, the sun, spicy foods, and stimulating products. Irritants and sensitizing ingredients can be essential oils, exfoliants, fragrances, color agents, and preservatives. All of these may cause skin

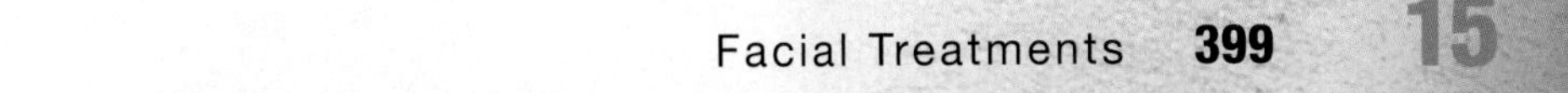

reactions and irritation. Home-care product recommendations should be designed for sensitive skin, but that is no guarantee they will not irritate the skin.

CAUTION!

Contraindications for Sensitive Skin or Redness

- Use of microdermabrasion, the vacuum suction, and the brush machine are too irritating for sensitive skin.
- Strong exfoliants and products with alcohol are also to be avoided.
- Less massage and a lighter touch should be used to avoid stimulating or irritating the skin.
- Hot steam or towels should not be used on reactive, sensitive skin. Use cool towels to calm the skin.

Rosacea

Rosacea is common for those with sensitive, mature skin. Some types of rosacea, like seborrhea, can be characterized by excessive oiliness of the skin. The nose and cheeks are the areas most frequently affected. The face will have a flushed appearance and, if neglected, the skin can become lumpy where the papules and pustules have formed. Although sometimes referred to as acne rosacea, this skin condition is not to be confused with acne. Rosacea is not the same type of skin condition that appears during adolescence, because it usually does not appear before the age of 35. Rosacea is more common in adult females than in males. However, when a male develops rosacea, it usually becomes quite severe.

Rosacea can be aggravated by alcohol and heavily spiced foods. The client should be advised to avoid squeezing or picking lumps that appear on any area of the face. In ordinary cases, soothing treatments will be helpful. The client should be encouraged to consult a dermatologist when experiencing severe rosacea flairs.

fyi

Cold globes are used for sensitive skin or acne to calm blood flow and reduce redness (Figure 15–21).

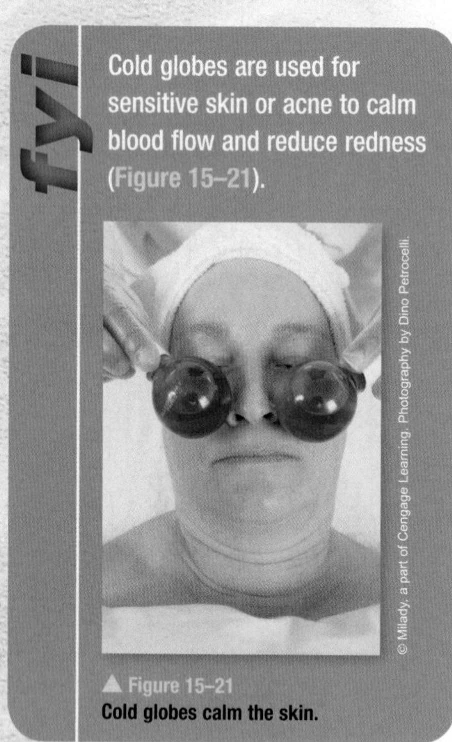

© Milady, a part of Cengage Learning. Photography by Dino Petrocelli.

▲ Figure 15–21
Cold globes calm the skin.

Sensitive Skin Treatment

Follow the facial procedure and incorporate the following guidelines:

- To soothe irritation, a gentle cleanser is the best type of cleanser. Foaming, detergent-based cleansers can strip the skin's lipids and barrier protection.
- Less steam and heat should be used. Make sure warm towels are not hot, or skip them altogether. Cold towels are **vasoconstricting**, which means they constrict capillaries and blood flow.
- An enzyme peel formulated for sensitive skin gently exfoliates the skin.
- A soothing gel mask is great for calming and toning down redness. Freeze-dried collagen masks are also excellent for redness or sensitive skin.
- Lipids protect the skin, and a serum or moisturizer with lipids is essential for treating sensitive and dry skin. Moisturizers with calming ingredients are also beneficial.

Treatments for Hyperpigmentation

Hyperpigmentation is a condition that affects many people. Sun exposure causes dark pigmentation areas on the skin that clients often want to diminish. Advise clients that the best preventative measures are to stay out of the sun and wear protective clothing and sunscreen daily. Chemical exfoliation and brightening agents can be effective in reducing some of these hyperpigmented areas. Melanin-suppressant agents are also used for this condition. Brighteners such as kojic acid, mulberry, licorice root, azaleic acid, bearberry, and citrus such as lemon are known to reduce pigmentation. These affect melanin production and are more effective when used with AHAs, BHAs, and other types of exfoliators that may lighten the pigment on the surface of the skin. Harsh skin-bleaching agents such as hydroquinone may damage the skin and are controversial. Remember that over-exfoliating can cause damage and make hyperpigmentation worse—or conversely, cause hypopigmentation.

Treatments for Oily Skin

Oily and combination skins need light, water-based products. Facial goals are focused on deep cleansing. This skin can usually tolerate more stimulation and stronger products, but be careful not to overdo it or overdry the skin. Aggressive products and treatments may make it worse. The trick is to apply the right products without irritating the skin. Most facial machines work well on oilier skin that is not irritated or red. Treatment for oily skin can be similar to the following acne treatments. ✓ LO4

Acne Facials

Acne facial treatments can significantly affect the skin's appearance. Extractions and a good mask can improve the skin, and clients will be greatly relieved to have clearer, smoother skin. A gentle, cautious approach is best, especially for first-time clients. Extractions must be done gently and without pain to the client. If it hurts, it is probably too rough and forceful. Treatment care and client education regarding acne can be challenging, but the results are rewarding for clients and the esthetician (Figure 15–22).

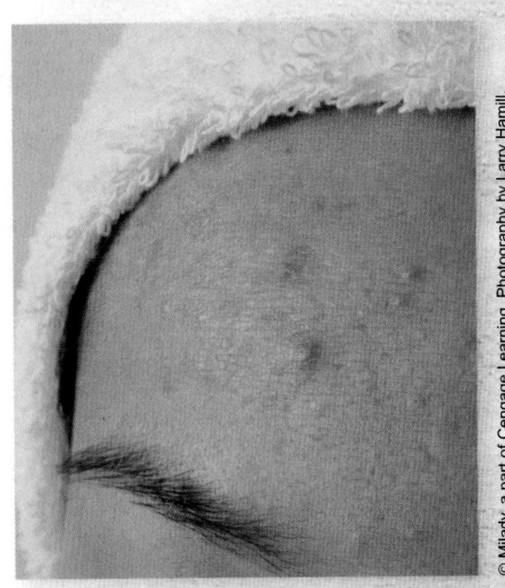

▲ Figure 15–22
Acne can be challenging to work with.

Acne Treatment Care

The esthetician can outline an acne treatment plan to balance the skin. Treatments are focused on clearing the follicles by deep cleansing and extractions. Physicians will prescribe medications that will work to suppress acne flare-ups; however, medications can have adverse side effects and, even with medication, acne can return. Working with problem skin is a continuous process, and clients need to follow regular skin care programs.

Acne treatments may include clay, oxygen, sulfur, or anti-inflammatory masks. Desincrustation, steam, and extractions are all part of an acne facial. AHA and BHA exfoliation treatments are also effective. Each client is treated individually according to his or her needs.

Here are some products and vitamins recommended for acne:

- **Beta hydroxy acids (salicylic acid).** These products work synergistically with AHAs to slough old cells and keep follicles open. BHAs are not as strong as AHAs, but they are effective when used alone, especially for sensitive skin (check for aspirin allergies before using salicylic acid).

- **Sulfur masks.** These are effective acne products that exfoliate skin, and heal and dry blemishes (check for sulfur allergies).
- **Vitamins.** These oral vitamins should include zinc and B-complex vitamins.
- **Increased vitamin C.** This oral vitamin has antioxidant value and healing effects.
- **AHAs (glycolic, lactic, malic, citric, and tartaric acids).** These products are used in different percentages and pH factors to dissolve the desmosomes between cells to keep skin cells exfoliated. Exfoliation also softens acne impactions and stimulates cell production.
- **Vitamin A.** This topical vitamin benefits the skin in several ways; it stimulates new cell production and clears up acne impactions and the skin in general.
- **Benzoyl peroxide.** This product releases oxygen that kills the bacteria and stops the irritating effects of the bacteria; it also irrigates and sloughs out acne impactions.
- **Healing creams.** These products encourage new cell growth.
- **Oxygen therapy treatments.** These products reduce bacteria; they also oxygenate and open impacted follicles for easier extractions.
- **Spot blemish treatments.** These include products such as tea tree oil and benzoyl peroxide that are applied just on blemishes after cleansing.

CAUTION!

Some minerals in multivitamins may aggravate acne because of iodides from sea-sourced products.

Acne Care Tips

Here are some suggestions for clients with acne.

- Eliminate comedogenic products. *Oil-free* does not mean "noncomedogenic." Examine the ingredients on product labels to determine if they are correct for problem skin. (Refer to Chapter 13, Skin Care Products: Chemistry, Ingredients, and Selection, for ingredient information.)
- Control oil through proper product usage. Do not irritate the skin with harsh products.
- Exfoliate the follicles. Keep follicles clean and exfoliated to keep sebum and cells from building up. Benzoyl peroxide or alpha hydroxy acids are beneficial. Do not overuse these products. Sometimes once a day is too much.
- Avoid environmental aggravators such as dirt, grease, sun, humidity, and pollution.
- Practice stress reduction and good nutrition.
- Have regular facials once a month or as needed.

Home-Care for Acne

Proper home-care can usually help keep acne under control. However, when clients cannot achieve results with their home-care, they may seek the aid of the esthetician or a physician. After the skin is analyzed, suggestions are given to the client specific to their needs. It is important for clients to follow the recommended home-care routine as outlined by the esthetician. Treatments must be accompanied by a real commitment from the client to maintain their home-care regimen.

The blue light of LED-light therapy is beneficial for the treatment of acne. (See Chapter 19, Advanced Topics and Treatments.)

It is important to ask clients not to "pick" at their blemishes. Explain to them that the internal membrane is delicate, and performing self-extractions will cause the infection to go deeper and spread more rapidly. Picking also is the cause of external bacterial infections and scarring, both under the skin and on the surface. When the skin shows signs of infection, it is important to treat the area as you would any inflamed area. A cold compress or towel will calm the infection by constricting blood flow to the area. Calm the skin down with anti-inflammatory products, and ice the lesions when necessary.

Home-care will include a cleanser, an exfoliant, a mask, a toner, and a light calming hydrator:

- Make sure recommended ingredients are not irritating or contraindicated.
- A foaming cleanser with an exfoliant (AHA, salicylic acid, or benzoyl peroxide) is the best choice. Use a soothing or antibacterial toner to calm skin, control oil, or kill bacteria.
- Use an AHA gel or benzoyl peroxide (BP) gel. Alternate using AHAs and BP. Use these at different times or on alternate days to avoid reactions or overdrying the skin.
- Apply a light, hydrating, oil-free moisturizer and sunscreen for balance and protection.
- A clay mask is recommended twice per week. A mask with sulfur also works well for acne.
- Other products may include a hydrating, soothing mask to balance the drying products.

All home-care includes an analysis of lifestyle to help the client better understand what some of his or her acne triggers might be. (See Chapter 11, Disorders and Diseases of the Skin.) By understanding the causes, the client is better prepared to follow a home-care program.

Extraction Techniques

In treating acne or blemished skin, the most important step for the esthetician is the effective removal and cleansing of blemishes. When the follicles are properly cleansed, the client's skin will begin to show marked improvement. It is important to explain to the client that you cannot always remove all blemishes during one treatment.

Training and caution are needed before performing extractions. The skin must be exfoliated and warmed before performing extractions. It is also imperative that the esthetician wear gloves during extractions and then change the gloves before performing the rest of the facial to prevent the spread of infection. It is recommended that gloves remain on the hands throughout the rest of the facial procedure. Protective eyewear is also recommended in some instances. Proper extraction procedures are necessary to safely extract oil and debris from the follicles. Do not practice extractions without prior instruction or training.

There are three methods to use for extractions: the forefingers wrapped with finger gloves and cotton (known as finger cots); cotton swabs; and comedone extractors (Figure 15–23).

1. Finger cots are individual finger "gloves" that are used with thin, dampened cotton wrapped around the gloved index fingers.
2. Comedone extractors are metal tools used for open comedones and sebaceous filaments.
3. Cotton swabs are smaller than fingertips and are especially useful around the nose area.

For all methods, press gently around the lesion.

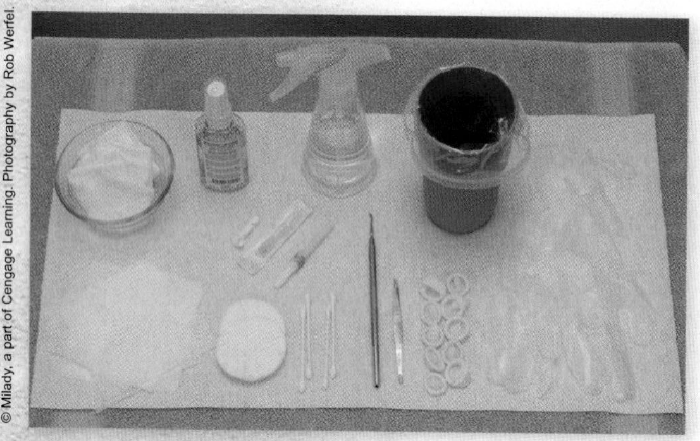

▲ Figure 15–23
Extraction supplies.

To achieve optimum success when performing extractions, you must put pressure on the skin surrounding the follicular wall so that you can extract the impaction with the least trauma to the surrounding tissue. Understanding the angle of the various follicles in the different locations on the skin will enable you to perform extractions easily and effectively.

All areas of the forehead, the top of the nose, the chin, and the jawline have follicular walls perpendicular to the surface of the skin. The follicles are positioned this way on all flat surfaces. All other areas of the skin, such as the sides of the nose and cheeks, have slanted follicular shafts.

Before extractions, the use of desincrustation fluid or an enzyme peel will help to prep the skin by softening the plug of dead cells, sebum, and debris from the follicular shaft.

After extractions, a calming, healing mask is beneficial. Antibacterial products and the high-frequency machine kill bacteria and help heal the skin. Cool water or skin globes can also calm irritated skin and redness.

Extraction of Open Comedones (Blackheads)

Desincrustation (des-in-krus-TAY-shun) is a process used to soften oil and comedones in follicles. Methods such as the galvanic current, enzyme peels, other exfoliating products, or lifting masks must be used before an extraction to soften sebaceous material. The follicles must also be prepared by using either the steam machine or warm, moistened towels to facilitate extractions. If the skin is dry and tight, extractions will not be effective and will damage the skin. The blackheads can usually be coaxed from the follicle with a minimum amount of pressure. Excessive pressure or force is not appropriate and will damage the skin and capillaries.

To avoid spreading infection elsewhere on the skin, it is important to follow proper cleansing procedures when extracting blemishes.

Wrap fingertips with wet cotton strips that have been lightly saturated with astringent. The fingertips are used to exert firm pressure on the skin directly surrounding the blackhead and to lift it from the follicle by pressing down, inward, and up on the sides around the follicle. Concentrating on one blackhead at a time, the esthetician must work gently and carefully so as not to bruise the tissue. Never use the fingernails on the skin or for extractions. Nails must be filed shorter than the finger tips to perform extractions properly.

When extracting blackheads from the nose, it is important not to press down on the cartilage that forms the semi-flexible part of the bridge of the nose.

To use the comedone extractor, place the loop over the lesion so that the lesion is inside the loop. Press gently next to the lesion to push it up and out. Be aware that the pressure exerted can traumatize tissues. The follicle walls can rupture, spilling sebum and bacteria into the dermis. This debris can cause infection and irritation that leads to the start of even more blemishes. Never force extractions.

Most clients will only tolerate 10 minutes of extractions. Check to make sure they are comfortable with the procedure if you intend to work longer. Once the skin becomes dry and resistive, it is time to stop the procedure. At the end of your service, rebook the client's next appointment to be able to continue their extractions during their next treatment.

Extraction of Closed Comedones, Whiteheads, and Other Blemishes

It is necessary to open closed lesions. Closed lesions are removed in the same manner as blackheads except that an opening in the dead-cell layer must first be made. This is done by placing a lancet almost parallel to the surface of the skin and pricking the top of the dead-cell layer to make an opening for the debris to pass through. The lesion is then removed by applying gentle pressure down, in, and then upward.

The lancet is a small, sharp, pointed surgical blade with a double edge used to pierce or prick the skin. Each lancet is sterilized and comes in a separate, sealed envelope. If the envelope is open, the lancet cannot be guaranteed to be sterile. A fresh lancet must be used for each client.

After extractions, wipe the area with an astringent. Do not transfer the fluid from one area to another. Wipe the cleanest area first: comedones, then papules, and finally pustules. Use a separate cotton pad for pustules as necessary.

REGULATORY AGENCY ALERT

Check with your local regulating agencies for extraction regulations which may not be legal in certain regions. Using a lancet in the extraction procedure may be illegal in some regions.

PAGE 422

Mini Procedure

THE ACNE TREATMENT PROCEDURE

The following general procedure can be used for problem skin. Most of the facial focuses on deep-cleansing and extracting impactions from the follicles. Some steps may be omitted or rearranged, depending on the treatment goals and the client's needs. See the facial machine procedures (Chapter 17, Facial Machines) for additional details. Treatments for the back are performed in much the same way as acne treatments for the face.

1. Cleanse with an acne-appropriate cleanser that rinses clean.
2. Exfoliate with an enzyme peel, an AHA or BHA peel, or an exfoliating mask. (Scrubs and brushes are too irritating on inflamed skin.)
3. Steam (can reverse steps 2 or 3, depending on the products and methods of choice).
4. **Optional desincrustation:** Use the galvanic machine with a desincrustation fluid to soften the follicles. (Alternate method: A desincrustation fluid can be used while steaming.)
5. Perform extractions.
6. After extractions, use an astringent/toner to kill bacteria.
7. **Optional:** Use the high-frequency mushroom electrode to spark blemishes to help kill bacteria and heal the lesions. An acne serum can also be applied after extractions to treat the skin.
8. **Optional:** Use light acupressure massage with less friction on noninflamed areas. **Note:** Massage is irritating to inflamed acne and is usually not part of the acne facial.
9. Apply a clay or soothing mask after extractions. Remove with towels.
10. Apply benzoyl peroxide on blemishes, if the client is not allergic to it. (If in doubt, send clients home with a sample for patch testing.)
11. Finish the treatment with a light, soothing, hydrating gel and any other appropriate product. ✓ LO5

Men's Skin Care

Men's skin care needs are just as important as women's. It is becoming more common for men to use spa services and to take care of their skin. Estheticians need to take a simple, direct approach when discussing skin care with their male clients. Men need the same skin care programs that women do, but most men will want to use only a few products.

Male clients are willing to follow suggestions and want a basic, consistent routine. They tend to be loyal customers. Male clients represent a growing percentage of a spa's business. The challenge is to attract male clients to make the initial visit in the first place. Using the term *skin treatment* rather than the term *facial* is a better way to promote men's services.

One way to attract male clientele is to offer special services designed just for them. Make them feel comfortable, and tactfully assure them that it is normal for men to have spa services and practice good skin care habits. Conduct consultations privately, without discussing products and treatments out in the reception area where other clients may be present. Some salons and spas cater to men only. The male client market will continue to grow as men feel more comfortable about receiving services (Figure 15–24).

Men's Skin Care Products

To build the market, a salon or spa could carry a specific line of men's skin care products. Most unisex product lines will work as long as packaging or fragrance is not overly feminine. Men typically have larger sebaceous glands and oilier skin. They also need sun protection. Men may tend to neglect their skin care because it is not considered masculine or a priority. Clients who are especially pleased with visible treatment results are more willing to try a home-maintenance program.

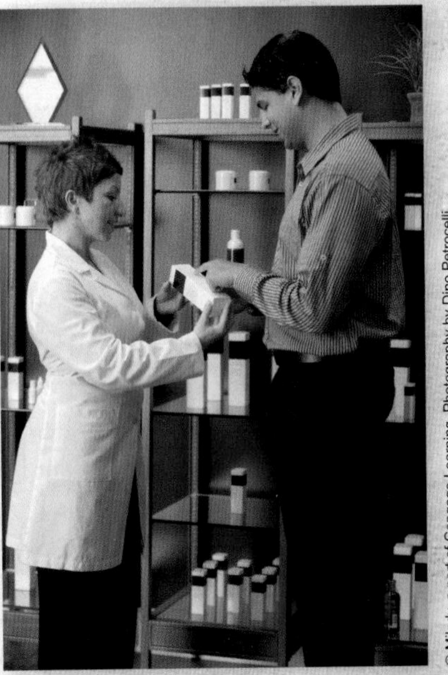

▲ Figure 15–24
The male client market continues to grow.

When considering a men's skin care line, keep in mind several key points. Be sure the products are basic and the routines are simple. Men do not want highly fragranced, feminine products. For instance, lotions need to be light, without fragrance, highly absorbent, and with a matte finish. Most men do not like the greasy feeling of some products.

Men prefer simple routines and multipurpose products. They would rather have a combined cleanser and toner. They also like the foaminess of soaps, so a foaming cleanser is a good choice. They can use a toner just like they would an aftershave lotion. They should then apply a light moisturizer with sunscreen. Give male clients specific instructions on how and when to use products.

Keep the following tips in mind when working with male clients:

- Tubes and pumps that are easy to open are more male-friendly than jars.
- His home-care regimen should begin with only two products: a cleanser and a hydrating lotion. If he wants three, add sunscreen.
- As he grows accustomed to the regimen and sees favorable results, he will most likely add to his regimen by purchasing a toner, eye cream, and a mask.
- Educate him on sun protection and skin-cancer facts, even if he chooses not to purchase sunscreen.
- Estheticians can suggest that male clients shave in a downward direction—in the direction of the hair growth pattern—because it is less irritating.

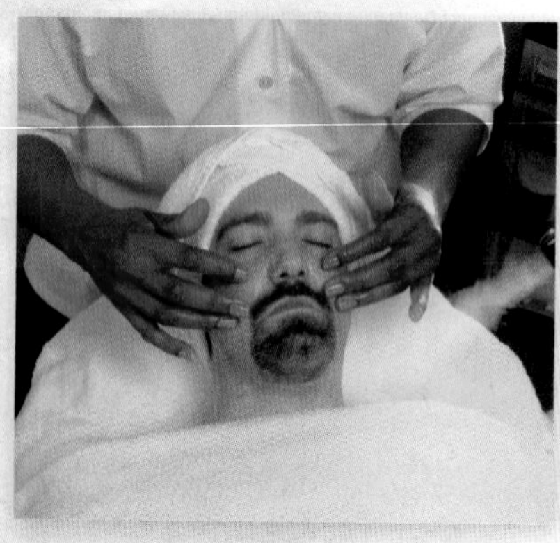

© Milady, a part of Cengage Learning. Photography by Paul Castle, Castle Photography.

▲ Figure 15–25
Most men love steam and the brush machine.

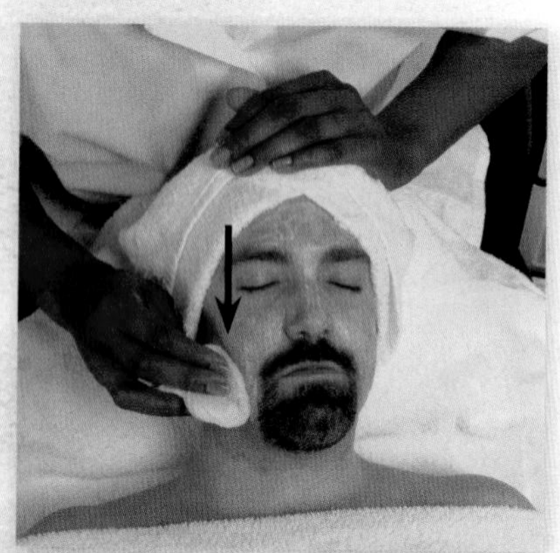

© Milady, a part of Cengage Learning. Photography by Paul Castle, Castle Photography.

▲ Figure 15–26
Most movements for the beard and moustache area should follow the hair-growth pattern.

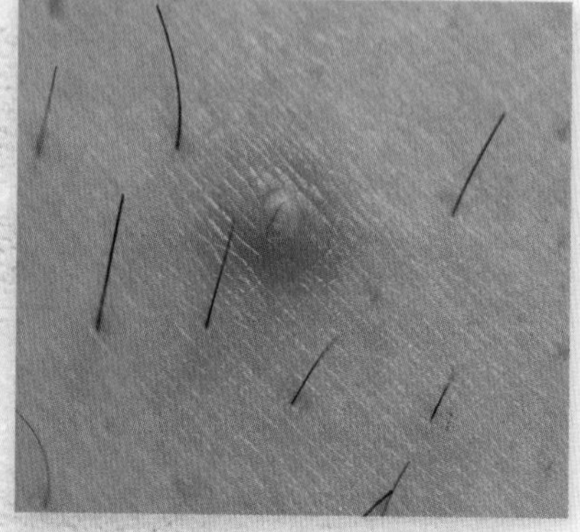

© C.F.G. 2011; used under license from Shutterstock.com.

▲ Figure 15–27
Folliculitis can be a problem for many men.

Web Resources

www.cosmeticsandtoiletries.com
www.milady.cengage.com
www.dayspa.com
www.lneonline.com
www.skininc.com

- Once he is accustomed to receiving treatments and using products, your male client will use an eye cream if he is taught how. While men may be conscious of lines and wrinkles around their eyes, they seldom request an eye product. Estheticians can point out the benefits of these and other products.

Professional Treatments for Men

Depending on the client's skin conditions, you can offer various treatments. Most men love steam and the brush machine (Figure 15–25). Even if a client's skin is slightly sensitive, he will prefer the assertiveness of a brush and foamy cleanser. A firmer touch and deeper massage are also needed on male skin.

There are some other important aspects of men's facials. First, sponges and towels are more appropriate for a man's face. Cotton pads or gauze will grab the beard hair, leaving particles clinging to the face. Shaving before a facial actually makes the skin more sensitive. On freshly shaven skin, exfoliating products or techniques, including strong sensitizing agents such as alpha hydroxy acids and microdermabrasion, may be contraindicated.

Professional movements during a man's facial should flow with the hair growth. For example, most massage movements in the beard area should move downward, not upward (Figure 15–26). This goes against the typical esthetic procedure of lifting movements up the neck and face. Overall, the beard area tends to be relatively sensitive due to shaving lotions that contain perfume, alcohol, or other similar substances. Shaving itself is also quite abrasive to the skin, so men need more calming and healing products.

Folliculitis

Folliculitis (fah-lik-yuh-LY-tis) is inflammation of the hair follicles. This can be a problem for many men, especially if they have very coarse or curly beard hair (Figure 15–27). Folliculitis is an infection characterized by inflammation and pus. Improper shaving may also cause folliculitis barbae (fah-lik-yuh-LY-tis BAR-bay), where the hair grows slightly under the skin and is trapped there, causing a bacterial infection. The treatment goal for this condition is to alleviate the irritation, dry up and disinfect the pustules, and desensitize the area. A soothing gel mask is probably the most comfortable product for a male client to use in this area.

Pseudofolliculitis (SOO-doe-fah-lik-yuh-LY-tis), also known as *razor bumps*, resembles folliculitis without the infection. This condition also results from improper shaving techniques.

There are products on the market for ingrown hairs that help exfoliate and keep the follicles clean. Exfoliating is necessary to keep the follicles open. A foaming cleanser will also help a man's beard area. Estheticians can help male clients by keeping them informed of how to take care of their skin on a regular basis. ☑ **LO6**

PROCEDURE

15-1

Eye Makeup and Lipstick Removal

IMPLEMENTS AND MATERIALS

- Disinfectant
- Hand sanitizer/antibacterial soap
- Covered waste container
- Bowl
- Spatula
- Hand towels
- Headband
- Clean linens
- Bolster

Single-use Items

- Gloves
- Cotton pads
- Cotton rounds
- Cotton swabs
- Plastic bag
- Paper towels
- Tissues

Products

- Eye makeup remover or cleanser
- Facial cleanser

Preparation

- **Perform** 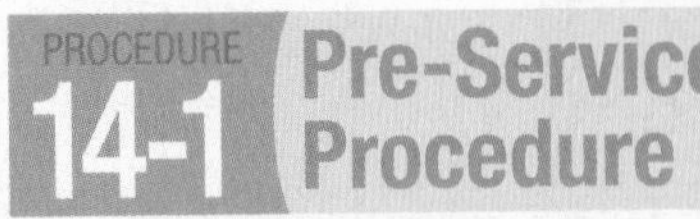

PAGE 372

Procedure

Eye Makeup Removal

Note: If the client is wearing contacts, do not remove the eye makeup. Be especially gentle when cleansing the eyes because the skin around the eyes is very sensitive and can become irritated. Do not get cleanser into the eyes.

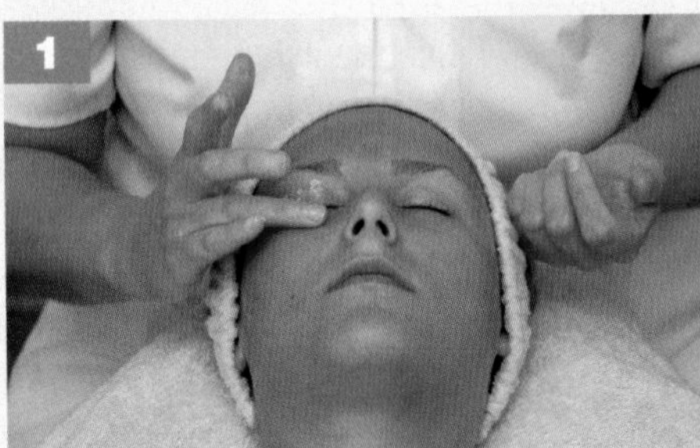

1 Apply a small amount of cleanser.

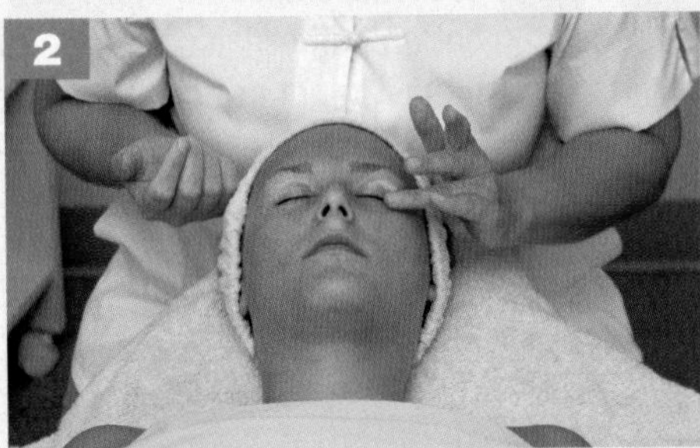

2 With the middle and ring fingers, apply the cleanser to the eyelids with gentle downward strokes. Use downward movements with the cleansing pad to cleanse the eyelid and lashes. Gently rinse with cotton pads.

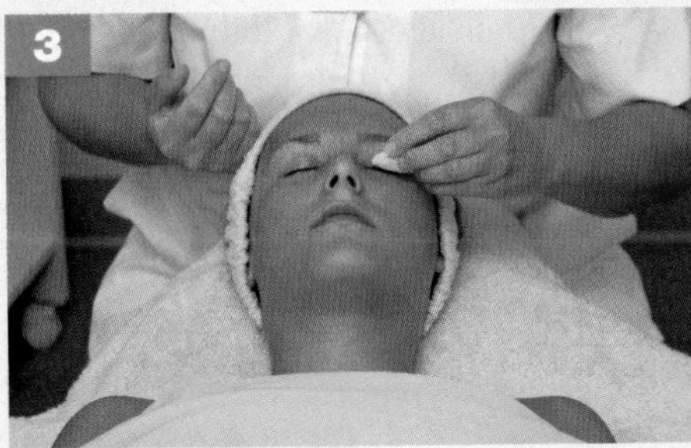

3 Repeat this step as necessary to remove eye makeup. While cleansing the eyes, rotate the pad to provide a clean, unused surface.

PROCEDURE

15-1 Eye Makeup and Lipstick Removal (continued)

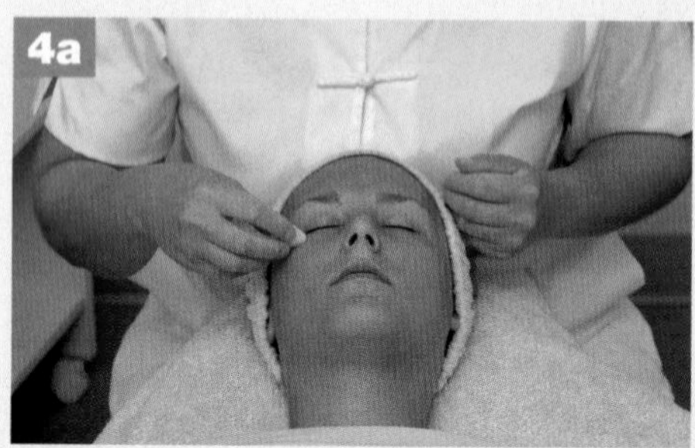

4a Rinse under the eyes sweeping in towards the nose. Remove any makeup underneath the eyes and along the lash line with a cotton swab or pad. Place the edge of the pad under the lower lashes at the outside corner of the eyes, and slide the pad toward the inner corner of the eyes. The mascara will gradually work loose and can be wiped clean. Always be gentle around the eyes; never rub or stretch the skin, as it is very delicate and thin.

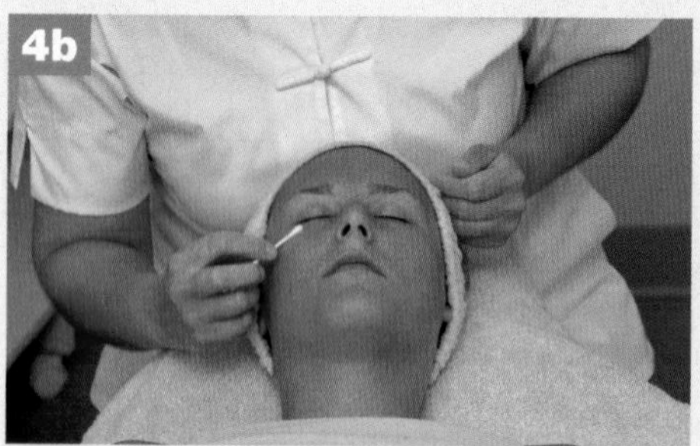

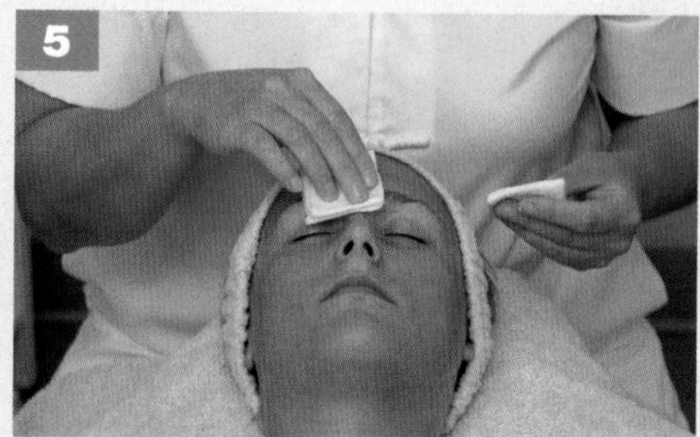

4b Make a complete circular pattern around the eye. Use the cotton pad or a cotton swab to wipe inward under the eye toward the nose and then outward on the top of the eyelid.

5 Rinse the eye area with plain water to remove the eye makeup remover. Make sure the remover is rinsed off thoroughly.

Lipstick Removal

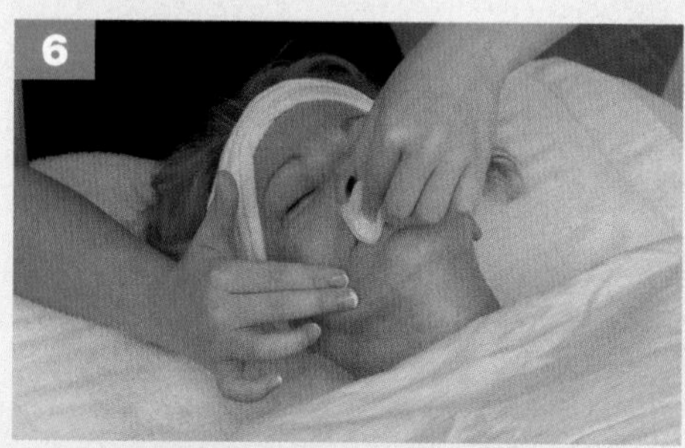

6 To remove lipstick, apply eye makeup remover or a cleanser to a damp cotton pad or tissue and remove the client's lipstick. Use a small amount and do not get cleanser in the mouth—it does not taste good.

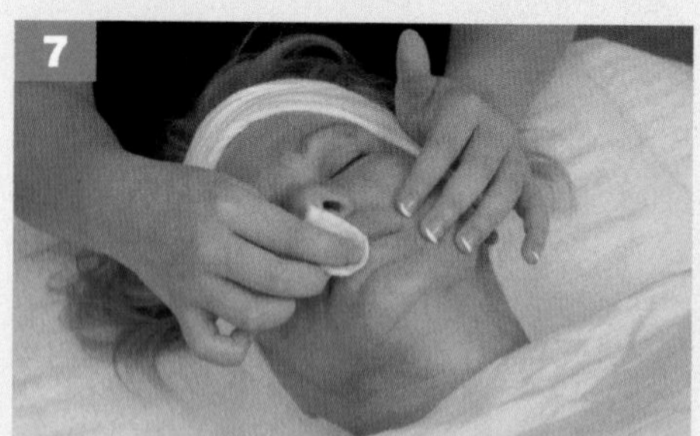

7 With the index and middle finger (either the left or right side) of one hand, hold on next to the outside edge of the lips to keep the skin taut so it does not move around; then remove the cleanser with the other hand using even strokes from the corners of the lips toward the center from both sides.

8 Repeat the procedure on the other side until the lips are clean.

Post-Service

- **Complete** 

PAGE 375

PROCEDURE

15-2 Applying a Cleansing Product

IMPLEMENTS AND MATERIALS

- Disinfectant
- Hand sanitizer/antibacterial soap
- Covered waste container
- Bowl
- Spatula
- Facial towels
- Headband
- Clean linens
- Bolster

Single-use Items

- Gloves
- Cotton pads
- Cotton rounds
- Cotton swabs
- Plastic bag
- Paper towels
- Tissues

Products

- Eye makeup remover or cleanser
- Facial cleanser
- Toner
- Moisturizer

The following method of application is used when applying cleansers, massage creams, treatment creams, and protective products. Most product removal requires rinsing each area at least three times. If possible, use both hands at the same time for a more even and efficient technique. Use either circular motions or straight, even strokes for cleansing.

Preparation

- **Perform** 

PAGE 372

Procedure

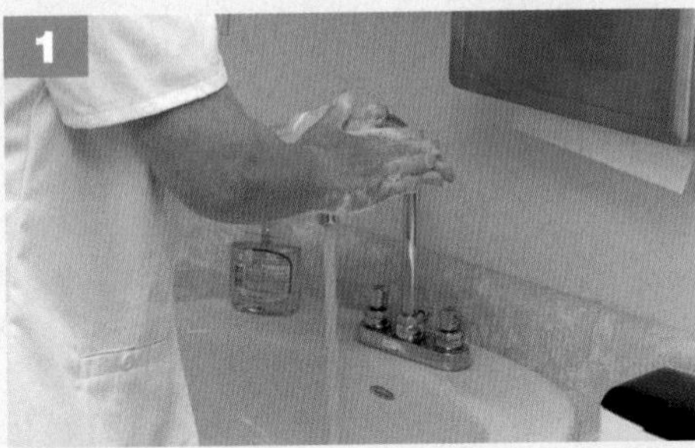

1 Cleanse the hands and apply gloves before touching the client's face. Apply warm towels. After checking the temperature, apply one towel to the décolleté and one to the face. Leave on at least 1 minute and then remove.

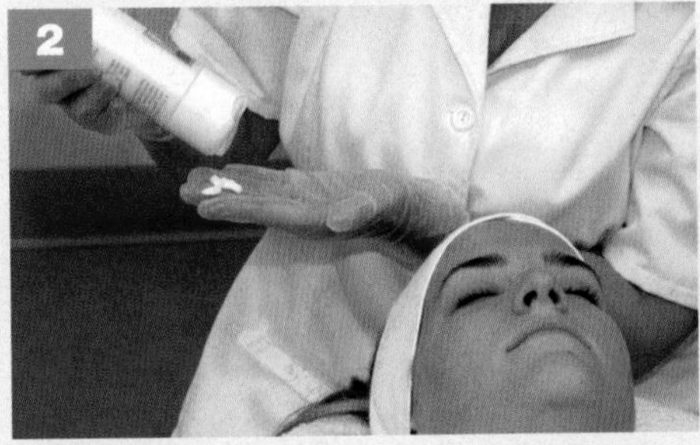

2 Apply approximately one-half teaspoon of the product to the fingers or palms of the hand. Water-soluble cleansing lotion is preferred over foamy cleansers when cleansing the face because it can be removed easier with moistened cotton pads or sponges.

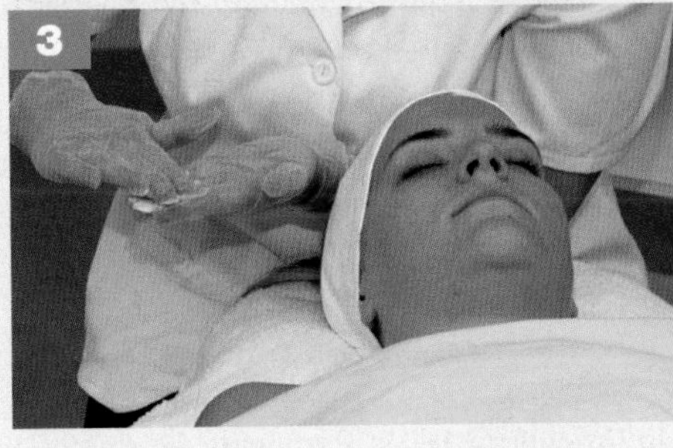

3 Use circular motions to distribute the product onto the fingertips. You are now ready to apply the product to the client's décolleté, neck, and face. Cleanse each area using six passes. If starting on the décolleté, start in the center and work out to the sides moving up to the neck. Be guided by your instructor.

PROCEDURE

15-2 Applying a Cleansing Product (continued)

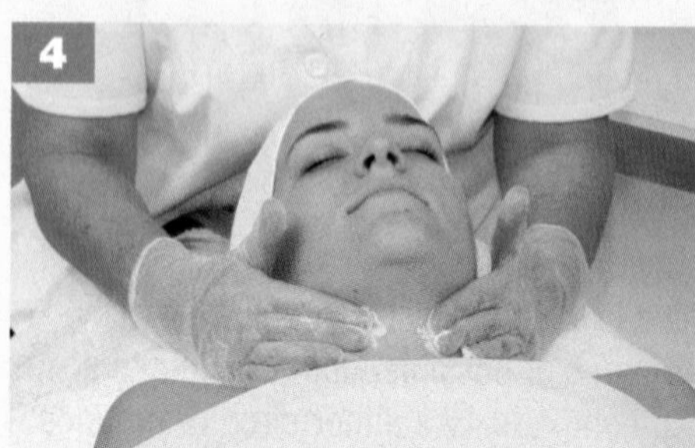

4 Start applying a small amount of the product by placing both hands, palms down, on the neck. Slide hands back toward the ears until the pads of the fingers rest at a point directly beneath the earlobes. While applying the product, it is suggested that hands are not lifted from the client's face until you are finished.

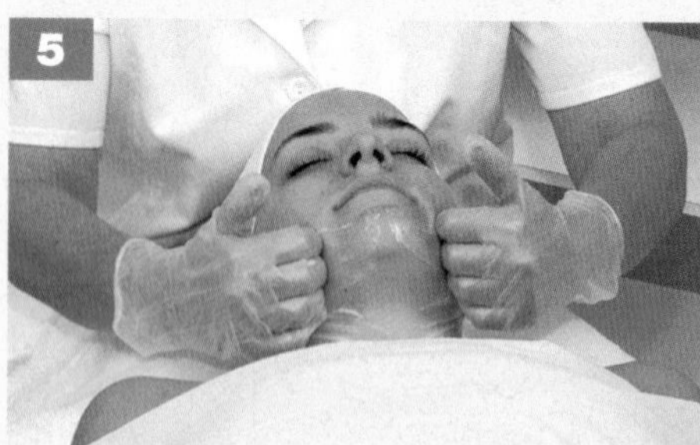

5 Reverse the hand, with the back of the fingers now resting on the skin, and slide the fingers along the jawline to the chin.

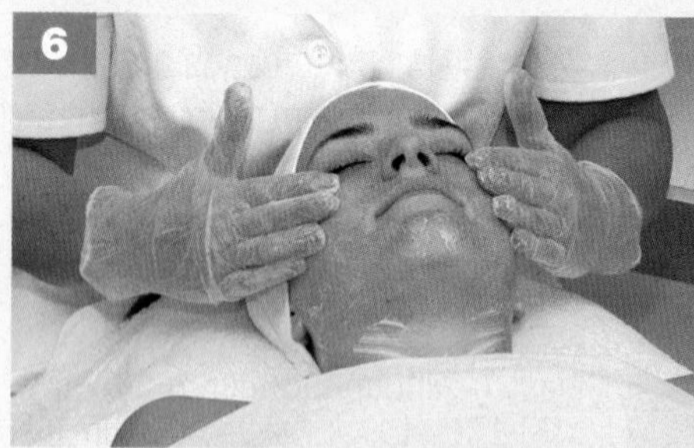

6 Reverse the hands again and slide the fingers back over the cheeks and center of the face until the pads of the fingers come to rest directly in front of the ears.

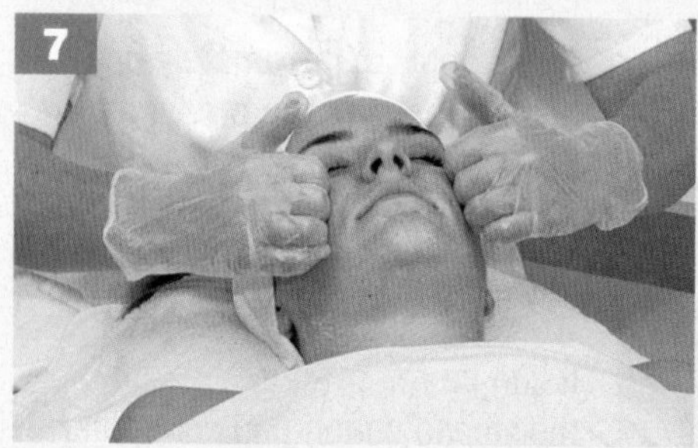

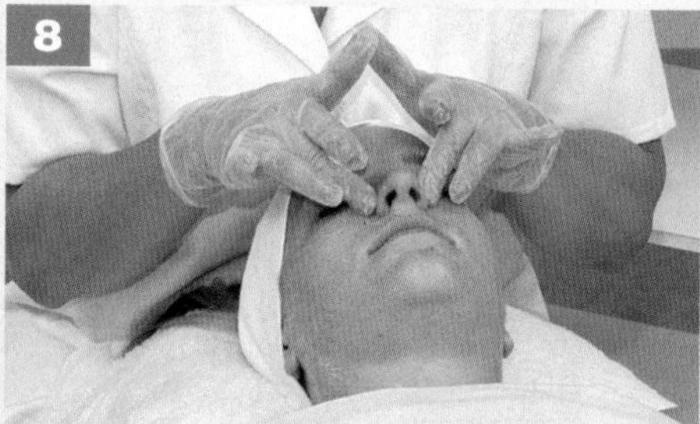

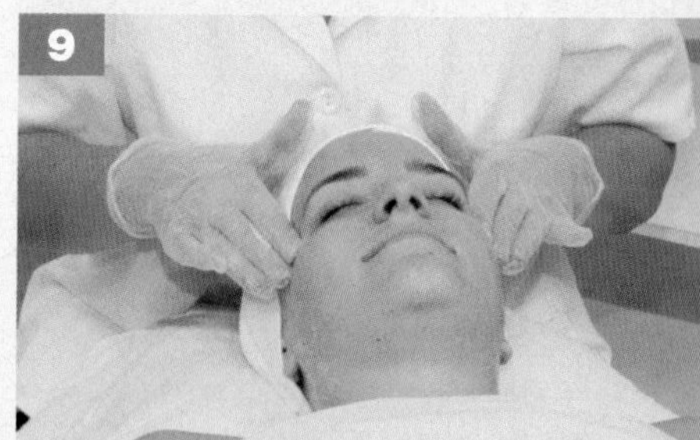

7 Reverse the hands again, and slide the fingers forward over the cheekbones to the nose. Cleanse the upper lip area under the nose with sideways strokes from the center area moving outward. Then slide up to the sides of the nose.

8 With the pads of the middle fingers, make small, circular motions on the top of the nose and on each side of the nose. Avoid pushing the product into the nose.

9 Slide the fingers up to the forehead and outward toward the temples, pausing with a slight pressure on the temples. Slide fingers across the forehead using circles or long strokes from side to side.

10 Continue to remove the product in Procedure 15–3, Removing Products.

PROCEDURE

15-3 Removing Products

IMPLEMENTS AND MATERIALS

- Disinfectant
- Hand sanitizer/antibacterial soap
- Covered waste container
- Bowl
- Spatula
- Facial towels
- Headband
- Clean linens
- Bolster

Single-use Items

- Gloves
- Cotton pads
- Cotton rounds
- Cotton swabs
- Plastic bag
- Paper towels
- Tissues

Products

- Eye makeup remover or cleanser
- Facial cleanser
- Toner
- Moisturizer

To remove products, rinse each area at least three to six times. Some estheticians prefer to use wet cotton pads or disposable facial sponges when removing product. Others prefer to use towels. Both methods are correct and equally professional, and many estheticians use both methods. For example, an esthetician who usually uses the sponges will use cotton pads when working on acne skin. Even when using sponges, an esthetician may need cotton pads during the treatment for eye pads or removing blackheads.

Facial movements are generally done in an upward and outward direction from the center to the edges of the face. Under the eyes, it is usually inward to avoid tugging on the eye area.

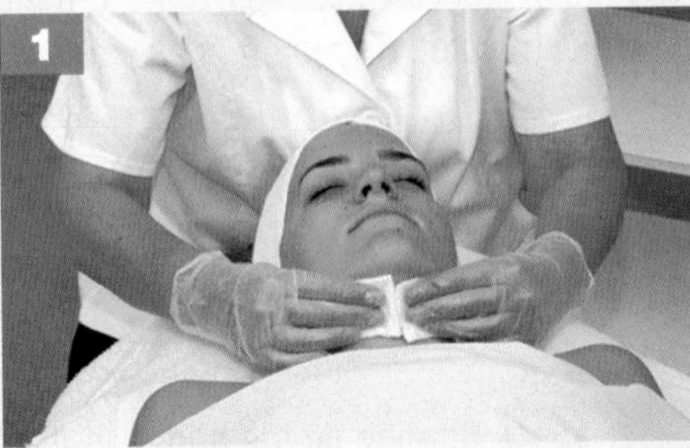

1 Starting at the décolleté, cleanse sideways and up to the neck. Cleanse the neck using upward strokes. To keep the pad from slipping from the hand, pinch the edge of the pad between the thumb and upper part of the forefinger. It is important that most of the surface of the pad remain in contact with the skin. Do not exert pressure on the Adam's apple in the center of the neck.

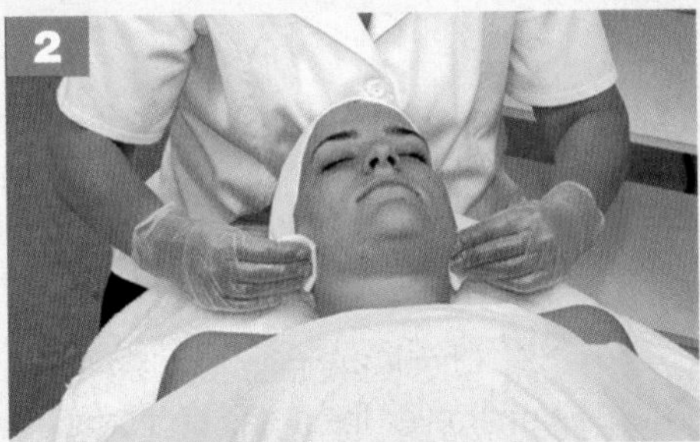

2 Place the pad directly under the chin and slide the pad along the jawline, stopping directly under the ear. Repeat the movement on the other side of the face. Alternate back and forth three times on each side of the face, or do the movement concurrently by using both hands at the same time.

15-3 Removing Products (continued)

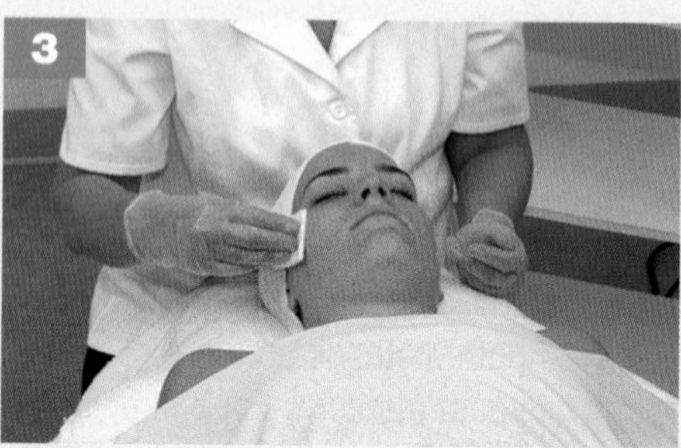

3 Starting at the jawline, use upward movements to cleanse the cheeks.

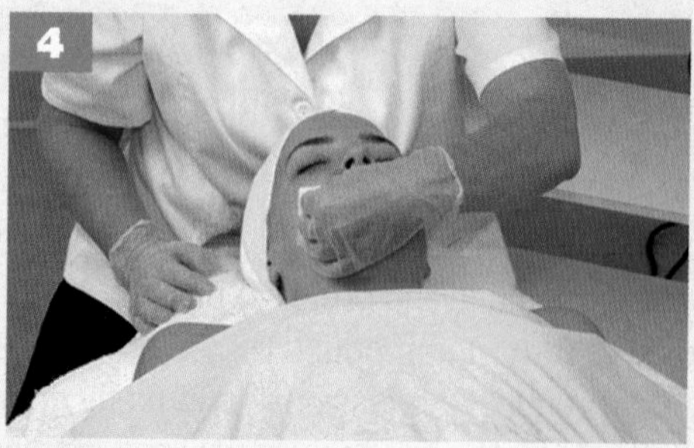

4 Continuing the upward movement and cross over the chin to the other cheek if you are only using one hand.

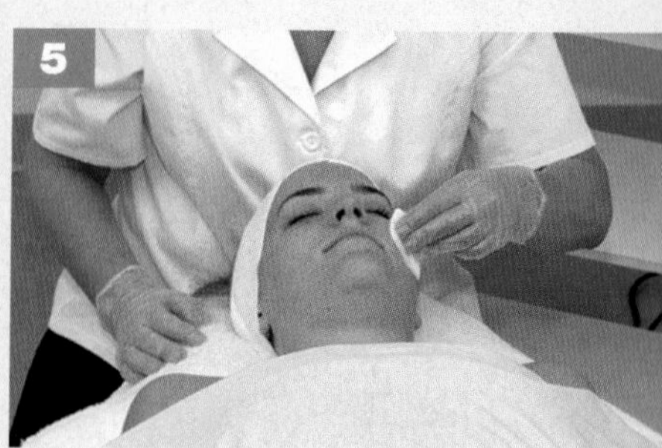

5 Continue the cleansing movement with approximately six strokes on each cheek.

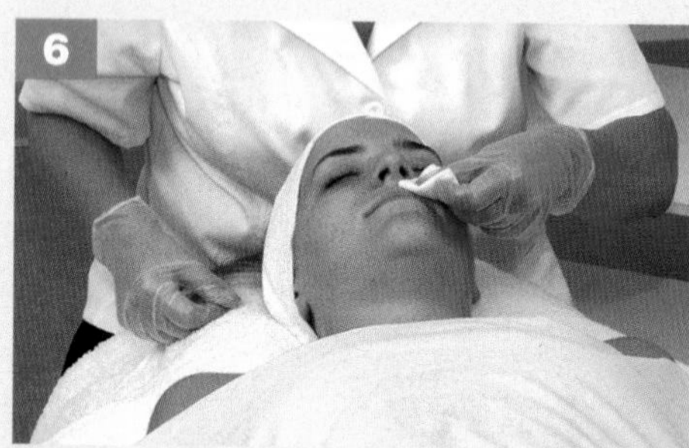

6 Cleanse the area directly underneath the nose by using downward and sideways strokes. Start at the center and work outward toward the corners of the mouth. Rinse at least three times on each side of the face.

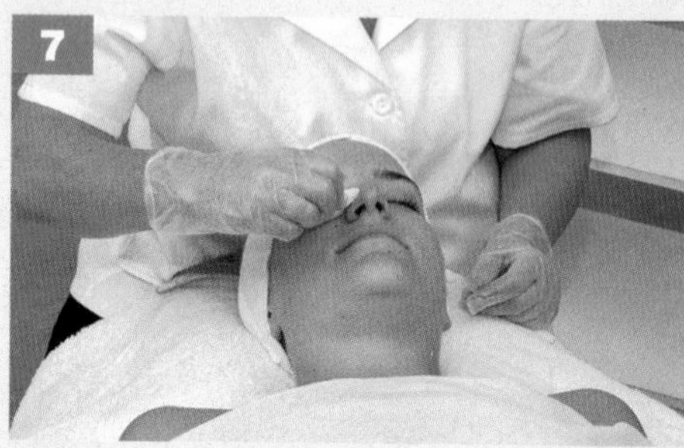

7 Starting on the bridge of the nose, cleanse the sides of the nose and the area directly next to it. Use light, outward movements.

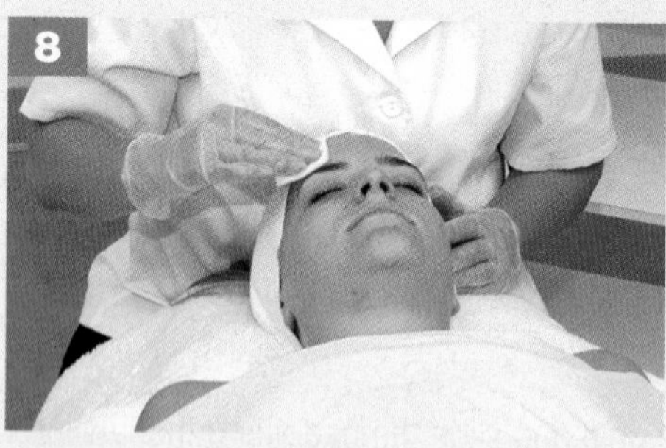

8 Place the pads flat on the center of the forehead, and slide them outward to the temples. Apply a slight pressure on the pressure points of the temples. Repeat the movement three times on each side of the forehead.

9 Check the face to make sure there is no residue left on the skin. Feather over the areas of the face with the finger tips to check that it is well rinsed.

Post-Service

- **Complete** 

PAGE 375

PROCEDURE

15-4 The Basic Step-by-Step Facial

IMPLEMENTS AND MATERIALS

Equipment

- Facial equipment (towel warmer, steamer, mag light)

Supplies

- Disinfectant
- Hand sanitizer/antibacterial soap
- Covered waste container
- Bowls
- Spatulas
- Fan and mask brush
- Implements
- Distilled water
- Sharps container
- Hand towels
- Clean linens
- Blanket
- Headband
- Client wrap
- Bolster
- Client charts

Single-use Items

- Cotton pads
- Cotton rounds
- Cotton swabs
- Paper towels
- Tissue
- Gloves/finger cots
- Sealable plastic bag

Products

- Cleanser
- Exfoliant
- Masks
- Massage lotion
- Toner
- Moisturizer
- Sunscreen
- Optional: serums, eye cream, lip balm, extraction supplies

Now that you have practiced the preliminary steps and cleansing, it is time to put it all together in a complete facial. The steps for performing a basic facial treatment are listed here. Facial procedures vary, so be guided by your instructor.

While not shown, wearing gloves may be required while performing facial services in your region.

Preparation

- **Perform** 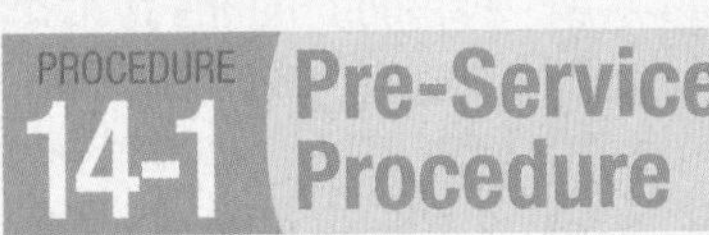

PAGE 372

Procedure

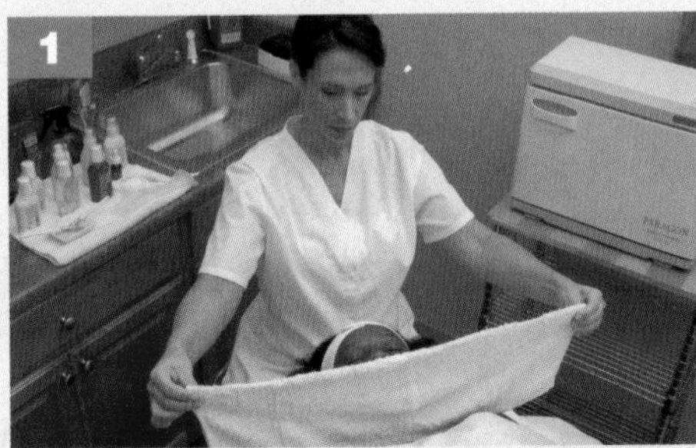

1 Cleanse your hands and apply warm towels. After checking the temperature, apply one towel to the décolleté and one to the face.

To apply warm towels: Hold the ends of the towels with both hands on either side of the face. Lay the center of the towel on the chin and drape each side across the face with the towel edges draped over to the opposite corner across the forehead. To remove, lift each end and remove. For product removal: use the towels over the hands as mitts. Be guided by your instructor on this method.

Optional: Remove eye makeup and lipstick. If your client has no makeup, skip this part and proceed to step 2. Remember to ask about contact lenses before putting product on the eyes. If the client is wearing contacts, do not remove the eye makeup.

PROCEDURE

15-4 The Basic Step-by-Step Facial (continued)

2 Cleanse

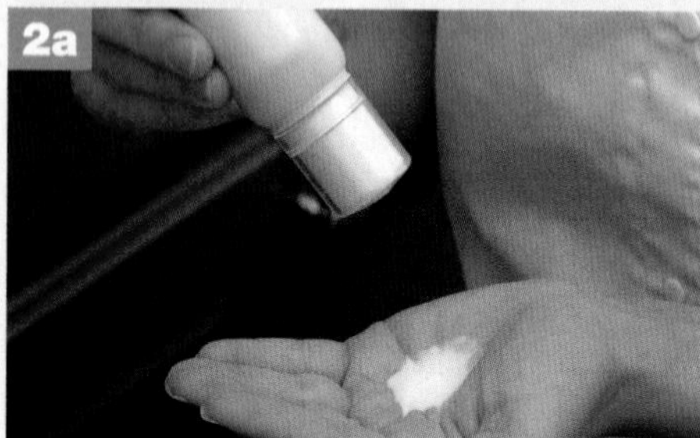

2a Remove about one-half teaspoon of cleanser from the container (with a clean spatula if it is not a squirt-top or pump-type lid). Place it on the fingertips or in the palm and then apply a small amount to your fingertips. This conserves the amount of product you use.

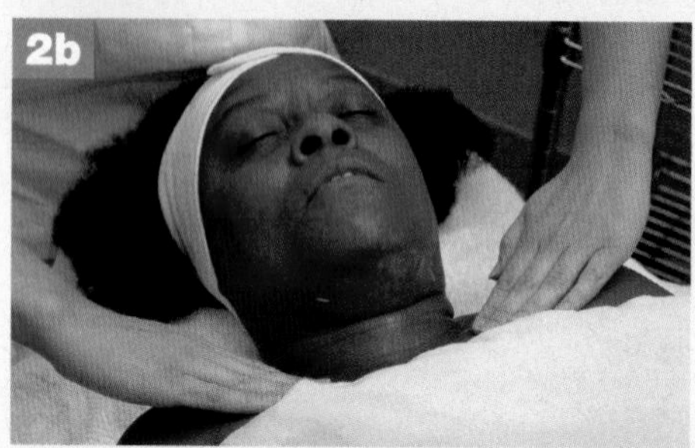

2b Starting at the neck or décolleté and with a sweeping movement, use both hands to spread the cleanser upward and outward on the chin, jaws, cheeks, and temples. Spread the cleanser down the nose and along its sides and bridge. Continue to the upper lip area. Cleanse the upper lip area under the nose with sideways strokes from the center area moving outward.

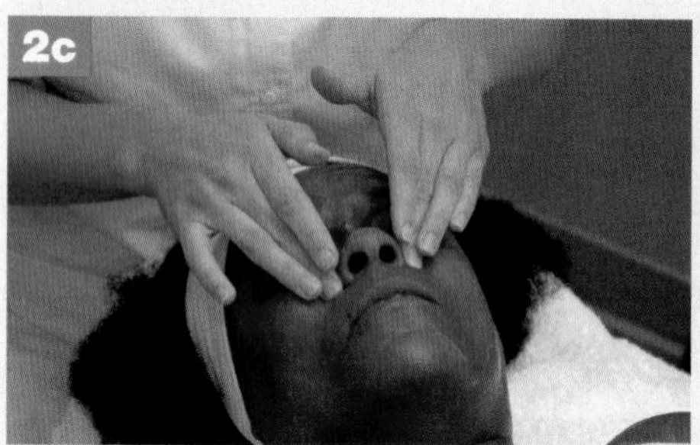

2c Make small, circular movements with the fingertips around the nostrils and sides of the nose. Continue with upward-sweeping movements between the brows and across the forehead to the temples.

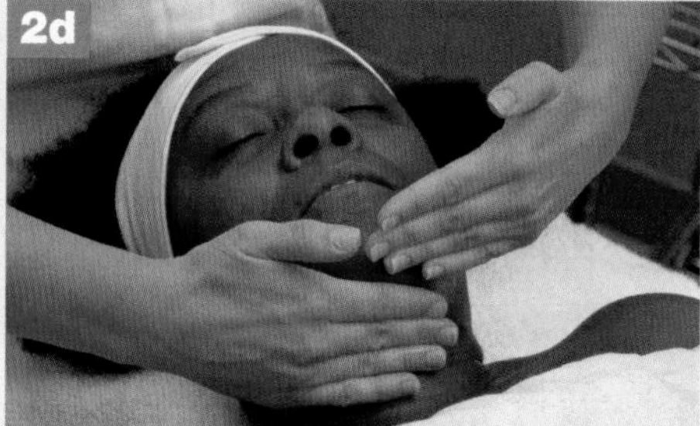

2d Apply more cleanser to the neck and chest with long, outward strokes. Cleanse the area in small, circular motions from the center of the chest and neck toward the outside, moving upward. Try to use both hands at the same time on each side when applying or removing product.

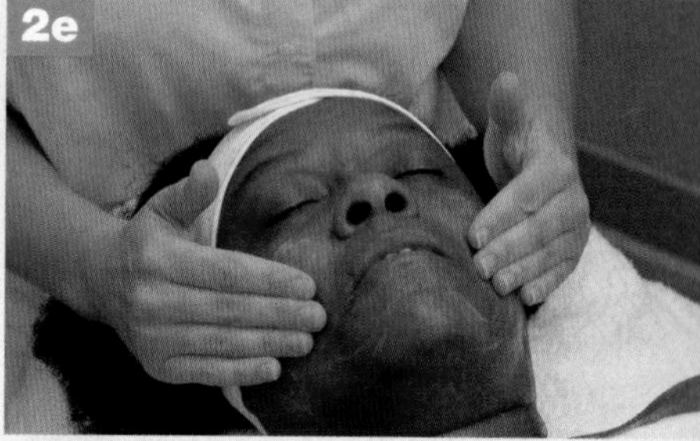

2e Visually divide the face into left and right halves from the center. Continue moving upward with circular motions on the face from the chin and cheeks, and up toward the forehead using both hands, one on each side.

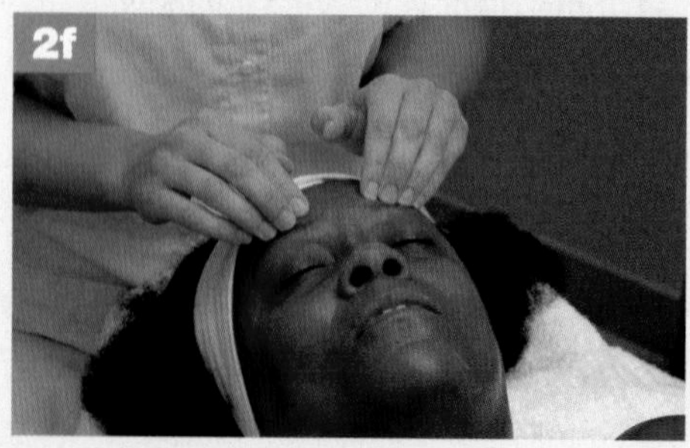

2f Starting at the center of the forehead, continue with the circular pattern out to the temples. Move the fingertips lightly in a circle around the eyes to the temples and then back to the center of the forehead. Lift your hands slowly off of the face when you finish cleansing.

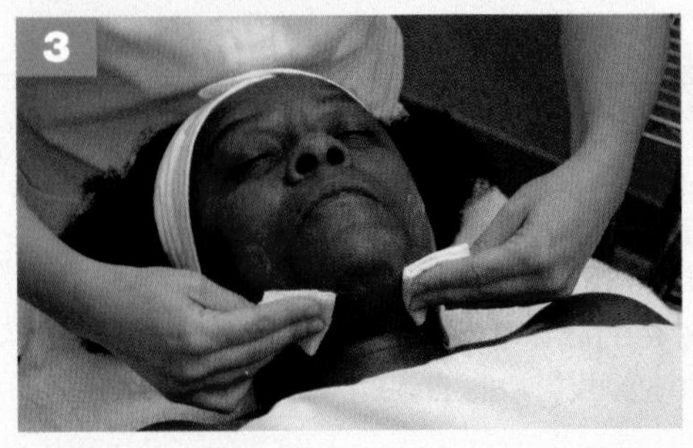

3 Remove the cleanser. Using moist cotton pads or disposable facial sponges, start at the neck or forehead and follow the contours of the face. Move up or down the face in a consistent pattern, depending on where you start according to the instructor's procedures. Remove all the cleanser from one area of the face before proceeding to the next. (Under the nostrils, use downward strokes when applying or removing products to avoid pushing product up the nose. This is uncomfortable and will make the client tense.) Blot your hands on a clean towel, and touch the face with dry fingertips to make sure there is no residue left.

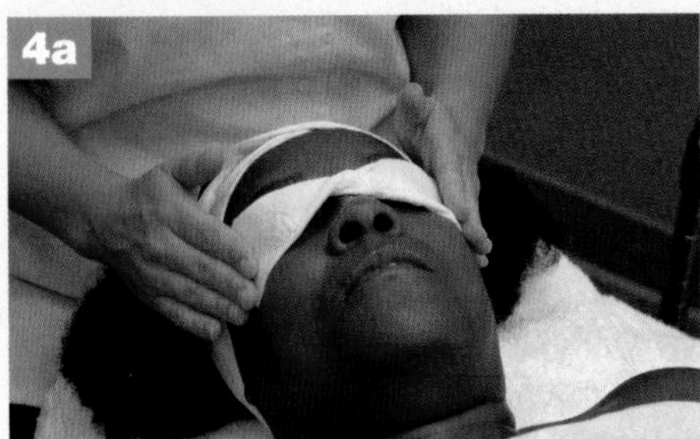

4a Analyze the skin.

Cover the client's eyes with eye pads.

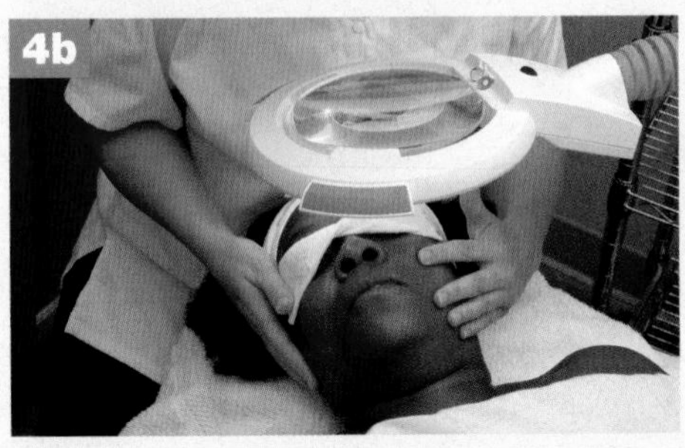

4b Position the magnifying light where you want it before starting the facial, so that you can swing it over easily to line up over the face. Note the skin type and condition, and feel the texture of the skin.

Optional: Cleanse the face again. Some treatment protocols do not include this second cleansing. Be guided by your instructor.

Optional: If exfoliation is part of the service, it could be done at this time before steaming. If eyebrow arching is needed, it could be done either at this time or following the steam and extractions to avoid irritation from the steam. Be careful what you apply to freshly waxed areas.

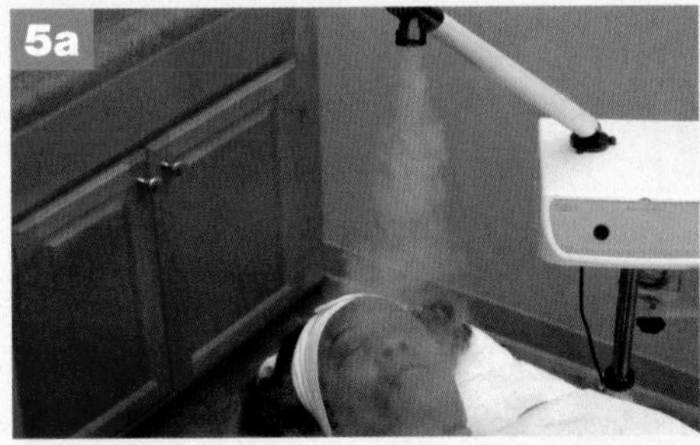

5a Steam the face.

Preheat the steamer before you need it. Check that the water level is at the appropriate fill line. Turn it on, wait for it to start steaming, and then turn on the second ozone button if applicable while steaming (review the section on steamers in Chapter 17, Facial Machines, for steamer operations and cautions).

Caution: Keep the steam facing away from the client until it is steaming to avoid potential spitting of water which may happen if the machine is overfilled or not maintained properly.

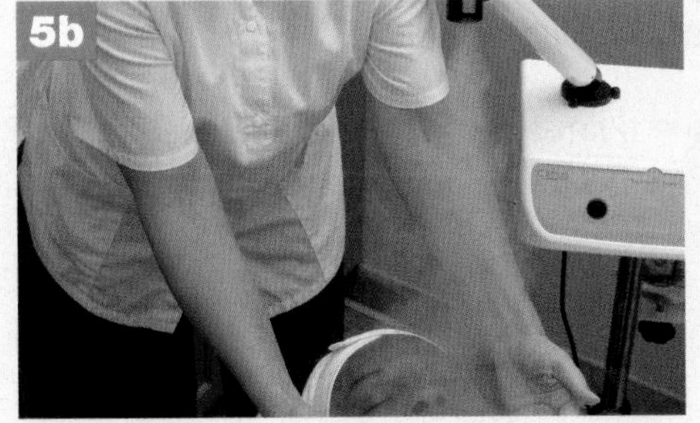

5b Check to make sure the steamer is not too close to the client (approximately 18 inches [45 centimeters] away) and that it is steaming the face evenly. If you hold your hands close to the sides of the client's face, you can feel if the steam is reaching both sides of the face. Steam for approximately 5 to 10 minutes.

PROCEDURE

15-4 The Basic Step-by-Step Facial (continued)

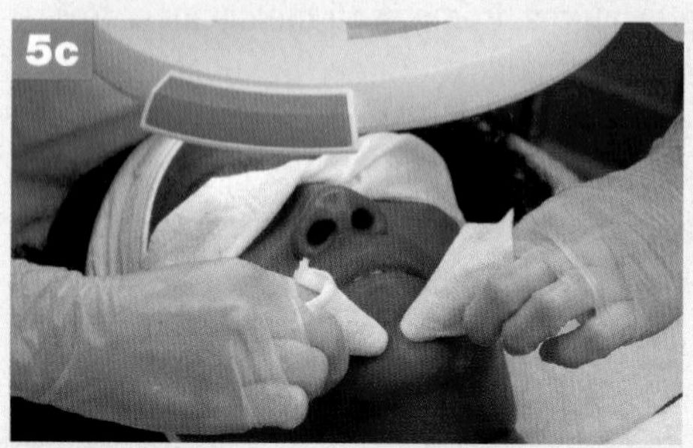

5c Turn off the steamer immediately after use. If using towels in place of steam, remember to test them for the correct temperature. Ask the client if she is comfortable with the temperature. Towels are left on for approximately 2 minutes. Steam or warm towels should be used carefully on couperose skin.

Optional: Extractions are done immediately after the steam, while the skin is still warm. Refer to the extractions section of this chapter to incorporate this step into your basic facial procedure if it is applicable to your facility.

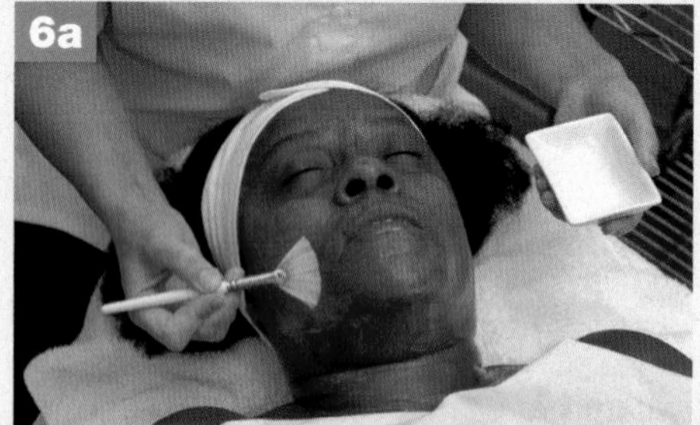

6a **Massage the face.** Use the facial manipulations described in Chapter 16, Facial Massage.

Select a water-soluble massage cream or product appropriate to the client's skin type. Use the same procedure as you did for product application to apply the massage cream to the face, neck, shoulders, and chest. Apply the warmed product in long, slow strokes with fingers or a soft fan brush, moving in a set pattern.

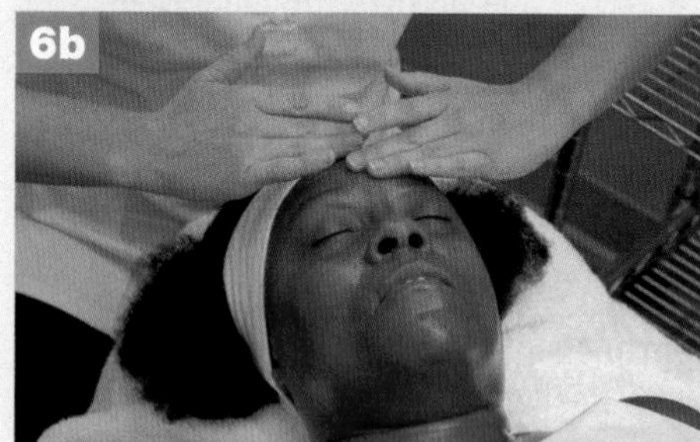

6b Perform the massage as directed.

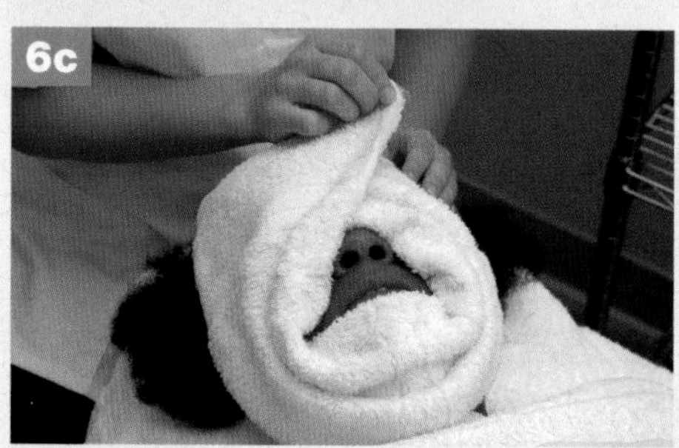

6c Remove the massage cream. Use warm towels or cleansing pads and follow the same procedure as for removing other products or cleanser.

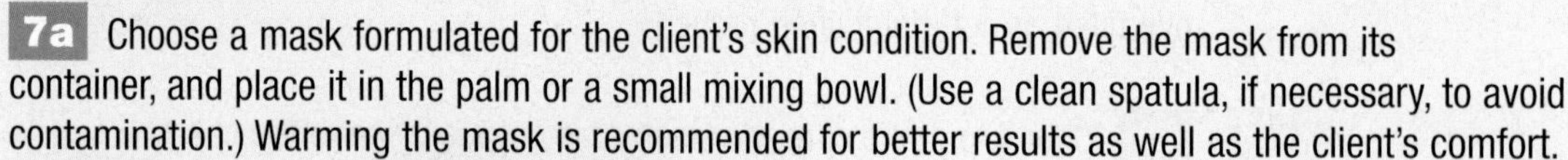

7a Choose a mask formulated for the client's skin condition. Remove the mask from its container, and place it in the palm or a small mixing bowl. (Use a clean spatula, if necessary, to avoid contamination.) Warming the mask is recommended for better results as well as the client's comfort.

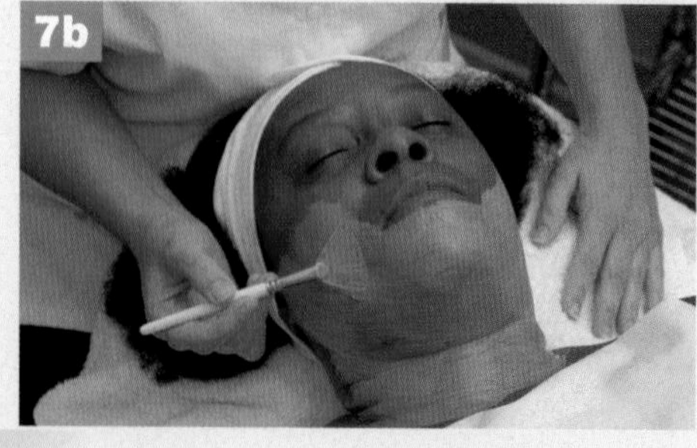

7b Apply the mask with fingers or a brush, usually starting at the neck. Use long, slow strokes from the center of the face, moving outward to the sides.

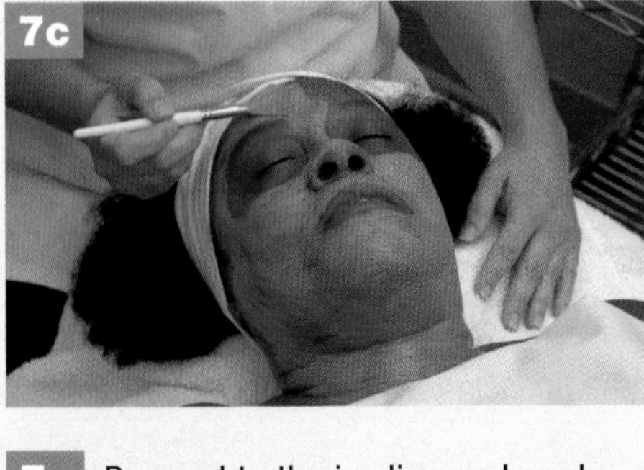

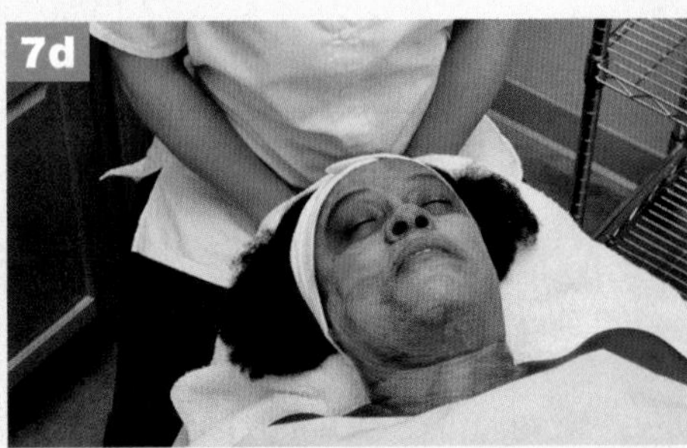

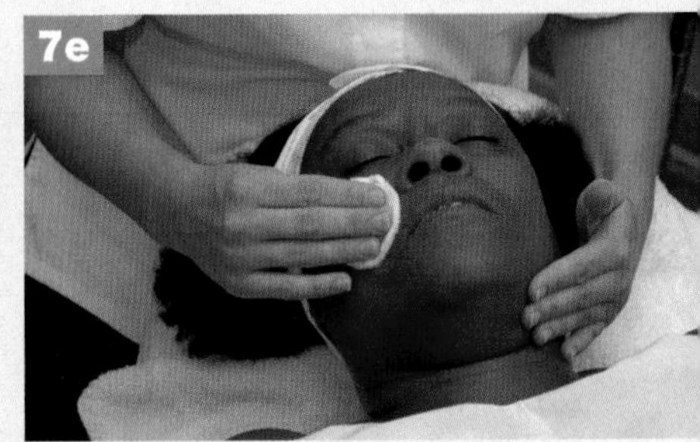

7c Proceed to the jawline and apply the mask on the face from the center outward. Avoid the eye area unless the mask is appropriate for that area.

7d Allow the mask to remain on the face for approximately 7 to 10 minutes.

7e Remove the mask with towels, followed by wet cotton pads or sponges.

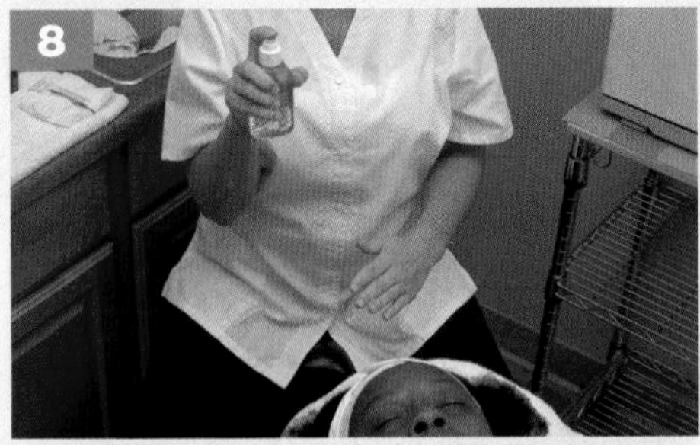

8 Apply the toner product appropriate for the skin type.

Note: Serums as well as eye and lip creams are optional for application before the final moisturizer.

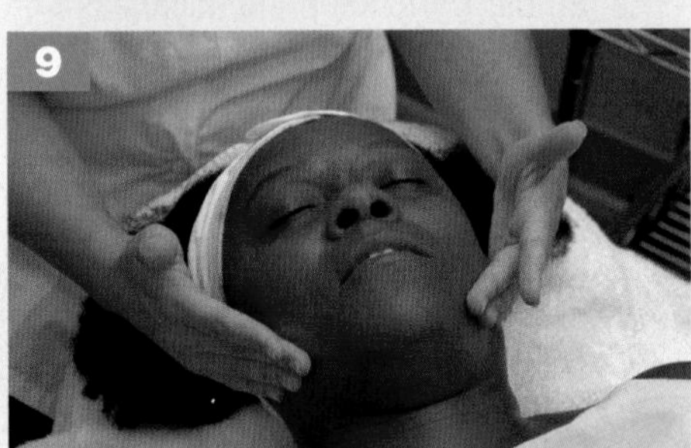

9 Apply a moisturizer (and an additional sunscreen as appropriate).

Never remove products from containers with your fingers. Always use a spatula. Do not touch fingertips to lids or openings of containers. Clean and disinfect product containers after each service.

10 End the facial by washing your hands and quietly letting the client know you are finished. Give the client instructions for getting dressed. Have the client come out to the reception area when they are ready to discuss the home-care products and regime.

Post-Service

- **Complete** 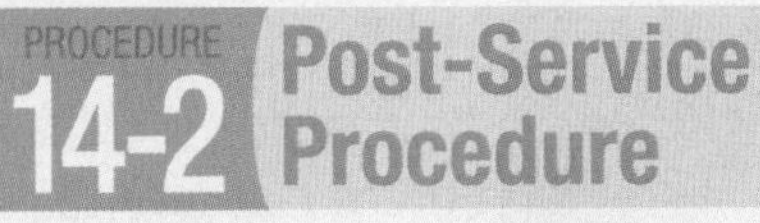

PAGE 375

☑ **L07**

FOCUS ON

Clients

The importance of following proper hygiene, health, and safety guidelines when giving facials cannot be overemphasized. As much as possible, wash your hands in the presence of your clients. When they see you doing this, they will have more confidence in your infection prevention.

PROCEDURE

15-5 Applying the Cotton Compress

IMPLEMENTS AND MATERIALS

- Cotton roll
- Scissors
- Basin of warm water
- Product

Note: This procedure is outdated but some licensing boards may still test on it.

Preparation

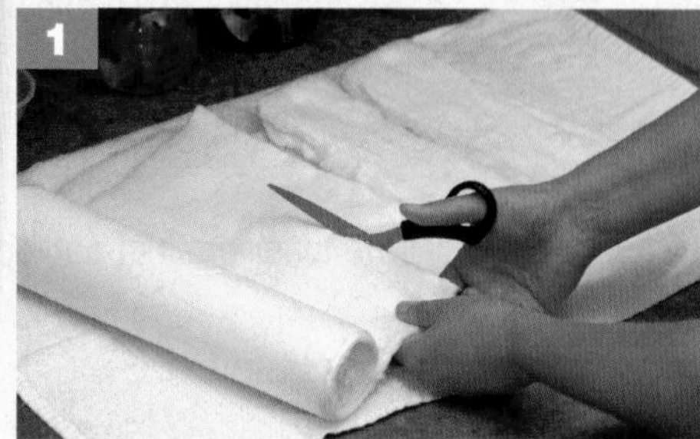

1 Prepare the cotton on a clean and disinfected work area.

2 Wet and unfold the cotton strip, and carefully divide it lengthwise into three separate strips. Try to keep the thickness of each strip as even as possible.

Procedure

The steps for applying a cotton compress alone or over a mask are as follows:

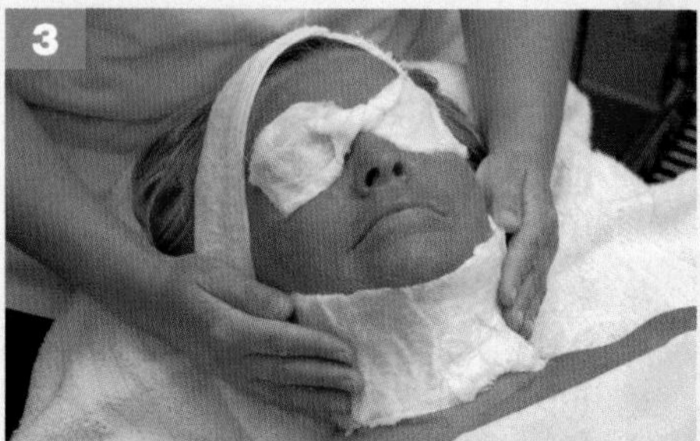

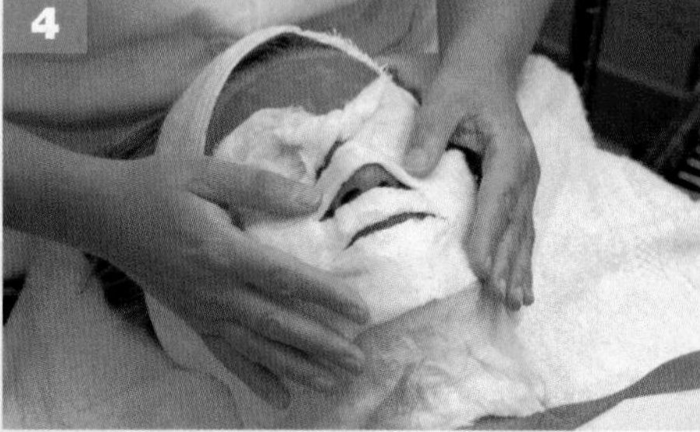

3 Secure eye pads on the client's eyes. Take the strip that feels the thinnest and mold it to the client's neck. Be sure the strip does not overlap on the underside of the chin and jawline.

4 Place the center of the second strip of cotton (saving the thickest piece for last) on the chin, under the lower lip. Mold the cotton under the jaw, chin, and lower part of the cheeks. Leave breathing access by molding the strips around the tip of the nose.

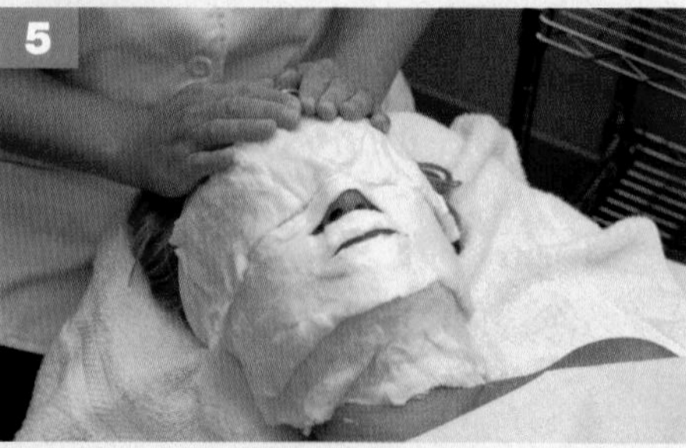

5 Place the third and thickest cotton strip over the upper portion of the face (eye pads remain in place). Carefully stretch the cotton.

PROCEDURE

15-6 Removing the Cotton Compress

IMPLEMENTS AND MATERIALS

- Cotton roll
- Cotton pads
- Ice cubes or face globes
- Waste container

1 **Optional step:** Massage over the surface of the compress mask with an ice cube or cool face globes if applicable, using circular movements. The ice will feel refreshing and will firm the skin. As the ice melts, the water seeps into the compress, helping to soften the mask underneath.

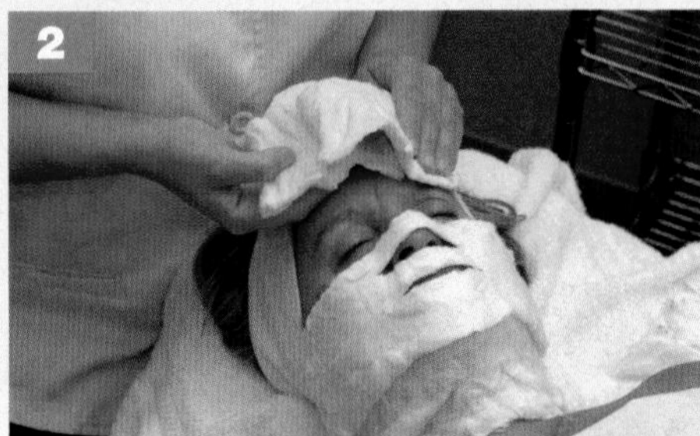

2 Starting on the upper part of the face, place the hands, palms down, on each side of the face. With one hand, slide the compress slowly toward the side of the face, picking up as much of the treatment mask as possible. The eye pads will come off at the same time and should be discarded.

3 Fold the strip in half, so that the side of the compress that has the treatment mask on it is inside and the compress strip has two clean surfaces. Squeeze the cotton over a waste container to remove any excess water.

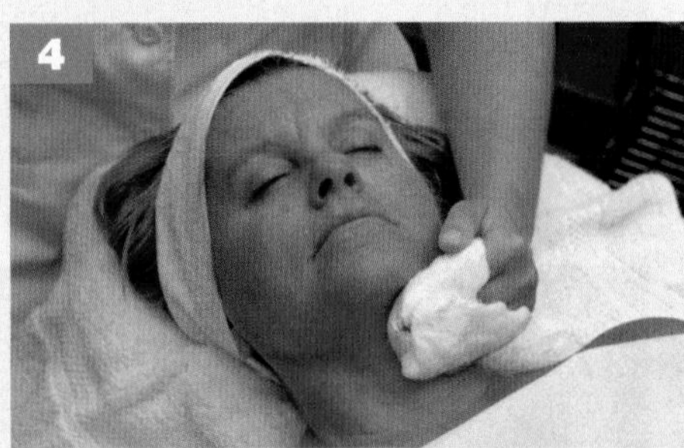

4 Tear a separate strip of wet cotton in half, wrapping around the first three fingers of the hand to form a cotton mitt. Use the cotton mitts to further remove remaining traces of the mask. If necessary, cotton pads, rather than finger mitts, can be used to cleanse the face.

PROCEDURE

15-7 Extractions

IMPLEMENTS AND MATERIALS

- Basin of water
- Cotton pads
- Gloves
- Astringent
- Sealable plastic bag
- Other appropriate facial supplies, products, and equipment

Preparation

Preparing the Fingers for Comedone Extractions

If you are using 4" × 4" (10 cm × 10 cm) or 2" × 2" (5 cm × 5 cm) premade pads, apply astringent to pads (without oversaturating them) and wrap around fingers. If you are not using four premade pads, prepare cotton as follows. Always wear gloves during extractions.

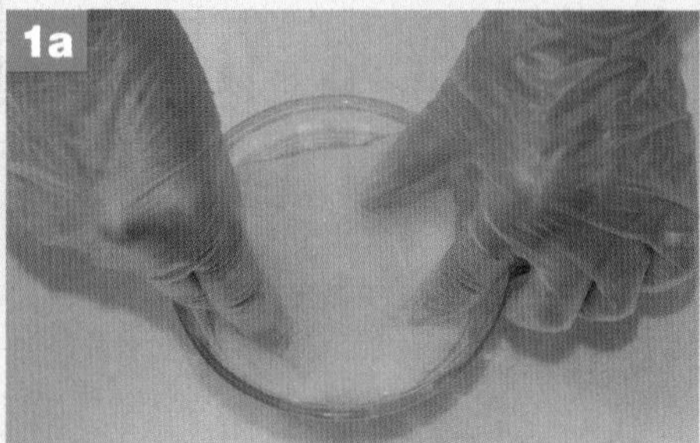
1a

1b

1 Dip strips of clean cotton in water and squeeze out the excess.

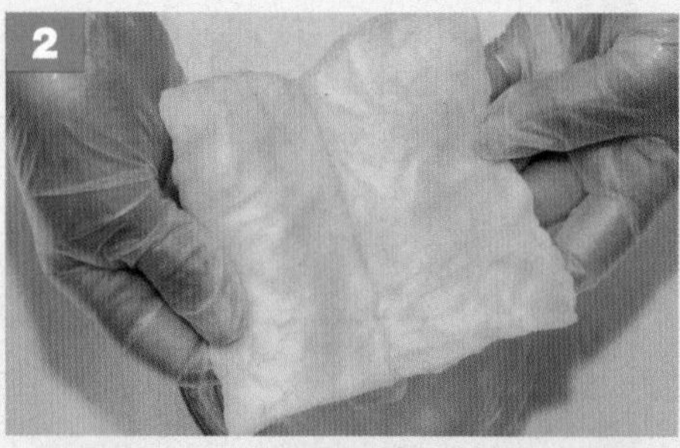
2

2 Unfold the pad and divide it into two thinner pieces. Place one-half of the pad back in the bowl that holds the cleansing pads. With astringent, lightly saturate the half of the pad you are holding. Squeeze out the excess astringent.

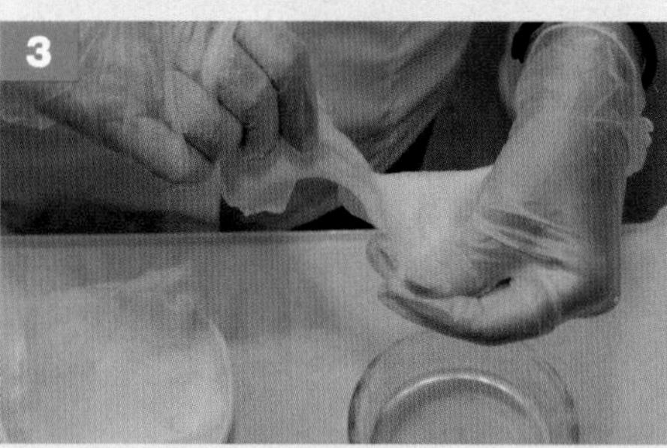
3

3 Tear small strips from the astringent-saturated cotton.

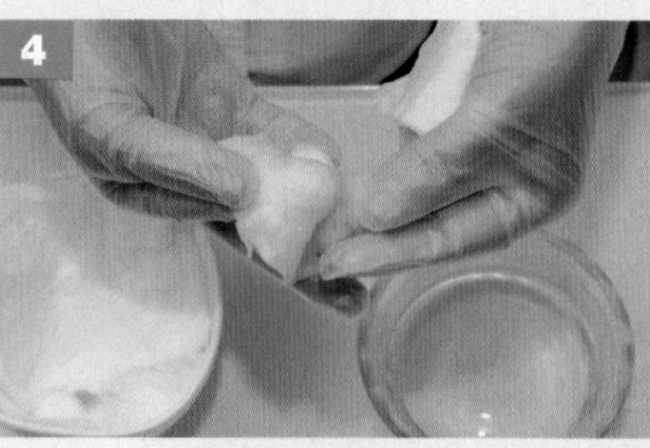
4

4 Wrap fingers with dampened pads. Wrap the strips smoothly around the end of each index finger. Repeat this step until the fingertips are well padded (approximately ⅛-inch [3 millimeters] thick).

Procedure

Performing Extractions

Prepare the client's skin. Extractions are performed during a treatment after the skin is warmed and prepared/softened with product. Never extract on unprepared dry, cold skin. Extraction procedures for different facial areas follow:

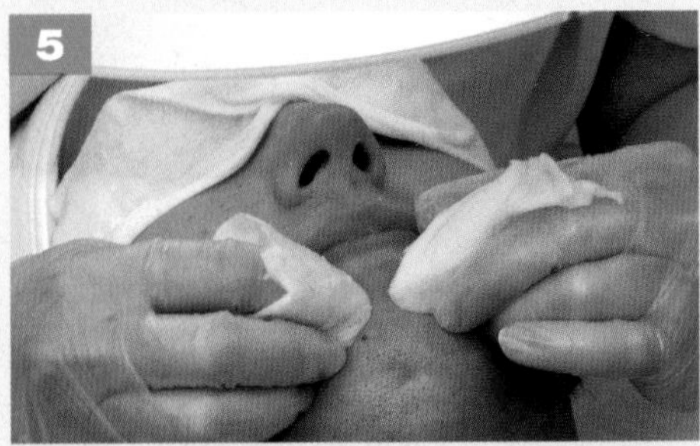

5 **Chin.** On a flat area, press down, under, in, and up. Work around the plug, pressing down, in, and up. Bring fingers in toward each other around the follicle without pinching.

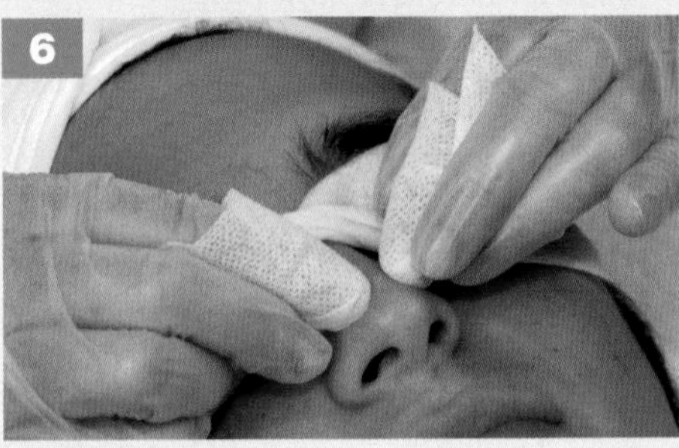

6 **Nose.** Slide fingers down each side of the nose, holding the nostril tissue firmly, but do not press down too firmly on the nose. The fingers on top do the sliding, while the other one holds close to the bottom of the follicle. Do not cut off the air flow to the nostrils.

7 **Cheeks.** Slide fingers together down the cheek, holding each section of the skin as you go. The lower hand holds and the other hand slides toward the lower hand.

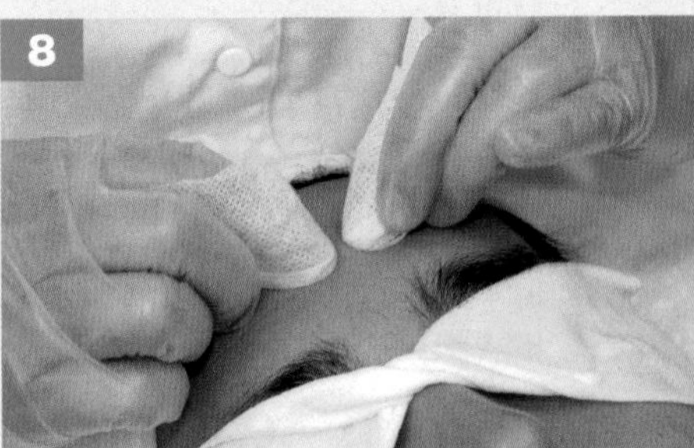

8 **Forehead; upper cheekbones.** Extract as on the chin: press down, in, and up.

Post-Service

- **Complete** 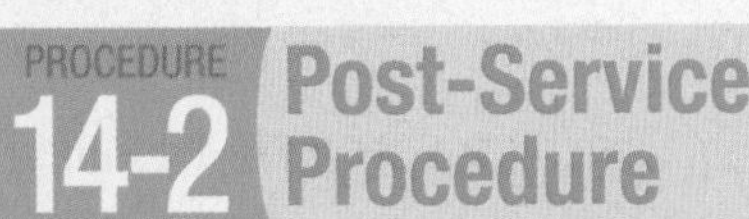

PAGE 375

9 **Note:** Dispose of gloves and supplies properly. Change gloves to continue the facial treatment.

fyi

Extractions with Lancets

When a lesion is sealed over, as in old blackheads and closed comedones, a small-gauge needle or lancet is used for extraction. The lancet should be inserted at a 35-degree angle or parallel to the surface of the skin. Slowly insert the needle just under the top of the plug, lift the top off, and open it gently. Never put the needle down into the follicle because it is painful and could damage it. Extract in the appropriate direction following the angle of the follicles to release sebum (Figure 15–28). Lancets are disposed of in biohazard containers. Remember to check with your regulatory agency to see if lancets are permitted in your area. ✓ LO8

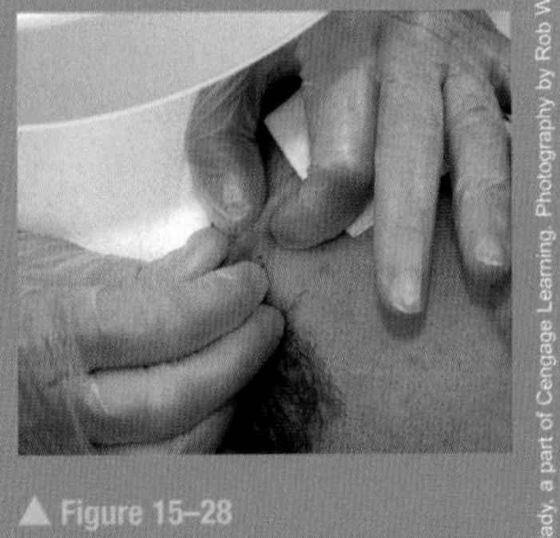

▲ Figure 15–28
Using a lancet.

PROCEDURE

15-8 Applying the Paraffin Mask

IMPLEMENTS AND MATERIALS

Equipment

- Paraffin wax and heater

Supplies

- Disinfectant
- Hand sanitizer/antibacterial soap
- Paraffin wax brush
- Covered waste container
- Plastic bag
- Bowl
- Spatula
- Bolster

Linens

- Hand towels
- Client wrap
- Sheets or other linens
- Blanket
- Headband

Single-use Items

- Gauze
- Paper towels
- Gloves
- Cotton pads
- Cotton rounds
- Tissues

Products

- Cleanser
- Serum
- Mask
- Toner
- Eye cream
- Moisturizer
- Sunscreen
- Lip balm

Note: Paraffin wax masks are not used much anymore, but it is helpful to be familiar with them and they are interesting to try. It is still popular for the hands and feet.

Service Tip

- The paraffin mask can be applied in a facial or alone.
- Unscented white paraffin should be used for the face.
- Serums and ampoules used under the mask are designed for specific skin conditions.
- Gauze is used to keep paraffin and gypsum/plaster masks from sticking to the skin and the tiny hairs on the face.

Preparation

- **Perform** 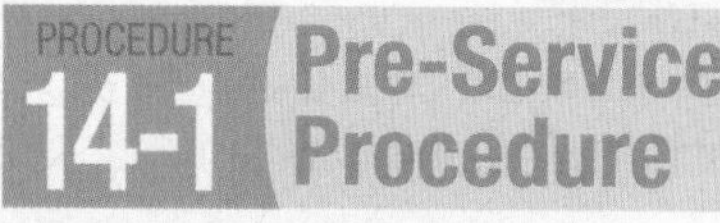

PAGE 372

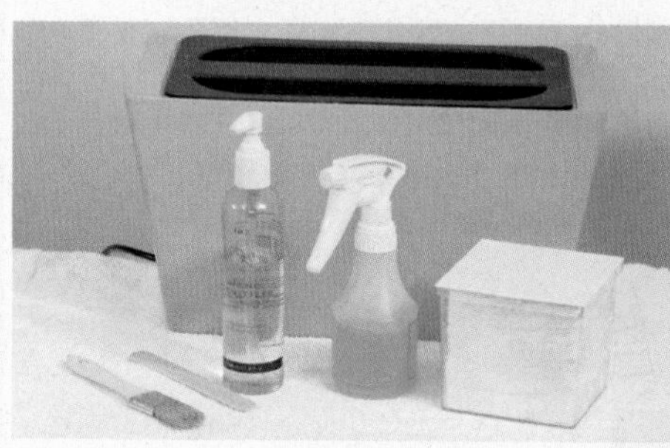

- Melt the paraffin in a warming unit to a little more than body temperature (98.6 degrees Fahrenheit or 37 degrees Celsius). The wax may take up to an hour to heat to the proper temperature.

Procedure

1 After draping and cleansing, place eye pads on client.

2 Apply an appropriate product, such as a serum or hydrating mask, under the paraffin mask.

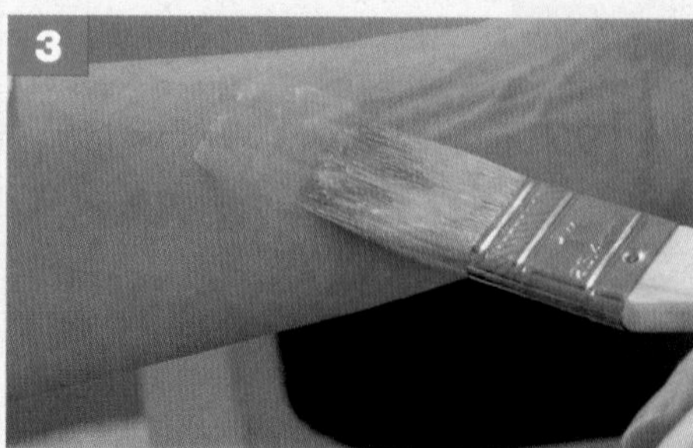

3 Test the temperature of the paraffin by applying to the inside of the wrist with a spatula. Discard any used wax in a plastic bag for waste disposal.

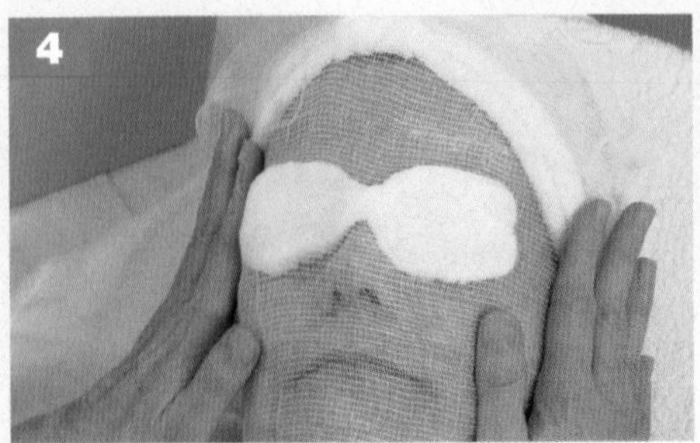

4 Cut the gauze to the desired size, and place it over the face and neck. It is not usually necessary to cut holes for the eyes and nose, because the gauze is woven very loosely. Occasionally, however, a client may feel claustrophobic. In that case, make slits in the gauze for the eyes, nose, and mouth before use. Precut gauze pads are available and are more efficient for this use.

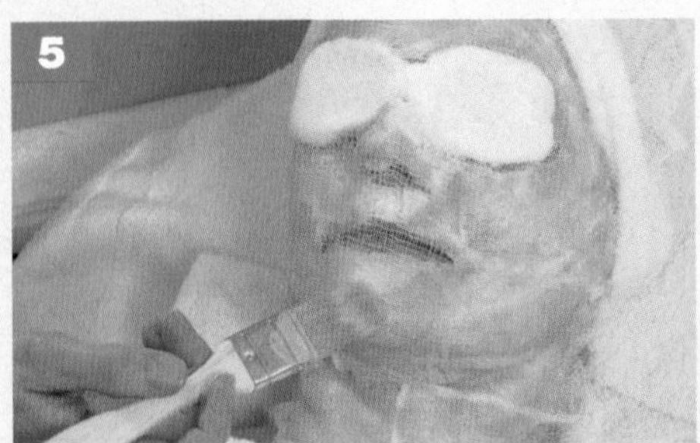

5 Apply the first coat of paraffin over the gauze with a brush, beginning at the base of the neck and working up to the forehead. Do not get wax in the hair as it is difficult to get out. Use a new spatula or brush for each layer to avoid contamination by double-dipping.

6 Continue adding layers of paraffin to the top of the gauze until the application is approximately ¼-inch (.6 centimeters) thick. The application of wax will take approximately 10 minutes.

7 After the wax application is completed, have the client relax until the wax is hardened and ready to remove (approximately 15 minutes).

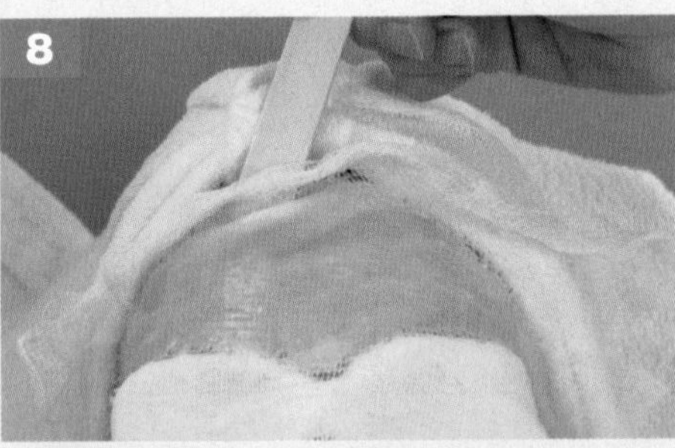

8 When ready to remove the mask, use a wooden spatula to work the edges of the mask loose from the face and neck.

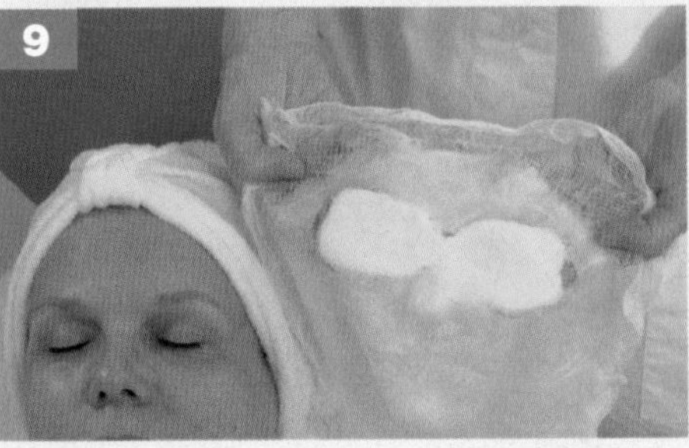

9 Carefully lift the mask from the neck in one piece.

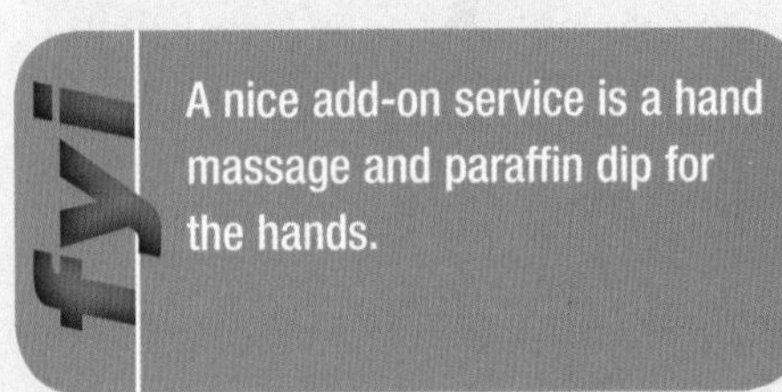

fyi
A nice add-on service is a hand massage and paraffin dip for the hands.

10 Finish the service with the appropriate products (toner, moisturizer).

Here's a Tip

To avoid double-dipping in the paraffin, put a small amount in a separate bowl and work out of that bowl with a brush. Work quickly as paraffin cools rapidly. After the service, the bowl and brush can be cleaned out and disinfected after the paraffin hardens and is removed from the bowl and brush.

Post-Service

- **Complete** 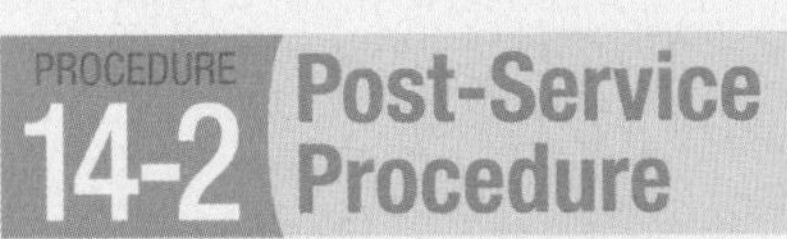

PAGE 375

Review Questions

1. Name six benefits of a facial.
2. What are five of the guidelines to follow in order to be successful and to maintain client loyalty?
3. List the steps in a basic facial.
4. What are three of the contraindications for facials?
5. How does a mini-facial differ from the basic facial?
6. List four treatments that are beneficial for mature skin.
7. What treatment procedures are contraindicated for sensitive skin?
8. List four ingredients that are recommended for treating acne.
9. What are the key points to consider when choosing skin care products for men?

Glossary

extraction	Manual removal of impurities and comedones.
facial	Professional service designed to improve and rejuvenate the skin.
vasoconstricting	Vascular constriction of capillaries and blood flow.

CHAPTER 16

Facial Massage

Chapter Outline

- Why Study Facial Massage?
- The Benefits of Massage
- Incorporating Massage During the Facial Treatment
- Massage Contraindications
- Types of Massage Movements
- The Dr. Jacquet Movement
- Alternative Massage Techniques
- The Basic Facial Massage Technique
- Procedures

Learning Objectives

After completing this chapter, you will be able to:

- ✓ LO1 Describe the benefits of massage.
- ✓ LO2 Understand the contraindications for massage.
- ✓ LO3 Explain the different types of massage movements.
- ✓ LO4 Describe alternative massage techniques.
- ✓ LO5 Perform a facial massage.

Key Terms

Page number indicates where in the chapter the term is used.

acupressure
pg. 436

chucking
pg. 433

Dr. Jacquet movement
pg. 435

effleurage
pg. 433

foot reflexology
pg. 437

friction
pg. 433

fulling
pg. 433

hacking
pg. 434

manual lymph drainage (MLD)
pg. 436

massage
pg. 429

pétrissage
pg. 433

rolling
pg. 434

shiatsu
pg. 436

slapping
pg. 434

tapotement (percussion)
pg. 434

vibration
pg. 434

wringing
pg. 434

Massage is one of the oldest therapeutic methods, dating back thousands of years (Figure 16–1). It has many physiological and psychological benefits. When the body senses touch, reflex receptors respond by increasing blood and lymph flow. The central nervous system is affected, resulting in a state of relaxation. **Massage** (muh-SAHZH) is defined as a manual or mechanical manipulation by rubbing, kneading, or other methods that stimulate metabolism and circulation. Massage also assists in product absorption and relieves pain. A thorough knowledge of muscles, nerves, connective tissues, and blood vessels is vital to performing a correct massage.

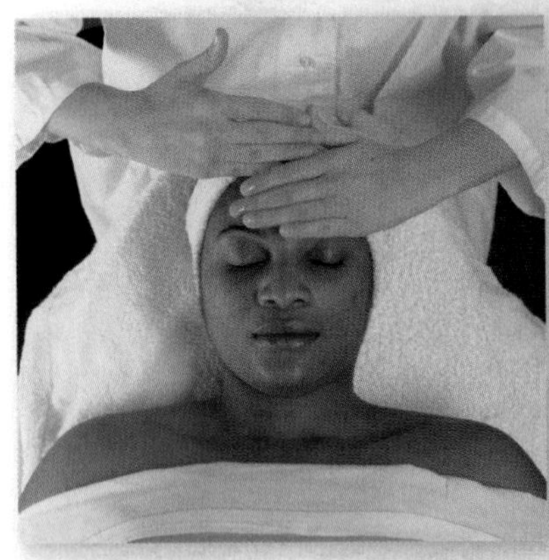

▲ Figure 16–1
Massage is one of the oldest therapeutic methods.

Why Study Facial Massage?

Estheticians should have a thorough understanding of facial massage as it is another foundational service that enhances product effectiveness, has both mental and physical benefits, and provides relaxation.

- It is important to know the physiological and psychological benefits of massage.
- Massage is a very relaxing part of the facial that keeps clients coming back.
- Knowing the proper techniques and the contraindications for massage is important for client safety.

The Benefits of Massage

Massage during facials benefits the client in many ways. A variety of techniques can be used to give the best massage for each client's individual needs. Massage should never be given too long or too deeply. Be mindful of the results you are trying to achieve when giving a facial massage. Stimulating muscle and nerve motor points will both contract muscles and relax the client. Massage is an enjoyable part of the facial that keeps clients coming back. It is relaxing and stress relieving. Most new clients are surprised at how relaxing a facial can be, and they enjoy the benefits of skin rejuvenation as well as an overall feeling of well-being (Figure 16–2).

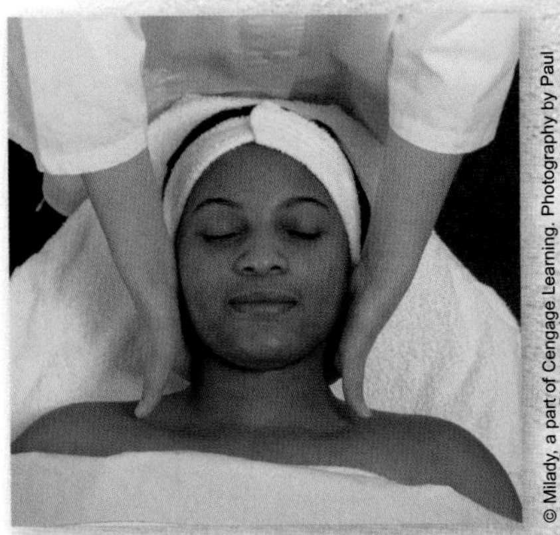

▲ Figure 16–2
The facial massage has numerous benefits.

The following are benefits of massage:

- Relaxes the client and the facial muscles.
- Stimulates blood and lymph circulation.
- Improves overall metabolism and activates sluggish skin.
- Helps muscle tone.

- Helps cleanse the skin of impurities and softens sebum.
- Helps slough off dead skin cells.
- Reduces puffiness and sinus congestion.
- Helps product absorption.
- Relieves muscle tension and pain.
- Provides a sense of physiological and psychological well-being. ✓ L01

fyi To maintain soft skin, keep hands moisturized and exfoliated. Frequent washing of hands has a drying and dehydrating effect, so routinely nourish them with lotion. Keep nails short and filed smooth in order to give a good massage without scratching the skin.

Incorporating Massage During the Facial Treatment

This chapter contains general guidelines that vary according to each specialized treatment. The massage procedure and when it is performed in the facial depends on many factors. A facial massage routine will change depending on the training or protocols established by the facility or product manufacturer. A facial massage is performed for approximately 10 to 15 minutes during a facial. Some treatments incorporate more massage, and others do not include a massage at all. Massage techniques also depend on the client's skin analysis and what you are focusing on in the treatment.

Technical Skills

A professional facial massage is one of the major differences between a professional treatment in a spa and a home-care regimen. When performed correctly, massage is relaxing and healthy. Massage movements need to flow and be consistent. Hand movements should be smooth and glide easily from one area to the next. Mental focus is important when giving a massage (**Figure 16–3**). Do not let mental distractions reduce your focus on the massage and your client.

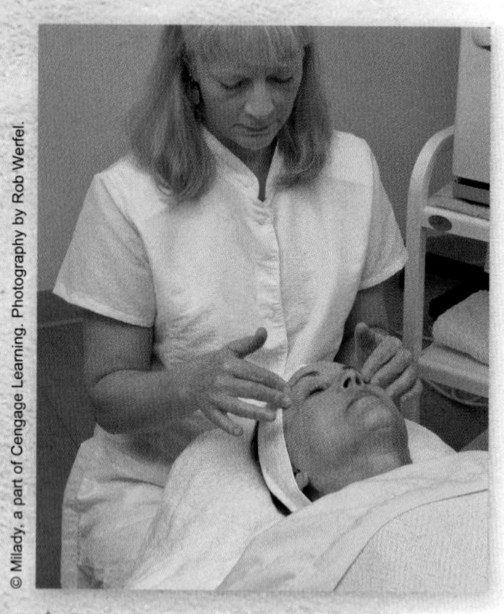

▲ Figure 16–3
Mental focus is important when giving a massage.

Communicate with clients, and adjust your touch according to their preferences. Remember: estheticians are not massage therapists (unless they are a licensed massage therapist: LMT) and cannot do deep tissue work. Too much pressure on the face can weaken elastin fibers and break down elasticity. Educate your clients so they understand that excessive or deep massage is too rough for facial tissue and couperose skin. Massage pressure, the direction of movements, and the duration will vary accordingly. It is helpful to explain to clients what you are trying to achieve with your facial massage techniques.

Always massage from muscle *insertion* to *origin*. The insertion is the portion of the muscle at the more movable attachment (where it is attached to another muscle or to a movable bone or joint). The origin is the portion of the muscle at the fixed attachment (to an immovable section of the skeleton). Know the correct direction to massage to avoid breaking down tissue and potentially causing premature aging.

Hand Mobility

A technician's hands need to be flexible and have a controlled and firm touch. Hands should be soft with short, well-filed nails. Hand mobility is important in maintaining a smooth rhythm and regulating the massage pressure. Both the left and right hands need to be synchronized using equal pressure on both sides. The correct balance comes with practice and being attentive to your touch.

Hand exercises can help strengthen hands and prevent repetitive motion problems, such as carpal tunnel syndrome. Therapists are susceptible to problems because of repetitive movements, muscle and tendon strain, and fatigue due to improper or poor posture. (Refer to Chapter 14, The Treatment Room, for hand-strengthening exercises.) Skin care therapists have a physical job, and stretching exercises maintain flexibility and can help alleviate aches and pains. Remember to take care of yourself with exercise and self-care maintenance, such as massage and yoga. They are necessary parts of a healthy lifestyle (Figure 16–4).

▲ Figure 16–4
Take care of yourself by exercising and stretching.

Massage Contraindications

Certain health problems and skin conditions contraindicate a massage. Facial massage contraindications, such as product allergies, are the same as facial contraindications in Chapter 15, Facial Treatments. If you cannot perform a massage, you can alter your service by substituting another step or leaving a mask on longer. It is appropriate to improvise in your facials. Contraindications include contagious diseases, inflamed acne, sunburn, or sensitive skin.

Other contraindications are open lesions, skin disorders, or severe redness. Additionally, clients with acne should not be massaged in any area that has breakouts. If your client has sensitive or redness-prone skin, avoid using vigorous or strong massage techniques.

Do not massage a client who has certain health problems, because massage increases circulation and may be harmful to clients with medical conditions. If a client has arthritis or other pain, be very careful to avoid vigorous massage. If a client is sick, the massage may be too stimulating and make the client feel worse. Of course, if the client has a cold and is contagious, it is not a good idea to work on them anyway.

Before performing a service that includes a facial massage, consult the client's intake or health screening form. During the consultation acknowledge and discuss any medical condition that may contraindicate a facial massage. Ask the client if he or she has discussed massage with a physician. If the client has not already sought a physician's advice as to whether or not a facial massage is advisable, encourage her to do so before you perform the service.

Traditionally contraindicated, it is now acceptable for many clients who have high blood pressure (hypertension), diabetes, cancer, or a circulatory condition to still have facial massage without concern, especially if their condition is being treated and carefully looked after by a physician. Full body massage is different, as it is much more stimulating. If your client expresses a concern about having a facial massage and has a medical condition, advise her to speak with a physician before having the service.

Facial massage is, however, contraindicated for clients with severe, uncontrolled hypertension. Excessive heat is also a concern. When in doubt, don't include massage as part of your service. Light acupressure massage is a good alternative to the stronger European style massage. ✓ L02

REGULATORY **AGENCY**
ALERT

Refer to licensing regulations regarding your scope of practice regarding massage services that are legal to perform under your license. Do not violate these regulations. Just because your employer encourages additional protocols outside of your scope of practice, such as a foot massage or someone is teaching back massage at a conference, does not mean it is legal. You may be fined or lose your license. Plus you risk injuring your client.

Get an additional massage license or nail technician license if you want to add additional services to your esthetics business.

Scope of Practice

An esthetician's massage services are limited to certain areas of the body: the face, neck, shoulders, and décolleté. Therapeutic massage, such as deep tissue massage and manual lymph drainage, should be performed only by therapists who specialize in these areas. Therapeutic body massage requires special training and, in most cases, licensure. If the client wants a full body massage, refer her or him to a licensed massage therapist.

Although skin treatments such as back facials and body treatments are part of esthetics services, massage is not performed when working on these treatment areas—only the application of products. Refer to licensing regulations regarding your scope of practice and services that are legal to perform under your license. Fully licensed cosmetologists and nail technicians can perform massage and additional treatments on the arms, hands, lower legs, and feet.

One advantage estheticians have over massage therapists for performing facial massage is the understanding of the skin and products. Massage therapists are not trained in esthetics and therefore are not familiar with correctly treating the skin conditions or whether they are applying potentially irritating ingredients. Massage therapists should not be performing facial treatments. This is a common concern in the industry from an esthetician's point of view. Body treatments for the skin are generally performed by both estheticians and massage therapists, but this will depend on local license regulations.

Here's a **Tip**

To keep the relaxing flow and connection, do not remove your hands from the client's face once you have started the massage. Choose instrumental music with a slow, even tempo.

Types of Massage Movements

Classic Swedish massage movements include effleurage, pétrissage, friction, tapotement, and vibration.

Effleurage

Effleurage (EF-loo-rahzh) is a soft, continuous stroking movement applied with the fingers (digital) and palms (palmar) in a slow and rhythmic manner (Figure 16–5). The gliding movement is soothing and relaxing. The fingers are used on smaller surfaces such as the forehead or face. The palms are used on larger surfaces such as the back or shoulders. Effleurage is often used to begin and end most massage sessions. It is used on the forehead, face, scalp, back, shoulders, neck, chest, arms, and hands.

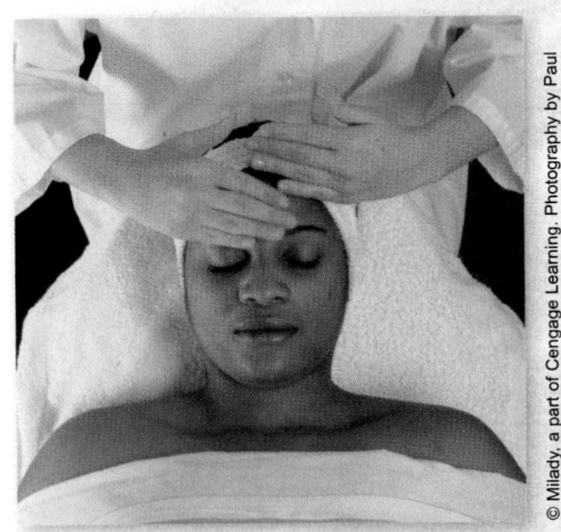

▲ Figure 16–5
Effleurage.

To correctly position the fingers for stroking, slightly curve the fingers with just the cushions of the fingertips touching the skin. Do not use the ends of the fingertips, because fingertips cannot control pressure and may scratch the client. To correctly position the palms for stroking, hold the whole hand loosely. Keep the wrist and fingers flexible, and curve the fingers to conform to the shape of the area being massaged. Effleurage, the most important of the five movements, is used in conjunction with other types of massage such as shiatsu (shee-AH-tsoo), which is a form of acupressure.

Pétrissage

Pétrissage (PEH-treh-sahzh) is a kneading movement that stimulates the underlying tissues (Figure 16–6). The skin and flesh are grasped between the thumb and forefinger. As the tissues are lifted from their underlying structures, they are squeezed, rolled, or pinched with a light, firm pressure. Pétrissage is performed on the fleshier parts of the face, shoulders, back, and arms. The pressure should be light but firm and the movements should be rhythmic. Pétrissage can stimulate sebum production and activate circulation and sluggish skin.

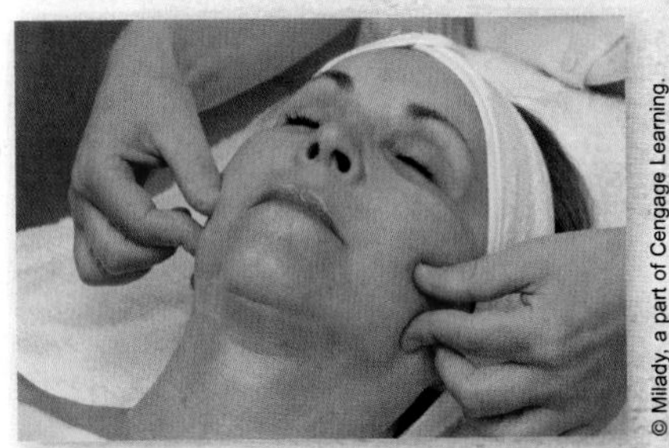

▲ Figure 16–6
Pétrissage.

Fulling is a form of pétrissage in which the tissue is grasped, gently lifted, and spread out. It is used mainly for massaging the arms. With the fingers of both hands grasping the arm, apply a kneading movement across the flesh, with light pressure on the underside of the client's forearm and between the shoulder and elbow.

Friction

Friction (FRIK-shun) is a rubbing movement. Pressure is maintained on the skin while the fingers or palms are moved over the underlying structures (Figure 16–7). Friction stimulates the circulation and glandular activity of the skin. Circular friction movements are usually used on the scalp, arm, and hands. Lighter circular friction movements are used on the face and neck.

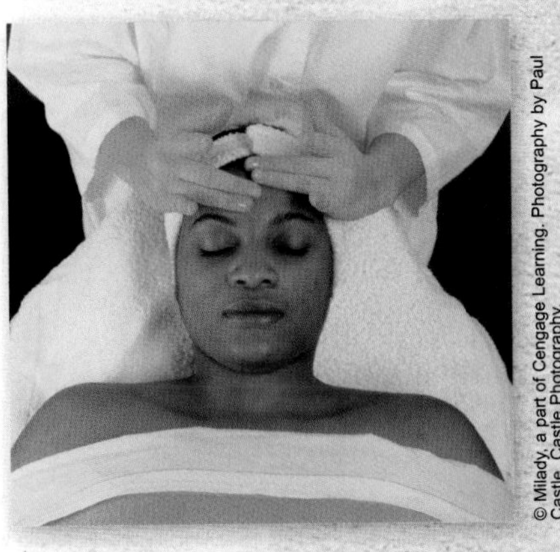

▲ Figure 16–7
Friction.

Chucking, rolling, and wringing are variations of friction movements used mainly on the arms or legs:

- **Chucking.** Grasp the flesh firmly in one hand, and move the hand up and down along the bone while the other hand keeps the arm in a steady position (Figure 16–8 on page 434).

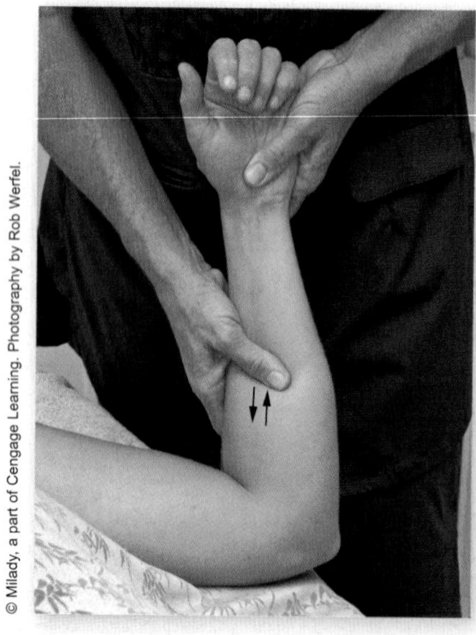

© Milady, a part of Cengage Learning. Photography by Rob Werfel.

▲ Figure 16–8
Chucking.

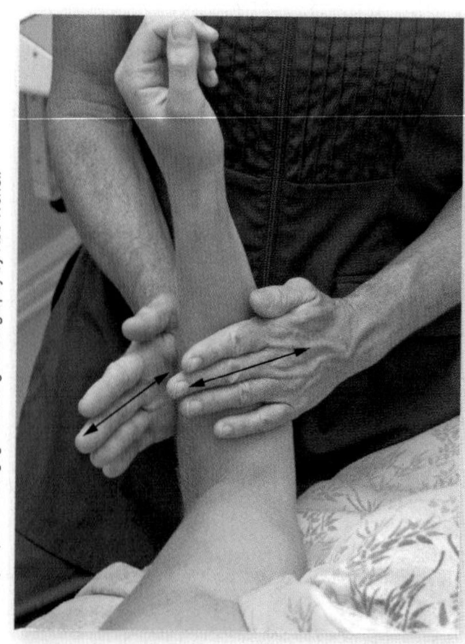

© Milady, a part of Cengage Learning. Photography by Rob Werfel.

▲ Figure 16–9
Rolling.

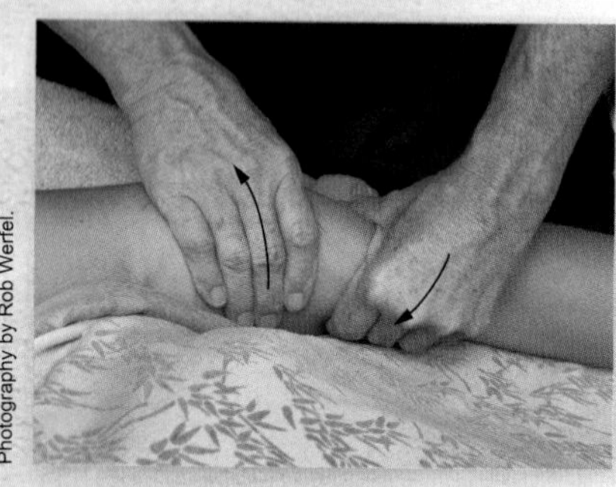

© Milady, a part of Cengage Learning. Photography by Rob Werfel.

▲ Figure 16–10
Wringing.

- **Rolling.** Used on the arms and legs to apply pressure to the tissues; press the tissues firmly against the bone, and roll your hands around the arm or leg with a rapid back-and-forth movement. Move both hands at the same time, opposite to each other, while rolling the flesh up and down the bone (Figure 16–9).
- **Wringing.** This is a vigorous movement with the hands placed a small distance apart on both sides of the arm. While the hands are working downward, the flesh is twisted against the bones in opposite directions (Figure 16–10).

Tapotement

Tapotement (tah-POT-ment), also known as **percussion**, consists of fast tapping, patting, and hacking movements (Figure 16–11). This form of massage is the most stimulating and should be applied carefully and with discretion. It is good for toning and is beneficial to sluggish skin. Only light, digital tapping should be used on the face. The fingertips are brought down against the skin in rapid succession. This movement is sometimes referred to as a *piano movement.*

Slapping and hacking movements are used by massage therapists on the back, shoulders, and arms. In **slapping** movements, keep the wrists flexible so that the palms come in contact with the skin in light, firm, and rapid strokes. One hand follows the other. With each slapping stroke, lift the flesh slightly. **Hacking** is a chopping movement with the wrists and outer edges of the hands. Both the wrists and fingers move in fast, light, firm, flexible motions against the skin in alternate succession.

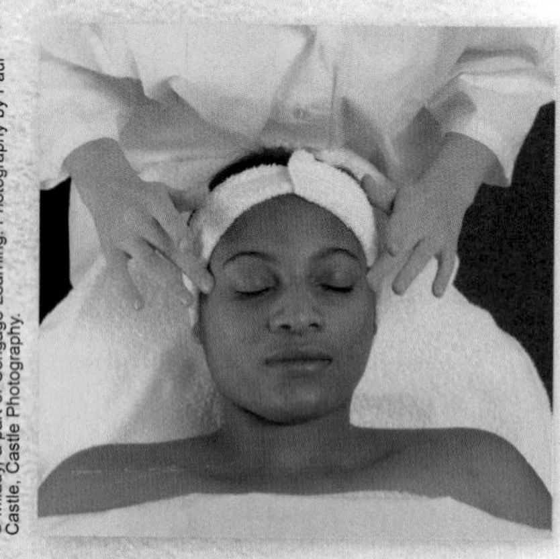

© Milady, a part of Cengage Learning. Photography by Paul Castle, Castle Photography.

▲ Figure 16–11
Tapotement.

Vibration

Vibration (vy-BRAY-shun) is a rapid shaking movement in which the technician uses her or his body and shoulders—not just the fingertips—to

create the movement. It is accomplished by rapid muscular contractions in the arms (**Figure 16–12**). The balls of the fingertips are pressed firmly on the point of application. Vibration is a highly stimulating movement, but it should be used sparingly and never for more than a few seconds on any one spot.

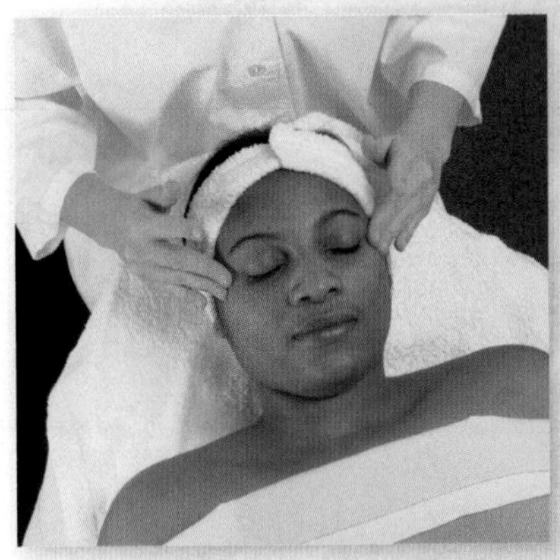

▲ Figure 16–12
Vibration.

The Dr. Jacquet Movement

Some years ago in Europe the famous dermatologist, Dr. Jacquet (zha-KETT), introduced a massage method that is especially effective in the treatment of oily skin and acne-blemished skin.

To perform this method, gather a small section of the skin between the thumb and forefinger and squeeze gently. At the same time, give the skin a slight twisting or kneading movement. This helps to empty the oil ducts. The movement is somewhat similar to squeezing the peel of an orange until a fine spray of oil is expelled, but it is much more subtle. The **Dr. Jacquet Movement** keeps the sebum moving forward and out of the follicles. When the movement is done as part of a facial treatment, it should follow the desincrustation step that softens and prepares the skin for extractions.

The following movements combine the Dr. Jacquet method with variations on the original technique, so that the client will receive the maximum benefits.

1. Start with a slight twisting or kneading movement on the chin (**Figure 16–13**).
2. Continue with a kneading movement on the cheeks moving horizontally.
3. When the skin on the forehead is too tight to twist between the thumb and forefinger, place the tips of the fingers parallel to one another approximately ¾ inch (3.75 centimeters) apart on the forehead. Push the fingertips toward one another, so that the skin is pinched gently between the fingers. Continue this horizontal movement across the entire forehead. ☑ LO3

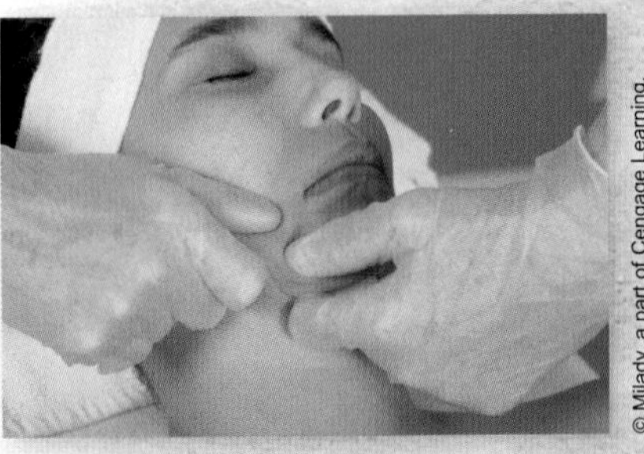

▲ Figure 16–13
The Dr. Jacquet massage is a form of kneading similar to pétrissage.

CAUTION!

The Dr. Jacquet Movement must be done with care because the pressure of the movement can cause pain, and too much kneading can stretch the skin. Do not use the movement in the eye area. If used close to the eye area, keep pressure to a minimum. Do not perform stimulating massage on couperose areas, or the capillaries could be damaged.

Do not perform the Dr. Jacquet Movement over areas of the skin that are infected or irritated. Too much pressure will rupture follicle walls and cause tissue damage.

Here's a Tip

Whatever movements you use, be consistent on the number of passes you make for each step. If you repeat a step three times or six times, repeat all of your steps the same number of times. Always perform the same routine on both the left and right sides of the area being massaged.

fyi

For your male clients, use downward movements in the area of beard growth. It feels uncomfortable when you massage against hair growth. Pressure point massage in the beard area works well.

Alternative Massage Techniques

Different types of massage are based on body structure and energy flow within the body. Most massage techniques are based on classical, or Swedish, massage movements. There are many additional advanced techniques that stimulate and detoxify the body. Massage techniques require additional training and study. A combination of techniques can be used in various treatments. Some of these are discussed more thoroughly in Chapter 19, Advanced Topics and Treatments.

- **Acupressure** is an Oriental technique of applying pressure to specific points of the body (acupressure points) to release muscle tension, restore balance, and stimulate *chi* (CHEE) (life force; energy). These points follow the same pattern of meridians in the body as acupuncture.
- **Shiatsu** is a form of acupressure, the Japanese technique using acupressure massage points to relax and balance the body. Many of the motor points on the face and neck are acupressure points (Figures 16–14 and 16–15). Every muscle has a motor point which is a specific spot on the skin over the muscle where pressure or stimulation will cause contraction of that muscle, nerve stimulation, and overall relaxation. The standard pressure-point technique is to pause briefly for a few seconds over the motor points using light pressure. This technique is also used on the scalp.
- **Pressure point massage** is similar to acupressure. On each point, the movement is repeated three to six times. Pause for 3 to 6 seconds on each point, moving from either top to bottom on the face, using light inward pressure at each point and then lifting the pressure to slide to the next point. Training is necessary to perform this massage correctly. Techniques and patterns vary with different methods (Figure 16–16). Pressure point massage is a form of acupressure, but the technique can be incorporated into treatments without being a true acupressure massage. There are other types of pressure point massage that do not follow the body's specific acupressure meridians, such as massage on motor points.
  - **Aromatherapy massage** uses essential oils applied to the skin during massage movements. These oils are often used during the facial massage to promote mental relaxation and to treat the skin in numerous ways.
  - **Manual lymph drainage** (MLD) massage uses gentle, rhythmic pressure on the lymphatic system to detoxify and remove waste materials from the body more quickly. It reduces swelling and is used before and after surgery for pre- and post-op care. It is a very light touch. For example,

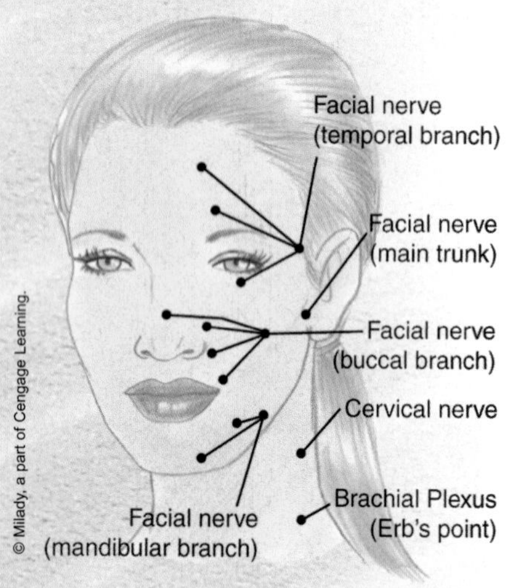

▲ Figure 16–14
Motor nerve points of the face.

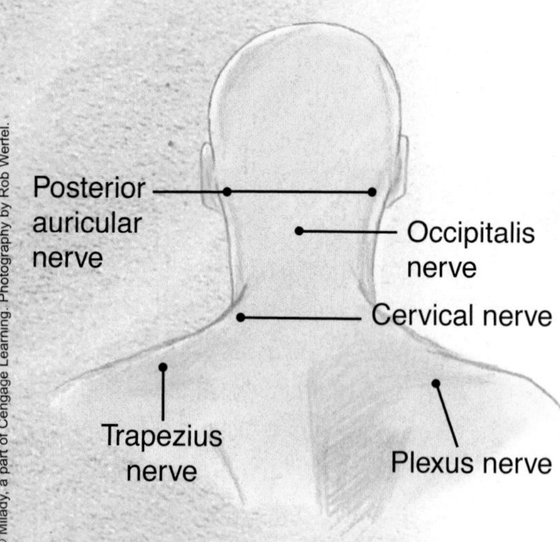

▲ Figure 16–15
Motor nerve points of the neck and shoulders.

moving down the side of the neck towards the collar bone helps drain fluid from the face to the lymph drainage channel in that area.

- **Foot Reflexology** (re-flexs-AHL-uh-jee) is the technique of applying pressure to the feet based on a system of zones and areas on the feet that directly correspond to the anatomy of the body. It causes relaxation, increased circulation, and balance to the entire body. Estheticians are not usually trained in reflexology, so be aware of your scope of practice and licensing regulations. There is a reflexology chart in Chapter 19, Advanced Topics and Treatments. ✓ LO4

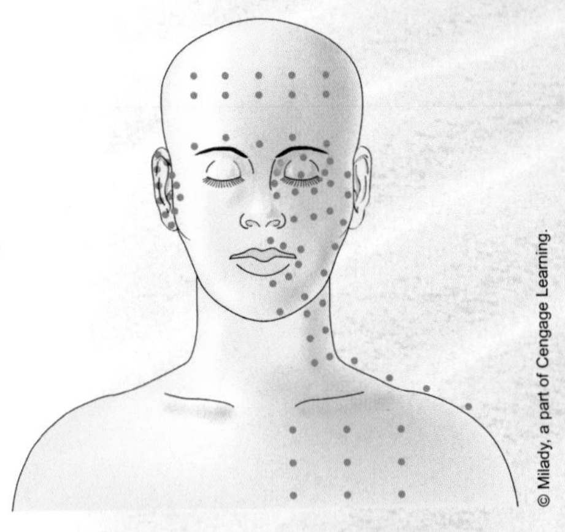

▲ Figure 16–16
Pressure point massage is very relaxing and therapeutic.

The Basic Facial Massage Technique

Different massage movements may be used on the various parts of the face, chest, and shoulders. Massage may be started on the chin, décolleté, or forehead. Most movements are repeated three to six times before moving on to the next one. Use both hands at the same time or alternate hands with a flowing rhythm, depending on the steps. Slide the hands back down to each starting point to repeat the movements in each step.

When performing facial massage, keep in mind that an even tempo, or rhythmic flow, promotes relaxation. Do not remove the hands from the client's face once you have started the massage. Should it become necessary to lift the hands from the client's face, feather them off (slowing down the movement is often called *feathering*), then gently replace them with feather-like movements. When coming back to the face, gently make contact on the side of the face or top of the head to avoid startling the client.

Keep one hand on the client's body at all times if it is necessary to take one hand away (if you need to apply more product, for example). The sequence of massage movements is designed for a smooth and graceful flow from one movement into another.

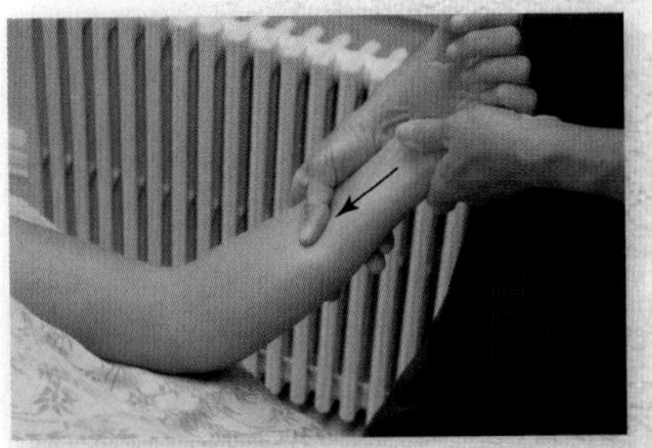

▲ Figure 16–17
Massage from muscle insertion to origin.

Remember that to avoid damage to muscular tissues, massage movements are generally directed from the insertion toward the origin of a muscle (Figure 16–17). Massage movements are also focused on using pressure so that the direction of blood flow is moved toward the heart from the extremities (legs, arms). For example, use more pressure when moving up the legs and arms than when moving towards the feet or hands.

One type of massage is a cleansing massage. The main purpose of a cleansing massage is to continue the cleansing process, help remove dead surface cells, and stimulate the skin to help increase blood circulation. These "massage" movements are more vigorous than those used for a slower, relaxing massage. Massage or cleansing cream that is not formulated to penetrate the skin is used for this cleansing massage technique. Deep-

FOCUS ON

Relaxation

Do not talk to clients when performing massage. Talking eliminates the relaxation therapy of the massage. If the client is talking, invite them to relax and enjoy the massage and don't continue the conversation. Speak in a quiet voice and only when necessary during the facial.

Put aside all distractions during a service. A technician's mood and mental disposition will affect the service and the client. Take a minute to clear your mind and forget about everything except giving a relaxing service. Many technicians close their eyes and take a few deep breaths before working on a client. The close contact in a massage is very personal and intimate. It is a service that can be calming to the technician as well as the client.

Check-in with the client about their comfort. Ask about the pressure of your touch and whether it should be more or less firm. Remember that the facial massage should be lighter than a body massage and let the client know that the skin on the face should be treated more carefully. We are not massage therapists, so it is important to educate clients about the reasons that we do not perform stronger deeper tissue massage on the face, so they are not disappointed if they expected a stronger touch. A light firm touch, when performed well, is more relaxing than a heavier one.

Ambience is another important part of creating a relaxing space. Soft music and a warm, comfortable room are essential for facial services.

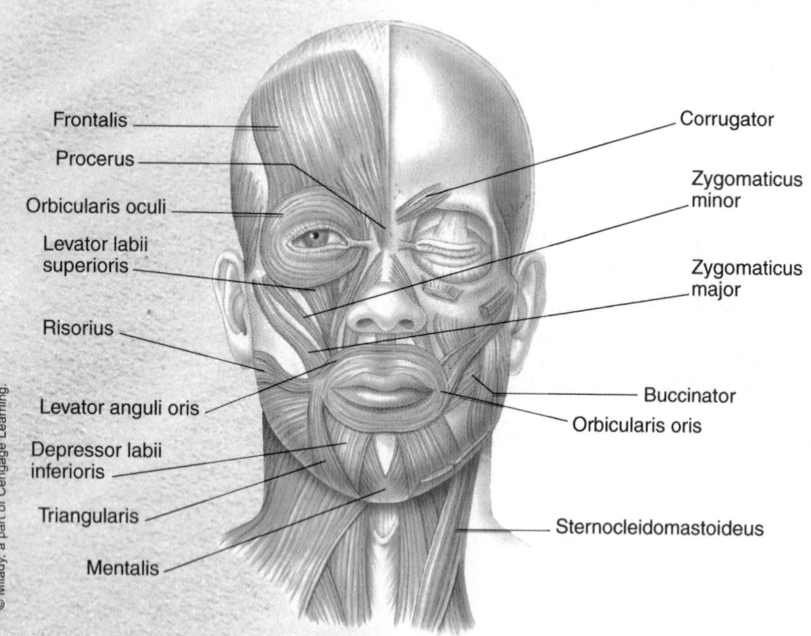

▲ Figure 16–18
Facial structure and muscles.

penetrating creams should not be used in this cleansing procedure, because they can act as vehicles to carry dirt and makeup deeper into the follicles. Other massage products are designed to penetrate into the skin and are applied to clean skin. These products range from serums to oils, lotions, and creams.

Massage is the most relaxing part of the facial and has many benefits. Various massage techniques can be incorporated into facial treatments. Appropriate massage movements are based on the anatomy of the facial structure, nerves, and muscles (**Figure 16–18**). Using the proper techniques is important. It is also necessary to know the contraindications for massage. Once the basic massage flows smoothly, other movements can be added to the routine.

Many estheticians find that giving a facial massage is also relaxing to them and one of the most enjoyable parts of their job.

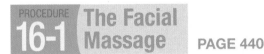

PAGE 440

Chest, Shoulder, and Neck Manipulations (Optional)

Some therapists prefer to treat these areas first before starting the regular facial massage. There are variations on this standard technique. Apply massage cream and perform the following manipulations:

- Chest and upper back movement—Use a rotary circular movement outward across the chest to the shoulders, and then inwards across the shoulders down to the spine. Slide your fingers up to the sides of the base of the neck. Rotate three times.
- Shoulders and upper back movement—Rotate on top of the shoulders three times. Glide your fingers in towards the spine and then to the base of the neck. Apply circular movement up to the back of the ear, and then slide your fingers to the front of the earlobe. Rotate three times. Slide down the neck to the shoulders and repeat three times.
- Shoulder massage—Use your thumbs and bent index fingers to grasp the tissue on top of the shoulders in a kneading-type movement. Rotate six times. Slide up to the neck and continue with the massage.

FOCUS ON

Sharpening Your Professionalism

If a client seems dissatisfied with a facial treatment, it could be due to the following reasons:

- **Offensive breath or body odor.**
- **Rough, cold hands or ragged nails that may have scratched the client's skin.**
- **Allowing cream or other substances to get into the client's eyes, mouth, nostrils, or hairline.**
- **Towels that are too hot or too cold.**
- **Talking too much.**
- **Manipulating the skin roughly or in the wrong direction.**
- **Being disorganized and interrupting the facial to get supplies.**
- **Sloppy product application or movements.**
- **Noise or distractions during the service.**

ACTIVITY

Briefly outline the massage steps on index cards to use when practicing and learning the massage. This will help you to remember the steps and to feel comfortable while practicing the massage until it is memorized.

Web Resources

www.acupressure.com

www.amtamassage.org

www.ayurveda.com

www.massagetherapy101.com

PROCEDURE

16-1

The Facial Massage

IMPLEMENTS AND MATERIALS

- Client intake form
- Disinfectant
- Hand towels
- Soap
- Covered waste container
- Bowls
- Spatulas
- Fan brush
- Bolster
- Clean linens
- Blanket
- Headband
- Client gown or wrap

Single-use Items

- Paper towels
- Cotton swabs
- Gloves/finger cots
- Cotton pads/4" × 4" pads (10 cm × 10 cm)
- Tissues
- Cotton rounds
- Plastic bag (for waste disposal)

Products

- Cleanser
- Massage lotion
- Toner
- Moisturizer
- Sunscreen for daytime
- Additional facial products if performing an entire facial

Equipment

- Facial bed/table
- Towel warmer as needed

Preparation

- **Perform** 

PAGE 372

It is recommended that you first practice the facial massage steps on a mannequin and write out the massage steps on an index card before doing the massage. By this point in your studies you will already have experience with the set up procedures, client consultation, and decontamination procedures.

Procedure

The following procedure is a standard relaxing massage.

- Use a product that will easily glide across the skin. Warm the product before applying.
- Start out with a light touch, gradually using firmer pressure where applicable.
- A good rule of thumb is to repeat each of the movements (each pass) consecutively three to six times.
- The number of movements to perform for each step may vary—these are only suggestions.
- Each instructor may have developed her own routine. Follow your instructor's lead.

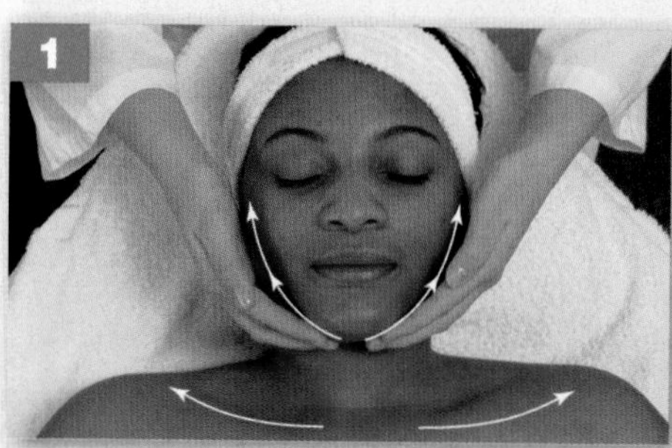

1 With clean, warm hands, evenly apply the warmed massage product to the décolleté, neck, and face by using the hands or a soft brush. One teaspoon (5 milliliters) should be enough product for the facial area.

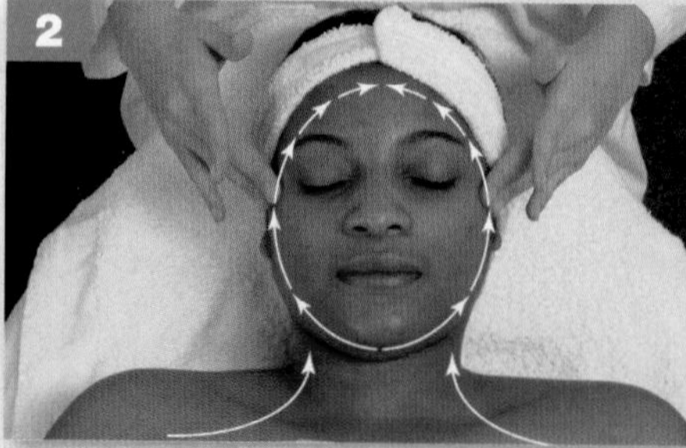

2 Start with hands on the décolleté. Move slowly up the sides of the neck and face to the forehead. Slide to each of the next steps without breaking contact or lifting fingers off the face.

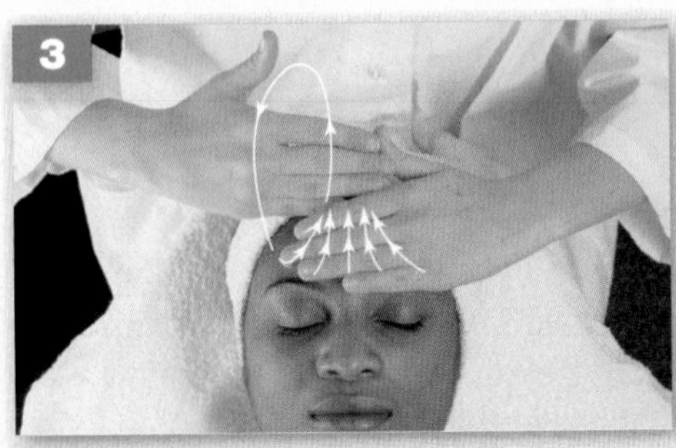

3 With the middle and ring fingers of each hand, start upward strokes in the middle of the forehead at the brow line. Working upward toward the hairline, one hand follows the other as the hands move over toward the right temple, then move back across the forehead to the left temple, and then move back to the center of the forehead. Repeat the movements three to six times.

4 With the middle or index finger of each hand, start a circular movement in the middle of the forehead along the brow line. Continue this circular movement while working toward the temples. Bring the fingers back to the center of the forehead at a point between the brow line and the hairline. Move up on the forehead towards the hairline for the final movements. Each time the fingers reach the temple, pause for a moment and apply slight pressure to the temple. Repeat three to six times.

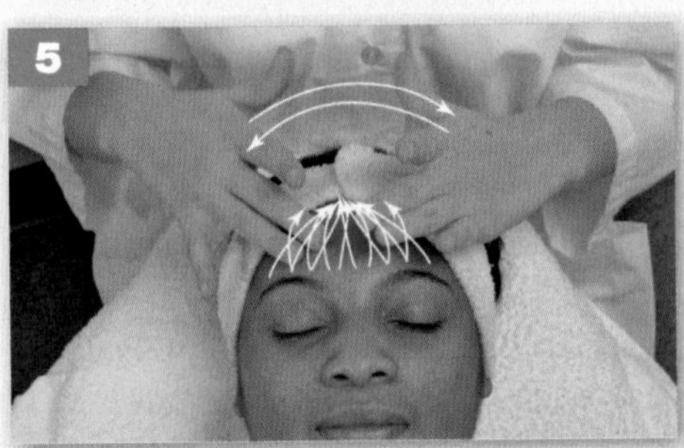

5 With the middle and ring fingers of each hand, start a crisscross stroking movement at the middle of the forehead, starting at the brow line and moving upward toward the hairline. Move toward the right temple and back to the center of the forehead. Now move toward the left temple and back to the center of the forehead. Repeat three to six times.

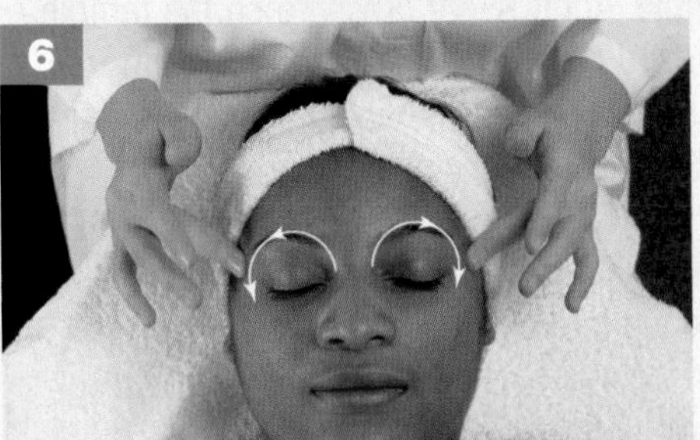

6 Place the ring fingers under the inside corners of the eyebrows and the middle fingers over the brows. Slide the fingers to the outer corner of the eye, lifting the brow at the same time. This movement continues with the next step.

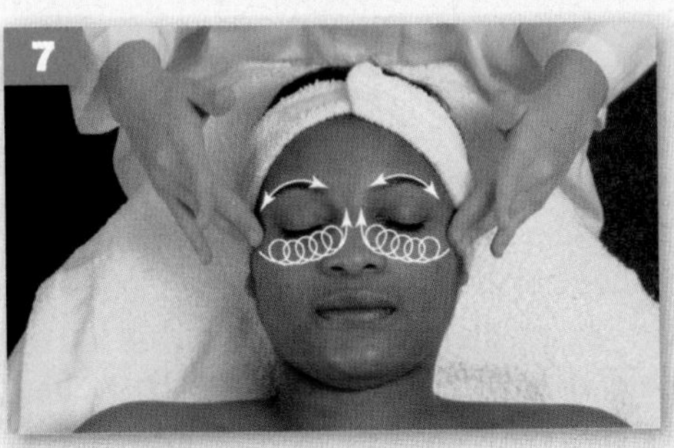

7 Start a circular movement with the middle finger at the outside corner of the eye. Continue the circular movement on the cheekbone to the point under the center of the eye, and then slide the fingers back to the starting point. Repeat six to eight times. The left hand moves clockwise, and the right hand moves counterclockwise.

PROCEDURE

16-1 The Facial Massage (continued)

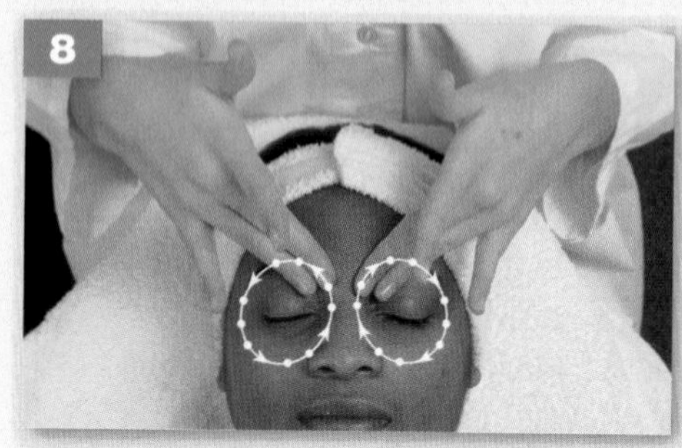

8 Start a light tapping movement with the pads of the fingers. Tap lightly around the eyes as if playing a piano. Continue tapping, moving from the temple, under the eye, toward the nose, up and over the brow, and outward to the temple. Do not tap the eyelids directly over the eyeball. Repeat six times.

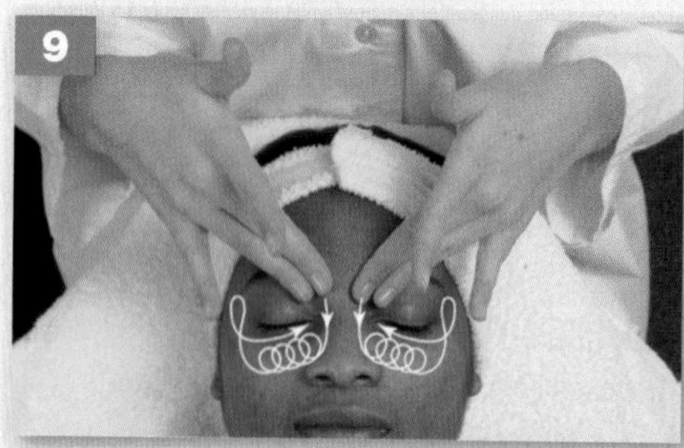

9 With the middle or index finger of each hand, start a circular movement down the nose and continuing across the cheeks to the temples. Slide the fingers under the eyes and back to the bridge of the nose. Repeat the movements six times.

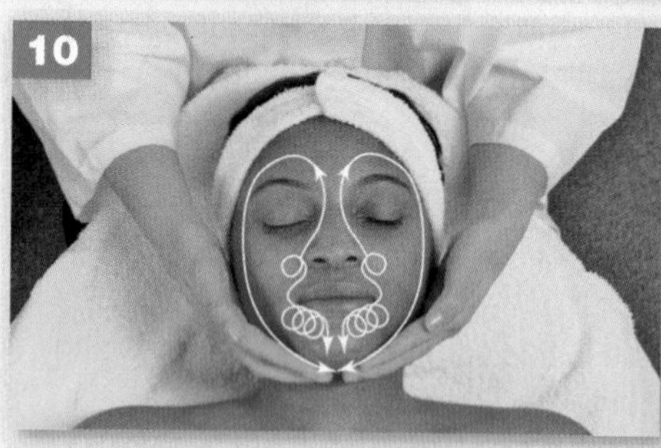

10 With the middle and ring fingers of each hand, slide the fingers from the bridge of the nose, over the brow (lifting the brow), and down to the chin. Start a firm circular movement on the chin with the thumbs. Change to the middle fingers at the corner of the mouth. Rotate the fingers five times, and slide the fingers up the sides of the nose, over the brow, and then stop for a moment at the temple. Apply slight pressure on the temple. Slide the fingers down to the chin, and repeat the movements six times. The downward movement on the side of the face should have a very light touch to avoid dragging the skin downward.

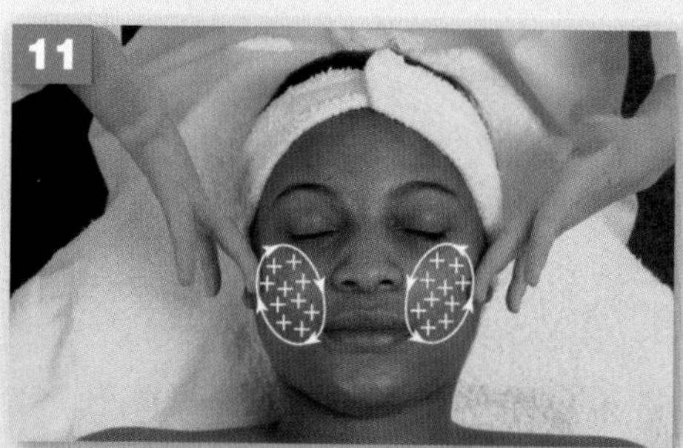

11 With the pads of the fingertips, start a light tapping movement (piano playing) on the cheeks, working in a circle around the cheeks. Repeat the movements six to eight times.

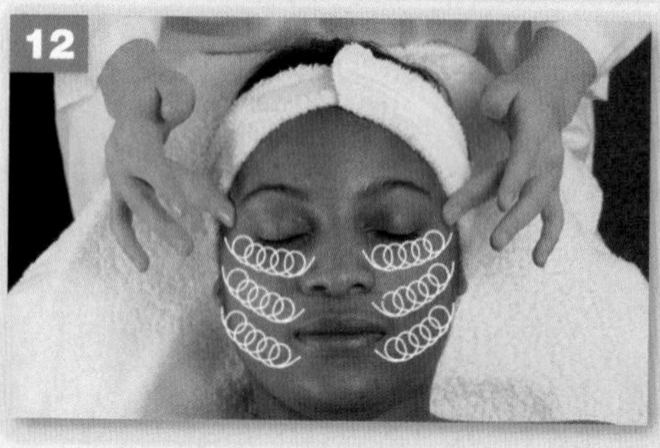

12 Slide to the center of the chin. Using a finger of each hand, start a circular movement at the center of the chin and move up to the earlobes. Slide the middle fingers to the corner of the mouth and then continue the circular movements to the middle of the ears. Return the middle fingers to the nose and continue the circular movements outward across the cheeks to the top of the ear. Repeat each of the three passes three to six times. Slide down to the mouth.

13 Place one finger above the mouth and one finger below the mouth. With the index and middle fingers of each hand, start the "scissor" movement, gliding from the center of the mouth, upward over the cheekbone, and stopping at the top of the cheekbone. Alternate the movement from one side of the face to the other, using the right hand on the right side of the face and then the left hand on the left side. As one hand reaches the cheekbone, start the other at the center of the mouth. Repeat eight to ten times.

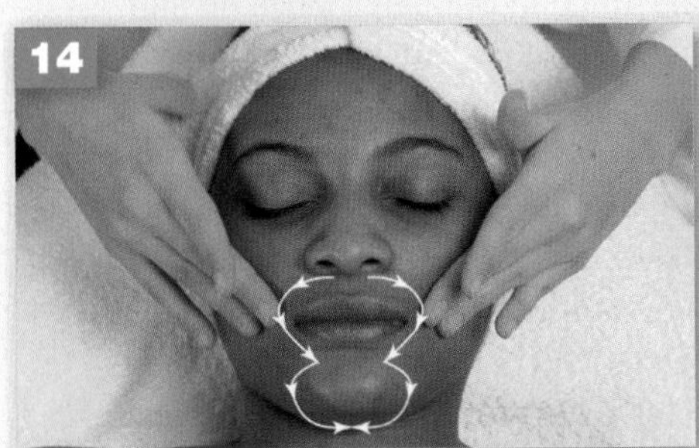

14 With the middle finger of both hands, draw the fingers from the center of the upper lip, around the mouth, under the lower lip, and then continue a circle under the chin. Repeat six to eight times.

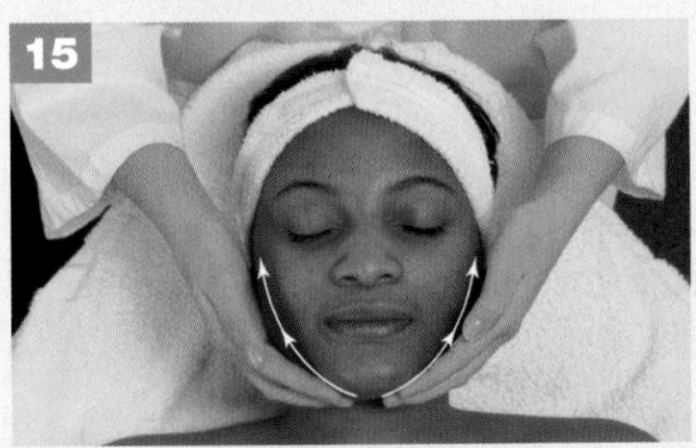

15 With the index finger above the chin and jawline (the middle, ring, and little fingers should be under the chin and jaw), start a scissor movement from the center of the chin and then slide the fingers along the jawline to the earlobe. Alternate one hand after the other, using the right hand on the right side of the face and the left hand on the left side of the face. Repeat eight to ten times on each side of the face. Slide down to the neck.

16 Apply light upward strokes over the front of the neck with both hands. Circle down and then back up, using firmer downward pressure on the outer sides of the neck. Repeat 10 times. Do not press down on the center of the neck.

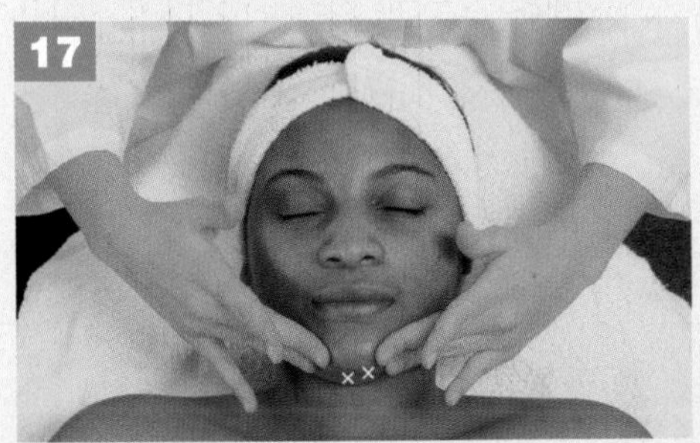

17 With the middle and ring fingers of the right hand, give two quick taps under the chin, followed with one quick tap with the middle and ring fingers of the left hand. The taps should be done in a continuous movement, keeping a steady rhythm. The taps should be done with a light touch, but with enough pressure so that a soft tapping sound can be heard. Continue the tapping movement while moving the hands slightly to the right and then to the left, so as to cover the complete underside of the chin. Without stopping or breaking the rhythm of the tapping, move to the right cheek.

PROCEDURE

16-1 The Facial Massage (continued)

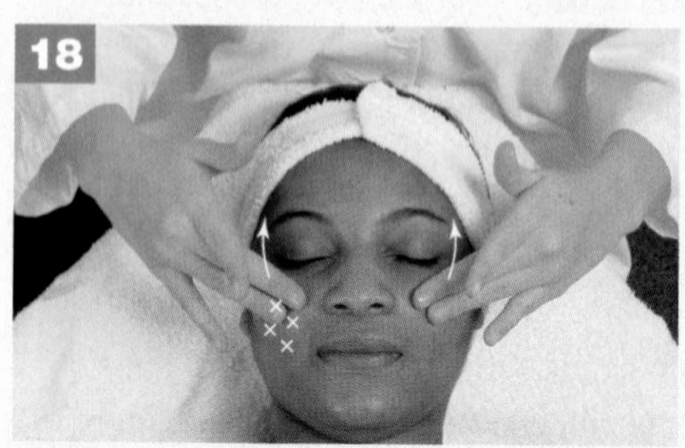

18 Continue the tapping on the right cheek in the same manner as under the chin, except the tapping with the left hand will have a lifting movement. The rhythm will be tap, tap, lift, tap, tap, lift, tap, tap, lift. Repeat this rhythmic movement 15 to 20 times. Without stopping the tapping movement, move the fingers back under the chin and over the left cheek, repeating the tapping and lifting movements. Move up and out on the area in a consistent pattern. Avoid tapping directly on the jawbone because this will feel unpleasant to the client.

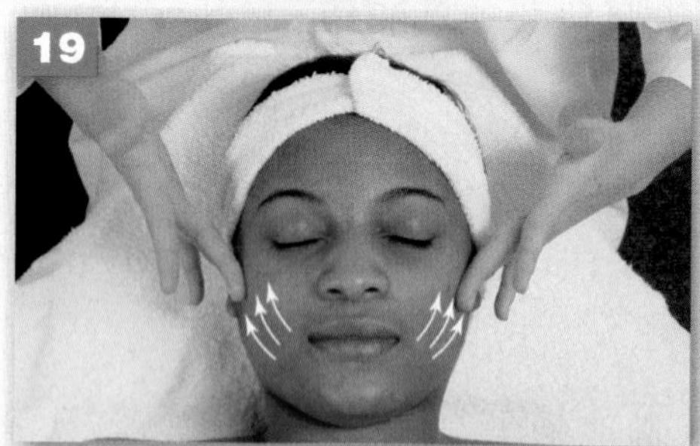

19 Without stopping the tapping movement, move the hands over to the corners of the mouth. Break into an upward, stroking movement with the first three fingers of each hand. One finger follows the other as each finger lifts the corner of the mouth. Use both hands at the same time or alternate each hand—as one hand ends the movement, the other starts. Repeat the stroking movement 15 to 20 times.

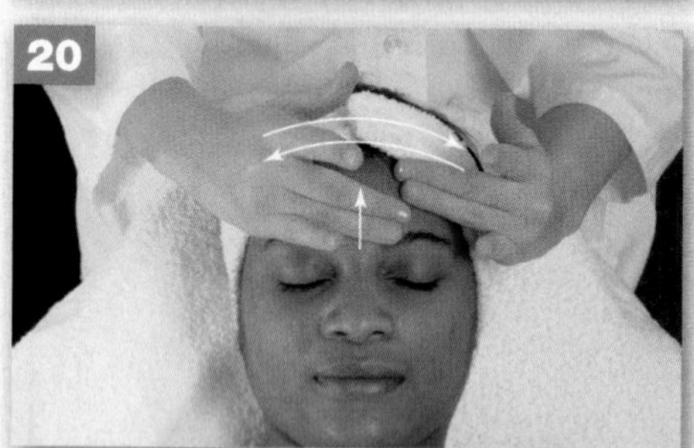

20 Without stopping the stroking movement, move up to the outside corner of the left eye and continue the stroking, upward movement. Continue the stoking movement across the forehead to the outside corner of the right eye. Continue this stroking movement back and forth 10 times in each direction.

21 Continue the stroking movement back and forth across the forehead, gradually slowing the movement. Let the movements grow slower and slower as the touch becomes lighter and lighter. Taper the movement off until the fingers are gradually lifted from the forehead. This slowing down of movement is often called *feathering*.

Optional: Glide down to the neck and chest and repeat the movements on these areas as directed by your instructor.

22 Finish the facial service, and complete your client consultation. ☑ L05

fyi

Blood returning to the heart from the head, face, and neck flows down the jugular veins on each side of the neck. All massage movements on the side of the neck are done with a downward (never upward) motion. Always slide gently upward in the center of the neck and circle out and then down on the sides. This also assists with fluid and lymph drainage.

Post-Service

- **Complete** 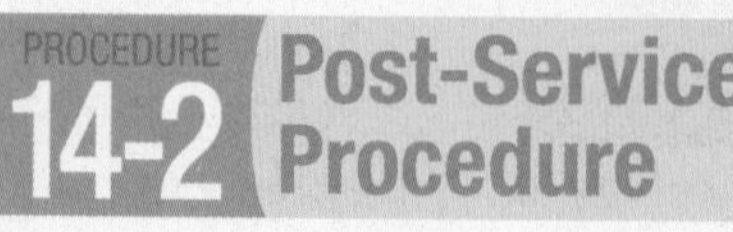

PAGE 375

Review Questions

1. What are five benefits of massage?
2. What are five of the massage contraindications?
3. How do you find out what the licensing regulations for massage are in your area?
4. List the five main types of classical massage movements, and briefly describe each of the movements.
5. What is the Dr. Jacquet Movement used for?
6. Define acupressure.
7. What is manual lymph drainage?
8. In what direction do you massage on the muscles?

Glossary

acupressure	Oriental technique of applying pressure to specific points of the body (acupressure points) to release muscle tension, restore balance, and stimulate *chi* (CHEE) (life force; energy).
chucking	Massage movement accomplished by grasping the flesh firmly in one hand up and down along the bone while the other hand keeps the arm or leg in a steady position.
Dr. Jacquet Movement	Beneficial for oily skin; it helps move sebum out of the follicles and up to the skin's surface by kneading.
effleurage	Light, continuous stroking movement applied with the fingers (digital) or the palms (palmar) in a slow, rhythmic manner.
foot reflexology	The technique of applying pressure to the feet based on a system of zones and areas on the feet that directly correspond to the anatomy of the body. Reflexology is also performed on the hands and ears.
friction	Deep rubbing movement requiring pressure on the skin with the fingers or palm while moving them under a underlying structure. Chucking, rolling, and wringing are variations of friction.
fulling	Form of pétrissage in which the tissue is grasped, gently lifted, and spread out. Used mainly for massaging on the arms.
hacking	Chopping movement performed with the edges of the hands in massage.
manual lymph drainage	Abbreviated MLD; gentle, rhythmic pressure on the lymphatic system to detoxify and remove waste materials from the body more quickly; reduces swelling and is used before and after surgery for pre- and post-op care.
massage	Manual or mechanical manipulation of the body by rubbing, gently pinching, kneading, tapping, and other movements to increase metabolism and circulation, promote absorption, and relieve pain.
pétrissage	Kneading movement that stimulates the underlying tissues; performed by lifting, squeezing, and pressing the tissue with a light, firm pressure.

Glossary

rolling	Massage movement in which the tissues are pressed and twisted using a fast back-and-forth movement.
shiatsu	The application of pressure on acupuncture points found throughout the body to balance the body's energy flow and to promote health. It originated as a form of physical therapy in Japan.
slapping	Massage movement in which the wrists are kept flexible so that the palms come in contact with the skin in light, firm, and rapid strokes; one hand follows the other; with each slapping stroke, the flesh is lifted slightly.
tapotement	Also known as *percussion*; movements consisting of short, quick tapping, slapping, and hacking movements.
vibration	In massage, the rapid shaking movement in which the technician uses the body and shoulders, not just the fingertips, to create the movement.
wringing	Vigorous movement in which the hands, placed a little distance apart on both sides of the client's arm or leg, working downward apply a twisting motion against the bones in the opposite direction.

CHAPTER 17

Facial Machines

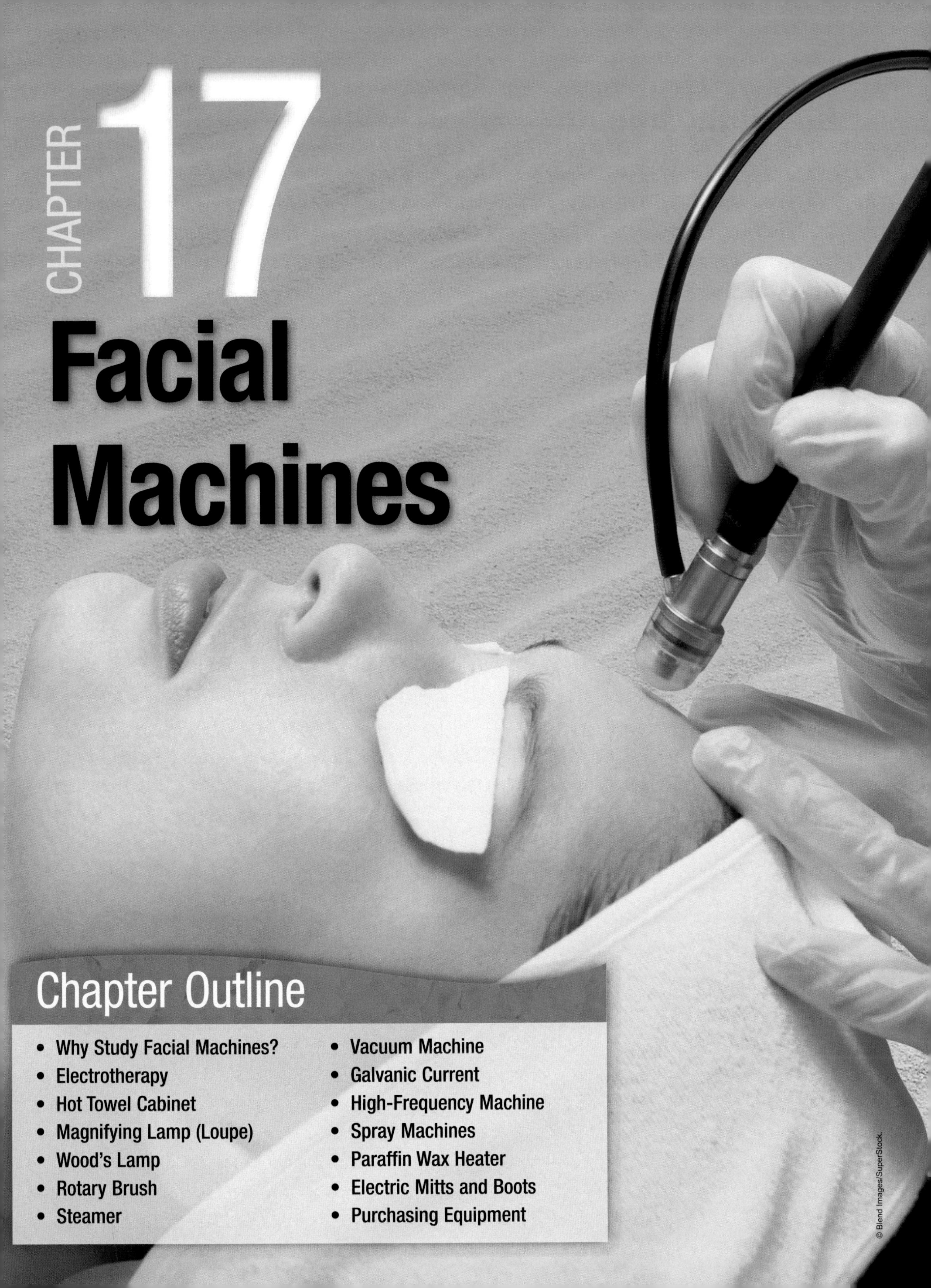

© Blend Images/SuperStock.

Chapter Outline

- Why Study Facial Machines?
- Electrotherapy
- Hot Towel Cabinet
- Magnifying Lamp (Loupe)
- Wood's Lamp
- Rotary Brush
- Steamer
- Vacuum Machine
- Galvanic Current
- High-Frequency Machine
- Spray Machines
- Paraffin Wax Heater
- Electric Mitts and Boots
- Purchasing Equipment

Learning Objectives

After completing this chapter, you will be able to:

- ✓ LO1 Identify the basic concepts of electrotherapy.
- ✓ LO2 Describe the contraindications for machines.
- ✓ LO3 Understand how to maintain a hot-towel cabinet.
- ✓ LO4 Use and maintain the magnifying lamp.
- ✓ LO5 Describe the purpose of the Wood's Lamp.
- ✓ LO6 Be familiar with the brush machine.
- ✓ LO7 Safely use and maintain the steamer.
- ✓ LO8 Explain how the vacuum machine is used.
- ✓ LO9 Understand how galvanic machines are used.
- ✓ LO10 Be familiar with the high-frequency machine.
- ✓ LO11 Explain how the spray machine is used.
- ✓ LO12 Make informed decisions when purchasing equipment.

Key Terms

Page number indicates where in the chapter the term is used.

high-frequency machine
pg. 463

Lucas Sprayer
pg. 467

rotary brush
pg. 453

saponification
pg. 459

sinusoidal current
pg. 463

spray machine
pg. 466

thermolysis
pg. 464

vacuum machine (suction machine)
pg. 458

Wood's Lamp
pg. 452

There are a variety of useful machines that will enhance the esthetician's services. Each machine has a specific benefit for the skin and makes clients feel as though they are receiving a specialized service. In this chapter you will learn how these tools are integrated into the facial experience. Although facial treatments can be performed effectively without electrical devices, even better results can be achieved with electrical tools and electrotherapy.

Why Study Facial Machines?

Estheticians should study and have a thorough understanding of facial machines so that they can operate the machines safely, provide the best results for their clients, and enhance their service menu.

- It is vital to understand how to safely use each machine and the potential contraindications in using machines.
- There are a variety of useful machines and new high-performance tools that will enhance the esthetician's services and it is important to be able to explain the benefits of each machine.
- To maintain professional credibility, estheticians must continue to be educated about the latest methods in skin care as new machines and technology emerge each year.
- Investing in high-quality machines will increase both your credibility and potential business revenue.

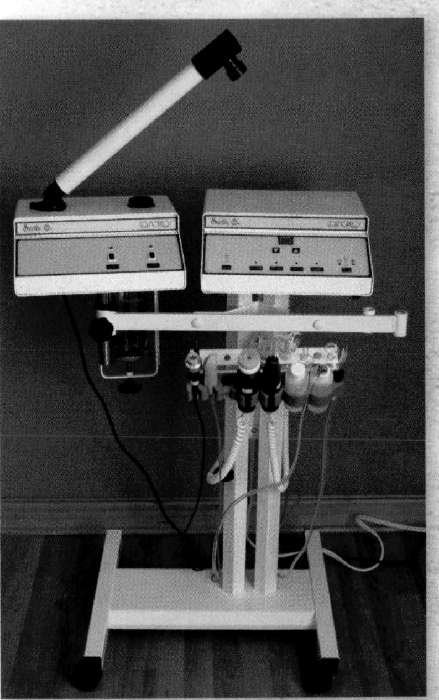

© Milady, a part of Cengage Learning. Photography by Rob Werfel.

▲ Figure 17–1
Multifunctional machines.

Electrotherapy

Electrotherapy is the use of electrical devices for therapeutic benefits. It is important to be familiar with machines even if you choose not to work with them. Electrical devices enhance the facial by making it easier to give a skin analysis, achieve better product penetration, or by exfoliating the skin. These tools are especially effective for more challenging skin conditions. Machines can be purchased separately or as multifunctional units with many of the modalities (machines) all on one unit (Figure 17–1).

Estheticians must continue to be educated about the latest methods in skin care, while being cautious of expensive, trendy machines. Lasers, light therapy, microdermabrasion, and microcurrent are some of the advanced machines discussed later in Chapter 19, Advanced Topics and Treatments. Today's clients are well educated and have greater access to information, and they will expect you to be knowledgeable about all skin care topics, trends, and tools. To maintain professional credibility, it is important that you are aware of current technology. ☑ L01

Contraindications

There are several contraindications for electrotherapy. These include the standard facial contraindications discussed in previous chapters. (See Chapter 12, Skin Analysis and Chapter 15, Facial Treatments.)

To prevent physical harm, some electrotherapy machines should never be used on: heart patients, clients with pacemakers, metal implants, or braces; pregnant clients; clients with epilepsy or seizure disorders; clients who are afraid of electric current; or those with open or broken skin.

If you ever have any doubts about whether the client can have electrotherapy safely, request that the client get a note from her or his physician approving electrotherapy treatment. Additionally, have clients remove jewelry and piercings before using electrical devices such as the galvanic machine. Use all machines as directed by the manufacturer, because similar machines may have different mechanisms and work differently. Most machines are used for approximately 5 to 10 minutes in a service. ✓ LO2

▲ Figure 17–2
The towel warmer.

Hot Towel Cabinet

Towel warmers, called *hot-towel cabinets* or *hot cabbies*, are commonly used in the treatment room (Figure 17–2). Hot towels are used for both face and body treatments. Towels provide a warm, soothing, and softening benefit to the skin and are utilized for removing facial masks and softening the skin before doing extractions. Cotton pads and products can also be warmed in a towel warmer or specialized product warmer. Some towel warmers are equipped with ultraviolet lamps. UV lamps in towel warmers may reduce bacteria but are not effective for disinfection.

CAUTION!

Plastic melts in hot-towel warmers—use heat-resistant dishes to warm products.

Hot Cabinet Maintenance

It is important to keep the hot-towel cabinet clean and free from mold or mildew. After each client session, clean the inside of the cabinet with a topical disinfectant. Give towel warmers a thorough cleansing at the end of the day. Leave the door open at night to allow the cabinet and rubber seals to dry thoroughly. Also empty and clean and disinfect the water catchment tray underneath the cabbie daily. ✓ LO3

Magnifying Lamp (Loupe)

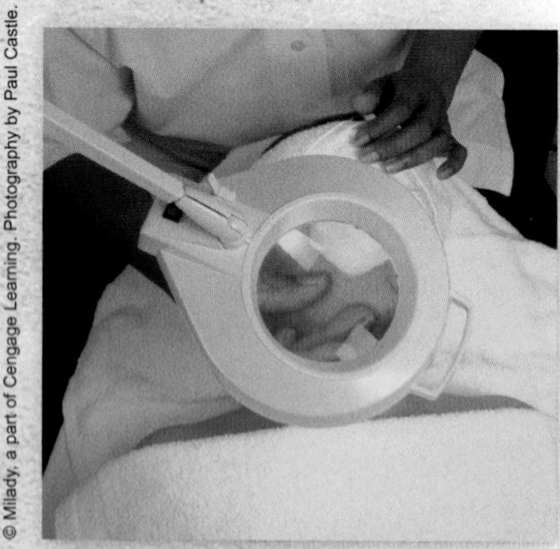

▲ Figure 17–3
The magnifying lamp is used to analyze the skin.

The magnifying lamp (also referred to as a *loupe*; pronounced "loop") magnifies the face to help the esthetician treat and analyze the skin (Figure 17–3). The lamp uses a cool fluorescent light bulb. The magnifying lamp has various powers of magnification known as *diopters*. Most lamps in the industry come in values of 3, 5, or 10 diopters which means 30 times the power magnification, 50 times the power magnification, or 100 times the power magnification respectively.

Five diopters is the most common magnification. A good-quality light should have a clear lens, free of distortion. Since you are using this light often, any distortion will add strain to your eyes and make it more difficult to see the skin.

Lamps are designed to sit on a floor base or attach directly to a facial cart. The base that it sits on may be sold separately from the lamp itself. Carts are not as mobile, so floor stands are preferred. It is worth getting a quality lamp that has good knobs that stay tight instead of one that hinges, as it will last longer due to all of the constant adjustments that are used in positioning the lamp correctly for each client and treatment.

It is important to loosen the adjustment knobs before moving the lamp arms up or down. If you force the lamp into positions without loosening the knobs first, you will wear out the light and then it will not stay in position at all. To avoid overreaching and hurting your back or wrists, you may need to stand up to move and adjust the lamp.

CAUTION!

Loosen the adjustment knobs on the lamp before moving the lamp arms up or down. If you force the lamp into positions without loosening the knobs first, you will wear out the light and then it will not stay in position at all.

Other skin analysis devices include handheld magnification tools, head visors, and cameras that view the skin at up to 200X magnification. Other tools are available to read the skin's hydration level. These can be hooked up to a computer and the data can be stored and viewed on the screen. These devices are especially useful to track treatment progress in medical aesthetics or when performing advanced treatments such as peels or microdermabrasion.

Magnifying Lamp Procedure

The procedure for using a magnifying lamp is as follows:

1. Place eye pads over the eyes to protect the eyes from the bright light. Make sure your eye pads are not too large, or they may block the eye area you need to analyze or treat.
2. Position the lamp where you want it during the room setup. Turn on the light and carefully bring it back over the face. If necessary, move it away from the face and loosen the adjustment knob to change the light's angle so you can see through it comfortably.
3. Once the lamp is adjusted, bring it back over the face. Avoid startling the client by suddenly shining the light directly into the eyes, or by losing control of the lamp.
4. Gently move the client's head back and forth to examine the sides of the face.

Magnifying Lamp Maintenance

Magnifying lamps can last up to 10 years if they are well constructed and maintained. Conversely, if they are abused and roughly handled, their longevity is compromised. If problems do occur, they typically involve the adjustment arm. The spring on the arm can wear out and may break if not used with care. Some less expensive magnifying lights have hinges rather than knobs that adjust, but these usually wear out

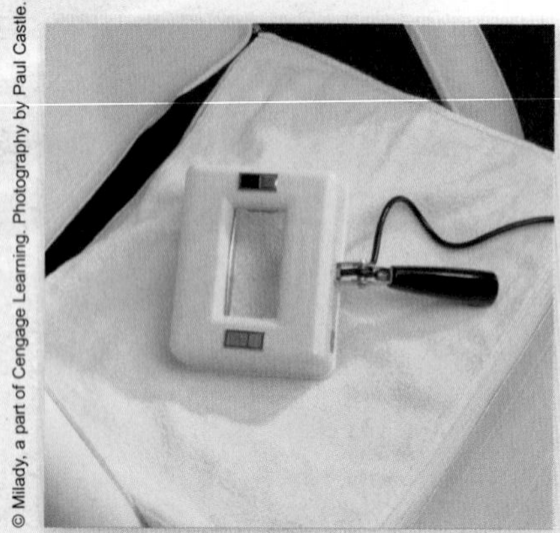

▲ Figure 17–4
The Wood's Lamp illuminates skin care problems that are ordinarily invisible to the naked eye.

faster. Periodically check the screws around the light to ensure that they are not loose. The arm and bolt underneath the base may also need tightening. A simple tool box with screw drivers and wrenches is handy to have in the facility.

- To clean the lens, turn off the lamp and spray it with a disinfectant and wipe with a soft cloth. Avoid using paper products because paper towels or tissues will scratch the lens.
- Clean and disinfect the entire lamp and base with a disinfectant. ✓ L04

Wood's Lamp

The **Wood's Lamp**, developed by American Physicist Robert Williams Wood, is a filtered black light that is used to illuminate fungi, bacterial disorders, pigmentation problems, and other skin problems (Figure 17–4). The Wood's Lamp allows the esthetician to conduct a more in-depth skin analysis, illuminating skin problems that are ordinarily invisible to the naked eye. Under the lamp, different conditions show up in various shades of color. For instance, the thicker the skin, the whiter the fluorescence will be. Pigmentation that shows up under the Wood's Lamp cannot be completely lightened with products or treatments, because the pigmentation is in the dermis.

Following are some examples of skin conditions and how they appear under the Wood's Lamp:

- Thick corneum layer—white fluorescence
- Horny layer of dead skin cells—white spots
- Normal, healthy skin—blue-white
- Thin or dehydrated skin—light violet/purple
- Acne or bacteria—yellow or orange
- Oily areas of the face/comedones—yellow or sometimes pink or orange
- Hyperpigmentation or sun damage—brown
- Hypopigmentation—blue-white or yellow-green

When using the Wood's Lamp, the room must be totally dark. Put small eye pads on the client, making sure the area around the eye is still visible. Turn on the light and hold it 4 to 5 inches (10 to 12.5 centimeters) above the client's face (Figure 17–5). The bulbs can get hot, so be careful not to touch the skin or have the lamp turned on too long. Note the corresponding skin conditions to the area of the face on the client's chart.

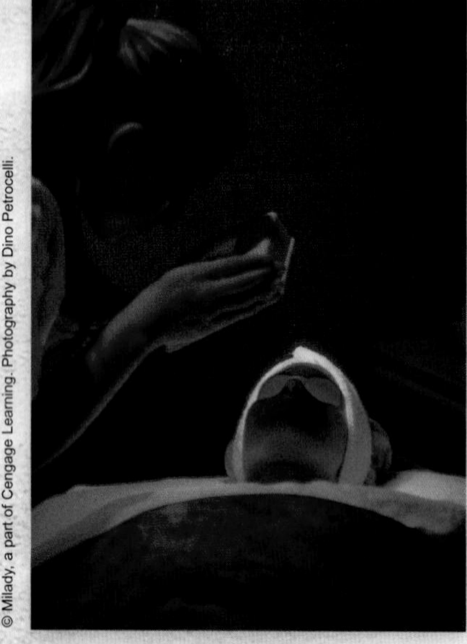

▲ Figure 17–5
Using the Wood's Lamp for skin analysis.

fyi

Pigmentation that shows up under the Wood's Lamp cannot be completely lightened with regular exfoliation treatments, because it is in the dermis. Only pigmentation on the surface of the skin can be potentially lightened by exfoliation treatments and lightening products.

Treat the Wood's Lamp carefully, as you would a magnifying lamp. Follow the manufacturer's directions for cleaning. To protect the bulbs, store the lamp in a safe place where it is protected from breakage. A small covered plastic tub and protective wrapping is helpful in storing the glass parts of various tools and machines.

Skin scopes are similar to a Wood's Lamp. These larger skin analysis tools use a UV light with an interior mirror. A client can look at their face on one side of the scope while the esthetician looks through the scope and examines them from the other side. These scanners use a magnifying lamp and black light to analyze skin features such as hydration and pigmentation. ☑ LO5

Rotary Brush

The main purpose of the **rotary brush** is to lightly exfoliate the skin (Figure 17–6). The brush machine also assists in the cleansing process. Brushes stimulate the skin and help soften excess oil, dirt, and cell buildup. Do not use brushes on acne, couperose, or inflamed skin. Brushes come in smaller sizes for the face and larger sizes for body areas, such as the back.

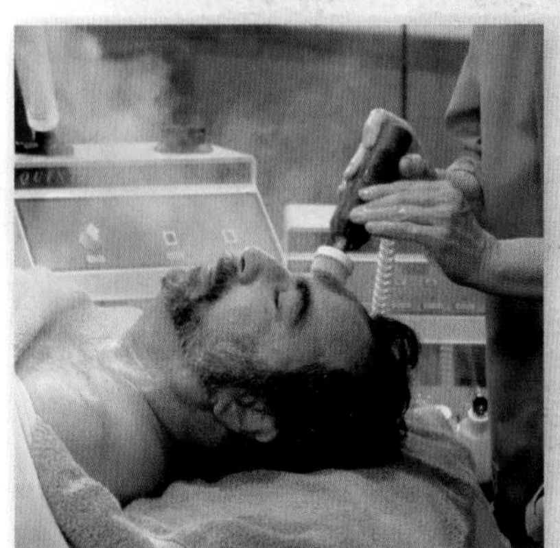

▲ Figure 17–6
Using the brush machine.

Mini Procedure

The Brush Machine

The following steps describe the safe and effective use of a rotary brush.

1. Before using the brush, lightly cleanse the client's skin.
2. Insert the appropriate size brush into the handheld device.
3. Apply more cleanser or water to the skin. Do not let water or cleanser drip down the face or into the eyes. Use a piece of cotton or a towel to catch any excess water.
4. Use the brush approximately three times on each area, or for approximately 3 to 5 seconds, unless directed otherwise. Keep the brush moving across the face without stopping.
5. Dip the head of the brush into water, adjust the speed, and begin a horizontal pattern across the forehead. The brush should be damp, not drippy. Wipe excess water on a towel if necessary.
6. Continue the rotation down to the cheeks, nose, upper lip, chin, jaw, and neck areas.
7. Do not apply pressure. Allow the rotating brush to do the work. The bristles of the brush should remain straight.
8. Lift the brush from the skin and turn off the machine.

Here's a Tip

Using the brush machine while cleansing the skin saves time for both you and your client.

Brush machines vary. Typically they have two or three small brushes with different textures ranging from soft to firm. The brushes can be rotated at different speeds and directions. Moisten the brush before each use to soften the bristles. More sensitive skin requires a slow, steady rotation and soft brushes. Thicker, oily skin can tolerate a faster speed and firmer brushes.

Brush Maintenance

Rotary brush machines come with detachable brushes for cleaning. Here are some guidelines for maintaining the brushes:

CAUTION!

To avoid damaging or further irritating the skin, do not use brushes or suction devices on acne, couperose, or inflamed skin.

- Remove the brushes after each use and wash them thoroughly with soap and water.
- After manual cleansing, immerse the brushes in a disinfectant for the time recommended in the manufacturer's instructions.
- It is important to clean, rinse, dry, and store the brushes so that they do not lose their shape when drying. If the bristles become bent or lose their shape, they will not rotate properly.
- Although they can be stored temporarily in a dry ultraviolet sanitizer, the brushes will break down if left in the light box too long. When they are completely dry, transfer them to a closed container. ✓ L06

Steamer

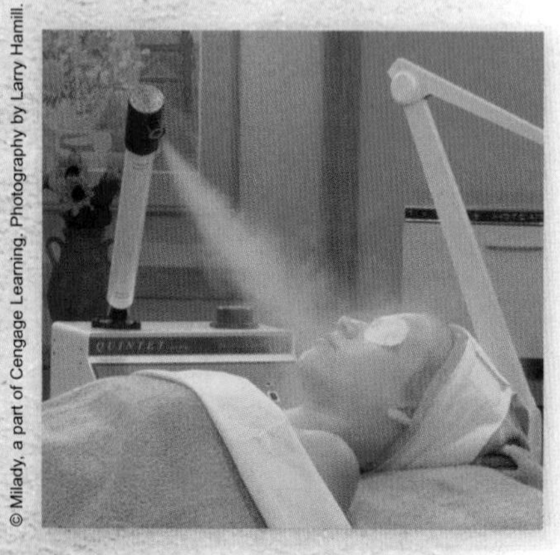

▲ Figure 17–7
The steamer provides many benefits during the facial treatment.

Many estheticians consider the steamer to be the most important machine used in esthetics. There are many benefits to steaming the skin (Figure 17–7). Steam helps to stimulate circulation, as well as softening sebum and other debris. The warmth relaxes the skin and tissues, making it easier for the esthetician to extract comedones. Steam can also be beneficial for the sinuses and congestion. Steamers with ozone (O_3) may have an antiseptic effect on the skin that is beneficial for acne and problematic skin. Do not use too much steam on couperose or inflamed skin, because it dilates the capillaries and follicles, causing more redness and irritation.

Professional steamers come in various sizes and models. Use only distilled or filtered water in the steamer, because the mineral and calcium deposits in tap water can damage the machinery. The vapor is directed onto the skin's surface by a nozzle at the end of the steamer's arm. Steamers usually have a place for an aromatherapy ring on the inside of the nozzle head, and they may have a special feature for using essential oils. A quality steamer will last for years, as inexpensive models break down quickly. It is worth the extra money to buy a good quality steamer that will last and be reliable.

Mini Procedure

USING THE STEAMER

When using a steamer, or any equipment, always read and follow the manufacturer's directions. Steam treatments are timed according to the client's specific needs and the type of facial procedure. Ordinarily, treatment time is between 8 and 10 minutes.

1. Place distilled water into the designated container through the fill opening in the top. Check that it is not too full and is level with the fill line.
2. Before giving the facial, position the steamer where you want it. Adjust the height.
3. Preheat the steamer before the facial. Do not let water steam or boil for more than a minute while preheating. If all of the water evaporates, the glass may break.
4. Place a towel under the client's neck and over the shoulders to protect these areas from the steam or dripping water and keep the nozzle completely away from the body.
5. Turn the machine away from the client, and flip the power switch to "on." Do not turn on the second switch, the ozone or vaporizer, until steam is visible.
6. When the water is boiling and steam is visible, flip on the second switch and slowly adjust the steamer arm close to the client. This will activate the generator inside the machine. You may hear the sound of a small motor. If the noise is too loud and the steam amount does not increase, turn the vaporizer switch back to "off" because the steamer is not ready yet.
7. Keep the steam approximately 15 to 18 inches (37.5 to 45 centimeters) from the face. Place the steamer farther away, if necessary, so that it is warm but not too hot on the face. If placed too close, steam can cause overheating of the skin, possible irritation, or burning. Always check the client's comfort level and ensure even distribution of the steam on the face. Never leave the client unattended while steaming as the water can spray out and burn the client.
8. When you are ready to discontinue the steam, move the steamer away from the client. Turn off the ozone/vaporizer switch first. Then turn off the power switch.
9. Clean and disinfect the steamer after each use. Do not spray the hot glass jar reservoir with disinfectant before it has cooled off, as this may cause it to shatter.

CAUTION!

To avoid burning yourself, never touch the glass jar on the steamer when it is hot—it takes a long time to cool down. Ask your instructor for a demonstration on how to safely remove and replace the glass jar.

Here's a Tip

If the steamer is positioned with the steam directed from below the nose and is too close for the client, try steaming from above the head. Reposition it a few times if necessary to get an even placement of steam across the face.

CAUTION!

- **Do not use too much steam on couperose or inflamed skin because it dilates the capillaries and follicles, causing more redness and irritation.**
- **Do not leave the room while steaming the client in case the steamer starts spraying water—this may burn the client.**
- **Do not overfill the steamer because the steamer may spray excess water and burn the client.**
- **Clean the steamer regularly to avoid mineral buildup that causes water to spray and burn the client.**
- **Do not let the water-level run low in the steamer—the glass may break.**

Steamer Maintenance

To ensure proper usage, always read and follow the manufacturer's directions for the steamer. Following these guidelines will keep your machine in peak working condition for years.

- After each use, wipe down the outside of the steamer with a disinfectant.
- At night, unscrew and empty the jar to let it dry. Make sure that the rubber seal along the rim of the jar is clean.
- Refill the steamer machine with fresh distilled water each morning. Do not overfill. Turn it on to give it a chance to warm up. This will save valuable time when treating your first client of the day.
- Water used inside the steamer should be as free of chemicals and minerals as possible; therefore, it is always recommended that distilled, not tap, water be used. Most tap water contains chlorine, other chemicals, and mineral deposits.
- Do not leave water in the steamer overnight or on weekends. If the steamer is not emptied regularly, deposits can collect on the heater element. Empty the jar and lightly clean with vinegar and then with soap and water. Allow the coils to dry.
- Neglected steamers tend to spit hot water due to the buildup of mineral deposits that occur with daily use. Mineral deposits may appear as a white or yellow crusty film on the heating element. The hot water can land on the client's face and may cause a serious burn.
- Some steamer models have solid tanks, preventing you from seeing the element; therefore, they need to be cleaned at least two times a month. Use a cleaning solution of plain vinegar and water.
- Never put essential oils or herbs directly into the water. Essential oils are highly active. When dropped directly into a closed jar with boiling water, they can cause excessive spitting of water or, even worse, clog the steamer or cause the glass to break from pressure. Some steamers are equipped with a wick-type apparatus that fits at the mouth of the nozzle. A couple of drops of essential oil can be placed here before the steamer is preheated. The steam picks up the aroma as it vaporizes out into the room.
- Other steamer models make use of a special container for herbs. These specialized steamers are normally more expensive; however, they provide the esthetician with the added benefit of incorporating therapeutic herbs into the steaming process. You can also put a few drops of essential oil on your hands or a cotton pad or swab and hold it close to the steam for aromatherapy.

- Do not leave the room when preheating the steamer or you may forget about it and run the water down too low and shatter the glass. Water levels must be kept above the safety line marked above the element on the glass jar. Not all steamers have automatic shutoffs.
  - Some machines may have automatic regulators that detect the water level. When it becomes too low or empty, a safety switch is triggered, turning off the machine.
  - Some machines have timers that shut off after the set time. Timers are useful but some may tick and then ding when the timer goes off, which can be a loud and distracting noise. Try before you buy. ✓ LO7

Mini Procedure

CLEANING THE STEAMER

The steamer should be trouble-free if you follow these general cleaning guidelines.

1. Add two tablespoons (10 milliliters) of white vinegar, and fill jar to the top fill line with water.
2. Turn on the steamer and let it heat to steaming. Do not turn on the ozone.
3. Let the machine steam for 20 minutes or until the water level is low, but make sure it stays above the bottom low-level line to avoid jar breakage.
4. Turn off the steamer and let the vinegar solution rest in the unit for 15 minutes. Because vinegar has a pungent smell, clean the steamer in your utility room or in an area away from the treatment rooms. Open a window, if possible, when performing maintenance to keep fumes from traveling to other areas of the salon.
5. After it cools, drain the steamer jar completely and then refill with water. Again let the steamer heat to steaming and operate for approximately 10 minutes. If there is still an odor, drain the unit and repeat the process.
   a. Do not allow the caustic vinegar and water solution to sit on the heating coil without steaming immediately. If left overnight, it will corrode the copper coils.
   b. Note that there is usually a reset button on steamers for additional safety in the event the steamer runs out of water. If the steamer is not running, check the reset button before you call for help. The reset button is ordinarily found on the back of the machine.

FOCUS ON

Ozone

Ordinary oxygen in the atmosphere consists of two oxygen atoms (O_2). Ozone consists of three oxygen atoms (O_3). Ozone is what is created after a lightning storm and has a distinct smell. Ozone also has antiseptic qualities. These molecules have the power to kill bacteria and other microorganisms; that being stated, ozone is also a strong oxidizer that creates free radicals. The third atom can detach from the O_3 molecule and reattach to other molecules.

Some steamers have ozone mechanisms. High-frequency machines also create ozone. According to the EPA, exposure to ozone affects the respiratory system, can irritate the eyes, and may cause shortness of breath and coughing. OSHA standards for normal exposure should not exceed .1 part per million (ppm). Ozone air purifiers are ineffectual and may exceed safe levels of O_3. Check the ozone output for machines before purchasing or using one to make sure they are under the maximum exposure limits.

Here's a Tip

You can place 1 to 2 drops of an essential oil onto two hot stones and place them beside the client's ears while steaming. Before choosing oils, check for client product allergies and preferences.

Vacuum Machine

The **vacuum machine**, also known as **suction machine**, serves two main functions. One is to suction dirt and impurities from the skin. The other is to stimulate the dermal layer and lymphatic and blood circulation. This function is thought to help reduce the appearance of creases, such as laugh lines, and improve the overall appearance of the skin (Figure 17–8).

This machine can be used after desincrustation and before extractions. It can also be used in place of massage. It should not be used on couperose skin with distended or dilated capillaries or on open lesions. Glass and metal suction cups come in different sizes and shapes, depending on their use.

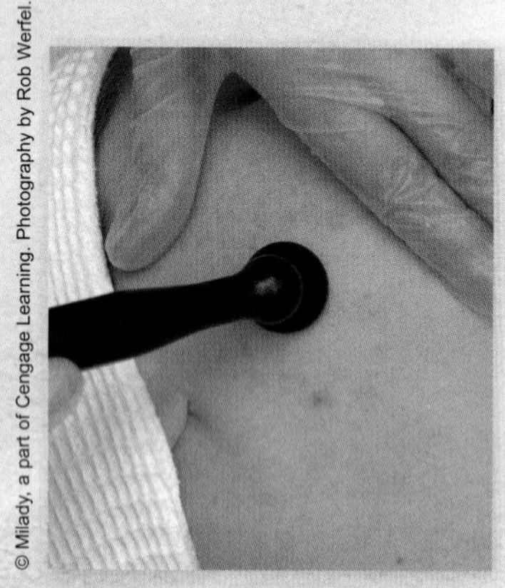

▲ Figure 17–8
The vacuum apparatus.

Mini Procedure

THE VACUUM PROCEDURE

Use the vacuum to remove impurities by following these guidelines.

1. Cleanse the face.
2. Attach the appropriate glass or metal tip to the hose after inserting a piece of cotton into the hand piece as a filter (without blocking the suction pressure).
3. Turn on the power and adjust the suction.
4. With the index finger, cover the finger hole on the hand piece when moving the suction across the skin starting at either the top or bottom of the face. Usually three to five passes on each area are enough.
5. Slowly move the device horizontally on moistened or damp skin. Keep moving across the face without stopping. Hold the skin taut with the other hand on each area of the face.
6. Switch to the small tip for the nose. Be sure to include the vertical creases near the nose.
7. To avoid pulling on the skin, lift the finger off the hole before lifting the device off the face.
8. Continue with the next step in the facial such as extractions or a mask.

CAUTION!

To avoid harming the client's skin, do not use suction on inflamed, rosacea, or couperose skin. Never suction liquids or oils into the suction device. Avoid using strong suction because it may cause tissue damage or bruising.

Vacuum Machine Maintenance

To clean and maintain the vacuum machine, follow these guidelines.

- Clean all glass devices with soap and water and soak them in a hospital-strength disinfectant.
- Follow manufacturer's directions to clean the hand pieces and hoses.
- Normally a filter is located at the end of the hose where the hose attaches to an orifice connected to the machine. The filter may have to be changed frequently, depending on use.
- Store the tips in a covered storage area to protect from breakage.

✓ LO8

Galvanic Current

Galvanic current is used to create two significant reactions in esthetics: chemical desincrustation (des-in-krus-TAY-shun) and ionic iontophoresis (eye-ahn-toh-foh-REE-sus). Desincrustation causes an alkaline reaction to soften the follicles for deep cleansing. Iontophoresis is used for introducing a water-soluble product into the skin (Figure 17–9).

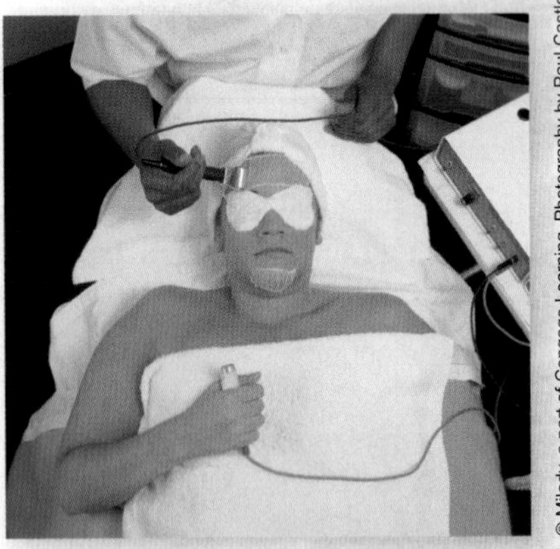

▲ Figure 17–9
The galvanic machine is used to create two significant reactions in esthetics: chemical (desincrustation) and ionic (iontophoresis).

The galvanic machine converts the alternating current received from an electrical outlet into a direct current. Electrons are then allowed to flow continuously in the same direction. This creates a relaxation response that can be regulated to target specific nerve endings in the epidermis. The machine can leave a metallic taste in the mouth, which is normal. To avoid harm to the skin, desincrustation should not be used on couperose skin, pustular acne, or inflamed areas. To avoid potential health complications, do not use galvanic current on clients who are pregnant or on those who have pacemakers, heart problems, high blood pressure, braces, or epilepsy.

Desincrustation

Estheticians use desincrustation, the infusion of a product that has a negative pH, to facilitate deep cleansing (Figure 17–10). During this process, galvanic current is used to create a chemical reaction that emulsifies or liquefies sebum and debris. This treatment is beneficial for oily or acne skin because it helps soften and relax the debris in the follicle before extractions.

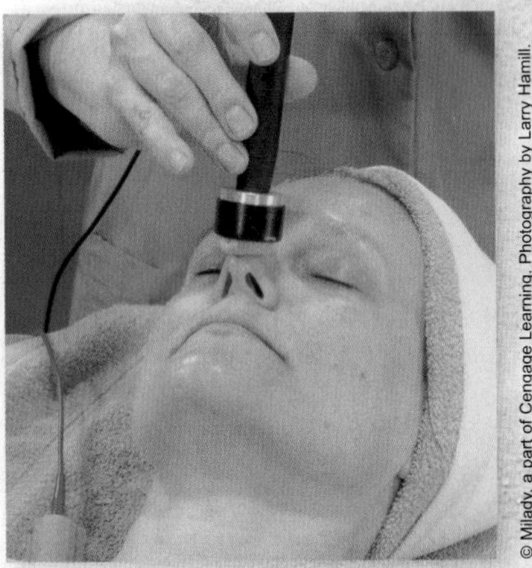

▲ Figure 17–10
The desincrustation process.

To perform desincrustation an alkaline-based, electronegative solution is placed onto the skin's surface. This product helps soften sebum and follicles for deep cleansing. The solution is formulated to remain on the surface of the skin rather than being absorbed. When the esthetician is conducting desincrustation, the client holds the positive electrode, the positive polarity. The esthetician uses the negative electrode, set on negative polarity, on the face. This creates a chemical reaction that transforms the sebum of the skin into soap—a process known as **saponification** (sah-pahn-ih-fih-KAY-shun). Soap is made from fat and lye (sodium hydroxide). When the electrical current interacts with the salts (sodium chloride) in the skin, it creates the chemical known as sodium hydroxide—or lye. This soapy substance helps dissolve excess oil, clogged follicles, comedones, and other debris on the skin, while softening it at the same time.

Various types of electrodes are available for the galvanic machine (Figure 17–11). The most common are the flat electrode and the roller. To make proper contact, each electrode must be covered with cotton, and the client must hold the electrode whose charge (either positive or negative) is the opposite of the electrode on the skin.

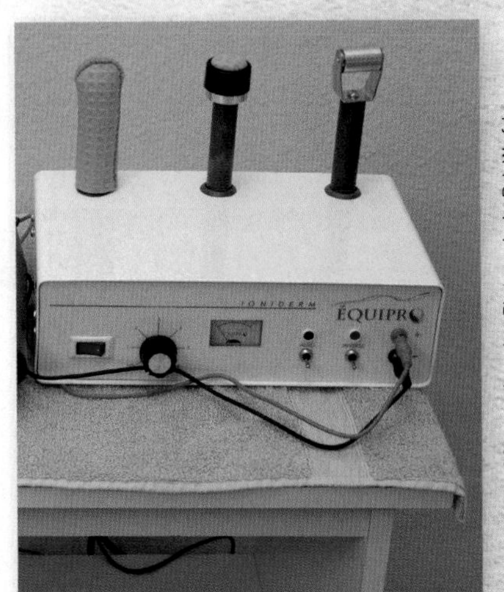

▲ Figure 17–11
A selection of electrodes for the galvanic machine.

CAUTION!

To avoid health complications or harm to the skin, do not use galvanic current on clients who have the following conditions, or contraindications:

- Metal implants or a pacemaker
- Braces
- Heart conditions
- Epilepsy
- Pregnancy
- High blood pressure, fever, or any infection
- Diminished nerve sensibility due to diseases such as diabetes
- Open or broken skin (wounds, new scars) or inflamed pustular acne
- Couperose skin or rosacea
- Chronic migraine headaches
- Apprehension about the use of electrical appliances

Baking soda in water can be used as a desincrustation fluid for anaphoresis.

Most water-based serums can be used as iontophoresis products for cataphoresis.

CAUTION!

Keep even contact with the skin once the galvanic machine is on. Electricity is flowing through the electrode and when it is lifted even slightly the client may feel a mild tingling or shock. To avoid this sensation, turn off the machine first and then remove the electrode from the skin.

Mini Procedure

DESINCRUSTATION

1. Gently cleanse the skin before treatment. Instruct the client to remove any jewelry and piercings, especially from the hand that will be used to hold the electrode.
2. Cover the entire positive electrode to be held by the client with a moistened sponge, or place a piece of dampened 4" × 4" (10 cm × 10 cm) cotton gauze around the electrode. Give this to the client to hold. This electrode is connected to the red wire (the positive wire).
3. Prepare the handheld flat electrode by placing a small, dampened sponge or round cotton pad over the electrode. Slide the ring back onto the electrode.
4. Apply product and gauze to the face as directed. Dip the electrode into the desincrustation solution. Apply the electrode to the client's forehead. Make sure the electrode is directly on the skin before turning on the galvanic current (Figure 17–12).
5. Turn the switch to negative and set at the appropriate level for the client.
6. Beginning on the forehead, gently rotate the electrode while gliding it over the client's forehead. Do not lift the electrode or break contact once the machine is on the skin, or it will be uncomfortable to the client. Keep the electrode as flat as possible and parallel to the skin's surface at all times.
7. Continue in the T-zone area down the nose and onto the chin area (or onto any area that is oily or needs desincrustation). Use desincrustation only in congested areas that need it, and avoid areas with dry skin conditions.
8. Keep the electrode constantly moving to avoid over-stimulating an area. Keep the skin moist and the pads wet. Add water to the pad or face if it gets too dry to glide over the skin.
9. When you are finished, turn off the machine first and then remove the electrode. Rinse the skin thoroughly with warm 4" × 4" (10 cm × 10 cm) cotton pads. Discard the pads.
10. Proceed with extractions or the next step in the treatment.

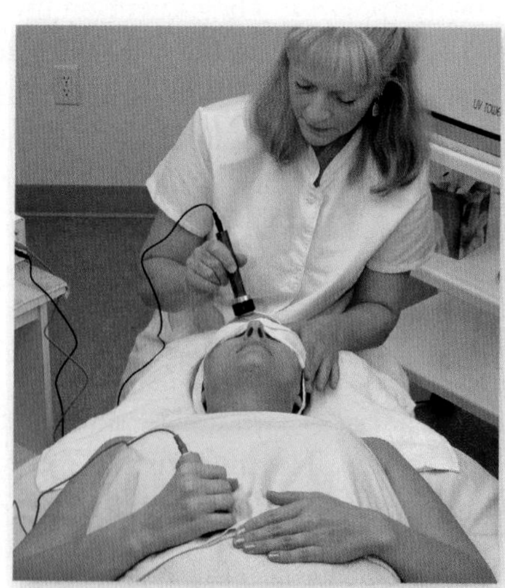

▶ Figure 17–12
Do not let the galvanic electrode break contact with the skin.

Iontophoresis

Iontophoresis is the process of using electric current to introduce water-soluble solutions into the skin. This process allows estheticians to transfer, or penetrate, ions of an applied solution into the deeper layers of the skin (Figure 17–13). Ions (EYE-ahns) are atoms or molecules that carry an electrical charge. Current flows through conductive solutions from both the positive and negative polarities. This process is known as ionization (eye-ahn-ih-ZAY-shun), the separating of a substance into ions.

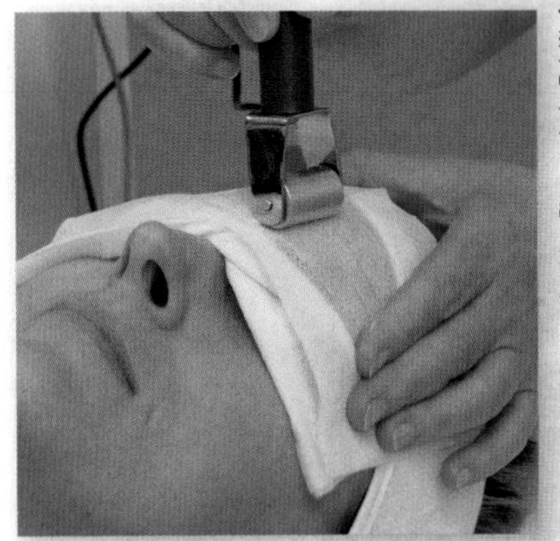
© Milady, a part of Cengage Learning. Photography by Rob Werfel.

▲ Figure 17–13
Iontophoresis can be relaxing.

Theoretically, iontophoresis is based on universal laws of attraction. For example, negative attracts positive, and vice versa. Similar to a magnetic response, iontophoresis creates an exchange of negative and positive ions or charges (Figure 17–14).

The process of ionic penetration takes two forms: cataphoresis (kat-uh-fuh-REE-sus), which refers to the infusion of a positive product; and anaphoresis (an-uh-for-EES-sus), which refers to the infusion of a negative product, such as a desincrustation fluid.

Some machines have a switch on the panel that controls the positive and negative modes so that you do not have to manually switch the red and black wires but instead move only the switch.

Polarity of Solutions

It is important to identify the polarity of an ampoule (AM-pyool) or solution. Products that have a slightly acidic pH are considered positive. Products with an alkaline (or base) pH are considered negative and are used for desincrustation. If the manufacturer indicates that the product is negative, the esthetician infuses the solution with the electrode set at negative and the esthetician holds the negative electrode. The client holds the positive electrode.

If the product were positive, the client and esthetician would use the opposite electrodes. The technician holds the positive and the client

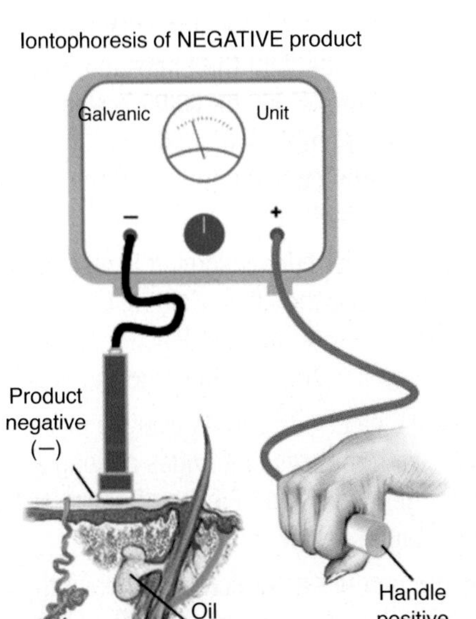

© Milady, a part of Cengage Learning.

◀ Figure 17–14
Iontophoresis infuses positive and negative products.

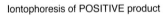

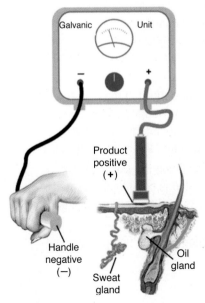

holds the negative. Some manufacturers may include ingredients in the same vial that are simultaneously positive and negative. In that case, the product should be ionized for 3 to 5 minutes on negative followed by 3 to 5 minutes on positive. If neither a negative nor positive polarity is indicated for an ampoule, as a general rule the esthetician should first use the negative and then the positive pole. This way you are stimulating and softening the skin first and preparing it for the treatment with anaphoresis, and then ending with the product penetration, skin tightening, and soothing with cataphoresis.

The molecular weight of a product is also a factor in permeability. Smaller molecules have greater penetration ability, while larger molecules cannot penetrate into the skin. Water-based products will also penetrate better than oil-based products. Several possible skin reactions can occur during ionization (Table 17–1).

▶ Table 17–1
Effects from the Galvanic Current: Iontophoresis.

EFFECTS FROM THE GALVANIC CURRENT: IONTOPHORESIS	
NEGATIVE POLE (CATHODE): ANAPHORESIS	POSITIVE POLE (ANODE): CATAPHORESIS
Negative Solutions:	***Positive Solutions:***
Causes an alkaline reaction	Causes an acidic reaction
Softens and relaxes tissue	Tightens the skin
Stimulates nerve endings	Calms or soothes nerve endings
Increases blood circulation	Decreases blood circulation

Mini Procedure

IONTOPHORESIS

The steps in iontophoresis are the same as those used for the desincrustation procedure.

1. Set the switch on the machine to the appropriate setting while the client holds an electrode with the opposite charge. When the client holds the handheld electrode, all the water molecules in the skin become charged with the polarity of the electrode. For iontophoresis to occur, the client must hold the polarity opposite to that of the product, otherwise there will be no attraction or reaction.
2. To ensure proper connections, it is also important to moisten the electrodes. Have the client hold an electrode that is wrapped with a moistened cover or sponge. Place a sponge or piece of cotton that has been dipped into the solution onto the electrode before applying to the skin.
3. No metallic electrode should ever be placed directly on the skin. Gels can be used with metallic electrodes as long as the skin is completely covered with the gel and gauze. Pieces of gauze can be moved around the face and held on each section as needed.
4. Apply the product as directed. You have the option of switching positive and negative poles when infusing solutions.

Galvanic Maintenance

Before attempting to clean the electrodes, always read and follow the manufacturer's directions for cleaning and disinfecting the equipment. Detach the electrode cord from the electrode. Remove any soiled sponge or cotton cover from the electrode and discard. Do not soak the electrode unless directed otherwise. Never place the metal electrode in an autoclave. The black plastic ring can be cleaned and then soaked in a disinfectant for the required time. In general, when cleaning rollers, detach the metal tip and then clean and soak it for 20 minutes in a disinfectant solution. Carefully spray and wipe the electrode attachment piece and machine with a disinfectant. ☑ LO9

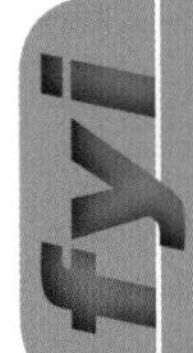

Galvanic treatments can actually be relaxing when using slow movements across the face.

Ionto Mask

The ionto mask works with galvanic current and can be used to facilitate either desincrustation (deep follicle cleansing) or ionization (penetration of product). Depending on treatment goals, different solutions can be used to target specific skin conditions. The face is first covered with moistened gauze. Water helps direct the current to the underlying tissue. The mask is then applied to the face and timed according to treatment parameters. Instead of the client holding an electrode, a wet pad is placed under the shoulder. The mask is then plugged into the source of the galvanic current. This mask is rarely used any more.

High-Frequency Machine

The **high-frequency machine** is an apparatus that utilizes an alternating or **sinusoidal current** (sy-nuh-SOYD-ul KUR-unt)— which is a smooth, repetitive alternating current and produces a heat effect. The high-frequency machine is a useful and versatile esthetic tool (**Figure 17–15a and b**).

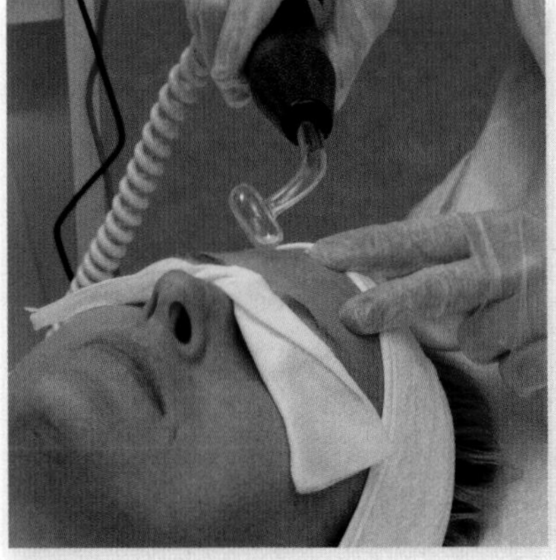

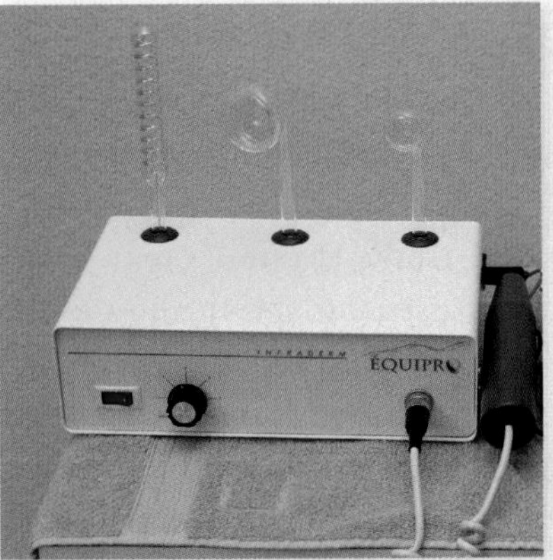

▲ Figure 17–15a and b
The high-frequency machine produces a heat effect that stimulates circulation and has an antiseptic effect on the skin.

It may be applied after extractions or used over a product. The machine also creates ozone and this has a germicidal action on the skin.

High frequency should not be used on couperose skin, inflamed areas, or on clients who are pregnant, epileptic, or have pacemakers or high blood pressure.

The high-frequency machine benefits the skin in the following ways:

- It has an antiseptic and healing effect on the skin.
- It stimulates circulation.
- It helps oxygenate the skin.
- It increases cell metabolism.
- It helps coagulate and heal any open lesion after extraction by sparking it with the mushroom electrode.
- It generates a warm feeling that has a relaxing effect on the skin.

The high-frequency machine creates noise and the ozone has a distinctive smell to it. Let clients know what to expect when using machines and that this is normal.

The high-frequency oscillating circuit passes through a device that allows for the selection of a *Tesla* pulse current. This current can produce a frequency of 60,000 to 200,000 hertz, depending on how it is regulated. The frequency indicates the repetition of the current per second. Because high-frequency current is capable of changing polarity thousands of times per second, it basically has no polarity and in effect does not produce chemical changes. This makes product penetration physically impossible. Product penetration is achieved instead by using the galvanic current.

The rapid oscillation created by the high-frequency machine vibrates water molecules in the skin. This can produce a mild to strong heat effect. It is important to note that esthetic high-frequency devices have a mild effect. An example of a stronger heat reaction is seen in **thermolysis** (thur-MAHL-uh-sus), which is used for electrolysis (permanent hair removal).

Electrodes

During the manufacturing process, most of the air is removed from high-frequency electrodes, creating a vacuum in the tube. The air is replaced, mainly with neon gas. However, some electrodes may also contain argon gas. As electricity passes through these gases, they emit visible shades of light. Neon gas produces a pink, orange, or red light. Argon or rarified gas produces blue or violet light. Sometimes these lights are inaccurately called *infrared* or *ultraviolet* because of their colors; however, there are no infrared or ultraviolet rays in high frequency.

Several types of direct or indirect electrodes are available with high frequency. Each of these electrodes has unique benefits and features that produce specific physiological reactions in esthetic treatments. If you use the high-frequency machine,

HIGH-FREQUENCY PROCEDURES AND ELECTRODES PRIOR TO USING HIGH FREQUENCY, APPLY DRY GAUZE TO THE SKIN AND HAVE CLIENTS REMOVE THEIR METAL JEWELRY.	
ELECTRODE	**GENERAL APPLICATION**
Small mushroom	(Pink/orange light) for sensitive skin or (violet light) for normal to oily skin. 1. Place electrode into the handheld device. Twist it gently into place. 2. Adjust the rheostat to the proper setting if the machine is not automatic. 3. Place an index finger on the glass electrode to ground it until it touches the skin, then remove. 4. Apply the electrode directly onto dry skin beginning at the forehead. Glide the electrode over the skin in circular movements (across the forehead area) and then to the nose, cheeks, and chin areas. Sometimes when skin is very clean, the electrode drags. In this case, place gauze between the skin and the electrode. 5. To remove from the skin, place an index finger on the electrode to ground it and then remove it. Turn the power switch off.
Large mushroom	(Violet light) normal to oily or (pink/orange) sensitive. 1. The large mushroom is used in the same way as the small mushroom. 2. Another effective way to use this apparatus is to open a piece of cotton gauze and glide the mushroom electrode over the gauze. This produces a small spray of sparks onto the skin. This treatment is ideal for acne or problematic skin. 3. Facial finish: High frequency may be used at the end of a treatment over cream. Place cotton gauze between the cream and the electrode. Glide in circular motions over the entire area.
Indirect electrode (spiral)	Used indirectly to stimulate the skin during massage. This treatment is ideal for sallow and aging skin. 1. Apply cream to the client's face. 2. Give the wire glass electrode to the client, who then holds it with both hands. 3. The operator places the fingers of one hand to the forehead. 4. With the opposite hand, turn the high frequency on and move to a low setting. 5. Using both hands, perform a piano finger motion, gently tapping the skin. Move around in a systematic manner over the entire face. 6. To discontinue, remove one hand from the skin and turn the power switch off. 7. Do not lose contact with the skin during this procedure in order to keep the current flowing.
Sparking (glass tip)	A glass tip electrode is used to direct sparking to a specific area such as an acne lesion. It helps disinfect and heal the lesion. Sparking is visible and creates an interesting zapping noise. 1. Place the electrode into the handheld device. 2. Place the glass electrode over the lesion area, removing the finger so that the area is sparked for a few seconds. Touch the electrode to the blemish for a few seconds and remove. Repeat this a few times. 3. Remove the electrode from the skin by placing the finger once more on the glass. Turn the power switch off.
Comb electrode (rake)	To apply, follow the directions for the mushroom electrode. It may also be used in a scalp treatment.

▲ Table 17–2 **High-Frequency Procedures and Electrodes.**

CAUTION!

High frequency should not be used on clients with the following conditions:

- Couperose skin
- Inflamed areas
- Pacemakers
- Heart problems
- High blood pressure
- Braces
- Epilepsy
- Clients who are pregnant

Be sure to know all the contraindications of using a machine before implementing it in treatments. To avoid being burned, the client should avoid contact with metal during electrical machine treatments. Clients should remove all jewelry and piercings prior to the treatment.

▲ Figure 17–16
The spray machine.

you will need to be trained in the procedure and on how to use the different electrodes (Table 17–2 on page 465).

High-Frequency Maintenance

Follow these maintenance guidelines for the high-frequency machine.

- After each use, clean the glass electrode by wiping it with a solution of soap and water. Do not use alcohol on electrodes.
- Do not immerse the electrode directly in water. Place only the glass end (not the metal) into a disinfectant solution for 20 minutes.
- Do not place electrodes in an ultraviolet machine or in an autoclave.
- Rinse the electrodes. Do not get the metal end wet. Dry with a clean towel and store in a covered container.
- Unless they break or are damaged, most electrodes do not need replacing, but keep in mind that the electrodes are very fragile. Take extra care to wrap them in a soft material and then store them in a drawer where they will not be knocked around or damaged. Some of the newer machines offer inserts for storing the electrodes right on the machine. Be sure to cover the electrodes so they remain clean and undamaged.
- The high-frequency coil should be replaced after a few years of use if it is losing power. Check with the manufacturer for additional service requirements. ✓ LO10

Spray Machines

Spray mists are beneficial in calming and hydrating the skin (Figure 17–16). The **spray machine** is part of the vacuum machine and is attached via a hose that is connected to a small plastic bottle with a spray nozzle. This bottle can be filled with a freshener solution or toner (1 part toner; 2 parts distilled water) to gently mist the client's face after cleansing or another treatment step, such as the massage.

Spray Machine Maintenance

Here are some general guidelines for spray machine maintenance.

- Follow the cleaning directions supplied by the manufacturer.
- Empty the bottle of fluid regularly to keep it fresh.
- Flush with distilled water regularly.
- Mineral buildup in the nozzle of the sprayer should be cleaned monthly or more often. ✓ LO11

Mini Procedure

THE SPRAY PROCEDURE

To mist the skin, use the following steps.

1. Place a towel under the client's chin to stop the mist from dripping down the neck. Remind the client to keep the eyes and mouth closed during the misting.
2. Turn on the power and adjust the velocity of the spray.
3. Hold the spray approximately 12 to 15 inches (30 to 37.5 centimeters) away from the face and mist for approximately 5 to 20 seconds. If necessary, pause and make sure the client can take a breath between the misting.
4. Turn off the power.
5. Gently pat or wipe off the product remaining on the skin with esthetic wipes/pads.

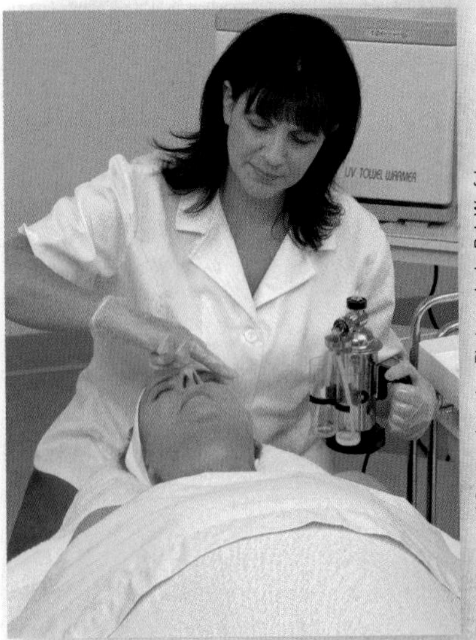

▲ Figure 17–17
The Lucas Sprayer.

The Lucas Sprayer

The **Lucas Sprayer** was invented by Dr. Lucas Championniere (1843–1913). It is the most unique of all atomizers and sprays. The Lucas Sprayer is used to apply a very fine mist of plant extracts, herb teas, fresheners, or astringents (Figure 17–17). The mist is excellent for treating dehydrated, mature, and couperose skins. The mist can be used warm to increase the blood flow to the skin's surface, or it can be used cool to calm couperose skin. While not common, it is still in use today.

CAUTION!

To avoid burning the client's skin, never heat paraffin in anything other than an approved paraffin heater.

Paraffin Wax Heater

The paraffin wax heater is used to create a warm paraffin mask for hydrating dry skin (Figure 17–18). This device allows the esthetician to provide a treatment that offers quick results, but it lasts only for a limited period of time. Heated paraffin is applied to the face, creating an occlusive mask to hold in body heat and promote penetration of underlying products. The result is a hydrating and relaxing treatment that gives clients a glowing complexion. This is popular with women who want to look their best instantly, especially for special occasions. The paraffin mask procedure is in Chapter 15, Facial Treatments.

Paraffin wax heaters stay warm at a safe, low level of heat. They must be replenished as you discard the used wax. These heaters

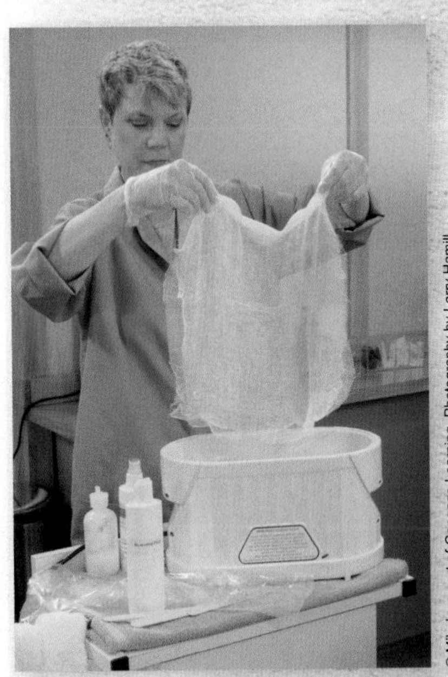

▲ Figure 17–18
The paraffin wax treatment.

tend to take a long time to heat up in the morning. Always use a professional wax bath machine that emits low heat. A substitute heater, such as an electric cooking pot, regulates heat differently and is not recommended.

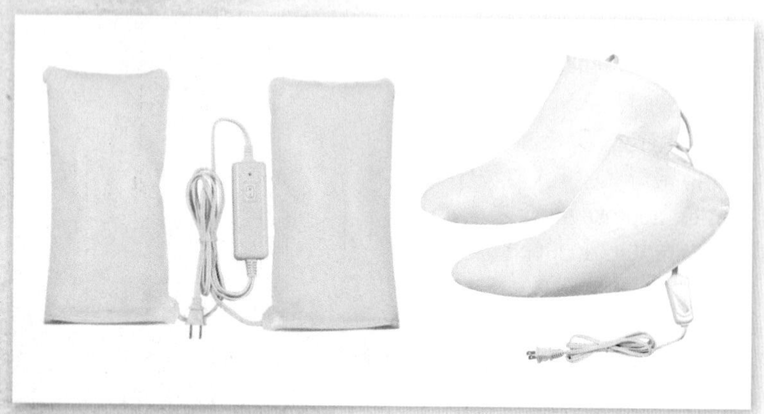

Courtesy of Equipro.

▲ Figure 17–19
Electric mitts and boots.

Electric Mitts and Boots

Boots and mitts heat the hands and feet to increase circulation and to promote overall relaxation (**Figure 17–19**). Often promoted as an add-on to a service, boots and mitts actually perform an important function. The heat helps lotion penetrate, and it soothes aching feet and hands. Paraffin wax is also used over lotion to warm and moisturize the skin.

To use these products, put lotion on the hands and/or feet and cover with plastic single-use liners before inserting into the warmers. Warm the mitts and/or boots for approximately 10 minutes. Make sure the warmers do not get too hot. If the client feels sweaty, then the lotion cannot penetrate. To clean the electric mitts and boots, wipe them with a disinfectant after each use.

Here's a Tip

It may be more affordable to purchase individual machines rather than the all-in-one machines that have the different modalities together on one unit. If anything needs to be repaired, you do not have to ship—or be left without—all of your machines.

Purchasing Equipment

Do your research before purchasing equipment. Regulations define what devices can be used within an esthetician's scope of practice. Another purchasing consideration is insurance coverage for the devices. Make sure the manufacturer claims are accurate and there is clinical evidence to support the claims. It is advisable to go slowly when considering purchasing expensive machines. Warranties and training provided from the manufacturer and distributor are two important considerations when purchasing equipment. Education and training are required for many high-tech machines.

Advances in science and technology have generated many new high-performance tools that enhance the esthetician's work. Estheticians must continue their education to keep abreast of the latest developments in therapeutic skin care. In this chapter, we have presented an overview of specialized tools and equipment designed to help the esthetician obtain the best results possible in skin care treatments. While some machines are not used on a regular basis, it is good to be familiar with them. See Chapter 19, Advanced Topics and Treatments, for additional information on the more advanced equipment.

Study and review the suggested guidelines for operating machinery, and practice your skills until you are comfortable working with equipment. Always be conscientious about safety issues and contraindications in using machines. Clients want instant results, so make sure you can deliver what you promise. Invest in high-quality machines and your investment will increase your credibility and revenue as an esthetician. What machines would you like to incorporate into your services? High-tech equipment just may be the wave of the future. ✓ LO12

ACTIVITY

Choose two machines that interest you. Think about what would be important in purchasing these machines. What should you look for in purchasing a machine? Compare at least three different manufacturers, the selling points of each machine, the prices, and the quality. Which machines would you purchase? Why?

Web Resources

www.epa.gov

www.nlm.nih.gov/medlineplus

www.osha.gov

www.skininc.com

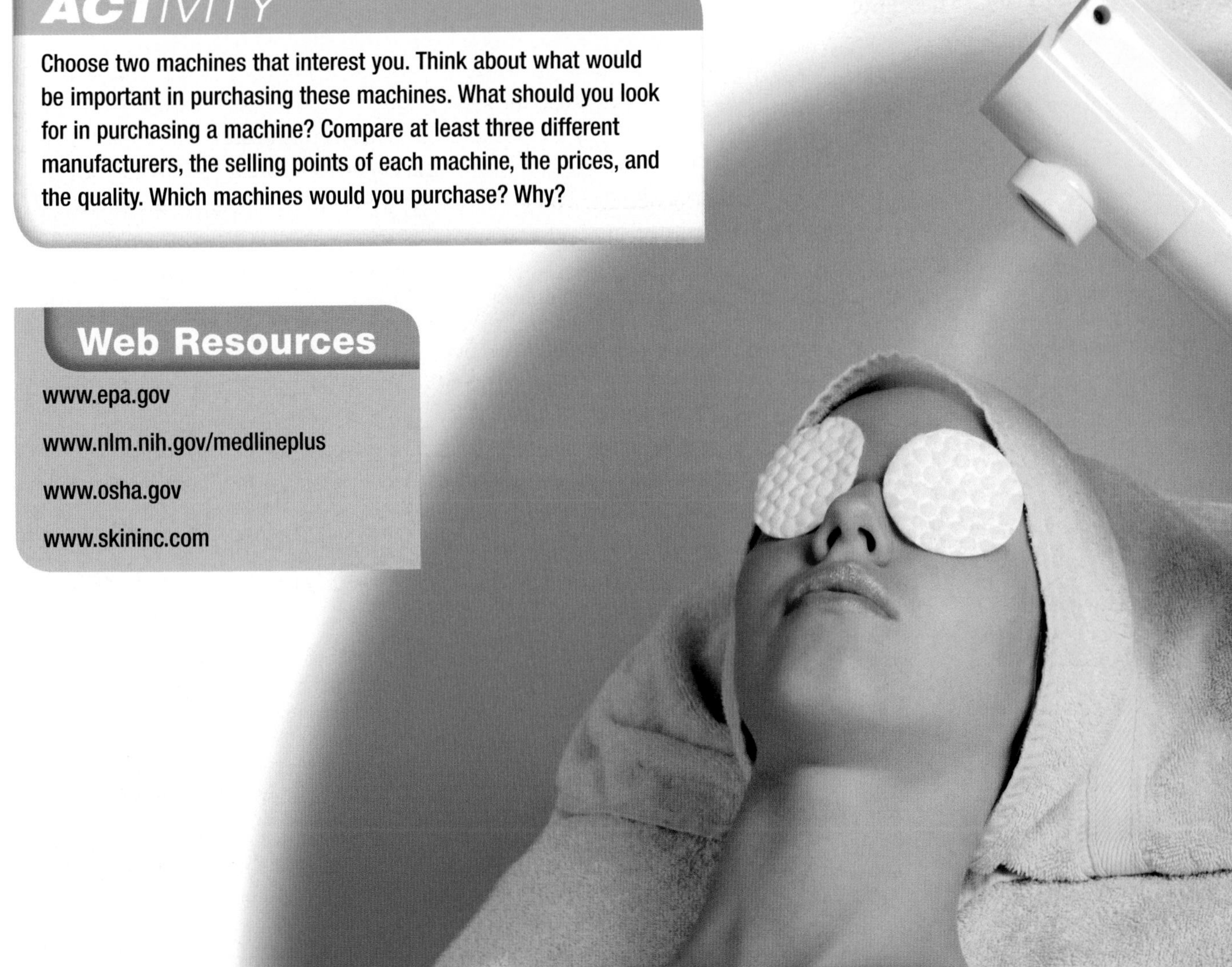

Review Questions

1. What are five of the contraindications for electrotherapy?
2. What skin conditions does a Wood's Lamp reveal?
3. What is the purpose of a brush machine?
4. What are the benefits of using a steamer?
5. What are the benefits of the vacuum device?
6. List and define the two main reactions of the galvanic current.
7. What are the contraindications for using a galvanic machine?
8. What are the effects on the skin from anaphoresis?
9. How does the negative pole of the galvanic current affect the skin?
10. Define cataphoresis.
11. How does the positive pole of the galvanic current affect the skin?
12. What is high frequency used for?
13. What are the benefits of the spray machine?
14. What are the benefits of electric mitts and boots?

Glossary

high-frequency machine	Apparatus that utilizes alternating, or sinusoidal, current to produce a mild to strong heat effect; sometimes called *Tesla high-frequency* or *violet ray*.
Lucas Sprayer	Atomizer designed to apply plant extracts and other ingredients to the skin.
rotary brush	Machine used to lightly exfoliate and stimulate the skin; also helps soften excess oil, dirt, and cell buildup.
saponification	Chemical reaction during desincrustation where the current transforms the sebum into soap.
sinusoidal current	A smooth, repetitive alternating current; the most commonly used alternating current waveform, used in the high frequency machine and can produce heat.
spray machine	Spray misting device.
thermolysis	Heat effect; used for permanent hair removal.
vacuum machine	Also known as *suction machine*; device that vacuums/suctions the skin to remove impurities and stimulate circulation.
Wood's Lamp	Filtered black light that is used to illuminate skin disorders, fungi, bacterial disorders, and pigmentation.

CHAPTER 18

Hair Removal

Chapter Outline

Learning Objectives

After completing this chapter, you will be able to:

- ✓ LO1 Understand the morphology of hair.
- ✓ LO2 Explain the hair growth cycle.
- ✓ LO3 Describe the methods of permanent and temporary hair removal.
- ✓ LO4 Identify different hair removal equipment, tools, and accessories.
- ✓ LO5 Name the contraindications for hair removal.
- ✓ LO6 Provide a thorough client consultation before hair removal.
- ✓ LO7 Safely perform basic face and body waxing techniques.

Key Terms

Page number indicates where in the chapter the term is used.

anagen
pg. 477

catagen
pg. 477

depilation
pg. 484

depilatory
pg. 484

electrolysis
pg. 481

epilation
pg. 484

hair bulb
pg. 476

hair follicle
pg. 475

hair papilla
pg. 477

hair root
pg. 475

hair shaft
pg. 475

hirsutism
pg. 480

hypertrichosis
pg. 480

lanugo
pg. 474

laser hair removal
pg. 482

photoepilation
pg. 482

pilosebaceous unit
pg 476

sugaring
pg. 486

telogen
pg. 478

threading (banding)
pg. 485

trichology
pg. 474

vellus hair
pg. 474

Throughout history, hair has been used for physical adornment and to enhance beauty. Different cultures have different views as to what is beautiful and attractive. Both social and personal preferences influence hair removal choices. Most women want smooth and hair-free bodies. Hair removal for cosmetic reasons has become very popular. Consumers in the U.S. spend millions of dollars per year on hair removal products and services.

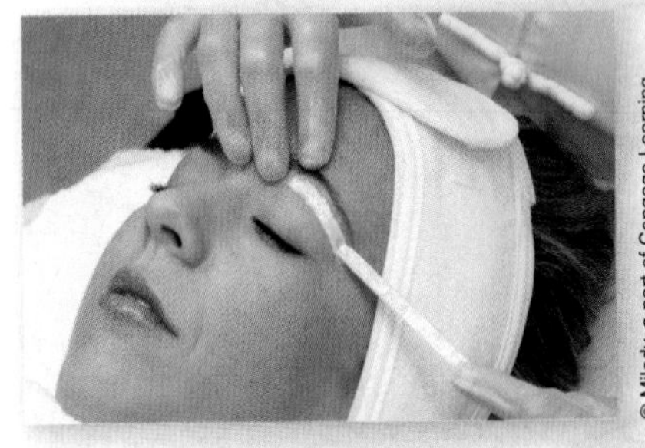

▲ Figure 18–1
Hair removal is a large part of an esthetician's business.

Throughout the ages, unwanted hair has been removed by a variety of methods. Excavations of Egyptian tombs indicate that abrasive materials such as pumice stones were used to rub away hair. Ancient Greek and Roman women were known to remove their body hair by similar methods. Native Americans may have used sharpened stones and seashells to rub off and pluck out hair. The ancient Turks used a chemical method—a combination of yellow sulfide made of arsenic, quicklime, and rose water—as a crude hair removal agent. Today, of course, the methods are more benign.

Excessive or unwanted hair is a common problem that affects both men and women. Fortunately, a variety of hair removal methods are available, ranging from procedures such as shaving and tweezing to more advanced techniques that require special training. Face and body hair removal has become increasingly popular as evolving technology makes it easier to perform with more effective results.

Women comprise the vast majority of hair removal clients. Most often, they want hair removed from the eyebrows, upper lip, underarms, bikini line, and legs. Hair removal for men is also on the rise. Men may choose to have hair removed from their back and chest. If they compete in sports like bicycling and swimming, they may want hair removed from their legs and arms to facilitate faster competition times. Hair removal makes up a large part of a salon's business (**Figure 18–1**). Waxing is the most common method of hair removal in salons. In some cases, up to 50 percent of the salon services involve hair removal.

Understanding the benefits, risks, and how to perform various techniques is vital to an esthetician's success in this potentially profitable market. In this chapter, you will learn hair removal procedures, what methods are used, and what is involved in room preparation. Safety, decontamination procedures, and Universal Precautions are an important part of hair removal procedures. Conducting services in a safe environment and taking measures to prevent the spread of infectious and contagious diseases are always primary concerns. Thorough client consultations and a careful review of hair removal contraindications are necessary before providing any service.

Why Study Hair Removal?

Estheticians should study and have a thorough understanding of hair removal because this is an essential service that estheticians must be able to perform effectively and safely.

- Learning how to safely perform face and body waxing techniques is vital to an esthetician's success as hair removal makes up a large part of a salon's business.
- Conducting services in a safe environment and taking measures to prevent the spread of infectious and contagious diseases protects clients and technicians.
- Providing thorough client consultations and reviewing hair removal contraindications is necessary before providing any hair removal service.
- Removing unwanted hair is a primary concern for many clients, and being able to advise them on the various types of hair removal services will enhance your professionalism.

Morphology of the Hair

Trichology (tri-KAHL-uh-jee) is the scientific study of hair and its diseases. *Trichos* is the Greek word for "hair." How much hair you have is predetermined by genetics. Hair growth is also affected by age and hormones. Not all follicles contain hair. Some are singular sebaceous follicles that connect directly to the surface of the skin. No hair grows on the palms of the hands, the soles of the feet, the lips, or the eyelids.

Hair formation actually begins before birth. The hair on a fetus is extremely soft and downy, known as **lanugo** (luh-NOO-goh) hair. The lanugo hair is lost and then replaced with either vellus or terminal hairs (stronger, pigmented hair) after birth. The shape, size, and normal function of the hair follicle is genetically determined, as is secretion activity and the depth of the hair shaft.

Vellus hair: Very fine, soft hair is referred to as **vellus hair** (VEL-lus) or *lanugo hair*. It is found in areas that are not covered by the larger, coarse terminal hairs. For example, vellus hair usually grows on women's cheeks (a.k.a. peach fuzz). Removing vellus hair can result in the follicles producing new terminal hairs, so it is not recommended to tweeze, shave, or wax these fine hairs.

Terminal hair: Terminal hair is the longer, courser hair found on the head, brows, lashes, genitals, arms, and legs. With hormone changes during puberty, follicles are naturally regulated to switch from producing vellus hairs to producing terminal hairs in these areas.

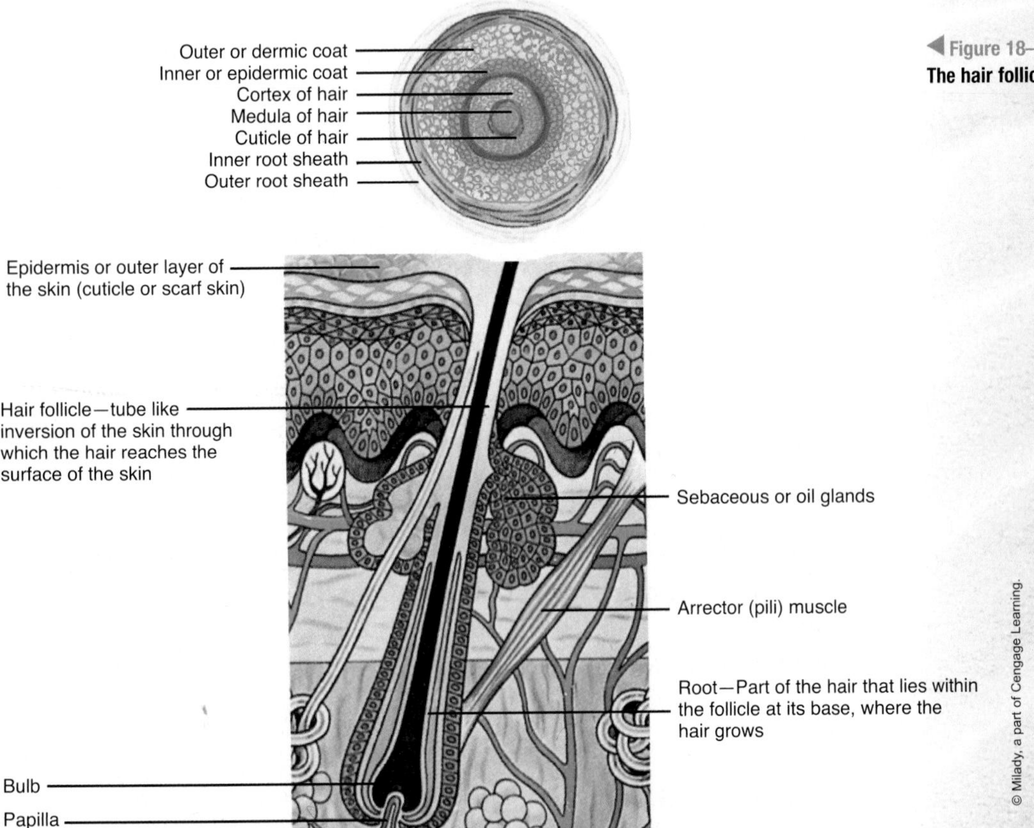

▲ Figure 18–2
The hair follicle and appendages.

The Hair Follicle

Hair is made from a hard protein called *keratin*, which is produced from the hair follicle. A **hair follicle** is a mass of epidermal cells forming a small tube, or canal (Figure 18–2). Follicles extend deep into the dermis.

The face contains many follicles per square inch (2.5 square centimeters). Only some of these follicles have hair. It is estimated that we have millions of hair follicles covering our bodies. It is interesting to note that as our bodies grow the follicle density we are born with does not change, but as we age it decreases because there is more surface area to cover once we grow larger and become adults. Hair follicles are slanted. Sometimes more than one hair will grow from a single follicle, and hair can grow in many different directions in one area (for example, under the arm). This hair growth pattern is important to know when providing hair removal services.

Hair Components

A mature strand of hair is divided into two parts: the hair root and the hair shaft.

The root: The **hair root** anchors hair to the skin cells and is part of the hair located at the bottom of the follicle below the surface of the skin.

The shaft: The **hair shaft** is defined as the part of the hair located above the surface of the skin. The shaft actually starts forming about halfway up to the surface near the sebaceous gland in the hair follicle. As the cell division within the hair matrix continues, hair grows and gets longer.

Keratinization is complete by the time these cells approach the skin's surface and the hair shaft starts. This is similar to skin-cell division and migration. Basal cells in the hair matrix divide and form the three main layers of the hair shaft: the cuticle, cortex, and medulla. The cuticle is the outermost layer, the cortex is the middle, and the medulla is the center or innermost layer of the hair shaft. The two outer layers of the shaft are hard keratin and the inner layer is soft keratin.

The Pilosebaceous Unit

The **pilosebaceous unit** contains the hair follicle and its appendages. The main structures of the hair unit (the area below the skin's surface) consist of the follicle, hair root, hair bulb, hair papilla, and the attached arrector pili muscle and sebaceous glands.

The main structures in the hair follicle are the root, bulb, and papilla. The arrector pili muscle and the sebaceous glands are appendages attached to the follicles (**Figure 18–3**). The follicle is lined with epidermal tissue. These epidermal cells produce the follicle and hair matrix. The matrix is where cell mitosis (division) happens.

The **hair bulb** is a thick, club-shaped structure made from epithelial cells that surround the papilla. This forms the lower part of the hair root. This is where hair grows from cell division. The lower part of the bulb fits over and covers the papilla. The hair bulb contains the dividing cells of the hair matrix that produces the hair and both the external root sheath (epidermal tissue) and internal root sheath lining the follicle. The external root sheath is the made of horny epidermal tissue. The

▼ Figure 18–3
Hair morphology.

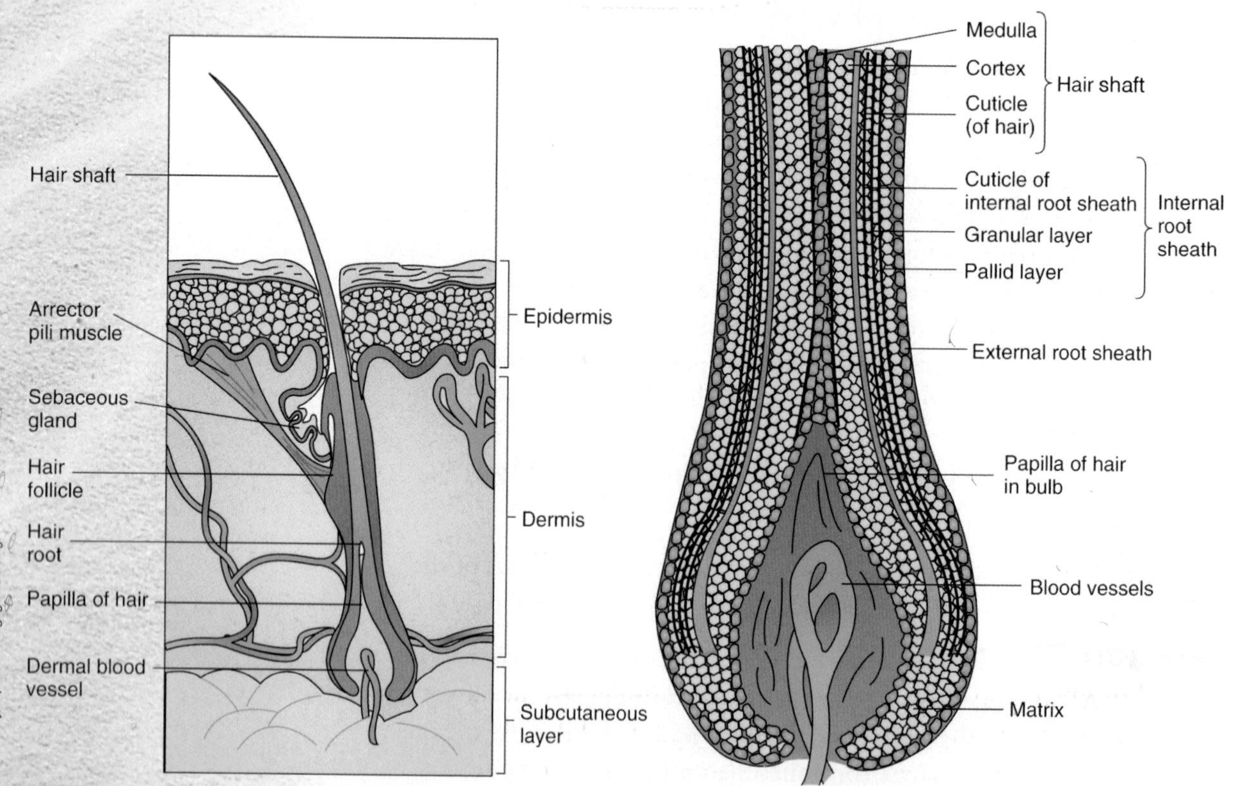

internal sheath is the innermost layer of the follicle closest to the hair. The internal sheath is the thick layer of cells you see attached to the base of a hair when epilating it.

The **hair papilla** (plural: papillae), a cone-shaped elevation at the base of the follicle, fits into the bulb. This is the dermal papilla, the connective tissue that contains the capillaries and nerves. Hair papillae are necessary for hair growth and nourishment of the follicle. Vitamins, minerals, and nutrients are needed for strong, healthy hair. The blood vessels bring nutrients to the base of the bulb, causing it to grow and form new hair. Sensory nerves surround the base of the follicle.

The arrector pili muscle (ur-REK-tohr PY-li) attaches to the base of the hair follicle. This muscle extends from the papillary layer of the dermis and attaches to the follicle.

When cold or other stimuli cause the muscle to contract, it pulls on the follicle and forces the hair to stand erect. The hair stands straight up, causing goose bumps. This reaction is also thought to keep skin warmer by creating an air pocket under the upright hairs. The muscle contraction also helps disperse the protective lipids from the sebaceous gland to the skin and hair. Sebaceous glands attached to the follicle are responsible for lubricating the skin and hair. Moderate amounts of sebaceous oil are necessary for healthy skin and hair. ☑ L01

Did You Know?

Pilus [PY-lus] means hair; *pili* [PY-lie] is the plural.

FOCUS ON

Hair

The hair unit consists of the follicle which includes the root, bulb, papilla, and the appendages: the arrector pili muscle and sebaceous gland. The hair shaft consists of the cuticle, cortex, and medulla.

Hair Growth Cycle

Hair growth is a result of the activity of cells found in the basal layer. These cells are found within the hair bulb. Hair growth occurs in three stages: anagen, catagen, and telogen (**Figure 18–4**, page 478). Use the acronym ACT to remember the growth stage sequence.

Did You Know?

The average hair growth on the scalp is one-half inch (1.25 cm) per month.

Anagen Phase

Anagen (AN-uh-jen) is the growth stage during which new hair is produced. New keratinized cells are manufactured in the hair follicle during the anagen stage. Activity is greater in the hair bulb, which pushes down into the dermis and swells with cell mitosis in the matrix. Stem cells at the junction between the arrector pili muscle and the follicle grow downward and stimulate cell mitosis in the matrix. New cells form hair and root sheaths while the older part of the hair is pushed upward. Once hair has reached its full length, it can remain there for weeks or years, depending on its location on the body. Hair on the scalp remains for years. Other areas have a growth cycle in weeks. The length of the anagen phase determines the length of the hair.

Catagen Phase

Catagen (KAT-uh-jen) is the transition stage of hair growth. In the catagen stage, mitosis ceases. The hair grows upward and detaches

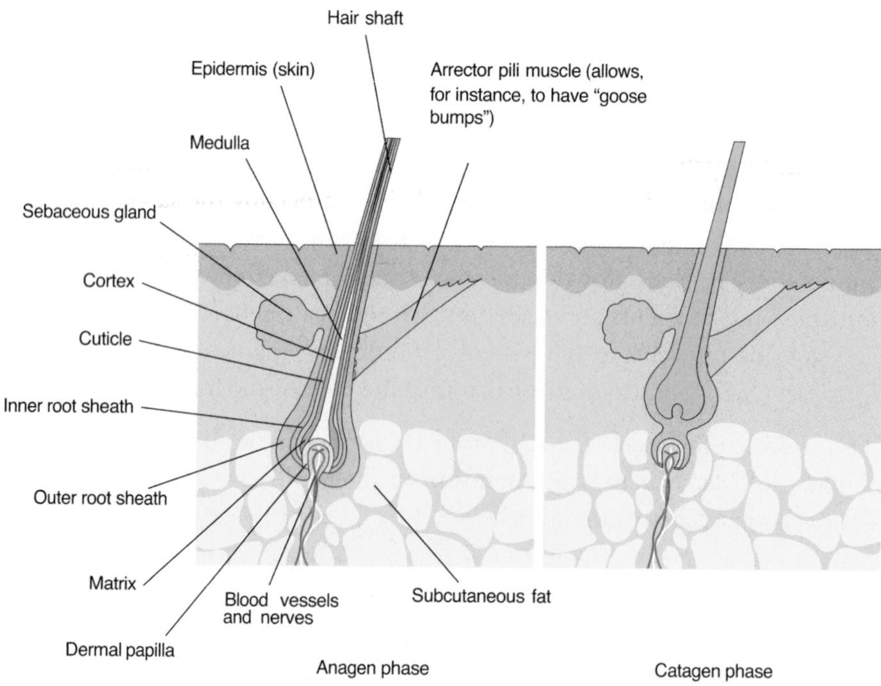

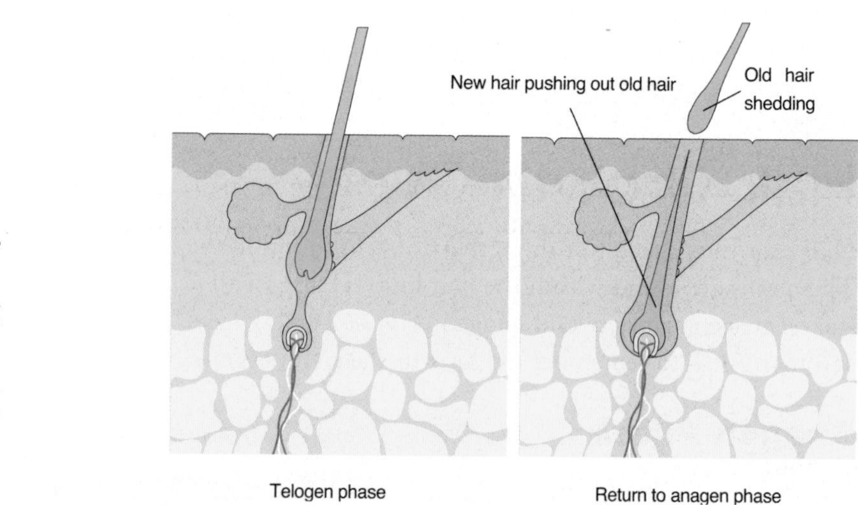

▲ **Figure 18–4**
Hair growth encompasses three stages: anagen, catagen, and telogen.

itself from the dermal papilla. The follicle degenerates and collapses as epidermal tissue retracts upward. Hair loses its inner root sheath and becomes dryer. The mature hair is now referred to as a *club hair* (the base looks like a club). This is the shortest part of the hair growth cycle.

Telogen Phase

Telogen (TEL-uh-jen) is the final, or resting, stage of hair growth. During the telogen stage, the club hair moves up the follicle and is ready to shed. The hair is at its full size and is erect in the follicle. It shows above the skin's surface. The hair bulb is not active, and the hair is released and is only attached by epidermal cells. Hair may sit in the follicle or fall out.

Latent Phase

After the telogen stage, the follicle is empty and dormant. The old hair sheds and the cycle then begins again. The follicle can be void of hair in the telogen stage until it cycles back into the anagen stage. If the hair does not fall out and the anagen stage begins again, two hairs can occupy the same follicle.

It is important to understand the three stages of hair growth. Two hairs can be growing next to each other and be at different stages of growth. It takes 4 to 16 weeks for the hair to grow from the papilla to the surface of the skin, depending in part on the area of the body. Hair growth is affected by many factors including age, genetics, hormones, and a person's health. When offering services, the practitioner takes into consideration these stages and schedules appointments according to these cycles. Repeat visits are normally necessary. Remind clients that not all hair grows at the same rate and that hairs are at different growth stages in the follicle. Hairs removed in the anagen stage, while the hair bulb is more "active," will be more effective for long-term hair reduction. ☑ L02

Characteristics and Differences in Hair Growth

Hair protects the body from environmental elements and ultraviolet rays. It guards the nose, ears, and reproductive areas with fine hairs to filter out dust and other particles. Hair is a conduit of sensation for the skin and acts as a wick in the follicle, allowing for sebum to move up and out onto the skin's surface. Everyone has millions of hair follicles on their body. One-fifth of the hair follicles on the body are on the scalp. Some estimate that there are 500,000 hairs on the head, which helps protect the scalp. Hair on the scalp grows an average of .33 millimeters (1/60 of an inch) per day.

As cultures moved from region to region, individuals acquired mixed traits of hair color and thickness (**Figure 18–5**). In northern regions of the world, fine hair and lighter skin tones are common. Blond hair is generally finer and easier to remove. Redheads can have coarse hair that can be more difficult to remove—these individuals generally have fair skin that tends to be sensitive, a very important point to remember when performing hair removal on them.

▲ Figure 18–5
Genetic differences in hair growth and coloring.

In warmer areas closer to the equator, the skin and hair are normally thicker and darker. These characteristics help protect the body from strong ultraviolet rays. Central and South American people, as well as those from Mediterranean regions and the Middle East, tend to have darker and more noticeable hair as it is coarser and thicker in diameter. Individuals from Western Europe (France, Spain, and Portugal) generally have dark hair, with average thickness. With thicker hair, the root is quite deep in the follicle, and thus very difficult to remove. With repeated removal, hair regrowth tends to become thinner and easier to remove.

Individuals with olive and darker skin tones can have major pigmentation problems if hair removal is not performed carefully. Those originating from Africa and Australia tend to have black, coarse, curly hair which has a tendency to become ingrown. The method of hair removal for these individuals needs to be chosen carefully. Native Americans and many Asians have thinner facial hair, but the roots tend to be deep.

Aging creates changes in the hair. Gray hair is a result of physiological and hormonal changes, causing it to be coarse with a deep root system. Before hair grays, it is easier to remove. With the changes that take place during the aging process, the hair root system increases on the face, making hair removal difficult. This explains the increase in coarse hairs on women's chins and lips. For many people, however, hair on other areas of the body and scalp gets thinner as we age.

Indicator of Health

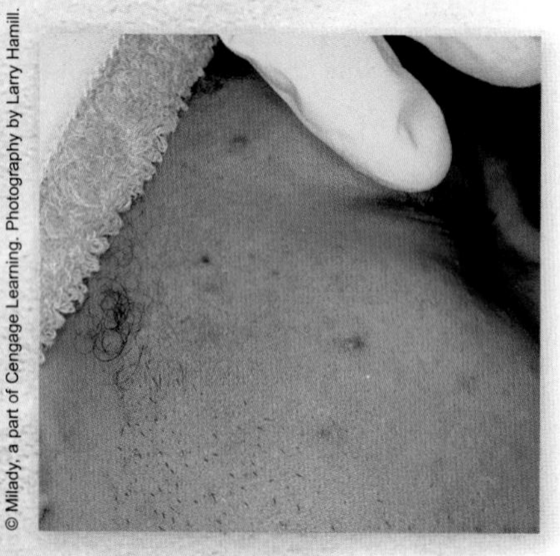

▲ **Figure 18–6**
Hirsutism.

Hair and skin are good barometers of an individual's state of health. Dull, lifeless hair and sallow, listless skin tone may signal a health warning. Strong, healthy hair and good skin tone are signs of good health. Hair also responds to the outside elements. For instance, hair grows faster in a warm climate. Excessive cold can dry the hair and reduce its luster. The rate of oil secretions from the follicle determines whether the skin is oily or dry. Excessive heat or damaging products such as haircolor will dry the hair and scalp. Medical conditions, disease, drug use, and the aging process affect the hair's growth and overall appearance.

Excessive Hair Growth

Two medical terms are applied to excessive hair growth. The first is **hirsutism** (HUR-suh-tiz-um), which is excessive hair growth on the face, arms, and legs, especially in women (**Figure 18–6**). The second is **hypertrichosis** (hy-pur-trih-KOH-sis), an excessive growth of hair. It is characterized by the growth of terminal hair in areas of the body that normally grow only vellus hair. The amount of hair an individual has differs from person to person. What would be normal hair growth in one person might be extreme in another. Excessive abnormal hair growth on a female body suggests an imbalance of hormones.

Hirsutism can be caused by various factors. A normal pregnancy increases adrenocortical activity, which may cause moderate hirsutism. Vitamin deficiency, certain diseases, particular drugs, and emotional shock or stress can result in glandular disturbances that stimulate excessive hair growth.

Excessive hair growth on a female face or body may be attributed to hormonal imbalances and excessive androgen production secreted from the ovaries or adrenal glands. One of the more notable and prevalent causes of this is Polycystic Ovarian Syndrome (PCOS). Menopause may also cause excess facial hair. The "menopause mustache," as it is often called, is a sign of menopause. These changes may dissipate with time. Other excessive androgen production conditions that affect hair growth are adrenogenital syndrome, Achard–Theirs syndrome, and Cushings syndrome. Client health and medical conditions are potential contraindications for hair removal.

Methods of Hair Removal

Methods of hair removal fall into two general categories: temporary and permanent. Temporary hair removal involves repeat treatments as hair grows. With permanent hair removal, the papilla is destroyed, making regrowth impossible. Salon techniques are generally limited to temporary methods such as waxing.

Permanent Hair Removal

Electrolysis

Electrolysis (ee-lek-TRAHL-ih-sis), the process of removing hair by means of electricity, is considered the only true method of permanent hair removal (versus permanent hair *reduction* with lasers). All electrolysis procedures are performed by inserting small needles into the hair follicles. Electrolysis should be performed by a certified and licensed (if the state requires it) electrologist. If the state does not license the profession, look for an electrologist who holds the designation "CPE" (Certified Professional Electrologist) from the American Electrology Association (AEA). Talk with your instructor for additional information about classes and licensing in electrolysis.

There are three methods of electrolysis: galvanic, thermolysis, and blend.

GALVANIC ELECTROLYSIS: This method uses direct current, which causes chemical decomposition of the hair follicle. The galvanic method decomposes the papilla, the source of nourishment for the hair. The needle is connected to the negative side of a direct current (DC) power source and is inserted into the follicle. The client holds the electrode connected to the positive side of the power source. When power is applied, the electrical charge begins transforming saline moisture inside the follicle into sodium hydroxide (lye) along with hydrogen and chlorine gas. Unstable sodium hydroxide destabilizes the follicle wall through a chemical action. It weakens the hold of the follicle wall on surrounding tissue. This allows the hair to be removed easily. In the case of galvanic electrolysis, the moisture content within the skin is important to conduct a proper current. This method is slower than thermolysis.

THERMOLYSIS: This method of electrolysis utilizes a high-frequency current to produce heat, which coagulates and destroys the hair follicle. Thermolysis, also known as *electrocoagulation*, destroys the hair by coagulating the papilla through heat. An alternating current (AC) passes through a needle causing vibration in the water molecules surrounding the hair follicle. This action produces heat, which destroys the papilla.

BLEND: This method combines both systems, sending a current through a fine needle or probe. The blend method combines the benefits of the galvanic and thermolysis methods by passing AC and DC current through the needle at the same time. Results are reported to be quicker than with the galvanic method alone.

Did You Know?

The word *laser* is an acronym for "light amplification by stimulated emission of radiation." Lasers use intense pulses of electromagnetic radiation.

Photothermolysis comes from three Greek root words meaning light, heat, and destruction (photo: light; thermo: heat; and lysis: destruction). This method is the precise targeting of a structure using a specific wavelength of light that absorbs light into that target area alone, which damages it with heat.

Permanent Reduction and Semipermanent Hair Removal

Methods of permanent hair reduction include laser as well as photo light hair removal systems. Laser and photo light are normally performed in a medical setting. Food and Drug Administration (FDA) guidelines require that these procedures be defined as permanent hair reduction. While these methods are sometimes called "permanent," the hair bulb must be destroyed completely or there may be some regrowth. This has led to the confusing, interchangeable terms of *permanent reduction* and *semipermanent removal* (both of these terms mean that hair removal is not permanent).

Laser and Pulse Light Technology

Photoepilation (FOH-toh-ep-uh-LAY-shun) uses intense light to destroy the growth cells of the hair bulb. Photoepilation includes both *laser hair removal* and *intense pulsed light* (IPL) to reduce hair growth.

Laser hair removal technology has been around since the early 1980s. A variety of lasers are available such as the diode, alexandrite, and Nd:YAG. The hair removal industry now has the ability to offer clients a choice of both treatments: epilation by traditional methods and photoepilation with intense pulse light and lasers. Clinical studies have shown that photoepilation can provide a 50 to 60 percent reduction of hair in 12 weeks.

LASERS: In **laser hair removal**, a laser beam is pulsed on the skin, impairing the hair follicles. It is most effective when used on follicles in the growth, or anagen, phase. As mentioned earlier, "permanent" laser hair reduction is defined as *semipermanent*. The laser will reduce the number of body hairs. It cannot be guaranteed that permanent hair removal will happen; however, in some clients the hair does not grow back and in other clients lasers slow hair regrowth. Regardless of these factors, laser hair removal is increasingly in demand by clients with excess hair problems.

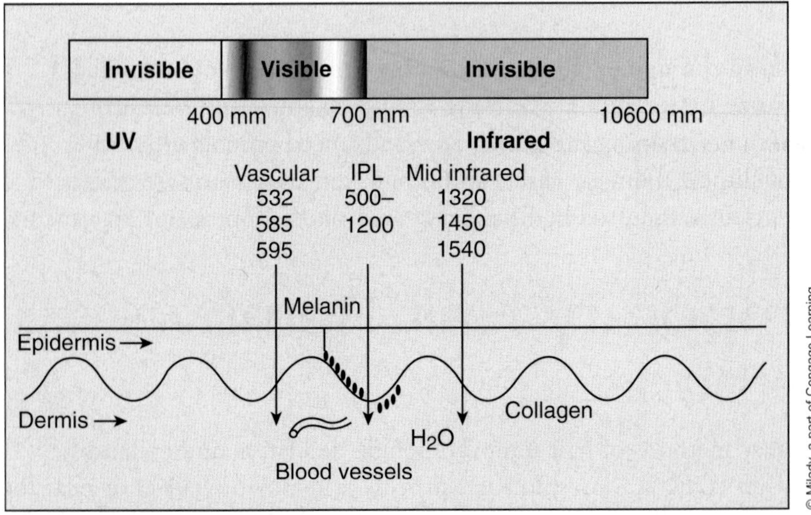

Figure 18–7
Lasers: light and the chromophores they target.

The laser method was discovered by chance when it was noted that birthmarks treated with certain types of lasers became permanently devoid of hair. Lasers are not for everyone. Some lasers work only if one's hair is darker than the surrounding skin. Coarse, dark hair responds better to laser treatments than light hair because the laser is designed to target the pigment in the hair.

Earlier-generation lasers restricted hair removal to Fitzpatrick Skin Types II, III, and sometimes Type IV. Darker skin ended up absorbing more energy, which often resulted in skin damage and postinflammatory hyperpigmentation (PIH). Individuals with a lack of contrast between hair and skin color are not good candidates for laser hair removal. Lasers are attracted to chromophores such as blood and dark hair color. *Chromophores* are defined as what lasers are attracted to. Laser hair removal uses what is called selective *photothermolysis* to target an area using a specific wavelength to absorb light only into that specific area (Figure 18–7). The pigment of the hair absorbs the light and thus destroys the dermal papilla.

REGULATORY AGENCY ALERT

Laws regarding photoepilation services vary by region and province. Be sure to check with your regulatory agency for guidelines.

INTENSE PULSED LIGHT: Different from a traditional laser, the first-generation lasers were a solid beam of light. Pulsed light (or photo light) produces a quick "flash" of light. These short, powerful pulses shatter their target without allowing heat to build up and burn the surrounding skin. IPL is used for hair reduction, as well as for vascular and pigmented lesions and skin treatments. The IPL used for skin tightening is referred to as *photorejuvenation*, or a photo facial. Improved since its introduction in the United States, it is widely used in the medical arena or in medi-spas. While there is always a risk of scarring with any laser procedure, this newer technology greatly reduces the risk of scarring, often to less than 1 percent.

All laser devices must have FDA approval. Most photoepilation hair removal machines must be used under the direct supervision of a physician. Each local regulatory agency regulates who can use these devices. Manufacturers of photoepilation equipment generally provide the specialized training for administering this procedure, but

fyi

To protect the eyes from damage, laser use requires eye protection goggles for the client and the practitioner. Additionally, do not have mirrors in the room in order to avoid reflections from the laser's light.

certification through an advanced training program is recommended and in some cases required. Training should be above and beyond manufacturers' training programs. Some advanced schools offer 60 hours of clinical training. Lasers and other light treatments are advanced treatments also discussed in Chapter 19, Advanced Topics and Treatments.

Temporary Hair Removal Methods

Temporary methods of hair removal include depilation and epilation. **Depilation** (DEP-uh-lay-shun) is a process of removing hair at or near the level of the skin. Both shaving and chemical depilation are included in this category. Another temporary method of hair removal is **epilation** (ep-uh-LAY-shun), the process of removing hair from the bottom of the follicle by breaking contact between the bulb and the papilla (Figure 18–8). The hair is pulled out of the follicle. Tweezing, wax depilatories, and sugaring are all methods of epilation. Waxing is the most common epilation procedure estheticians perform and is the focus of this chapter.

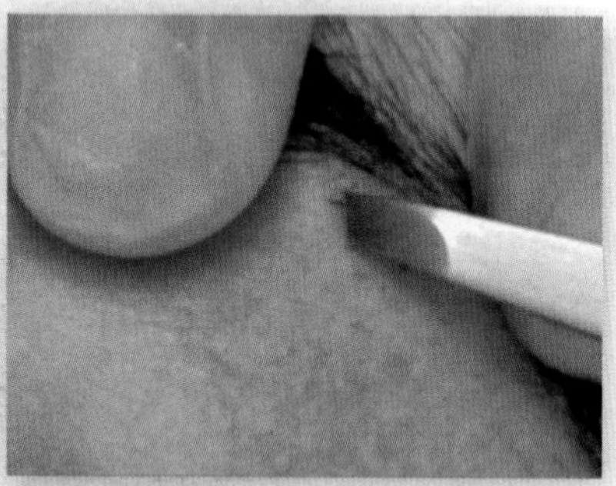

▲ Figure 18–8
Epilation removes hairs from the follicles.

Depilation

The main method of depilation is shaving. How long it takes for hair to grow back after removal depends on a person's hair growth pattern. After removal by any method, hair can take from days to weeks to reappear.

Shaving

Shaving is a daily ritual for most men and women. Many women shave the underarms, legs, and bikini area. As in any depilation method, the hair is removed down to the skin's surface. Shaving is a temporary method of hair removal that can also irritate the skin. Ingrown hairs are an additional problem with shaving. *Folliculitis* (fah-lik-yuh-LY-tis) is a term for infected follicles or ingrown hairs from shaving or other hair removal methods such as waxing. This problem can be corrected by changing the direction of shaving. Contrary to popular belief, shaving does not cause hair to grow back thicker or stronger. It only seems that way because the razor blunts the hair ends and makes them feel stiff. *Pseudofolliculitis* refers to razor bumps or ingrown hairs without pus or infection.

Depilatories

A **depilatory** (dih-PIL-uh-tohr-ee) is a substance, usually a caustic alkali preparation, used for temporarily removing superfluous hair by dissolving it at the skin level. During the application time, the hair expands and the disulfide bonds of the hair (protein and cystine) break as a result of using such chemicals as sodium hydroxide, potassium hydroxide, thioglycolic acid, or calcium thioglycolate. Although depilatories are not commonly used, you should be familiar with them in case your clients have used them.

Chemical depilatories are applied in a thin coating on the surface of the skin. Any chemical depilation cream should be patch tested first on the inside of the arm to make sure there are no allergic or sensitivity reactions. Normally, if there is no reaction—swelling, itching, or redness—within the first 10 minutes, the substance can then be applied to a larger area. A chemical depilatory causes skin irritation and is generally not recommended for use on the upper lip or other sensitive areas.

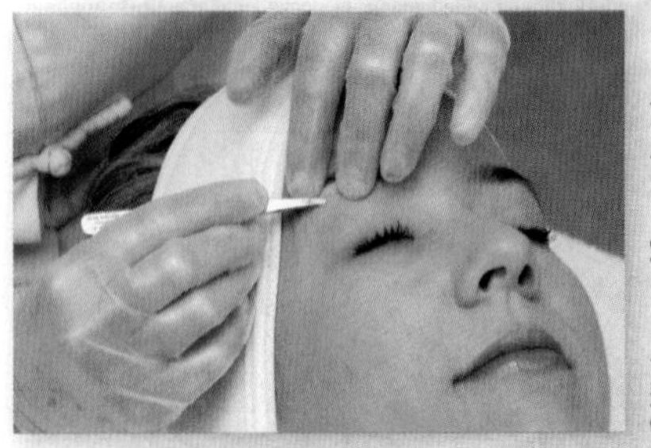

▲ Figure 18–9
Tweezing hair from the eyebrows.

Methods of Epilation

Epilation methods and products continue to improve and become more effective.

Tweezing

The method of using tweezers to pull hair out by the root one at a time is called *tweezing*. Eyebrows can be shaped and contoured by tweezing (Figure 18–9). Tweezing is also used on remaining hairs after waxing. If clients are sensitive to waxing, tweezing is a slower, but effective, alternative for removing the dark, coarse hair on the face.

PAGE 506

Electronic Tweezers

Another tweezing method used in the past was the electronically charged tweezers. This method transmits radio-frequency energy down the hair shaft into the follicle area. The papilla is thus dehydrated and eventually destroyed. The tweezers are used to grasp a single strand of hair. Electronic tweezers are not a method of permanent hair removal and the process is slow. Certain licensing is usually required to perform electronic tweezing.

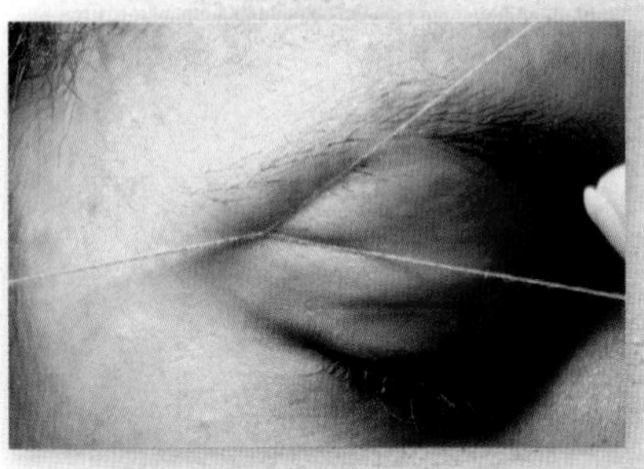

▲ Figure 18–10
An example of threading.

Threading

An ancient method of hair removal is threading (Figure 18–10), which is still common practice in many Middle Eastern cultures today. Threading, also known as **banding**, works by using cotton thread that is twisted and rolled along the surface of the skin, entwining the hair in the thread and lifting it out of the follicle. There are two main threading techniques: *hand and mouth threading*, using both hands and the mouth to hold the thread; and *two-handed threading*, using just the hands (Figure 18–11). A third technique uses the neck instead of the mouth to hold and maneuver the piece of thread.

Threading is a fast, inexpensive method of hair removal and requires minimal products and supplies. The thread is discarded after use, so it is more sanitary than waxing.

▼ Figure 18–11
Threading techniques.

Open end placed in mouth

Twist snags hair

Open end placed between thumb and forefinger

A clean thread is used and the skin is prepared as it is for waxing. The thread is 24- to 30-inches (60 to 75 centimeters) long. The ends of the thread are tied together to form a loop. The middle is twisted and captures the hair inside the two twisted threads. The hair only needs to be 1⁄16 (1.5 millimeters) of an inch long to be removed with threading.

Threading is mainly used for the facial area. It is not recommended to remove vellus hair as this may result in terminal hairs and can distort the natural angle of the follicles over time. The skin usually reacts with a little redness and slight soreness. The discomfort level is similar to tweezing, as multiple hairs are removed at once. Threading is considered an effective hair removal method for clients unable to tolerate waxing due to the use of exfoliation treatments or products like glycolic acid and Retin A®. Do not use the threading method on irritated skin. Threading has become increasingly popular as an option to other methods and requires specialized training. Some regions require special licensing to perform threading.

Sugaring

Sugaring is another ancient method of hair removal, dating back to the Egyptians. It is an alternative for those who have sensitive skin or who react to waxes with bumps and redness. The sugaring solution is water soluble, meaning that it is easily removed with water. The original basic recipe is a mixture of sugar, lemon juice, and water. It is heated to form a syrup, which is then molded into a ball and pressed onto the skin and quickly stripped away.

Sugaring is similar to waxing methods except that it uses a thick, sugar-based paste and is especially appropriate for more sensitive skin types. One advantage with sugar waxing is the hair can be removed even if it is only 1⁄16- to 1⁄8-inch (1.5 to 3 millimeters) long. It can be removed in the direction of the hair growth, which is less irritating than waxing. It can be used for some who have certain wax contraindications. Always do a consultation and do not perform sugaring on irritated skin. Follow the manufacturer's instructions.

Sugar mixtures are now manufactured in large quantities and sold in small containers ready to be placed in a heater. There are also homemade recipes. The sugar mixture melts at a very low temperature. The sugar paste adheres only to the hair, making removal more comfortable. The sugar can be used over and over on the same client until the hair left in the product interferes with the process. It is hygienic because it is only used on a specific client and then discarded. True sugar products should be natural and resin-free. Additives in the formula will change the results and effects on the skin.

Sugaring uses both directions of applying and removing the product: with the hair growth and against the hair growth. The application and removal depends on the product and the manufacturer's instructions. There are two types of sugaring methods: hand-applied and spatula-applied. The hand method is performed with room temperature sugar wax and the spatula applied method is with warm sugar wax.

Hand Method: With the hand method, the product is applied against the hair growth and removed in the direction of the hair growth using a thicker application. The application is similar to hard wax. It can be applied either warm or at room temperature with the hands (Figure 18–12).

Spatula Method: The product is applied with the hair growth (as with soft wax) and removed against the hair growth with the spatula and a strip (Figure 18–13).

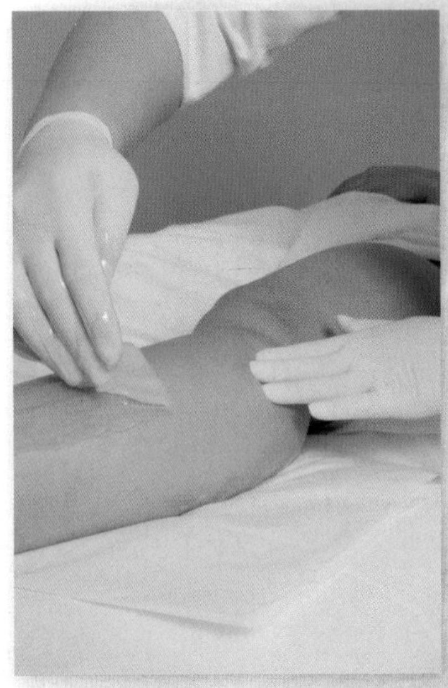

▲ Figure 18–12
Sugaring: hand method.

Waxing

The primary hair removal method used by estheticians is waxing. Wax is a commonly used epilator, applied in either soft or hard form as recommended by the manufacturer. Both products are made primarily of resins and beeswax. Wax is applied evenly over the hair and then removed. Hard wax is thicker than soft wax and does not require fabric strips for removal. The benefit of waxing is that the hair takes longer to grow back and the skin feels smoother without the hair or stubble. The recommended time between waxing appointments is generally 4 to 6 weeks. ✓ L03

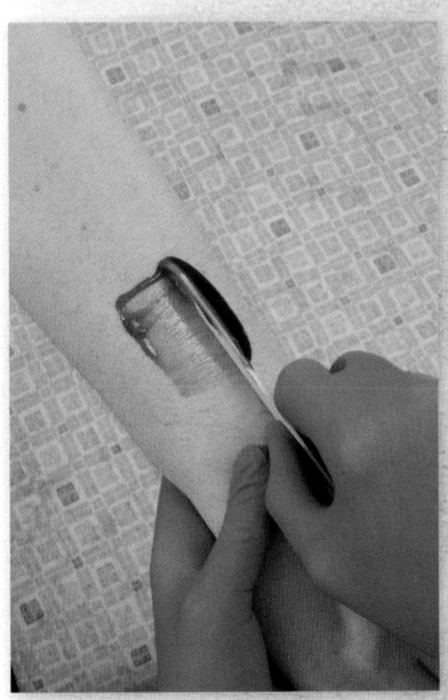

▲ Figure 18–13
Sugaring: spatula method.

Waxing Techniques and Products

Correct waxing techniques, appropriate materials, and proper wax temperatures are all factors in obtaining positive results from waxing services. Wax is designed to adhere to the hair as close to the skin as possible. When the wax is removed, it should adhere to the hair and remove the hair and bulb from the follicle.

If the wax is not applied correctly, is applied at the wrong temperature, or if the skin is not cleansed well, the hair will not be removed. If the wax is too hot, it can cause skin irritation and burns severe enough to cause blistering. If not performed correctly during removal, the skin can be pulled off as well.

The skin must be held as taut as possible to avoid skin damage. As with all esthetic methods, proper technique is the key to successful waxing. Understanding the "whys and hows" of proper waxing techniques and checking for contraindications that might cause injury is crucial to providing a satisfactory, safe, and comfortable hair removal service.

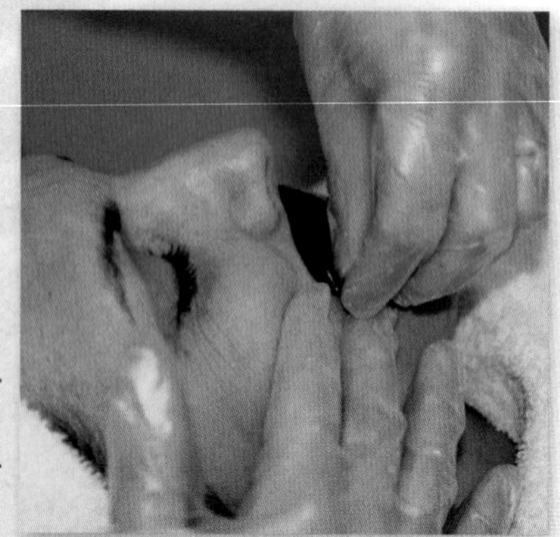

Courtesy of Shelley Lotz.

▲ Figure 18–14
Hard wax application on the face.

Types of Wax Products

There are two types of waxes: *hard* (no strip is used) and *soft* (a strip is used). Hard "*stripless*" waxes are applied directly to the skin in a thick, "wet" layer that hardens as it cools (Figure 18–14). The technician then uses the fingers to lift the wax off the skin while it is still tacky-feeling. Soft "*strip*" waxes are applied in a thin layer and covered with a strip of pellon or muslin material, which removes the hair as it is pulled off quickly. All soft wax is applied in the same direction as the hair grows out of the follicle and is removed in the opposite direction of the hair growth. Pulling wax off in the wrong direction with soft wax can have serious consequences. Hard wax is the only wax that may be removed in the direction of the hair growth, but additional training is needed to use this method.

Wax product consistencies vary, as do melting points. Waxes require a heater to liquefy them. Cold hard waxes are also available, primarily for home use. It is important to keep the wax at the right temperature so it works correctly. It has to be exactly the right temperature and consistency for hair removal use. Do not leave the wax unit on overnight or overheat the wax. This changes the effectiveness of the wax product.

Wax formulas are made from rosins (derived from resins of pine trees), beeswax, paraffin, honey, and other waxes and substances. Waxes may include additives to address the needs of different skin types. For example, azulene or chamomile may be used for sensitive skin. Tea tree oil may be added for its soothing and antiseptic benefits. Some waxes are water soluble and wipe off easily with water. Others, such as resins, are oil soluble. Excess wax is removed with an oil-based solution if it is not soluble in water.

© Milady, a part of Cengage Learning. Photography by Rob Werfel.

▲ Figure 18–15
Hard waxes are available in blocks, disks, pellets, or beads.

Hard Wax

Hard waxes are available in blocks, disks, pellets, or beads (Figure 18–15). They are considered a no-strip wax. They must be liquefied before they can be used. Hard waxes are available at different melting points to address the needs of normal and sensitive skin. The harder the wax, the more heat it requires to melt it. Small, individual wax heaters are available and can be placed in each treatment room. The used wax is discarded after each service.

Some estheticians prefer hard waxes. They are gentle enough for the face area, yet strong enough to be used on hard-to-remove, coarse hairs. Some like to use it on the bikini and underarm area. Estheticians generally use soft wax in larger areas, such as the back and legs, and hard wax in smaller areas, such as the eyebrow.

Hard wax is thicker than soft wax. It is first applied against the hair growth, then back in the opposite direction in a figure eight pattern. The hair is gripped as the wax dries and tightens and lifts off without sticking to the skin. The follicle is not distorted when pulled in the same direction as the hair growth pattern. Hard wax is especially effective in areas where hair grows in multiple directions or skin is thin or fragile. Some estheticians apply and remove the hard wax in the same direction as the soft wax. Application depends on the area to be waxed and how coarse the hair is. The direction for pulling the hard wax off is more forgiving than soft wax. Hard wax is the only wax recommended for Brazilian waxing.

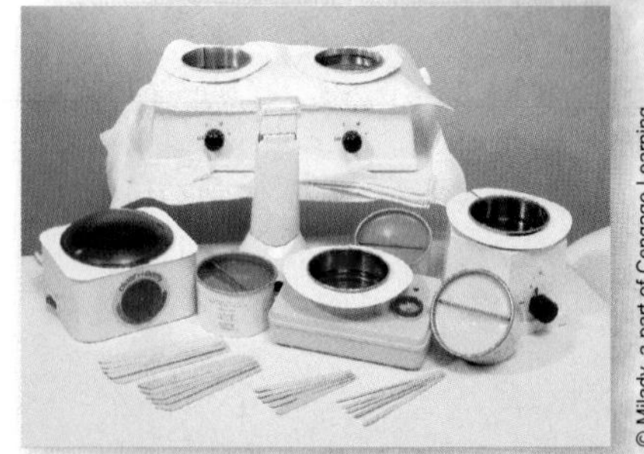

▲ Figure 18–16
Soft wax products.

Soft Wax

One of the most common methods of hair removal is soft, or strip, waxing. Soft waxes have a lower melting point and come in tins or plastic containers. If they come in plastic containers, they can be melted slightly in the microwave to make it easier to pour the wax into a wax heater or warming pot (Figure 18–16). With this method, a thin coat of wax is applied on the skin and removed immediately with a muslin, pellon, or cotton strip before it cools.

One of the benefits of soft wax is that it feels warm on the skin and the heat dilates the follicle for easier removal. The quick application of soft wax is known as *speed waxing* and is more comfortable for the client. Faster procedures save time, lead to more revenue, and more satisfied clients.

The main detractor to using soft wax is that it can be irritating to the skin because the ingredients, such as rosins, can adhere to the skin. Additionally, the removal has to be precise against the hair growth. Removing against the hair growth can distort the follicles. A negative effect of removing vellus hair is that this can stimulate the growth of coarser hair. Waxing may also lead to more ingrown hairs.

All wax techniques take practice and can be messy at first. Practice working with the wax to avoid leaving stringy trails of wax where you do not want them. There are many little details to keep track of, and wax sets up fast, so be ready to work quickly.

REGULATORY AGENCY ALERT

Some regions may prohibit the use of roll-on wax due to concerns with cross-contamination in the wax and the proper disinfection of the applicators.

Roll-On Wax

Another type of soft wax method uses roll-on applicators (Figure 18–17). The applicators contain wax and have roll-on heads. Applicators are warmed in a heating unit designed to fit the applicators. This method is very efficient and clean to work with. Many estheticians prefer to use the roll-on wax because it can be less messy and more efficient. Be sure to clean and disinfect applicators and rollers properly. There are concerns with cross-contamination and disinfection with the use of roll-on wax applicators.

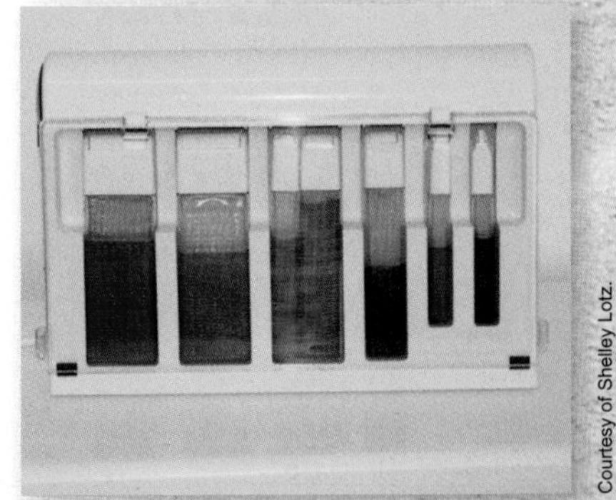

Courtesy of Shelley Lotz.

▲ Figure 18–17
Roller-type waxes are convenient for various waxing applications, but may be prohibited in some regions.

Room Preparation and Supplies

The waxing room and equipment should be immaculately clean, with appropriate covers on the waxing table. The room should be warm and comfortable. The music can be livelier than the music that is played during the more relaxing treatments.

Furniture and Accessories

Some spas and salons have separate rooms for waxing. Others perform waxing services in the facial rooms. Waxing, especially on larger body areas such as the legs, is labor intensive. Furniture should be ergonomically designed so that both the technician and client are comfortable. Ideally, the waxing table should be adjustable to different heights. This allows each technician to adjust the table to the correct height that is comfortable for their back. Straining or bending over is bad for the technician's back. Client comfort is also a priority, and disrupting the service with too many table adjustments is slow and less efficient. Test the setup and think about the positioning needs of the client before the service.

A multitiered wheeled cart is useful for holding waxing pots and supplies (**Figure 18–18**). The cart can be moved near the client, keeping tools and supplies close at hand. A covered waste container is necessary for the proper disposal of all used supplies as you work. A stool should also be available to help the client safely get on and off of the table.

Tools and Supplies

Appropriate tools and supplies need to be replenished every day. Many items, such as applicators, are available as single-use items that are

▶ Figure 18–18
The wax cart setup.

both convenient and sanitary. The cart should be stocked with items such as the wax and warmer, cleansers, pre- and post-epilation solutions, tweezers, scissors, applicators, cotton supplies, and gloves. Follow the same cleaning and decontamination procedures for all esthetic services, whether it is for facials or waxing.

Tweezers

Professional tweezers are available in different point sizes. Slant-tipped tweezers are best for general tweezing. A more pointed tip is ideal for ingrown hairs. Tweezers should be made of stainless steel so they will not corrode when disinfected in solution or in the autoclave. Plastic breaks down quickly. Always purchase the highest-quality tweezers and accessories you can afford. Tweezers are an important tool that will help make your work more precise and efficient. The result will be a more satisfied client.

Applicators

Single-use wax applicators are wooden, flat sticks, either large, medium, or small. These are similar to Popsicle sticks, metal pushers, and tongue depressors. A stainless steel or hard plastic 5-inch (12.5 centimeter) spatula is ideal for spreading a thin coat on larger areas such as the legs. The spatula must be cleaned and disinfected after each use. All single-use applicators are used once and are not double-dipped. If they are, wax is exclusively used on each client, any leftovers are discarded, and the container must be disinfected and refilled or replaced.

Wax Strips

There are two popular types of wax strips: cotton muslin, which comes in rolls or precut packets, and pellon. Pellon® is a fiber-like material. Strips can be used a few times on a client before disposal. When using a strip wax, prepare your strips ahead of time. Cut smaller strips for the eye and face areas. Trim a strip to the size of the area you are going to wax, plus an inch or two (2.5 to 5 centimeters) on the end to hold onto. With correct strip sizes, less material is wasted and more effective pulling is ensured. Estimate the number of strips needed for each service and prepare these ahead of time.

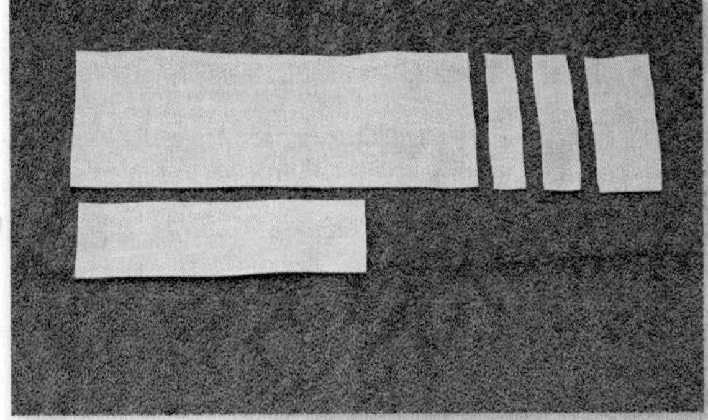

▲ Figure 18–19a and b
Wax strips and sizes.

Wax strip sizes: If strips are not precut, cutting the wax strip to the right size is important for client safety and proper technique. If the strips are too large, they interfere with your waxing technique. It is not safe to wax too much surface area at one time. Your instructor will give you specific dimensions to use. The strips should be cut straight with no stray edges. The width for leg strips is the size of the wax roll, approximately 3 inches (7.5 centimeters) (Figure 18–19a and b). Cut smaller sizes from the leg strips or roll. The length of the small face strips match the roll's width, so only the widths need to be cut for these.

These are approximate sizes:

- ***Leg*:** 3" (7.5 cm) wide × 8" (20 cm) in length (cut one-half to three-quarters of the leg strip length for the knees).
- ***Brow/lip*:** ½" (1.25 cm) to ¾" (2 cm) wide to 1" (2.5 cm) wide × 3" (7.5 cm) in length.
- ***Face (chin)*:** 1½" (3.75 cm) wide × 3" (7.5 cm) length.
- ***Bikini/underarm*:** 1½" (3.75 cm) to 2" (5 cm) wide × 5" (12.5 cm) to 6" (15 cm) length (half of the roll's width and three-quarters of the leg strip length). As an option, you can use part of a small leg strip for larger areas.

Linens/Roll Paper

To keep the area clean, place a clean sheet or sheet of paper on the waxing table for each new client. Roll paper for waxing is normally ordered through esthetics or medical suppliers. You can also use bath towels or sheets. Keep wax linens separate from nicer facial linens.

Pre- and Post-Epilation Products

Various products are available for treating the skin before and after waxing. A prep solution is applied to thoroughly clean the skin before waxing. Both pre- and post-waxing solutions may have antiseptic or calming ingredients such as witch hazel, arnica, chamomile, or calendula. Other desensitizing lotions ease discomfort. Powder and other pre-wax products protect the skin while waxing.

Post-waxing products contain antiseptic or soothing properties, such as azulene or aloe. Other post-waxing products are hair-growth inhibitors. Use caution when applying products to skin after waxing. Fragrances and other ingredients such as alcohol can be irritating to the skin. Irritation, reactions, and breakouts can occur. Unfortunately, some aloe and other post-wax products are not always soothing—most are not pure and contain irritating ingredients. Just because a product comes with a wax kit does not mean you have to use it. Products to prevent ingrown hair are used after the skin has recovered from waxing and help keep the follicle open.

Infection Control

Waxing stations and supplies must be kept clean and disinfected. Wax drips on the side of a heater are unsightly. Waxing needs to be done carefully to avoid drips on the floor, linens, and furniture. Wipe excess wax off the spatula before taking it from the pot and move the spatula carefully from the pot to the client. Do not double-dip the spatula unless you are disposing of the entire pot of wax after treating that individual client. Otherwise, use a new spatula each time to dip into the pot of wax. Place the waxing unit and all your accessories on a roll cart that can be pulled close to the client.

Keep the clean single-use wooden applicators and cotton supplies in covered containers when not in use. Do not put contaminated hands or gloves into clean containers. Use clean gloves or disinfected tongs to open and reach into a drawer if more supplies are needed.

Always wear gloves. Use gloves other than latex. Latex tends to get sticky and breaks down easily. Change your gloves if they become excessively sticky during a waxing service. Hair removal often causes trauma to the follicle. When the hair is forcefully pulled out of the follicle, spot-bleeding may occur and fluids may rise to the surface of the skin. This is normal—this is the blood that has been nourishing the dermal papilla.

All blood-stained gauze and materials should be discarded in a biohazard waste container and disposed of properly. When there is slight bleeding or even red bumps, place a small amount of antiseptic on a cotton 4" × 4" (10 cm × 10 cm) or 2" × 2" (5 cm × 5 cm) pad and gently press it on the area. This helps stop the bleeding and calms the skin. A cold, wet cotton compress is also soothing and constricts the follicles after waxing. A bowl of ice or cold water is useful to have on hand for certain clients and procedures.

The liquid-disinfectant container is normally a small, rectangular box with a lid. Tweezers and any other multiuse items should be thoroughly cleansed, dried, and placed into a wet disinfectant following the manufacturer's instructions. Place the instruments into an EPA-registered, hospital-strength disinfectant solution that is designated to kill all microbes, including staphylococcus, tuberculosis, pseudomonas (a pathogen), fungus, and the HIV virus. These solutions are often listed in catalogs for the esthetics industry or are available at a medical supply house. Stainless steel instruments can be sterilized in an autoclave. ☑ L04

Contraindications for Hair Removal

The main reason for the client consultation is to determine if the client has any contraindications for hair removal (**Table 18–1**, page 494). It is also helpful to know if they have been waxed before and if they had any problems or reactions from past waxing experiences. ☑ L05

Client Consultations

Before any hair removal service, a consultation is always necessary. A client assessment form (**Figure 18–20** on page 495) should be completed by each new client and kept in the client's file folder. Ask the client to complete a questionnaire that discloses all products and medications, both topical (applied to the skin) and oral (taken by mouth), along with any known skin disorders or allergies. Allergies or sensitivities must be noted and documented.

Keep in mind that many changes can occur between client visits. This is why many facilities have clients read, update, and sign their release form on every visit

CONTRADICTIONS FOR WAXING PROCEDURES

- Leg waxing should not be performed on clients who have varicose veins.
- Body waxing should not be performed on clients with phlebitis, skin disorders, epilepsy, diabetes, or other contraindicated medical conditions.
- Facial waxing should not be performed on clients who have any of the following contraindications:

Recent Treatments or Product Use

- Recent chemical exfoliation using glycolic, salicylic, or other acid-based products
- Recent microdermabrasion or injectables (Botox® or other dermal fillers)
- Recent cosmetic or reconstructive surgery, laser, or IPL treatments
- Recent use of exfoliating topical medication including Retin-A®, Renova®, Tazorac®, Differin®, Azelex®, other peeling agents, or vitamin A topical products on the area
- Recent use of hydroquinone for skin lightening
- Recent use of topical or oral cortisone medication

Medical Conditions or Medications

- Recent use of acne medications (do not wax within 1 year for some)
- Recent use of blood-thinning medications (Coumadin®, warfarin)
- Circulatory disorders (phlebitis, thrombosis)
- Chemotherapy or radiation
- Epilepsy, diabetes, hemophiliacs (face and body waxing)
- Autoimmune disorders (AIDS, lupus)
- Medications such as tetracycline may have an adverse reaction with wax

Skin Conditions

- Rosacea or very sensitive skin
- Sunburn, inflamed skin, bruising
- History of fever blisters or cold sores (herpes)
- Presence of pustules or papules on area to be waxed

Other Cautions and Contraindications

- Do not wax over scar tissue, moles, skin tags or warts or varicose veins.
- Do not wax over skin disorders (eczema, seborrhea, psoriasis).
- Do not wax papery-like or over-thinned skin.
- Do not wax inside the nose, ear, or over the nipples or eyelids.
- Check for product allergies to wax ingredients.
- Contraindicated topical products and treatments should be stopped at least 1 month to 6 weeks prior to waxing. With harsher products and treatments, it can take up to 3 months or longer after healing before the skin is ready to be waxed.
- This is only a guideline and medical information needs to be carefully reviewed.

▲ Table 18–1 **Contraindications for Waxing Procedures.**

CLIENT ASSESSMENT FORM

(Sample form)

(assessment should be performed/reviewed prior to each treatment)

Name ____ Date ________

Phone ____________________ Address ______________________________

E-mail ____

Have you been waxed before? Yes ___ No ___

The following are potential contraindications for waxing:

Any chemical exfoliation treatment such as a glycolic acid peel or any other AHA treatment? (wait at least two weeks before waxing): Yes ___ No ___ If yes, when: __________

Applied any topical products containing AHAs (glycolic or lactic acid), BHAs (salicylic acid), or lightening or bleaching gels? (wait at least 48 hours; a week is better) Yes ___ No ___

Have you had microdermabrasion, laser resurfacing, light therapy, or injectable treatments? (wait 4 weeks or longer—treatment dependent) Yes ___ No ___ If yes, when: __________

Are you taking acne drugs and/or using exfoliating topical products such as Retin-A® or other vitamin A products ? (wait at least 3 months or longer—drug dependent) Yes ___ No ___ If yes, what type: ______

Exposure to continuous sun, or shaved, scrubbed, or experienced any recent peeling or irritation in the last 48 hours? Yes ___ No ___

Skin treatments: ______________________________ Date(s): ____________________

Currently using, or has used, the following topical products on face and neck:

____

Medical conditions: ____

Currently taking, or has taken, the following medications: ____________________

Pregnant or lactating? Yes ___ No ___

Seen or seeing dermatologist? Yes ___ No ___ Date:________

Name of doctor: ____

Allergies to products or medications: __________________________________

History of fever blisters or cold sores? Yes ___ No ___

Tanning regime or use of tanning booths? ____________________ Frequency: __________

Client initials: __________

WAX TREATMENT RECORD

(esthetician to fill out chart notes on back of assessment form for each service)

Client Name: ____

Date	Esthetician	Wax Service	Notes
9/8/12	*Teresa*	*Brow w/soft wax*	*New client: shaping for more arch, close-set eyes* *Tweezed chin* *No redness*

▲ Figure 18–20

A client assessment form.

Wax Release Form

(Sample form)

Name ______________________________ Date ______________

Phone ____________ Address ______________________________

E-mail ____

I understand that topical creams, medical conditions, and medications can affect the results of waxing. I understand that I cannot be waxed if I have certain contraindications such as taking topical acne drugs or if I am using Retin-A® (or other peeling agents) topical prescription products.

I understand that I am accepting full responsibility for skin reactions if I do not inform my technician of contraindications prior to waxing.

Certain medications, products, and treatments used prior to waxing may result in irritation, skin peeling, blotchiness, pigmentation, and sensitivity.

I understand that some redness and/or sensitivity may result. I agree to avoid sun exposure, excessive heat (saunas, hot tubs), and all active products for the next 48 hours or as instructed by the technician.

The hair removal process has been explained and I have had an opportunity to ask questions and receive satisfactory answers.

I consent to be waxed and will not hold the salon or technician responsible for any adverse reactions from treatments or products.

Name (print) ____________________ Signature ______________________

Initial below for each visit:

Date: _______ Client initials: _______ Date: _______ Client initials: _______

Date: _______ Client initials: _______ Date: _______ Client initials: _______

Date: _______ Client initials: _______ Date: _______ Client initials: _______

▲ Figure 18–21
A sample wax release form.

(**Figure 18–21**). Since the last time you saw them, clients may be taking new medications such as antidepressants, hormones, cortisone, medicine for blood pressure or diabetes, or such topical prescriptions as Retin-A®, Renova®, and hydroquinone. A client on any one of these prescriptions may not be a candidate for hair removal, because the client is more sensitive and the skin can actually be pulled off if waxed. See Table 18–1 on page 494 for contraindications. Always refer to this contraindication list to make sure clients are safe to receive hair removal services.

It is imperative that every client fills out a release form for the hair removal service you are going to provide. Have clients review their forms before every service because it reminds them to think about any topical or oral medication they may have started since the last visit. If you neglect to do this, a potential accident may occur.

Give clients post-wax precautions: avoid sun exposure, exfoliation, creams with fragrance or other ingredients that may be irritating, and excessive heat (hot tubs, saunas) for at least 24 to 48 hours after waxing.

Fitzpatrick skin typing and the skin's response to UV light are important to keep in mind due to how the skin reacts with treatments. This helps

Here's a Tip

If a client comes in for face waxing and you are unable to wax due to contraindications, offer to tweeze or trim a small amount of hair for them instead. Or offer a substitute service such as a mini-facial. They will appreciate getting at least some hair removal or other service completed. Most clients will appreciate a cautious approach in caring for their skin. Don't be talked into waxing if you are in doubt about the contraindications.

predict how the skin will respond to chemical peeling, microdermabrasion, waxing, and laser treatments. The possibilities of pigmentation problems or sensitivities are serious issues. Postinflammatory hyperpigmentation (Figure 18–22) from injury to the skin is common from waxing for darker skin types. Refer to the Fitzpatrick Skin Type Scale and note it on the client chart before waxing new clients. ✓ LO6

CAUTION!

Never wax if you are in doubt about how a client's skin will react. Do a patch test on a tiny area if you are concerned about the results or reactions from a procedure or product.

Waxing Safety Precautions

Please note the following safety precautions for wax treatments:

- Before beginning a wax treatment, be sure to complete a client consultation card and have the client read and sign a release form.
- Wear single-use gloves to prevent contact with any possible bloodborne pathogens.
- The hair should be at least ¼-inch (.6 centimeters) to ½-inch (1.25 centimeters) long for waxing to be the most effective. Trim hair before waxing if it is longer than ¾ inch (2 centimeters).
- Do not remove vellus hair; doing so may cause the hair to lose its softness and uniformity.
- Beeswax has a relatively high incidence of allergic reaction. Before every service, always do a small patch test of the product to be used.
- To prevent burns, always test the temperature of the heated wax on the inside of the wrist before applying it to the client's skin.
- Use caution so that the wax does not come in contact with the eyes. Have the client keep their eyes closed for face waxing as wax may drip or "string" off the spatula.
- Do not apply wax over warts, moles, abrasions, or irritated or inflamed skin. Do not remove hair protruding from a mole since the wax could cause trauma to the mole.
- Cover the scalp hair with a headband for face waxing and protect clothes to avoid wax drips near the area you are waxing.
- Never wax over curves—always do one side of an area at a time or the top and bottom separately. Waxing over curves damages the skin because the pull is not parallel to the skin when going over the curved surface.
- The skin under the arms and other areas is very sensitive. If sensitive, use hard wax.
- Redness and swelling sometimes occur on sensitive skin. Apply aloe gel or cortisone cream to calm and soothe the skin after waxing.
- Give clients post-wax precautions: avoid sun exposure, exfoliation, creams with fragrance or other ingredients that may be irritating, and excessive heat (hot tubs, saunas) for at least 24 to 48 hours after waxing.

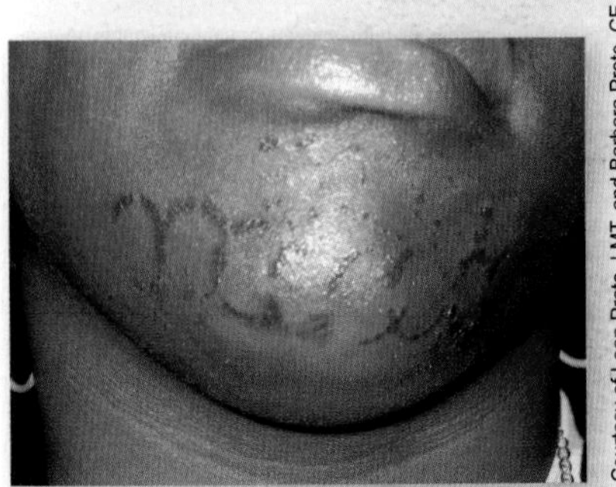

▲ Figure 18–22
Postinflammatory hyperpigmentation.

FOCUS ON

Waxing

Frequent waxing does weaken the hair follicle and slow down hair growth. Conversely, with frequent waxing, follicles may grow deeper into the dermis and closer to a richer blood supply. This stimulates stronger, thicker hairs. As women age, the excess androgens (from less estrogen) also stimulate the hair growth. The hair growth in the chin may become so coarse that only tweezing will remove it. Ingrown hairs from hair removal and more fragile skin is common with mature skin, so treating facial hair is more complicated. Sugaring or hard wax is gentler on the face. Laser is also a consideration for those with waxing contraindications.

Here's a Tip

Unlike facials, waxing procedures need to flow quickly, so make sure you are ready to quickly apply and remove the wax immediately. Keep up a fast pace to avoid client discomfort and problems with the product consistency and removal.

Here's a Tip

To safely cover an area such as a blemish or abrasion that cannot be waxed that is close to where you are removing hair, apply an occlusive balm such as petroleum jelly over the area so wax will not adhere to it.

CAUTION!

Wax expands out beyond the edges when pressing down the strip, so stay inside the border and do not put wax anywhere hair should not be removed.

General Waxing Procedures

Here is an overview of waxing procedures to review before performing the hands-on procedures.

Client Preparation

Provide the client with a gown, single-use panties, or other items, depending on the service provided. Draping is important for client's modesty.

Prepare the skin per the instructor's directions.

- ***Brows/face.*** The client's eyes should be closed. Completely remove any traces of makeup with a gentle cleanser. Follow with a preparation solution to remove any residue on the area. Allow the area to dry for a few moments. Some states or regions require the use of client eye pads before some services, such as waxing or tweezing.
- ***All areas.*** Clean the skin thoroughly with a pre-epilation solution such as witch hazel on a cotton pad. Powder is applied if a moist area needs to be dried (especially underarms). Powder can also protect the skin and make hairs more visible. However, it can interfere with waxing if too much powder is applied. Do not use talcum powder. Many talcs contain fragrances and other particles that can cause an allergic reaction. Cornstarch is a good alternative.
- ***Excess body hair.*** Trim any thicker or longer hair areas with scissors before applying wax. This allows the wax to adhere better with fewer traumas to the follicles and is more comfortable for the client. Trim hair to no shorter than ½ inch (1.25 centimeters).

Wax Application and Removal Techniques

- All wax applications are either soft wax used with strips or hard wax without strips.
- Hold spatulas or applicators at a 45-degree angle or less while applying the wax.
- Hold the skin taut next to where the wax is first applied for a smoother application.
- The most important points in all wax removal techniques are to hold the skin *taut* (tightly stretched) next to where starting the pull and to remove it *quickly* while pulling *parallel* to the skin. Stretch the skin out while holding, rather than applying too much pressure downward on the skin.

Soft Wax Application

- Dip the end of the spatula into the warm wax. Following the direction of the hair growth, apply a very thin coat along the area to be waxed (Figure 18–23). Be careful not to drip wax on areas that are not being waxed.

Soft Wax Removal

- Apply the muslin or Pellon® strip evenly over the wax and with light pressure. Rub the strip firmly in the same direction as the wax application. Do not use too much pressure, or you could cause bruising. Leave approximately 1inch (2.5 cm) of the strip free to grip for removing.
- Check under the edges of the strip to make sure the wax did not migrate out beyond the border or line—especially for brows.
- Hold the skin taut next to the end you will be pulling with one hand, and remove the wax quickly with the other hand using one continuous pull in the direction opposite the hair growth. If the end of the hair is pointing to the left, pull to the right. Because follicles do not grow vertically, but at an angle, the hair is "popped" out at an angle. The pulling method and direction are critical. When pulling, keep the strip parallel to the skin without lifting to avoid skin damage (Figure 18–24).
- Follow through on the pull to avoid slowing down. Do not pull straight up, or you will remove skin or cause bruising or the hair to break off. Immediately after you remove the strip, place your other hand or fingers quickly over the area and apply pressure to block the nerves from sensing pain.

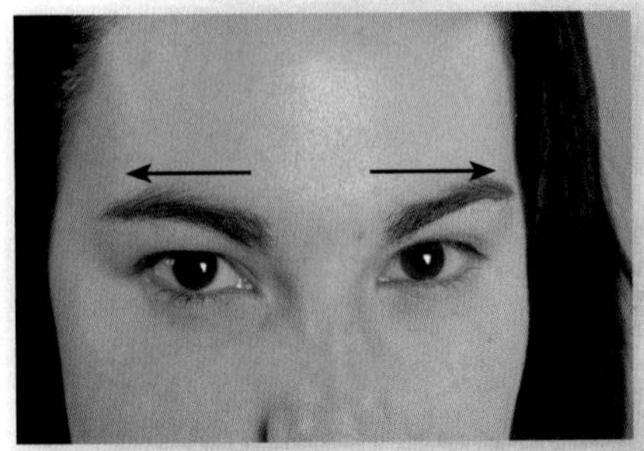

▲ Figure 18–23
Wax application in the direction of the hair growth.

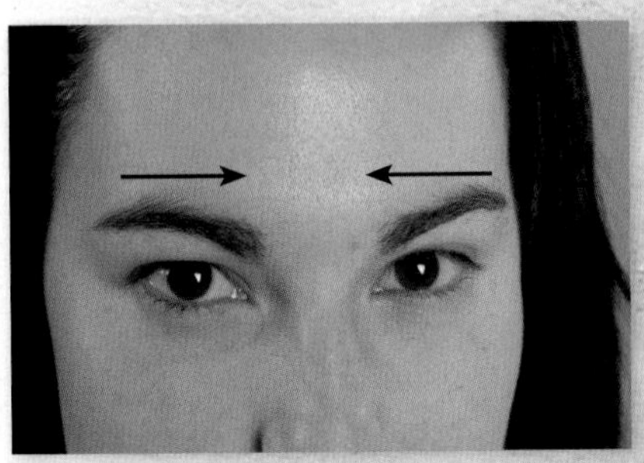

▲ Figure 18–24
Wax removal opposite to the hair growth.

Hard Wax Application and Removal Techniques

Hard Wax Application

- Dip a spatula into the wax and apply it first in the opposite direction of hair growth, then in the same direction of the hair growth in a smooth or figure-eight pattern over the area to be waxed. Apply to the thickness of a nickel. For the body use 2-inch (5 centimeter) wide strips of hard wax. Length should not exceed 9 inches (22.5 centimeters). Use smaller sections when first learning how to wax.
- Apply a thicker area on the end to pull up with, lifting it up before it completely hardens to make a tab that can be grasped between the thumb and index finger. It is best to have the pull tab end where there is no hair underneath.
- Wait a few moments for the wax to set up. If hard wax becomes too dry or cool, it will be brittle and break off when you attempt to remove it. Try to end the wax where there is no hair when flicking up the end to make a tab (to grasp on to for the pull). It's very uncomfortable when hair is pulled

Here's a Tip

Especially for brow waxing: Only apply the strip where hair removal is desired. If soft wax is accidently placed where the hair should not be removed, then do not put the strip over it. You can later remove the wax with a wax remover or oil for the skin. Always make sure you can see the brow area outside of the wax and strip to avoid removing too much hair. Use smaller strips and place them carefully to avoid covering the entire brow with the strip so you have a clear view.

ACTIVITY

Before attempting the actual wax application, practice a mock application. Using a mannequin head or other body part, pretend you are applying and pulling off wax for an actual client. Use a pencil or practice applicator to mimic applying the wax, and then apply scotch or masking tape as a practice strip to pull off of the area. *Remember the mantra: hold taut, pull fast, keep it parallel and follow through (don't slow down) on the motion.*

Removing wax is a similar sort of action to throwing a Frisbee without the wrist action.

CAUTION!

Never apply hard wax as thinly as soft wax. Hard wax must be at least as thick as a nickel. If it is too thin, it will be brittle and the only way to get it off is one tiny painful piece at a time using lots of oil or petroleum jelly.

on under the tab. Small plastic pull tabs are now available to slide under the edge of the wax before it sets up, to make the removal easier.

- Hard wax is a slower method, and the technician has to wait for the applied wax to set. With experience, one should be able to apply the second application to another part of the area (although not immediately adjacent) while waiting for the first application to set. If the procedure is too slow, it becomes inefficient, laborious, and uncomfortable for the client.

Hard Wax Removal

- Follow the previous removal steps for the soft wax, only without the strips. Once the wax has set, grasp the thick edge firmly between the thumb and index finger. Pull off the wax in the appropriate direction according to instructions. Immediately put your other hand over the area to soothe nerve endings.

Post-Wax Treatment

Tweezing

- After waxing, visually check the waxed area with the magnifying light. All hair should have been removed in the pull.
- Remove any residual hair with tweezers. If there are ingrown hairs, pointed tweezers can be used to loosen them or remove them. Carefully slide the point of the tweezers just under the skin close to the hair and lift it out. It is recommended not to remove ingrown hairs right away. Release them from under the skin and let the follicle heal, so the hair does not become trapped under the skin again. Tweeze them a few days later or wax them at the next appointment.

Here's a Tip

Have the client take a *deep breath in* just before removing the wax while you rub over the strip and *exhale and blow out* during the pull when removing the wax. This decreases the discomfort.

Post-Wax Product Application

- Remove residual wax with a wax remover made for the skin. Gently apply to the waxed area, removing any wax residue. Rub with a cotton pad to remove excess wax and product.
- Apply an after-wax soothing product (such as azulene or aloe) as directed. After waxing, open, irritated follicles are susceptible to

more irritation. Keep epilated areas clean and free from any debris. If you are applying a hair-growth inhibitor cream, follow the manufacturer's directions.

- If skin is especially sensitive, a cold compress with baking soda mixed in water can be applied to calm the skin and help neutralize reactions from products.

Here's a Tip

To calm down the skin for sensitive clients apply a cool, wet cotton pad to waxed areas.

Post-Wax Clean Up

Follow all cleaning and decontamination procedures. Give the client post-wax instructions and precautions. Prepare the station for the next service.

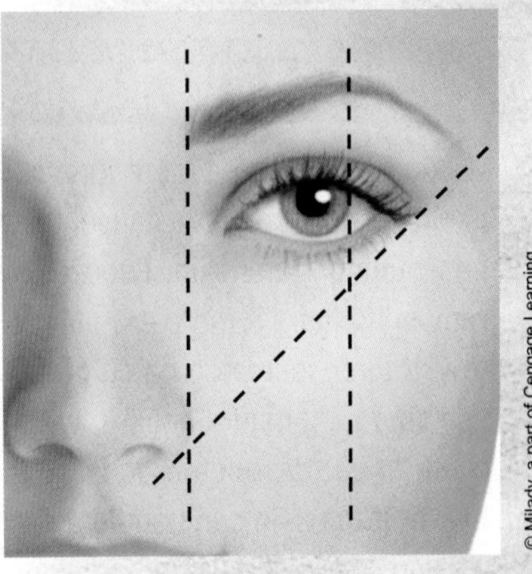

▲ Figure 18–25
Brow shaping guidelines.

Shaping Eyebrows

Correctly shaped eyebrows have a strong, positive impact on the overall attractiveness of the face (Figure 18–25). The natural arch of the eyebrow follows the top of the orbital bone, or the curved line above the eye socket. Most people have hair growth above, between, and below the natural line. These hairs can be removed to give a cleaner, more attractive appearance. Correctly shaping brows is an art, and a good brow artist attracts loyal clients who trust their esthetician. Initial brow shaping takes detail work and more time than just maintenance appointments (Figure 18–26a and b).

As with any procedure, always perform a client consultation before tweezing or waxing the eyebrows. Determine the client's wishes as to the final eyebrow shape. If you remove too much hair, it will generally grow back, but the process takes a long time. You will also end up with an unhappy client who is not likely to return for your services. Conducting a thorough consultation beforehand will help you avoid such mistakes.

Reshaping is common, and sometimes there is a need for hair to grow back in spots. This regrowth stage takes patience to not remove hair outside the current line, even if it is the wrong shape. Use a mirror and brow brush to show the client where hair should or should not be removed before they lay down on the table.

Encourage the client not to tweeze between appointments. Recommend a brow pencil or powder and a shaping gel to enhance the brow shape and

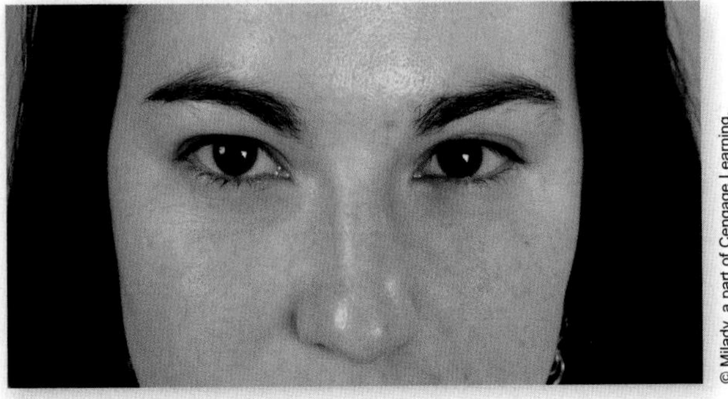

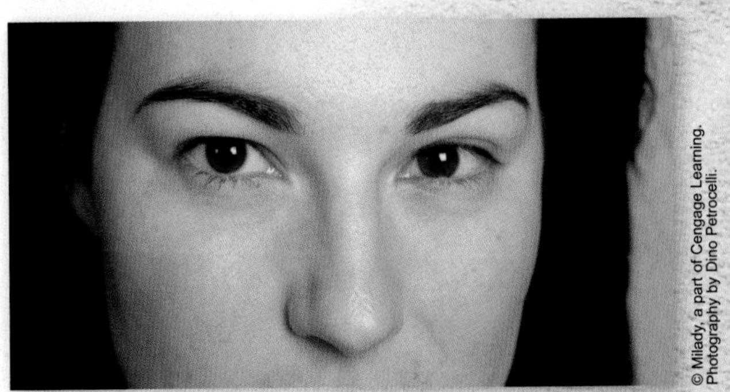

▲ Figure 18–26a and b
Brow design: before and after.

help clients achieve the look they desire, especially if brows are sparse or uneven. Demonstrate for clients how to use these products for the best results.

PROCEDURE 18-2 Eyebrow Waxing with Soft Wax PAGE 509

Brow Waxing Tips

Here are some guidelines to use when waxing the eyebrows.

- ***Men's eyebrows:*** Most men want the brows left natural with just cleaning-up underneath and between the brows. Do not make an even line or tweeze to define unless the client requests it.
- ***Sculpting:*** Brows are arched according to the standard diagram.
- ***Corrections:*** If brows are uneven or too thin, leave the stray hairs to grow back in to match the shape the client wants. Recommend letting the hair grow back to achieve the desired shape. If hairs are removed, they may not always grow back. Hair density gets thinner with time, so in 10 or 20 years, there may be less hair in areas. Let clients know that over-thinning now can affect the brow shape for years to come.
- Check the balance, length, width, and arch for the correct brow shape.
- Use a pencil liner to help mark the boundary lines or points of where to remove (or not remove) the hair.
- Chapter 20, The World of Makeup, provides more information about corrective brow shaping.

CAUTION!

Waxing over an area more than once is not recommended because it can be irritating to the skin. Tweeze any remaining hairs if there are only a few. If there is a large patch of hair, use your judgment. Check-in with the client to decide whether to leave the hair or if the skin can handle a second waxing, but only if using hard wax.

Face, Chin, and Lip Waxing Tips

Hard wax is the preferred wax method for face waxing. It is gentler on the follicles than soft wax and can be removed in the direction of hair growth. It is not recommended to wax vellus hair. The skin is also more delicate on the face. The lip area is especially sensitive.

PROCEDURE 18-3 Lip Waxing with Hard Wax PAGE 512

PROCEDURE 18-4 Chin Waxing with Soft Wax PAGE 514

Tweezing

Tweezing takes practice. It can be very painful if not performed correctly. To remove hair with tweezers, first hold and stretch the skin very taut around the area where you are removing the hair. Then place the tweezers at the base of a hair and gently but firmly pull the hair out, matching the direction of the hair growth (Figure 18–27). A pair of quality tweezers is necessary for professional services.

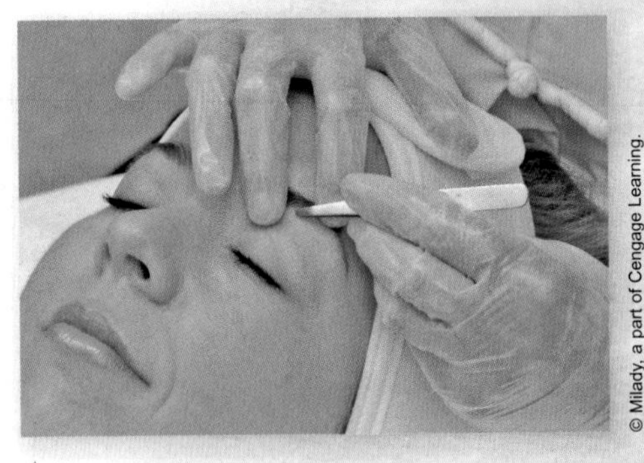

▲ Figure 18–27
Tweezing techniques.

Always check your work with the magnifying lamp. Some estheticians prefer to use their magnifying light while doing hair removal to allow for very detailed work.

Whether you are tweezing or waxing brows, the order of the procedure can be altered. The area between the brows can be tweezed or waxed first, then the areas underneath the brow line. It is more efficient to wax one brow, and then move over to the other one, and then proceed to tweeze as necessary. Some estheticians tweeze between the brows and above the brow line first because the area under the brow line is much more sensitive; others prefer to start underneath.

Body Waxing Procedure Preparation

- Use the same equipment as for the eyebrow waxing procedure, with the addition of larger strips and a larger metal or single-use wooden spatula. A metal spatula holds the heat longer, but it must not touch the client's skin as you apply the wax and must not be used if prohibited by your regulatory agency. You may find single-use spatulas more convenient. Prepare the correct strip sizes.
- Make sure the treatment table is at the right height for the technician and that it is comfortable and easy to move around the table.
- Drape the treatment bed with single-use paper, or use a bed sheet with a towel or paper over the top.
- Conduct the consultation and review the client release form and contraindications.
- Instruct the client on how to prepare, and be mindful of her or his modesty and comfort.
- If bikini waxing, offer the client single-use panties or a small towel for draping.
- If waxing the underarms, have the female client put on a facial gown or wrap. Offer a wrap or towel when waxing the legs or back as well.
- Assist the client onto the treatment bed and drape the client with towels.
- Tuck in a paper towel or wax strip into a bikini bottom or on the edge of the pants to protect any clothing from the wax.
- If trimming excess hair, put an extra single-use paper towel under the area to catch the hair and discard it before waxing. This keeps the extra hair from interfering with the wax and getting all over the table and floor.

PAGE 516

REGULATORY **AGENCY**
ALERT

Laws regarding waxing services vary by region and province. Be sure to check with your regulatory agency for guidelines.

PROCEDURE 18-6 Underarm Waxing with Hard Wax PAGE 518

PROCEDURE 18-7 Bikini Waxing with Hard Wax PAGE 520

Bikini Waxing Variations

Bikini waxing can be categorized in three ways: American (or standard) bikini wax, French bikini wax, and Brazilian bikini wax. The waxing method used depends on the client's preference and the extent of hair to be removed.

Standard *American* bikini waxing is the removal of hair outside the normal bikini line. *French* bikini waxing leaves only a small patch of hair on the front pubis area—everything else is removed.

With *Brazilian* waxing, all of the hair on the genital area is removed—both front and back. Because of the different hair growth directions, hair coarseness, and delicate skin in that area, hard wax is the preferred method used. Blood spots are normal when waxing the bikini area.

The client needs to be positioned to remove hair from the front and back of the bikini area, so everyone needs to be comfortable with the different client positions. These include holding the legs up in a frog position while holding the feet, or being face down while holding themselves up on the arms and legs. Think of them as stretching and yoga poses. You can remove most of the hair and get a very clean shape with normal bikini waxing techniques without doing a full Brazilian wax.

Brazilian waxing is a very popular service. This "extreme" waxing requires practice, competency, and being comfortable working with private areas on the body. Advanced training is required. Refer to the *Milady Standard Esthetics: Advanced* textbook for more information on this procedure.

FOCUS ON

The Client

Be mindful of your client's modesty. Try to make her as relaxed as possible, and do not expose the bikini area any more than she is comfortable with.

CAUTION!

Especially when using hard wax, start with the lower or last sections of hair so the end section or "handle" of wax does not have hair underneath it. Each section then has a bare area at the bottom to form the next handle of the wax as you work up. Avoid pulling the hair underneath when first lifting or flicking the edge to grasp onto—it is very uncomfortable to initially lift the hair underneath with the wax stuck on it.

FOCUS ON

Details

Details are important in any esthetic service. Make sure the wax line is not obvious and blends into the next section of the body with hair. For example, on arm waxing the line between the waxed and nonwaxed area should be gradual and natural looking, not a straight line or abrupt area that has been waxed. Leave some partial hair on the area next to the hairless area. Using a magnifying light and tweezing is another important detail in making sure all the hair is removed after waxing. Clients expect every hair to be gone after a service.

Waxing for the Male Client

The main areas men have waxed are the brow area and the nape of the neck (base of the back of the neck). Another common area that men have waxed is the back (Figure 18–28). The chest waxing procedure is similar to back waxing. Estheticians must proceed with caution in all cases. Men may be sensitive to waxing as the hair is dense and coarse. The skin may become red and irritated. With regular services, your male clients typically get used to waxing. Men may grow wiry hair on the edges of their ears and on the inside of the nose. This growth tends to increase with age. It is not advisable to wax these sensitive areas, but trimming the external hair is helpful. Since men's body hair is thicker and denser, more wax strips are needed to perform men's waxing services.

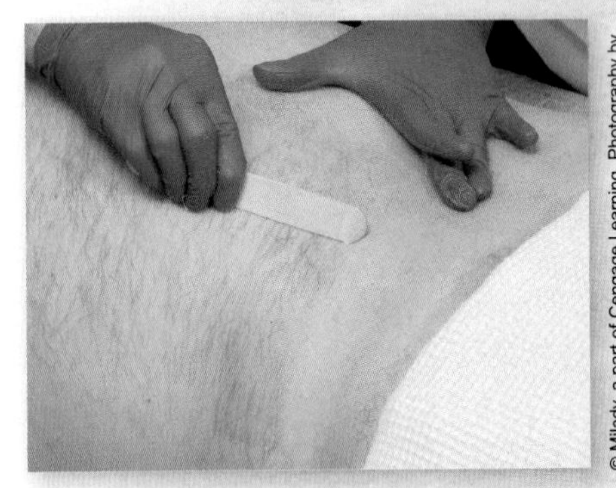

▲ Figure 18–28
Waxing of the back and neck is common for many men.

PROCEDURE 18-8 Men's Waxing with Soft Wax PAGE 523

Scheduling Services

- Face waxing procedures take from 15 minutes to 30 minutes. For example, for both a brow and lip wax, it normally takes 30 minutes. Add time for each additional area that is waxed.
- First time clients, consultations, and shaping with detail work takes longer.
- Body waxing procedures take from 30 minutes to an hour. A basic bikini or lower leg wax takes 30 minutes each; a full leg wax can take an hour. Add time for each additional area.
- The time depends on the amount of hair and area to be waxed.

Preparation time and clean-up time is usually scheduled for 15 minutes before and 15 minutes after the service (refer to Table 18–2 for average times and prices). Body waxing takes more preparation and clean-up time. Proper decontamination takes time.

REGULATORY AGENCY ALERT

Some states or provinces require estheticians to (1) clean the skin before tweezing or waxing and (2) apply an antiseptic at the end of the procedure. Always check with your regulatory agency to be sure you are complying with the requirements.

WAXING TIMES AND PRICES

These times and prices obviously vary by region and facility, but this is a partial example of a menu with average pricing. Times and prices are usually adjusted by the amount of hair to be waxed.

WAXING SERVICE	TIME	PRICE
Eyebrow Maintenance or Design	15–30 minutes	$25–$50
Lip or Chin	15 min. each	$15–$25 each
Under Arms	30 min.	$25–$35
Half Leg	30–45 min.	$35–$50
Full Leg	60 min.	$65–$75
Basic Bikini	30 min.	$40–$50
Back, Chest, or Shoulders	30–45 min.	$30–$50

▲ Table 18–2 **Waxing Times and Prices.**

CAUTION!

To avoid injuring or irritating the client's skin, remember these important points about the wax removal technique: You must hold the skin taut, remove the wax quickly, and not pull upward when removing the wax strip. Always pull parallel along the skin's surface. Parallel pulling means following the same plane as the body: keeping the entire motion at a constant and equal distance to the skin's surface.

PROCEDURE

18-1 Eyebrow Tweezing

IMPLEMENTS AND MATERIALS

- Station and cleaning supplies
- EPA-registered disinfectant
- Hand sanitizer
- Towels
- Tweezers
- Small hair scissors
- Small hand-held mirror
- Cotton pads
- Eyebrow brush or comb
- Emollient cream
- Antiseptic lotion
- Gentle eye makeup remover
- Astringent
- Single-use gloves
- Client release form and chart
- Client headband
- Plastic bag for disposables

Preparation

- **Perform** 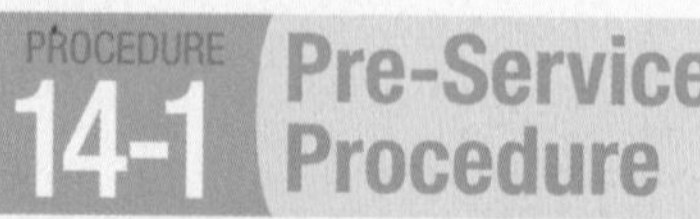

PAGE 372

1 Discuss with the client the type of eyebrow arch suitable for her facial characteristics.

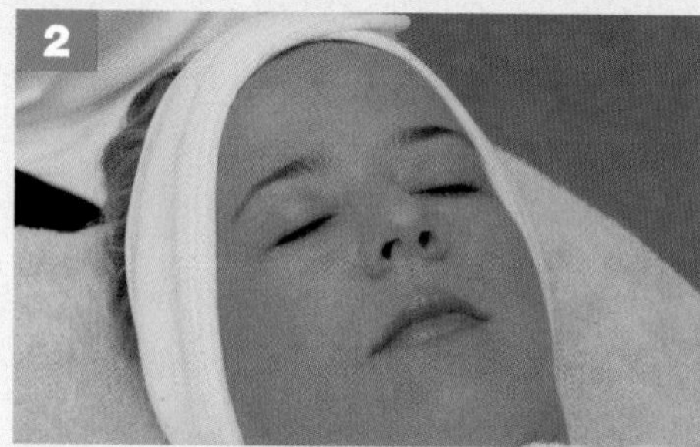

2 Seat the client in a facial chair in a reclining position, as for a facial massage. Or, if you prefer, seat the client in a half-upright position and work from the side if it is comfortable for both you and the client. The head needs to be supported and held steady to get a firm grip and hold the skin taut. The brows should be easy to reach and visible under adequate lighting, preferably with a magnifying light.

3 Drape a towel over the client's clothing.

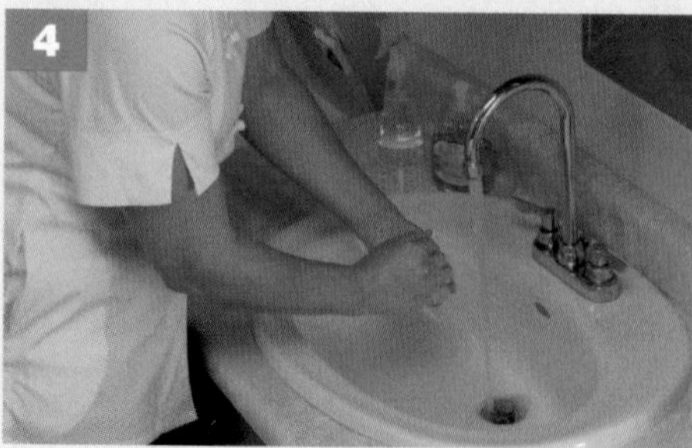

4 Wash and dry your hands, and put on single-use gloves. Washing your hands thoroughly with soap and warm water is critical before and after every client procedure you perform. The importance of proper cleaning in these procedures cannot be overemphasized.

Procedure

The eyebrow tweezing procedure involves the following steps:

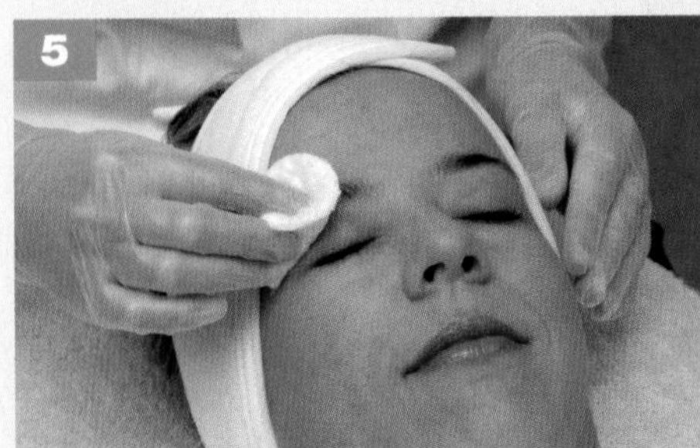

5 Prepare the skin: use a mild antiseptic on a cotton pad before tweezing to clean and prepare the area.

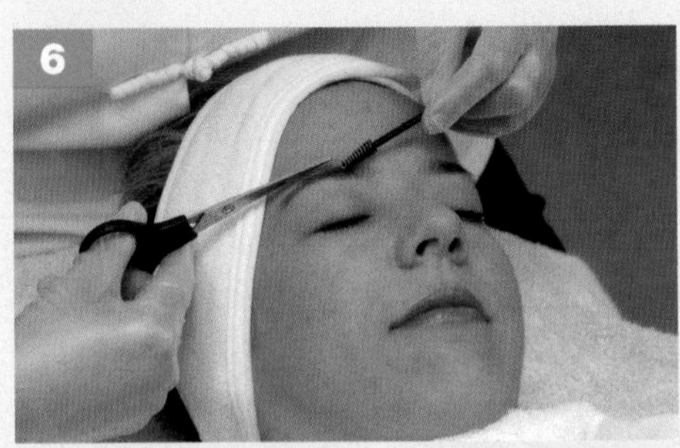

6 Measure the brows to check the shape (in-between the brows, the arch, and the end of the brow). Brush the eyebrows with a small brush. Carefully trim long hairs outside the brow line now or after tweezing. Brush the hair upward and into place to see the natural line of the brow. Observe the stray hairs and what needs to be removed.

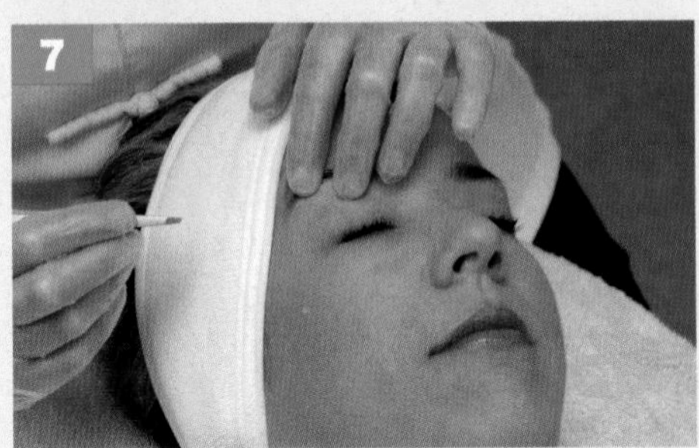

7 Stretch the skin taut next to the hair with the index finger and thumb (or index and middle fingers) of your other hand while tweezing. Hold each area taut next to the hair being removed.

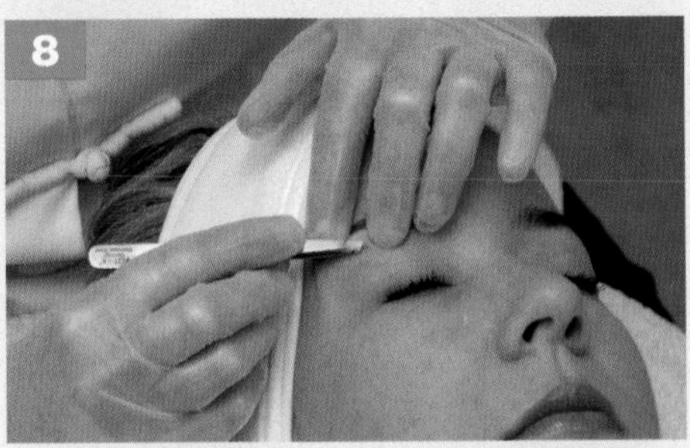

8 Remove hairs from under the eyebrow line. Shape the lower section of one eyebrow, then shape the other. Grasp each hair individually with tweezers and pull with a quick, smooth motion in the direction of the hair growth. Carefully grasp the hair at the base as close to the skin as possible without pinching the skin and pull in the direction of the hair growth, not straight up or out.

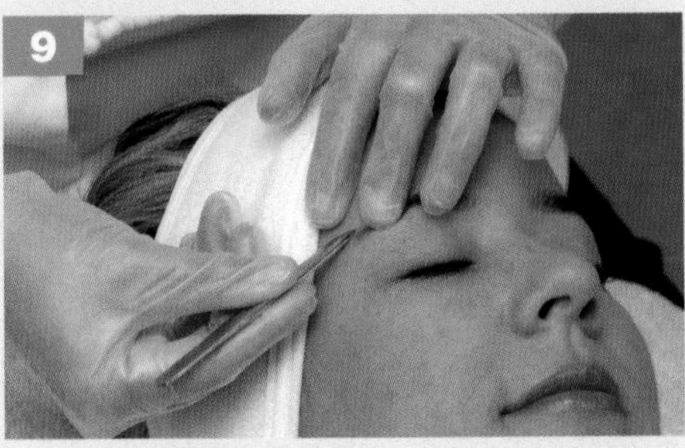

9 Brush the hair downward. Remove hairs from above the eyebrow line if the predetermined shape deems it neccessary. Shape the upper section of one eyebrow; then shape the other.

PROCEDURE

18-1 Eyebrow Tweezing (continued)

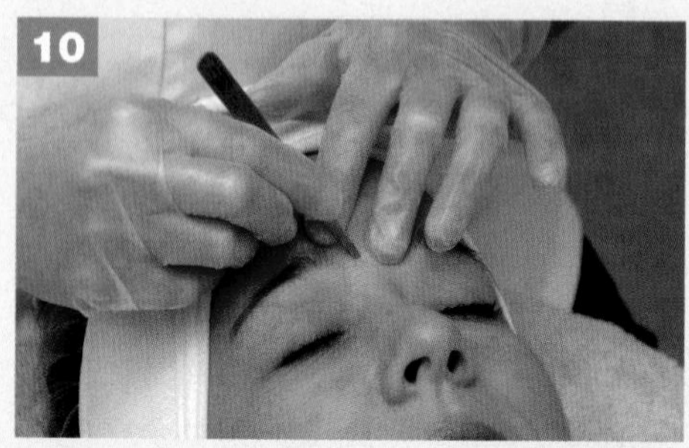

10 Remove hair from between the brows.

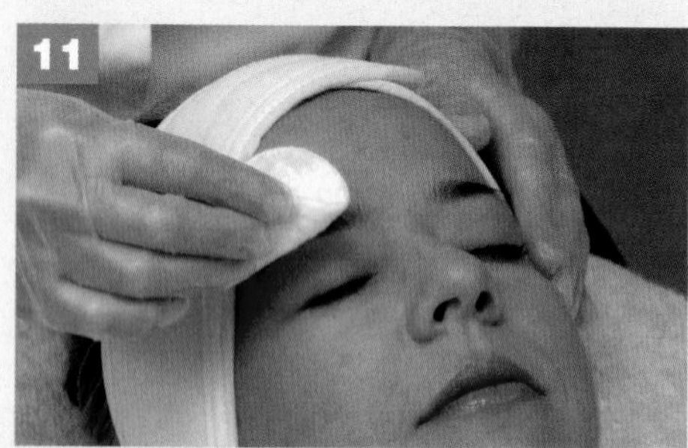

11 Wipe the tweezed areas with a cotton pad, moistened with a nonirritating antiseptic lotion, to contract the skin and avoid infection.

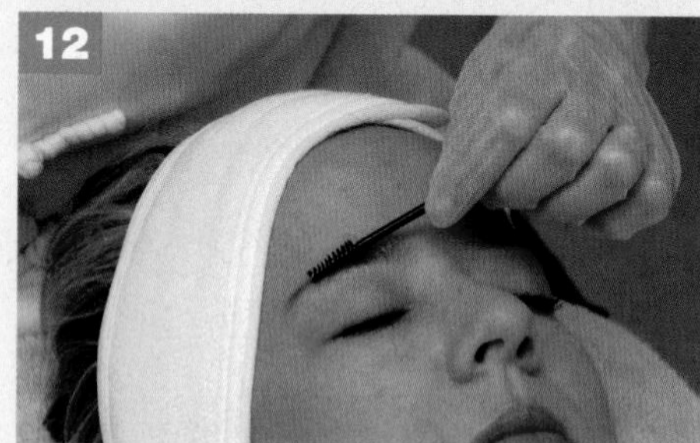

12 Brush the eyebrow hair in its normal position.

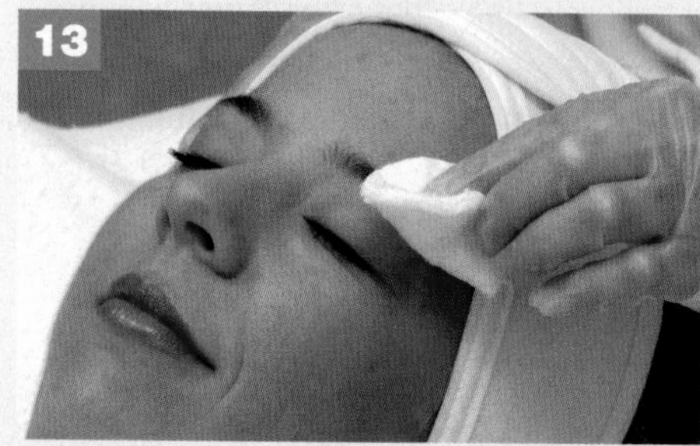

13 ***Optional:*** Apply a soothing cream. Gently remove excess cream with a cotton pad.

fyi

Always wash your hands before preparing and setting up for a service, after draping, immediately after any service before walking the client out, and after finishing the post-service procedures.

14 If eyebrow tweezing is part of a makeup or facial service, continue the procedure. If not, complete the next step.

Post-Service

- **Complete** 
PAGE 375

PROCEDURE

18-2

Eyebrow Waxing with Soft Wax

IMPLEMENTS AND MATERIALS

The following list applies for all waxing procedures.

- Facial chair or treatment table
- Technician stool
- EPA-registered disinfectant
- Hand sanitizer
- Roll of single-use paper or paper towels
- Closed, covered waste container
- Cart
- Implement tray
- Containers for supplies
- Wax product
- Wax heater
- Wax remover
- Small single-use applicators (brow size spatulas)
- Wax strips (for soft wax)
- Single-use gloves
- Sealable plastic bags for waste disposal
- Cotton pads and swabs
- Powder
- Mild skin cleanser
- Emollient or antiseptic lotion
- Brow brush
- Tweezers
- Small scissors
- Hand mirror
- Tongs (to retrieve clean supplies during a service)
- Surface cleaner (oil to remove wax from the equipment)
- Wax cleaning towels/supplies
- Table linens/towels
- Hair cap or headband for face waxing
- Towels for draping
- Wax release form and client chart
- Biohazard container, especially for underarm, bikini, and back waxing (the potenial for blood spots from follicles is normal)

This procedure for eyebrow waxing employs the use of a strip to remove soft wax. Hard wax may also be used. Adapt this procedure and supply list for all other body areas to be waxed. Review the wax application and removal techniques in the chapter before performing this procedure.

Preparation

- **Perform** 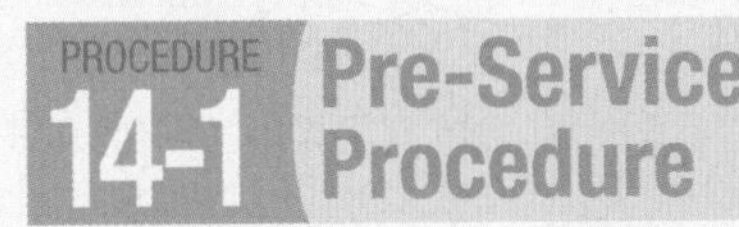

PAGE 372
- For the waxing procedures, melt the wax in the heater. The length of time it takes to melt the wax depends on the product, temperature, and how full the wax holder is: approximately 30 minutes if it is full; 15 minutes if it is a quarter to half full. Be sure the wax is not too hot.
- Complete the client consultation, release form, determine any contraindications, and determine what hair you need to remove.
- Lay a clean towel over the top of the facial chair and then a layer of single-use paper under the head (if applicable).

Procedure

The soft pot wax procedure with strips includes the following steps:

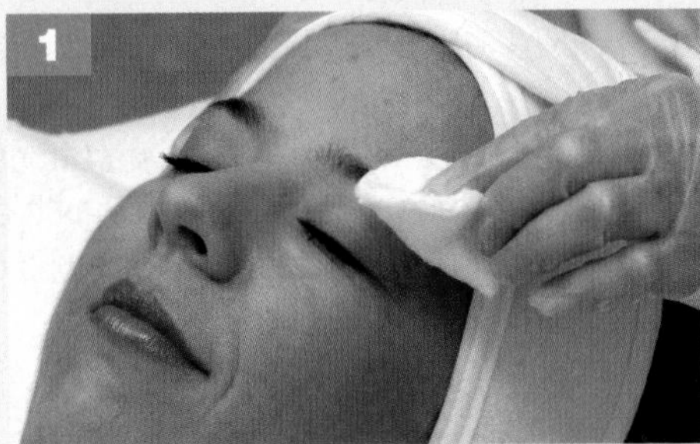

1 Prepare the skin: remove makeup on the area to be waxed. Cleanse the area thoroughly with a mild astringent cleanser, and dry.

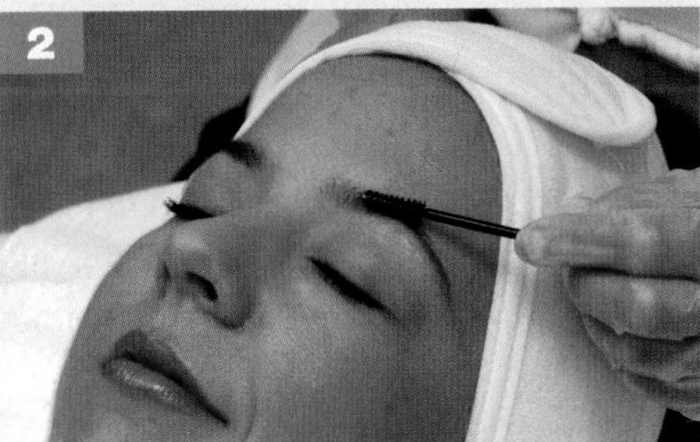

2 Apply a non-talc powder, if applicable. Brush the hair into place to see the brow line. Measure the three lines for shaping and examine what hair needs to be removed.

PROCEDURE

18-2 Eyebrow Waxing with Soft Wax (continued)

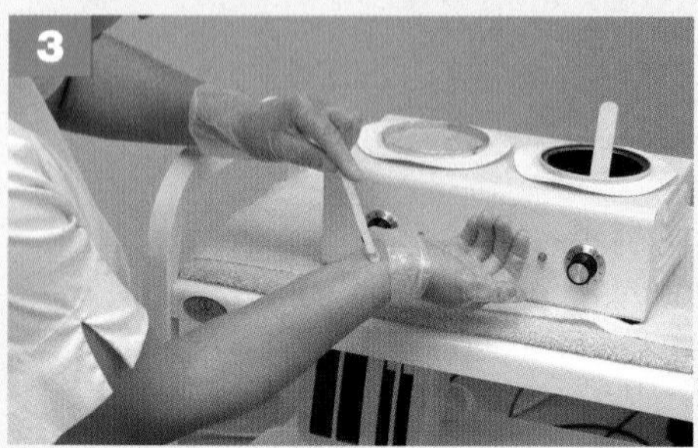

3 Test the temperature and consistency of the heated wax by applying a small (dime size) drop on the inside of your wrist. It should be warm but not hot, and it should run smoothly off the spatula. Remove with a strip as you would while waxing.

4 Wipe off one side of the spatula on the inside edge of the pot, so it does not drip. Carefully take it from the pot to the brow area. If it is dripping off the spatula, there is too much wax, or it is too hot. Correct the problem to avoid drips or hurting the client.

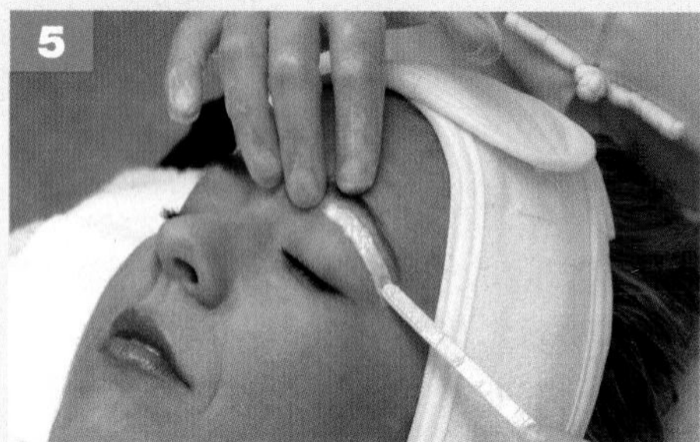

5 Apply the wax: with the spatula at a 45-degree angle, spread a thin coat of the wax evenly over the area to be waxed, following the direction of the hair growth. Hold the skin taut near the edge where the wax is first applied. Be sure not to put the spatula in the wax more than once (do not double-dip). Do not use an excessive amount of wax, because it will spread when the fabric is pressed and may cover hair you do not wish to remove.

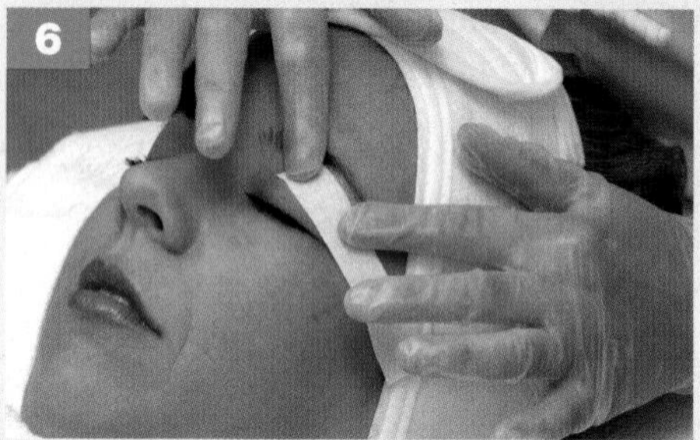

6 Apply a clean fabric strip over the area to be waxed. Start the edge of the strip at the edge of the wax where you first applied it. Do not cover the rest of the brow with the strip. This way you can see the exposed area that you do not want to wax. Leave enough of the strip to hold on to for the pull. Press gently in the direction of hair growth, running your finger over the surface of the fabric three to five times so the wax adheres to the hair. Remember to check to make sure wax has not spread where you do not want it.

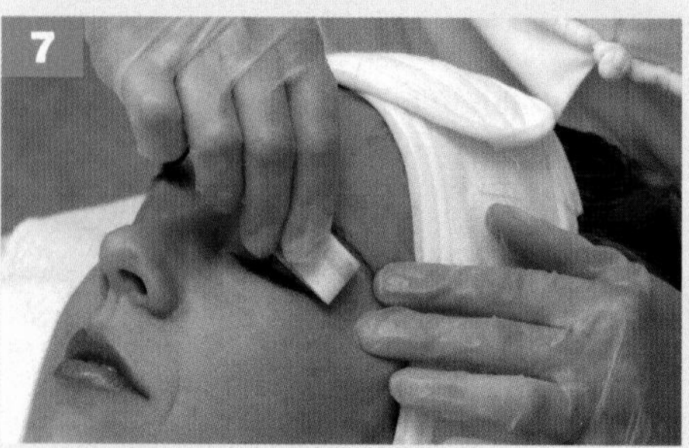

7 Remove the wax: gently but firmly hold the skin taut, placing the index and middle fingers of one hand on next to the strip as close as possible to where you will start to pull. Hold the loose edge of the strip at the end and quickly remove the strip by pulling in the direction opposite to the hair growth. Do not lift or pull straight up on the strip; doing so could damage or remove the skin.

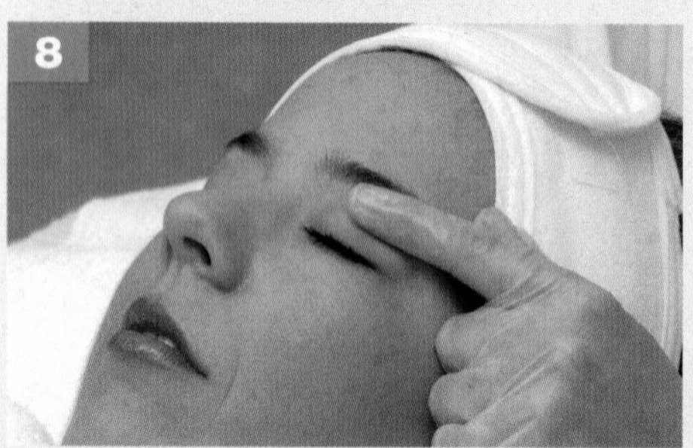

8 Immediately apply pressure with your finger to the waxed area. Hold it there for approximately 5 seconds to relieve the painful sensation.

9 Remove any excess wax residue from the skin with the strip by gently lifting it sideways in the same direction as the hair growth. To avoid removing additional hair, do not let the strip accidently touch any hair while doing this. A clean part of the strip can be folded over and used for this, or use a new strip.

10 Repeat the wax procedure on the area around the other eyebrow.

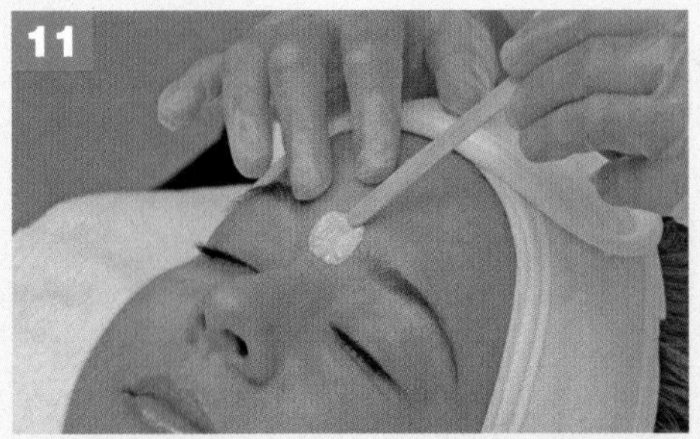

11 For the area between the brows, apply the wax (generally in an upward direction between the nose and the forehead). Line the bottom of the strip up to the bottom edge of the wax. Hold the skin taut on both sides of the strip above the brows with the middle and ring fingers.

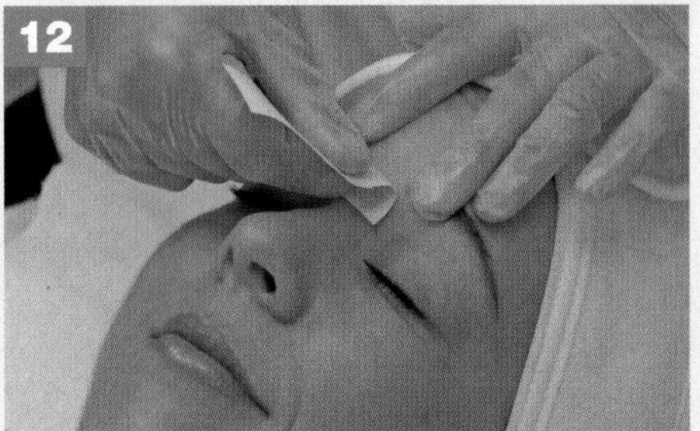

12 Hold the top of the strip and pull the strip straight down close to the nose without lifting. This area can be done all in one section or in two halves—the right and the left.

CAUTION!

Never leave the wax heater on overnight, because it is a fire hazard and can affect the quality of the wax.

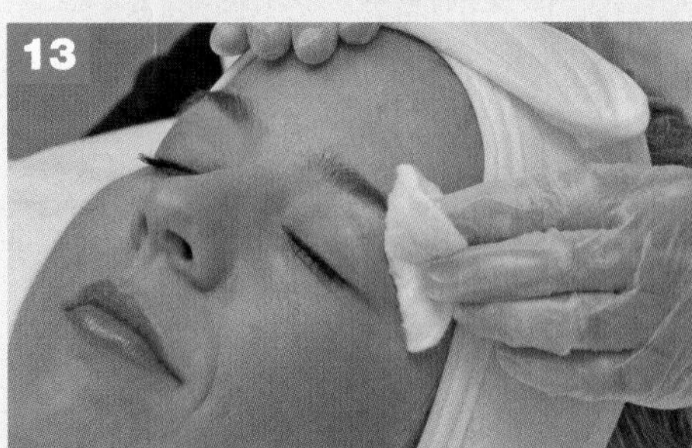

13 Cleanse the waxed area with a mild wax-remover, and apply a post-wax product or antiseptic lotion.

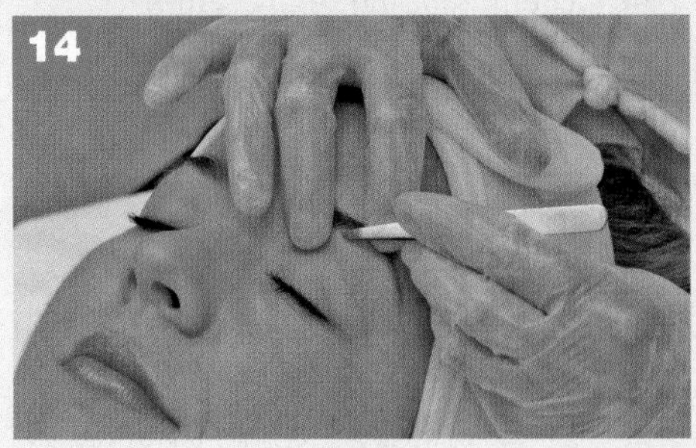

14 Tweeze the remaining stray hairs, and apply a cold compress if necessary. If it is too slippery or there is wax residue, apply the post-wax products after tweezing or rinse the area with water and pat dry before tweezing.

Service Tip

Excess wax will get on the tweezers and interfere with tweezing. Remove all wax and post-products with a moist cotton pad before tweezing, and reapply soothing products after tweezing.

15 Remove the gloves and wash your hands.

Post-Service

- **Complete** PROCEDURE 14-2 Post-Service Procedure PAGE 375
- Discard all used single-use materials in a sealable plastic bag and closed waste container.
- Never reuse wax.
- Do not place the used spatula, muslin strips, wax, or any other materials used in waxing directly on the counter. Use a tray or paper towel.
- Complete a post-wax consultation and discuss post-wax precautions.

CAUTION!

If the wax strings and lands in an area you do not wish to treat, remove it with lotion designed to dissolve and remove wax. Always cover clients' hair and clothes to protect them from wax.

PROCEDURE

18-3

Lip Waxing with Hard Wax

IMPLEMENTS AND MATERIALS

- Facial chair or treatment table
- Technician stool
- EPA-registered disinfectant
- Hand sanitizer
- Roll of single-use paper or paper towels
- Closed, covered waste container
- Cart
- Implement tray
- Containers for supplies
- Wax product
- Wax heater
- Wax remover
- Single-use applicators (medium size spatulas)
- Wax strips (for soft wax)
- Single-use gloves
- Sealable plastic bags for waste disposal
- Cotton pads and swabs
- Powder
- Mild skin cleanser
- Emollient or antiseptic lotion
- Tweezers
- Small scissors
- Hand mirror
- Tongs (to retrieve clean supplies during a service)
- Surface cleaner (oil to remove wax from the equipment)
- Wax cleaning towels/supplies
- Table linens/towels
- Hair cap or headband for face waxing
- Towels for draping
- Wax release form and client chart
- Biohazard container, especially for underarm, bikini, and back waxing (the potenial for blood spots from follicles is normal)

Be guided by your instructor for hard wax application and removal. Some apply and remove hard wax differently than soft wax. For example: Only with hard wax can you apply opposite to the hair growth and remove with the direction of the hair growth. It is best to learn the soft wax techniques first to avoid incorrect pulls and injuring the skin.

Preparation

- **Perform** 

PAGE 372
- Melt the wax in the heater.

Note: Soft wax may be used with strips for the same procedure. The lip waxing procedure with hard wax includes the following steps:

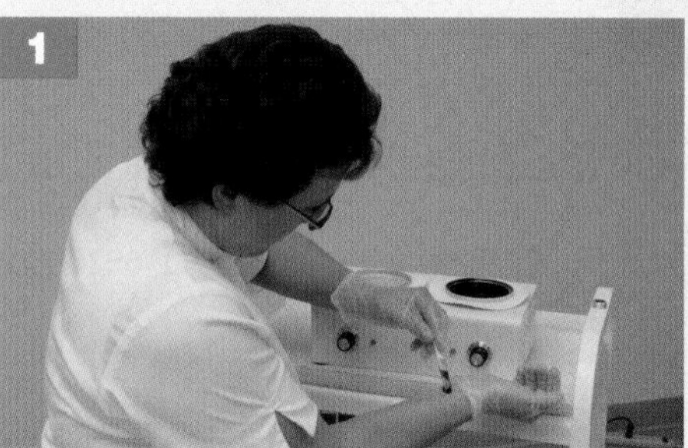

1 After draping the client, test the temperature and consistency of the wax on the inside of your wrist.

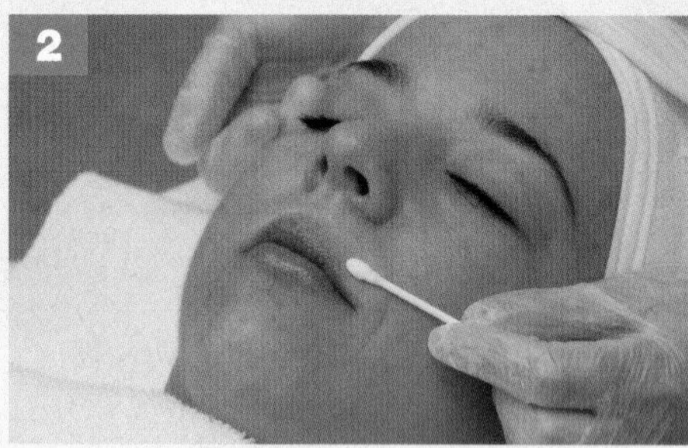

2 Prepare the skin by cleansing. For lip waxing, have the client hold the lips tightly together to avoid pulling the skin.

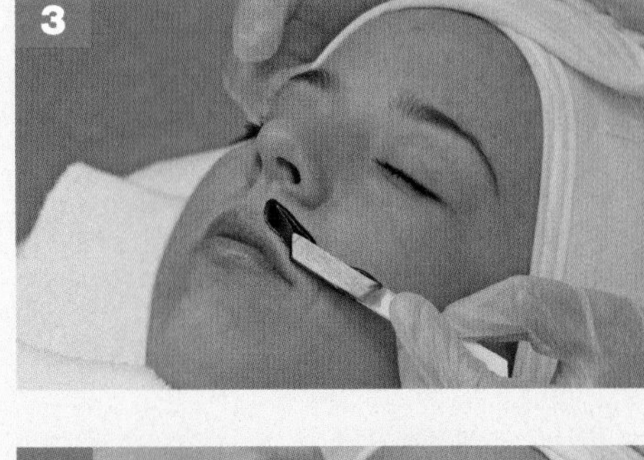

3 Apply wax to one side of the upper lip outward from the center to the corner, leaving a "tab" or "handle" to grasp. Make sure there is a thicker layer of hard wax and the consistency is right before removing. It should be firm and feel tacky, but not hard or brittle. (If using soft wax, apply the strip.)

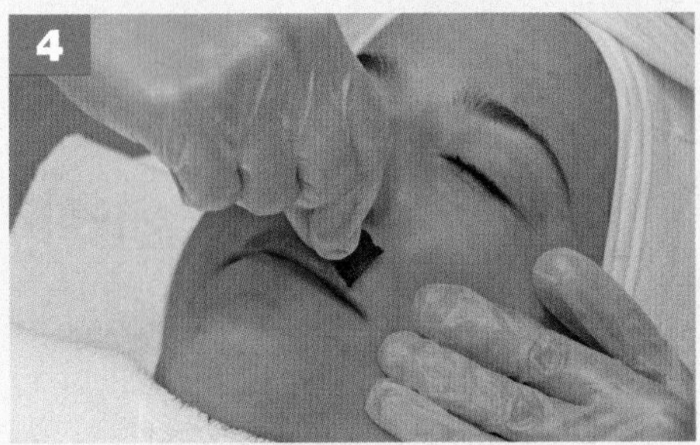

4 Remove the wax: hold the skin taut, and quickly pull parallel to the skin without lifting up.

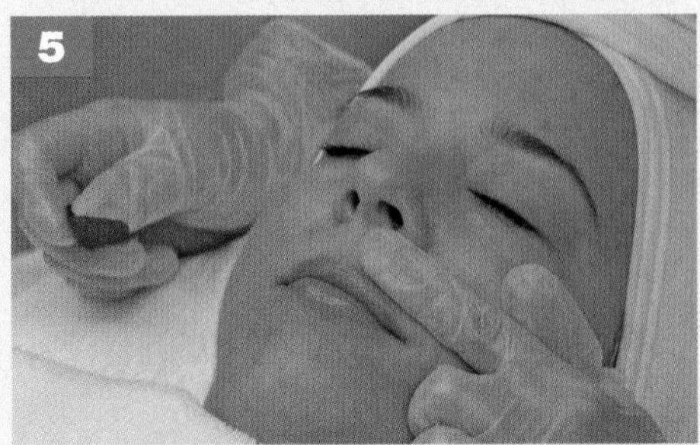

5 Immediately apply pressure to the waxed area to ease any discomfort.

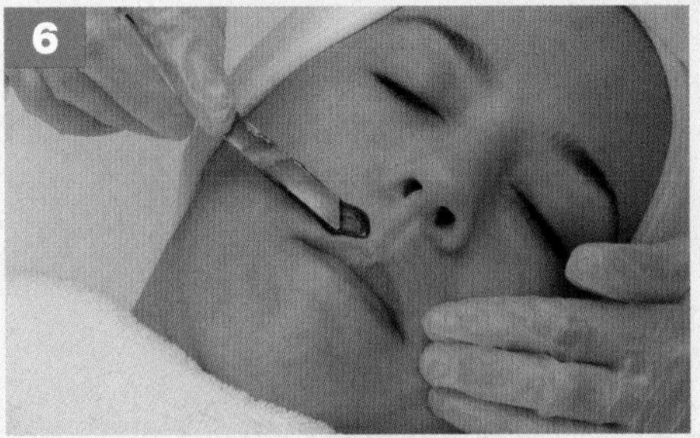

6 Repeat on the other side of the lip.

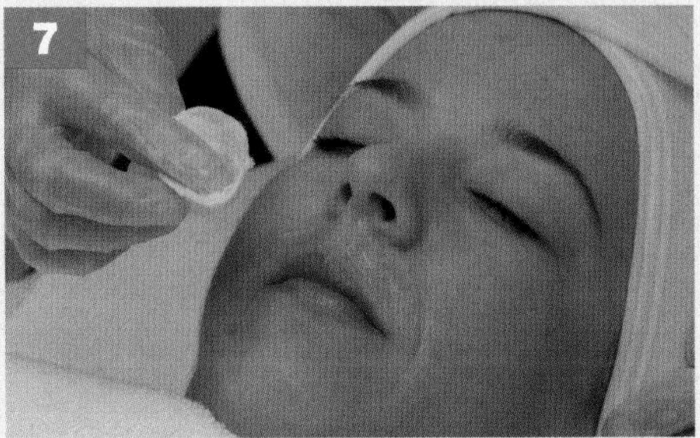

7 Apply after-wax soothing lotion.

Post-Service

- **Complete** 

PAGE 375

- Complete a post-wax consultation and discuss post-wax precautions.

PROCEDURE

18-4

Chin Waxing with Hard Wax

IMPLEMENTS AND MATERIALS

Note: Make sure you have the correct strip sizes ready if you are using soft wax instead of hard wax.

The following list applies for all waxing procedures.

- Facial chair or treatment table
- Technician stool
- EPA-registered disinfectant
- Hand sanitizer
- Roll of single-use paper or paper towels
- Closed, covered waste container
- Cart
- Implement tray
- Containers for supplies
- Wax product
- Wax heater
- Wax remover
- Single-use applicators (medium size spatulas)
- Wax strips (for soft wax)
- Single-use gloves
- Sealable plastic bags for waste disposal
- Cotton pads and swabs
- Powder
- Mild skin cleanser
- Emollient or antiseptic lotion
- Tweezers
- Small scissors
- Hand mirror
- Tongs (to retrieve clean supplies during a service)
- Surface cleaner (oil to remove wax from the equipment)
- Wax cleaning towels/supplies
- Table linens/towels
- Hair cap or headband for face waxing
- Towels for draping
- Wax release form and client chart
- Biohazard container, especially for underarm, bikini, and back waxing (the potenial for blood spots from follicles is normal)

Preparation

- **Perform** 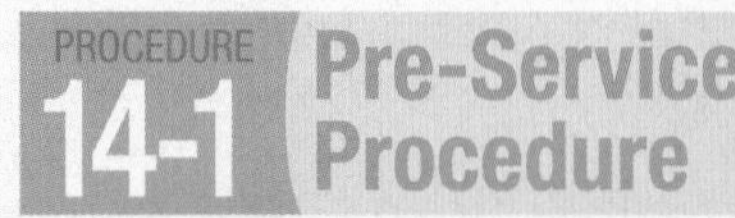 PROCEDURE 14-1 Pre-Service Procedure PAGE 372
- Melt the wax in the heater. Be sure the wax is not too hot.
- Complete the client consultation, release form, determine any contraindications, and determine what hair you need to remove.
- Lay a clean towel over the top of the facial chair and then a layer of single-use paper under the head (if applicable).

Procedure

1 Test the wax temperature.

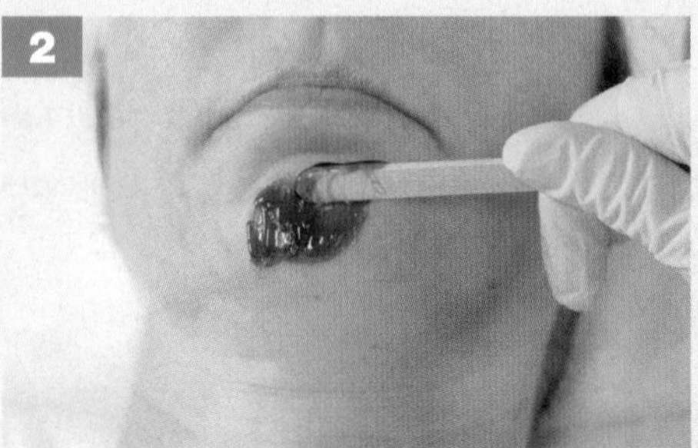

2 Apply the wax in small sections above the curve of the jawline from the top to bottom ending at the jawline. Do not go over the curve. Wax above the jawline, then below it using separate pulls. Or you can wax below the jawline first, then above it. Make sure to leave enough wax beyond the area for a handle/pull tab. Lift up the pull tab to grasp onto. Check that the wax consistency is "tacky" before removal.

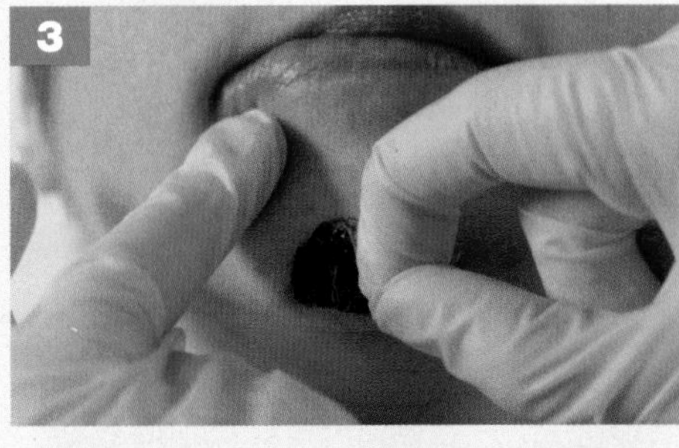

3 Remove the wax: hold the skin taut close to the end of the wax where you start the pull, and pull opposite to the hair growth and parallel to the skin.

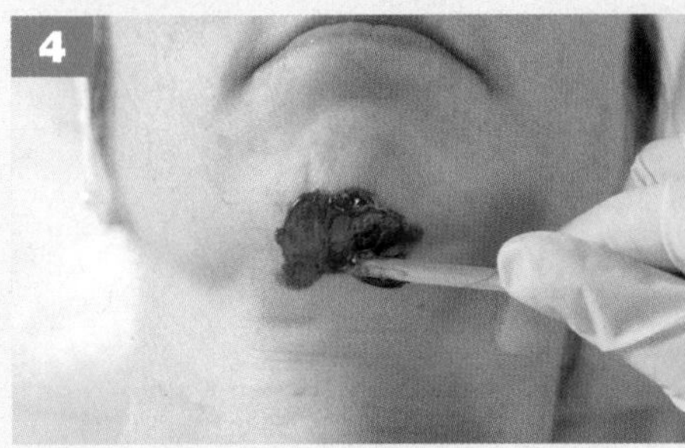

4 Apply the wax in small sections below the curve of the jawline.

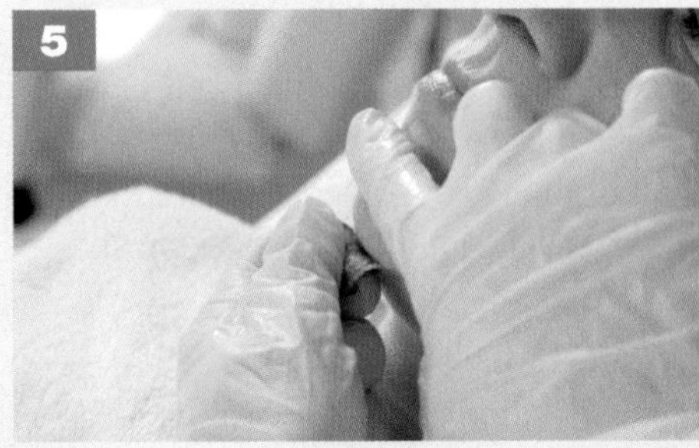

5 Remove the wax: hold the skin taut, and pull parallel to the skin.

6 Apply light pressure on the waxed area without pressing down hard on the throat or neck.

7 Continue the procedure and apply the post-wax products.

Post-Service

- **Complete** PROCEDURE 14-2 **Post-Service Procedure** PAGE 375
- Complete a post-wax consultation and discuss post-wax precautions.

PROCEDURE

18-5 Leg Waxing with Soft Wax

IMPLEMENTS AND MATERIALS

Note: Make sure you have the correct strip sizes ready if you are using soft wax instead of hard wax.

The following list applies for all waxing procedures.

- Facial chair or treatment table
- Technician stool
- EPA-registered disinfectant
- Hand sanitizer
- Roll of single-use paper or paper towels
- Closed, covered waste container
- Cart
- Implement tray
- Containers for supplies
- Wax product
- Wax heater
- Wax remover
- Single-use applicators (large spatulas)
- Wax strips (for soft wax)
- Single-use gloves
- Sealable plastic bags for waste disposal
- Cotton pads and swabs
- Powder
- Mild skin cleanser
- Emollient or antiseptic lotion
- Brow brush
- Tweezers
- Small scissors
- Hand mirror
- Tongs (to retrieve clean supplies during a service)
- Surface cleaner (oil to remove wax from the equipment)
- Wax cleaning towels/supplies
- Table linens/towels
- Hair cap or headband for face waxing
- Towels for draping
- Client wrap for body waxing
- Wax release form and client chart
- Biohazard container, especially for underarm, bikini, and back waxing (the potential for blood spots from follicles is normal)

Preparation

- **Perform** PROCEDURE 14-1 Pre-Service Procedure PAGE 372
- Melt the wax in the heater. Be sure the wax is not too hot.
- Complete the client consultation, release form, and determine any contraindications.
- Place a clean sheet or sheet of paper on the waxing table for each new client.

Procedure

Leg waxing can be started with either the front or the back of the legs. Visually divide the front of the legs in quarter sections (below the knees) and use a set pattern, starting removal at the bottom half of the lower legs. Make sure the skin is held taut while removing the wax, especially around the ankle, which is more sensitive.

Start the application on the front (or back) side of the leg 7 inches (17.5 centimeters) below the knee and apply down to the just above the ankle. Work across to the other side of the leg using two or three strips. Then do the next section from the middle of the lower leg to the knees. The entire front leg should be waxed, including the knees, and lotion applied to the front before having the client turn over and continue on the back of the legs.

1 If skin is moist or oily, cleanse the area to be waxed with a mild astringent cleanser and dry. If skin is dry and flaky, a tiny amount of lotion may be applied and then removed. Apply a light dusting of powder if necessary.

2 Test the temperature and consistency of the heated wax.

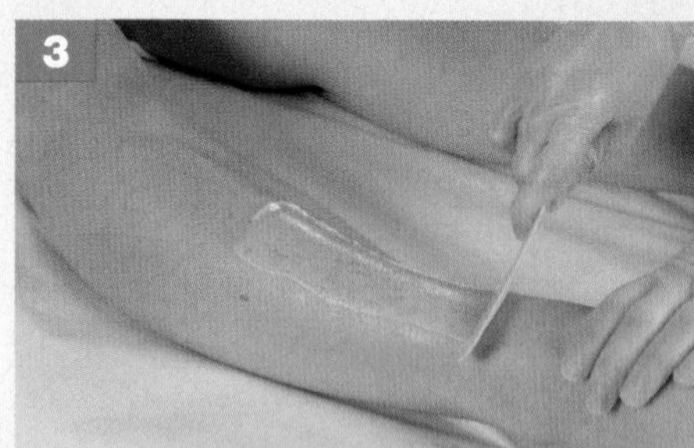

3 Apply the wax using a spatula. Spread a thin coat of warm wax evenly over the skin surface in the same direction as the hair growth.

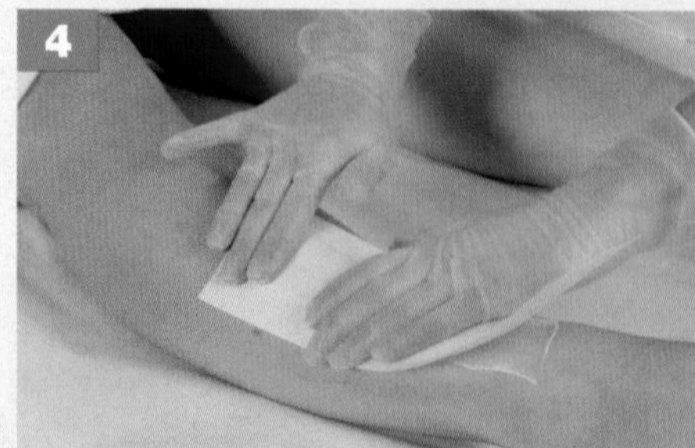

4 Apply a fabric strip over the wax in the same direction as the hair growth. Press gently but firmly, rubbing your hand back and forth over the surface of the fabric three to five times.

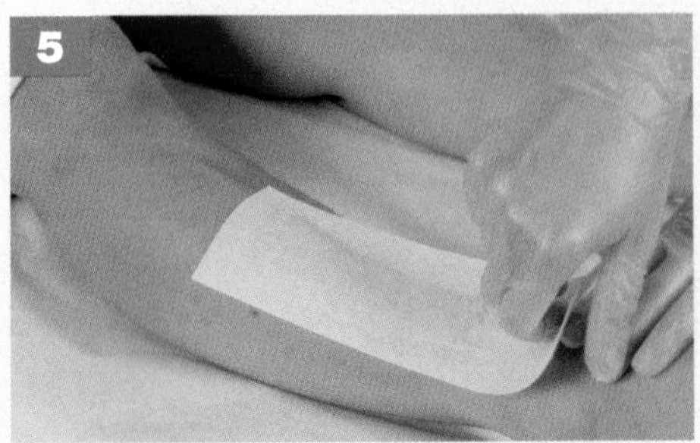

5 Remove the wax: hold the skin taut with one hand close to where you will pull with the other hand, and quickly remove the wax in the opposite direction of the hair growth without lifting.

6 Quickly put your hand down to apply pressure to the waxed area for approximately 5 seconds.

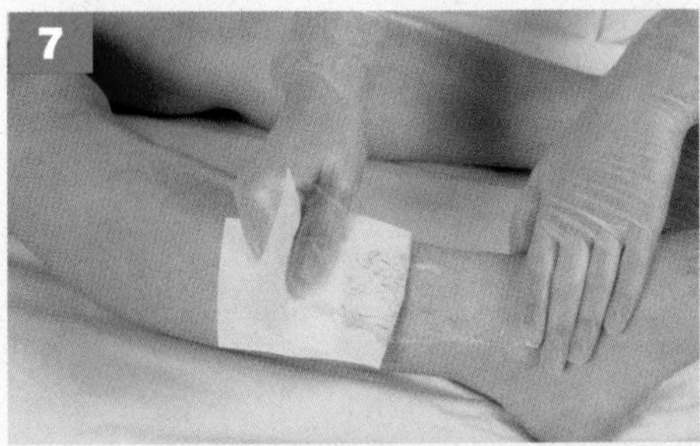

7 Repeat, using a fresh fabric strip as each strip becomes too thick with wax or hair.

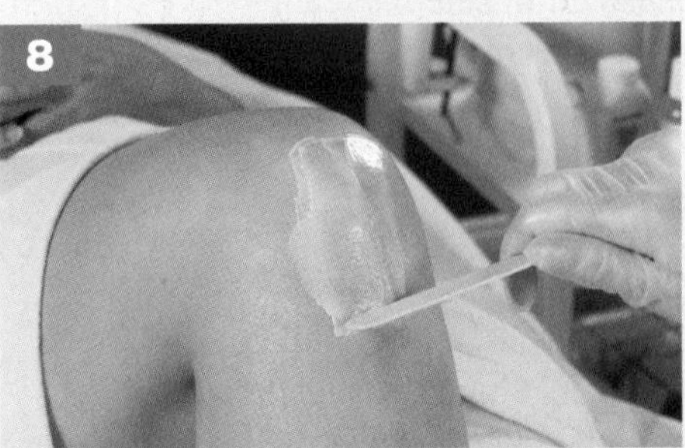

8 Wax the knees. Have the client bend the knee and place the foot on the table. Wax below the curve of the knee working in three sections across from one side to the other: left, middle, and right sides. Then wax the top of the knees above the curve using the same pattern in three sections.

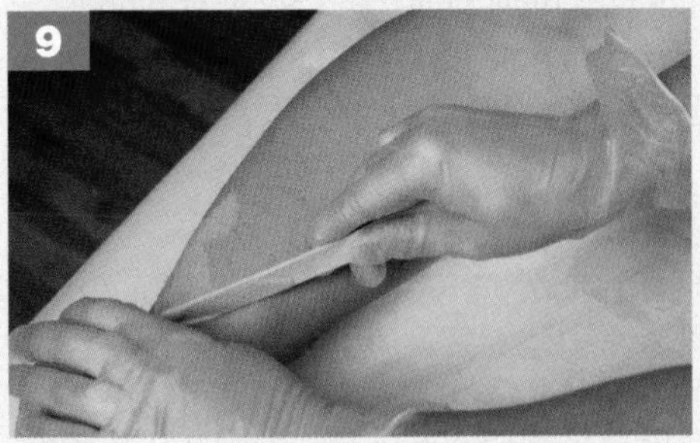

9 To keep the client's skin from sticking to the table, apply the soothing wax remover (made for the skin) only where the wax was applied before having the client turn over to wax the back of the legs. Have the client turn over, and repeat the procedure on the backs of the legs.

10 Remove any remaining residue of wax from the skin, and apply an emollient or antiseptic lotion. Check for stray hairs. Remove gloves and wash your hands after the service.

Service Tip

If skin is too dry or cold, wax may stick and will not come off properly. A tiny amount of lotion or oil may be used to pre-treat the skin. Conversely, too much product will prevent the wax from sticking. Make sure the room is warm so both the wax and client are at the right temperature. Check the wax consistency and machine temperature knob while setting up for services so adjustments can be made before starting a service.

Post-Service

- **Complete** PROCEDURE 14-2 **Post-Service Procedure** PAGE 375
- Complete a post-wax consultation and discuss post-wax precautions.

PROCEDURE

18-6

Underarm Waxing with Hard Wax

IMPLEMENTS AND MATERIALS

The following list applies for all waxing procedures.

- Facial chair or treatment table
- Technician stool
- EPA-registered disinfectant
- Hand sanitizer
- Roll of single-use paper or paper towels
- Closed, covered waste container
- Cart
- Implement tray
- Containers for supplies
- Wax product
- Wax heater
- Wax remover
- Single-use applicators (large)
- Wax strips (for soft wax)
- Single-use gloves
- Sealable plastic bags for waste disposal
- Cotton pads and swabs
- Powder
- Mild skin cleanser
- Emollient or antiseptic lotion
- Brow brush
- Tweezers
- Small scissors
- Hand mirror
- Tongs (to retrieve clean supplies during a service)
- Surface cleaner (oil to remove wax from the equipment)
- Wax cleaning towels/supplies
- Table linens/towels
- Hair cap or headband for face waxing
- Towels for draping
- Client wrap for body waxing
- Wax release form and client chart
- Biohazard container, especially for underarm, bikini, and back waxing (the potential for blood spots from follicles is normal)

Preparation

- **Perform** 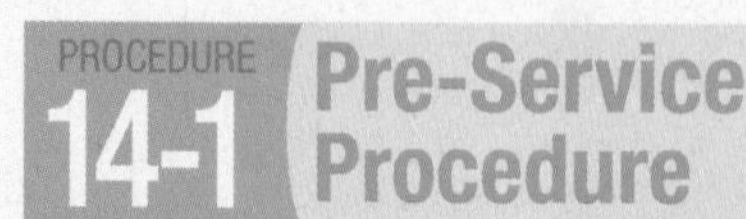 PAGE 372

- Melt the wax in the heater. Be sure the wax is not too hot.
- Complete the client consultation, release form, determine any contraindications, and determine what hair you need to remove.

Procedure

Because the hair under the arms grows in several different directions, it is important to first determine the number of different growth patterns and then to wax in sections following those patterns. Cut strips to the appropriate size if using soft wax. Divide the underarm area into multiple sections or as hair growth patterns allow. Follicles under the arm have fluids and spots of blood that come to the surface after hair removal, so apply a cold compress to calm the follicles after the hair is removed from the area.

1 Wearing gloves, cleanse the underarm area.

2 Apply a small amount of powder (or pre-wax product) to the area to dry the area and facilitate the adherence of wax. Have the client hold the skin taut next to the area to be waxed and place her hands where it does not interfere with the waxing pull. Hold the skin taut next to the edge of the wax strip where applying and removing the wax.

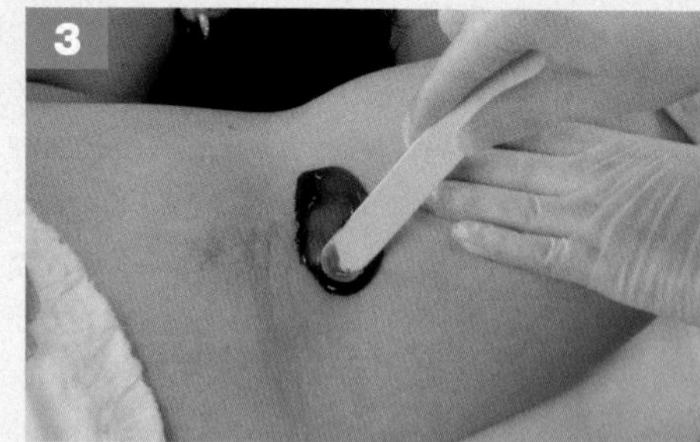

3 Apply wax to the first area, usually on the top or outer edge of the underarm. Leave a tab to grasp onto and check the consistency for removal.

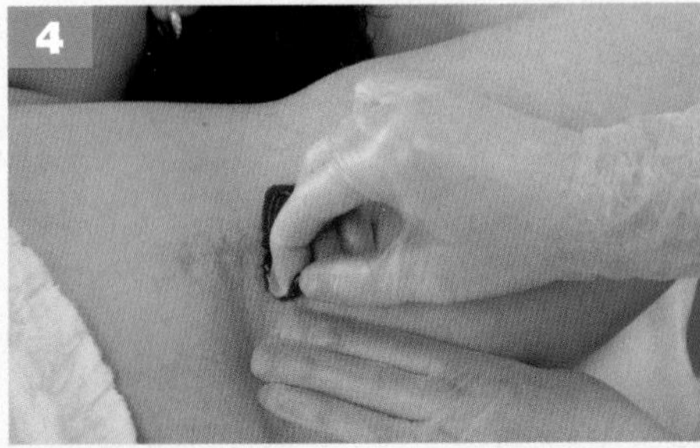

4 Remove wax: grasp the wax "handle" or strip and quickly pull. Hold and stretch the skin taut when removing the wax.

5 Apply pressure immediately after wax removal to ease any pain.

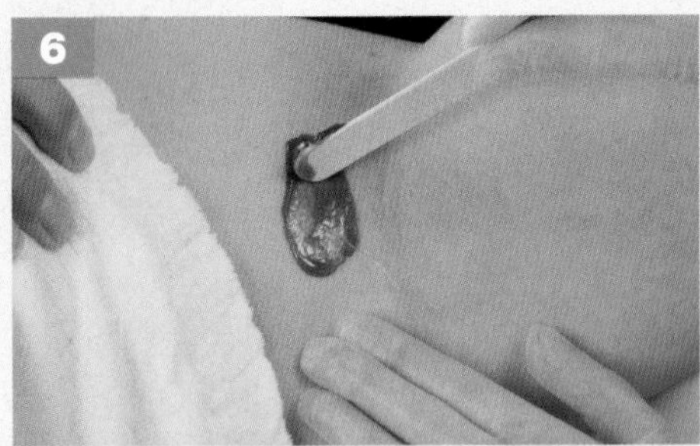

6 Repeat the procedure on the last growth area, or the center of the underarm. Remove any other stray hairs. Check-in with the client to make sure she is comfortable and can handle any tweezing. This is a sensitive area, so the faster the procedure, the better.

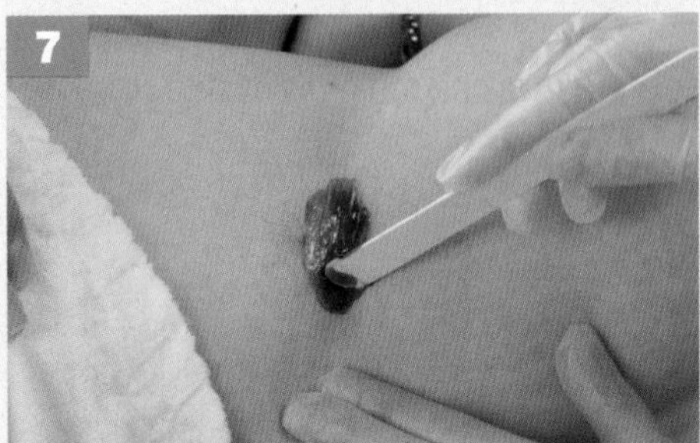

7 Repeat the procedure on the next growth area.

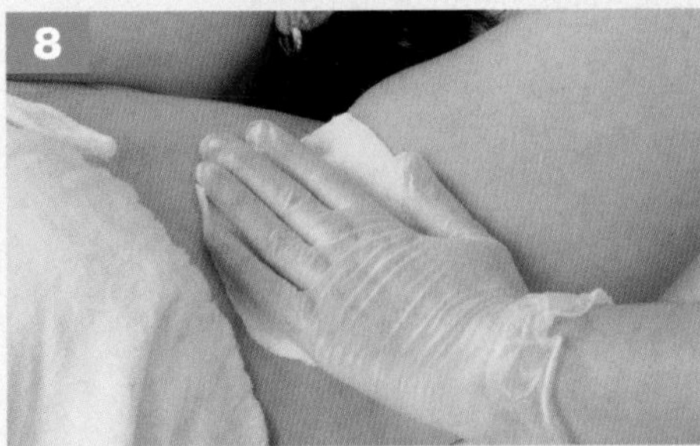

8 Apply a soothing after-wax lotion; cold compresses are also nice to soothe the skin.

Post-Service

- **Complete** 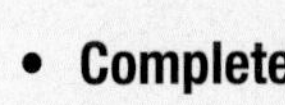 PROCEDURE 14-2 Post-Service Procedure PAGE 375
- Complete a post-wax consultation and discuss post-wax precautions.

PROCEDURE

18-7

Bikini Waxing with Hard Wax

IMPLEMENTS AND MATERIALS

Supplies will depend on the type of bikini waxing service to be performed (basic or Brazilian).

- Facial chair or treatment table
- Technician stool
- EPA-registered disinfectant
- Hand sanitizer
- Roll of single-use paper or paper towels
- Closed, covered waste container
- Cart
- Implement tray
- Containers for supplies
- Wax product
- Wax heater
- Wax remover
- Single-use applicators (large)
- Wax strips (for soft wax)
- Single-use gloves
- Sealable plastic bags for waste disposal
- Cotton pads and swabs
- Powder
- Mild skin cleanser
- Emollient or antiseptic lotion
- Brow brush
- Tweezers
- Small scissors
- Hand mirror
- Tongs (to retrieve clean supplies during a service)
- Surface cleaner (oil to remove wax from the equipment)
- Wax cleaning towels/supplies
- Table linens/towels
- Hair cap or headband for face waxing
- Towels for draping
- Client wrap for body waxing
- Wax release form and client chart
- Biohazard container, especially for underarm, bikini, and back waxing (the potential for blood spots from follicles is normal)
- Disposable underwear

Note: Soft wax with strips may be used in place of hard wax for the same procedure if performing an American or French bikini waxing (not a Brazilian wax).

Preparation

- **Perform** 

PAGE 372
- Melt the wax in the heater. Be sure the wax is not too hot.
- Complete the client consultation, release form, and determine any contraindications.
- Place a clean sheet or sheet of paper on the waxing table for each new client.

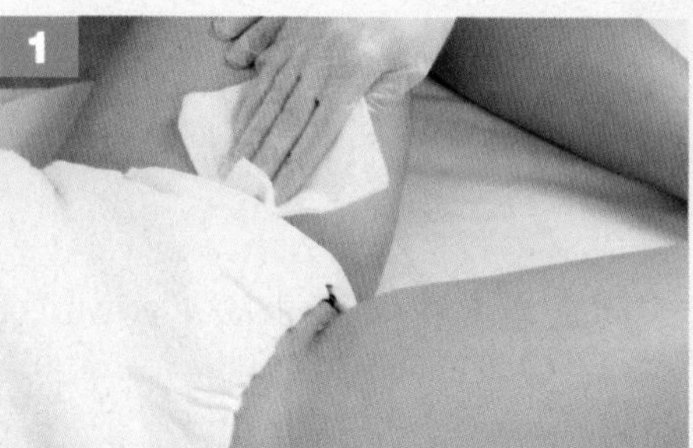

1 Wash hands and wear gloves. Drape the client. Tuck in a paper towel or wax strip along the edge of the client's bikini line. Cleanse the area.

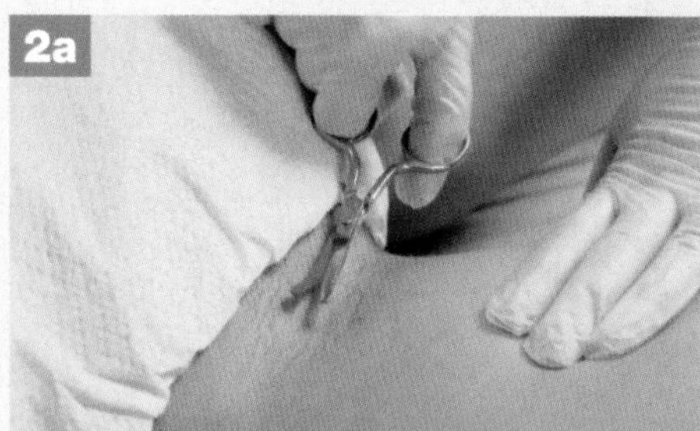

2a Trim the hair to ½" to ¾" (1.25 cm to 2 cm) in length if necessary.

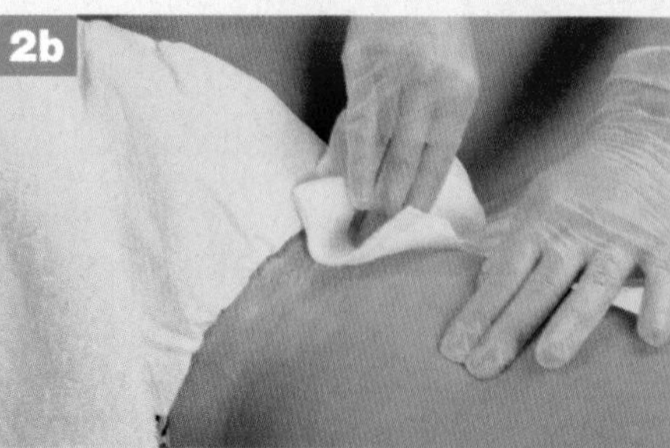

2b Apply a small amount of a pre-epilating product.

3 Bend the client's knee with the leg facing out. This position assists in reaching the inner bikini area and stretches the skin tighter. Be confident in moving the client's body position around to reach the right angle for waxing, but make sure they are comfortable in the different positions.

Service Tip

When waxing sensitive areas such as underarms or bikini lines, trim the hair with scissors if it is more than ½" (1.25 cm) to ¾" (2 cm) long.

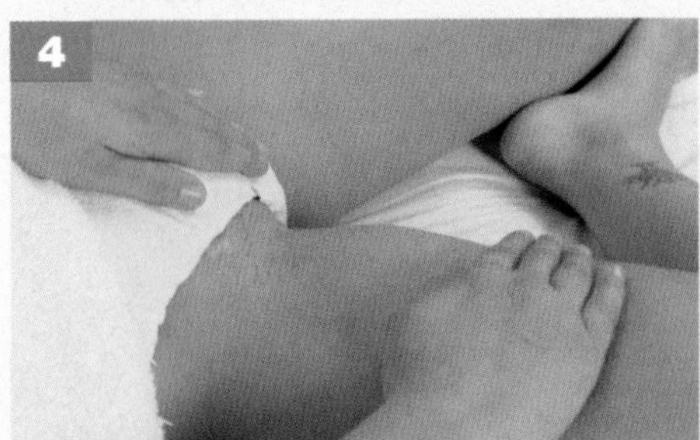

4 Have the client hold her skin taut next to the area being waxed. Show her where to place her hand and make sure that the hand is not in the way of the parallel pull used for removal.

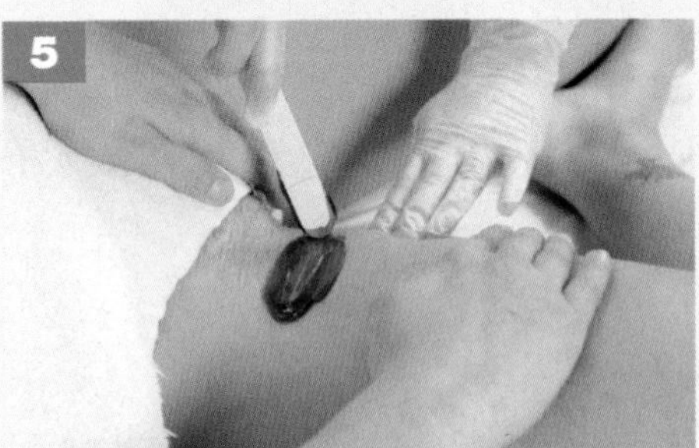

5 Apply wax to the first growth area, usually on the upper, outer edge of the bikini line. Extend the wax beyond the hair to make the pull tab and check wax consistency for removal.

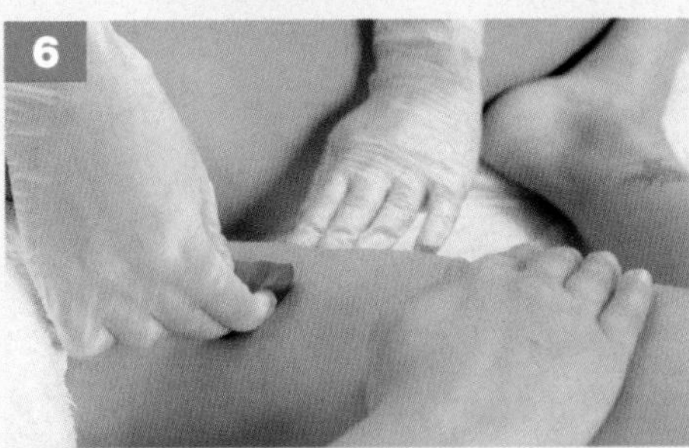

6 Remove the wax: hold the skin taut, grasp the wax "handle," and quickly pull. Pull back parallel to the skin.

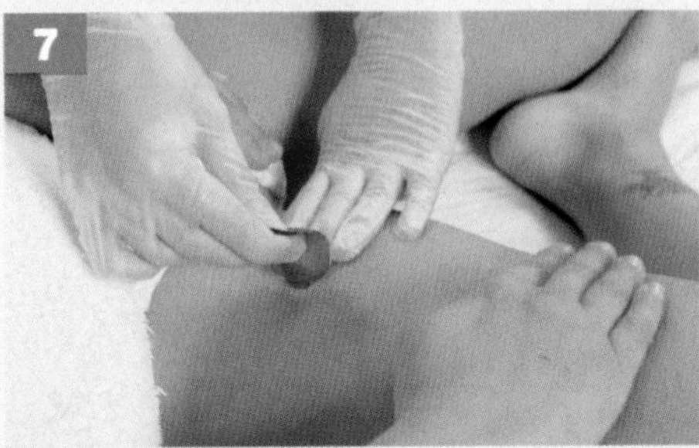

7 Apply pressure immediately to alleviate any discomfort.

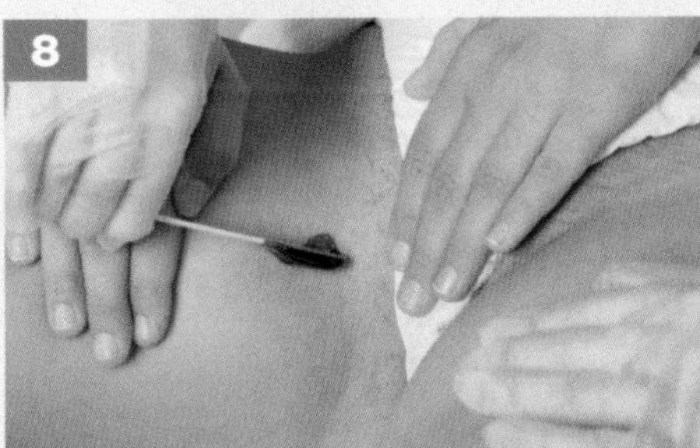

8 Work in and down to the femoral ridge in sections. Do not wax over the curve of the femoral ridge (tendon).

PROCEDURE

18-7 Bikini Waxing with Hard Wax (continued)

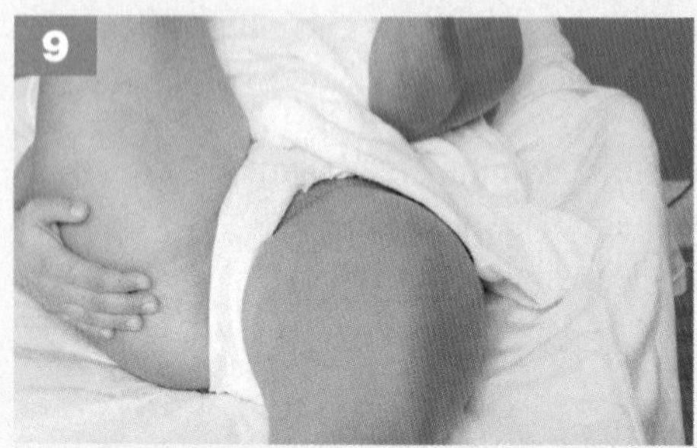

9 To wax the underside and the back side of the bikini area in separate sections have the client lift her leg toward her chest, grasping the ankle if possible. This position also holds the skin taut.

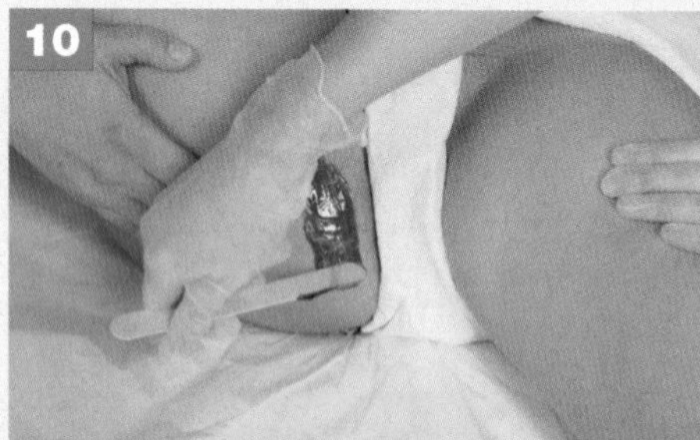

10 Apply the wax.

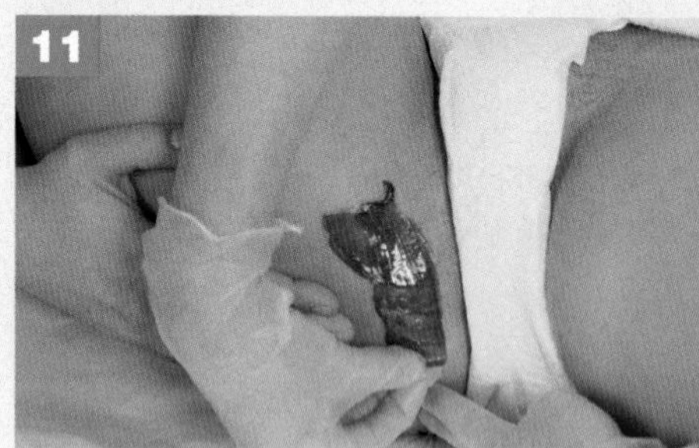

11 Remove it parallel to the body without lifting up while pulling.

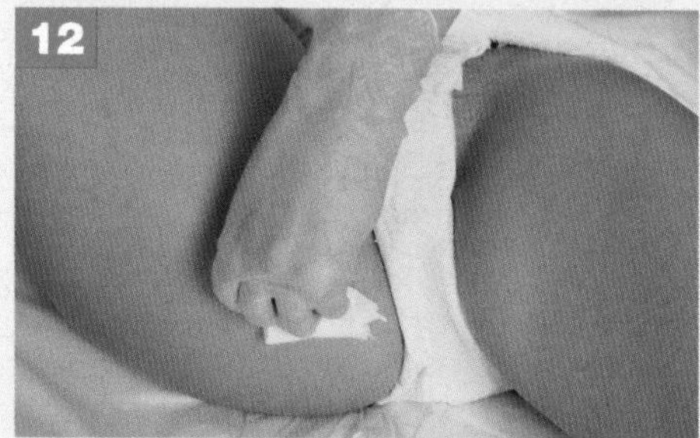

12 Apply a soothing after-wax lotion. (Cold compresses are also nice to soothe the skin.)

CAUTION!

Never go over the curve of the femoral ridge. Wax the top and bottom of the bikini area separately.

Post-Service

- **Complete** PROCEDURE 14-2 Post-Service Procedure PAGE 375
- Complete a post-wax consultation and discuss post-wax precautions.

PROCEDURE

18-8

Men's Waxing with Soft Wax

IMPLEMENTS AND MATERIALS

- Facial chair or treatment table
- Technician stool
- EPA-registered disinfectant
- Hand sanitizer
- Roll of single-use paper or paper towels
- Closed, covered waste container
- Cart
- Implement tray
- Containers for supplies
- Wax product
- Wax heater
- Wax remover
- Single-use applicators (large)
- Wax strips (for soft wax)
- Single-use gloves
- Sealable plastic bags for waste disposal
- Cotton pads and swabs
- Powder
- Mild skin cleanser
- Emollient or antiseptic lotion
- Brow brush
- Tweezers
- Small scissors
- Hand mirror
- Tongs
- Surface cleaner (oil to remove wax from the equipment)
- Wax cleaning towels/supplies
- Table linens/towels
- Hair cap or headband for face waxing
- Towels for draping
- Client wrap for body waxing
- Wax release form and client chart
- Biohazard container, especially for underarm, bikini, and back waxing

Due to the hair density, back waxing generally requires more wax strips. Strips fill up with hair quickly. Sometimes a partial wax will be requested and the time and price varies with the amount of waxing that is needed. Waxing of the back and neck is a common procedure for many men. First determine the number of different growth patterns, and then wax in sections following those patterns. Do not wax large strips of areas at one time—it's uncomfortable and traumatizes the follicles. Leg strip sections are generally too large. Cut the leg strips to three-quarters of the length. Save the unused leftover part of the strip for other body parts.

Preparation

- **Perform** 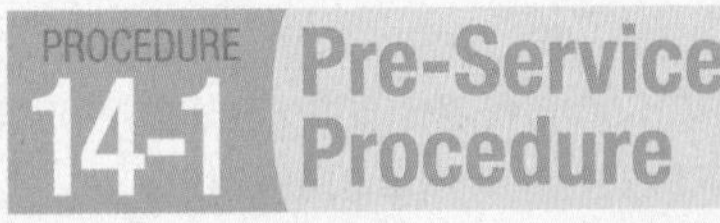

PAGE 372
- Melt the wax in the heater. Be sure the wax is not too hot.
- Complete the client consultation, release form, and determine any contraindications.
- Place a clean sheet or sheet of paper on the waxing table for each new client.

1 Have the client remove any uncomfortable clothing (belts) or give them a wrap to put on. Tuck a paper towel into the waist band to protect the clothing or wrap from wax. Have the client lay face down and start at the lower back area working up to the shoulders. Then have him sit up for the top of the shoulder area if necessary.

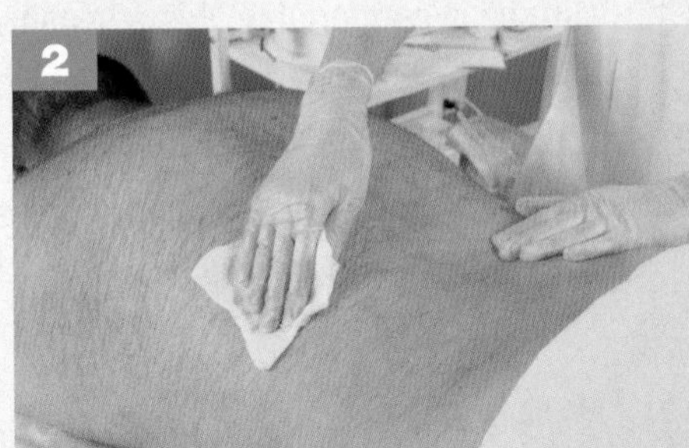

2 Cleanse the area to be waxed and trim hair as necessary. Brush excess hair onto a paper towel and discard before starting.

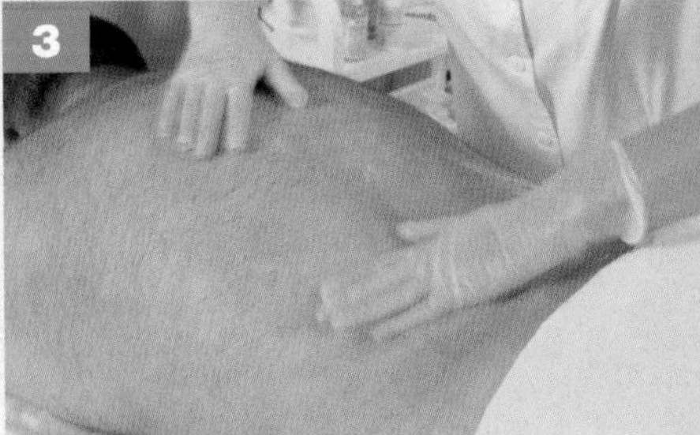

3 Apply a small amount of powder all over the area to be waxed. Check the hair growth pattern to decide on the pattern of removal before starting.

PROCEDURE

18-8 Men's Waxing with Soft Wax (continued)

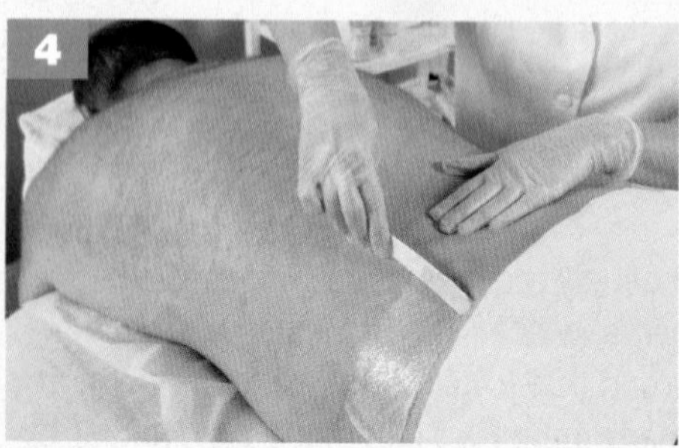

4 Apply wax to the first growth area. Start at the bottom of the lower back on the outside edge. Work in sections on one side of the body, working up towards the shoulders. Do the outside edge, then the center. Follow the hair growth and a set pattern.

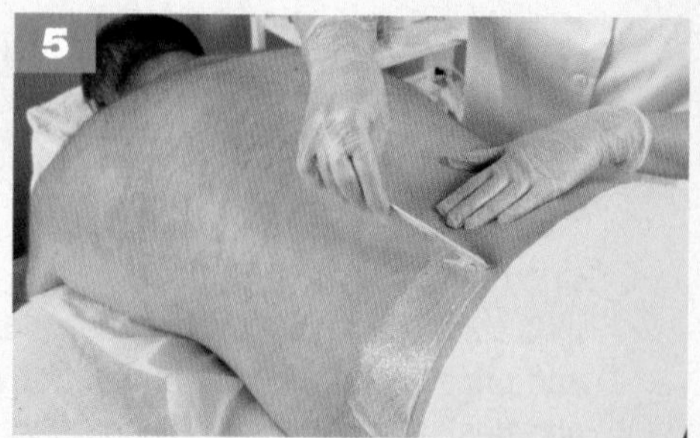

5 Apply the strip. Do not use too big of a strip, as a large section is painful and the parallel removal is not as easy to control. Follow the directional changes. The client may need to turn onto their hip to wax the curved edge next to the bed, if the bed is in the way of the pull and follow through.

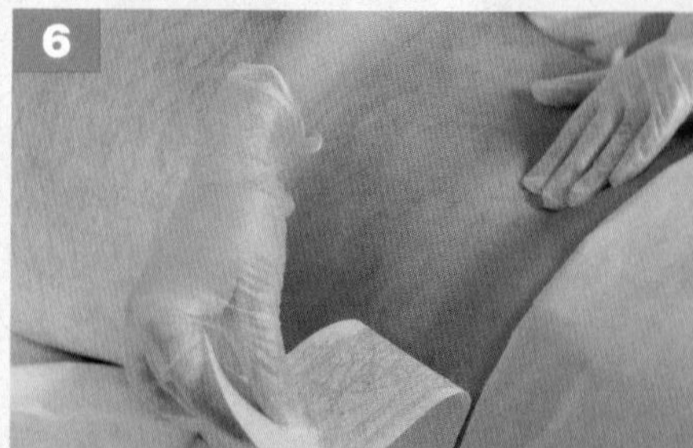

6 Grasp the strip, hold skin taut, and quickly pull parallel against the hair growth.

7 Apply pressure immediately after wax removal for at least 3 to 5 seconds to ease any pain. Apply cold compresses and soothing lotion as needed after completing a large section during the procedure.

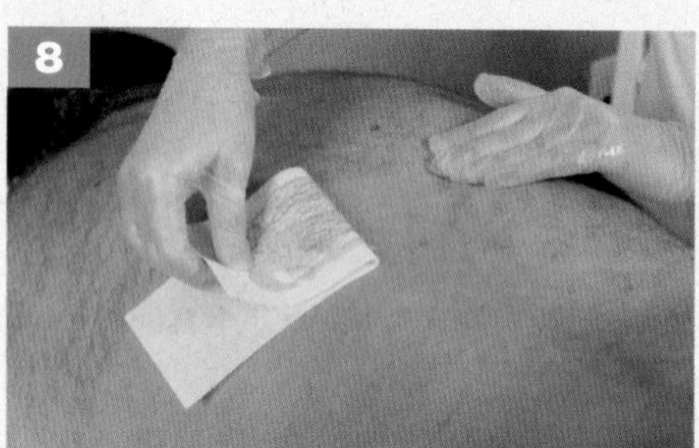

8 Repeat the procedure until all hair is removed, working up one side and then the other side of the body (this is more efficient to avoid changing sides during the waxing)

Service Tip

To wax a male client's shoulder and neck area, have him sit up and do the work from behind him.

Web Resources

www.dermatology.about.com

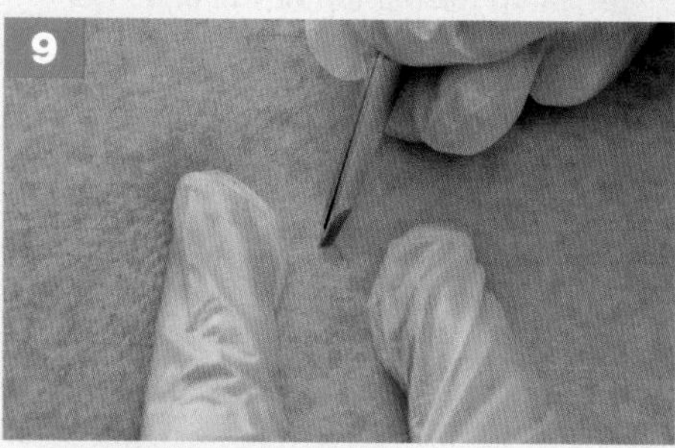

9 Remove any other stray hairs. Check-in with the client to make sure he is comfortable. It is a sensitive area, so the faster the procedure, the better.

10 Sit the client up to remove hair from the curve of the shoulder area. Blend the end of the waxed area to the front so there is not an abrupt line where the hairless area ends. Some trimming may be necessary here.

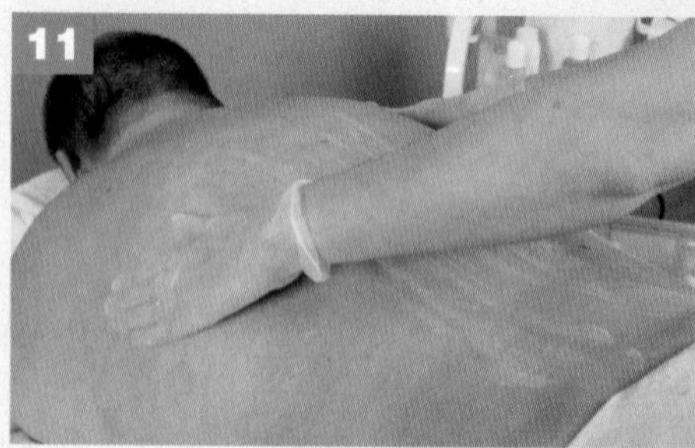

11 Apply a soothing after-wax lotion; large cold compresses (paper towels or cotton) are also used to soothe the skin. It is normal for hives and redness to appear after waxing such a large area of thick, coarse hair.

Post-Service

- **Complete** 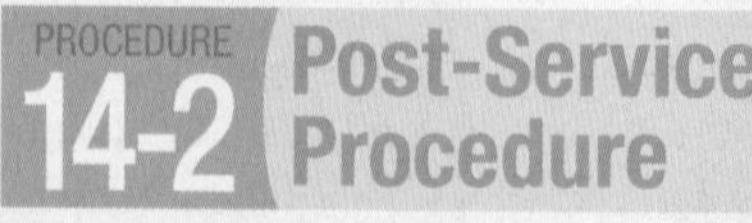

PAGE 375
- Complete a post-wax consultation and discuss post-wax precautions. L07

Review Questions

1. What structures are part of the pilosebaceous unit?
2. What are the main structures of the hair follicle?
3. Explain the three stages of the hair-growth cycle.
4. Define the terms hirsutism and hypertrichosis.
5. Define electrolysis.
6. Define threading and sugaring.
7. What is photoepilation?
8. What is the difference between depilation and epilation?
9. What are the two main types of waxing products?
10. What are six of the conditions, treatments, and medications that contraindicate hair removal?
11. List four of the safety precautions that must be followed for waxing.
12. What are the three most important points in safe wax removal techniques?
13. When should you use a biohazard container for waste disposal?
14. Why is hard wax better than soft wax for sensitive areas?

Glossary

anagen	First stage of hair growth during which new hair is produced.
catagen	Second transition stage of hair growth; in the catagen stage, the hair shaft grows upward and detaches itself from the bulb.
depilation	Process of removing hair at skin level.
depilatory	Substance, usually a caustic alkali preparation, used for temporarily removing superfluous hair by dissolving it at the skin level.
electrolysis	Removal of hair by means of an electric current that destroys the hair root.
epilation	Removes hairs from the follicles; waxing or tweezing.
hair bulb	Swelling at the base of the follicle that provides the hair with nourishment; it is a thick, club-shaped structure that forms the lower part of the hair root.
hair follicle	Mass of epidermal cells forming a small tube, or canal; the tube-like depression or pocket in the skin or scalp that contains the hair root.
hair papilla (plural: papillae)	Cone-shaped elevations at the base of the follicle that fit into the hair bulb. The papillae are filled with tissue that contains the blood vessels and cells necessary for hair growth and follicle nourishment.

Glossary

hair root	Anchors hair to the skin cells and is part of the hair located at the bottom of the follicle below the surface of the skin; part of the hair that lies within the follicle at its base, where the hair grows.
hair shaft	Portion of the hair that extends or projects beyond the skin, consisting of the outer layer (cuticle), inner layer (medulla), and middle layer (cortex). Color changes happen in the cortex.
hirsutism	Growth of an unusual amount of hair on parts of the body normally bearing only downy hair, such as the face, arms, and legs of women or the backs of men.
hypertrichosis	Also known as *hirsuties*; condition of abnormal growth of hair, characterized by the growth of terminal hair in areas of the body that normally grow only vellus hair.
lanugo	The hair on a fetus; soft and downy hair.
laser hair removal	Photoepilation hair reduction treatment in which a laser beam is pulsed on the skin using one wavelength at a time, impairing hair growth; an intense pulse of electromagnetic radiation.
photoepilation	Also known as *Intense Pulsed Light* (IPL); permanent hair removal treatment that uses intense light to destroy the growth cells of the hair follicles.
pilosebaceous unit	The hair unit that contains the hair follicle and appendages: the hair root, bulb, dermal papilla, sebaceous appendage, and arrector pili muscle.
sugaring	Ancient method of hair removal. The original recipe is a mixture of sugar, lemon juice, and water that is heated to form a syrup, molded into a ball, and pressed onto the skin and then quickly stripped away.
telogen	Also known as *resting phase*; the final phase in the hair cycle that lasts until the fully grown hair is shed.
threading	Also known as *banding*; method of hair removal; cotton thread is twisted and rolled along the surface of the skin, entwining hair in the thread and lifting it out of the follicle.
trichology	Scientific study of hair and its diseases and care.
vellus hair	Also know as *lanugo hair*; short, fine, unpigmented downy hair that appears on the body, with the exception of the palms of the hands and the soles of the feet.

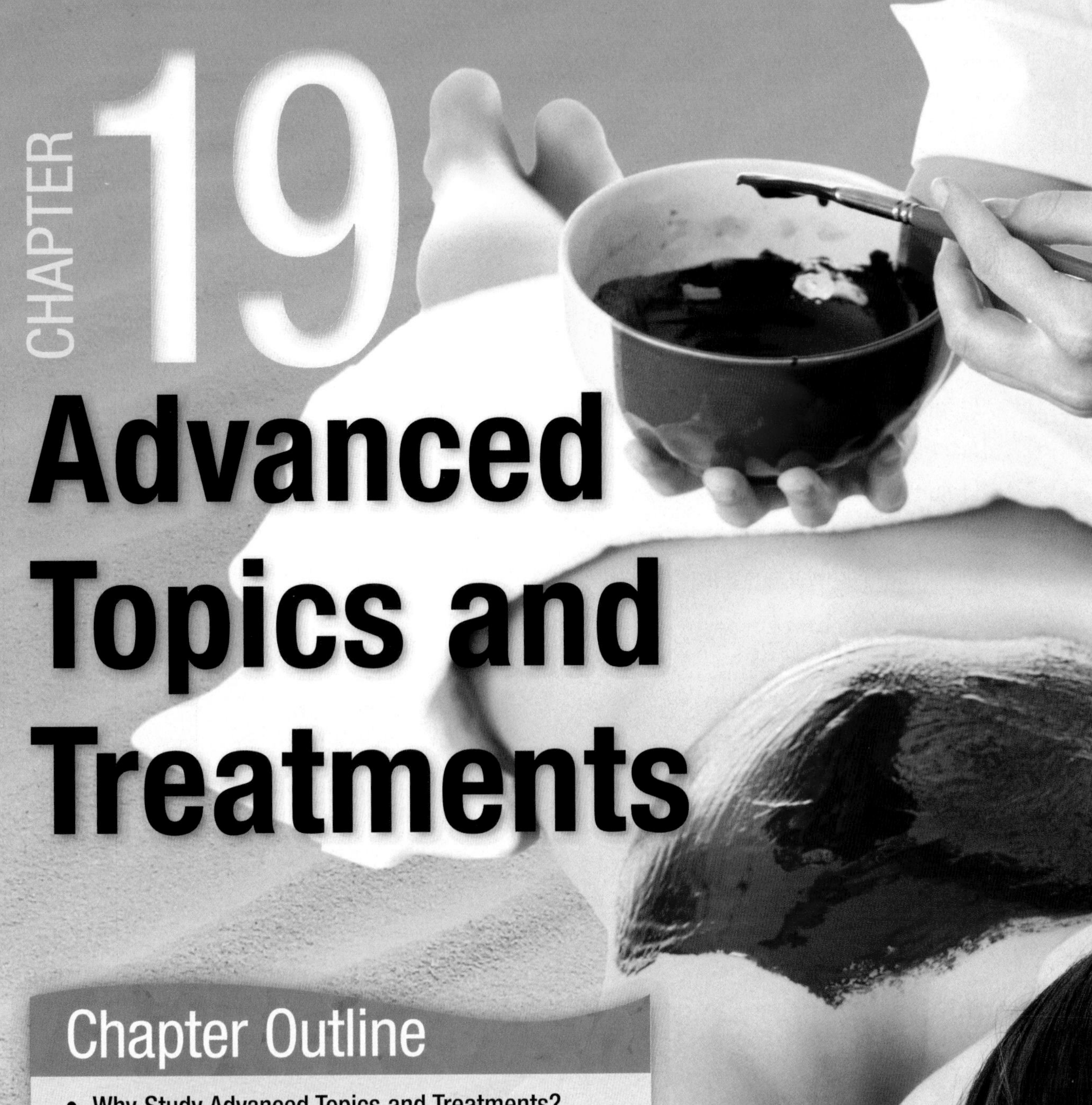

CHAPTER 19

Advanced Topics and Treatments

Chapter Outline

- Why Study Advanced Topics and Treatments?
- Chemical Exfoliation
- Microdermabrasion
- Laser Technology
- Light Therapy
- Microcurrent Machines
- Ultrasound and Ultrasonic Technology
- Spa Body Treatments
- Cellulite
- Manual Lymph Drainage
- Medical Aesthetics

Learning Objectives

After completing this chapter, you will be able to:

- ☑ LO1 Recognize the contraindications of chemical exfoliation procedures.
- ☑ LO2 Explain chemical peels.
- ☑ LO3 Describe the benefits of AHA peels and microdermabrasion.
- ☑ LO4 Understand light therapy and lasers.
- ☑ LO5 Be familiar with microcurrent and ultrasound technology.
- ☑ LO6 Describe spa body treatments and services.
- ☑ LO7 Be familiar with medical aesthetics.
- ☑ LO8 Be familiar with injectables.
- ☑ LO9 Be familiar with various surgical procedures.

Key Terms

Page number indicates where in the chapter the term is used.

abdominoplasty
pg. 553

ayurveda
pg. 543

balneotherapy
pg. 542

blepharoplasty
pg. 552

body masks
pg. 542

body scrubs
pg. 541

body wraps
pg. 541

Botox®
pg. 550

cell renewal factor (CRF)
pg. 530

cellulite
pg. 547

cosmetic surgery (esthetic surgery)
pg. 551

dermabrasion
pg. 552

dermal fillers
pg. 551

endermology
pg. 544

foot reflexology
pg. 543

hydrotherapy
pg. 542

injectable fillers
pg. 550

Jessner's peel
pg. 530

laser resurfacing
pg. 552

liposuction
pg. 553

mammoplasty
pg. 553

microcurrent (device)
pg. 539

microdermabrasion
pg. 534

nonablative
pg. 550

phenol
pg. 552

reconstructive surgery
pg. 551

Reiki
pg. 546

rhinoplasty
pg. 552

rhytidectomy
pg. 551

stone massage
pg. 542

transconjunctival blepharoplasty
pg. 552

trichloroacetic acid (TCA) peels
pg. 552

ultrasonic
pg. 540

ultrasound
pg. 541

Advanced esthetics is an ever-expanding subject (Figure 19–1). There are many interesting topics to study and techniques to utilize. Advanced esthetics goes beyond the basics and is traditionally part of postgraduate studies. Chemical exfoliation, microdermabrasion, light therapy, clinical skin care, and spa body treatments are just some of the specialized services offered in the world of esthetics. This chapter presents an overview of some of the advanced esthetic topics. Estheticians can incorporate many of these treatments into their service menus.

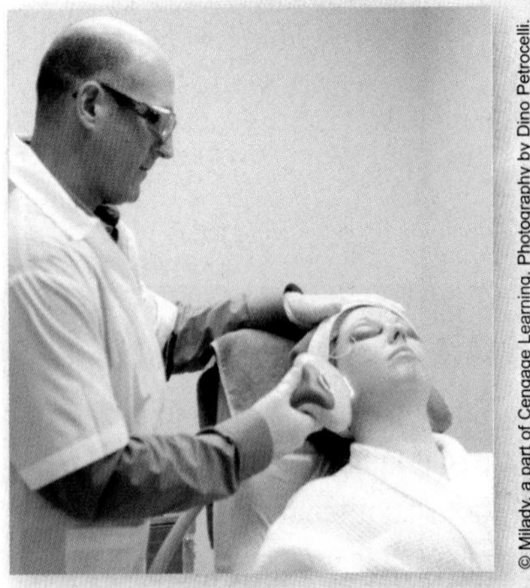

▲ Figure 19–1
The world of advanced esthetics continues to grow.

The public's growing interest in maintaining the health of the body, coupled with tremendous scientific advances, has generated a trend toward integrating beauty, health, and therapeutic services. As a result, estheticians are required to be more knowledgeable about new tools and technology. Procedures such as microdermabrasion have expanded the esthetician's repertoire to include more results-driven services.

Why Study Advanced Topics and Treatments?

Estheticians should study and have a thorough understanding of advanced topics and treatments so they can better serve their clients while increasing their service revenues and menus. Advanced treatments have expanded the esthetician's repertoire to include more results-driven services such as chemical exfoliation and microdermabrasion.

- Chemical exfoliation, microdermabrasion, light therapy, clinical skin care, and spa body treatments are just some of the specialized services estheticians are expected to be knowledgeable about, including the benefits and contraindications of the treatments.
- The public's growing interest in maintaining the health of the body, coupled with tremendous scientific advances, has generated a trend toward integrating beauty, health, and therapeutic services.
- Offering advanced treatments will keep technicians competitive in the market place.

Chemical Exfoliation

Offering chemical exfoliation in your skin care practice will be one of the most exciting and financially rewarding areas of your treatment "bag of tricks." In the field of skin care, we define the process of removing excess accumulations of dead cells from the corneum layers of the epidermis as *superficial peeling, exfoliation, keratolysis,* and *desquamation.* These are all interchangeable terms. This process can be accomplished mechanically (microdermabrasion), manually (scrubs), or chemically by the use of specific products (glycolic acid) formulated to achieve these results.

Physicians use procedures designed to penetrate deeper into the skin (the dermal layer) that are referred to as *medium* or *deep peels.* Skin care therapists, in contrast, use procedures designed to penetrate only the epidermis. These are referred to as *light peels,* or *chemical exfoliation.* These light "peels" are noninvasive and nonaggressive in nature and are designed to treat the epidermis—not the dermis, or living tissue.

CAUTION!

Chemical exfoliation and peels can result in burns that may require medical attention and can scar a client. It is important to obtain as much training as possible in working with chemicals. Make certain that you consult with the client before applying a chemical exfoliant, follow the manufacturer's instructions, and always patch test (inside the arm or behind the ear) 24 to 48 hours before giving a treatment to watch for adverse reactions to the product.

Peel History

More than 5,000 years ago, the Egyptians used a form of chemical peeling. They understood the value of lactic acid from milk and the various fruit acids for skin conditioning. Thus, when Cleopatra relaxed in her milk bath, she was actually using a method of chemical exfoliation.

Physicians began using deeper peels in 1882, employing resorcinol, trichloroacetic acid (TCA), salicylic acid, and phenol. These procedures became very popular in the 1930s and 1940s, when Antoinette la Gasse brought the procedures from France to the United States. In the 1980s, the practice of superficially peeling clients by estheticians was just beginning. Alpha hydroxy acid (AHA) peels were the buzzword of the 1990s, and they are even more popular today.

The Cell Renewal Factor (CRF)

The **cell renewal factor (CRF)**, or *cell turnover rate,* is the rate of cell mitosis and migration from the dermis to the top of the epidermis. This process slows down with age. The average rate of cell turnover rate for babies is 14 days; for teenagers, 21 to 28 days; for adults, 28 to 42 days; for those 50 and older, 42 to 84 days. Keeping the cell mitosis going is one of the goals for skin preservation.

Factors influencing the CRF include genetics, the natural environment, and one's medical history, lifestyle, personal care, and exfoliation methods. The keratinized corneum layer is composed of approximately 15 to 20 layers and varies in thickness in different body areas.While exfoliating is great for the skin, a hydrolipidic balance must be maintained, especially for alipidic (dry) skins. Over-peeling is detrimental to the skin.

Deep Peels versus Light Peels

Deep peels are administered by physicians and make use of the following chemicals: resorcinol, phenol (carbolic acid, also called *Baker's peel*), trichloroacetic acid (TCA), glycolic acid (50 percent or more), and Jessner's peel (4 to 10 coats). **Jessner's peel** contains lactic acid, salicylic acid, and resorcinol in an ethanol solvent. It is very strong. TCA is a medium-depth peel that removes the epidermis down to the dermis. Phenol is a highly acidic deep peel that peels down into the dermis.

Light peels (chemical exfoliators) are esthetician administered. These make use of glycolic acid (30 percent or less), lactic acid (30 percent or less), enzyme peels, and in some cases Jessner's solution (1 to 3 coats). *Chemical exfoliation* is used in place of the word peel to differentiate between the deeper clinical *peels* and the lighter chemical exfoliation with AHAs used in salons and spas.

REGULATORY AGENCY ALERT

Each regulatory agency is different, so check your local laws to see what is acceptable in performing exfoliation services under your esthetics license.

AHAs and BHAs

Alpha Hydroxy Acids (AHAs) and Beta Hydroxy Acids (BHAs) are mild acids. **Glycolic acid** is the strongest alpha hydroxy acid and is derived from sugar cane. Acids are used in different percentages and pH factors to dissolve the desmosomes between cells to keep skin cells exfoliated (Figure 19–2). Other AHAs promote superficial peeling as well. Beta hydroxy acids, while milder, are also used to effectively exfoliate the skin.

AHAs penetrate the corneum via the intercellular matrix and loosen the bonds between the cells. The intercellular matrix between the skin cells consists of ceramides, lipids, glycoproteins, and active enzymes. AHAs also stimulate the production of intercellular lipids. Glycolic acid can penetrate into the epidermis more effectively because it has the smallest molecular size of the AHAs.

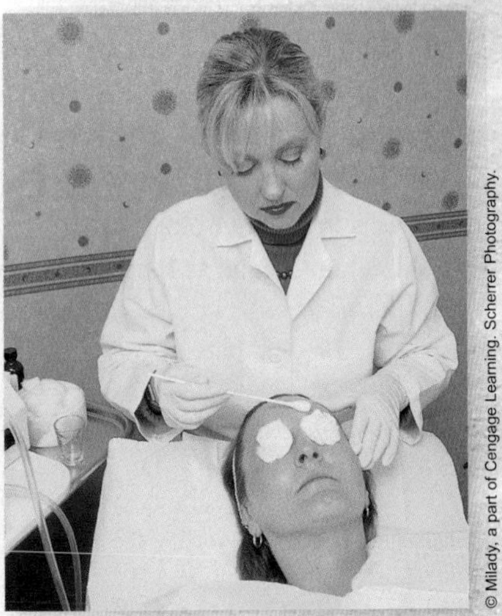

▲ Figure 19–2
A glycolic acid exfoliation treatment.

AHAs include glycolic acid derived from sugar cane; lactic acid derived from milk; tartaric acid derived from grapes; citric acid from citrus fruit; and malic acid derived from apples. Citric acid is now considered an AHA, rather than a BHA.

BHAs (salicylic acid) also dissolve oil and are used for oily skin and acne. Salicylic acid—derived from sweet birch, willow bark, and wintergreen—has antiseptic and anti-inflammatory properties. Aspirin is derived from salicylates, so those clients allergic to aspirin may be allergic to salicylic ingredients.

Acid, Alkaline, and pH Relationships

The pH is an important consideration in peel products. Acids have a pH of 1 to 6, neutral is 7, and alkalies range from 8 to 14. The average pH of skin ranges from 4.5 to 5.5. Acids penetrate into the skin and can be a cause of irritation. A pH of less than 3 is not recommended for salon peels; most states do not allow using a lower pH. A 30 percent concentration of glycolic acid is usually formulated to have a pH of 3 if buffered properly.

Buffering agents are ingredients added to products to help make them less irritating. Products with a higher percent of acid and a lower pH are more irritating. The acid needs to have a pH lower than the skin's pH to be effective (Figure 19–3, page 532). Over the counter (OTC) AHA product formulations contain from 2 to 15 percent of an acid. The most common AHAs sold by salons range from 5 to 10 percent. Physicians carry products with higher percentages.

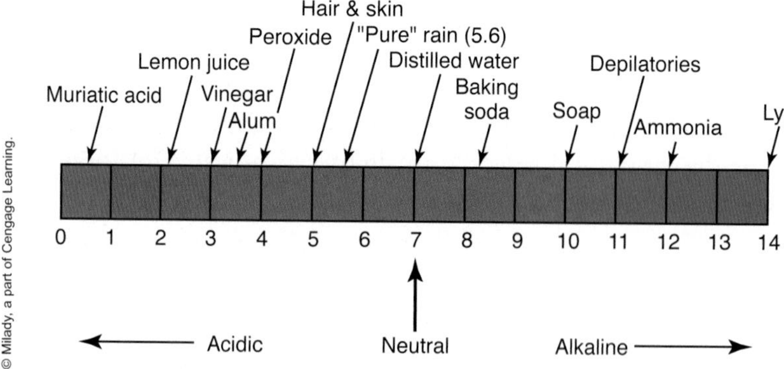

▶ **Figure 19–3**
pH relationships.

CAUTION!

Exfoliated skin needs to be protected from sun exposure or tanning to avoid hyperpigmentation and damage to the skin. Sunscreen must be used daily when using AHAs or other strong exfoliating products or treatments.

Peels and Chemical Exfoliation Benefits

Peels and chemical exfoliation result in:

- Improved texture of the skin, barrier function, and moisture retention.
- Increased CRF, hydration, and intercellular lipids.
- Reduced fine lines, wrinkles, and surface pigmentation.
- Skin that looks and feels smoother and softer.
- Improved skin conditions such as acne, hyperpigmentation, clogged pores, and dry skin.
- Potentially stimulating elastin and collagen production.

Who Should Have a Chemical Exfoliation Treatment?

Who are the best candidates for chemical exfoliation? When determining whether a series of treatments is appropriate for a client, consider the following factors: skin type, sebaceous gland activity, skin conditions, the client's philosophy of sun exposure, her cosmetic and product use, whether she is using Retin-A® or other acids/AHAs, or acne drugs such as tetracycline.

Contraindications

Chemical exfoliation contraindications include the following:

- Recent cosmetic surgeries, laser resurfacing, chemical peels, or dermabrasion
- Recent injectables, fillers, or Botox®
- Use of Retin-A or other medications that exfoliate or thin the skin
- Allergies or sensitivities to products or ingredients
- Pregnancy
- Herpes simplex
- Hyperpigmentation tendencies

- Inflamed rosacea or acne
- Infectious diseases
- Open sores or suspicious lesions
- Sunburn or irritated skin
- Photosensitizing medications (makes skin very sensitive to sun)
- Other contraindicated drugs or medication ✓ LO1

Here's a Tip

Because sun is stronger during the summer and outdoor exposure is more frequent, chemical exfoliation and other exfoliation procedures (microdermabrasion) are not recommended during those months.

Before a chemical exfoliation service, discuss the issues and contraindications during the client consultation. Explain the procedures, the expected outcome, and realistic goals. In a diagnostic facial or skin analysis before scheduling treatments, note the condition of the skin, dehydration, hyperpigmentation, open lesions, and any other skin conditions on the client intake form. Also choose the type of exfoliant based on the client's skin condition and the results desired. Additional ingredients added to formulas include pigment lighteners, acne ingredients, moisturizers or hydrators, and others (Table 19–1).

The Procedure for AHAs

Your regulatory agency will determine the guidelines regarding the strength and pH of the product. The treatment selection will include the type of acid, the procedure time, strength, and the assisting ingredients. Protocols vary depending on the product line. Advanced training and certification are necessary to perform glycolic treatments. The basic process consists of applying the product and removing it within a few minutes. Exfoliation services are efficient and take less time than the more relaxing, in-depth facials.

CAUTION!

To prevent skin damage, warn your clients to avoid sun exposure, scrubs, rubbing, pulling dead skin, depilatories, waxing, benzoyl peroxide, and exfoliating or glycolic acid products for at least 24 to 48 hours before or after any chemical exfoliation procedure. Recommend a longer period of time if the client's condition warrants it.

Treatments can be scheduled in a series of four to eight sessions, one time per week for 4 to 8 weeks. More than eight weekly treatments in a row is not recommended. A series of treatments every 3 or 4 months is the typical recommendation. Treatments can also be scheduled once a month or as needed. The optimum facial maintenance schedule is once a month or every 6 weeks. The schedule will depend on the product strength and the client's tolerance to AHAs.

BENEFICIAL INGREDIENTS TO COMBINE WITH CHEMICAL EXFOLIATION

SKIN CONDITION	BENEFICIAL INGREDIENTS
Mature and/or sensitive skin	glycolic acid, lactic acid, ceramides, hyaluronic acid, phospholipids, linoleic acid, aloe vera, allantoin, kojic acid, licorice root, peptides
Hyperpigmentation	glycolic acid, kojic acid, licorice root, mulberry extract, bearberry extract, azelaic acid, ascorbic acid
Acne	glycolic acid, lactic acid, salicylic acid, azelaic acid, citric acid

◀ Table 19–1
Beneficial Ingredients to Combine with Chemical Exfoliation.

Mini Procedure

CHEMICAL EXFOLIATION

Do not perform this procedure without advanced training and instructor supervision. It is included here as it is important to be familiar with the basic procedure. See *Milady Standard Esthetics: Advanced* textbook for the full procedure on peels and other advanced treatments.

Follow the manufacturer protocol for the strength and timing of the procedure.

1. Prepare and cleanse the skin.
2. Let the skin dry and put protective eye pads on.
3. Set the timer and give clients a fan to keep the skin cool if it feels itchy or warm during the peel.
4. Apply the product carefully with a large disposable cotton swab, two small disposable cotton swabs, or brush. Avoid the eyes.
5. Remove the product with cool cotton pads saturated with water. Rinse at least six times.
6. Ask the client if there are any warm or itchy areas to make sure all of the product is neutralized.
7. Apply a soothing product such as aloe vera or a calming cucumber mask.
8. Finish with a high-performance serum, moisturizer, and a sunscreen.
9. Rebook the next weekly treatment and remind the client how to take care of freshly exfoliated skin.

Post-Chemical Exfoliation Home-Care

Discussion of home-care with clients includes issuing precautions and product advice. Clients should avoid the sun and additional exfoliation outside of the recommended home-care program. An example of a glycolic home-care product is a 5 percent cream in a moisturizer base. This product may be used approximately every other day. It is put on under sunscreen or at night on dry skin (not damp). Water or moisture on the skin can make the cream more active and cause it to tingle or sting. Strong exfoliation does make the skin drier on the surface because the top layer is sloughed off, so keeping the skin hydrated is important. Make sure to communicate these points clearly to your clients.

It can take approximately 6 weeks to notice a difference in the skin, but sometimes improvements are visible after only one session or 1 week of using the home-care products. ✓ L02

CAUTION!

Machines can do more harm than good if used improperly. To avoid injuring clients, estheticians performing services using machines should receive thorough training, including clinical practice, before using any machine. Advanced training is recommended because manufacturer training alone is generally not enough education to use machines safely. Advanced equipment should be used only by licensed, well-trained skin care professionals.

Microdermabrasion

Microdermabrasion (my-kroh-der-mah-BRAY-shun) is a form of mechanical machine exfoliation that originated in Europe. Some of the first machines entered the U.S. market around 1995. Today, many microdermabrasion models are available for both the esthetician's and physician's use. These machines are utilized in many skin care clinics, spas, and medical offices (Figure 19–4).

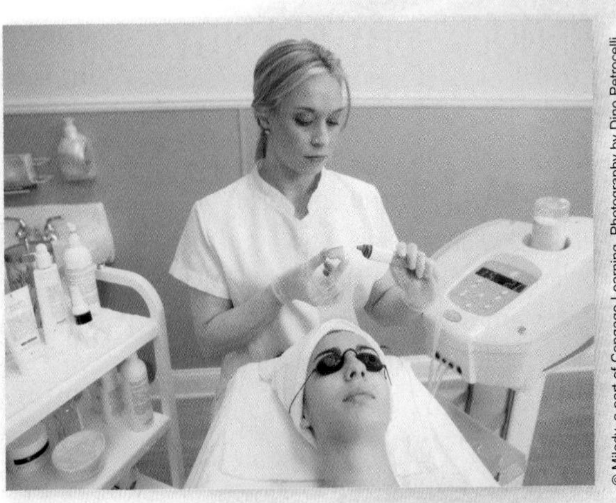

▲ Figure 19–4
The microdermabrasion machine.

The microdermabrasion machine is a powerful electronic vacuum. Microdermabrasion is achieved by spraying high-grade microcrystals, composed of corundum (kah-RUN-dum) powder or aluminum oxide, across the skin's surface through a hand piece (Figure19–5). Crystals can also be used manually without the machine—this process is considered gentler on the skin. Other machines have hard applicators, such as diamond tips, applied without crystals.

The microdermabrasion technique is similar to running the vacuum/suction machine across the face. Crystals are first sprayed on the skin through the hand piece, and then are vacuumed off after the spraying application is complete. Microdermabrasion treatments are quick 30-minute services that can be offered alone or as part of a facial. A quick hydrating and nourishing mask is usually part of exfoliation treatments.

Microdermabrasion Benefits

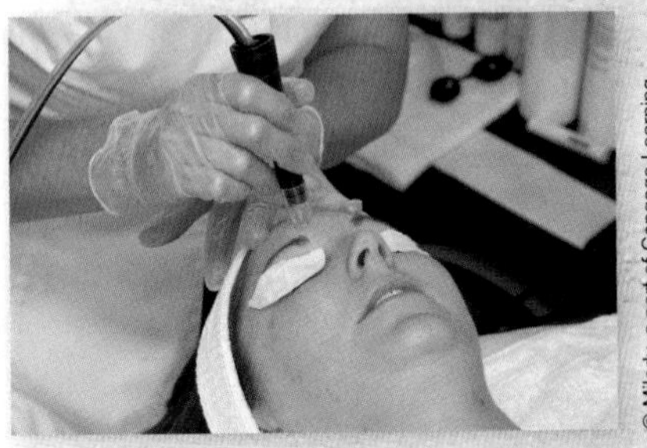

▲ Figure 19–5
Microdermabrasion machines exfoliate the skin.

Microdermabrasion can be used to diminish the following conditions: sun damage, pigmentation, open and closed comedones, fine lines and wrinkles, enlarged pores, and coarsely textured skin. In addition to the typical exfoliation benefits, the vacuum mechanism stimulates cell metabolism and blood flow. Those who cannot tolerate acids may be candidates for microdermabrasion.

The difference between AHAs and microdermabrasion is that AHAs are chemical and penetrate into the epidermis. The AHA product and its penetration into the skin have many benefits. Microdermabrasion is a mechanical method of exfoliation. It exfoliates the epidermis more effectively than a 30 percent AHA product does, but the benefits of the chemical products are not produced. For example, acids penetrate into the skin and stimulate cell mitosis and the cell turnover rate more than microdermabrasion. The vacuum used in microdermabrasion does stimulate cell metabolism and circulation. Generally, you can think of microdermabrasion as a more effective tool for surface exfoliation and AHAs as more effective below the surface. Using both peels and microdermabrasion in a treatment series is a common practice. ☑ L03

Microdermabrasion Cautions

Technique plays a vital role in creating a positive outcome with the microdermabrasion machine. Proper use of the hand piece, rate of crystal flow, and vacuum setting all contribute to a successful treatment. Do not use microdermabrasion so aggressively that the

CAUTION!

To avoid eye damage or breathing in crystals during microdermabrasion, technicians need to wear eye glasses and protective masks. Clients must keep eyes closed at all times. Avoid getting crystals in client's eyes, mouth, nose, or ears.

REGULATORY **AGENCY ALERT**

Check with your regulatory agency about laws governing advanced machine use such as microdermabrasion and light therapy. Many areas require special licensing and training to legally operate certain equipment.

ACTIVITY

Research microdermabrasion machines and chemical exfoliation products. See what is offered in salons. Which product or manufacturer do you like? Why do you think one is better than the others? What services would you choose to offer? How much would you charge per treatment?

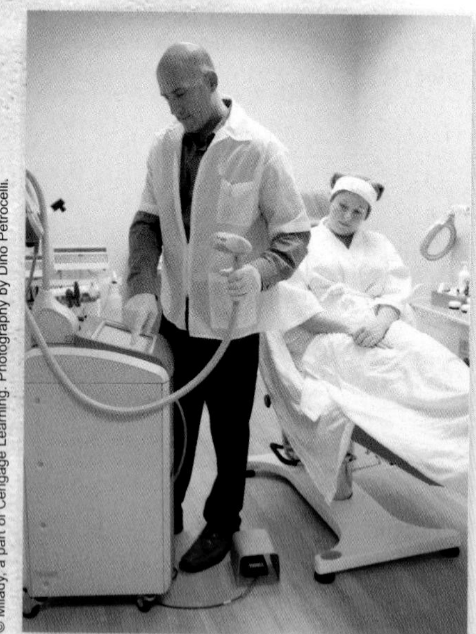

▲ Figure 19–6
Lasers are medical devices.

client is uncomfortable. Once the skin shows erythema or redness, this is considered the stopping point for the procedure.

A series of treatments that incorporate complementary products, along with a complete home-care program, makes the difference in obtaining the best results. Topical vitamins and antioxidants are even more effective when used after exfoliation procedures. The esthetician's professional expertise in analyzing the skin and recommending the best program help make these procedures safe and effective.

Improper use of microdermabrasion can actually cause hypopigmentation and hyperpigmentation. It can also lead to sensitivity and other problems. Any strong exfoliation procedure requires sun abstinence and daily sunscreen. Microdermabrasion is not recommended for sensitive or couperous skin, rosacea, or for those with a predisposition to pigmentation problems.

Reading a manual does not provide instant experience in using this machine. Training and certification are absolutely mandatory. Microdermabrasion machines should be used by licensed, trained skin care professionals only. New technology for microdermabrasion devices and those similar to microdermabrasion is constantly emerging.

Microdermabrasion Equipment Maintenance

Daily care and proper use prevents unnecessary machine repairs. Microdermabrasion machines consist of internal motors, hoses, filters, and hand pieces. Hoses and hand pieces must be dry so that the crystals will flow properly. Use only the crystals recommended by the manufacturer. It is not necessary to overuse crystals to obtain good results. A constant, even flow of crystals will give a smooth and effective treatment. Crystals should flow onto the skin's surface only. Avoid breathing the crystals or getting them in the eyes or the nose.

Carefully clean up crystals while wearing rubber gloves and a mask. Machines that have separate crystal containers for both clean and used crystals are preferred. This way the used crystals stay contained and do not come into contact with the technician. These sealed containers are safer to dispose of properly. Follow the manufacturer's directions for disposal and maintenance. The treatment room and linens also need to be cleaned and checked for crystal residue and contamination.

Laser Technology

Lasers (LAY-zurs) are medical devices used for hair removal and skin treatments (Figure 19–6). Lasers are high-powered devices that use intense pulses of electromagnetic radiation and a single wavelength at one time. Different wavelengths affect different components of the skin. These different treatments can stimulate collagen production, reduce spider veins, reduce hair growth, or peel the skin (Figure 19–7). Some lasers target specific substances—such as melanin, dark hair, blood vessels, skin growths, and pigmentation—that absorb the energy from the laser.

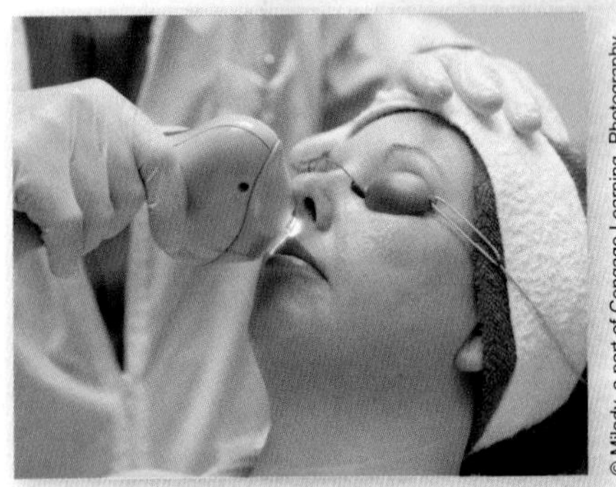

▲ **Figure 19–7**
Laser treatments.

All lasers and light therapy methods use selective *photothermolysis*. Lasers emit lightwaves of the same wavelength, while non-laser photo devices, such as IPL, use a spectrum of different wavelengths. For skin rejuvenation, heating and damaging the dermal tissue stimulates fibroblasts to repair and rebuild tissue such as collagen. The laser is a precise tool used for surgical procedures. In laser skin resurfacing, pulsed lasers are so precise that they can be directed to "burn" off the surface of the skin without ever touching the lower dermis.

A laser produces colored light. Wavelengths are selected to treat a range of skin conditions. For instance, one laser is designed to produce yellow light. Yellow light will selectively absorb into the color red. Laser light passes harmlessly through the skin and targets only the hemoglobin of the red blood cell. The laser energy then heats and destroys the cell, leaving the normal skin cell completely intact.

Lasers are now more commonly used for noninvasive procedures. Lasers include the alexandrite, diode, and Nd:YAG lasers. Another treatment is referred to as *photodynamic* therapy and is best for primarily treating actinic keratoses. Many manufacturers have different names for their devices and specific treatments, which can be confusing. New devices are constantly coming on the market.

Lasers combined with radio frequencies are considered to be even more effective. This combined energy technology targets and heats connective tissue to stimulate collagen production and produce a firming effect. Radio waves of a certain frequency penetrate and are absorbed by the tissues. The strong damaging heat effect is what promotes skin healing and tightening. It is also effective for hair removal and used for cellulite reduction. The effect of using radio waves in the skin is a similar process to how a microwave cooks food. Medical devices that use this technology are very strong, while those sold for home use are much weaker.

Lasers and light therapy are advanced topics. It is not necessary at this stage to learn all of the details concerning these devices. They are mentioned to familiarize you with the technology, which continues to evolve. See Chapter 18, Hair Removal, for additional information on lasers used for hair removal.

Did You Know?

Lasers produce a powerful beam of light that creates heat. The direct beam of radiation penetrates the dermis and creates a reaction. Some beams are thin enough to make holes the size of a pinhead. Some lasers are forceful enough to pierce a diamond, and others can produce a nuclear reaction. Bursts of laser light can record music or store data on a compact disk. Lasers can be used over long distances with no loss of power and are used in fiberoptic communications. Electrical signals are changed into pulses (bursts) of laser light. An optical fiber is about as thin as a human hair and can carry as much information as several thousand copper wires. Using laser technology, a tremendous amount of information can be carried relatively inexpensively over telephones, televisions, and computers.

Light Therapy

Light therapy is the application of light rays to the skin for the treatment of wrinkles, capillaries, pigmentation, or hair removal. Light therapy uses different types of devices: lasers, intense pulsed light

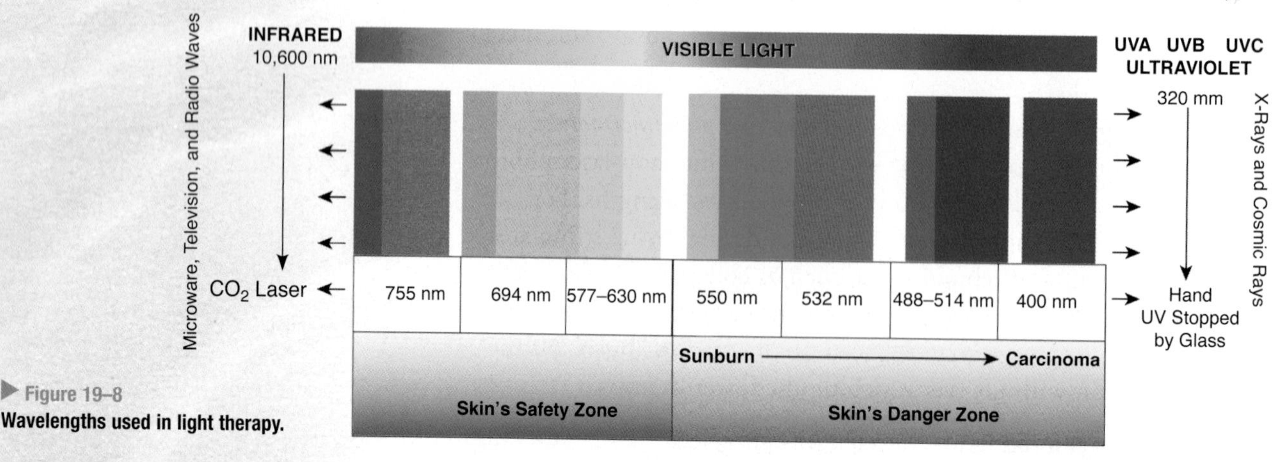

Figure 19–8
Wavelengths used in light therapy.

(IPL), and light-emitting diode (LED) technologies. The power and effectiveness of the machines vary and depend on such factors as the wavelength, heat, and penetration power. Lasers and IPL are strong machines that are rated as Class IV medical devices by the Food and Drug Administration (FDA). LED is rated as a safer Class I or II device and is regulated less strictly.

The range of wavelengths used in light therapy are visible, infrared, and far infrared (**Figure 19–8**). Lasers such as Nd:YAG tighten skin and reduce wrinkles and spider veins. Intense pulse light devices use pulses of multiple wavelengths to reduce pigmentation, remove surface capillaries, and rejuvenate the skin. Intense pulse light emits light absorbed by hemoglobin (vascular), melanin (pigmented lesions), or hair follicles (hair removal).

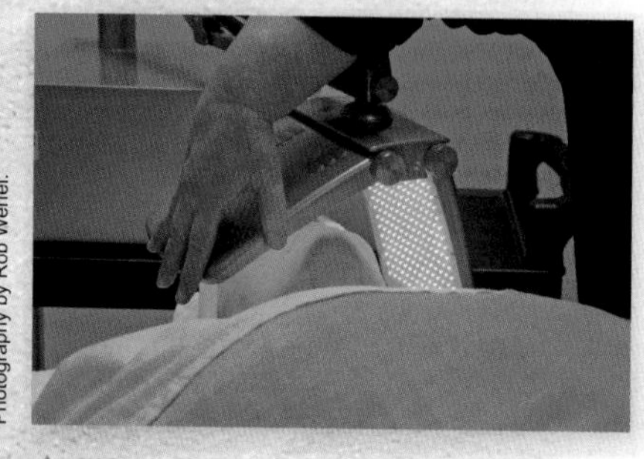

Figure 19–9
LED light therapy.

LED technology is nonthermal, meaning it does not use heat. Estheticians use LED light for skin rejuvenation. LED individual wavelengths are used at low intensity and are not as strong as the laser and intense pulse light modalities. LED uses visible light such as blue, red or amber, and infrared (invisible). Different colors of light produce different effects on the skin. Blue light is considered effective in treating acne. Amber and red are used for muscles and healing. Infrared is used for rejuvenation. Infrared light is also used to detoxify the body and reduce pain. LED is used for photosynthesis because it converts light to cellular energy that stimulates the body's collagen and metabolism (**Figure 19–9**).

Photorejuvenation (FO-toh-rih-joo-vin-A-shun) is another term used for the growing technology that utilizes light therapy to enhance the skin (**Figure 19–10a** and **b**). Light therapy such as infrared heat has been used for years to treat physical conditions such as pain and to promote healing. LED has been shown to help the lymph system and increase ATP energy production in the cells.

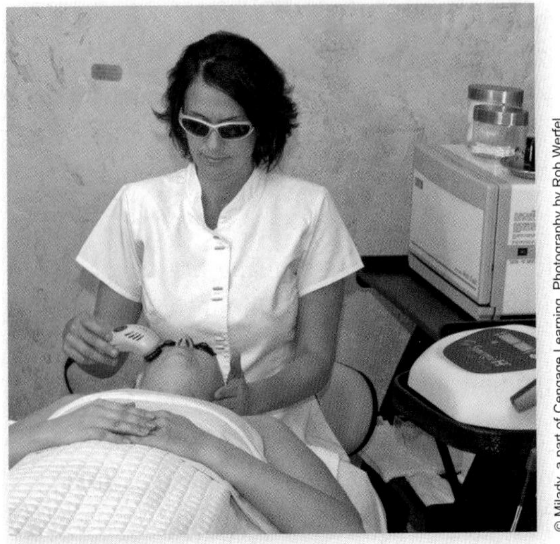

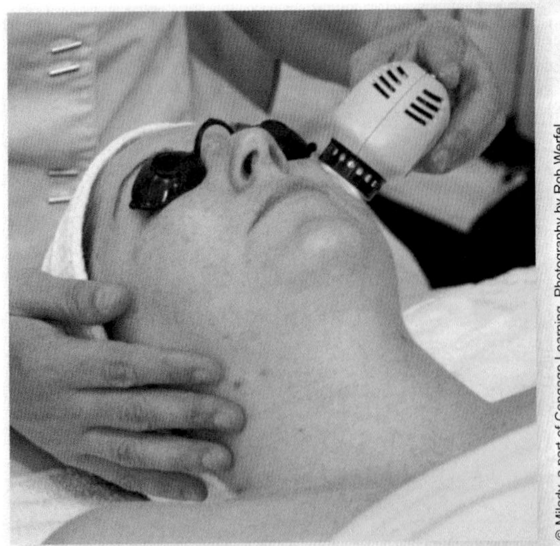

▲ Figure 19–10a and b
LED light therapy.

Therapeutic lamps are also used for light therapy. Color therapy uses different colors of light for various psychological effects: red is considered stimulating, while green is calming (Figure 19–11).

LEDs are used in facials for approximately 15 minutes. Eye goggles are used to protect both the technician's and client's eyes. Hand-held devices are increasingly popular. The use of machines, light therapy, and medical aesthetics continues to develop. Scientific discoveries and advances are changing the face of the antiaging industry. ☑ L04

▲ Figure 19–11
Color therapy has psychological benefits.

Microcurrent Machines

Modern medicine utilizes microcurrent to treat many conditions, such as Bell's palsy and stroke paralysis. The growing uses of microampere electrical neuromuscular stimulation include healing muscles and wounds, controlling pain, and even fusing bones. There is even greater potential for this type of therapy. In the esthetics realm, microcurrent is used to tone the muscles by stimulating motor nerves and contracting the muscles.

Facial Benefits of Microcurrent

Microcurrent (MY-kroh-kur-runt), or wave therapy, devices mimic the way the brain relays messages to the muscles. In esthetics, microcurrent is used primarily to tone and stimulate facial muscles. Considered a passive form of exercise, this therapeutic technique helps stimulate motor nerves until a contraction of the muscles can be seen. Microcurrent has the ability to firm muscles and boost cellular activity. It improves blood and lymph circulation and can also assist with product absorption. In the past, faradic current has been used to stimulate motor nerves.

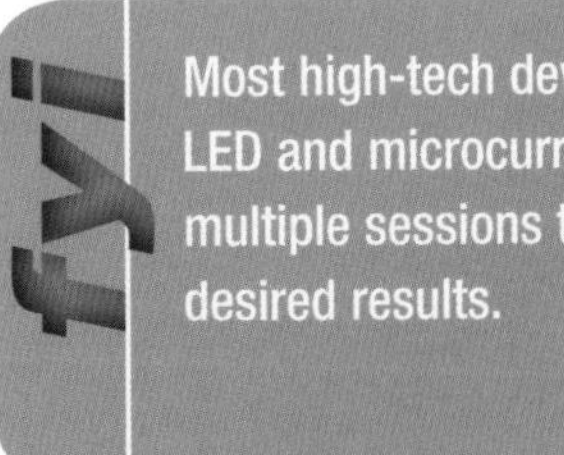

fyi

Most high-tech devices such as LED and microcurrent require multiple sessions to achieve desired results.

Many biological processes are associated with electrical impulses. Facial skin tone and muscles are all related to this system. As we age, impulses slow down, causing the skin to sag. Muscles may not completely contract after use, such as in the case of sagging jowls (jaw muscles). The same effect can be seen on the rest of the body as well. That is why exercise and stretching are extremely important as one ages.

Microcurrent is thought to aid in the healing and repairing of tissue and to influence metabolism. It works gently and helps speed up the natural regenerative processes of the body when the correct intensity of current and frequency is used. Treatment results are expected to show firmer and healthier skin.

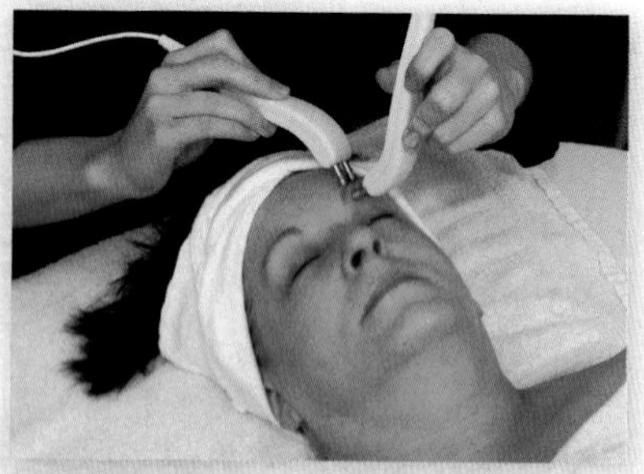

▲ Figure 19–12
The microcurrent machine.

Microcurrent devices are designed to work in harmony with the natural bioelectrical currents found in the body. The standard technique utilizes two hand-held probes placed on facial muscle groups (**Figure 19–12**). A specific movement technique is used on all of the designated facial points. A gel, such as a collagen ampoule, is placed on the skin before beginning the treatment. The electrical current is regulated according to the skin's resistance. Treatments are given one time per week for at least 10 sessions to see visible results. Treatments must be given every 4 weeks to maintain the benefits and results.

Some models of hand-held devices are combined with ultrasound technology (**Figure 19–13**) for additional penetration and added exfoliation effects.

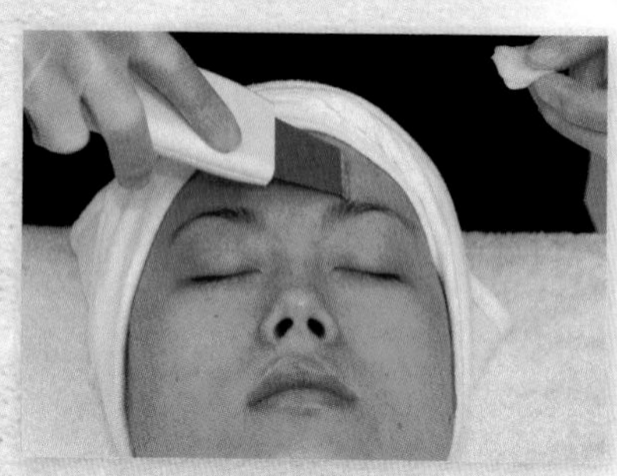

▲ Figure 19–13
Ultrasound technology.

Microcurrent combined with light therapy can be even more effective. When using any electrical device, you should obtain a complete client health history and conduct a consultation before treatment. Contraindications are the same as those described for other electrical devices.

As with all electrical current devices, microcurrent should not be used on clients with the following health conditions: pacemakers, epilepsy, cancer, pregnancy, phlebitis, or thrombosis; or on anyone currently under a doctor's care for a condition that may be contraindicated.

Ultrasound and Ultrasonic Technology

Ultrasound and *ultrasonic* are synonymous terms referring to a frequency that is above the range of sound audible to the human ear. This equipment uses noninvasive sound waves to create results-oriented treatments. **Ultrasonic** equipment is based on high-frequency mechanical oscillations produced by a metal spatula-like tool. The vibrations, created through a water medium, help cleanse and exfoliate the skin by removing dead skin cells. Ultrasound contraindications include epilepsy, pregnancy, and cancerous lesions. Like all machines, overuse can be damaging.

Ultrasound technology in esthetics is also used for product penetration and for cellulite reduction. Ultrasound is deep-penetrating—it stimulates tissue, increases blood flow, and promotes oxygenation. Keep in mind that the lower the frequency, the greater the penetration; conversely, a higher frequency has less penetration. Cellulite is affected through the heat manipulation of the tissue and lymphatic movements performed with the device. Heat is created, and the vibration in the cells stimulates circulation, metabolism, and lymph drainage. The heat damage from ultrasound and other modalities (such as lasers) is what stimulates collagen production.

Ultrasound also sends waves through the skin to assist in product penetration. This process is called *sonophoresis* (SAHN-oh-for-EE-sus), which is similar to iontophoresis (iontophoresis uses electrically charged ions, so an electrical charge is needed from electrodes). Some esthetic ultrasound equipment is rated as an FDA Class II device and may not be within an esthetician's scope of practice outside of a medical facility. Advanced training and technical research on equipment claims are necessary before using any advanced esthetic machine. Different frequencies of ultrasound are also used for medical imaging, physical therapy, and pain management. Lower-frequency ultrasonic devices are used for toothbrushes and jewelry cleaners.

Hand-held devices for a consumer's personal skin care that are used at home are milder but should be used in moderation to avoid damaging the skin. ☑ **LO5**

FOCUS ON

Dermal Rolling

Cosmetic and medical rolling are forms of collagen induction therapy (CIT). This procedure causes tiny needle pricks across the skin from rollers that induce collagen formation from the wound healing process. This also improves the skin's appearance in other ways. Studies conclude that the .05 mm (3/64 in) needles achieve the best results. In conjunction with dermal rolling, oral and topical vitamins, amino acids, and other nutrients are required for collagen synthesis. These are not used on acne or other skin lesions.

Spa Body Treatments

Spa treatments provide a wonderful, relaxing experience. Body treatments have a therapeutic effect and treat the skin of the whole body. They include wraps, scrubs, and masks. Be mindful of contraindications and allergies to ingredients (seaweed, nuts) before working on clients.

- **Body wraps** are treatments where product is applied on the body and then covered or wrapped up. Wraps are used for various reasons and can either remineralize, hydrate, stimulate, detoxify, or promote relaxation. The product used will determine the effects and results. Aloe, gels, lotions, oils, seaweed, herbs, clay, or mud products can all be used for wraps. Linens or plastic can be used to wrap clients and to promote product penetration. Blankets or sheets are the cocoon of the "wraps." Inch-loss wraps, another type of wrap, are designed to flush toxins out of the body and promote inch loss. Inch-loss wraps have a diuretic effect and are controversial in their effectiveness. If done properly, detoxifying the body may aid in weight reduction (**Figure 19–14**).
- **Body scrubs** use friction to exfoliate and hydrate, increase circulation, and nourish skin using a combination of ingredients such as ground

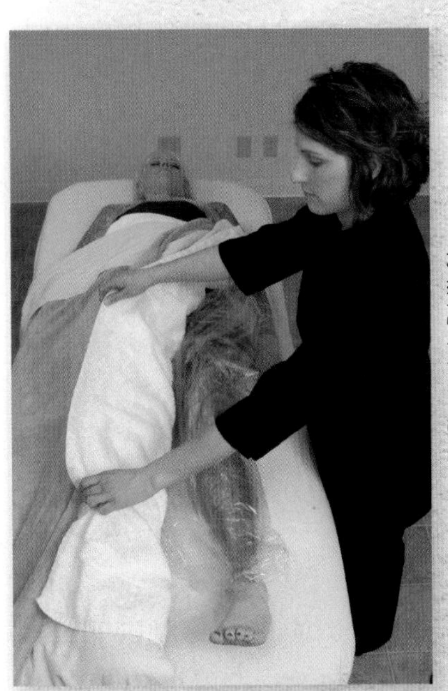

▲ Figure 19–14
A body wrap.

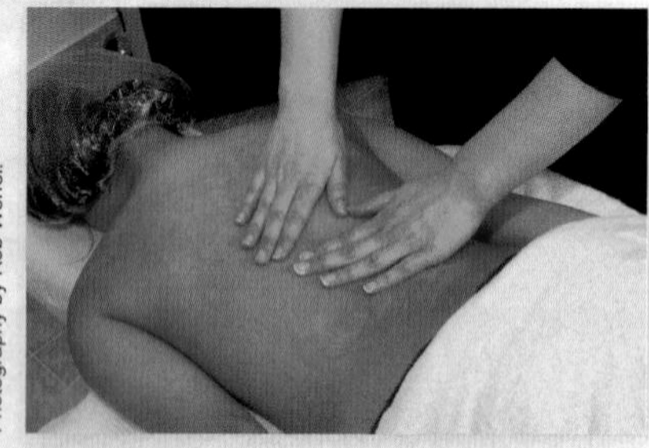
© Milady, a part of Cengage Learning. Photography by Rob Werfel.

▲ Figure 19–15
A salt glow.

nuts, apricot kernels, cornmeal, jojoba beads, honey, salt, or sugar combined with oil or lotion. Exfoliation treatments are also called *polishes* and *glows* (Figure 19–15). Exfoliation prepares the skin to receive additional products or treatments. Dry brushing is also beneficial and is used to exfoliate and stimulate the skin.

- **Body masks** remineralize and detoxify the body using primarily clay, mud, or seaweed mixtures. Certain body masks are used to treat cellulite. Clients are usually wrapped up after the mask application, and thus masks are similar to wraps. The ingredients and procedure used in the treatment determine whether the process is called a *mask* or a *wrap* (Figure 19–16).

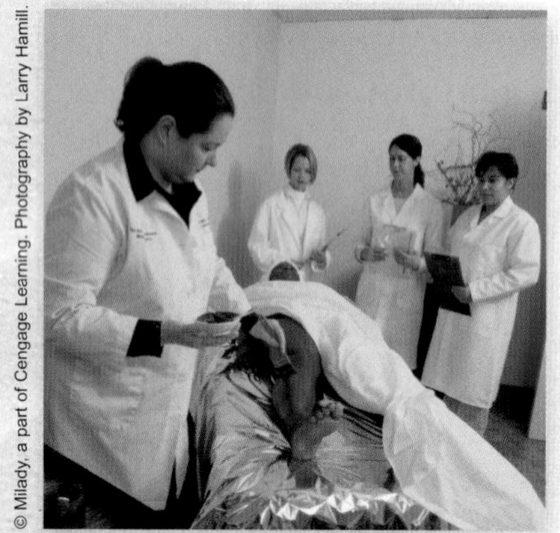
© Milady, a part of Cengage Learning. Photography by Larry Hamill.

▲ Figure 19–16
A body mask.

- **Hydrotherapy** (hy-druh-THAIR-uh-pee) is another spa treatment that uses water in its three forms (ice, steam, and liquid). Hydrotherapy tubs, the Scotch hose, Vichy (VIH-shee) shower (Figure 19–17), Watsu® massage, hot tubs, steam rooms, saunas, the cold-plunge pool, foot soaks, and whirlpool baths are all different forms of hydrotherapy found in spas.

All spa treatments, especially intensive hydrotherapy treatments, can be powerful, so proper training is important before offering these services.

- **Balneotherapy** (bal-nee-oh-THAYR-uh-pee) is the treatment of physical ailments using therapeutic water baths (Figure 19–18). Mineral, mud or fango, Dead Sea salt, seaweed, enzymes, or peat are all used in baths (*balneum* is Latin for bath).
- **Stone massage** is the technique of using hot stones and cold stones in massage or other treatments (Figure 19–19). Facial stone massage can be incorporated into regular facials.

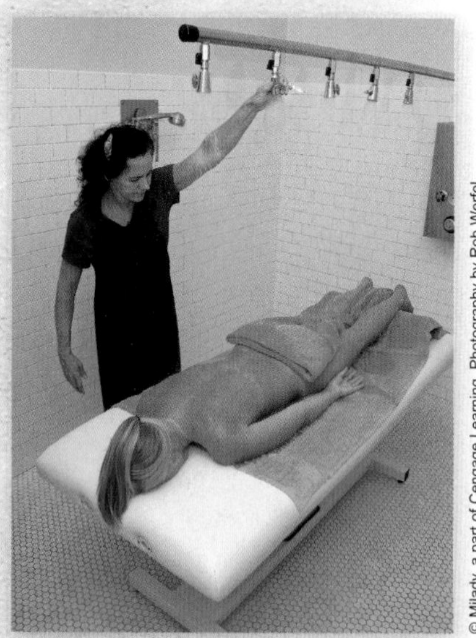
© Milady, a part of Cengage Learning. Photography by Rob Werfel.

▲ Figure 19–17
The Vichy shower.

© Khoroshunova Olga, 2011; used under license from shutterstock.com.

▲ Figure 19–18
Balneotherapy.

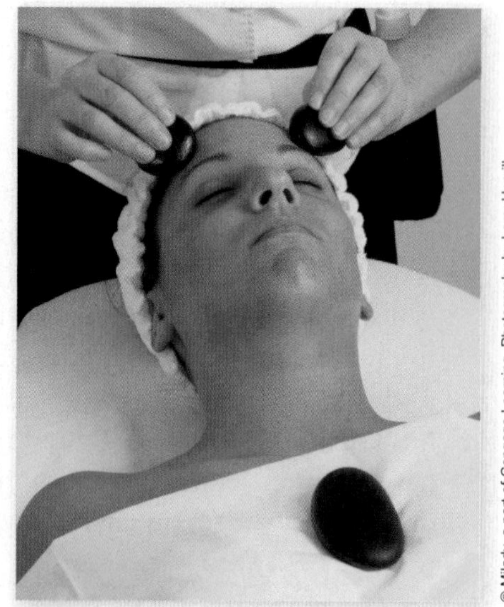
© Milady, a part of Cengage Learning. Photography by Larry Hamill.

▲ Figure 19–19
Stone therapy on the face.

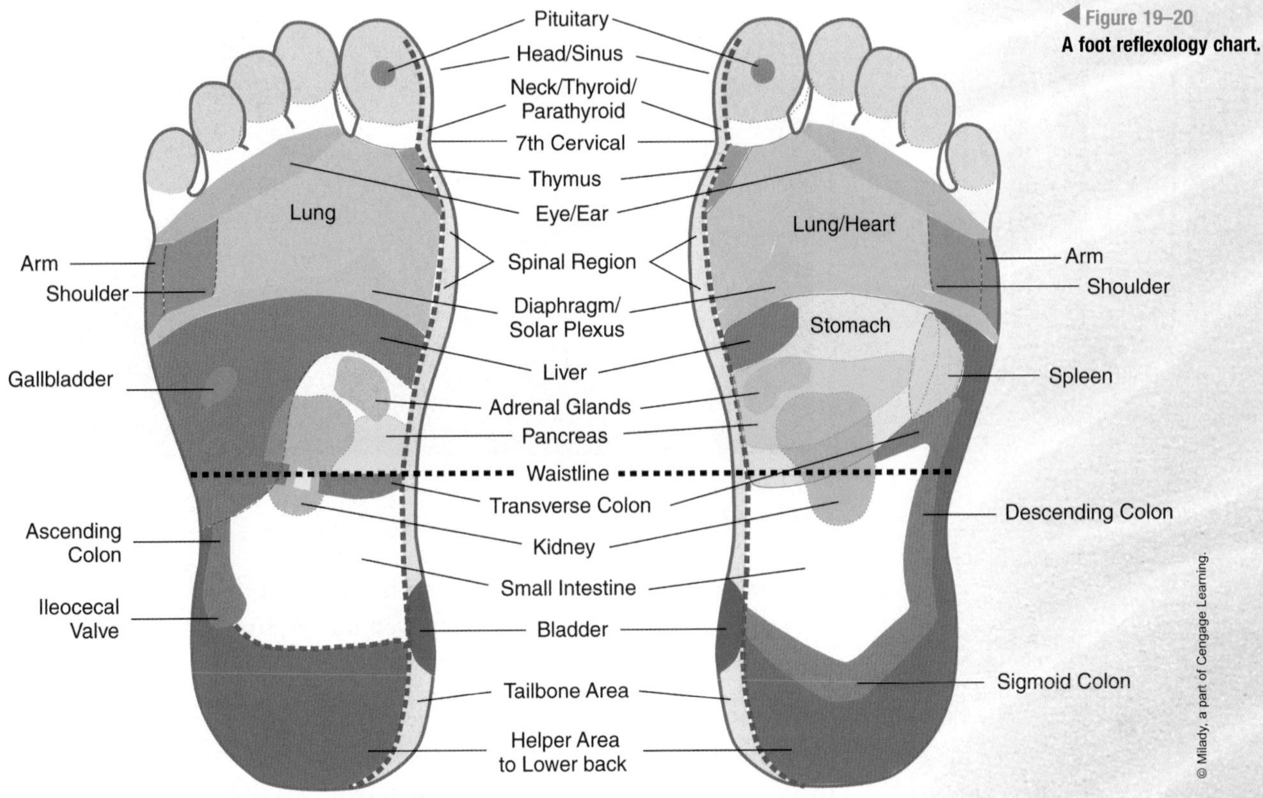

◀ Figure 19–20
A foot reflexology chart.

- **Foot reflexology** (ree-flex-AHL-uh-jee) is the technique of applying pressure to the feet based on a system of zones and areas on the feet that directly correspond to the anatomy of the body (Figure 19–20). Reflexology is performed on the feet, hands, and ears as these are the areas that correspond to the body zones. It causes relaxation, increased circulation, and balance to the entire body. Estheticians are not usually trained in reflexology, so be aware of your scope of practice and licensing regulations. Reflexology is generally performed by licensed massage therapists. Massage can be dangerous if performed incorrectly.
- Ayurvedic (eye-ur-VAY-dic) concepts are based on three *doshas,* or mind and body types. Treatments include *Shirodhara* (Figure 19–21), massage, and facials using ancient Indian concepts and ingredients suited to the three body/mind types: *pitta, kapha,* and *vatta.* **Ayurveda** originated over 5,000 years ago in India. It is a philosophy of medicine and balancing life and the body through various methods ranging from massage to eating habits. *Ayur* means "life, vital power"; *Veda* means "knowledge." *Ayurveda* translates from Sanskrit as "science of health or wellness." Shirodhara is an ayurvedic treatment that consists of running warm oil on the third-eye area of the forehead for 30 minutes. This relaxing, meditative process releases stress and calms the mind.

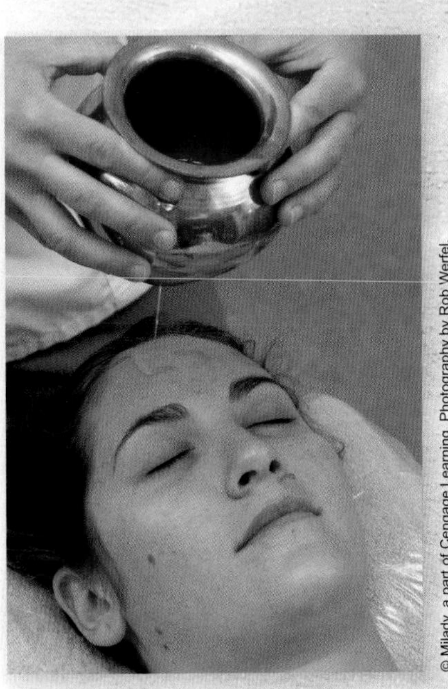

▲ Figure 19–21
Shirodhara.

Sandalwood is a wonderful scent and is a main component of the body polish used with Shirodhara treatments.

© sunlessinc.

▲ Figure 19–22
A spray tan booth.

© Milady, a part of Cengage Learning. Photography by Rob Werfel.

▲ Figure 19–23
Sunless spray tanning.

- **Sunless tanning** product application is a service offered as an alternative to tanning (Figure 19–22). It is sprayed on (Figure 19–23) or applied manually.
- Endermology (en-dur-MAHL-uh-gee) is a treatment for cellulite. It helps stimulate the reduction of adipose tissue by a vacuum massage that combines a vigorous massage along with suction. Machines and other endermology methods are used in spas and in medical facilities (Figure 19–24).

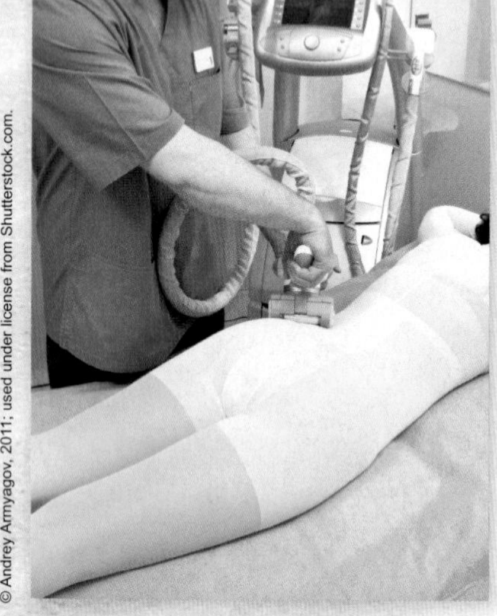
© Andrey Armyagov, 2011; used under license from Shutterstock.com.

▲ Figure 19–24
Endermology.

Body Treatment Procedures

The following procedures briefly outline how the spa treatments are performed. Advanced training is needed to perform these treatments safely and efficiently. There are contraindications to be aware of and many variables in body treatments. Body services are wonderful treatments to offer clients.

CAUTION!

Instruct your clients to drink lots of water to flush the system and rehydrate the body after detoxifying body treatments. If they do not replenish the water in the body, clients may feel tired or sick. Additionally, detoxifying treatments are not as effective when the body is not flushed or rehydrated with water.

FOCUS ON

Ayurveda

Pitta, kapha, and vatta are the three doshas or body/mind types of ayurveda. Doshas are combinations of energy from the five elements: Earth, Water, Fire, Air, and Ether.

- *Vatta* is a combination of air and ether. It is responsible for movements of the body, mind, and senses. The skin type is typically dry/mature.
- *Pitta* is a combination of fire and water. It is responsible for heat, metabolism, energy production, and digestive functions. The skin type is typically sensitive.
- *Kapha* is a combination of earth and water. It is responsible for physical stability, body structure, and fluid balance. The skin type is typically prone to congestion.

Mini Procedure

THE BODY SCRUB

This procedure outline describes a basic body scrub. Follow the instructor's and manufacturer's directions for preparing the scrub. Prepare the supplies per the instructions.

1. Use a prepackaged body exfoliating product, or mix either salt or sugar with lotion or oil. Mix until the desired consistency is reached. Add two drops of aromatherapy oil if desired. A high-quality unrefined salt or sugar is recommended.
   - Make sure the product is not too coarse or rough.
   - Make sure your product rinses off easily because this treatment generally does not require a shower after the service.
   - Prepare the bed with linens while the product and towels are warming in the hot cabbie. It is important to keep the room warm for the client's comfort.
2. Use a set pattern to apply the warmed product, starting with the lower legs and using circular motions upwards toward the heart (Figure 19–25).
   - Exfoliate the body using the hands, a brush, or a mitt (keep adding warm water if necessary).
   - Most body products are applied first to the legs, followed by the arms, then the torso and back. Work on the right side first, then the left. Move from the bottom to the top of each area.
   - To keep the client warm, cover each area with a sheet or body towel before proceeding to the next area.
3. Remove the scrub in the same order (legs, arms, torso) with warm, wet towels (Figure 19–26). Pat dry and cover each area before moving to the next to keep the client warm.
4. ***Optional:*** Finish by spraying the treated areas with a skin freshener and apply lotion if time permits.

   Note: A body wrap treatment can also follow the scrub.

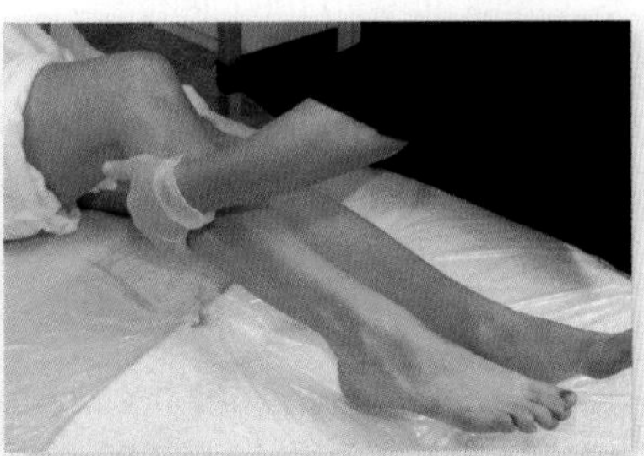

▲ Figure 19–25
Applying a body scrub to the legs.

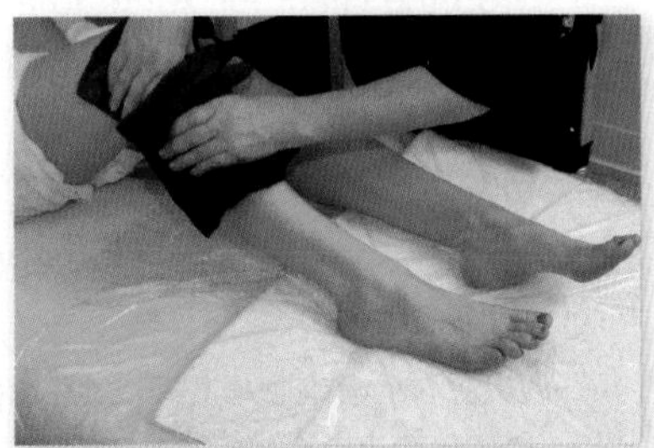

▲ Figure 19–26
Removing the body scrub with towels.

ACTIVITY

To learn more about spa treatments, here is a research idea: Check out the spa menus and brochures in your area or on Internet sites. Professional trade journals and spa suppliers offer excellent information on a variety of treatment procedures. Many spa magazines are also good resources to gain insight into the industry. What body treatment services are you most interested in learning about? A nice way to learn is to experience the treatment yourself. Book an appointment to have a spa research day!

FOCUS ON

Energy

Reiki and Other Treatments

Reiki is a Japanese technique for stress reduction and relaxation that also promotes healing. It is administered by "laying on hands" and is based on the idea that an unseen "life force energy" flows through us and is what causes us to be alive.

Other energy practices include energy balancing and chakras. According to ancient Hindu philosophy, our bodies have seven major vortexes through which we process our life force energy (sometimes known as *ki*, or *chi*). A block in any of these power centers can create unbalance, disease, or an overwhelming sense of tiredness and feeling "stuck." The focus of the chakra balancing is to identify any blocks in the chakras, open them up, and reconnect your energy body.

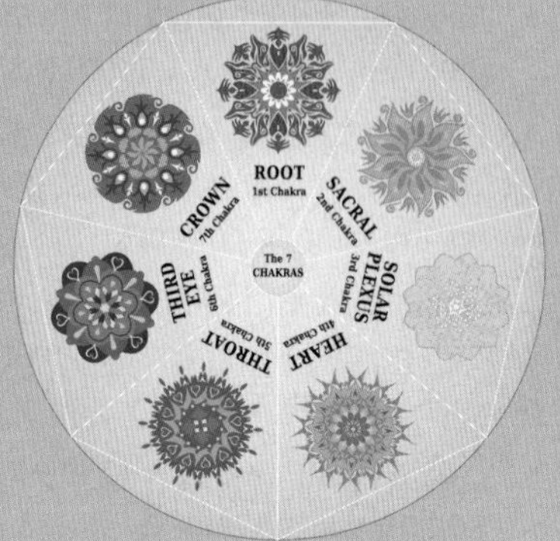

Mini Procedure

THE BODY WRAP OR MASK

Use a body lotion, seaweed, or mud.

1. A dry brush or body scrub can be performed before the wrap or mask.
2. Apply the product (per manufacturer's instructions) with hands or a body "paint" brush. Follow the same pattern as the scrub application.
3. Wrap the client for 20 to 30 minutes. Check-in with the client regarding their comfort level. Are they warm enough or too warm? Do they feel claustrophobic?
4. Add a facial or foot treatment, if desired, during the wrap.
5. Remove the product with warm towels if applicable, or have the client shower.

   Note: Never leave the client alone in the room as they may become uncomfortable or react to the product. An add-on service can be performed to the face or feet while the wrap is processing. This saves time and increases the value of the service.

Did You Know?

Physical therapists Emil and Estrid Vodder created manual lymph drainage (MLD) in 1932 in Europe.

Cellulite

Cellulite (SEL-yoo-lyt) appears as dimpled or bumpy skin caused primarily by female hormones and genetics. Cellulite consists of fat cells. Dermal fat cells do swell, but that is not the only cause of cellulite. Cellulite is visible when dermal fat cells are closer to the surface of the skin (Figure 19–27). This occurs from damage to the dermis. If water is lost and the tissue is weakened, then dermal fat begins to push into the dermis. Additionally, if the epidermis is weakened or dehydrated, cellulite is more visible.

Keeping collagen and elastin healthy helps reduce cellulite. To repair cellulite, cells and connective tissue need to be strengthened and hydrated through nutrients and water intake. Drinking water is not enough—our cells have to be able to hold onto the water. Wasted water in the body builds up and leads to water retention and puffiness. Blood flow and the circulation of nutrients through blood vessels up to the skin also affect cellulite. Repairing cell damage, connective tissue damage, and stratum corneum damage is important in treating cellulite.

The following recommended nutrients and ingredients may be beneficial for cellulite reduction:

- Lecithin and lipids for cell walls
- Glycosaminoglycans (GAGs) for moisturizing and firming
- Glucosamine to build GAGs and connective tissue
- B vitamins to retain moisture and provide nutrients
- Amino acids for building collagen and elastin
- Essential fatty acids to attract water for the connective tissue
- Antioxidants
- Anti-inflammatories
- Aloe vera is anti-inflammatory, improves hydration, and contains enzymes and minerals
- AHAs
- Alpha lipoic acid

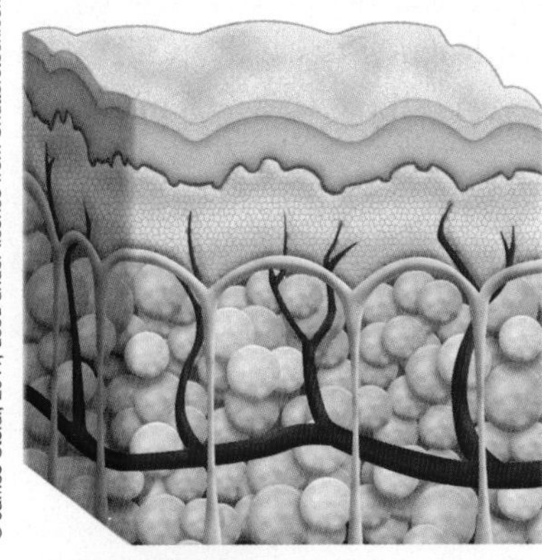

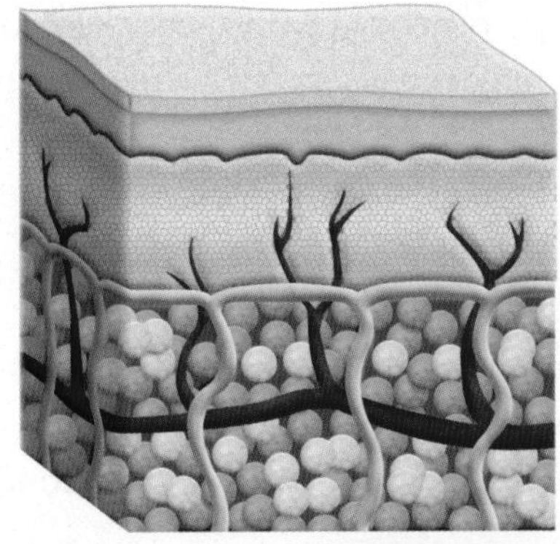

◀ Figure 19–27
Cellulite skin versus smooth skin.

The effectiveness of some endermology treatments is controversial. Detox diets, liposuction, and muscle-stimulating systems do not minimize cellulite. Some body wraps result in only a temporary water loss. Electronic devices with vacuums may reduce cellulite temporarily.

Manual lymph drainage, mesotherapy (microinjection to the dermis to melt fat), dermal fillers, lasers, chemical peels, and microdermabrasion have all been tried to help reduce cellulite. Most of these techniques are considered temporary, and their effectiveness varies. Increasing blood flow, stimulating collagen and elastin, attracting water to cells, and repairing cell membranes are recommended to reduce cellulite. Additionally, reducing wasted water, preventing free radical damage, and reducing inflammation is part of a healthy approach to treating cellulite and the skin. Exercise, along with a healthy low-fat diet with a reduced intake of processed foods, is thought to help reduce cellulite.

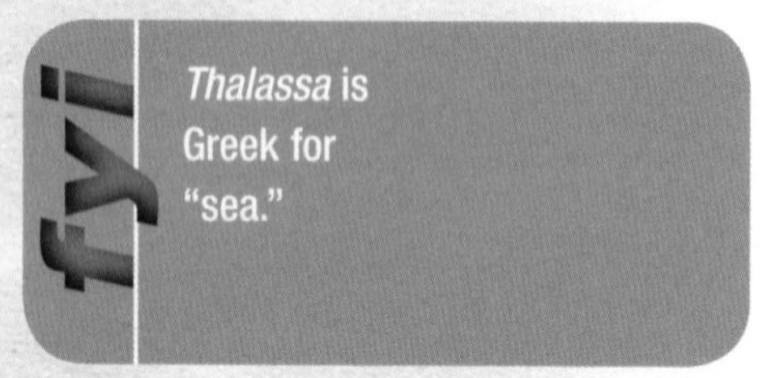

Professional cellulite treatments must be performed consistently in continuous sessions. A common spa treatment consists of exfoliation with a scrub or dry brushing followed by a detoxifying mask and wrap. These stimulate the metabolism and circulation. To finish the service, a cellulite treatment cream is applied.

Exfoliation and skin brushing is also good for vessels and circulation. Another popular treatment is *thalassotherapy* (thuh-LA-soh-THAIR-uh-pee). Thalassotherapy is the use of seawater as a form of therapy. Therapeutic benefits from sea and seawater products include many minerals and nutrients. Massage can also help soften hardened cellulite. Cellulite is a common condition for most women, and improving the health of the skin is a continual process.

Manual Lymph Drainage

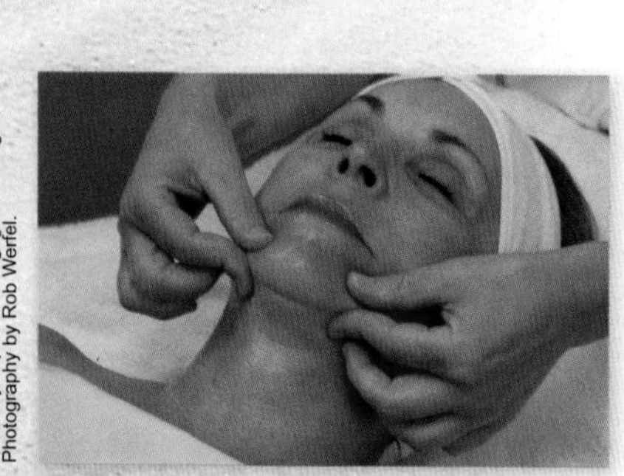

▲ Figure 19–28
Manual lymph drainage.

Manual lymph drainage (MLD) (MAN-yoo-ul LIMF DRAY-nij) stimulates lymph fluid to flow through the lymphatic vessels. This technique helps to cleanse and detoxify the body. Congestion, water, and waste in the vessels create edema in the tissue. Moving this fluid out of the body with light massage movements will decrease the swelling from excess fluid (**Figure 19–28**). MLD is a great addition to a facial. It is also used both before and after surgery because it expedites healing and enhances cell metabolism. Mechanical lymph drainage is a very beneficial MLD service performed with machines. Advanced training courses in MLD are available for both estheticians and massage therapists. ☑ L06

Medical Aesthetics

Medical aesthetics is a multibillion-dollar industry. The industry is constantly developing new products and services for our youth-oriented society. Plastic surgery, laser treatments, and injectables focus on maintaining a youthful appearance. Medical aesthetics integrates surgical and nonsurgical procedures with esthetic treatments. Estheticians also perform services such as peels, microdermabrasion, and light therapy (Figure 19–29). Some assist in the medical procedures and monitor patient recovery.

Additionally, recommending home-care products help patients heal faster and maintain their skin's health. Because medical aesthetics is evolving, the esthetician's role can be shaped to fit the facility's needs. Each setting varies, so it is important to define the responsibilities included in the esthetician's job description.

▲ **Figure 19–29**
There are many opportunities for a medical aesthetician.

Medical aestheticians are well trained, experienced, and in some cases certified; however, not all estheticians must be certified to work in medical aesthetics. Most clinical procedures must be done in a medical office under a physician's supervision. Medi-spas are medical clinics and spas combined in one location and offer both esthetic and medical services.

The most popular medical spa services are chemical peels, microdermabrasion, Botox®, fillers, laser hair removal, and light therapy/photorejuvenation. Estheticians are not qualified to perform certain procedures, but it is important to be familiar with all of them because many clients will be asking questions and utilizing these procedures. Society is now flooded with information on medical aesthetics. It is part of modern society's continued quest for instant gratification and maintaining physical beauty. Medical spas are a fast-growing segment in the beauty industry.

Pre- and Postoperative Care

Estheticians perform pre- and postoperative treatments and provide patient education before cosmetic surgery. These are important for faster patient recovery time. Estheticians also provide facials, light peels, extractions, and microdermabrasion prior to surgery. Camouflage makeup, retail sales, and patient home-care counseling are other responsibilities in medical aesthetics.

Preoperative care focuses on preparing the skin for the procedure. Getting the skin in its optimum state and as healthy as possible makes the surgery less traumatic on the tissue and shortens recovery time. Increasing the skin's metabolism and reducing cellular debris on the surface are part of conditioning the skin. Helping the patient stay calm is also a role the esthetician can fill. A plan and schedule for pre- and post-op care are outlined by the medical staff before a patient's surgery.

Post-op care includes providing skin care for rapid wound healing and the avoidance of infection. Decreasing inflammation, soothing and moisturizing, and providing for sun protection are the goals. Massage, hydration, protection, and camouflage makeup are all part of post-op care. Home-care instructions for long-term maintenance are also important. Permanent makeup, sometimes referred to as *micropigmentation*, is another technique utilized in clinical aesthetics.

Microdermabrasion and Chemical Peels

Glycolic (gly-KAHL-ik) treatments can be performed to precondition the skin before laser resurfacing or surgery. These "lunchtime peels" can enhance the strength and barrier function of the epidermis. Microdermabrasion benefits to the epidermis are similar to those provided by AHA treatments, although the effects are more superficial.

Documentation

The patient charts are a record of what the patient conveys, what the esthetician observes, the assessment and analysis, and a plan of action for treatment. Protocols from clinical procedures are followed. Patient informed-consent forms and treatment records are required and are part of the standard charting procedure.

Other Clinical Procedures

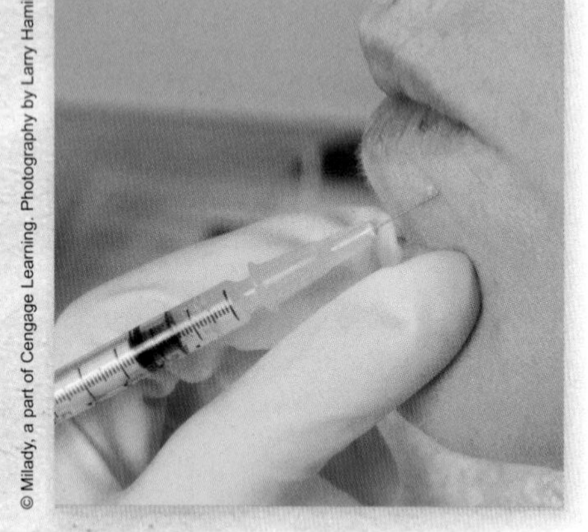

▲ Figure 19–30
Botox®.

Numerous opportunities for estheticians are found in specialized clinical settings. Laser and medical centers offer hair reduction, spider vein removal, nonablative wrinkle treatments, and other types of laser procedures. **Nonablative** (non-uh-BLAY-tiv) procedures do not remove tissue. Nonablative wrinkle treatments use intense pulsed light (IPL) to bypass the epidermis and stimulate collagen in the dermis to promote wrinkle reduction. Estheticians can assist physicians in these procedures if the technician is properly trained and certified.

Other common procedures performed by physicians include injectables of dermal fillers and Botox®. ☑ L07

Injectables

Botox® and dermal fillers are injectables that are a large part of the industry. Injectables have become the fastest-growing product in the medical spa industry. **Injectable fillers** are substances used in nonsurgical procedures to fill in or plump up areas of the skin. FDA-approved fillers are nontoxic, durable, biocompatible, and easy to use—these are the necessary attributes of a safe filler.

▲ Figure 19–31
The glabella is the most common site for Botox® injections.

BOTOX: Botox injection is a popular nonsurgical clinical service. **Botox®** is a neuromuscular-blocking serum (botulinum toxin) that paralyzes nerve cells on the muscle when this serum is injected into it. Botox is injected into the muscles to cause paralysis or diminished movement by blocking neurotransmitters (Figure 19–30). This relaxes tissues and diminishes lines. The glabella (gluh-BEL-uh) is the area between the eyebrows where muscles cause creasing from squinting or frowning. The glabella has strong muscles and is the most common site for Botox injections (Figure 19–31). Millions of Botox injections are performed annually in the United States.

DERMAL FILLERS: **Dermal fillers** are used to fill lines, wrinkles, and other facial imperfections. As we age, dermal collagen, hyaluronic acid, and fat (lipotrophy) are lost and skin loses its shape. The first fillers were from animal sources, specifically bovine collagen. Collagen treatments use a filler, usually a bovine (cow) derivative, to fill in wrinkles or to make lips larger. Dermal fillers will last longer when used in conjunction with Botox.

Today's fillers are obtained from a variety of sources. Many are combined substances and materials. Collagen may be derived from human or animal sources. Synthetic sources are silicone and hyaluronic acids (HAs). The newest trend is to use both non-animal (Restylane®) and animal-based (Hylaform®) hyaluronic acid fillers. Juvéderm® is one of the many cross-linked HA fillers. Hyaluronic acid is a polysaccharide found in the body and connective tissues. A component of the skin's natural moisturizing function, it holds up to 1,000 times its weight in water. Cross-linking is a process where ingredients are combined to increase the stability and durability of the products.

Another type of filler is aqueous calcium (Radiesse® FN), which is calcium-based. Another injectable is not a filler, but a dermal stimulator called poly-L-lactic acid (PLLA). This product (marketed as Sculptra®) increases fibroblast activity and collagen production. New products are coming on the market regularly. ✓ LO8

Surgical Procedures

There are two types of surgery: reconstructive and cosmetic.

- **Reconstructive surgery** is defined as "restoring a bodily function." This type of surgery is necessary for accident survivors and those with congenital disfigurements or other diseases.
- **Cosmetic surgery**, also known as **esthetic surgery**, is elective surgery for improving and altering the appearance.

Cosmetic Surgical Procedures

Common plastic surgery procedures are face lifts, forehead lifts, eye lifts, nose reconstruction, laser resurfacing, and deep peels.

- A **rhytidectomy** (rit-ih-DEK-tuh-mee) is a face lift. This procedure removes excess fat at the jawline; tightens loose, atrophic muscles; and removes sagging skin (Figures 19–32a and b).
- A forehead lift, also called a *brow lift*, can be performed separately or in combination with an eye lift.

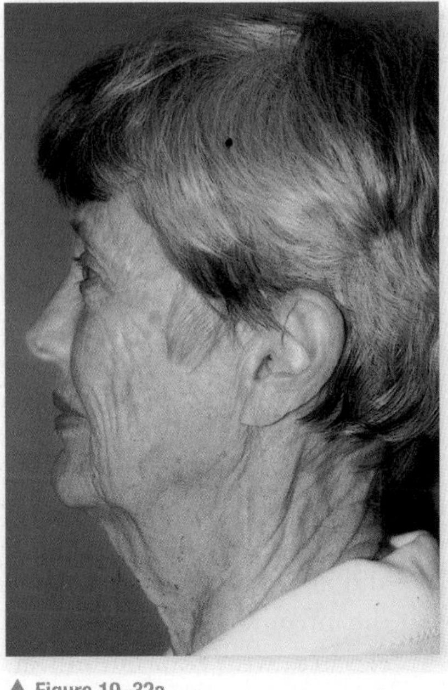

▲ Figure 19–32a
Before a face lift.

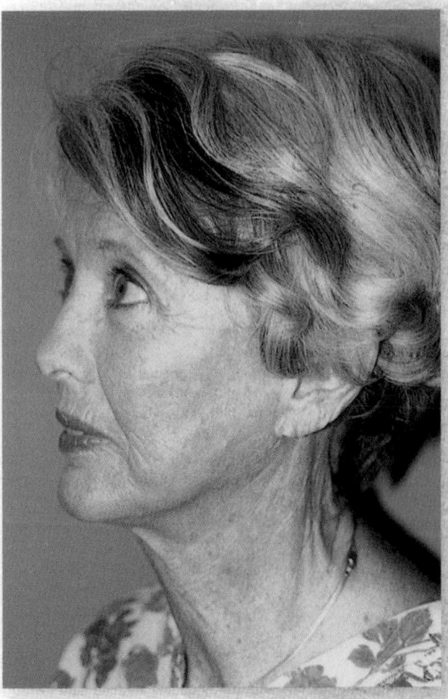

▲ Figure 19–32b
After a face lift.

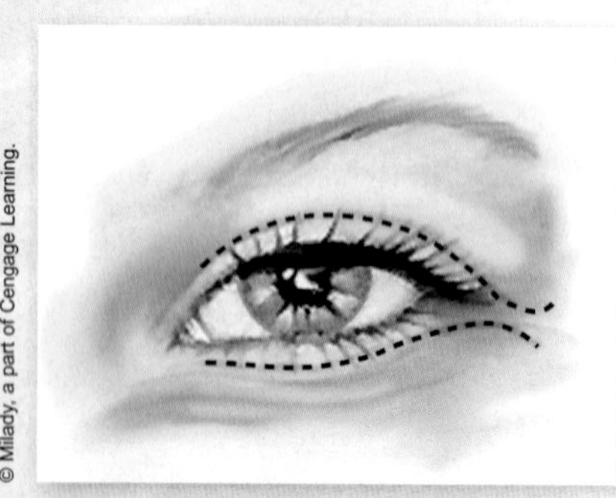
© Milady, a part of Cengage Learning.

▲ Figure 19–33
Blepharoplasty.

- A **blepharoplasty** (BLEF-uh-roh-plas-tee) is an eye lift. It removes fat and skin from the upper and lower lids, making them less baggy and crinkled-looking (Figure 19–33). When sagging eyelids impede a patient's ability to see, it is a medical condition that may be covered by insurance.
- A **transconjunctival blepharoplasty** (trans-kon-junk-TIE-vul BLEF-uh-roh-plas-tee) is performed inside the lower eyelid to remove bulging fat pads, which are often congenital.
- **Rhinoplasty** (RY-noh-plas-tee) is nose surgery that makes a nose smaller or changes the appearance in some way. Sometimes rhinoplasty is necessary for health reasons and to improve the patient's breathing ability.
- **Laser resurfacing** (LAY-zur ree-SIR-fuh-sing) is used to smooth wrinkles or lighten acne scars. Collagen remodeling stimulates the growth of new collagen in the dermis (Figures 19–34a and b). This type of laser treatment removes the epidermal layer and requires a recovery period.

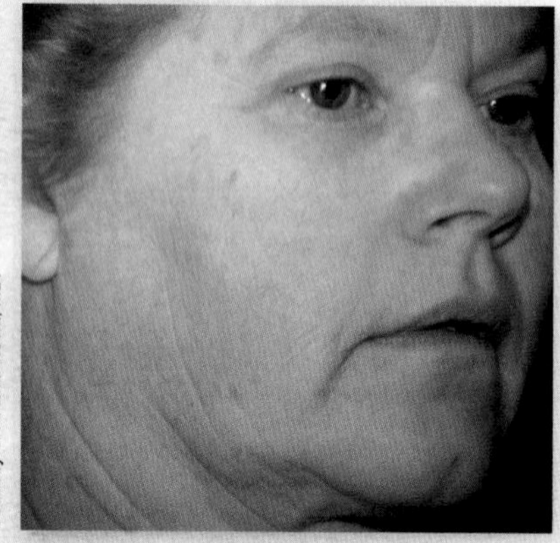
Courtesy of R. Emil Hecht, MD.

▲ Figure 19–34a
Before laser resurfacing.

- **Dermabrasion** (dur-muh-BRAY-zhun) is a strong exfoliation method that uses a mechanical brush to physically remove tissue down to the dermis. It is a very deep exfoliation used primarily on scars. Lasers are replacing the use of this medical procedure.

  Do not confuse dermabrasion with microdermabrasion. Microdermabrasion is a mild, superficial mechanical exfoliation method.
- **Trichloroacetic acid (TCA) peels** (TRY-klor-oh-uh-SEE-tik AH-sid peels) are deep peels used for sun damage and wrinkles.
- **Phenol** (FEE-nohl) peels are the strongest peels and can be toxic. They are still used and are less expensive, but they require a longer recovery period than TCA peels or laser resurfacing.

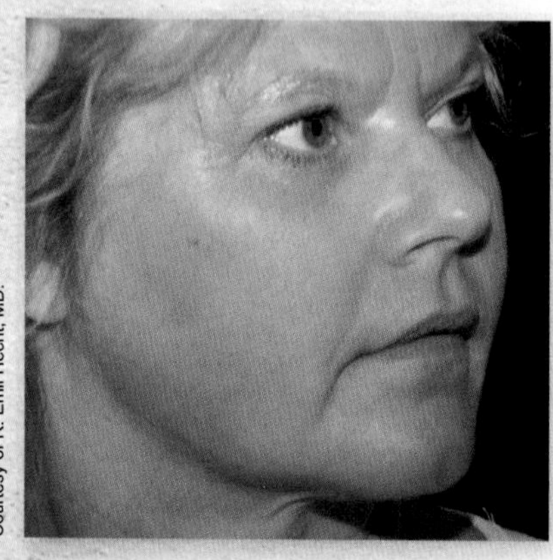
Courtesy of R. Emil Hecht, MD.

▲ Figure 19–34b
After laser resurfacing.

Body Procedures

Many individuals are having elective surgeries. It is therefore important to be familiar with these procedures, especially if you are offering body treatments.

- **Sclerotherapy** (sklair-oh-THAIR-uh-pee) minimizes varicose veins (dilated blood vessels) and other varicosities by injecting chemical agents into the affected areas. Lasers are a secondary method of vein therapy. Over 50 percent of women have varicose veins and smaller spider veins (telangiectasia) on their legs. Potential causes are heredity, race, gender, posture, hormones, and pregnancy. Trauma and injury causes inflammation to vessels. Phlebitis (fluh-BY-tus) is the inflammation of a vein. To take pressure off of veins keep the legs elevated, wear compression stockings, avoid crossing the legs, exercise, and avoid being in stationary positions for long periods of time.

- **Mammoplasty** (MAM-oh-plas-tee) is breast surgery that enlarges the breasts or reconstructs them. This procedure is also referred to as breast augmentation, or implants. Breast reduction reduces or repositions the breasts. This is sometimes performed for health reasons, primarily to alleviate back pain.
- **Liposuction** (LY-puh-suck-shun) is the procedure that surgically removes pockets of fat.
- An **abdominoplasty** (ab-DOM-un-oh-plas-tee) removes excessive fat deposits and loose skin from the abdomen to tuck and tighten the area. ☑ L09

The Clinical Aesthetician

Working as a clinical aesthetician in medical aesthetics can be enriching (Figure 19–35). This specialty requires compassion and patience because you will work with people who are in pain or who are experiencing physical trauma. Many patients feel more comfortable with the esthetician than they do with a physician, who may not have time for more personal and empathetic discussions. Remember to stay focused on the treatment goals and maintain a professional role at all times. The role of an esthetician can be invaluable in a medical setting in providing pre- and postoperative care and other patient services and education.

A career in esthetics is always exciting and fascinating. Advanced areas of study range from medical aesthetics to exotic body treatments. Utilizing AHAs and light therapy for skin care are two of the most effective tools available today to estheticians. The opportunity for advanced training is limitless.

There are many services one can specialize in. As the industry continues to grow, keep up with new technology and changes, even if they are not on your service menu. After basic esthetic techniques are mastered, it is a natural progression to add advanced treatments to the services currently offered. This is the beauty of esthetics: The increased ability to improve the health of the skin as the industry evolves. Educated and skilled technicians will always be in demand.

Web Resources

Here are some great Web sites for more information:

American Society of Plastic Surgeons: www.plasticsurgery.org

eMedicine: www.emedicine.com

Mayo Clinic: www.mayoclinic.com

The medical journal for skin care professionals: www.pcijournal.com

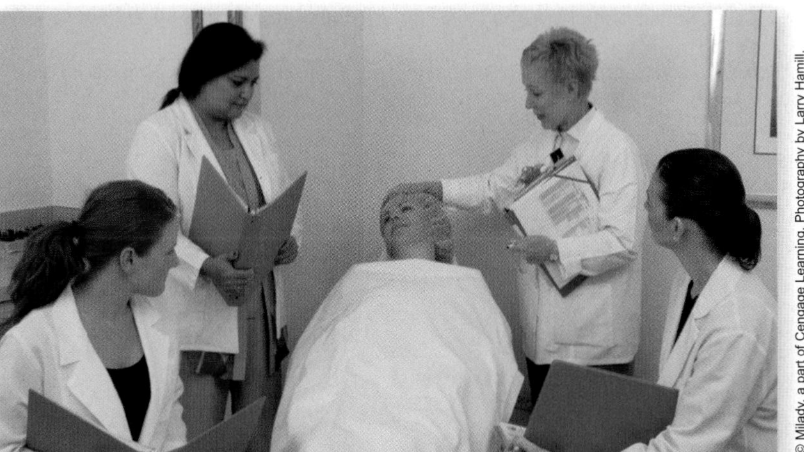

Figure 19–35
Working in a medical clinic can be rewarding.

Review Questions

1. How do alpha hydroxy acids exfoliate the skin?
2. What are the benefits of chemical exfoliation?
3. What are the contraindications for chemical exfoliation?
4. What benefits does microdermabrasion have on the skin?
5. What types of skin conditions do lasers treat?
6. What is light therapy?
7. What is light therapy used for?
8. What is LED used for?
9. What is microcurrent and what does it do for the skin?
10. What is ultrasound and what is it used for in esthetics?
11. What are body wraps used for?
12. What is endermology?
13. What services do medical aestheticians provide?
14. What are injectable fillers used for?
15. What are the medical terms for a face lift, eye lift, and nose surgery?

Glossary

abdominoplasty	Procedure that removes excessive fat deposits and loose skin from the abdomen to tuck and tighten the area.
ayurveda	One of the world's oldest holistic healing systems. It originated in India and is thought to be as much as 5,000 years old. Ayurveda translates from Sanskrit as "science of health or wellness."
balneotherapy	Body treatments that use mud or fango, Dead Sea salt, seaweed, enzymes, or peat baths.
blepharoplasty	A plastic surgery procedure that removes excess skin and/or fat in the upper or lower eyelids.
body masks	A body treatment involving the application of an exfoliating, hydrating, purification, or detoxification mask to the entire body. Masks may include clay, cream, gel, or seaweed bases.
body scrubs	Use of friction and products to exfoliate, hydrate, increase circulation, and nourish the skin.
body wraps	Wraps remineralize, hydrate, stimulate, or promote relaxation by using aloe, gels, lotions, oils, seaweed, herbs, clay, or mud.
Botox®	Neuromuscular-blocking serum (botulinum toxin) that paralyzes nerve cells on the muscle when this serum is injected into it.
cell renewal factor	Abbreviated CRF; cell turnover rate.

Glossary

cellulite	Dimpling of the skin caused by protrusion of subcutaneous fat; is due to an irregularity in distribution of fat in the area, usually found on the thighs, hips, buttocks, and abdomen.
cosmetic surgery	Also known as *esthetic surgery*; elective surgery for improving and altering the appearance.
dermabrasion	Medical procedure; strong exfoliation method using a mechanical brush to physically remove tissue down to the dermis.
dermal fillers	Products used to fill lines, wrinkles, and other facial imperfections.
endermology	Treatment for cellulite.
foot reflexology	Technique of applying pressure to the feet based on a system of zones and areas on the feet that directly correspond to the anatomy of the body. Reflexology is also performed on the hands and ears.
hydrotherapy	Spa treatments that use water.
injectable fillers	Substances used in nonsurgical procedures to fill in or plump up areas of the skin. Botox® and dermal fillers are injectables.
Jessner's peel	Light to medium peel of lactic acid, salicylic acid, and resorcinol in an ethanol solvent.
laser resurfacing	A laser procedure utilizing the CO_2 or erbium laser that involves vaporization of the epidermis and/or dermis for facial rejuvenation; used to smooth wrinkles or lighten acne scars and stimulate growth of new collagen.
liposuction	A surgical procedure used to remove stubborn areas of fat.
mammoplasty	Surgery to alter the shape or contours of the breast.
microcurrent (device)	A device that mimics the body's natural electrical energy to reeducate and tone facial muscles; improves circulation and increases collagen and elastin production.
microdermabrasion	Form of mechanical exfoliation.
nonablative	Procedure that does not remove tissue; wrinkle treatments that bypass the epidermis to stimulate collagen in the dermis for wrinkle reduction are nonablative.
phenol	Carbolic acid; a caustic poison; used for peels and to disinfect metallic implements.
reconstructive surgery	Defined as: restoring a bodily function; necessary surgery for accident survivors and those with congenital disfigurements or other diseases.
Reiki	Universal life-force energy transmitted through the palms of the hands that helps lift the spirits and provide balance to the whole self: body, mind, and spirit.
rhinoplasty	Plastic or reconstructive surgery performed on the nose to change or correct its appearance.

Glossary

rhytidectomy	A face-lift procedure that removes excess fat at the jawline; tightens loose, atrophic muscles; and removes sagging skin.
stone massage	Use of hot stones and cold stones in massage or in other treatments.
transconjunctival blepharoplasty	Procedure performed inside the lower eyelid to remove bulging fat pads, which are often congenital.
trichloroacetic acid (TCA) peels	A strong peel used to diminish sun damage and wrinkles.
ultrasonic	Frequency above the range of sound audible to the human ear; vibrations, created through a water medium, help cleanse and exfoliate the skin by removing dead skin cells; contraindications include epilepsy, pregnancy, and cancerous lesions; synonymous with ultrasound.
ultrasound	Frequency above the range of sound audible to the human ear; vibrations, created through a water medium, help cleanse and exfoliate the skin by removing dead skin cells; also used for product penetration; cellulite reduction; stimulating tissue, increasing blood flow, and promoting oxygenation.

CHAPTER 20

The World of Makeup

Chapter Outline

- Why Study Facial Makeup?
- Color Theory
- Makeup Products and Formulations
- Makeup Brushes
- Products, Tools, and Supplies
- Infection Control
- Client Consultations
- Selecting Makeup Colors
- Makeup Application Techniques
- Face Shapes and Proportions
- Corrective Makeup
- Special-Occasion Makeup
- Makeup for the Camera and Special Events
- Camouflage Makeup
- Artificial Eyelashes
- Lash and Brow Tinting
- Other Eyelash Services
- Permanent Cosmetic Makeup
- A Career as a Makeup Artist
- Freelance Makeup Artistry
- Retailing
- Procedures

Learning Objectives

After completing this chapter, you will be able to:

- ✓ LO1 Demonstrate an understanding of cosmetic color theory.
- ✓ LO2 Describe warm and cool colors.
- ✓ LO3 Describe the different types of cosmetics and their uses.
- ✓ LO4 Prepare the makeup station and supplies for clients.
- ✓ LO5 Perform a makeup consultation, determine a client's needs, and fill out a client chart.
- ✓ LO6 Demonstrate how to choose products and colors and then apply them using the appropriate techniques.
- ✓ LO7 Identify different facial features.
- ✓ LO8 Identify the ideal brow shape measurements.
- ✓ LO9 Demonstrate procedures for basic corrective makeup.
- ✓ LO10 Perform a basic makeup procedure for any occasion.
- ✓ LO11 Perform decontamination and cleanup procedures.
- ✓ LO12 Demonstrate the application and removal of artificial lashes.
- ✓ LO13 Complete a lash and brow tinting procedure.

Key Terms

Page number indicates where in the chapter the term is used.

band lashes (strip lashes)
pg. 601

cake makeup (pancake makeup)
pg. 564

complementary colors
pg. 561

concealers
pg. 565

cool colors
pg. 562

eye tabbing
pg. 601

foundation (base makeup)
pg. 563

greasepaint
pg. 564

individual lashes
pg. 601

matte
pg. 565

primary colors
pg. 560

secondary colors
pg. 561

tertiary colors
pg. 561

warm colors
pg. 562

Makeup artistry is a fun, creative career choice. This is an area of esthetics where one can be artistic and expressive. Different makeup looks can show off an individual's unique style. A wide range of makeup styles can be created, from basic daytime applications to makeup for dramatic photoshoots. It is both interesting and enjoyable to experiment with different colors and looks.

▲ Figure 20–1
An attractive makeup station.

Makeup plays an important role in the fashion world and constantly changes with the seasons. Society has always taken great interest in the latest trends in fashion, hair, and clothing styles. The fashion and film industry continue to influence these trends. Makeup is also an important feature of weddings, proms, and other glamorous events. With ever-changing formulas and colors, each year brings increased sophistication to the art and science of makeup.

The world of makeup offers a variety of opportunities. Makeup artists work in salons or spas offering makeup applications, makeovers, and lessons (Figure 20–1). Weddings are also a big part of makeup services. Other opportunities include working with photographers, television stations, or video companies. Some artists become stylists on photoshoots or work in film and video production. Theaters also use makeup artists for theatrical stage makeup. Providing camouflage makeup applications for clinics or plastic surgeons is another avenue for makeup artistry.

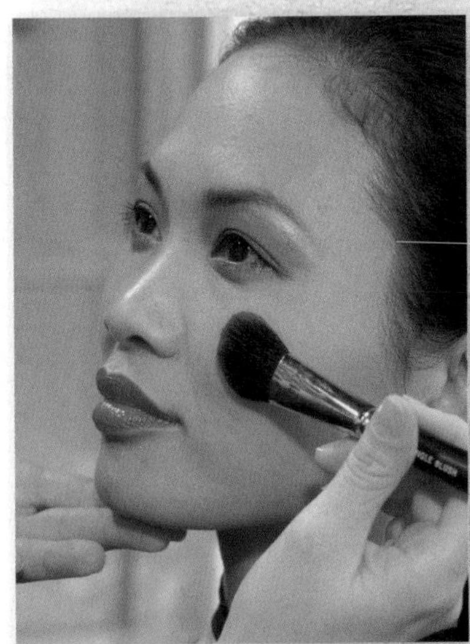

▲ Figure 20–2
Makeup helps enhance a client's natural beauty.

The primary goal of makeup is to enhance the client's natural beauty by bringing out the most attractive features of the face, while minimizing those that are less attractive (Figure 20–2). Makeup is a tool that helps create a certain look. Every woman wants to look her best. Through the consultation, the client's individual needs can be determined. The natural skin tone, hair color, eye color, and face shape are all taken into consideration. A person's lifestyle and preferences are also factors in determining the look. For most clients, makeup application should be subtle. The client's natural beauty can be enhanced by a blend of makeup artistry, hairstyle, and clothing choices.

This chapter covers all aspects of makeup artistry. Knowledge of color theory, analyzing facial features, and corrective makeup techniques are all part of being a successful makeup artist. Client consultations, the makeup station, products, application techniques, and lash procedures are all included in this comprehensive chapter. The key to creating beauty is in the details.

This is a large chapter, and you will not be expected to comprehend or memorize all of the information in one study session. The tables are included as guidelines that you can refer to again and again. The great thing about makeup is that it is not permanent—it washes off! There is room to color outside the lines and be creative with makeup. After trying a few practice applications, you will find that the concepts will all come together.

Why Study Facial Makeup?

Estheticians should have a thorough understanding of makeup because makeup skills and knowledge add another element of expertise to enhance your reputation, grow your clientele, and increase menu services and revenues.

- Knowledge of products, color theory, analyzing facial features, and corrective makeup techniques are all part of being a successful makeup artist.
- Educated estheticians will be confident when providing consultations, product recommendations, makeup applications, and lash procedures.
- In addition to salons offering makeup services, the world of makeup offers a variety of career opportunities in areas such as fashion and video.
- Makeup Artistry is part of being an esthetician: Clients will rely on you to advise them on tips and techniques that will help them look their best.
- Makeup is a natural and lucrative addition to an esthetician's repertoire.

FOCUS ON

Beauty

The most beautiful thing about a person is her or his inner beauty—a radiant smile and a positive attitude.

Color Theory

An understanding of how color works is essential for makeup application. Everyone sees color a little differently, and it may take a while to learn to see color shades naturally and easily. Primary, secondary, and tertiary colors as well as warm, cool, and complementary colors are shown in the color wheels (Figure 20–3). Once you understand these basics of color theory, you can use your creative instincts to invent any color palette you desire.

- **Primary colors** are fundamental colors that cannot be obtained from a mixture. The primary colors are yellow, red, and blue (Figure 20–4). These are the main spectral colors of light seen in a prism from sunlight.

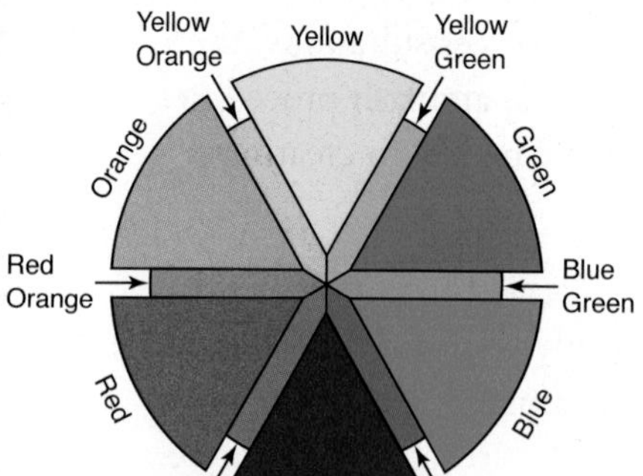

▲ Figure 20–3
The color wheel.

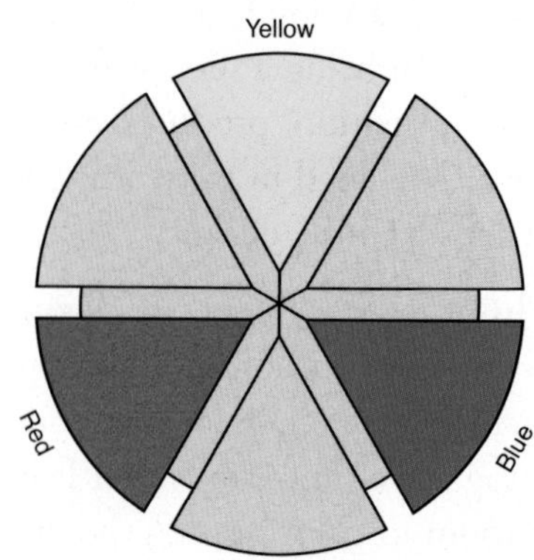

▲ Figure 20–4
Primary colors.

- **Secondary colors** are obtained by mixing equal parts of two primary colors. Yellow mixed with red makes orange. Red mixed with blue makes violet. Yellow mixed with blue makes green (Figure 20–5).
- **Tertiary colors** (TUR-shee-ayr-ee KUL-urz) are formed by mixing equal amounts of a primary color and its neighboring secondary color on the color wheel. These colors are named by primary color first, secondary color second. For example, when we mix blue (a primary) with violet (a neighboring secondary), we call the resulting color blue-violet (Figure 20–6).
- A primary and secondary color directly opposite each other on the color wheel are called **complementary colors**. These complementary colors are defined as two colors that, when mixed together, produce a neutral gray or white. When mixed, these colors cancel each other out to create a neutral brown or gray color. When complementary colors are placed next to each other, each color makes the other look brighter, resulting in greater contrast (Figure 20–7). For example, if you place blue next to orange, the blue seems bluer, the orange brighter. The concept of complementary colors is useful when determining color choices. The use of complementary colors will emphasize eye color, making the eyes appear brighter.

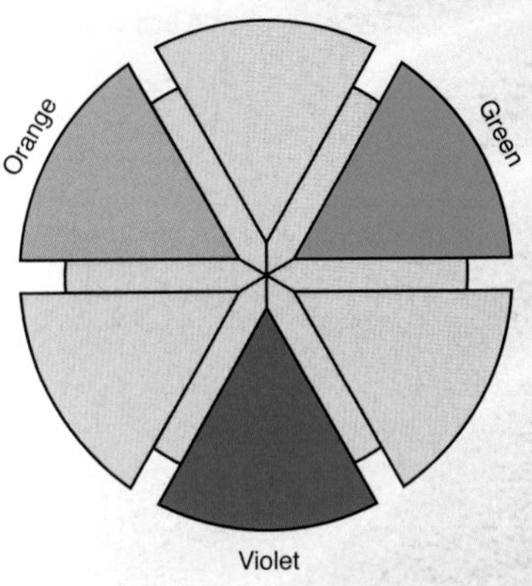

▲ Figure 20–5
Secondary colors.

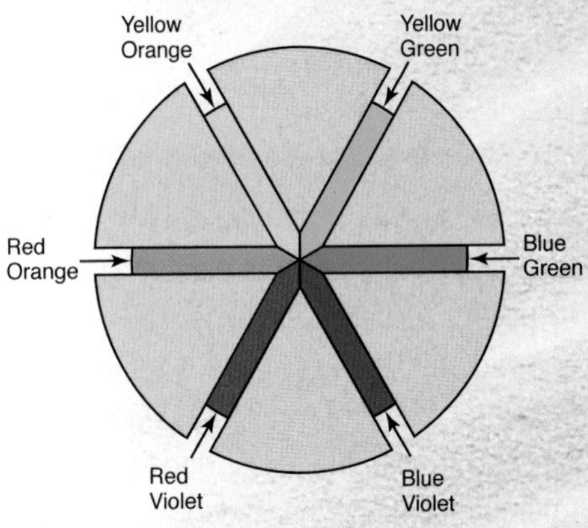

▲ Figure 20–6
Tertiary colors.

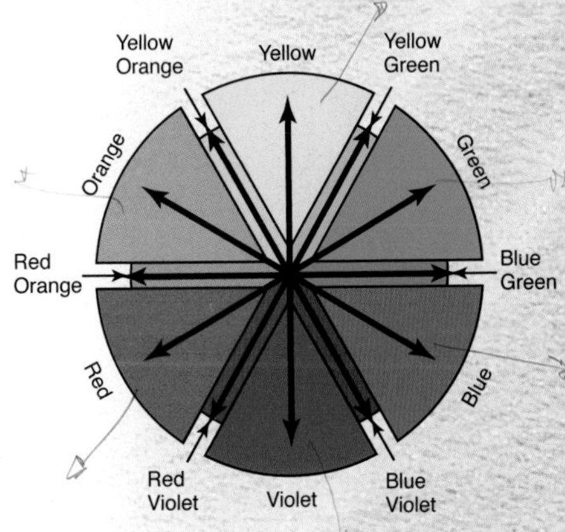

▲ Figure 20–7
Complementary colors.

FOCUS ON

Makeup Choices and Self-Confidence

Many women are attached to their makeup kits and believe their attractiveness depends on their makeup. Others avoid makeup altogether. There are strong beliefs associated with makeup. What do you believe? Do you like makeup? Is it fun? Intimidating? Many women are not comfortable wearing makeup. Others play in front of the mirror every day, trying out different looks and colors. Adding color to our lives with cosmetics can be uplifting and give us a positive feeling. Makeup artists have an opportunity to help clients feel better about themselves not just through makeup alone, but also by boosting the client's self-confidence and helping each one focus on their natural beauty. By finding out what clients believe about makeup, you can gain insight into what look will most satisfy them.

Makeup can give people a lift and make them feel more attractive, thereby enhancing their self-esteem. For those with disfigurements, camouflage makeup can be a wonderful tool that allows them to be more comfortable and live normal lives. For example, the American Cancer Society and National Cosmetology Association sponsor the Look Good . . . Feel Better programs that help those with cancer by hosting hair and makeup clinics. Professionals volunteer their time, helping cancer patients look and feel better by applying makeup and styling their hair or working with wigs. For more information visit the Look Good . . . Feel Better Web site at www.lookgoodfeelbetter.org.

▶ Figure 20–8
Warm and cool colors.

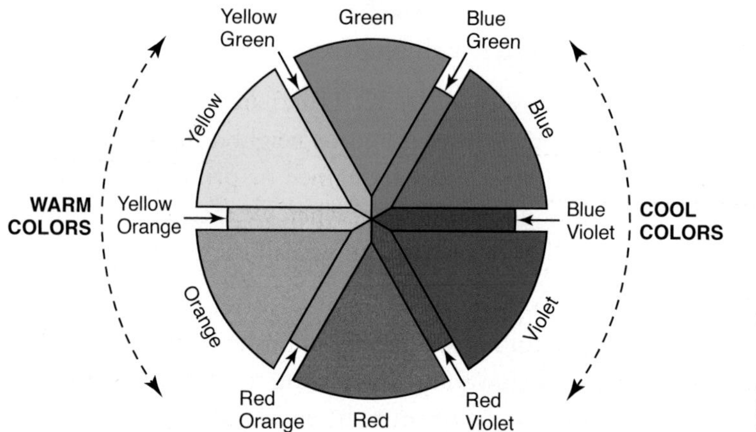

- ***Hue*** is the actual color we see that distinguishes red from yellow from blue. Hue is the distinct characteristic of the color. Colors can be mixed with white, black, or gray to yield other colors, or hues. Hues depend on the dominant wavelength of light emitted or reflected form an object.
- ***Tint:*** White added to a pure hue is called a tint.
- ***Shade:*** Adding black to a pure hue is referred to as a shade.
- ***Tone:*** Adding gray to a pure hue is a called a tone.
- ***Saturation*** is the intensity, or strength, of a color. Colors are either pale or strong.
- The ***value*** or brightness of a color is how light or dark it is. This depends on the amount of light emanating from the color. If it is lighter and closer to white, the color is brighter and higher in value. LO1

ACTIVITY

Try placing colors next to each other by using pencils, magic markers, or different sheets of colored paper to compare how they look together. An artist's color wheel is a good reference tool for color theory. Swatches of cloth are also good to experiment with.

Warm and Cool Colors

Learning the difference between warm and cool colors is essential to your success as a makeup artist. This is the basis of all color selection, and understanding the difference will enable you to properly enhance your client's coloring (Figure 20–8).

- **Warm colors** have a yellow undertone and range from yellow and gold through the oranges, red-oranges, most reds, and even some yellow-greens.
- **Cool colors** have a blue undertone, suggest coolness, and are dominated by blues, greens, violets, and blue-reds.
- Reds can be both warm and cool. If the red is orange-based, it is warm. If it is blue-based, it is cool.
- Greens are also warm and cool and can be tricky: if a green contains more gold, it is warm; if it contains more blue, it is cool. LO2

Makeup Products and Formulations

Warm colors have a yellow undertone (sunshine). Cool colors have a blue undertone (water).

Choosing a makeup product line is similar to choosing a skin care line. Makeup product choices range from private-label brands to exclusive spa lines. There are some good-quality, private-label cosmetics. Quality is important when choosing products and supplies. There is a difference between high-quality makeup and less expensive brands. The quality of the ingredients, products, and brushes makes a big difference in how makeup application will turn out—smoothly or not so smoothly. Pigment quality, packaging, and applicators all vary. Advertising costs and overhead costs play a part in the cost of makeup lines. More advertising may mean more expensive products.

Explain to clients why they should buy quality makeup and brushes. Why are they better? Is quality going to make a difference on their skin? Will quality products glide on easier and not tug on the delicate eye tissue? Clients will be more satisfied with products that are easier to work with and will discover that quality is worth the extra money.

You will be better equipped to offer your professional expertise when you have learned about the products, supplies, and tools used in makeup application and services. The cosmetics industry offers a wide range of products designed to improve the skin's appearance as well as its condition. The cosmetics available today meet the needs of every skin type.

Most products come in several forms, including powders, creams, and liquids, in an assortment of containers and packages (Figure 20–9). Makeup formulations are evolving and are now healthier for the skin than products of the past. The product formulations, application techniques, and facial features are introduced here before beginning the hands-on procedures.

▲ Figure 20–9
Makeup products and color choices are unlimited.

Foundation

Foundation, also known as **base makeup**, is a tinted cosmetic used to even out skin tone and color, conceal imperfections, and protect the skin from the outside elements of climate, dirt, and pollution. Dark circles, blemishes, pigmentation, redness, and other facial features can be toned down with foundation. Face makeup comes in different forms—mainly cream, liquid, powder, and mineral. Most people need different makeup colors in the summer (darker) and winter (lighter).

Foundations that usually contain mineral oil or other oils are referred to as ***oil based***. These products are a good choice for normal to dry skin.

Oil-free products are referred to as ***water based***. Water-based foundations generally give a more ***matte*** (nonshiny, dull) finish and help conceal minor blemishes and discolorations. These foundations are preferred for oily skin.

Product ingredients continue to improve and advance. The ingredients of a foundation consist mainly of water, emollient bases, humectants, pigments, binders, fragrances, and preservatives. Sunscreen, plant extracts, vitamins, and other ingredients beneficial to the skin are also added to some face makeup.

For example, foundations may contain ingredients such as oil, stearic acid (fatty acid used as an emulsifier or lubricant), cetyl alcohol (emollient, emulsion stabilizer), butylene or propylene glycol, glycerine (humectant), lanolin derivatives, waxes, and insoluble pigments. Many foundations now contain barrier agents, such as sunscreen and silicone, to protect the complexion from environmental damage (Figure 20–10).

▲ Figure 20–10
A wide selection of foundations.

Primers are liquids or silicone-based formulas designed to go underneath foundations and other products to prepare the skin for makeup and to help keep the product on the skin.

Some ***liquid*** foundations are suspensions of organic and inorganic pigments in alcohol and water-based solutions. Bentonite (a clay base) is added to help keep the products blended. The liquid formulation is generally suited for clients with oily to normal skin conditions who desire sheer to medium coverage. Other liquid foundations are oil based.

Cream foundations are thicker and give medium to heavier coverage. These are generally suited for dry to normal skin. Pancake makeup is oil based and heavy.

Cake makeup, also known as **pancake makeup**, is a heavy cream foundation. It is normally applied to the face with a moistened cosmetic sponge. It gives good coverage and is generally used to camouflage scars and pigmentation defects. It is also used for theater, film, and video applications. **Greasepaint** is a term for heavy cream makeup used for theatrical purposes.

Powder foundations, which consist of a powder base mixed with a coloring agent (pigment) and perfume, are good for oily skin. Cream-to-powder foundations are moist on application but dry to a powdery finish.

Mineral Makeup

Mineral makeup is composed of minerals and other ingredients and is designed to be healthy for the skin. A mineral-based foundation is considered more noncomedogenic (less likely to clog pores) and natural than liquid foundations. This makeup is not as heavy as other types of products. Mineral pigments are found in a range of products including powders, eye shadows, and blush. Mineral foundations give good coverage yet are lightweight. If lightly applied, mineral makeup can refract light from lines and creases and minimize imperfections. Mineral makeup is popular to use as camouflage makeup after surgery.

> **Here's a Tip**
>
> Some makeup products may contain ingredients that are comedogenic, so it is best to avoid them. Also, to help your clients avoid skin problems and keep skin healthy, remind them to remove makeup at night.

Many companies offer a mineral makeup line. The quality of ingredients and type of minerals used in formulas will affect the coverage, look, and feel of the makeup. Some formulas have a tendency to be shiny and can also be too drying for some mature clients who prefer liquid foundation. If applied too heavily, it can actually set in wrinkles, which makes them more noticeable. Mineral makeup ingredients may include titanium dioxide, zinc oxide, mica, silica, magnesium stearate, bismuth oxychloride, iron oxides, kaolin clay, and rice powder. Other beneficial ingredients such as ascorbyl palmitate (vitamin C) are added to some products as preservatives and antioxidants. Synthetic preservatives, fragrances, talc, and dyes are commonly used in cosmetics, but are not recommended ingredients.

Concealer

Concealers (kahn-SEEL-urs) are used to cover blemishes and discolorations and may be applied before or after foundation. They are available in pots, pencils, wands, or sticks in a range of colors to coordinate with or match skin tones (Figure 20–11). Concealers may contain moisturizers or control oil, depending on the formulation. The chemical composition of concealers is similar to that of cream foundation.

▲ Figure 20–11
Concealers help to cover minor imperfections.

Face Powder

Face powder is used to add a **matte**, or nonshiny, finish to the face. It enhances the skin's natural color, helping to conceal minor blemishes and discolorations, and diminish excessive color and shine. Face powder is also used to set foundation.

Two forms of face powder are widely used: loose powder and pressed powder (Figure 20–12). Both types have the same basic composition. Pressed powders are compressed and held together with binders so that they will not crumble. Face powders are available in a variety of tints and shades and in different weights (sheer to heavy). Coverage depends on the weight and formulation.

▲ Figure 20–12
Powders come in two forms—loose and pressed.

Face powders consist of a powder base mixed with a coloring agent (pigment) and perfume. Ingredients in powders may include talc, zinc oxide, titanium dioxide, dimethicone, kaolin, tocopheryl acetate, zinc stearate, and magnesium stearate.

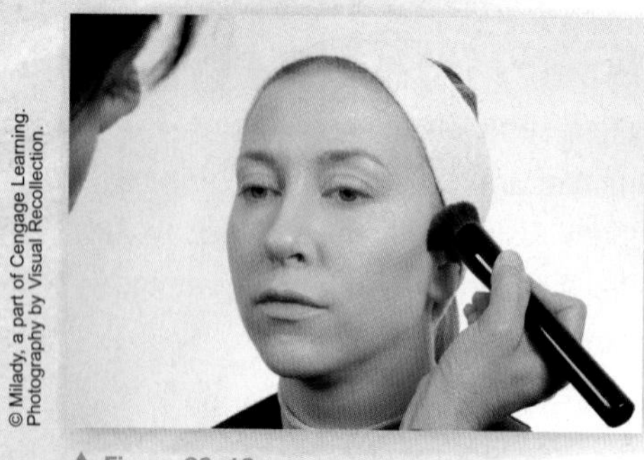
© Milady, a part of Cengage Learning. Photography by Visual Recollection.

▲ Figure 20–13
Blush contours cheekbones.

Blush

Cheek color is available in cream, liquid, dry (pressed), or loose powder form. ***Blush*** gives the face a natural-looking glow and helps create facial contours (Figure 20–13).

Powder blush is the most common cheek color and consists of ingredients similar to powders with colorants added. Cream or gel cheek colors resemble cream foundation and are generally preferred for dry and normal skin. Cream and liquid blush fall into two categories: oil based and emulsions.

Oil-based formulations are combinations of pigments in an oil or fat base. Blends of waxes (carnauba wax and ozokerite) and oily liquids (isopropyl myristate and hexadecyl stearate) create a water-resistant product. In addition, cream cheek colors contain water, dyes, thickeners, and a variety of surfactants or detergents that enable particles to penetrate the hair follicles and cracks in the skin. Because these ingredients can potentially clog the follicles, it is important to remind clients to remove their makeup each night.

Eye Shadow

The eyes are the focal point in makeup design. ***Eye shadows*** accentuate and contour the eyes. They are available in almost every color of the rainbow—from warm to cool, neutral to bright, and light to dark. Some powder eye shadows are designed to be used either wet or dry. They also come in a variety of finishes including matte, frost, or shimmer.

© Milady, a part of Cengage Learning. Photography by Dino Petrocelli.

▲ Figure 20–14
Eye shadows come in a variety of colors and forms.

Eye shadow is available in cream, pressed, and dry powder form (Figure 20–14). Stick and cream shadows are water based with oil, petrolatum, thickeners, wax, perfume, preservatives, and color added. Water-resistant shadows have a solvent base, such as mineral spirits. Pressed and dry powder eye shadow ingredients are similar to pressed face powder, mineral makeup, and powdered cheek color.

Eyeliners

Eyeliner is used to emphasize the eyes. It is available in pencil, liquid, and pressed (cake) form. With eyeliner, you can create a line on the eyelid close to the lashes to make the eyes appear larger and the lashes fuller. Pencil is the most commonly used liner. Liquid or gel eyeliners create a more dramatic look. Powder liners or eye shadows can be applied wet or dry. Powder forms applied wet are more vivid and stay on longer than when applied dry.

Eyeliner pencils consist of a wax (paraffin) or hardened oil-base (petrolatum) with a variety of additives to create color. Pencils are available in both soft and hard form for use on the eyebrow as well as the eye. Eyeliners contain ingredients such as alkanolamine (a fatty alcohol), cellulose ether, polyvinylpyrrolidone, methylparaben, antioxidants, perfumes, and titanium dioxide.

Eyebrow Color

Eyebrows frame the eye. The correct brow shape enhances the face and the entire makeup look. ***Eyebrow pencils*** or ***shadows*** are used to add color and shape to the eyebrows. They can be used to darken the eyebrows, correct their shape, or fill in sparse areas. For the best results, match the natural brow color or use a close shade of brown. The chemistry of eyebrow products is similar to that of eyeliner pencils and eye shadows (Figure 20–15).

Mascara

Mascara darkens, defines, and thickens the eyelashes (Figure 20–16). It is available in liquid, cake, and cream form in various shades and tints. The most popular mascara is a liquid formula in black or brown. These colors enhance the natural lashes, making them appear thicker and longer.

Mascaras are polymer products that contain water, wax, thickeners, film formers, fragrance, and preservatives in their formulations. The pigments in mascara must be inert (unable to combine with other elements) and are made with carbon black, carmine, ultramarine, chromium oxide, and iron oxides. Some wand mascaras contain rayon or nylon fibers to lengthen and thicken the hair. Lash conditioners and gels are also popular products. Lash enhancers are products designed to stimulate the actual lash growth.

▲ Figure 20–15
Pencils are used for the lips, eyes, and brows.

Eye Makeup Removers

Makeup removers are either oil based or water based. Oil-based removers are generally mineral oil with a small amount of fragrance added. Water-based removers are a water solution to which witch hazel, boric acid, oils, lanolin or lanolin derivatives, and other solvents have been added. Most products will come off with cleansers. It is not recommended to remove eye makeup while wearing contacts.

▲ Figure 20–16
Mascara emphasizes the eyelashes.

Lip Color

Most women have very definite ideas about their lip color. ***Lip color***, lipstick, or gloss give color to the face and finish a makeup design. Lip color worn alone enhances the face like no other product can. Some lip colors contain sunscreen to protect the lips from the harmful effects of the sun. Most contain moisturizers to keep lips from becoming dry or chapped.

▲ Figure 20–17
Lipsticks come in a variety of colors, textures, and forms.

Lip color is available in several forms: creams, glosses, pencils, and sticks (Figure 20–17). All are formulas of oils, waxes, and dyes. Castor oil is a common ingredient in lipsticks. Other oils used are olive, mineral, sesame, cocoa butter, petroleum, lecithin, and hydrogenated vegetable oils. Waxes commonly included in the ingredients are paraffin, beeswax, carnauba, and candelilla wax. D&C Red No. 27, D&C Orange No. 17 Lake, and related tints are examples of common coloring agents. Lakes are organic pigments that are formulated to be insoluble. Iron oxides, mica, and annatto are natural colorants sometimes used in lip colors. Lip gloss, plumpers, and stains are also popular. ☑ L03

Makeup Brushes

Makeup brushes come in a variety of shapes and sizes (Figure 20–18). Commonly used makeup brushes are shown in Table 20–1. Choosing quality makeup brushes is important. Brushes are made of three parts: the hair (bristles), the handle, and the ferrule. By running the brush hair across the hand, you can test the hair for softness and the bristles for shedding.

▲ Figure 20–18
Quality brushes are important tools for the makeup artist.

Brush hairs are either natural animal hair or synthetic. Sable, squirrel, mink, goat, pony, and other blends are used for brushes. These are softer and gentler than synthetic. The soft, natural-hair brushes are more expensive than the synthetic ones. The "first-cut" hair is a better quality and considered cruelty-free because it is sheared from the tips of the fur. "Blunt cuts" are less expensive and more coarse and prickly. Synthetic nylon and Taklon are stiffer bristles used for brow, concealer, and foundation brushes.

A hard wood handle is the most durable type of handle. Lengths vary and 7 inches (17.5 centimeters) is a standard length for brushes. If the handle is too long, it is harder to control.

The ***ferrule*** is the metal part that holds brushes intact. Look for double-crimping of the ferrule to avoid loose handles that come apart faster.

Caring for Makeup Brushes

If you invest in high-quality makeup brushes, you will have them for years. Take good care of your brushes by cleaning them gently.

MAKEUP BRUSHES		
STANDARD BRUSH	**TYPE OF BRUSH**	**DESCRIPTION AND USE**
Most brushes can be interchanged and used for more than one purpose.		
	Powder brush	Large, soft brush used for blending and to apply powder or blush.
	Blush brush	Smaller, more tapered version of the powder brush used for applying powder blush; can be angled.
	Concealer brush	Usually narrow and firm with a flat edge; used to apply concealer around the eyes, on blemishes, and other areas.
	Kabuki brushes	Short brushes with dense bristles for powder or blush. These are mainly used in a circular motion to apply and blend powders.
	Eye shadow brushes	Available in a variety of sizes and ranging from soft to firm. The softer and larger the brush, the more blended the shadow will be. A firm brush is better for depositing dense color than for blending it. Small brushes are best for dark colors.
	Eyeliner brush	Fine, tapered, firm bristles; used to apply liner to the eyes.
	Angle brow brush	Firm, thin bristles; angled for use on the eyebrows or for eyeliner.
	Lash and brow brush	The comb-like side is used to remove excess mascara on lashes, and the brush side is for brows. Metal lash combs are also useful tools.
	Lip brush	Similar to the concealer brush, but smaller and with a more tapered, rounded edge; also used to apply concealer.

▲ Table 20–1
Makeup Brushes.

A commercial cleaner can be used for quick cleaning, although spray-on instant sanitizers contain a high level of alcohol and will dry brushes over time. A gentle shampoo or brush solvent should be used to thoroughly clean the brushes. These products will not hurt brushes and may actually help them last longer.

Brushes must be cleaned and disinfected properly after each client with liquid antibacterial soap and an EPA-registered disinfectant. Standard brush cleaners may not be enough to disinfect brushes for clients. The brush should always be put into running or still water with the ferrule (the metal ring that keeps the bristles and handle together) pointing downward. If the brush is pointed up, the water may remove the glue that keeps the bristles in place.

fyi

Do not leave the brushes in the disinfectant longer than necessary, because it will wear them out much faster. Time this according to the manufacturer's instructions.

Rinse brushes thoroughly after cleaning. Do not pull on the brush bristles. Because they will dry in the shape they are left in, reshape the wet bristles and lay the brushes flat to dry. Cover brushes with a towel while drying to keep them clean and put them in a clean, closed covered container or drawer when dry.

Products, Tools, and Supplies

Supplies and Accessories

Numerous supplies and accessories are useful for makeup applications (Figure 20–19; Table 20–2). These supplies include the following:

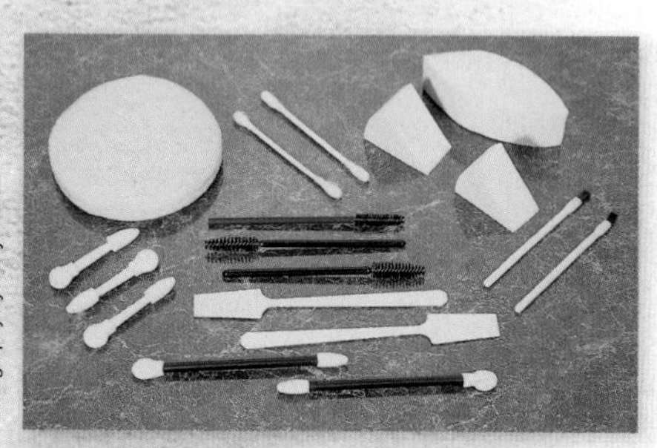

▲ Figure 20–19
Single-use applicators are necessary for client's safety.

- ***Sponges*** are good for blending foundation, concealer, and powder. Wedge shapes are the most versatile. Use the large, thicker end of the sponge for foundation to get more coverage and control. Use the smaller sides to blend around the eyes.
- ***Brushes*** to blend powder, blush, and eye shadows work better than sponge tips or fingers. Brushes allow for better control and better blending. They also feel nicer to the skin and are more professional. Make sure you clean and disinfect brushes between clients. Be prepared and have enough brushes on hand for multiple uses throughout the day. Buy good-quality brushes. Art stores or brush wholesalers are good places to buy brushes.
- For straight lashes, a ***lash curler*** can be used before applying mascara.
- Use a clean, single-use ***wand*** to dip into the mascara. Do not double-dip. Roll the wand around in a circle rather than pumping it in and out because this dries out the mascara.
- A ***lash comb*** separates lashes so lashes look finished and are not clumpy or messy looking. Metal combs work the best. Do not point combs or brushes toward the eyes or poke the skin. Point the prongs down or up away from the eye. If necessary, you can gently rest the

MAKEUP SUPPLIES CHECKLIST		
SKIN CARE	**MAKEUP**	**SUPPLIES/ACCESSORIES**
cleanser	concealer	cape and draping items
toner	highlighter	EPA-registered disinfectant/cleaning supplies
moisturizer	contour color	tweezers
	foundation	hair clip/headband
	powder	brushes
	eye shadow	pencil sharpener
	eyeliner	mirror
	mascara	lash comb
	blush	lash curler
	lip gloss	single-use items: spatulas, cotton swabs, mascara wands, mixing cups, sponges, tissues, applicators
	lip liner	hand towel
	lipstick	artist tray/palette
		gloves
		client chart

◀ Table 20–2
Makeup Supplies Checklist.

side of the little pinky finger on the face to steady the application. If the client is sensitive around the eyes, let her apply the mascara.

- Use ***hair clips*** or a ***headband*** to hold the hair away from the face. Remove these items and fix the client's hair before showing her the finished look.
- Use a ***cape*** or towel around the client's neck to protect her clothes. Have her lean toward you to protect clothing from powder application. Put a tissue or single-use ***neck strip*** under the collar and around the neck to keep the cape clean for other clients, or wash the cape each time.
- Use a ***cleaning agent*** to clean hands, surfaces, and tools.
- Use ***tissue*** for blotting lipstick or powder. It can also be used to hold under the eye when applying dark shadow, so it does not flake onto the skin.
- Use ***spatulas*** to remove products such as concealer or lipstick from jars and containers. Do not put fingers into products. Use a clean spatula each time. Do not double-dip.
- ***Cotton swabs*** are great for fixing mistakes. They are useful for blending under the eyes and especially when fixing mascara or other smudges. Put a little foundation on the cotton swab, place it on your fingertip, and roll off the excess before using.

Here's a Tip

Use an artist's palette to distribute your makeup products into once you narrow your color choices. This keeps the original product clean and free of bacteria and it is easy to work with. A palette is especially helpful when using loose mineral makeup. Remember the colors you used, so you can recommend and record them on your client charts. Do not put the colors away until they are recorded.

- ***Mixing cups*** can be used for blending foundation colors together or mixing foundation and moisturizer for a lighter tinted foundation. Artist's ***palettes*** are also great for holding products. LO4

Infection Control

For all products:

- Do not touch product containers to hands or previously used applicators. Distribute onto clean palettes, brushes, or sponges.
- Scrape powders with clean brushes or spatulas onto a tissue or clean tray.
- Scrape off powders and other products before and after use if contaminated.
- Do not apply lipstick or gloss directly to the lips from the container or tube. Use a spatula to remove the product, and then apply with a clean brush.
- If the product is accidentally contaminated, follow your supervisor's directions either to throw away the product or give it to your client. Do not put it back with your clean products to reuse.

For applicators, pencils, testers, and so forth, follow these cleaning guidelines:

- ***Applicators.*** Use new or clean applicators, brushes, and spatulas to distribute products. Disinfect these after each use. Do not double-dip dirty spatulas, wands, or brushes back into products. Discard single-use applicators such as sponge tips, as these are porous and cannot be disinfected.
- ***Pencils.*** Sharpen pencils, spray to disinfect, and wipe with tissue—if they cannot be sharpened, they cannot be cleaned. Pencils with auto-rollers cannot be sharpened.
- ***Testers.*** Keep testers clean. To avoid contamination, assist clients who are using testers. Using fingers and double-dipping applicators are not proper infection control practices.
- ***Palettes and supplies.*** Wash and disinfect artist trays, brushes, sharpeners, and mixing cups after each use.

REGULATORY **AGENCY** **ALERT**

Check your local regulations for proper makeup product and brush cleaning. Facilities do not always follow proper disinfection standards for makeup station testers and applications. If you see incorrect practices, bring this to the attention of the staff to help them be in compliance. A staff training session may be necessary to remind everyone of the correct procedures. Clients will appreciate knowing testers and applicators are clean; otherwise they may be hesitant to try products or have a makeover.

Client Consultations

The first step in the makeup process, as with all services that take place in the salon, is the client consultation. A service should always begin with a warm introduction to your client. Visually assess the client to understand her personal style. This will give you cues as you continue your consultation. Ask the client questions that will elicit her preferences

◀ Figure 20–20
The makeup consultation.

and concerns (Figure 20–20). Have the client fill out a questionnaire to get insight into her makeup needs (Table 20–3, page 574). Listen closely and try not to force your own opinion upon them.

If the client chooses not to act on your recommendations, do not take it personally. In time, perhaps she will. Record the client's needs and make recommendations based on the general application guidelines.

Gather information on the client's skin condition, how much or how little makeup she wears, the amount of time spent applying makeup, colors she likes or dislikes, and any makeup problem areas. Record this information on a client consultation card. Also write down the colors you use and your recommendations on the client chart (Table 20–4, page 575) so that you can refer to them at the end of the makeup application. Reviewing and restating your written advice with the client at the end of the service will also help you recommend the retail products that would be beneficial for her.

After the service, escort your client to the retail or reception area, where you can assist her in choosing the products you have recommended. Ask if the client has any other questions. If applicable, set up a time for the next appointment. Present a business card with your name on it and thank the client as you say good-bye.

▼ Figure 20–21
A professional makeup kit.

The Makeup Station and Consultation Area

The area that you use for services and consultations must be clean and organized. No one wants to see a messy makeup unit or dirty brushes. Clean and organize your makeup kit and area daily (Figure 20–21). Also keep a portfolio in the consultation area that includes photographs of your own work or pictures from magazines. The client can go through your portfolio to find styles and colors that appeal to her. This also builds her confidence in your ability. Try to have the makeup station in a visible yet semiprivate area of the salon for client privacy.

THE CLIENT QUESTIONNAIRE

Confidential Makeup Questionnaire

PLEASE PRINT

Today's Date: ____________________

First Name: ____________________ Last Name: ____________________ Birthday ______/______

Street ____________________ Apt# __________ City ____________________ State __________ Zip __________

Phone: Home ( ) __________ Work ( ) __________ Cell ( ) __________ E-mail: ____________________

Referred by □ Friend □ Mailer □ Walk-by □ Yellow Pages □ Gift Certificate □ Other

____

- Have you ever had a professional makeover? □ Yes □ No
- If yes, what did you like (dislike) about the session? ____________________
- What are some of your goals today? ____________________
- What special areas would you like to focus on? ____________________
- What are your favorite makeup and clothing colors? ____________________
- Describe an ideal look for your makeup. ____________________
- Do you wear contact lenses? □ Yes □ No If yes, are they □ Hard □ Soft
- Do you take any medications that cause your eyes to be dry or itch? □ Yes □ No
  If yes, what? ____________________
- Are you currently taking prescription drugs that affect your skin or have you taken any in the past? □ Yes □ No
  If yes, describe the course and length of treatment. ____________________
- Do you have any health condition that may cause sensitivity in your skin or eye area? □ Yes □ No □
  If yes, what? ____________________
- Do you have any allergies? □ Yes □ No If yes, please indicate. ____________________
- Do you have any allergies to skin care products? □ Yes □ No If yes, what? ____________________

I fully acknowledge that I do not have any known allergies to makeup products or have listed them above.

Signature: ____________________

Salon Policies

(Note: this is just an example of policies that may be used.)

1. We require a 24-hour cancellation notice.
2. Please arrive on time for appointments.
3. There is a $25 charge for a no-show appointment.
4. Health regulations do not allow us to accept returned products unless they are unopened and in their original packaging.
5. Returns are given salon credit only. No cash refunds.

I fully understand and agree to the above salon policies.

Client's Signature: ____________________ Date: ____________________

▲ Table 20–3 **The Client Questionnaire.**

THE CLIENT CHART

Name: ____________________ Date: __________

Skin Care

Makeup remover ____________

Cleanser ____________

Freshener ____________

Moisturizer ____________

Makeup

Note: Matte, dewy, or frost/shiny products?

Foundation ☐ Liquid ☐ Wet/dry ☐ Mineral

Color ____________

Concealer ____________

Powder ____________

Brow color ____________

Eye shadows ____________

Orbital area ____________

Crease ____________

Lid ____________

Other ____________

Eyeliner ____________

Mascara ____________

Lip conditioner ____________

Lip pencil ____________

Lipstick ____________

Lip gloss ____________

Special Instructions

____

____

____

▲ Table 20–4
The Client Chart.

Lighting

Adequate and flattering lighting is essential for the application. Natural daylight is the best choice. If it is necessary to use artificial light, it should be CFL (compact fluorescent light) bulbs in the warm- or natural-color temperature range. Fluorescent lights (overhead tube lights) are not as flattering, but now come in more bulb choices than the previous technology offered. The best artificial lighting for makeup application is to have even light on both sides of the face without shadows, with the lights at eye level. Makeup mirrors and stations have bulbs placed on the top and sides of the mirror for the best lighting.

Make sure that the light always shines directly and evenly on the face. Check the makeup on both sides of the face for evenness, and take the client over to a window if necessary to check the final look in natural light. Clients who can see the finished look in natural light are more comfortable with purchasing the products you recommend. Makeup changes with the lighting, so it is important to use the appropriate lighting to match the lighting that the makeup is being applied for, such as an outdoor wedding or indoor photosession.

Makeup Lessons

Lessons are services that are offered to teach application techniques to clients and introduce new colors to them. This helps clients expand their confidence in applying their own makeup. Lessons are a step beyond *makeovers*, which focus on giving clients a new look. In a lesson, clients are shown how to apply makeup.

Explain the techniques and make sure they can see you perform the steps in the mirror. Let them practice on one side of the face during the lesson so that you can guide them. These services are more time-consuming and expensive because you are sharing your knowledge. Lessons are a good opportunity to retail the products which will allow clients to reproduce the look you have created for them at home. ✓ LO5

Selecting Makeup Colors

Now that products, basic color theory, and consultations have been introduced, it is time to learn more about choosing colors for your clients. Keep in mind this is simply one way of choosing colors. The art of the makeup application allows for more than one way to achieve the result you desire. Once you learn the rules of basic color selection, you can then go on to expand them. With practice, these concepts and guidelines will become second nature—you will just automatically know what matches and looks good.

As you look at the color wheel, think of it as a tool for determining color choice. There are three main factors to consider when choosing colors for a client: skin color, eye color, and hair color. Assess the client's features during the consultation.

You may hear people refer to a color as having blue in it. For example: "This lipstick has a blue base/undertone" or "That is more of a cool blush than a warm one." This does not mean that the color is truly blue. Rather, it means that when the pigments were mixed to create that cosmetic, more blue color was added. Cool colors will be more pink or purple rather than peach or orange (Table 20–5).

COLOR TEMPERATURES	
MAKEUP COLOR/ TEMPERATURE	DESCRIPTION
Pink—cool/warm	We think of pink as being a warm, rosy color, but a pastel (tint) is cool. When more red is added to white, the pink becomes warmer. Pink is flattering to skin tones unless the skin is ruddy. Pink combines well with other shades and tints of blue, black, green, yellow, gray, purple, brown, beige, and white.
Blue—cool	Blue is complementary to most skin tones. Lighter blues enhance darker skin, while darker blue brings out color and is complementary to lighter skin. Blue combines well with almost all other colors.
Purple—cool/warm	Mixed with pale tints of orchid and lavender, purple is cool. Darker shades (plum) with red undertones are warm. Purple is not kind to blemished or reddish skin tones and should be studied against the skin before using. Purple combines well with pink, white, gray, soft blue, beige, black, and pale yellow.
Green—cool/warm	Green is easy on the eyes and flattering to many skin tones. Bright green can intensify red in the skin. Blue-greens are cool and generally attractive for both light and dark skin. Green combines well with other greens, blue, yellow, orange, beige, brown, white, and black.
Brown—warm	Brown is a good basic color and can be kind to many complexion tones. Other reflecting or accent colors can be worn near the face if the skin is dark brown. Brown combines well with warm colors, green, beige, blue, pink, yellow, orange, gold, white, and black. Reddish browns may not be flattering for the same reason that purples and reds may make the skin or eyes look ruddy or tired.
Red—warm/cool	Red is a vibrant color. Red with blue undertones is cool; with yellow undertones it is warm. Red of a specific tint or shade may not be kind to a ruddy complexion. Freckles will look darker when red is reflected onto the face. Red combines well with many other colors. Among them are black, white, beige, gray, blue, navy, green, and yellow.
Black—neutral	Black combines well with all other colors. A black costume can create a contrast for light skin and hair. When the skin and hair are dark, a lighter color contrast near the face acts as a frame or highlight for the face.
White—cool/neutral	White is easy to wear, but be cautious of its undertones. Some materials reflect beige or yellow undertones (off-white is warm), while others appear slightly blue. White combines well with all other colors.
Gray—neutral	A cool-based neutral gray combines well with many other colors, especially cool colors.

▲ Table 20–5 **Color Temperatures.**

Determining Skin Color

When determining skin color, you must first decide if the skin is light, medium, or dark. Then determine whether the tone of the skin is warm or cool (use Table 20–6, page 578 as a guide). You may not see true skin colors in the beginning. Give yourself time and practice to develop your eye. Skin color comes from the pigmentation in the skin and the blood showing through the skin.

A neutral skin tone contains equal elements of warm and cool, no matter how light or dark the skin is. Match the foundation color to the color of the skin, or use the corrective techniques discussed later in this chapter. You can choose eye, cheek, and lip colors to match the skin color level, or try contrasting colors for more impact. Most skin tones and levels (light to dark) can wear a surprisingly wide range of eye, cheek, and lip colors. The majority of the population has a

SKIN TONES	
TONE	**UNDERTONES**
Ivory to fair	Fair, light skin with creamy or slightly pink undertones
Beige or medium	Medium skin with pink or yellow
Olive or warm	Olive skin with gold/yellow or orange/red
Deep or dark	Dark skin with brown/yellow, brown/red, or brown/blue

▲ Table 20–6 **Skin Tones.**

warm skin color with yellow undertones.

- If skin color is light, you can use light colors for a soft, natural look. Medium to dark colors will create a more dramatic look.
- If skin color is medium, medium tones will create an understated look. Light or dark tones will provide more contrast and will appear bolder.
- If skin color is dark, dark tones will be most subtle. Medium to medium-light or bright tones will be striking and vivid.
- Be cautious when choosing colors lighter than the skin. If the color is too light, it will turn gray or chalky on the skin. Look for translucent, shimmery colors if you are choosing these colors.

For various reasons, some clients may wish to alter their skin tone. In terms of corrective makeup, you will be dealing with two basic skin tones: ruddy and sallow.

- For ***ruddy*** skin (skin that is red, wind burned, or affected by rosacea), apply a yellow- or green-tinted foundation to affected areas, blending carefully. You can then apply a light layer of foundation with a yellow base over the entire complexion. Set it with translucent or yellow-based powder. Avoid using red or pink blushes. The skin color should still be natural-looking.
- For ***sallow*** skin (skin that has a yellowish hue), apply a pink-based foundation on the affected areas and blend carefully into the jaw and neck. Set with translucent powder. Avoid using yellow-based colors for eyes, cheeks, and lips.

Complementary Colors for Eyes

As you begin recommending eye, cheek, and lip colors, *neutrals* will always be your safest choice. They contain elements of warm and cool and work well with any skin tone, eye, or hair color. They come in variations of brown or gray. For instance, they may have a warm or cool base with brown tones. Or you might choose a plum-brown, which would be considered a cool-neutral. An orange-brown would be considered a warm-neutral. Charcoal gray is a cool-neutral color, as is blue-gray.

The following are guidelines for selecting eye makeup colors. Refer to the color wheel for additional help in determining complementary colors.

Here's a Tip

Be careful with orange or red tones in eye shadows because they can make the eyes look tired.

- **Complementary colors for blue eyes.** Orange is the complementary color to blue. Because orange contains yellow and red, shadows with any of these colors in them will make your eyes look bluer. Common choices include gold, warm orange-browns like peach and copper, red-browns like mauves and plum, and neutrals like taupe or camel. Orange is a warm color and not flattering to all skin tones, so use it sparingly.
- **Complementary colors for green eyes.** Red is the complementary color to green. Because red shadows tend to make the eyes look tired or bloodshot, pure-red tones are not recommended. Instead, use brown-based reds or other color options next to red on the color wheel. These include red-orange, red-violet, and violet. Popular choices are coppers, rusts, and purples.
- **Complementary colors for brown eyes.** Brown eyes are neutral and can wear any color. Recommended choices include such contrasting colors as greens or blues. Gray (cool) is not as flattering when combined with brown (warm), because warm and cool colors together will clash.

Cheek and Lip Color Selection

After choosing the eye makeup, determine whether your choices are warm or cool. Next, coordinate the cheek and lip makeup in the same color family as the eye makeup. For example, suppose your client has green eyes, and you recommended plums for her, which are cool. Now you should stay with cool colors for the cheeks and lips, so they will coordinate with the eye makeup. You could also choose neutrals because they contain both warm and cool elements and coordinate with any makeup colors.

It is not recommended to mix warms and cools on a face. They will compete with each other and create an "off" and unflattering appearance. Staying within the color ranges you have chosen will ensure a balanced, beautiful look.

Hair Color Considerations

Hair color needs to be taken into account when determining makeup colors. For example, if a woman has blue eyes, your instinct might be to select orange-based eye makeup as the complementary choice. But if she has cool blue-black hair, the orange will not be flattering. In this case, you would choose cool colors to coordinate with the hair color. Red-violets (plums) would be a more flattering choice. Look at orange on the color wheel: it is warm. Go around the wheel toward the cool end. Red-violets are the closest to orange on the color wheel while still remaining cool. There are a range of colors to choose from for any client and many times it is based on personal preferences.

Did You Know?

For most women, applying eye makeup is the hardest and most intimidating part of applying makeup. Many women also have trouble applying makeup without their glasses and need magnifying mirrors.

ACTIVITY

Apply makeup to a partner using color theory to choose and coordinate makeup colors. Have fun and experiment. Fill out a client chart and questionnaire. Use the color selections and write down which colors enhance her appearance and coordinate with her wardrobe, and which ones do not. And remember, a haircut or haircolor may represent a big commitment, but makeup does not. If you do not like it, just wash it off and try again!

Here's a Tip

To save time and confusion, do not give the client too many color choices—start with two or three choices for each product.

Reviewing Color Selections

To review color selection, follow these steps:

1. Determine skin level: light, medium, or dark.
2. Determine skin undertone: warm, cool, or neutral.
3. Determine eye color: blue, green, brown, other.
4. Determine complementary colors.
5. Determine hair color: warm or cool.
6. Choose eye makeup colors based on complementary or contrasting colors.
7. Coordinate cheek and lip colors within the same color family: warm, cool, or neutral.
8. Apply makeup based on client preferences from two or three color choices per product.

The best thing about choosing colors is the unlimited number of choices you have. Try one or all methods of choosing color. You can choose colors based on eye color and skin tone, or you might find that working with complementary colors makes you feel more comfortable.

ACTIVITY

Color Selections

You will not be getting into such details with every client, but this exercise will help you practice making color selections.

Use these steps to determine color selections and write in client information here:

Complete These Steps	Note Client Features (circle or fill in)	Note Makeup Product and Color Choices
Determine skin level:	light, medium, or dark	Foundation:
Determine skin undertone:	warm, cool, or neutral	Concealer:
Determine eye color:	Eye Color:__________	Eye shadow: Eyeliner:
Determine hair color:	warm or cool Hair Color: __________	Blush: Lipstick:
Determine complementary colors from the color wheel:	For Eyes: For Hair:	Other product options:

Makeup Application Techniques

Read through these techniques before practicing the makeup application procedure. They are explained here in-depth so that the concepts can be understood prior to performing the hands-on application.

> **Here's a Tip**
>
> For a smoother makeup application, remember to have clients exfoliate their skin to remove dead skin cells and prepare the face for product application before their appointment.

Foundation Application

The success of makeup application depends on the correct color selection and begins with the application of the foundation (base makeup). When correctly applied, foundation creates an even canvas for the rest of the makeup application. Skin tone determines the selection of foundation color. Skin tones are generally classified as warm, cool, or neutral. Warm tones have yellow undertones. Cool tones have blue undertones. Neutral skin has equal amounts of warm and cool tones.

Foundation should always be matched as closely as possible to actual skin tone. If the foundation color is too light, it will have a chalky or ghostly appearance and will "sit" on top of the skin. If the color is too dark, it will look dirty or artificial on the skin. The best way to determine the correct foundation color for your client is to apply a 1- to 2-inch (2.5 to 5 centimeter) vertical stripe of color below the cheek down onto the jawline. Blend slightly and then try other colors if necessary. The color that "disappears" and blends in is the correct one. Avoid creating a contrast between the color of the face and the color of the neck. Makeup should blend smoothly with no visible line (no line of demarcation). Two different colors can be mixed together to custom-blend a color. Base makeup colors may need to be changed with the seasons and sun exposure—darker in the summer, lighter in the winter.

> **Here's a Tip**
>
> **Mineral Makeup Application**
>
> Loose mineral products are easy to spill. Tap jars before opening to settle the product and only take out a tiny amount (a little goes a long way) to use. A partial brushful of product is usually more than enough. Use a clean brush or spatula to remove products from the container and tap the product onto a palette to use. Replace the caps right away to avoid spillage and keep products clean.

Foundations are applied to the face with the fingertips, a makeup sponge, or brush, using short strokes. The sponge can be moist or dry. Patting (called "stippling"), rather than rubbing, gives better coverage where it is needed. Avoid excessive rubbing and use gentle pressure while blending. Using higher-quality sponges and applicators are definitely worth it. Primers underneath makeup help the product go on smoother and stay on longer.

Concealer Application

Concealer is usually one to two shades lighter than foundation. You can apply this under or over the foundation beneath the eyes and on other areas to conceal. Concealer is removed from the container with a spatula and may be applied with a concealer brush, fingertips, or a sponge. Place it sparingly over blemishes or areas

of discoloration and blend. It is important to match concealer color to skin color as closely as possible.

Concealer that is noticeably lighter than the skin can appear obvious and can actually draw attention to a problem area, such as dark circles. If covering a blemish, match skin tone closely to avoid highlighting the blemish. Yellow- and green-toned concealers must be well blended and covered with foundation.

The principles that apply to choosing foundation colors also apply to concealer colors. Concealer may be worn alone, without foundation, if chosen and blended correctly. Be sure to use it sparingly and soften the edges so that the complexion looks natural.

Concealer products can also be used as a highlighter if the concealer is lighter than the skin color to accentuate and bring out features. A darker shade of concealer can be used for contouring. Light shades bring out the features, and dark shades cause them to recede.

Highlighting and Shading

Highlighters are lighter than the skin color, and they accentuate and bring out features such as the brow bone under the eyebrow, the temples, the chin, and the cheekbones. Highlighters are used more extensively in photography than in everyday use.

Contouring colors are darker shades used to define the cheekbones and make features appear smaller. Dark colors recede or diminish features.

These highlighting and shading (contouring) products are found in both liquid and powder forms. Depending on placement, these are applied in a variety of ways similar to shadow, blush, or concealer application.

Face Powder Application

Face powder should match the natural skin tone and work well with the foundation. It should never appear caked or obvious. ***Translucent powder*** (colorless and sheer) blends with all foundations and will not change color when applied.

> **Here's a Tip**
>
> **Pressed products can be turned into loose powder by loosening it up with a spatula or brush. This is a faster way to remove more of the pressed product out of the container.**

Powder sets the foundation and finishes the makeup blending. This is usually applied after the foundation and before the rest of the makeup. It is also applied again after the blush to help blend and set the blush. Do not use too much powder as it can make skin appear dry and draw attention to wrinkles. Make sure the clients eyes are closed to avoid getting powder in the eyes.

Apply face powder using a brush. Use a brush to blend and remove the excess powder. To apply, sweep in circular or downward motions. Recommend both loose and pressed powders when suggesting products to a client. Pressed powder is compact and easy to carry for quick touch-ups during the day. Loose powder is best used at home because it is easy to spill.

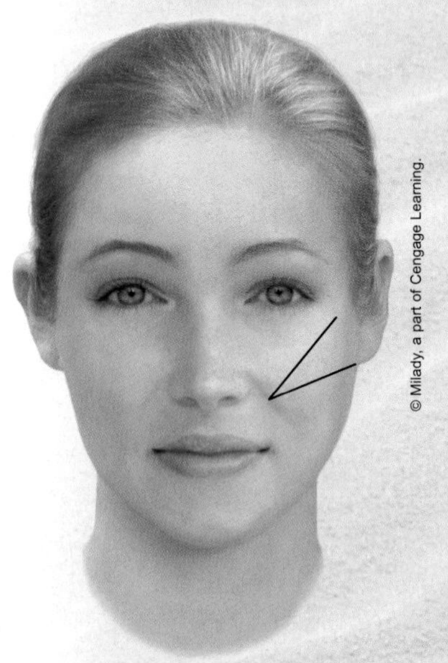

▲ Figure 20–22
Measuring blush placement.

Blush Application

Blush gives color to the face and accentuates cheekbones. Apply blush just below the cheekbones, blending on top of the bones toward the top of the cheeks (Figure 20–22).

Depending on the formulation, blush is usually applied with a brush. Creams are applied with a stiff brush, fingers, or sponges. Blend the color along the cheek bone so that it fades softly into the foundation. Keep blush placement away from the nose and below the temples.

Eye Shadow Application

Choose colors to bring out the eyes, even if the application is subtle. When applied to the lids, eye shadow makes the eyes appear brighter and more expressive. Matching eye shadow to eye color creates a flat field of color and should generally be avoided. Using color other than the eye color (that is, a contrasting or complementary color) can enhance the eyes. Using light and dark contrasts also brings attention to the eyes.

Here's a Tip

Look at the flecks of color in the iris of the eyes and use eye shadow colors to match or coordinate with these colors in the iris.

Generally, a darker shade of eye shadow makes the natural color of the iris appear lighter, while a lighter shade makes the iris appear deeper. The only set rules for selecting eye makeup colors are that they should enhance the client's eyes and color choices should be flattering. If desired, eye makeup color may match or coordinate with the client's clothing color. Blending is the key, especially when using dark colors.

Eye shadow colors are generally referred to as highlighters, bases, and contour/dark colors (Figure 20–23).

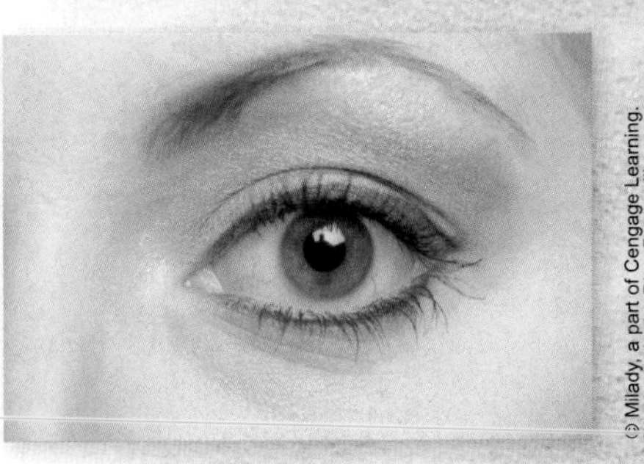

▲ Figure 20–23
Eye makeup techniques.

- A ***highlight*** color is lighter than the client's skin tone. Popular choices include matte (nonshiny) or iridescent (shiny). These colors highlight a specific area, such as the brow bone. A lighter color such as white will make an area appear larger.
- A ***base*** color is generally a medium tone that is close to the client's skin tone. This color is used to even out the skin tone on the eye. It is often applied all over the lid and brow bone—from lash to brow, before other colors are applied—thus providing a smooth surface for the blending of other colors. If used this way, a matte finish is preferred.
- A ***contour*** color is deeper and darker than the client's skin tone. It is applied to minimize a specific area, to create contour in a crease, or to define the eyelash line.

Did You Know?

You can use an artist's tray or palette to hold different makeup products and color choices during a service. This can be a more efficient way to work and to blend colors.

To apply eye shadow, remove the product from its container with a spatula and then use a fresh applicator or clean brush. Unless you are doing corrective makeup, apply the base eye color close to the lashes on the eyelid, sweeping the color slightly upward and outward. End the color inside the outer edge of the brow. Highlighters are used under the eyebrow and on the lid. Darker colors are used in the crease. Blend to achieve the desired effect. Some people like to use a primer on the eyelids before the eye makeup.

Eyeliner Application

Eyeliner accentuates the eyes. Eyeliner can be applied before or after eye shadow. Some clients prefer eyeliner that is the same color as the lashes or mascara, for a more natural look. More intense colors may be preferred to match shadow colors or seasonal color trends.

Did You Know?

Eye shadows can be used as either a brow color or an eyeliner.

As an alternative to pencils, eye shadow used with a thin brush dipped in water works well as a wet liner. Dry shadow applied with a thin, firm brush also works well. Gels and liquids are also popular. Liner is applied to the top and bottom edge of the eye on the outside of the lashes, not the inner part of the eye. Applying it on the inner mucous membrane can be unhealthy for the eye and can lead to infections.

CAUTION!

According to the American Medical Association, eye pencils should not be used to color the inner rim of the eyes. Doing so can lead to infection of the tear duct causing tearing, blurring of vision, and permanent pigmentation of the mucous membrane lining the inside of the eye.

Be extremely cautious when applying eyeliner. You must have a steady hand and be sure that your client remains still. Sharpen the eyeliner pencil and wipe with a clean tissue before and after each use. Also, remember to clean the sharpener after each use.

Apply short, even strokes and gentle pressure. The most common placement is close to the lash line. For powder shadow liner application, scrape a small amount onto a tissue or tray and apply to the eyes with a single-use applicator or clean brush. If desired, wet the brush before dipping into the color for a more intense and lasting color.

Eye shadow may be applied as eyeliner with an eyeliner brush to create a softer-lined effect. Whether you are using shadow or pencil liner, it may be helpful to gently pull the skin taut—from right below the eyebrow and out or upward without distorting the shape of the eye—to ensure smooth application.

Mascara Application

Dip a single-use wand into a clean tube of mascara and apply from close to the base of the lashes out toward the tips, making sure your client is comfortable throughout the application. Rest the hand lightly on the face for more control. The lower or upper lashes can be coated first. Have the client look up at the ceiling to apply mascara to the lower lashes. Let the mascara sit for a few seconds before having them look down to apply to the upper lashes.

For more coverage, use a side-to-side motion with the wand when applying it from the base to the tip of the lashes. The end of the wand can also be used to apply more mascara to the tips of the lashes. Hold the wand sideways, not pointing towards the eye. Apply mascara carefully. The most common injury with mascara application is poking the eye with the applicator. Practice applying mascara repeatedly until you feel confident enough to apply it on clients.

Dispose of each wand into the lined waste receptacle. Never double-dip the same wand back into mascara used on different clients. Comb with a lash separator before the mascara dries to avoid clumps.

Lash curlers: If you are using an eyelash curler, you must curl the lashes before applying mascara. If lashes are curled after mascara, eyelashes may be broken or pulled out. Use extreme caution whenever you use an eyelash curler. It is easiest to learn how to use this tool by first observing its use. Ask your instructor to demonstrate before attempting to use an eyelash curler on someone else. Clients may prefer to curl their own lashes.

Eyebrow Color Application

Measure the brow shape and follow the shaping guidelines as closely as possible (refer to Table 20–11, page 594). Check the brows before beginning the service to tweeze any stray hairs.

Avoid harsh contrasts between hair and eyebrow color, such as pale-blond or silver hair with black eyebrows. Taupe or gray are good color choices. Brown is usually a good choice, but reddish-browns can be an unflattering tone. To color in the brows, use a sweeping motion to follow the pattern of the hair. Blend back and forth inside the brow line to achieve a natural look.

Lip Color Application

Consider the client's preferences, eye color, skin tone, and lip shape before selecting and applying lip color. The current fashion trend may be lighter or darker lipstick colors, or a certain style such as glossy, lightly stained, or matte.

Light colors make lips appear larger; dark colors make lips look smaller; however, brighter colors show up more. Lip color can be tricky. Clients can be very selective about their lip color. Give them two or three shades to choose from.

> **FOCUS ON**
>
> **Retailing**
>
> **Lip colors create a good opportunity for retail sales. Most women own several lipsticks, glosses, and pencils. Some carry more than three in their purse. Suggest a few colors and finishes to your clients. Lip color is a simple way to change a look. It is an easy way for your client to complete her look and brighten her day.**

Lip gloss can give a shiny, moisturized look to the lips.

Lip conditioner: Put on a lip moisturizer (or gloss) when starting the makeup application, so it can soak in and moisturize before starting to apply the liner. If the lips have too much gloss, the liner will not stick. A primer, foundation, or plumper can be applied prior to the lip color.

Lip liners are colored pencils used to line and define the lips. Lining the lips also helps keep lip color on and keeps it from feathering. Lip liner is often used when doing corrective makeup. Lip liner comes in thin- or thick-pencil form, and the formulations are similar to eye pencils. Some lip liners can double as lipstick.

To define and shape the lips, lip liner is usually applied before the lip color. Choose a lip liner that coordinates with the natural lip color or lipstick. The liner color should not be dramatically darker or brighter than the lip shade. If a darker liner is desired, fill in most of the lip with the liner and blend the lip color and lip liner to avoid harsh lines.

Did You Know?

Lip liner used as a base for lipstick and applied all over the lips helps color last much longer than lipstick alone. It also helps color look more natural, as it fades without leaving an obvious line around the lips.

To fix any mistake with the lip color and help define the lines, use a small amount of foundation or powder on a cotton-tipped swab or small brush to erase and blend the lined area as necessary.

Sharpen the lip liner pencil and wipe with a clean tissue before each use. Also remember to clean the sharpener before every use.

Lipstick: Lip color must not be applied directly from the container unless it belongs to the client. Use a spatula to remove the lip color from the container and then take it from the spatula with a lip brush. Use the tip of the brush to follow the lip line. Connect the center peaks using rounded strokes, following the natural lip line. For long-lasting color, use a liner and then a lipstick with gloss over the lipstick.

Makeup Application Tips and Guidelines

The following guidelines should be considered in applying makeup:

- Fingernails should be short with smooth edges. Be especially cautious when working around the client's eyes!
- Blending and evenness are the most important factors in a good makeup application.
- Apply creams or liquids before powders, not afterward (Table 20–7). Creams over powders do not blend, and you might end up with a big mess.
- Avoid tugging on the skin or rubbing too hard. If the client's head is moving or you have to hold it to keep it steady, your touch is too heavy.
- Do not hold the client's head or lift the eye skin unless it is absolutely necessary. Holding the head can feel too rough to the client. Lifting the skin will change the look when you let go of the skin around the eyes.
- To avoid getting products in the client's eyes, be sure they are closed when applying powder or eye shadow.
- Makeup is one area in esthetics where you have to apply downward, with the hairs on the face, when applying foundation and powder for better blending. ✓ L06

If nothing else, mascara and lipstick are the two items that can enhance and give color to the face and eyes. Most women say these are the products they can't live without.

MAKEUP APPLICATION STEPS
(The order of the steps can be changed.)
1. Cleanse, tone, moisturize
2. Lip conditioner
3. Concealer (before or after foundation)
4. Foundation
5. Highlight
6. Contour
7. Powder
8. Eyebrows (before or after eyes)
9. Eye shadow
10. Eyeliner
11. Mascara
12. Blush (before or after eyes)
13. Lip conditioner
14. Lip liner
15. Lipstick (optional: gloss)

▲ Table 20–7 **Makeup Application Steps.**

Face Shapes and Proportions

Focusing on specific face shapes is not as popular as it used to be, because you mainly want to use light and dark to accentuate or diminish features. The rules are more relaxed with makeup, and just about anything goes.

Analyzing Face Shapes

The basic rule of makeup application is to emphasize the client's attractive features while minimizing the less appealing features. Learning to see the face and its features as a whole and determining the best makeup for an individual takes practice. While the oval face with well-proportioned features has long been considered the ideal, other face shapes are just as attractive in their own way (Table 20–8, page 588). The goal of effective makeup application is to enhance the client's individuality and unique beauty, not to "remake" her image according to some ideal standard.

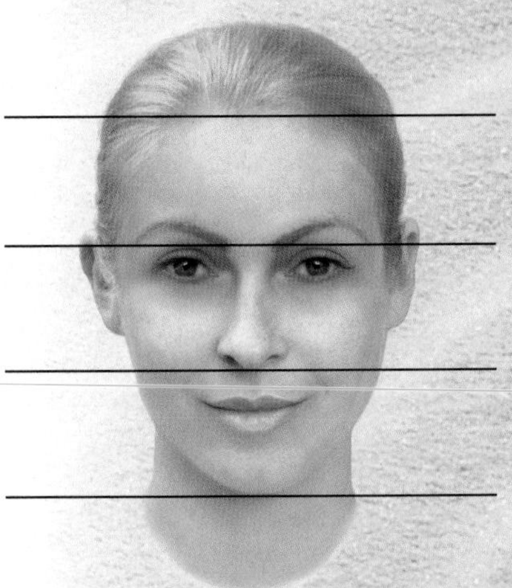

▲ Figure 20–24
The oval face is divided into three equal horizontal sections.

An Oval-Shaped Face

The artistically ideal proportions and features of the oval face are the standard you can refer to when learning the techniques of corrective makeup application. The face is divided into three equal horizontal sections (Figure 20–24). The first third is measured from the hairline to the top of the eyebrows. The second third is measured from the top of

FACE SHAPES		
FACE SHAPE		**CHARACTERISTICS**
Oval 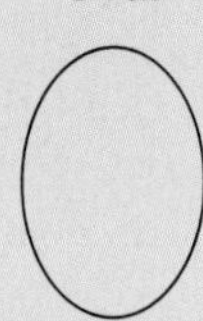		Widest at the temple and forehead, tapering down to a curved chin. This is considered the ideal facial shape because of its balance and overall look of symmetry.
Round 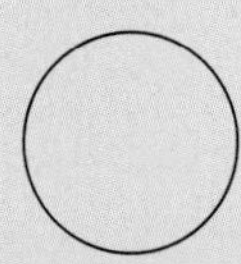		This face is widest at the cheekbone area, and is usually not much longer than it is wide, having a softly rounded jawline, short chin, and a rounded hairline over a rather full forehead.
Square 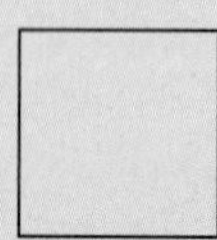	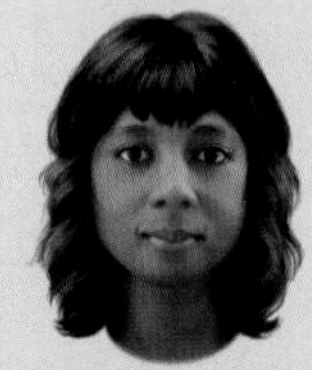	This face has a wide, angular jawline and forehead; the lines of this face are straight and angular.
Rectangle (oblong) 		This face shape is long and narrow; the cheeks are often hollowed under prominent cheekbones. Corrective makeup can be applied to create the illusion of width across the cheekbone line, making the face appear shorter and wider.
Triangle (pear-shaped) 		Like a pyramid, this face is widest at its base or jawline, tapering up to slightly narrower cheeks, and reaching its apex at a narrow forehead. A jaw that is wider than the forehead characterizes the pear-shaped face. Corrective makeup can be applied to create width at the forehead, slenderize the jawline, and add length to the face.
Heart 		This facial shape is wide at the temple and forehead area that tapers down to a narrow chin, forming a heart shape (inverted triangle). It is usually soft rather than angular, and has some prominence in the cheekbone area.
Diamond 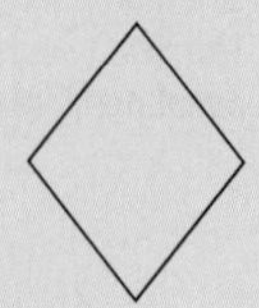		Widest at the cheekbones, this face has a narrow chin and forehead. It is angular in form, and the measurements of the jaw and hairline are approximately the same.

▲ Table 20–8
Face Shapes.

the eyebrows to the end of the nose. The final third is measured from the end of the nose to the bottom of the chin. The ideal oval face is approximately three-fourths as wide as it is long. The distance between the eyes is the width of one eye (Figure 20–25).

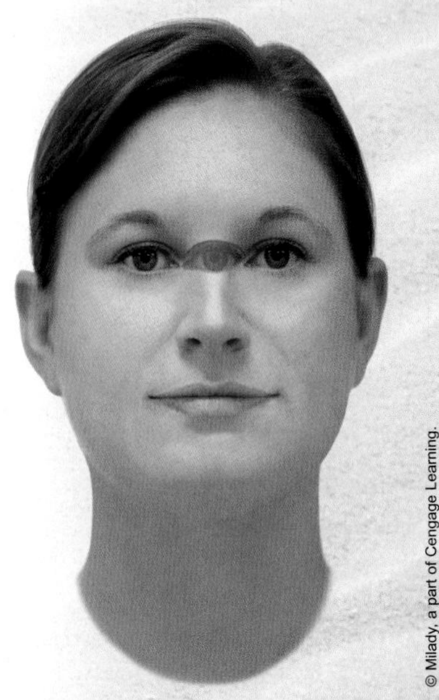

▲ Figure 20–25
The standard distance between the eyes is the width of one eye.

Corrective Makeup

Corrective makeup mainly involves using light and dark colors to highlight and contour features (Figure 20–26). All faces are interesting in their own special ways, but none are perfect. When you analyze a client's face, you might see that the nose, cheeks, lips, or jawline are not the same on both sides; one eye might be larger than the other; or the eyebrows might not match. These tiny imperfections can make the face more interesting if treated artfully.

Facial makeup can create the illusion of better balance and proportion when desired. Corrective makeup can be very effective if applied properly; however, a new makeup artist should proceed with caution because improper application, insufficient blending, or the wrong choice of colors can make the face look artificial.

Facial features can be accented with proper highlighting, subdued with correct shadowing and shading, and balanced with the proper hairstyle. A basic rule for makeup application is that highlighting emphasizes a feature, while shadowing minimizes it. A highlight is produced when a cosmetic, usually a concealer or pencil that is lighter than the original foundation, is used on a particular part of the face. Conversely, a shadow is formed when the product is darker than the skin color. The use of shadows (dark colors and shades) minimizes prominent features so that they are less noticeable.

Before you undertake any kind of corrective makeup application, you should have a clear sense of how to contour and highlight the shape of the faces you will be working with (Table 20–9, page 590). Products for highlighting and contouring are similar to foundations and powders. It is basically using lighter and darker shades to achieve the desired effects.

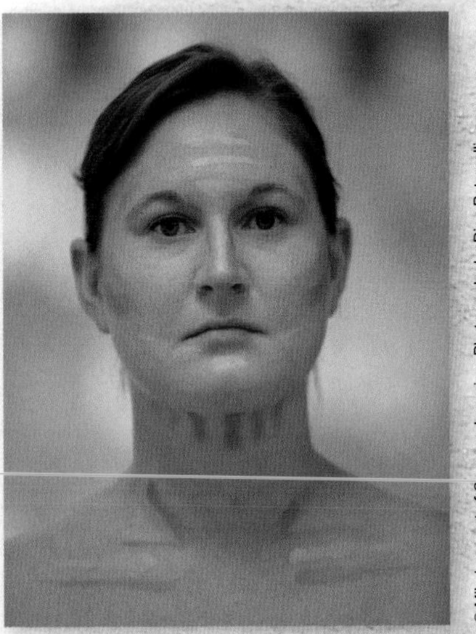

▲ Figure 20–26
Shading and highlighting.

Jawline and Neck Area

When applying makeup, you can blend the foundation onto the neck so that the client's color is consistent from face to neck. Always set with a translucent powder to avoid transfer onto the client's clothing.

For a small face and a short, thick neck use a slightly darker foundation on the side of the neck than the one used on the face. This will make the neck appear thinner.

Corrective Makeup for the Eyes

The eyes are very important when it comes to balancing facial features. Proper application of eye colors and shadow can create the illusion

CORRECTIVE MAKEUP TECHNIQUES		
FACIAL FEATURE		CORRECTIVE TECHNIQUES
Round/square face	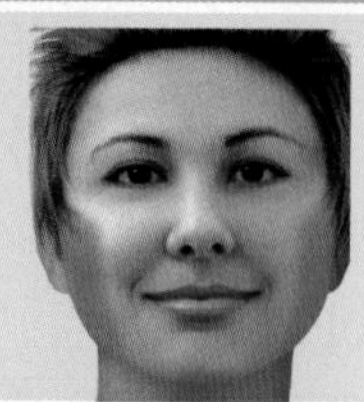	Use two foundations, light and dark, with the darker shade blended on the outer edges of the temples, cheekbones, and jawline, and the light one from the center of the forehead down the center of the face to the tip of the chin.
Triangular	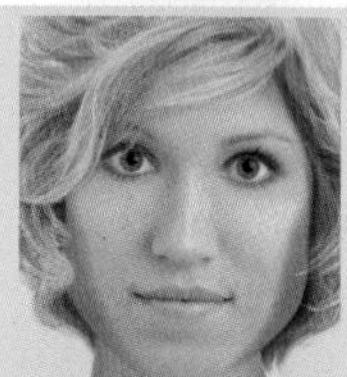	Apply a darker foundation over the chin and neck and a lighter foundation through the cheeks and under the eyes to the temples and forehead, and then blend them together over the forehead for a smooth and natural finish.
Narrow face		Blend a light shade of foundation over the outer edges of the cheekbones to bring out the sides of the face.
Wide jaw	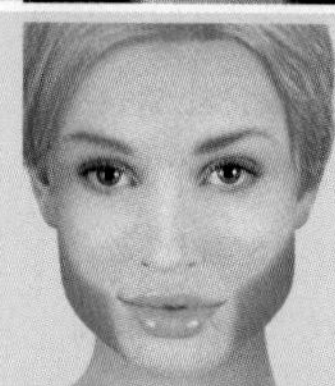	Apply a darker foundation below the cheekbones and along the jawline; blend into the neck.
Double chin	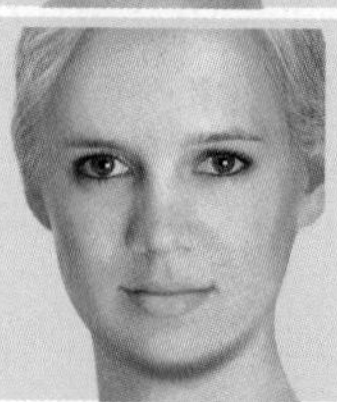	To minimize a double chin, apply shading under the jawline and chin over the full area.
Long, heavy chin		To make a long or heavy chin appear less prominent, apply darker foundation over the area.
Receding chin	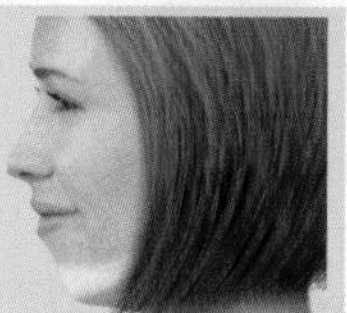	Highlight the chin by using a lighter foundation than the one used on the face.
Protruding forehead		Apply a darker shade of foundation over the forehead area.

▲ Table 20–9
Corrective Makeup Techniques.

CORRECTIVE MAKEUP TECHNIQUES

FACIAL FEATURE	CORRECTIVE TECHNIQUES
Narrow forehead 	Apply a lighter foundation along the hairline and blend onto the forehead.
Wide nose 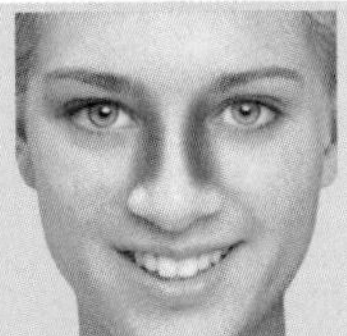	Apply foundation a shade lighter to the center of the nose. Apply darker foundation on both sides, and blend them together.
Short nose 	A lighter shade of foundation is blended onto the tip of the nose and between the eyes.

▲ Table 20–9 **continued**

of the eyes being larger or smaller and will enhance the overall look (Table 20–10, page 592).

- Round eyes can be lengthened by extending the shadow beyond the outer corner of the eyes.
- Close-set eyes are closer together than the width of one eye. For eyes that are too close together, lightly apply darker shadow on the outer edge of the eyes and light on the inside near the nose.
- Protruding eyes can be minimized by blending a dark shadow carefully over the prominent part of the eyelid, carrying it lightly toward the eyebrow. Use a medium to deep shadow color.
- For heavy-lidded eyes, shadow evenly and lightly across the lid from the edge of the eyelash line to the small crease in the eye socket. Use a light color on the lid and a medium to dark color (sparingly) above the crease.
- To make small eyes appear larger, extend the shadows slightly beyond the side of the eyes.
- To correct wide-set eyes, apply the shadows to the inner side of the eyelid toward the nose, and blend carefully.
- For deep-set eyes, use bright, light, reflective colors. Use the lightest color in the crease, and a light to medium color sparingly on the lid and brow bone.
- To diminish dark circles under the eyes, apply concealer over the dark area, blending and smoothing it into the surrounding area. Set lightly with translucent powder. ✓ LO7

▼ Table 20–10 **Eye Shapes.**

EYE SHAPES	
EYE SHAPES	**CORRECTIVE TECHNIQUES**
Hidden lids	1. With a darker color, create a crease in the middle of the upper lid. Avoid strong colors. 2. Highlight the brow bone and hidden area. 3. Softly line upper and lower lashes using a thin line (or skip the upper liner). 4. Apply light (brown) mascara.
Small eyes	1. Place a lighter shadow over the lid, blending it out toward the temple and up to the eyebrow. 2. Apply a darker shadow to the crease and outer corners of the lower lids. 3. Blend eyeliner softly from the center to the outer corners of both eyes along the eyelashes. 4. Apply mascara, brushing the lashes carefully.
Round eyes	1. Apply a medium shade of shadow, blending it over the eyelid out towards the edge of the eyebrow. 2. Apply dark shadow onto the crease and blend it out toward the temple. 3. Line the eye with an eyeliner pencil. 4. Extend and blend the colors applied in steps 1 and 3 toward the outer corner of the eye. 5. Apply mascara to the lashes heavier at the outer corners of the eyes.
Protruding eyelids	1. Apply a medium shading color on the entire eyelid, and blend it toward the eyebrow. 2. Highlight the brow bone area. 3. Line the eye. 4. Apply mascara.
Deep-set eyes	1. Apply a light eye shadow along the crease of the lid. 2. Blend in a medium color next to the outer corners of the eyelids. 3. Use a soft color to accentuate the eyes. 4. Clearly outline the eyes along the lashes. 5. Choose a dark shade of mascara.
Close-set eyes	1. Apply a paler shade to the lid and a darker shade to the outer corner. 2. Line the eye from the middle out to the corner, and blend the shadow outward. 3. Apply mascara in an upward and outward motion.
Wide-set eyes	1. Extend a darker shadow to the inner corner of the eye toward the nose so eyes appear closer together. 2. Blend a lighter shadow from the middle toward the outer corner. Blend the light and dark colors together in the middle, so it's not obvious. 3. Apply liner all the way to the inside edge of the eye by the nose. 4. Apply mascara with an inward motion toward the nose.
Drooping eyes	To offset the droop of the eye, which is often accompanied by a low bone structure or low lid fold, it is suggested to give the appearance of a lift to the entire eye area. 1. Tweeze the under-area of the outer portion of the brow to give a more prominent arch. 2. Lightly apply a medium-color shading shadow across the fold and smudge it up and outward. 3. Apply highlighter directly under the arch of the brow. 4. Apply eyeliner (if used) in a very thin line, and thicken it very slightly at the outside edge in a wedge-like point to give a lift to the eye.

Eyebrows

Reshaping and defining eyebrows can be an art unto itself. Well-groomed eyebrows are part of a complete makeup application. The eyebrow is the frame for the eye (Figure 20–27). Over-tweezed eyebrows can make the face look puffy or protruding, or they may give the eyes a surprised look. Subtle changes in the shape of the brows can make a big difference in the overall look. Adjustments to eyebrow shape can also be used to enhance other facial features (Table 20–11, page 594).

When a client wants to correct her eyebrow shape, begin by removing all unnecessary hairs and then demonstrate how to use the eyebrow pencil or shadow to fill in until the natural hairs have grown in again. When there are spaces in the eyebrow hair, they can be filled in with hair-like strokes of an eyebrow pencil or shadow applied with an angled brush. Use an eyebrow brush or makeup sponge to soften the pencil or shadow marks.

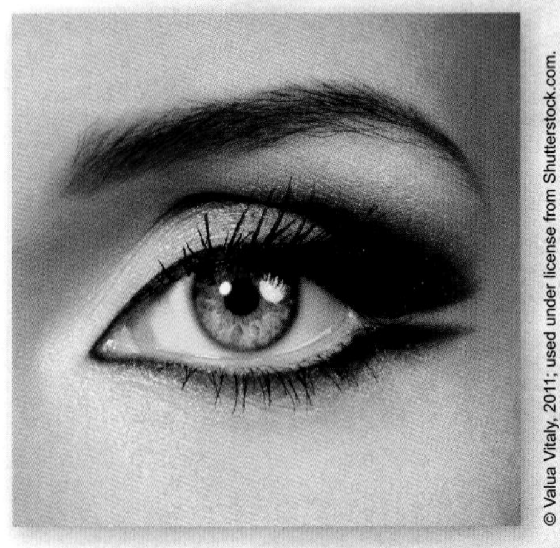

▲ Figure 20–27
An example of a nice eyebrow look.

The Ideal Eyebrow Shape

The ideal eyebrow shape can be measured by using three lines (Figure 20–28). The first line is vertical, measuring from the widest side of the nose and inner corner of the eye upward. This is where the eyebrow should begin. The second line is from the outer corner of the nose to the outer corner of the eye. This is where the eyebrow should end. The third line is vertical, from the outer circle of the iris (colored part of the eye) upward to the highest point of the brow arch. The client should be looking straight ahead as you determine this line. This third line is where the highest part of the brow arch would ideally be.

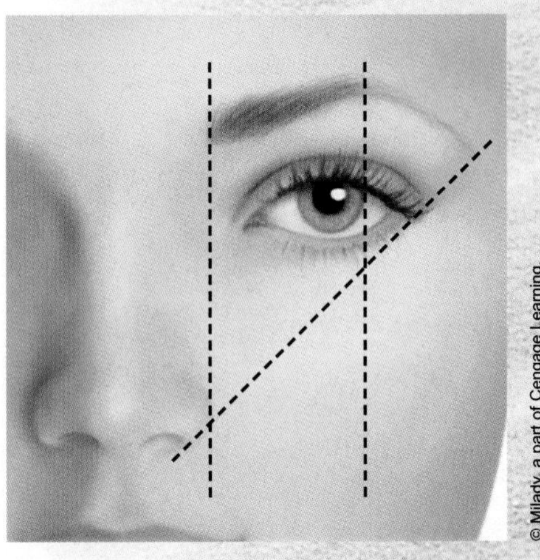

▲ Figure 20–28
The ideal eyebrow shape.

Of course, not everyone's eyebrows fit exactly within these measurements, so use them only as guidelines. Use the thin edge of a tool such as a small ruler, brow brush, pencil, or mascara wand to measure these lines. If desired, use a brow pencil to draw little dots and mark the three points. This also helps marks the area for hair removal. ☑ LO8

Here's a Tip

For a more natural look and better blending, brush or rub the brow color in the opposite direction of the hair growth (in towards the nose). Stay inside the brow line while blending.

The Lips

Lips are usually proportioned so that the curves or peaks of the upper lip fall directly in line with the center of each of the nostrils. In some cases, one side of the lips may differ from the other. Various lip colors and techniques can be used to create the illusion of better proportions (Table 20–12, page 595 to 596). It is best to follow the natural lip line as closely as possible. ☑ LO9

ACTIVITY

Draw several kinds of incorrect brows and different face shapes on a piece of paper. Next, sketch in some lines and your makeup ideas showing how you would correct or reshape them.

PAGE 608

BROW SHAPES	
BROW SHAPES	**CORRECTIVE TECHNIQUES**
High arch	When the arch is too high, remove the superfluous hair from the top of the brow and fill in the lower part with eyebrow pencil or shadow. Build up the shape by layering color lightly until the desired effect is achieved.
Low (small) forehead	A low arch gives the illusion of more height and space to a low forehead.
Wide-set eyes	The eyes can be made to appear closer together by extending the eyebrow line closer together past the inside corners of the eyes; however, care must be taken to avoid giving the client a frowning look.
Close-set eyes	To make the eyes appear farther apart, widen the distance between the eyebrows and extend them slightly outward beyond the outside of the eyes.
Round face	Arch the brows high and more angular to make the face appear narrower.
Long face	Making the eyebrows almost straight (less arch) can create the illusion of a shorter face. Do not extend the eyebrow lines farther than the outside corners of the eyes.
Square face	The face will appear more oval if there is a higher brow arch.

▲ Table 20–11 **Brow Shapes.**

LIP SHAPES

LIP SHAPE	CORRECTIVE TECHNIQUES
Thin lower lip	Line just outside the lower lip to make it appear fuller. Fill in with lip color to create balance between the lower and upper lips.
Thin upper lip	Use a liner to outline the upper lip and then fill in with lip color to balance with the lower lip.
Thin upper and lower lips	Outline the upper and lower lips slightly fuller, but do not try to draw far over the natural lip line. Use a lighter color to make lips appear larger.
Cupid bow or pointed upper lip	To soften the peaks of the upper lip, use a medium-color liner to draw a softer curve inside the points. Extend the line to the desired shape. Fill in with lip color.
Large, full lips	Draw a thin line just inside the natural lip line. Use soft, flat lipstick colors that will attract less attention than frosty or glossy lip colors.
Small mouth and lips	Outline both the upper and lower lips. Fill in lips with soft or frosted colors to make them appear larger. 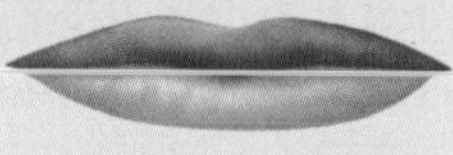
Drooping corners	Line the lips to build up the corners of the mouth. This will minimize the drooping appearance. Fill in lips with a soft color. 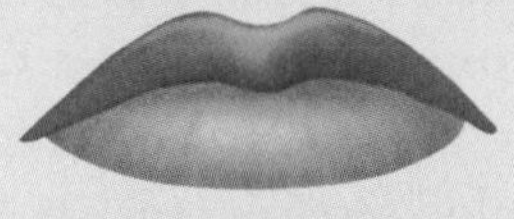 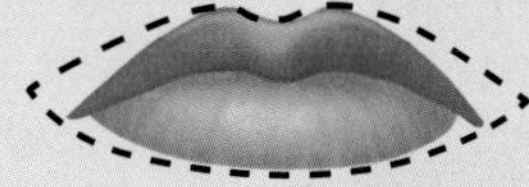 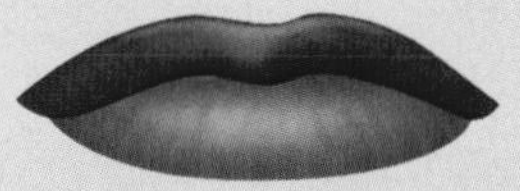
Uneven lips	Outline the upper and lower lips with a soft color to create the illusion of matching proportions. 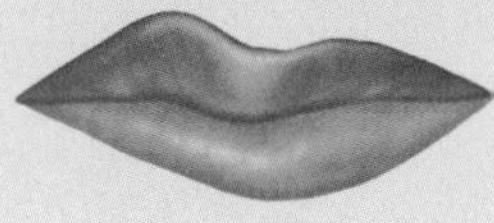 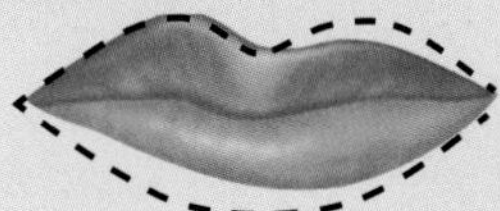 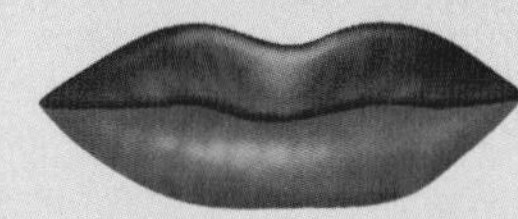

▲ Table 20–12 **Lip Shapes.**

LIP SHAPES	
LIP SHAPE	**CORRECTIVE TECHNIQUES**
Straight upper lip	Use liner to create a slight dip in the center of the upper lip, directly beneath the nostrils. Fill in with a flattering color.
Fine lines around the lips	Outline the lips with a long-lasting lip pencil, and then fill in with a product formulated to keep lip color from running into fine lines. Lighter colors work better and do not show the lines as much as dark or red colors do.

▲ Table 20–12 **continued**

Here's a Tip

Color Choices

If you first hold a few colors of a product up next to the face, it will give you an idea if the colors would be a good potential choice. This is especially useful for foundations, eye shadows, and blushes.

Special-Occasion Makeup

When a client asks for makeup for a special occasion, it is an opportunity to use your creativity. Special occasions often come with special conditions to consider, such as the lighting. For instance, many of these events take place in the evening, when lighting is subdued. That means more definition is required for the eyes, cheeks, and lips. You may also add drama by applying false lashes and using more shimmery colors on the eyes, lips, cheeks, or complexion.

If the special occasion is a wedding, though, where photography is an issue, matte colors are recommended because shimmer may reflect light too much. Follow the basic makeup procedure and expand on it. It is not recommended that you intensify every feature, because this will result in an overdone and harsh look. For example, you can intensify the eyes and lips but not the eyes, cheeks, and lips (Figure 20–29).

▲ Figure 20–29
Bold eyes and lips.

Remember to offer waxing and facial services before a special occasion. Waxing and facials are not recommended the day of the special event, but these are important treatments for achieving the best look and results. When someone schedules for a makeup service, remind them about other salon services that are available such as waxing, facials, hairstyling, and body treatments. Cross-promoting services is beneficial for everyone.

Special-Occasion Makeup for Eyes

Evening Makeup

Follow these techniques for more glamorous eyes (Figure 20–30):

1. Apply the base color from the lashes to the brow with a shadow brush or applicator.
2. Apply a colorful medium tone on the lid, blending from lash line to crease with the shadow brush or applicator.
3. Apply medium to deep color in the crease, blending up toward the eyebrow but ending below it. Take the color further—just outside of the eye.
4. Apply a shimmery highlight shadow under the brow bone with the shadow brush or applicator.
5. Apply eyeliner (liquid or dry) on the upper lash line from the outside corner in, tapering as you reach the inner corner. Blend with the small brush or applicator.
6. Apply shadow in the same color as the liner, directly over the liner. This will give longevity and intensity to the liner. Repeat on the bottom lash line, if desired.
7. Apply two coats of mascara with a single-use mascara wand. Do not "double-dip" the wand.

▲ Figure 20–30
Glamorous eyes!

Dramatic Smoky Eyes

The techniques for dramatic smoky eyes (Figure 20–31) include the following:

1. Encircle the eye with dark gray, dark brown, or black eyeliner.
2. Smudge with a small shadow brush or single-use applicator.
3. Apply dark shadow from the upper lash line to the crease, softening and blending as you approach the crease. The shadow should be dark from the outer to inner corner. You can choose either shimmery- or matte-finish eye shadows. Blend out towards the edge of the brow (in a wedge shape from thickest near the eye to thin on the outside edge of color placement).
4. Apply shadow over the liner on the lower lash line, carefully blending any hard edges.
5. If desired, add a highlight color in a shimmering or matte finish to the upper brow area with the shadow brush or applicator.
6. Apply heavier mascara with a disposable wand.
7. Add individual or band lashes if desired.

▼ Figure 20–31
Dramatic smoky eyes.

Makeup Application for the Camera and Special Events

Makeup for photography, film/video, or weddings essentially uses the same basic application techniques, but with additional special features.

Bridal Makeup

Bridal makeup is an important part of the bride's wedding (Figure 20–32).

▲ Figure 20–32
Bridal makeup is a specialty-makeup service.

Try to have a consultation and practice makeup session before the wedding day. There is no time on the wedding day to deal with personal preferences, color choices, or makeup product quality issues. Record the colors and products used to reproduce the look on the wedding day. Have the bride bring in examples of the looks she wants and her own makeup kit if she wants to use her own makeup or colors. Have her wear a shirt color close to the dress color.

A classic, timeless look is best for weddings. Proper scheduling is important and an hour is recommended for the bridal makeup on the wedding day. Then if anything goes wrong or the bride is late, there is enough time to complete the application. Wedding makeup should be applied after the hair and is the last thing to do before she puts on her dress.

Makeup should be finished as close to the time of the wedding as possible, especially the lipstick. Put a scarf carefully over the hair and face to protect the dress or clothing while it is put on over the head. During the wedding, it is helpful for the main attendant to carry the bride's touch-up kit that includes lipstick and powder.

ACTIVITY

Make your own portfolio and try more dramatic highlighting and contouring. Take before and after pictures. Look at some makeup books to see how professional artists have created dramatic looks.

Photography and Video Applications

More product, color, and powder are generally used for photography and for print work such as newspaper or magazine ads. For photos or film/video, the main difference is the powder and depth of color. Lighting will also influence the look. Learning about lighting differences is essential. The amount of makeup applied does not show up in photos and videos, so a heavier application is needed for these occasions. Theatrical and fantasy makeup must be seen throughout the theater, faraway from the stage, and it is the most exaggerated type of makeup application (Figure 20–33a and b). Airbrush makeup is a spray-on technique popular for video and photography (Figure 20–34).

High-definition makeup is designed to be invisible to high-definition cameras. This makeup is formulated with super-fine micro particles that blend into the skin to provide a flawless complexion. The photochromatic pigments react with all types of lighting so skin

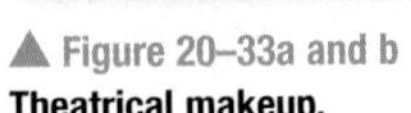

▲ Figure 20–33a and b
Theatrical makeup.

▲ Figure 20–34
Airbrush makeup.

looks natural and flawless. The optical correctors and liquid crystal pigments reflect both natural and artificial lights. "High def" primers, foundations, and powders diffuse pores and smooth out the skin tone.

Airbrush Makeup

Airbrush makeup is used for photography, film, theater, fantasy, and bridal makeup.

Airbrush makeup is sprayed on and techniques include both freehand and stencil (Figure 20–35).

Airbrushing has the following benefits:

- Hygienic, long-lasting, rub- and water-resistant, yet simple to remove
- More efficient and faster to apply than traditional makeup
- Lightweight, natural, and a flawless look

▲ Figure 20–35
Airbrush makeup techniques.

FOCUS ON

Services

Weddings and special occasions are a great opportunity for client services and retail sales. Brides and those attending special events will want to look their best. Facials, good skin care products, and waxing are an important part of preparing for a big day!

If possible, schedule the first consultations, facials, and waxing appointments at least 8 weeks before the event. Give plenty of time to start a beauty-maintenance program, and make sure products are effective and there are no negative skin reactions.

▲ Figure 20–36
Camouflage makeup—before.

▲ Figure 20–37
Camouflage makeup—after.

ACTIVITY

Using a model (or yourself) and two different color applications, divide the face in half. Try various foundations, colors, and intensity on each side. This will give you a visual example of how different makeup will look on the same face.

Airbrush makeup is used for the following applications:

- Face and body art, washable tattoos, and tropical tans (lasting 4 to 5 days)
- Makeup application: foundations, shading and highlighting, use of stencils
- Hair- and nail-art application: hair adornments, coloration, and scalp covering
- Popular for photography, film, theater, fantasy, and bridal makeup

Camouflage Makeup

Camouflage makeup is another area where makeup artists can utilize their skills (**Figures 20–36 and 20-37**). Post-surgery patients often need camouflage makeup to conceal their healing facial scars. Working with patients in medical offices after surgery is important to help clients look better and thus feel better about themselves. Individuals with permanent scars or disfigurements can benefit greatly from camouflage makeup.

Teaching clients how to apply their own makeup is important. Camouflage makeup is challenging, and advanced training is recommended. Heavier makeup and corrective techniques are used for camouflage makeup, although mineral makeup may be better in some instances. Makeup and skin care needs are always based on individual situations.

Artificial Eyelashes

Artificial eyelashes are still popular makeup and fashion accessories. Clients with sparse lashes and clients who want to enhance their eyes for special occasions are most likely to request this service. Unless they want a dramatic look, the objective is to make the client's own lashes look fuller, longer, and more attractive without appearing unnatural.

Two types of artificial eyelashes are commonly used: band and individual lashes.

© Milady, a part of Cengage Learning. Photography by Larry Hamill.

▲ Figure 20–38
False eyelash kit.

Band lashes, also known as **strip lashes**, are eyelash hairs on a strip that are applied with adhesive to the natural lash line (Figure 20–38).

Individual lashes are separate artificial eyelashes that are applied on top of the upper lashes one at a time. These are more natural-looking than band lashes (Figure 20–39). Individual eyelashes attach directly to a client's own lashes at the base. This process is sometimes referred to as **eye tabbing**.

Eyelash adhesive is used to make artificial eyelashes adhere, or stick, to the natural lash line. Some clients may be allergic to adhesive. When in doubt, give the client an allergy test before applying the lashes.

This test may be done in one of two ways:

- Put a drop of the adhesive behind one ear.
- Attach a single individual eyelash to an eyelid.

In either case, if there is no reaction within 24 hours, it is probably safe to proceed with the application.

Artificial lashes are available in a variety of sizes and colors. They can be made from human hair, animal hair, or synthetic fibers. Synthetic-fiber eyelashes are made with a permanent curl and do not react to changes in weather conditions. Artificial eyelashes are available in natural colors, ranging from light to dark brown and black or auburn, as well as in bright, trendy colors. Black and dark brown are the most popular choices.

© Milady, a part of Cengage Learning. Photography by Rob Werfel.

▲ Figure 20–39
Individual and band lashes.

Removing Artificial Eyelashes

To remove artificial eyelashes, use pads saturated with special lotions. The lash base may also be softened by applying a facecloth or cotton pad saturated with warm water and a gentle facial cleanser. Hold the cloth over the eyes for a few seconds to soften the adhesive. Starting from the outer corner, remove the lashes carefully to avoid pulling out the client's own lashes. Pull band lashes off parallel to the skin, not straight out. Use wet cotton pads or swabs to remove any makeup and adhesive remaining on the eyelid.

PAGE 614

Lash and Brow Tinting

Lash and brow tinting is used to darken lashes and brows. It is nice for clients with light hair to have some color that lasts a few weeks, rather than penciling in brows or having light eyelashes without mascara. Tint is effective for those who have enough hair to darken. If the hair is sparse, tinting may not show up enough to be effective. Tinting is a quick procedure and can be a great add-on service to facials or waxing.

The application must be precisely placed inside the brow shape. It is very important to keep the tint off of the skin unless requested for the brow area. Color takes very quickly, so any excess on the skin must be removed within seconds or it could remain there for weeks. Lashes or brows can be tinted—clients do not always want both areas tinted.

REGULATORY **AGENCY ALERT**

Do not use tints with aniline derivatives (coal-tar based). These are not FDA approved and can cause blindness. Some tints are illegal in the United States, but they are still available from retailers for use. Do not use them if they are not legal in your region. You may be fined and lose your license. Permanent haircolor should not be used on brows. Vegetable dyes are allowed in some regions but do not work as well or last as long. Some regions prohibit eyelash and eyebrow tinting using any type of coloring product. Check with local laws and regulations to see what is legal in your area.

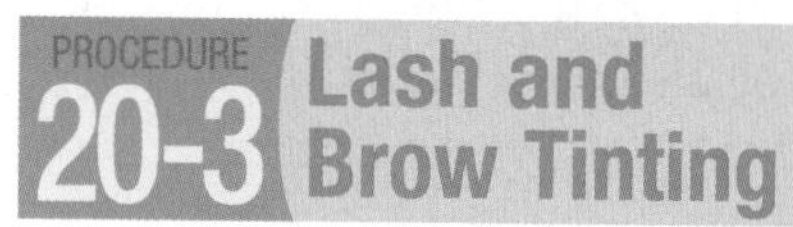

PAGE 616

Other Eyelash Services

Lash Extensions

Lash extensions are single synthetic or natural hairs that are applied one-by-one to the client's natural lashes with a special adhesive. Fine-tipped forceps or tweezers are used to apply the lash extensions, and it can take up to 2 hours to apply a set. Partial applications and touch-ups take less time. Clusters or groups of hairs should not be applied as extensions, because doing so can damage the natural hairs.

The bond will last for the life cycle of the natural lash—approximately 2 months. Fills, or touch-ups, are necessary as the hair grows and the extension needs to be replaced. For extensions to last, makeup application and cleansing should be gentle around the lash area. Research on the adhesive quality and safety is recommended. Advanced training and practice are necessary before performing this intricate procedure on clients.

Lash Perming

Lash perming is the process of curling the lashes. Research on the quality and safety of the perm solution is recommended. Advanced training and practice are necessary before performing this delicate procedure on clients. Always check with your regulatory agency about the legalities of performing lash services. ☑ LO10

Permanent Cosmetic Makeup

Permanent cosmetic makeup is cosmetic tattooing. The specialized techniques used for permanent cosmetics are often referred to as *micropigmentation, micropigment implantation,* or *dermagraphics*. The cosmetic implantation technique deposits colored pigment into the upper reticular layer of the dermis. Eyeliner and eyebrow tattooing are the most popular services (**Figure 20–40**). Scar camouflage and body art are also offered as permanent cosmetic services.

Permanent cosmetic procedures are performed using various methods, including the traditional tattoo machines, the pen or rotary machine, and the hand method. The process includes an initial consultation, then application of pigment, and at least one or more follow-up visits for adjusting the shape and color or density of the pigment.

Technically, permanent cosmetic procedures are considered permanent because the color is implanted into the upper reticular part of the dermal layer of the skin and cannot be washed off. As with any tattoo, however, fading can and often does occur, requiring periodic maintenance and touch-ups.

Estheticians, tattoo artists, and medical technicians perform these services. Licensing and training requirements vary from state to state. A thorough training program and hands-on experience are necessary to perform these technical services. It is recommended that clients choose a technician carefully by considering their training and experience and by looking at their portfolio. It is important to remember that the shape and proper placement of the procedure is as important as the right color.

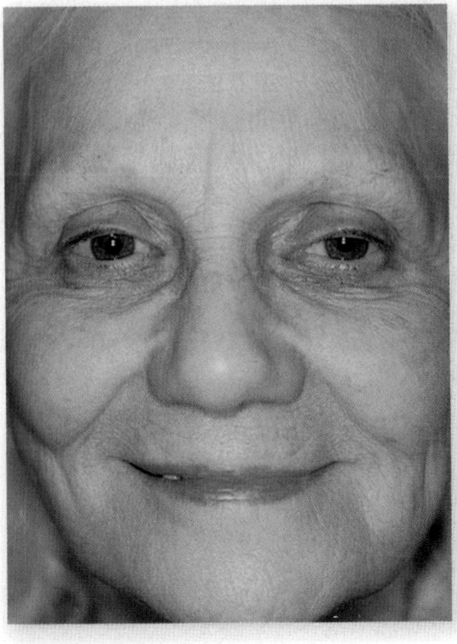

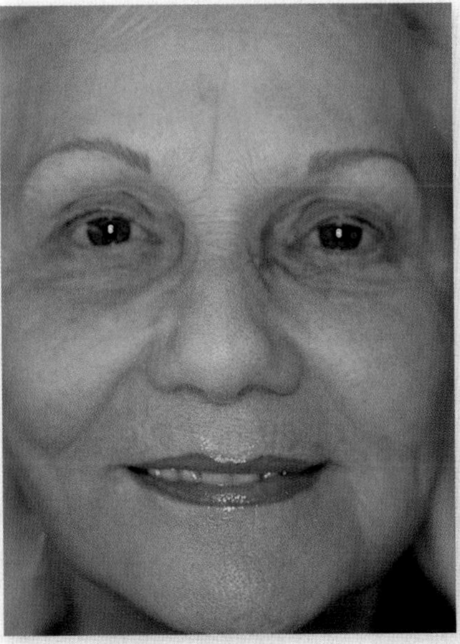

▲ Figure 20–40
Permanent "tattoo" makeup.

ACTIVITY

Examine industry journals or women's magazines:

- **Find five pictures of makeup-looks that you like and five that you dislike. Note why you like or dislike them.**
- **Find one example of each look: natural, business, evening, and dramatic looks.**
- **Find a brow-look you like and one you dislike.**
- **What is in style right now for makeup? Present an example in class.**
- **Find two professional articles about techniques on applying makeup.**

It is permanent and there is absolutely no room for error. One must have a steady hand and an attention to detail to perform this service.

The initial procedure will generally take approximately 1 to 2½ hours to perform. Touch-up procedures do not usually require as much time. Most clients experience some discomfort. This varies according to an individual's pain threshold as well as the skills of the technician performing the service. Generally, there is some swelling of the treated area. While eyebrows may show little after-effect, eyeliner and lips may show more, and the edema (inflammation) may last from 2 to 72 hours. During the procedure, there may be some bleeding and or bruising. There is usually some tenderness for a few days. The color is much darker for the first 6 to 10 days.

A Career as a Makeup Artist

Makeup artists play an important role in the esthetics field. Many opportunities are available for makeup artists in clinical offices, film/video, theater, and fashion. These art forms give individuals a chance to be creative. A natural part of the full-service menu for spas and salons, makeup services are complementary to other services offered by estheticians.

To thrive in this business, it is important to keep up with current styles, sell yourself, and present yourself well. The key to building up a loyal client base is staying professional. Be punctual and prepared. Makeup artistry is a great addition to your repertoire of services.

Makeup services are another opportunity to work with facial and waxing clients and assist them with their makeup needs in a professional, clean environment. Clients benefit from the personalized service offered during a professional makeover. Each client is different, and that keeps the job interesting and challenging—because what may look good on one person does not often look good on another.

Enhancing our appearance through makeup is also a fun and easy way to boost our self-image. The satisfying part of working as an artist is client satisfaction—the look on their faces when they see how much they can improve their appearance. This gives them encouragement and helps them feel better about themselves. Makeup is not simply a trend or fashion statement. It has evolved over the years into a natural finishing touch to healthy skin.

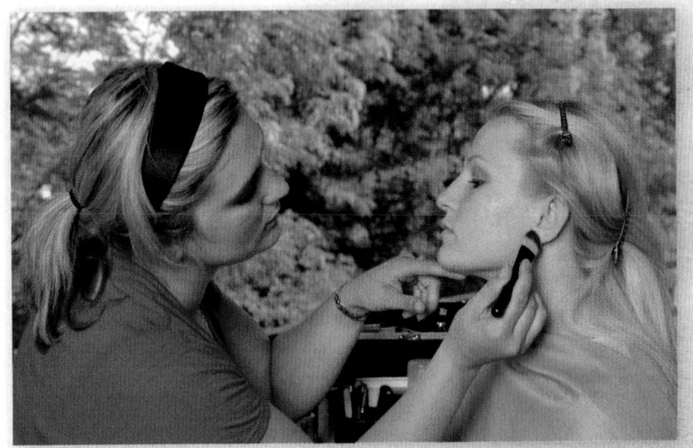

▲ Figure 20–41
On-location makeup.

Freelance Makeup Artistry

Freelance makeup artists provide services outside of the salon for photography, video, and events (Figure 20–41). Studios, movies, theater, fashion shows, and special events all require on-location makeup services. Men also need makeup for video, fashion, and print work (Figure 20–42). Foundation, concealer, powder, lip conditioner, and sometimes even additional products are used for men's basic makeup. It depends on the occasion and desired look.

Freelance makeup artistry is an exciting, fast-paced part of the makeup business. It can be challenging to work on-location. You need to be flexible, quick, and organized to keep up with the crew and schedule. The work area can be limited and correct lighting is not always available, but it is rewarding to see the fruits of your labor in action. It can be an interesting and lucrative career choice to be a freelance makeup artist.

▲ Figure 20–42
Men's makeup is used for film and video.

A good eye for detail is important because once the photo or video session is completed, it is captured forever. You may be the only one checking details and acting as a stylist for the event. Check the hair, clothes, jewelry, lighting, shadows, and background areas behind the models. The crew and models sometimes turn to the makeup artist/stylist to help them with other details. Don't be shy about speaking up if you notice something that would not look right through the camera. Being able to provide needed supplies or an eye for detail adds value to your services. This experience broadens your horizon and may lead to other opportunities.

Marketing Freelance Makeup Services

The best marketing is word of mouth and through people you know. After getting a professional portfolio and brochure together, make contacts at photo and TV studios, bridal shops, theaters, event centers, high schools (senior portraits), and other avenues where makeup artists may be needed. Offer some free services to get your foot in the door. There is no substitution for making that personal connection face-to-face.

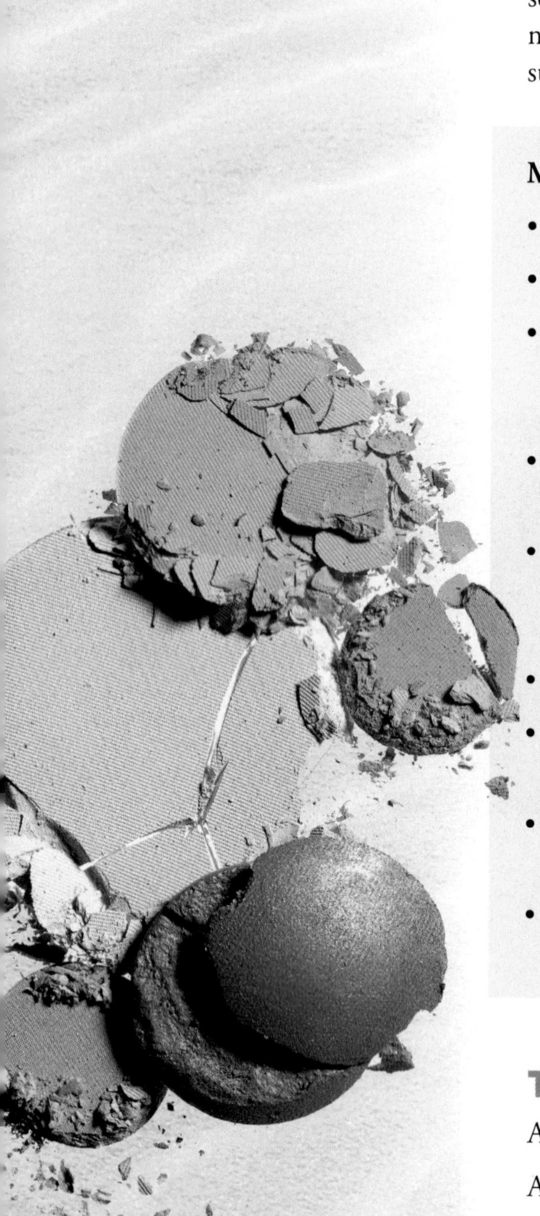

Makeup Marketing Tips:

- Promote makeup services to facial clients.
- Offer free consultations.
- Visit and hand out your business cards and brochures to photographers, bridal shops, TV studios, ad agencies, and high schools. Think of other places where clients are looking for makeup artists.
- Establish a relationship with physicians' offices (dermatologists, cosmetic surgery).
- Create a quality portfolio to share with potential clients. It is worth having a professional photo session to create your portfolio if you are going to specialize in freelance makeup.
- Attend bridal fairs and place ads in bridal publications.
- Market yourself at event locations and venues where large functions are held.
- Think of other retail stores and locations where you could offer free consultations at, or host a special "free makeover day."
- Take advantage of all the social network, media, and Internet marketing avenues.

The On-Location Makeup Kit

A makeup kit starts with a good case—this is your tool box.

Add these essentials to your basic makeup kit (see Table 20–2, page 571):

- Make sure you have color choices for each product: two warm colors, two cool colors, and two neutral colors. You can mix shades together for even more selection.
- Palette for mixing colors, plenty of brushes, single-use applicators, and supplies.
- Enough powder and foundation choices: powder is important for print and video makeup.
- For more creative looks: use theatrical makeup and cream foundations.
- Hair supplies: clips, headbands, hair spray, brush, comb, hairpins.
- Other supplies: tweezers, scissors, safety pins, skin oil, hand sanitizer, mirror, wash cloths, drinking straws (a lipstick saver).
- Eyelash kits (one lash set for each model as needed).

- Body camouflage products (don't forget the neck, chest, back, arms).
- Outdoors: umbrella for shade, sunscreen, water.
- As needed: small portable table, chair, shower curtain and tape for privacy screen, duct tape, lights and lighting.
- Other stylist accessories and on-location supplies: paper towels, snacks, mints, eye drops, etc.

ACTIVITY

Put together an "on-location" makeup kit to carry with you for special-event makeup.

Retailing

Retailing cosmetics is a significant part of the business. It is also an effective way to increase your income. Most salons will pay you 5 to 10 percent of every product you retail. If you focus on retailing to every client, this amount will add up quickly. You will be helping your client by giving her professional advice, and it is convenient to shop for makeup while receiving salon services.

One of the biggest challenges women face when purchasing cosmetics is finding the correct colors and finishes. Focus on consultative selling by recommending products. Set out what you used for the service, show the client the products, and then recommend the items you think they need or would benefit from.

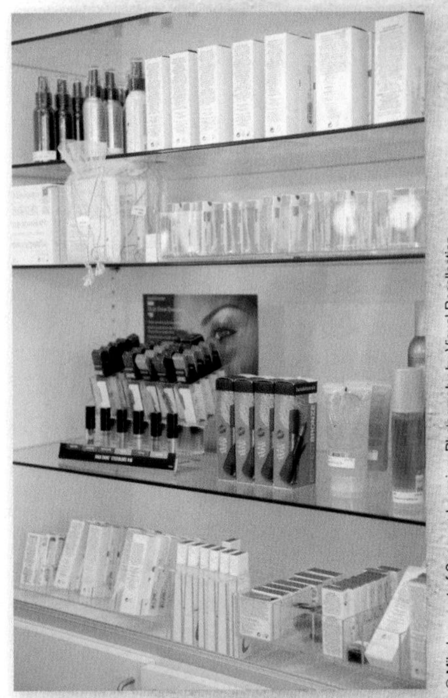

▲ Figure 20–43
Displays should stimulate interest in products.

When you start to use specific and "colorful" language, you will see a great improvement in your selling technique. Consider complimentary and persuasive phrases such as these:

- "This cocoa shadow will make your green eyes look even more beautiful."
- "You have a great smile. This new peach lipstick will really show it off."
- "What a great dress! This silver eyeliner would look beautiful with it."

While retailing is important, always keep a person's best interests in mind. Never sell anything that you honestly feel will not benefit clients. Genuine advice is the best advice, and clients know the difference. If they trust you, they will return and recommend you to their friends, which is the best business advertisement.

Makeup displays should be attractively presented and should stimulate interest in retail products (Figure 20–43). Make testers accessible and let clients enjoy "playing" with the products. Assist them with keeping testers clean and using single-use applicators to avoid contamination.

The price of services and products will vary depending on the geographical location of the salon and client demographics. Lessons, makeovers, and special-occasion applications cost more than basic applications.

Web Resources

www.makeupabout.com

www.safecosmetics.org

PROCEDURE

20-1 Professional Makeup Application

IMPLEMENTS AND MATERIALS

Skin Care Products
- Cleanser
- Toner
- Moisturizer (skin primer optional)
- Lip conditioner

Makeup
- Concealer
- Highlighter
- Contour color
- Foundation
- Powder
- Eye shadow
- Eyeliner
- Mascara
- Blush
- Lip liner
- Lipstick
- Lip gloss
- Other: bronzers, specialty items

Supplies
- Cape and draping supplies
- EPA-registered disinfectant
- Lined waste receptacle
- Tweezers
- Hair clip/headband
- Makeup brushes
- Pencil sharpener
- Mirror
- Lash comb
- Lash curler
- Hand towel
- Client charts

Single-use Items
- Spatulas
- Cotton (swabs and rounds)
- Mascara wands
- Sponges
- Tissues
- Applicators
- Paper towels

This is a basic makeup application. Your instructor may prefer a different method that is equally correct. Completing a makeup application includes the consultation, setup, application, and cleanup procedures (refer to Tables 20–2 and 20–3). Some artists prefer to apply the makeup working from the top to the bottom of the face—eyes, cheeks, and then lips. There are pros and cons to every method. You will likely come up with your own prefered application procedure. If you miss a step, go back and perform it later if it does not complicate the application. The finished "painted" face is what is important, not how you get there. You may need to go back and change or add to your canvas once it is complete. It is, however, beneficial to develop a regular and efficient routine.

Preparation

- **Perform** 

PAGE 372
- Start by setting out a few color selections: neutrals, cools, warms.

Procedure

1 Determine the client's needs, and choose products and colors accordingly. Focus on your client's features and preferences. Discussing skin care or waxing is appropriate with a makeup client. Record these on the client chart. Ask the following questions:

- Do you wear contacts or have allergies?
- What look do you want?
- What makeup products do you normally wear?
- What are your typical clothing colors?
- What is the special occasion or event?

2 Wash your hands.

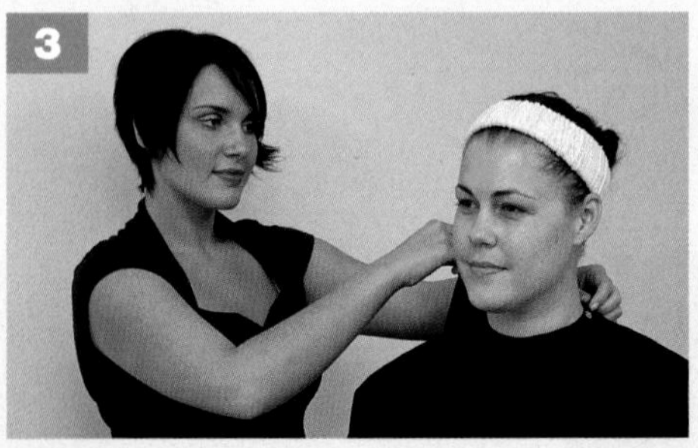

3 **Drape** the client and use a headband or hair clip to keep her hair out of her face.

Service Tip

Preparing the Canvas for Makeup
Preparing the face is like preparing a painting canvas for the palette of colors. The skin needs to be exfoliated and hydrated for the makeup to be applied successfully. This should happen before the procedure, but if there is extra time the client can wash and exfoliate their face at a sink. You might ask them to come in early for this.

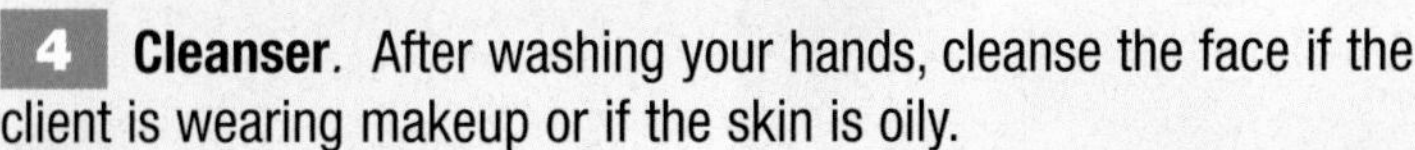

4 **Cleanser**. After washing your hands, cleanse the face if the client is wearing makeup or if the skin is oily.

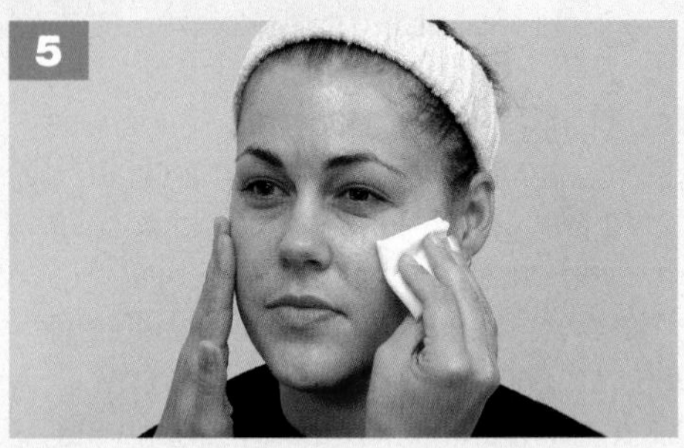

5 **Freshener**. Use a cotton pad to apply the freshener (or toner/witch hazel) to cleanse the skin.

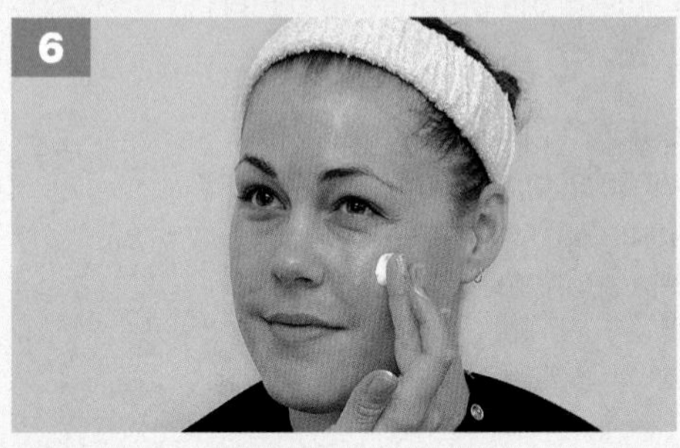

6 **Moisturizer.** Apply a small amount of moisturizer to prepare the skin for makeup. Apply a primer if applicable.

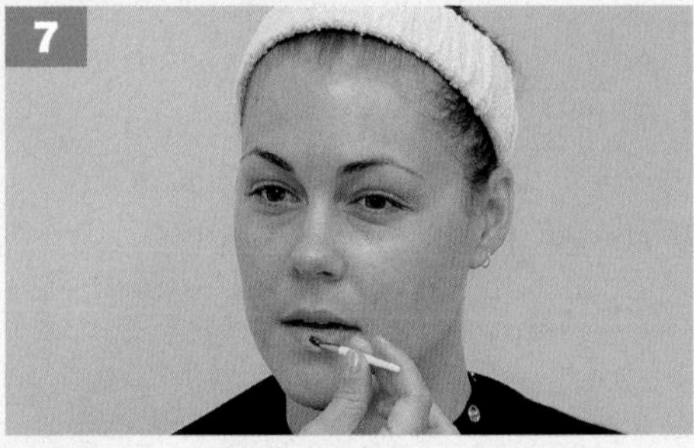

7 **Lip conditioner**. Use a spatula to remove the product from the container. Apply with a brush. To give it more time to soak in and moisturize, put on the lip conditioner when starting the makeup application.

Note: If lips are chapped, have clients rub off the dry skin with a wet wash cloth, esthetic wipes, or a lip scrub before starting the service. Tissue or paper towels are drying and leave lint on the lips so are not recommended for this.

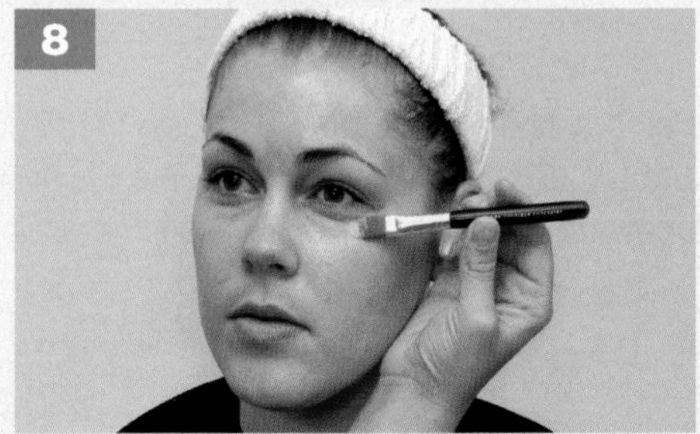

8 **Concealer**. Use a spatula to get the product out of the container. Choose a color one to two shades lighter than the foundation. You can apply this under or over the foundation beneath the eyes with a brush, sponge, or finger. Depending on the color, it can also be used as the highlighter (light) and to cover blemishes if it matches the skin tone. Apply using short strokes.

Note: Always use creams and liquids before applying powders, or they will not blend. If you are using a powder concealer or contour powder, apply these after the foundation.

20-1 Professional Makeup Application (continued)

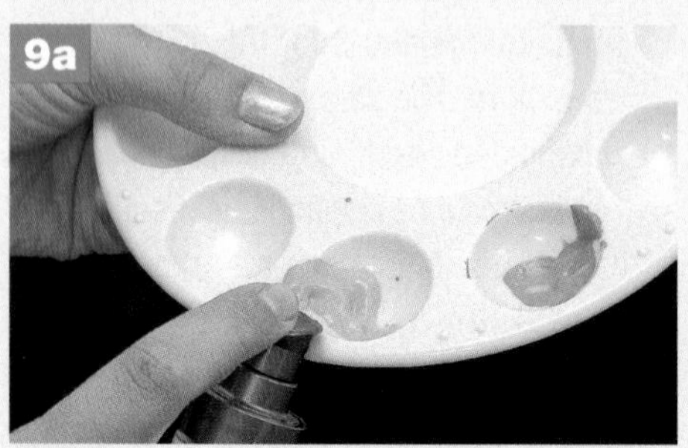
9a

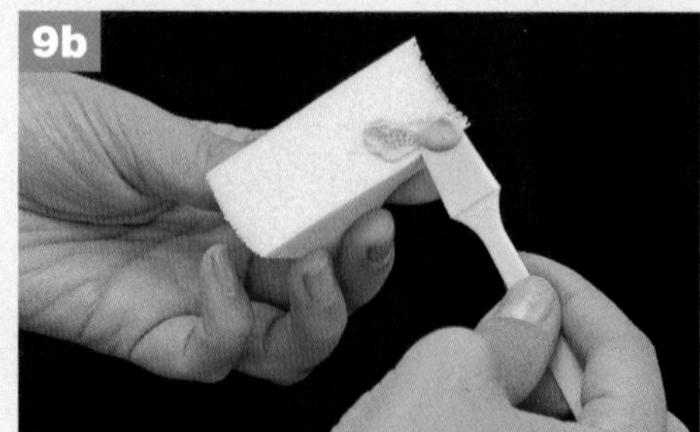
9b

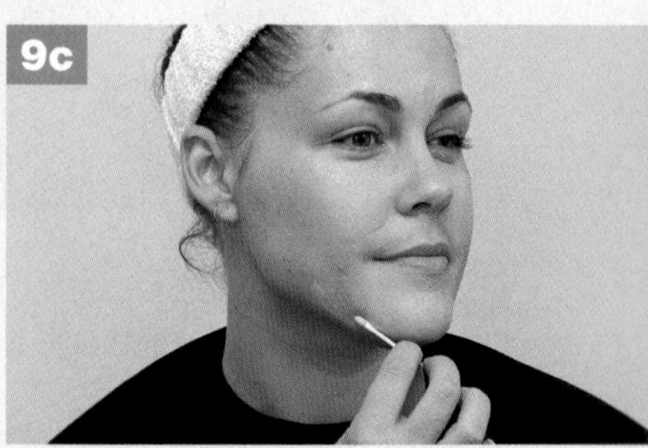
9c

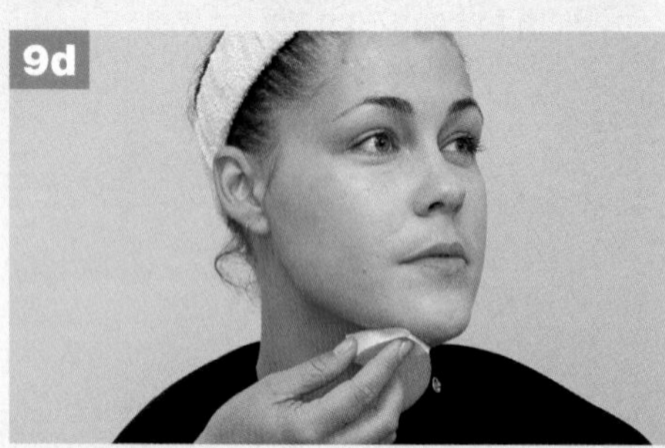
9d

9 **Foundation**. First choose a few colors to match the right shade. Use a spatula to get the product out of the container, or put some on a clean sponge or in a small container. Apply to the jawline to match the skin color. Cover the skin using short strokes to even out the skin tone and cover imperfections without over-rubbing the skin. Blend along the jaw and edges of the face. Blend downward to blend with facial hair and up around the hairline so the product does not stick in the hairline. Pat gently around the eyes. Pressing, rather than rubbing, keeps the product on better.

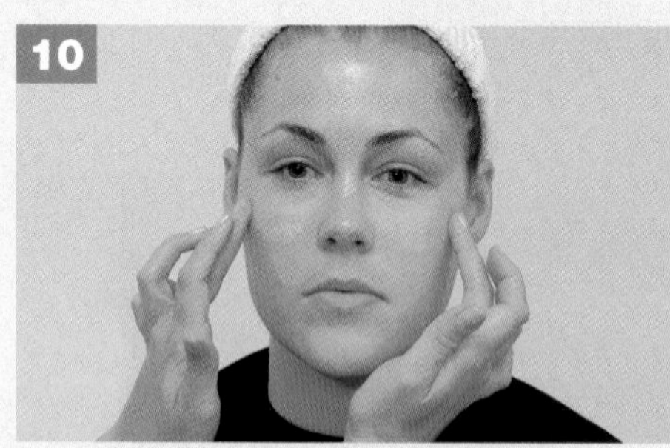
10

10 **Highlighter**. Use a spatula to get the product out of the container. Apply a white or light color to accentuate and bring out features along the brow bone, the temples, chin, or above the cheekbones. Blend with your brush, a sponge, or your finger.

11

11 **Contouring**. Use a spatula to get the product out of the container. Using a small amount, apply a darker shade under the cheekbones and to other features you want to appear smaller. Blend well.

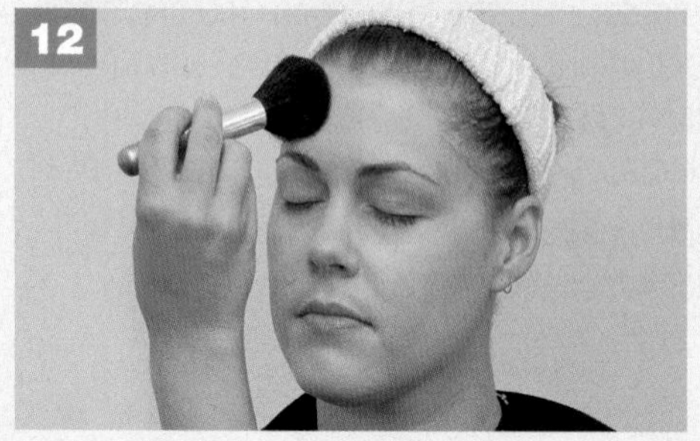
12

12 **Powder**. Pour a little powder on a tissue or tray to avoid cross-contamination. Apply to the brush and tap off excess powder onto the tissue (not the floor or table). Use a powder brush and sweep all over the face to set the foundation.

13 **Eyebrows.** Use a shade that is close to the hair color, or a shade the client likes. Apply color by using short strokes with a pencil or eye shadow with a brush. Smudge with a brush or a makeup sponge, going in the opposite direction of the hair growth to blend. Then smooth brows back into place with a brow brush.

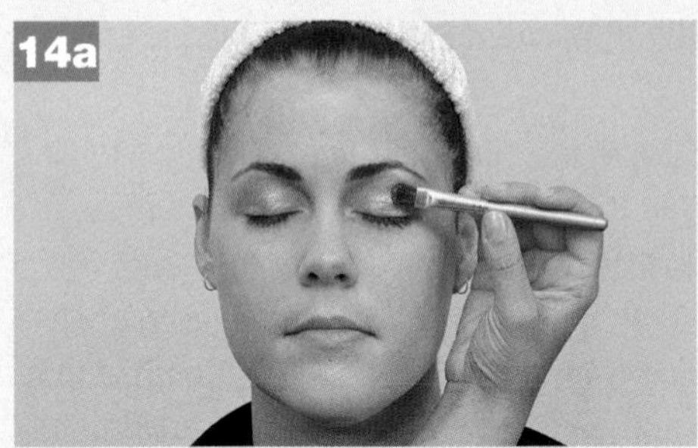

14a **Eye shadow.**

Light: Choose a light-base color and apply all over the eyelid, from the lash line up to the brow. Stop color at the outside corner of the eye up to the outside corner of the brow.

14b *Dark:* Apply a darker shade to the crease: partially on top of the crease and partially underneath the crease. First tap the excess powder off the brush. Apply the most color from the outside corner of the eye into the crease area above the inside of the iris.

14c This dark color covers three-quarters of the way above the outside part of the eye. Blend the color.

Optional: Apply the eyeliner before applying the dark shadow color.

15a **Eyeliner**. Sharpen the liner before and after use.

Shadow as wet liner can also be used for liner and applied with a single-use or clean brush. Eye shadow can be applied as liner with a thin brush dipped in water. Dry shadow can also be applied with a thin, firm brush for a more natural look. Make sure the liner is not too rough or so dry that it drags on the eye. Liquid liners require applicators that are disposable or that can be disinfected.

Have the client shut her eyes when you apply the liner on top of the eyelids next to the lashes. Then have her look up and away as you apply the lower liner under the eyes. Apply the liner underneath the lower lashes.

15b Bring the liner three-fourths of the way from the outside edge of the eye in towards the center of the eye, ending softly at the inside of the iris. Blend so that the color tapers off. Bringing the liner in closer to the nose can make the eyes appear closer together. Lining only the outside corner makes the eyes appear farther apart. Make sure the line does not abruptly stop. Blend the liner with a firm, small liner brush.

PROCEDURE

20-1 Professional Makeup Application (continued)

16 **Mascara.** Dip a single-use brush into the mascara. Move the wand from side-to-side from the base of the lashes out to the tips. Hold the wand at an angle (not pointing towards the eye) and apply more to the tips of the lashes.

Note: Some artists prefer to do the lower lashes first to avoid mascara touching the tops of the eye area when the client looks up for the lower application.

Bottom lashes: Wipe off the excess. Have the client put her chin down while looking up at the ceiling with her eyes to apply mascara to the bottom lashes. Comb and separate before the mascara dries.

Upper lashes: Have the client look down and focus on a fixed point to apply mascara to the upper lashes, brushing from the base to the tip. Comb with a lash comb before the product dries and before the client looks in a different direction to avoid smudging.

Use a cotton-tipped swab or small stiff brush with a little foundation or powder on it to fix or erase smudges.

Optional: Curl the lashes before applying mascara. Hold the curler on the base of the lashes without pulling and release the curler before moving it away from the lashes. Do not curl after mascara as lashes can be damaged and may fall out.

Optional: Apply false lashes following the mascara. Refer to Procedure 20–2, Applying Artificial Lashes, later in the chapter.

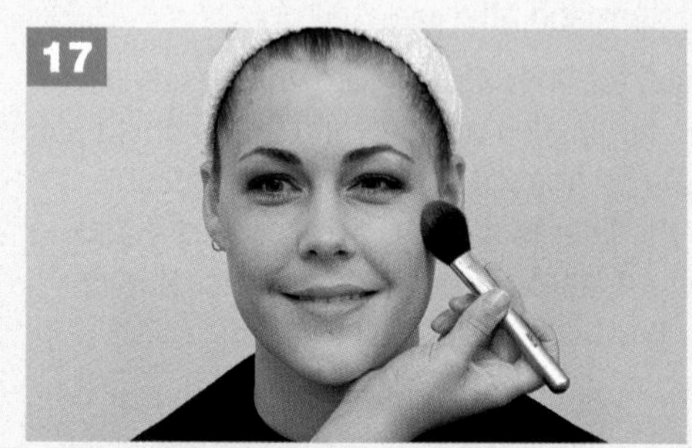

17 **Blush**. This can be done before the eyes. The blush color will depend on whether you choose a warm or cool color scheme. Tap off the excess powder on the brush. Apply blush just below the cheekbones, blending on top of the bones toward the top of the cheeks. Blend back and forth along the cheekbones. The color should stop below the temple and not be closer than two fingers away from the nose. It should not go lower than the nose, because this can "drag down the face." Blush should blend to the hairline, but not into it.

Do not apply too much blush on the apple of the cheek; this makes the face look fatter. A horizontal line makes the face appear wider, whereas a vertical line makes it look thinner. Following the cheekbones usually works best.

18 ***Optional:*** **Lip conditioner.** This step applies if lips are dry or you did not already apply lip moisturizer earlier. Use a spatula to get the product out of the container. Use a brush to apply. Put on a lip moisturizer when starting the makeup application so it can soak in and moisturize before you start applying the liner. If the lips have too much gloss or product, the liner will not go on or stick.

Optional: Some artists use a primer or foundation on the lips under the lip color to help keep it on, but these may be drying.

19 Lip liner. Sharpen the liner. Have the client smile and stretch her lips. With the lips pulled tight, the liner and lipstick brush glide on more smoothly. Line the outer edges of the lips first with small firm strokes; then fill in and use the liner as a lipstick. This keeps the lipstick and color on longer. Use a natural color for those clients who do not like liner. Lipstick will not last long without it.

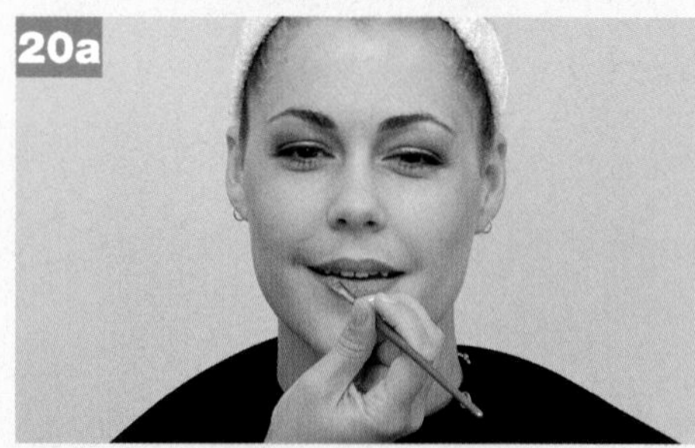

20a Lipstick. Use a spatula to get the product out of the container. Have the client select a color from among two or three choices. Apply the lipstick evenly with a lip brush. Rest your ring finger near the client's chin to steady your hand. Ask the client to relax her lips and part them slightly. Brush on the lip color. Then ask the client to smile slightly so that you can smooth the lip color into any small crevices.

20b Blot the lips with tissue to remove excess product and set the lip color. Finish with gloss if desired.

21 Show the client the finished application. Remove the cape and hair clips so you can see the finished look. Discuss the colors and any product needs she may have.

Post-Service

- **Complete** PROCEDURE 14-2 Post-Service Procedure PAGE 375
- After the service is completed (and before the cleanup), fill out the client chart and make retail product suggestions and sales. ✓ LO11

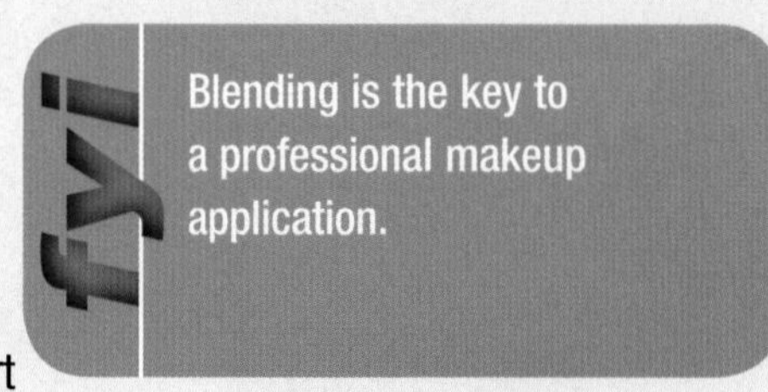

Blending is the key to a professional makeup application.

PROCEDURE

20-2 Applying Artificial Lashes

IMPLEMENTS AND MATERIALS

Supplies

- Disinfectant
- Headband or hair clip
- Tweezers
- Eyelash comb/brush
- Eyelash curler
- Hand mirror
- Small (manicure) scissors
- Adjustable light
- Adhesive tray or foil to put adhesive on
- Makeup cape
- Hand sanitizer
- Waste container

Products

- Artificial eyelashes
- Eyelid and eyelash cleanser
- Lash adhesive
- Eyelash adhesive remover
- Eye makeup remover

Single-use Items

- Cotton swabs
- Cotton pads
- Toothpick or hairpin
- Mascara wand
- Paper towels

Preparation

- **Perform** 

PAGE 372
- Discuss with the client the desired length of the lashes and the effect she hopes to achieve.
- Wash your hands.
- Place the client in the makeup chair with her head at a comfortable working height. The client's face should be well and evenly lit; avoid shining the light directly into the eyes. Work from behind or to the side of the client. Avoid working directly in front of the client whenever possible.
- Prepare for the makeup procedure, if applicable.
- If the client wears contact lenses, she must remove them before starting the procedure.
- If the client is only having artificial lashes applied and you have not already done so, remove mascara so that the lash adhesive will adhere properly. Work carefully and gently. Follow the manufacturer's instructions carefully.

  Note: If the artificial lash application is in conjunction with a makeup application, complete the makeup either with or without applying mascara to the lashes, and then finish with the false lashes.

Procedure

1 Brush the client's eyelashes to make sure they are clean and free of foreign matter, such as mascara particles (unless this is part of a makeup application). If the client's lashes are straight, they can be curled with an eyelash curler before you apply the artificial lashes.

2 Carefully remove the eyelash band from the package. Tweezers work well for this.

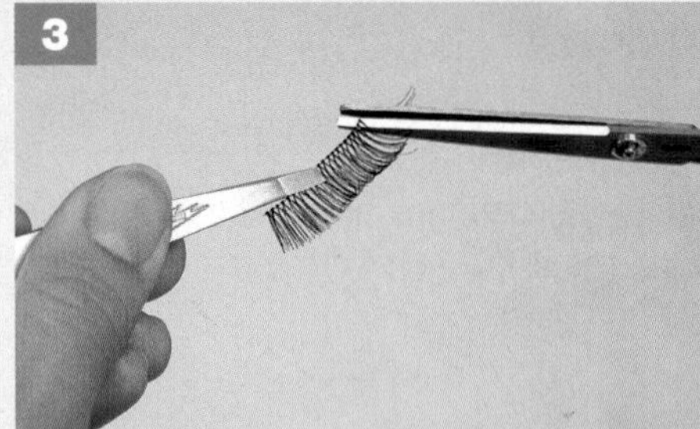

3 Start with the upper lash. If the band lash is too long to fit the curve of the upper eyelid, trim the outside edge. Hold this up to the eye to measure the length. Use your fingers to bend the lash into a horseshoe shape to make it more flexible so it fits the contour of the eyelid.

4 Feather straight band lashes to make uneven lengths on the end ("w" shapes) by nipping into it with the points of your scissors if desired. This creates a more natural look.

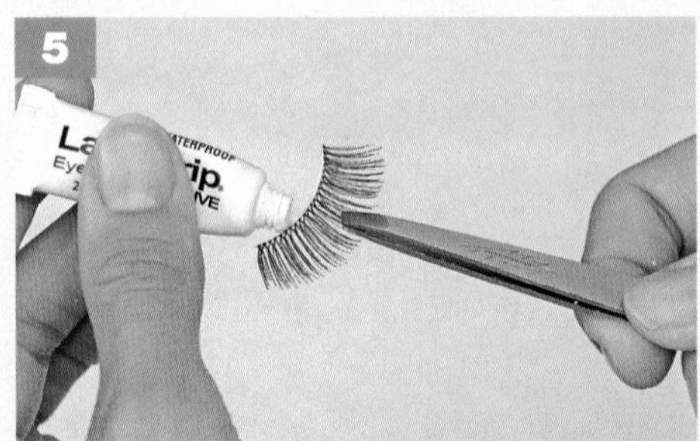
5

5 Apply a thin strip of lash adhesive to the base of the false lashes with a toothpick or hairpin and allow a few seconds for it to set.

6a

6b

6 Apply the lashes by holding the ends with the fingers or tweezers. Make sure there is not an excess of glue and that the client can open their eyes once applied. Remove any excess glue and reposition the lashes as necessary.

For band lashes: Start with the shorter part of the lash and place it on the natural lashes at the inner corner of the eye, toward the nose. Position the rest of the artificial lash as close to the client's own lash as possible, not on the skin.

For individual lashes: Apply five or six lashes, evenly spacing each one across the lash line. Use longer lashes on the outer edges of the eye, medium length in the middle, and short on the inside by the nose. Cut lash lengths as needed.

Use the rounded end of a lash liner brush, the round side of a hairpin, or tweezers to press the lash on without adhering it to the glue. Be very careful and gentle when applying the lashes. Remove any excess glue and recomb or reposition lashes as necessary.

Note: Apply eyeliner before the lash is applied. An additional liquid liner may be used to finish the look if it does not affect the false lash adhesion. Adding a coat of clear mascara can help false lashes adhere to natural lashes.

7 ***Optional:*** Apply the lower lash, if desired. Lower lash application is optional; it tends to look more unnatural. Trim the lash as necessary, and apply adhesive in the same way you did for the upper lash. Place the lash on top or beneath the client's lower lash. Place the shorter lash toward the center of the eye and the longer lash toward the outer part.

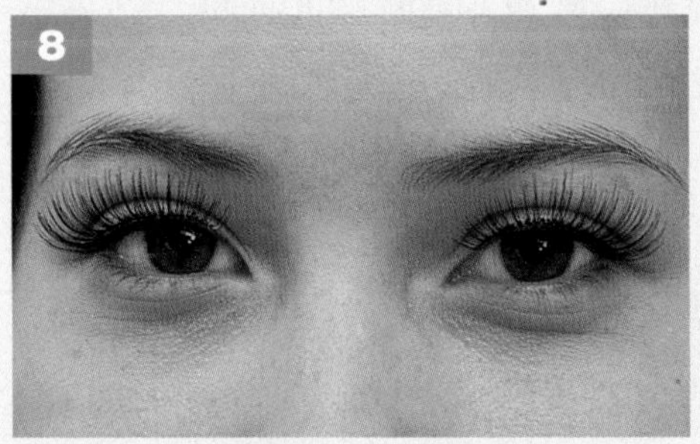
8

8 Check the finished application and make sure the client is comfortable with the lashes. Remind the client to take special care with artificial lashes when swimming, bathing, or cleansing the face. Water, oil, or cleansing products will loosen artificial lashes. Band lash applications last one day and are meant to be removed nightly. Individual lashes may last longer.

Post-Service

- **Complete** 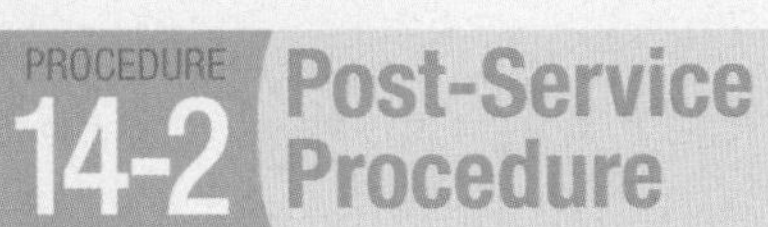

PAGE 375 ✓ L012

PROCEDURE 20-3

Lash and Brow Tinting Procedure

IMPLEMENTS AND MATERIALS

Supplies

- EPA-registered disinfectant
- Headband
- Hand towels
- Plastic mixing cup
- Distilled water
- Small bowl of water
- Timer
- Brow comb or mascara wand
- Eyeliner brush
- Small scissors
- Lined waste container

Products

- Cleanser or eye makeup remover
- Witch hazel
- Petroleum jelly/occlusive cream
- Lash tint kits: black for lashes and brown for brows unless client requests otherwise

Single-use Items

- Cotton swabs (12)
- Round cotton pads (8)
- Protective paper sheaths (1 under each eye)
- Sealable sandwich bag (to discard waste in)

Preparation

- **Perform**  PROCEDURE 14-1 Pre-Service Procedure PAGE 372

Procedure

1 Wash hands.

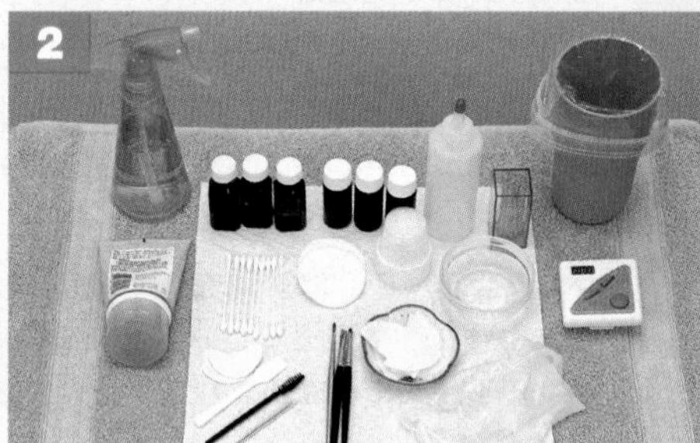

2 Gather and set out supplies.

3 Wet cotton pads and cotton swabs. Cut supply amounts in half if doing only one procedure on either the brows or lashes.

4 Conduct the client consultation, and have the client sign the release form.

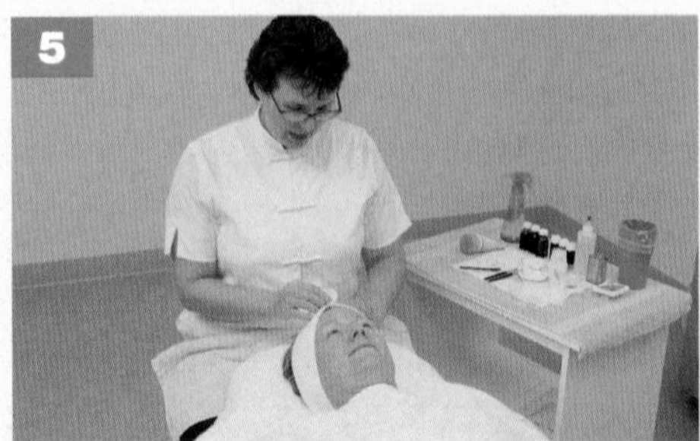

5 Drape the client with a headband and towel around the neck.

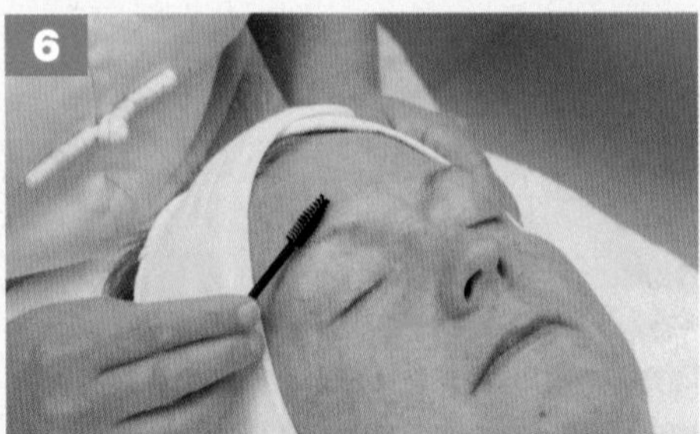

6 Wash your hands and cleanse the brow and/or lash area. All makeup must be removed and the area clean and dry before applying tint. Brush brows into place.

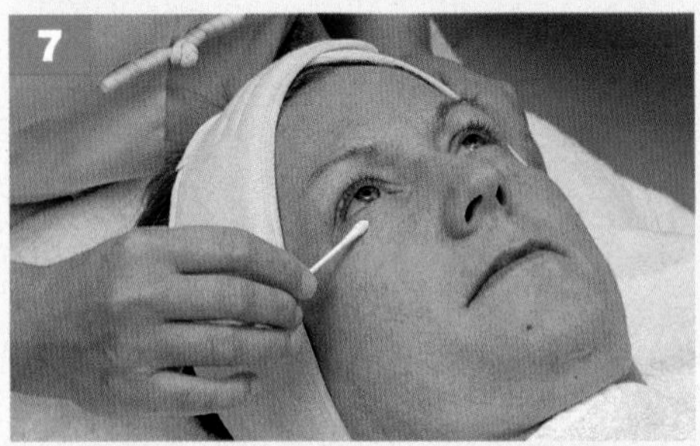

7 Apply protective cream with a cotton swab directly next to the area where you are tinting to protect the skin, covering the area where you do not want the tint. Do not touch the hairs with cream because this interferes with the color. Apply cream around the brow area. Apply under the eyelashes on the skin below the eye and above the lashes, just next to the lash line.

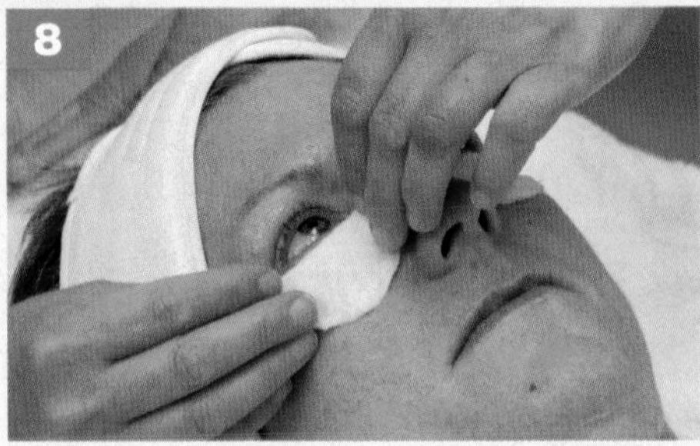

8 ***For lash tinting:*** Apply pads under the eyes and over the cream to keep tint from bleeding onto the skin. Use the paper sheaths in the tint kit, or you can make thin cotton pads from cotton rounds.

You may have to cut or adjust pad shapes to fit under the eyes. Pads should be under the lashes as close to the eye as possible without hoiding or interfering with the lower lashes.

To make cotton pads: Wet the pads and squeeze out excess water, tearing them so they are half as thick. Then fold in half to make half-moon shaped pads.

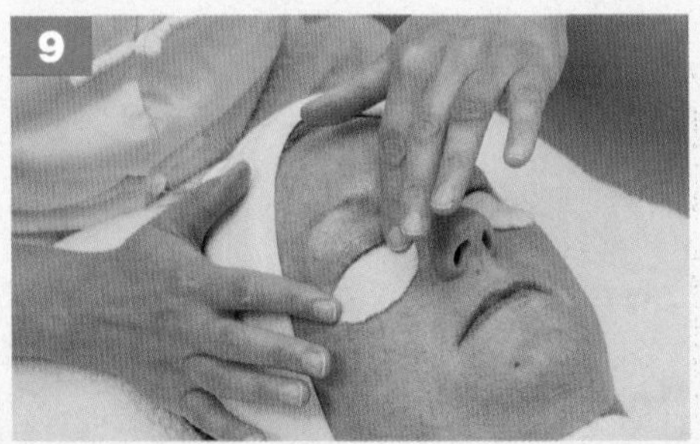

9 ***For lash tinting:*** Have the client close her eyes, and adjust the pad so it sits next to the eye—not bunched up too close to the eye. If the pad is too close or too wet, tint may wick into the eye and onto the skin.

Note: You can start with the lashes and do the brows while the lash tint is processing. Generally, tint can sit on the lashes longer than the brows if you are going for a natural brow-look.

PROCEDURE

20-3 Lash and Brow Tinting Procedure (continued)

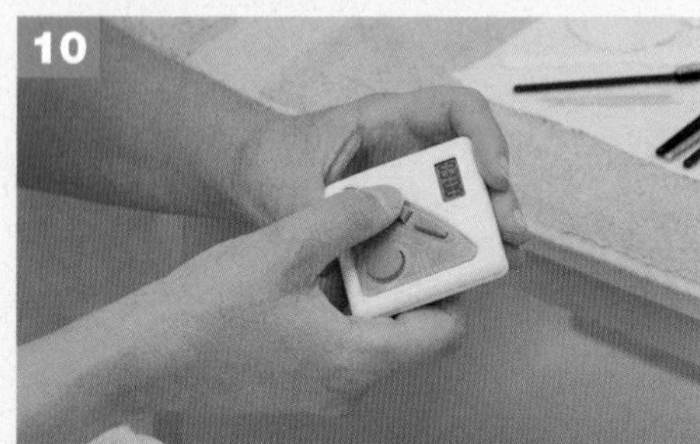

10 Set timer according to manufacturer's directions and have wet pads and cotton swabs ready to use for rinsing.

11 ***For brows:*** The tint can be diluted with water in a 1:1 ratio in a mixing cup to lighten the color.

Caution: Brows can absorb color quickly, so be ready to remove it right away to avoid excess color. Make sure you do not get your colors mixed up if using both brown (brows) and black (lashes).

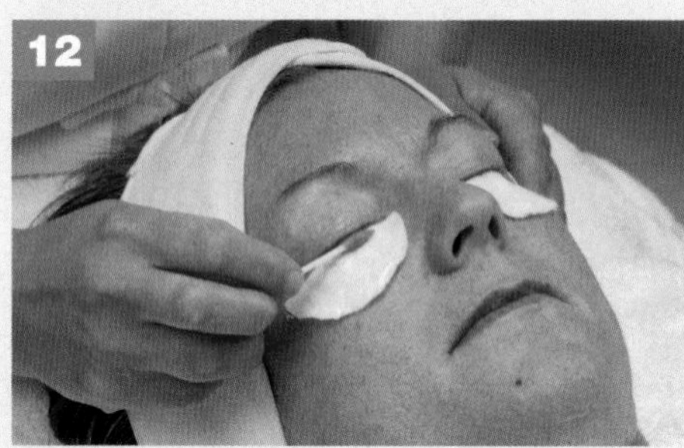

12 ***Apply tint:*** Dip cotton swab or brush applicator into tint (bottle #1), blot excess, apply and carefully saturate the lashes or brows. Brush on lashes from base to tip. Brush on brows from the inside out to the edge. A toothpick can be used to hold up the brow hair off of the skin while applying to avoid getting the product on the skin. Hold up different sections and work across the brow.

13 Leave on for 3 minutes or as directed. Some tint kits have only one bottle and combine the tint and developer into one application. Alter the procedure accordingly. Do not double-dip—use a new applicator each time to reapply.

CAUTION!

To avoid eye damage, do not let tint or water drip into the client's eyes. Have the client keep her eyes closed the whole time.

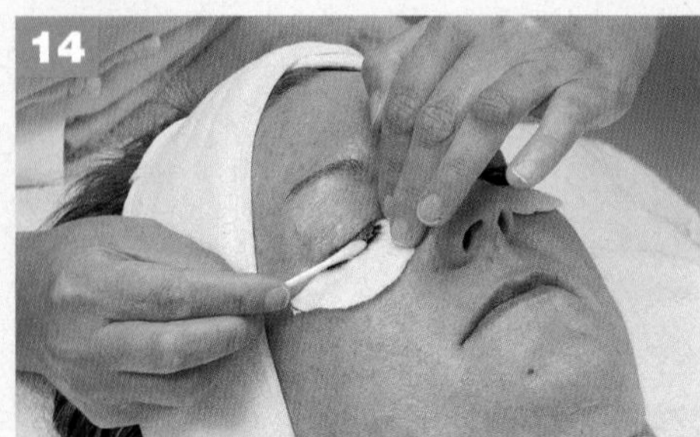

14 With a new applicator, carefully apply the developer (bottle #2 for some kits) for 1 minute or as directed.

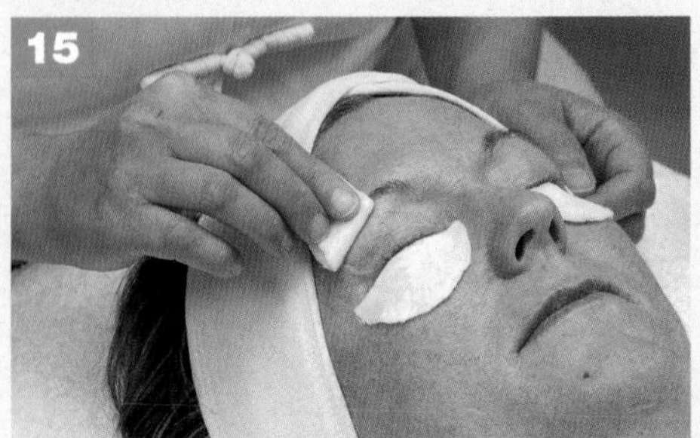

15 Rinse each area with water at least three times with wet cotton swabs and cotton pads without dripping water into the eyes.

Tip: Before rinsing, you can replace the under-eye shields if necessary (if color is bleeding through the pads to the skin). Make sure the tint does not touch the skin.

16 Ask the client if she feels any discomfort, and have her flush the eyes with water at the sink if necessary. It is common for the eyes to feel a little grainy after tinting, so rinsing is a good idea.

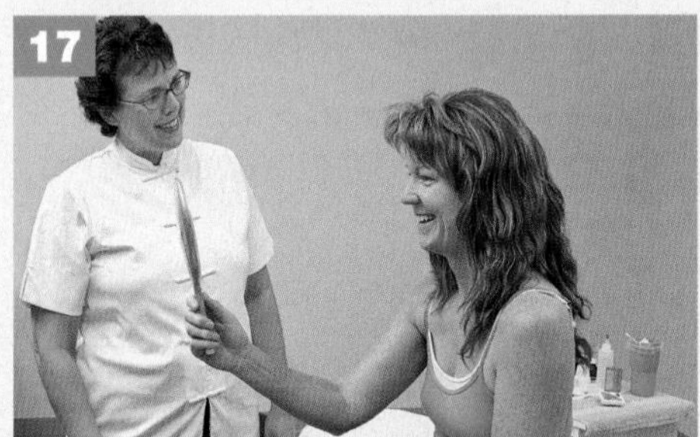

17 Show the application to the client.

Post-Service

- **Complete** PROCEDURE 14-2 **Post-Service Procedure** PAGE 375
- After the service is completed (and before the cleanup), fill out the client chart, and make any product suggestions and sales. ✓ LO13

Review Questions

1. What is the primary goal of makeup application?
2. List the primary and secondary colors.
3. What are complementary colors?
4. Define warm and cool colors.
5. Give two examples each of warm and cool colors.
6. List at least five safety measures that should be followed when applying makeup to avoid product contamination.
7. What are five of the makeup questions you ask the client in a makeup consultation?
8. List the 15 steps of makeup application in the typical order they are performed.
9. What colors are used to tone down red?
10. What are the eight color selection steps used to choose makeup colors?
11. What is shading, or contouring, used for?
12. Where on the face could you apply a highlighter?
13. How do you measure the ideal eyebrow shape?
14. Name and describe the two types of artificial eyelashes.
15. What ingredient found in lash tint products should not be used?

Glossary

band lashes	Also known as *strip lashes*; eyelash hairs on a strip that are applied with adhesive to the natural lash line.
cake makeup	Also known as *pancake makeup*; a heavy-coverage makeup pressed into a compact and applied to the face with a moistened cosmetic sponge.
complementary colors	Primary and secondary colors opposite one another on the color wheel.
concealers	Cosmetics used to cover blemishes and discolorations; may be applied before or after foundation.
cool colors	Colors with a blue undertone that suggest coolness and are dominated by blues, greens, violets, and blue-reds.
eye tabbing	Procedure in which individual synthetic eyelashes are attached directly to a client's own lashes at their base.
foundation	Also known as *base makeup*; a tinted cosmetic used to cover or even out skin tone and coloring of the skin.
greasepaint	Heavy makeup used for theatrical purposes.
individual lashes	Separate artificial eyelashes that are applied on top of the lashes one at a time.
matte	Nonshiny; dull.
primary colors	Yellow, red, and blue; fundamental colors that cannot be obtained from a mixture.
secondary colors	Colors obtained by mixing equal parts of two primary colors.
tertiary colors	Intermediate color achieved by mixing a secondary color and its neighboring primary color on the color wheel in equal amounts.
warm colors	The range of colors with yellow undertones; from yellow and gold through oranges, red-oranges, most reds, and even some yellow-greens.

Business Skills

PART 5

CHAPTER 21
Career Planning

Chapter Outline

- Why Study Career Planning?
- Preparing for Licensure
- Preparing for Employment
- Preparing Your Resume
- The Job Search
- On the Job
- The Job Description
- Employee Evaluation
- Compensation
- Independent Contractors
- Managing Money
- Finding the Right Role Models
- Continuing Your Education
- Planning Your Success

Learning Objectives

After completing this chapter, you will be able to:

- ☑ **LO1** Explain the steps involved in preparing for and passing the licensing exam.
- ☑ **LO2** Discuss the essentials of becoming test-wise.
- ☑ **LO3** Describe those qualities that are needed to be successful in a service profession.
- ☑ **LO4** List and describe the various types of esthetics practices and determine your employment options.
- ☑ **LO5** Demonstrate effective techniques for writing a good resume.
- ☑ **LO6** Discuss methods for exploring the job market and researching potential employers.
- ☑ **LO7** Be prepared to complete a successful job interview.
- ☑ **LO8** List the habits of a good salon player.
- ☑ **LO9** Recognize the importance of a job description.
- ☑ **LO10** Describe the different methods of compensation that are utilized in esthetics.
- ☑ **LO11** Explain the importance of meeting financial responsibilities and managing money well.
- ☑ **LO12** List several ways you can benefit from good role models.
- ☑ **LO13** Understand the importance of continuing your education.

Key Terms

Page number indicates where in the chapter the term is used.

commission
pg. 658

deductive reasoning
pg. 626

franchised salon or spa
pg. 637

independent contractor
pg. 660

information interview
pg. 638

job description
pg. 653

networking
pg. 640

quotas
pg. 659

resume
pg. 631

role model
pg. 662

salary
pg. 657

test-wise
pg. 625

transferable skills
pg. 634

A desire to help people is often at the top of the list of reasons why individuals choose a career in esthetics. Esthetics is a caring, nurturing profession that helps others to feel positive about their appearance. However, there are many facets of esthetics to consider in planning your career.

Whether this is your first job or you are making the transition from another occupation, defining your reasons for entering the field of esthetics is an important first step in developing long-term goals and short-term objectives.

As you embark on your newly chosen career path, take some time to think about your personal goals. Begin by naming at least three reasons why esthetics appeals to you. Next list three services that you especially like to perform. What other aspects of being an esthetician do you enjoy? For example, do you like to consult with clients or recommend products, track your sales progress, or make follow-up phone calls to see how clients are doing with a new skin care program? Name at least two tasks that are not hands-on that you find rewarding. Finally, state what you would like to be doing 5 years from now. Perhaps this involves moving on to another aspect of skin care, such as education, running your own salon, or becoming a sales representative. Developing a better understanding of your long-term goals and short-term objectives will help you to make the best choices as you plan your esthetics career.

FOCUS ON

Career Goals

To be successful in the field of esthetics you must be passionate about your work and committed to achieving your goals. Defining your reasons for becoming an esthetician, finding out what you like most about your work, and planning your career goals will help you to stay focused on achieving them.

1. State three reasons why esthetics appeals to you.
2. List the three services you most like to perform.
3. Name two tasks that are not hands-on that you find rewarding.
4. What does your dream job look like upon graduation?
5. Where would you like to be 5 years from now?

Why Study Career Planning?

There are many employment options available to estheticians today. Careful preparation for your licensing exam and a good understanding of the job requirements will give you the confidence you need to excel at interviews and become gainfully employed.

- A successful employment search is a job in itself, and there are many tools that can give you the edge—as well as mistakes that can cost you an interview or a job.
- You must pass your State Board Exam to be licensed and you must be licensed to be hired; therefore, preparing for licensure and passing your exam is your first step to employment success.
- The ability to pinpoint the work environment that is right for you is an important prerequisite in targeting potential employers.
- Proactively preparing the right materials, such as a great resume, and practicing your interviewing skills will give you the confidence that is needed to secure a job in a salon or spa that you love.

Preparing for Licensure

The preparation period before you enter the workforce is an exciting time. But before you can actually apply for a job, you must first fulfill the required number of hours for esthetics training and pass your state licensing exam (**Figure 21–1**).

Hopefully, you have developed good study habits and practice skills during the course of your esthetics program. These will come in handy as you prepare for the exam. Your school may offer additional assistance for test preparation. If so, you should take advantage of these options. However, there is no substitute for a solid understanding of the material. Mastery of the course content is essential to passing the exam. As you become comfortable with the various testing methods used in your program, your confidence will increase and you will be better prepared for taking the final licensing exam.

▲ **Figure 21–1**
Developing good study habits and practice skills now will help you prepare for the state licensing exam.

Preparing for the Test

Test anxiety can be a real issue for many students. If you are subject to pre-test jitters, there are several simple strategies that can help to alleviate much of the stress involved. A **test-wise** student begins to prepare for taking a test by practicing the good study habits and time management skills outlined in Chapter 2, Life Skills, that are such an important part of effective studying. The following are some tips that will help you to gain control of the test situation.

- Read content carefully and become an active studier.
- Take effective notes during class.
- Organize your notebook and class handouts for easy review.
- Separate vocabulary lists and study these carefully.
- Scan your text and review end-of-chapter questions.
- Take advantage of any audio tapes and interactive CDs that are available to help you review the material.
- Listen carefully in class for any cues and clues about what questions could be expected on the test.
- Use any study guides that are available from the state board of examination or in conjunction with your text.
- Review tests or quizzes taken as part of your course work.
- Plan your study schedule so that you are not cramming the night before the test.
- Pay attention to any tips offered by your instructors.

In addition to good study habits, there are other, more holistic test-wise habits to keep in mind as you prepare to take the test.

- Take good care of yourself in the days and weeks before an exam; eat right, exercise, and get plenty of rest.

- Maintain a positive attitude that supports passing the test as a necessary and useful step in the process of achieving your goal of becoming a licensed esthetician.
- Anticipate feeling some anxiety but note that a certain amount of anxiety may actually help you to do better. ✓ L01

Did You Know?

If you have a physician-documented disability, such as a learning disability, your state may allow you extra time to take the test, or even provide a special examiner. Ask your instructor and check with your state licensing board. Be certain to make any special arrangements well in advance of the test date.

Taking the Test

Many techniques can be useful in preparation for testing. For instance, it may help you to practice relaxation methods or to arrive early to become familiar with the surroundings. But the most important thing to keep in mind is that you must have knowledge of the test material. If you are unsure of certain information, take time to review the material beforehand.

Deductive Reasoning

One of the best techniques that students should learn to use for better results is called deductive reasoning. **Deductive reasoning** is the process of reaching logical conclusions by employing logical reasoning.

Some strategies associated with deductive reasoning follow.

- **Eliminate options known to be incorrect.** The more answers you can eliminate as incorrect, the better your chances of identifying the correct one.
- **Watch for key words or terms.** Look for any qualifying conditions or statements. Keep an eye out for such words as *usually, commonly, in most instances, never, always,* and the like.
- **Study the stem.** The stem is the basic question or problem. It often provides a clue to the answer. Look for a match between the stem and one of the choices.
- **Watch for grammatical clues.** For instance, if the last word in a stem is *an,* the answer must begin with a vowel rather than a consonant.
- **Look at similar or related questions.** They may provide clues.
- **In answering essay questions, watch for key words.** Look for words like *compare, contrast, discuss, evaluate, analyze, define,* or *describe* and develop your answer accordingly.
- **In tests that contain long paragraphs of reading followed by several questions, read the questions first.** This will help you identify the important elements in the paragraph.

Understanding Test Formats

Tests are developed using numerous styles and formats. These commonly include *true or false, multiple choice, matching,* and *essay* questions. Here are some important points to consider when answering each of these kinds of questions.

True or False

True or false questions offer only two choices. Sometimes the question can be presented so that it seems there is an element of truth in each answer. But it is important to remember that for an answer to be true, the entire sentence must be true. In general, long statements are more likely to be true than short statements because it takes more detail to provide truthful, factual information. When in doubt, look for qualifying words such as *all, some, no, none, always, usually, sometimes, never, little, equal, less, good,* or *bad.* For the most part, questions that use absolutes such as *all, none, always,* or *never* are generally not true.

Multiple Choice

Multiple-choice questions typically offer the tester a selection of four to six responses. However, in some cases more than one choice may be true, so it is always important to look for the best answer. A process of elimination can be helpful in determining the right choice. Note that when two choices are close or similar, one is probably right; when two choices are identical, both must be wrong; when two choices are opposites, one is probably right and one is probably wrong. However, this also depends on the other choices. Often, but not always, if one of the choices states "all of the above," it is the correct answer. If you are unsure, it is helpful to pay attention to qualifying words such as *not, except,* and *but.* It is also possible to find the answer to one question in the stem of another. As you work through the answer it can be helpful to cross out wrong answers, provided you are allowed to write on the test exam booklet.

Multiple choice is the most commonly used test format and has been adopted by the majority of state boards for written and theory-based examinations.

Matching Questions

Matching questions to answers is a relatively straightforward method of testing, because the right answer is always available; however, these questions assume that you have knowledge of the material. Sometimes the matching responses to different questions can be similar or confusing. It may be helpful to check off items from the response list as you use them to eliminate the number of choices as you go along.

Essay Questions

Essay questions are open-ended and allow the test taker some leeway in how she or he can present an answer. Before putting pen to paper, always take a few moments to organize your thoughts. Frequently, the question itself will suggest a method for organizing your response. Look for cue words in the question to help you, and begin by creating an outline to structure your response. For example, if you are asked to compare and contrast two items, make a list of the characteristics of each. This will help you to frame your response. It is also important to remember that essay questions are designed to test your reasoning skills. When you have completed your answer, always review what you have written. Be sure you have addressed the question asked completely and accurately and that you have provided the information in an organized and clear manner.

On Test Day

When you are taking written exams, it is always wise to do the following:

- Listen carefully to all verbal directions given by the examiner.
- Do not hesitate to ask the examiner questions if something is not clear.
- Enter identifying information, such as your name, before you begin answering questions.
- Read all written directions carefully before you begin.
- Scan the entire test before you start.
- Wear a watch to monitor your time.
- Read each question carefully before answering.
- Answer those questions you are sure about first.
- Save difficult questions or ones you are unsure of for last.
- Mark any questions you skip, so that you can find them easily later.
- Answer as many questions as possible.
- If you have time at the end of the exam, review your answers. If you feel compelled to change an answer, make sure there is sufficient reason to do so.
- Check that you have entered all pertinent information correctly.

The Practical Examination

Although requirements vary, in most states you must also be prepared for a test of your practical or hands-on skills. If your state requires a practical examination, you will probably receive some notice of the materials that you will be required to bring to perform this portion of the test, including whether it is necessary to bring a model. Always take time to review any notices, materials, or pamphlets you receive. This information will give you a good idea of what to anticipate. Your instructors can also be useful resources in helping you to prepare for this part of the test. If a trial run is available, take advantage of any opportunities to participate. If you do not, it is a good idea to perform your own trials, paying close attention to timing, infection control, and safety procedures. Finally, make sure you are familiar with the location of the test site and the amount of time it will take you to get there on time. Arriving late will only increase your anxiety level and may even prevent you from taking the exam. ☑ **LO2**

Preparing for Employment

When you chose a career in esthetics, your primary goal was to get a good job. To fulfill that goal, you will need to showcase your best qualities to prospective employers. To define these qualities, you will need to answer two very important questions:

1. What are my strongest practical skills?
2. What personal qualities do I possess that will make me a good hire?

The inventory of personal characteristics and technical skills (**Figure 21–2** on page 630) will help you to answer these questions. After you have completed this inventory and identified the areas that need further attention, you can then determine where to focus the remainder of your training. ☑ **L03**

Surveying Your Options

Deciding on the type of esthetics practice that is right for you is an important part of the job search. Traditionally, the field of skin care grew out of the beauty salon business, where the main focus was on hair and nail services. Since acquiring separate licensing, the field of esthetics has expanded to include several new business opportunities. While there are many variations of skin care practices, the following general categories highlight those that are referenced frequently.

- ***The independent skin care clinic*** or ***day spa*** offers a variety of skin care treatments and may include facial and body treatments, hair removal, makeup artistry, nail care services, massage therapy, and other holistic health practices.
- The ***full-service salon*** provides a total beauty experience including hair services, makeup artistry, and nail and skin care; it also may offer a combination of other holistic health practices similar to those available at the skin care clinic or day spa.
- The ***wellness center*** or ***spa*** is focused on maintaining optimal health and may combine several holistic, complementary, or alternative health-care practices with more traditional medical practices, exercise and nutrition counseling, medical aesthetic procedures, beauty treatments, skin care, and spa services to promote an inclusive wellness program. The wellness center or spa may exist as an independent operation or can be incorporated within a health, fitness, or destination-type spa facility.
- The ***medical spa*** integrates a variety of medical aesthetic and surgical procedures with esthetic skin care treatments and spa services. The *medi-spa,* as it is often referred to, may exist in a hospital setting, laser center, or independent medical practice, such as a cosmetic surgery or dermatology office. The medical aesthetic practice employs a diverse, well-trained staff that can include physicians, nurses, estheticians, and other professionals such as massage therapists and electrologists. Treatments in the medical spa are mainly focused on clinical procedures, such as dermal filler injection therapy, chemical peels, laser treatments, and dermatological

INVENTORY OF PERSONAL CHARACTERISTICS

PERSONAL CHARACTERISTIC	Excellent	Good	Avg.	Poor	Plan for Improvement
Posture, Deportment, Poise					
Grooming, Personal Hygiene					
Manners, Courtesy					
Communications Skills					
Attitude					
Self-motivation					
Personal Habits					
Responsibility					
Self-esteem, Self-confidence					
Honesty, Integrity					
Dependability					

INVENTORY OF TECHNICAL SKILLS

TECHNICAL SKILLS	Excellent	Good	Avg.	Poor	Plan for Improvement
Skin Analysis					
Skin Conditions					
Fitzpatrick Scale					
Basic Facials					
Advanced Skin Care					
Body Treatments					
Use of Equipment					
Waxing					
Makeup					
Retail Sales					
Other					

After analyzing the above responses, would you hire yourself as an employee in your firm? Why or why not?
State your short-term goals that you hope to accomplish in 6 to 12 months:
State your long-term goals that you hope to accomplish in 1 to 5 years:

▲ Figure 21–2
Inventory of personal characteristics and technical skills.

and cosmetic surgery procedures that require pre- and postoperative skin care (**Figure 21–3**).

- The ***destination spa*** is an all-inclusive spa retreat that offers patrons a wide range of health, beauty, and wellness programs such as fitness, nutrition, massage, skin care, beauty treatments, educational classes, and more. This environment, as the name implies, involves travel to a specific location and includes hotel accommodations.
- The ***resort*** or ***hotel spa*** is an amenity spa that provides guests with a variety of spa services that may include skin care, massage, and hair and nail services. The amenity spa may also be available to local patrons and residents who wish to receive services on a regular basis.
- ***Booth rental*** establishments, or the practice of leasing a room to provide services independently, is an option in some states. Opportunities may exist in a variety of skin care salon and spa businesses. If your state board allows you to operate under this business structure, this may be the least expensive way of owning your own business. ✔ L04

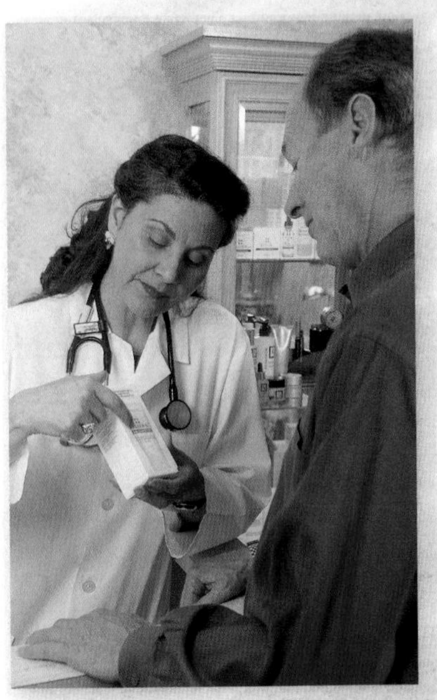

▲ Figure 21–3
The medical spa integrates medical aesthetics and surgical procedures with skin care and spa services.

Preparing Your Resume

The **resume** (REH-zuh-may) provides employers with a summary of your education and work experience, highlights relevant accomplishments and achievements, and is your ticket to employment. Before you begin the task of writing your resume, you should consider that, on average, a potential employer spends about 20 seconds scanning your resume to decide whether to grant an interview.

To create a positive reaction, it is a good idea to know as much as possible about the culture you are targeting and tailor your resume accordingly. For example, if you are interested in working in a medical aesthetics practice, you should use terminology that is commonly accepted in the medical profession and highlight any experience you have that is relevant to this setting. You may also want to take a more conservative approach in your presentation style. However, if you are interested in working for a chic day spa, you might want to take a more stylish approach that demonstrates your knowledge of the latest trend-setting spa techniques.

Formatting Your Resume

There are many styles of resumes. Finding the format that works best for you will require a bit of research. Fortunately, there are numerous resources available to help you. Some esthetic training programs provide vocational guidance counseling or include resume development as part of the curriculum. If your program does not, many resources can be easily accessed at your local library, located on-line, or purchased from a bookstore.

Once you have determined the resume style and format that is right for your needs, you can begin to address more functional requirements. To be effective, your resume should be neat, concise, easy to read, grammatically correct, and error free. Ideally it should fit on one page and be formatted in a type size and font that is easy on the reader's eye. The content of your resume should incorporate several important areas, including practical knowledge, interpersonal skills, administrative and management skills, and sales abilities. In general, this information is integrated using a structure that includes the following information:

- Name, street address, telephone number, and e-mail address
- Career goals and objectives
- A summary of professional qualifications
- A history of employment or experience
- Any awards or achievements that highlight your credentials

Rather than providing a detailed account of your duties and responsibilities, it is often a good idea to focus on presenting your accomplishments (**Figure 21–4**). The goal is to get the reader's attention in a way that demonstrates your broad-based skills. Notice the difference in impact in the following statements:

- Performed facials on individuals with varying skin types and conditions.
- Developed and retained a personal client base of over 75 individuals of all ages, both male and female, with various skin types and conditions.

If you are applying for your first position as an esthetician, you may be concerned that your qualifications are inadequate compared to those of more seasoned estheticians. Do not let this discourage you; many employers are looking for eager self-starters. Highlighting student achievements such as attendance, academic awards, clinic performance, or volunteer work can also stimulate the interest you need to obtain an interview.

CAUTION!

If your state board allows you to rent space from a salon or spa owner to practice skin care independently, proceed with caution. An esthetician renting space in a salon or spa is considered self-employed and is responsible for adhering to all of the rules and regulations associated with owning and operating his or her own business. Responsibilities include but are not limited to: developing your own clientele, purchasing equipment and supplies, maintaining inventory, client record-keeping, and all of the accounting and tax obligations associated with running a small business. Before going this route conduct an honest assessment of your individual skills and abilities. Are you ready for business ownership? More importantly, are you in a position to forego the benefits commonly associated with being an employee such as health insurance, vacation time, or paid time off? Starting out, this may not be the most wise or lucrative option.

The Resume Checklist

A well-written resume is an excellent marketing tool. As you tackle putting the right words on paper, the following checklist will help you avoid problems and make the most of your individual skills.

- Use clear, concise language and avoid elaborate or cliché phrases.
- Think about writing separate resumes to target different markets if you are applying for positions that have distinct requirements, for example one that targets a medical spa and another for a skin care salon.
- Consider your audience, and use specific words they can relate to.
- Highlight your accomplishments and the methods you used to achieve them. For example, were you selected student of the month for your academic performance or for exemplary attendance?

MARY SMITH
m.smith@gmail.com

143 Fern Circle
Anytown, USA 12345

Home: (320) 555.1234
Mobile: (987) 654.3210

An esthetician with excellent technical, sales, and customer service skills who works well with people of all ages.

ACCOMPLISHMENTS

ACADEMICS Achieved an "A" average in theoretical requirements and "Excellent" ratings in technical requirements, exceeding the number of practical skills required for graduation.

Named "Student of the Month" for best attendance, best attitude, highest retail sales, and most clients served.

SALES Increased add-on services to 30 percent of my clinic volume by graduation.

Achieved an average client sales ticket comparable to $45.00 in the area salon market.

Increased retail sales of cosmetic products by over 18 percent during part-time employment at local department store.

CLIENT RETENTION Developed and retained a personal client base of over 75 individuals of all ages, both male and female, with various skin types and conditions.

MANAGEMENT Lead a student salon team in developing a business plan for opening a full-service salon. The project earned an "A" and was recognized for thoroughness, accuracy, and creativity.

As President of the Student Council, organized fundraising activities including car washes, bake sales, and yard sales which generated enough funds to send 19 students to a skin care show in El Paso.

IMAGE CONSULTANT Certified as an Image Consultant to assist in coordinating wardrobe, makeup, and hairstyles for clientele of all ages in a full-service salon.

EXTERNSHIP Trained 1 day weekly at the salon for 10 weeks under the state-approved student externship program.

SPECIAL PROJECTS Reorganized school facial room for more efficiency and client comfort.

Organized the school dispensary, which increased inventory control and streamlined operations within the clinic.

Catalogued the school's library of texts, books, videos, and other periodicals by category and updated the library inventory list.

EXPERIENCE

Salon Etc. Spring 2010
Student Extern in Esthetics

Dilberts Summer 2010
Retail Sales, Cosmetics

Food Emporium 2007–2009
Cashier

EDUCATION

Graduate, New Alamo High School, 2009
Graduate, Best Institute for Image Consultants, January 2010
Graduate, Milady Career Institute of Cosmetology, August 2011
Licensed as Esthetician, September 2011

ORGANIZATIONS

National Skin Care Association for Esthetic Professionals
American Cancer Society, "Look Good...Feel Better" Program Volunteer

▲ Figure 21–4
A sample resume for an esthetician with limited work experience.

- Present your career goals in a nonthreatening manner that encourages trust in your willingness to work cooperatively in the position that is available.
- Emphasize any **transferable skills**, such as sales training, customer service, or administrative abilities that you have mastered at other jobs and can apply to a new position.
- Choose your words carefully, using action or power words such as *established, accomplished, increased, managed, developed,* or *coordinated* for emphasis.
- Avoid making any reference to salary levels or requirements.
- State only professional references, and include the person's title, phone number, and business name on a separate page.
- Be honest in the way that you present yourself, stating only those experiences and achievements that are valid.
- Avoid including personal commentary and hobbies that are not directly related to business.

Writing Your Resume

Many people find it difficult to start the actual resume writing process. With a little organization and the right materials, writing your resume can be a lot easier than you might imagine. A computer or word processor is an ideal tool if you are creating your own materials. If you are not computer literate or do not have access to a computer, other resources are available. Try searching your local community directory for print shops or individuals that specialize in formatting resumes. Libraries are also a good resource and typically have several computers available for public use if you are without one. Some schools have computer labs and will allow students time to work on their resumes during study periods. When working on your resume at a remote location, remember to save your work on a separate disk or e-mail the information to a personal address where it can be accessed at a later time.

A good way to start organizing the content of your resume is to compile all of the documents in your possession relating to your education or work experience. These can include diplomas, continuing education or training certificates, copies of previous job applications, achievement awards or letters of recommendation, and memberships in professional organizations. Using this information, you can begin to create an outline listing pertinent information under each of the headings discussed previously. For example, make a list of your accomplishments and achievements, professional qualifications, and career objectives. Condensing this information into small bulleted phrases is a good way to begin developing sentences. Next, you can focus on choosing the best words to define your experience. A dictionary and thesaurus can be useful tools in performing this task.

When you have completed a rough draft, have someone with knowledge about resume writing review it for you. An objective opinion can lend valuable insight, pointing out areas that you may have overlooked. You should also double-check your spelling and grammar for errors. In this technological age, resumes are often delivered electronically via the Internet. If you are mailing a hard copy of your resume, the right stationery and envelopes are also important in creating a positive impression. Remember to keep your target market in mind when selecting paper, and be sure to buy enough for a coordinating cover letter. A good quality white, buff, or grey bond paper is generally a good way to go. ☑ L05

The Cover Letter

Your cover letter completes the presentation of your professional qualifications and should be written using a professional letter format (**Figure 21–5**). Begin your letter with a statement that identifies the position you are interested in, and include the reason you are interested

Your Name

Your Address

Your Phone Number

*Ms. (or Mr.)*__________________

Salon Name

Salon Address

Dear Ms. (or Mr.)__________________,

We met in August when you allowed me to observe your salon and staff while I was still in skin care training. Since that time, I have graduated and have received my license, which allows me to practice esthetics. I have enclosed my resume for your review and consideration.

I would very much appreciate the opportunity to meet with you and discuss either current or future career opportunities at your salon. I was extremely impressed with your staff and business, and I would like to discuss with you how my skills and training might add to your salon's success.

I will call you next week to discuss a time that is convenient for us to meet. I look forward to meeting with you again soon.

Sincerely,

(your name)

▲ **Figure 21–5 A sample resume cover letter.**

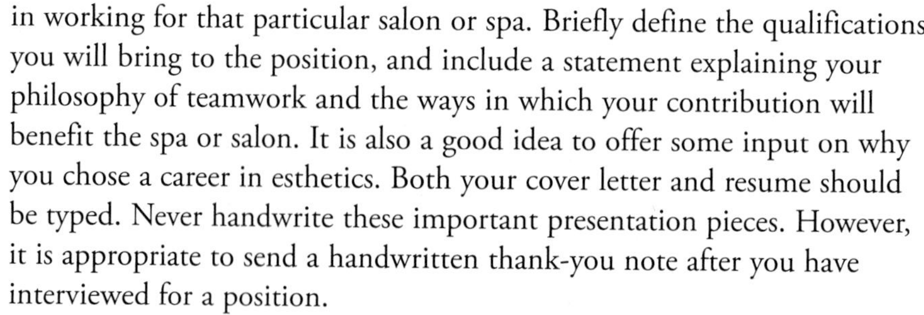

in working for that particular salon or spa. Briefly define the qualifications you will bring to the position, and include a statement explaining your philosophy of teamwork and the ways in which your contribution will benefit the spa or salon. It is also a good idea to offer some input on why you chose a career in esthetics. Both your cover letter and resume should be typed. Never handwrite these important presentation pieces. However, it is appropriate to send a handwritten thank-you note after you have interviewed for a position.

In addition to your written resume, you may also have a portfolio of your work that includes before and after photos relating to skin care or makeup artistry, award certificates, or letters of recognition for community service or volunteer work. Materials of this nature should not be included with your resume; however, they make an excellent presentation when interviewing. If you intend to use such materials, arrange them in a neat portfolio so the interviewer can review them easily.

Job Application

PRE-EMPLOYMENT FORM
EQUAL OPPORTUNITY EMPLOYER

Personal Information
NAME (LAST NAME FIRST)
ADDRESS
PHONE NO.
CITY
SOCIAL SECURITY NO.
STATE
REFERRED BY
ZIP CODE

Employment Desired
POSITION
DATE YOU CAN START
SALARY DESIRED
ARE YOU EMPLOYED? Yes No
IF SO, MAY WE INQUIRE OF YOUR PRESENT EMPLOYER? Yes No
EVER APPLIED TO THIS COMPANY BEFORE? Yes No
WHERE?
WHEN?

Education History

	NAME OF SCHOOL	YEARS ATTENDED	SUBJECTS STUDIED	DIPLOMA/DEGREE
GRAMMAR SCHOOL				
HIGH SCHOOL				
COLLEGE				
TRADE, BUSINESS OR CORRESPONDENCE SCHOOL				

General Information

OR NAVAL SERVICE
RANK

Employers

YEAR	NAME & ADDRESS OF EMPLOYER	SALARY	POSITION	REASON FOR LEAVING
TO				
TO				
TO				

The Job Search

With a completed resume in hand, you are now ready to present yourself to prospective employers. The job search is an exciting process that will open up many new doors. To make the most of your efforts, it is a good idea to be clear about any personal prerequisites you may have and to gather as much information as possible before calling on employers.

Finding the Salon or Spa That Is Right for You

Finding the right work environment takes careful planning and preparation. With loans to repay and living expenses to meet, of course you are eager to earn real wages. But money does not necessarily guarantee satisfaction. Before you accept the first job opportunity that comes along, take time to find out as much as possible about a salon's history and philosophy. This will help you to make critical choices about whether you will be happy working there.

When searching for a good job fit, ask yourself the following important questions.

- ***What is the most important consideration for me in terms of work conditions?*** Each individual will have his or her own agenda; however, things to think about might include flexibility in scheduling, salary, benefits, opportunity for advancement, safety, or ethical considerations.
- ***Am I in agreement with the salon or spa's philosophy?*** Learning that you are opposed to meeting a sales quota, performing a particular treatment, or using certain products after you have accepted a position makes it hard to exit gracefully. By taking a look at all aspects of a company's philosophy or policies, the types of products they use and the primary focus of their treatments, you can decide what you are comfortable with beforehand.

- ***Do I have any other obligations that may interfere with the demands of this particular situation?*** It is always best to be honest. Trying to work around other duties or responsibilities may become a burden that will compromise your ability to do a good job and jeopardize your position. If you are unavailable at certain times or days of the month, make sure your employer is informed and willing to consent to your schedule.
- ***What support will I need to ensure my success?*** The salon or spa industry has become increasingly competitive. To maintain credibility, you must continue to keep abreast of new treatments and techniques. Finding the support you need to do your job well can become a critical issue after you have graduated. Mentors may not be readily available, and workshops and seminars could become prohibitively expensive. It is always best to find out what options are available to continue your education before you start a job. Learning that your employer is not invested in providing you with opportunities to enhance your performance may ultimately become a lesson in frustration.
- ***Are there any causes that you feel passionate about?*** Some people have ethical or moral issues that are compelling enough to make them take a stand. These may be related to personal, cultural, or political differences. For example, you may have strong feelings about working on Sundays or using products that are tested on animals. If you hold certain opinions or views that you feel strongly about, be sure these are a good fit and can be tolerated within the environment where you will be working. Becoming a crusader for certain rights or privileges may or may not make you employee of the month.

Qualifying Your Options

Many people enter the field of esthetics with the dream of working in a particular setting. Some might want to work at a chic urban day spa or a health and wellness center, while others will crave a more intimate atmosphere. Understanding more about the qualitative differences in salon and spa environments will help you to narrow your search and find the best fit for your personality and style.

There are many variations of the general categories stated previously. Skin care salons and spas range from basic to glamorous, and prices vary according to location and clientele. These options can exist in urban, suburban, or rural settings. Salons or spas may be franchised, independent, or corporately owned. They can be full service, specialized, or health oriented, and they may be categorized as skin care clinics, salons, and day spas, destination, or medical spas. A **franchised salon or spa** (FRAN-chyzed suh-LON or SPAH) is owned by individuals who pay a certain fee to use the company name, and it is part of a larger organization or chain of salons. The franchise operates according to a specified business plan and set protocols and is able to offer certain advantages associated with more corporate environments, such as national marketing campaigns and employee benefits packages. Important decisions such as the size, location, décor, and menu of services are dictated by the parent company.

Small ***independently owned skin care clinics*** and ***day spas*** afford the owner greater freedom and control in decision making, which in turn can allow them to be more flexible in their dealings with employees. Benefits may be fewer; however, this does not necessarily mean that income is inadequate. Practitioners who prefer a more intimate setting and like to work closely with a smaller group of practitioners may find this experience very rewarding. Many also associate the small skin care clinic, salon, or spa with a greater opportunity to build long-lasting relationships with clientele.

The ***full-service salon*** or ***day spa*** can be a fast-paced hub of activity appealing to those who appreciate the full spectrum of beauty and the opportunity to become part of a larger team or network. Chic, high-end image salons or day spas may appeal to more cosmopolitan personalities who like to be on the cutting edge of beauty and fashion.

The ***resort*** or ***destination spa*** is associated with a hotel facility and can be just the right fit for the esthetician who likes to work with a constantly changing clientele. This climate may also afford more corporate-style benefits and educational opportunities.

Finally, the ***medical spa*** or ***wellness center*** may be an ideal situation for those estheticians who are more focused on the health benefits or age-management aspect of skin care.

Before you decide on the setting that is best for you, take time to visit and research a variety of operations (**Figure 21–6**). If you do not find the type of spa or salon you are looking for in your locale, there are many trade publications, consumer magazines, and Web sites that can provide you with more in-depth information to help you make your decision.

The Salon Visit or Information Interview

One of the best ways to learn about a salon or spa is to request an **information interview**, a scheduled meeting or conversation whose sole purpose is to gather information. Whether in person or over the telephone, having a chat with the owner, employees, or clients who frequent a salon you are interested in is a good place to start. Asking questions without the added pressure of being a job candidate may also be a less stressful approach to getting the answers you want. Just be sure to be diplomatic and prepared; remember those granting an information interview have taken valuable time to help you. In turn you should be prompt, courteous, and respectful of any boundaries they may impose.

Visiting salons before you graduate is also a good way to network. Many salon owners or managers are eager to meet students looking for employment. At the same time, this will give you the opportunity to compare different types of esthetic salons, service menus, pricing, and styles of management. When requesting an information interview, always use professional telephone etiquette. Begin the conversation by identifying yourself as a student interested in learning more about salon operations. Ask to speak to the owner or manager, and politely request a few moments

SALON VISIT CHECKLIST

When you visit a salon, observe the following areas and rate them from 1 to 5, with 5 considered being the best.

_____ SALON IMAGE: Is the salon's image pleasing to you and appropriate for your interests? Is it neat and clean? Is the decor warm and inviting? Is the physical layout user-friendly? If you are not comfortable, or if you find it unattractive, it is likely that clients will also.

_____ PROFESSIONALISM: Do the employees present the appropriate professional appearance and behavior? Do they give their clients the appropriate levels of attention and personal service or do they act as if work is their time to socialize?

_____ MANAGEMENT: Does the salon show signs of being well managed? Is the phone answered promptly with professional telephone skills? Is the mood of the salon positive? Does everyone appear to work as a team?

_____ CLIENT SERVICE: Are clients greeted promptly and warmly when they enter the salon? Are they kept informed of the status of their appointment? Are they offered a magazine or beverage while they wait? Is there a comfortable reception area? Are there changing rooms, attractive smocks?

_____ PRICES: Compare price for value. Are clients getting their money's worth? Do they pay the same price in one salon but get better service and attention in another? If possible, take home salon brochures and price lists.

_____ RETAIL: Is there a well-stocked retail display offering clients a variety of product lines and a range of prices? Do the estheticians and receptionist (if applicable) promote retail sales?

_____ IN-SALON MARKETING: Are there posters or promotions throughout the salon? If so, are they professionally designed and relevant to contemporary skin care treatments?

_____ SERVICES: Make a list of all services offered by each salon and the product lines they carry. This will help you decide what earning potential estheticians have in each salon.

SALON NAME: ______________________________

SALON **MANAGER:** ______________________________

▲ **Figure 21–6 Salon visit checklist.**

of his or her time. Remember that an information interview is not the same as a request for a job interview, although managers frequently will consider enthusiastic students for positions that become available.

If your request for an information interview is turned down or limited, do not be offended. Some salon owners may have time for only a brief telephone conversation or may be unwilling to disclose what they consider privileged information. Others may generously offer you an opportunity to visit the salon and meet them in person. If you are lucky enough to be granted an interview, it is a good idea to prepare very specific questions, limiting topics to key areas that will give you a general idea of how the salon or spa operates. Possible subjects might include:

- The duties and responsibilities required of estheticians on staff.
- How management makes important decisions related to product selection, new techniques, pricing, and other policies.
- What customer service policies the manager believes are critical to operating a successful salon or spa.

▶ Figure 21–7
A sample thank-you note for the salon visit or information interview

Dear Ms. (or Mr.) ______________________,

It was a pleasure to observe your salon/spa in operation last Friday. Thank you for the time you and your staff gave me. I was impressed by the efficient and courteous manner in which your estheticians served their clients. The atmosphere was pleasant and the mood was positive. Should you ever have an opening for a professional with my skills and training, I would welcome the opportunity to apply. You can contact me at the address and phone number listed below. I hope we will meet again soon.

Sincerely,

(your name, address, telephone)

- How the salon attracts new customers or markets its services.
- Who is responsible for retail sales, and if there are any sales quotas that estheticians must meet.
- Whether there are specific policies or procedural guides for employees.

If you would like to solicit additional information directly from employees or clients afterward, always ask permission from the salon owner first. After your visit, it is considered proper professional etiquette to send a handwritten thank-you note (**Figure 21–7**).

Those who are uncomfortable with conducting an information interview with the owner or manager may choose to gather information anonymously, frequenting different salons and spas as a client. Interacting with estheticians and other patrons will give you the opportunity to ask questions indirectly in a relaxed and nonthreatening fashion. In such situations, remember that you should always practice professionalism, tact, and diplomacy.

▼ Figure 21–8
Networking is a good way to increase contacts that can enhance your career.

Networking

Establishing contacts that eventually lead to employment opportunities is another important part of the job search. There are many ways to network or build relationships to further your career; finding the one you are most comfortable with is part of the process (**Figure 21–8**).

Networking is a subtle approach to increasing the breadth and scope of your contacts. It is far less intimidating than a direct request for a job interview and is a useful exercise in developing important communication skills. Students can begin to develop networking skills in many ways. The following list of suggestions will help you to get started.

- Join professional organizations. Most offer student discounts and encourage membership.
- Attend industry trade shows and educational seminars. Talk to presenters and participants.
- Create a list of ideal affiliations (for example, dermatologists, massage therapists, and nutritionists). Develop a "script" for introducing yourself.
- Find out who's who in the area of skin care, and request a 10-minute information interview. This can be conducted over the phone or by e-mail.
- Subscribe to trade publications and get in the habit of checking into calendars of events.
- Ask your instructors about local, regional, and national happenings.
- Investigate on-line communities and social media networks in which you can participate.
- Participate in field trips sponsored by your school.
- Keep a list of guest speakers who have visited your school, for future reference.
- Become involved in a charity project.
- Be open-minded and attend business functions or health seminars that will provide positive learning experiences, even if they are not completely focused on skin care. ☑ **L06**

The Employment Interview

The first step in getting hired is to arrange an employment interview. Hopefully, you have spent some time narrowing your search and getting in touch with your personal job requirements. Now you are ready to focus exclusively on finding a job.

Many students have a list of spas and salons where ideally they would like to work, but it is always a good idea to begin your search by scouting the many advertised positions that are available. Your school's job board is generally the best place to begin your search. If your school offers job-search counseling take advantage of it. School counselors who are familiar with your work style and know the management style of potential employers can be very helpful in developing leads that are a good match for your skills.

To land an interview you must first send your resume, prefaced by a cover letter, to those salons and spas you are interested in. Even if you have general knowledge about a salon or spa before sending your resume, it is wise to review the salon's brochure or menu of services beforehand. This information is generally available on-line via the salon's Web site which may contain other important information, such as a virtual tour of the facility, professional bios, and treatment videos that will help you to frame your cover letter and resume

Here's a Tip

To help you stay organized during the employment search, create a chart that lists the name of the salon or spa, the contact person responsible for hiring, the date you sent your resume or called to inquire about a job, a planned time to follow up, and a brief summary of your results (Figure 21–9).

Name of Salon	Position Available	Web site	Brochure	Contact Person	Contact Date	Resume Sent	Follow-up Date	Results
Best Salon Ever	Entry Level Esthetician	www.bestsalonever.com	✓	Joan Smith, Manager	7/5/2011	7/6/2011	7/16/2011	Interview scheduled for 7/22/2011
Next Best Salon	None Advertised	www.nextbestsalon.com	✓	Kim Jones, Owner	7/8/2011	7/10/2011		Called. No jobs available currently; Owner suggested sending resume and calling back in the Fall.

▲ Figure 21–9 **Interview checklist.**

accordingly. Demonstrating knowledge of the employment setting shows prospective employers that you are genuinely interested in making a good impression.

You may need to send several resumes and make many phone calls before you are actually granted an interview. Do not get discouraged; you may not begin your career in your dream job, but the right job will come along. Just speaking with someone responsible for hiring over the phone is a move in the right direction. Often, salon managers will not have an immediate position available but may be interested in having a copy of your resume or meeting you in case an opening becomes available later. Do not consider this effort a waste of your time. Each interview is a valuable learning experience that will help you build confidence in your interpersonal skills and become familiar with what to expect. Interviews can also be an excellent occasion to network. Whatever the outcome, always be polite and thank those in charge for their time and consideration. If you are granted an interview, following up with a handwritten thank-you note is standard protocol. This should include a positive statement about why you want the job, if in fact you do want it. Even if you are not interested in a position, always put your best foot forward. The salon community is close-knit and employers may be in communication with other potential hiring managers for whom you might be a good fit.

Preparing for the Interview

Does the thought of being interviewed make you anxious? If so, you are not alone. It is common to feel a bit nervous when preparing for a job interview.

There are many ways to alleviate the pressure of being interviewed. Being organized and prepared with the appropriate documents will put you at ease and help you make a positive first impression. Even if you have already mailed your resume, be sure to have an additional copy in case the interviewer has misplaced it or in the event that there are multiple interviewers. You should also have some form of identification, such as your driver's license and your social security card. Other important documents include a copy of your esthetics license, any other pertinent licenses you may hold, training certificates or awards, professional memberships, references or letters of recommendation from former employers, and any photos of your work that may enhance your status. Presenting these in a covered binder or portfolio is a good way to appear efficient and organized (**Figure 21–10**).

We have already discussed the importance of personal appearance in the esthetics industry in Chapter 3, Your Professional Image. This is especially

PREPARING FOR THE INTERVIEW CHECKLIST

RESUME COMPOSITION

1. Does it present your abilities and what you have accomplished in your jobs and training?
2. Does it make the reader want to ask, "How did you accomplish that?"
3. Does it highlight accomplishments rather than detailing duties and responsibilities?
4. Is it easy to read, short, and does it stress past accomplishments and skills?
5. Does it focus on information that's relevant to your own career goals?
6. Is it complete and professionally prepared?

PORTFOLIO CHECKLIST

____ Diploma, secondary and post-secondary

____ Awards and achievements while in school

____ Current resume focusing on accomplishments

____ Letters of reference from former employers

____ List of, or certificates from, trade shows attended while in training

____ Statement of professional affiliations (memberships in esthetics organizations, etc.)

____ Statement of civic affiliations and/or activities

____ Before and after photographs of technical skills services you have performed

____ Any other relevant information

Ask: Does my portfolio portray me and my career skills in the manner that I wish to be perceived? If not, what needs to be changed?

GENERAL INFORMATION

1. Describe specific methods or procedures you will employ in the salon/spa to build your clientele.
2. Describe how you feel about retail sales in the salon/spa and give specific methods you would use in the salon/spa to generate sales.
3. State why you feel consumer protection and safety is so important in the field of esthetics.
4. Explain what you love about you new career.
5. Describe your passion for esthetics.

◀ **Figure 21–10**
Interview preparation checklist.

important when presenting for a job interview. Employers will expect you to reflect healthy skin care practices.

Keep perfume subtle and your makeup simple, with the focus on a natural glow. Nails should be clean, short, and manicured. If you wear polish, choose a neutral shade. Your jewelry and hairstyle should be unpretentious and conform to the practice of esthetics. If you have long hair, it is a good idea to style it neatly away from your face, particularly if you will be performing a facial. Wear a flattering neutral-colored suit that is cleaned and pressed, and make sure your shoes are polished and in good condition (**Figure 21–11**). To complete your professional appearance, carry a briefcase or portfolio to store your documents. Do not carry a handbag if you are using a briefcase. Too much baggage can be cumbersome and often ends up looking unprofessional. If you do not have a briefcase, a simple handbag and a folder for your materials are appropriate.

▲ Figure 21–11
A professional appearance is important when presenting yourself for a job interview.

There is always an element of surprise when it comes to the interview, however, there are certain commonly asked questions. For example, expect to answer questions related to the following issues:

- Your previous job experience or academic performance
- Your attendance record
- What you liked best about your esthetics training program
- Your individual strengths and weaknesses
- Ways that your skills will contribute to the success of the salon or spa
- Your ability to be a team player
- Your method for handling common problems or conflicts
- How flexible you are willing to be in terms of scheduling
- Your philosophy of skin care
- Your product preferences
- Any services that you are unable to or do not like to perform
- Your approach to customer service
- Your methods for increasing client retention
- Your retail sales philosophy
- Your plan for meeting retail sales goals
- Your long-term career goals and objectives

Many prospective employers will also ask you to perform a facial. This situation can be stressful for some, although others may find the opportunity to demonstrate practical skills a plus. Whichever category you fall into, it is ultimately in your best interest to cooperate. If by chance you do falter, do your best not to bring attention to your mistake.

Another very important area of concern for salon owners is retail sales. In fact some salon owners may be more interested in your sales ability than they are in your technical skills. When interviewing for a job it is important to remember that recommending and providing clients with quality skin care products and additional facial services is a professional responsibility. Expect questions on this topic and be prepared to discuss how you will educate clients and promote additional services. This topic will be addressed further in Chapter 23, Selling Products and Services.

> **Here's a Tip**
>
> If you are unfamiliar with the location of the salon, it is always a good idea to map out the most direct route and conduct a trial run. Whether you are driving or taking public transportation, calculate how long it will take you to get there and add a little extra time should you run into any unexpected delays, like highway road construction or traffic. Knowing what to expect will help to eliminate additional stress.

Other difficult questions, such as those in which you are asked about your weaknesses, have the potential to make or break an interview. When responding to such questions, it is important to frame your answer in a positive manner. For example, if you are asked about things that you found challenging in your program or past employment, be prepared to discuss what you learned about yourself in the process and how you have grown. Staying focused on the positive can make all the difference in how the interviewer perceives you.

The Interview

Finally, the moment you have been waiting for has arrived: you have been granted an interview (**Figure 21–12**). Many books are available that offer lengthy discussions on the do's and don'ts of interviewing. You may want to spend some additional time browsing through a few of them. Here are a few basic survival tips.

- Dress professionally.
- Carry breath mints, tissues, and cleansing wipes.
- Be prepared with a compact umbrella that can be tucked into your briefcase or purse.
- Be on time; or better yet, arrive 10 to 15 minutes early.

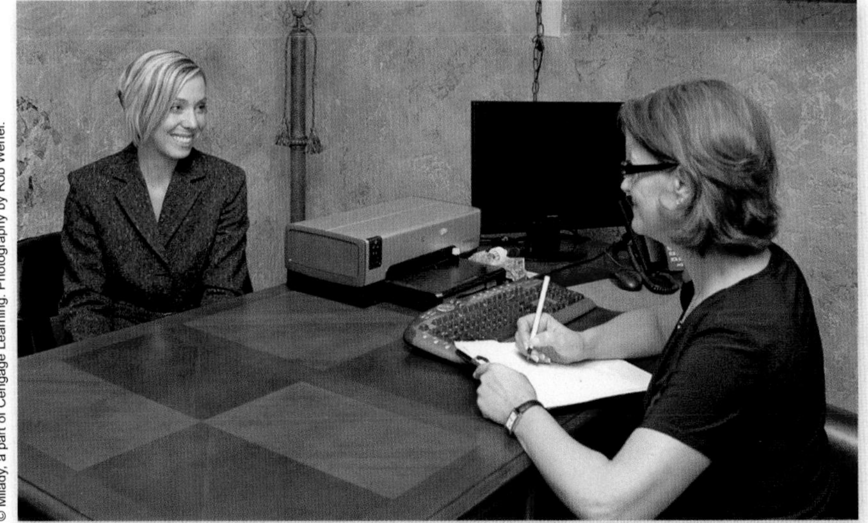

Figure 21–12
An interview is an opportunity to demonstrate your qualifications.

- Use good manners. Be polite and courteous at all times to everyone you come in contact with.
- Do your best to appear relaxed and confident.
- Project a warm, friendly smile.
- Never smoke or chew gum, even if one or the other is offered to you.
- Do not come to an interview with a cup of coffee, a soft drink, snacks, or anything else to eat or drink.
- Do not bring children, friends, or significant others with you.
- Never lean on or touch the interviewer's desk. Some people do not like their personal space invaded without an invitation.
- Listen respectfully without interrupting.
- Answer questions thoughtfully, but do not elaborate for more than two minutes at a time.
- Be honest with your answers.
- Frame all of your answers, even those that address weaknesses, in a positive context.
- Speak clearly, and use good language.
- Do not make critical remarks about previous employers or instructors.
- Always thank the interviewer for the opportunity to present your skills.

Web Resources

Many women find it difficult to afford the two or three outfits necessary to project a confident and professional image when going out into the workplace for a job interview. Fortunately, several nonprofit organizations have been formed to address this need. These organizations receive donations of clean, beautiful clothes in good repair from individuals and manufacturers. These are then passed along to women who need them. For more information, visit Wardrobe for Opportunity at www.wardrobe.org and Dress for Success at www.dressforsuccess.org.

Another crucial part of the interview comes when you are invited to ask the interviewer questions of your own. You should think about those questions ahead of time and bring a list if necessary. Doing so will show that you are organized and prepared. Some questions to consider include the following:

- Is there a job description? May I review it?
- Is there a salon manual?
- How frequently does the salon advertise?
- How long do practitioners typically work here?
- Are employees encouraged to grow in skills and responsibility? How so?
- Does the salon offer continuing education opportunities?
- Is there room for advancement? If so, what are the requirements for promotion?
- What benefits does the salon offer, such as paid vacations, personal days, and medical insurance?
- What is the form of compensation?

- When will the position be filled?
- Should I follow up on your decision, or will you contact me?

Do not feel you have to ask every question on your list. The point is to create as much dialogue as possible. Be aware of the interviewer's reactions, and stop when you think you have asked enough questions. By obtaining answers to at least some of your questions, you can compare the information you have gathered about other salons and then choose the one that offers the best package of income and career development.

Legal Aspects of the Interview

While the opportunity to be interviewed can elicit a response to tell all, you should know that many questions are considered inappropriate or illegal. As a job applicant, you have certain rights as established by the Equal Employment Opportunity Commission (EEOC) and federal and state laws. It is important to be aware of those questions that cannot be asked either on an application form or during an interview. These include questions about your age or date of birth, race, religion, national origin, marital status, number of children, disabilities, medical conditions or health problems, and citizenship status. Employers are permitted to inquire about drug use or smoking habits and may also obtain an applicant's consent to conform to the company's drug and smoking policies or to submit to drug testing.

Sometimes interviewers are unaware when they are crossing a boundary that is illegal. You can always choose not to answer inappropriate questions; however, it is in your best interest to be tactful and diplomatic regardless of whether or not you want the job.

The Employment Application

Even if you have submitted a resume, you should also expect to fill out an employment application. Forms can vary; however, most request the same basic information—such as name, address, telephone and Social Security number, education and employment history, the position you are applying for, languages you speak, references, and emergency contacts. Your resume and portfolio will help you to answer the employment application form quickly and efficiently. To ensure credibility, be sure that the information you supply is the same on all documents. ☑ L07

On the Job

Congratulations! You have worked hard to finish your esthetics training program, pass your licensing exam, and gain employment—your career as an esthetician is about to begin. This is your opportunity to put your learning to the test.

To make the transition from school to work successfully, you will need to establish and prioritize your goals. Now more than ever, you will need to practice putting your best self forward. Learning to discipline and conduct yourself in a positive and professional manner will help you develop a standard of behavior that will last throughout your career (**Figure 21–13**).

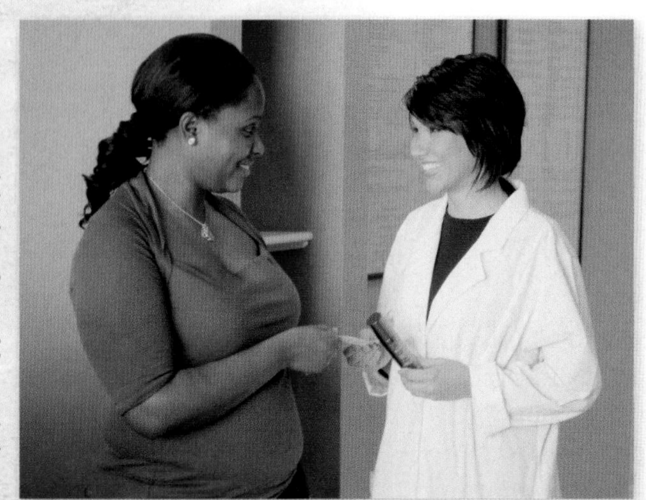

▲ Figure 21–13
Getting off to a good start.

Moving from School to Work

Entering the workforce is an exciting time. Amongst this new found excitement, keep in mind that earning a salary commands a new level of responsibility.

As a student, chances are you were given many opportunities to perfect your skills by performing a procedure several times before you got it right. Having instructors to guide you and peers to support you no doubt gave you a good deal of security as you learned the trade. School may also have afforded you a more flexible schedule that allowed you to juggle personal or work commitments to complete your training program. When you become an employee of a salon or spa, you will be expected to conform to a new set of rules.

Thriving in a Service Profession

The most important thing to remember as you embark on a career in esthetics is that your work revolves around serving clients. Although some people consider the idea of serving the public demeaning in some way, many find this type of work extremely rewarding.

As you continue on your journey to provide quality customer service, the following key points are emphasized to help guide you in providing client-focused service.

- ***A professional appearance.*** Maintain a clean, neat work environment and a polished personal appearance. These are important considerations in building client confidence.
- ***Courteous behavior.*** Use good manners when interacting with clients. Practicing proper etiquette is an important part of conducting yourself professionally.
- ***Prompt service.*** Remember that no one wants to wait. Punctuality shows clients that you value and respect their time.
- ***Personal consideration.*** Give each client your undivided attention. Respectful listening demonstrates a genuine interest in the client's concerns.
- ***Honesty.*** False claims damage the client's trust. Be sure to tell the truth when it comes to the products and services you provide.
- ***Competence.*** Clients need to know they can rely on your expertise. Make sure you are knowledgeable about the treatments you are practicing and the products you use. When in doubt, seek support from supervisors, manufacturers, or other educational sources.

- ***Positive attitude.*** A pleasant and helpful attitude makes clients feel welcome and cared for. If you cannot provide a particular service or certain information, make an effort to find out how the client can obtain it.

Joining a Successful Business

Joining a successful team is an incredible opportunity to use the training and skills that you have worked so hard to obtain.

Estheticians should always remember that the main goal of a salon or spa is to promote business. Maintaining work habits that foster this goal, such as keeping a schedule that benefits the salon's clients, will become a top priority. You will also be responsible for producing good work and following set standards. Learning to put the needs of the salon and its clients ahead of your personal concerns and performing whatever services and functions your job requires, regardless of personal circumstances, is an ordinary part of the working world.

Being a Team Player

Most skin care businesses employ several individuals and are dependent upon their working cooperatively to achieve success. In today's fast-paced and competitive business environment, salon and spa owners simply cannot tolerate individual agendas that would undermine their prosperity. Skin care services are expensive, and customers are demanding. There are bills to pay and quotas to meet to earn a profit. To increase productivity and keep customers satisfied, smart managers realize that all employees must be equally invested in achieving a common goal (**Figure 21–14**).

Unless you intend to be a one-person operation, it is important to understand how to get along with others and work productively. Salon management is responsible for creating a climate that promotes teamwork and encourages each person's success in the most stress-free and supportive atmosphere possible. It is your job to understand and implement the traits that support these efforts. The following behavioral characteristics are crucial to being a good team player.

FOCUS ON

Professionalism

Once you have accepted employment, follow through on your commitment. Employers invest a considerable amount of time and money seeking viable candidates for a position. Many will spend more marketing dollars on business cards, photos, and announcements before you even begin to work. A failure to show up on the scheduled start day, a decision to quit abruptly without a proper notice, or a condescending remark via social media can result in a tarnished reputation that has the potential to destroy your prospects with other employers for years to come.

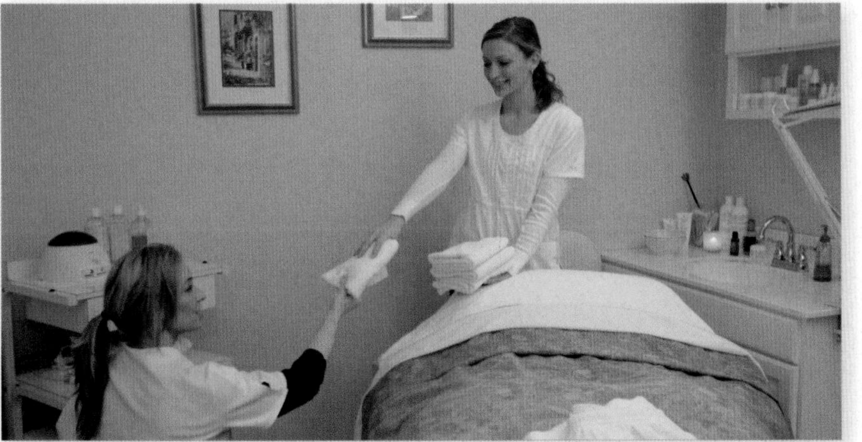

◀ Figure 21–14
Teamwork makes all the difference.

Be Dependable

It is important for all team members to have a sense of being able to depend upon one another. Be punctual, keep your word, and be willing to help out whenever a colleague needs your assistance.

Be Cooperative

Understand what your boss expects of you, and work hard to meet those objectives. If you have finished your own work, be willing to pitch in and help others to meet team goals. Sharing the workload in a cooperative and pleasant manner benefits everyone.

Be Supportive

If you are knowledgeable in a particular area, be willing to share that information with others. Offering support in a humble and genuine fashion is a good way to earn the respect of coworkers and receive positive recognition from your employer.

Be Responsible

For a salon to be successful, each employee must be successful. Be ready, willing, and able to pull your own weight and accept additional responsibilities whenever necessary.

Be Caring

Show an interest in others. At times your coworkers may be stressed or overwhelmed with their duties and responsibilities. When you encourage and support your teammates to do their best, particularly through difficult times, everyone wins.

Did You Know?

In some cases, those working for someone else may be held liable for errors in professional judgment. It is always best to understand the limits of your employer's liability protection and to seek additional insurance coverage when applicable.

Be Respectful

Each of us has unique talents and methods of doing things. At times you may disagree with another's approach. However, it is important to be patient and work to solve problems in a kind and productive way. As you learn to value differences in others, you will no doubt find new ways to approach tasks and increase your ability to express yourself positively (**Figure 21–15**). ☑ **LO8**

Recognizing the Value of Policies and Procedures

Knowing what the rules are is an important part of functioning in the work world. Rules and regulations help us navigate many situations. For example, rules and guidelines help us maintain a healthy and productive existence by telling us how fast we can drive on the highway, what forms of payment are acceptable when purchasing goods and services, or what our rights are when applying for health insurance, credit cards, or loans.

Successful businesses also recognize the need for clear directives and work hard to see that all employees are aware of expectations. To keep

Figure 21–15
Staff meetings are essential for building high-functioning teams.

personnel informed and maintain quality control, most well-run businesses will provide a written statement of their policies and procedures. These may come in the form of an employee handbook or company manual. Rules and regulations are instrumental in keeping operations running smoothly; they also help to guarantee customer satisfaction. It is every employee's responsibility to be aware of company policy; ignorance is no excuse for not following the rules.

Chances are you will receive some explanation of how your employer expects you to behave when you are hired. Whether this comes in the form of a verbal discussion or written statement, you will want to be clear about what your duties and responsibilities are. The following list targets critical issues every employee should know about.

- Correct protocol for calling in sick or late
- Number of sick days allowed
- Length of vacation time and number of days that can be accrued over time
- Paid and unpaid holidays
- Dress code
- A detailed job description highlighting specific duties and responsibilities
- Insurance plan and payment procedure
- Person responsible for human resource issues
- Person responsible for your direct supervision

Many salons incorporate a mission statement or philosophy in their company manual. This may explain their vision for the future as well as their position on various issues, such as what products they believe in or how they feel about supporting employee education. This statement can help you determine whether your own goals and objectives will be a good fit.

If you are working for a large organization, the manual may include an organization chart. Understanding who is in authority and how you fit into the company's "big picture" is important in terms of diplomacy. Knowing who's who may save you from an embarrassing moment or give you the motivation you need if you are looking to advance within the company.

Some salons may also insist on performing treatments in a certain way. Do not be surprised if the salon you work for dictates exactly how a procedure should be performed. Because estheticians work closely with the public, it is imperative in our litigation-oriented society for businesses to provide specific guidelines on such topics as cleaning, disinfecting, sterilization, and Standard Precautions. It also makes sense to have a set way of administering a treatment or task to ensure that each customer receives the same quality of treatment and is ultimately satisfied with whomever performs the service.

▼ **Figure 21–16**
Always exercise care and caution to ensure the safety of your clients.

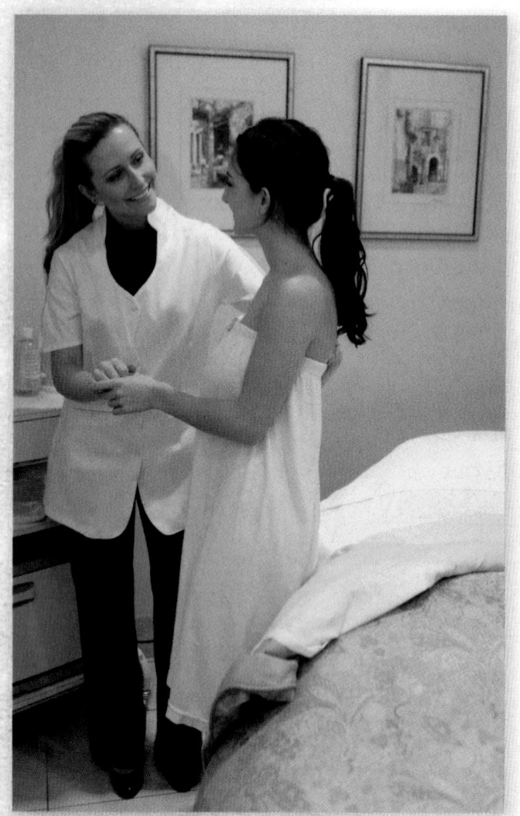

Liability Issues

Liability is a topic that deserves a good deal of attention. The skin care business has become increasingly sophisticated, incorporating treatments that are far more aggressive and complex than they were 10 years ago. And while no one looks for problems, accidents do happen. Reactions or sensitivities to cosmetic products are commonplace. Clients may not fully disclose information, or they may suddenly develop an allergic reaction to a substance they have been using without a problem for some time. Therefore, it is in everyone's best interest, employers and employees alike, to take a cautious approach (**Figure 21–16**).

Ideally, the esthetician should have the opportunity to practice using a new product or treatment several times under direct supervision before administering it to a paying customer. This helps businesses avoid more costly errors. Still, smaller salons and spas may not be able to afford such practices—the cost of products may be high, and management may be limited in their capacity to bring in professional consultants. To ensure the safety of your clients and to protect yourself and your employer from liability issues, take time to consider these recommendations.

- Before beginning any new procedure, be sure to take a complete client history, noting any contraindications, allergies, or sensitivities.
- Administer patch tests before allowing a client to undergo the complete treatment process.
- As a general rule, when in doubt, don't! Whenever you have a question, seek supervision from someone more knowledgeable than you.
- Always have the client sign the intake form and/or a consent form that explains the procedure and what to expect, as well as the benefits and possible side effects or risks.
- Review the intake and/or consent form, and go over any special instructions with clients before beginning the procedure.

- Be sure to have clients sign the intake form and/or a consent form each time they undergo a procedure, updating information as necessary.
- Should a problem arise, inform your supervisor immediately and document the incident carefully, noting specific side effects and client concerns in the client's profile.

As a professional working for someone else, it is your duty to practice with care and caution. Although you should expect to be covered against any claims that may arise, you should know that, in some cases, even those working for someone else could be held liable for errors in professional judgment. To be safe, it is always best to ask your employer for documentation of the business's professional liability insurance and the limits of protection. Regardless of coverage, it is also a good idea to make inquiries about the cost of obtaining an additional individual professional liability insurance policy. Professional organizations, training schools, and small business associations can be helpful in referring you to appropriate resources.

The Job Description

The **job description** is an important tool that is a specified list of duties and responsibilities that are required of an employee in the performance of his or her job.

Once you are hired as an employee, you will be expected to conduct yourself professionally and perform those services required of you as an esthetician in compliance with salon or spa policy. To carry out your responsibilities to the best of your ability, you should be given a job description. If the salon or spa you are working for does not provide one, it is a good idea to write down those duties that were discussed during your interview or training and review them with your employer or manager. This way you will both have a clear understanding of the requirements. If you do have any questions or some areas seem vague, this would be a good time to clarify them with your boss.

Job descriptions are as varied as the types of salons that exist, and they are typically based on the needs of the salon or spa. Expect that the small clinic or day spa will have a different set of demands than a large resort spa or medical aesthetics practice. The number of employees may also determine which tasks you are required to perform. In most instances, estheticians are expected to perform some variation of the following duties and responsibilities.

- Analyze skin types and conditions.
- Perform facials and other specialized skin care treatments.
- Develop therapeutic skin care programs to treat certain skin conditions.
- Explain treatment protocols and review possible side effects with clients.
- Apply facial masks.
- Apply basic and corrective makeup.
- Conduct hair removal services.

- Conduct spa/skin care services such as body wraps and polishes.
- Recommend skin care products.
- Educate clients on new treatment programs.
- Advise clients on home-care programs.
- Make follow-up phone calls.
- Investigate new products and techniques.
- Advise management on new methods, products, and services.
- Educate staff on products and services.
- Encourage salon clients to try new services.
- Promote retail sales.
- Participate in sales events or promotional activities.
- Refer clients to colleagues for additional services or other professionals whenever appropriate.
- Create retail displays and perform merchandising tasks.
- Clean and disinfect the treatment room and utensils.

Estheticians may also be asked to perform other administrative duties such as the following.

- Answer the telephone.
- Schedule appointments.
- Confirm appointments.
- Initiate and update the client profile or intake questionnaire.
- Record client information and treatment results.
- File client data.
- Review consent forms with clients.
- Maintain product inventory.
- Supervise new employees.

Some salons and spas may incorporate other objectives in their job descriptions. These can specify the attitudes that are expected and the opportunities for growth that are available to employees (**Figure 21–17**). ☑ **LO9**

Employee Evaluation

Developing a productive process for measuring an employee's progress is critical to setting employee and business standards. The esthetician's evaluation is likely to begin with a reference to her or his job description.

The job description provides an excellent standard for evaluating the functional aspects of employee performance, that is, how well you perform the practical tasks that are expected of you. Keep in mind that attitude is a critical factor in evaluating employee performance and may be specified in your job

▼ Figure 21–17
A sample job description for an entry-level esthetician.

Job Description: Entry-Level Esthetician

Every Entry-Level Esthetician must have an esthetic's license as well as the determination to learn and grow on the job. All estheticians are expected to follow specified skin care protocols, and must attend all training seminars and workshops proposed by management for their job level. In addition, Entry-Level Estheticians must report weekly to an assigned Senior-Level Esthetician for a period of 6 weeks to review skin care protocols and raise any questions they may have regarding salon operations or procedures. This helps the Salon to maintain quality control, a significant factor in client satisfaction and repeat business. As an Esthetician, you must be willing to cooperate with coworkers in a team environment, which is most conducive to learning and to good morale among all employees. You must display a friendly yet professional attitude toward coworkers and clients alike.

Excellent time management is essential to the operation of a successful salon. All estheticians must perform services in accordance with set time allowances for each treatment. This helps to keep all service providers on schedule. Estheticians should be aware of clients who arrive early or late and should also keep track of other scheduled service providers who may be running ahead or behind in their schedule. In those situations, the esthetician should be willing to make the appropriate adjustments to their schedule if needed. Be prepared to stay at work up to an hour late when necessary. Keep in mind always that everyone needs to work together to get the job done.

The Responsibilities of an Entry-Level Esthetician include the following:

1. Analyze skin types and conditions.
2. Perform facials and other entry-level exfoliation and specialized skin care treatments.
3. Develop therapeutic skin care programs in accordance with set salon protocols for specific skin types and conditions.
4. Explain treatment protocols and review possible side effects with clients.
5. Apply facial masks.
6. Apply basic and corrective makeup.
7. Conduct hair removal services.
8. Demonstrate knowledge of cosmetic ingredients.
9. Recommend skin care products.
10. Educate clients on new treatment programs.
11. Advise clients on home-care programs.
12. Encourage salon clients to try new services.
13. Promote retail sales in accordance with specified sales goals for your job level.
14. Participate in sales events or promotional activities.
15. Refer clients to colleagues for additional services or other professionals whenever appropriate.
16. Clean and disinfect the treatment room and utensils after each use.
17. Supervise the client intake questionnaire.
18. Review the appropriate consent forms with clients as necessary.

19. Record client information and treatment results.
20. Maintain inventory control in treatment room at regularly scheduled daily and weekly intervals set by management.
21. Inform management of any equipment malfunctions, treatment room, or building maintenance problems that would impact the safety of clients and/or service providers.

Continuing Education

Your position as an Entry-Level Esthetician is the first step toward becoming a successful member of the salon's skin care team. In the beginning, your training will focus on set protocols and procedures. Once you have mastered these, your training will focus on the sales skills you will need to promote proper client home-care. As part of your continuing education in this salon, you will be required to:

- Attend all salon classes as required for your job level.
- Attend our special Sunday sales seminars four times a year.
- Meet the established retail sales goals set for all Entry-Level Estheticians.

Advancement

Upon successful completion of all required classes and seminars and your demonstration of the necessary skills and attitudes, you will have the opportunity to advance to the position of a Level II Esthetician. This advancement will always depend upon your successful performance as an Entry-Level Esthetician as well as the approval of management. Remember: How quickly you achieve your goals in this salon is up to you!

▲ Figure 21–17 *(continued)*

description. Maintaining a running checklist of your job requirements will help to ensure that you are meeting these important obligations.

Most salons today also use computerized information systems to analyze retail and service sales. This generally includes a detailed account of each employee's productivity levels. Be prepared to review the results of your individual sales performance with your supervisor in an open-ended manner. When queried, try not to respond to questions with a simple yes or no. This approach may not supply you with the feedback you will need to move forward in the best way possible. Whenever you have the opportunity, it can also be helpful to ask your employer for suggestions that will help you to do your job better. This demonstrates that you are willing to grow and learn and are mature enough to handle constructive criticism.

Although the evaluation process may take some getting used to, it should ultimately supply employees with incentive for performing their duties in a way that also helps management to meet their goals, creating a win–win situation for both. In general, estheticians starting out should expect to be evaluated 90 days or 3 months after they are hired, and on a yearly basis thereafter. In the meantime, developing a method for critical self-analysis and soliciting important feedback from management can help you to become comfortable with the process.

Employers generally appreciate personnel who are proactive in assuming responsibility for their own success and may automatically supply monthly sales and service reports to help individuals evaluate their progress. If your employer does not, consider requesting such information or keep track on your own. You may also want to ask a trusted colleague to critique your sales technique, or you can ask clients for suggestions about how to provide better service. Understanding your productivity and client-satisfaction levels can validate those things that you are doing right and provide additional incentive for making necessary changes. Learning to use this information wisely will help you fulfill job requirements and develop solid career management skills.

Compensation

Just as the bottom line for salons is making money, getting paid is the primary incentive for estheticians. You undoubtedly enjoy what you do, but it is not likely that you would go to work if you did not receive a paycheck. *How much* an esthetician is paid varies from salon to salon and is subject to a variety of factors, such as current economic conditions, the type and size of the salon, the method of compensation, and so on. While estheticians should not base employment decisions solely on salary, compensation is typically a strong factor in whether an esthetician accepts a position. All things considered, you must be able to meet your living expenses.

Historically, esthetics grew out of the salon industry, which used a percentage-based or commission-based wage structure. As a result, many skin care salons and day spas adopted this method of compensation. Since acquiring separate licensing, estheticians have gained entry to many other professional arenas. This has opened the door to new ways of thinking about how to pay estheticians.

Methods of Compensation

Skin care salons, day spas, and other businesses that employ estheticians differ in how they compensate employees. Pay structures may be based on salary, commission, or on some combination of both.

Salary

Salary can be based on either a *flat* or *hourly* rate. If you are compensated using a flat rate, you can expect to be paid a certain amount that has been agreed upon per week. Salary levels for estheticians vary, and in some cases are negotiable, but remember: If you are offered a set salary each week, instead of an hourly rate, it must be equal to at least minimum wage; and you are entitled to overtime pay if you work more than 40 hours per week. The only exception would be if you were in an official salon-management position.

ACTIVITY

Go through the budget worksheet and fill in the amounts that apply to your current living and financial situation. If you are unsure of the amount of an expense, put in the amount you have averaged over the past 3 months or give it your best guess. For your income, you may need to have 3 or 4 months of employment history in order to answer, but fill in what you can.

- **How do your expenses compare to your income?**
- **What is your balance after all your expenses are paid?**
- **Were there any surprises for you in this exercise?**
- **Do you think that keeping a budget is a good way to manage money?**
- **Do you know of any other methods people use to manage money?**

The hourly rate is a popular method of payment for estheticians and is generally based on company standards. For example, a senior-level esthetician may earn a higher rate of pay than does an entry-level esthetician. Those compensated using this method can expect to be paid only for those hours they work. For example, if you worked 35 hours at the rate of $10 per hour, you would be paid $350. If you worked more hours you would earn more money; conversely, you would earn less money for working fewer hours.

Commission

Commission wages are directly related to your performance, which means that you earn a certain percentage of whatever services you perform. In the salon industry straight-commission rates typically fluctuate and can range anywhere from 25 to 60 percent depending on the length of your employment, your performance level, and the benefits that are part of your employment package. This means that if you take in $1,000 in services for the week and your commission is 25 percent, your gross earnings (before taxes) would be $250. If your commission rate were 50 percent, your gross earnings would be $500. At 60 percent, your gross earnings would be $600. In addition to a commission on services, a percentage of retail sales, generally between 10 and 15 percent, is also calculated.

This compensation method continues to appeal to a number of salon owners, however, as newer methods of compensation become more readily accepted, and salon owners recognize inherent differences in the role of individual service providers and the costs of services, many of those using this system of payment to pay estheticians are establishing lower commission rates and implementing tiered schedules to motivate staff to increase their income. This means the service provider must meet a certain volume of sales and services dollars to earn higher commission rates. Others are implementing a fixed percentage or flat rate for each service. If you are comfortable with this method of payment, be aware that the commission-based model varies according to the employer and may or may not include additional benefits or other bonuses. In addition, some salons may apply surcharges to cover the cost of products used to perform services. This policy can make earning a living difficult for the esthetician who is starting out and has yet to develop a clientele.

Hybrid Pay Structures

Many salons are now using a combination of salary and commission-based structures. Generally speaking, these incorporate a base salary plus a certain commission on services and/or products. Again, the salary-plus-commission model varies and is dependent on the philosophy of the individual salon owner. Typically, this model offers a salary that is established by an hourly or flat rate, plus anywhere between 10 and 20 percent commission on products and/or services. Some salons also incorporate bonuses or other incentives that are fixed according to performance **quotas,** a method for gauging the amount of sales and targeting production levels. In some cases these quotas will be based on team rather than individual performance. ☑ L010

Other Factors Affecting Wages

Estheticians can also expect wages to vary according to several criteria, such as an individual's level of training and experience. Other business factors, such as the type of salon (that is, full service, day or resort spa, skin care clinic, or medical practice), geographic location (urban or suburban), and pricing (moderately priced or high end) will come into play.

Today, many opportunities are available to estheticians in a variety of work environments. Each will have its own basis for establishing wages. Although pay scales and methods continue to vary, there appears to be a growing movement toward establishing more professional salary levels and benefits. As you make important decisions about employment, it is a good idea to analyze all aspects of compensation considering salary, health benefits, vacation pay and allowances for sick days, and any retirement benefits that might be included.

FOCUS ON

The Goal

Always put the team first. While each individual may be concerned with getting ahead and being successful, a good teammate knows that no one can do it alone.

Gratuities

Similar to other service oriented industries such as the hair, hotel, and restaurant business, in the esthetics world, tips or gratuities have become a customary way of expressing appreciation for satisfactory service. Be aware that not all salons and spas allow tipping. Most salons and spas today make their policy on gratuities clear to clients before they purchase a service by posting a sign at the front desk or checkout area or by incorporating their position in a brochure or menu of services.

Estheticians can expect the amount a client tips to vary, with most gratuities ranging between 15 and 20 percent of the total service ticket. For example, if a client spends $120 on a facial treatment, and tips 15 percent, then the tip to the service provider would be about $18. The most important thing for estheticians to remember about tips is that the Internal Revenue Service (IRS) considers tips additional income. As such, tips must be tracked and reported on your income tax return. While this may seem like a nuisance, it can actually prove beneficial in some situations, for example when applying for a loan or mortgage, where you want your income to appear stronger than it might be otherwise.

CAUTION!

Some businesses choose to use independent contractors to avoid paying mandatory insurance and taxes, such as Social Security taxes, Medicare, Workers' Compensation, federal and state income taxes, and liability insurance.

An esthetician who meets the lawful IRS definition of an independent contractor is considered self-employed and is responsible for paying all of his or her own insurance, federal and state income taxes, plus an additional self-employment tax. Other periodic estimated income taxes may apply. IRS Form SS-8 "Determination of Worker Status for Purposes of Federal Employment Taxes and Income Taxes Withholding" is an excellent resource for determining employee versus independent contractor status. More information on this topic can be found in *Milady Standard Esthetics: Advanced* text.

Independent Contractors

The use of independent contractors is widespread in the salon and spa industry; however, estheticians must be cautious when accepting employment under this status.

According to the IRS, an **independent contractor** is someone who sets his or her own fees, controls his or her own hours, has his or her own business card, and pays his or her own taxes. In effect, estheticians working as independent contractors are free to operate their skin care practice however they choose within legal parameters. What you must know if you elect to work in this way is that you are also responsible for adhering to all laws set forth by your state licensing board and any other local, state, and federal rules and regulations that apply to small business owners. This means paying your own insurance and taxes. If you are offered a position as an independent contractor it is wise to investigate all of the legal ramifications before entering into a binding agreement.

Managing Money

Once you are earning a salary, you will want to keep careful track of what you are spending. Understanding the value of a dollar that you have earned is a valuable lesson in economics and long-term financial success. Particularly if this is your first job, you will need to learn to plan and budget your money according to your needs.

Meeting Financial Responsibilities

Perhaps you took out a loan to pay for your esthetic's education or you need to purchase a car to get to work. How will you pay for these expenses? Creating a personal budget is an important task that will help you to meet your financial obligations responsibly.

Money management is a complex issue that often generates a great deal of anxiety for people. But with careful planning and thoughtful deliberation, learning to manage your money can actually be fun. Many businesses provide automatic mechanisms for taking care of important basics such as depositing an employee's salary into his or her personal checking account, managing savings, planning for retirement, and paying health and dental insurance. Unfortunately, smaller salons and spas may not be able to afford these types of employee benefits. If you work for such an organization, you will need to learn to manage most of these things for yourself.

Keeping track of where your money goes is the first step in financial planning. To get started, write down all of your expenses and then weigh these against your total income (**Figure 21–18**). Once you understand the amount of money you have coming in and going out, you can make critical choices about your spending habits. Cutting down on certain unnecessary expenses can help you obtain other, more desirable items. Perhaps you would like to save for a special trip or purchase your own home. Learning to manage your money well can make these dreams a reality.

▼ **Figure 21–18**
A personal budget worksheet.

PERSONAL BUDGET WORKSHEET

A. Expenses $ ______________

1. My monthly rent (or share of the rent) is ______________
2. My monthly car payment is ______________
3. My monthly car insurance payment is ______________
4. My monthly auto fuel/upkeep expenses are ______________
5. My monthly electric bill is ______________
6. My monthly gas bill is ______________
7. My monthly health insurance payment is ______________
8. My monthly entertainment expense is ______________
9. My monthly bank fees are ______________
10. My monthly grocery expense is ______________
11. My monthly dry cleaning expense is ______________
12. My monthly personal grooming expense is ______________
13. My monthly prescription/medical expense is ______________
14. My monthly telephone is ______________
15. My monthly student loan payment is ______________
16. My IRA payment is ______________
17. My savings account deposit is ______________
18. Other expenses: ______________

TOTAL EXPENSES $ ______________

B. Income ______________

1. My monthly take-home pay is ______________
2. My monthly income from tips is ______________
3. Other income: ______________

TOTAL INCOME $ ______________

C. Balance ______________

Total Income (B) ______________

Minus Total Expenses (A) ______________

BALANCE ______________

Maintaining important obligations such as car loans, mortgage payments, and other bills will also help you establish good credit. Although some individuals may take a nonchalant attitude toward meeting financial responsibilities, it is ultimately in everyone's best interest to be mature and responsible about handling money. Defaulting on loans or claiming bankruptcy can have serious consequences for your personal and professional credit rating—an important consideration for those planning to own or operate their own business someday.

> **FOCUS ON**
>
> **The Goal**
>
> **Always remember that success does not just come to you. You make it happen. How? By being a team player, having a positive attitude, and keeping a real sense of commitment to your work foremost in your mind.**

Seek Professional Advice

Finally, if you have difficulty managing money or feel unsure about how to handle certain areas of finance, such as putting money away for retirement, it may be helpful to seek professional advice. Your local bank may offer such services or be able to refer you to other resources. There are many qualified financial advisors who can offer sound advice on such topics as investing, retirement planning, and credit card debt. If you decide such a service could be helpful to you, it is always best to be cautious. Take time to investigate the person's credentials, and do not feel obligated to act on anything that you are uncomfortable with. ☑ **LO11**

Finding the Right Role Models

As a student, you are given the opportunity to practice techniques and perfect skills under the umbrella of a supportive environment that includes teachers and fellow students. Once you are in a work environment, at times you may feel isolated or insecure about your ability to handle certain situations. Seeking the advice of someone more experienced than you can be a good way to alleviate concerns and gain the support you need.

Take a look around you. Is there anyone whose career status impresses you? Finding role models who inspire and invigorate you is an important part of career development. A **role model** is a person whose behavior and success you would like to emulate. People often think of role models only as those who have acquired significant fame or status within their industry. But the truth is, you may not have to look very far to find people with skills and habits worth imitating.

Perhaps there is a more experienced coworker or boss you admire. Take note of how she handles situations with clients and colleagues. Are there any special techniques she uses to enhance her job performance? What character traits does she possess that keep clients coming back?

Does she read certain publications or attend trade shows to keep herself informed? Paying attention to the habits that have made those in your immediate environment successful is a good place to begin your search. But do not limit yourself: the world is full of positive role models unaffiliated with the field of esthetics whose work habits or character traits are worth modeling. Consider them as well when you focus on how you can apply success strategies to your personal goals.

If you are lucky enough to find a role model who is willing to share her knowledge, use the time wisely. Be thoughtful in the way you present your questions and listen attentively without interrupting, even if you take issue with what the individual is saying. Remember: You asked for this person's advice. ☑ **LO12**

Continuing Your Education

Upon graduation, you will have a solid base of knowledge to use in building your success. Where you go from here depends largely on your willingness to grow and develop new skills. Esthetics is a dynamic industry that has made great strides over the past several decades. Advances in equipment and product technology have introduced sophisticated new skin care methods that have changed the way estheticians work and heightened media attention. Greater awareness of treatment options has resulted in a more educated consumer who expects estheticians to have answers to more complex questions about skin care treatments and techniques. In today's continually evolving esthetics market, there is every reason to expect that this trend will continue.

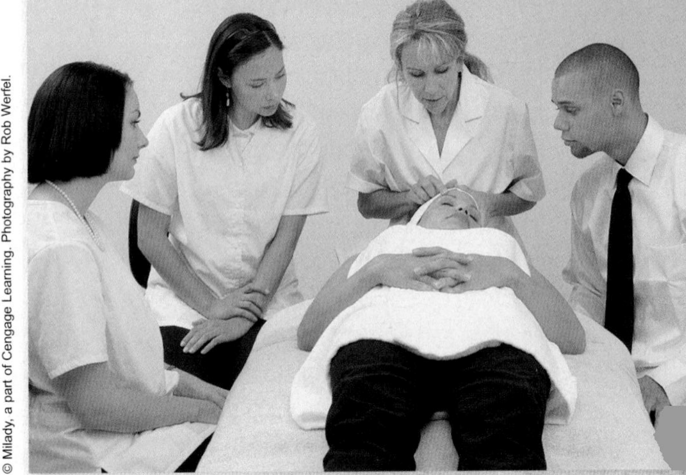

▲ **Figure 21–19**
Make continued education part of your long-term planning.

To keep up with consumer demands and job requirements, estheticians must find other sources of advanced education once they have graduated. In fact some states may demand that estheticians fulfill a certain number of continuing education units, or CEUs, to maintain their license. Fortunately, there are many opportunities available to those interested in increasing their knowledge. Alumnae and trade associations are a good place to start and are often good resources for accessing other information. Manufacturers and distributors are another viable source of education about new products and techniques, although you should be aware of vested interests and take care to substantiate all scientific data using unbiased methods. Subscribing to trade publications and professional newsletters will help you to keep up with important news and trends on a regular basis. You can also benefit from attending workshops and seminars sponsored by allied health professionals (**Figure 21–19**).

This will not only increase your knowledge of associated therapies, but it can also be an excellent opportunity to network.

If you are interested in learning more about management or operating your own salon or spa, you might also consider enrolling in other business-related courses such as those offered at local adult-education centers and community colleges. Becoming Internet savvy is another way to broaden your information base, although it is a good idea to follow through with additional research, particularly if topics are promotion or advertising based. Many books and videos are available that can be purchased or borrowed for independent reading and study. Of course, all of these options involve a certain expenditure of time, effort, and money. People that are committed to success understand that taking responsibility for advancing their education is ultimately worth the investment. ✓ **L013**

Web Resources

Continuing education requirements or CEUs (Continuing Education Units) for estheticians vary from state to state. Associated Skin Care Professionals (ASCP) provides a listing of all continuing education seminars along with the CE requirements for each state and a direct link to each state board. For a complete listing of requirements and seminars across the United States go to www.ascpskincare.com.

Planning Your Success

Many factors contribute to a successful career. We have already discussed several of them, including having a clear vision of the type of environment that best suits you, meeting the demands of your job description, and being committed to advancing your education. With that in mind, always remember that an important area that should not be overlooked is character or personality development.

We already know that efficient time management and a strong work ethic are important ingredients for success. But there are other qualitative factors to consider. Take a closer look at those who have made it. Successful people are *motivated* or driven to achieve their goals. This requires discipline and, at times, a great deal of flexibility. Success is not something that happens overnight. It requires hard work and dedication. There will be times when you hit roadblocks and need to rethink your plan. When this happens, it is important not to give up. Learn to use your setbacks as opportunities for growth, and stay focused on your goals. As you find your own way, it is also important to maintain a code of conduct that you can be proud of. Be clear about what you stand for, and remain ethical in your dealings with others. This will establish you as a person of integrity and credibility. Finally, it is important to remember to be true to yourself—there is no stopping success if you believe in yourself.

Review Questions

1. Name several ways you can begin to investigate job opportunities as a student.
2. Discuss the best methods for preparing for your state licensing exam.
3. List several techniques that can be utilized to improve your results when taking written exams.
4. What is the best way to approach your response to multiple-choice questions on a test? True and false questions?
5. List the topics that should be covered in a resume and identify the general categories they apply to.
6. Name at least five things that should not be included in your resume.
7. List the components of a good cover letter. Practice writing a cover letter that includes these criteria.
8. What should you look for in determining whether a salon or spa is right for you?
9. What is the purpose of an information interview?
10. Describe four types of salon or spa environments. Comment on the one that suits you best, and state the reasons for your decision.
11. Create a list of possible questions that you might ask during an information interview based on your target environment.
12. Name eight possible ways to network.
13. Discuss several practical steps you can take to prepare for a job interview.
14. What questions are not allowed during a professional interview?
15. What is the purpose of a job description?
16. Name and describe two ways in which the esthetician is compensated for his or her work. Which method do you consider the most advantageous? State your reasons.
17. Name several possible candidates for role models, and discuss the best way to approach these individuals for an information interview. List at least three questions that you would like to ask these people.
18. What is the primary reason for estheticians to continue their education?

Glossary

commission	A method of compensation that is percentage-based and is directly related to the employee's performance; for example, the employee earns a certain percentage of whatever services he or she performs and/or a certain percentage of the amount of product he or she sells.
deductive reasoning	The process of reaching logical conclusions by employing logical reasoning.
franchised salon or spa	A salon or spa owned by an individual(s) who pays a certain fee to use the company name and is part of a larger organization or chain of salons. The franchise operates according to a specified business plan and set protocols.
independent contractor	Is someone who sets his or her own fees, controls his or her own hours, has his or her own business card, and pays his or her own taxes.
information interview	A scheduled meeting or conversation whose sole purpose is to gather information.

Glossary

job description	Specified list of duties and responsibilities that are required of an employee in the performance of his or her job.
networking	A method of increasing contacts and building relationships to further one's career.
quotas	A method for gauging the amount of sales and targeting production levels.
resume	A written summary of education and work experience that highlights relevant accomplishments and achievements.
role model	A person whose behavior and success are worthy of emulation.
salary	A method of compensation that specifies a certain amount of pay based on either a flat or hourly rate.
test-wise	Refers to a student who begins to prepare for taking a test by practicing good study habits and time management as part of an effective study program.
transferable skills	Those abilities, such as sales training or administrative skills, that were mastered at other jobs and can be applied to a new position.

CHAPTER 22

The Skin Care Business

Chapter Outline

- Why Study The Skin Care Business?
- Going into Business for Yourself
- The Importance of Keeping Good Records
- Operating a Successful Skin Care Business
- Public Relations

Learning Objectives

After completing this chapter, you will be able to:

- ☑ **LO1** Describe the qualities necessary to be successful in a service profession.
- ☑ **LO2** Name and describe the types of ownership under which a skin care salon or spa may operate.
- ☑ **LO3** Evaluate options for going into business for yourself.
- ☑ **LO4** List the most important factors to consider when opening a salon.
- ☑ **LO5** Understand the importance of the business plan.
- ☑ **LO6** Explain why it is necessary to keep accurate business records.
- ☑ **LO7** Discuss the importance of the front desk and receptionist to a salon's success.
- ☑ **LO8** Demonstrate the best practices for telephone use.
- ☑ **LO9** Describe methods for managing personnel.

Key Terms

Page number indicates where in the chapter the term is used.

booth rental
pg. 672

business plan
pg. 675

capital
pg. 670

consumption supplies
pg. 685

corporation
pg. 671

demographics
pg. 674

employee manual
pg. 693

fixed costs
pg. 675

partnership
pg. 670

personnel
pg. 693

procedural guide
pg. 693

profit
pg. 676

public relations (PR)
pg. 695

retail supplies
pg. 685

revenue
pg. 676

sole proprietorship
pg. 670

variable costs
pg. 675

Over the past several decades, the beauty business has grown tremendously, becoming a multibillion-dollar industry that has moved beyond traditional hair and nail care to include total body services. This more holistic approach to beauty has given birth to a new era that has broadened treatment options and created a much stronger connection between beauty, health, and wellness, expanding the role of the salon and spa. From this new perspective, professional skin care has emerged from what traditionally has been a minor role in the U.S. beauty market to become the focus of many new business opportunities (**Figure 22–1**).

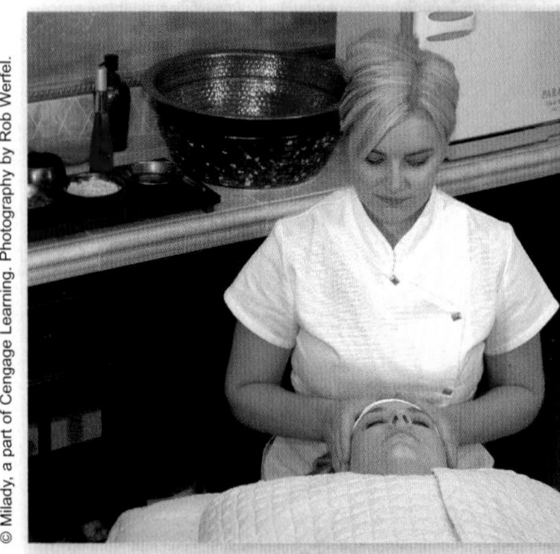

▲ Figure 22–1
Professional skin care has become a significant part of the health, beauty, and wellness movement.

Why Study The Skin Care Business?

Skin care is an ever-evolving industry with new and more sophisticated products and procedures continually entering the market.
To be competitive you must have knowledge of all facets of operations and business management.

- Starting your own skin care business has its risks and rewards. The successful entrepreneur weighs both carefully *before* going into business on their own.
- Planning is critical to establishing and growing your business. When you begin with a detailed business plan, you have a better chance of staying on track and reaching your goals.
- Deciding which type of business ownership you will use to operate your business is an important consideration that affects liability, finances, and taxes.
- The front desk is the center of business operations. What happens here will impact two of the most important factors in establishing a profitable salon or spa: customer satisfaction and retail sales.
- Skilled workers are an invaluable asset to the profitability of any skin care business. When you provide employees with clear expectations your chances of developing long and fruitful relationships increase.

Going into Business for Yourself

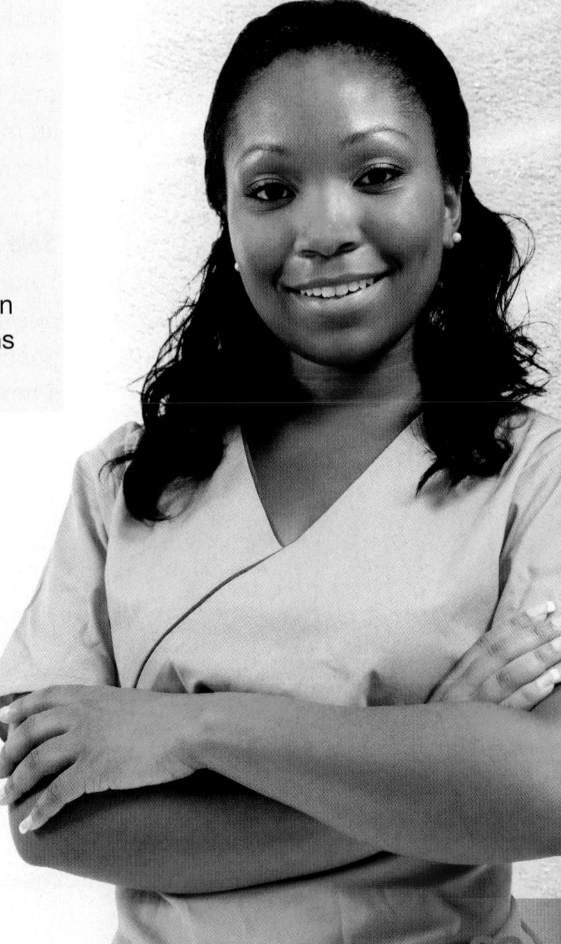

Perhaps you are thinking about starting your own business. Many service providers enter the field of skin care with the thought of owning their own salon or spa one day. If you are focused, disciplined, and driven to achieve your goals this may be a viable option for you. You need to keep in mind that motivation and commitment are only the beginning. To be successful, you will need to have lots of energy, a clear vision of what you would like to accomplish, and solid business skills. Education is critical to gaining the knowledge you will need to operate a profitable business. You should also have some real, practical experience in the business before taking the leap to spa or salon ownership. Hands-on familiarity with daily operations is a valuable lesson for anyone starting out in the industry, especially those with little or no business management experience

Operating your own business is a big responsibility, and it will involve many hours of careful planning and preparation. You will need to become familiar with several basic business principles such as accounting, finance, business and tax laws, insurance, human resource management, sales, and marketing. Managing day-to-day operations will also require the ability to solve employee, customer, and business management problems on a regular basis. Even if you have experience in the business world, there is always a learning curve. Be prepared to address any number of issues such as scheduling employees, booking appointments, managing dissatisfied clients, tracking inventory, and ordering supplies. Those who take the time to study the industry, focus their intentions, and develop critical thinking skills are generally in a better position to achieve success. ✓ **L01**

Ownership Options

There are various options available to those interested in becoming a salon owner. To choose the one that is right for you, it is important to understand the specific parameters associated with each. An attorney who specializes in such matters can be an invaluable resource in helping you reach a decision. Before you seek legal advice, it is a good idea to conduct your own research. This will help you formulate the right questions, thus saving time and money. A salon can be owned and operated by an individual, a partnership, or a corporation. The following are brief descriptions of each type of ownership.

Sole Proprietorship

Under individual ownership, or **sole proprietorship**, the proprietor acts as sole owner and manager. A *sole proprietor* is responsible for determining all policies and making all of the necessary decisions associated with running a business. In turn, a sole proprietor is also accountable for all expenses, receives all profits, and bears all losses. If you are an independent, self-motivated individual who likes to be in charge and does not mind assuming all of the duties and obligations associated with operating a business, this may be the best arrangement for you.

▼ **Figure 22–2**
A partnership can be a mutually satisfying experience.

Partnership

In a **partnership** two or more people share ownership, although this does not necessarily mean an equal arrangement (**Figure 22–2**). There are several benefits to a partnership, including increased **capital** (money) for investment in the business, a greater pool of skills and talent to draw from, and the added advantage of shared responsibilities and decision making. It is important to remember that when it comes to sharing, partners also divide and share profits. In a partnership, each partner also assumes the other's unlimited liability for debt.

If you like the security of working jointly with others and you are willing to assume the risk of liability, a partnership may be ideal for you. A partnership can be a mutually satisfying experience for the right partners. It can also be a lesson in frustration if you find yourself affiliated with the wrong partner. To avoid any long-term repercussions seek qualified legal counsel. Also, before entering any binding agreement, learn as much as possible about your prospective partner's ethics and philosophies.

Corporation

Incorporating is one of the best ways that a business owner can protect his or her assets. Most people choose to incorporate for solely this reason, but this form of ownership has other advantages. For example, the corporate business structure saves you money in taxes, provides greater business flexibility, and makes raising capital easier. It also limits your personal financial liability if your business accrues unmanageable financial debts or otherwise runs into financial trouble.

A **corporation** raises capital by issuing stock certificates or shares. Stockholders (people or companies that purchase shares) have an ownership interest in the company. The more stock they own, the larger their interest becomes. You can be the sole stockholder (or shareholder) or have many stockholders. In a corporation, income tax is limited to the salary that you draw, not the real profits of the business; however, a stockholder in a corporation is required to pay unemployment insurance, whereas a sole proprietor or partner is not.

Corporations are managed by a board of directors who determine policies and make decisions according to the corporation's charter and bylaws. Corporate formalities such as director or stockholder meetings are required to maintain a corporate status. The corporation also costs more to set up and run than a sole proprietorship or partnership does. For example, there are the initial information fees, filing fees, and annual state fees; however, many people believe the advantages of incorporating outweigh any necessary legal and accounting obligations. Should you decide that a corporation is right for you, many resources—including computer software—are available to guide you through the process of incorporating. Additionally, you will require the services of a competent lawyer and tax accountant to be sure your business complies with more complex state rules and regulations. Nevertheless, corporations can offer excellent benefits and opportunities, particularly for businesses with a larger number of employees.

Other corporate models and business entities, such as the S corporation and the limited liability company (LLC), may be better suited to your needs. A competent business attorney familiar with the laws in your state is the best resource for answering more specific questions about these models. ☑ **LO2**

Booth Rentals

For many, renting a booth or space within an established salon is a good way to gain the experience of operating a business on a much smaller scale. Booth rentals, as they are commonly called, have become popular in various settings including beauty salons, skin care clinics, and day spas. They offer the practitioner an opportunity to be his or her own boss within a certain set of parameters. In **booth rental**, the esthetician is required to pay the owner a set rental fee, along with payment of utilities as agreed upon, to operate in a specific space within the owner's establishment. The renter is responsible for conducting all necessary business functions, such as managing her own clientele, supplies, and records. With that being stated, keep in mind that renting space does not necessarily mean that you have complete control over your situation.

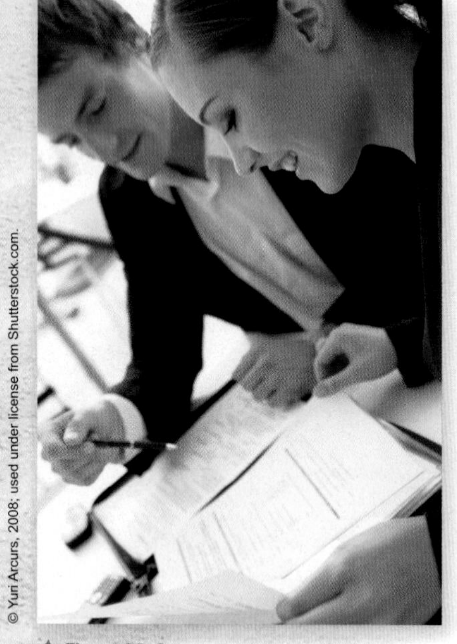

© Yuri Arcurs, 2008; used under license from Shutterstock.com.

▲ Figure 22–3
There are many factors to consider when opening your own salon.

Before you agree to a booth-rental arrangement, take time to investigate the many legal and business aspects of conducting business as a booth renter. The first thing you will want to determine is whether it is lawful to operate as a booth renter in your state. Some states require a separate license for booth rentals. Other states may not recognize this business structure at all. So it is important to check with all of the state regulating agencies that apply, including your esthetic licensing board, before adopting this model. Note that some state boards require an apprenticeship before an esthetician can be self-employed. Renting a space from a qualified practitioner may or may not meet the criteria, so be sure to learn whether your current esthetician license is sufficient to operate on your own. Other state business and licensing requirements for operating a separate business may also apply to you. It is also imperative that you have a complete understanding of Internal Revenue Service (IRS) laws governing this form of business ownership. Remember that as a booth renter you are responsible for paying all taxes associated with being self-employed, including higher Social Security taxes which are double that of an employee (**Figure 22–3**).

Once you are clear about the legalities, weigh the pros and cons of this business structure carefully. There are several advantages to booth rentals. For example, booth rentals offer the individual practitioner an opportunity to establish his or her own business with minimal investment, generally require lower maintenance fees, and give the practitioner the flexibility of creating his or her own schedule. In some situations, the booth renter may be allowed to engage in joint advertising efforts, sharing costs at a lower rate. Additionally, there may be an opportunity to access clients from the owner's existing clientele. These benefits can be appealing, but it is wise to learn as much as you can about the business and owner before signing any contracts. Take a close look at the owner's track record. How many years has the establishment been in business? What is its turnover rate for booth renters and/or employees? Do you agree with the accepted practices of the salon owner? Sharing similar philosophies goes a long way in resolving any problems that may arise.

There are other practical matters to consider. For some, the idea of keeping records for legal and tax purposes can be a challenge. Being the sole person responsible for all day-to-day operations such as scheduling appointments, managing clients, purchasing products, and maintaining inventory is a huge undertaking when there is no partner or team to support you. If you do not enjoy working alone, this arrangement may not suit you. Keep in mind that you will be required to retain separate malpractice and health insurance, and you will not have the luxury of additional benefits that are typically supplied by employers, such as paid vacation time and sick days. In addition, you may be limited to certain hours during which you can conduct business, and you will be responsible for marketing and developing your own clientele.

If, after exploring all angles, you decide this business model is right for you proceed cautiously, and be sure to obtain the appropriate legal advice before signing any documents or contracts. Carefully researching all matters before you act can help to avoid problems. ☑ **LO3**

REGULATORY AGENCY ALERT

Some state boards require a special license for booth rentals. Before entering a booth-rental arrangement, always check with local and state board officials to determine rules and regulations as they apply to your individual situation.

Developing a Plan of Action

Everyone has a different vision of the type of esthetics practice he or she would enjoy. For some, results are most important; for others, health and wellness are the top priority. Deciding which treatments you would like to offer will help you determine the type of facility, products, and equipment that will be most effective in accomplishing your goals.

Once you are clear about your overall concept, you will be ready to develop a strategic business plan. Many factors go into operating a successful business and are far beyond the scope of this chapter. It is a good idea to read and research your ideas extensively before making any final decisions. A review of the following basics will help you to get started.

Location

"Location, location, location!" How often have you heard that phrase? While no one location can guarantee success, deciding where to conduct business is an important consideration that requires careful deliberation. The right location for your business model can significantly affect your success.

Two of the most important factors in determining a location are *visibility* and *accessibility*. Ideally, a good location is easy to get to and highly visible. Most people are juggling busy schedules and being close to other thriving businesses, such as supermarkets, restaurants, department stores, or specialty shops, offers clients the added convenience of "one-stop" shopping that is so crucial. High-traffic areas offer access to a larger number of potential clients. More remote locations generally require a good deal of advertising to attract business, and this can be costly for the new small business owner. Before deciding on a location it is wise to conduct a complete marketing and demographic analysis, or feasibility study. This should include a thorough examination of the finances needed to develop a profitable business in the desired area (**Figure 22–4**).

▲ Figure 22–4
Visibility and accessibility are two of the most important factors to consider when searching for a business location.

Here's a Tip

A building that is highly visible is not necessarily easy to access. Be sure the facility you are renting has a convenient way to enter and leave during the salon's regular business hours. Learning that the building's main entry opens after or closes before your salon's doors may make it difficult for you to conduct business and can require extra security measures. Snow removal and sidewalk maintenance are other important safety considerations, especially for those with mobility issues. Be sure to consider these factors when negotiating the terms of a lease.

Parking Facilities

A critical element in attracting business is parking. Frequently, clients may be pleased with your services but become frustrated over the inability to find convenient or affordable parking. Particularly in these uncertain times, safety and convenience are important marketing features. As spa and salon hours become increasingly flexible, it is only natural for clients to want to feel safe walking in an area, especially at night or in bad weather. Well-lit, ample, and affordable parking is a good way to alleviate these concerns.

Target Market

In searching for various places to open your salon or spa, it is important to keep your target market in mind. If you want to attract a high-end clientele, explore high-income areas. If you are interested in attracting a variety of clients with moderate incomes, search for a high-volume area that is conveniently located and offers easy access to public transportation. While many people starting small businesses like the convenience of being close to home, understand that you may have to travel a bit to reach the market your spa or salon hopes to attract.

Demographics

How do you know if an area meets the criteria of your target market? One of the best ways to find out is to study the demographics. The term **demographics** (DEM-uh-GRAF-iks) refers to particular identifying characteristics of an area or population, such as the specific size, age, sex, or ethnicity of its residents; average income; and buying habits. This important information is available from various sources including town census bureaus, the government, local chamber of commerce and real estate agents, and special marketing agencies. Information may be obtained in a variety of formats including electronic media such as CD-ROM or print publications that distribute "cluster snapshots" or demographic synopses.

From a more subjective perspective, you can also gain valuable information by speaking with other business owners in the area or by attending local meetings and events. Learning more about who lives in a particular area, what they like to do, how they spend their money, and what they value, need, or want will help you to decide if the type of salon or spa you would like to open is a good fit.

Competition

The skin care and spa industry has grown tremendously in recent years, creating a far more competitive marketplace than the one existing even a decade ago. While it is important to investigate the services being offered at other salons in your area, do not let your findings intimidate you. The mainstay of business in the United States is competition, and in many cases it has played a positive and motivating role in driving successful businesses.

Nevertheless, it is usually in your best interest to look for an area that has a limited number of salons or spas. It is also wise to develop a unique menu of services that will attract your specific target market. There is always room for a different approach that does not directly compete with those of existing businesses. In fact, similar businesses often exist side by side quite successfully simply because they are targeting different markets.

Before you sign a lease, it still makes good sense to conduct a thorough investigation of what others are offering and the prices they are charging. You may also want to visit several reputable and established salons that are not in your general vicinity. It never hurts to find out what other successful businesses are doing right. As you conduct your research, keep a journal of those practices that make a positive impression. Then create a list of ways you might improve upon those ideas. ☑ L04

Here's a Tip

If your experience is limited there are many resources available, including computer software, that provide several methods for developing a business plan. Alternatively, hiring a professional consultant might ultimately be the most cost-effective way to approach this task. If you are unsure about how to locate a professional in this area, consider asking other small business owners for referrals or call the professional organizations to which you belong. Your local chamber of commerce or small business association is usually a good place to start.

The Small Business Administration (SBA) is another independent federal agency set up to help small businesses succeed. In addition to information on financial management and business planning, the SBA provides links to training programs and other resources such as the Service Core of Retired Executives (SCORE). More information on the SBA and its resources can be accessed at www.sba.gov.

The Business Plan: Costs, Revenue, and Profits

How will you get to your destination if you do not know where you are going? The **business plan** is a basic business tool that provides a strategy for understanding key elements in developing business. It is a written description of your business as you see it today, and as you foresee it in the next five years (detailed by year). It serves as a sort of map or blueprint to help guide you in making informed decisions and should include several important categories: an executive summary, a marketing plan, a strategic design and development plan, an operations plan, and a financial plan.

There are many variations of the business plan. Each will differ in style. Any plan you develop should include a general description of your business; the legal structure you will use to operate your business; the products and services you will provide; how you will market those products and services; a detailed explanation of how you will finance your operation; the accounting methods and technology you will use to control finances; and a discussion of the business administration policies and procedures you will use to manage two of the most important aspects of business operations: clients and employees.

Financial management is the cornerstone of a successful business plan. Be prepared to identify all costs related to operations, including a price structure for products and services, employee salaries, the cost of any additional benefits, and other ordinary expenses such as the cost of equipment, supplies, rent, utilities, insurance, taxes, and marketing and advertising.

Learning to think in terms of *costs, revenues,* and *profits* can help you gain a more global perspective of business functions as you develop your plan. Expenses related to operating your salon can be broken down into fixed and variable costs. **Fixed costs** are operating costs that are constant, for example, rent and loan payments. **Variable costs** are expenses that can fluctuate, such as utilities, supplies, and advertising. To a certain extent, you will have some control over variable costs. **Revenue** is the income generated from selling services and products; that is, money coming in. **Profit** is the amount of money available after all expenses are subtracted from all revenues.

As you become familiar with the specific costs related to running your business and the number of services or products you must sell to meet costs and earn a profit, you will be able to forecast, or make projections, about your business. Of course, to make viable projections, you will need to consider many variables on a weekly, monthly, or yearly basis. The smart businessperson also factors in changing circumstances such as economic trends and down periods. An in-depth analysis of the actual business you do over a certain time period versus forecasting will give you a more accurate idea of your situation and also help you make good business decisions (Table 22–1). ☑ LO5

▼ Table 22–1
An Income Statement.

AN INCOME STATEMENT				
	1ST QTR	2ND QTR	3RD QTR	4TH QTR
Net Sales or Revenues:	______	______	______	______
Less the Cost of Goods Sold	______	______	______	______
Gross Profit:	______	______	______	______
Operating Expenses:				
Salaries, Wages, & Commissions	______	______	______	______
Operating Supplies	______	______	______	______
Repairs & Maintenance	______	______	______	______
Laundry	______	______	______	______
Advertising & Promotion	______	______	______	______
Loan Interest	______	______	______	______
Rent	______	______	______	______
Utilities	______	______	______	______
Telephone	______	______	______	______
Insurance	______	______	______	______
Payroll Taxes	______	______	______	______
Benefit Costs	______	______	______	______
Administrative Costs	______	______	______	______
Legal Fees	______	______	______	______
Licenses	______	______	______	______
Training & Development	______	______	______	______
Depreciation	______	______	______	______
Total Operating Expenses:	______	______	______	______
Profit [or Loss] before Taxes:	______	______	______	______
Taxes:	______	______	______	______
Net Profit [or Loss] after Taxes:	______	______	______	______

Planning the Physical Layout

Creating an efficient and user-friendly workspace requires careful planning. To obtain the best results, you will need to work closely with other experts such as architects, contractors, electricians, plumbers, and product and equipment vendors. You will also need to establish a positive working relationship with local planning board officials and state licensing agents. This can be an exciting time. With so many critical decisions to be made, it can also be a stressful time when you must think quickly and act decisively.

Your business plan will serve as a useful tool throughout the planning process. You will want to have this plan readily available and refer to it often during the various stages of construction. It will help you to stay on task and within budget as you make all the necessary decisions and purchases associated with operating your salon on a day-to-day basis.

Before construction begins, think carefully about the primary services you will offer as well as the ambiance you would like to create. Follow up by carefully researching all of the equipment that is needed to provide your services. Certain apparatus and design features may require special handling or modifications. You will want to be aware of any hidden costs, such as special power sources, that will be needed to operate mechanical or technological devices. Naturally, the safety and comfort of both clients and practitioners should always be a top priority as you make these important decisions (**Figure 22–5**). A review of the information on ergonomics and treatment room setup in Chapter 3, Your Professional Image and Chapter 14, The Treatment Room, will be helpful here.

As you plan your spa or salon (**Figures 22–6** and **22–7** on page 678), the following checklist may be helpful.

- Does the layout provide maximum efficiency and a safe environment for practitioners and clients?
- Does the style of the salon evoke a professional ambiance that instills client confidence?
- Is the color scheme inviting to a broad spectrum of clients (men and women, older and younger clients)?
- Are amenities such as refreshments, music, and reading materials conducive to a friendly, relaxed, and professional ambiance?
- Does the reception area give clients a warm and welcoming first impression?
- Do services flow easily from the reception area to each treatment room?

Did You Know?

Mention the word *marketing* and most people immediately think about sales or advertising; however, marketing is more than advertising and sales promotions. It is a complex business strategy that is planned according to what are commonly referred to as the *Four P's: Product, Price, Promotion,* and *Place* or the marketing mix.

In skin care the word *Product* refers to your complete business concept. *Price* is the monetary value assigned to the goods and services you sell. *Promotion* refers to all of the communication methods you use to persuade customers to purchase your products and services. *Place* is the distribution channel or method for delivering your goods and services to clients. These factors are outlined in greater depth in the chapter on Marketing in the *Milady Standard Esthetics: Advanced* text, where you will also find a detailed explanation of the various promotional strategies used in marketing. We'll talk more about several of these in the next chapter.

What is important for anyone interested in owning and operating their own skin care salon or spa to remember is marketing drives business. Failure to set aside appropriate funding for this critical business strategy often means the difference between success and failure.

▲ Figure 22–5
The safety and comfort of both clients and practitioners should be a primary concern when planning the treatment room.

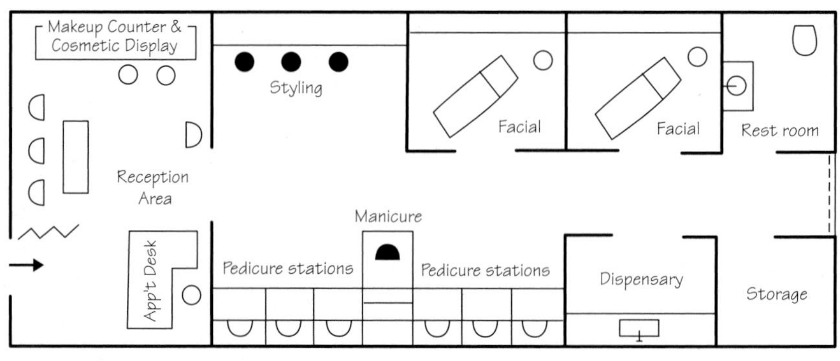

▲ **Figure 22–6**
Layout for a full-service salon.

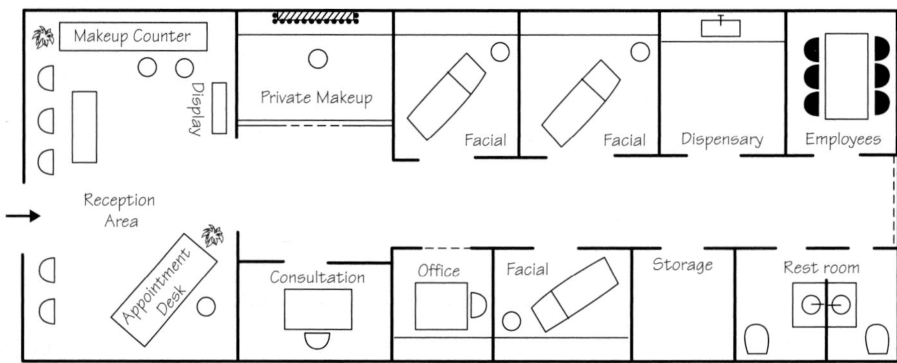

▲ **Figure 22–7**
Layout for a facial and makeup salon.

ACTIVITY

Create a physical plan for your own salon, designating the equipment that you will need to conduct facial and body services. Then estimate the cost of equipment. Be sure to include the cost of any special design or construction considerations.

- Is aisle space adequate for safety and efficiency?
- Is there enough space to allow for each piece of equipment that will be used in the treatment room?
- Have you chosen furniture, equipment, and fixtures on the basis of cost, durability, safety, utility, and appearance?
- Have you purchased the appropriate warranties or insurance necessary to protect your initial investments?
- Does your dispensary supply adequate storage space and ease of mobility?
- Are plumbing, lighting, and utilities adequate for the services that you intend to provide?
- Do air conditioning and heating systems supply adequate ventilation and comfort?
- Are restrooms clean and easily accessible?

Regulations, Business Laws, and Insurance

Understanding the law is critical to operating a successful business. Before opening the doors to your salon, be sure you are in compliance with all local, state, and federal regulations. You should be aware that laws vary from state to state. It is your responsibility to check into the specific laws that govern business owners in the state you are working in, particularly as they apply to your licensing or ability to establish your own business. In some states there are levels of licensure that may require a practitioner to work under another experienced and licensed professional for a certain period of time before being allowed to operate independently.

After confirming your ability to own and operate a salon, you must contact local authorities to investigate other necessary business licenses and regulations. Ordinarily, local officials supervise building renovations and business codes. You should seek information regarding sales tax, licenses, and employee compensation laws from state administration. The federal government oversees laws regarding Social Security, unemployment compensation or insurance, cosmetics, and luxury taxes. Although some people may be annoyed by the idea of complying with so many rules and regulations, keep in mind that regulations and laws exist to protect the consumer and enforce fair and reasonable standards for best business practices. Prospective business owners should also be aware that failure to comply with state and federal regulations and tax obligations can result in serious legal consequences. If you do not understand your obligations as a business owner, seek the advice of a qualified business attorney and certified public accountant (CPA).

As a small business owner you will be responsible for the payment of several business taxes. Your tax obligations will vary depending on the legal structure of your business and should be reviewed with a qualified business attorney and/or certified public accountant when setting up your practice.

Every small business should have a complete overview of the various tax obligations associated with business ownership. The Internal Revenue Service (IRS), a bureau of the U.S. Department of Treasury, publishes a complete guide to taxes for this purpose: "Publication 334, Tax Guide for Small Business." This publication is free and can be accessed on-line at www.irs.gov. A more complete summary of business taxes is covered in the chapter on financial business skills in *Milady Standard Esthetics: Advanced* text.

Insurance is another primary concern for business owners. You will need it to guard your business against such unforeseen events as malpractice, liability, disability, fire, burglary, theft, and business interruption. Before purchasing insurance, it is always best to seek professional advice to determine the right amount and type of coverage for your particular business needs. It is also a good idea to contact the department of insurance in your state to learn more about laws regulating insurance. You will need to comply with certain insurance obligations that are required by law, such as workers' compensation.

Although insurance may give the business owner some peace of mind, it should not be considered protection against inappropriate conduct. If you decide to become a business owner, it will be your job to ensure that everyone in your salon practices within the boundaries of their license. Always review the limitations of your insurance policy carefully, and take time to establish appropriate guidelines for your employees.

Salon owners must also be aware of state and federal guidelines for regulating sanitation and occupational safety. The Occupational Safety and Health Administration (OSHA) is a government agency responsible for overseeing safety in the workplace. Those working in the skin care industry should be familiar with OSHA guidelines, particularly as they apply to the correct procedure for handling bloodborne materials, instruments, and equipment. For more information on this topic or other issues more specific to skin care, visit one of OSHA's numerous Web sites on the Internet or contact the Department of Public Health in your state.

Purchasing an Established Salon

Buying an existing salon or spa is often advantageous. For example, you will have the opportunity to begin working right away and will not have to worry about buying furnishings or fixtures. Before you buy, however, thoroughly investigate what you are buying. Most buyers are concerned about the initial return on their investment and the possibility of increasing future sales. Many become disappointed when an existing clientele fails to frequent the salon under new ownership or when equipment does not operate as expected. This does not mean that buying an established business is out of the question. You should simply understand that some risk is involved and take preventive measures wherever possible. For example, you may be able to obtain an extended warranty for equipment that is several years old, or you could negotiate the owner's staying on for a certain time period to ease the transition. Another important consideration is finding out whether current employees will continue to work for you. If that is your desire, it is wise to develop a protocol that keeps staff informed during the process.

▲ Figure 22–8
It is best to seek the appropriate legal advice when making important business decisions.

If you decide to purchase an established salon, always seek the professional advice of an accountant and business lawyer (**Figure 22–8**). You may also want to consider a broker who specializes in the transfer of business ownership. In general, any agreement to buy an established salon should include the following parts:

- A formal written and legal purchase and sale agreement that dictates the terms of your agreement, noting any specific arrangements in detail
- A complete and signed statement of inventory that includes all products, equipment, fixtures, furnishings, and so forth and indicates the value of each article
- Information that clearly establishes the owner's identity
- Free and unencumbered use of the salon's name and reputation for a defined period of time
- Complete disclosure of all information, records, and files regarding the salon's clientele, purchasing, and service habits
- A noncompete clause stating that the seller will not compete directly with the new owner, work in, or establish a new salon within a specified distance of the present salon location

Finally, whenever there is a transfer of a note, lease, mortgage, or bill of sale, the buyer should always conduct a thorough investigation to be sure there has not been any default in payments.

Leases

Owning your own business does not necessarily mean that you own the building where your salon or spa is located. Many businesses rent or lease space in buildings owned by others. When renting or leasing space, be prepared to negotiate the terms of your agreement with your landlord.

The final agreement should be clearly written and should specify who owns what and who is responsible for which repairs and expenses. If this is your first time renting commercial space, it may be helpful to seek guidance from a commercial real estate broker. It is also wise to have an attorney who specializes in real estate review the contract for you. Here are some points to consider as you negotiate your lease:

- Allow an exemption for fixtures or appliances that might be attached to the salon so that they can be removed without violating the lease
- Specify how any necessary renovations and repairs—such as painting, plumbing, fixtures, and electrical installation—will be handled, clearly stating who is responsible for what
- Include an option that allows you to assign the lease to another person; in this way, the obligations for the payment of rent are kept separate from the responsibilities of operating the business should you need to bring in another person or owner

Did You Know?

In some states, estheticians must practice under another licensed professional for a certain period of time before being allowed to operate on their own.

Protecting Your Business Against Fire, Theft, and Lawsuits

Once your salon is up and running, you will want to do everything possible to protect it from any unfortunate mishaps or incidents. To avoid more costly dilemmas, consider taking the following precautions:

- Install adequate locks, a fire alarm, and a burglar alarm system. It can also be helpful to create a security checklist so that those responsible for closing or opening the salon are aware of all the necessary measures required to lock and secure the premises.
- Maintain adequate amounts of liability, fire, malpractice, and burglary insurance. Note the expiration dates of your policy and take special care not to allow a lapse in coverage during the course of business.
- Make certain that all personnel practice within the boundaries of their professional license, performing only those services they are properly trained for. Licensed professionals must never offer advice or make recommendations outside of their area of expertise. Never violate the medical practice laws of your state by attempting to diagnose, treat, or cure a disease or illness. Always refer clients to a physician for diagnosis and treatment.
- Ignorance of the law is no excuse for violating it. Make sure you are familiar with and adhere to all laws governing the practice of esthetics in your state, including any sanitary codes that may apply in the city or state where you are operating. If you are an esthetician operating a full-service salon or spa that employs other licensed professionals, such as cosmetologists or massage therapists, be aware of all laws and any limitations pertaining to their supervision or practice. If you have any questions about a law or regulation, always check with the appropriate regulatory agency.

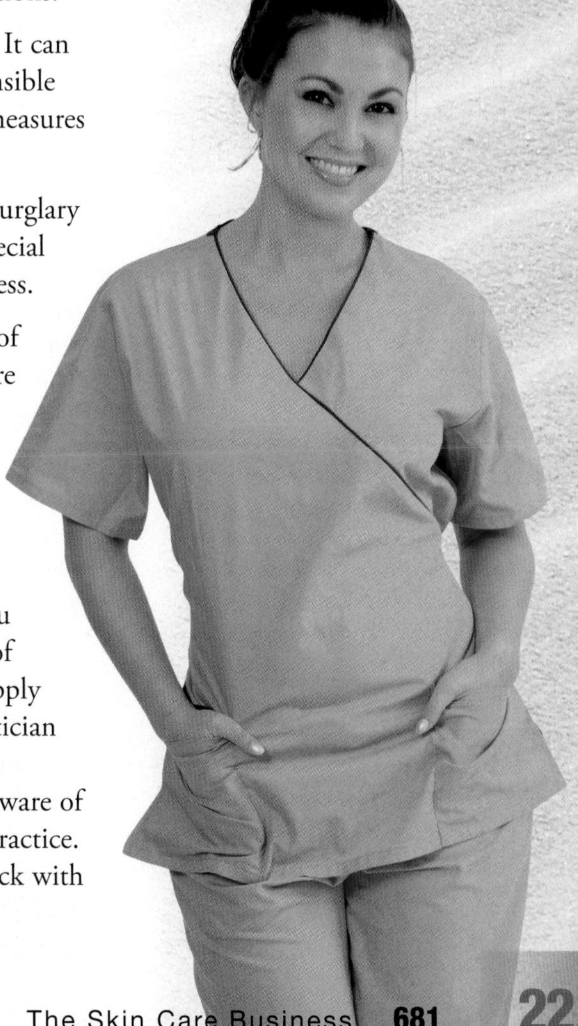

- As an employer, it is your duty to keep accurate records of the number of people you employ as well as their salaries, length of employment, and Social Security numbers. You must also be aware of and comply with various state and federal regulations as required by law to monitor the welfare of workers.

REGULATORY **AGENCY** **ALERT**

Ignorance of the law is no excuse for violating it. Always check with your regulatory agency if you have any questions about a law or regulation.

Business Operations

To operate a successful salon, you will need a variety of business and management skills. Owning your own skin care business can be extremely demanding. There are employees to manage, customers to please, appointments to schedule, services to perform, and business issues to address. For many, the list of tasks can seem endless, leaving even the most motivated individual feeling overwhelmed occasionally. Be patient: it takes time, discipline, and focus to become a good business manager.

As you develop a clear understanding of your business objectives, you can begin to address more practical requirements. Start by making a list of all the functions necessary to operate your salon successfully. Follow this with a critical self-analysis. If you find yourself lacking in certain areas, decide how you will address these issues. The smart businessperson recognizes that she or he cannot be all things. Perhaps you will enroll in a course to learn more about a subject, or you might decide to outsource certain responsibilities. For example, you could hire an accountant to manage your bookkeeping or a marketing consultant to handle advertising and promotions.

To keep your business running smoothly, consider the following successful business strategies.

Manage Finances Well

Working from your business plan, carefully determine how much capital or money you will need to operate your salon for at least 2 years. Understanding the amount of money that will be required to meet your expenses before you open your salon will help you develop a strategic plan for financing your operation and managing your money. We discussed costs, revenues, and profits earlier. Tracking these on a regular basis is vital to an established business. A reliable accounting system will help you to access this information and plan the allocation of your funds to maintain good business practices.

Develop Solid Business Management Skills

When starting out, you often will need to know more than you do. Running a successful business will require you to make thoughtful decisions. This means carefully researching your options and/or consulting with other professionals who can give you the information or support you need. When in doubt, do not be afraid to ask for help. As you become more informed, you will be able to make better choices and develop an effective management program.

Create Pricing Based on Value

Before you can determine a price for goods and services, you need to understand their value. Proper pricing begins with exact knowledge of what it costs to provide each service and retail product. Keeping in mind the old adage "You get what you pay for," set your prices according to the level and quality of the service or goods you are providing. In general, the type of salon and the clientele it serves determine the cost of goods and services. For example, you must understand what your clients need, want, and value as well as the price they are willing to pay for these products or services. It also makes good business sense to explore the competition, compare pricing, and regularly make appropriate adjustments to remain competitive.

Work Cooperatively with Employees

To stay in business and accomplish your goals, you must learn to work cooperatively with your staff. This requires effective management and communication skills. To develop harmonious working relationships, you must set clear boundaries and objectives, communicate respectfully, and resolve conflicts quickly and diplomatically. A good manager sets an appropriate example, includes staff in decision-making whenever possible, and encourages employees to achieve individual and salon goals that will keep clients coming back. To attract quality and experienced help, you must also be willing to offer competitive salaries and benefits, such as continuing education.

Develop Positive Customer Relations

Working with people in a service-oriented business such as skin care requires a variety of interpersonal skills. Clients come to you for a professional service. They should expect to receive quality care in a confidential, respectful, and courteous manner. Good communication is essential to reassuring clients and building a reputation for exemplary business practices. The well-run salon offers clear, concise policies and makes them highly visible—for example, by displaying them in the reception area, posting them on their Web site, and stating them directly in their brochure or menu of services (**Figure 22–9**). Although misunderstandings and conflicts are still bound to occur, if handled well, they can be an opportunity for you to develop a reputation for tact and diplomacy. To ensure client satisfaction and a positive outcome, be prepared to address common problems such as cancellations, no-shows, late arrivals, and product returns before they happen. The communication guidelines outlined in Chapter 4, Communicating for Success, will help you to accomplish this goal. When you follow through with clear directives, training all members of your staff to treat each client with dignity and respect, you will be well on your way to developing positive customer relations.

▲ **Figure 22–9**
Salon policies should be displayed in a highly visible area.

The Importance of Keeping Good Records

Keeping track of daily, weekly, and monthly records pertaining to your business may seem like one of the more mundane tasks associated with owning your own salon. This information is invaluable to you in understanding how well your business is functioning. Accurate records will help you determine income, expenses, profits, and loss. This information is also useful in assessing the net worth of your business and in arranging financing. Maintaining proper business records is also necessary for meeting the requirements of local, state, and federal laws regarding taxes and employees.

▲ Figure 22–10
Accurate records are crucial to understanding how well your business is functioning.

Many useful computer programs can simplify the task of keeping good records (**Figure 22–10**); however, it is recommended that you hire a professional accountant and skilled bookkeeper to assist you. (A bookkeeper is someone who is trained in financial record-keeping and follows proper bookkeeping standards.) To ensure that information is accurately applied, it should always be recorded clearly, correctly, concisely, and completely. Income is generally recorded as receipts from sales and service. Expenses include but are not limited to rent, utilities, salaries, insurance, advertising, equipment, supplies, and repairs. Be sure to retain all receipts, cancelled checks, check stubs, and invoices associated with your income and expenses. You will need these to manage your accounts efficiently and correctly.

Daily Records

A day-to-day accounting allows the business owner to measure various important functions. Most importantly, accurate daily records supply key information regarding gross income and the cost of operations. Whether you choose a computerized program or manual method, you will need to keep track of all sales on a daily basis. A review of your daily sales slips and appointment book will allow you to determine the number of products and services sold at your salon each day and the amount of income generated from these products and services. You will also want to note expenses that have been paid out. These should be registered in the appropriate accounting system and checkbook. Do not forget to document any miscellaneous or cash expenses for tax reporting purposes. This information may be kept in a cash journal or petty cash notebook. Your accountant can instruct you on the best way to handle daily slips and receipts. In general, cancelled checks, payroll, and monthly and yearly records are held for at least 7 years.

Weekly and Monthly Records

Certain financial records are easier to assess on a weekly or monthly basis. These reports may be used to compare the salon's performance to previous years, gauge promotional efforts, or check the demand for a service or product. Understanding the amount and types of services that are being performed in your salon can also serve as a check-and-balance system for utilizing products and staff more efficiently, controlling expenses, and eliminating waste.

Purchase and Inventory Control

Tracking inventory and supplies is an important part of conducting business. Inventory and purchase records will help you to prevent shortages, avoid overstocking, and alert you to any signs of pilfering. They are also important factors in measuring the net worth of your business at the end of the year.

Inventory can be broken down into two categories: consumption and retail supplies. **Consumption supplies** are items used to conduct business operations on a daily basis. Items available for sale to clients are referred to as **retail supplies**. Starting out you will need to base these purchases on projected sales revenue; however, it is important not to overstock items. Investing in products that might sit on your shelf for an extended period of time will tie up valuable dollars that could be better spent on other things. Accurate records can help you determine which items are used or sold most frequently. This information will help you to reorder supplies in a timely and cost-effective way (**Figure 22–11**).

Most business owners use a computerized system to track and control inventory. Be aware that you will need to conduct a physical count of all of the products on your retail and supply shelves as well. Monitoring the use of consumption products and supplies is an extremely important task that helps to control costs. All staff should be trained on the proper amount of product and supplies for each treatment and strict controls should be put in place to dispense product and supplies for day-to-day consumption. An analysis of service sales will help you to compare the amount of product being used to the number of services sold. This should correlate directly to the number of treatments being performed. Counting the items in every shipment and rotating newly purchased items when stocking your shelves is another important part of the process. If products expire before you can sell or use them, you have thrown valuable dollars right out the window.

▼ Figure 22–11
Tracking inventory and supplies helps owners prevent shortages and avoid overstocking.

Client Service Records

Maintaining accurate client records serves several business objectives, including customer service and performance analysis. Building relationships is an important factor in the service industry. To ensure client satisfaction, all service records should include key facts such as a client's name, the date and type of each treatment or product purchased, the amount charged, and the results obtained. It is also wise to note a client's particular preferences. In today's impersonal world, the simplest of details can significantly affect how the client perceives your efforts.

Client records are also instrumental in measuring the overall performance of a salon or individual practitioner. Analyzing sales and service can provide useful information for tracking customer trends and performing marketing tasks. Understanding what services and products clients need or want and when they are most likely to purchase them will ultimately increase sales and improve client satisfaction. ☑ **L06**

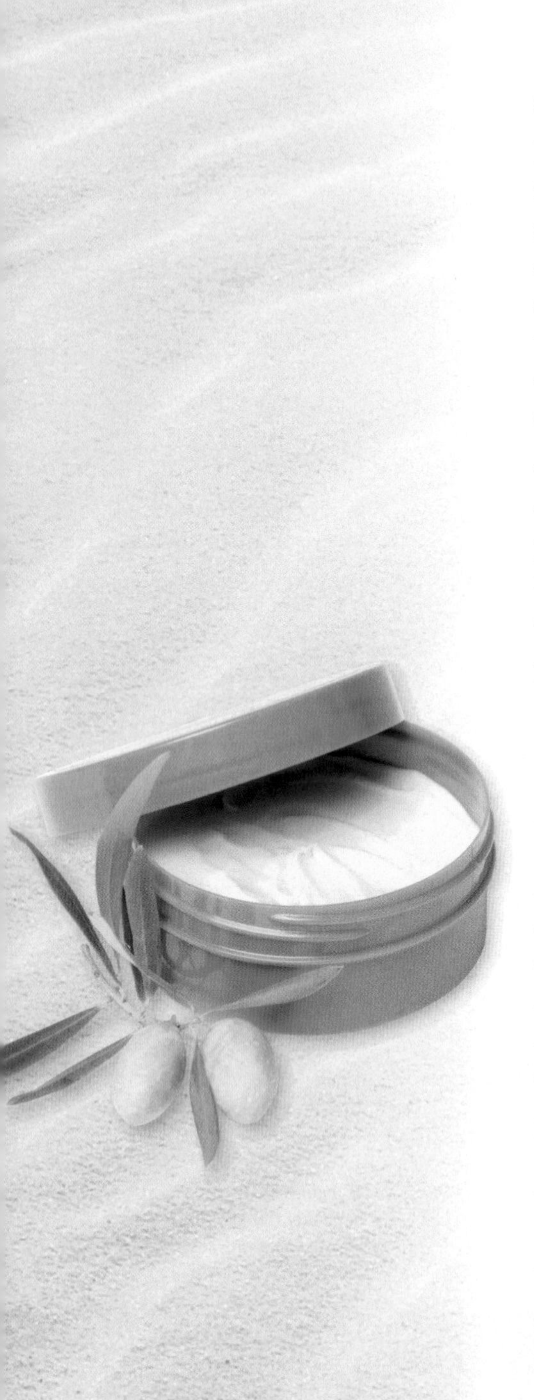

Operating a Successful Skin Care Business

Ask anyone operating a successful business what the key to his or her success is, and he or she will probably mention several things: the quality of services and staff, an efficient and pleasant workspace, eagerness to learn more about new treatments and techniques, and consistent marketing efforts; that being stated, one thing all owners likely have in common is the willingness to work hard. Certainly an element of luck is involved, you might be thinking—and indeed, in some cases, luck may be a factor. We have all had someone tell us, "I was just in the right place at the right time." Given the possibility that fate plays a role, we must still consider that without a great deal of planning, dedication, and continued hard work most businesses would ultimately fail.

The Front Desk

We have already mentioned the importance of developing positive customer relations in the esthetics industry. Establishing a caring, nurturing, and trusting relationship with clients is a key factor in building any skin care practice. It is important to recognize that client relations are not limited to interactions with the esthetician. A good salon owner or manager understands that a salon must consistently provide quality treatments and products to achieve success. More importantly, he or she knows that how well the front desk is managed has just as much to do with client satisfaction as the practitioner's performance does.

The Reception Area

In the reception area, your clients get that all-important first impression of your salon. Take extra care to make a positive impression by keeping the area attractive, neat, clean, and comfortable. Clients need to feel confident when they walk through your doors. To assure them, you must create a sense of calm, order, and organization. The front desk should be easily accessible and clutter free, allowing clients to check-in and out with a minimum amount of effort and confusion. While waiting for service, clients should be kept as comfortable as possible. Offer refreshments and reading materials for their pleasure. These should reflect the ambiance of your salon; for example, you will want to have educational materials that encourage good skin care habits (**Figure 22–12**).

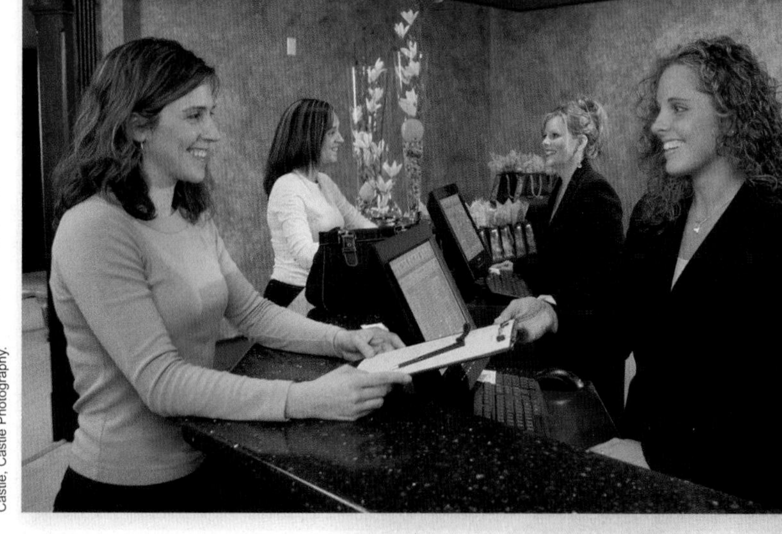

▲ Figure 22–12
An attractive reception area helps to create a positive first impression.

But the reception area offers more than a polished image. It is the hub of salon operations, where the receptionist does his or her job, appointments are made, retail merchandise is displayed and sold, and communication systems are located. To manage all these functions effectively, the reception area should be stocked with ample resources for accomplishing tasks quickly and efficiently. Essential items such as business and appointment cards, brochures, gift certificates, product guides, and price lists should be readily accessible at all times. The reception area is also the ideal place to display your menu of services, pricing information, spa policies, and promotional materials (**Figure 22–13**).

The Receptionist

The receptionist is instrumental in managing a well-run salon. He or she should be a valued member of your team and a resource for all products and services. It is imperative that you hire the right person for the job and train him or her well. This should include a complimentary sampling of all salon services. Having firsthand experience with all treatments will help the receptionist do a better job of selling them to clients.

▲ Figure 22–13
The reception area is the hub of salon operations.

The receptionist performs a variety of tasks that are critical to maintaining the flow of business. These include greeting clients, answering the telephone, booking appointments, keeping staff informed and on schedule, recommending services and products, and informing customers about policies and procedures. In many salons, the receptionist also performs other business functions. For example, he or she might maintain inventory, generate sales reports, perform marketing-related tasks, conduct follow-up or reminder phone calls, and prepare staff schedules.

It is the receptionist's job to promote goodwill, instill client confidence, and ensure customer satisfaction. To do the job well, he or she should enjoy working with people and have excellent interpersonal communication and public relations skills. The receptionist's work can be demanding and stressful, requiring the ability to juggle tasks simultaneously. The phone may be ringing, colleagues may have questions, and several clients may be standing in front of the desk waiting for service. Nevertheless, the receptionist must remain calm, courteous, and pleasant. He or she should also be conscious of personal presentation. As the first person clients come in contact with, the receptionist should reflect the image of the salon. A friendly smile and neat, clean appearance help create that all-important positive first impression. ✔ LO7

Scheduling Appointments

To generate business, you must book appointments. To do the job well, you should be aware of all scheduling parameters and time constraints. Managing time well is the key to successful business operations, particularly in the esthetics industry. In this fast-paced world, clients simply do not want to wait. To keep customers satisfied, those responsible for scheduling appointments should be aware of several crucial factors.

In most salons the receptionist is the primary person responsible for booking appointments. Whether appointments are made over the telephone or in person, the receptionist must be able to communicate clearly and effectively. Clients often have several questions when making decisions about appointments. The receptionist should be prepared to provide concise, direct, and courteous answers to such frequently asked questions such as the cost of a service and how long it takes to perform that service. There may be additional information that goes along with scheduling a treatment; for example, a client may need to be prepared to arrive early or dress in a certain way. This means the receptionist must be knowledgeable about all treatments and procedures and know how long it takes each practitioner to provide the requested service.

Appointments may be written in an actual book that is kept at the reception desk. In this day and age, most contemporary salons use computerized programs to schedule appointments. In many busy or larger salons, appointment information is networked to other areas of the facility to help staff stay on schedule. Whichever method is used, the receptionist must take care to enter information precisely. It is critical to obtain the client's first and last names, phone number, and the service they have requested.

To keep business flowing smoothly, most salons have specific policies for confirming and canceling appointments as well as for handling late arrivals. There may also be general guidelines for assigning services. In larger facilities, requesting a particular practitioner may not be an option. Smaller salons may honor such requests; however, it is sometimes difficult to fulfill a client's desire for a certain time or practitioner. In such cases, the receptionist should always give the client other options that may include suggesting another practitioner, offering to reschedule at another time, or putting the client on a waiting list for cancellations. Some clients may insist on being "squeezed in" for a special occasion or event. The receptionist must be careful not to overbook services, stating policies in an assertive but diplomatic way. Staying on schedule is crucial to the ease and flow of operations and ultimately promotes customer satisfaction. The receptionist must also consider how each practitioner works. In turn, practitioners must do their part to stay on schedule and work cooperatively with the receptionist. If schedules change or rotate monthly or weekly, the receptionist should be informed and display this information in a prominent place as a general reminder to others who may require it.

Scheduling appointments is generally the receptionist's main job. At times others may be required to answer the phone. It is important for management to instruct all staff members responsible for answering the phone in all aspects of booking appointments. Presenting the wrong information or keeping clients waiting for answers does not instill confidence.

© Milady, a part of Cengage Learning. Photography by Paul Castle, Castle Photography.

▲ Figure 22–14
Scheduling repeat appointments is an important aspect of generating business.

As a final note, those scheduling appointments should remember that repeat business is essential to maintaining a full appointment book. It should be standard practice to remind clients to book their next appointment (**Figure 22–14**). Some salons offer incentives for rebooking, such as special discounts or frequent-buyer programs. A good receptionist will make clients aware of any valuable savings when making appointments.

Telephone Skills

Although many businesses are becoming comfortable with e-commerce, using the Internet effectively to schedule appointments and make purchases on-line, the telephone is still considered the lifeline of business operations, offering direct personal service to clients. Therefore, proper training in the correct procedure for handling calls is essential.

For quality control purposes, it is often helpful to identify the specific language that should be used when answering calls and to supply examples of the best way to handle common problems. Many well-run businesses will print this information and store it in a strategic location near the telephone along with other important administrative manuals. Planning ahead in this way can prevent the necessity of urgently training a substitute for the receptionist. It also provides easy access to the correct protocols should employees who answer the telephone occasionally need a quick reminder.

The telephone is an important part of the salon's business. It is regularly used to do the following:

- Answer questions and provide friendly service
- Make, change, or confirm appointments
- Receive messages
- Promote client services
- Handle complaints
- Follow up with clients
- Order equipment and supplies from vendors

- Seek new business opportunities

Here are some suggested guidelines for making the most effective use of the telephone.

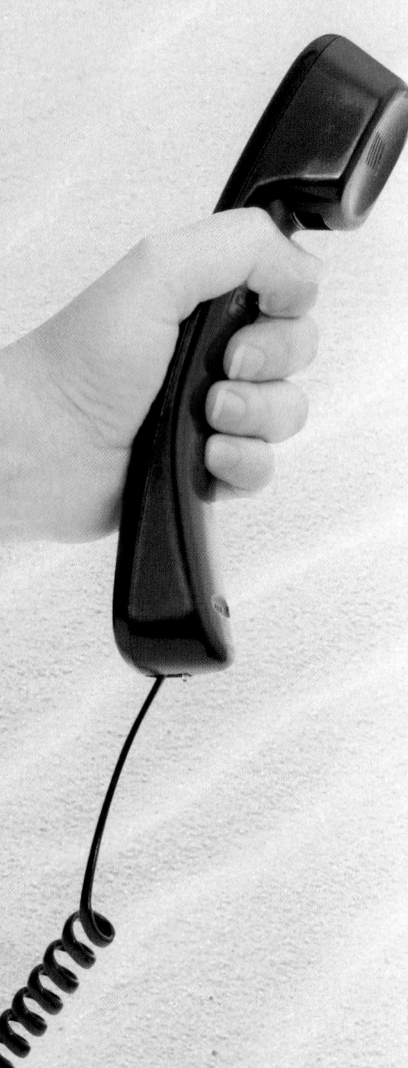

- Assign a specific person to answer the phone.
- Answer calls promptly, and return messages directly.
- Locate the telephone in a convenient and quiet area.
- Keep the necessary tools near the phone: pens, pencils, and a pad of paper for taking notes; directories; a list of important numbers; client records; and the salon's appointment book (or computer displaying the salon's appointment screen).
- Make business calls at a quiet time.
- Use a pleasant, natural tone of voice, speak clearly at a moderate pace, and use correct professional language. Do not use slang.
- Be polite, respectful, courteous, and attentive.
- Handle price objections or complaints with patience and tact. Do not say anything that might be construed as irritating or annoying.
- Practice appropriate greetings and answers to frequently asked questions.
- Plan and practice a "script" for marketing and business calls. This helps project an image of confidence and efficiency.
- Take notes so you will remember the main points of a conversation and be able to respond intelligently.

Incoming Calls

Salons spend a good percentage of their earnings on marketing. Getting the phone to ring is critical to stimulating business. Once your phone is ringing, you will want to make every effort to show how important that call is to you. Although voice mail and answering machines have become standard practice and are used in many smaller salons that may not be able to afford a full-time receptionist to answer the phone, proper etiquette still applies.

The following general guidelines are suggested as professional telephone etiquette:

- ***Answer your phone within three rings.*** No one likes to wait. Show clients you care by answering calls promptly.
- ***If you must place a caller on hold, be polite.*** Always ask permission before placing a caller on hold, allowing enough time for a response.
- ***Program your voice-mail system to be user-friendly.*** Your message should be brief, but provide enough information for clients to identify the salon. Use simple, easily understood instructions that encourage clients to leave their name, telephone number, and reason for calling.
- ***Return calls promptly.*** Check your messages often, and respond as quickly as possible. If you will be away from the telephone for any length of time,

let clients know how long and specify when you will return calls. Waiting longer than 24 hours to respond to a call is inappropriate.

- ***Project a positive attitude.*** Let clients know you are eager to serve them by greeting them in a sincere, welcoming tone of voice. Remember: a first-time caller is your first opportunity to make a good first impression.
- ***Be courteous and attentive.*** Use polite words and phrases such as *please, thank you,* and *excuse me.* Never chew gum or eat while engaged in a conversation. This is extremely unprofessional.
- ***Listen respectfully.*** Give the caller your undivided attention; carrying on a conversation with someone else while the caller is on the line is impolite. If you need to obtain additional information for a client, ask to place him or her on hold or take his or her number to return the call.
- ***Confirm appointments 24 to 48 hours in advance.*** Reminder calls show customers you value their business. Whether speaking directly to a client or leaving a message, be sure to state the details of the appointment including the exact time, date, day of the week, and service scheduled.
- ***When leaving messages, always address the client properly by name.*** Clearly identify yourself and the salon. Keep your message simple and to the point, providing exact information in a polite voice. ✓ **LO8**

Cell Phones and Other Electronic Devices

The use of cell phones and other electronic devices, such as iPhones and iPads, in spas and salons is a real concern today. Although skin care salons may vary in terms of the level of quietude that is expected, most are invested in creating an atmosphere of relaxation and privacy for their guests. This makes the restriction of cell phones and other technology tools a must for both clients and service providers.

Your policy on cell phone and electronic device usage should be clearly stated in any literature or promotional materials that alert guests to salon policies and etiquette prior to their appointment, such as your brochure and Web site. It should also be placed in highly visible areas in the salon, such as at your front desk, restrooms, waiting, and relaxation areas. A separate policy for employees should be incorporated into your employee manual and should also be written into other important documents, such as job descriptions or performance evaluations, where employees would be required to sign-off on their understanding of the policy.

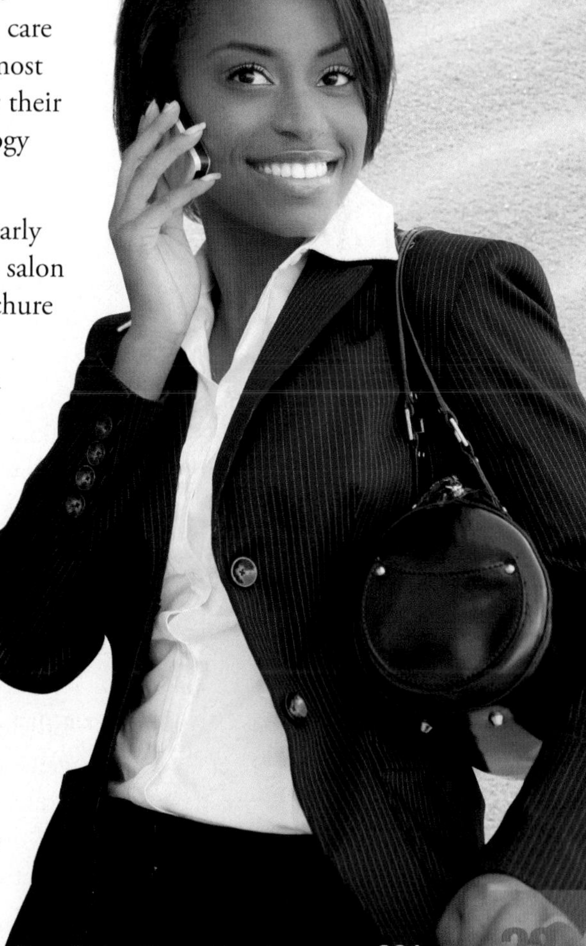

Some salons and spas designate special areas where the use of cell phones and other electronic devices is permissible. This often helps to alleviate complaints from clients who simply cannot part with their technology. Still you are likely to face challenges. If your salon has trouble enforcing its cell phone policy, you might consider implementing a policy that requires guests to turn off their cell phones, iPhones, and so forth as part of a routine check-in.

It is equally inappropriate for employees to allow their cell phones to ring during work hours. Under no circumstance should a service provider answer or use their cell phone, check personal e-mail, or send or respond to a text message during client treatments. Some employers may designate a special area, such as a breakroom, as a free-zone for cell phone and technology use. Others may ask that you step outside the building to make personal calls. It is important to remember that any conversations in or around the salon area run the risk of being heard by others. Estheticians should never discuss personal or private information in places where it can be overheard by clients, coworkers, and supervisors.

CAUTION!

The use of cell phones and other electronic devices, although commonplace in our culture, can be extremely disruptive to the quality of service in the salon or spa. Under no circumstance should a service provider answer or use their personal cell phone, check personal e-mail, or send or respond to a personal text message during client treatments. Repeated violation of the salon's cell phone policy for employees is likely to result in disciplinary action and could ultimately cost you your job.

Personnel

Skilled workers are an invaluable asset to any salon. How do you hire and keep good workers? The answer to that question is a multifaceted one that deserves special attention. How many times have you heard a business owner say, "It is not easy to find good help these days"? Although the phrase may seem overworked, it certainly highlights the frustration many salon owners feel when looking for new employees.

Searching for good employees is expensive. Advertising can be costly, and the process of reading resumes and interviewing takes a good deal of time, effort, and energy. To maximize your efforts, develop a list of questions and criteria for evaluating prospective employees beforehand. You will want to consider such factors as experience, skill level, overall attitude, communication skills, personal presentation, and philosophy of skin care as it relates to your practice. If you are interested in a candidate, you will want to follow up by requesting references from previous employers or supervisors. When dealing with more inexperienced candidates, you may wish to ask for recommendations from the school they attended and a demonstration of the required skills.

For some salons, the opportunity to increase clientele is an important prerequisite for employment. If that is a priority for hiring in your salon, you will want to learn more about a prospective employee's clients and the possible number of clients that will follow him or her to your spa or salon. Bear in mind that for various reasons, clients may be unwilling to follow an esthetician to a new establishment.

After determining that a candidate is a good fit for your salon and completing the hiring process, you will need to teach the new employee the way you would like things done. Training new staff takes time and patience. To get the best return on your investment, you will want to establish sensible rules and direction.

Efficiently run salons provide employees with clear expectations. These generally come in the form of job descriptions and employee manuals on policies and procedures. As we learned in Chapter 21, Career Planning, job descriptions are extremely useful in helping employees understand exactly what is expected of them. They can also provide a reasonable standard for evaluating an employee's performance. But it is important to remember that job descriptions vary from salon to salon. Larger salons or spas may hire a greater number of employees to perform very specific functions, while smaller salons may employ fewer **personnel**, or staff members, and require them to perform a greater number of services. For example, depending upon licensing regulations, an esthetician may be hired to perform facials as well as hair removal, body treatments, and makeup services.

Employee manuals have very distinct purposes. The **employee manual** or handbook may cover general information about salon operations: the number of sick days or amount of vacation time allowed, holiday closings, the procedure for calling in late or sick, the appropriate dress code for estheticians, the policy on purchasing goods or services from the salon, and how the company's health insurance plan works. A **procedural guide** is designed to standardize operations and may include specific protocols for conducting individual services, such as the expected method for performing a glycolic or microdermabrasion treatment. Although some may find this approach restrictive, keep in mind that guidelines are generally put in place to maintain a certain quality or standard of care. They may also address specific safety concerns such as cleaning, disinfecting, sterilization, or Universal Precautions that are intended to protect the consumer as well as the practitioner.

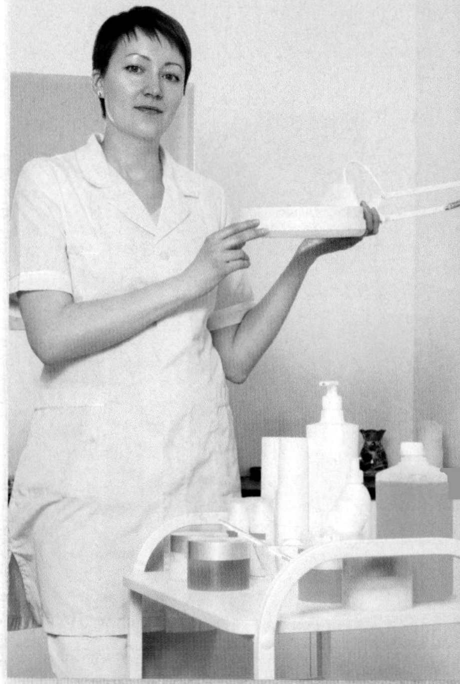

Hopefully, your relationship with employees will be long and fruitful, satisfying the needs of both parties. To encourage mutually beneficial, lasting, and profitable relationships, you must work hard to develop fair and ethical employee practices. This requires excellent communication skills and a good deal of patience. Expect that it will take time to build trust, cooperation, genuine caring, and respect. The following guidelines are suggested to encourage good employee relations:

- ***Begin each new employee relationship with the proper orientation.*** This should include a complete and thorough review of the company's mission statement, individual job descriptions, the employee manual or handbook, and procedural guidelines.
- ***Treat employees with dignity and respect.*** Acknowledge good work and reward exemplary behavior whenever possible. This may come in the form of verbal praise or a tangible bonus.
- ***Practice positive communication skills and take time to guide workers through difficulties.*** Learn to actively listen, and provide positive feedback whenever the opportunity arises.
- ***Let employees know you appreciate them.*** If the company does well, share as much of the wealth as possible by offering profit sharing or year-end bonuses.
- ***Meet payroll obligations on time.*** Remember that employees have bills to pay and personal obligations to meet. Make the payroll a top priority.
- ***Offer as many benefits as possible, and cover as much of the cost as possible.*** If you are a small business and cannot afford certain benefits such as health insurance, at least consider the option of making it available.

- ***Set clear goals and objectives, and be consistent.*** Knowing what the expectations and consequences are encourages trust. To be recognized as a person of your word, be sure to create salon policies that you can stick to. Set standards for how you will pay employees. Everyone wants to be acknowledged for his or her contribution. Let employees know what your standard of measurement is. For example, is salary based on knowledge, ability, experience, or training? Also, if you intend to incorporate commissions for specific sales or services, put this information in writing and provide a copy for each employee.
- ***Evaluate productivity, and furnish pay increases fairly.*** Establishing set criteria for pay increases sets the tone for a fair and equitable system.
- ***Learn to motivate your employees.*** Create incentives for employees by offering bonuses—money, prizes, or tickets to educational conferences or trade shows.

Managing Personnel

Managing your staff can be a difficult but rewarding job. Motivating others to do their job well may be a challenge at first. However, if you are patient and dedicated to building a team, you will succeed. To become a good manager, you will need a variety of interpersonal and communication skills. Not all of these skills will come naturally, and they may require additional education on your part (**Figure 22–15**). Management skills can be learned from various sources, including other salon managers or business owners. Do not be afraid to seek support from others more seasoned than you are. Joining managerial support groups or enrolling in courses designed specifically for new managers can be excellent opportunities for personal growth and development. As you acquire new methods for managing your team, think about the character traits that are most important to you in becoming a quality manager. The following suggestions may be helpful.

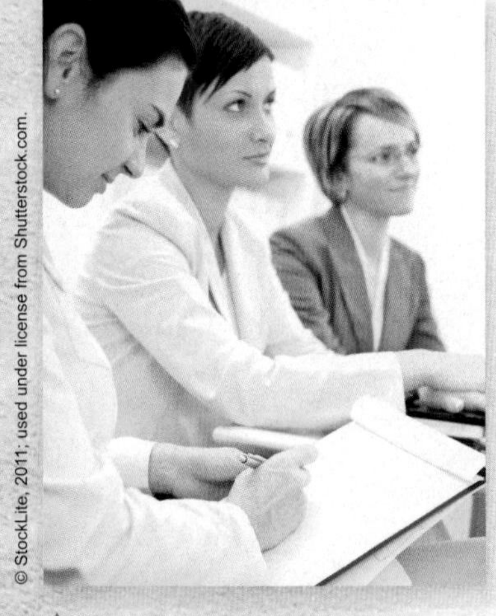

▲ **Figure 22–15**
Management skills can be learned by enrolling in courses for new managers or joining managerial support groups.

- ***Honesty is always the best policy.*** You will frequently have to share difficult information with employees, such as letting them know that their performance is not up to par. Learn to provide truthful, constructive feedback.
- ***Act decisively.*** Do not let situations linger. When issues and differences arise, address them as quickly and diplomatically as possible.
- ***Learn to expect the best.*** Before jumping to a negative conclusion, give your employees the benefit of the doubt and listen to all the facts. Good intentions may not always result in a positive outcome.
- ***Show leadership.*** Your employees will view you as the leader of the team. It is your job as the manager of your salon to support, guide, motivate, and mentor your staff.
- ***Share information.*** Show your employees that they are valuable members of your team by keeping them aware of important salon decisions. This does not mean you should tell all; some matters may cause employees

to become overly concerned or worried. Share only pertinent and appropriate information on a need-to-know basis (Figure 22–16).

- ***Follow the rules.*** Rules are important to a well-run organization. To enforce them, you must set a positive example. Be sure to follow your own rules: employees will have greater respect for them if you provide a good example.
- ***Be reliable.*** Keeping your word builds credibility and trust. Employees need to know they can depend and rely on you. To promote confidence, do not make promises you cannot keep.
- ***Teach them well.*** Learn to share your methods and reasoning for performing tasks or making certain judgments. This will help employees to understand that business decisions are determined in a thoughtful and rational way. It is also a good idea to provide a forum for employee input. Showing your employees you also value their opinion promotes mutual respect and strengthens relationships. ☑ **LO9**

Here's a Tip

One of the best ways to recruit talented estheticians is to develop relationships with quality schools in your area. Take advantage of any internship programs, job boards, and career days that are available through educational institutions. You might also invite esthetic instructors to bring students into your salon for a field trip, volunteer your time as a speaker, or participate in continuing education programs. Becoming a familiar and friendly face on campus will not only increase your access to students, it will help to establish you as a reputable and caring employer who is invested in education.

Public Relations

Developing a reputation for quality service and fair business practices will increase your standing not only with employees and clients but also in the community where you work. Although we hear the term *public relations* often, many are not clear about its meaning. **Public relations,** also known as **PR,** is all about planning and developing relationships to achieve a certain desired behavior. We'll talk more about this complex marketing strategy in Chapter 23, Selling Products and Services. It is important to understand that public relations impacts all aspects of business development and should be considered part of a total communication plan that includes all of your business relationships.

In operating your own skin care business, you will have many opportunities to interact with a wide variety of people including clients, employees, vendors, colleagues, business leaders, and local officials. To maintain productive relations and positive outcomes, you will need to work on developing effective communication and management skills. Your customer and employee policies will guide you in this process. When reviewing these materials, think earnestly about how comfortable you are with enforcing your "rules." If there are certain issues that you regularly dismiss, decide whether you can continue to stand behind them. You may decide to make changes to your commitments and philosophies over time. As you think about the many topics discussed in this chapter, take stock of how you handle difficult situations and treat others. Ongoing and critical self-evaluation is instrumental to the growth and development of a successful salon.

▲ Figure 22–16
Sharing pertinent information with employees promotes understanding and strengthens relations.

Review Questions

1. List the advantages and disadvantages of a booth-rental arrangement.
2. List the types of ownership under which a skin care salon may operate. Define each.
3. What should you look for when considering a location to open your own skin care salon?
4. Why are demographics important to the prospective salon owner?
5. How can a business plan help you to make good business decisions?
6. How do local, state, and federal government regulations affect the small business owner?
7. Why is it important for the small business owner to keep accurate records?
8. List several factors to consider when planning the physical layout of your salon.
9. Discuss the importance of insurance to the salon owner.
10. List several ways that you can safeguard your business.
11. Name several things you should look for when hiring employees.
12. Describe the qualities of a good manager.
13. List the qualifications that are important in a good receptionist.
14. Develop a script for receiving incoming calls and discuss the best way to place clients on hold.
15. What important information should you provide when leaving a telephone message on a machine or service?
16. How can employee manuals and procedural guides help you manage personnel?
17. How might public relations affect the way you operate your own skin care salon?

Glossary

booth rental	Arrangement in which the esthetician is required to pay the owner a set rental fee, along with payment of utilities as agreed upon, to operate in a specific space within the owner's establishment.
business plan	Strategy for understanding key elements in developing business; also serves as a guide to making informed business decisions; a written description of your business as you see it today, and as you foresee it in the next 5 years (detailed by year).
capital	Money needed to invest in a business.
consumption supplies	Supplies used to conduct daily business operations.
corporation	Form of business ownership whereby one or more stockholders share ownership; the corporation is considered an independent legal entity separate and distinct from its owners with its own rights, privileges, and liabilities.
demographics	The particular identifying characteristics of an area or population, such as the specific size, age, sex, or ethnicity of its residents; average income; educational attainment; and buying habits.
employee manual	Handbook or guide for employees; contains important general information about salon operations, such as the number of sick days or vacation time allowed, holiday closings, how to call in late or sick, and the appropriate dress code for estheticians.

Glossary

fixed costs	Operating costs that are constant, for example, rent and loan payments.
partnership	Form of business ownership in which two or more people share ownership, although this does not necessarily mean an equal arrangement. In a partnership, each partner assumes the other's unlimited liability for debt. Profits are shared among partners.
personnel	Employees; staff.
procedural guide	Manual or set of instructions designed to standardize operations; supplies specific protocols for conducting individual services, such as the expected method for performing a glycolic or microdermabrasion treatment.
profit	Amount of money available after all expenses are subtracted from all revenues.
public relations	Also known as *PR*; planning and developing of relationships to achieve a certain desired behavior.
retail supplies	Items available for sale to clients.
revenue	Income generated from selling services and products, or money taken in.
sole proprietorship	Form of business ownership in which an individual acts as sole owner and manager and is responsible for determining all policies and making all of the necessary decisions associated with running a business.
variable costs	Business expenses that fluctuate, such as utilities, supplies, and advertising.

CHAPTER 23

Selling Products and Services

Chapter Outline

- Why Study Selling Products and Services?
- Selling in the Skin Care Salon
- Know Your Products and Services
- Merchandising
- Marketing
- Client Value
- Building a Clientele
- Client Retention
- Closing the Sale
- Tracking Your Success

Learning Objectives

After completing this chapter, you will be able to:

- ☑ **LO1** List the basic principles of selling products and services in the salon.
- ☑ **LO2** Explain the purpose of marketing and promotions.
- ☑ **LO3** Name several methods of advertising to promote sales in the salon.
- ☑ **LO4** Explain the importance of understanding client value in selling products and services.
- ☑ **LO5** List the most effective ways to build a clientele.
- ☑ **LO6** Discuss the importance of closing the sale.

Key Terms

Page number indicates where in the chapter the term is used.

advertising
pg. 708

client record keeping
pg. 710

closing consultation
pg. 714

consultative selling
pg. 701

direct marketing
pg. 708

marketing
pg. 706

merchandising
pg. 705

promotion
pg. 707

publicity
pg. 709

questionnaire (intake form)
pg. 709

retailing
pg. 703

upselling services
pg. 704

Selling products and services is critical to the financial success of a skin care salon or spa. Sales keep business flowing and revenues coming in. A confident esthetician, who is comfortable with selling, is a valuable asset to any salon or spa and is likely to increase his or her income. The esthetician should not forget that the products and services he or she sells should benefit the consumer and meet their skin care needs. The right products increase the value of services and help to reinforce client goals on a daily basis. Those who place the client's best interests at the forefront of any sale can also take pride in basing the sale on ethical practices. As you review this chapter, keep an open mind. The rewards of selling may surprise you, both personally and financially.

Why Study Selling Products and Services?

The right skin care products and correct treatment protocols increase client satisfaction and support salon productivity. Estheticians who accept selling as a professional responsibility play a critical role in fostering these goals.

- An educated esthetician committed to selling with integrity promotes credibility and increases the client's trust.
- A successful sales and marketing program satisfies the needs of both buyer and seller, creating a mutually satisfying exchange between both parties.
- Businesses that employ a variety of advertising strategies are in a better position to increase sales. Estheticians are expected to do their part by bringing the client's attention to sales promotions.
- For marketing to be successful, the product must be something the client wants and/or needs. A knowledgeable esthetician tuned into client concerns can provide valuable information to the sales and marketing team.
- Repeat customers keep business flowing. To keep clients coming back, the esthetician must provide excellent service each and every time a client visits the salon.
- A close relationship with the client gives estheticians the edge in personal selling techniques. Excellent consultation skills are crucial in educating clients and recommending products and services.

Selling in the Skin Care Salon

Selling products and services is a fundamental objective in the esthetics business. Unfortunately, many estheticians fail to make the connection between selling and skin care. In many cases, the esthetician's aversion to selling stems from negative associations that portray sales agents as pushy or aggressive people who are interested only in making money. To move beyond this negative connotation, estheticians must learn to recognize the value in selling, viewing it as a reputable endeavor that supplies salon and spa-goers with certain valued benefits.

To frame the concept of sales positively, the esthetician must first accept that recommending and providing clients with quality skin care products and services is a professional responsibility. Esthetics is a personal-service business that promotes beautiful, healthy skin. When estheticians sell treatments and products that are in alignment with this goal, they are also promoting the client's best interest (**Figure 23–1**). ✓ L01

© Milady, a part of Cengage Learning. Photography by Paul Castle, Castle Photography.

▲ **Figure 23–1**
Recommending products is a professional responsibility.

Principles of Selling

Once you have accepted selling as a necessary and reputable part of your work as an esthetician, you can begin to work on developing principles that promote ethical sales practices.

To be successful selling products and services, you must first be educated. When you understand the benefit of each product and treatment, you will be motivated and committed to their value. You must also develop the client's trust in your competence and credibility. Looking the part and practicing your own philosophies is a good way to advertise the benefits of healthy skin care. Placing the client's needs and wants at the forefront is another important way of assuring your clients that you have their best interests in mind.

Consultative Selling

Because you are an expert on skin care, clients place their trust in your professionalism. They expect you to have the answers to their skin care concerns and will look to you for guidance in recommending the best treatments and products for their use. From this perspective, you are not simply selling—you are advising or consulting—to clients. This practice is known as **consultative selling**. If you begin by recommending only those products and services that meet the client's needs and goals, you will be perceived as a knowledgeable and caring practitioner interested in nurturing skin health. This ultimately builds trust and raises the level of the client–practitioner relationship, creating a sales concept the esthetician can be proud of.

The 10-step consultation method outlined in Chapter 4, Communicating for Success, sets the tone for a positive exchange between esthetician and client. Adapting your sales technique to accommodate the client's style is another technique that will help you to sell in a professional manner. Some clients respond best to a "soft sell," in which you inform them about which products are best for them without stressing that they purchase it. Others will prefer a "hard sell" that focuses emphatically on why they should buy the product. There are many books, tapes,

FOCUS ON

Meeting the Client's Needs and Goals

The following are basic principles of consultative selling.

- Know the benefits and features of your products and services.
- Recommend only those products and services that will benefit the individual client.
- Introduce products at a time that does not interfere with the relaxation benefit of the treatment.
- Whenever possible, demonstrate the use of products and treatments.
- Personalize your approach to meet the needs and personality of each client.
- Present a confident, helpful, and pleasant attitude when recommending products and services.
- Find out what your clients want and/or need, and make every effort to fulfil that need.
- Never make false or unrealistic claims about products or services. This will only lead to client disappointment and will ultimately destroy your credibility.
- Respect your client's intelligence and acknowledge her efforts to advocate for herself.
- Know when to close the sale without overselling once the client has decided to purchase a product or service.

and seminars devoted to each of these topics that may be beneficial in helping you to develop your approach. Whichever technique you use, keep in mind that it is important not to interfere with the relaxation benefit of the treatment. No one wants to hear what might be perceived as a sales pitch during a relaxing massage. As you develop experience, you will perfect your timing and learn which approach works best for each client.

The Psychology of Selling

What makes people buy? Understanding the consumer's motivation for purchasing products or services will help you refine your sales approach and directly meet client needs. In your work as an esthetician, you will encounter many different personalities with various skin care concerns. Some clients may come to you to correct a particular skin condition or problem; others may want to feel better about the way they look; while some may simply have issues of vanity. There are also those who simply want to experience every new product and treatment they hear about. Sometimes the client is unsure about which product or service will best suit his or her needs. Whatever circumstances the client presents, the esthetician must always remember to keep the client's best interests in mind. It is your job to help him or her resolve the issues presented in the most productive way.

Know Your Products and Services

It is important to have an extensive and thorough understanding of the products and services offered by your salon. A comprehensive knowledge of products and services makes it easier to educate clients and increase retail sales.

Promoting Retail Sales

Clients will rightfully assume that you, as the expert on skin care, are recommending the right products for their skin care needs. This makes **retailing** products, the act of recommending and selling products to clients for at-home use, a major part of the esthetician's training.

Sorting through the huge number of products available on the market today can be a challenge. To instill client confidence, the esthetician should develop a broad-based knowledge of chemical ingredients, their properties, and their effects on skin. The most important knowledge that the esthetician can have is, of course, the specific benefits and features of the retail products available for sale in the salon (**Figure 23–2**).

▲ Figure 23–2
Product knowledge is crucial to the success of retail sales.

Recommending Products

It takes time to develop confidence in recommending products. With so many sophisticated new products boasting fantastic technology, the novice esthetician can be easily intimidated. How do you explain such phenomena as *free radicals, liposomes,* and *cosmeceuticals* to clients if you have difficulty understanding these concepts yourself?

Breaking down product knowledge into more manageable categories is a good way to begin sorting through the overwhelming amount of information about products that exists today. The first step is to find out as much as you can about the manufacturer's philosophy. For example, is the manufacturer a proponent of natural ingredients, or does the company support the use of synthetic or chemical sources? Does the company conduct clinical studies, publicize the source of key ingredients, or test products on animals? This information can be easily accessed through promotional materials such as brochures, pamphlets, the company's Web site, or advertisements in trade publications.

Once you have defined a company's philosophy, you can assess the quality of its products and methods of research and development. Most companies provide literature explaining the theory behind their products and techniques. This may come in the form of marketing materials, instruction booklets, or procedural guides. After reading the manufacturer's literature, conduct your own research using unbiased sources to substantiate the data. Finding out more about key ingredients and the technology used in creating a product will help you understand and explain how it works.

FOCUS ON

Professionalism

In the relationship between esthetician and client, there must be a balance between what the client is asking for and what the professional knows is in the client's best interest. After all, one reason clients patronize professionals is to be advised of what is best for them. This is a delicate communication, but it is vital to satisfying the client. If it appears that the client does not fully realize that her choice will not benefit her, it is your obligation to find a tactful way to let her know.

FOCUS ON

Retailing

For quick reference, keep these five points in mind when selling.

1. Establish rapport with the client.
2. Determine the client's needs.
3. Recommend products and services based on those needs.
4. Emphasize benefits.
5. Close the sale.

Vendor Education

Many manufacturers and distributors offer seminars to attract new business and educate professionals about their products. Take advantage of these classes whenever possible. This is an excellent opportunity to have technical questions answered by a knowledgeable individual in a give-and-take format. It will also give you a chance to speak with other professionals who are using the product. Learning firsthand about the results other professionals are getting is a good way to assess the credibility of a product. Furthermore, manufacturers who promote this type of exchange realize the benefit of educated salespeople and demonstrate an investment in your success.

Although your personal knowledge is paramount in recommending products, you should also find out what is available from the manufacturer to enhance the client's understanding. Estheticians often need help in explaining a product's advantages and contraindications. Look for companies that supply a simple format for explaining the benefits and features of a product and that address frequently asked questions associated with its use. Using this information as a basis for discussion may help to alleviate some of the pressure you feel as you begin to recommend products to clients.

All of these suggestions will help you to recommend products with ease and confidence. It is important to note that the best marketing materials and educational support are no substitute for your professional endorsement. To promote a product successfully, you must first believe in it yourself. Take time to conduct your own trials by testing products that are appropriate for your skin type and condition. You might also consider asking other members of the salon team to try products that are likely to benefit their skin type. Clients will have a greater appreciation of the benefits of a product if they know you are genuinely supporting its use.

▼ **Figure 23–3**
Recommending other services to clients keeps business flowing smoothly.

Upselling

While the esthetician is the primary person responsible for recommending skin care products and services in a skin care salon or spa, it is also important for other members of the salon team to be knowledgeable about the different products and treatments available (**Figure 23–3**). In the salon, selling is everyone's business (**Figure 23–4**). Suggesting a client try something new, or **upselling services**, which is the practice of recommending or selling additional services to clients that may be performed by you or other practitioners in the salon, keeps business running smoothly.

◀ **Figure 23–4**
In the salon, selling is everyone's business.

Merchandising

Your extensive knowledge of products and services, along with the support of staff members and vendors, will help you to build a strong retail program. You must also give clients an opportunity to see, touch, smell, and feel a product before purchasing it.

Merchandising, or how retail products are arranged and displayed in your salon, has a direct impact on the guest experience that can help to increase product sales. Estheticians have the distinct advantage of being personally and professionally involved with their clients. This gives them a significant edge when making product recommendations, but they are still in competition with larger retail outlets, on-line shopping carts, home shopping networks, and specialty boutiques devoted to personal care products. How will you compete? Many practitioners enjoy the creative aspect of merchandising. If you have an interest in art and design, you may want to explore using these skills to help organize retail displays in the salon.

Creating a shopping experience that welcomes clients begins with a strategic plan. That plan should take into account the salon's mission, image, and marketing goals. If the main focus of the salon is to provide services that make clients look better, products that demonstrate dramatic results should take center stage. If health and well-being are more in sync with the salon's philosophy then it would be more appropriate to make this the focal point of your merchandising. All retail displays should match the ambience of the salon. If the tone of the salon is soft and restful using natural elements—like plants, flowers, seashells and sand, crystals or stones that blend gently with the surroundings—will complement nicely. If the salon is modern and trendy, funky art objects and chic novelty items such as hats and sunglasses can be added for a touch of glamour.

Of course the primary goal is to entice clients to buy, so retail displays should synchronize with the salon's marketing plan. When planning your promotional calendar take advantage of natural timelines such as monthly manufacturer specials, seasons, and holidays to create themes that generate automatic retail responses. Holidays like Christmas, Valentine's Day, Mother's Day, and Father's Day lend easily to sales promotions and gift packages; keep in mind that there are many other noteworthy occasions such as graduations, marathons, back to school, and so forth that you can use. Be creative and consider any charity efforts that you are involved with, for example bringing attention to skin cancer during skin health month in May. You can also tie retail displays to seasonal skin care concerns such as summer sun exposure and winter dehydration. All products should be carefully arranged so that it is easy for clients to find the right products for their skin type and condition. For example, products might be arranged for Normal, Dry, and Oily Skin or for Age Management, Face, Body, Men's, Teen products, and so on.

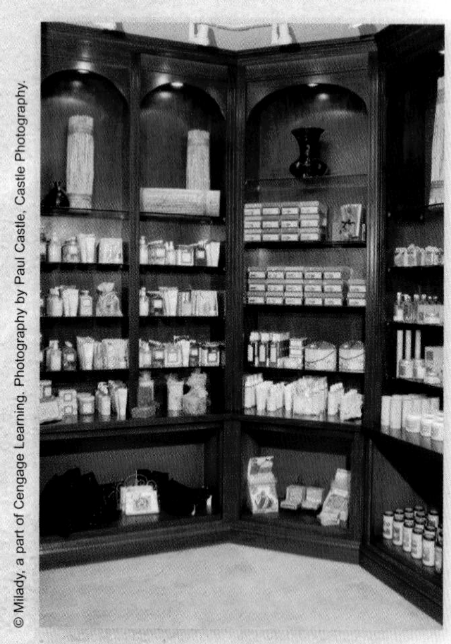

▲ Figure 23–5
Attractive retail displays have a direct impact on product sales.

Creating beautifully organized and artful retail displays does not have to be costly (**Figure 23–5**). Take advantage of any current salon advertising and marketing pieces or posters, shelf-talkers, and retail displays that are available from vendors and display these throughout the salon to bring attention to your retail products. Pay special attention to the check-out area. This is the ideal location for featuring new product information and sales promotions. It is also the perfect spot for displaying smaller impulse purchases such as lipsticks, nail polishes, hand lotions, and sun protection products. A front desk with a glass enclosure is ideal for displaying more expensive retail products. Be sure to take full advantage of this prime retail exposure.

If your creativity needs a boost scan fashion and health magazines, go window shopping, or visit art museums, boutiques, and department stores for ideas and then shop party goods, thrift stores, and yard sales for bargain items. Nature is a bountiful source of cost-effective items like berries, greenery, seashells, sand, and much more that can be changed with the seasons. Add product-testers, candles, and scents to create a sensory experience that lures your guests in, and you are bound to capture the attention of those who would rather sample, sniff, and browse than talk to a salesperson. Salons with window space are in an excellent position to extend retail themes to attract passersby.

Marketing

Most salon and spa owners understand the value of a good marketing program to stimulate business. **Marketing** provides a strategy for how goods and services are bought and sold, or exchanged. This is an involved process that was introduced with a general description of the marketing mix in Chapter 22, The Skin Care Business, and goes beyond the scope of this text, still it is important for estheticians to realize that marketing is more than a sales technique.

To market skin care products and services successfully, you must first recognize that marketing serves both buyers and sellers. Framing marketing within the context of skin care, we can see that consumers have certain needs and wants when it comes to solving their skin care problems. As businesses looking to satisfy consumers, salons and spas provide certain products and services to help resolve their concerns. What estheticians should remember is that the whole concept is based on an exchange that ultimately benefits both the client and the service provider (**Figure 23–6**).

▲ Figure 23–6
Some salons and spas hire freelance marketing consultants or agencies to help them with marketing.

Promotion

All marketing programs involve some form of promotion. **Promotion** is aimed at getting the consumer's attention, with the goal of increasing business. Several different methods of promotion can be employed to market products and services, such as *advertising, public relations, publicity, direct marketing, personal selling,* and *sales promotions*. Most marketing programs incorporate several of these techniques using a variety of media such as newspapers, magazines, television, the Internet, and direct mail to create a broad-based campaign.

The following are just a few examples of promotions salons and spas typically use to create excitement and increase sales. They can be applied using a variety of media and techniques.

- Use seasonal themes and holidays to promote packages at special prices.
- Endorse frequent-buyer programs or series-savings discounts.
- Reward clients who refer new customers with a gift certificate or free service.
- Introduce new customers to services with a special introductory offer.
- Demonstrate customer appreciation by giving clients a discount or complimentary service during their birthday month.
- Add value to an existing treatment. For example, tie product discounts to the purchase of a related skin care treatment or add-on to a service.
- Limit sales promotions to a certain time frame. For example, a winter-escape package may be offered only during the months of January and February.
- Introduce new products with trial-size samples and a gift certificate that can be applied toward the client's first purchase.
- Offer discounts or add value to services on slower days.
- Host special events to launch a new product or service.
- Team up with other professionals to cross-merchandise. ✔ LO2

fyi

The various communication methods used in marketing are commonly referred to as the "promotion mix." These include *advertising, public relations, publicity, direct marketing, personal selling,* and *sales promotions.* More detailed information on these topics can be found in the chapter on Marketing in *Milady Standard Esthetics: Advanced* text.

Advertising

Advertising is one of the more familiar and popular methods of promotion. In the broad sense of the word, advertising encompasses any activity that promotes the salon or spa favorably. For example, engaging in a charity event can be a good way to advertise a salon's services. Most of us can also identify with the popular phrase, "the best form of advertising is a satisfied customer." When it comes to marketing, **advertising** typically refers to promotional efforts that are paid for and are directly intended to increase business.

Some of the more popular methods of paid advertising used by salons include *classified, newspaper, magazine, radio* or *television, the Internet,* and *direct mail* (**Figure 23–7**). If you work at a salon or spa that employs a variety of advertising strategies, consider yourself lucky. Advertising helps to build business and increase sales. A good esthetician will take advantage of these efforts by becoming knowledgeable about special promotions and bringing them to the attention of clients.

▲ **Figure 23–7**
A sample direct mail piece.

Direct Marketing

Direct marketing refers to any attempt to reach the consumer directly with an offer. Historically, marketers have relied on the distribution of direct mail *postcards, coupons, newsletters, sales letters,* and *telemarketing* to achieve this goal. The use of traditional print media and human resources often made this a costly marketing expenditure. Technology has changed all that, introducing more cost-effective solutions like *electronic mail* and *text messages*. Although direct marketing may seem like a fairly simple and straightforward strategy, there are many factors that go into managing a successful campaign. Many spas and salons outsource this function to marketing experts.

The advanced use of the Internet for social networking, commonly referred to as Web 2.0, is another phenomenon that is having a significant impact on the direct market landscape. New social-media tools such as *blogs, podcasts,* and *viral marketing* provide the salon and spa owner with cost-effective methods for spreading the word about their salon or spa directly to the consumer. These, combined with other technology tools for sharing information and making connections—like Facebook, Twitter, and LinkedIn—have created more efficient ways for business owners to study and interface with millions of consumers and prospective business partners. Establishing a business identity using social media is not an easy task. If you decide to incorporate social marketing strategies, it is wise to seek professional help.

Public Relations

The term *public relations* is often associated with charitable giving, but there is more to "PR" than donating time or a percentage of salon profits to good causes to generate publicity. As we learned in Chapter 22, The Skin Care Business, public relations is a complex marketing-communications strategy aimed at planning and developing key relationships to achieve consistently positive results. More importantly, PR takes an ethical approach to marketing by supporting product and service claims with factual information.

Businesses typically hire PR consultants or agencies to help them develop a public relations program. This usually involves publicizing information about your business, products and services, planning events, and encouraging businesses to do good works rather than paying for advertising. Skin care professionals can do their part to promote good public relations by promoting excellent service and developing good client and employee relations. Getting involved in the community, networking with other local business owners, speaking, writing articles, and hosting seminars on important skin care topics are several other proactive methods that can be used by salon owners to generate **publicity**, or free media attention. When you act like a skin care ambassador and maintain professional standards in all of your endeavors, you not only foster good will for the salon you work in or own, the entire esthetic profession benefits. ✓ LO3

Did You Know?

Electronic mail is used by 97% of all consumers, making it a reliable and cost effective direct-marketing tool that is used by 94% of marketers.

Like any other promotional strategy careful planning, measurement, and evaluation are crucial to success. Spa and salon owners interested in using this popular method should be aware that excessive use of electronic mail can result in blocked e-mails and/ or requests to be removed from their mailing list.

Client Value

You can have the right marketing approach and the right intention, but the ultimate product-sales test is whether your clients want or need it. To successfully market products and services to clients, you must first determine if a product is something that clients are likely to buy. Discovering that a company's philosophy is not in sync with clients' values or skin care needs or that clients are unwilling to spend $70 on a facial moisturizer will ultimately shortchange sales efforts. ✓ LO4

Collecting Client Information

As you learned in Chapter 4, Communicating for Success, good communication skills are a critical part of client relations. The 10-step consultation method recommended in Chapter 4 sets the tone for a positive client interaction that will help you to improve communication and better understand the needs and wants of your clients, factors that will ultimately help you to increase sales.

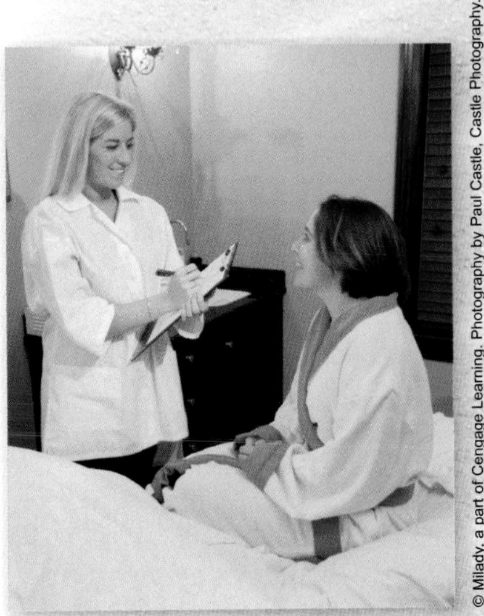

▲ Figure 23–8
The intake questionnaire supplies the esthetician with valuable information about the client's skin care habits and goals.

The Questionnaire

The **questionnaire**, also known as an **intake form**, is an important tool that allows the esthetician to learn about the client's overall skin condition (**Figure 23–8**). This form, an example of which appears in Chapter 4, Communicating for Success, documents the client's health history and gives the practitioner a way to open dialogue, discuss client goals, and determine the best products and treatments for meeting these objectives safely and effectively. As you gain experience using this form, you will begin to develop your own interviewing style. You may also adapt the client intake interview to gather additional information that supports your sales efforts.

Client Record Keeping

Client records serve a distinct purpose in building the client relationship, and should not be confused with the intake questionnaire. **Client record keeping** refers to a method of taking personal notes that helps the esthetician to remember important data and serve client needs better.

Every client wants to feel special; however, the truth is that unless the esthetician has a photographic memory, he or she will have a hard time maintaining a detailed mental account of each client's history. To establish a caring and nurturing bond with the client, the esthetician must find a way to recollect client information easily.

Each salon will have its own method for recording important client data. Most salons utilize technology for this purpose, though some may use a paper filing system. If the salon you work in does not offer either, it is a good idea to create a system of your own. You should always record the following client information:

- Name
- Address
- Telephone number
- Date of treatment
- Services performed
- Products used
- Treatment results
- Products purchased

Additional information that identifies a client's particular preferences, what products she or he uses at home, special anniversary dates, and personal anecdotes will also help to develop rapport and assure the client's comfort during subsequent visits. Smart estheticians will get in the habit of reviewing this information at a convenient time before the client's visit. This, along with a careful analysis of any computerized sales reports that show the client's product and service history, will improve client relations and ultimately increase satisfaction.

FOCUS ON

Developing Good Communication

It is a good idea to keep track of what your clients like and dislike, along with important events in their lives. Your awareness of these details will make them feel important. Include the following information on client records:

- Client's birthday
- New baby
- Upcoming wedding
- Job held and job promotions

Also include whatever else you think matters most to that client . . . within reason. Estheticians must exercise caution when it comes to documenting very personal information that could be construed as privileged or might embarrass a client. As a general rule, limit your personal anecdotes to general information that would be part of any casual, polite conversation.

Client Education

It seems that most people suffer from information overload these days. This is also true in skin care. With so much data available, it is nearly impossible for the average person to digest it all. That is why clients seek the advice of the esthetician.

As a licensed professional, you will be expected to be knowledgeable about the many different products and techniques that are currently on the market. While it is humanly impossible to be an expert on every cosmetic brand and skin care technique, the esthetician can support the client in finding the correct treatments and products for her or his particular needs. Before you inundate the client with a lot of detailed or unnecessary information, consider the following suggestions.

- ***Find out what the client already knows about her or his own skin.*** What products is the client now using, and what other treatments has she already tried? A thorough review of the intake form will increase your awareness of the client's understanding of their skin type and conditions and their goals and preferences. Some clients may be quite happy with their current regime and products. If so, you should introduce them to any new products or treatments slowly. Developing rapport is an important prerequisite to clients being open to your suggestions.
- ***Provide information when you have the client's full attention.*** Often, estheticians make the mistake of supplying clients with too much information during the treatment process. While it is important to let clients know what to expect, it is ultimately in the client's best interest to relax and enjoy the treatment. Save explanations for a time when you have the client's full attention; for example, during the skin analysis or closing consultation. The latter is also an ideal time to review product recommendations, prepare a home-care program for the client to follow, and provide any additional literature on other treatment options (**Figure 23–9**).
- ***Be honest about what you do not know.*** There may be times when a client requests information about a product or procedure that is not offered at your salon or about which you know very little. Do not be alarmed at such requests. When this happens, it is perfectly acceptable to tell the client you are unfamiliar with the product or procedure and would be happy to find out more about it. On the positive side, this may ultimately give you the incentive to introduce a new treatment option.

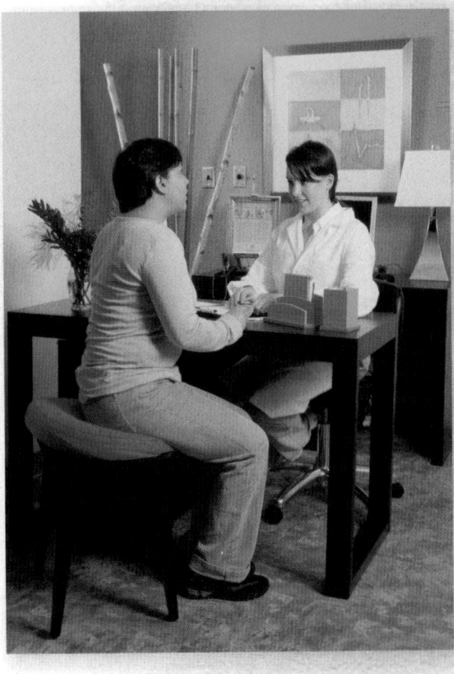

▲ **Figure 23–9**
It is best to educate clients when you have their full attention.

Building a Clientele

There is any number of reasons for a client's first visit to the salon. Perhaps he or she received a gift certificate, responded to an ad in the newspaper, or noticed that the salon is conveniently located on the route home from work. In any case, a client's initial visit should be considered the salon's first opportunity to make a good first impression and build a lasting relationship. To accomplish this goal, the salon must ensure that the client leaves with two important reasons for returning. First, the client must be happy with the results of treatment and feel he or she derived some benefit from these services. Second, he or she must have confidence in the professional's expertise.

The successful salon owner knows that repeat clients keep the business going. He or she also knows that developing a bond with clients has a great deal to do with whether they will continue to come back. The esthetician is instrumental in this process and should be considered a major partner in building a salon's clientele.

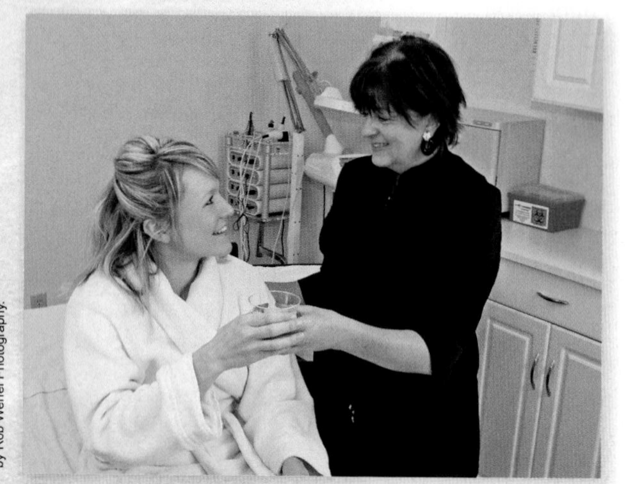

▲ **Figure 23–10**
To keep clients satisfied and loyal, the esthetician must continually provide quality service.

To be successful in developing a clientele, the esthetician must make every effort to provide good service *each* and *every* time a client visits the salon. Frequently, the esthetician will work hard at first to impress a client with her skills only to fall short of the client's expectations once she becomes accustomed to his or her rebooking. A client's business should never be taken for granted. The goal of every treatment should be to provide the highest-quality service. ✓ **L05**

Client Retention

Salons employ a variety of marketing efforts to support a steady stream of business. One simple strategy supersedes all others in the service industry: personal attention. We live in an impersonal world where consumers are often starved for a personal connection. In fact, some clients may visit spas for just that reason. Of course, estheticians would be naïve to think that clients are uninterested in their professional expertise or the benefit they derive from quality skin care treatments. To satisfy the need for both, estheticians are encouraged to adopt the following standards:

- ***Continually provide quality service.*** Once you have won a customer over, it is easy to become complacent. To avoid this common pitfall, estheticians must work hard to maintain their skills and provide excellent service *all the time* (**Figure 23–10**).
- ***Understand what the client wants, and provide it to her or him.*** Never forget that each client has a unique agenda. Always set aside time to update information and address client concerns. This lets clients know you are genuinely interested in understanding and fulfilling their individual skin care needs.
- ***Give each client your personal, undivided attention.*** Again, everyone wants to feel special. Get in the habit of treating clients as if they are special guests. Be warm, welcoming, and cordial. Offer refreshments and practice proper salon etiquette.
- ***Develop good listening skills.*** There is no substitute for the genuine respect that comes from actively listening to another person. A professional yet friendly and confidential manner will encourage

clients to share their concerns openly. This will enable the esthetician to provide a more effective treatment plan.

- ***Give clients incentives to rebook appointments.*** Most salons specifically train the front desk staff to rebook clients. Without the esthetician's support, though, clients may view this as just another sales tactic. Encouraging clients to book their next appointment is a good way to let them know you are dedicated to improving the condition of their skin. Keeping them informed of any special offers or programs that can save them money is also a good way to show that you have their best interests at heart.

Client Referrals

Marketing-savvy salon owners know that word of mouth is one of the best forms of advertising. They make every effort to promote their business through networking and public speaking opportunities. Estheticians should be willing to do their part as well.

Getting clients, coworkers, and other people to refer clients to you is an excellent way to enhance an existing clientele and increase business. Keeping your coworkers abreast of new products and treatments will help to create a buzz about your services. Whenever possible, offer to provide your colleagues with a treatment or new service.

Widening your circle of contacts to include other beauty and allied health professionals is another way estheticians can help spread the word. Beauty professionals, such as nail technicians and hairdressers, who do not offer additional skin care treatments can be an excellent source of referrals. Likewise, broadening this base to include allied health professionals such as massage therapists, fitness instructors, personal trainers, chiropractors, dermatologists, plastic surgeons, and nutritionists can be another mutually beneficial way to increase your clientele.

Community organizations, such as the local women's or garden club, church or parent groups, sports teams, and the chamber of commerce or small business association, are other good contacts. Many times, such organizations have a need for speakers, or they may be willing to distribute literature for members of their organization. If you are involved with or have contacts in these types of organizations, be sure to give them an ample supply of business cards and the salon's brochures.

Current clients are always a primary source of referrals and one of the best methods of advertising for a salon. A satisfied client is a vote of confidence in your abilities and should always be rewarded in some tangible way. Many salons implement reward programs to purposely encourage client referrals. Others simply reward clients with a free facial, gift certificate, discount on products or services, or special gift when they learn a client has been referred (**Figure 23–11**). If the salon you work

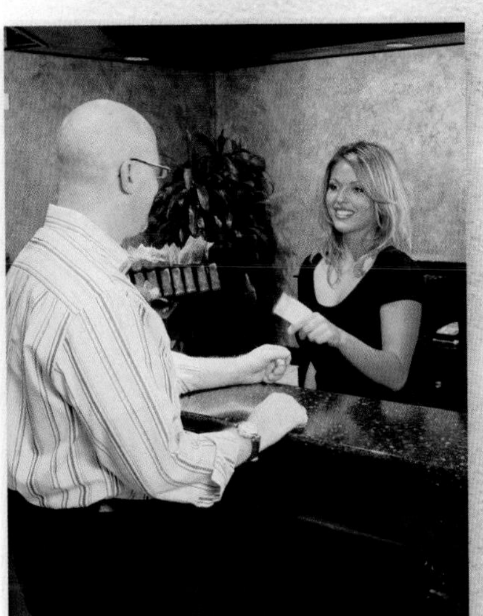

▲ Figure 23–11
Rewarding clients who refer new customers with a complimentary service or added value is a good way to build your client base.

at does not offer these types of rewards, do not hesitate to suggest them; it is always a good policy to let clients know you value their recommendation. Other social-media strategies, like a "fan page," can be ideal for generating word-of-mouth referrals.

On a final note, it cannot hurt to be prepared with business cards wherever you go. We already know that getting involved in the community and generating positive publicity are good ways to inform the public about your services. The chance encounter with an influential person can be equally beneficial. Practicing a nonthreatening introduction that can be used at social or business gatherings will help you to make the most of everyday situations that could eventually result in a new client.

Closing the Sale

One of the most important parts of the esthetician's job actually occurs after the treatment is complete. The **closing consultation** gives the esthetician and client a valuable opportunity to review client concerns and discuss an appropriate home-care program. This should be considered a natural part of an effective marketing program that helps clients to derive the most benefit from salon treatments.

Estheticians are fortunate because they are able to work one-on-one with clients. This gives them ample opportunity to interject valuable information that will help them to close the sale throughout the treatment process. To be successful the esthetician must be able to communicate his or her recommendations clearly and effectively. The closing consultation is a time to educate clients about their options and listen to their concerns. At times, clients may be overwhelmed by the mention of sophisticated product ingredients and technology. Elaborate explanations may cause further confusion. It is the esthetician's job to motivate and reassure clients and provide them with a personal program that they can follow each day.

Keep it simple. A simple reference to products during the treatment process is an excellent way to begin introducing the products you will review during the closing consultation. For example, you might say, "Ms. Smart, I am appling the vitamin C mask now. There are several coordinating treatment products that will help you

to maintain the results you achieve today. I'll write these down for you and go over them with you at the end of the treatment. Right now, just relax and soak in all of the benefits of the mask."

Many salons supply estheticians with a worksheet or prescriptive-type memo for use in summarizing product recommendations and explaining proper home usage. This is an excellent way to communicate specific directions about when and how to use products. Be sure to leave at least 10 minutes to go over the program. Clients may have questions about whether a product is best used in the morning or at night. They may also be confused about whether special treatments should be applied before or after a moisturizer or sun protection product. Writing down this information is a convenient way to help clients remember exactly what to do when they get home (**Figure 23–12** on page 716). If the salon you work for does not provide a model, consider creating one of your own. A simple format that utilizes generic headings such as *cleanser, toner, moisturizer, specialty treatments*, and so forth—followed by brief instructions and a reminder of when to use the product (for example, day or night)—can also be a great reference tool for clients when making future purchases. ☑ **LO6**

Follow-Up

After earning the client's trust, the esthetician will need to work hard to keep it. There is a great deal of competition in the esthetics market today, making it necessary to go that extra mile to let clients know you care. A simple follow-up phone call can make all the difference in maintaining a positive working relationship with the client.

Calling clients takes a considerable amount of time and organization. Even though this is so, many salons and spas realize it can substantially affect client loyalty. These salons are implementing specific call-back times for estheticians to follow up with clients.

Generally speaking, the esthetician should call clients back anywhere from 24 hours to 1 week after their salon visit, depending on the type of treatment they received and their skin care program. It is a good idea to call clients who receive more aggressive treatments within 24 hours. Clients starting a new home-care regimen should be called within 48 hours. All others should be called within 1 week. The esthetician may also wish to designate a special call-in hour to address client concerns. Some estheticians also choose to drop clients a note or send a message via the Internet. However the esthetician chooses to follow up with clients, the time is sure to be well spent.

Here's a Tip

Sometimes clients may not be interested in purchasing all of the products the esthetician recommends. If this happens, the esthetician should not be too assertive. Perhaps the client is happy with his or her current skin care products—or, because of the cost, would like to ease into a new program gradually as he or she runs out of the products currently being used. It is always best for the esthetician to build the client's trust first. Once this is established, the client may be more open to modifying his or her home-care program.

CUSTOMIZED SKIN CARE PROGRAM

Client's Name: ______________________ Date: __________

Esthetician: ______________________

Phone: __________ E-mail: __________

Treatment Goals: ______________________

Next Scheduled Appointment: ______________________

Professional Treatment Plan

	Treatment Schedule
Facials	
Acne	*Example: 1 hr facial 1x/week*
Age Management	______
Deep Pore Cleansing	______
Hydrating	______
Other	______
Specialized Skin Care	
Peels	______
Microdermabrasion	______
Light Therapy	______
Microcurrent	______
Ultrasound	______
Other	______

	Treatment Schedule
Spa Body Treatments	
Body Scrub	______
Body Wrap	______
Body Mask	______
Hydrotherapy	______
Massage	______
Other	______
Pre and Post Surgical Care	
Pre-Operative	______
Post-Operative	______
Other	______

Home-Care Program

Morning

- Cleanse ______
- Balance ______
- Correct ______
- Hydrate ______
- Protect ______

Evening

- Cleanse ______
- Balance ______
- Correct ______
- Nourish ______
- Hydrate ______

Weekly

- Exfoliating Scrub, Mask, Enzyme ______
- Clarifying Mask ______
- Nourishing Mask ______
- Other ______

Detailed Notes

1. ______
2. ______
3. ______
4. ______

▲ Figure 23–12
An example of a home-care guide.

Tracking Your Success

At first it may be difficult to think of sales as a meaningful part of the esthetician's work. Once you realize the benefit to the client and the success it brings to the salon, you will probably look forward to assessing your own contribution.

Sales are a significant source of a salon's revenue and a great way for estheticians to increase their profitability. In some salons, the owner or manager may install a sales quota system to stimulate growth. As mentioned in Chapter 21, Career Planning, a quota system is a method for gauging the amount of sales and targeting production levels. This is a great way to help individuals become more productive, and it can also be a great way to encourage team efforts. Therefore, many managers not only set individual objectives but also provide incentives for meeting team goals. If such a system is not in place at the salon where you work, it is a good idea to formulate your own sales objectives.

As you become comfortable with the idea of setting sales goals, keeping track of the number of salon services you perform and products you sell on a weekly and monthly basis will help you to evaluate your own personal success rate. Most salons use software programs to accomplish this goal and are willing to share this information with service providers. Good managers know that numbers allow you to take an honest and objective look at your performance. They know that unbiased measures can also motivate you to do your job better. Occasionally, sales may be higher or lower, depending on market conditions, promotional efforts, or your personal selling technique. Take all of these factors into consideration, and seek guidance when necessary. Your manager or supervisor and other more experienced colleagues can be valuable sources of information and inspiration that can help you to reach your goals. Pay attention to their advice and learn to work with them to make the most of promotions and boost your productivity level. Whenever possible, enroll in classes that help you to educate clients better. Those who keep the focus on consultative selling, described earlier in this chapter, can take pride in the fact that the ability to meet sales quotas is not simply about increasing earnings. When looked at from a qualitative perspective, it is another measure of the service provider's effectiveness as a caring and knowledgeable practitioner. At some point, you may find that others will seek your opinion. When this happens, you will know you have met with success.

Review Questions

1. Define the term consultative selling, and discuss how this approach differs from other methods of selling.
2. List the basic principles involved in selling products and services ethically.
3. Why are retail sales important to the salon or spa business?
4. Develop an outline for gathering information about a product line.
5. Discuss how the client's needs and wants (client value) influence the marketing process.
6. What is the best approach to educating clients?
7. Explain the difference between the *questionnaire* or *intake form* and *client record keeping*.
8. Discuss the esthetician's role in client retention.
9. What are the main methods of promotion in marketing?
10. List several different methods that a salon can use to promote business, and provide examples of each.
11. Name several of the more popular forms of advertising used by salons and spas.
12. List several ways businesses can promote good public relations.
13. Explain how merchandising influences client sales.
14. Describe several methods that can be used to build a clientele.
15. Name several ways you can reward clients who refer other clients.
16. Discuss the best approach to closing the sale.
17. Explain the importance of recommending products and encouraging clients to comply with a home-care program.
18. Why is follow-up with clients important in esthetics? Identify the three methods of follow-up described in this chapter.

Glossary

advertising	Promotional efforts that are paid for and are directly intended to increase business.
client record keeping	A method of taking personal notes that helps the esthetician to remember important data and serve client needs better.
closing consultation	An opportunity at the end of a treatment session to review product recommendations, prepare a home-care program for the client to follow, and provide any additional literature on other treatment options that the client may be interested in.
consultative selling	A method of advising or consulting to clients and recommending the best treatments and products for their use.
direct marketing	Any attempt to reach the consumer directly with an offer such as direct mail postcards, coupons, newsletters, sales letters, telemarketing, electronic mail, and text messages.
marketing	A strategy for how goods and services are bought, sold, or exchanged.
merchandising	How retail products are arranged and displayed in your salon.
promotion	The process of getting the consumer's attention, with the goal of increasing business.
publicity	A marketing strategy used to gain free media attention.
questionnaire	Also known as *intake form*; form that provides the esthetician with a complete client profile, including important information about a client's skin care habits and health.
retailing	The act of recommending and selling products to clients for at-home use.
upselling services	The practice of recommending or selling additional services to clients that may be performed by you or other practitioners in the salon.

Appendix A: Resources

Publications

Alberts, B. et al. (2002). *Molecular Biology of the Cell*, 4th edition. New York: Garland Science.

Barrett-Hill, F. (2009). *The Aesthetic Clinicians Pictorial Guide*, Vol 1. New Zealand: Virtual Beauty Corporation, Ltd.

Cook, A. R. (1997). *Skin Disorders Sourcebook*. Detroit, Michigan: Omnigraphics, Inc.

D'Angelo, J. (2010). *Spa Business Strategies: A Plan for Success, Second Edition*. New York: Cengage Learning.

D'Angelo, J. et al. (2003). *Milady's Standard Comprehensive Training for Estheticians*. New York: Cengage Learning.

Fitzpatrick, T., Johnson, et al. (1997). *Color Atlas and Synopsis of Clinical Dermatology*. New York, NY: McGraw-Hill.

Fulton, J. E. (2001). Acne Rx. Self-published by James E Fulton, MP, Phd.

Hill, P. (2006). Botox, *Dermal Fillers, and Sclerotherapy*. New York: Cengage Learning.

Hill, P. (2008). *Milady's Aesthetician Series: Advanced Hair Removal*. New York: Cengage Learning.

Hill, P. (2007). *Milady's Aesthetician Series: Permanent Makeup*. New York: Cengage Learning.

Kunz, K. & B. (1993). *The Complete Guide to Foot Reflexology*. Albuquerque NM: Reflexology Research Project.

Lees, M. (2007). *Skin Care Beyond the Basics: Third Edition*. New York: Cengage Learning.

Martini, F. et al. (2007). *Anatomy and Physiology*. Prentice Hall.

Milady. (2010). *Milady Standard Esthetics Advanced*, First Edition. New York: Cengage Learning.

Murad, H. (2005). *The Cellulite Solution*. New York, NY: St. Martin's Press.

Perricone, N. *The Wrinkle Cure*.

Pugliese, P. (2001). *Physiology of the Skin II*. Carol Stream, IL: Allured Publishing.

Pugliese, P. (2005). *Advanced Professional Skin Care*, Medical edition. Bernville, PA: The Topical Agent, LLC.

Sachs, M. (1994). *Ayurvedic Beauty Care*. Twin Lakes, WI: Lotus Press.

Turkington, C., & Dover, J. (1998). *Skin Deep*. New York, NY: Facts on File, Inc.

Winter, R. (1999). *A Consumer's Dictionary of Cosmetic Ingredients*. New York, NY: Three Rivers Press.

Worwood, V.A. (1991). *The Complete Book of Essential Oils and Aromatherapy*. San Rafael, CA: New World Library.

Web Sites

About.com: Dermatology, www.dermatology.about.com

About.com: Makeup, www.makeup.about.com

Acupressure.com: The Official Website for Acupressure, www.acupressure.com

Agricultural Marketing Service, www.ams.usda.gov

American Academy of Dermatology, www.aad.org

American Cancer Society, www.cancer.org

American Society of Plastic Surgeons, www.plasticsurgery.org

Centers for Disease Control and Prevention, www.phil.cdc.gov/phil/home.asp

Colorcube, www.colorcube.com

Cosmetic Ingredient Review, www.cir-safety.org

Dermnet: Skin Disease Image Atlas, www.dermnet.com

EWG's Skin Deep Cosmetics Database, www.cosmeticsdatabase.org

Gov.com, www.fda.gov

MedicineNet, Inc., www.medicinenet.com

Medline Plus, www.nlm.nih.gov/medlineplus

Medscape Reference, www.emedicine.com

Medscape, www.medscape.com

National Center for Biotechnology Information, www.ncbi.nlm.nih.gov

National Center for Complementary and Alternative Medicine, www.nccam.nih.gov

NSF International, www.nsf.org

Occupational Safety and Health Administration, www.osha.gov

Paula's Choice, www.paulaschoice.com

Rosacea.org, www.rosacea.org/index.php

Skin Cancer Foundation, www.skincancer.org

The Ayurvedic Institute, www.ayurveda.com

United States Environmental Protection Agency, www.epa.gov

Appendix B:Conversions

U.S. Measurement-Metric Conversion Tables

The following tables show standard conversions for commonly used measurements in Milady Standard Esthetics: Fundamentals, 11th Edition.

Conversion Formula for Inches to Centimeters: (number of) inches x 2.54 = centimeters

LENGTH	
INCHES	**CENTIMETERS**
⅛ inch (.125 inches)	0.317 centimeters
¼ inch (.25 inches)	0.635 centimeters
½ inch (.50 inches)	1.27 centimeters
¾ inch (.75 inches)	1.9 centimeters
1 inch	2.54 centimeters
2 inches	5.1 centimeters
3 inches	7.6 centimeters
6 inches	15.2 centimeters
12 inches	30.5 centimeters

Conversion Formula for U.S. Fluid Ounces to Milliliters:
(amount of) U.S. fluid ounce (fl. oz.) x 29.573 milliliters (ml)
Conversion Formula for U.S. Fluid Ounces to Liters:
(amount of) U.S. fluid ounce (fl. oz.) x .029573 liters (l)

VOLUME (LIQUID)	
U.S. FLUID ONCES	**MILLILITERS/LITERS**
1 fluid ounce (⅛ cup)	29. 57 milliliters/.02957 liters
2 fluid ounces (¼ cup)	59.14 milliliters/.05914 liters
4 fluid ounces (½ cup)	118.29 milliliters/.11829 liters
6 fluid ounces (¾ cup)	177.43 milliliters/.17743 liters
8 fluid ounces (1 cup)	236.58 milliliters/.23658 liters
16 fluid ounces (1 pint)	473.16 milliliters/.47316 liters
32 fluid ounces (1 quart)	946.33 milliliters/.94633 liters
33.81 fluid ounces (1 liter)	1,000 milliliters/1 liter
64 fluid ounces (½ gallon)	1,892.67 milliliters/1.8926 liters
128 fluid ounces (1 gallon)	3,785.34 milliliters/3.78534 liters

Conversion Formula for Degrees Fahrenheit (°F) to Degrees Celsius (°C): °C = (°F-32) x (5/9) ***

TEMPERATURE	
DEGREES FAHRENHEIT (°F)	**DEGREES CELSIUS (°C)**
32°	0°
40°	4.444°
50°	10°
60°	15.556°
70°	21.111°
80°	26.667°
98.6°	37°
200°	93.333°
300°	148.889°
400°	204.444°

*** If you have a Fahrenheit temperature of 40 degrees and you want to convert it into degrees on the Celsius scale: Using the conversion formula, first subtract 32 from the Fahrenheit temperature of 40 degrees to get 8 as a result. Then multiply 8 by five and divide by nine (8 x 5)/9 to get the converted value of 4.444 degrees Celsius.

Glossary/Index

A

Albinism, absence of melanin pigment in the body, including skin, hair, and eyes; the technical term for albinism is congenital leukoderma or congenital hypopigmentation, 266, 277
Alcohol (ethanol), antiseptic and solvent used in perfumes, lotions, and astringents. SD alcohol is a special denatured ethyl alcohol, 324, 347
Alcohol abuse, 296, 472
Alcohol-based antiseptics, 96
Algae, derived from minerals and phytohormones; remineralizes and revitalizes the skin, 326, 347
Alipidic, lack of oil or "lack of lipids." Describes skin that does not produce enough sebum, indicated by absence of visible pores, 285, 302
Alkalis, also known as *bases*; compounds that react with acids to form salts; have a pH above 7.0 (neutral), taste bitter, and turn litmus paper from red to blue, 167, 175
 in chemical exfoliation, 531
Allantoin, an anti-inflammatory compound isolated from the herb comfrey; it is used in creams, hand lotion, hair lotion, aftershave, and other skin-soothing cosmetics for its ability to heal wounds and skin ulcers and to stimulate the growth of healthy tissue, 326, 348
Allergic contact dermatitis, 264–265
Allergy, reaction due to extreme sensitivity to certain foods, chemicals, or other normally harmless substances, 86, 88, 109
 allergic contact dermatitis, 264–265
 anaphylactic shock from, 265
 atopic dermatitis, 263, 277
 food, 207
 lavender as antiallergenic, 320, 326, 350
 leukocyte response to, 244, 252
 no-fragrance policy due to, 41
 quaternium 15 causing, 325, 351
 to salon products, 321
 as topic for client consultation, 297, 458
 urticaria (hives) from, 264, 281
 wheals from, 259, 260, 281
Aloe vera, most popular botanical used in cosmetic formulations; emollient and film-forming gum resin with hydrating, softening, healing, antimicrobial, and anti-inflammatory properties, 321, 326, 348, 547
Alpha hydroxy acids, abbreviated AHAs; acids derived from plants (mostly fruit) that are often used to exfoliate the skin; mild acids: glycolic, lactic, malic, and tartaric acid. AHAs exfoliate by loosening the bonds between dead corneum cells and dissolve the intercellular matrix. Alpha hydroxy acids also stimulate cell renewal, 8, 315, 316, 347, 547
chemical exfoliation procedure using, 533–534
Alpha lipoic acid, a natural molecule found in every cell in the body; it is a powerful antioxidant and is soluble in water and oil, 319, 348
Alternating current (AC), rapid and interrupted current, flowing first in one direction and then in the opposite direction, 182, 195
Alum, compound made of aluminum, potassium, or ammonium sulfate with strong astringent action, 324, 348
American Cancer Society, 271
American Society for Aesthetic Plastic Surgery, 9
Amino acid, organic acids that form the building blocks of proteins. Twenty amino acids are used within the human body, nine of these are essential amino acids and must be supplied by the diet, 202, 223
Ampere Abbreviated A and also known as *amp*; unit that measures the amount of an electric current (quantity of electrons flowing through a conductor), 182, 195
Ampoules, small, sealed vials containing a single application of highly concentrated extracts in a water or oil base, 340, 348
Anabolism, constructive metabolism; the process of building up larger molecules from smaller ones, 120, 148
Anagen, first stage of hair growth during which new hair is produced, 477, 525
Anaphoresis, process of infusing an alkaline (negative) product into the tissues from the negative pole toward the positive pole, 186, 195
Anaphylactic shock, 265
Anatomy, the study of human body structure that can be seen with the naked eye and how the body parts are organized and the science of the structure of organisms or of their parts, 118, 148
Angular artery, artery that supplies blood to the side of the nose, 141, 148
Anhidrosis, deficiency in perspiration, often a result of a fever or skin disease that requires medical treatment, 262, 277
Anhydrous, describes products that do not contain any water, 308, 348
Anion, an ion with a negative electrical charge, 167, 175
Anode, positive electrode; the anode is usually red and is marked with a P or a plus (+) sign, 186, 195
ANS. *See* Autonomic nervous system
Anterior auricular artery, artery that supplies blood to the front part of the ear, 142, 148
Antibiotics
as LED therapy contraindication, 194
MRSA and, 82, 112
Antioxidants, used to stabilize skin care products by preventing oxidation that would otherwise cause a product to turn rancid and decompose. They are vitamins such as A, C, and E, which can be applied topically in products or taken internally to increase healthy body functions, 170, 175, 547
 alpha lipoic acid, 319, 348
 benefits to skin, 212
 coenzyme Q10, 319, 321, 349
 DMAE, 319, 349
 grapeseed extract, 326, 350
 green tea, 316, 321, 326, 350
 skin benefits, 212
 in skin care products, 319, 321
 vitamin A, 209, 211–212, 224, 317–318, 321, 351
 vitamin C, 216–217, 224, 319
 vitamin E, 210, 213–214, 224, 321
Antiperspirant, 41
Antiseptics, chemical germicides formulated for use on skin; registered and regulated by the Food and Drug Administration (FDA), 96, 109
Antoinette, Marie (queen), 7
Aorta, the arterial trunk that carries blood from the heart to be distributed by branch arteries through the body, 140, 148
Apocrine glands, coiled structures attached to hair follicles found in the underarm and genital areas that secrete sweat, 243, 251

B

C

Cathode, negative electrode; the cathode is usually black and is marked with an N or a minus (-) sign, 186, 195

Cation, ion with a positive electrical charge, 167, 175

Cell membrane, part of the cell that encloses the protoplasm and permits soluble substances to enter and leave the cell, 119, 150

Cell renewal factor (CRF), cell turnover rate, 530, 554

Cell turnover, 234

Cells, basic unit of all living things; minute mass of protoplasm capable of performing all the fundamental functions of life, 118, 150
basic structure of, 119
metabolism, 120
reproduction and division, 119
skin, 147, 229–230

Cellulite, dimpling of the skin caused by protrusion of subcutaneous fat; is due to an irregularity in distribution of fat in the area, usually found on the thighs, hips, buttocks, and abdomen, 547–548, 555

Cellulose gum, 320

Central nervous system (CNS), cerebrospinal nervous system; consists of the brain, spinal cord, spinal nerves, and cranial nerves, 132, 150

Ceramides, glycolipid materials that are a natural part of skin's intercellular matrix and barrier function, 244, 251, 321

Cerebellum, lies at the base of the cerebrum and is attached to the brain stem; this term is Latin for "little brain", 133, 150

Cerebrum, makes up the bulk of the brain and is located in the front, upper part of the cranium, 133, 150

Certificate or license, esthetician's, 625
as business expense, 676
FDA, FTC, and CPSC regulations, 32–33
scope of practice, 432
state regulatory agencies, 77–78
test and practical exam for, 626–628

Certified colors, inorganic color agents known as metal salts; listed on ingredient labels as D&C (drug and cosmetic), 314, 348

Cervical cutaneous nerve, nerve located at the side of the neck that affects the front and sides of the neck as far down as the breastbone, 137, 150

Cervical nerves, nerves that originate at the spinal cord, whose branches supply the muscles and scalp at the back of the head and neck; affect the side of the neck and the platysma muscle, 137, 150, 436

Cervical vertebrae, the seven bones of the top part of the vertebral column, located in the neck region, 122, 124, 125, 150

CEUs. *See* Continuing Education Units

Chamomile, plant extract with calming and soothing properties, 321, 326, 348

Championniere, Lucas, 467

Cheekbones, 139, 158

Chelating agent, a chemical added to cosmetics to improve the efficiency of the preservative, 313, 348

Chelating soaps, also known as *chelating detergents*; detergents that break down stubborn films and remove the residue of products such as scrubs, salts, and masks, 95, 110

Chemical change, change in the chemical properties of a substance that is the result of a chemical reaction in which a new substance or substances are formed that have properties different from the original, 165, 175

Chemical compounds, combinations of two or more atoms of different elements united chemically with a fixed chemical composition, definite proportions, and distinct properties, 165, 176

Chemical exfoliation, chemical agent that dissolves dead skin cells and the intercellular matrix, or "glue," that holds them together (desmosomes), 330, 336–337, 348, 529–534
acid, alkaline, and pH relationships, 531
AHAs and BHAs for, 531
benefits, 532
cell renewal factor and, 530, 554
contraindications for, 532–533
deep compared to light peels, 530–531
history of, 530
home-care after, 534
procedure for AHAs, 533–534

Chemical properties, those characteristics that can only be determined by a chemical reaction and a chemical change in the identity of the substance, 165, 176

Chemical reaction, a reaction between two elements or two compounds that results in chemical changes. The change is in the chemical and physical properties of the substance, 169–171
examples of, 170
solutions, suspensions, and emulsions comparison, 171

Chemical-free product, 164

Chemistry, science that deals with the composition, structures, and properties of matter and how matter changes under different conditions, 161, 176
applied to cosmetics, 171–174
chemical reactions, 169–171
internet resources for, 170
matter, 162–166, 176
periodic table, 162
pH, 166–169, 177, 201, 314, 320, 351, 531
reasons to study, 161

Chest bones, 125

Chewing muscles, 128–129

Chicken pox. *See* Herpes zoster

Chin waxing, 502

China, ancient, 6

Chloasma (liver spots), condition characterized by hyperpigmentation on the skin in spots that are not elevated, 266, 278, 290

Cholesterol, a waxy substance found in your body that is needed to produce hormones, vitamin D, and bile; also important for protecting nerves and for the structure of cells, 206–207, 223

Chromium, 210, 218

Chromophore, the colored cells or target in the epidermis or dermis that absorbs the laser beam's thermal energy, causing the desired injury or destruction of the material, 146, 148, 193, 195, 483

Chucking, massage movement accomplished by grasping the flesh firmly in one hand up and down along the bone while the other hand keeps the arm or leg in a steady position, 433, 445

Circuit breaker, switch that automatically interrupts or shuts off an electric circuit at the first indication of overload, 184, 195

Colorants, substances such as vegetable, pigment, or mineral dyes that give products color, 314, 349
ancient, 4
Combustion, rapid oxidation of any substance, accompanied by the production of heat and light, 170, 176
Comedo (plural: comedones), mass of hardened sebum and skin cells in a hair follicle; an open comedo or blackhead when open and exposed to oxygen. Closed comedos are whiteheads that are blocked and do not have a follicular opening, 261, 278
Comedogenic, tendency for an ingredient to clog follicles and cause a buildup of dead skin cells, resulting in comedones, 274, 278
Comedogenicity, tendency of any topical substance to cause or to worsen a buildup in the follicle, leading to the development of a comedo (blackhead), 311, 348
Commission, method of compensation that is percentage-based and is directly related to the employee's performance; for example, the employee earns a certain percentage of whatever services he or she performs and/or a certain percentage of the amount of product he or she sells, 658, 665
Commission wages, 658
Common carotid arteries, arteries that supply blood to the face, head, and neck, 141, 150
Communicable disease. *See* Contagious disease
Communication, the act of successfully sharing information between two people, or groups of people, so that it is effectively understood, 52, 70. *See also* Client consultation
basics, 51–54
with boss, 650
compliments, 52
with coworkers, 65–67
with difficult people, 64–65
to earn client trust and loyalty, 53, 701, 715
for employee evaluation, 69, 654–657
getting too personal, 65
Golden Rules of human relations, 51–52
human relations based on, 49–51
iPhone and iPad, 67
with managers, 67–69
for marketing, 707
nonverbal cues, 53
pheromones and, 243
reasons to study, 49
scheduling mix-ups, 61–62
with tardy clients, 60–61
with unhappy clients, 62–64
vocabulary, 26
Community involvement, 709
Compensation, 660
commission wages, 658, 665
gratuities, 659
hybrid pay structures, 658–659
salary, 657–658, 666
Complementary colors, primary and secondary colors opposite one another on the color wheel, 561, 620
Complementary foods, combinations of two incomplete foods; complementary proteins eaten together provide all the essential amino acids and make a complete protein, 203, 223
Complete electric circuit, the path of an electric current from the generating source through conductors and back to its original source, 181, 195
Complex carbohydrates, 204, 205, 207
Compliments, 52
Compound molecules, also known as *compounds*; a chemical combination of two or more atoms of different elements in definite (fixed) proportions, 163, 176
Compounding pharmacies, 9
Concealers, cosmetics used to cover blemishes and discolorations; may be applied before or after foundation, 565, 581–582, 620
Concentrate
aromatherapy essential oils, 313, 330, 348, 436
disinfectant, 89
mask (pack, masque) products, 99, 337–339, 350
serums, 340, 352, 392, 460
Conduct, professional, 44–45, 368, 648, 649–650
Conductor, any substance, material, or medium that easily transmits electricity, 180, 196
Confidential Skin Health Intake Form, 56
Confidentiality
for client consultation, 56, 299
for high-profile client, 56
on iPhone and iPad, 67
Conflicts, coping with, 45
Conjunctivitis (pinkeye), very contagious infection of the mucous membranes around the eye; chemical, bacterial, or viral causes, 268, 278
Connective tissue, fibrous tissue that binds together, protects, and supports the various parts of the body such as bone, cartilage, and tendons. Examples of connective tissue are bone, cartilage, ligaments, tendons, blood, lymph, and fat, 120, 150
Consent form, a (customary) written agreement between the client and esthetician (salon/spa) for applying a particular treatment, whether routine or preoperative, 54, 70
Consultation area, 57
Consultative selling, a method of advising or consulting to clients and recommending the best treatments and products for their use, 701, 717, 718
Consumer Product Safety Commission (CPSC), 32
Consumption supplies, supplies used to conduct daily business operations, 685, 696
Contact dermatitis, inflammatory skin condition caused by contact with a substance or chemical. Occupational disorders from ingredients in cosmetics and chemical solutions can cause contact dermatitis (a.k.a. dermatitis venenata). Allergic contact dermatitis is from exposure to allergens; irritant contact dermatitis is from exposure to irritants, 263, 278
allergic contact dermatitis, 264–265
irritant contact dermatitis, 265
Contagious disease, also known as *communicable disease*; a disease that is spread from one person to another person. Some of the more contagious diseases are the common cold, ringworm, conjunctivitis (pinkeye), viral infections, and natural nail or toe and foot infections, 82, 85, 110, 111, 268–269. *See also* Virus
Contamination, the presence, or the reasonably anticipated presence, of blood or other potentially infectious materials on an item's surface or visible debris or residues such as dust, hair, and skin, 83, 110
Continuing education, 663–664, 676
Continuing Education Units (CEUs), 664
Contraindications, factor that prohibits a treatment due to a condition; treatments could cause harmful or negative side effects to those who have specific medical or skin conditions, 189, 284, 293, 302

F

Fatty alcohols, emollients; fatty acids that have been exposed to hydrogen, 310, 349
Fatty esters, emollients produced from fatty acids and alcohols, 310, 349
FDA. *See* Food and Drug Administration
Feathering, 437
Federal Trade Commission (FTC), 32
Feet. *See also* Foot reflexology
electric boots, 468
human papillomavirus, 84, 111
safe footwear, 43
tinea pedis (athlete's foot), 85, 113
toe bones, 122
Fever blisters. *See* Herpes simplex virus 1
Fibroblasts, cells that stimulate cells, collagen, and amino acids that form proteins, 230, 238, 252
Fibula, 122
Fifth cranial nerve (trifacial, trigeminal nerve), it is the chief sensory nerve of the face, and it serves as the motor nerve of the muscles that control chewing. It consists of three branches, 136, 151
Fingers
bones of, 122, 126, 155
exercise for, 44
massage techniques using, 433–434, 445
muscles of, 131, 148, 151
radial artery to, 143, 156
sensory-motor nerve to, 137, 151
Fire extinguishers, 101
Fire insurance coverage, 681–682
First aid, 100–102
First digit, 122
First impressions, 52, 372
First-degree burns, 101–102
Fissure, crack in the skin that penetrates the dermis. Chapped lips or hands are fissures, 260, 278
Fitzpatrick, Thomas, 288
Fitzpatrick Scale, scale used to measure the skin type's ability to tolerate sun exposure, 59, 288–289, 302
Five food groups, 201–203
Fixed costs, operating costs that are constant, for example, rent and loan payments, 675, 697
Flagella, also known as *cilia*; slender, hair-like extensions used by bacilli and spirilla for locomotion (moving about), 80, 111
Flexors, extensor muscles of the wrist, involved in flexing the wrist, 131, 152
Fluoride, 211, 218
Folacin, 209, 215
Folic acid, 209
Follicles, hair follicles and sebaceous follicles are tube-like openings in the epidermis, 232, 241, 252
Folliculitis, also known as *folliculitis barbae, sycosis barbae*, or *barber's itch*. Inflammation of the hair follicles caused by a bacterial infection from ingrown hairs. The cause is typically from ingrown hairs due to shaving or other epilation methods, 264, 278
Food allergy, 207
Food and Drug Administration (FDA)
antiseptics registered and regulated by, 96, 109
on color agent ingredients, 314
on cosmetics, 307
esthetician certificate or license, 32–33
on lasers, 483
regulations, 32
on sunblock, 319
Food consumption, 201. *See also* Nutrition
Foot reflexology, technique of applying pressure to the feet based on a system of zones and areas on the feet that directly correspond to the anatomy of the body. Reflexology is also performed on the hands and ears, 437, 445, 543, 555
Footwear, 43
Forgiveness, 52
Format, of resume, 632
Fortified, a vitamin has been added to a food product, 213, 224
Foundation (base makeup), a tinted cosmetic used to even out skin tone and color, conceal imperfections, and protect skin, 563, 591, 620
Fourth digit, 122
Fourth-degree burns, 101–102
Fragrances, give products their scent, 313, 320, 349
salon no-fragrance policy, 41
Franchised salon or spa, a salon or spa owned by an individual(s) who pays a certain fee to use the company name and is part of a larger organization or chain of salons. The franchise operates according to a specified business plan and set protocols, 637, 665
Free radicals, unstable molecules that cause inflammation, disease, and biochemical aging in the body, especially wrinkling and sagging of the skin. Free radicals are *super* oxidizers that cause an oxidation reaction and produce a new free radical in the process that are created by highly reactive atoms or molecules (often oxygen), 170, 176
carotenes and, 212
skin aging from, 293
in skin care products, 318–319
Frequent-buyer programs, 707
Fresheners, skin-freshening lotions with a low alcohol content, 334, 349
Friction, deep rubbing movement requiring pressure on the skin with the fingers or palm while moving them under a underlying structure. Chucking, rolling, and wringing are variations of friction, 433–434, 445
Front desk, 686–688
for retail exposure, 706
Frontal artery, artery that supplies blood to the forehead and upper eyelids, 142, 152
Frontal bone, bone forming the forehead, 122, 123, 124, 152
Frontalis, front (anterior) portion of the epicranius; muscle of the scalp that raises the eyebrows, draws the scalp forward, and causes wrinkles across the forehead, 128, 129, 152
Frowning, as nonverbal cue, 53
Fruits, 210, 212, 216–217
FTC. *See* Federal Trade Commission
Fulling, form of pétrissage in which the tissue is grasped, gently lifted, and spread out. Used mainly for massaging on the arms, 433, 445

Full-service salon, 629

Functional ingredients, ingredients in cosmetic products that allow the products to spread, give them body and texture, and give them a specific form such as a lotion, cream, or gel. Preservatives are also functional ingredients, 307, 349
list of, 320–321

Fungi (singular: fungus), microscopic plant parasites, which include molds, mildews, and yeasts; can produce contagious diseases such as ringworm, 85, 111

Fungicidal, capable of destroying fungi, 79, 111

Furniture
dispensary room or area, 95–96, 360, 380
hair removal room, 490–493
treatment room, 357–359, 360–362, 367

Furuncle (boil), a subcutaneous abscess filled with pus; furuncles are caused by bacteria in the glands or hair follicles, 261, 278

Fuse, a special device that prevents excessive current from passing through a circuit, 196

fuse box, 183

G

Galvani, Luigi, 186

Galvanic current, 459–460
contraindications for, 460
ionto mask, 463
iontophoresis, 461, 462
maintenance and cleaning of electrodes, 463

Galvanic current, a constant and direct current (DC); uses a positive and negative pole to produce chemical reactions (desincrustation) and ionic reactions (iontophoresis), 186, 196
polarity of solutions, 461–462

Game plan, the conscious act of planning your life, instead of just letting things happen, 24, 28, 37

Gamma ray, 189

Gases, matter without a definite shape or size. No fixed volume or shape; takes the shape of its container, 164, 176

Gastrointestinal system, 145, 151

Geisha, 6

Gellants and thickeners, 313, 320

Genetic and hereditary factors
characteristics and differences in hair growth, 479–481
DNA damage and skin cancer, 269
personal appearance, 120
skin aging, 293, 313, 320
skin color, 231, 236, 237, 252

Genital herpes. *See* Herpes simplex virus 2

Gift certificates, 707

Glabella, 550

Glands, specialized organs that remove certain elements from the blood to convert them into new compounds, 144, 152, 242–243

Glogau scale, 288–289

Glossopharyngeal nerve, 135

Gloves, 300
for disinfectants, 92–93
Universal and Standard Precautions on, 98
for various chemicals, peels, and products, 167

Glucose, 205

Glycation, caused by an elevation in blood sugar, glycation is the binding of a protein molecule to a glucose molecule resulting in the formation of damaged, nonfunctioning structures, known as Advanced Glycation End products(a.k.a. AGES). Glycation alters protein structures and decreases biological activity, 248–249, 252
skin aging from, 293

Glycerin, formed by a decomposition of oils or fats; excellent skin softener and humectant; very strong water binder; sweet, colorless, oily substance used as a solvent and as a moisturizer in skin and body creams, 321, 324, 349

Glycoproteins, skin-conditioning agents derived from carbohydrates and proteins that enhance cellular metabolism and wound healing, 317, 349

Glycosaminoglycans, a water-binding substance such as a polysaccharide (protein and complex sugar) found between the fibers of the dermis, 203, 224, 249–250, 547

Goal setting, the identification of long-term and short-term goals that helps you decide what you want out of your life, 28, 30, 37
career, 624
real-life, 28, 30, 37
sample of short-term, 29
short-term and long-term, 28
understanding client goals, 57

Golden Rules, human relations, 51–52

Gommage (roll-off masks), exfoliating creams that are rubbed off the skin, 337, 349

Goose bumps, 242

Gown, Universal and Standard Precautions on using, 99

Granular layer, hair root, 241

Grapeseed extract, powerful antioxidant with soothing properties, 326, 350

Gratuities, 659

Greasepaint, heavy makeup used for theatrical purposes, 564, 620

Greater auricular nerve, nerve at the sides of the neck affecting the face, ears, neck, and parotid gland, 137, 152

Greater occipital nerve, nerve located in the back of the head, affects the scalp as far up as the top of the head, 137, 152

Greece, ancient, 5, 473

Green leafy vegetables, 210

Green light, a light-emitting diode for use on clients with hyperpigmentation or for detoxifying the skin, 190–194, 196, 539

Green tea, powerful antioxidant and soothing agent; antibacterial, anti-inflammatory, and a stimulant, 316, 321, 326, 350

Green/sustainable resources, 368–371
LOHAS, 371, 380

Gross profit, 676

Ground substance, 239

Grounding, the *ground* connection completes the circuit and carries the current safely away to the ground, 184, 196

H

Hacking, chopping movement performed with the edges of the hands in massage, 434, 445

Hair
anatomy of, 234, 240–241
components of, 475–477
excessive growth, 480–481
growth cycle, 477–479

Hair bulb, swelling at the base of the follicle that provides the hair with nourishment; it is a thick, club-shaped structure that forms the lower part of the hair root, 476, 525

Hair conditioner, 171

Hair follicle, mass of epidermal cells forming a small tube, or canal; the tube-like depression or pocket in the skin or scalp that contains the hair root, 475, 525

Hair papilla (plural: papillae), cone-shaped elevations at the base of the follicle that fit into the hair bulb. The papillae are filled with tissue that contains the blood vessels and cells necessary for hair growth and follicle nourishment, 239, 252, 477, 525

Hair removal
- characteristics and differences in hair growth, 479–481
- client consultations, 493–497
- contraindications for waxing procedures, 493
- hair growth cycle, 477–479
- methods of, 481–484
- morphology of hair, 474–477
- procedures
  - bikini waxing with hard wax, 520–522
  - chin waxing with hard wax, 514–515
  - eyebrow tweezing, 506–508
  - eyebrow waxing with soft wax, 508–511
  - leg waxing with soft wax, 516–517
  - lip waxing with hard wax, 512–513
  - men's waxing with soft wax, 523–524
  - underarm waxing with hard wax, 518–519
  - waxing (general), 497–505
- reasons to study, 474
- room preparation and supplies, 490–493
- temporary, 484–487
- waxing techniques and products, 487–489

Hair root, anchors hair to the skin cells and is part of the hair located at the bottom of the follicle below the surface of the skin; part of the hair that lies within the follicle at its base, where the hair grows, 475, 526

Hair shaft, portion of the hair that extends or projects beyond the skin, consisting of the outer layer (cuticle), inner layer (medulla), and middle layer (cortex). Color changes happen in the cortex, 233, 475, 526

Hand washing
- procedure for proper, 108
- waterless, 96–97

Hands
- blood supply to, 142, 143, 149, 156, 158
- bones, 125–126
- chapped, 260, 278
- electric mitts for, 468
- gestures as nonverbal cues, 53
- mobility of, for massage, 431
- muscles, 131
- radial artery to, 143, 156
- reflexology for, 437, 445
- safeguarding your, 167
- structures of skin of, 147

Handshake, 51, 52

Hazard Communication Standard (HCS), 75

HDLs. *See* Lipoproteins

Head. *See also* Face
- arteries and veins, 141–142, 151, 152
- bones, 122, 123, 124, 152, 157
- cervical nerves, 137, 150, 436
- muscles, 128–129
- nerves, 135–137

Head lice, 86

Headband, 300

Healing agents, substances such as chamomile or aloe that help to heal the skin, 314, 321, 350

Heart, muscular cone-shaped organ that keeps the blood moving within the circulatory system, 121, 138–139, 152
- client's pacemaker, 188
- endocrine glands and, 145

Heat
- as irritant, 275
- skin receptors for, 231

Hebrews, ancient, 5

Hemoglobin, iron-containing protein in red blood cells that binds to oxygen, 141, 152

Henna, a dye obtained from the powdered leaves and shoots of the mignonette tree; used as a reddish hair dye and in tattooing, 17

Hepatitis, a bloodborne virus that causes disease and can damage the liver, 84, 111
- EPA-registered disinfectant against, 90

Herbs, hundreds of different herbs that contain phytohormones are used in skin care products and cosmetics; they heal, stimulate, soothe, and moisturize, 321, 324, 350

Herpes simplex virus 1, strain of the herpes virus that causes fever blisters or cold sores; it is a recurring, contagious viral infection consisting of a vesicle or group of vesicles on a red, swollen base. The blisters usually appear on the lips or nostrils, 268, 279

Herpes simplex virus 2, strain of the herpes virus that infects the genitals, 268, 279

Herpes zoster (shingles), a painful viral infection skin condition from the chickenpox virus; characterized by groups of blisters that form a rash in a ring or line, 268, 279

High-frequency machine, apparatus that utilizes alternating, or sinusoidal, current to produce a mild to strong heat effect; sometimes called *Tesla high-frequency* or *violet ray*, 463–466, 470

Hirsutism, growth of an unusual amount of hair on parts of the body normally bearing only downy hair, such as the face, arms, and legs of women or the backs of men, 480, 526

Histology (microscopic anatomy), the study of the structure and composition of tissue, 118, 152
- reasons to study physiology and, 228

History, of style, skin care, and grooming, 4–9

HIV. *See* Human immunodeficiency virus

Hives. *See* Urticaria

Holiday sales promotions, 705–706

Home care
- for acne, 403
- after chemical exfoliation, 534
- in closing consultation, 714, 718
- Customized Skin Care Program form, 716
- skin care instruction sheet, 344
- skin care products, 343–344

Hormone replacement therapy (HRT), 250

Hormones, secretions produced by one of the endocrine glands and carried by the bloodstream or body fluid to another part of the body, or a body organ, to stimulate functional activity or secretion, such as insulin, adrenaline, and estrogen, 144–145, 146, 152
- as acne trigger, 273–274
- aging and, 249–250
- pheromones, 243
- reproductive, 147
- skin aging from, 293
- skin functions controlled by, 229
- telangiectasia and, 250

Horsechestnut, extract containing bioflavonoids; also known as vitamin P. Helps strengthen capillary walls; used for couperose areas or telangiectasia, 326, 350

Hospital disinfectants, disinfectants that are effective for cleaning blood and body fluids, 76, 111
 EPA-registered, 90

Hot towel cabinet, 450

Hotel spa, 631

HPV. *See* Human papillomavirus

HRT. *See* Hormone replacement therapy

Human immunodeficiency virus (HIV), a pathogen that is most often the precursor to acquired immune deficiency syndrome (AIDS). By impairing or killing the immune system affected with it, HIV progressively destroys the body's ability to fight infections or certain cancers, 84, 109, 111
 EPA-registered disinfection of, 90

Human papillomavirus (HPV, plantar warts), a virus that can infect the bottom of the foot and resembles small black dots, usually in clustered groups, 84, 111

Humectants, ingredients that attract water. Humectants draw moisture to the skin and soften its surface, diminishing lines caused by dryness, 314, 321, 350

Humerus, uppermost and largest bone in the arm, extending from the elbow to the shoulder, 125, 152

Humor, personal, 52

Hyaluronic acid, hydrating fluids found in the skin; hydrophilic agent with water-binding properties, 239, 252, 321

Hybrid pay structures, 658–659

Hydration. *See also* Water
 facial masks for, 337
 for healthy skin, 296

Hydrators, ingredients that attract water to the skin's surface, 314–315, 321, 350

Hydraulic chair, 44

Hydrogen, colorless, odorless, tasteless gas; the lightest element known, 165, 176

Hydrogen peroxide, chemical compound of hydrogen and oxygen; a colorless liquid with a characteristic odor and a slightly acid taste, 166, 176
 chemical composition of, 163
 solution of, 171

Hydrolipidic, hydrolipidic film is an oil-water balance that protects the skin's surface, 230–231, 252

Hydrophilic, easily absorbs moisture; in chemistry terms, capable of combining with or attracting water (water-loving), 172, 176

Hydrophilic agents, ingredients that attract water to the skin's surface, 314, 350

Hydropower (water-powered) plants, 180

Hydroquinone, 316

Hydrotherapy, spa treatments that use water, 542, 555

Hydroxide, an anion (an ion with a negative electrical charge) with one oxygen and one hydrogen atom, 167, 176

Hygiene, personal, 41

Hyoid bone, u-shaped bone at the base of the tongue that supports the tongue and its muscle, 124, 125, 152

Hyperhidrosis, excessive perspiration caused by heat, genetics, medications, or medical conditions; also called diaphoresis, 262, 279

Hyperkeratosis, thickening of the skin caused by a mass of keratinized cells (keratinocytes), 267, 279, 290

Hyperpigmentation, over-production of pigment, 265, 279
 green light therapy for, 193–194

Hypertrichosis, also known as *hirsuties*; condition of abnormal growth of hair, characterized by the growth of terminal hair in areas of the body that normally grow only vellus hair, 480, 526

Hypertrophy, abnormal growth of the skin; many are benign, or harmless, 267, 279

Hypodermis, 239

Hypoglossal nerve, 135

Hypoglycemia, a condition in which blood glucose or blood sugar drops too low; caused by either too much insulin or low food intake, 205, 224

Hypopigmentation, absence of pigment, resulting in light or white splotches, 265, 279

I

Identity, business, 708

Ilium, 122

Imidazolidinyl urea, 320

Immiscible, liquids that are not capable of being mixed together to form stable solutions, 171, 176

Immunity, the ability of the body to destroy and resist infection. Immunity against disease can be either natural or acquired and is a sign of good health, 86, 111

Impetigo, contagious bacterial infection often occurring in children; characterized by clusters of small blisters or crusty lesions, 268, 279

Implements, tools used by technicians to perform services. Implements can be reusable or disposable, 365, 380

Inactive electrode, opposite pole from the active electrode, 186, 196

Income Statement sample, 676

Independent contractor, someone who sets his or her own fees, controls his or her own hours, has his or her own business card, and pays his or her own taxes, 660, 665

Independent day spa or skin care clinic, 10, 629

India, Ayurvedic healing system from, 395, 543, 554

Indirect transmission, transmission of blood or body fluids through contact with an intermediate contaminated object such as a razor, extractor, nipper, or an environmental surface, 80, 111

Individual lashes, separate artificial eyelashes that are applied on top of the lashes one at a time, 601, 620

Infection, the invasion of body tissues by disease-causing pathogens, 78, 111

Infection control, the methods used to eliminate or reduce the transmission of infectious organisms, 78, 111
 aseptic procedure, 106–107
 for bacteria, 79–82
 disinfecting nonelectrical tools and implements, 104–105
 federal and state regulation of, 75–78
 for fungi, 85
 guidelines for salon and spa, 102–103
 makeup, 572
 for parasites, 86
 principles of prevention, 86–97
 proper hand washing procedure, 108
 reasons to study, 75
 terms related to disease, 83
 universal and standard precautions for, 97–102
 for viruses, 82–85

Infectious, caused by or capable of being transmitted by infection, 77, 111

Infectious disease, disease caused by pathogenic (harmful) microorganisms that enter the body. An infectious disease may or may not be spread from one person to another person, 78, 111

Inferior labial artery, supplies blood to the lower lip, 141, 152
Inflammation, condition in which the body reacts to injury, irritation, or infection; characterized by redness, heat, pain, and swelling, 81, 111
skin, 263–265
as treatment contraindication, 463
yellow light therapy for, 193
Information interview, a scheduled meeting or conversation whose sole purpose is to gather information, 638, 665
Infraorbital artery, artery that originates from the internal maxillary artery and supplies blood to the eye muscles, 142, 152
Infraorbital nerve, nerve that affects the skin of the lower eyelid, side of the nose, upper lip, and mouth, 142, 152
Infrared light, infrared light has longer wavelengths, penetrates more deeply, has less energy, and produces more heat than visible light; makes up 60 percent of natural sunlight, 189, 190, 196
Infratrochlear nerve, nerve that affects the membrane and skin of the nose, 136, 152
Ingestion, eating or taking food into the body, 145, 152
Inhalation, breathing in through the nose or mouth, and thus oxygen is absorbed by the blood, 146, 152
Injectable fillers, substances used in nonsurgical procedures to fill in or plump up areas of the skin. Botox® and dermal fillers are injectables, 550, 555
Inorganic chemistry, the study of substances that do not contain the element carbon, but may contain the element hydrogen, 162, 176
Inositol, 209
Insertion, point where the skeletal muscle is attached to a bone or other more movable body part, 127, 152
massage from, to muscle origin, 430–431
Insulator (nonconductor), substance that does not easily transmit electricity, 181, 196
Insulin, 205
Insurance coverage, 45, 56, 650, 652–653
as business expense, 676
exposure incidents, 99
fire, theft, lawsuits, 681–682
independent contractor, 660, 665
regulations, business laws, insurance, 678–679
Integumentary system, the skin and its accessory organs, such as the oil and sweat glands, sensory receptors, hair, and nails, 121, 146–147, 152, 229
Intense pulse light, abbreviated IPL; a medical device that uses multiple colors and wavelengths (broad spectrum) of focused light to treat spider veins, hyperpigmentation, rosacea and redness, wrinkles, enlarged hair follicles and pores, and excessive hair, 194, 196, 538
Intercellular matrix, lipid substances between corneum cells that protect the cells from water loss and irritation, 230, 233, 252
Internal carotid artery, artery that supplies blood to the brain, eyes, eyelids, forehead, nose, and internal ear, 141, 152
Internal jugular vein, vein located at the side of the neck to collect blood from the brain and parts of the face and neck, 142, 152
Interstitial fluid, blood plasma found in the spaces between tissues, 143, 152
Interview, employment, 638–640
employment application, 647
legal aspects of, 647
obtaining, 641–642
preparation for, 642–645
Interview Checklist, 642
Preparation Checklist, 643
tip for travel time, 645
your questions for interviewer, 646–647
Intestines, 121, 145
as digestive system component, 201
excretion by, 146
Intravenous drug users, 84
Introducing yourself, 53
Introductory offers, 707
Inventory control, 685
Inventory of Personal Characteristics, 630
Invisible light, light at either end of the visible spectrum of light that is invisible to the naked eye, 190–191, 196
Involuntary muscles, 126, 154
Iodine, 210, 218, 219, 402
Ion, an atom or molecule that carries an electrical charge, 167, 176
Ionization, the separation of an atom or molecule into positive or negative ions, 167, 176
Ionto mask, 463
Iontophoresis (ionization), process of infusing water-soluble products into the skin with the use of electric current, such as the use of positive and negative poles of a galvanic machine or a microcurrent device, 186, 196, 461, 462
IPad, 67
IPhone, 67
IPL device. *See* Intense pulse light device
Iron, 210, 218
Irritant contact dermatitis, 265
Isopropyl alcohol, 320
Isotretinoin (Accutane®), 188, 276

J

Japan, ancient, 6. *See also* Reiki; Shiatsu
Jessner's peel, light to medium peel of lactic acid, salicylic acid, and resorcinol in an ethanol solvent, 530, 555
Job. *See* Career planning; Careers
Job description, specified list of duties and responsibilities that are required of an employee in the performance of his or her job, 653–656, 666
Joint, connection between two or more bones of the skeleton
number in human body, 122
pain in, 122
Jojoba, oil widely used in cosmetics; extracted from the bean-like seeds of the desert shrub. Used as a lubricant and noncomedogenic emollient and moisturizer, 320, 326, 350
Junk food, 207

K

K. *See* Kilowatt
Keloid, thick scar resulting from excessive growth of fibrous tissue (collagen), 260, 279
Keratin, fibrous protein of cells that is also the principal component of skin, hair, and nails; provides resiliency and protection, 210, 233, 234, 252
Keratinocytes, epidermal cells composed of keratin, lipids, and other proteins, 234, 252
aging and, 249–250

Keratolytic, agent that causes exfoliation, or sloughing, of skin cells, 318, 350

Keratoma, acquired, superficial, thickened patch of epidermis. A callus is a keratoma caused by continued, repeated pressure or friction on any part of the skin, especially the hands and feet, 267, 279

Keratosis (plural: keratoses), abnormally thick build up of cells, 267, 279
retention hyperkeratosis, 272, 280

Keratosis pilaris, redness and bumpiness common on the cheeks or upper arms; it is caused by blocked hair follicles. The patches of irritation are accompanied by a rough texture and small pinpoint white milia, 267, 279

Kidneys, one of the body organs which supports the excretory system by eliminating water and waste products, 121, 128, 152
endocrine glands and, 145
excretion by, 146

Kilowatt (K), 1,000 watts, 183, 196

Kojic acid, skin-brightening agent, 316, 321, 326, 350

Kosmetikos (skilled in use of cosmetics), 5

L

Lachium bone, 122

Lacrimal bones, small, thin bones located in the anterior medial wall of the orbits (eye sockets), 123, 124

Lakes, insoluble pigments made by combining a dye with an inorganic material, 314, 350

Langerhans immune cells, guard cells of the immune system that sense unrecognized foreign invaders, such as bacteria, and then process these antigens for removal through the lymph system, 235, 238, 252

Lanolin, emollient with moisturizing properties; also an emulsifier with high water-absorption capabilities, 324, 350

Lanugo, the hair on a fetus; soft and downy hair, 474, 526

Laser (light amplification stimulation emission of radiation), a medical device that uses electromagnetic radiation for hair removal and skin treatments, 189–194, 196, 324, 351
chromophores and, 146, 148, 193, 195, 483
FDA on, 483
hair removal, 482–483, 526
photothermolysis, 192, 197, 482
resurfacing, 552, 555
technician, 11
technology and procedures, 536–537
types of, 191–192

Laser hair removal, photoepilation hair reduction treatment in which a laser beam is pulsed on the skin using one wavelength at a time, impairing hair growth; an intense pulse of electromagnetic radiation, 482–483, 526

Laser resurfacing, a laser procedure utilizing the CO_2 or erbium laser that involves vaporization of the epidermis and/or dermis for facial rejuvenation; used to smooth wrinkles or lighten acne scars and stimulate growth of new collagen, 552, 555

Lateral pterygoid, muscles that coordinate with the masseter, temporalis, and medial pterygoid muscles to open and close the mouth and bring the jaw forward; sometimes referred to as chewing muscles, 128, 152

Latissimus dorsi, large, flat, triangular muscle covering the lower back, 130, 153

Laundry and linens, 367, 676

Laurel PCA, 320

Lavender, antiallergenic, anti-inflammatory, antiseptic, antibacterial, balancing, energizing, soothing, and healing, 320, 326, 350

Laws. *See* Regulations, business laws, insurance; Regulatory agencies

Learning disability, 626

Leases, 680–681

Lecithin, 547

LED (light-emitting diode), a device used to reduce acne, increase skin circulation, and improve the collagen content in the skin, 193, 196, 538
effects of, 194

Legal issues. *See also* Certificate or license, esthetician's; Skin care business
for employment interview, 647
exposure incidents, 99
fire, theft, lawsuits, 681–682
for independent contractor, 660, 665
insurance coverage, 45, 56, 99, 650, 652–653, 660, 665, 676, 681–682
legal fees as business expense, 676
regulations, business laws, insurance, 678–679

Legs
hirsutism, 480, 526
tinea versicolor on, 85, 113
varicose veins and vascular lesions on, 264, 281
waxing with soft wax, 516–517

Lentigo, freckles; small yellow-brown colored spots. Lentigenes that result from sunlight exposure are actinic, or solar, lentigenes. Patches are referred to as *large macules*, 266, 279

Lesions, mark, wound, or abnormality; structural changes in tissues caused by damage or injury, 279
primary, 258–260
secondary, 260–261, 280

Lesser occipital nerve, 137, 157

Leukocytes, 141, 158, 238

Leukocytes, white blood cells that have enzymes to digest and kill bacteria and parasites. These white blood cells also respond to allergies, 244, 252

Leukoderma, skin disorder characterized by light, abnormal patches; congenital, acquired, post-inflammatory, or other causes that destroy pigment-producing cells. Vitiligo and albinism are leukodermas, 266, 279

Levator anguli oris (caninus), is a muscle that raises the angle of the mouth and draws it inward, 129, 153

Levator labii superioris (quadratus labii superioris), is a muscle that elevates the lip and dilates the nostrils, as in expressing distaste, 129, 153

LGFB. *See* Look Good . . . Feel Better

Liability issues, 650, 652–653

License, esthetician. *See* Certificate or license, esthetician's

Licensed massage therapist (LMT), 430

Licorice, anti-irritant used for sensitive skin; helps lighten pigmentation, 316, 321, 327, 350

Life skills. *See also* Communication
building on your strengths, 21–22
design your mission statement, 27–28
dress for success, 41
good habits, 26–27
personality development, 33–35
reasons to study, 20

rules for success, 24–25
self-care test, 23
study skills, 26–27
time management, 29–31
your game plan for success, 24, 28, 37
Lifestyle
creating your own balance, 42, 52
skin health and, 247–248
treatment options and, 58
Light therapy, also known as *phototherapy*; the application of light rays to the skin for the treatment of acne, wrinkles, capillaries, pigmentation, or hair removal, 192, 194, 197
Lighteners, 316
LinkedIn, 708
Linoleic acid, omega 6, an essential fatty acid used to make important hormones; also part of the skin's lipid barrier, 206, 224
Lip treatments, 392
Lipids, fats or fat-like substances; lipids help repair and protect the barrier function of the skin, 315, 350
in cosmetics, 321
Lipophilic, having an affinity for or an attraction to fat and oils (oil-loving), 173, 176
Lipoproteins (HDLs), 207–208
Liposomes, closed-lipid bilayer spheres that encapsulate ingredients, target their delivery to specific tissues of the skin, and control their release, 316, 350
Liposuction, a surgical procedure used to remove stubborn areas of fat, 553, 555
Lips
chapped, 260, 278
corrective makeup for, 593, 595–596
digestive system component, 201
herpes simplex virus 1, 268, 279
inferior labial artery, 141, 152
waxing tips for, 502
waxing with hard wax, 512–513
Lipstick, 585–586
Liquids, matter that has volume, no definite shape and will take the shape of its container, such as water, 164, 176
Listening
nod to demonstrate you're, 53
as relationship builder, 52
to show you care, 51
understanding client's goals, 57
Liver, one of the organs which supports the excretory system by removing toxic waste products of digestion, 121, 153
as digestive system component, 201
excretion by, 146
Liver spots. *See* Chloasma
LMT. *See* Licensed massage therapist
Loan interest, 676
Local infection, an infection, such as a pimple or abscess, that is confined to a particular part of the body and appears as a lesion containing pus, 81, 111
Location, business, 673–674
Logarithmic scale, a method of displaying data in multiples of 10, 168, 176
LOHAS (Lifestyle of Health and Sustainability), forward-thinking consumers who consider the impact on the environment and society when making purchasing decisions, 371, 380
Long wavelengths, 189–190
Look Good . . . Feel Better (LGFB), 15
Loupe. *See* Magnifying lamp
Lubricants, coat the skin and reduce friction. Mineral oil is a lubricant, 310, 350
Lucas Sprayer, atomizer designed to apply plant extracts and other ingredients to the skin, 467, 470
Lungs, spongy tissues composed of microscopic cells in which inhaled air is exchanged for carbon dioxide during one respiratory cycle, 121, 153
adverse chemical reactions in salon, 265
airways of, in miles, 147
excretion by, 146
Lymph, clear, yellowish fluid that circulates in the lymph spaces (lymphatic) of the body; carries waste and impurities away from the cells, 143, 153
Lymph capillaries, lymphatic vessels that occur in clusters and are distributed throughout most of the body, 144, 153
Lymph nodes, gland-like structures found inside lymphatic vessels; filter the lymphatic vessels and help fight infection, 143, 153
Lymph vessels, located in the dermis, these supply nourishment within the skin and remove waste, 238, 252. *See* Manual lymph drainage
Lymphatic/immune system, a vital factor to the circulatory and to the immune system made up of lymph, lymph nodes, the thymus gland, the spleen, and lymph vessels that act as an aid to the blood system; the lymphatic and immune system are closely connected in that they protect the body from disease by developing immunities and destroying disease-causing microorganisms, 121, 143–144, 153
Lymphocyte, 238

M

mA. *See* Milliampere
Macronutrients, nutrients that make up the largest part of the nutrition we take in; the three basic food groups: protein, carbohydrates, and fats, 202, 224
Macule (plural: maculae), flat spot or discoloration on the skin, such as a freckle. Macules are neither raised nor sunken, 259, 279
Magnesium, 210, 217
Magnifying lamp (loupe), 450–452
Magnifying lamp/light, 297, 299
Makeup
application techniques, 581–587
blush, 583
concealer, 581–582
eye shadow, 583–584
eyebrow color, 585
eyeliner, 584
face powder, 582
foundation, 581
highlighting and shading, 582
lip color, 585–586
mascara, 584–585
steps, 587
tips and guidelines, 586
artificial eyelashes, 600–601
brushes, 568–570
for camera and special events
airbrush, 599–600
bridal, 598
photography and video applications, 598–599
special occasion (general), 596–597

Occipitalis, back of the epicranius; muscle that draws the scalp backward, 128, 154, 436
Occipitofrontalis, 127, 151
Occlusive, occlusive products are thick and lay on top of the skin to reduce transepidermal water loss (TEWL); helps hold in moisture, and protect the skin's top barrier layer, 286, 302
Occupational disease, illness resulting from conditions associated with employment, such as prolonged and repeated overexposure to certain products or ingredients, 83, 112
Occupational Safety and Health Administration (OSHA), 75
  on ozone, 457
Oculomotor nerve, 135
Ohm (O), unit that measures the resistance of an electric current, 183, 197
Oil glands, 233
  secretory nerves, 242
Oil soluble, compatible with oil, 312, 316, 351
Oil-in-water (O/W) emulsion, oil droplets dispersed in water with the aid of an emulsifying agent, 171, 173, 177
  examples of, 174
Olfactory nerve, 135
Olfactory system, gives us our sense of smell, which is the strongest of the five senses, 331, 351
Olive oil, 320
Omega-3 fatty acids, alpha-linolenic acid; a type of "good" polyunsaturated fat that may decrease cardiovascular diseases. It is also an anti-inflammatory and beneficial for skin, 206, 224
Onyx, 241
Operating expenses, business, 676
Ophthalmic nerve, branch of the fifth cranial nerve that supplies the skin of the forehead, upper eyelids, and interior portion of the scalp, orbit, eyeball, and nasal passage, 136, 154
Optic nerve, 135
Orbicularis oculi, ring muscle of the eye socket; closes the eyelid, 129, 154
Organelle, small structures or miniature organs within a cell that have their own function, 119, 155
Organic chemistry, study of substances that contain carbon, 161, 177
Organic compounds, 177
Organs, structures composed of specialized tissues designed to perform specific functions in plants and animals, 120, 155
  nine major, 121
Origin, part of the muscle that does not move; it is attached to the skeleton and is usually part of a skeletal muscle, 127, 155
Os, means *bone* and is used as a prefix in many medical terms, such as osteoarthritis, a joint disease, 122, 155
OSHA. *See* Occupational Safety and Health Administration
Osteology, study of anatomy, structure, and function of the bones, 122, 155
Osteoporosis, a thinning of bones, leaving them fragile and prone to fractures; caused by the reabsorption of calcium into the blood, 213, 224
Ovaries, function in sexual reproduction as well as determining male and female sexual characteristics, 145, 155
  endocrine glands and, 145
Overweight, 219
  fad dieting, 220
  nutrition and portion size, 201
O/W emulsion, oil–in–water emulsion
Ownership, business, 670–672
Oxidation, either the addition of oxygen or the loss of hydrogen; a chemical reaction that combines a substance with oxygen to produce an oxide, 165, 177
  examples of, 170
Oxidation-reduction, also known as *redox;* chemical reaction in which the oxidizing agent is reduced and the reducing agent is oxidized, 170, 177
Oxidize, to combine or cause a substance to combine with oxygen, 171, 177
Oxygen, the most abundant element on Earth, 165, 177
  smoking and reduced, 247–248
Ozone, 457

P

PABA (para-aminobenzoic acid), 209
Pacemaker/heart conditions/high blood pressure
  high frequency machine contraindicated for problems with, 463
  treatments contraindicated for, 188
Pacinian corpuscle, 233
Pain
  joint, 122
  massage to relieve, 429, 445
  nerve endings to register, 147, 231
  sensory nerve messages, 242
Palatine bones, two bones that form the hard palate of the mouth, 123, 124, 155
Pallid layer, hair root, 241
Pancreas, secretes enzyme-producing cells that are responsible for digesting carbohydrates, proteins, and fats. The islet of Langerhans cells within the pancreas control insulin and glucagon production, 144, 155
  as digestive system component, 201
  endocrine glands and, 145
Pantothenic acid, 209, 216
Papaya, natural enzyme used for exfoliation and in enzyme peels, 321, 327, 351
Papillary layer, top layer of the dermis next to the epidermis, 229, 233, 237, 239, 240, 252
Papule, pimple; small elevation on the skin that contains no fluid but may develop pus, 259, 280
  acne and sebaceous follicles, 273
Parabens, one of the most commonly used groups of preservatives in the cosmetic, pharmaceutical, and food industries; provide bacteriostatic and fungistatic activity against a diverse number of organisms, 320, 324, 351
Paraffin wax heater, 467–468
Paraffin wax masks, mask used to warm the skin and promote penetration of ingredients through the heat trapped under the surface of the paraffin, 339, 351
Parasites, organisms that grow, feed, and shelter on or in another organism (referred to as the host), while contributing nothing to the survival of that organism. Parasites must have a host to survive, 86, 112
Parasitic disease, disease caused by parasites, such as lice and mites, 83, 112

Parasympathetic division, part of the autonomic nervous system, it operates under normal nonstressful situations, such as resting. It also helps to restore calm and balance to the body after a stressful event, 132, 155

Parathyroid glands, regulate blood calcium and phosphorus levels so that the nervous and muscular systems can function properly, 144, 145, 155

Parietal artery, artery that supplies blood to the side and crown of the head, 142, 155

Parietal bones, bones that form the sides and top of the cranium, 122, 123, 124, 155

Parking facilities, 673–674

Partnership, form of business ownership in which two or more people share ownership, although this does not necessarily mean an equal arrangement. In a partnership, each partner assumes the other's unlimited liability for debt. Profits are shared among partners, 670, 697

Patella, 122

Pathogenic, harmful microorganisms that can cause disease or infection in humans when they invade the body, 79, 112

Pathogenic disease, disease produced by organisms, including bacteria, viruses, fungi, and parasites, 83, 112

PDAs. *See* Personal digital assistants

Peanuts, 207

Pectoralis major and minor, muscles of the chest that assist the swinging movements of the arm, 130, 155

PEG. *See* Polyethylene glycol

Peptides, chains of amino acids that stimulate fibroblasts, cell metabolism, collagen, and improve skin's firmness. Larger chains are called polypeptides, 317, 321, 351

Percussion. *See* Tapotement

Perfectionism, an unhealthy compulsion to do things perfectly, 24, 37

Performance ingredients, ingredients in cosmetic products that cause the actual changes in the appearance of the skin, 306, 351

Performance, to improve cell metabolism, 316–317

Perfume, 372

Pericardium, double-layered membranous sac enclosing the heart; made of epithelial tissue, 138, 155

Periodic table, 162

Perioral dermatitis, acne-like condition around the mouth. These are mainly small clusters of papules that could be caused by toothpaste or products used on the face, 263, 280

Peripheral nervous system (PNS), system of nerves and ganglia that connects the peripheral parts of the body to the central nervous system; has both sensory and motor nerves, 132, 155

Peristalsis, moving food along the digestive tract, 145, 155

Permanent cosmetics, 603–604. *See also* Cosmetic surgery

Personal digital assistants (PDAs), 32

Personal hygiene, 41

Personal hygiene, daily maintenance of cleanliness and healthfulness through certain sanitary practices, 41, 46

Personal protective equipment (PPE), protective clothing and devices designed to protect an individual from contact with bloodborne pathogens; examples include gloves, fluid-resistant lab coat, apron, or gown, goggles or eye shield, and face masks that cover the nose and mouth, 97, 112

Personality development, 33–35

Personnel, employees; staff, 676, 692–695, 697

Perspiration
- to create barrier on skin surface, 168
- excretion by, 146

Petri dish, 78

Pétrissage, kneading movement that stimulates the underlying tissues; performed by lifting, squeezing, and pressing the tissue with a light, firm pressure, 433, 445

Petroleum jelly, occlusive agent that restores the barrier layer by holding in water; used after laser surgery to protect the skin while healing, 324, 351

pH, the abbreviation used for potential hydrogen; relative degree of acidity and alkalinity of a substance. pH represents the quantity of hydrogen ions, 166–169, 177
- in chemical exfoliation, 531
- pH Worksheet Form, 169

pH adjusters, acids or alkalis (bases) used to adjust the pH of products, 314, 320, 351

pH scale, a measure of the acidity and alkalinity of a substance; the pH scale has a range of 0 to 14, with 7 being a neutral. A pH below 7 is an acidic solution; a pH above 7 is an alkaline solution, 166–167, 177, 201

pH test papers, 168

Phalanges (digits), the bones in the fingers, three in each finger and two in each thumb, totaling 14 bones, 122, 126, 155

Phenol, carbolic acid; a caustic poison; used for peels and to sanitize metallic implements, 552, 555

Phenolic disinfectants, powerful tuberculocidal disinfectants. They are a form of formaldehyde, have a very high pH, and can damage the skin and eyes, 91, 112

Pheomelanin, a type of melanin that is red and yellow in color. People with light-colored skin mostly produce pheomelanin. There are two types of melanin; the other is eumelanin, 237, 252

Pheromones, 243

Phospholipids, 321

Phosphorus, 210, 217

Photoaging
- Glogau scale evaluation of, 288–289
- Rubin's Classifications of Photodamage, 290
- from ultraviolet light, 191–193

Photoepilation, also known as *Intense Pulsed Light;* permanent hair removal treatment that uses intense light to destroy the growth cells of the hair follicles, 482, 526

Photography
- to demonstrate product results, 56
- makeup application for, 598–599

Photorejuvenation, 538

Photosensitivities, 194

Photosensitizers, medications and topical products as, 211, 224, 295, 317–318

Photothermolysis, process by which light from a laser is turned into heat, 192, 197, 482

Physical change, change in the form or physical properties of a substance without a chemical reaction or the formation of a new substance, 165, 177

Physical layout planning, 677–678

Physical mixtures, combination of two or more substances united physically, not chemically, without a fixed composition and in any proportions, 165–166, 177

Physical presentation, a person's physical posture, walk, and movements, 43, 46

Physical properties, characteristics that can be determined without a chemical reaction and that do not cause a chemical change in the identity of the substance, 165, 177
Physiology, study of the functions or activities performed by the body's structures, 118, 155
reasons to study histology and, 228
Phytotherapy, use of plant extracts for therapeutic benefits, 330, 351
Piercings, 188
Pigmentation, 452. *See also* Melanin
disorders, 190–194, 196, 265–267, 277–278, 280, 290, 400–401, 483, 497, 537–539
PIH. *See* Post-inflammatory hyperpigmentation
Pilosebaceous unit, the hair unit that contains the hair follicle and appendages: the hair root, bulb, dermal papilla, sebaceous appendage, and arrector pili muscle, 476, 526
Pineal gland, a gland located in the brain. Plays a major role in sexual development, sleep, and metabolism, 144, 145, 155
Pineapple, 321
Pinkeye. *See* Conjunctivitis
Pituitary gland, a gland found in the center of the head. The most complex organ of the endocrine system. It affects almost every physiologic process of the body: growth, blood pressure, contractions during childbirth, breast-milk production, sexual organ functions in both women and men, thyroid gland function, and the conversion of food into energy (metabolism), 144, 145, 155
Plantar warts, 84, 111
Plasma, fluid part of the blood and lymph that carries food and secretions to the cells and carbon dioxide from the cells, 141, 155
Platelets (thrombocytes), much smaller than red blood cells; contribute to the blood-clotting process, which stops bleeding, 141, 155
Platysma, broad muscle extending from the chest and shoulder muscles to the side of the chin; responsible for depressing the lower jaw and lip, 128, 156
Plexus nerve, 436
Plug, two- or three-prong connector at the end of an electrical cord that connects an apparatus to an electrical outlet, 182, 197
PNS. *See* Peripheral nervous system
Podcast, 708
Poison ivy, 265
Polar cavity, 316
Polarity, negative or positive pole of an electric current, 186, 197
Polyethylene glycol (PEG), 320
Polyglucans, ingredients derived from yeast cells that help strengthen the immune system and stimulate the metabolism; they are also hydrophilic and help preserve and protect collagen and elastin, 317, 321, 351
Polymers, chemical compounds formed by combining a number of small molecules (monomers) into long chain-like structures; advanced vehicles that release substances onto the skin's surface at a microscopically controlled rate, 316, 351
Polysaccharides, carbohydrates that contain three or more simple carbohydrate molecules, 204, 224
Polysorbate, 320
Polyunsaturated fats, 205–206
Pons, 134
Pores, tube-like opening for sweat glands on the epidermis, 229, 232, 233, 253
Porous, made or constructed of a material that has pores or openings. Porous items are absorbent, 93, 112
Positive and negative nonverbal cues, 53
Positive attitude, 649, 662
Posterior auricular artery, artery that supplies blood to the scalp, behind and above the ear, 142, 156, 436
Posterior auricular nerve, nerve that affects the muscles behind the ear at the base of the skull, 137, 156
Postinflammatory hyperpigmentation (PIH), 483, 497
Posture, your, 43–44
Potassium, 210, 217
Potassium hydroxide, strong alkali used in soaps and creams, 324, 351
Potential hydrogen. *See* PH
PPE. *See* Personal protective equipment
PR. *See* Public relations
Precursors, 212
Pregnancy. *See also* Melasma
breast milk, 98
high frequency machine contraindicated for problems with, 463
nutrition during, 201–202
treatments contraindicated during, 188, 194
vitamin deficiency during, 213
Preservatives, chemical agents that inhibit the growth of microorganisms in cosmetic formulations. These kill bacteria and prevent products from spoiling, 313, 320, 351
Prickly heat. *See* Miliaria rubra
Primary colors, yellow, red, and blue; fundamental colors that cannot be obtained from a mixture, 560, 620
Primary lesions, primary lesions are characterized by flat, nonpalpable changes in skin color such as macules or patches, or an elevation formed by fluid in a cavity, such as vesicles, bullae, or pustules, 258–260, 280
Prioritize, to make a list of tasks that need to be done in the order of most-to-least important, 30, 37
Prism, light spectrum in, 190–191
Private labeling, 9
Probe. *See* Electrode
Procedural guide, manual or set of instructions designed to standardize operations; supplies specific protocols for conducting individual services, such as the expected method for performing a glycolic or microdermabrasion treatment, 693, 697
Procedures
after facial decontamination procedures, 364–368
making butterfly eye pads, 379
making cleansing pads, 378
post-service procedure, 375–376
pre-service procedure, 372–374
Procerus, muscle that covers the bridge of the nose, depresses the eyebrows, and causes wrinkles across the bridge of the nose, 129, 156
Procrastination, putting off until tomorrow what you can do today, 23, 37
Product. *See also* Makeup
allergic reaction to, 321
chemical-free, 164

Q

R

Redox reactions, chemical reaction in which the oxidizing agent is reduced and the reducing agent is oxidized, 170, 177
Reduction, the process through which oxygen is subtracted from or hydrogen is added to a substance through a chemical reaction, 170, 177
Referrals, client, 713–714
Reflective listening, listening to the client and then repeating, in your own words, what you think the client is telling you, 58, 70
Reflex, automatic reaction to a stimulus that involves the movement of an impulse from a sensory receptor along the sensory nerve to the spinal cord. A responsive impulse is sent along a motor neuron to a muscle, causing a reaction (for example, the quick removal of the hand from a hot object). Reflexes do not have to be learned; they are automatic, 134, 156
Registered nurse (RN), 10
Regulations, 56, 650, 652–653, 678–679. *See also* Certificate or license, esthetician's; Insurance coverage; Skin care business
Regulatory agencies
  on booth rentals, 673
  on electrotherapy services, 188
  esthetician's certificate or license, 32–33
  infection control, 75–78
  for infection control, 75–78
  on operating advanced machines and equipment, 536
  record keeping for disinfection, 95
  for safe footwear, 43
  on using disinfectants and autoclaves, 94
  on using skin-penetrating implements, 86
  on waxing services, 504
Reiki, universal life-force energy transmitted through the palms of the hands that helps lift the spirits and provide balance to the whole self: body, mind, and spirit, 546, 555
Relaxation
  aromatherapy, 313, 330, 348, 436
  body wraps, 541, 554
  facial massage, 438
  galvanic treatments, 463
  shirodhara, 543
Remineralization, 326, 347, 541, 554
Renaissance, 7
Rent, as business expense, 676
Repairs, as business expense, 676
Reproductive system, body system that includes the ovaries, uterine tubes, uterus, and vagina in the female and the testes, prostate gland, penis, and urethra in the male. This system performs the function of producing offspring and passing on the genetic code from one generation to another, 121, 147, 156
  herpes simplex virus 2, 268, 279
Resort spa, 631
Respiration, process of inhaling and exhaling; the act of breathing; the exchange of carbon dioxide and oxygen in the lungs and within each cell, 121, 156
  in breathing cycle, 146
Respiratory system, body system consisting of the lungs and air passages; enables breathing, which supplies the body with oxygen and eliminates carbon dioxide as a waste product, 121, 146, 156
Resume, a written summary of education and work experience that highlights relevant accomplishments and achievements, 631–636, 666
  cover letter, 635
  sample of, 633
Resume Checklist, 632, 634
Retail supplies, items available for sale to clients, 685, 697
Retailing, the act of recommending and selling products to clients for at-home use, 703, 718
  makeup, 607
Retention, client, 712–714
Retention hyperkeratosis, hereditary factor in which dead skin cells build up and do not shed from the follicles as they do on normal skin, 272–273, 280
Reticular layer, deeper layer of the dermis containing proteins, collagen, and elastin that give the skin its strength and elasticity, 229, 239, 240, 253
Retin-A®. *See* Retinoic acid; Tretinoin
Retinoic acid (Retin-A®), vitamin A derivative that has demonstrated an ability to alter collagen synthesis and is used to treat acne and visible signs of aging; side effects are irritation, photosensitivity, skin dryness, redness, and peeling, 211, 224, 276, 317–318
Retinoids, 188, 212
Retinol, natural form of vitamin A; stimulates cell repair and helps to normalize skin cells by generating new cells, 209, 211, 224, 317–318, 321, 351
Retinyl palmitate polypeptide, 212
Revenue, income generated from selling services and products, or money taken in, 675–676, 697
Rhinoplasty, plastic or reconstructive surgery performed on the nose to change or correct its appearance, 552, 555
Rhytidectomy, a face-lift procedure that removes excess fat at the jawline; tightens loose, atrophic muscles; and removes sagging skin, 551, 556
Riboflavin, 209, 215
Ribs, twelve pairs of bones forming the wall of the thorax, 122, 125, 156
Rickets, 213
Ringworm. *See* Tinea corporis
Risorius, muscle of the mouth that draws the corner of the mouth out and back, as in grinning, 129, 130, 156
RN. *See* Registered nurse
Role model, a person whose behaviour and success are worthy of emulation, 662–663, 666
Rolling, massage movement in which the tissues are pressed and twisted using a fast back-and-forth movement, 434, 446
Roll-off masks. *See* Gommage
Rome, ancient, 5–6, 473
Root, hair, 241
Rosacea, chronic condition that appears primarily on the cheeks and nose and is characterized by flushing (redness), telangiectasis (distended or dilated surface blood vessels), and, in some cases, the formation of papules and pustules, 250, 253, 264, 280, 288
Rose, credited with moisturizing, astringent, tonic, and deodorant properties; found in the forms of rose extracts, oil, or water, 327, 351
Rotary brush, machine used to lightly exfoliate and stimulate the skin; also helps soften excess oil, dirt, and cell buildup, 453–454, 470
Rubin's Classifications of Photodamage, 290

S

Serratus anterior, muscle of the chest that assists in breathing and in raising the arm, 130, 157
Serums, concentrated liquid ingredients for the skin designed to penetrate and treat various skin conditions, 340, 352, 392, 460
Service Core of Retired Executives (SCORE), 675
Sesame oil, 320
Seventh cranial nerve (facial nerve), the chief motor nerve of the face. It emerges near the lower part of the ear and extends to the muscles of the neck, 137, 157
Shang dynasty, 6
Sharps, Universal and Standard Precautions on, 99
Sharps container, plastic biohazard containers for disposable needles and anything sharp. The container is red and puncture-proof and must be disposed of as medical waste, 359, 380
Shaving, 264, 278, 484
Sheath, hair root, 241
Shiatsu, the application of pressure on acupuncture points found throughout the body to balance the body's energy flow and to promote health. It originated as a form of physical therapy in Japan, 436, 446
Shingles. *See* Herpes zoster
Shirodhara, 543
Shoes, work-appropriate, 43
Short wavelengths, 189–190
Shoulder
  bones, 125, 156
  exercise, 44
  massage, 439
  motor nerve points of, 436
  muscles, 130–131
Show and tell, of treatment options, 58
Silicones, oil that is chemically combined with silicon and oxygen and leaves a noncomedogenic, protective film on the surface of the skin, 310, 320, 352
Single-use, also known as *disposable*; items that cannot be used more than once. These items cannot be properly cleaned so that all visible residue is removed or they are damaged or contaminated by cleaning and disinfecting in exposure incident, 93, 96, 113
  for treatment room, 360–362, 367
Sinusoidal current, a smooth, repetitive alternating current; the most commonly used alternating current waveform, used in the high frequency machine and can produce heat, 463, 470
Sitting posture, correct, 44
Skeletal system, physical foundation of the body, composed of the bones and movable and immovable joints, 121, 122, 124, 125–126, 157
  osteoporosis, 213
  primary functions of, 123
Skin, external protective coating that covers the body. The body's largest organ; acts as a barrier to protect body systems from the outside elements, 121, 157
  adverse chemical reactions in salon, 265
  antioxidants and, 212
  bioflavonoids and, 217
  blood vessels of, 147, 241
  excretion by, 146
  facts about, 229
  functions of, 230–233
  health, 243–250
  layers of, 233–240
  natural pH of, 168
  nutrition for healthy, 200, 202
  as part of immune system, 243–250
  structures of, 147, 230–231
  Universal and Standard Precautions on broken, 98
  vitamin D and, 192, 210, 213, 224
Skin analysis
  client consultation, 296–297
  Client Consultation Form, 298
  client with open wound or abrasion, 96
  contraindications for service, 295–296
  diverse skin pigmentation, 290–291
  factors affecting skin, 293–295
  Fitzpatrick Scale for, 59, 288–289, 302
  genetic determination of skin type, 285–287
  healthy habits for skin, 295
  performing, 297–299
  procedure, 300–301
  reasons to study, 285
  sensitive skin, 287–288
  skin type compared to skin condition, 291–292
Skin cancer, 192, 237
  from damage to DNA, 269
Skin care business, 686
  company owner, 14
  Customized Skin Care Program form, 716
  going into, 669
    action plan for, 673–675
    booth rentals, 672–673
    business operations, 682–683
    business plan: costs, revenue, profits, 675–676
    leases, 680–681
    ownership options, 670–672
    physical layout planning, 677–678
    protection against fire, theft, lawsuits, 681–682
    purchasing established salon, 680
    regulations, business laws, insurance, 678–679
  operation of
    appointment scheduling, 688–689
    front desk, 686–688
    Income Statement sample, 676
    personnel, 692–695
    telephone skills, 689–692
  public relations, 695
  reasons to study, 669
  record keeping, 684–686
    client service records, 686, 708, 710
    for disinfection, 95
    purchase and inventory control, 685
Skin care products, 307
  as acne trigger, 274
  aromatherapy, 330–331
  choosing product line, 344–346
  history of, 4–9
  home-care products, 343–344
  ingredients, 323–330
    color agents, 314
    delivery systems, 316
    emollients, 308–311
    exfoliation, 315
    fragrances, 313
    free radicals, 318–319
    gellants and thickeners, 313
    hydrators and moisturizers, 314–315

Spinal cord, portion of the central nervous system that originates in the brain, extends down to the lower extremity of the trunk, and is protected by the spinal column, 134, 157

Spirilla, spiral or corkscrew-shaped bacteria that cause diseases such as syphilis and Lyme disease, 80, 113

Spray machine, spray misting device, 466–467, 470

Squalane, derived from olives; desensitizes and nourishes; an emollient, 325, 352

Squamous cell carcinoma, type of skin cancer more serious than basal cell carcinoma; characterized by scaly, red or pink papules or nodules; also appear as open sores or crusty areas; can grow and spread in the body, 270, 281

Stain, brown or wine-colored discoloration with a circular and/ or irregular shape. Stains occur after certain diseases, or after moles, freckles, or liver spots disappear. A port wine stain is a birthmark, which is a vascular type of nevus, **266, 281**

Standard of ethics, 32–33

Standard Precautions (SP), precautions such as wearing personal protective equipment to prevent skin and mucous membrane where contact with a client's blood, body fluids, secretions (except sweat), excretions, nonintact skin, and mucous membranes is likely. Workers must assume that all blood and body fluids are potential sources of infection, regardless of the perceived risk, 97–102, 113
  Universal Precautions compared with, 98

Standing posture, 43

Staphylococci, pus-forming bacteria that grow in clusters like a bunch of grapes. They cause abscesses, pustules, and boils, 80, 113

State board member, 15

State license or certificate. *See* Certificate or license, esthetician's

State licensing inspector, 15

States of matter, the three different physical forms of matter: solid, liquid, and gas, 164, 177

Steamer, 454–457

Steatoma, sebaceous cyst or subcutaneous tumor filled with sebum; ranges in size from a pea to an orange. It usually appears on the scalp, neck, and back; also called a *wen*, 262, 281

Stem cells, derived from plants to protect or stimulate our own skin stem cells; for health and antiaging benefits, 317, 352

Sterilization, the process that completely destroys all microbial life, including spores, 88, 113

Sternocleidomastoid (SCM), muscle of the neck that depresses and rotates the head, 128, 157

Sternum (breastbone), the flat bone that forms the ventral support of the ribs, 122, 125, 157

Sterols, 321

Stomach, 121
  as digestive system component, 201
  endocrine glands and, 145

Stone massage, use of hot stones and cold stones in massage or in other treatments, 542, 556

Stratum corneum (horny layer), outermost layer of the epidermis, composed of corneocytes, 229, 233, 234, 240, 253

Stratum germinativum (basal cell layer), active layer of the epidermis above the papillary layer of the dermis; cell mitosis takes place here that produces new epidermal skin cells and is responsible for growth, 229, 235, 240, 253

Stratum granulosum (granular layer), layer of the epidermis composed of cells filled with keratin that resemble granules; replace cells shed from the stratum corneum, 229, 233, 235, 240, 253

Stratum lucidum, clear, transparent layer of the epidermis under the stratum corneum; thickest on the palms of hands and soles of feet, 229, 233, 235, 240, 253

Stratum spinosum (spiny layer), layer of the epidermis above the stratum germinativum layer containing desmosomes, the intercellular connections made of proteins, 229, 233, 235, 240, 253

Streptococci, pus-forming bacteria arranged in curved lines resembling a string of beads. They cause infections such as strep throat and blood poisoning, 80, 113

Stress, 43, 132, 155, 157
  skin aging from, 293
  vitamin C and resistance to, 216–217

Striated muscles (skeletal, voluntary), attached to the bones and make up a large percentage of body mass; controlled by the will, 126, 157

Study skills, 26–27

Subcutaneous layer (hypodermis), subcutaneous adipose (fat) tissue located beneath the dermis; a protective cushion and energy storage for the body, 23, 229, 233, 239, 253

Subcutis tissue (adipose tissue), fatty tissue found beneath the dermis that gives smoothness and contour to the body, contains fat for use as energy, and also acts as a protective cushion for the outer skin, 239, 253

Submental artery, artery that supplies blood to the chin and lower lip, 141, 157

Success
  chart of skills for, 384
  dress for, 41
  guidelines for, 21–23
  habits for, 26–27
  life skills for, 24–25, 28, 37, 41
  on-the-job, 664
  role model's, 662, 666
  rules for, 24–25
  tracking your, 717

Suction machine. *See* Vacuum machine

Sudoriferous glands (sweat glands), excrete perspiration, regulate body temperature, and detoxify the body by excreting excess salt and unwanted chemicals, 147, 168, 229, 232, 233, 242–243, 253
  disorders of, 262–263

Sugaring, ancient method of hair removal. The original recipe is a mixture of sugar, lemon juice, and water that is heated to form syrup, molded into a ball, and pressed onto the skin and then quickly stripped away, 486, 526

Sulfur, sulfur reduces oil-gland activity and dissolves the skin's surface layer of dry, dead cells. This ingredient is commonly used in acne products, 211, 325, 352

Sun protection factor (SPF), ability of a product to delay sun-induced erythema, the visible sign of sun damage. The SPF rating is based only on UVB protection, not UVA exposure, 294–295, 319, 352

Sun spots, 85, 113

Sunlight. *See also* Cancer; Ultraviolet radiation
  effect on skin, 294–295

photoaging from, 191–193, 288–289, 290
types of electromagnetic radiation in, 190–191
Sunscreen
after facial treatment, 392
ingredients, 319–320
sun protection instructions, 59
Superficial temporal artery, a continuation of the external carotid artery; artery that supplies blood to the muscles of the front, side, and top of the head, 141, 157
Superior labial artery, artery that supplies blood to the upper lip and region of the nose, 141, 157
Supinator, muscle of the forearm that rotates the radius outward and the palm upward, 131, 157
Supraorbital artery, artery that supplies blood to the upper eyelid and forehead, 142, 157
Supraorbital nerve, nerve that affects the skin of the forehead, scalp, eyebrow, and upper eyelid, 136, 157
Supratrochlear nerve, nerve that affects the skin between the eyes and upper side of the nose, 136, 157
Surfactants, acronym for surface active agent: reduce surface tension between the skin and the product to increase product spreadability; allow oil and water to mix, or emulsify, 172, 177, 311–312, 320
Suspensions, unstable mixtures of two or more immiscible substances, 171, 172, 177
Sustainability, meeting the needs of the present without compromising the ability of future generations to meet their needs. The three facets of sustainability are the three E's: the *Environment*, the *Economy*, and social *Equity*, 368–371, 380
Sweat glands. *See* Sudoriferous glands
Sweat pore, 233
Swedish massage movements, 432–434
Sympathetic division, part of the autonomic nervous system that stimulates or speeds up activity and prepares the body for stressful situations, such as in running from a dangerous situation, or competing in a sports event, 132, 157
Synthetic ingredients, 320–321
Systemic disease, disease that affects the body as a whole, often due to under-functioning or over-functioning of internal glands or organs. This disease is carried through the blood stream or the lymphatic system, 83, 113
Systemic or general circulation, circulation of blood from the heart throughout the body and back again to the heart, 138, 157
Systems. *See* Body systems

Tan, increase in pigmentation due to the melanin production that results from exposure to UV radiation; visible skin damage. Melanin is designed to help protect the skin from the sun's UV radiation, 266, 281
Tanning beds, 191, 192
Tapotement (percussion), movements consisting of short, quick tapping, slapping, and hacking movements, 434, 446
Tarsals, 122
Taxes, 660, 665, 676
Tazarotene (Tazorac®), 276, 317–318
TCA peels. *See* Trichloroacetic acid peels
T-cells, identify molecules that have foreign peptides and also help regulate immune response, 244, 253
TEA (triethanolamine), 320
Tea tree, soothing and antiseptic; antifungal properties, 327, 352
Team work
with boss, 650
with client, 52
with coworkers, 36, 52, 649–650
pitching in when needed, 45
success due to, 662
Telangiectasia, capillaries that have been damaged and are now larger, or distended blood vessels; commonly called *couperose skin*, 250, 253, 264, 287, 302, 326, 350, 463
Telephone calls
as business expense, 676
for follow-up with client, 715
skill at, 689–692
texting, 31
Telogen, also known as *resting phase;* the final phase in the hair cycle that lasts until the fully grown hair is shed, 478, 526
Temperature control, 372
Temporal bones, bones forming the sides of the head in the ear region, 123, 124, 157
Temporal nerve, nerve affecting the muscles of the temple, side of the forehead, eyebrow, eyelid, and upper part of the cheek, 137, 157
Temporalis muscle, temporal muscle; one of the muscles involved in mastication (chewing), 128, 157
10-step consultation method, 57–58
consultative selling, 701–702
Terminal differentiation, 236
Terminal hair, 474
Tertiary colors, intermediate color achieved by mixing a secondary color and its neighboring primary color on the color wheel in equal amounts, 561, 620
Tesla high-frequency current (violet ray), thermal or heat-producing current with a high rate of oscillation or vibration, 186, 188, 190, 197
direct and indirect application methods, 189
Test taking, for licensure, 625, 666
deductive reasoning, 626
practical examination, 628
test day, 628
understanding test formats, 626–628
Testes, male organs which produce the male hormone testosterone, 145, 157
Test-wise, refers to a student who begins to prepare for taking a test by practicing good study habits and time management as part of an effective study program, 625, 666
TEWL. *See* Transepidermal water loss
Texting, 31
Thank You Note sample (job search), 640
Thermal masks. *See* Modelage masks
Thermolysis, also known as *electrocoagulation;* heat effect; a high-frequency AC current that produces heat and destroys the follicle; a method of electrolysis used for permanent hair removal, 464, 470
Thiamine, 209, 215
Third digit, 122
Third-degree burns, 101–102
Thorax, also known as *chest* or *pulmonary trunk;* consists of the sternum, ribs, and thoracic vertebrae; elastic, bony cage that serves as a protective framework for the heart, lungs, and other internal organs, 125, 157

Twitter, 708

Two-prong plug, 184

Tyrosinase, the enzyme that stimulates melanocytes and thus produces melanin, 237, 253, 316

T-zone, center area of the face; corresponds to the "T" shape formed by the forehead, nose, and chin, 285, 302

U

UL. *See* Underwriter's Laboratory

Ulcer, open lesion on the skin or mucous membrane of the body, accompanied by pus and loss of skin depth. A deep erosion; a depression in the skin, normally due to infection or cancer, 260–261, 281

Ulna, inner and larger bone of the forearm, attached to the wrist on the side of the little finger, 122, 125, 126, 158

Ulnar artery, artery that supplies blood to the muscle of the little-finger side of the arm and palm of the hand, 143, 158

Ulnar nerve, sensory-motor nerve that, with its branches, affects the little-finger side of the arm and palm of the hand, 138, 158

Ultrasonic, frequency above the range of sound audible to the human ear; vibrations, created through a water medium, help cleanse and exfoliate the skin by removing dead skin cells; contraindications include epilepsy, pregnancy, and cancerous lesions; synonymous with ultrasound, 540–541, 556

Ultrasound, frequency above the range of sound audible to the human ear; vibrations, created through a water medium, help cleanse and exfoliate the skin by removing dead skin cells; contraindications include epilepsy, pregnancy, and cancerous lesions; synonymous with ultrasonic, 540–541, 556

Ultraviolet (UV) radiation, invisible rays that have short wavelengths, are the least penetrating rays, produce chemical effects, and kill germs, 189–191, 197
- effects on skin, 294–295
- types of, 191

Ultraviolet (UV) sanitizers, 93

Underarms
- deodorant, 41
- waxing, 518–519

Underwriter's Laboratory (UL), 184–185

Universal Precautions (UP), a set of guidelines published by OSHA that require the employer and the employee to assume that all human blood and body fluids are infectious for bloodborne pathogens, 97–102, 113
- Standard Precautions compared with, 98

Unsaturated fats, 205–206

UP. *See* Universal Precautions

Upselling services, the practice of recommending or selling additional services to clients that may be performed by you or other practitioners in the salon, 704, 718

Urea, properties include enhancing the penetration abilities of other substances; anti-inflammatory, antiseptic, and deodorizing action that protects the skin's surface and helps maintain healthy skin, 320, 325, 352

Urticaria (hives), caused by an allergic reaction from the body's histamine production, 264, 281

USDA. *See* Department of Agriculture, U. S.

Utilities, as business expense, 676

UV sanitizers. *See* Ultraviolet sanitizers

UVA radiation (aging rays), longer wavelengths ranging between 320 to 400 nanometers that penetrate deeper into the skin than UVB; cause genetic damage and cell death. UVA contribute up to 95 percent of the sun's ultraviolet radiation, 245, 253

UVB radiation (burning rays), these wavelengths range between 290 to 320 nanometers. UVB rays have shorter, burning wavelengths that are stronger and more damaging than UVA rays. UVB cause burning of the skin as well as tanning, skin aging, and cancer, 245, 253

V

V. *See* Volt

Vacuum machine (suction machine), device that vacuums/suctions the skin to remove impurities and stimulate circulation, 458, 470

Vagus nerve, 135

Valves, structures that temporarily close a passage or permit flow in one direction only, 138, 158

Variable costs, business expenses that fluctuate, such as utilities, supplies, and advertising, 675, 697

Varicella-zoster virus. *See* Herpes zoster

Varicose veins, vascular lesions; dilated and twisted veins, most commonly in the legs, 264, 281

Vascular system, body system consisting of the heart, arteries, veins, and capillaries for the distribution of blood throughout the body, 138, 158

Vasoconstricting, vascular constriction of capillaries and blood flow, 400, 426

Vasodilation, vascular dilation of blood vessels, 264, 281

Vegetables, green leafy, 210

Vegetarian diet, 202, 203

Vehicles, spreading agents and ingredients that carry or deliver other ingredients into the skin and make them more effective, 316, 352

Veins, thin-walled blood vessels that are less elastic than arteries; they contain cuplike valves to prevent backflow and carry impure blood from the various capillaries back to the heart and lungs, 139, 143, 147, 149, 158, 241
- of head, face, and neck, 140–142, 150, 151, 152
- layers of skin and, 229
- varicose, 264, 281

Vellus hair, also known as *lanugo hair;* short, fine, unpigmented downy hair that appears on the body, with the exception of the palms of the hands and the soles of the feet, 474, 526

Ventricle, a thick-walled, lower chamber of the heart that receives blood pumped from the atrium. There is a right ventricle and a left ventricle, 138, 158

Venules, small vessels that connect the capillaries to the veins. They collect blood from the capillaries and drain it into veins, 140, 158

Verruca (wart), hypertrophy of the papillae and epidermis caused by a virus. It is infectious and contagious, 268, 281

Vertebral column, 122, 125

Vesicle, small blister or sac containing clear fluid. Poison ivy and poison oak produce vesicles, 259–260, 281

Vestibulocochlear nerve, 135

Vibration, in massage, the rapid shaking movement in which the technician uses the body and shoulders, not just the fingertips, to create the movement, 434–435, 446

Vichy shower, 542

Victoria (queen), 7
Victorian Age, 7
Video makeup, 598–599
Violet ray, 190, 197
Viral marketing, 708
Virucidal, capable of destroying viruses, 79, 113
Virus (plural: viruses), a parasitic submicroscopic particle that infects and resides in the cells of biological organisms. A virus is capable of replication only through taking over the host cell's reproductive function, 81, 113. *See also* Hepatitis; Herpes simplex virus 1; Herpes simplex virus 2; Herpes zoster; Human immunodeficiency virus; Human papillomavirus
  principles of infection, 82–85
  types of, 82–83
Visceral muscles, 126, 154
Visibility, business location, 673–674
Visible light, the primary source of light used in facial and scalp treatments, 182, 190–191, 197
Vitamin A (retinol), an antioxidant that aids in the functioning and repair of skin cells, 209, 211–212, 224, 317–318, 321, 351. *See also* Carrot
Vitamin B. *See* B vitamins
Vitamin C (ascorbic acid), an antioxidant vitamin needed for proper repair of the skin and tissues; promotes the production of collagen in the skin's dermal tissues; aids in and promotes the skin's healing process, 216–217, 224
  in skin care products, 319
Vitamin D, fat-soluble vitamin sometimes called the sunshine vitamin because the skin synthesizes vitamin D from cholesterol when exposed to sunlight. Essential for growth and development, 210, 213, 224. *See also* Cholesterol
  UV therapy for, 192
Vitamin E (tocopherol), primarily an antioxidant; helps protect the skin from the harmful effects of the sun's rays, 210, 213–214, 224, 321
Vitamin F, 210
Vitamin K, vitamin responsible for the synthesis of factors necessary for blood coagulation, 210, 214, 224
Vitamin P (bioflavonoids), 210, 217, 223. *See also* Horsechestnut
Vitamins, 208–217, 318
  skin aging from deficient, 293
Vitiligo, pigmentation disease characterized by white patches on the skin from lack of pigment cells; sunlight makes it worse, 267, 281
Vocabulary, 26
Voice volume, as nonverbal cue, 53
Volt (V, voltage), unit that measures the pressure or force that pushes the flow of electrons forward through a conductor, 182, 197
Voluntary muscles, 126, 157
Vomer bone, flat, thin bone that forms part of the nasal septum, 123, 139, 158

W

W. *See* Watt
Warm colors, the range of colors with yellow undertones; from yellow and gold through oranges, red-oranges, most reds, and even some yellow-greens, 562, 620
Wart. *See* Verruca
Water, most abundant of all substances, comprising about 75 percent of the Earth's surface and about 65 percent of the human body, 166, 177, 308. *See also* Balneotherapy; Oil-in-water emulsion; Water-in-oil emulsion
  chemical composition of, 163
  electrical equipment and avoidance of, 185
  fluoridated, 211
  as functional ingredient, 320
  in human body, 120
  hydrolipidic film, 230–231, 252
  skin and, 220–221
Water soluble, mixable with water, 312, 316, 352
Water soluble vitamins, 214–217
Water-in-oil (W/O) emulsion, droplets of water dispersed in an oil, 171, 174, 177
Waterless hand washing, 96–97
Watt (W), measurement of how much electric energy is being used in one second, 183, 197
Wavelength, distance between two successive peaks of electromagnetic waves, 190, 197, 538
Wax products
  beeswax, 487
  hard wax, 488–489
  roll-on wax, 489
  soft wax, 489
  wax strips, 491–492
Waxing
  bikini, 504, 520–522
  body, 503
  chin, with hard wax, 514–515
  eyebrow, 502, 508–511
  eyebrow shaping guidelines, 501–502
  face, lip, chin, 502, 512–513
  general procedure, 497–505
  laws regarding services, 504
  legs, with soft wax, 516–517
  male clients, 505
  times and prices, 505
  underarm, with hard wax, 518–519
Wellness center or spa, 629
Wheal, itchy, swollen lesion caused by a blow, insect bite, skin allergy reaction, or stings. Hives and mosquito bites are wheals. Hives (urticaria) can be caused by exposure to allergens used in products, 259, 260, 281
White blood cells (white corpuscles, leukocytes), perform the function of destroying disease causing germs, 141, 158, 238
White light, referred to as *combination light* because it is a combination of all the visible rays of the spectrum, 191, 197
Whole grains, 203–205, 209–211
Witch hazel, extracted from the bark of the hamanelis shrub; can be a soothing agent or, in higher concentrations, an astringent, 327, 352
Wood's Lamp, filtered black light that is used to illuminate skin disorders, fungi, bacterial disorders, and pigmentation, 297, 452–453, 470
Work ethic, 36
Wringing, vigorous movement in which the hands, placed a little distance apart on both sides of the client's arm or leg, working downward apply a twisting motion against the bones in the opposite direction, 434, 446

Wrinkle treatments, 550–551

Wrist. *See* Carpus

Xanthan gum, 320

Xiphoid bone, 122

X-ray, 189

Yawning, as nonverbal cue, 53

Yellow light, a light-emitting diode which aids in reducing inflammation and swelling, 190–191, 193, 197
  beneficial effects of, 194

You are what you eat, 202, 212

Zinc, 211, 218

Zinc oxide, inorganic physical sunscreen that reflects UVA radiation. Also used to protect, soothe, and heal the skin; is somewhat astringent, antiseptic, and antibacterial, 325, 352

Zygomatic bones (malar bones, cheekbones), bones that form the prominence of the cheeks; the cheekbones, 123, 139, 158

Zygomatic nerve, nerve that affects the skin of the temple, side of the forehead, and upper part of the cheek, 137, 158

Zygomaticus major and minor, muscles on both sides of the face that extend from the zygomatic bone to the angle of the mouth. These muscles elevate the lip, pull the mouth upward and backward, as when you are laughing or smiling, 130, 158